HISTORY OF THE SECOND WORLD WAR

HISTORY OF THE SECOND WORLD WAR

Editor-in-chief **Sir Basil Liddell Hart**

Exeter Books

NEW YORK

in association with Phoebus

This edition © 1980 Phoebus Publishing
Company/BPC Publishing Limited,
52 Poland Street, London W1A 2JX

This material first appeared in
HISTORY OF THE SECOND WORLD WAR
© 1979/1974/1972/1966 Phoebus
Publishing Company/BPC Publishing
Limited

First published in USA 1980 by
Exeter Books, distributed by
Bookthrift, Inc
New York, New York 10018

Made and printed in Hong Kong

ISBN 0-89673-065-4
Library of Congress 80-80953

INTRODUCTION

When Adolf Hitler unleashed his tanks eastwards against Poland in the summer of 1939 and put into practice the Blitzkrieg theory, he started a global conflict which was to rage unabated for some six years. His decision to declare war had been caused in part by his megalomania, and in part by the confidence that the Allies' prewar appeasement policy had given him.

Germany's forces soon overran Poland, and there followed a period aptly called the 'Phoney War', when the whole world waited for the British and French reply. However, the entire Allied strategy was based on defence and the economic wearing-down of Germany. The initiative had to come from Hitler.

It came suddenly in April 1940, when the Germans bulldozed their way into Holland and Belgium and quickly outflanked the Maginot Line to subdue the French, and clear the continent of the British. The latter's hasty evacuation of Dunkirk was hailed at the time almost as a victory, and although large numbers of men were saved, the amount of equipment lost was almost total. Only the crucial Battle of Britain, in September 1940, prevented catastrophe and kept the hopes of England, and democracy, alive.

Gradually, British forces, under Churchill's magnificent leadership, fought back and especially in North Africa, the scene of many bloody yet brilliant skirmishes. But the decisive land battles, and the most costly in men and materials, were destined to take place between Germany and the Soviet Union.

The same year saw the American and Japanese entry into the war, with the monumental Japanese decision to attack Pearl Harbor, on December 7, 1941. The Japanese lost no time in assuming almost total command of the entire South-East Asia region, attacking Thailand, Malaya, Wake Island, Guam, the Philippines, Burma and Hong Kong before the end of 1941. The US Pacific Fleet replied in 1942 with raids on Japanese shipping culminating in the decisive Japanese defeat in June. However with the massive resources of the hitherto 'sleeping giant' of America at the Allies' command, the Axis death knell was sounded. The end was not swift, however. Millions of men lost their lives in Africa, Europe, the Mediterranean and the Pacific before the horrors of Nagasaki and Hiroshima signalled the end of the war.

History of the Second World War is written by established military and historical experts, and contains many exciting and original colour photographs, especially of the German campaign in eastern Europe, and the American battles in the Pacific.

In a series of well researched articles, this book tells the story of every decisive development of the war, of how in the end it was eventually won—and lost.

CONTENTS

Before the Blitzkrieg

Europe March/September 1939

Donald C Watt

The five months separating Britain's guarantee to Poland from Germany's onslaught on that country were hectic ones. Throughout that long summer the diplomats bluffed, blandished, threatened, parleyed, bargained; the stakes were high, the tension enormous. At first it looked as if Hitler might be contained; then came the diplomatic shock which paralysed the West, the *volte-face* of Soviet Russia. Finally, when it became too late for negotiations, smaller nations found themselves the pawns of greater powers — and the major powers seemed themselves to be the pawns of fate

On March 15, 1939, German troops invaded Czechoslovakia and occupied Prague. Two days later Chamberlain, in a public speech at Birmingham, accused Hitler of breaking his word. On March 22, German troops occupied the old German city of Memel in Lithuania, forcing that state to sign a treaty conceding Memel's return to Germany. Recognising a parallel between Memel and the old German port of Danzig in Poland, the Poles announced, on March 28, that any German attempt to alter Danzig's status without Polish consent would lead to war. On March 31, Britain extended to Poland a unilateral guarantee against German aggression. Diplomatic talks began between the West and the Soviet Union.

THE LAST SIX MONTHS OF PEACE

April 7: Italy invades the Balkan state of Albania.

April 17: Diplomatic talks begin between Germany and the Soviet Union.

April 28: Hitler cancels the Anglo-German naval agreement of 1935 and the German-Polish non-aggression agreement of 1934.

May 4: Molotov replaces Litvinov as Soviet Foreign Minister.

May 22: Ribbentrop and Ciano sign the 'Pact of Steel' to weld together Europe's strongest Fascist dictatorships; Japan is asked to join the alliance.

June 3: Nazi-controlled Danzig complains of too many Polish customs officials. Poland's caustic reply meets with a new barrage of Nazi propaganda, and rumours of an impending Nazi *coup* sweep the country.

July 24: Britain, France, and Russia agree to offer mutual assistance should any of the three be attacked. But the pact is not to come into operation until corresponding military agreements are reached.

August 23: Ribbentrop and Molotov sign a non-aggression pact between Berlin and Moscow. The pact includes a secret annex that divides eastern Europe between Germany and the Soviet Union.

August 25: Hitler schedules the attack on Poland for the next day, but revokes the orders when Mussolini informs him that Italy is not prepared for war.

August 31: Hitler again orders the attack on Poland.

September 1: At 0445 hours, without declaring war, Germany launches its attack on Poland.

September 2: Chamberlain sends his ultimatum to Hitler: if Germany does not withdraw her troops immediately she must consider herself at war with Britain.

September 3: Hitler receives the ultimatum and ignores it. Britain is at war with Germany.

Central Press

APRIL:

BIDS FROM THE KREMLIN

The British action in guaranteeing Poland completely transformed the scene; it upset the Soviet authorities, who saw in it a further indication of British unwillingness to treat them as a serious partner. Litvinov declared that the Soviet government had had enough and would stand apart from any further commitments. He made a further attempt to negotiate on his own with the Baltic states, and instituted further soundings in south-eastern Europe. But this reaction was short-lived. The realisation in the Kremlin that the British guarantee was meaningless without Russian support encouraged the Soviets to raise their demands on Britain, and on April 6 their Foreign Minister raised the question of Anglo-Russian staff agreements. On April 18 Litvinov proposed a ten-year alliance between Britain, France, and the Soviet Union.

◀ Russian Foreign Minister Litvinov (left) tried hard to secure co-operation between Russia and the Allies

Molotov, right, shown shaking hands with his German counterpart Ribbentrop, was much tougher than Litvinov, the man he replaced ▶

Hitler's target

If Britain was really determined to defend Poland against Germany then, the Soviet authorities must have reasoned, she had to have an alliance with Russia. Without it Poland could not be defended. If Britain was still hoping for an accommodation with Hitler, then she would refuse the offer of the alliance. At the same time, however, the Soviet authorities seem to have determined to test their assumption, formed from their knowledge of the German negotiations with Japan, that Hitler's real target was the Western democracies. Early in April Russian diplomatic representatives began hinting in Berlin that the Soviet Union was interested in improving her relations with Germany, still strained as they were by Ribbentrop's attempt to get an agreement with the Poles.

Italy invades Albania

Nor was this the end of the repercussions of the occupation of Prague and the British guarantee to Poland. Hitler's action in Prague had outraged Mussolini—who took great pride in the role of peacemaker he had played at Munich. Italian prestige made it essential, in his view, for Italy not to be outdone by Hitler in the use of force to advance national interests. He felt, moreover, bitterly insulted by Hitler's failure to give him any reasonable warning before the move against Prague. He decided, therefore, without warning Germany, to put an end to the semi-protectorate Italy had long enjoyed over Albania, the small Slav mountain state on the borders of Greece and Yugoslavia, just across the Adriatic from the heel of Italy itself. On April 5 General Keitel and General Pariani, the chiefs of the German and Italian armed forces, met in Innsbruck to discuss the division of operations in the event of a war with the Western democracies; no mention of Italy's designs on Albania was made to the Germans—yet even as General Pariani's train left Innsbruck for Italy the Italian forces moved to the attack.

The Italian invasion of Albania at once led the British to widen the scope of their guarantees, since they were convinced that Mussolini must have concerted it with Hitler. They had already been considering the possi-

bility of linking a guarantee for Rumania with a strengthening of the old Polish-Rumanian alliance. Now they were in the process of trying to persuade Rumania's partners in the so-called 'Balkan Entente' —Yugoslavia, Greece, and Turkey—to come into a collective guarantee of Rumania. So far as their negotiations with the Soviet Union were concerned, the outright refusal of the Polish Foreign Minister, Colonel Beck, during his visit to London at the beginning of April, to be party to any agreement with Soviet Russia, seemed to them to leave them no alternative but to play down their negotiations with the Soviets and try to find some way of keeping them in reserve, without driving Poland and, still more, Rumania into Germany's arms. The reaction of the three Baltic states in rejecting Litvinov's approaches in favour of agreement with Germany only strengthened them in their views.

Italy's action (which the British wrongly presumed to have been co-ordinated with Hitler) now seemed to demand the extension of their guarantee system to Greece and even to Turkey. To some extent this would make their guarantees even less credible; but on the other hand it offered the chance of producing a solid Balkan bloc against the Axis powers. This would especially be the case if Bulgaria could be persuaded to drop her old enmity with Rumania and Greece and enter the Balkan pact. On April 13 Anglo-French guarantees were therefore issued to Rumania, and Greece and Turkey replied to enquiries that in principle they would be prepared to exchange similar guarantees with Britain. The Turks further undertook to approach the Bulgarian government with a view to her possible inclusion in the proposed bloc.

The French hand

In the meantime the French government tried to play its own hand in the negotiations for an alliance with the Soviet Union. Georges Bonnet, the French Foreign Minister, suggested on April 15 that an annex be signed to the Franco-Soviet pact of 1935, pledging Russia to come to France's aid if she were attacked by Germany as a result of her giving assistance to Poland and Rumania. This, however, conflicted both

with Britain's desire for urgency, and with a certain anxiety the British Foreign Office was beginning to feel at the absence of any Soviet equivalent to the British guarantees of Poland, Rumania, and Greece and to the projected guarantee for Turkey. Seen from London, the Soviet government seemed to be giving remarkably little in return for the indirect guarantees of her own security involved in the British underwriting of Poland and Rumania. On April 15, therefore, the British ambassador in Moscow, Sir William Seeds, invited Litvinov to declare a parallel guarantee of Poland and Rumania, one to match that given already by Britain.

The proposal was an unhappy one in itself, being so much less than the offer of assistance which the Russians were convinced they had already made. But when taken with the evidence of British involvement in Turkey, it raised ancestral Russian fears of British entry into the Black Sea and British hegemony in the Balkans. On April 22 the Soviet Deputy Foreign Minister, Vladimir Potemkin, was dispatched on a tour of the Balkan capitals to investigate how far the plans to develop a Balkan bloc under British leadership had gone. In the meantime, Litvinov made what was to be his last proposal for a collective pact against Germany. On April 18 he proposed a ten-year Anglo-Franco-Soviet alliance against German aggression whether against the signatories themselves or against the states of eastern Europe.

An unwelcome alliance

Litvinov's proposal was rejected. The British were trying to create a state of affairs which would lead Hitler to a conference table, not a military alliance to destroy him. In their view an Anglo-Franco-Soviet alliance would be unwelcome to Poland and Rumania; it would take much too long to negotiate, and was unnecessary anyway, since Britain was already firmly committed to Poland, Rumania, and to Turkey. Hitler's policy, as they saw it, was to create the maximum degree of apprehension among Germany's neighbours for the minimum effort, but not to move against them, unless he thought he could avoid provoking general war. A strengthening of the Balkan Entente and the Polish-Rumanian alliance with British backing and the promise of Soviet aid—if it should be needed and wanted—would be quite enough, in the British view, to restrain him.

MAY:
WEBS OF DIPLOMACY

The rejection of Litvinov's proposal—when taken with the evidence of British diplomatic success in the Balkans and of Balkan resistance to Soviet help against Germany—must have seemed suspicious in Moscow, even though Potemkin said he was satisfied. Everywhere the Soviets were being welcomed only as an adjunct to British policy, an insurance against its failure to bring Hitler to see reason; everywhere British initiative and leadership were paramount —in the Baltic, in the Balkans, and in Poland and Rumania. The Soviet Union was

still outside the circle. On Potemkin's arrival in Ankara on April 29, he remained virtually inactive for four days. On May 4 the news of Litvinov's dismissal from office and replacement by Stalin's right-hand man, Vyacheslav Molotov, burst upon a startled world.

It was as startling to the Germans as to the West. During April, Hitler must have begun to feel a little hemmed in by what German propaganda persisted in calling the British encirclement policy. His diplomats, it is true, did score a minor success in the north by blocking the Russian attempt to negotiate non-aggression pacts with Latvia, Estonia, and Lithuania, and getting them to accept non-aggression pacts with Germany instead. But similar pressure on the Turks in Ankara and on the Rumanian Foreign Minister failed to detach either from the

British-inspired 'front'. And to make matters worse, the British made their commitment to a continental war clear on April 26 when the Minister for War, Mr Leslie Hore-Belisha, announced the introduction of conscription in Britain. And, in addition, the German diplomats were getting no further with their alliance negotiations with the Japanese.

Denunciation by Hitler

Hitler reacted as might have been expected to the British introduction of conscription. On April 28, at Wilhelmshaven, he denounced both the German-Polish non-aggression pact and the 1935 naval agreement with Britain—the two treaties he had always cited when rebutting accusations that he did not keep his word in treaty

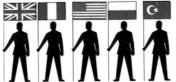

Europe on the eve of war. Britain is allied with France, Poland, and Turkey and has an understanding with the USA. Germany is allied with Italy, and has an understanding and non-aggression pact with the USSR

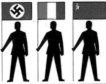

obligations. In fact, there were good technical reasons from Germany's point of view why the naval agreement had to be denounced: Germany was just about to lay down two new battleships which the agreement's terms clearly prohibited. The gesture was no doubt a satisfying one for Hitler, but it could not have been said to have improved his diplomatic position. Indeed, he was rapidly losing patience with diplomacy.

On May 6 Ribbentrop was to meet his Italian opposite number, Count Ciano, in Milan, to propose a bilateral German-Italian alliance to which Japan could accede when her internal disagreements had finally been resolved. But Hitler saw that a German-Italian alliance was hardly likely on its own to restrain Britain and France and leave him free to attack Poland, so long as Britain and France could rely on the prospect of Soviet support. If he could detach the Soviet Union from the West, this would be quite a different matter.

Feelers to Russia

The idea of a German-Soviet pact had never been completely abandoned in German military and diplomatic circles. There was always a small group who remembered how Germany—when she was forbidden to possess tanks or other heavy weapons on her own soil—had conducted tank exercises in the 1920's with the Red Army and had manufactured poison gas, with Soviet connivance, on Russian soil. In those days enmity towards Poland had been the strongest link between Germany and Soviet Russia, and there were always those who regretted the ending of German-Soviet collaboration and the conclusion of the non-aggression pact with Poland in the first year after Hitler's coming to power in 1933.

It is hardly surprising, then, that the deterioration of German-Polish relations at the end of March 1939 should have turned people's minds to the idea of reviving the old friendship with the Soviet Union. In fact, the idea first seems to have been ventilated in Hitler's *entourage* at the end of March. It received added support when on April 15 Mussolini roundly advised Göring that Germany should take up good relations with the Soviet Union. Hitler and Ribbentrop, however, must have regarded the idea as quite unrealistic, as Litvinov's sudden dismissal seems to have taken them quite by surprise.

Anxious debate in Berlin

It seemed to them, however, that they ought to exploit the removal of Litvinov—whom they disliked as much for his Jewishness and his British wife as for his support for the League of Nations and collective action against aggression. The German ambassador in Moscow, von Schulenburg, was hastily recalled from Teheran, where he had been acting as German representative at an official Persian function, and there followed ten days of anxious debate in Berlin before it was decided to test the ground. Schulenburg returned to Moscow to seek an interview with Molotov. At this interview, on May 20, he very diplomatically broached the idea of reopening the conversations on the conclusion of a German-Soviet trade agreement which had been broken off in March. Molotov's answer, that commercial

talks were meaningless without a political agreement, was so rudely phrased as to cause a fresh wave of indecision in Berlin. So it was not until May 30 that Schulenburg again approached Molotov—this time in a spirit of desperation rather than expectancy. For, in the meantime, on May 24, Chamberlain had announced that agreement between Britain and the Soviet Union was imminent.

Two days before this, however, Ribbentrop and Ciano had finally signed the treaty of alliance known as the 'Pact of Steel'. At the same time an urgent telegram had been sent to Tokyo asking for Japanese accession to the treaty. On May 23 Hitler felt sufficiently sure of himself to reveal his plans to his generals; his speech made it clear that he had decided to attack Poland 'at the first available opportunity'. The conquest of Poland would open the way to the Baltic states, give Germany large extra areas of agricultural land and slave labour, and remove the danger of Polish attack in the event of a show-down with the West.

War was inevitable; but first Poland must be isolated. If Britain and France intervened, then the fight must be primarily with them; if Russia came in on their side then Britain and France must be attacked with 'a few devastating blows' synchronised with the occupation of the Belgian and Dutch air bases. ('Britain is our enemy and the show-down with Britain is a matter of life or death.') If Russia came in, it would also be possible to restrain her by inciting Japan against her. On the other hand, Hitler added, it was not impossible that Russia might show herself uninterested in Poland.

Hitler's war plans

Hitler then ordered the formation of a small planning staff, drawn from all three services, to consider the problems of war with Britain. As he saw it, the first task was to defeat France and occupy Belgium and the Netherlands; after this all German war production could be turned to the Luftwaffe and the fleet, with the aim of blockading Britain into surrender. In the meantime 1943-44 was set as the completion date for the German armaments programme.

In his speech Hitler thus made it clear that he intended to attack Poland that year and that he hoped to be able to do it without drawing in Britain and France. Poland had to be isolated, and it was to this task that German diplomacy was now turned. The isolation of Poland involved essentially three tasks: the detachment of Rumania from the alliance with Poland, the detachment of the Soviet Union from the Western democracies, and the weakening of support for Poland in Britain and France. On the wider plane German diplomacy continued to do its best to keep the Polish question on the boil; to press Yugoslavia, Bulgaria, and Rumania to abandon any idea of a neutralist bloc in the Balkans; to stir up trouble in the Middle East and to wean Turkey away from her new attachment to Britain; to further its attempts to bring Japan into the Pact of Steel.

In the meantime the military planning against Poland went steadily forward; and there was a certain amount of trouble with the new state of Slovakia—which had been formed from the remains of Czechoslovakia

after Munich—over the concentration of German troops building up opposite Poland's southern frontier.

The British government, for its part, had been severely shaken by Litvinov's fall. Everything seemed up to that point to have been going reasonably successfully in the negotiations with Russia. Britain had, in fact, just been about to propose to the Russians a formula which would have ensured a maximum deterrent effect without seeming to commit Poland and Rumania to direct relations with the Soviet Union. It would also, it was believed, have allayed Russian fears, since the proposed Russian declaration of support for the Western allies was only to become operative once Britain and France had honoured their guarantees to Poland or Rumania.

On May 6 Sir William Seeds was instructed to put the plan to Molotov—an experience he found to be profoundly disturbing. Molotov cross-examined him relentlessly, especially on whether there were to be staff conversations with Russia. Three days later *Izvestiya*, one of the Soviet Union's two leading papers, attacked the new British formula as one which would leave the brunt of any resistance to German aggression to the Soviet Union, and revived for the first time the question of a direct German attack on Russia through the Baltic states of Lithuania and Latvia.

Russia seeks a pact

As the Soviet ambassador in London told Halifax the same day, there was no reciprocity. The Soviet Union would be obliged to help Britain and France if Hitler attacked Poland or Rumania, but Britain and France were under no obligation to help the Soviet Union. A formal reply on these lines, arguing that a direct Anglo-Franco-Soviet alliance with concrete military agreements was essential, was presented on May 15. The following day the Soviet ambassador made it clear that the point about a possible German attack through the Baltic states was mainly included to strengthen the argument. The real point was the Soviet demand for a pact of mutual assistance.

Price of Soviet support

What was the Soviet government up to? A clue is provided by an *Izvestiya* article on May 11. The German-Italian alliance, it said, was not directed against the Soviet Union but against Britain and France. Yet British policy (this argument implied) was based on an attempt to get the Soviet Union to do Britain the favour of completing the dam she was trying to build against Germany. In return for what? Nothing. The whole policy pursued by Molotov from May 7 onwards was one of trying to see what could be extracted from the two sides—both of which, according to the Soviet way of thinking, were capitalist, both imperialist, and both obviously set in head-on collision courses.

This Soviet attitude the British government took some time to appreciate. The idea of negotiating with the Soviet Union was itself distasteful to some members of the British government and embarrassingly difficult to reconcile with the wishes of those countries Britain had guaranteed—Poland and Rumania. Others—among them

Churchill, Eden, Vansittart, and their supporters in Parliament—were so obsessed by the need to contain Germany that their normal critical powers were blunted. They could see only the need for speed, and feared that the Soviets would elude Britain's invitation.

No one seems to have seen that the price of Soviet support in eastern Europe would prove one that the Western allies could not, and Germany could easily, afford: Soviet supremacy over the Baltic states and parts of Poland. It took Molotov ten weeks to realise that he was not going to extract from Britain hegemony over the whole of Poland and Rumania—and that he might as well settle for what Germany had to offer.

The British dilemma

In these ten weeks he was to exert himself to raise the British and French offers as much as he could. The first step came on May 27. Molotov's rejection of the British guarantee formula had put the British in an embarrassing dilemma; it appeared that a direct pact with Russia was now unavoidable, for an agreement with Russia now seemed the only way that Poland and Rumania could be aided and Hitler restrained. If negotiations broke down now, at the very least Hitler would feel that he had a free hand again, and there might even be a direct Nazi-Soviet agreement. If Germany was going to attack in the west it seemed essential to the Western powers that the Soviet Union should join their side in the war.

On the other hand, it was argued, a direct pact with Russia would look as if Britain had decided that war was inevitable and that she was forming an ideological bloc against Germany. In such a case Italy, Franco's Spain, Portugal, Finland, and Yugoslavia might well join Germany. Vatican influence could well be thrown to the anti-Soviet—that is, the German—side. Japan would be thoroughly hostile. Would the British public urge Britain to come to Russia's aid if Germany attacked her? The British Chiefs-of-Staff did not rate Russian aid very highly in the event of war with Germany. And there was the continuing refusal of Poland, Rumania, and the Baltic states to be associated in any way with the Soviet Union; if a British alliance with the Soviets were to drive them all over to the German camp, the whole point of concluding such an alliance would be destroyed.

The British solution was to draft a pact which linked to the League of Nations Covenant any aid given to Russia by Britain and France (or vice versa) and to add this pact to their earlier drafts providing for Soviet aid to Britain and France if they were involved in war with any power, as a result of its aggression against any state they had guaranteed or which appealed for their assistance. Provision was made for staff talks—but none, however, for advance Soviet consultation with the states that Britain and France had guaranteed. These, in deference to their susceptibilities were not named, and the rights and position of other powers were expressly reserved. The Soviet ambassador in London liked the draft and remarked that agreement should now be possible. On the strength of this assur-

ance, Chamberlain announced to the House of Commons—where embarrassing questions had been raised about the seriousness of British purpose in negotiating with the Soviet Union—that the conclusion of an agreement with the Soviet Union was imminent.

He was to be rudely disabused of this notion. On May 27 Molotov rejected any mention of the League. Britain, he said, was apparently satisfied with a pact which would allow Russia to be bombed from the air while at Geneva some minor state like Bolivia blocked all counteraction. To Molotov the British proposals seemed calculated to ensure the maximum of talk and the minimum of results.

Molotov's real intentions were revealed in his attack on the clause which reserved the rights and position of the states Britain and France had guaranteed. He demanded that further guarantees be extended to cover these Baltic states and Finland, and reiterated this point strongly on May 31 in a widely publicised speech to the Supreme Soviet. The British ambassador in Moscow commented ruefully on his interview: 'It is my fate to deal with a man totally ignorant of foreign affairs and to whom the idea of negotiation as distinct from imposing the will of his party leader is utterly alien.'

JUNE:
STALEMATE WITH RUSSIA

On June 2 Molotov presented the Soviet counter-proposals. First, the states to be guaranteed must be enumerated in the text of the treaty; the list included three states in the east—Finland, Estonia, and Latvia—and Belgium in the west, all of which had repeatedly declared their unwillingness to accept any guarantees. Second, the Russians demanded that the political terms of any agreement between the Soviet Union and the Western powers should not come into force until an agreement on military assistance and co-operation had been concluded between the three powers.

Much disturbed, Lord Halifax, the British Foreign Secretary, recalled Sir William Seeds for consultations; and, when illness prevented Seeds from travelling, a senior official in the Foreign Office was dispatched to aid him in explaining Britain's standpoint to Molotov. At their first meeting on June 15, they had to face a new barrage of questions from Molotov on the attitude of Poland, Rumania, and the Baltic states. The next day, a new Soviet note accused the British of refusing to consider coming to the Soviet's aid if the Soviet Union supported the Baltic states against Germany. On June 22 Molotov rejected fresh British proposals as 'carelessly drafted' and, on June 29, none other than Stalin's right-hand man on internal matters, Zhdanov, voiced Russia's impatience in an article in *Pravda*. The Soviet insistence that a common guarantee of the three Baltic states should be included in the treaty, despite the strong protests of those states against such guarantees being made, led Seeds to presume that what the Soviet leaders really wanted was an international warrant enabling them to intervene in the Baltic states without the consent—and contrary to the wishes of—their governments.

JULY:
FOCUS ON DANZIG

In a further interview on July 1, Molotov provided Seeds with more material for his suspicions. Seeds had been instructed to yield to the Soviet demands on the Baltic but to ask in return that the treaty be extended to cover the Netherlands and Switzerland. Molotov at once objected to this as a further extension of Soviet commitments and demanded compensation in the form of Polish and Rumanian alliances with the Soviet Union—a proposal which the governments of these countries, allied with each other against the Soviets as they had been since the 1920's, would never have conceded, since they feared Russian aid as much as or more than German aggression.

Molotov further demanded that the treaty should be operative in the event of 'indirect aggression' against the countries named—a concept which he defined as 'an internal *coup d'état* or a reversal of policy in the interests of the aggressor', and which he justified by referring to the German *coup* in Prague in March. It needed little imagination in London to see that Molotov's definition could also cover Soviet action against any government they disliked and distrusted.

But Molotov stuck to this point and to his demand for the simultaneous conclusion of a military agreement, despite British protests throughout July; on July 23, however, he suddenly demanded that military talks should begin forthwith, expressing the belief that these points would present little difficulty once the military got together.

In the meantime, the other British negotiations to secure a front against Hitler were running into difficulties. Agreement with Turkey was fairly easily secured, but the Rumanians were easily scared by German and Hungarian pressure into making specific demands which had the effect of rendering the British guarantee virtually inoperative. The Italians remained at odds with France, for no amount of pressure could make the French see any point in yielding to Italy's demands for territorial concessions—a point of view strongly supported by the new British ambassador in Rome, tough-minded Sir Percy Loraine.

Japanese fury

In the Far East, elements of the Japanese army, furious at the resistance put up by the Japanese Foreign Office and navy in Tokyo to the conclusion of an anti-British alliance with the Axis, tried to force a state of war between Britain and Japan by blockading the British settlement at Tientsin in northern China and subjecting British citizens who attempted to pass through these posts to vulgar and humiliating indignities. Fortunately, the skill of the British ambassador in Tokyo, Sir Robert Craigie, was sufficient to avoid a total breakdown of Anglo-Japanese relations.

Danzig killing

German-Polish relations were meanwhile deteriorating steadily—especially in the always tense area of relations between the Poles and the Nazi-dominated government of the Free City of Danzig. On May 20, a Danziger was shot after an organised demonstration against the Polish customs house inside the boundary of Danzig. The dead man subsequently turned out to have been a member of the Danzig SA; the killer was the chauffeur of the Polish Acting Commissioner in Danzig. On June 3 the President of the Senate of Danzig complained of the increasing number of Polish customs officials (31 had been added since May 20 to the existing total of 75) and ordered Danzig officials to accept no further instructions from them. A week later the Poles replied by refusing to restrict the activities of their customs inspectors and even threatened to increase their number still further.

This retort provoked a rush of German propaganda attacks on Poland, especially during the visit of Dr Goebbels, then Nazi Minister of Propaganda, in mid-June; the attacks were so violent that by the end of June there was a new 'week-end scare' with widespread rumours that the Germans were going to stage a *coup* in Danzig. These rumours became more worrisome when it became known that the Danzig Senate had allowed the formation of a volunteer defence corps and had imported arms from East Prussia.

Comment in the Polish press gained in intensity and, on June 29, Lord Halifax felt impelled to give a strong public warning,

made in a speech to the Royal Institute of International Affairs in London, that Britain would resist any new act of aggression in Europe. On July 19 the Poles complained again of the difficulties placed in the way of the Polish customs officials in Danzig and announced economic reprisals against a Danzig margarine factory, and against the import of Danzig herrings into Poland. At the end of July their complaints were rebutted by the Danzig authorities. During all this turmoil, preparations continued in Danzig for a German take-over at Hitler's command, and the German press continued its propaganda barrage against Poland and Britain.

It was under these circumstances that elements in the British government made a singularly ill-advised attempt to bring to a culmination the policy of appeasement embarked upon two years before. The motive behind this policy had been to convince Hitler that Britain would block any attempt to obtain his way by force, but would not stand in the way of peaceful change in Europe. The policy thus depended on the belief that Hitler would respond to a judicious combination of the stick and carrot.

The aim of British policy since March 31, 1939, had been to convince Hitler that any further aggression would run into the

combined opposition of all the other powers in Europe. By June some people felt that perhaps he should be given another sight of the carrot. Contact was therefore made, not with Ribbentrop, who was believed to be an out-and-out war-monger, but with Göring.

A bait for Göring

The bait held out was participation in a grandiose scheme for joint Anglo-German exploitation of the wealth and markets of Africa and other under-developed areas of the world. Behind this offer lay the notion that the world was divided into 'have' and 'have-not' powers, and that it was this division, with Germany among the latter, which was threatening peace—a naive misconstruction of Nazi ideas which had found wide acceptance in the world in the late 1930's. News of the talks held in London between Dr Wohltat (Göring's representative), Sir Horace Wilson, head of the Treasury and Chamberlain's personal adviser, and Mr Hudson, President of the Board of Trade, leaked out at the end of July and led to bitter attacks on the British government both at home and in the German and Italian press.

This, then, was the situation in the last week of July, when the German plans for

△In the inflamed sector of Tientsin, White Russian soldiers and Chinese demonstrated against Great Britain— 'enemy of the new Asian order'

△Danzig was the real powder-keg, and during the last few months before war broke out Germany laid down a heavy barrage of propaganda: this funeral was for two German soldiers said to have been shot by the Poles on the Danzig frontier

◁ The result of their discussions was announced on August 23, 1939, when an amazed world learned that Russia and Germany, sworn enemies, had signed a ten-year non-aggression pact. Molotov signs while Ribbentrop and Stalin watch

attack on Poland began to mature. Britain was still chasing the will-o'-the-wisp of agreement with the Soviets. On July 27 the dispatch of an Anglo-French military mission to Moscow was announced. The diplomatic front against Italy was in reasonable shape; that against Germany still consisted only of the British and French guarantees to Poland – an increasingly bellicose and determined Poland – while the Soviet Union was still holding out for an offer from Germany. Appeasement of Germany therefore depended on the faint hope of unofficial contacts with Göring.

Germany had still failed to bring off the negotiations for an alliance with Japan. The Italian government still believed that it had assurances from Germany that 1939 would pass without war with the West; the Balkans were in disarray, with Hungary and Bulgaria on the German side, and Yugoslavia leaning towards her. In the Far East Japan was further embroiled in China and was being subjected to increasing economic pressure from America, where President Roosevelt was beginning, gingerly, to flex America's muscles.

In the military field, Anglo-French cooperation was now well advanced, and while Britain was beginning to overtake Germany in the field of war production, France was doing her best, with Roosevelt's aid, to buy modern aircraft from America. Germany's war plans were nearly mature. By this time Hitler needed only to detach the Soviet Union from the West and to provide himself with an excuse for an attack on Poland. He remained convinced that once the British and French saw their hopes of Russian support collapse, they would in turn abandon their support of Poland.

AUGUST: SOVIET SHOCK

The preliminary German approaches to the Soviets, to see if their constant hints of the possibility of an agreement were seriously intended, were made at the end of July, and turned out to be quite satisfactory. On August 3 Ribbentrop followed them up by dropping what he called a gentle hint as to the possibility of an understanding on the fate of Poland, and again there was a positive reaction from the Soviet side.

With that assurance, Hitler proceeded to the next stage – the fabrication of an excuse for war. At the end of July the Danzig Senate, on Hitler's orders, dispatched a deliberately provocative note to the Polish authorities on the customs inspector dispute, threatening reprisals against Polish officials. The Polish reaction was quite as violent as the German authorities could have wished: on August 4 the Polish government told the Danzig Senate that any physical action against the Polish customs officials in Danzig would be regarded as an act of violence against officials of the Polish state.

Hitler now had his excuse for action against Poland, an excuse made more plausible by the violent reaction of the Polish press to the threats made by the Danzig Senate. He summoned the Nazi Gauleiter of Danzig to Berchtesgaden, and gave him instructions on when and how to step up the pressure on Poland, so that a Polish military action against Danzig would

be provoked at the right time for German military preparations, which were then set for any date after August 24.

On August 9 the Polish ambassador in Berlin received a German note protesting Polish intervention in the internal affairs of Danzig. 'Any repetition,' it said, 'would lead to an aggravation of German-Polish relations for which the Poles would be directly responsible.' The following day came the Polish reply; again it was violent and uncompromising. The Poles were determined not to be bullied like the Czechs; and they genuinely believed that they could defeat Germany. Any German intervention in Poland's dispute with Danzig, so ran the reply, would be regarded as an act of aggression. Hitler could now proceed to the next phase of his plan – the isolation of Poland.

At this point, however, things began again to go a little wrong. Since the signing of the Pact of Steel the Italians had been mainly concerned with trying – with rather less success than the Germans – to disrupt the British front in the Balkans and the Mediterranean. Mussolini and his Foreign Minister, Count Ciano, still believed that they had Hitler's promise that no general war should be provoked against the West before 1942; but as August opened, Count Ciano suddenly realised where German policy was going. On the news of the Polish note he descended on Berchtesgaden in an agony of apprehension, where he was met with what he took to be arrogance and deceit. Ribbentrop and Hitler both lectured him for hours; his warnings, that this time Britain was not going to stand aside, were hardly even listened to. He returned to Rome furious with German treachery, convinced that Italy in her own interests must stand aside.

His visit left little impression on Hitler's mind. On August 14 Hitler harangued selected military leaders on the timidity of Britain and France, and that same day the German ambassador in Moscow saw Molotov and proposed that Ribbentrop should come to Moscow to settle matters between them. Molotov replied by proposing a non-aggression pact.

Slow boat to Moscow

In the meantime the Anglo-French military mission was proceeding slowly (by sea, as the French refused to fly and the British to travel by train through Germany) to Moscow. At its first meeting with the Soviet military authorities, on August 12, the mission was confronted at once with three embarrassing questions. Did its members have authority to conclude a military agreement? How did the Western powers propose to react to German aggression against Poland? How did the Western powers envisage the Russians coming to the aid of Poland and Rumania?

Some elements in Russia may have still hoped that the Western replies would show they meant business, and there may even have been some who still thought the Western allies could be brought to force the Poles and the Rumanians to admit Soviet forces *before* war broke out. Others, probably taking the Western answer to this question as the touchstone by which to judge British and French resolution to defend Poland and stand up to Hitler, seem to have

agreed with Hitler that resolution was lacking, that Britain and France were bluffing, and that at the last moment they would desert Poland, or else negotiate another Munich-style settlement at her expense.

Again, the Soviet leadership may have simply taken the inability of the West to force a way for them into Poland as confirmation of what they knew already – that to conclude an alliance with the West meant at best a European settlement for which the credit would go to Britain, at worst an unrewarding war with Germany. Only the Germans offered the chance of a major Soviet advance to the shores of the Baltic and into east central Europe.

Hitler prepares a coup

Hitler certainly thought he detected signs of British unwillingness to back Poland to the bitter end. He devoted himself therefore to preparing everything for the diplomatic *coup* which, in his view, would enable the British to withdraw their guarantee to Poland. On August 15 the Japanese were reported to be still at odds over allying themselves with Germany. The crisis over Tientsin – which had looked at one moment as if it would lead the Japanese into a conflict with Britain sufficient to drive Japan to ally herself with Germany – was fizzling out. Still worse, the Japanese army in northern China, always the most violent and ultra-nationalist, had embroiled itself with the Soviet army at Nomonhan on the borders of Outer Mongolia. In a series of engagements in which several divisions were committed on each side, and which reached their climax in mid-August, the Japanese were defeated with severe losses. The Japanese army's credit sank to an all-time low.

The bombshell

Hitler had, in fact, already turned to Russia. In a series of messages he beat down Russian procrastination and secured Stalin's permission for Ribbentrop to visit Moscow. The news of his visit burst on a startled world late in the evening of August 21. The Nazi-Soviet non-aggression pact was signed in the evening of August 23, together with a secret protocol putting all the Baltic states (except Lithuania), the eastern half of Poland, and the Rumanian province of Bessarabia into the Soviet sphere of influence. The rest of eastern Europe went to Germany.

In the meantime Hitler had already given the order for Danzig to provoke a break with Poland over the customs inspectors' dispute; and he set 4.30 am on August 26 as zero hour for the German attack on Poland. On August 22 he addressed his generals. Britain, he said, was so tied down in the Mediterranean, the Middle East, and the Far East, that it was most unlikely that she would intervene. The pact with Russia had struck the last weapon from her hands. The men he met at Munich would never go to war over Poland, and his only anxiety was that some state might again try to mediate. Poland must be brutally, pitilessly crushed. The next few days were to prove his judgement of Britain and France completely at fault.

The crucial day was August 25, the day on which Hitler had to confirm the order to attack, and at 3 pm that day his order was given. Then came two disasters in rapid succession: at 4.30 pm Hitler heard that the

Europe's Changing Alliances May/September 1939

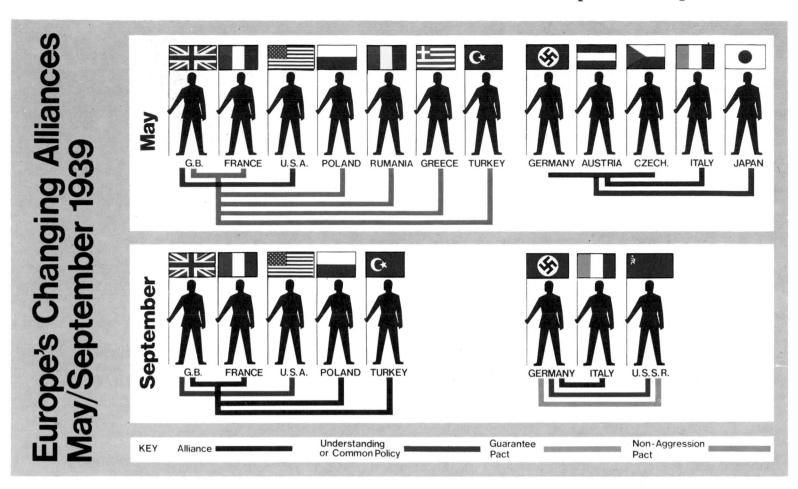

May

G.B. FRANCE U.S.A. POLAND RUMANIA GREECE TURKEY   GERMANY AUSTRIA CZECH. ITALY JAPAN

September

G.B. FRANCE U.S.A. POLAND TURKEY   GERMANY ITALY U.S.S.R.

KEY   Alliance ▬▬▬▬   Understanding or Common Policy ▬▬▬▬   Guarantee Pact ▬▬▬▬   Non-Aggression Pact ▬▬▬▬

alliance between Britain and Poland which embodied formally the guarantee of March 31 had been signed in London. (So Britain was not going to stand aside after all.) And at 6 pm Mussolini, torn between his own feeling of loyalty to Hitler and Ciano's fury at Ribbentrop's double-dealing, told Hitler that Italy could not support Germany without German supplies on a scale which Ciano made sure was well beyond Germany's capacity to fulfil.

A military observer described Hitler as 'considerably shaken' by Mussolini's defection, and at 7.30 pm the order to attack was withdrawn: the German invasion forces had tamely to return to their barracks. As it happened, Japan broke off the alliance negotiations with Germany on the same day, and three days later a new cabinet took over in that country. Hitler's hopes of Britain being distracted by anxieties in the Far East disappeared. The Nazi-Soviet pact had backfired.

The cancellation of the order to attack Poland put Britain and France momentarily in a very strong position. It was, however, one that proved impossible to exploit, since Hitler soon recovered his initiative, and the British government could only proceed on the assumption that the German-Polish conflict was a genuine one which would yield to mediation, and not a trumped-up, stage-managed excuse for war.

Their apparent willingness to mediate, and the increasing evidence of divided purpose in France, gave Hitler heart for a new plan—to lure the Poles into negotiations which could then be broken off in such a way as to put all the blame on the Poles, and to give the British government every conceivable excuse thereafter for backing

down. These proposals were put to the British through a neutral intermediary named Birger Dahlerus, a Swedish businessman who lived in Britain and was related to Göring.

SEPTEMBER:
THE BLITZKRIEG BREAKS

Meanwhile, the German armed forces were commanded to be ready for attack by September 1. The final order was given on August 31. The attack on Poland was begun at 4.45 am the next day.

The German attack on Poland ended any hope of peace with Britain; but the French were still clutching at the hope of evading war, and they persuaded Mussolini to propose a new four-power conference. All through September 1 and the following day, while German bombs were falling on Poland and the Panzers were rolling into action against the Polish cavalry, the British were doing their utmost to get the French into line. Unaware of this back-stage manoeuvring, opinion in the British Parliament and in the country was reaching boiling point. On the afternoon of September 2 the House of Commons, suspicious that a new Munich was under preparation, broke into open revolt, and the Cabinet followed them.

An ultimatum

At 10.30 that evening its members descended *en masse* on Neville Chamberlain as he dined with Halifax, Sir Horace Wilson, and the head of the Foreign Office, Sir Alexander Cadogan. The meeting was brief and accompanied by tremendous peals of thunder. Chamberlain was left no option but to abandon the attempt to get France into line, and leave her only to follow. As

the meeting broke up, a telegram was sent to Sir Nevile Henderson in Berlin instructing him to deliver an ultimatum to Hitler at 9 am the following morning. If German troops did not end all aggressive action against Poland and begin to withdraw from Polish territory by 11 am that day, September 3, then Britain and Germany would be at war. At 9 am on September 3, Henderson arrived at the German Foreign Ministry, but Ribbentrop refused to see him and he was received instead by the Foreign Ministry interpreter, Dr Schmidt. After Henderson left, Schmidt hurried over to Hitler's headquarters; while he translated the British ultimatum the Führer sat 'like one turned to stone'. Finally he turned to Ribbentrop with an angry 'What now?'. As Schmidt left the room to break the news to the crowd of ministers and high-ranking Nazis that thronged the antechamber, Göring turned to him. 'If we lose this war,' he said, 'may heaven be merciful to us.'

Two hours later, as church bells rang in Britain for morning service, the British ultimatum expired. Britain and Germany were at war. The Second World War had begun.

A typical application of the Blitzkrieg technique

Phase 1

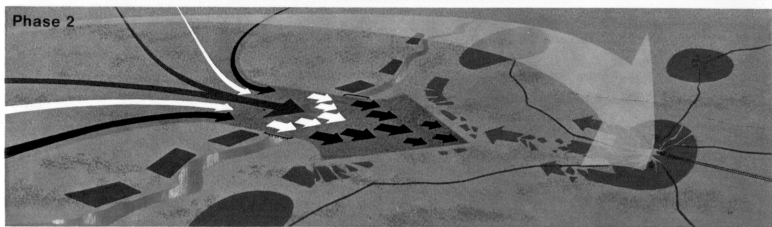

Phase 2

Phase 3

Phase 4

■ Armour	□ Mobile Artillery	■ Motorised Infantry	Dive-bombers and Paratroops	■ Holding Infantry	■ Path of Attack	Defending Armies

Peter Warrington

Blitzkrieg!

Poland September 1/October 6, 1939

Barrie Pitt

The *Blitzkrieg,* with its tactics of speed and shock, was a fresh approach to war, and the overwhelming success of its debut in the Polish campaign surprised not only the Poles but the Germans themselves. Never before had a nation's military capacity been so utterly annihilated in so short a time, with so few losses to the victor

'Blood is the price of victory,' wrote the German military theorist Clausewitz. 'Philanthropists may easily imagine that there is a skilful method of disarming and overcoming the enemy without great bloodshed, and that this is the proper tendency of the Art of War. . . . That is an error which must be extirpated.'

His dictum was seized upon so avidly by the political and military leaders of the world that mankind had to pour out rivers of blood, and to wait over a hundred years, for a practical demonstration of the falsity of Clausewitz's conclusions which might relieve them of the philosophical necessity to try to win their wars by nothing less than the physical obliteration of their enemy's armies. As late as 1917, the British were still attempting to break the German forces opposite them by the simple application of the principle of attrition – using up three British lives to neutralise two Germans, and relying on a numerical superiority of thirteen to eight to leave a British residue when there were no Germans left. This was attrition at its most brutal, and the degree of success it achieved is still a matter of argument.

Military technique

Twenty-three years later, Germany completely destroyed Poland, whose total armed forces exceeded 3,000,000 men, at a cost of less than 10,000 fatal casualties – and did so in so effective a manner that even now it can hardly be claimed that the defeated nation has as yet regained her former status. The explanation of the astonishing difference in military efficiency which this comparison indicates lies in the enormous development in military technique which occurred between 1918 and 1940.

This development was largely the result of the studies and activities of a small group of military thinkers in England, led by Captain B. H. Liddell Hart, who depicted the action of their theories in terms of the play of lightning. Ironically, it was their country's chief military antagonist, Germany, who translated their theories into action – and called the result 'Blitzkrieg'.

An army is composed of men, and has in itself many of the attributes and requirements of a human being. It needs food and drink to keep alive, tools in the shape of weapons to carry out its work, and a constant flow of basic material – ammunition – to produce its finished product – an impotent enemy. Perhaps most important of all, it needs a brain in the shape of a High Command, and a nervous system in the shape of a communications and control network.

The basic principle behind the *Blitzkrieg* technique is that it is simpler, easier, and cheaper to reduce the strength of an enemy army by starvation (cutting off its supplies) or by paralysis (destroying its High Command or cutting its communication and control lines) than by battering it to

Phase 1 Holding infantry keep defenders occupied along whole length of front, and lay smoke-screen to blind them and to conceal mass of attacking armour. Dive-bombers act as long-range artillery to isolate the battleground, cutting off defenders' reserves and silencing defending guns. Armoured spearhead with sappers and shock troops advances to first obstacle – here, a river. Under cover of smoke, artillery, and dive-bombers concentrated at the planned bridgehead, shock troops cross river in rubber boats while sappers erect pontoon bridges. Paratroops may be dropped to disrupt rear areas

Phase 2 Assault troops and demolition squads destroy defending strongpoints where possible and widen bridgehead, as armour crosses river and then moves up through them. Motorised infantry and artillery follow armour, clear up remaining opposition, and hold the flanks. Dive-bombers clear area in advance of armour and keep up attack on communications and reserves
Phase 3 Armoured spearhead has broken through defences, fans out, and by-passes defensive strongpoints. Some engage the enemy rear till motorised infantry comes up; main armour sweeps around key road and rail junctions, paralysing supply, reserve, and

command units. Main infantry crosses river when defenders are demoralised by the chaos behind them. (Every attempt must be made to capture or encircle defenders, not to drive them back.
Phase 4 The first three phases have been carried out at intervals along the whole front: spearheads now plunge deep into enemy territory towards key towns and cities; motorised infantry follows to maintain communications and reduce strongpoints; marching infantry moves in to collect prisoners, surround defending pockets, etc. Second-line infantry moves up to original front, carries out administrative and supply tasks for the forward units

Blitzkrieg: chaos inside the trap

a bloody pulp. It is a recognition of the fact that the judo expert can often defeat a far bigger and more powerful opponent by speed, agility, and efficiency; and above all by attacking him when and where he least expects it. The campaign in Poland was the first practical demonstration of this technique in modern times—in times, that is, since the development of armoured vehicles reintroduced the possibility of movement on a field of battle dominated before by the rifle, the machine-gun, and accurate, long-range artillery.

Vulnerable frontiers

Poland was well suited to such a method of warfare, for in addition to being fairly flat (and at the time of the German invasion, dry and hard-surfaced) her frontiers were much too long for every mile of them to be defended. She was, moreover, flanked by her enemy on both sides—in East Prussia to the north and in the recently occupied provinces of Czechoslovakia to the south—and as it happened, the most valuable areas of the country lay within those flanks. Poland, in fact, protruded like a tongue into hostile territory, and unfortunately it was considered politically necessary for her armies to be deployed in that tongue in order to safeguard the country's prestige and morale despite the military wisdom of deploying them instead behind defences along the wide river-lines of the Vistula and the San.

But Poland's most fatal weakness was in the quality of her armed forces. Though her soldiers were hardy, and brave to a degree which elicited the highest admiration of her enemies, they were in great majority slow-moving, foot-marching infantry; alongside 30 Polish infantry divisions there were only two motorised *brigades* and eleven cavalry *brigades*—and horses are as vulnerable to bullets as any other flesh and blood.

Against this force, spread in defensive positions along that enormous frontier, were to be launched six armoured *divisions,* four light *divisions* consisting of motorised infantry accompanied by armoured units, and four motorised *divisions*—plus 27 infantry divisions whose main role would be to hold the attention of the Polish infantry while the mobile forces raced around the flanks and struck at the vital rear centres of control and supply.

Systematic destruction

But even before the armoured columns had broken through any defensive crust which might impede their progress, the attack on the nerve centres would begin. At 0445 hours on September 1, 1939, bombers and fighters of the German Luftwaffe crossed the frontier and began their systematic destruction of Polish airfields and aircraft, of road and rail centres, of concentrations of troop reserves, and of anything which intelligence or observation indicated as likely to house command headquarters of any status. Within two days they had established German air superiority over Poland, and could then revert to the more purely tactical role of concentrated bombing immediately ahead of the probing tank columns.

These had followed the Luftwaffe across the frontier one hour later. The main German concentration had been along the

southern quarter of the original German-Polish frontier, and at the western end of the old Czechoslovak-Polish frontier. Here had lain Army Group South under General von Rundstedt, comprising from north to south the VIII Army under General Blaskowitz, the X Army under General von Reichenau and the XIV under General List. On the left wing, the VIII Army was to break through between two Polish armies (the Poznan and the Lodz), isolate the Poznan Army in the west, and guard Reichenau's left flank; on the right wing, List's army would break through towards Krakow and then swing east to isolate the Polish Carpathian Army against the mountains.

In the centre, Reichenau's X Army, with the bulk of the German armoured forces, would engage the Lodz Army with infantry while the armour raced around the southern flank, turned north and made contact with Blaskowitz's forces, and then advanced with them on Warsaw. Thus would the main Polish armies be first isolated from each other and their own supplies, and then cut up piecemeal.

In the meantime, Army Group North would have struck—the IV Army eastwards from Pomerania across the Polish corridor into East Prussia where it would join forces with III Army and then strike south, *east* of Warsaw and the Vistula, eventually to join forces with List's armour coming up from the south. Thus two vast encircling movements would be carried out, and any Polish forces which managed to escape the trap west of the Vistula would be caught in the outer trap.

Even Germans confused

It is rare that military plans can be carried out as exactly as was the German plan for the invasion of Poland. By September 4, Reichenau's spearheads were 50 miles into Poland, and two days later they were past Lodz and the whole of the Polish army based on that town was thus isolated. To the south, List's armour had crossed the Dunajec, the Biala, and the Wisloka in turn and then swept on to reach the San on each side of Przemysl, thus opening the way to the city of Lwow and also outflanking the San defences. They then turned north to meet the armoured spearhead of Army Group North, commanded by General Guderian, already across the Narew and storming southwards towards Brest Litovsk over 100 miles behind the battlefront.

At the end of the first week of the invasion, therefore, the confusion in Poland

The inner and outer pincers

was so great that even the instigators of the confusion were baffled. From the German point of view, their inner pincers had met successfully, but the chaos inside the trap was such that they could make little of it. Polish columns marched and counter-marched in their frantic efforts to make contact either with the enemy or their own support, and in doing so raised such clouds of dust that aerial observations could report nothing but general movement by unidentified forces of unknown strength, engaged in unrecognisable activity in pursuit of incomprehensible ends.

A bitter battle

There was thus some argument at German Supreme Headquarters as to whether the bulk of the Polish forces had managed to escape across the Vistula or not. In the event, Rundstedt's view that they had not—in which he was correct—prevailed, and Reichenau's army was as a result wheeled north to form a block along the Bzura, west of Warsaw. Here was fought one of the most bitter battles of the campaign, but one for which there could be only one end. Despite the desperate bravery of the Poles, the odds were too great for them, for they were fighting in reverse, they were cut off from their supplies and bases, and they were coming into action in sections instead of together, against an enemy who had only to hold his position to win. And after the first day of the Bzura battle they were being harried from behind by troops under Blaskowitz along their southern flank, and part of the German IV Army which had swung south-east before actually reaching East Prussia, along their northern flank. The Poles were thus cut off from even the divisional control and supply organisations which had originally accompanied them into their deployment areas. It is hardly surprising that only a very small number managed to break through Reichenau's screen (at night) and join up with the garrison in Warsaw.

The trap closes

The Battle of the Bzura sealed the inner ring in which the Polish armies of the centre were trapped; and the trap itself was formed of armour and sprung by speed—the two essentials of the *Blitzkrieg*. Reichenau's spearhead had reached the outskirts of Warsaw in eight days, having travelled 140 miles in that time, always along the line of least resistance and least expectation—and there it halted and formed a solid bar against which the Poles hammered in vain for another week, while 100 miles to the east the two prongs of the outer trap met as Guderian's armoured corps from the north made contact with Kleist's armour coming up from the south.

From this double encirclement only a small fraction of the Polish army could hope to escape—and this hope faded when, on September 17, the Russian army moved in from the east to take her share of the spoils which had been agreed between the two dictatorships the previous month. Poland ceased to exist and a new international frontier ran from East Prussia, past Bialystok, Brest Litovsk, and Lwow, to the Carpathians.

There had been extended common frontiers between Russia and Germany before, and rarely had they proved anything but sources of constant friction and animosity. In October 1939 a sense of history prompted many to wonder how long such bellicose neighbours could live in harmony.

INVASION OF HOLLAND AND BELGIUM

May 10/May 28, 1940   *Jean-Léon Charles*

Although the Low Countries had the best of reasons for suspecting that they were included in the Nazi plan of conquest—for German military plans had fallen into their hands—they still clung to the hope that somehow their neutrality could protect them from the inevitable. But geography had placed them squarely in the Wehrmacht's path. By moving directly forward across the frontiers in the north, one German army group held the attention of the Dutch and Belgian armies and tempted the French and British forward, while the Panzers of another army group thrust through in the south and reached the sea

German storm troops strike at the Albert Canal in Belgium, one of the Wehrmacht's first targets

Blitz in the west

At 0130 hours on May 10, the Luftwaffe was laying mines off the British and Dutch coasts. At dawn German bombers made fierce attacks on Dutch airfields, destroying a large number of aircraft on the ground, and Army Group B crossed the frontier. The main campaign in the west had opened.

Supported by the II Air Fleet, German airborne troops took the bridges of the Moerdijk and various keypoints of the Vesting Holland (in particular Rotterdam airfield), thus blocking the movement of the reserves for the Dutch forward troops. By evening the German XVIII Army had entered Deventer, Arnhem, and Nijmegen without encountering much resistance—even taking intact one bridge over the Meuse and also penetrating the Peel position. This position was pierced the next day together with the Zuid-Willemsvaart, and at about 1300 hours on May 11 the Germans at last met up with the motorised forward units of the 7th French Army on the move in the vicinity of Tilburg. Having been surprised while on the move, the French had to withdraw on the next day to the line Breda-St Léonard, merging their movement in with the Belgian disposition.

The Germans were thus meeting with success, and this success continued. On the evening of the next day, the IX Panzer Division joined the Moerdijk paratroops, leaving the Dutch command no alternative but to order a withdrawal during the night of the 13th/14th to the Vesting Holland. In order to drive home this success and force a surrender of the Vesting Holland, the Luftwaffe subjected Rotterdam to very heavy bombing during the afternoon of the 14th, and threatened to destroy Amsterdam. The Hague, and Utrecht if resistance continued.

Resistance in the Vesting Holland did in fact cease on the evening of the 14th, and at 1145 hours the next day the Dutch army laid down its arms—except for a few units in Zeeland, which were to continue fighting until the 17th. The units of the Dutch navy, together with Queen Wilhelmina and her government, crossed to Britain to continue the fight there. In the meantime Giraud's 7th Army, now in danger of encirclement, withdrew into Zeeland. Thus, in four days the fate of the Dutch army had been decided at the hands of Küchler's XVIII Army.

Meanwhile, General von Reichenau's VI Army was busy chalking up great successes on the Belgian front. By 0500 hours on May 10, 53 of Belgium's 179 operational aircraft had been destroyed on the ground, and the most important centres of communication had all been bombed. Chaos reigned in Limburg. The population was panic-stricken, refugees were pouring on to the roads, and even some of the military units were in a state of terror. The news reaching GHQ was unbelievable. The Veldwezelt and Vroenhoven bridges on the Albert Canal had apparently already fallen into the hands of the enemy intact, and—most alarming of all—airborne troops were landing on the superstructure of the Eben-Emael fort. Here, just as in Holland, vertical envelopment came as a complete surprise.

However, not all the German operations achieved such immediate success. At Canne, north of Eben-Emael, the gliders landed too far from the objective and the bridge was blown up in time, as were the other bridges on the Albert Canal which the Germans had not attacked immediately. Things were rather touch and go at the Maaseik bridge, however, as the result of a ruse by which the Germans prevented the destruction of the Dutch part of the bridge by dressing up in the uniform of the Dutch constabulary. The Belgian officer on guard, however, succeeded in blowing up his half of the bridge.

Other more orthodox German operations, however, were successful. Paratroops landed between the first and second echelons of the Belgian 7th Division, holding a 19-kilometre front behind the Albert Canal. Stuka dive-bombers harassed the positions and the troops' quarters without respite, preventing any co-ordinated counterattack, and eventually the defences crumbled. In this way the Germans succeeded by the end of the day in setting up two bridgeheads, 2 kilometres deep, fed respectively by the Vroenhoven and Veldwezelt bridges.

The Germans cross the Albert Canal

The news of the German airborne attacks came like a bombshell, and throughout Belgium it produced a psychosis among the population which was fostered unwittingly by the authorities through its warning of infiltration by the Fifth Column. People saw 'paratroops' everywhere, had priests and nuns arrested, and organised search parties. In this way many military organisations were to wear themselves out all through the campaign to no purpose, in the pursuit of imaginary enemies.

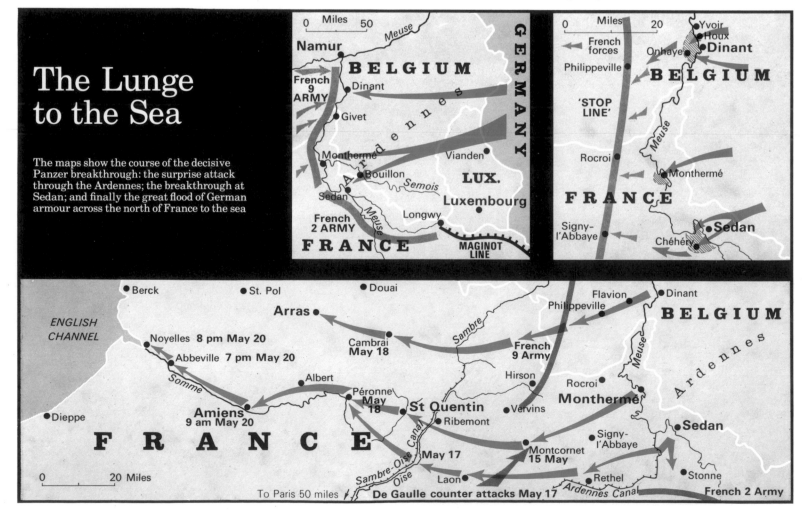

The Lunge to the Sea

The maps show the course of the decisive Panzer breakthrough: the surprise attack through the Ardennes; the breakthrough at Sedan; and finally the great flood of German armour across the north of France to the sea

As a result of their capture of the two bridges, and with the Eben-Emael fort out of action, the Germans were now strongly established on the left bank of the Albert Canal, although the tanks of III and IV Panzer Divisions were held up in Maastricht itself, where the bridges over the Meuse had been blown, until the following day, May 11, by which time a military bridge had been constructed.

This bridge, and those of Vroenhoven and Veldwezelt, were bombed on the morning of the 11th by a squadron of Belgian Fairey Battles, each of which carried eight 50-kg bombs – a ludicrously small armament in view of the size of these bridges which were heavily defended by anti-aircraft artillery. Ten machines of the 15 sent into the attack were lost on this occasion, and later 15 French aircraft carrying 100-kg bombs, followed by 24 Blenheims of the RAF, made other fruitless attacks, both with very heavy losses.

Meanwhile the German tanks were crossing the reconstructed bridge in Maastricht, passing out through the bridgeheads, and reaching Tongres by midday without difficulty. Once beyond this town they arranged themselves in fan order, and by the afternoon one formation arrived at Waremme, thus threatening Liège from the rear.

It was at this moment that Hitler published a communiqué proclaiming the fall of the Albert Canal and the Eben-Emael fort. There can be no doubt that coming as it did at this particular time the proclamation had severe repercussions on Belgian morale and did much to dampen public opinion, many faint hearts seeing in it clear confirmation of German invincibility.

In actual fact, however, matters were progressing according to plan and penetration of this covering line had been expected. By dawn on May 10, the Allied armies were on their way to the main Dyle position, to which the Belgian army began to withdraw on the 11th and *this* was the line of defence which had been selected in order to fight the defensive battle and to block the enemy advance. The position as regards the number of forces to the north of the Sambre-Meuse area clearly favoured the Allies, for they

The withdrawal proceeds according to plan

had almost 40 divisions, including the Belgians, against Bock's 30. The loss of the Albert Canal was therefore really no more than a tactical incident – compared with what was to happen 36 hours later between Sedan and Dinant.

In the Ardennes seven Panzer divisions had been on the move since dawn on the 10th, gaining their main attack positions on the Meuse. In the face of this advance across the provinces of Liège and Luxembourg, the Belgian frontier units and the *Chasseurs Ardennais* destroyed everything as planned (except at Butgenbach) and fell back according to orders in a north-westerly direction to make way for the covering troops of the 9th and 2nd French Armies. Some units, not informed of the withdrawal, even managed seriously to delay the Panzers.

On the evening of the 10th, the French cavalry met up with the Germans in the vicinity of Marche, Saint-Hubert, and Etalle, but the following day they withdrew across the Meuse. Meanwhile Kleist concentrated his resources for a spectacular crossing of the river, which he began immediately, thus piercing the centre of the Allied front. It was here, and not at the Albert Canal, that everything was at stake for the Allied forces.

While the Belgians were at grips with airborne troops on the Albert Canal, the Allied forces had taken up their positions north of the Meuse in accordance with the Dyle Plan. Preceded by light troops who had arrived the evening before, three British divisions dug in on the morning of the 11th on the Dyle, between Wavre and Louvain. Blanchard's army took up positions on the railway between Wavre and Namur, the Prioux Cavalry Corps, which had preceded it, moving on in front to the rivers Mehaigne and Gette, extending the line held by the 2nd Belgian Cavalry Division. There had been some delay in the movement of Blanchard's army because the echelons below divisional level had not been acquainted with the Dyle Plan. On May 10 many of the division commanders were on leave and their deputies had no knowledge of the secret dossier before this date.

Meanwhile the Belgian GHQ had also begun to regroup the army at the 'KW' position. The two divisions of *Chasseurs Ardennais* were withdrawn to Namur and the two Liège divisions were also pulled back – but not without some difficulty, for the Panzers had reached Tongres by midday on the 11th and were threatening the Belgian rear. Fortunately the Germans did not take full advantage of their position and the remnants of the Belgian units where the enemy had broken through retired behind the Gette. This movement, which became general on the 12th, was covered by rearguards on the

Continued on page 25

British machine-gunners in Belgium wait for the assault

A light German gun is wheeled into position — unlike the French artillery the German was geared to mobile warfare

branch canal and the Albert Canal up to Genebos. Meanwhile the Belgian cavalry corps held fast on the Gette, and two French mechanised divisions remained in position on the Mehaigne.

During the afternoon of the 12th, when systematic Luftwaffe bombing of the rear communications took place, French positions between Tirlemont and Huy successfully held off advance units of the XVI Panzer Corps, but elsewhere along the line the only contact with the Germans was with their reconnaissance units.

The infantry units of the German VI Army were in fact rather slow to follow up their armoured screen. They thus failed to exploit one or two confused situations — notably the premature abandonment of some rear-

The Panzers win the first tank battle of the war

guard positions between the Demer and the Albert Canal — and thus gave the Belgian command time to avert a real crisis. Moreover, Reichenau's army seemed to be experiencing difficulty in linking up with Küchler's XVIII Army in the north, and in the zone between them there were few German troops.

This same afternoon of the 12th a conference was held at Casteau, near Mons, attended by King Léopold, M Daladier, Generals Georges and Billotte, and Lord Gort's Chief-of-Staff, Sir Henry Pownall. There was dire need at this moment for an effective organisation of command, and it was now agreed that: 'General Billotte, Commander of 1st Army Group, will act as delegate of General Georges, Commander-in-Chief on the north-east front, to co-ordinate the actions of the Allied forces in Belgian territory'. This vague solution, however, still did not provide the necessary effective command, and it was to cause considerable difficulties later. Indeed, Billotte was to find himself overloaded with work and could do little 'co-ordinating', so that the Belgian command and Lord Gort were left virtually without directives.

Thus the price paid for unpreparedness rose even higher. At Louvain on the evening of May 10, for instance, there had been two divisions, one Belgian and one British, each of which had received orders to occupy the sector; only on May 12, during the Casteau conference, was it decided to give Louvain to the British.

Similarly there was virtually no liaison between the Belgians and the French Light Mechanised Division on the Gette at the very moment the Panzers were attacking in force on May 13. It was the soldiers, thrown hastily into battle amid such confusion, who were to have to pay for such mistakes.

At this stage the front, almost continuous, ran along a part of the Albert Canal, the Winterbeek barrier position, Diest, the Gette, and the Mehaigne. At 1100 hours on the 13th, covered by Stuka dive-bombers and by fierce artillery fire in the area of Hannut, Merdorp, and Jandrain, an attack was led by III and IV Panzer Divisions. The French Somua and H-35 tanks were disposed along the line in small groups, their value wasted by ignorance of their potential

strength when concentrated and by over-confidence in the superiority of their guns and their armour.

This, the first battle of the war to be fought between tanks, clearly underlined the superiority of the offensive manoeuvre — lost from the field of battle for a century — and the advantages of movement over stationary guns. Followed closely by their infantry, the Panzers operated flexibly, surrounding centres of resistance, attacking on the flanks and in the rear, dodging hither and thither when necessary, and infiltrating by another route when one was blocked.

By 1745 hours the French position was overrun, and General Prioux decided to fall back with his light mechanised divisions behind the Belgian anti-tank obstacle of Perwez. The heavy losses incurred by these divisions at such an early stage of the campaign were irretrievable, for this had been the only body of tanks on which the command had relied. But on the other hand losses had indeed been inflicted on the enemy, and the action did at least give the 1st Army, hurrying up behind but delayed by the flood of refugees and by the harrying of the Luftwaffe, time to get into position.

During that night of May 13/14 the Belgian Cavalry Corps fell back to the 'KW' position and in the meantime the infantry had occupied the battle position. On the evening of the 14th the disposition of the troops was as follows:

● From Breskens at the mouth of the Schelde to the north of Antwerp the front was held by three divisions of the 7th French Army, which had been ordered back from its vain mission to Holland. (The off-shore islands were being defended by a few French and Dutch units.) The front then ran south-east to the northern outskirts of Louvain, for 50 kilometres, and this stretch was manned by the Belgian army with three echelons of divisions — eight in the first echelon, three in the second echelon, and two behind the Willebroek Canal, with a general reserve consisting of the Cavalry Corps and the 1st *Chasseurs Ardennais* Division.
● From Louvain to Wavre the front was defended by the British army with five divisions on the Dyle (two in reserve) and four more lying back (one on the Senne, one on the Dendre, and two on the Schelde). This deep disposition was designed to enable Lord Gort to carry out delaying manoeuvres, if required, with the minimum of risk. The wisdom of this deployment was to be confirmed later.
● The front from Wavre to Namur was manned by six divisions of the 1st French Army, with two mechanised divisions in reserve, which were to fight a fierce last-minute covering action in the region of Gembloux-Ernage before withdrawing. Two Belgian divisions defended the Namur position, with the support of the fortress artillery.

Thus the front appeared to be firmly held from the Schelde to the Meuse, and the future seemed bright — except for the alarming news being received from the southern Meuse area, where dislocation was occurring in the face of Kleist's armoured attacks. Could it be that the Allies had played into the enemy's hands after all?

Certainly the German GHQ was overjoyed to see how perfectly its trap had worked. The pivoting of the French 1st Army Group and its immobilisation had allowed complete freedom of action for the proposed

scything operation already started at Sedan. On the evening of May 14 General von Reichenau received the following order: 'Attack the enemy position between Louvain and Namur on the 15th, so as to prevent consolidation of the Allied forces in this position.' But at the same time the possibility of an orderly Allied withdrawal was to be prevented in view of the potential danger it would pose to the racing armour in the south. Hence the Allied armies were to be both attacked and held in position by aggressive fighting.

The III and IV Panzer Divisions, together with a number of infantry divisions, therefore attacked the 1st French Army, the main thrust being made in the direction of Gembloux. The French positions withstood the attack in the main, but their paltry reserves had all been expended in protecting the southern right flank, where the break-up of the 9th French Army was presenting a serious danger. Further north, the Germans succeeded in penetrating into Louvain, in the sector of the 3rd British Division commanded by Major-General B. L. Montgomery, but were dislodged by a counter-attack strongly sustained by artillery early in the afternoon of the 15th, and no other section of the line was threatened. Things were thus going quite well for the Allies on the 'KW', and it will never be known how long this disposition could have withstood a frontal attack, for none developed.

But the fate of these armies was soon to be settled in the south. On the evening of the 15th, realising that the breach in the Sedan front was irremediable, General Billotte made a decision of extreme gravity: the Allied forces in Belgium would withdraw to the line of the Schelde and the old frontier position. This meant abandoning the Dyle Plan and a return to the Schelde project — one of the first solutions contemplated before May 10. However inevitable this decision may have been, it should have been communicated immediately to the Belgians and the British — but Lord Gort only learned of it at 0500 hours on the next day (and then only through an officer whom he had sent to Billotte's HQ and who happened to read the order there before its dispatch). The order did not reach the Belgians until 1000 hours that morning, on the initiative of the Belgian liaison mission.

The Belgians greeted the order with bitterness. To quote the Belgian Deputy Chief-

The Belgians and British are ordered to withdraw

of-Staff, General Derousseaux: 'It came like a shot out of the blue, and, with the subsequent surrender, it is my worst memory of the campaign. The General Staff was stunned by it. We had to shake ourselves back into action and make the necessary preparations for execution of this order.'

The Belgian and British armies now had to carry out an extensive withdrawal over a distance of over 50 miles. The conditions were quite favourable, because the enemy was not yet in a position to mount a systematic attack on the retiring forces, and moreover was deprived, from May 16 onwards, of the XVI Panzer Corps, which had moved south to take part in the great armoured envelopment.

The withdrawal of the northern section of the Belgian forces and the whole British force took place that night in three stages, and was covered by rearguards installed on the waterways along the route – the Willebroek Canal, the Senne, and the Dendre. It also became necessary to protect the northern flank of the withdrawal, as the French 7th Army Division had been ordered south from the mouth of the Schelde. As they cut at right angles across the British and Belgian lines of withdrawal, they created such chaos that they themselves eventually broke up and their commander, General Giraud, was captured on May 18 by a German patrol. Their place on the northern flank was taken by the Belgian Cavalry Corps operating in the Waas country. The two Belgian fortress divisions at Namur were ordered to make their way towards Ghent; the other force to the north, the 1st French Army, withdrew to the Schelde extended by the Sensee, on a line Maulde-Bouchain-Arleux, thus evacuating Belgian territory.

The Germans followed the withdrawal at a respectful distance. According to General von Bock, he was continuously restrained by Halder, who was anxious to limit the role of the VI Army to that of 'protecting the right flank'. Indeed, a surprising slackness was evident in most of the units of the German VI Army. They did not resume any systematic attack before the 17th, for they were actually hampered a good deal by the absence of bridging equipment; General von Bechtolsheim confessed after the war to Captain Liddell Hart: 'The only real difficulty was the crossing of rivers and canals – not from opposition. When the XVI Panzer Corps was taken away, most of the bridging units went with it. . . .'

Action did take place however on the Nethe, the Rupel, the Willebroek Canal, the Schelde – where a surprise crossing was effected by the Germans at Antwerp on May 19 – and on the Dendre, where the 1st *Chasseurs Ardennais* Division was involved in bitter fighting.

The atmosphere was grim at the new Belgian HQ in Bruges during these times. The King had had them installed in an old and uncomfortable castle, in a remote position at the end of a lane and surround-

A crisis of confidence in the Allied Command

ed by water. Only the operations section had proper quarters in which to work, the other sections making do in the entrance hall. It was impossible to check the alarming rumours circulating at once, because of the lack of adequate communications. But as these improved confidence was renewed for a time. After all, the withdrawal could be said to have gone off without a hitch – which was better than had been expected.

On May 20 the Belgian army held the front from Terneuzen to Oudenarde, with 11 divisions in the line and seven in reserve. The British army was positioned on the Schelde from Oudenarde to the frontier, with seven divisions in the front and one in reserve. Anxious about his communications and with little news reaching him of the position on his right flank, Lord Gort now resolved to reinsure this sector himself. He

installed units on the Scarpe, around Arras, and on the La Bassée Canal behind the 1st French Army, as well as other small forces along the canal right up to the coast, thus giving himself some measure of all-round protection.

The British Commander's unease was quite understandable, in view of the atmosphere prevailing at this time in the French GHQ, where, it seemed, nobody fully understood the scale of the disaster. A crisis of confidence therefore arose, one which was to grow incessantly during the next few days.

Meanwhile in France, General Gamelin had been dismissed from office on May 19 at the very moment of issuing orders for a counteroffensive on the flank of the Panzer breakthrough. As it happened, these orders were futile, because of the impossibility of assembling anything like an effective 'mass of manoeuvre' in the short time available. There were, in fact, no reserves left worthy of the name, as Winston Churchill had noted on the 16th during his visit to Paris.

The ageing General Weygand now replaced Gamelin as French Commander-in-Chief; his first acts on assuming office were to cancel his predecessor's instructions for a counteroffensive, and to fly over to the front on the morning of the 21st to see for himself how things were going. In this he ignored one essential point, which was that the II Panzer Division had reached Abbeville at 2100 hours the previous evening, and so the encirclement of the Allied forces to the north was now complete.

Amid the turmoil on May 20, General Ironside, Chief of the Imperial General Staff, visited Lord Gort and General Billotte and conferred with them. Just as ignorant of the position as Weygand, he gave Lord Gort the order to open up the road to Amiens by sheer force, if possible in conjunction with the French and the Belgians, and so restore continuation of a single Allied front.

At first sight this order appeared logical: certainly between May 18 and 21 the Panzers, too far ahead of the infantry, were highly vulnerable to attack, and a gap had formed in their rear. Hitler's ill-advised decision to reverse the roles assigned to his XII and II Armies had delayed the arrival of the support troops by two days. Nevertheless, however good Ironside's idea was (it had actually been mentioned earlier by Gamelin, and was finally to be adopted by Weygand on his own) the time and the resources required for it were sadly lacking.

For his part, Gort reckoned simply on carrying out an operation around Arras with a limited objective, using his 5th and 50th Divisions and his armoured brigade (all sadly depleted by this time), under the command of General Franklyn. The latter had also agreed to concert his attack with one by Generals Blanchard and Prioux, the French even hoping to make a thrust towards Cambrai, there linking up with the new French 3rd Army Group, which was preparing to attack on May 23 from the west.

However, the actual attack, which began at 1400 hours on the 21st, was only on a small scale. The British moved off on their own as the French had not completed their forming up, and General Martel, who was in command of the assault, could mount a raid of only three infantry battalions and 74 tanks – 58 of which were light ones. Nevertheless, the operation, carried out forcefully, came as a complete shock to the forward units of General Rommel's division and the *Totenkopf* ('Death's-head') group. It gained

16 kilometres and destroyed a large number of enemy tanks, before being blocked at about 2000 hours by large-scale Stuka attacks, in the face of which Martel was forced to withdraw his forces that evening.

The psychological effect which this counterattack at Arras had on the German command was staggering. The surprise had been such that Rommel signalled that evening: 'Very heavy fighting took place between 1530 and 1900 hours with *hundreds* of enemy tanks and their supporting infantry . . .', and panic set in at the German GHQ, for the British forces were estimated at five divisions! Hitler undoubtedly felt himself at bay, and sent Keitel to the site of the attack, where the whole disposition was revised. The V and VII Panzer Divisions with the *Totenkopf* and *Schutzen* motorised brigades remained in position as if mesmerised by events – while the VI and VIII Panzer Divisions countermarched in an easterly direction.

Moreover, from this moment onwards the German conduct of operations became ner-

General Weygand plans his counterattacks

vous. Rundstedt was later to say that the Arras attack was the only Allied action which inspired any fear in him in May 1940, and certainly the élan of the Panzer force was badly shaken. They made no more mass attacks after this date and it certainly seems that the action by the 'Frank Force' sowed the seeds of the success of Dunkirk.

It was on this same afternoon, May 21, in the drawing-room of the Chatellenie d'Ypres, that General Weygand called the first – it was also to be the last – conference of the Belgian, French, and British commanders-in-chief of the campaign.

General Weygand had had some difficulty in reaching Ypres himself, for after leaving le Bourget he had touched down near Béthune at 0940 hours to find the airfield utterly deserted: it had been evacuated two days earlier. 'I was thus alone in the country with my ADC,' Weygand writes, 'with no means of contacting those expecting me.' He decided to fly on to Calais airport, which was still functioning, and there he landed at 1300 hours. Once there a telephone call brought a car to take him finally to Ypres, but he found that only King Léopold and his military adviser, General Van Overstraeten, had arrived. Billotte came in later, but Lord Gort was not in time to meet Weygand at all.

Without delay, Weygand presented his plan: his object was to close the present breach by simultaneous counterattacks from both north and south – from the encircled forces and from those on the Somme. This required a withdrawal of the Belgian troops to the Yser in order to gather enough units for the counterthrust, and in any case he considered that the Belgian army had 'stayed too long in the east'. General Van Overstraeten, however, was against this plan. 'The new withdrawal will have a serious effect on morale,' he said. 'The Yser position is not prepared, the rear is paralysed by hundreds of thousands of refugees, the Belgian army is weary and some of its units are breaking up. Our army will put up

Continued on page 29

Below: **Stuka strafes refugees.** *Below right:* **Refugees block French armour.** *Bottom:* **Waffen SS troops in Belgium**

27

German infantry were not baulked by Holland's water obstacles

a good fight in its present disposition, but if it has to undertake a further extensive withdrawal, I can't guarantee anything.'

In the course of the conversation which followed, it suddenly became apparent that Weygand was unaware that the Germans had actually reached Abbeville the previous evening, and this unexpected news completely disconcerted him. Moreover, in the meantime Billotte had arrived and gave a realistic account of the disastrous position of his army group, which made it clear that the British army was now the only effective offensive instrument to hand. Weygand himself then admitted the difficulty of withdrawing the Belgians to the Yser, and agreed to their remaining on the Ghent-Terneuzen Canal, and the Schelde, provided that British divisions earmarked for the counterattack could be relieved—for he still felt that only by this counterattack could the situation be saved.

It now remained only to persuade Lord Gort to agree to the plan—but by the time he finally arrived at Ypres, General Weygand had been forced to leave, for he had promised Reynaud, the French President of the Council, that he would return to Paris that evening. Lord Gort brought news that the Germans had crossed the Schelde near Oudenarde. In his opinion a withdrawal to the Lys was now inevitable—especially since the water level of the Schelde had fallen dangerously low, a result of flooding operations carried out upstream by the French in an effort to check the German advance. Lord Gort also thought the Allies incapable of mounting a strong and immediate counteroffensive, for the British divisions were strung out over incredibly broad fronts, while the French armies were already cut to shreds.

When the discussions ended around 2000 hours, it had been decided to move the Allied forces to a new front marked by Valenciennes, the French Schelde (the Escaut), the old frontier position from Maulde to Halluin, and the Lys. The Belgians and the French were to relieve three of the British divisions, but even then no more than five divisions could be mustered for the offensive to the south, decided on for the 23rd.

Unfortunately, this already delicate situation was now made even worse. While returning to his HQ from the conference, General Billotte was fatally injured in a road accident and thus the principal figure of the conference vanished from the scene without being able to give his orders: it was noon the following day before his successor at 1st Army Group, General Blanchard, learned of the decisions made at the conference, and the steps which had been taken. As it happened, further co-ordination proved impossible. Events moved so fast that Generals Weygand and Blanchard were unable to exercise any control over the northern forces, and each army thus operated separately for the rest of the campaign.

The Panzers had therefore covered the 380 kilometres separating Bastogne from the coast in barely ten days. Their scything operation, conducted up to May 21 with remarkable adroitness, completely routed their opponents; yet despite this impetus, the German forces were still to take 16 more days to cover the last 30 miles between Abbeville and Dunkirk.

Nevertheless, during the night of May 22/23 at the German GHQ, General von Brauchitsch summed up the situation correctly, fearing little from the Allied armies, and ordering his army groups to continue vigorously with the envelopment. Army Group A was to swing rapidly northwards to a line through Armentières, Ypres, and Ostend; Army Group B was to wheel its left flank around to face the north, thus strengthening the walls of the trap.

General von Rundstedt, commander of Army Group A, showed no enthusiasm for a move northwards, however. Disturbed by the deployment of the re-formed French 7th Army, now on his southern flank, and by the Arras counterattack, he decided on the evening of the 23rd, in conjunction with Kleist, to regroup his armour on the line Gravelines, Saint-Omer, Béthune—where it temporarily halted. This at least gave the British another day in which to strengthen defences along their western flank.

That same evening of May 23, Brauchitsch at the German GHQ, totally unaware of Rundstedt's decision, resolved to transfer Klüge's army from Rundstedt's Army Group A to Bock's Army Group B, thus placing under a single command all units charged with the task of liquidating the encircled pocket of Allied forces. The order was to come into force at 2000 hours on the following day, and may well have sealed the fate of the Allies. But at this point Hitler intervened. At 1130 hours on May 24, on a visit to Rundstedt's HQ at Charleville, he learned of Brauchitsch's instruction and straightaway cancelled it—not only approv-

Hitler intervenes to halt Rundstedt's armour

ing Rundstedt's decision to halt the armour, but also giving orders for the halt to be made permanent and not temporary.

Meanwhile the pocket of encircled Allied forces was proceeding with the withdrawal decided on at Ypres. The British army re-established itself on a line marked by Maulde and Halluin (which it had occupied before May 10) and on the Lys up to Menin. Threatened with encirclement at Arras, General Franklyn took shelter behind the 'canal line' along the western flank of the pocket. The Belgian army withdrew in two stages to behind the Lys and the branch canal from Deynze to Heist on the coast, covered by units left in the Ghent bridgehead and on the Terneuzen Canal. Behind the front conditions were becoming impossible, for the obstruction caused by the mass of fleeing refugees, the bombing raids all along the coast, and the first hasty stages of evacuation were all contributing to the chaos.

Twelve divisions of German Army Group B were now assembled for the 'last round' of the battle. General von Küchler's XVIII Army, extricated from the Netherlands, regrouped on the line of the Terneuzen Canal, which it crossed on the afternoon of May 23. That evening the Germans were in position all along the Lys and were infiltrating into the Ghent bridgehead, which was then to be abandoned. In addition, the Luftwaffe had by now achieved complete command of the air.

By dawn on the 24th the Belgian army was arranged in an arc 95 kilometres long, extending from Menin to the sea and in contact everywhere with the enemy. The Lys, only 20 to 30 metres wide, offered them no real protection: its water level was low, the dikes and curves of the river complicated the defence, while the south bank was higher than the north and thus gave more cover to the Germans. The morale of some Belgian units, despite severe losses of men and material, remained excellent, but in other units defeatism had found a foothold. The Luftwaffe was dropping thousands of sketch-maps showing the desperate position of the encircled armies, and the crowds of refugees cast a profound gloom over the troops.

During the night of May 23/24 and the next morning, German artillery pounded the positions between Courtrai and Menin, while Stukas extended the attack to the rear areas. At the beginning of the afternoon the attack on the main defensive positions was launched by four divisions which crossed ·the Lys on both sides of Courtrai, breaking through the Belgian 1st and 3rd Divisions.

From a strategic point of view, the place of attack had been well chosen. Close to the joint of the Belgian and British armies, it threatened Belgo-British liaison and—if it succeeded—could cut off the centre and northern sections of the Belgian army from its allies. However, the command realised the danger and reacted rapidly: the breach was plugged that evening by the remaining reserves—a manoeuvre which has since been unjustly criticised on the grounds that those reserves should not have been engaged so early in the battle. But what else was the command to do?

Lord Gort certainly realised the danger of the threat, especially after a patrol of the British 3rd Division had carried out a daring raid and captured the German VI Army orders, which revealed that Menin was the axis of the German thrust. For the British, a breakthrough on the Belgian front would be critical, for it was essential to keep open a line of communication to the coast, and the corridor through which it passed was now shrinking hour by hour. On May 25 Lord Gort therefore decided to utilise the reserves, which were still held back for the southern counterattack, to occupy a barrier position along the canal from Comines to Ypres, and along the Yperlée up to the Yser. In the meantime the Belgians held the line to which they had been forced back by the German attacks, between Roulers and Menin.

King Léopold had meanwhile issued a *proclamation pathétique* to the troops: 'The great battle which we feared has begun. It will be hard. We shall fight with all our strength and with supreme courage. We shall struggle on this soil where we victoriously halted the invader in 1914. Belgium expects you to honour the flag. Soldiers, whatever the outcome, my fate is with you.'

At 0700 hours on May 25 the Germans had broken through and formed a new bridgehead further to the north, on the branch canal just north of Deynze; and although the King's hopes were to be dashed by one division which had been soured by propaganda and showed no inclination to fight, on the other hand his call was answered by a splendid counterattack by the *Chasseurs Ardennais*, which slowed the enemy attack.

The front was not pierced elsewhere that day, but by the evening two pockets were beginning to form—one around Courtrai, over a 25-kilometre front 6 to 8 kilometres

Continued on page 32

'Widespread paratroop drops spread panic across the countryside'   'The news of the German airborne attacks came like a bombshell

deep, and the other on both sides of Deynze, 5 kilometres wide and 3 kilometres deep.

The hours of the Belgian army were now numbered, and on the following day, May 26, the fatal crisis loomed up. In the west, the Germans attacked at dawn, with venom, on a line between Gheluwe and Iseghem. The Mandel Canal was crossed near Ingelmunster, and the two bridgeheads set up the previous day were thus united, while further away to the north, the Deynze-Heist branch

The Admiralty signals 'Operation Dynamo must begin'

canal was forced above Eeklo. The air was never empty of German aircraft, which now terrorised the rear areas, bombing Roulers, Tielt, and Ostend, and dispersing the population and choking the roads with fleeing refugees.

Appeals for reinforcement streamed into the GHQ, which now had to contend with danger on six different fronts. There were only the remnants of three divisions in reserve, and all had suffered rough treatment in the last few days. The 3rd Division, for example, could muster only 1,250 men; all its heavy weapons had been abandoned or destroyed in battle, and the merging of units within the division created inextricable confusion, making the job of exercising command increasingly more difficult.

It was in fact a matter of surprise that there was still a continuous front—but although the Germans had made effective

breaches at many points, each time the opening had been plugged at the last minute.

On the afternoon of May 26 the King sent Blanchard the following message: 'The Belgian command requests you to inform the Commander-in-Chief of the Allied armies that the situation of the Belgian army is grave and the Belgian command intends to continue the fight to the very end. Nevertheless, the limits of resistance have now practically been reached.'

Lord Gort had also been told that 'the Belgians now have no forces available to block the advance on Ypres. The idea of withdrawal to the Yser should therefore be discounted, for it would destroy our units more rapidly than a battle, and without loss to the enemy. The order has been given to extend the inundations to the east bank of the Yser, prolonged by the Yperlée, but it should be noted that the waters will only rise slowly because we are now in the period of low tides.'

Meanwhile the British command had taken the ultimate decision. At 1857 hours the Admiralty signalled 'Operation Dynamo must begin'—the signal to begin evacuating troops from the Belgian and French coasts.

It was in these tragic circumstances that the last day of fighting of the Belgian army dawned. The main weight of the German attack was now concentrated on the centre of the Belgian front, towards Tielt, where an opening 5 miles wide was breached by the end of the morning. There were no means for plugging this breach, so the road to Bruges was open.

King Léopold then sent the following message to Lord Gort at 1230 hours on May 27: 'The army is very discouraged. It has been fighting continuously for four days under intensive bombardment, and the moment is approaching when it will be unable to continue the fight. In these circumstances, the King will find himself

forced to surrender to avoid a collapse.' The French military mission also received a warning in this vein at 1430 hours.

Very early that same morning, Admiral Keyes, head of the British military mission to Belgium, had passed on a message from the King of England to King Léopold urging him to leave Belgium and continue to lead Belgian resistance from England. The latter had retired immediately he received this, with Queen Elizabeth the Queen Mother, and shortly afterwards he informed Admiral Keyes that this was simply a repetition of the arguments which his own ministers had used a few days earlier. King Léopold and the Queen Mother had steadfastly resolved to stay in Belgium. Keyes then went to La Panne, where he telephoned Churchill, telling him of King Léopold's decision and reporting that the Belgian army was incapable of continuing the resistance further, even for a single day.

At 1600 hours the Belgian command concluded that since all their fighting power was now exhausted, the dispatch of a truce mission would gain for their allies a little extra

The Führer demands unconditional surrender

time: the night of May 27/28 and part of the morning of the 28th—which was, as it happened, exactly what would have been gained by continuing the struggle, but in that case at the cost of catastrophic dislocation.

The heads of the Allied missions were immediately informed that a truce mission was leaving to learn the conditions of a cessation of hostilities between the Belgian and the German armies. The French General Champon protested because the Allies had not been called in to state their views and in

A bridge is blown up in Louvain before advancing Germans

his opinion the negotiations should only be begun by common consent. But he was told that the mission was being sent simply to enquire the 'conditions' for a suspension of arms. Nevertheless, at 1830 hours Champon sent a telegram to General Weygand, who then sent to General Blanchard the following instructions: 'The French and British governments are agreed to order General Blanchard and Lord Gort to defend the honour of their flags by disassociating themselves completely from the Belgian army.'

At 1700 hours Major-General Derousseaux, the Belgian Deputy Chief-of-Staff, had left for the German lines. By a devious and protracted route he eventually reached the command post of an army corps general, who passed on his message directly to the German GHQ. The reply was clear and to the point: the Führer demanded unconditional surrender.

It was 2230 hours before General Derousseaux got back to the Belgian GHQ by the same devious route and after an eventful journey. At 2300 hours King Léopold, in conjunction with his Chief of General Staff, decided to accept the conditions and proposed that the cease-fire should come into operation at 0400 hours on May 28. Meanwhile the 60th French Division, still under Belgian command, was moved across the Yser by trucks and that evening the French military mission left the Belgian GHQ for La Panne.

Admiral Keyes, who had also gone to La Panne to inform London of what was happening, returned to see King Léopold in Bruges at 2300 hours, with a new and pressing invitation from Churchill to go to England. When the King again declined, the Admiral took his leave and went to Nieuport, where Colonel Davy awaited him, and there the Admiral and his staff searched for means of departure. They found a fishing

vessel, but soon afterwards heard the engines of a torpedo-boat, so the name 'Keyes' was signalled by means of a torch, and the next instant three torpedo-boats pulled in. The mission's vehicles were then driven into the deep waters of the port, and by dawn the British military mission to Belgium was on its way to Harwich.

Firing ceased along the Belgian front at

Germans receive Rotterdam's surrender

0400 hours on May 28, 1940, except in the Roulers-Ypres sector, where units without communications continued fighting for two more hours.

At 1030 hours the Belgian command received a message from the German High Command—via its truce mission at the command post of General von Reichenau, near Renaix—requesting unhindered passage for German columns in the direction of the sea. A copy of this message was sent

immediately by dispatch-rider to the French mission at La Panne—telephone communications being out of order—but it was brought back, as General Champon had already left Belgium. By 1100 hours the German columns were moving towards Dixmude and Ostend.

From then on the only resistance to Bock's forces in the area from Nieuport to Comines was to come from General Alan Brooke's 2nd Corps, reinforced by the British 3rd and 4th Divisions, the artillery of the British 1st Corps, and the 60th French Division.

And it was here, on the ground where thousands of British soldiers of the First World War lay buried, that the heroic defence of the Dunkirk perimeter began.

JEAN-LÉON CHARLES was born at Quaregnon, Belgium, in 1922 and studied at the Athénée Royal (at Antwerp) and at the Flemish Cadet School. During the war he served in the Belgian Resistance Intelligence (Groupe Bayard), and was mentioned in dispatches and decorated. At the liberation he volunteered for the Belgian infantry as a regular officer, and in 1960 he passed into the cadres of the reserve, where he is now a major. From 1953 to 1955 J. L. Charles was Professor of Military History and Tactics at the Preparatory School for Second-Lieutenants, and from 1957 to 1963 he taught history at the Royal Military School in Brussels, where he became Deputy-Professor in historical critique, military history, and contemporary history. In 1962 he was awarded his doctorate in philosophy and letters by the University of Liège. He is the author of numerous articles on military/ historical subjects.

The centre of Rotterdam was destroyed by an artillery and air bombardment on May 14, 1940

Dunkirk May 24/June 4 1940 *Christopher Hibbert* Operatio
Dunkirk (below) – could have been one of the worst disasters i
the Blitzkrieg, the BEF appeared to be at the mercy of the Luftwaff
army. But Göring had not reckoned on the nullifying effect of th
or on the gallant and unstinting efforts of the civilians who helped t

OPERATIOI

ynamo — the attempt to evacuate the Allied troops besieged at
ilitary history. Trapped within a tiny perimeter and exhausted by
hich, Göring claimed, could annihilate them without help from the
and on his bombs, or on the brilliant direction of Admiral Ramsay —
scue over 330,000 troops in nine days.

N DYNAMO

△ Queues of British and French troops waiting to be rescued   ▽ Part of the varied armada that rescued the trapped BEF from Dunkirk

'These orders from the top just make no sense,' General Franz Halder, Chief of the German General Staff, wrote angrily in his diary on the morning of May 26, 1940, 'the tanks are stopped as if they were paralysed.'

The anger was real and justified. Two days before, the Führer had visited the headquarters of Rundstedt's Army Group A at Charleville. At that time the German armies were still maintaining their astonishing success—the Belgian front was close to collapse, and in the south Kleist's Panzer group, comprising the two armoured corps of General Reinhardt and the brilliant Heinz Guderian, had reached the mouth of the Somme at Abbeville and after sweeping round to take Boulogne and envelop Calais had come to within a dozen miles of Dunkirk. Caught in the trap between this armour and the German armies advancing remorselessly from the north-east were the Belgian army, ten divisions of the French 1st Army, and the bulk of the BEF. The Germans were poised for their final and spectacular victory. Yet shortly after Hitler's arrival at Charleville an order was issued to stop the armour dead in its tracks.

For days, so Halder had noted in his diary, the Führer had been 'terribly nervous'. 'He is worried over his own success,' Halder went on, 'will risk nothing, and insists on restraining us. . . . He rages and screams that we are on the way to ruining the whole operation and that we are courting the danger of a defeat. He won't have any part in continuing the drive westward, let alone south-west.'

Hitler's nervousness was increased and his opinions confirmed when he arrived at Charleville on May 24 to be advised by Rundstedt that the Panzer divisions ought to be brought to a temporary halt on the line of the canalised river Aá until more infantry could be brought up. For Rundstedt, like most of the other higher German generals, had not really believed in the possibility of the Panzers' triumphant thrust; he was haunted by the fear that it could not be continued, and had, in fact, made no plans for the immediate further use of the Panzers once they had reached the sea. And so, despite the fact that at this time there was only one British battalion covering the Aá between Gravelines and St Omer, Rundstedt strongly urged that a pause was needed to make up depleted strength and regain lost balance before the 'last act' of the 'encirclement battle' which the Commander-in-Chief, von Brauchitsch, had ordered him to complete. Already there had been a strong British counterattack southward from Arras which Rommel's VII Panzer Division had had difficulty in checking. Furthermore, nearly half Army Group A's armoured vehicles had been put out of action either by the enemy or by wear and tear. In fact, instructions for a temporary halt to give time to close up and regroup had been issued the evening before. Hitler immediately agreed with Rundstedt's arguments; and the instructions for a temporary full stop became the fateful order for a definite full stop.

It was not only, though, that Hitler was anxious that his armour should be conserved for the later operations that he felt would be necessary against the French south of the Somme, rather than become involved in the bad tank country further north, where canals, dykes, and floods rendered movement so limited and hazardous. For, so General Blumentritt, Rundstedt's chief of operations, said after the war, Hitler had a political motive, too. He believed that after he had concluded 'a reasonable peace with France, the way would be free for an agreement with Britain'. It would not benefit Germany to bring Britain to her knees; and a painful humiliation would merely make it more difficult to come to terms with her.

'Hitler astonished us,' Blumentritt said, 'by speaking with admiration of the British Empire, of the necessity for its existence, and of the civilisation that Britain had brought into the world . . . He said that all he wanted from Britain was that she should acknowledge Germany's position on the Continent . . . His aim was to make peace with Britain on a basis that she would regard as compatible with her honour to accept.'

Generals accuse Göring

But apart from political considerations, however influential they may have been; apart from his fear of a reversal that loomed over his joy at his initial success; and apart from his anxiety to conserve the army's strength for the final crushing of the French in the south, there was another reason behind Hitler's order which so frustrated Halder and Brauchitsch. That reason, as the generals became convinced during the following week, was Hermann Göring.

'Göring, who knew his Führer well, took advantage of his anxiety,' Halder believed. 'He offered to fight the great battle of encirclement alone with his Luftwaffe, thus eliminating the risk of having to use the valuable Panzer formations . . . He wanted to secure for *his* air force, after the surprisingly smooth operations of the army up to then, the decisive final act in the great battle, and thus gain the glory of success before the whole world.'

If the victory could be claimed exclusively by the army generals, 'the prestige of the Führer in the German homeland would be damaged beyond repair. That could be prevented only if the Luftwaffe and not the army carried out the decisive battle.'

While the Luftwaffe prepared to fight this battle, Lord Gort prepared to fight his. Still under orders to carry out the Weygand Plan of a breakout towards Cambrai, Gort realised by the 25th that such an attack had little chance of success. With Belgian resistance crumbling fast, and with no sign of a complementary attack northwards by the French, the British Commander-in-Chief could no longer be in doubt that his only hope for survival lay in breaking out to the sea while an escape route was still open.

Already, to General Weygand's annoyance, Gort had had to order Major-General Franklyn to withdraw from the Arras area with the 5th and 50th (Northumbrian) Divisions. And now, further north on either side of Courtrai, units of General von Bock's Army Group B had opened a heavy new attack on the Belgian line. If this attack were successful, as seemed likely, the flank of the British 2nd Corps, commanded by Lieutenant-General Brooke, would be laid dangerously bare. For the moment the BEF line facing north-west was relatively quiet—the 48th (South Midland) Division around Cassel, the 44th (Home Counties) Division near Aire, and the 2nd Division on the right of the French near Carvin were all benefitting from Hitler's order to stop and regroup. But who could say when the attack would be resumed? Even then the French 1st Army was under attack in the area of Denain.

At 0700 hours on May 25, Sir John Dill, Vice-Chief of the Imperial General Staff,

Some survivors from the *Bourrasque* managed to clamber aboard a nearby ship

Paul Popper

arrived from London at Gort's headquarters in the chateau at Premesques. The previous day Churchill, who was anxiously awaiting the news of a British counterattack, had sent a message to Lord Ismay criticising the conduct of Lord Gort and his troops—a message which he later admitted did 'less than justice' to them. But it was immediately clear to Dill that there was 'NO blinking the seriousness of the situation'.

'BEF,' he reported back to the Prime Minister, 'is now holding front of 87 miles with 7 divisions . . . Germans in contact along whole front and are reported to have penetrated Belgian line north-east Courtrai yesterday evening . . .'

That evening Gort made up his mind. Shortly after 1800 hours he came out of the drawing-room of the chateau where he had spent a long time alone studying his map. According to the British historian, David Divine, he then walked next door into the office of his Chief-of-Staff, Henry Pownall.

'Henry,' he said, 'I've had a hunch. We've got to call off the 5th and 50th Divisions from the attack to the south and send them over to Brookie on the left.'

'Well, you do realise, sir,' General Pownall said, 'that that's against all the orders that we've had and that if we take those divisions away, the French 1st Army is very unlikely to attack without British support?'

'Yes, I know that quite well. All the same it's got to be done.'

So the decision was finally taken. It had been an agonising decision to make. But it saved the BEF.

Admiral Ramsay takes charge

Five days before, on May 20, a meeting had been called at Dover in the deep galleries of the east cliff below the castle. Here, in a large room which had held an electrical plant during the First World War and was consequently known as the 'Dynamo Room', Vice-Admiral Bertram Ramsay had opened a discussion of the 'emergency evacuation across the Channel of very large forces'.

Ramsay, an enterprising, clear-headed, somewhat aloof and decidedly didactic officer of 57, whose career had been impeded by an inability to accommodate himself to the idiosyncrasies of his superiors, knew the Straits of Dover well. He had served there in the First World War, and in 1938 had been called from the Retired List to examine the harbour and port and the state of their defences. On the outbreak of war he had taken over command as Flag Officer in Charge.

His first main problem, of course, was to find enough ships to evacuate so large a number of men in the short time which would be allowed him. At the time of this conference on May 20, it was believed that although three French ports would be available—Calais and Boulogne, as well as Dunkirk—no more than 10,000 men could be taken from each of them in any 24 hours and that even this number could not be reached if there were more than 'moderate interference'.

Heavy ships could not be used because of the tortuous channels and shoals off the coast, and because the threat from shore batteries would be greatly increased by the threat from the air. Of lighter ships, though, there was a serious shortage. Over 200 destroyers had been in service when war was declared, but many had since been lost or damaged and many more could not be spared from duty elsewhere.

Fortunately, in addition to the passenger-ferry steamers, most of which had ▷

After the last of the little ships had
gone the beaches of Dunkirk were
littered with the debris of an army

been specially built to operate in the Channel ports, and in addition to the self-propelled barges which could also operate in these waters, there were available 40 Dutch coasters *(schuits)* which had steamed over after the fall of Holland and which were now manned by crews of the Royal Navy. With the help of these and other smaller ships, including paddle-steamers and pleasure craft (a list of which was already being prepared) it was hoped that Operation Dynamo—the code name given to the proposed evacuation—could be carried out with some degree of success.

The plans had rested, however, on the assumption that three ports would be available. But by May 23 the II Panzer Division had begun its irresistible attack on Boulogne; and three days later, after a stubborn defence against dive-bombers, fighters, tanks, and infantry, the remnants of Brigadier Nicholson's force were captured in Calais Citadel. The whole concept of Operation Dynamo was already in jeopardy.

The protracted defence of Calais, described by Guderian himself as 'heroic, worthy of the highest praise', had, however, given Lord Gort time in which to develop his plans for the BEF's fight for its existence.

As early as May 19 he had given an evacuation by sea as one of the possible courses open to the BEF and soon afterwards General Pownall had ordered Colonel Lord Bridgeman to prepare the necessary plans. At that time the Channel ports were open all the way from Boulogne to Zeebrugge. Now the only stretch of coastline still in Allied hands was the 30 odd miles between Gravelines and Nieuport, either side of Dunkirk. The difficult task that faced Gort was to keep open the corridor by which his men might reach it.

By the evening of May 25 the Belgians had expended their last reserves and their front had been broken between Geluwe and the River Lys. The next day the British 5th Division, which had now been moved up to General Brooke's support in this area, was being threatened by three of Bock's divisions, and, on the western front, Hitler had authorised the resumption of Rundstedt's advance by 'armoured groups and infantry divisions in the direction Tournai-Cassel-Dunkirk'. A new pincer movement had thus been started which threatened completely to encircle the French around Lille and the whole of the BEF.

Only one course

There could be no doubt in London now that Gort's decision, which he had taken entirely on his own initiative, would have to be endorsed. On May 26 Anthony Eden, Secretary of State for War, sent Gort a telegram in which he said that if the information he had received was true 'only course open to you may be to fight your way back to west where all beaches and ports east of Gravelines will be used for embarkation. Navy will provide fleet of ships and small boats and RAF would give full support. As withdrawal may have to begin very early, preliminary plans should be urgently prepared'.

Preliminary plans already had been prepared. Lieutenant-General Sir Douglas Brownrigg, the Adjutant General, had been ordered to organise the evacuation of all administrative and training units and other non-combatant troops which would prove an embarrassment to the withdrawal of the front-line troops. And a scheme had been drawn up with the French General Blanchard, commanding Army Group 1, for a withdrawal behind the Lys Canal west of Lille and for the subsequent formation of a bridgehead with its base along the Lys. Here, it was at first intended, a stand could be made against the Germans with—the phrase is Blanchard's—'no thought of retreat'.

It soon became clear, however, that it would be impossible to hold a perimeter on the Lys. By midday on the 26th, when Hitler's order for the resumption of the attack had taken its effect, heavy fighting had broken out along the western front in the area held by the 2nd Division; and further to the south-east Brigadier Churchill's brigade in the 50th Division, which had not yet left to reinforce Brooke, was drawn into the battle at Carvin.

The 5th Division, with Muirhead's brigade of the 48th Division under command, had been transported through the night to fill the gap between the Belgians and Brooke's left flank. But no sooner had they arrived in position there than they, too, were under heavy attack, and three battalions of the 1st Division were drawn into their battle, which raged all day.

And all day long, behind them to the west, the 2nd Division fought furiously against dive-bombers, artillery, and the armour of General Hoth to keep the narrowing corridor open. By dusk the division had been reduced to the size of a single brigade. But there was still a gap between them and Franklyn's reinforced 5th Division holding bravely on to the line between Comines and Ypres. And through this gap the 1st, the 3rd, the 4th, and the 42nd Divisions of the BEF, together with a third of the French 1st Army, were able to escape. Two days later the pincers firmly closed.

How the Germans found Dunkirk. Both sides hailed Dunkirk as a triumph. In a stirring speech on June 4, Winston Churchill told the House of Commons: 'The tale of the Dunkirk beaches will shine in whatever records are preserved of our affairs'

But by then a tighter perimeter around Dunkirk had been organised. This perimeter had been mapped out by the 3rd Corps Commander, Sir Ronald Adam (acting on Gort's orders) and by the French General Fagalde (deputy of Admiral Abrial, who, as *Amiral Nord,* was responsible for the defence of Dunkirk). It stretched from Nieuport in the east, along the canals through Furnes and Bergues, to Gravelines in the west. The French were to be responsible for the western sector between Bergues and Gravelines, the British for the eastern.

The British sector was divided into three—one segment for each corps—and each segment had its own strip of beach for the evacuation, and its own ammunition and food dumps inside the perimeter with a collecting area outside it. To solve the problem of traffic congestion, all vehicles, with very few exceptions, were to be abandoned beyond the canals. Brigadier Lawson was given the task of organising the troops already in the perimeter and of strengthening the defences along the canals as the remainder came in.

It would be a long time yet, though, before the remainder *could* get in. For in the early hours of the 28th the Belgian army surrendered, and for 20 miles to the sea Gort's left flank was laid open. General Brooke's 2nd Corps, fighting hard to hold back the onslaughts of the German VI Army, now had to do so on a greatly extended front. The 50th Division was brought up to extend the line northwards; and then the 4th and 3rd Divisions—two of the four divisions just withdrawn from the area of Lille where Rommel had been so confident of surrounding them—were rushed up by motor transport to expand the defences of the eastern wall of the corridor leading to Dunkirk.

Threats to the perimeter

Before they could close the gap that the Belgian collapse had exposed, however, the German 256th Division, which had been driven fast towards the coast in improvised transport, launched an attack on the eastern end of the Dunkirk perimeter at Nieuport, threatening to break out on to the beaches behind the main body of the BEF. But at Nieuport the Germans came up against the armoured cars of the 12th Lancers, who succeeded in bringing them to a halt. And by the time a heavier attack was launched, Brigadier Lawson had been able to reinforce the Lancers with a scratch force of gunners and engineers fighting as infantry; units of the French 60th Division had been brought into the battle; and General Brooke had diverted a brigade of the British 4th Division from Dixmude.

For the rest of the day the fighting went on all along the eastern wall of the pocket from Nieuport to Comines and along the western wall where the remaining divisions of the BEF struggled furiously to hold back the driving German armour from Merville up to Gravelines.

The battle along this western wall was both savage and confused. There was little or no cohesion between the British divisions, nor could there be: contact was lost, communications were cut. Repeatedly German tanks broke through the wall between the stop points, through a barrage of artillery and small-arms fire, forcing a withdrawal to other temporary stop points further back, while the south end of the pocket was gradually being bitten off by claws of a fresh pincer movement formed by Rommel's VII Panzers driving in from the west and by Bock's VII

Infantry Division pressing inwards from the east. The jaws closed and six divisions of the French 1st Army were surrounded southwest of Lille, where for four days they bravely continued a hopeless struggle under the leadership of General Molinié, pinning down seven German divisions well away from the Dunkirk perimeter.

Farther to the north, throughout the afternoon of May 28, eight other infantry divisions pressed forward against General Brooke's eastern front, while five Panzer and four motorised divisions attacked the western wall, forcing the British divisions back towards this small perimeter of marsh and dyke and sand.

The 44th Division, suffering heavy losses on its way, withdrew to a new position on the Mont des Cats; the remnants of the 2nd Division fell back through Poperinghe; units of the 48th Division were slowly eaten away as they fought desperately to cling to Cassel.

The next day the withdrawal continued as the British artillery fired their remaining ammunition at the Germans so remorselessly closing in. As it grew dark the rearguards of the 50th Division and Major-General Montgomery's 3rd Division withdrew from the Poperinghe Line; the 42nd and the 5th pulled back from the upper waters of the Yser; and elsewhere, all along the ever-constricting front, down the increasingly congested roads, the brigades, sometimes still more or less intact, but more often fragmented into separate battalions or even separate companies, fought their way back into the perimeter and took up their positions to defend it behind the high banks of the canals.

By midnight on the 29th the greater part of the BEF and nearly half of the French 1st

The German ring closes around Dunkirk: 'The British army, which has been compressed into the territory around Dunkirk, is going to its destruction before our concentric attack.' The photo shows part of the armada which saved the BEF

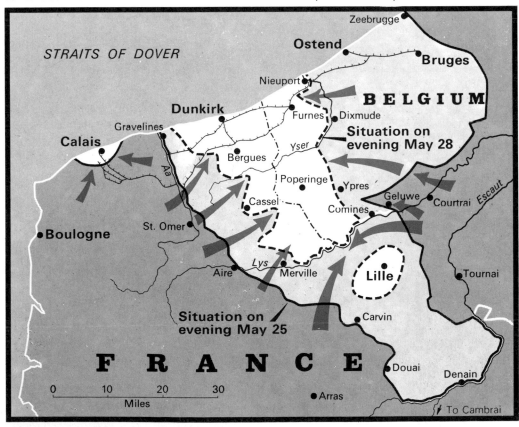

338,000 ESCAPED

After the last
ship had left:
on June 3 the
Germans broke
out on to the
beaches and into
Dunkirk at last

Army had managed to reach these canals; and although a few days before it had seemed impossible to believe that they would not spend the rest of the war in a German prison camp, there now seemed a slender chance that they might get away to England.

Crisis of logistics

Some, at least, had already gone. Most of the casualties from the base hospitals had been embarked four days before; and on May 25 large numbers of base personnel and other non-combatant troops, with more wounded, had followed them. The next day, at 1857 hours, the Admiralty signalled to Dover: 'Operation Dynamo is to commence'.

Admiral Ramsay's problems were truly formidable. Dover, with its eight berths for cross-Channel steamers, and its 50-odd mooring buoys, was not adapted for the congestion of shipping that Operation Dynamo entailed. Soon at these berths as many as 20 ships were to be moored in tiers three deep, while at the buoys ship after ship came up to fuel or take on stores. At Dunkirk the position was far worse. The town and the quays had been subjected to fierce aerial bombardment for several days now. The waterworks and mains had been destroyed and the docks had been rendered useless. A guiding jetty and two moles—the West Mole that led out from the oil storage area and the more important East Mole, a narrow plank-way that stretched out over three-quarters of a mile into the roadstead—were all that remained. And the berthing of ships against the East Mole, for which it had not in any case been designed, was difficult enough even when there was no enemy interference to contend with.

In the Channel between Dunkirk and Dover there were grave problems of a different sort: how to cover the route of the evacuation ships, how to provide counter-bombardment against the German batteries now established at Calais, how to provide anti-aircraft protection, how to sweep the approach channels for mines, how to deal with the enemy ships operating from Flushing and the U-boats reported approaching from the North Sea—how to do all these things as well as lift 'up to 45,000 of the BEF within two days'. These were the Admiralty's orders, for after those two days it was expected that the Germans would have made further evacuation impossible.

For the crews of the ships themselves, the worst of all the hazards was the shellfire from the Calais area and the air bombardment.

Captain Duggan, master of the Isle of Man packet, *Mona's Queen*, who made the crossing to Dunkirk on the first evening of the operation, reported how 'hell was let loose' on his ship when he was 'shelled from the shore by single guns and also by salvoes' from shore batteries. He continued:

Shells were flying all around us. The first salvo went over us, the second astern of us. I thought the next salvo would hit us, but fortunately it dropped short, right under our stern. The ship was riddled with shrapnel, mostly all on the boat and promenade decks. Then we were attacked from the air. A Junkers bomber made a power dive towards us and dropped five bombs, but he was off the mark too, I should say about 150 feet from us. All this while we were still being shelled, although we were getting out of range. The Junkers that bombed us was shot down and crashed into the water just ahead of us (no survivors). Then another Junkers attacked us, but before he reached us he was brought

down in flames. Then the tension eased a little.

Owing to the bombardment, I could see that the nerves of some of my men were badly shaken. I did not feel too well myself, but I mustered the crew and told them that Dunkirk was being bombed and was on fire. On being asked if they would volunteer to go in they did so to a man and I am glad to say we took off as many as Mona's Queen could carry.

Entering Dunkirk was already not merely hazardous but sometimes impossible. In the town oil tanks and warehouses, sheds and quayside offices were ablaze, the flames now seen leaping up over the wrecked town, now hidden by the thick black smoke; and in the harbour the many wrecks made navigation perilous. The bombing was ferocious.

Need for smaller craft

It was clear that soon the men would have to be embarked not in the harbour but along the sandy beaches that stretched away on either side of it, to Nieuport in the east and to Gravelines in the west. But Ramsay had as yet few small craft, and small craft would be essential to transport the men from the shallow waters to the bigger ships which would be unable to get in close. He signalled urgently for more to the Admiralty, where Captain Wharton of the Small Vessels Pool had been collecting boats on his own initiative for almost a week and already had 40 moored in the Thames near Westminster Pier. Soon many more were on the way from yachting centres, boatyards, and private moorings all over the south and east coasts and from the banks of the Thames.

Throughout Sunday night the evacuation went on, and by midnight a total of nearly 30,000 men had been brought safely back to Dover. At dawn on Monday, however, both the shellfire from Calais and the attacks from the air had increased in intensity, and several more ships were damaged and some turned back. Aboard the *Mona's Isle* 23 men were killed and 60 wounded when the ship came under fire from the German batteries on shore as well as from the Luftwaffe; and SS *Yewdale* was sunk off Calais.

It was now painfully clear, in fact, that the short mine-swept route to Dunkirk, which took the ships within range of the Calais batteries, would have to be abandoned, and that the longer channel which ran north of the Goodwin sands to the Kwinte Buoy north-west of Ostend would have to take its place. This route (Route Y) was, however, 87 miles long—48 miles longer than the one which had been previously used—and to use it meant a serious loss of time and a dangerously extended period during which the ships would be endangered by the Luftwaffe. RAF Fighter Command allotted 16 squadrons to patrol the route; but the loss of time did not permit of so seemingly straightforward a solution.

When Captain Tennant came ashore at Dunkirk in the late afternoon, as Senior Naval Officer, he realised immediately how little time there was. A report from the BEF indicated that their position was precarious; and the position at Dunkirk was obviously so. The air bombardments continued (there were 12 separate raids this day) and the town was burning more fiercely than ever; almost all the harbour facilities had been destroyed. At 2000 hours he sent this signal to Dover: 'Please send every available craft to beaches east of Dunkirk immediately. Evacuation tomorrow night is problematical.'

Evacuation even on this night was hazardous enough. The cross-Channel steamer,

Queen of the Channel, arrived alongside the pier to find an air raid in progress. In his report the chief officer wrote:

Our guns with others were in action. We landed a man on the pier to hang on to our ropes. About 8 pm Lieutenant-Commander Williams, RN, came on board and told the captain to proceed out of the harbour, lower his boats and get the men on board from the beach. We got to the anchorage. . . . When I was about to lower the fourth boat we received the information that there were a number of troops arriving at the pier. With the remainder of the crew we still had on board we proceeded alongside the pier. We got about 600 men on board. They were arriving in batches. About 11 pm we were told there were no more men in the vicinity, so we cut our mooring ropes. On hearing more men running along the pier we got the ship alongside the pier again and got about 80 more men on board. During our stay alongside the pier we had four air raids. While we were leaving the pier the enemy dropped illuminated parachutes which lit up the whole sea front. Our Captain backed the vessel up the harbour under the smoke screen made available to us from the burning town of Dunkirk.

We then proceeded to try and pick up our boats and crew . . .

Hazards and heavy losses

As well as being hazardous, the work off the beaches was fearfully slow. Ships had to use their heavy, unwieldy lifeboats, and the naval vessels their cutters and whalers; and hard as the crews worked, less than 2,500 men were taken up from the beaches that night. Only the prompt arrival of more suitable small craft could save the situation from disaster. So in the meantime Captain Tennant felt that he had no alternative but to attempt the embarkation of men from the East Mole. The tide beneath the piles made berthing there highly dangerous, but the attempt must be made. Tennant ordered a ship to try, and the brave attempt was successful: men could be more quickly embarked.

The next day, May 28, full use was made of it. Early in the morning Tennant signalled for ships to come there, and within a few hours six destroyers, later followed by cross-Channel and Irish Sea packets, had berthed, loaded troops, backed away, and returned to Dover. Soon, in spite of the difficulties and dangers of the off-shore channel, the air bombardment, and the shells of the German guns now approaching ever closer from the landward side, and in spite of the hazards to their thin side-plating of scraping and running against the concrete walls and the sides of other ships, destroyers were taking off as many as 900 men each trip, stowing them below deck and on deck, opening compartments usually left shut in such conditions and even opening watertight doors to make more space available. 'So crowded were their upper decks at times,' David Divine has written in his *The Nine Days of Dunkirk*, a fine, accurate, and moving account of the whole operation, 'that they could not fire their guns; so top-heavy were they that, as they took avoiding action against falling bombs, they heeled over to wild and impossible angles.'

Often, too often, these bombs could not be avoided. In the narrow off-shore channel, filled with the wrecks of ships, water-logged boats, bits of hawser, broken planks, and floating bodies, there was not enough room in which to manoeuvre effectively and once berthed the congestion was appalling.

The *Lochgarry*, for instance, loading under heavy fire in the harbour, could not only do nothing to avoid the bombs, she could not for a time even get out—a destroyer was loading across her decks alongside her, and three others were loading astern.

The losses this day were very heavy. Those ships that survived the bombing at the mole were frequently damaged or sunk as they steamed back down the off-shore channel. The *Queen of the Channel* was dive-bombed and sunk on her way out; the French cargo vessel *Douaisien*, with 1,000 men on board, struck a magnetic mine at the side of the channel and slowly disappeared; and the old paddle-minesweeper *Brighton Belle* noisily making for home, her great wheels churning in their boxes, when she hit a hidden wreck that ripped her bottom out.

But now, on the beaches, the first of the small ships were arriving, tows of whalers and ships' lifeboats, yard craft and coasters — and among them the *Gipsy King*, a beach motor-boat from Deal, with a crew of three:

We went to Dunkirk on May 28th. We stayed there about 48 hours. We were under shellfire and machine-gun fire. We stayed there till every British soldier was off the beach. I should like to mention Harry Brown who did a brave action. We just loaded the boat with troops. We saw a pontoon with soldiers in being swamped with waves. Brown, being the swimmer, decided to go over the side with a rope; he tied it to the pontoon and saved the soldiers from being drowned. I am writing this as Fred Hook and Harry Brown are in the minesweepers.

Havoc on the docks
The following day, May 29, the losses were even greater than the day before. In the early hours of the morning the destroyer *Wakeful* was struck amidships by a torpedo and broke in two; she sank in 15 seconds with most of her load of troops below. Soon afterwards another destroyer, the *Grafton*, was also hit by a torpedo which exploded under the wardroom, killing 35 army officers who were lying there exhausted; her captain was killed by machine-gun bullets as he stood on deck; and soon she, too, sank. These were only two of three destroyers sunk and six damaged on this one day.

The losses among the other ships were even more severe. The *Clan MacAlister*, the largest merchant vessel used at Dunkirk, was bombed from the air and was soon in flames; the *Fenella* was holed by lumps of concrete which were blasted off the mole and hurtled through her side below the water-line; another paddle-steamer, the *Crested Eagle*, which took up the *Fenella's* survivors, was also hit and set on fire and grounded on the beach to the east of the mole; the *Mona's Queen* was mined and sank within two minutes; the trawlers *Polly Johnson, Comfort, Nautilus,* and *Calvi* all soon followed her; many other ships, including the French destroyer, *Mistral*, were badly damaged.

Most of the havoc was caused by a ferocious air bombardment launched on the mole soon after 1600 hours, when the wind changed, blowing inshore the heavy pall of smoke which up till then had screened the harbour and roadstead. By 1900 hours all activity on the mole had stopped and Admiral Ramsay was informed from Dunkirk that the harbour was 'blocked by damaged ships and all evacuation must therefore be effected from the beaches'.

The attacks off the beaches, however, were by now quite as relentless as those on the harbour. Two Southern Railway ships, the *Normannia* and the *Lorina*, were both bombed and sunk; and soon after leaving La Panne beach between Dunkirk and Nieuport with 750 troops on board, the minesweeper *Gracie Fields* was hit by a bomb which burst her pipes and jammed her rudder. Her engines could not be stopped and she circled round and round until eventually she sank. Another minesweeper, the *Waverley*, was attacked by 12 Heinkels and was sunk by a bomb which wrecked the wardroom and passed through the bottom of the ship, after her one 12-pounder, her Lewis guns, and the rifle fire of the troops on board had failed to drive the Heinkels off.

In the face of this fearful toll, the Admiralty decided that all modern destroyers must be withdrawn from Dunkirk. For if losses were to continue at this rate, the sea life-lines of Britain would be seriously endangered. So the position looked bleak indeed when, on the morning of May 30, Rear-Admiral Wake-Walker, sent over with two commodores to strengthen the naval organisation off Dunkirk, faced his first day's duties. With only 15 of the older and smaller destroyers left available for Operation Dynamo, and with so many other ships now damaged or sunk, it seemed impossible that a rate of lifting could be maintained that would evacuate the bulk of the BEF before the army's perimeter collapsed. By noon Admiral Ramsay at Dover had been made acutely aware of this fact; and in the early afternoon he telephoned the First Sea Lord. His representations were effective: at 1530 hours six of the modern destroyers were ordered to return immediately to Dunkirk.

As it happened the numbers brought home that morning, even without the help of the modern destroyers, were encouragingly high. Conditions at Dunkirk had greatly improved. The seas were quieter, the low cloud ceiling and the smoke from the still burning oil tanks were providing an adequate screen. Despite the damage it had suffered, it was still possible to use the mole; and army engineers had constructed makeshift jetties out of all the trucks that could be found and were capable of being driven down into the sea.

Initiative and sacrifice
The ships' crews, both British and French, made the most of their opportunity. Seven old British destroyers carried over 1,000 men each this day. The passenger steamer, the *Isle of Guernsey*, took back nearly 500 wounded. The *Royal Sovereign*, which had taken two full loads on Wednesday, took two more today. And most significant of all, perhaps, the little ships were now working off the beaches, ferrying the troops to the deeper-draught vessels, with splendid initiative and effect. The variety of these boats was extraordinary. There were lifeboats, dockyard launches, cockle boats, river tugs, French and Belgian fishing boats, pleasure craft, Pickford's little transport ships made for their trade between the Solent ports and the Isle of Wight, oyster dredgers, yachts, Thames barges, even the Thames fire-float, *Massey Shaw,* which sailed out of the river for the first time in her career.

The experiences of a man who sailed in one of these little ships were characteristic of many. Allan Barrell, of the pleasure-boat *Shamrock*, wrote:

We stared and stared at what looked like thousands of sticks on the beach and were amazed to see them turn into moving masses of humanity. I thought quickly of going in, picking up 70 to 80 and clearing off. With the sun behind me I calculated I should find some East Coast town. We got our freight, so did the Canvey Queen, *when I realised it would be selfish to clear off when several destroyers and large vessels were waiting in deep water to be fed by small craft, so I decided what our job was to be.*

We could seat sixty men and with those standing we had about eighty weary and starving British troops, some without boots, some only in their pants, but enough life left in them to clamber on board the destroyers. Again and again we brought our cargo to this ship until she was full . . .

Navigation was extremely difficult owing to the various wreckage, upturned boats, floating torpedoes, and soldiers in the water trying to be sailors for the first time. They paddled their collapsible little boats out to me with the butts of their rifles, and many shouted that they were sinking; we could not help them. I was inshore as close as I dare . . .

Later I took in two or three large Carley floats one behind the other. These were filled to capacity, about fifty men in each standing up to their waists in water in the net inside. My craft was loaded, too. We were just making for our destroyer when I was brought to a standstill; my engine stopped, the propeller had fouled, I believe, a human obstruction. There were many of these in the shallow water. Naval men came down and tried to free the obstruction but without success. I was too weak to dive under the thick black oil which surrounded us, so rather than be left sitting on our useless craft I asked to be taken on HM ship. This was the last straw, having to leave my vessel which constituted my life savings . . . I took one more glance at the beach and sat down beneath a gun with my hands over my face and prayed.

All along that beach men were standing or swimming in the water, shouting for help, rushing at boats and swamping them until the skippers had to take out revolvers and threaten to shoot the panic-stricken soldiers.

'Things were getting bad,' wrote the coxswain of the Margate lifeboat, *Lord Southborough*. 'Troops were rushing out to us from all directions and were being drowned close to us and we could not get to them and the last time we went in to the shore it seemed to me we were doing more harm by drawing the men off the shore, as, with their heavy clothing on, the surf was knocking them over and they were unable to get up.'

Yet for all the difficulties, by the end of that day 53,823 men had been landed in England—6,500 more than the day before.

Next day, however, the wind dispersed the smoke and haze, and the shelling and aerial bombardment and machine-gunning, which had slackened much on Thursday, increased to a new intensity. German artillery brought the La Panne beaches under heavy shellfire from beyond Nieuport; and the Luftwaffe came back in force once more, sinking the French destroyer *Sirocco* and badly damaging two other French destroyers.

The RAF lost 28 aircraft in the course of their counter-activities. But the RAF's losses the following day—31 to a German loss of 29—were even greater.

For on Saturday the Luftwaffe launched the heaviest attack of the entire operation. There were furious bombardments of the whole length of La Panne beaches along which fighters made constant strafing runs. Out at sea and in the harbour dive-bombers swooped down from 10,000 feet to attack the congested shipping. Within a few hours one French and three British destroyers had been lost—together with two cross-Channel steamers, a minesweeper, and a gunboat—and four destroyers had been hit.

'In these circumstances, it was apparent,' as Admiral Ramsay wrote, 'that continuation of the operation by day must cause loss of ships and personnel out of all proportion to the number of troops evacuated, and if persisted in, the momentum of the evacuation would automatically and rapidly decrease.'

The inevitability of this was recognised. And the Admiralty ordered all operations by daylight to stop. The exhausted crews, some of which were near to physical and mental collapse (a few of them had collapsed and been replaced), prepared to work again through another night.

Shrinking perimeter

As the crews prepared for another night's unremitting work, the troops defending the perimeter withdrew to a new and shorter line round Dunkirk where, it was proposed, a bridgehead would be held 'with all available anti-aircraft and anti-tank guns and with such troops as had not yet embarked'.

The perimeter had been contracting by degrees ever since Thursday morning, when the War Office had received a message from

Admiral Ramsay: mastermind of Dunkirk

the Army Headquarters in the village of La Panne to the effect that 'the perimeter cannot be held for long'. During the course of this day, however, the German pressure had eased and only one attempt was made to cross the canals. This attack was temporarily successful north of Furnes, but the Coldstream Guards had counterattacked and driven the enemy out of their bridgehead. And elsewhere along the line of the canals, the British and French defences were strengthened and the infantry dug in, while the German attack faltered.

For up till now the German Command had failed to recognise the full significance of what was happening at Dunkirk. A belief had long persisted that the surrounded armies were doomed. As late as May 29 a communiqué had complacently recorded: 'The fate of the French army in Artois is sealed . . . The British army, which has been compressed into the territory . . . around Dunkirk is also going to its destruction before our concentric attack.'

This belief, complicated by a fatal indecision as to how best to press the attack and where, had led to a state which was close to inertia. 'There is an impression here that nothing is happening today,' the Operations Officer at IV Army HQ complained impatiently on May 30, 'an impression that no one is any longer interested in Dunkirk.'

At the same time General Halder, Chief of the General Staff, was writing in his diary: 'The disintegration of the enemy which we have encircled continues.' Their forward units, which were in touch with German troops still, to be sure continued to fight 'with tooth and nail'. But the rest were 'fleeing to the coast and trying to get across the Channel on anything that floats'.

Later that day it was realised at German army headquarters that the dismissive term, 'anything that floats', scarcely comprehended the importance of the armada of little ships that were bobbing about so elusively in the Channel. And it was at last decided that an all-out effort must be made to break through the line of the BEF's defences. So, early the next day, German pressure in the Furnes area was so greatly increased that a further constriction of the perimeter was made necessary. The Allies were forced to withdraw to the line of the defences along the Franco-Belgian frontier—a withdrawal that meant a loss of 9 miles of coastline between Dunkirk and Nieuport and the opening up of the beaches west of La Panne to German shelling.

The withdrawal had also meant that Lord Gort had no further excuse to evade the instructions he had received to return home as soon as his command was so reduced that he could hand over to a corps commander. He had asked permission to remain till the end, but this had been refused; and on May 31 he handed over command of the rearguard, which was to be provided by 1st Corps, to Major-General Alexander. He and General Brooke returned to Dover.

The German pressure on the perimeter continued throughout the day, but after six Albacores and 18 Blenheims had bombed the concentrations of Army Group B in and beyond Nieuport, there seemed less danger of a breakthrough. General Alexander felt sure, however, that the present perimeter line could not be held until 'all the troops were embarked', as Admiral Abrial had hoped. And, indeed, early in the morning of Saturday, June 1, while the Luftwaffe began its massive assault, the first German land attacks were launched. The line was penetrated at Bergues and at Hoymille, necessitating a further withdrawal which took the British into their final bridgehead.

Nerves taxed to limit

Saturday night was dark and the loading in the wreckage-cluttered harbour was more confused than ever. Ships collided and blocked each other's passage; the crowds of French and British soldiers were so thick on the mole that at 0200 hours the commander at Dunkirk decided it was 'essential that rearguard BEF embarks from the beaches'.

Once more the crews of the small boats were required to work to the limits of their endurance. And their problems were even greater now, for French troops were by this time in the majority, and the difficulty in making men understand the dangers of rushing and swamping the boats increased.

The persistent bombing, the constant fear, the hunger, and exhaustion had broken the nerve of a few men completely. For days they had been existing in a world that only the strongest willed and least imaginative could endure without appalling strain.

During the early stages of the evacuation, discipline in some of the units which had been split up by the withdrawal had broken down. There was a good deal of drunkenness in Dunkirk and several bombed shops and warehouses were looted. Men came down on to the beaches with all manner of acquisitions—from cases of brandy to cartons of cigarettes, from toys and bicycles to wireless-sets. And having got on to the beaches, they made little effort to co-operate with those who were doing their best to set up some sort of beach organisation. Indeed, they often failed to find any organised leadership at all. The system drawn up at General Adam's headquarters had seemed orderly enough; but the division of the beach into separate sectors was of no help to men who had become separated from their units and had no idea where to go. Thousands of men wandered about from one group to the next trying to find a friendly face, an embarkation officer who would tell them what to do, where to form a queue. Most of them were utterly exhausted, 'scarcely able', the master of a ship noticed, 'to walk along the pier'.

Once they had found a boat able to take them off they were all too often inclined to wade in the sea towards it, blindly trusting that the navy would do the rest.

The experiences recorded by one of the Oriole's officers were far from uncommon. The Oriole, a paddle-minesweeper, had no adequate boats with which to take the men off the beach, so the captain decided to run her aground and then use her as a pier along which the men could climb to other ships in the deeper water astern:

Everybody went aft to raise the bows as much as possible, and we went lickity-split for the shore and kept her full ahead until we jarred and came to a full stop. As we went in we dropped two seven-hundredweight anchors from the stern, to kedge off with. The men waded and swam out and many of them had to be hauled over the rails. The snag was that when a rope was thrown to a man, about six grabbed it and just hung on looking up blankly with the water breaking over their shoulders, and it was a hell of a job getting any of them to let go so that the rest could get pulled overboard.

Once they had landed on board the relief was overwhelming. 'A curious sense of freedom took possession of me,' one army officer said. 'All the accumulated strain of the last few hours, of the last day or so vanished. I felt that my job was over. Anything else that remained to be done was the navy's business.'

For some, though, there was no such contentment. And as the hours and days passed the strain proved too much. Hungry, thirsty, and desperately tired, their minds tortured by the screeching of the dive-bombers' whistles, the ships' sirens, the exploding bombs, the rattle of machine-guns, the shouts and screams of men, they broke down.

But there were few. Most men soon noticed how little damage the German bombers were actually doing on the beaches; the exploding bombs shot up tall plumes of sand, yet they sank deep and their blast was muffled and deadened. A foxhole, particularly one sheltered by a bank or, even better, an old mattress, afforded ample protection from everything but a direct hit. So gradually a spirit of confidence and self-possession came over the beaches. The early evacuations had been, for the most part, limited to the army's 'tail' or troops unused to fighting; but during the subsequent days the troops remaining had all had their baptism of fire. Now dive-bombers were met not only by the guns of the ships at sea, but the rifle fire of the men on the beaches.

Humour and pathos

There was a resurgence, too, of the British serviceman's traditional humour, at times grimly sardonic, at others blithely facetious — a sailor calmly fishing over the stern of the *Medway Queen* as she lay off the mole, waiting for his turn to go in, and calling back when told there were no fish about and, if there were, they would be dead, 'You never can tell, sir. I might catch a bloody Boche helmet'; naval officers standing on ships' gangways and bawling out like pierhead barkers, 'Any more, any *more* for the *Brighton Queen!*'; army gunners from Yorkshire singing as they waited for their turn, 'Oh, I *do* like to be beside the seaside!'. And a young sub-lieutenant thinking what a 'jamboree' it all was, though

rather a desperate business at times in the boats crammed with troops, trying to handle them in the swell and the wash of bombs. A bomb overturned a whaler fifty yards away from us on one occasion and we went over to pull the fellows out of the drink. We pulled out all those we could reach — some sank with all the ridiculous ironmongery tied on to them — and we were just shoving off when we heard a faint tapping from inside the boat which was upside down, and a faint voice was heard. 'What shall I do?' So we told him to duck his head under and come up outside and not to waste time playing hide and seek at such a time.

So there was a bit of a giggle and up came a tin hat and under it an overcoat, a gasmask, picks and shovels and all the rest of the gie-guys those chaps carry; so we pulled him in, purple in the face — a little Cockney — and he gasped like a landed fish: 'Gawd, what a bloody nightmare!'

A bloody nightmare it was; but there was far less muddle towards the end. On the night of Saturday, June 1, Mr R. B. Brett waded ashore from one of the ships' boats towed by the *Medway Queen*, and called out 'I want sixty men!' For some time he received no reply.

'I sighted a causeway about eight feet wide heading out into the water. To my surprise I found it to be a perfectly ordered straight column of men about six abreast, standing as if on parade. When I reached them a sergeant stepped up to me and said, "Yes, sir. Sixty men, sir?" He then walked along the column, which remained in perfect formation and detailed the required number to follow me.'

He placed the hand of one of them in Mr Brett's. The man had been blinded. He was told he was being taken to safety. He said simply and politely, 'Thanks, mate' and followed Brett out into the deeper water.

'BEF evacuated'

By midnight the total of men brought home that day, June 1, was no less then 64,429. And the next night Operation Dynamo was completed. General Alexander was picked up by Admiral Wake-Walker and at 2330 hours Captain Tennant signalled from Dunkirk a short, triumphant message: 'BEF evacuated.'

On Monday, June 3, the Germans closed in on the shrunken perimeter. The French rearguard fought bravely against heavy odds but the enemy forced them back to a new line on the outskirts of the town little more than 2 miles from the base of the East Mole. It was agreed between the British and French Admiralties that this French rearguard, estimated to number 30,000 men, should be taken away that night. Admiral Ramsay made his plans and the necessary shipping was sent. But there were far more than 30,000 French troops in Dunkirk. And as General Barthélémy's men disengaged and came down to the sea, what the French historian Jacques Mordal described as a 'vast crowd of troops, materialised suddenly as the news of the last departure spread. Out of the cellars and the holes streams of unarmed men appeared, emerging everywhere, converging on the mole with no intention of giving up their chances of escape to those who had been fighting for them.'

And so, as the old destroyer, *Shikari*, the last ship out of Dunkirk, sailed for England at 0340 hours, 40,000 men were left to be captured by the Germans who broke out on to the beaches at last. 338,226 men, however, had been brought away.

In London when the full measure of this remarkable triumph became known, the relief of the government was profound. At the beginning of the previous week, the Prime Minister had felt it necessary to warn the House of Commons in sombre tones that the country must 'prepare itself for hard and heavy tidings'. But now, as he later wrote, 'in the midst of our defeat, glory had come to the Island people, united and unconquerable . . . there was a white glow, overpowering, sublime, which ran through our island from end to end . . . and the tale of the Dunkirk beaches will shine in whatever records are preserved of our affairs.'

Basking in this glow and in the pride that had been engendered, the people of Britain began to believe that they had, in some way, won a great victory.

But it was a good deal less than that. And Britain's position was perilous. The BEF (with the loss of 68,111 killed, wounded, and taken prisoner) had been saved, but immense quantities of its equipment had been lost (including 2,472 guns, 63,879 vehicles, 20,548 motorcycles and well over 500,000 tons of stores and ammunition) and it was in no condition to defend the island from attack. The Royal Navy was still a powerful force, but the operations off the Norwegian coast had demonstrated only too clearly how vulnerable its big ships were to aircraft flying from inland bases; and of the 243 ships sunk at Dunkirk (out of more than 1,000 engaged) six were British destroyers and 19 other destroyers had been damaged. The RAF had acquitted itself well, but it had been seriously weakened; and its achievement was, indeed, far less gratifying than the accepted figures seemed to indicate. The Prime Minister, in a magnificent speech in the House of Commons on June 4, took particular pains to praise the work of the air force. He had been deeply disturbed by reports of the army's dissatisfaction with the cover and support they had received at Dunkirk and of how men in RAF uniform had been insulted by returning soldiers.

We must be very careful not to assign to this deliverance the attributes of a victory. Wars are not won by evacuations. But there was a victory inside this deliverance which should be noted. It was gained by the air force. Many of our soldiers coming back have not seen the air force at work; they saw only the bombers which escaped its protective attack. They underrate its achievements. I have heard much talk of this; that is why I go out of my way to say this; I will tell you about it.

This was a great trial of strength between the British and German air forces. Can you conceive a greater objective for the Germans in the air than to make evacuation from these beaches impossible, and to sink all these ships which were displayed, almost to the extent of thousands? Could there have been an objective of greater military importance and significance for the whole purpose of the war than this? They tried hard, and they were beaten hard; they were frustrated in their task. We got the army away; and they have paid fourfold for any losses which they have inflicted.

When the figures were checked and analysed, however, this was seen to be far from the truth. During the operation Fighter Command lost 106 aircraft; but the German losses over Dunkirk were nothing like four times this figure. In fact, they were between 130 and 140, and of these the French navy shot down a few and the Royal Navy claimed to have destroyed 35. There can be no doubt that the RAF fought bravely and skilfully. It is time now to recognise, though, that the Luftwaffe did so too, and that although 129 German officers were lost to the Luftwaffe between May 21 and 31 there was no such wholesale slaughter as the propaganda of 1940 suggested.

But if Dunkirk, even in the limited sense which Churchill mentioned, could not be considered a victory, it did achieve something of inestimable value: for the first time, perhaps, since the war began, the British people were wholeheartedly determined to fight and to win. They had seen for themselves what modern mechanised warfare meant; how right those prophets such as Basil Liddell Hart had been to propound the arguments for deep strategic penetration by independent armoured forces and to insist that this penetration could be checked by concentrated counterstrokes by similar forces; they had seen how woefully incapable the BEF and the French armies were of subduing the force of the Panzer thrusts; how close Britain had come to the sudden and shameful defeat that threatened so soon to overtake France. But they had seen, too, a brilliant display of improvisation, an inspiring example of fortitude and self-sacrifice. The realisation that catastrophe had been so narrowly avoided, that the enemy's guns could even now be heard across the Channel provided the sudden shock that they had long needed.

And so it was that when Churchill in that great speech of June 4 told the House of Commons that the British should fight on the beaches and on the landing-grounds, in the fields and in the streets and in the hills, and that they should never surrender, he was not forming public opinion — he was reflecting it. The Dunkirk spirit was born.

It had been a close-run thing. But now at least there was a chance of survival.

 CHRISTOPHER HIBBERT was born in Leicestershire in 1924. Educated at Radley and at Oriel College, Oxford, he joined the army in the ranks of the Sherwood Foresters in 1943, later transferring to the 60th Rifles. Commissioned in 1944, he served in Italy as a platoon commander in the London Irish Rifles. After being wounded at Commachio he was awarded the MC and appointed Staff Captain at Allied Force Headquarters; later he became Personal Assistant to General Duff. His published works, which have been translated into most west European languages, include studies of the Battle of Agincourt, Wolfe at Quebec, the retreat to Corunna, Lord Raglan, the Crimean War, Mussolini, and the Battle of Arnhem. He is a fellow of the Royal Society of Literature.

FALL OF FRANCE

France May 20/June 25, 1940   *Colonel Adolph Goutard*

After the shock of the German armoured thrust through the Ardennes to the French coast, followed immediately by what looked to many Frenchmen as the desertion of their British allies via Dunkirk, it is hardly surprising that resistance to the invading forces when they turned south was sporadic and inefficient. Many specious excuses and reasons have been given for the disaster to French arms which followed. But this account by a leading French historian—in addition to its main, historical narrative—does not try to avoid the inevitable conclusion that the reasons for the Fall of France lay just as much in France herself as in the prowess of the enemy

After the battle of Dunkirk, General Weygand, who had taken command of the French troops on May 19 after his recall to service from Beirut, was able to take stock of the situation. The French army in the field was sadly depleted as a result of the losses incurred in the fighting, the capture of hundreds of thousands of prisoners in the Meuse and in the north, the surrender of the 1st Army at Lille, and finally the evacuation of more than 100,000 French troops from Dunkirk.

The losses included 24 infantry divisions (13 of them active, including six of the seven motorised divisions which had been in the field on May 10), all three light mechanised divisions, two light cavalry divisions, and one armoured division. In addition, we had lost the valuable support of the British divisions, except for the 51st Infantry Division and the Armoured Division, which, isolated from the rest of Lord Gort's army, had missed the evacuation and was to continue fighting in the lower Somme sector before returning finally to England.

Along the 225 miles of front stretching from the coast to the Maginot Line, we had at our disposal 43 active or 'Series A' infantry divisions (some of which had suffered heavy losses), three light cavalry divisions with only 36 armoured vehicles between them (out of their original 112), and three armoured divisions, all with less than 40 of their original 200 tanks left.

To hold the Maginot Line from the Moselle to the Jura mountains, we had a mere 17 divisions—only one of which was active—together with the troops immobilised in the forts. Meanwhile, in the interior, the remnants of the Belgian and Meuse armies were being re-formed into seven light infantry divisions scheduled to be ready by June 15. By this date, General Weygand considered that the forces available would total 60 divisions, as against 130 German divisions, ten of them armoured. But would the enemy give us even until June 15 to regroup? At all events, in view of this great inferiority of numbers and equipment, the battle was indeed going to be a hopeless one for us, and only one conclusion was possible.

'After Dunkirk,' wrote General Gamelin, and with good reason, 'we couldn't hold the Somme-Aisne front long with the forces left to us. There were thus two solutions: either to ask for an armistice or to withdraw to the empire. Only the second solution was worthy of France, but there should be no delay; bridgeheads should be set up covering our ports, and evacuations should be begun immediately.... We depended on the empire and Britain for our recovery.'

A defensive battle along the Somme-Aisne thus appeared to be necessary, for this, followed by a withdrawal along the major axes, would give us a month to transport our forces to North Africa over the ditch of the Mediterranean and to consolidate the resources of our empire. Such resources could have changed the face of things at the end of June 1940 and later.

But General Weygand did not envisage this. On May 24 he told Baudouin, Secretary of the War Cabinet, that 'the 50 divisions left to us would only form a sand embankment which, when pierced, would impede both an orderly retreat and the setting up of a withdrawal line, even one prepared in advance'. And he concluded: 'The army must resist firmly in the Somme-Aisne position, and when this resistance is broken, the fragments must stand fast to the end, to save our honour.'

On May 25 at a War Council meeting, he opened the proceedings by discussing an unlikely solution: 'shorten the front, choosing either a line running from the coast to the Loire, with the right-hand flank left in the air and the Maginot Line abandoned, or a line taking in the Maginot Line, and abandoning Paris.' This meant building half an embankment, either on the right or on the left, to stop the flood!

'Defence to the death'

After himself dismissing this solution, General Weygand also rejected that of withdrawal from the Somme-Aisne Line to the Seine-Marne Line, 'because of lack of reserves to carry out an orderly retreat'—although many withdrawals with no more reserves had been effected before, and would be again between 1941 and 1945. He thus returned to his solution of the previous day: 'The present position must be maintained. It may crumble. . . . The fragments will form breakwaters. Each part of the army must fight to the end in defence of honour.'

In his memoirs, General Weygand explained: *'I had had this solution in mind from the first: defence to the death in the Somme-Aisne position.'* And on May 26 it found expression in his General Order beginning thus:

I. The battle on which the fate of the country depends will be fought on our present position, without thinking of withdrawal. All the leaders, down to the platoon leaders, must be imbued with a fierce desire to fight to the death.

But what would happen after the ensuing partial surrender—

◁ **Previous page:**
A dying French
soldier, assisted
by the man who
shot him

△ After the Allied
evacuation at
Dunkirk, Rommel
and his VII Panzer
Division (left)
wheeled south,
crushing all French
opposition. French
heavy artillery
(right) failed to halt
the fresh offensive.
As a last resort a
system of defence
sites, bristling with
anti-tank weapons
and called
'hedgehogs', was set
up. But nothing
could stop the
onrush of German
infantry and
armour

▷ Panzer General
Erwin Rommel, seen
here with General
Fortune, captured
commander of the
British 51st
Highland
Division at St
Valery en Caux.
The picture comes
from Frau Rommel's
personal diary

Germans:
1. Keitel: Chief of the OKW
2. Brauchitsch: C-in-C of the Army
3. Jodl: head of the General Staff Office

for surely not everybody would fight to the death? On May 26 the general told Baudouin: 'If we succumb, I shall have the ghastly job of meeting the Germans, just as at Rethonde 22 years ago, but with the position reversed.' (Weygand was present when the 1918 Armistice was signed in a railway carriage at Rethonde.)

What were Hitler's plans? After Dunkirk would the Germans attack Britain under the shelter of a 'safety corridor' provided by the Luftwaffe, mines, and U-boats—or would they concentrate on the destruction of the French? Hitler, who longed to form an alliance with Britain, as he had stated at Rundstedt's headquarters in Charleville on May 24, undoubtedly preferred to destroy her 'continental sword', France, and then get Britain to ally herself with him. At all events, as early as May 29, at Cambrai, he had informed the army group commanders of his decision 'to regroup the armoured forces rapidly for action in a southerly direction, to settle the French army's account'.

The Panzers were then withdrawn from Flanders, and Bock, leaving to his XVIII Army the job of liquidating Dunkirk, took his IV, VI, and IX Armies to the Somme to extend the front of Rundstedt's army group (II, XII, and XVI Armies), already positioned on the Aisne and the Ailette. The ten Panzer divisions were reorganised into five armoured corps, three of which were given to Bock and two to Rundstedt.

Under Bock, Hoth's XV Panzer Corps took up a position on the lower Somme, between the coast and Amiens, towards the lower Seine. The other two armoured corps, the XIV and the XVI (Kleist's group), occupied the middle Somme, and moved from the Amiens and Péronne bridgeheads towards Paris. In a second phase, Guderian's armoured group (XXXIX and XLI Panzer Corps) crossed the Aisne and pushed towards the south-east, via Châlons and Langres, in the direction of the Swiss frontier, to take the Maginot Line and the French eastern armies from the rear.

For his part, Weygand had adopted the following disposition:
● **On the left,** the 3rd Army Group (Besson) would block the routes to the lower Seine and Paris with the 10th Army (Altmayer) in the lower Somme area, the 7th Army (Frère) in the Amiens and Péronne Somme area, and the 6th Army (Touchon) on the Ailette and Aisne to Neufchâtel.
● **In the centre,** of the 4th Army Group (Huntziger) the 4th Army (Requin) on the Aisne was to block the route to Langres, while the 2nd Army (Freydenberg) would remain south of Sedan.
● **On the right,** the 2nd Army Group (Prételat) was to defend the Maginot Line and the Rhine with its three armies—the 3rd (Condé), the 5th (Bourret), and the 8th (Laure).

Although the Maginot Line was strong, our new front facing the north, between the Meuse and the sea, was weaker, and became increasingly so towards the west. On the Aisne, which our troops had occupied since May 16, there had been time to get organised, but on the Somme there had not. They could not hold the breach, because the Germans had large and impregnable bridgeheads at Amiens and Péronne on the south bank, from which they were liable to launch an attack at any time. Furthermore, the density of the French troops was low: only one division to every 7 to 9 miles.

The last resort: 'hedgehogs'

But the French reserves capable of carrying out general counterattacks were even weaker. To offset the inadequacy of the effective forces and to resist the Panzers, therefore, General Weygand gave instructions for a checkerwork of closed operational bases called 'hedgehogs' to be set up; these, installed in the villages and woods and packed with 75-mm guns housed as anti-tank weapons, would hold for a time even when encircled and outflanked. 'This system,' wrote General Requin, 'was only a last resort to enable these weak but brave troops to resist with honour before being overwhelmed.'

'It was necessary, therefore,' wrote General de Gaulle afterwards, 'not simply to enter into a further merely defensive battle in the fashion of 1918, but to give up the idea of a continuous front, and to

manoeuvre, to manoeuvre . . .' He had in fact proposed to General Weygand the formation, with the 1,200 up-to-date tanks still remaining and several infantry divisions, of two counterattack groups, one to the north of Paris, and the other to the south of Rheims, 'to attack the flanks of the advancing German armoured corps, which would more or less be strung out and disarranged'.

At dawn on June 5, the Luftwaffe carried out a fierce attack on the front and rear of the French 3rd Army Group, the Panzers then emerging from the Péronne and Amiens bridgeheads, over the bridges still remaining intact west of Amiens. The Führer was soon announcing to the world on the radio: 'The second great offensive is starting today with formidable new resources!' General Weygand, for his part, made a moving appeal to the French army: 'May the thought of our afflicted country inspire in you an unflinching resolve to stand firm. The fate of our country and the future of our children depend on your firmness.'

The Germans were not slow to observe that something had changed on the opposite side. By now battle-hardened, and enclosed in their 'hedgehogs', our soldiers resisted firmly, and our 75s, used as anti-tank guns, massacred the Panzers. 'The French are putting up strong opposition,' wrote General List. 'No signs of demoralisation are evident anywhere. We are seeing a new French way of fighting.'

At 1300 hours, General Besson gave General Georges an optimistic report, for although the Germans had penetrated our front position, our 'hedgehogs' were holding. In the west (10th French Army), the XV Panzer Corps, halted to begin with by the Hangest and Quesnoy breakwaters, finally came up to the second position (Molliens-Vidame), only some 7 miles south of the Somme. In the centre (7th Army), the XIV and XVI Panzer Corps from the Amiens and Péronne bridgeheads failed to make any further advance. And in the east (6th Army) the IX German Army infantry infiltrated across the Ailette, but was held back in front of the Chemin des Dames. 'Our operational bases held,' wrote General Weygand. 'There was only one agonising question: would intervention by our reserves in fact permit their relief, and the destruction of the armour which had penetrated our disposition? This was the crux of the entire battle.'

It was indeed a vital problem, for on the following day, June 6, although the 7th Army was still holding back the XIV and XVI Panzer Corps, on the flanks the resistance had weakened. In the west, Hoth's XV Armoured Corps liquidated the 'hedgehogs' of the 10th Army and in the evening reached Hornoy and Orival, outflanking and isolating the two left-hand divisions—including the 51st British Division—which had to abandon Abbeville in order to withdraw to the Bresle. In the east, between the Ailette and the Aisne, the IX German Army took the Chemin des Dames, forcing the 6th Army back to the south bank of the Aisne. 'By 6 pm,' wrote General Weygand, 'in the face of these enemy successes on the flanks, I had to accept a withdrawal of defence to the line Bresle-Avre-Aisne. With our system of unlimited resistance by closed operational bases, it was vital to avoid enemy thrusts into our disposition. But our reserves were too weak to do this.'

On the morning of June 7 Rommel, who commanded the VII Panzer Division and had learned a lesson from the two preceding days, resolved to avoid the 'hedgehogs' and push forward straight to the south-west over open ground. In this way he reached Forges-les-Eaux, 37 miles south of the Somme, by the end of the day. He was now no more than 25 miles from the Seine at Rouen.

A counterattack by a hastily formed group—consisting of the remains of an armoured division, three light cavalry divisions, and an infantry division under General Petiet—proved abortive, and to the west of the Forges-les-Eaux breach, the 51st British Infantry Division and the 9th Corps were cut off from the rest of the 10th Army. In the east we still held the Avre, the second Montdidier-Noyon position, the Oise, and the lower Aisne. But at 2200 hours Colonel Bourget of the C-in-C's department telephoned Baudouin, informing him that 'a tactical accident occurred this afternoon' and that the Panzers had reached Forges-les-Eaux. 'I hung up with a trembling hand,' wrote Baudouin, 'and advised the President of

4   5

the War Council, M Reynaud. "Can it be that our hope is fading?" he exclaimed, his voice changing. "No, it can't be! And yet I know that the battle is lost!" '

And indeed the Battle of the Somme was lost. On June 8, breaking through a British curtain spread over Béthune and Andelle, Rommel pushed towards Elbeuf, and our 10th Army then allowed the breach to widen, the forces isolated on the left withdrawing towards Le Havre while the bulk of the army retired towards Pontoise. The lower Seine was now wide open, and General Weygand ordered General Duffour, Commander of the 3rd Region in Rouen, to improvise a barrier across the river with his regional units. He also gave orders for the 'Paris Military Government' to be turned into a 'Paris Army', under General Hering, to defend the Seine between Vernon and Pontoise and the western part of the 'Paris advanced position', while the eastern part was to be defended by the 7th Army.

In the east, after the Germans had crossed the Aisne and set up a bridgehead at Soissons, our 6th Army withdrew to the Marne, east of the Ferté. The 3rd Army Group then re-formed in the lower Seine sector, the Paris advanced position, and the Marne. 'If this line is crossed,' declared the C-in-C, 'then a co-ordinated defence of the territory will be impossible.'

On June 8 Rommel had engaged in a raid on the Elbeuf bridges. After passing through villages during the night (amid the acclamation of the inhabitants who, awakened by the roar of the 'caterpillar' vehicles, mistook them for the British), the Germans were outside Elbeuf by dawn on the 9th—just in time to see the bridges blown up! Yet they had managed to reach the Seine.

Completely isolated, the western flank of the French 10th Army dug in at St Valéry-en-Caux, on the coast, to attempt an evacuation by sea; but, under attack by the VII Panzer Division, it had to surrender on June 12 after heroic resistance—particularly by the British 51st Highland Division under General Fortune.

Our disposition was then as follows: from the sea to Vernon, the 10th Army; in the Paris advanced position, the Paris Army and the 7th Army; on the Marne east of Ferté-sous-Jouarre, the 6th Army. By the morning of June 9 the battle extended eastwards to the Aisne; it was now the turn of Rundstedt's army group to assume the attack, and as a result of the resistance which had held up the German XIV and XVI Armoured Corps for two days south of Amiens and Péronne, these had now been transferred from Bock's to Rundstedt's army group. Now Rundstedt had four of the five armoured corps, and was to thrust against Champagne. The main scene of the battle had moved to the east.

General Weygand then issued the following Order of the Day: 'The enemy offensive now covers the whole of the front. . . . The order to fight with no thought of withdrawal still stands. The enemy has suffered considerable losses. His forces will soon be exhausted. We are now at the eleventh hour. Hold fast!'

The Aisne battle

On the Somme, thanks to their bridgeheads, the Germans had been able to throw their Panzers directly into the attack. On the Aisne, German infantry had to blaze a passage for the tanks, and at 0500 hours on June 9 the XII German Army infantry attacked the French 4th Army positions on the Aisne, between Neufchâtel and Attigny.

On the right, the 14th Infantry Division of General de Lattre de Tassigny threw back the German units which had started to cross the river, taking 800 prisoners. In the centre also, at various points near Rethel, the 2nd Infantry Division fought off every attack, and it was in this sector that the XXXIX and XLI Panzer Corps of the Guderian group should have crossed the Aisne to make an onslaught on Champagne.

During the morning, from a hill to the north of the Aisne, General Guderian observed the fruitless assault of the German infantry. In his words he was 'anxious not to misjudge his intervention', but the way was still closed that afternoon, and Guderian was seething with

impatience; as the last straw General List, the army commander, made some biting comments to him about the inactivity of his tanks on the north side of the river!

But at the end of the afternoon, on learning that a small bridgehead had been set up farther to the west at Château-Porcien, Guderian decided to move the I Panzer Division there overnight for an attack at 1000 hours next day, followed by the II Panzer Division. On the evening of June 9 at the OKH (Land Army HQ) List wrote: 'The French resisted firmly, and the attack did not proceed beyond a few bridgeheads.'

However, General Weygand did not appear to think that prolonged resistance was possible. At a conference on the 9th he stated: 'Our armies are fighting the last possible defensive battle. If this attempt fails, they are doomed to rapid destruction.' That evening he prepared a note which he delivered to the President of the War Council next day, saying that 'the ultimate failure of our lines may occur at any moment. . . . Our armies would then fight to the end, but their collapse would only be a question of time.'

At 0600 hours on June 10 the I Panzer Division left the Château-Porcien bridgehead, followed by German infantry, and marched on the Retourne, the French 4th Army's second position. 'Our Panzers are not meeting any opposition on open ground,' wrote Guderian, 'because the new French tactics are concentrated on the defence of the villages and the woods, and at these operational bases our infantry is meeting firm house-to-house, barricade-to-barricade resistance.'

But by 1600 hours the French 'hedgehogs' had fallen and the Panzers were crossing the Retourne. About one hour later a flanking counterattack by Buisson's armoured group commenced. 'But,' wrote the Chief of General Staff of the north-east front, 'our tanks came too late. They were soon spotted, and the element of surprise was lost.' A wild *mêlée* of the armoured forces ensued, in which our heavy 'B' tanks—the strongest in the world at the time—inflicted heavy losses on the Panzers. Guderian, who was himself caught up in the scuffle, described the scene: 'At one point I was trying in vain to immobilise a "B" tank with a captured French 47-mm anti-tank gun, but all the shells ricochetted off the thick plate of the French tank! The French 37- and 25-mm guns were also ineffective. Because of this we had to take severe losses.'

To the north of the Retourne the French tanks advanced about 2 miles, rescuing a regiment encircled in the village of Perthes and destroying some 100 German armoured vehicles. But the enemy had had time to re-form his rear, and because of the delay in mounting it, the French armoured counterattack was indecisive. 'Here, as at Sedan and Dinant,' wrote the Chief of General Staff of the north-east front, 'our mechanised units had no opportunity of putting their shock strength into effect.' In the face of the overwhelming numerical superiority of the enemy, our tank forces and infantry were powerless to alter the course of the battle, despite their brilliant local successes.

Meanwhile the II Panzer Division in its turn left the Château-Porcien bridgehead and by the afternoon was on the northern outskirts of Rheims, driving the French 6th Army towards the Marne. Outflanked on the left, our 4th Army had to abandon the Rethel-Aisne and withdraw overnight to Rheims Mountain, in touch with the 6th Army at Damery on the Marne on the left, and the 2nd Army, south of Vouzier, on the right. Unfortunately, only depleted and exhausted units reached the new Marne-Rheims Mountain-Argonne front—which marked the end of organised resistance.

On the same day—June 10—to the west of Paris, the Germans were crossing the lower Seine and in the east they were pushing from the Ourcq to the Marne. Paris was thus threatened with an outflanking movement on two sides. The government decided to leave the capital that evening for Tours, the first step towards Bordeaux (where a displaced government had been set up in 1870), and General Weygand ordered the GHQ to be withdrawn to Briare. Then, at 1700 hours, it was learned that Italy would enter the war at midnight. Mussolini had knifed the 'Latin Sister' in the back.

51

By the morning of the next day, the Germans had already established three bridgeheads on the lower Seine at Elbeuf, les Andelys, and Louviers, and in the east they crossed the Marne at Château-Thierry. The double outflanking movement was now in progress. Further to the east, Kleist's armoured group crossed the Aisne at Berry-au-Bac, and there were now eight armoured divisions in Champagne. Rheims fell; the enemy pushed towards Rheims Mountain.

There was now no hope of defending Paris. At 1100 hours, by agreement with the President of the War Council, the C-in-C declared Paris an 'open city', and ordered: 'General Hering will command the Paris Army and watch over its fate, while General Dentz, to whom he will delegate the functions of governor, will stay behind right until the Germans enter the city.' Paris was abandoned, and the French army was ordered to retreat without a strategic aim: it prepared for nothing, because no recovery was possible in metropolitan France, and covered nothing, because the C-in-C was not envisaging a withdrawal across the Mediterranean. The roads along which our units would sink in the flood of refugees were roads leading inevitably towards total surrender – whatever names it was given on the way.

On the morning of June 11 at the GHQ set up in Briare, General Weygand counted the losses: we still had 52 divisions on paper, but they were equivalent to about only 30. In fact, 11 divisions had no more than 50% of their theoretical strength; 13 had 25%, while 10 were only remnants. Finally, the GHQ had only one reserve division.

Only two solutions could be seen at Briare: either to maintain the Maginot Line and withdraw our centre and left-hand armies southwards, which would eventually lead to encirclement of all our forces; or else to beat a retreat of all the armies. This was the solution which General Weygand adopted. He therefore sent General Georges a 'personal and confidential instruction' which laid out the basic organisation for a retreat, without as yet ordering its execution. The aim was stated at the outset: 'to ensure that the centre of the country is covered *for as long as possible*' – this was only a stay of execution – and the axes of withdrawal were fixed as follows:

● **10th Army:** axis Rouen-Argentan;

● **3rd Army Group** (Paris Army and 7th Army): axis Paris-Orleans-Vierzon;

● **4th Army Group** (6th, 4th, and 2nd Armies): Châlons-Troyes-Nevers;

● **2nd Army Group** (3rd, 5th, and 8th Armies): from the Maginot Line to Épinal-Dijon.

'The ultimate withdrawal line,' continued Weygand, 'will be the line Caen-Alençon-the Loire from Tours to Briare-the Morvans-the Côte d'Or-the Juras. On the Maginot Line some garrisons instructed by General Prételat will carry on resisting until the withdrawal of the bulk of the forces is complete.'

At 1900 hours on June 11 a meeting of the Supreme Council of Briare – which was later to become famous – opened at the Château of le Muguet, attended by Marshal Pétain, Generals Weygand and de Gaulle for France, and Churchill, Eden, and Generals Ismay and Spears for Britain. Weygand depicted the situation in dark colours and declared that 'the last line of defence has been overrun and all the reserves are used up. We are on a knife-edge, and don't know which way we may fall from one minute to the next.' After General Weygand had finished speaking, General Georges was called in, and said that 'if the enemy renews his attacks based on armour and aerial bombardment, there is a risk of dislocation of our order of battle'. Finally, General Weygand gave a warning: 'Once our disposition is upset, and that won't be long now, there is no hope of re-forming it, because of our lack of reserves. In this case I could see no way of preventing an invasion of the whole of France.'

'These three hours of discussions achieved nothing,' writes General de Gaulle. 'I thought how empty this chatter was, because it was not directed towards the only viable solution: recovery across the sea.'

On June 12 the situation deteriorated. The Paris advanced position was not attacked, but in the west the enemy crossed the lower Seine in force. To the east, south of the Marne, they reached Montmirail, while in Champagne the thrust of the Panzers came like lightning. In the morning, Guderian crossed the Champagne Mountains and threw Schmidt's XXXIX Armoured Corps against Châlons, covering it to the east by Reinhardt's XLI Armoured Corps.

'The limit was reached,' wrote General Weygand, 'our last line of defence was cracking everywhere. The battle of France was lost. My resolution was firm. In a few hours I would ask the government to conclude an armistice.'

From now on the C-in-C lost all interest in the military operations, and turned his efforts instead towards asking for an armistice. He himself wrote: 'I had provided the best conditions for the retreat, but at this juncture my role at GHQ was taking a back seat. My duties of advising the government were becoming all-important, and would take up most of my time.' But while our highest leaders waged battle in the councils, the retreat had still to continue until an armistice had been sought and obtained from the victor.

The fall of Paris

On June 13 the enemy, after crossing the Seine to the west of Paris, reached Évreux, and pushed towards Dreux, driving the French 10th Army westwards, where it withdrew to Brittany. That same day the Paris Army and the 7th Army abandoned the Paris advanced position and moved round the capital on the east and the west, so as to re-form provisionally along a line marked by the Rambouillet Forest, the Chevreuse Valley, and the Corbeil Seine. 'Our armies,' wrote General Georges in his report, 'are starting their withdrawal under attack from the air and the constant threat of encirclement by the Panzers.' Their general condition was like that of his 4th Army:

'The disposition has failed. Exhausted by four days of battle and night marches, the troops no longer have the appearance of organised units. On the 13th, some divisions have no more than several hundred men. Communications have broken down. The orders, carried by officers bogged down in the columns of refugees, can no longer be carried out when they at last arrive at their destination.'

Thus Paris was completely cleared of our armies. On June 14, a day of mourning, the Germans entered Paris . . . and they were to stay there for four years. The abandoning of Paris was accompanied by an exodus of the population, along the roads to the south, joining those already fleeing from Belgium and northern France. On the 14th the German GHQ ordered a pursuit in three directions:

● **South-westerly** towards the Loire: the XIV Panzer Corps to cut off the retreat of the French troops withdrawing to Bordeaux;

● **South-easterly** towards Dijon and Lyon: the XVI Panzer Corps to help the Italians cross the Alpine passes by attacking the defending army from the rear;

● **Easterly** towards the Langres Plateau and the Swiss frontier: Guderian's armoured group to cut off the retreat of the French armies in the Maginot Line.

On the French side, that evening the GHQ withdrew to Vichy. The 7th Army and the Paris Army fell back to the Loire, leaving voids in the east and the west. At 1900 hours on June 15, General Georges reported to General Weygand in Bordeaux that 'the armies are completely split up'. It was becoming impossible to organise fronts to prevent deep incisions by the enemy; all we were doing was mobilising scratch forces to try to 'plug' the incisions.

In the west the enemy was pushing towards the 'Brittany redoubt', while in the east the Panzers were bearing down on Dijon and Langres to imprison the 2nd Army Group, which had only started its withdrawal from the Maginot Line the day before.

Not surprisingly, General Prételat had some caustic comments to make, for when he had asked for authority to prepare for the withdrawal of his armies on May 26, and again on June 2, General Weygand had refused, because he wanted, he said, 'to stake everything on the existing line, with no thought of retreat'. General Prételat wrote: 'In refusing to consider the possibility of a withdrawal or to authorise its preparation, a decision which he was to

reconsider only on June 12—far too late—the Commander-in-Chief had sealed the fate of the eastern forces.'

The retreat, which was ordered on June 12, did not in fact begin until the 14th. In order to escape encirclement the armies of the east would have to cross the line Langres-Gray-Besançon before the arrival of the enemy. The 45th Corps was sent in this direction to keep the way open, but Guderian's Panzers were already in Langres and Gray on the 15th; they reached Besançon on the 16th and the Swiss frontier at Pontparler on the 17th. Our armies were thus completely cut off. As for the 45th Corps, they were to cross into Switzerland and be interned there.

Meanwhile, the I German Army, which had emerged from the breach of the Sarre at Sarrebourg on the 15th, was marching on the Vosges from north to south, while the VII Army, which crossed the Rhine at Neuf-Brisach, was bearing down on the Vosges from east to west. Pressed on all sides and with all avenues of retreat cut, the 3rd, 5th, and 8th French Armies drew together in the Vosges. On June 22 General Condé, who had taken over command of this group of armies, was authorised by General Weygand to capitulate with his 400,000 men.

'From the 17th onwards,' wrote General Roton, 'the German thrust is overwhelming. There is no longer any co-ordinated defence except on the Loire.' By now, it was simply a question of waiting for the armistice. Indeed, the previous night, June 16/17, the Reynaud Cabinet had fallen and had been replaced by a Pétain government and this government's first thought was to ask the Germans for an armistice. On the 17th the Marshal broadcast a message to the French people saying: 'It is with a sad heart that I tell you we must stop fighting.' 'This,' wrote General Georges, 'finally broke the spring of the French army's resistance'—and that evening, because of the effect the sentence had produced, Baudouin, now Minister of Foreign Affairs, amended it for the press to: 'We must *endeavour* to stop fighting.'

On the 17th the Führer declared in a special order that 'the occupation of Cherbourg and Brest is a *matter of honour* for the German army'. General Hoth, commanding the XV Armoured Corps, which preceded the IV Army in the direction of the lower Loire, immediately brought Rommel's VII Panzer Division around to Cherbourg and the V Panzer to Brest. On the 18th the armoured troops entered Rennes, where they captured the headquarters of the 10th Army together with its commander, so liquidating the 'Brittany redoubt'. The next day the two armoured divisions easily took Cherbourg and Brest, and then continued southwards towards the lower Loire and Rochefort. In the bend of the Loire, meanwhile, the enemy began to cross the river at La Charité-sur-Loire and at Briare.

On the 19th between Tours and Saumur, the enemy broke down the last resistance on the river—despite the efforts of the cadets of the cavalry school at Saumur, who on this day wrote a page of glory into French history. General Besson withdrew the remnants of his armies to the Cher. In the east, the Germans were reaching Vichy and Lyon. From June 21 to 25—despite occasional pockets of resistance with rearguards sacrificing themselves to cover the retreat, and even isolated groups who, having had enough of constantly withdrawing, lay in ambush alongside the roads and met death where they lay—the Germans continued their remorseless march, bringing them to a line Royan/Angoulême/Clermont-Ferrand/St Étienne/northern approaches to Tournon/and finally Grenoble. Then the armistice was finally secured.

But we had been at war with Italy since June 10, and another battle, a Franco-Italian one, was already in progress on the southeast front where the French Alpine Army, despite its extremely low manpower, was contributing a notable chapter to history.

On June 10 in Rome, from his balcony high above the Piazza Venezia, and amid the delirious acclamations of his supporters, the Duce had announced to the world that Italy had entered the war to 'liberate' Savoy, Nice, Corsica, and so on. But his armies, massed along the frontier of the Alps, had delayed their attack until the Germans reached the Rhône valley on the heels of the small French Alpine Army commanded by General Olry. So it was not until June 20 that the Italians took the offensive with two armies (I and IV) consisting of a total of 24 divisions, of which 19 were in the first echelon. In the rear, eight divisions of the VII Army were ready to engage—making a total of 32 Italian divisions on the Alpine front.

Against this, General Olry's French Army of the Alps numbered only three divisions of the 'B' series—the 64th, 65th, and 66th Infantry Divisions—and three 'Fortress Sections' (the garrisons of the fortified sectors of the Alpes-Maritimes, Dauphine, and Savoy), each equivalent to a fortress division. Six French divisions therefore faced 32 Italian. But the very accumulation of Italian divisions in the narrow valleys of the high mountains, where they were unable to deploy, was only to increase their losses under the fire of the French artillery which had prepared its 'beaten zones' and had at its disposal excellent observation posts on the summits. Moreover, from June 11 General Olry had put into effect a very efficient plan for destroying the mountain passes, so that when the Italians came to cross the frontier, they would have the greatest difficulty in advancing and revictualling.

Every Italian attack made on the frontier passes in the Tarente, Maures, Briançon, Queyras areas failed. In some cases, and especially on the Mont Genevre pass, a few companies of reserve Alpine Rifles posted on the ridges sufficed to block the formidable Italian forces thrusting into the high valleys.

On the 21st, however, the Italians did achieve several local successes, although on this day the powerful Italian fort of Chaberton, which had fired on Briançon, was silenced by our batteries. On the 22nd, in the Maures area, the Italians passed Lanslebourg, and in the Briançon area they reached—but did not succeed in penetrating—the frontier pass of Mont Genevre towards Briançon. On the 23rd, on the Côte D'Azur, the Italians launched an attack to 'liberate' Nice. At the frontier, alongside the mountain, they infiltrated into Menton; but on the coastal road the St Louis bridge fort, on the actual frontier, which was only defended by a dozen men, held fast right up to the armistice. When the armistice brought hostilities to an end, our resistance position was still intact from Switzerland to the sea.

In order to understand this lack of verve on the part of the Italians, we should remember that the Italian nation, bulldozed into the war by Mussolini's megalomania, was averse to fighting against France. Moreover, the Germans—who had to throw open the passes to their allies by taking the Alpine Army from the rear—were themselves held in check up to the armistice by isolated regional elements on the Isère, in Chartreuse, and on the Lac du Bourget. One such element was a hastily formed group, under the remarkable General Cartier, which successfully prevented the Germans from entering Grenoble until the end.

Alas, all this gallantry was not enough to prevent our defeat.

No faith in victory

How could France have fallen so quickly? In the First World War French officers and soldiers had won the admiration of the world through their tenacity and the scale of their sacrifice: 1,500,000 dead. In the Second World War, the sons were a credit to their fathers. They proved this on the Aisne and elsewhere, and were to prove it again in Africa, at Bir-Hakeim and in Tunisia, and later in Italy, where they were in the vanguard of victory, opening the road to Rome for the Allies, and finally in France and Germany, up to the Rhine and the Danube.

But in 1940, inadequately armed, badly deployed tactically in accordance with the precepts of 1918, badly disposed strategically, and led by commanders who had no faith in victory, they were defeated in the first round of the battle. The first C-in-C, Gamelin, watched the catastrophe approach with fatalism. 'Things are going to be terrible,' he said, and once battle had been joined he gave no orders, for this was not 'his battle', but that of General Georges.

Ullstein

The second C-in-C, Weygand, urged only a 'fight for honour, to the last', and then armistice. Furthermore, on June 19 he was to tell enquirers: 'I was only called in when everything was balled up!'

France in 1940 lacked someone of the calibre of Joffre, who had not despaired at the end of August 1914, when everything appeared lost. Above all what France needed was a Clemenceau or a Churchill at its head. The fatalistic acceptance of defeat by our highest leaders had been indicated very soon after the first setbacks. As early as June 5, the day of the Battle of the Somme, General Weygand had told the War Council that 'if the battle then beginning were lost, there would be no cowardice in negotiating with the enemy' – which might seem a rather odd way of putting it. However, Marshal Pétain agreed, and said that he 'supported General Weygand absolutely'.

By June 8, with Rommel raiding Elbeuf, the battle was considered lost, and General Weygand referred at the morning conference to the 'gaping wound' which had been opened in the 10th Army. That afternoon General de Gaulle, recently appointed Under-Secretary of State for War, visited him at the Montry GHQ. He reported the interview as follows:

'A few moments' conversation suffices to show me that General Weygand is resigned to defeat and has decided on an armistice. The conversation went as follows:

"You see," he said to me, "the Germans are passing the Somme, I can't stop them."

"Right, they're passing the Somme. And then?"

"Then it's the Seine and the Marne."

"Yes, and then?"

"Then, but it's finished!"

"How is it finished? And the world? The empire?"

"The empire! That's nonsense! As for the world, after my fight here, it won't be a week before Britain is negotiating with the Reich!"'

Marshal Pétain, for his part, told Louis Marin, Minister of State, that 'he was not a bit afraid of meeting Hitler, he would gladly approach him as between soldiers, and in this way he would obtain more than from a discussion between diplomats'.

However, there was a further solution, other than this ultimate passive collapse of the French army. During the night of June 9/10, the President of the War Council, M Reynaud, summoned General de Gaulle, advising him of the threat overhanging Paris and of the imminence of the Italian declaration of war. 'In the face of this bad news,' wrote General de Gaulle, 'I had only one suggestion to make: to go it the hard way and get to Africa as soon as possible, adopting a war of coalition. . . . With the bases and the plan to which we were committed, there was no way out except surrender. Instead of resigning ourselves to this, as some (and not the least important) were already doing, it was necessary to change the plan and the bases. A recovery, as on the Marne in 1914, was still possible on the Mediterranean.'

But General Weygand did not envisage this solution. At 1800 hours on the 10th he too visited the President of the War Council. General de Gaulle was also present and recorded the interview thus:

'General Weygand sits down and proceeds to set forth the situation as he sees it. His conclusion is patent; we must ask for an armistice without delay. . . . The President tries to dispute this opinion, but Weygand sticks to it. The battle of metropolitan France is lost. We must surrender.'

At 1800 hours on June 12, after giving orders for a general retreat, Weygand told the War Council for the first time of the need for an armistice. 'The main thing is to avoid a total disintegration of the army,' he said, 'and so we should ask the German government for an armistice forthwith.' He added: 'France can now request an armistice without blushing. I am proud to have fought on the Somme a battle restoring the true honour of the French army. It has defended honour, and henceforward negotiation will no longer be unworthy of it.'

Marshal Pétain then read – as usual – a prepared note, concluding with 'the necessity for requesting an armistice to save what remains of France and to permit rebuilding of the country'.

It was evident that if the government moved to Africa to continue the fight there alongside the Allies – with the fleet intact, the aircraft still remaining to us (almost the same in number as on May 10, because of the output from the factories and the deliveries of American aircraft), and the forces abroad – then Hitler would not agree either to a free zone in 'what remained of France', or to a small army to ensure order there and enable us 'to rebuild the country'. Thus from now on the prevention of the departure of the government would be the main aim of the military commanders and, in the wings, of Pierre Laval.

On the 13th, at the Council of Ministers held in the afternoon at Cangey, Weygand repeated his request of the previous day.

Far left: French prisoners stream down the roads of France. On June 22 General Weygand authorised the surrender of the army group in the east—a total of 400,000 men

◁German soldiers help themselves to petrol on their drive through France

▷ The Luftwaffe kept pressure on the fleeing French by attacking key roads, bridges, and railway lines ahead of the thrusts of armour and infantry

▽Near the Franco-German border—as here, in Strasbourg —the French were often quick to adjust to occupation

Ullstein

Ullstein

Ullstein

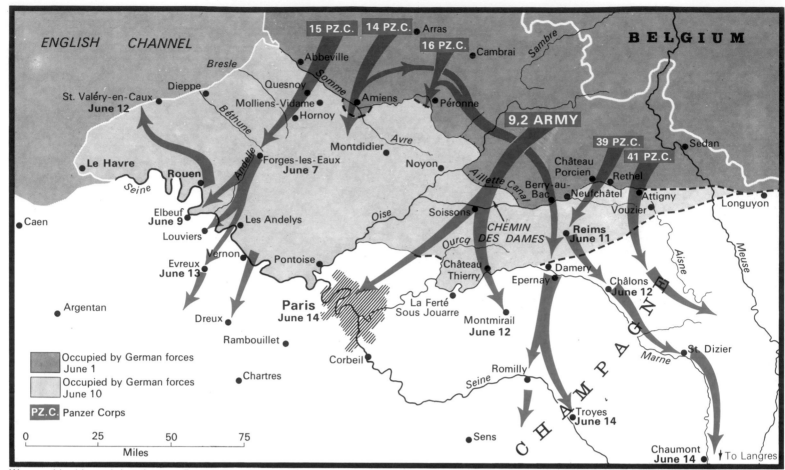

Weygand had hoped that the new French line along the Somme and the Aisne would hold the Germans, but the Panzers broke through in many places

By June 8 the Germans were breaking deep into France

'If we wish to save the discipline of the army,' he said, 'we must rapidly obtain a cessation of hostilities.' Marshal Pétain then rose and took a note from his pocket which he proceeded to read. 'The armistice is inevitable,' he said, 'it should be requested without delay.'

The next day, the government moved to Bordeaux. Before leaving, the President of the War Council sent a final appeal to the President of the United States, asking him 'in order to save France, advanced guard of the democracies, to throw the weight of American power into the scales'. Yet, in the chaos of the hour, Baudouin, who had visited Marshal Pétain, was told that 'the 15th of June had been fixed as the final date for the request for an armistice. He will send General Weygand a message telling him that his presence at Bordeaux is necessary'.

Despite this, on the evening of the 14th President Reynaud was continuing to make preparations for transporting recruits and depot personnel to North Africa. In agreement with Campbell, the British ambassador, he decided to send General de Gaulle to London the next day with our tonnage requirements, reckoned at 500,000 tons over a fortnight. But Pierre Laval, who had arrived in Bordeaux on the 14th, was already at work making arrangements which would lead eventually to foreign domination of his country. 'On my arrival,' he was to say two days later, 'I saw the Spanish ambassador, de Lequerica, and arranged formalities for an armistice request. I was able to do this through my numerous previous contacts. The following night I saw the Marshal and explained to him my ideas on how he would be made Chief of State.'

At 1500 hours President Reynaud made a proposal which caused a great flutter among the partisans of the armistice. He asked General Weygand to follow the example of the Dutch Chief of General Staff, and surrender with the one army on metropolitan soil, while the government went to North Africa to continue the struggle there alongside Britain, with our powerful fleet intact and the aircraft and troops which could be saved from metropolitan France. 'I rejected the proposal with indignation,' wrote General Weygand. 'I will never agree to inflicting such shame on our flag! . . . This would have been the ultimate crime, damning and doing irreparable harm to the military honour of our nation, a crime which the Military Code of Justice punishes with death! . . . I cannot think of such an ignominious proposal without a shiver of disgust!'

What 'ignominy' Weygand saw in this proposal is difficult to follow. He apparently considered it less dishonourable to give up

the common fight of our entire sea, air, and overseas forces *in combat order,* than to surrender only the forces on metropolitan soil—which was, in fact, soil no longer under French control. And at that moment, what did this 'metropolitan' force amount to, whose surrender would have been so ignominious? In his evidence at the Pétain trial after the war, General Georges was to state: 'At the moment when we were about to stop fighting, five armies were partly imprisoned. In the groups which had fought step by step over a depth of 281 miles, the trained effective strengths still available were of the order of three to four hundred thousand men'—or, with the Alpine Army, about 500,000 men.

Furthermore, on June 22, the C-in-C saw no ignominy in authorising the army group in the east, with its 400,000 men, to 'ask for a cessation of fighting with war honours'—and in any case, what *is* punishable with death, according to Article 233 of the French Code of Military Justice, is 'surrender without having exhausted all means of defence', which was by no means the case here.

Then Chautemps—Vice-President of the War Council—intervened. He proposed asking Hitler his conditions for ending fighting, to prove that nothing acceptable could be expected of him—an attractive-sounding proposal which contained, however, the danger of being the first step in a downhill slope towards capitulation. Georges Mandel, Minister of the Interior, cautioned the Council against the dangers of this step, adding: 'We are losing precious time for transporting a large contingent of troops to Africa. All this delay is aimed at one thing: keeping us from resisting.'

Fall of the Reynaud Cabinet

On June 16, at the council at 11 am, Marshal Pétain rose and read out his letter of resignation. 'We have delayed too long,' he said. 'It's time to stop.' But when Paul Reynaud asked him to wait for America's reply, he consented and sat down again. This respite did not last long, however. At a further council at 4 pm, Reynaud read out President Roosevelt's reply, which was disappointing because, while certainly promising arms and equipment, it declared that Roosevelt could not undertake any military engagement without a decision by Congress.

The President of the War Council then made known a 'plan of indissoluble union' between Britain and France of which General de Gaulle had just told him on the telephone from London. But, wrote

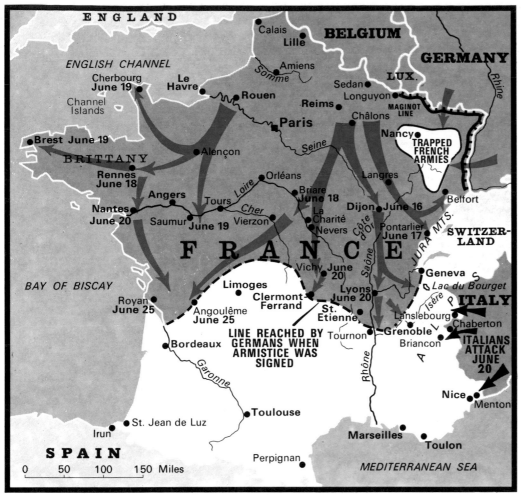

In the north the Germans broke the Weygand line; in the south Italy struck

May 10: The Germans launch their offensive against Belgium, Holland, and Luxembourg.
May 15: Holland capitulates.
May 19: General Weygand takes command of the French army.
May 20: German tanks break through to the Channel, cutting off the Allies in the north.
May 26: Operation Dynamo—the evacuation of Allied forces from Dunkirk—begins.
May 28: Belgium capitulates.
June 5: The Germans launch their major offensive against France, beginning the Battle of the Somme.
June 7: Rommel's VII Panzer Division, avoiding the French 'hedgehogs', drives to Forges-les-Eaux—37 miles south of the Somme.
June 8: French forces withdraw from the Somme sector.
June 10: Mussolini declares war on France.
June 11: A German pincer movement threatens Paris, which the French C-in-C declares an 'open city'. French and British leaders—among them Pétain, de Gaulle, Churchill, and Eden—meet at Briare to discuss the situation.
June 13: French troops abandon Paris.
June 14: German troops enter Paris.
June 16: The Reynaud Cabinet falls at Bordeaux, to be replaced by a Pétain government.
June 17: Marshal Pétain broadcasts to the French people to 'stop fighting'. Notes to the Germans and Italians, asking them for their armistice terms, are sent via Madrid and the Vatican.
June 20: The Italians take the offensive on the Alpine front.
June 21: A French delegation meets with Hitler at Rethonde.
June 22: General Weygand authorises the signing of the armistice convention; in the east, the 3rd, 5th, and 8th French Armies—a total of 400,000 men—surrender.
June 24: In Rome, a French delegation signs an armistice with Italy.

the President of the Republic, Albert Lebrun: 'The Council was greatly surprised at this. . . . In such an unfavourable atmosphere this project only met with a tepid welcome, despite the support of the President of the Council and myself.'

Ybarnegaray, Minister of State, protested against such a union, 'which would make France a dominion', and the Marshal, convinced that Britain was going to be beaten, declared that he didn't want to 'unite with a corpse'. The discussions on the Chautemps project then resumed with a clear majority favouring it. But at this point, the President of the War Council, realising that his own opinion was being overruled, announced the resignation of his Cabinet. At 10 pm the meeting ended. No vote had been taken.

At 11 pm President of the Republic Lebrun met Mm Reynaud, Herriot, and Jeanneney—Presidents of the War Council, of the Chamber, and of the Senate. He asked the President of the War Council to apply Chautemp's proposal and when Reynaud refused, a new leader of the government had to be appointed.

'But who?' asked Lebrun.

'You won't be embarrassed,' replied Reynaud. 'The Marshal told me this morning that he had his Cabinet in his pocket!'

'I summoned the Marshal then,' wrote Lebrun. 'I asked him to form a Cabinet. A pleasant surprise for me! He opened his briefcase and presented me with the list of his collaborators!'

At 11.30 pm the President of the Republic signed the decree nominating the new Ministers who, already under pressure, met immediately. This council lasted ten minutes. Baudouin, now Minister for Foreign Affairs, was instructed to ask the Germans and Italians for their armistice terms through the intermediary of Madrid and the Vatican, respectively. He then summoned the two ambassadors. Charles Roux, Secretary-General at the Ministry of Foreign Affairs, wrote: 'There was no risk of the summons addressed to de Lequerica, the Spanish ambassador, taking him unawares! He was expecting and waiting for it.'

'At 12.30 am,' wrote Baudouin, 'I send the note to de Lequerica. He telephones St Jean-de-Luz, where two attachés are waiting at the end of the line. They will go to Irun, from where they will telephone Madrid.' So everything was arranged! But was it really an armistice, that is, a suspension of hostilities, that they wanted?

In Madrid, the French note was passed to Colonel Beigbeder, Spanish Minister of Foreign Affairs, to Baron von Stohrer, the German ambassador who, on receiving this message, forwarded the following text to Wilhelmstrasse in a telegram:

'The government of Marshal Pétain requests the Spanish government to act with all possible speed as an intermediary with the German government, to ask for a cessation of hostilities and for their peace terms. The French government hopes that on receipt of this note the German government will order its aircraft to stop the bombing of towns. *Signed:* Baudouin, Minister of Foreign Affairs.'

A second telegram followed: 'The Spanish ambassador in Bordeaux supplements his report of the French request for peace with the following telegram:

"At midnight M Baudouin telephoned, asking me to call immediately at the Presidency. There he told me that the French government hoped the Spanish government would pass on to Germany, with all possible speed, their request for an immediate cessation of hostilities and for peace terms. I asked him if he meant armistice terms, or peace terms, or both. He replied that an armistice was obviously a temporary expedient, but that the French government was interested in learning the peace terms." '

Two hours later, at 9.30 in the evening of the 17th, Baudouin broadcast to the nation, giving the government's reasons for the defeat and saying: 'This is why the Marshal's government had to ask the enemy for his "peace terms".' How was Hitler going to receive this request?

On June 15 General Keitel, Chief of the German General Staff, had already instructed Colonel Bohme to draw up a draft armistice convention 'to prevent any resumption of hostilities by the French'. 'The first draft, which I completed in the evening of the 16th,' wrote General Bohme, 'provided for total occupation of metropolitan France and total disarmament of the French forces.'

But on the 17th, on receipt of the Bordeaux request via Madrid, Hitler gave fresh instructions to Generals Keitel and Jodl, and to Colonel Bohme, which the latter relates as follows:

'The Führer said that France had to be cut off from Britain and that, to do this, she must obtain terms appearing to make up for this. Since the Pétain government appeared to be favourably disposed, it had to be given a "golden bridge"; otherwise there would still be a risk of the French government escaping to North Africa with its fleet and some of its aircraft, to continue the war there. This would strengthen Britain's position and stir up the war in the Mediterranean, where Italy was in an isolated position.'

◁ June 21, 1940: the meeting for the Armistice. Now the wheel had come a full circle. It was in this same coach that the 1918 Armistice was signed

▷ Triumphal German march through Paris

Hitler then specified his directives:

1. The French government must survive as a sovereign power. Only in this way can we be certain that the French colonial empire will not go over to Britain.

2. Thus a total occupation of metropolitan France is inadvisable. The French government must retain a sphere of sovereignty.

3. The French army will be taken to the free zone and demobilised there. The preservation of some units in a free zone must be permitted in order to maintain order. The fleet must be neutralised. Under no circumstances must we demand its hand-over, otherwise it would withdraw overseas or to Britain.

4. The territorial demands are a matter for the peace settlement, which cannot be discussed at present.

5. No demand concerning the empire will be formulated for the moment. This would only drive the colonies to Britain. Moreover, in case of refusal, we could not put these demands into effect by force at present.

But Hitler still needed to have all this approved by Mussolini, and this was the object of the conference now held at Munich between Hitler and Mussolini.

'At Munich,' General Bohme wrote, 'despite strong opposition from the Italians, Hitler won acceptance for his moderate terms. His aim was, he said, to get an armistice at any price. Mussolini yielded.

'The fleet was the main question. Hitler played on "the great increase in power which this fleet would represent to Britain", and concluded: "It is preferable therefore to reach an agreement with the French government, in order to neutralise the fleet in the French ports, under German or Italian control."

'As a bait, the French would be given a guarantee that their fleet would be restored to them when peace was proclaimed. Ribbentrop and Ciano were now brought in, and Hitler repeated that "the main thing was to prevent any departure of the French fleet for Britain". The Duce approved.'

On the morning of June 19, the German government declared itself ready 'to announce the terms for a cessation of hostilities', and requested the names of the plenipotentiaries. At 10 am on the 20th, Baudouin sent a list to de Lequerica, announcing that the delegation would be led by General Huntziger, with Ambassador Léon Noël as his deputy. At 2 pm the delegation left Bordeaux.

Meanwhile, the Germans had continued their advance on Bordeaux, and Marshal Pétain, at the insistence of the Presidents of the Chamber and the Senate, agreed that the government, to avoid capture, should withdraw to Perpignan, within reach of North Africa. He himself would remain in France 'to come between the victor and the country' and would delegate his powers to Chautemps, the Vice-President. But on the 20th, the Marshal decided to defer the departure. At 10 pm he received a delegation of members of parliament led by Laval, and brought them up to date as regards the military situation. He favoured an early peace, because of Britain's desperate position. At 8 am the next day he cancelled the departure of the government.

The same railway coach

At 3.30 pm on June 21 the French delegation was shown into the same railway coach as that in which the Armistice of 1918 had been signed, and where Hitler and the top leaders of the Third Reich now awaited them. After reading the preamble, Hitler raised his arm and left the coach, after which Keitel handed the French the text of the convention, which he said could not be altered. Our delegation then retired into a tent to study the document. At 8.30 pm, General Huntziger was allowed to telephone General Weygand in Bordeaux. Dr Schmidt, the Führer's interpreter, who listened in, reported the conversation as follows:

'General Huntziger began by saying that he had not been acquainted with any peace terms, the German delegation having refused to discuss this subject. He had simply been handed an armistice convention of 24 articles, which they said could not be altered.'

On June 22, after discussions which resulted only in an agreement that units of the French navy could be stationed in overseas ports, plus a few other minor concessions, at 6.34 pm Keitel handed the French delegation an ultimatum. They had until 7.30 pm to sign it, 'otherwise the delegation will be led back to the outposts'.

At 6.42 pm General Huntziger signed the convention on telephoned orders from General Weygand, but as the convention was only to come into force after an armistice with Italy, it was then necessary for our delegation to leave on the 23rd for Rome, to be received by Marshal Badoglio, who was conciliatory and courteous in the discussions. Signatures were exchanged at 7.10 pm on the 24th. Hostilities would cease at 1.35 am.

Why did Hitler refuse to divulge his peace terms? Otto Meissner, head of the Reich Chancellery, explained: 'In 1940, Hitler often

said that he would not enter into an engagement with France, because he wanted to see what Britain would do. An engagement with France would only complicate the peace arrangements, the crux of which would be the German-British relations.'

Later, at Nuremberg, Admiral Raeder was to say: 'The Führer wanted to leave every possibility open for demanding more or less large indemnities from France, depending on what he could get from Britain.' Furthermore, as General Halder was to note in his diary on September 23, 1940: 'Hitler will never abandon the idea of making not Britain but France pay the costs of the war.'

What then would be the bill? Otto Abetz revealed: 'At the time of the armistice, Hitler was envisaging a fairly elaborate division of France: incorporation of the northern departments into a future Flanders, autonomy for Brittany, the Lorraine frontier carried well beyond that of 1861, and a Burgundy incorporated in Germany.'

Although Hitler wanted to conclude an armistice with France, he obviously could not present her with such demands! As Goebbels wrote in his diary: 'We have to keep the French holding on and extract all we can in the meantime.'

On June 25, the moment the armistice came into force, Marshal Pétain proclaimed over the radio: 'Honour is saved! We must now turn our efforts to the future. A new order is beginning!'

On July 11 this 'new order' found concrete form in the 'First Bill of the Constitution', couched in regal terms: 'We, Philippe Pétain, Marshal of France, in accordance with the Constitutional Law of the 10th of July, hereby assume the functions of Head of the French State.' The Republic was abolished; Parliament was dismissed.

Later, Pétain spoke of 'National Revolution' and the 'rebirth of France' – as if all this were possible in the middle of a world war, in a country two-thirds occupied by the enemy, from Vichy, a spa only 25 miles from the Panzers. The 'battle for an armistice' had thus led at the same time to an assumption of power for a 'new order', which was destined for a short – but tyrannical – life.

Errors are not treason

The main error had been that our highest leaders were convinced that a rapid German victory was pre-ordained. France, the leading military power on the Continent, had therefore been defeated. 'Britain', General Weygand repeated incessantly in his vivid language, was to have her 'neck wrung like a chicken', while Russia,

he maintained, was Germany's 'ally'. And America refused to intervene.

What – in their eyes – could stop Hitler remodelling Europe as he liked? Was it not better to get him to formulate his peace terms before he had defeated Britain, his last enemy – because his terms would doubtless be worse when he was in the rapture of a total victory? Moreover, would not Hitler be more indulgent to a France with an authoritarian regime like those of Germany and Italy, and *after* it had entered into the 'new European order' deliberately?

It was therefore not a question of treason, against either France or the Allied cause. The men asking Hitler for peace were French patriots who on the contrary wished to save their country from total destruction, so that it could survive and gradually make its mark in the new Europe which was to arise. As for the Allied cause, nobody could betray it for it was lost! Thus it was all simply a question of errors in calculation, errors which President Lebrun defined perfectly as follows:

'Two errors were committed: there was a conviction of German victory, and Marshal Pétain believed that his prestige would suffice to protect the country and defend it.'

A misapprehension of the possibility of a German victory in a war which was destined to become worldwide, plus a deplorable ignorance of the nature of Hitler's megalomania, was therefore responsible for the tragedy.

COLONEL ADOLPH GOUTARD was born in Annonay in 1893. He served in the infantry during the First World War, was wounded twice, and finished the war as a lieutenant with the Cross of the Legion of Honour with three citations. Between the wars he served with the Army of the Rhine, with the Corps Français in Constantinople, with the 159th Alpine Infantry Regiment at Briançon, and at the Special Military School of St-Cyr for six years – during three of which he was Professor of History. During the Battle of France he was stationed in North Africa; when the African Army took up arms beside the Allies, he took part in the Tunisian campaign. He then went on to take part in the Italian campaign, the liberation of France, and the campaign in Germany. In 1947, he was made Commander of the Legion of Honour. Colonel Goutard's books include *Kemmel – 1918, The Expeditionary Corps in the Italian Campaign* (prefaced by Marshal Juin), *The War of Lost Opportunities* (prefaced by General de Gaulle), and *The Battle of France* (prefaced by Captain Sir Basil Liddell Hart).

◁ War reaches the outskirts of Paris. On June 13 the Paris Army and the 7th Army abandoned the French capital

▷ The Germans in Paris: a triumphal parade down the Avenue Foch in June 1940

60

OPERATION SEA LION
THE PLAN TO INVADE BRITAIN

Germany, May/October 1940. There was one flaw in the German plan that no one could disguise: it would not work unless the Luftwaffe controlled the skies, and would be unnecessary if they did. *David Elstein*
Göring (second from right) and his staff gaze out over the straits of Dover

> Hitler astonished his hearers when he spoke 'with great admiration of the British Empire, of the necessity for its existence, and of the civilisation that Britain had brought into the world . . .'

Since 1892, when General Schlieffen had been appointed Chief of the German Great General Staff, the basic German war strategy had remained the same: France had to be demolished by one quick thrust, after which Germany could turn to the East. In 1914 the strategy failed, and for three years Germany had to fight a war on two fronts. In 1940, after the brilliant victories of May and June, it seemed to have succeeded. Apart from Britain, the West was crushed; and even Britain had been forced to evacuate her Expeditionary Force from France, with the loss of practically all its equipment. Since Hitler was prepared to offer Britain fairly generous peace terms, he had every reason to be confident that the war in the West was over.

And then the possibility arose that Britain would not sue for peace. In that event, Hitler had been ready, since May 1939, to wage long-term economic warfare against Britain, using the Luftwaffe and the navy to cut her supply lines. But on May 21, 1940 – the day after the crucial breakthrough to the Channel coast by the II Panzer Division – Hitler's attention was drawn by Admiral Raeder, C-in-C of the navy, to the idea of an invasion. The attractions of such a plan must have been very great for Hitler. Instead of spending months and years in squeezing Britain slowly into submission by economic warfare, he could finish her off in a matter of weeks, and turn to face Russia (at this time, still Germany's nominal ally).

It was to be another six weeks before Hitler ordered even tentative preparations for an invasion to begin, but in fact all three services had considered the possibility as far back as 1939, and in tracing the curious fate of Sea Lion, it is as well to start there.

In November 1939 the navy had prepared a report on the subject of invasion: it was not over-optimistic. Before a landing could take place, according to the Naval War Staff, which drew up the report, all the British coastal defences – artillery, anti-aircraft, and troops – had to be eliminated, the RAF had to be destroyed, and the Royal Navy had to be kept away from the approaches to the landing area. A choice would have to be made between a short sea crossing from the French Channel ports, which were open to British air attacks, or a long sea crossing from ports beyond British bombing range – in the Low Countries, North Germany, or the Baltic. Finally, if German troops were to be landed in sufficient numbers, a beach landing would be too slow: a major British port on the east coast would have to be captured by paratroops first.

These difficulties were not insuperable. But, the navy reasoned, if the conditions they thought necessary for the invasion were fulfilled – such as the elimination of the RAF and Royal Navy – these would in themselves induce the British to surrender: further resistance would be pointless. An invasion, as such, would surely be unnecessary?

The navy, however, was not the only military arm involved. In December 1939 the army had also put forward an invasion plan – one that envisaged a surprise attack across the North Sea to the East Anglian coast by 16 or 17 divisions, backed up by all the paratroops available. This was the signal for inter-service rivalry to begin. The navy objected to this plan on the grounds that they could not simultaneously provide cover for the invasion *and* keep the British navy occupied elsewhere (as the army had hoped). They also pointed out the need for continuous good weather, without which the Luftwaffe would be unable to operate, and without which the invasion force might well be cut off without supplies.

The Luftwaffe, too, was unhappy: the East Anglian landing would 'run into the strongest point of the enemy air defence', said their memorandum, prepared at the end of December. And they sounded a note which was to be repeated many times in the summer of 1940. The invasion 'could only be the last act of a war against England which had already taken a victorious course'. It could not itself bring about victory.

Lack of confidence

So the matter rested for the first five months of 1940. There is no evidence that invasion was seriously considered again by any of the services, or by the Wehrmacht High Command, which co-ordinated the activities of the armed forces, until the meeting between Hitler and Raeder on May 21, 1940. As a result of that meeting, however, the navy, acting on its own initiative, reopened the question of invasion. Again, the basic dilemma emerged: the short Channel crossing would put the embarkation ports within range of British bombers, but the longer North Sea crossing would endanger the invasion fleet itself, and greatly increase the difficulties of reinforcement.

The navy plumped for the Channel crossing; but the same conditions as in the November 1939 report were required – the grounding of the RAF, good weather during the invasion and for some days after it. Working on the hypothesis that these could be fulfilled, the navy planners for the first time applied themselves to the detailed problems of invasion. They promptly encountered their first major practical difficulty. Investigations revealed an almost complete lack of landing craft; and even ordinary barges, which could be towed by tugs across the Channel, would take many weeks to reinforce for the sea voyage.

It is a curious fact that while the navy was trying to solve some of the practical problems of invasion, Hitler and the Wehrmacht High Command seem to have displayed scant interest in the whole idea. On June 17, 1940, the navy was informed that 'with regard to a landing in Britain, the Führer has not up to now expressed such an intention, as he fully appreciates the unusual difficulties of such an operation. Therefore, even at this time, no preparatory work of any kind has been carried out in the Wehrmacht High Command'. And on June 21 the navy was told that the Army General Staff 'is not concerning itself with the question of England. Considers execution impossible. Does not know how the operation is to be conducted from southern area. Presumably 20 divisions in England, that is, at least 40 divisions required by us. Is absolute air superiority attainable in view of the very strong defence? General Staff rejects the operation.'

But now there were pressures in the other direction: the army advisers were by no means unanimous, and General von Bock, C-in-C of Army Group B, thought that serious preparations for an invasion should be made. Moreover, Hitler had discussions in mid-June with Mussolini and Raeder on the question of operations against Britain, including the possibility of a sea and air attack, and at the end of June General Jodl sent in a paper on 'The Continuation of the War against England'. In this, while recognising the advantages of long-term economic warfare, he showed more interest in the short-term strategic possibilities.

Basically, he wanted an attack on the RAF, to be linked with an assault on Britain's food supply and occasional terror raids on population centres. The cumulative effect of these measures, he argued, would be to break the people's will to resist. Finally, he suggested a landing operation; but this, he thought, 'should not have as its objective the military conquest of England, a task that could be left to the Luftwaffe and navy. Its aim should rather be to give the death-blow to a country already economically paralysed and practically incapable of fighting in the air – if it should still be necessary.' This was a distinct echo of two of the memoranda of December 1939, which had described invasion as the last stage of an already victorious war.

What was probably the most decisive factor in turning Hitler's mind to the possibility of invasion was the diminishing likelihood of a peaceful settlement with Britain. Hitler's desire for such a settlement was no bluff: about the time that he issued the order halting the advance on the armies trapped at Dunkirk, he astonished his advisers (according to General Blumentritt, who was present) 'by speaking with great admiration of the British Empire, of the necessity for its existence, and of the civilisation that Britain had brought into the world. . . . He said that all he wanted from Britain was that she should acknowledge Germany's position on the Continent. The return of German colonies would be desirable but not essential. . . . He concluded by saying that his aim was to make peace with Britain on a basis that she would regard as compatible with her honour to accept.' On a number of occasions in June and July, Hitler spoke

German troops practise for the landing on the beaches. Army Chief-of-Staff Halder thought a landing on the south coast was like putting his troops 'straight through a sausage machine'

of his willingness to make peace, and of his reluctance to wage war on the Empire, from whose destruction he expected only Japan and America to benefit. But all the feelers put out by the Germans and by potential mediators were rejected or ignored by the British government, and as June wore on, prospects of an early peace grew more remote.

Hitler asks for plans

This diplomatic setback was a bitter blow for Hitler, and made him much more responsive than before to invasion proposals. On July 2, three days after receiving the paper prepared by General Jodl, Hitler issued the tentative directive 'that a landing in England is possible, providing that air superiority can be attained and certain other necessary conditions fulfilled. . . . All preparations must be undertaken on the basis that the invasion is still only a plan, and has not yet been decided upon.' In the next fortnight, Hitler held a series of meetings with his military advisers, but, as before, they were by no means agreed as to the feasibility of an invasion. On July 11 Admiral Raeder outlined the difficulties of the project — such as sweeping and laying mines, and preparing an invasion fleet — and he thought he had persuaded Hitler that invasion should only be attempted as a last resort. But on the next day General Jodl sent in a memorandum suggesting that the difficulties could be overcome if the invasion took 'the form of a river crossing in force on a broad front. . . . In this operation, the role of the artillery will fall to the Luftwaffe; the first wave of landing troops must be very strong; and in place of bridging operations, a sea lane completely secure against naval attacks must be established in the Dover Straits.'

The next day, July 13, Jodl's memorandum was followed by a more comprehensive document when the army chiefs, who had become much more optimistic about the prospects of an invasion, presented their rather ambitious plan of operations. It envisaged landing 13 divisions in three days

— six from Army Group A between Ramsgate and Bexhill, four more from Army Group A between Brighton and the Isle of Wight, and another three, from Army Group B, farther west in Lyme Bay. This initial body would be supplemented by 28 other divisions, including Panzer, motorised, and airborne divisions.

After the first connected bridgehead, about 13 to 19 miles from the coast, had been established by the A Group divisions, these were to make for the first major objective, a line from Gravesend to Southampton. They would then, after reinforcement, press on to their second objective, a line from Maldon, on the Essex coast, to the Severn estuary, leaving London unconquered but sealed off. Meanwhile, the B Group divisions would break through to Bristol from Lyme Bay, cutting off the south-west. From this base, which would by then comprise most of southern England, the army expected to take the rest of the country within a month.

As a result of all this planning activity, there emerged, on July 16, a directive entitled 'Preparations for a Landing Operation against England'. It read: 'As England, in spite of her hopeless military situation, still shows no sign of willingness to come to terms, I have decided to prepare, and if necessary to carry out, a landing operation against her. The aim of this operation is to eliminate the English mother country as a base from which the war against Germany can be continued, and, if it should be necessary, to occupy it completely.' The operation — which Jodl had called 'Lion' in his memorandum of July 12 — was to bear the code name 'Sea Lion'.

This did not mean that Hitler had given up all idea of peace. On July 19 he made another offer to Britain (which Halifax, the Foreign Secretary, rejected on the 22nd), claiming that he could see no reason why the war must go on. But the captured German records leave little doubt (despite the testimony of certain generals after the war) that from this point onwards the invasion was intended to take place: in fact, it was

the Wehrmacht's major objective in the summer of 1940, and preparations for it took precedence over all other activities.

However, the navy, which had first raised the idea of Sea Lion and then had kept it going when the other services lost interest, was now paradoxically becoming increasingly pessimistic as it probed the project in detail. In a memorandum written only three days after the directive of July 16, the naval planners expounded the 'exceptional difficulties' with which they were faced. The embarkation ports had been damaged in the previous campaign. Weather conditions in the Channel were unpredictable. The plan for beach landings meant that the transport fleet would have to be specially converted. Most significant of all, the navy now asserted that it could not guarantee protection of the sea passage after the initial assault.

Hitler did not ignore these warnings; indeed, at a conference of service chiefs on July 21 he described Sea Lion as an 'exceptionally daring undertaking', of which 'the most difficult part will be the continued reinforcement of equipment and stores'. He also recognised the need for the first-wave landings to be over by mid-September; otherwise, worsening weather would prevent the Luftwaffe from participating in the operation. But Hitler's natural caution was outweighed by his desire to finish off Britain as quickly as possible, and at this conference he explicitly stated that he wanted to attack his ally, Russia, at the earliest opportunity, and only Sea Lion, he thought, could bring the Western campaign to a swift conclusion. Admiral Raeder was asked to report back again stating the earliest date on which the navy would be prepared to invade.

The navy urges caution

On July 25 the conscientious admiral duly listed the difficulties which he thought could be overcome: given air cover, he could clear enemy mine-fields and lay his own, prepare the embarkation ports, and provide barges whenever necessary. But he was nonetheless inclined to caution, and he warned Hitler that the shipping problem was still the big headache, especially the provision of the main transports — the steamers.

On July 29 the trend of naval thinking became even more apparent in a memorandum submitted by the Naval War Staff, which made it clear that invasion could not even begin until after mid-September (by which time Hitler had wanted the main operation to be over), and that even then the navy could not guarantee protection. Schniewind, Chief of the Naval War Staff, wrote that 'no responsibility can be accepted for execution this year . . . and the possibility of carrying out the operation at all appears extremely doubtful.' This memorandum convinced the army chiefs that Sea Lion would be abandoned; and they

DAVID ELSTEIN was born in Slough in 1944, and was educated in London and at Gonville and Caius College, Cambridge, where he was an open scholar specialising in modern European, English, and American history. He graduated in 1964, having gained a double first in the historical tripos, and joined the BBC. He has lectured, written, and broadcast on a variety of subjects, including 'Operation Sea Lion'. He has written many historical articles.

decided, without actually dropping their own invasion proposals, to advise Hitler to open up a Mediterranean offensive instead, aimed at Gibraltar, Haifa, and the Suez Canal.

An even more telling blow was struck at the invasion plans by Raeder at a major conference on July 31, when he gave full details of the transport problem, and of the disruption that Sea Lion would cause through the withdrawal of steamers, tugs, and barges from the merchant and inland shipping fleets. Iron ore and coal—vital to the war economy—had to be shipped from Sweden during the summer and autumn; and distribution of food, as well as of the iron ore and coal, depended heavily on the internal shipping system. He argued further that if Sea Lion were to take place in autumn 1940, preparations would not be ready till mid-September, and that the only period during which tide and moon would be right was September 19-26, by which time three clear days' good weather could not reasonably be expected. He asked, moreover, for the landing front to be confined to the Dover Straits, and finally suggested that Operation Sea Lion be postponed until May 1941.

These arguments had persuaded the army, but they did not convince Hitler, who, paradoxically, now upheld the army's original plan. He was prepared to consider a Mediterranean diversion, but he still wanted a 'decisive result' as soon as possible, which could 'only be achieved by an attack on England. . . . An attempt must be made to prepare the operation for September 15, 1940'. Sea Lion was to go ahead, provided that air superiority was attained; and the next day he ordered that 'the German Air Force is to overcome the British Air Force with all means at its disposal and as soon as possible'. Operation Sea Lion therefore became dependent on the success of Operation Eagle, the attack on the RAF. Together with the rest of the world, the invasion staffs fastened their immediate attention on the course and probable outcome of the Battle of Britain.

Time passed, but it was only a matter of days before it was realised that—whatever the outcome of the air battle—Hitler's latest decision had entirely ignored the navy's demand for a narrow-front invasion, and when Raeder discovered that the broad front was still the basis of the army's plans, he reaffirmed the navy's opinion that protection could be provided only for a landing between Folkestone and Eastbourne. To Brauchitsch, C-in-C of the army, this was completely unacceptable: 'the landing in this sector alone presents itself as a frontal attack against a defence line, on too narrow a front, with no good prospects of surprise, and with insufficient forces reinforced only in driblets.' His subordinate, Halder, was more forceful: 'I utterly reject the navy's proposal. From the point of view of the army I regard it as complete suicide. I might just

as well put the troops that have been landed straight through a sausage machine.' Although the Lyme Bay and Deal landings might have been dispensed with, the Brighton landings were vital. Jodl, who intervened at this stage, thought the invasion 'an act of desperation' if a certain rate of reinforcement were not achieved—and the army claimed that this depended on there being landings in Brighton Bay.

In the face of such basic divergencies, Hitler had to adjudicate: the Lyme Bay landing was abandoned, and the navy agreed to provide 50 steamers for a single crossing to Brighton.

But this concession did not satisfy the army chiefs. They wanted 70 steamers making *several* crossings and declared that a military operation of the size originally planned was now impossible. Halder told Jodl: 'It can only be a question . . . of finishing off an enemy defeated by the air war'—which is how Jodl had seen it in the first place. All these modifications to the invasion plan had clearly dampened the army's enthusiasm for the whole operation: their first plan had spoken in terms of 250,000 men landing in the first three days, and now this figure was halved. And the first three waves would be eight divisions weaker than had been planned, and would take longer to arrive.

By this time Brauchitsch was becoming sceptical about Sea Lion's chances of even being launched, and in the instructions he issued to the army on August 30 for the preparation of Sea Lion, he noted that 'the order for execution depends upon the political situation'.

Raeder too was pessimistic about Sea Lion's prospects; but he dutifully gathered together the armada for the invasion, and, like the army chiefs, transferred to the Luftwaffe the responsibility for the success of the operation. The illogicality of such an attitude must have been apparent to all. The very first naval report in 1939 had ruled out invasion on the grounds that its success depended on such complete air superiority that the British would have surrendered before Sea Lion could get under way. If the RAF were destroyed, Britain would be defenceless against bombing, and resistance would be futile. Even as a *coup de grâce*, invasion would be needlessly risky. And if it *were* necessary—for instance, as a quick follow-up to massive air assaults—it would have to be on a large scale. The final plan simply did not make strategical sense.

Despite this, the preparations for it went ahead, and on September 4 the Naval War Staff reported to Raeder that 'the assembly of personnel and material requested for Sea Lion had been successfully carried out in time or can be completed in the period of preparations still available: thus the operation can be carried out by the date envisaged as the earliest possible one'—which was September 21. The army and the SS

were also more or less in a state of readiness. Everything now depended on the Luftwaffe.

All-out Luftwaffe effort

The C-in-C of the Luftwaffe, Göring, had expected to demolish the fighter defences in southern England in four days, and the whole of the RAF in two to four weeks. He, at least, was logical about Sea Lion: if the Luftwaffe could achieve all that was expected of it, Sea Lion would be unnecessary. In fact, as late as September 5 the Wehrmacht Operations Branch was told that 'the Reichsmarschal is not interested in the preparations for Operation Sea Lion as he does not believe the operation will ever take place'. Göring's confidence was in part justified by the enormous numerical superiority of the Luftwaffe over the RAF; but this advantage was largely offset by radar, and by the sudden change in focus of the German air attack during the Battle of Britain.

From August 23 till September 6 the Luftwaffe launched an all-out assault on the fighter defences; but just as they seemed to have gained the upper hand, the attack was switched to the cities. This change in tactics caused great hardship to the civilian population, but it allowed Fighter Command to recover from its losses sufficiently well to inflict heavy casualties on a daylight German raid on September 15.

The failure to subdue the RAF forced Hitler to push back the date for Sea Lion. According to the schedule, he was due to decide on September 11 whether or not to launch the invasion on the 21st; but on the 10th he announced that he would not make this decision until the 14th, on the grounds that air superiority was not yet attained—though there was full expectation that this could only be a matter of days. This postponement meant that the invasion could not begin till the 24th, as it required ten days' notice to put into operation. Then, on the 13th, according to Jodl, Halder, and Raeder, Hitler suddenly decided to call Sea Lion off, and curiously enough, the reason he gave was not that Göring had failed, but that the air attack was so successful it would do the trick alone. Without realising it, Hitler was now coming round to the point of view that Sea Lion was impossible without air supremacy, and superfluous if air supremacy were achieved.

But this was by no means the end of the affair; by the 14th, Sea Lion was on again. Hitler's reason for reversing his decision was simply that he had realised after all that the invasion would hasten the collapse of Britain: the change of mind shows how marginal Sea Lion was compared with the real task—the air war. Success in that, he thought, required only five days' clear weather, although somewhat inconsistently (and against Raeder's advice) he pushed back the decision to invade only *three* days to the 17th, and the landing itself to the 27th. But on the 17th there was still no sign of a

How the Germans intended to invade and conquer Britain. The object of Operation Sea Lion was: 'to eliminate the English mother country as a base from which the war against Germany can be continued'

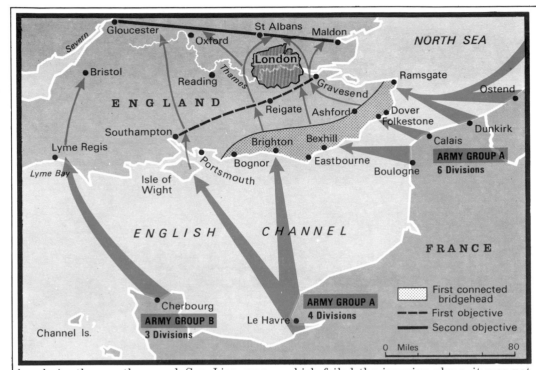

Map labels:
Severn · Gloucester · St Albans · Maldon · NORTH SEA · Oxford · London · Ramsgate · Bristol · Reading · Thames · Gravesend · Ostend · ENGLAND · Reigate · Ashford · Dover · Folkestone · Southampton · Brighton · Bexhill · Calais · Dunkirk · Lyme Regis · Bognor · Eastbourne · ARMY GROUP A 6 Divisions · Portsmouth · Boulogne · Lyme Bay · Isle of Wight · ENGLISH CHANNEL · FRANCE · Channel Is. · Cherbourg · ARMY GROUP B 3 Divisions · Le Havre · ARMY GROUP A 4 Divisions · First connected bridgehead · First objective · Second objective · 0 Miles 80

break in the weather, and Sea Lion was postponed 'until further notice'.

Meanwhile, other tactical considerations had arisen. The RAF was itself carrying out raids on the invasion fleet, and Raeder persuaded Hitler of the necessity to stop the build-up of shipping, and allow a limited dispersal of the transports. This did not mean that the invasion was off: although no definite embarkation date could be issued, Hitler insisted that the invasion forces remain at ten days' readiness. In fact, once limited dispersal was allowed, such a state of readiness was impossible to maintain, as Hitler was eventually forced to recognise in a directive issued on October 2. Even before then, the navy and army had been urging Hitler to cancel Sea Lion so as to avoid unnecessary casualties from British air raids on the massed fleet, and on October 12 Sea Lion was at last postponed until 1941.

From the series of postponements—always on the grounds that bad weather and Fighter Command had prevented the Luftwaffe from gaining air superiority—it is evident that the action with the RAF on September 15 was not in itself decisive. The postponement on the 17th had not been abandonment: Hitler still meant to carry out the plan, though every delay gave the RAF further opportunities to attack the transports. That the postponement on the 17th had been 'until further notice' was as much a result of the lack of possible invasion dates as winter drew on, as of lack of success in the air. Indeed, well into September the Luftwaffe still hoped to achieve the promised air supremacy. By that time, however, winter was too close for an invasion in 1940.

Although, in the event, it was the Luftwaffe's failure to achieve a breakthrough

which foiled the invasion plans, it was not just the RAF which saved Britain: if there had been no British army, the Germans could have afforded to plan for a much smaller invasion force. Above all, it was the weakness of the German navy—weak in 1939, crippled after the Norwegian campaign—which made the full-scale invasion plan a non-starter. And the very need for air superiority, upon which the modified plan depended, arose from the dominance of the British navy—the same dominance which had saved Britain from invasion by Philip of Spain, Louis XIV, Louis XV, and Napoleon. Because of the strength of the British navy, the original Sea Lion plan had to be modified until it was a mere appendage of the air war. Just as Napoleon's invasion from Boulogne was made impossible by the battles of Aboukir, Copenhagen, and Trafalgar, so Sea Lion foundered, along with half of Germany's destroyers, in the actions at Narvik and Trondheim.

Lessons from Napoleon

In a wider sense, too, Hitler failed to learn the lessons of Napoleon. Like Napoleon, he fully expected Britain to stand aside from the Continent, if he allowed her full play overseas. But Britain could never be content with a simple balance between land power and sea power: only a balance of power on the Continent itself would satisfy her. This had been true since the days of Elizabeth I; and the thinking behind the proposal made by the British government to Stalin in July 1940 was relevant to any time in the previous 400 years: 'The British government is convinced that Germany is striving for hegemony in Europe. . . . This is dangerous to the Soviet Union as well as

to England. Therefore both countries ought to agree on a common policy of self-protection against Germany and on the re-establishment of the European balance of power.' Although Halifax and Churchill often spoke of restoring freedom to the nations of Europe, what really concerned them was restoring the balance of power. Because Hitler failed to understand the traditions of British foreign policy, he deceived himself into thinking that Britain would settle peaceably with him after his stunning victories. Quite the opposite was true: the more stunning the victories, the greater the threat to the isolated sea power.

The misunderstanding was bad enough; but the delay it caused—while Hitler was waiting for a response to his peace moves—was probably crucial. Raeder raised the idea of invasion on May 21; yet not until July 2 did Hitler order preparations to be made. Had that directive come six weeks earlier, all sorts of possibilities might have presented themselves: the Luftwaffe could have attacked the RAF earlier, and in better weather. And even if they had achieved only parity in the air, Hitler could well have gambled on a surprise invasion, which would probably have succeeded. For by the end of July 1940 there were not very many British divisions sufficiently equipped to put up powerful resistance; and, until September, most of these troops were deployed in East Anglia, away from the projected invasion front. An August invasion might well have won the war in the West.

Like Napoleon, Hitler realised eventually that Britain was not prepared to stand aside from Europe, and that alliance with Russia could only be a preliminary to her conquest; but he repeated Napoleon's mistake of trying to crush Russia before he had settled with Britain. Yet he had no need to adopt this strategy. Stalin was his ally. He was confident that Russia would make no attempt to start a war with Germany. He had two or three years in which to starve Britain into submission (and in fact the abandonment of Sea Lion forced Hitler to revert to the strategy of blockade). Ironically, it was the short war strategy, as much as his own ambitions, which made him turn on Russia: 'If Russia is smashed,' he said, 'Britain's last hope will be shattered.' But this scheme grotesquely reversed the old Schlieffen strategy: the whole point of the short war in the West, and of Sea Lion, was to avert the nightmare of a war on two fronts if and when Hitler decided to attack Russia. The Führer, however, lost sight of this: he was impatient: he needed quick and crushing success. It was not until March 1942 that Operation Sea Lion was put on the basis of a year's notice, which meant, in effect, cancellation. But long before then—even before the invasion of Britain had proved impossible—Hitler's imagination had been captured by the idea of invading Russia: Operation Barbarossa.

In the harbours along the French coast the invasion barges began to mass menacingly. British bombers were commanded 'to go in and flatten them', and they did so with excellent effect

June 17: Marshal Pétain asks for an armistice.
June 22: Germany and France sign an armistice at Rethonde.
June 24: Italy and France sign an armistice.
July 3: British Task Force H attacks the Vichy fleet at Oran and Mers el Kébir in Algeria.
July 16: Hitler issues Directive 16, *Preparations for a Landing Operation against England.*
August 13: On 'Eagle Day' the Luftwaffe launches the Battle of Britain with 1,485 sorties.
September 13: *Italy invades Egypt.*
September 15: The RAF claims to have shot down 183 German aircraft during daylight Luftwaffe raids on Britain — a figure subsequently found to have been greatly exaggerated.
September 17: Hitler postpones Operation Sea Lion 'until further notice'.
September 23/25: *British and Free French forces attempt to take Dakar in French West Africa.*

Germans at work on the invasion barges. Aircraft engines were to power this type. The RAF bombing was so effective that Hitler was soon forced to order a dispersal of his invasion fleet

German SS troops wait on the beaches. They waited in vain. For like Philip of Spain, Louis XIV, Louis XV, and Napoleon before him, Hitler failed to gain control of the English Channel

BATTLE OF BRITAIN

Hitler's plan was to soften up Britain for the proposed invasion. But he was not dealing with the same Britain that signed away Czechoslovakia at Munich. Fortified and inspired by their war leader, the British knew that the fate of the West could very well hinge on their courage on land, and on their aggressive spirit in the skies

BRITAIN AUGUST/SEPTEMBER 1940   **DENIS RICHARDS**

In its element: the Spitfire, symbol of the battle

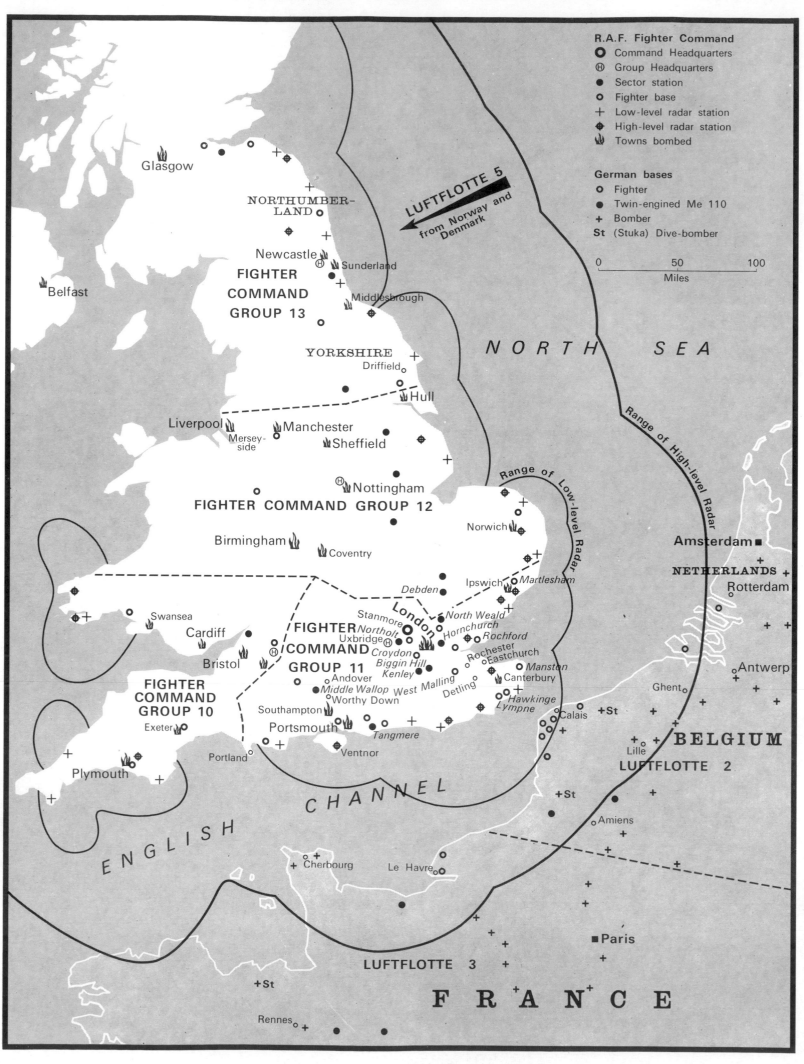

R.A.F. Fighter Command

○ Command Headquarters
⊕ Group Headquarters
● Sector station
○ Fighter base
+ Low-level radar station
✛ High-level radar station
🔥 Towns bombed

German bases

○ Fighter
● Twin-engined Me 110
+ Bomber
St (Stuka) Dive-bomber

0   50   100
Miles

LUFTFLOTTE 5
from Norway and Denmark

Glasgow

NORTHUMBER-LAND

Newcastle
Sunderland
Middlesbrough

FIGHTER COMMAND GROUP 13

Belfast

YORKSHIRE
Driffield
Hull

Liverpool
Mersey-side
Manchester
Sheffield

NORTH   SEA

Range of High-level Radar

Nottingham

FIGHTER COMMAND GROUP 12

Birmingham
Coventry

Norwich

Range of Low-level Radar

Amsterdam
NETHERLANDS
Rotterdam

Swansea
Cardiff
Bristol

Debden
Ipswich
Martlesham

Stanmore
London
North Weald
Hornchurch
Rochford
Northolt
Uxbridge
Croydon
Rochester
Eastchurch
Biggin Hill
Kenley
Manston
Andover
West Malling
Canterbury
Middle Wallop
Detling
Worthy Down
Hawkinge
Southampton
Lympne
Calais
Portsmouth
Tangmere
Ventnor

FIGHTER COMMAND GROUP 11

FIGHTER COMMAND GROUP 10

Exeter
Portland

Plymouth

Antwerp
Ghent

St

BELGIUM

Lille
LUFTFLOTTE 2

Amiens

ENGLISH   CHANNEL

Cherbourg
Le Havre

St

Paris

LUFTFLOTTE 3

St

FRANCE

Rennes

72

The moment drew near for the Luftwaffe's great assault

From the very outset of the war a great German air assault had been expected in Britain. It was for fear of this that mothers and children had been evacuated from the big cities, the blackout enforced, gas masks and Anderson shelters distributed, thousands of beds held vacant in the hospitals. But no 'knock-out blow' from the air, or indeed any kind of blow at all—other than minelaying and raids on Scottish naval bases and east coast convoys—had disturbed the uncanny peace of the British Isles during the autumn and winter of 1939-40.

This quiet remained unbroken even when, in the spring of 1940, the war in the west came abruptly to the boil. Strange as it seemed at the time, there were in fact good reasons for Britain's unexpected immunity. Britain herself had not launched a strategic bombing offensive against Germany during the 'Phoney War' for fear of retaliation while the Allies were still the weaker side in the air. Germany had not launched any such offensive against Britain because she did not think she could achieve decisive results from German bases and because the Luftwaffe was largely cast for the role of military support. This support the Luftwaffe had given, with exemplary effectiveness, during the campaign in Poland; and now, as the Germans struck in the west, it operated in similar fashion in Norway, the Low Countries, and France. Meanwhile, it did not waste its strength in irrelevant activity against England.

This self-imposed restriction lasted until the German army entered the smoking ruins of Dunkirk. Within less than 48 hours, on the night of June 5/6, the Luftwaffe began to show a more lively interest in the British homeland. Some 30 German bombers—far more than on any previous occasion—crossed the east coast to attack airfields and other objectives; and the following night similar forces repeated the experiment. Then came a lull while the German armies in France struck southwards, again supported by the Luftwaffe. It lasted until the French sought an armistice, whereupon within a few hours German aircraft resumed night operations over Britain. From then on until the opening of their full daylight air offensive in August, the Germans repeatedly dispatched bombers—70 of them on the busiest night—against widely separated targets in England. Their intention was to give their crews experience in night operations and the use of radio navigational aids, to reconnoitre, and to maintain pressure inexpensively (their usual losses were one or two aircraft each night) until captured airfields in France and the Low Countries could be made ready for operations of a more intensive kind.

Meanwhile there was always the chance—or so it seemed to Hitler—that such operations might not be necessary. The Führer accordingly put out 'peace-feelers', at the same time encouraging preparations for the next stage of hostilities. This next stage, the invasion or occupation of Britain, was not one to which the Germans had already devoted long thought. The speed and completeness of the German victory in France had taken even the optimistic Hitler by surprise; and though his armed forces had given some casual attention in the autumn of 1939 to the general problems of invading Britain, it was not until German troops actually reached the Channel coast on May 20, 1940, that the project really came to life. From then on the German navy, anxious not to be caught out by Hitler, began serious planning; but the German army showed comparable interest only after the total defeat of France. On July 2 Hitler formally directed his services to proceed with this invasion planning, though on a purely provisional basis. On July 19 came his public peace offer; on the 22nd, its rejection.

If the Germans were to take advantage of the 'invasion season' in the Channel that year, their three services would now have to formulate and agree plans with extraordinary speed. This difficulty struck the German naval and military chiefs more forcibly than it did Hitler, who declared to his paladins that only the rapid elimination of Britain would enable him to complete his life's work by turning against Russia. On July 31 he accordingly disregarded the fast-waning enthusiasm of the German navy and army and ordered that an attempt must be made to prepare the invasion operation, to which the code-name 'Seelöwe' ('Sea Lion') was given, for September 15. The following day, August 1, he issued a directive concerning the only part of the venture on which all three German services were thus far agreed. It was for the preliminary stage, which must consist of the subjugation of the RAF. 'The German air force is to overcome the British air force with all means at its disposal, and as soon as possible.' With these words, Hitler finally decreed the Battle of Britain.

600 RAF sorties a day

While the plans for Sea Lion and the preliminary air battle were taking shape, the Luftwaffe was not of course idle. From its captured airfields it continued to harass Britain by night, and from July 10 onwards it waged increasing war by day against British shipping in the Channel. The German bombers were usually detected by the British radar stations, but since the attacks were delivered at the periphery of the British defensive system they set the Fighter Command a difficult problem. In such circumstances it was highly creditable to the command that the British fighters inflicted more casualties than they themselves suffered: between July 10 and August 10, as we now know, the Germans lost 217 aircraft, Fighter Command 96. On the other hand the German attacks, though sinking only a modest tonnage of British shipping, imposed a severe strain on Fighter Command, which was compelled to fly some 600 sorties a day at extended range at a time when it was trying to build up resources for the greater trials clearly soon to come. As Air Chief Marshal Sir Hugh Dowding, Air Officer C-in-C of the Fighter Command, pointed out to the Air Ministry and the Admiralty, if constant air protection was to be given to all British shipping in home waters, the entire British fighter force could be kept fully employed on that task alone.

These German attacks on shipping, how-ever, were only a prelude to the air battle which the Luftwaffe had now to induce. The prerequisite of Sea Lion was that the Germans should gain air supremacy over the Channel and southern Britain. Only if the RAF were put out of business could the Germans hope to cross, land, and maintain communications without an unacceptable rate of casualties; for the destruction of the RAF would not only obviate British bombing attacks, but would also enable the Luftwaffe to deal, uninterrupted from the air, with the Royal Navy. And beyond this there was always the hope, ever present in the minds of Hitler and his service chiefs alike, that the Luftwaffe's success alone might be so great as to bring Britain to submission, or very near it. In that case, an invasion about which neither the German navy nor army was really happy could become something much more to their liking—a virtually unresisted occupation.

As the moment drew near for the Luftwaffe's great assault, the forces arrayed stood as follows. On the German side there were three *Luftflotten,* or air fleets. The main ones were Luftflotte II, under Field-Marshal Kesselring, in northern Germany, Holland, Belgium, and in north-eastern France; and Luftflotte III, under Field-Marshal Sperrle, in northern and western France. By day, these two air fleets threatened the entire southern half of England, up to and including the Midlands; and by night they could range still farther afield. In addition, to disperse the British defences and to threaten Scotland and north-eastern England there was also a smaller force, Luftflotte V, under General Stumpff, based in Denmark and Norway. Between them, the three air fleets on August 10 comprised over 3,000 aircraft, of which about three-quarters were normally serviceable at any one time. Roughly 1,100 of the 3,000 were fighters—for the most part Messerschmitt 109E's, virtually the equal of the opposing Spitfires of that date, but handicapped in a protective role by their limited range.

To escort bombers to the more distant targets, including those to be reached across the North Sea from Norway, there were some 300 Messerschmitt 110s; but these twin-engined fighters, though sturdy, could not compare in manoeuvrability with the single-engined Spitfire or Hurricane. The remaining 1,900 German aircraft were almost entirely bombers, mainly the well-tried if slow Heinkel 111, the slim, pencil-like Dornier 17, and the fast and more recent Junkers 88, but including also about 400 Junkers 87s—the Stukas, or dive-bombers. These had established a legendary reputation on the battlefields of Poland and France, but their range was very short and they had yet to face powerful and sustained opposition.

On the British side, the situation was a great deal better than it had been a few weeks earlier. On June 4, following the heavy losses of Hurricanes in France, Fighter Command had been able to muster only 446 modern single-engined fighters—Spitfires and Hurricanes—with another 36 ready in the Aircraft Storage Units (ASUs) as replacements. But on August 11, on the eve of the main air battle, Fighter Command had 704 of these aircraft in the squadrons and 289 in the ASUs. Its fighting strength had been virtually doubled during those ten critical weeks since Dunkirk, thanks to the fruition of earlier Air Ministry plans and the tremendous efforts of the air-

The Luftwaffe was able to use the entire coastline of occupied Europe: the British resources were to be strained to their furthest limits ◁

craft industry under the stimulus of the newly appointed Minister of Aircraft Production, Lord Beaverbrook.

Strengthening the shield

During those same ten weeks the British air defence system, built up against an enemy operating from Germany and possibly the Low Countries, had also been extended, thanks to schemes already worked out and in progress, to deal with forces operating from France and Norway. To the existing groups within Fighter Command—No. 11 Group, guarding the south-east, No. 12 Group, guarding the east and Midlands, and No. 13 Group, guarding the north-east up to the Forth—had been added another: No. 10 Group, guarding the south-west. The intermittent defences of the north-west, including Northern Ireland, had been thickened, as had those of Scotland.

This was not only a matter of providing more fighter aircraft and the pilots to fly them. It was also a matter of extending the main coastal radar chain, adding special radar stations to detect low-flying aircraft, extending Observer Corps posts for inland tracking over the south-western counties and western Wales, adapting more airfields for fighter operations, installing guns, searchlights, balloon barrages. All this was the concomitant, on the air defence side, of the gun-posts and the pill-boxes, the barbed wire and the dragon's teeth, that the inhabitant of southern England, enrolled perhaps in the newly formed Local Defence Volunteers and on watch at dawn and dusk for the arrival of German paratroops, saw springing up before his eyes along his familiar coasts and downlands.

The island's air defences had grown stronger and more extensive, but many grave deficiencies remained. Of the 120 fighter squadrons which the Director of Home Operations at the Air Ministry considered desirable in the new situation created by the German conquests, Dowding had less than 60—and eight of these flew Blenheims or Defiants, no match for the Me-109s. Of the 4,000 anti-aircraft guns deemed necessary even before the German conquests, Anti-Aircraft Command still had less than 2,000. The early warning and inland tracking systems were still incomplete in the west and over parts of Scotland. There was a shortage of fighter pilots: new planes could be produced quicker than new skilled men to fly them. But whatever the deficiencies of the air defence system by day, they were as nothing compared with its alarming weaknesses by night, when ordinary fighters were useful only in the brightest moonlight, and when the men of the Observer Corps had to rely on ineffective acoustical detectors instead of their clear eyesight and a pair of binoculars.

Britain, however, had assets not yet mentioned. Among others, there was RAF Coastal Command, prepared both to carry out reconnaissance and to help in offensive operations; and there was RAF Bomber Command. Most of the latter's aircraft could operate safely only by night, and by night it was by no means certain that they could find and hit the more distant targets. The daylight bombers—about 100 Blenheims—were capable of much greater accuracy; but they needed fighter support, which could be supplied only at short range (assuming that Hurricanes or Spitfires could be spared). Against targets near at hand—airfields, ports, and shipping just across the Channel

—the British bombing force was capable of playing a vital part. Against distant objectives, its effectiveness at that date was more problematical.

In sum, the opposing forces, disregarding reconnaissance aircraft and units still stationed in Germany, consisted of about 1,900 bombers assisted by 1,100 fighters on the German side, and of about 700 fighters assisted to a limited extent by 350 bombers on the British side. The Germans had the advantage not only of numbers but of the tactical initiative—of the fact that they could strike anywhere within their range—while the British defences could react only to the German moves.

The British air defence system, however, though incomplete, was the most technically advanced in the world. The early warning supplied by the radar stations (which in the south-east could pick up enemy formations before they crossed the French coast), the inland tracking by the Observer Corps, the control of the British fighters from the ground in the light of this information and the continuous reporting of the fighters' own position—all this, designed to obviate the need for wasteful standing patrols, meant that the British fighters could be used with economy and could take off with a good chance of making interception.

One other factor, too, helped the British: the Luftwaffe's offensive against Britain was largely an improvised one; and Luftwaffe C-in-C Göring, though an able man, was also a vainglorious boaster who in technical proficiency was not in the same class as the opposing commander. The single-minded Dowding, in charge of Fighter Command since its formation in 1936—the man whose obduracy had preserved Britain's fighter resources against the clamour to squander them in France—knew his job. Göring, as much politician as airman, scarcely knew his; while theoretically controlling and co-ordinating the entire offensive, in practice he was incapable of more than occasional acts of intervention. On the next level of command, Kesselring, in charge of the main attacking force—Luftflotte II—was for all his successes in Poland and France a novice in the forthcoming type of operation; while Air Vice-Marshal Keith Park, commanding the main defending force—Group 11—had earlier been Dowding's right-hand man at Headquarters, Fighter Command. Unlike their opposite numbers, the two principal British commanders had lived with their problem for years. Their skill, experience, and devotion, like those of their pilots, offset some of the British inferiority in numbers.

Operation Eagle

By August 10 the three Luftflotten stood ready to launch the major assault—Operation Eagle ('Adler')—which would drive the RAF from the skies of southern Britain. Four days, in the opinion of the German Air Staff, would see the shattering of the fighter defences south of the line London-Gloucester, four weeks the elimination of the entire RAF. Allowing for the ten days' notice required by the German navy for minelaying and other final preparations before the actual D-Day, the date of the invasion could thus be set for mid-September.

August 11 was a very cloudy day, and the Germans confined their activity to bombing Portland and some east coast shipping. On the following day came what seemed to the British to be the beginning of the main attack: five or six major raids and many

minor ones, involving several hundred aircraft, including escorted Ju-87s, struck at airfields and radar stations along the south coast and at shipping in the Thames Estuary. Of the six radar stations they attacked, the raiders damaged five but knocked out only one—that at Ventnor on the Isle of Wight. It could not be replaced until August 23—a sharp blow. Among the airfields, they hit Lympne, a forward landing ground, and Manston and Hawkinge, two important fighter stations in Kent, but all were·back in action within 24 hours. Fighters from No. 11 Group challenged all the major raids, and frustrated completely one aimed at Manston. In the course of the fighting the Germans lost 31 aircraft, the British 22.

According to the German records, the next day, August 13, was Eagle Day itself—the opening of the Eagle offensive proper. The attack went off at half-cock in the morning, when a message postponing operations till later in the day failed to get through to some of the German squadrons. In the afternoon the main assault developed with a two-pronged thrust, Luftflotte II attacking over Kent and the Thames Estuary, while Luftflotte III, challenged by No. 10 Group, attacked over Hampshire, Dorset, and Wiltshire. The raiders hit three airfields severely—Eastchurch, Detling, and Andover—but none of these belonged to Fighter Command; their attacks on fighter stations such as Rochford were beaten off.

In the whole day's operations—which witnessed 1,485 German sorties and ended with a successful night attack on a Spitfire factory at Castle Bromwich, near Birmingham—the Germans lost 45 aircraft, Fighter Command only 13 (with six of the British pilots saved). This was a poor sort of Eagle Day for the Germans, but they were nevertheless well satisfied with their progress. They calculated that between August 8 and 14, in addition to successful attacks on some 30 airfields and aircraft factories, they had destroyed more than 300 British fighters in combat. In fact, they had destroyed less than 100.

After lesser activity on August 14—a matter of some 500 German sorties, directed mainly against railways near the coast and against RAF stations—the Luftwaffe on August 15 attempted the great blow with which it had hoped to open the battle some days earlier. In clear skies the Germans sent over during the day no less than seven major raids, using all three Luftflotten in a series of co-ordinated attacks on widely separated areas. The first clash came at about 1130 hours, when some 40 escorted Ju-87s of Luftflotte II struck at Lympne and Hawkinge airfields in Kent. Then, about 1230 hours some 65 He-111s escorted by 35 Me-110s of Luftflotte V, operating from Stavanger in Norway, headed in to the Northumberland coast in an attempt to bomb airfields in the north-east. These formations were barely retiring when at 1315 hours another force of Luftflotte V, consisting of about 50 unescorted Ju-88s operating from Aalborg in Denmark, approached the Yorkshire coast on a similar mission. Little more than an hour later at 1430 hours, and once more at 1500, Luftflotte II struck again, on the first occasion north of the Thames Estuary against Martlesham airfield and on the second against Hawkinge and Eastchurch

▷ **Seen through German eyes: a British fighter pilot bales out of his stricken Hurricane; his parachute canopy is about to open (top)**

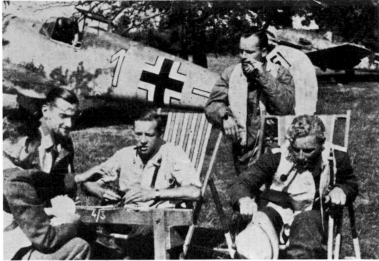

A seat in the sun—but both sides are at instant readiness for take-off. On RAF and Luftwaffe bases, the youth, the pipes, and the flying-kit were much the same. There is little to distinguish these pilots except the national markings on their aircraft

airfields and aircraft factories at Rochester.

Next it was the turn of Luftflotte III: at 1720 hours some 80 bombers, heavily escorted, came in to the south coast at Portland, bombed the harbour, and then attacked airfields at Middle Wallop and Worthy Down. Finally, at 1830 hours, 60 or 70 aircraft of Luftflotte II again penetrated over Kent, hitting West Malling airfields and the airfield and aircraft factories at Croydon. To round off the day's work, another 60 or 70 bombers made sporadic attacks during the hours of darkness.

All this German effort was fiercely challenged. Though the bombing had its successes, notably at Middle Wallop, Martlesham, and Driffield (Yorkshire) airfields and at Croydon, in no case did the British fighters allow the raiders to operate unmolested, and in many cases the primary objectives escaped unscathed. Especially significant was the fighting in the north-east, where No. 13 Group, involved for the first time in the battle, intercepted the formations from Norway well out to sea, and with the help of the anti-aircraft guns on Tyne and Tees destroyed eight He-111s and seven Me-110s, with no British losses. A little farther south, too, No. 12 Group and the local guns, tackling the formations from Denmark, brought down eight of the enemy with no loss on the British side. The Germans thus failed in their main hope—that Dowding, in his anxiety to protect the vital and heavily threatened south-east, would have left the north almost undefended. Instead, they discovered, to their cost, that their attacks across the North Sea were met before they reached the British coast, and that the Me-110s in a long-range escorting role were useless against Spitfires and Hurricanes. The lesson was sufficiently expensive to convince the Germans not to launch any further daylight attacks from this area.

The fighting on August 15 was the most extensive in the whole Battle of Britain. With 520 bomber and 1,270 fighter sorties, and attacks stretching from Northumberland to Dorset, the German effort was at its maximum. But so too was the German loss—75 aircraft as against 34 British fighters. This did not prevent an effort of almost equal magnitude on the following day, when the Germans sent across some 1,700 sorties, attacked a number of airfields (with particular success at Tangmere), and lost 45 aircraft in the process. With Fighter Command losing 21, the balance remained in the British favour.

The Luftwaffe switches strategy
The four days of intensive attack calculated to clear the skies of southern England were now over, and the Germans took stock. In the opinion of their Intelligence, Fighter Command, if not exhausted, was down to its last 300 aircraft. This appreciation was very wide of the mark, for Dowding still had nearly twice that number of Hurricanes and Spitfires in the front line, in addition to another 120 or so Blenheims, Defiants, and Gladiators. However, it encouraged the Germans to believe that another day or two of major effort might see the end of British opposition. On August 18 the Luftwaffe accordingly struck again in full force, chiefly against airfields in Kent, Surrey, and

A Ju-87: the legendary Stuka, the terror of Europe—now, matched at last by comparable fighter opposition, now the hunted and not the hunter ◁

Sussex; but in doing so they lost 71 aircraft while the British lost no more than 27. Clearly Fighter Command was still unsubdued. After a few days of minor activity owing to bad weather, the Germans therefore made their first great change of plan.

Up till then, the main German objectives had been airfields fairly near to the coast; after August 12 they had given up intensive attacks on radar stations—fortunately for Fighter Command—because they found them difficult to destroy. The airfields and other coastal targets they had continued to attack, partly to deny the airfields to the British during the proposed invasion period, but still more to force Fighter Command to join battle in their defence. The German theory was that by such attacks they might, without severe losses to themselves, inflict heavy losses on the RAF—for raids on coastal targets or those not far inland did not involve prolonged exposure to the British defences—while at the same time the Me-109s would be free from worries on the score of endurance and accordingly able to give maximum protection to the German bombers. Such was the German strategy when the battle began. It had not disposed of Fighter Command, so it was now changed in favour of attacks farther inland.

The first phase of the battle was thus over. So far, Fighter Command had more than held its own: 363 German aircraft had been destroyed between August 8 and 18, as against 181 British fighters lost in the air and another 30 on the ground. The period had also seen what proved to be the last daylight attack by Luftflotte V, and the last attempt by Luftflotte II to make regular use of its Ju-87s—both notable successes for British defences.

At the same time, however, there was one aspect of the struggle which gave Dowding and the Air Ministry acute anxiety. During the same ten days, when Fighter Command had lost 211 Spitfires and Hurricanes, the number of replacements forthcoming from the aircraft industry had fallen short of this total by at least 40. In the same period, Fighter Command had lost 154 experienced fighter pilots: but the output of the training schools had been only 63—and those less skilled than the men they replaced. Fighter Command, while inflicting nearly twice as many casualties as it was suffering, was thus in fact being weakened—though not, as yet, at anything like the speed desired by the enemy.

It was to increase the rate of destruction of the British fighter force—which unchanged would have left Fighter Command still in existence in mid-September—that the Germans now switched to targets farther inland. They reckoned that by making their prime objective the fighter airfields, and in particular the sector airfields of No. 11 Group from which the British fighters in the south-east were controlled, they would not only strike at the heart of the British defences, but would also compel Fighter Command to meet their challenge with all its remaining forces. In the resulting air battles, they hoped to achieve a rate of attrition that would knock out Fighter Command within their scheduled time: though they also knew that in penetrating farther inland they were likely to suffer greater losses themselves. To guard against this, and to destroy as many Hurricanes and Spitfires as possible, they decided to send over a still higher proportion of fighters with their bombers.

The sector stations of No. 11 Group stood

in a ring guarding London. To the south-west, in a forward position near Chichester, lay Tangmere. Nearer the capital and south of it there were Kenley in Surrey and Biggin Hill in Kent, both on the North Downs. Close to London in the east lay Hornchurch, near the factories of Dagenham; and round to the north-east was North Weald, in metropolitan Essex. Farther out there was Debden, near Saffron Walden. The ring was completed to the west by Northolt, on the road to Uxbridge, where No. 11 Group itself had its headquarters—which in turn was only a few minutes' drive from that of Fighter Command at Stanmore. All the sector stations normally controlled three fighter squadrons, based either on the sector station itself or on satellite airfields.

Strikes at the source
The Germans had already severely damaged two of the sector stations—Kenley and Biggin Hill—on August 18. Now, on August 24, they struck hard at North Weald and Hornchurch. On August 26 they attempted to bomb Biggin Hill, Kenley, North Weald, and Hornchurch, were beaten off, but got through to Debden. On August 30 they hit Biggin Hill twice, doing great damage and killing 39 persons. The following day—the most expensive of the whole battle for Fighter Command, with 39 aircraft lost—they wrought great damage at Debden, Biggin Hill, and Hornchurch.

On September 1 Biggin Hill suffered its sixth raid in three days, only to be bombed again less than 24 hours later; and on September 3 the attack once more fell on North Weald. On the 5th the main raids again headed towards Biggin Hill and North Weald, only to be repelled, while on the 4th and 6th the attacks extended also to the Vickers and Hawker factories near Weybridge. The Hawker factory, which produced more than half the total output of Hurricanes, was a particularly vital target. Its selection showed that the Germans, perplexed by the continued resilience of Fighter Command, were also trying to cut off the British fighter supply at its source.

Between August 24 and September 6 the Germans made no less than 33 major raids, of which more than two-thirds were mainly against the sector and other stations of Fighter Command. This assault imposed on the command a still greater strain than the preceding one, against targets in the coastal belt. The fighting was more difficult for the British pilots, in that the proportion of German fighters to bombers became so high, and sections of the fighter escort so close; and over the whole fortnight a daily average of something like 1,000 German aircraft, of which 250 to 400 were bombers, operated over England. Twice, on August 30 and 31, the number of intruders was nearer 1,500.

In the course of the combats and the ensuing night operations the British defences destroyed 380 German aircraft, as against a Fighter Command loss of 286: but many other British fighters were seriously damaged, and no less than 103 fighter pilots were killed and 128 wounded out of a fighting strength of not much more than 1,000. In addition six of the seven sector stations of No. 11 Group sustained heavy damage: and though none was yet out of action, Biggin Hill could control only one squadron instead of its normal three.

So Fighter Command was being steadily worn down, and at a faster pace than in the opening phase. The wastage, both of fighters

Keystone

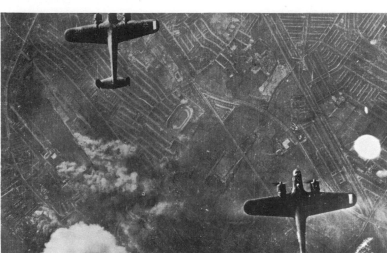

Imperial War Museum

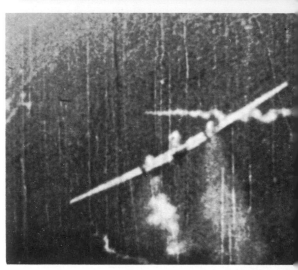

◁ A Dornier in action: a stick of bombs streams from its bomb-bay

▷ Target and tracer-fire: camera-gun film from a British fighter records the end of an Me-110 fighter. The 110, at full throttle, streams smoke trails from its twin engines (top); tracer fire misses the starboard wing, then the first hit glows on the port engine which explodes (bottom)

◁ Two Dorniers fly over fires started by the first wave

▽ The Luftwaffe strikes at Fighter Command: on an RAF fighter base, a Spitfire in its bomb pen survives a low-level strafing run

Ullstein

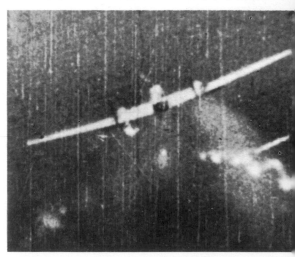

Imperial War Museum

and of pilots, was far exceeding the output. In one sense the command was winning the battle; in another – if the Germans could maintain the pressure long enough – it was losing it.

The Germans, however, were not intending to fight a prolonged battle. They, too, could not afford heavy losses indefinitely – as may be seen from their decision after August 18 to hold back most of the vulnerable Ju-87s for the actual invasion, from their caution in employing Me-110s, and from their increasingly closer and more numerous fighter escort. Their attack, as we have seen, was meant to be a brief one, geared to Operation Sea Lion; and for Sea Lion they were now running short of time. This Hitler recognised at the end of August when he agreed that D-Day, provisionally set for September 15, should be postponed to September 21. For this date to be kept the German navy had to receive the executive order by September 11: and Göring's Luftwaffe had thus to administer the *coup de grâce* to the British fighter forces within the next few days. The attack on sector stations and other inland targets might be doing well, but in itself it was not proving decisive. On September 7 the Germans accordingly switched to another target, farther inland than most of the sector stations and, as they believed, still more vital – London.

Target London

The German decision to attack London was inspired by three beliefs. In the first place, operations against London could be expected to bring about still greater air battles and so – the Germans hoped – still higher wastage in Fighter Command. It was for this reason that Kesselring, though not Sperrle, strongly supported the change of plan. Second, an assault on the capital, if reinforced by attacks during the night against other main cities as well, might paralyse the British machinery of government in the final period before the invasion, or even terrorise the British people into submission. Third, an attack on the British capital would be, as the Germans saw it, an act of retribution. On the night of August 24/25, during the course of the Luftwaffe's usual scattered night operations, some badly aimed or jettisoned bombs had fallen on central London – the first of the war. Churchill and the War Cabinet had immediately ordered retaliation against Berlin; and during the following nights RAF bombers had found and hit the German capital – an occurrence which Göring had assured Hitler could never happen. The enraged Führer promptly vowed revenge and with Göring's eager concurrence unleashed the Luftwaffe against its supreme target.

On the night of September 4 German bombers laid flares over London; on the following two nights small numbers of aircraft dropped bombs on Rotherhithe and other places near the docks. These were the warming-up operations.

In the late afternoon of September 7 some 300 German bombers escorted by 600 fighters crossed the Kent and Sussex coasts or penetrated the Thames Estuary in a series of huge waves. A few bombed the oil installations at Thameshaven, still burning from earlier attacks; the rest, instead of bombing the sector stations, which the British fighters were alert to guard, held on until they reached the outskirts of the capital itself. Though nearly all the British squadrons ordered up eventually made contact, most of the raiders were able to put down their high explosive and incendiaries before they were molested. The attacks fell in full force on London's dockland east of the City. Huge fires sprang up among the dockside warehouses, especially at Silvertown, and these the Germans used as beacons to light their way to further attacks during the ensuing hours of darkness. That night, when 250 German bombers ranged over the capital in a prolonged assault from dusk to dawn, millions of Londoners had their first experience of what they imagined was Blitzkrieg, and what they were soon to call 'The Blitz'.

The climax of the battle was now approaching. Göring took personal charge of operations, and the bombers from Norway and Denmark joined Kesselring's forces for what were meant to be the final and deciding blows. Meanwhile, however, the German invasion preparations had not gone unobserved: since August 31 Spitfires and Hudsons of RAF Coastal Command had been returning with an impressive photographic record of the growing number of barges and other invasion craft in the ports and estuaries across the Channel. On August 31 in Ostend, for instance, there were 18 barges; by September 6 there were 205.

As the concentrations increased, Bomber Command began to attack them, using at first its daylight Blenheims. By September 6 the enemy preparations were sufficiently obvious for the British authorities to order Invasion Alert 2: 'Attack probable within three days.' The following day, when the German bombers turned against London, it seemed that the hour of supreme trial might be at hand. Alert 2 then gave place to Alert 1: 'Invasion imminent, and probable within twelve hours.'

That night, as the German bombs began to crash down on London, the code-word 'Cromwell' went out to the Southern and Eastern Commands of Britain's Home Forces, bringing them to immediate readiness. In the prevailing excitement a few commanders of Home Guard units rang church bells to call out their men, so spreading the impression that German paratroops had actually landed. Meanwhile, forces of the Royal Navy waited at immediate notice, and the Hampdens of Bomber Command – 'heavy' bombers of the time – joined Blenheims, Hudsons, and Battles in intensified attacks on French and Belgian ports.

It was with the British fully alert to what the next few hours or days might bring that the Luftwaffe now strove to repeat the hammer blows of September 7. On September 8 bad weather limited their daylight activity; but at night Luftflotte III was able to send 200 bombers against London in a lengthy procession lasting more than nine hours. The zone of attack now extended from dockland to the capital as a whole, with special attention to railways and power stations, and by the morning every railway line running south of London was for a brief time unserviceable.

On the next day, September 9, clouds again restricted activity in the morning, only for a further assault to develop in the late afternoon. More than 200 bombers with full escort headed for London; but such was the promptness and vigour of the interception that less than half reached even the outskirts of the capital, and the bombs fell widely over the south-eastern counties. No. 12 Group's Duxford wing of four squadrons, led by the legless pilot Squadron Leader Douglas Bader, enjoyed a notable success. All told, the British pilots shot down 28 German aircraft for the loss of 19 of their own.

Very different once more was the story at night. Again nearly 200 aircraft bombed the capital in attacks lasting over eight hours; this time some 400 Londoners were killed and 1,400 injured – all with negligible loss to the Luftwaffe.

Hitler again shifts D-Day

September 10 was a day of cloud, rain, and light German activity – though at night there was the usual raid on London, while other German bombers attacked South Wales and Merseyside. The next afternoon, while the Germans tried to jam some of the British radar stations, Luftflotte III attacked Southampton, and Luftflotte II sent three big raids against London. Many of the bombers got through to the City and the docks; and the balance of losses – 25 German ones, against 29 by Fighter Command – for once tilted against the British. On their return, some German pilots reported that British fighter opposition was diminishing. But though the Luftwaffe still hoped to complete its task, the date was now September 11, and Fighter Command was still in existence. With the German navy requiring ten days' notice before D-Day, an invasion on September 21 thus became impossible. Accordingly Hitler now gave the Luftwaffe three more days' grace, till September 14, in the hope that a decision could then be taken to invade on September 24.

As it happened, September 12 and 13 were days of poor visibility, unsuitable for major attacks. Even the nightly efforts against London – which was now enjoying the heartening noise of greatly reinforced gun defences – were on a reduced scale. When September 14 came, Hitler could only postpone the decision for a further three days, till September 17. This set the provisional D-Day for September 27 – about the last date on which the tides would be favourable until October 8. The Führer's order was contrary to the advice of his naval chiefs, who urged indefinite postponement – a tactful term for abandonment. Their worries had been sharply increased by the mounting intensity of the RAF's attacks on the invasion barges, large numbers of which had been destroyed the previous evening.

The Luftwaffe now strove to clinch the issue in the short time still at its disposal. Despite unfavourable weather, on the afternoon of September 14 several raids struck at London. Some of the German pilots reported ineffective opposition, and Fighter Command lost as many aircraft as the enemy. The night proved fine, but on this occasion no more than 50 German bombers droned their way towards London. The Luftwaffe was husbanding its efforts for the morrow.

Sunday September 15 was a day of mingled cloud and sunshine. By 11 am the British radar detected mass formations building up over the Pas-de-Calais region. Half an hour later the raiders, stepped up from 15,000 to 26,000 feet, were crossing the coast in waves bent for London. Park's fighters met them before Canterbury, and in successive groups – two, three, then four squadrons – challenged them all the way to the capital, over which No. 12 Group's Duxford wing, now five squadrons strong, joined the conflict. In the face of such opposition, the raiders dropped their bombs inaccurately or jettisoned them, mainly over south London.

Two hours later a further mass attack developed. Again British radar picked it up well in advance: and again—since they had had time to refuel and rearm—Park's fighters challenged the intruders all the way to, and over, the capital. Once more the Germans jettisoned their bombs or aimed them badly, this time mainly over east London, and, as before, further British formations harassed the raiders on their way back. Meanwhile a smaller German force attacked Portland. Later in the day other raiders—some 20 Me-110s carrying bombs—tried to bomb the Supermarine aircraft works near Southampton, only to meet spirited and effective opposition from local guns. When darkness fell, 180 German bombers continued the damaging but basically ineffectual night assault on London, while others attacked Bristol, Cardiff, Liverpool, and Manchester.

So closed a day on which Göring had hoped to give the death-blow to Fighter Command. In all, the Germans had sent over about 230 bombers and 700 fighters in the daylight raids. Their bombing had been scattered and ineffective, and they had lost the greatest number of aircraft in a single day since August 15—no less than 60. Fighter Command had lost 26, from which the pilots of 13 had been saved.

This further German defeat on September 15—combined with the attacks of British bombers against barge concentrations—settled the issue. When September 17 came, Hitler had no alternative but to postpone Sea Lion indefinitely. A few days later, he agreed to the dispersal of the invasion craft in order to avoid attack from the air. The invasion threat was over.

Göring orders more raids

Göring, however, was not yet prepared to admit failure: he still clung to the belief that given a short spell of good weather the Luftwaffe could crush Fighter Command and thereafter compel Britain to submit, even without invasion. Between September 17 and the end of the month his forces strove to attack London by day, whenever weather permitted, in addition to aircraft factories elsewhere. On only three days—September 18, 27, and 30—was he able to mount a major assault on the capital, and on each occasion British fighters prevented intensive bombing and took a heavy toll of the raiders. The loss of 120 German aircraft during these three days (as against 60 by Fighter Command) was not one which afforded Göring much encouragement to continue.

Had the Luftwaffe's corpulent chief known them, he would not have derived any greater encouragement from the casualty figures during the whole three weeks his air force had been attacking London. Between September 7 and 30 Fighter Command had lost 242 aircraft, the Luftwaffe 433. Equally important, though Dowding was still gravely worried by the continuing loss of pilots (on September 7 his squadrons had only 16 each instead of their proper 26), his anxieties about aircraft were diminishing. From the time the Germans abandoned their attack on sector airfields in favour of an assault on London, the wastage of Hurricanes and Spitfires had been more than counterbalanced by the output of the factories.

The prize of victory had thus eluded Göring's grasp. On October 12 Hitler recognised this by formally postponing Sea Lion

until the spring of 1941. In fact, this meant abandonment: Hitler's mind was now fixed on Russia. Until the German war machine could roll east, however, there was everything to be said, from the German point of view, for maintaining pressure on Britain, so long as it could be done inexpensively. During October the Luftwaffe, assisted by a few Italian aircraft, kept Fighter Command at stretch in daylight by sending over fighters and fighter-bombers, which did little damage but were difficult to intercept. At night the German bombers, operating with virtual impunity, continued to drop their loads on London.

The story of the 'Night Blitz' is one of civilian suffering and heroism, of widespread yet indecisive damage—and of slowly increasing success by the British defences. In the battle of wits against the intruders, perhaps the most vital developments were the discovery (and distortion) of the German navigational beams, the provision of dummy airfields and decoy fires, and the advances in radar which made possible accurate tracking overland.

Radar advances resulted in gun-laying radar that gave accurate readings of heights, and so permitted the engagement of the target 'unseen', and in ground-controlled interception (GCI) radar stations which brought night fighters close enough to the enemy for the fighters to use their own airborne radar (AI) for the final location and pursuit. It was only towards the end of the Blitz, however, that the GCI/AI combination emerged as a real threat to the attackers, who began to lose three or four aircraft in every 100 sorties, instead of merely one.

Meanwhile, the Luftwaffe was able to lay waste the centres of a score or more of British cities. After the early raids in August, the weight of attack by night fell for a time almost entirely on London. Between September 7 and November 13 there was only one night on which London escaped bombing, and the number of German aircraft over the capital each night averaged 163. With the final postponement of Sea Lion, the attack then extended also to longer-term, strategic objectives—the industrial towns, and later mainly the ports, so linking up with the blockading actions of the German submarines.

On November 14 the devastation of Coventry marked the change of policy; thereafter Southampton, Birmingham, Liverpool, Bristol, Plymouth, Portsmouth, Cardiff, Swansea, Belfast, Glasgow, and many other towns felt the full fury of the Blitz. In the course of it all, until Luftflotte II moved east in May 1941 and the attacks died away, the Germans killed about 40,000 British civilians and injured another 46,000, and damaged more than 1,000,000 British homes, at a cost to themselves of some 600 aircraft. On the economic side, they seriously impeded British aircraft production for some months, but in other directions the damage they did was too diffuse to be significant.

Hitler's first setback

The 'Blitz' ceased not because of the increased success of the British defences, but because most of the German aircraft were needed elsewhere. Had Russia collapsed within the eight weeks of the German—and the British—estimate, they would doubtless have returned quickly enough, to clear the way for invasion or to attempt to pulverise Britain into submission. As it was, Russia held, and though the British people were

subjected to further bombardments, they were not again called upon to face a serious threat of invasion.

Though the Night Blitz was inconclusive, the daylight Battle of Britain was thus one of the turning points of the war: it was the air fighting of August and September 1940, together with the existence of the Royal Navy and the English Channel, which first halted Hitler's career of conquest. The 1,000 or so pilots of Fighter Command who bore the brunt of that fighting—including the 400 or more who lost their lives—saved more than Britain by their exertions. By earning Britain a great breathing space in which the further progress of events was to bring her the mighty alliance of Russia and the United States, they made possible the final victory and the liberation of Europe from the Nazi terror.

DENIS RICHARDS took a first-class honours degree in history at Cambridge, and before the war taught history at public schools. After serving in the RAF, he was appointed in 1942 to the Air Ministry to write confidential studies on the war-time operations, and from 1942 to 1946 was in charge of all such work within the Air Ministry Historical Branch. In 1950 he returned to education as principal of Morley College, London. He left this position 1965, holding the Longmans Fellowship in history at Sussex University until 1968. In collaboration with the late Hilary St George Saunders, he wrote the officially commissioned, three-volume war history of the RAF, and he has also written the text for the *Illustrated History of Modern Europe*, books on British history, a history of Morley College, and contributions to encyclopedias and the *Dictionary of National Biography*.

1940

August 1: Hitler decrees the Battle of Britain with the command: 'The German air force is to overcome the British air force with all means at its disposal, and as soon as possible.'

August 13: 'Eagle Day': the Luftwaffe launches its air offensive against Britain, with 1,485 sorties. The Germans lose 45 aircraft, the RAF 13.

August 15: In the most intense attack of the Battle of Britain, the Luftwaffe sends a total of 1,790 sorties over England. They lose 75 aircraft, while Britain loses 34.

August 17: The Germans establish an 'operational area' around Britain; in it, all ships are to be sunk without warning.

August 25: The RAF conducts its first raid on Berlin.

September 3: Britain cedes to the USA bases in the West Indies and elsewhere in exchange for 50 destroyers.

September 7: Some 300 German bombers, escorted by 600 fighters, head for the British capital and bomb London's dockland.

September 13: *Italy invades Egypt.*

September 15: The RAF claims to have shot down 183 German aircraft during daylight Luftwaffe raids on Britain—a figure subsequently found to have been greatly exaggerated.

September 17: Hitler postpones Operation Sea Lion 'until further notice'.

September 23/25: *British and Free French forces attempt to take Dakar.*

October 12: Operation Sea Lion is postponed until 1941.

A formation of the much-vaunted Me-110s; they had long range but rather poor manoeuvrability, and thus they suffered heavy losses in the battle ▷

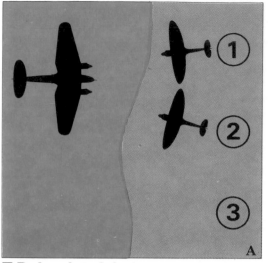
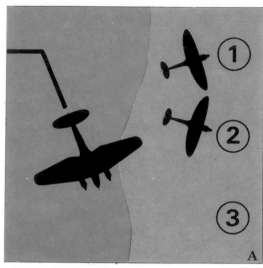
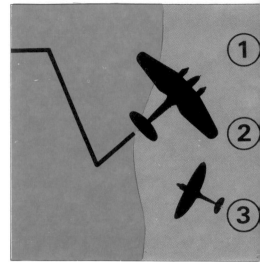

▽ Radar plotted the incoming bomber formations, alerting the AA defences and RAF Headquarters. Fighter Command had to anticipate feints by the incoming bombers in addition to the weight of the German attack itself

Fighter reports ■ Auto radio plots ■ Radar reports ■ AA land line ■ Observer reports ■ Combat orders

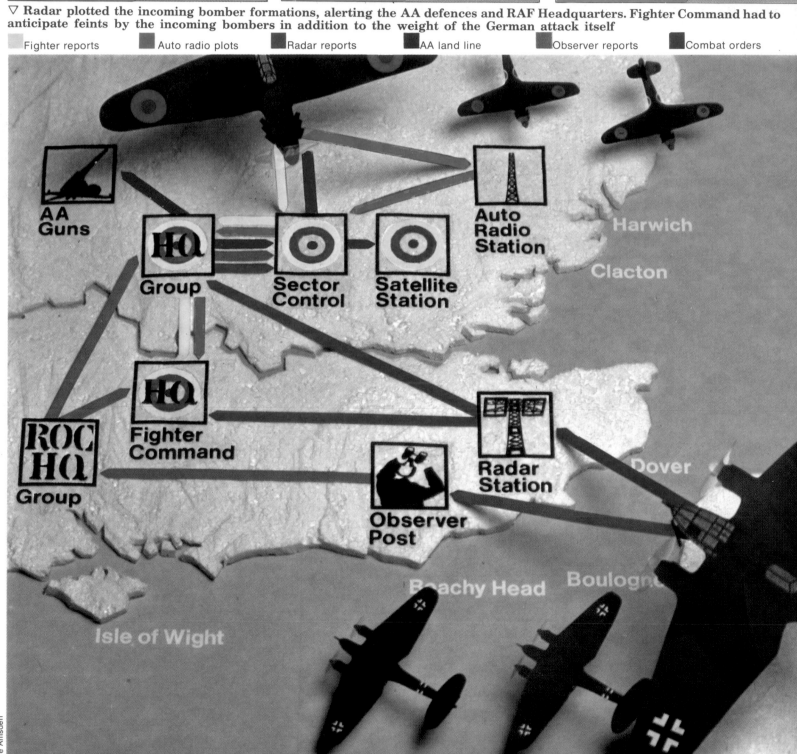

AA Guns

HQ Group

Sector Control

Satellite Station

Auto Radio Station

Harwich

Clacton

HQ Fighter Command

ROC HQ Group

Radar Station

Observer Post

Dover

Beachy Head

Boulogne

Isle of Wight

Deirdre Amsden

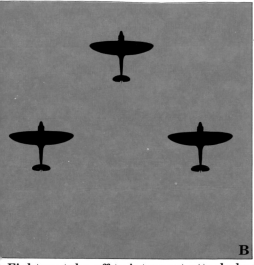
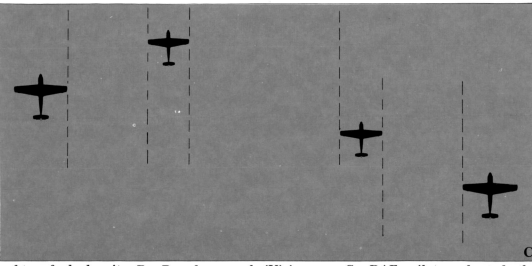

B

C

Fighters take off to intercept attack, but land to refuel when it heads for 3. Attack swings away from fighters at 3, returning to 1 and 2, where the fighters are still grounded

B: Parade-ground 'Vic' was rigid and inadequate for the needs of modern air fighting

C: RAF pilots adopted the German 'Schwarm': better known as the 'Finger-four'

RAF Commander (X THEATRE OF WAR)	**Luftflotte** (EQUIVALENT OF ARMY GROUP)
Group	**Fliegerkorps**
Wing Fighter Command Bomber Command Coastal Command	**Geschwader** Kampfgeschwader – Bomber Jagdgeschwader – Fighter Stukageschwader – Dive-bomber
(No Direct Equivalent)	**Gruppe**
Squadron	**Staffel**

Air Marshal Sir Hugh Dowding

WAAFs plot the battle

Reichsmarschall Göring (centre), with Luftwaffe officers

1. Messerschmitt 109E
Known to Luftwaffe pilots as the 'Emil', the 109E was at least as fast as the Spitfire but was found to be less manœuvrable, though more so than the Hurricane. Always handicapped by its short range, its performance as a fighter was further restricted by a bomb load later in the battle, when pressed into service in a fighter/bomber role.
Armament: Two 7·9-mm machine-guns and two 20-mm cannons.
Max speed: 357 mph

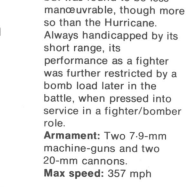

2. Messerschmitt 110
Göring's folly: the cream of the Luftwaffe fighter strength was deployed in 'destroyer' units, intended to smash through the fighter defences and provide long-range escort for the bombers. Against the Spitfire and Hurricane, however, the Me-110s had finally to be provided with escorts themselves, for their lack of manœuvrability meant that their powerful armament was all too often useless.
Armament: Two 20-mm cannons, four 7·9-mm machine-guns, one free-mounted 7·9-mm gun.
Max speed: 349 mph

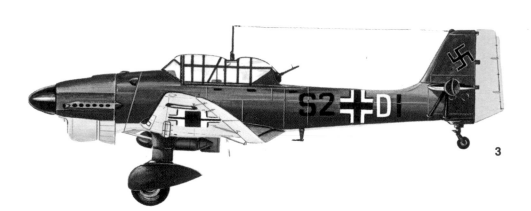

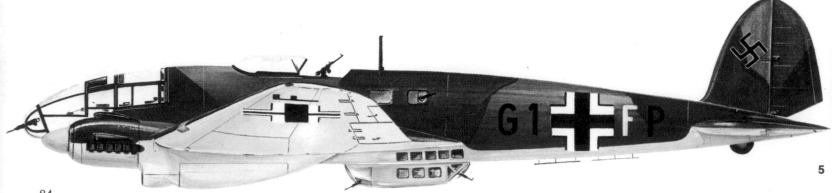

8. Supermarine Spitfire

The Spitfire fighter was the most agile machine in the battle—it could out-manoeuvre even the Me-109E. Another vital superiority was its fire-power: eight wing-mounted Brownings which, though out ranged by the German cannon, held a decisive concentration of rounds per second. In the Battle of Britain the Spitfire also held the advantage of fighting on home ground, unfettered by the range handicap of the 109E.
Armament: Eight ·303-inch machine-guns.
Max speed: 361 mph

9. Hawker Hurricane

Britain's first monoplane fighter was the numerical mainstay of RAF Fighter Command in the Battle of Britain. The Hurricane's ideal role was that of bomber-interceptor; as a rule, only the Spitfire could tackle the Me-109 on level terms, though the Hurricane scored notable successes against the Me-110. During the battle the Hurricane was already being replaced by the Spitfire as the standard RAF fighter.
Armament: Eight ·303-inch machine-guns.
Max speed: 328 mph

8

9

3. Junkers 87

The famous gull-winged Stuka was the main weapon which Göring turned against the RAF fighter bases. But the easy victories of past campaigns had been won in the absence of adequate fighter opposition, and RAF pilots found the Stuka an easy prey. Severe losses in operations throughout August destroyed its reputation as the all-conquering weapon of the Luftwaffe, and the Ju-87 was withdrawn from the spearhead of the attack.
Bomb load: One 1,102-lb, four 110-lb bombs.
Max speed: 217 mph

4. Junkers 88

The Ju-88 was the most versatile aircraft in the Luftwaffe's armoury for the entire war, serving as level bomber, dive-bomber, and night-fighter, as well as carrying out valuable reconnaissance duties. It was used by the Luftwaffe as a medium bomber in the Battle of Britain; but neither speed nor its comparatively high number of defending machine-guns was adequate protection from the fire-power of Spitfires and Hurricanes.
Bomb load: 5,510 lb
Max speed: 292 mph

5. Heinkel 111

The standard level bomber of the Luftwaffe at the time of the Battle of Britain, the He-111 suffered from its design as a medium bomber ideal for Continental operations but handicapped—as were all German twin-engined bombers—by the distances to targets in the north of England. Göring was convinced that its use in mass would prove decisive; but the He-111, it was found, was unable to beat off determined RAF fighter attacks.
Bomb load: 5,510 lb
Max speed: 258 mph

6. Dornier 17

The Do-17 was the Luftwaffe's veteran bomber: the type first saw service in the Spanish Civil War. Despite subsequent modifications, it was very weak in defensive fire, especially to attacks from below and to the rear. Known as the 'Flying Pencil' from its slim fuselage, the Do-17 was often confused with the British Hampden bomber, many of which were fired at by their own anti-aircraft guns. Its slender lines dictated a light bomb load.
Bomb load: 2,210 lb
Max speed: 270 mph

7. Dornier 215

This variant was a development of the basic design of the Do-17 with the installation of more powerful Daimler-Benz engines. The Do-215 was faster than the Do-17—fast enough to tax the lower-rated British engines of the early Spitfires and Hurricanes in a chase. In its light bomb-load and weak defence armament, however, the Do-215 was as handicapped as the Do-17.
Bomb load: 2,215 lb
Max speed: 311 mph

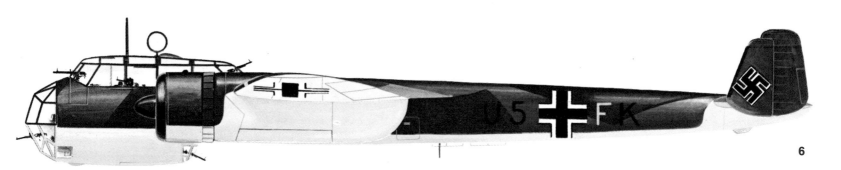

6

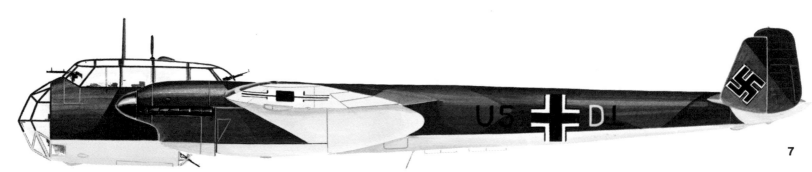

7

John Batchelor

△ Old Bailey in ruins: many landmarks were hit by the Blitz

△ Rescue workers bring out a man buried by rubble for 14 hours

△ Adding to the havoc of the bombing were the fires that raged in the Blitz's wake: firemen work while others hunt for survivors

By May 1941 bombs had killed some 40,000 British civilians

△ Street damage like this often cut power and water lines

△ The bombing of Coventry marked a shift to strategic targets

Keystone

Ullstein

Artillery in action in front of Tobruk in March 1941

WAVELL'S 30,000

Western Desert December 1940/February 1941   Wavell (on right) with O'Connor, his 'architect of victory'
In a short and memorable campaign, the British defeated the Italians in Egypt, Libya, and Cyrenaica in the last weeks of 1940 and the beginning of 1941. It was the first British offensive of the Second World War, and the first victory on land. Its practical and psychological consequences were enormous. As it was happening, it was transformed into a legend; and then other events which loomed much larger at the time—victories and defeats—pushed it into the background of men's minds   *John Connell*

Italian machine-gunners on the desert front

When the half-forgotten legend of Wavell's desert campaign is brought out into the light of history, and the quite simple, true facts are told, it shines as brilliantly as some gem which has lain for years buried in the desert sand or in a rocky cleft in the escarpment. And in its glow we see reflected the qualities and the calibre of Britain and the old Empire and Commonwealth—India, Australia, and New Zealand, South Africa and Rhodesia—as they appeared to the men, by far the greater part of them volunteers, whose soldierly skill, courage, and endurance brought victory in a time when it was sorely needed.

It is essential to think of this desert warfare not in the terms of the late 1960's, but in those of more than a quarter of a century ago, before 'empire' was a word unusable in civilised society. This was an imperial campaign, fought between empires and by imperial troops, on political and strategic grounds which were of the utmost importance to those who directed the affairs of the clashing empires.

The British Empire was old, strong, and well tested in peace and war. The Italian Empire was new, brash, on the surface very self-confident, underneath, deeply lacking in assurance or strength of purpose. Mussolini, the Italian dictator, who had begun in the 1920's with a protracted honeymoon period of excellent relations with Britain, had convinced himself, as his own imperial ambitions expanded, that the British were decadent and feeble. Italy had come late into the general European scramble for territory in Africa; but from the frontier of Egypt westward she controlled a vast, if thinly-populated, region—partly desert, partly cultivated—divided into Libya, Cyrenaica, and Tripolitania, and sharing its western frontier with Tunisia in French North Africa. In 1935-36 the Italian conquest of the ancient and independent East African country of Ethiopia—virtually unopposed by both Britain and France—whetted Mussolini's appetite; but it drove him into closer and closer association with Nazi Germany, and was one of the final stepping-stones to the Second World War. The Axis (Germany, Italy, and Japan) was never a very closely knit alliance, but in the Mediterranean and the Middle East it had its greatest chance of proving effective. It was there that the Axis was first badly dented by the British; and British victories there were the inevitable prelude to the final destruction of the Axis as a whole, and each of its three member-nations separately.

In 1940, however, the Axis appeared to be a most menacing challenge. The Middle East was the fulcrum of the British Empire. Here, in Iraq and in south-west Persia, were its main sources of oil for transport and industry, for the Royal Navy, the Royal Air Force, and for an army which was rapidly being mechanised. Here, in Egypt—nominally independent since 1936 but linked to Britain by a treaty which guaranteed British forces a great many essential facilities—was established the biggest military base outside the United Kingdom, and the centre of a network of communications with India, the Far East, the rest of Africa, Australia, and New Zealand. In Alexandria and in Haifa, Palestine, the Royal Navy had harbours and extensive dock and repair facilities.

The retention of this strategically vital region was obviously a primary British objective. To use it as a springboard for an assault, or a series of assaults, which could destroy the Italian Empire, would be a bold

strategy; and if achieved and fully exploited, it might even shorten the war by as much as two years.

Wavell takes command

The importance of holding the Middle East was realised by the Chamberlain government in the summer of 1939. On August 2 General Sir Archibald Wavell took up the appointment of General Officer Commanding-in-Chief all British land forces in Egypt, the Sudan, Palestine and Transjordan, and Cyprus. When war broke out early in the following month, his command was extended to include British Somaliland, Aden, Iraq, and the shores of the Persian Gulf. Wavell, then 56 years old, was regarded within the army as one of its ablest soldiers. He had just had a few months at Southern Command in England, after having headed the sizeable formations which had dealt with the protracted Arab rebellion in Palestine. He had served on General Allenby's staff in this area in the First World War, and had written Allenby's biography and a study of the Palestine campaign of 1917-18. Though he came of an old Hampshire family, his regimental service had been with a Scottish regiment, The Black Watch. He was resourceful, robust, and extremely well-read—far beyond the boundaries of his profession. His outlook was fresh and original, his mental processes were rapid; but in speech he was laconic. His reserve was as great as his resilience.

For more than nine months, while Italy dallied over her entry into the war, while Poland was defeated and overwhelmed, throughout the twilight period of the Phoney War, and even after the Nazis launched their onslaught on Denmark and Norway, Wavell's was only a watching brief. But from the moment he assumed his command he thought, planned, and worked as best he could outside the rigidly defensive directive which the Chamberlain government gave him; and from the outset he was convinced that the Middle East was bound to be one of the major battlefields of the war. All his ideas for taking any initiative anywhere on the perimeter of his vast command were rejected; his efforts to build up an efficient intelligence network in the Italian colonies and in the Balkans were persistently frustrated by the Foreign Office; and even his own freedom of movement within his command (a facet of his duties to which he attached great importance) was gravely impeded by Whitehall's refusal to allow him his own personal aircraft.

Nevertheless, in spite of all these difficulties, Wavell's tireless efforts achieved results in four separate fields of his authority, all of which were to be of momentous consequence in the campaigns which he waged in 1940-41. First, he travelled the length and breadth of his command, seeing for himself, getting to know subordinate commanders and officials, and reconnoitring the terrain as far as he was able. Second, with the invaluable help of a very energetic and able administrative officer, General Sir Balfour Hutchison, he turned Egypt into a base which could supply the logistical requirements of an army of 300,000 men. Third, he insisted that the combatant formations at his disposal, small and ill-equipped as they were, should be as highly trained and as aggressively-minded as possible. And fourth, one of his first operational instructions, issued within a few weeks of arriving in Cairo, was to General Maitland Wilson, the

General Officer Commanding British Troops in Egypt, to prepare plans for an invasion of Italian Libya, paying particular attention to the problems of supply and maintenance for a mobile force driving westward across the desert.

On May 10, 1940, the Germans launched their great *Blitzkrieg* against the Low Countries and France. Winston Churchill became Prime Minister of the United Kingdom, in a coalition government pledged to victory, whatever the cost; and a new, resolute, aggressive spirit, at a time of supreme crisis, was breathed into every area of the nation's activity. It was a mood to which Wavell was eager to respond, for he had waited for it long and impatiently.

Exactly one calendar month later, Italy, choosing a moment when it seemed that a swift and total German victory in the west was inevitable, declared war on Britain and France. France, already broken by the Nazi onslaught, was to sue for an armistice within ten days; and her large forces in her colonial empire in North Africa and in Syria and Lebanon—though ultimately of great strategic importance—were to be for many months out of the battle. In essence in the Mediterranean and the Middle East the crunch was to be between Britain and Italy alone.

Three days before the Italian entry into the war Major-General Richard O'Connor, who was then commanding British forces in southern Palestine with his headquarters in Jerusalem, was ordered to report to Lieutenant-General Maitland Wilson in Cairo. He flew down at once and was told that he was to command a formation called the Western Desert Force, whose headquarters were at Marsa Matrûh, the railhead village and small port some 120 miles east of the Egypt-Libya frontier. His task, as outlined to him by Wilson, was to protect Egypt from Italian attack, a directive which he received with surprise mingled with pride.

O'Connor was short, slight, and seemingly diffident; gentle of speech, tireless in action, and great of heart; Anglo-Irish by ancestry and a product of the conventional military background of his time, Wellington and Sandhurst; an officer in the Cameronians (the Scottish Rifles), he had served with the Italians in the First World War and had been given an Italian Silver Medal for valour; he had been an Instructor at the Staff College in the 1920's, and a graduate of the Imperial Defence College in 1935.

He was a commander of remarkable quality beneath his quiet manner. While Wavell's is the credit for the strategic direction of the campaign, O'Connor's achievement was the tactical victory. Without his ability and his leadership it *might* not have been won.

The 'Desert Rats'

Immediately upon the outbreak of war with Italy O'Connor's Western Desert Force, consisting of the 7th Armoured Division (minus a brigade), a support group of two regiments of Royal Horse Artillery, and two motor battalions, took the initiative. The quality of the 7th Armoured Division bore testimony to the influence and vigour of the man who had raised it. In September 1938 Major-General Percy Hobart had been sent to Egypt at short notice to take command of the troops in the desert and to form them into what they then called 'The Mobile Division'. His invaluable experience with modern mobile forces linked with a ruthless,

Italian troops under RAF attack during their retreat in the desert

driving energy had rapidly welded an incoherent group of tank, artillery, infantry, and administrative units into a formation that not only understood its task, but was thoroughly accustomed to moving among and enduring the frightening mysteries of the unfamiliar desert wastes. They were as at home in the desert as the little jerboas upon which they modelled their shoulder-flash. They were, as Major-General O'Connor himself wrote in the autumn of 1939, 'the best-trained division I have ever seen'.

The opinion of Brigadier Gott (who was to command the division later in the war) that so many of Hobart's tactical ideas proved sound and true, was quickly vindicated. During less than a fortnight's offensive patrolling they inflicted heavy casualties on the Italians, captured 25 officers (including an engineer general) and 500 other ranks; and their RAF comrades destroyed, in air combat and ground attack, more than 50 enemy aircraft. O'Connor's little force stayed on the offensive for the rest of June and throughout most of July, harassing the Italians so much that they had to keep at least four divisions in defensive readiness near the frontier.

Meanwhile, earning Churchill's praise for this bold and cavalier activity, Wavell was beginning to ponder the possibilities of a much more ambitious operation. To understand what he planned and what he achieved, it is necessary to have a clear picture of the territory over which the campaign was fought, and the composition, equipment, and character of the forces engaged.

The campaign was unique of its kind, in that it was fought in a virtually empty but well-defined arena. It was pure theoretical war-game soldiering, turned by the chances of world strategy into real fighting, with real communications, real guns, real armoured fighting vehicles. Nothing like it had happened before in modern history; but it offered a classic example—unhappily not yet followed—of nations fighting a war without making it total. If ever limited war was shown to be practical, in modern terms and with modern weapons, it was in the Western Desert.

The desert stretched almost exactly 500 miles as the crow flies—from El Alamein on the coast of Egypt 80 miles west of Alexandria, to El Agheila on the Gulf of Sirte, on the border between Cyrenaica and Tripolitania. Such inhabited areas as existed were scattered along the coastline which, for the soldiers (though not for the sailors and airmen), was the northern edge of the board. The only communications, road and rail, kept close to the coast. The desert itself was a plateau which shelved steeply down to sea level; this shelf was known in desert-warfare terminology as the 'escarpment'. Where the coastline bulged between Derna and Benghazi, the escarpment became a range of hills, cultivable and wooded. Southward the desert stretched for many hundreds of miles, its rocky, barren wastes broken by a few widely-separated oases—the ancient and famous Siwa within the Egyptian frontier, and Jarabub and Jalo in Cyrenaica. Its eastern boundary, providing a natural defence system, was the great Qattara depression, impassable for vehicles and infantry alike; but between the depression and the coast at El Alamein there was a small, 40-mile-wide gap of open, traversable desert—the gateway to the Nile Delta, metropolitan Egypt, and the Suez Canal

zone. To the west the desert shaded, through dune and marshland, into the cultivated, colonised country of Tripolitania.

Over the years the desert became a single, huge battlefield, whose emptiness, so far as logistics were concerned, was absolute. If you wanted anything, you brought it with you, or (if you were lucky) you captured it from the enemy. The needs of an army and of its accompanying air force in the Second World War were numerous and diverse, but they were summed up under five main headings: ammunition, fuel, food, water, and repairs. The ranges at which both fighter aircraft and tanks could operate without refuelling and workshop maintenance were short by the standards of a quarter of a century later; and their requirements added to the neat mixture of rigidity and flexibility which characterised the tactics and techniques of Western Desert fighting—learned by the contestants, for the most part, as they went along.

British forces dwarfed

Facing each other across this curious chess-board, in the summer and autumn of 1940, were forces remarkably disproportionate in numbers. Wavell's principal opponent, Marshal Graziani, had under his command along the Egypt-Libya frontier and in depth behind it, in Cyrenaica and Tripolitania, almost 250,000 men: nine 'metropolitan' (or regular) divisions, each numbering some 13,000 men; three Blackshirt and two Libyan native divisions, of some 8,000 men each; a proportion of army and corps troops, and various other Libyan units and frontier guards. Under the Marshal's North African Supreme Headquarters, this huge force was organised as two armies—the X in Cyrenaica, consisting of one regular and one Blackshirt corps, each of two divisions, and a 'group' of two Libyan divisions; and the rest forming the V Army in Tripolitania. With the defeat of France, Graziani was released from the anxiety of having to fight on two fronts and could, if he chose, concentrate his whole effort against Wavell in Egypt.

This he proved noticeably reluctant to undertake, despite the fact that, for the whole of his far more widely scattered command, Wavell could muster a total force of only 86,000. Of these, 36,000 were in Egypt—short of equipment, artillery of all calibres, ammunition, AFVs (armoured fighting vehicles), and transport. There was the 7th Armoured Division, commanded by Major-General O'Moore Creagh, two of whose brigades consisted of two instead of three regiments of tanks, and these by no means fully equipped. There was the 4th Indian Division, commanded by Major-General Noel Beresford-Peirse, consisting of only two brigades, and with its reconnaissance regiment and its artillery far below strength. There was the New Zealand division, commanded by Major-General Bernard Freyberg, consisting of one infantry brigade, a cavalry regiment minus one squadron, a machine-gun battalion, and a regiment of field artillery. There were also 14 British infantry battalions and two regiments of artillery.

In Palestine Wavell had 27,000 troops: the 1st Cavalry Division, two more cavalry regiments (still horsed), two Australian brigades with two regiments of field artillery and some divisional troops, and a British infantry brigade and two other battalions. It was unlikely that either the British

cavalry or the Australians would be fully equipped and trained before the end of 1940.

If numbers were all that mattered in war, Wavell had not a chance, even in defence; to go on to the offensive would surely be to court disaster. Yet this is just what he was determined to do, not because he was a reckless romantic, but because he had calculated, quite coolly, that he could bring it off.

The hard core of his small force consisted of British and Indian professional soldiers of high quality, officers, NCOs, and men. His subordinate commanders and senior staff officers had nearly all been young regimental officers in the First World War, and had learned their rigorous profession the hard way, as he had himself. The impression that some of them were to give of being amiable amateurs was both disarming and inaccurate. The best of them were men of above average intellect, of an alert and unprejudiced temper, capable of considerable originality of thought as well as boldness of action. So far as the army was concerned, they were the pick of their generation, in qualities of mind and spirit as much as in a certain physical hardiness which desert warfare evoked and sustained. The troops they led were good because *they* were good; and the victory they won did not come to them by accident.

In August Wavell was summoned to London for consultations with Churchill—whom he had never met before—and with the Chief of the Imperial General Staff (CIGS), General Sir John Dill, who was one of his oldest and closest friends. Their conferences were held while the crucial first phase of the Battle of Britain was being fought, and the invasion of Britain seemed likely any day. It is against that sombre yet splendid background that the decisions taken must be considered. After several days of strenuous discussion in the War Cabinet and the Chiefs-of-Staff Committee, the CIGS was able to tell Churchill on August 15 (a day during which every fighter squadron in Britain was engaged in resisting the Luftwaffe's onslaught), that the War Office were arranging to send at once to Egypt one cruiser-tank battalion of 52 tanks, one light-tank regiment of 52 tanks, and one infantry-tank battalion of 50 tanks, together with 48 anti-tank guns, 20 Bofors light AA guns, 48 25-pounder field guns, 500 Bren-guns, and 250 anti-tank rifles, all with the necessary ammunition. Churchill wrote afterwards: 'The decision to give this blood transfusion while we braced ourselves to meet a mortal danger was at once awful and right. No one faltered.'

The value of these timely reinforcements was immeasurable. To send them was an act of high faith and courage on the part of the British government. Wavell flew back to the Middle East on the evening of August 15, fortified by the knowledge that his political chiefs were doing all they could to back him.

Graziani's irresolute advance

Four weeks later Graziani made a ponderous, fumbling, and irresolute advance, which could hardly be construed as a massive invasion of Egypt. O'Connor's small force responded with a skilful fighting withdrawal to a defence line which had been constructed at Marsa Matrûh; and the Italians, bombed by the RAF, shelled by artillery, and harassed by mines, took four comfortless days to make the 65-mile march to Sidi Barrani—at that time nothing more than a

Crossing the frontier-wire into Libya

Fort Capuzzo, captured on June 14, 1940

On patrol: British light tank at speed

collection of a few mud huts and a landing ground—where they halted and began laboriously to dig themselves in. From Rome there came a boastful communiqué announcing Graziani's victorious advance, and claiming that 'all is quiet and the trams are again running in the town of Sidi Barrani'.

Thereafter Graziani was frequently prodded by Mussolini to resume his attack, and became more and more reluctant to do as he was told—and more and more exasperated in his protests about his paucity of equipment, tanks, and guns. If he could not be budged, Wavell decided, O'Connor must go out and hit him. On September 21 Wavell gave his Chief-of-Staff, General Arthur Smith, a directive outlining a four-stage advance in the recapture of Sidi Barrani, the establishment of a sufficient force along the frontier, the occupation of Bardia and the Jarabub oasis, and finally the capture of Tobruk. If the operation continued, the next move would be to Derna in Cyrenaica.

From this starting point (in the middle of Graziani's attack, be it noted) the plan built itself up in Wavell's mind, and in the minds of his staff and subordinate commanders. The convoy of much-needed tanks and guns reached Egypt safely in mid-September. Churchill began to fret lest they were not used promptly in the aggressive kind of fighting he longed for. In the middle of October Anthony Eden (Lord Avon), then Secretary of State for War, went out to the Middle East to discuss with Wavell the various developments that were likely to take place within the command.

The months of watching and waiting were nearly over. Wavell's responsibilities widened suddenly and vastly. There were plans for a major attack on the Italians in Ethiopia. The Royal Navy took the offensive in the Mediterranean. And when on October 28 the Italians, moving in from Albania, launched a major attack on Greece, the RAF in the Middle East was told to send three squadrons of Blenheims and one of Gladiators to help the Greeks deal with the Regia Aeronautica (Italian Air Force). Wavell was also asked to send two AA batteries to Athens and an infantry brigade to Suda Bay, in Crete, to assist in the defence of the Greek islands.

So slender were Wavell's resources at this time that these demands made it necessary to confide in Eden his ideas for a Western Desert offensive, which hitherto he had kept as secret as possible. Eden was delighted. Meanwhile, Generals Wilson and O'Connor were working out their plans for the operations which Wavell wanted. In parenthesis, the command structure in the Middle East at this time was undoubtedly cumbrous. Wavell, as Commander-in-Chief, gave his strategic orders to Wilson, as commander of British troops in Egypt; and Wilson, putting if need be his own tactical interpretation on them, passed them on to O'Connor in command of the Western Desert Force—the formation that had in fact to carry out the job. The system worked as smoothly as it did only because the men concerned knew and liked and understood one another very well.

On November 2 Wavell wrote to Wilson:

In continuation of my Personal and Most Secret letter of 29 October, I wish you to inform your senior commanders in the Western Desert as follows:

I have instructed Lieut.-Gen. O'Connor, through you, to prepare an offensive operation against the Italian forces in their present positions (if they do not continue their advance) to take place as soon as possible.

I realise the risks of such an operation and am fully prepared to accept them, and the possibility of considerable casualties to personnel and to AFVs. I consider that the advantages of the operation entirely justify the risks run. Nor do I consider the risks excessive. In everything but numbers we are superior to the enemy. We are more highly trained, we have better equipment. We know the ground and are better accustomed to desert conditions. Above all we have stouter hearts and greater traditions and are fighting in a worthier cause.

I need hardly point out that a striking success, which I consider can well be won, will have an incalculable effect not only on the whole position in the Middle East, not only on the military situation everywhere, but on the future of freedom and civilisation throughout the world. It is the best way in which we can help our Greek allies in their gallant struggle.

We have waited long in the Middle East; when our chance comes let us strike hard. We have been on the defensive; we must accustom our minds to the offensive which only can bring victory.

The Prime Minister has sent us every good wish in this battle with Italy and his assurance that 'all acts and decisions of valour and violence against the enemy will, whatever their upshot, receive the resolute support of His Majesty's Government'. I need not add that all commanders will have my full support in acting boldly and with determination. We have other large reinforcements on the way and can afford to take some of the risks without which battles cannot be won. I have the greatest confidence in the commanders and troops in the Western Desert and am sure that a striking success is possible, with good fortune which only boldness can bring.

One of our most powerful aids to victory will be surprise. Every means by which we can preserve secrecy and deceive the enemy must be studied. The plan and intentions must be confined till the last moment to as few persons as possible; and everyone must understand that the lives of his comrades and the success of the war may be imperilled by carelessness.

These seven paragraphs were the only formal written directive for the operation which, given the code name 'Compass', was to be so brilliant a victory and so far-reaching in its effects.

Operation Compass

Back in London on November 8 Eden unfolded the 'Compass' plan to Churchill and the CIGS. Churchill, as he himself said, 'purred like six cats'. He wanted to know the exact date of the operation's launching; he grew excited at the thought of extending its purpose; and he fretted because Wavell, in a manner which was permitted to no other commander in the Second World War, kept his own secrets—even from the War Cabinet.

Wavell had various objects in mind, which were very difficult to adjust and reconcile: he wanted to make Compass appear nothing more than a large-scale, five-day raid, a reconnaissance in strength; he would thus have room for strategic manoeuvre; if it succeeded, he could (if he had the troops) exploit it to the full, and go on to Cyrenaica; if the Italians' resistance proved tough, he could hold such gains as he might have made, and prepare to go on later in greater

strength; but at the same time he wanted to get preparations for the attack on Eritrea and Italian-occupied Ethiopia under way. And he had one trained infantry division—the 4th Indian—which he believed to be capable of playing a full part in both operations. He therefore planned that this division, having fought in the first phase of Compass, should be shifted off at once, if the shipping were available, to the Sudan, there to join 5th Indian Division for the East African campaign. *He told nobody about his intentions except Arthur Smith, his CGS, and Maitland Wilson.* Wilson therefore had the difficult task of participating in and supervising the tactical planning of Compass, alongside O'Connor and his staff, even though in all probability one of O'Connor's key formations would be snatched from him just as his operation was building up its impetus.

Nor did Wavell allow a hint to escape him that, if O'Connor achieved success in the first phase—which was all he was told to plan for—he might be allowed to exploit his victory and go on as far and as fast as he could.

This mixture of purposes in Wavell's mind must be understood if the real magnitude of the victory is to be appreciated. A basic element in it was secrecy. In GHQ in Cairo not more than half a dozen of the staff were aware of the plan at all; and similar precautions were taken in all the other headquarters involved. The impression was spread that the forces in the Western Desert had been seriously weakened by the sending of reinforcements to Greece, and that there would soon be more withdrawals.

Against this background Wilson and O'Connor, and the two divisional commanders, O'Moore Creagh and Beresford-Peirse, had to do their tactical planning. The operation they proposed was remarkably unorthodox, a mixture of drive and deception, boldness and bluff. It was preceded by a full-dress rehearsal on November 26—on a plateau near Matrûh—called Training Exercise Number 1. All that the troops who took part in this exercise knew was that 'on a day in the second week in December' they would have Training Exercise Number 2. Not even when they moved off on December 6, but only on December 7—after their first night's bivouacking in the desert—were they told that this was the real thing and not just one more exercise.

The Italians had, on paper, fairly formidable forces assembled round and in front of Sidi Barrani. In six fortified camps (four at Nibeiwa, Tummar, and a place called Point 90, all south of the coast road; one at Maktila just north of the road; and one to the east of Sidi Barrani itself) they had two Libyan divisions, the IV Blackshirt Division, and (in Nibeiwa camp) a formation, to all intents and purposes as strong as a division, known as 'General Maletti's Group'. In reserve they had a division in four more fortified camps around Sofafi and Rabia, south-west of Sidi Barrani, and along the southern fringe of the escarpment. They had another division south of the coastal road, between Buq Buq and Sidi Barrani, and two more further west near Sollum, Sidi Omar, and Capuzzo, on the far side of the soon-to-be-famous Halfaya Pass.

O'Connor had for his assault a total force of some 30,000 men: the 4th Indian Division, the 7th Armoured Division, and a formation known as 'Selby Force'—consisting of three mobile columns of infantry, one troop of

armoured cars, and some field and light AA guns—which numbered 1,750 men of all ranks, and had been part of the garrison of Matrûh, under the command of Brigadier A. R. Selby.

Western Desert Force's headquarters were at Maaten Bagush, on the coast 25 miles or so east of Matrûh. Maitland Wilson moved in here during the first week in December, and O'Connor, with his chief staff officer, Brigadier John (later Field-Marshal Lord) Harding, went forward on December 6 with his troops.

Undetected move

The approach march in the first two days, some 60 miles across open, treeless country, was made by day—two divisions, with hundreds of vehicles—without the Italians getting an inkling of what was happening. For two nights the force laagered in the desert some 10 miles west of Bir el Kenayis, on the Matrûh-Siwa road. Then, during the afternoon of Sunday, December 8, they set out—luckily protected by low cloud which made air reconnaissance difficult for the Italians—for their final pre-battle rendezvous in an area which the troops nicknamed 'Piccadilly', in the desert due south of Maktila and about 50 miles west of the Matrûh-Siwa road. By 1700 hours they were all assembled, prepared to make the final leap forward by moonlight.

Hitherto the two divisions had gone forward together. During the night of December 8/9, they split. The 7th Armoured Division headed further west, to be able to operate over a wide area, well behind the Italians' camps, to the south of the road between Sidi Barrani and Buq Buq. The initial attack on the Nibeiwa and Tummar camps was to be made by 4th Indian Division, coming in on them from the west; and Selby Force, which left Matrûh on December 9, heading due west along the road, was to immobilise Maktila and press on towards Sidi Barrani itself.

While this final approach was under way, the Royal Navy, with the heavily gunned monitor *Terror*, and the more lightly armed gunboats *Aphis* and *Ladybird*, bombarded Sidi Barrani and Maktila.

The night turned bitterly cold. Until about midnight the Italians in Nibeiwa were on the alert; there was some rather wild rifle fire and flares went up. A little before 0500 hours a temporarily detached battalion of 4th Indian Division opened fire on the camp from the east, and successfully diverted the Italians' attention in their direction. They kept up this exercise for nearly an hour, and then let a deceptive quiet reign. At 0715 hours the 72 guns of the divisional artillery began a brief, intensive bombardment, again from the east. Within ten minutes the infantry ('I') tanks of the 7th Royal Tank Regiment (RTR) swept down on the north-west corner of the camp, putting out of action *en route* some 25 Italian medium and light tanks parked outside the perimeter. Two squadrons of infantry tanks (known as 'Matildas') broke at once into the camp, tackling the Italian artillery and infantry at close quarters. General Maletti, the Italian divisional commander, was killed by a burst from one of the tanks' guns as he emerged from his dug-out. Through the breach there followed almost immediately two battalions of infantry from the 4th Indian Division—the 1/6th Rajputana Rifles and the 2nd Cameron Highlanders—who mopped up with zest. It was by no means easy; there

'Operation Compass' begins: the British barrage hammers an Italian desert fort to the south of Sidi Barrani

was some hard fighting; but within two hours the camp was in British hands.

While this was going on the 5th Indian Infantry Brigade (the 1st Royal Fusiliers, the 3/1st Punjab Regiment, and the 4/6th Rajputana Rifles) and one of the division's regiments of field artillery were moving in a big arc west of Nibeiwa, to be ready to attack the next objective, Tummar West.

Westward again, on an even wider arc, 7th Armoured Division had been on the move since first light, with its leading formation, the 4th Armoured Brigade, heading unopposed for the coastal road, some 35 miles north of the starting line.

Before 1100 hours the tanks had done their job in Nibeiwa; the final business could be left to the Rajputana Rifles and the Camerons. They had more than 2,000 prisoners to deal with, and ample supplies, tanks, guns, and water, all of which were useful. British casualties had been under 100.

Tummar West, some 13,000 yards from Nibeiwa, had not been reconnoitred at all. Some time had therefore to be spent in reconnaissance, and it was not until the afternoon that the attack could be launched. In the meantime 4th Armoured Brigade crossed the coastal road some 12 miles east of Buq Buq and captured 100 lorries and several hundred soldiers; and Selby Force, after going hard towards Maktila, swung south in

order to try to prevent the Italian garrison from escaping. However, a severe sandstorm blew up, and under its cover the Italians in Maktila pulled out and dug themselves in some 6 miles westwards, presumably to try to defend Sidi Barrani.

At Tummar West things went much as they had at Nibeiwa, though there were fewer tanks, and there was no longer any chance of surprise. Nevertheless by dusk Tummar too was in British hands, and the capture of personnel and material was again considerable, though at a slightly heavier cost in casualties.

O'Connor himself arrived in the camp at 1700 hours, and there encountered Beresford-Peirse. The divisional commander was in high spirits; O'Connor was satisfied with the first day's fighting, and full of quiet hope for the morrow. He went back to his operational headquarters on the escarpment south-east of Sidi Barrani. Harding, his General Staff Officer (GSO.1), sat up late writing his situation reports for Cairo; and by 0900 hours on December 10 Wavell was able to signal to Dill in London a detailed account of the state of play five-and-a-half hours earlier. Plans for the next phase had to be flexible, and Wavell finished his telegram with the cautionary words: 'It will be necessary to do some clearing up today and further operations cannot at present be foreseen.'

It was a sensible warning, because the first news of victory immensely excited the Prime Minister, and his buoyant optimism was reflected in the British Parliament and Press. This was excellent, but Wavell was determined to keep the operation in perspective: if the five-day raid could be extended, very well, and the congratulations and rejoicings would be merited. Meanwhile, the first battle was still to be won.

The sandstorm which had held up Selby Force was the beginning of a long period of bad weather, chilly enough by day, bitterly cold by night; and high winds whipped up the dust and alternated with torrential, driving rain. On the morning of December 10 two of Beresford-Peirse's brigades, the 5th Indian (which had taken Tummar West the day before) and the 16th British (which had hitherto been in reserve) fought their way northward to Sidi Barrani against stiffening Italian opposition. There was heavy fighting throughout the evening. The 7th RTR sent ten of its tanks round on 16th Brigade's left flank, and even further west the 4th Armoured Brigade came into action. The dust storm reduced visibility severely; communication and infantry/tank co-operation grew more and more difficult; and water ran short. The leading battalion of 16th Brigade (the 1st Argyll and Sutherland Highlanders) reached the road at Alam el Dab, had a stiff fight with an entire Black-

An Italian strong-point on the perimeter of Bardia: a 47-mm anti-tank crew in action, December 1940

shirt division, and had fairly heavy casualties. Nevertheless by 1330 hours the brigade had gained its objectives. The Italians' escape routes to the south and west were bolted and barred.

Beresford-Peirse kept up the pressure. Sixteenth Brigade, with the addition of the Camerons from the 11th Indian Brigade, as many 'I' tanks as were still serviceable, some more help from the 4th Armoured Brigade, and the whole weight of the division's artillery, attacked Sidi Barrani from the west at 1600 hours. They were through the hamlet and its surrounding encampments in half an hour; and before dusk they and Selby Force, coming up from Maktila, had hemmed in the remains of two Libyan and one Blackshirt divisions. Throughout the day 7th Armoured Division, ready to help if the Sidi Barrani situation did not clear up, cruised in the desert south of the road and west of the Sidi Barrani-Bir Enba track. In the evening O'Connor ordered it to advance on Buq Buq as soon as possible. Some of 4th Armoured Brigade's advance patrols were indeed already 15 miles west of Buq Buq.

During the night of December 10/11, Wavell took what was for him the most difficult decision of the whole campaign. The shipping was available at Suez; the 4th Indian Division (less the 16th British Brigade) could now be moved to the Sudan.

He issued the order. O'Connor woke up in his operational headquarters on the morning of December 11 to be given this surprising and very unwelcome news. True, the Indian division was to be replaced by the 6th Australian; but only one of the latter's brigades was even in the desert area, and it was generally short of transport, guns, and equipment. O'Connor took the shock philosophically and without reproach to the Commander-in-Chief; but he realised that the impetus of his offensive was bound to be blunted for several weeks while the change-over took place and the new arrivals fitted themselves into the campaign.

He went up to see Beresford-Peirse, who now had his divisional headquarters less than 3 miles south of Sidi Barrani. It was a considerable consolation to hear the news, within a few minutes of his arrival, that the battle in this area was now over. All the remaining Italian detachments had either surrendered or were in the process of doing so. This wholesale collapse included the Maktila garrison which, less than three days earlier, had presented so prickly a problem.

Seventh Armoured Division was now completely astride the road from Sidi Barrani to Buq Buq, and, ranging rapidly further west towards Halfaya, had an almost equally successful day, marred by only one lapse, due to a never-explained delay in the receipt

of orders. The 8th Hussars went into the desert west of Sofafi, to prevent the escape of the fairly large number of Italians (the bulk of two divisions) in the Sofafi and Rabia group of camps. But during the night their prey slipped out to the west and shortly after noon next day were discovered by British infantry patrols (from the 2nd Rifle Brigade) on the top of the escarpment about 10 miles south of the Halfaya Pass. They moved rapidly westward.

Apart from this one sizeable fish which had escaped the net, O'Connor—with remarkable speed, skill, and economy of effort—had now finished the first phase of the campaign. He had brought it off with a completeness which exceeded his own expectations—though not perhaps Wavell's, and Wavell always kept his own counsel on such matters—and the count of the victory was impressive and (in terms of the dark, arduous winter of 1940) very heartening.

The IV Blackshirt, the I and II Libyan Divisions, and the Maletti Group (the equivalent of a division) had been destroyed, and the II Blackshirt and 64th Divisions had been very roughly handled. And in the three days' fighting, Western Desert Force had captured no fewer than 38,000 Italian and Libyan prisoners, 237 guns, and 73 light and medium tanks. Among the prisoners, incidentally, were four generals. The total of captured vehicles was never recorded (throughout the war, units were notoriously reticent on this theme), but more than 1,000 were at least admitted to be in British hands—and they were badly needed. O'Connor's total casualties were 624 killed, wounded, and missing.

By the evening of December 12 the only Italians (other than prisoners) left in Egypt were those blocking the immediate approaches to Sollum and a force of some strength in the neighbourhood of Sidi Omar. Churchill sent Wavell a telegram offering his heartfelt congratulations on 'your splendid victory'. They were well merited.

The 4th Indian Division departed at once, exultant but mystified. Such pursuit and mopping-up as was necessary had to be done by the 7th Armoured, since O'Connor's only available infantry, the 16th British Brigade, had their hands full guarding and escorting the huge mass of Italian prisoners.

Axis dismay was considerable. Graziani (with Mussolini's approval) gave orders that Bardia and Tobruk were to be held at all costs. The commander in Bardia was a glamorous, handsomely bearded officer, General Bergonzoli, to whom the Duce addressed a personal message: 'I am sure that "Electric Beard" and his brave soldiers will stand at whatever cost, faithful to the last.'

The name delighted British and Commonwealth troops, who, however, altered it slightly to 'Electric Whiskers', and as such the gallant general marched into the headlines in London and Sydney. The Australians were moved up as quickly as possible; but there were administrative and transport difficulties which, though they did not take the edge off O'Connor's zest, imposed at the minimum a two weeks' delay on the strategic development of the campaign. This was in the end to prove of crucial significance.

Tactically Wavell, Wilson, and O'Connor were determined to maintain the impetus. Sollum, which the Navy heavily bombarded on the night of December 11, Capuzzo, and Sidi Omar, were all pockets of Italian resistance. O'Connor decided, with Wavell's firm support, that Bardia would be his next objective. What, however, should be done with these Italian pockets *en route*? How long would it take before the forward supply depots (of food, ammunition, and petrol) could be laid down and ready for use? How soon could the Australians come into action, even if their equipment was not up to the proper standard? How hard would the Italians fight?

Fourth Armoured Brigade was kept at it relentlessly, isolating and subduing the pockets and ranging boldly westwards; and 7th Armoured Brigade had the task of capturing Capuzzo and Sollum. Fourth Armoured, spotted by Italian reconnaissance aircraft on the move, was heavily bombed on December 14, and suffered a good many casualties in the worst day of enemy air attack in the campaign. Nevertheless, by mid-day on December 15, with Sidi Azeiz firmly in their hands, they were astride the Bardia-Tobruk road, and it looked as if Capuzzo would be cut off. On December 17, Sidi Omar was successfully attacked; its guns were captured and some 1,000 more Italian POWs joined their compatriots in a disconsolate trudge eastwards. But Bergonzoli and Graziani were now becoming increasingly anxious about Bardia; Bergonzoli assured his Commander-in-Chief that without these troops he would not be able to hold Bardia.

Graziani was looking even further over his shoulder towards Tobruk. If Bergonzoli tried to stand at Bardia and failed, what hope would there be of retaining Tobruk? And if Tobruk were lost. . . . The Marshal was so depressed that he signalled Mussolini asking if it would not be wiser to concentrate all his available forces for the defence of Tobruk, and so gain time for the arrival of the troops and aircraft which, he hoped, would be sent from Italy. The Duce replied sternly that everything possible must be done to delay and exhaust the British, and that a prolonged resistance at Bardia would be a useful contribution to this end.

Seventh Armoured Division was a magnificent mobile formation; but it had neither the equipment nor the men to contain a force the size of that which, moving mostly by night, Bergonzoli was able to pull out of Capuzzo and Sollum. By December 20 both these places were in British hands, but the Italians had got away enough of their infantry and their artillery to be able to assemble within the Bardia perimeter the equivalent of four divisions, totalling with fortress troops and frontier guards 45,000 men and more than 400 guns—slightly over double the estimate offered to O'Connor by his intelligence staff, who had calculated that there ought to be some 20,000 men and 100 guns at the Italian commander's disposal.

On December 21 Major-General I. G. Mackay, commander of the 6th Australian Division, took over in the Sollum area. His was the first contingent of Australian volunteers to go overseas in the Second World War, and they were proud of and eager to rival the fighting reputation of their fathers, uncles, and elder brothers of the First World War. Their training in Palestine had been good, and their morale was high. But they suffered from the chronic deficiencies of this phase of the desert war: too few guns and too few carriers, a good deal of obsolescent equipment, and a shortage of transport spare parts. Mackay himself, Australian-born of Scots-Canadian parents, and in civilian life the headmaster of a big school in Sydney, was also an experienced soldier, a month older than Wavell and with a first-class First World War record. His relations with Wavell and O'Connor were always exemplary.

His task at Bardia was similar to Beresford-Peirse's at Nibeiwa and Tummar, though on a bigger scale, and deprived of the advantage of strategic surprise. In close concert with O'Connor he chose, as Beresford-Peirse before him had chosen, to go in from the west. When Wavell went up to the battle area just after Christmas he found the final preparations well in hand, and everyone from the generals downwards in high spirits—in spite of increasing fatigue and shortage of sleep on the part of the 7th Armoured Division.

Bardia's perimeter, some 17 miles in extent, defended by a continuous anti-tank ditch, numerous wire obstacles, and concrete blockhouses at intervals covering the wire, was a far more formidable proposition than Nibeiwa, Tummar, Sollum, or Capuzzo. As at Sidi Barrani, the solution lay in getting the tanks—the 7th RTR once again—into the perimeter. This time O'Connor and Mackay planned to send in a battalion of infantry first, in order to establish a bridgehead on the far side of the anti-tank ditch and the wire, then to bridge the ditch and

clear the wire and the minefields for the passage of the tanks. The tanks would then be shepherded within the perimeter and fan out in attack, with two more infantry battalions close behind them. O'Connor and Mackay agreed on delivering the assault where they believed that the Italians—because of, rather than in spite of, their previous experience—would least expect it: the centre of the western face of the perimeter. The 7th Armoured Division stood to the north and north-west to block the garrison's escape routes; and the Support Group was to be ready to break through the defences in this area if a chance to do so showed itself.

Bardia falls

On December 28 Mackay decided that zero hour was to be 0530 hours on January 2; but two days later he had to postpone it for 24 hours because the ammunition he needed arrived late. Despite this delay, the plan worked out almost without a hitch. It was the Australians' blooding in the Second World War. From the outset they fought with the utmost dash and self-confidence. The tank ditch was bridged by the infantry in less than one hour. Crossing-places were quickly made and nearly 100 mines removed, and the tanks were into the bridgehead by 0700 hours on January 3. By noon the Italians were surrendering in scores. Offshore, the battleships *Warspite*, *Valiant*, and *Barham* joined in with their heavy guns. There were two days of mopping-up and on January 5 the fortress surrendered. 'Electric Whiskers' himself slipped through the cordon, and walked to Tobruk; but the new bag was impressive: some 38,000 troops, 33 coast-defence and medium guns, 220 field guns, 26 heavy AA guns, 40 infantry (65-mm) guns, 146 anti-tank guns, 120 tanks, and more than 700 trucks and cars. The total Commonwealth casualties, mostly Australian, were 500, with under 150 killed.

Once again there were rows and recriminations on the Axis side. Several of the generals who had not been taken prisoner were sacked; Graziani complained that he was waging a war of 'the flea against the elephant', and Rome radio proclaimed that 250,000 men with 1,000 aircraft had attacked Bardia.

Now the hunt was up. The Australians whistled 'Waltzing Matilda' as they swirled into Bardia, but to many of the British regular officers in the battle the attitudes and the metaphors of fox-hunting came with natural ease—to Wavell not the least. And the elderly Anglo-Irish writer, Lord Dunsany, who was in Athens lecturing for the British Council, was moved to compose a poem for Lady Wavell, full of elegant and stirring classical allusion.

Western Desert Force was renamed 13th Corps on New Year's Day, and at once—even before Bardia fell—set about rapid preparations for the next phase of the chase. On the morning of January 5, 7th Armoured Brigade was on the move towards El Adem—the Italians' main airfield in Libya—and by the next day was operating to cut off Tobruk from the west. On the evening of January 6 the 19th Australian Brigade Group, of Mackay's division, pulled out of Bardia and by next morning was exchanging fire with the eastern sector of the Tobruk defences. The 16th British Brigade came up on its left; and 4th Armoured Brigade, the Support Group, and 7th Armoured Brigade created an arc of investment to the south and west of the fortress. Once again emphatic Italian orders were issued that it was to be held to the last. Once again the Commonwealth forces were determined to annihilate the Italian defence.

True, the Italians' losses were already huge. In just under a month, *eight* divisions had been completely destroyed, and out of all the squadrons with which the Regia Aeronautica had begun the campaign, Graziani now had available a grand total of 119 aircraft, of which half were fighters, operating not even from Derna but from Marawa, 80 miles farther west in central Cyrenaica. The capture of Bardia had greatly reduced the number of troops at his disposal to build up a garrison for Tobruk; all he had there now was some 25,000 men (the 61st Division, and about 9,000 other stragglers and survivors from formations that no longer existed), 220 guns, and between 60 and 70 medium and light tanks. Farther west, he

mustered the 60th Division at Derna, the XVII at Benghazi and an armoured group at Mechili.

O'Connor, however, was also beginning to feel the strain—even if of advance rather than retreat. The establishment of supply dumps was growing more and more difficult; petrol and ammunition took stern precedence over food, and forward formations were down to half-rations for days at a time. The number of 'I' tanks, which had been so invaluable at both Sidi Barrani and Bardia, was now down to 18. But morale remained high. The questions now to be answered were: how soon could O'Connor take Tobruk, and what would be the next move after he had done it?

On the day Bardia fell, 3,000 miles away in London Churchill reached a decision which was to have a profound effect on the rest of the Western Desert campaign: the western flank of Egypt, he told the Chiefs-of-

Staff, was to be made secure, and by this (he made it clear) he meant that he was looking no farther than Benghazi; thereafter the support of Greece against Italian attack and the increasing likelihood of a German assault had to have priority. From this time onwards Wavell was pressed—and he accepted the pressure—to go ahead with large-scale preparations for a British expeditionary force to be sent from Egypt to Greece. He had to do this from his own immediate resources: no sizeable reinforcements in men, guns, or AFVs would come to him from Britain.

Thus while O'Connor, O'Moore Creagh, and Mackay could, for another month at least, concentrate on shattering the Italians in North Africa, Wavell was faced with an increasingly tight dilemma. He knew, though Churchill shut his mind to it, that the demolition of the East African half of the Italian Empire was bound to use up consider-

General Bergonzoli goes into captivity

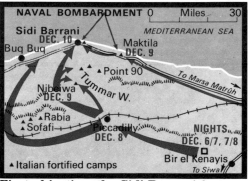

First objective: the Sidi Barrani forts

Horizons widen: Bardia/Tobruk/Derna

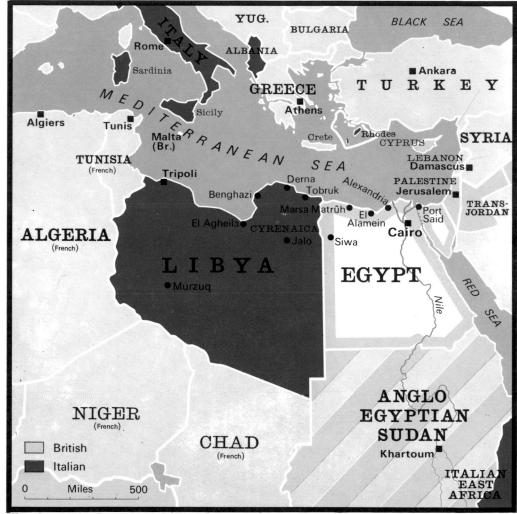

The threat: in June 1940, Italian Libya menaced Egypt and the Suez Canal

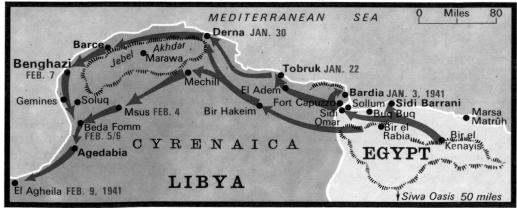

The final achievement: Wavell's original attack became a landslide conquest

Desert Armour

ITALIAN
M13/40 (above): standard Italian medium tank during and after the 'Wavell campaign'. Armour: 40-mm. Turret gun: 47-mm. **Autoblinda 40** (right): medium armoured car of the Italian desert army. Turret gun: 20-mm. Machine-gun: 8-mm.

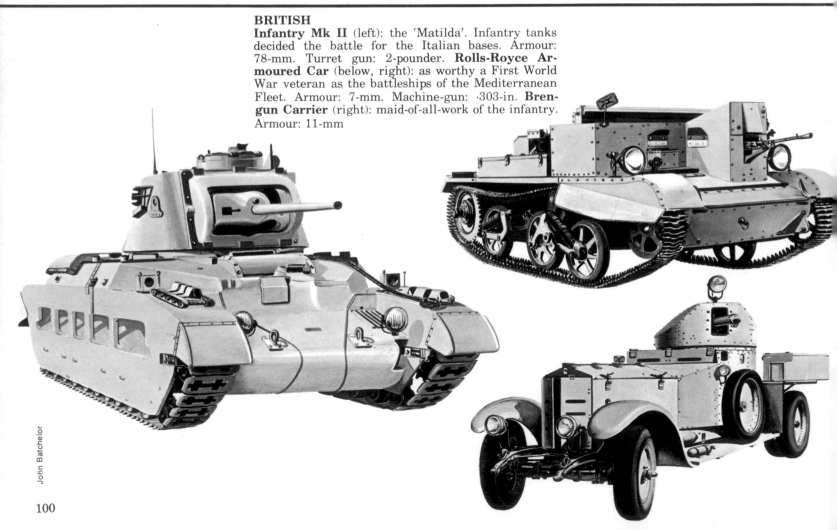

BRITISH
Infantry Mk II (left): the 'Matilda'. Infantry tanks decided the battle for the Italian bases. Armour: 78-mm. Turret gun: 2-pounder. **Rolls-Royce Armoured Car** (below, right): as worthy a First World War veteran as the battleships of the Mediterranean Fleet. Armour: 7-mm. Machine-gun: ·303-in. **Bren-gun Carrier** (right): maid-of-all-work of the infantry. Armour: 11-mm

John Batchelor

able forces; he knew too, as did Churchill and the War Cabinet, that there were growing threats to his northern flank, in Palestine and Iraq. Turkey would not budge from her jealously guarded neutrality; in Syria and Lebanon a Vichy French regime was being pressed to increasingly open collaboration with the Axis; and the Germans, even more than the Italians, were busy stirring up Arab nationalism and awakening their own old dreams of a *Drang nach Osten,* a new German sphere of influence from the Balkans to Baghdad and beyond.

The Greek expedition, however, was Wavell's chief preoccupation, and its effect on O'Connor's single-minded drive to victory was immediately apparent. While preparations were being made for the assault on Tobruk, Wavell flew off to Athens to confer with the Greek Cabinet and army commanders; and Air Chief Marshal Sir Arthur Longmore, the RAF Commander-in-Chief in the Middle East, received a blunt order from the Chief of the Air Staff to cut air support to 13th Corps far below the minimum necessary, by at once sending to Greece three squadrons of Hurricanes and one of Blenheims. Joint protests, by Wavell and Longmore, got the peremptory edge removed from this directive; but it was more and more clear in headquarters in Cairo—though not to the commanders in the field—that a limit would have to be set to O'Connor's advance. The farther west he went, the greater the prize that seemed to be in his grasp, but the fewer became his chances of taking it.

Attack on a bigger scale

The plan for the attack on Tobruk was very similar to that of the attack on Bardia, though on a bigger scale. Not quite 18 months later the plan of a German general, Erwin Rommel, which resulted in Tobruk's recapture by the Axis and his own promotion to Field-Marshal, was almost identical.

O'Connor on this occasion had available 7th Armoured Division, three brigades of Mackay's 6th Australian Division, two machine-gun battalions, the 7th RTR (to whose few tanks no addition had yet been made), and a heavy concentration of artillery. For 12 days after the fall of Bardia there was constant movement around the perimeter of Tobruk; ammunition came up, gun positions were made ready, and there were aggressive patrols which continually harassed and confused the Italians.

After a 24-hour postponement caused by one of the most severe sandstorms of the whole campaign, O'Connor's attack went in at 0830 hours on January 21. The 16th Australian Brigade and the 'I' tanks broke through the perimeter at the south-eastern corner, under cover of a heavy and accurate artillery barrage; and they were closely followed by the 19th Brigade. Both brigades reached their first objectives, with few losses, by mid-day; but then the Italians brought their coastal and AA guns into action, and there were several hours of fierce fighting around and about the middle of the perimeter. By dusk, however, the Commonwealth forces were ranged along the edge of the escarpment overlooking the town. Nearly half the defended area had been won.

All night long the attacking troops saw fires flaring in the town, and heard the crump and rumble of explosions. When dawn broke they went in without resistance. There were more troops in the town than had been estimated: nearly 30,000, including a great many specialists, and a naval detachment of more than 2,000. There were, once again, so many motor vehicles that nobody bothered to count them; there were 87 tanks and more than 200 guns. Thirteenth Corps' casualties were just over 400, of whom 355 were Australians. Attempts had been made to put the harbour out of action, but the Royal Navy had it ready to receive shipping within 48 hours of the Italian surrender. There was a complete bulk-petrol installation and there were 10,000 tons of stored water. There was tinned food for the garrison for two months—fruit and vegetables galore, boxes of spaghetti and pulped tomatoes, several hundred tons of flour, and a cold-storage plant well filled with meat.

Thirteenth Corps had been stretched to the limit for the past month. Now it got fresh wind for a final gallop. On the day that the assault was launched against Tobruk, the Chiefs-of-Staff told Wavell that the capture of Benghazi was now regarded as of great importance. O'Connor was already making his plans for this next leap forward. He had already arranged for 7th Armoured Brigade to press on towards Derna, and for 4th Australian Brigade to begin its 100-mile move to Mechili. By the evening of January 22 the former was in contact with the enemy 20 miles from Derna, while the latter had patrols across the tracks leading west, south, and south-east from Mechili.

Immense new distances, and a country hitherto untraversed by any British soldier—it was to become very familiar to thousands of them in the next two years—now opened up ahead of 13th Corps. From the seemingly endless vistas of sand and rocky desert, and the barren ravines and corries of the escarpment, the land shelved gradually into the green, cultivable region of the Jebel Akhdar. Between the Gulf of Bomba and the Gulf of Sidra the coastline bulged northwards into the Mediterranean. The bulge—and the prosperous and settled Italian colony of Western Cyrenaica—extended some 200 miles from east to west; the hills rose to a height of well over 2,000 feet; there were roads; there were two small stretches of railway; there was a considerable farming population, and there was the city and port of Benghazi, with a population of 65,000, one-third of whom were Italian. The two principal roads from the east were of great tactical importance. One kept close to the coast from Tobruk to Gazala, Tmimi, Martuba, and Derna, then struck west-south-west through the Jebel to Barce, Benina, and Benghazi. The other, from the junction of El Adem, due south of Tobruk, ran to Mechili on the southern ridge of the Jebel, then turned south-west to Msus, Antelat, Agedabia, and El Agheila, with a branch track heading west from Msus to Solluch, and back to the main coastal road which ran due south from Benghazi to Agedabia.

The pounce on Benghazi

On the evening of January 22 it appeared that of all the vast army that Graziani had had at his disposal at the beginning of December there now remained: the 60th Division (less one infantry brigade group) in position just east of Derna; an armoured brigade of about 160 tanks, and the infantry brigade group from 60th Division, at or near Mechili under the command of General Babini; and farther west—whether in Cyrenaica or Tripolitania was not certain—two more divisions, XVII and XX.

The Italian C-in-C: Marshal Graziani

Paul Popper

101

British night barrage on Tobruk

The northern force in Cyrenaica held the coast road to Benghazi, while the southern lay at the main junction of the roads out of the desert, out of the Jebel, and from the coast. Wavell, just as clearly as O'Connor, saw the chance for a rapid advance on Benghazi and a decisive victory.

O'Connor achieved both in just under three weeks. The pace of this final phase of the campaign was breathless. Men drove themselves and their vehicles to the limit of their capacity. The weather was wintry; reliable maps and the chances of careful reconnaissance were both few. O'Connor's determination and energy overcame the fatigue and stomach trouble that had nagged at him throughout the whole enterprise. His leadership was quiet but intensely efficient. He seemed able, like Wavell, always to be at the spot where he was most wanted when he was most wanted.

On January 24 at Mechili occurred one of the first tank battles of the campaign, in which 7th Armoured Division destroyed eight medium tanks and captured one for the loss of one cruiser and six light tanks of their own. O'Connor decided first to crush what remained of Italian strength in this area, while containing the 60th Division at Derna. He therefore left two brigades of the 6th Australian Division near Derna, took the third away, sent it south to join 7th Armoured Division and the Support Group, and on January 25 gave explicit orders that General Babini and his troops were not to be allowed to escape from Mechili.

Large parts of this force, however, were held up by shortage of petrol until the morning of January 27; and during the previous night, to O'Connor's disappointment, Babini had slipped away to the north. When air reconnaissance discovered the Italians, using a road shown on no map in British hands and moving as fast as they could through the wooded, ravine-slashed country, the 4th Armoured Brigade set out on a two-day pursuit, and fighters swooped down with machine-gun fire and light bombs. But by the afternoon of January 28

bad going, heavy rain, numerous mechanical breakdowns, and a shortage of petrol brought the chase to a halt.

On January 29 the Italians withdrew from Derna. It looked, for the moment, as if they might make a stand in the heights of the Jebel Akhdar. The Australians took Derna on January 30. O'Connor had a fleeting hope that he might rest some of his officers and men and overhaul some of his battered tanks and equipment. To outflank the enemy in the Jebel, a wider movement for 7th Armoured Division than an approach march by the direct westward track from Mechili would be necessary.

During the next two days operations against the Australians in the north began to slacken notably, and reports came in that the Regia Aeronautica was abandoning its few remaining airfields. Early on February 1, these reports of withdrawal were confirmed when long columns of transport were seen moving westward to Barce and tanks were spotted being entrained at Barce station.

On the evening of January 31 O'Connor, O'Moore Creagh, and John Harding had a conference with a special liaison officer whom Wavell had sent up (since he himself, seriously concerned with the Greek venture, could not spend the time to go) to report to him on the whole situation. This was Brigadier Eric Dorman-Smith, who had been Wavell's Brigade-Major (and close friend) at Aldershot in the 1930's, and was now commandant of the highly successful staff school at Haifa. This talented officer played a key part in the concluding stages of the Western Desert advance.

At this conference O'Connor concluded that the Italians were preparing to quit not just the coastal sector but the whole of Cyrenaica. The greatest speed in following them up was essential. He could not afford to wait for reinforcements, which could not reach him before February 10 at the earliest. The 7th Armoured Division would have to go on as long as its vehicles could move; but it must have petrol, and O'Connor's

administrative staff, after long consultation and a good deal of vigorous encouragement, declared that they could get the division to the Benghazi road with enough petrol to take it into battle.

Early next morning, at O'Connor's urgent request, Dorman-Smith flew to Cairo to see the Commander-in-Chief and get his authority for a rapid advance to intercept the Italian retreat. Wavell saw him that same evening. When Dorman-Smith had completed his report Wavell said, 'Tell Dick he can go on, and wish him luck from me. He has done well.'

Dorman-Smith flew back to give O'Connor this message on February 2. By the time he arrived 7th Armoured Division, without waiting for any reinforcements, had gone ahead, with orders from O'Connor that they simply must move until they could move no longer. So far as maintenance was concerned, the first convoys loaded at Tobruk were beginning to arrive at Mechili, and by February 4 it would be just possible for the division to set out with their supply vehicles full; they could be followed by a convoy containing two days' supplies, water, petrol, food, and two refills of ammunition. They had already had their first warning telling them to be prepared to leave for Msus.

On February 4 Wavell himself flew up to Cyrenaica. Back in Cairo before nightfall, he signalled the CIGS, telling him that what remained of 7th Armoured Division—one brigade with between 40 and 50 cruiser tanks, some 80 light tanks, and the Support Group, whose vehicles were wearing down and whose men were exhausted—was heading for Msus and might reach it that evening. Meanwhile, as the Australians were following up on the main road to Barce and Benghazi, the RAF was attacking the Italians' line of retreat. Unless O'Connor's information was inaccurate, or something unforeseen happened, he should therefore 'be at the gates of Benghazi in the next few days'.

British armoured cars occupied Msus on that day; but the battered remnants of 7th

An RAF aircraft after a forced landing behind the enemy lines

Armoured Division found the going hard over very rough country, and it was not until daybreak on February 5 that they could report that they were in position just east of Msus.

All that day the pursuit continued. A good many of the light tanks broke down. Officers and men had two days' rations, and as much ammunition as they could carry. The most perplexing question was: how long would the petrol last? By dusk O'Connor's forces were ranging deep into the south of Cyrenaica and far to the west. Fourth Armoured Brigade, indeed, was approaching Beda Fomm, where the Italians were gathering hurriedly for what might be their last stand. A column of some 5,000 of them, mainly gunners with their guns, but including a good many civilians, surrendered south-west of Beda Fomm. O'Connor brought his Advanced HQ up to Msus, and by dawn on February 6 it was obvious that the Italians were going to make a final attempt to shoot their way out of the ring that had swiftly formed around them. They fought hard and bravely throughout that day, but when evening came their position was desperate. Seventh Armoured Division pinned down a mass of vehicles and men in complete confusion along some 20 miles of the one possible escape road from Solluch to Agedabia. In repeated attempts to break through, the Italians lost more than 80 tanks. Meanwhile, O'Connor ordered the Australian 6th Division to send a fast-moving detachment – about a brigade group in strength – along the main road from Barce to Benghazi and on to Ghemines, to complete the encirclement of the Italians. The Australians pressed on as fast as they could and received the surrender of Benghazi during this eventful day.

Dawn broke cold and clear. A force of some 30 Italian tanks made a last, unavailing assault on the ring of British armour. When this broke, the surrender was immediate and unconditional.

O'Connor was at 7th Armoured Division's headquarters when the news came to him.

He and Dorman-Smith had known and liked each other for many years. O'Connor left it to him to draft a signal to Wavell. It began, 'Fox killed in the open. . . .'

Then, through the bright winter morning, under the great sweep of the African sky, with the small gazelles bounding through the scrub across which they drove, they came down to Beda Fomm. The sea sparkled in the distance, and the kites circled overhead.

O'Connor's own comment, made in a report which he wrote four months later, when by a swift reversal of fortune he himself was a prisoner of war, was austere and accurate: 'I think this may be termed a complete victory, as none of the enemy escaped.'

In just two months his force – no more than two divisions, of a total strength of 31,000 men – had advanced 500 miles, destroyed an Italian army of ten divisions, took some 130,000 prisoners, and captured 850 guns, 400 tanks, and thousands of lorries and other vehicles. Their casualties totalled under 2,000: 500 killed, 1,373 wounded, and 55 missing. There have been few greater victories recorded in all military history.

O'Connor was eager to exploit his own achievement and go on to Tripoli. If he had been allowed to make the attempt, who can tell whether he would have succeeded? It is orthodox to argue that logistically and administratively he had no chance. His vehicles could go no farther; the RAF and the Royal Navy were stretched to their limits; Benghazi would have taken too long to repair and get into working order. But he believed that he could have done it. By the evening of February 8 the 11th Hussars, sending out patrols 40 or 50 miles along the coast to Sirte, encountered no resistance of any kind. O'Connor sent Dorman-Smith to obtain permission to try once more. Bad weather delayed the emissary, and it was not until the morning of February 12 that he walked into Wavell's office.

By this time it was too late. New formations had been ordered to replace the

battered and weary victors who had set out at the beginning of December on a five-day raid. Wilson was appointed Military Governor of Cyrenaica and Libya; O'Connor himself was ordered back to Cairo to be General Officer Commanding British Troops in Egypt; and – at the insistence of the War Cabinet and the Chiefs-of-Staff – a thin covering force was left to hold the huge expanse of conquered territory. All eyes were turned on Greece, which was suddenly developing signs of crisis.

But on February 5, the first day of the battle of Beda Fomm, Hitler had written to Mussolini expressing his displeasure at the conduct of the North African campaign as a whole, and offering the assistance of a complete armoured division, on condition that the Italians stood firm and did not pull back to Tripoli. Five days later Mussolini accepted. On February 11 Lieutenant-General Erwin Rommel arrived in Rome, to be assured that the first line of defence in Tripolitania would be at Sirte. Three days after that a German reconnaissance battalion and an anti-tank battalion reached Tripoli. A new and formidable factor had entered the Desert War.

JOHN CONNELL was born in 1909 and educated at Loretto and at Balliol College. In 1933 he joined the staff of the London *Evening News,* for whom he was leader-writer and book critic until 1959. Interested in all forms of education, he served on the LCC Education Committee from 1949-58 and was Deputy Mayor of St Pancras 1951-52. His greatest interest, however, lay in military affairs, and his biography of General Auchinleck was widely acclaimed. This was followed by a finely analytical account of Wavell's Middle East campaigns, published in 1965. On October 5, 1965, shortly after finishing this article, John Connell suddenly collapsed and died. In a letter to his widow, one of his admirers wrote: 'The loss which history has suffered is very great, for there are only too few Jack Connells to illuminate the past with the humanity and understanding which he always showed.'

Derna: a British Vickers machine-gun crew in action on the perimeter of the Italian defence zone

Imperial War Museum

Victory in the Desert

1939 August 2: Wavell takes command as C-in-C of British land forces in Egypt, the Sudan, Palestine, Transjordan, and Cyprus.
September 3: Wavell's command extended to British Somaliland, Aden, Iraq, and the shores of the Persian Gulf.
September 6: South Africa declares war on Germany; Egypt breaks off relations with Germany.

1940 January 12: First Anzacs reach Suez.
June 10: Italy declares war.
June/July: Frontier skirmishing between British 7th Armoured Division ('Desert Rats') and Italian units.
August 3: Italians invade British Somaliland.
August 5: Italians capture Hargeisa.
August 16: British begin evacuation of Berbera, Somaliland.
September 13: Italian army under Marshal Graziani crosses the Egyptian border and occupies Sollum.
September 18: Italians occupy Sidi Barrani; their offensive halts.
October 28: Italian invasion of Greece.
December 9: 'Operation Compass', the first British offensive in the Western Desert, begins. Wavell's 'Thirty Thousand' cut off Graziani's army at Sidi Barrani.
December 11: British capture Sidi Barrani.
December 17: British occupy Sollum.

1941 January 3: British air and naval bombardment of Bardia.
January 5: British and Australians capture Bardia.
January 22: British and Australians capture Tobruk.
January 29: South African forces enter Italian Somaliland.
January 30: Australian troops occupy Derna.
February 3: British occupy Cyrene.
February 4: British armoured column leaves Mechili to encircle the Italian forces south of Benghazi.

Imperial War Museum

February 6: British and Australians enter Benghazi **(above)**.
February 7: Complete collapse of the surrounded Italian forces at Beda Fomm.
February 10: Mussolini accepts Hitler's offer of a German armoured division.
February 14: First German units arrive in Tripoli. South Africans capture Gobuen in Somaliland.
February 20: British cross River Juba in Somaliland.
February 25: British Nigerian troops occupy Mogadishu in Somaliland.

Alfredo Zennaro

Italian troops in action at El Agheila

TOBRUK SURVIVES

From their bases minutes away from Tobruk, Stukas hammer the defences of the Fort Pilastrino strongpoint

Cyrenaica, April/November 1941
John Foley

In April 1941, Rommel's dash into Cyrenaica soon found itself flanked by the Allied forces holding out in Tobruk — a constant menace to his supply lines to the Egyptian frontier. Thanks to the courage and fighting skill of the Australian, British, and Polish garrison, and the motley collection of small ships which fought to keep open the British sea-route to Tobruk, Rommel's attempts to storm Tobruk were defeated. And the siege became a legend ranking with those of Malta and Leningrad

Tobruk is a small but important port on the coast of Cyrenaica. Its pre-war population numbered about 4,000 people, living in a few hundred white buildings standing out starkly against the sun-baked, rocky ground sloping down to a tiny quay. The square in the centre of the town boasted a few dusty palm trees; and in times of peace the busiest installation in Tobruk was probably the water distillation plant which, with one or two wells, produced 40,000 gallons a day.

The importance of Tobruk lay in the fact that its harbour was the only safe and accessible port for over 1,000 miles, between Sfax in Tunisia and Alexandria in Egypt, apart from the even tinier harbour at Benghazi. Like Benghazi, Tobruk had been built by the Italians as one of the principal defences of Libya from the east and as a naval base.

In peace, it was important as the main outlet for the products of a vast area of hinterland. But in war, during the struggle for North Africa, its importance was greatly increased because any advance beyond it, either to the east or west, was doubly imperilled. First, the possession of Tobruk was essential as an unloading point for supplies and reinforcements, which otherwise had to be brought along difficult and lengthy lines of communication, either from Alexandria in one direction, or Benghazi in the other. Secondly, in the hands of a determined and aggressive garrison, it could represent a serious offensive threat to the flank of any advance which by-passed it.

Winston Churchill himself described it as a 'sally port' and declared: 'Nothing but a raid dare go past Tobruk.'

The original Italian maps of the Tobruk defences show two lines of strong-points, completely sunk into the ground. These covered a perimeter of some 35-40 miles with a radius of about 20 miles (see map). The outer defences consisted of a series of heavily concreted dugouts — many cleverly improvised from natural caves — each holding 30 to 40 men. These dugouts were interconnected by trenches with locations every few hundred yards for machine-guns, mortars, or anti-tank guns. The trenches were roofed in with thin boarding and covered lightly with sand so that they were invisible from even a few yards away. In front of the outer defences barbed wire was laid, varying in some places from a single coil in width to a belt 30 yards wide elsewhere.

In front of the barbed wire the Italians had built an anti-tank ditch, often cleverly adapting an existing natural ravine. Straight-sided, and averaging 7 feet deep and 10 feet wide, the ditch was designed to thwart any attempted crossing by a tracked vehicle. The inner defence line was some 2,000 to 3,000 yards behind the outer line and constructed

to the same pattern, but without the anti-tank ditch.

When Rommel launched his forces against the Western Desert Force in April 1941, and the opposition crumbled before him, one of his first thoughts was to capture Tobruk so as to eliminate it as a hazard, and to shorten his lines of communication for his drive into and beyond Egypt.

He did not anticipate any great difficulty. Wavell's forces had captured it from the Italians in two days, and the confident Rommel thought that it would not take much longer — if as long — to wrest it back.

The story of his first attempts to rush the defences of Tobruk at the end of his precipitate drive from Mersa Brega has been well documented. It has been shown how, even in their infancy, the improvised defence by the 9th Australian Division — augmented by 18th Brigade from 7th Australian Division and the remnants of 3rd Armoured Brigade, with field and anti-aircraft regiments, all under Major-General Leslie Morshead — was more than a match for the dying momentum of Rommel's push.

Siege warfare — modern style
From then on, Tobruk was in a constant state of siege. But it was not a siege in the same sense as those of Ladysmith and Mafeking in the Boer War, or of Lucknow in the Indian Mutiny, where isolated garrisons were surrounded by a numerically superior enemy and completely cut off from friendly forces. Constant contact was maintained between Tobruk and the main Allied forces by the Royal Navy — although it should not be imagined that this was in any way a 'milk run'.

Yet it was certainly a siege in the sense that Tobruk was a fortified position under continuous attack by the enemy. Every inch of the defended area was within range of the German and Italian artillery, and the harbour working-parties came under fire almost as much as the troops in the outer perimeter.

Beyond dispute the survival of Tobruk depended upon the harbour being kept in working order and the continuance of supplies along the tenuous sea-lane leading to it from Egypt. Nothing of use to the survival of an army was indigenous to Tobruk except for the shelter given by the natural caves. Everything had to be brought in from Egypt; and Rommel, realising this, concentrated almost as much on neutralising the harbour and interrupting the sea life-line as he did on planning a landward assault.

Since the days of Wavell's offensive the British army in Cyrenaica had been supported and supplied from the sea by ships of the Inshore Squadron, a heterogeneous armada comprising anything from a destroyer to a monitor, sloop, gunboat, trawler, sponge-fisher, or lighter. In Tobruk's most heated hour, these ships, supported sometimes by the Mediterranean Fleet, as often as possible covered by fighter aircraft, regularly braved the perils of mines, shells, bombs, and torpedoes to run men, machines, and supplies (including water), along the enemy-held coast to the besieged fortress.

Sometimes their support was of the direct kind, such as the bombardment of enemy transport on the coastal road, or the conveyance of commandos in a somewhat ineffective raid on Bardia on the night of April 19.

No matter what kind of operation it was, it almost certainly took place at night, for

by day the medium and dive-bombers of the Luftwaffe dominated the skies. Only from June 1941 onwards could sufficient British fighters be gathered to mount a worthwhile day light escort from Egyptian airfields.

When first the siege began, the sea supply service was as heavily improvised as the perimeter defences and the anti-aircraft barrage which endeavoured to defend unloading in the anchorage. For the first time, 'A' Lighters (the original tank landing-craft) came into service, those ugly diesel-engined vessels transporting in their cavernous holds anything from tanks to shells or food, carried on board through the lowered bow ramps just like a car ferry. Having the ability to 'beach', they stood a better chance of survival in Tobruk than the conventional ships which had to tie up alongside the one, obvious quay.

Small craft led adventurous careers and were crewed by individuals of strong character, who did not give up easily. This strange collection of men and ships (with names like *Waterhen*, *Stuart*, and *Eskimo Nell*) worked as a team, rushing to each others help in time of need, defending themselves with desperate heroism when the enemy struck, and mourning their losses collectively, especially when the casualty happened to be a hospital ship. Indeed, after three hospital ships had been hit by dive-bombers all the wounded were carried in destroyers.

Losses among the Inshore Squadron were heavy, particularly by day, and at times it became permissible to voyage only on the moonless nights. Daylight attacks such as those aimed at the anti-aircraft sloops *Auckland* and *Paramatta* on June 24, when they were escorting the valuable petrol-carrier *Pass of Balmaha*, give an indication of the scale of Axis efforts. On this occasion, combined raids by torpedo-bombers and 96 dive-bombers accounted for *Auckland* and stopped *Pass of Balmaha*. At the other end of the scale, a captured Italian fishing schooner *Maria Giovanni*, skippered by an Australian, Lieutenant Alfred Palmer, ran the gauntlet night after night until tricked into disaster by the Germans. In common with others, Palmer guided himself into Tobruk harbour by a shaded green light at the entrance, but he was not to know that one night the Germans had lit a decoy to the east. To his surprise Palmer ran himself hard ashore and was taken prisoner by the Germans as he and his crew were industriously digging a channel through which to refloat the ship.

German E-boats lurked at night, hoping to catch the supply convoys and eventually, quite inevitably, U-boats too made their appearance, engaging the lighters from the surface and swapping cannon fire in savage actions at close range. On October 10 an 'A' lighter (one of four) charged U-34 and forced her to dive. The next night two 'A' lighters, returning from Tobruk, fell in with U-75, commanded by Lieutenant Eckleman, but this time the U-boat commander made no mistake. Positioning himself in the shadow of the land, Eckleman established his fire-power superiority at once and sank both lighters.

Full-dress assault
Against the backcloth of coastal sea and air battle, the fight on land muttered and grumbled amid bombardments and patrol-scuffles while Rommel, chastened by his first rebuffs, raised his strength for a full assault. He was becoming impatient. Any   ▷

△ German armoured cars in a night battle for Tobruk: Rommel was becoming impatient, and threw his forces into a full assault

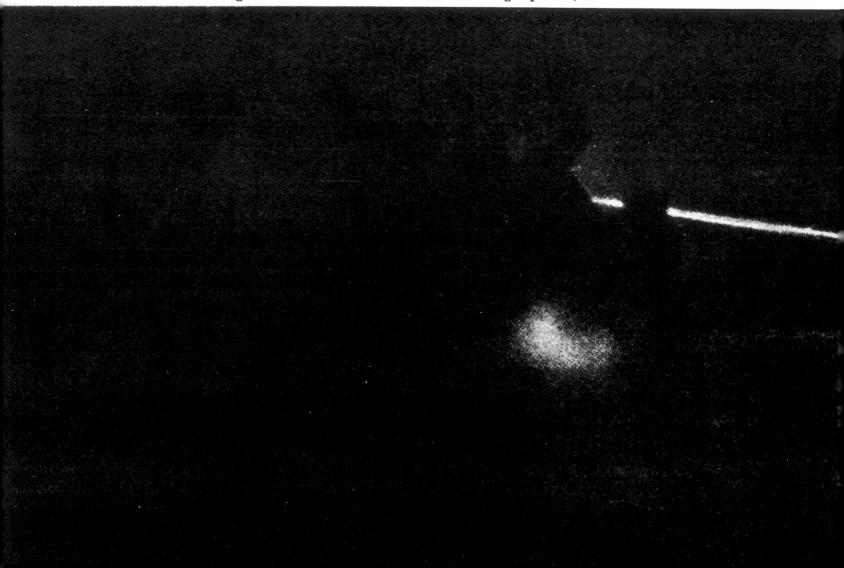

▽ German tracer strikes home: Rommel's biggest attack knifed 2 miles through the Tobruk perimeter, but could advance no farther

advance beyond the frontier was out of the question until Tobruk had been taken, but he was not ready until April 30.

The attack on that day began with a continuous pounding from Stuka dive-bombers and artillery, against which the defenders' powers of retaliation were limited. They engaged the dive-bombers with anti-aircraft and small-arms fire, and the British artillery put down counter-fire on the enemy gun-positions. But because the garrison could not expect fresh supplies of ammunition until the next moonless night—a week away—ammunition had to be husbanded and every shot made to count.

The German dive-bombers were unchallenged in the air, for the RAF Hurricane squadron, unable to operate from airstrips under continuous fire—with their runways frequently cratered and with workshops and petrol-dumps shelled every day—had been withdrawn on April 25.

As the dive-bombers drew off from their targets, the attacking infantry and tanks moved in against the western sector of the defences. But the defenders were far from subdued, and the Germans and Italians were met by ferocious fire from the British artillery and tanks and the Australian infantry.

It was a grim and bitter battle. Writing of it later Rommel said: 'The Australians fought with remarkable tenacity. Even their wounded went on defending themselves with small-arms fire, and stayed in the fight to their last breath. They were immensely big and powerful men, who without question represented an élite formation of the British Empire, a fact that was also evident in battle.'

By the end of the day the Germans and Italians had succeeded in penetrating the defences of Tobruk and had established a 2-mile salient into the Australian positions on the western sector of the perimeter. The salient included the important hill of Ras el Madauar, which dominated a large part of the defended area.

Still determined to subdue Tobruk, Rommel next day put in fresh troops, to exploit the Ras el Madauar salient, but although the fighting raged unabated until May 4, the attackers were unable to advance farther.

The salient of Ras el Madauar, however, remained a constant threat to the besieged garrison and—although there was sporadic activity on the other sectors of the defended perimeter—from May 4 onwards the defence of Tobruk was, in essence, the defence of its western sector. Here the hard outer shell of permanent defence works had been breached, and the opposing forces faced one another from hastily improvised foxholes. It was, in a way, the soft under-belly of Tobruk: the Germans and Italians expected that if the breakthrough came anywhere it would come in the western sector, and this was the area to which they devoted most of their attention.

By the time Tobruk had been under siege for a month the area around the town was littered with burned-out tanks, vehicles, and all the debris of war. The town itself was reduced to a heap of rubble in which only one house remained standing, and in this—despite the fact that it stood out among the flattened buildings like a sore thumb—General Morshead maintained his operational headquarters.

For the defenders of Tobruk each day brought a fresh crop of problems. Problems, that is, in addition to those normally associated with desert fighting—the strange disorientation brought on by a featureless landscape which induced a tendency to walk in circles; and daily temperatures in the hundreds, so that to touch a tank left standing in the sun meant a burned hand. There were problems of food; not a shortage, perhaps, but a monotonous sameness with everything coming out of cans. There was, like elsewhere in the desert, a shortage of water, and what little there was was salty. There was an almost total absence of bread, and a superabundance of fleas, flies, and rats.

Added to these discomforts was a problem rare in the annals of defended strongholds. The Axis airfields from which sorties were made against Tobruk were sufficiently close for the defenders to hear the aircraft starting up prior to take-off. Two of the airfields, El Adem and Acroma, were only about 10 miles away, and some of the defenders swore that in the still, desert night air they could hear the ground crews singing as they worked on the aircraft.

There was only one permanent line of defence against the bombers once the RAF fighters had been withdrawn on April 25, and that was the anti-aircraft guns of the Royal Artillery, supplemented by the guns of ships in harbour. Two regiments of 3·7-inch and captured Italian 102-mm guns, plus three regiments with 40-mm Bofors stayed during the siege, pitting their wits against each new variation and combination of attack by high-level and dive-bombers. Throughout countless raids the gunners emulated their colleagues at Malta by maintaining a miniature 'Grand Barrage' in the face of the fierce bravery of German pilots who sometimes swept at less than 500 feet over the gun pits. By July the dive-bombers actually began to let up, and it became possible even to unload ships in daylight. Alone, the anti-aircraft gunners prevented bombing with impunity and so they, above all, enabled the supply vessels to unload and maintain the garrison.

The western sector, around the Ras el Madauar salient, had its own special problems. The rocky nature of the ground made deep digging almost impossible and, on those days when fighting was not actually taking place, both sides lay in their shallow trenches unable to move. A German account of conditions in the salient at the time says: 'The Australians were crack shots. Their sniping was superb. Even the most trivial movement from the foxhole—rump too high—and ping! You'd had it.'

Although conditions in the western sector were grim, in the other two sectors (southern and eastern) it was by no means a case of sitting comfortably in a concrete dugout and repulsing the odd attack. Offensive patrolling was an almost permanent night operation for both sides.

For night patrolling, the Australians wore crêpe-soled shoes, long trousers, pullovers, and berets. They were armed with sub-machine guns and grenades, and their objective in most cases was a single enemy stronghold. They would descend on it silently on a moonless night, throw their grenades and empty the magazines of the sub-machine guns into the enemy emplacement, then disappear back into their own positions as swiftly and silently as they had arrived. The Germans used much the same technique against the Australians and British, and on occasions a patrol from either side would encounter one another in No-Man's-

Land, and a short sharp action would develop, often involving fierce, hand-to-hand fighting.

Conditions worsen

As time went on, conditions in the besieged area became steadily worse, a fact of which Rommel himself was very much aware. Writing home to his wife in June he said: 'Water is very short in Tobruk, the British troops are getting only half-a-litre a day. With our dive-bombers I'm hoping to cut their rations still further. The heat is getting worse every day and . . . one's thirst becomes almost unquenchable.'

It seems clear from the frequency with which Rommel mentioned Tobruk in his letters home that the capture of the port became almost an obsession with him. Throughout May, June, and July he constantly referred to his determination to subdue the fortress. Indeed, in one of his letters he wrote about there being 'signs of attack from Tobruk from mid-June', when it seems clear from the context of the rest of the letter that he meant Sollum, 70 miles to the east.

Churchill, too, was highly sensitive to the importance of Tobruk, and the role it should and could play in the Middle East campaign. After Tobruk had successfully beaten off one of the many attacks by the Axis forces, he cabled: 'Bravo, Tobruk! We feel it vital that Tobruk should be regarded as a sally port.'

This the Australians and British did, although often their efforts were overshadowed by events elsewhere. The eyes of the world were on the airborne invasion of Crete, the German assault on Russia, and—somewhat nearer to the beleaguered garrison—the abortive Operation 'Battleaxe'. Nevertheless, the Australian and British troops in Tobruk continued to play a decisive part in the tactical moves of both sides in the Western Desert.

Then, in August, Churchill began to receive demands from the Australian government for the withdrawal of their troops from Tobruk. Already, in response to this pressure, Auchinleck had relieved one Australian brigade by the Polish Carpathian Brigade (Lieutenant-General S. Kopanski), but this was not enough. By early September the Prime Minister of Australia (Mr Fadden) had become firmly determined that the Australian troops must be withdrawn from Tobruk. The reason he put forward at the time was: '. . . in order to give them an opportunity for refreshment, restoration of discipline and re-equipment, and to satisify public opinion in Australia.' The Australian government was also said to be 'anxious about the decline in health resistance of their troops in the fortress and the danger of catastrophe resulting from further decline and inability to withstand a determined attack'.

There seems to be no evidence that the Australian troops were themselves clamouring to be relieved. They had fought with vigour and determination under the most trying conditions for five months, but they would probably have borne the strain longer if called upon to do so. Nevertheless, during September the rest of the Australians were replaced by the 70th British Division (Major-General R. M. Scobie, who also assumed command of the garrison).

It was not an easy change-over. The ships which brought in the 70th Division and took out the Australians were subjected to severe air attack in the process, the minelayer

Latona being sunk and the destroyer *Hero* damaged.

When the Polish Brigade arrived in mid-August, General Morshead allocated them at first to the comparatively quiet southern sector, but after a few weeks they took over, with the Durham Light Infantry and Black Watch, the western sector with the salient.

By then the sector was showing all the signs of the four months' siege. The 'No-Man's-Land' between the forward posts was thickly carpeted with mines and booby-traps, and strewn with the unburied bodies of soldiers of both sides. But the defences—if such they could be called—were still in the same primitive condition; narrow and shallow trenches in which there was no room for the occupants to sit or kneel. In some places there was nothing but small, improvised stone breastworks.

The exposed nature of the forward defences in the western sector made any daylight approach to them impossible. Once

the sun had risen, the defenders could not move out, nor could their reserves or supplies get up to them. Life would have been impossible had it not been for the fact that, by one of those unspoken mutual arrangements which sometimes come about in war, both sides observed an unofficial two-hour armistice, beginning at dusk. During this period, neither side opened fire on the other and the troops on both sides could emerge safely from their cramped positions. Food, water, and ammunition could be brought up to forward defended positions and life could be made slightly more bearable on both sides.

Each night the Germans signalled the end of the two-hour armistice by a burst of tracer-bullets fired straight up into the air, and from then on it was 'business as usual'.

Another mutually accepted custom was the raising of a Red Cross flag when a man was wounded. Fire immediately switched from that point and stretcher-bearers could safely approach to remove the wounded

man. Indeed, on one or two occasions when casualties were heavier than usual, ambulances were allowed to drive up unmolested to the Red Cross flag to remove the wounded.

When the Poles took over the western sector from the Australians, their first instinct was to reject these cease-fire arrangements. They were all men who had, at great risk to themselves, escaped from a Poland occupied by the Germans, who were applying barbarian methods of treatment. There was a powerful emotional barrier inhibiting the Poles' acceptance of anything in the nature of a pact with the Germans.

However, General Kopanski realised that any change in the established customs would alert the Germans to the fact that a change of units had taken place, and this, of course, the defenders wished to keep secret as long as possible. Accordingly he ordered his battalion commanders to continue to observe the armistice and cease-fire arrangements of the Australians and this they did,

September, 1941: wrecked ships litter Tobruk harbour as another German raid explodes on the town and its defences

Keystone

The defence of Tobruk was a genuine achievement, and was a welcome boost to Allied morale; but it was inevitable that the hardships of the siege should become glamorised by the cheery defiance of British propaganda. The original news-agency caption to this photograph states: *Modern-age cavemen, the British Empire forces defending Tobruk fortress spend much of their time in their dugouts, shelters dug from the solid rock. Some* *of the defenders are pictured before a typical Tobruk mansion. Notice those ventilators. The lower photograph shows where they were obtained — Tobruk harbour is a clutter of wrecked ships, both British and Axis. Salvage from the vessels has been incorporated into the Tobruk defences, or used by defenders to make life a bit easier. The Tobruk garrison is playing a major role in the current British attack in Libya.* These men were the 'rats of Tobruk'

although with some reluctance. After a few days in the sector, however, they began to appreciate the practical value of the two-hour nightly armistice, realising that without it the forward companies would inevitably have died from thirst and starvation. But they discontinued the hoisting of the Red Cross flag as soon as possible. Each section was equipped with medical supplies and with the aid of these, plus some improvised surgery, it was possible in the majority of cases for the wounded to wait for evacuation until the two-hour armistice at dusk.

Nevertheless, on their side the Germans and Italians continued the custom of hoisting a Red Cross flag and evacuating wounded in daylight, and although the Poles did not fire on the casualty clearing party, the flag—as General Kopanski put it—'greatly facilitated our pinpointing their strongholds, and destroying them very efficiently and inflicting new casualties later on'.

Improving the defences

The Poles also took energetic steps to improve the defensive positions. Chipping away at the rock with improvised tools—often old leafsprings from wrecked vehicles—they sweated and laboured to deepen the trenches, a difficult operation from a prone position. It says much for their energy and determination that by the time they left the western sector, in December, the trenches were deep enough to allow men to walk along them, out of view of the enemy. But what it cost in sweat and blisters, only the Poles knew.

With the relief of the 9th Australian Division by the 70th British Division complete, there were now in Tobruk three infantry brigades (14th, 16th, and 23rd), a tank brigade (32nd, comprising 1st and 4th Royal Tank Regiments and a squadron each from 7th Royal Tank Regiment and the King's Dragoon Guards), seven artillery regiments, plus an anti-aircraft artillery brigade, a Czech battalion, a machine-gun battalion of the Royal Northumberland Fusiliers, an Australian battalion and—later on—two New Zealand battalions with supporting artillery.

This was the force with which General Scobie intended to break out from Tobruk and link up with a co-ordinated offensive by the 8th Army: Operation 'Crusader'.

Meanwhile, Rommel was himself planning a special operation to capture Tobruk, for until this was done he could advance no farther towards the Nile. The XV Panzer Division (General Neumann-Sylkow) formed a 'Tobruk Assault Unit' which undertook training exercises outside Acroma, where the ground had been prepared to simulate the defensive arrangements of Tobruk, and were given special instructions in the use of demolition charges against reinforced dugouts. The date fixed for this attack was November 23.

But early in November British Intelligence in Cairo acquired (by means which are still veiled in uncertainty) a sketch map, in what looked like Rommel's hand, showing complete details of the proposed attack on Tobruk—units taking part, timings, routes, strong-points—everything was there, *except the date of the attack*.

There was a good deal of argument at Auchinleck's headquarters about whether or not the plan was genuine—and, if it was a genuine Rommel map, whether or not it represented his real intentions, or was a 'plant' to fox the British. Eventually it was decided that the plan *was* genuine; Auchinleck moved his forces into position, so that they could launch themselves against Rommel as soon as he attacked Tobruk—and for once catch the 'Desert Fox' off balance.

Days passed while the 8th Army waited tensely for Rommel to make the first move. But back in London Churchill found waiting irksome, and eventually he issued direct orders that the offensive—Operation 'Crusader'—should start on November 18.

Inside the besieged fortress General Scobie decided that the Tobruk garrison should break through the lines of the enemy on the eastern sector, in order to meet the approaching units of the 8th Army. This was to be the task of the 14th Infantry Brigade (Black Watch, Bedfordshire and Hertfordshire Regiment, York and Lancaster Regiment) under its commander Brigadier B. H. Chappel, with the support of the tanks of the 32nd Tank Brigade and the machine-gunners of the Royal Northumberland Fusiliers.

The break-out was planned for dawn on November 22. But three hours before the break-out, the Polish Brigade was to launch a feint break-out from the western sector, preceded by a heavy artillery barrage.

During the hours of darkness on the night November 21/22, the Tobruk troops moved to their arranged jumping-off points. In the distance they could hear the sounds of the fierce battle in the Sidi Rezegh area, where the 8th Army was fighting to reach them.

All those awaiting zero hour—British, Poles, Czechs, New Zealanders, and Australians—were hopeful that the siege was about to be ended. But much hard fighting lay ahead. Operation 'Crusader' was destined to continue for many weeks and the siege of Tobruk was not to end until December 10, when land communications between the garrison and the main body of the 8th Army were once again firmly established. Then the Royal Navy could relax from its task of being the only link between Tobruk and the rest of the Allies—a task which had included delivering to the garrison 34,000 men, 72 tanks, 92 guns, and 34,000 tons of stores over a period of 242 days.

JOHN FOLEY is an ex-regular soldier who served with various armoured regiments from 1936 to 1954. His last post was in the War Office, as a major, after which he left the army to take up a career in writing. His books include *Mailed Fist, Bull and Brass, Death of a Regiment, No Need to Go Home*, and *The Boilerplate War*. He was a contributor and military adviser to Granada Television's comedy series *The Army Game* and has written several short stories and articles on military and non-military themes.

Frontier duels with the Afrika Korps

1941 **April 9/12:** Rommel's advance encircles Tobruk: the siege begins.
April 25: German forces occupy Halfaya Pass, the key to the eastward land-route into Egypt.
April 30/May 4: *German forces complete the occupation of Greece.* Rommel's first large-scale assault on Tobruk is defeated, but pushes a salient into the western perimeter defences.
May 12: 'Tiger' Convoy docks at Alexandria, bringing 238 tanks for Wavell's Western Desert Force.
May 15: Operation 'Brevity' begins the repair

of the British position on the Egyptian frontier by recapturing Halfaya Pass, but pulls back from Sollum and Capuzzo after initial successes.
May 16: Halder, as Chief of OKH, orders Rommel to leave the siege of Tobruk to the Italian forces, and concentrate his own forces near Sollum.
May 27: Rommel recovers Halfaya Pass and fortifies it.
June 14: British forces advance from Sidi Barrani to begin Operation 'Battleaxe'—the

offensive in Cyrenaica to relieve Tobruk.
June 15: British forces skirt the German defences at Halfaya Pass and reach Capuzzo, but are held by Rommel's skilful defensive tactics and the vulnerability of the British tanks.
June 17: Rommel's thrust towards Halfaya Pass forces the British to head back towards Egypt to avoid the loss of their communications.
June 21: Churchill decides to replace Wavell with Auchinleck as C-in-C Middle East.
June 22: *Germany invades the USSR in Operation 'Barbarossa'.*

◁ **The commanders of Tobruk: Major-General Morshead (left) and Major-General Scobie**

▷ **Tobruk was threatened by the German salient at Ras el Madauar, but Rommel had underestimated the strength of the western defences. The perimeter was more vulnerable to attack from the south-east corner**

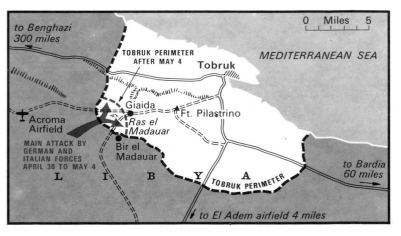

BARBAROSSA *THE SHOCK*

Russia June 21/22, 1941

Lieutenant-General N. K. Popel. The German Blitzkrieg stunned the Russian frontier armies with the brutal realities of invasion. General Popel, at the time an officer with the Red Army, recalls the nagging suspicion and apprehension which accompanied the last hours of peace in eastern Europe

On Saturday June 21, 1941, the night before the German invasion, there was as usual an evening entertainment in the garrison house of the Red Army; this time a Red Army song and dance ensemble had come from district HQ. I had barely had time to go home and change, and when I entered the hall the concert had already begun. From the stage came the tank men's song. As I listened to it, I looked round the hall where our men were sitting, and thought of the events of the last few days.

I had spent these days in one of the divisions of the corps. Only a week before, our tank stock, which consisted of obsolete T-26, BT, T-28, and T-35 tanks, had been supplemented by six KVs and ten T-34s. A complete renewal of our equipment was to proceed from day to day.

After the concert, the Corps Commander, Lieutenant-General Dmitri Ivanovich Ryabishev and I — in accordance with army tradition — invited the artists to dinner. I did not arrive home until 3 am; and although Sunday had already begun, and my Saturday duties were behind me, I hadn't been able to have a bath. I didn't want to wait while the bath filled up, so I stood under the shower. The warm streams washed my fatigue away. My brain was working clearly, and all the time my thoughts kept coming back to the same point: What's happening

now on the opposite bank of the San?

No, it wasn't a premonition. How many times afterwards did I hear of that night 'my heart told me', or 'my mind felt it'? Neither my heart nor my mind told me anything. It was just that I — like many of the senior officers in the frontier formations — knew more facts than I could explain. And so, when returning from Vasiliev's division that day, I had made a small detour and gone to Lwow. There was the staff of the neighbouring combined-arms army, commanded by Lieutenant-General Muzychenko, a friend of mine since the Finnish campaign. The pretext for my visit was that we had to clarify some details of the recent exercises; but both the general and I understood that this was not why I had come.

'Now then, to business,' Muzychenko had interrupted. He was a direct and open man, who had been a commissar in the civil war, did not care for beating about the bush, and despised diplomatic artifice in official relationship — and even more in personal ones.

I told him about the recent dispute between General Ryabishev and Colonel Varennikov, the Chief-of-Staff of the army to which we were subordinate. Ryabishev pointed out the continual arrival of German divisions which was marked on the map, and said that Hitler was preparing to start war. Varennikov replied curtly: 'I guarantee there'll be no war for another year — you can cut my hand off if there is.'

There were many facts on Ryabishev's side. Not only the concentration of German forces, but the suspicious violations of our air space by German aircraft, the increasing boldness of German Intelligence, and the revival of the Ukrainian nationalists. Varennikov was relying on the Soviet News Agency statement. He explained the concentration of German divisions on our frontiers by the version put about at the time — that the Germans were bringing divisions from France for a rest there.

'What have they been doing there that they need a rest?' replied Ryabishev, reasonably enough. Varennikov boiled over. He said we were judging world events just by what was happening on our corps' front, without having any information on the situation along the whole Soviet/German frontier.

When I told him this, General Muzychenko rose from behind his desk, went over to the wall, and drew back the map-curtain. 'I think Ryabishev is right, not Varennikov. There's a concentration of German troops on our front, too — and what a concentration!' Muzychenko did not sit down again, but walked round the office. With a sharp movement he drew back the curtain covering the map, and closed it again.

'I think Ryabishev's on the right scent. I too, at my own risk, am cooking something up. There were to be district artillery competitions here. I persuaded the command to hold army ones instead, and ordered my men not to concentrate the artillery in one place but to take the regiments out on to the range one at a time. And between ourselves, I moved the infantry out from their barracks to the fortified areas. I'm in no hurry to tell command about it, in case they call me a panic-monger.'

A sharp insistent knocking on the bathroom door interrupted my reflections. 'You're wanted on the telephone.' My wife watched silently as I crossed the room and picked up the instrument. 'Comrade Brigade Commissar, this is the Operations Duty Officer. The Corps Commander asks you to come to the staff. I am sending a car.'

My wife couldn't contain herself: 'Well, what is it?'

'Nothing in particular. General Ryabishev is calling me to the workhouse.' Our staff was located in the former workhouse and I thought this joke should calm my wife. Frankly speaking, I really didn't think that anything in particular had happened. Night calls are not so rare for our brother, the soldier.

Ryabishev met me as if we had not parted after dinner. He told me, in a businesslike way, that 15 minutes ago the Army Commander, Lieutenant-General Kostenko, had telephoned and said: 'Get ready and wait for orders.' 'I don't know what this means,' added Ryabishev, 'but anyway I've given the order to stand to, and commanded the units to go out to their areas.'

The officers of the staff, who had been summoned by the alarm, took their places behind their desks. Alongside them they put their suitcases—the 'alarm cases', as they were sometimes called at home: two changes of underwear, shaving gear, and a small stock of food—the minimum necessary to go off to war without first returning home. The staff officers were grumbling. Really, what can be more unpleasant than an alarm on the eve of Sunday. The day is spoiled, the plans which the family has been making all week are broken. How could they not grumble!

'The concert's still on,' one of them joked despondently.

'No,' replied the other, 'it's the beginning of the sports festival—running with suitcases over broken ground.'

Everything seemed as usual. Neither Ryabishev, myself, nor any of the staff officers supposed that this was war. How strange it was! The day before I had gone to General Muzychenko to confirm that the commander's and my own surmises were correct. Three days before, on his own authority, Ryabishev had moved some of his regiments from barracks to the concentration area—but nevertheless we did not suppose that the war was already beginning.

We knew well enough that throughout the entire district units were being intensively formed and re-formed; that two days ago the district staff had moved from Kiev to Tarnapol. But despite all these facts—above all else, despite the conviction that war with Hitler was inevitable, which had never left any of us in recent years—the approaching reality of the war itself was a catastrophe which we could not even conceive. To some extent this could be explained by the fact that our corps was not ready to fight. We had not finished re-forming and had not

managed to find all our new equipment. We lacked repair equipment and spare parts. How could our minds reconcile themselves to beginning a war in such unfavourable conditions?

But whether they could or not, Army Chief-of-Staff Varennikov—the same one who had said we could cut his hand off—telephoned at 4.30 am and told us that the German artillery was firing along the whole frontier, that Przemysl was under fire from close range, and that in places they were crossing the frontier. Yet he warned us 'Do not fall for provocation, do not fire on German aircraft—wait for orders!'

And precisely at that moment, the heavy, tearing roar of motors reached our ears. We all sprang out into the street. It was already light. 'June 22, the longest day!' flashed across my mind. The sun was rising—and to meet it came Hitler's heavily-loaded bombers. They turned over the town and came down. The crosses on the wings—which we knew from the recognition albums and diagrams—could be seen with the naked eye. So could the black dots which separated from the aircraft. They bombed with precision: the railway station, the approach roads, the oil refinery, our barracks (German Intelligence did not know that they had been emptied some days before). When they had dropped their bombs, they circled slowly over the town. Why should they hurry? Not one of our fighters was there; our anti-aircraft guns had not fired a single shot.

The first wave was followed by a second. This time the town centre was bombed, including the blocks where the officers' families lived. Ryabishev seized me by the hand. 'Let's go!' While still running, he threw some words at the Operations Duty Officer: 'Connect me with the anti-aircraft brigade!' He shut the office door behind him and looked me in the eyes. We had already known each other for more than a year; the relationship between us was defined by the short but adequate formula—heart to heart. We did not need long explanations. I nodded silently. Ryabishev lifted the telephone, hesitated a second, then gave the command: 'Open fire on the enemy aircraft.'

We froze at the window, listening intently as the explosions of anti-aircraft shells mingled with the roar of the bombs. And only then did it become completely clear to us—the war had begun!

The bombing went on for a relatively short time. It seemed that our anti-aircraft artillery was not to the German pilots' taste. (We later found out that although the gunners did not shoot particularly well, they shot down four aircraft just the same.)

Ryabishev and I went out into the corridor. Here stood the officers and political workers of the corps directorate, who only a few minutes ago had been exchanging jokes about yet another night alarm which had spoiled their Sunday. Now they were silent, concentrating, worried, grim. They looked at us, waiting for us to speak, but we knew little more than they. We didn't even have orders.

LIEUTENANT-GENERAL NIKOLAY KIRILLOVICH POPEL was Chief Political Officer of the 8th Mechanised Corps of the Red Army at the outbreak of war; he subsequently became Chief Political Officer of the 38th and 28th Armies, and his wartime service included participation in the Stalingrad offensive.

Barbarossa: The Southern and Central Thrusts

1941 June 22: Operation Barbarossa begins: Army Group North (Leeb), Army Group Centre (Bock), and Army Group South (Rundstedt) invade Soviet territory and head for Leningrad, Moscow, and Kiev respectively. Easy progress is made in the north and centre, but Rundstedt meets desperate Soviet resistance in the south.
June 26: In the centre, Brest Litovsk falls after a four-day siege. *Manstein's Panzers of Army Group North enter Daugavpils.*
June 24/30: Army Group Centre seals off Soviet resistance into pockets at Bialystok, Novogrudok, and Volkovysk.
July 1: In the centre, Guderian's Panzers cross the Berezina. *Panzer spearheads of Army Group North cross the Dvina and advance on Pskov.*
July 4: *Army Group North captures Ostrov and reaches the pre-1939 Russian frontier.*
July 9: Army Group Centre ends Soviet resistance in the Minsk pocket and captures Vitebsk.
July 10/11: Panzers of Army Group Centre cross the Dniepr. In the south, a Soviet counter-offensive by 5th and 6th Armies fails; Kleist's Panzers approach to within 10 miles of Kiev.
July 15: A breakthrough in the centre leads to the encirclement and fall of Smolensk, cutting off a Soviet concentration of 300,000 men between Orsha and Smolensk.
July 20: In the centre, Bock orders Guderian to close the ring at Smolensk before any further advance to the east.
July 22: *After a month's scorching advance, Army Group North is checked west of Lake Ilmen by the exhaustion of the troops.*
July 30: In the south, Kleist begins to seal off the Soviet concentration at Uman.
August 3: In the south, Kleist and Stülpnagel seal off the Uman pocket: the inner pincers close.
August 5: End of Soviet resistance in the Smolensk pocket: Army Group Centre has succeeded in breaking out of the Smolensk 'land-bridge' but is still faced with determined Soviet counterattacks. In the south, Rumanian forces begin the 73-day siege of Odessa.
August 12: Hitler insists on the destruction of the Soviet South-West Front before resuming the advance in the centre, as Guderian heads south towards Gomel and Starodub. *Army Group North advances on Leningrad from the Luga bridgehead.*
August 23/30: Guderian heads south; belatedly, the Soviet front commander Yeremenko prepares to forestall the threat to Kiev from the rear.
August 25: Panzers of Army Group South consolidate the Dniepr crossing at Dnepropetrovsk; path cleared for the southern arm of the German pincer movement to engulf the Uman/Kiev concentration.
August 30/September 2: Failure of Yeremenko's counteroffensive against Guderian's flank.
September 12: Kleist heads north from the Cherkassy/Kremenchug beach-heads.
September 15: The outer pincers close: Panzer spearheads of Kleist and Guderian meet at Lokhvitsa, trapping four Soviet armies.
September 17: STAVKA belatedly orders Soviet withdrawal from Kiev.
September 18/27: In the south, slaughter and surrenders inside the Kiev pocket. Nearly two-thirds of the Red Army's strength on the outbreak of war has already been eliminated.

In the centre, Bock's two Panzergruppen pass Brest Litovsk and Bialystok and probe deep into Belorussia, heading for the first target: Smolensk

BARBAROSSA *DRIVE TO SMOLENSK*

**White Russia
June 22/July 17, 1941**

Generalmajor (AD) Alfred Philippi. The waiting was over: Bock's Army Group Centre plunged into White Russia, with Moscow as its key objective. The Russians fought and lost the 'battle of the frontiers', as the Germans had hoped; and the German victories of encirclement at Minsk and Smolensk netted vast numbers of prisoners. But it was a long way to Moscow — and Russia's reserves seemed inexhaustible

Shortly after 0300 hours on June 22, 1941, the whole of the German front line, from the Carpathians to the Baltic, moved forward after a short artillery bombardment across the demarcation line, while air squadrons above them flew far into Russia.

Army Group Centre reported good progress soon after the beginning of the attack. Most of the bridges over the Bug fell into German hands intact — for the Russian frontier units fought without cohesion, their artillery fire was weak, and there seemed to be no plans either for organised defence or for organised retreat. Wherever Soviet forces put up a local resistance, they were outflanked, and tactical surprise was achieved (see maps).

The Russian lack of preparations for invasion was quite astonishing, especially as the extensive and lengthy German preparations can hardly have escaped the notice of the Soviet leaders. Perhaps they did not expect an early German offensive in view of the Balkan campaign, where they knew considerable German forces to be involved, and the transport of which to the Eastern Front must take some time. Or did they think that the movement of troops in Poland and East Prussia was a mere political demonstration? One is left in ignorance of Stalin's thoughts. Did he recognise the German peril too late?

It was only in the fortress of Brest Litovsk and in the field-works to the north of that city that the enemy put up a tough resistance; but after four days the fortress was captured by a German division left behind for the purpose. The main crossing of the River Bug on the south wing of Army Group Centre was blocked until June 26, and this had an adverse effect on the deployment of the units of II Panzergruppe, leading to much congestion in the area. The programme for this important river-crossing was upset, and the traffic police were at first unable to deal with the jams; motorised units had to be diverted south of the fortress area to assault bridges thrown hastily across the Bug. But here, too, there were further delays, caused by the bad and marshy approach roads. Nevertheless, General Heinz Gude-

118

Following up the deep penetration of the Panzer units came the infantry armies; their first big battle was the four-day fight for Brest Litovsk

rian, II Panzergruppe's commander, urged on his tanks tirelessly, and some of his advanced units reached the two important roads near Kobrin and Pruzhany during the night of June 23. Meanwhile, to the north of Brest Litovsk, IV Army penetrated enemy territory to a depth of nearly 10 miles. Simultaneously, farther to the north, III Panzergruppe captured intact the Niemen bridges at Alitus and to the south of it. Grodno fell on June 23.

Luftflotte II made surprise raids on the Russian airfields, and inflicted severe losses. The Luftwaffe established a superiority over the Russian air force which was of vital importance at the outset of the offensive.

These initial successes opened the way for the thrusts of the motorised units on the two wings of Army Group Centre, planned to bring about a wide encirclement of the enemy in the general direction of Minsk. The Russian forces overrun in the Bialystok region were to be dealt with by shorter pincers thrown out from IV and IX Armies.

On June 23 air reconnaissance reported many enemy columns retreating eastwards from the Bialystok area. Had the disorganisation caused by the initial surprise been so quickly overcome? Had the Soviet High Command taken the reins back into its

hands, and made up its mind to withdraw its forces eastwards, to avoid the danger of encirclement and to regain freedom of movement? Bock was inclined to take this view, although reports of the growing resistance of local fighting units were coming in simultaneously. The latter were apparently intended to cover the general retreat which Bock suspected.

He was afraid that strong enemy contingents might escape into the marshlands of the Berezina before the ring around them could be closed near Minsk. He therefore planned on the evening of the 23rd that III Panzergruppe, which had advanced the farthest, should forthwith occupy the Dvina crossings at Polotsk and Vitebsk, in order to prevent in good time the enemy from building up a new front on the Dvina. The northern arm of the pincer movement near Minsk could safely be left to IX Army. However, in an exchange of views with OKH, the latter saw no advantage in such a deep and isolated thrust by III Panzergruppe, but rather an unnecessary risk. OKH insisted on the junction of the two Panzergruppen near Minsk, in accordance with the original 'Barbarossa' plan.

Further developments showed that this decision was the right one. On June 24, the

spearheads of the two Panzergruppen reached Slonim in the south and Wilno in the north. Always edging farther to the east, IV and IX Armies swung gradually to the north and south respectively, pushing into the circular trap the Soviet forces which had been overrun by the tanks.

The Soviets fought in separate, unco-ordinated groups, apparently without unified leadership; obstinate resistance alternated with withdrawal. Some Red Army units disappeared into the vast forests, only to turn up again in the rear of the advancing German troops. The result was a series of local engagements, carried out by day and night, with severe losses to both sides. Again and again portions of the Russian forces succeeded in breaking out eastwards, at points where the gaps in the net drawn around them were widest. There was no question of surrender. Nevertheless, the general view was that such tactics would be unable to prevent the planned encirclement and the elimination of the Soviet forces.

But now the creation of a great pocket extending from Bialystok to Minsk had become a difficult problem. The original scheme was therefore quickly altered to conform with the course of events. The old plan had depended on the speed   ▷

This sequence shows a single shot fired by a German 50-mm gun crew against a Soviet strongpoint. In the third photograph, the shell can be seen while still in the air

of the armour. Tanks had indeed disrupted the Soviet forces along their lines of attack and had cut their rearward communications. But they were unable, in their unceasing forward thrusts, to create a solid ring around the encircled pockets. The Panzergruppen expected the infantry corps to do this, but for all their efforts the latter could not maintain the pace. To deal with the enemy forces driven off the main lines of attack, the Germans needed more time than had been anticipated, especially as their tanks had moved on.

The result was that the gaps between the infantry and the tank columns became progressively wider, and that the enclosing ring was very thin on the east side. The enemy soon discovered the weak spots, and strong forces tried to break out through Volkovysk and Slonim. At Volkovysk they succeeded. As a result, II Panzergruppe (advancing partly on Minsk and partly on the Dniepr) found its overstretched left flank threatened—its rearward communications were even in danger. Differences arose between the impetuous Guderian and the more cautious Kluge, because the infantry was held up by the unexpectedly bad roads, and by the unexpectedly tough fighting on the edges of the pocket. Bock was from June 23 onwards looking beyond Minsk to the Dniepr and the Dvina, and he took the side of Guderian. But on June 25 Hitler expressed his misgivings about the Minsk pocket, which seemed to him altogether too large. Bock, on the other hand, was furious at this damaging deviation from the master plan. Finally, on the same evening, OKH prevailed on Hitler to issue an order that the two Panzergruppen should confine their attentions to the Minsk area.

However, II Panzergruppe was compelled, though unwillingly, to leave part of its force at Slonim in order to join the expected infantry corps of IV Army in buttressing the pocket which was being formed around Volkovysk, farther to the east. As the encircling forces of IX Army on the north side of the pocket were—thanks to better movement conditions—stronger than those of IV Army on the south-eastern side, the Soviet attempts to break out were naturally directed towards the points of least resistance. For a time, several corps of IV Army, with detachments of II Panzer Corps, were in a serious predicament.

On June 25 OKH insisted on strengthening the pressure exercised by IX Army on the north and IV Army on the south sides of the pocket. Thus it came about that, instead of one huge pocket as originally planned, several fragmentary pockets were created in desperate fighting, first around Bialystok, then around Volkovysk. Again and again in this phase of the fighting, one saw the ability of the tough Russian soldier to make use of the dense and trackless forests to filter through the German lines. His supplies from the interior of Russia had long since been cut off by the Germans, but there were ammunition and ration dumps that he could use. Largely self-sufficient, he could live on the land; and when ammunition failed, he was not afraid of hand-to-hand combat in mass formation.

Before the bolt was shot on the eastern side of the Volkovysk pocket on June 29, large numbers of Red troops had slipped north-eastwards · through the thin net to Novogrudok; but they found themselves entangled and encircled again on June 29. On this day the spearhead of II Panzer-

gruppe joined up near Minsk with units of III Panzergruppe, which had arrived there on the previous day after a bitter struggle. It was mainly the task of III Panzergruppe, in the last days of June, to ward off attacks of fresh Soviet tank units thrown in from the east with the intention of helping the encircled forces to fight their way out of the German pocket.

Thus by June 28 the preliminary objective of the two Panzergruppen had been attained—although behind them IV and IX Armies were still fighting hard to clear up the pocket. By June 30 the fighting around Bialystok and Volkovysk was more or less over. The 3rd and 10th Soviet Armies, comprising about ten rifle divisions, two cavalry divisions, and six armoured brigades, had been destroyed or scattered.

This victory set free a number of German infantry corps, which were used to relieve the Panzergruppen in the great encirclement near Minsk. In the area between Novogrudok and Minsk there were trapped not only the remnants of forces retreating from the west, but also considerable Soviet reserves from the rear—a total of 13 rifle divisions, two cavalry divisions, and four tank squadrons.

But once again the patience of the German tank leaders, anxious to forge ahead, was sorely tested by the lagging infantry. For an entire week part of the tank forces had to be left on the front of the pocket, in a crescent on either side of Minsk; for in spite of forced marches, the infantry could not maintain the desired speed on the rough and dusty byroads between the hard roads used by the motorised units. It was not until July 9 that the battle of Minsk was won by IV and IX Armies.

On July 9 Army Group Centre reported the results of operations to OKH. Of the four Soviet armies, composed of 43 divisions and six brigades, they had succeeded in destroying 22 infantry divisions, three cavalry divisions, seven armoured divisions, and six motorised brigades. In all, 300,000 prisoners, 2,500 tanks, 1,400 guns, and 250 aircraft had been captured.

At Minsk the Germans had succeeded in stopping almost completely the Soviet attempts to break out of the pocket. Admittedly, the German armoured forces had been obliged to leave behind about one-third of their strength, until relieved by the infantry. The Soviet forces, badly affected by the earlier fighting, were now more inclined to surrender, a state of mind to which a shortage of ammunition and other supplies may well have contributed.

Nevertheless, a large number of Soviet troops were left behind in the forests, out of control; and in the later stages of the campaign, when partisan warfare became increasingly rife, this was to produce very disturbing effects. There were not enough German security divisions available to mop up the areas behind the front line, and so Army Group Centre had to employ some of the reserve fighting divisions on the task. Even they were only partially successful.

After the defeat at Bialystok and Minsk, the centre of the Soviet front was left wide open. At first, Russian troops were seen retreating eastwards across the Dniepr as a result of the battle, but the OKH had realised some days before that the Soviets had decided against any general retreat into the depths of the country. This was confirmed by air reports, from June 29 onwards, of large-scale troop movements by road and railway *westward* from the Smolensk area. It seemed highly probable that the Soviet High Command had resolved to set up a new defence line on the Dniepr and Dvina, and on the 'land bridge' between the two rivers.

This was a proof that Marshal Timoshenko, Soviet Commander-in-Chief, had retaken the reins of command firmly and energetically into his own hands. Fresh Russian forces, put in in these days to oppose III Panzergruppe, were doubtless intended to relieve their hard-pressed comrades, but their arrival could also be interpreted as an attempt to gain time for the build-up of the Dniepr defences. If so, it showed that Bock's fears of June 23 were far from illusory: it explained why he and his tank commanders were so keen on pushing forward without delay to the Dniepr and Dvina, and why, because of their long-term aims, they were so reluctant to take any part in the engagements connected with the encirclements.

Tank thrust to the Dniepr
Time was short. Every day lost in tactical warfare helped the Red Army, enabling them to bring up reserves and build up a new defence line on the Dniepr and Dvina. If one made a present of these days to the Red Army, having to break through a fresh front would cause unnecessary German losses and more valuable time would be lost before the Orsha/Smolensk/Vitebsk 'land-bridge', the first great objective of the campaign, could be reached. This area was the essential base for the final attack on Moscow. That was the reason why the field commanders had from the beginning fixed their gaze far ahead, on the Dniepr and Dvina; and that was why they had correctly kept large parts of the two Panzergruppen moving eastwards, without letting them take part in the fighting around the pockets.

The situation of Army Group Centre at the beginning of July was the starting-point for the next advance to the east. One corps of II Panzergruppe on its right wing, had crossed the Berezina; encountering only slight resistance, it had reached the Dniepr near Rogachev. On the north wing, another corps had reached the Berezina near Borisov, and after a hard struggle had established a bridgehead on the motor-road to Smolensk. The third corps was still waiting for the infantry to relieve it on the encirclement front at Minsk.

The part of IV Army not tied to the Minsk pocket was advancing in forced marches with the bulk of its divisions; but with distances of up to 125 miles to the Berezina alone, it could hardly be expected there in much less than a week. Marching along roads deep in dust was exhausting in the extreme for both man and beast.

At the far end of Army Group Centre's south wing, on the edge of the Pripet marshes, I Cavalry Division was holding the long flank by reconnoitring skirmishes among the swamps. It was known that on the south side of the River Pripet comparatively strong enemy bands were operating skilfully, and were proving a considerable nuisance to VI Army of Army Group South. OKH therefore ordered Army Group Centre to detach an infantry corps to comb the Pinsk marshes. With both its corps, III Panzergruppe was thrusting towards the Dvina near and above Polotsk, whereas the southern wing of Army Group North had already crossed that river near Daugavpils (Dvinsk). In the tracks of III Panzergruppe, IX Army, with the bulk of its infantry, was following up. Its routes to the Dvina were shorter than those of IV Army to the Dniepr. Parts of this army, too, were employed at the Minsk pocket.

There had been no great supply problems, not even in the matter of fuel. Advanced dumps had been established at Slutsk and Molodechno and in the Minsk area, and the conversion of the railway to normal gauge had been completed as far as Baranovichi. The Luftwaffe still dominated the sky, although it was discovered that the number of enemy aircraft had been much underestimated.

As far back as June 26 a discussion on the strategy to be followed in the next phase of the operations had taken place between Bock and the Army Commander-in-Chief, Field-Marshal Walther von Brauchitsch. Both were of the opinion that no time was to be lost in engaging the enemy around Smolensk and beginning the thrust towards Moscow. Brauchitsch advocated the merging of the two Panzergruppen into one, under the command of Field-Marshal von Kluge — a step that would allow better use to be made of the fast-moving armoured units amid the vicissitudes of battle.

Bock, on the other hand, had misgivings, based mainly on the self-willed personalities of Kluge and Guderian, which had already given rise to serious tension. But Brauchitsch dismissed this objection as of no great significance. The new arrangement would come into force on July 3. The former High Command of IV Army was therefore renamed 'Panzer-AOK IV' (Armour/Army High Command IV), to occupy a place in the heirarchy of command between Army Group Centre Command and II and III Panzergruppen Commands. The IV Army units were taken over by the new High Command of II Army, with General Maximilian Freiherr von Weichs at its head.

On July 1 a new instruction was sent out to Army Group Centre. In it, the sub-commands received the following orders:
● IV Panzer Army must be in a position on July 3 'to break through in the direction of Moscow';
● II Panzergruppe, with this object in view, was to force a crossing of the Dniepr in the Rogachev/Orsha sector, and its spearhead, following the line of the Minsk/Moscow motorway, was to capture the heights of Yelnya on the Desna;
● III Panzergruppe was to by-pass the marshes of the upper Berezina and, following the line of the Dvina between Polotsk and Vitebsk, break into the region north of Smolensk;
● II and IX Armies were to follow the fast-moving units with all possible speed and send forward mobile detachments to support them. The quick capture of the Orsha/Vitebsk 'land-bridge' was of vital importance to both armies;
● Co-operation with the Luftwaffe was to remain as before. Both II Army and II Panzergruppe were to be supported by II Fliegerkorps, and IX Army and III Panzergruppe by VIII Fliegerkorps.

On the first day, July 3, the attack of the new IV Panzer Army met with tough resistance on the river-courses and was held up. This time the surprise element had failed. On the outer wings, near Rogachev on the Dniepr and Polotsk on the Dvina, bridgeheads were formed; but between the two, on the Berezina, the Soviets put up a stubborn defence and showed intense activity near Borisov. This energetic behaviour, with German air reconnaissance reports of further troop movements from the rear, led to the conclusion that the Soviet leaders were at last trying to halt the German invaders at the river barriers. Here, it seemed certain, the approach to Moscow via Smolensk was to be stopped.

Thus on the first evening Bock was faced with an urgent dilemma: should the attack be continued by IV Panzer Army alone, entailing the inevitable use of the fast-moving, vital armoured units; or should he await the arrival of II and IX Armies? The first divisions could be expected in a week at the earliest. The advanced detachments with artillery, which had been ordered, might provide some slight reinforcement at an earlier date — but that consideration did not justify the vital loss of time, and once again time was the vital factor.

Bock resolved to act at once. In agreement with Kluge, he ordered the units of II Panzergruppe, which were too scattered, to concentrate on either side of Mogilev in order to deliver a strong attack both there and at Borisov. He was less anxious about III Panzergruppe, because its advance had been shorter and it could count on earlier reinforcement by divisions from IX Army.

Although the consequent regrouping had been hindered and delayed by heavy rainfalls which softened the roads, the situation was greatly improved by a fortunate success on the part of III Panzergruppe. Fighting hard beyond Polotsk, it was able to roll up the Dvina defences in an easterly direction

Marshal Budenny, C-in-C South-West Front

Field-Marshal Bock, C-in-C Army Group Centre

and to occupy Vitebsk on July 9. This was a key success, and the staff of both the army and the army group, seizing the opportunity, decided to transfer the spearhead of the operation to the north wing by moving units from II Panzergruppe to III Panzergruppe. But this idea was abandoned because of the difficulties caused by bad weather and bad roads. Nor was it necessary after all: very soon afterwards, on July 10/11, II Panzergruppe succeeded in crossing the Dniepr on both sides of Mogilev, at Stary Bykhov and at Shklov.

Sudden raid on Smolensk

The fighting was extremely hard on these days, both there and near Vitebsk; but on July 13 a double breakthrough on the wings set in motion the operation for the encirclement of Smolensk. By-passing the Russian forces along the Orsha/Smolensk road, which had been strongly reinforced, the armoured spearheads approached their goal with surprising speed. On July 15 one division of III Panzergruppe, coming from the northwest, reached the Smolensk/Moscow highroad at Yartsevo and blocked it. Next day, in a bold raid, a division of III Panzergruppe made a surprise attack on Smolensk and captured the city. The strong enemy forces between Orsha and Smolensk, a number eventually estimated at about 300,000, were thus cut off. The essential next step was to protect the spearhead by establishing a wider defence to the east. By July 17 II Panzergruppe, which had left its XLVII Corps on the south edge of the Smolensk pocket, sent XLVI Corps to the River Desna on either side of Yelnya, and XXIV Corps to the River Sozh on either side of Krichev. Meanwhile III Panzergruppe, with its two corps (XXXIX and 57th), constituted the northern section of the ring trap, fighting its way forward to the Yartsevo/Nevel line.

The fast armoured units, even bolder and more reckless than in their thrust for Minsk, were dispatched to deal with the Soviet forces threatening the German tanks' lines of attack. It looked like a race for time. Strong Soviet forces had been left behind by the German tank columns near Mogilev (six or seven divisions) and north-east of Vitebsk (three or four divisions), apart from several groups on both sides of Nevel—some ten divisions in all. To deal with them, and also to mop up the huge pocket at Smolensk, it was essential for the Germans to await the arrival of the infantry corps of II and IX Armies.

Unfortunately, it was not possible to seal off Smolensk entirely. A small gap was left in the tangled valley of the Dniepr, and through it the enemy could and did percolate eastwards. Guderian, who was responsible for this sector, tried to close the gap with artillery fire and air raids. When urged by the army group to effect a definitive junction with III Panzergruppe, he replied that with all the tasks he had in hand he simply had not enough tanks to comply. In fact, he was less interested in closing the gap than in continuing his thrust eastwards and creating a springboard for the advance on Moscow. But when on July 20 he established a bridgehead across the Desna near Yelnya and proposed to follow this up with further thrust to the east, Bock intervened, reminding him in no uncertain terms of his prior duty—to close the Smolensk gap.

This was not done until July 27, and it was not until August 5 that the enemy in the Smolensk pocket was finally liquidated.

In the fighting since July 10, some 310,000 prisoners, 3,205 tanks, and 3,120 guns had been taken. The Soviet 16th Army and parts of the 19th and 20th Armies were destroyed. These large numbers, and the length of their resistance are explained by the fact that the gap so tardily closed was used less for escape than for bringing in supplies, and by the strategy of the Soviet leadership—to which reference will be made later.

This was the situation on July 17. In a vast curve, some 500 miles from the starting-line, stretched the loose front of the fast-moving units of IV Panzer Army, which were fanning out with the support of the infantry divisions of II and IX Armies. The first main objective of Army Group Centre had been obtained, in the break-out from the Orsha/Smolensk/Vitebsk 'land-bridge'. The Soviet forces had been crushed and scattered on a wide front, and their attempts to form a fresh line along the Dniepr and Dvina had been foiled.

From mid-July onwards, the German staffs were aware of the new battle-order of the Soviet 'fronts', or army groups, and that Marshal Timoshenko had assumed the leadership of the 'West Front', opposite Army Group Centre. It was becoming clear that the new Soviet Commander-in-Chief was displaying a new spirit of strong will and initiative. If there was any recompense to be retrieved from the loss of six Soviet armies, it was that their sacrifice had at least given the Soviet High Command time to conjure up fresh (if partly improvised) forces from their immense reservoir of manpower, and to place them in the front line. These were now coming into action, chiefly on the wide flanks of the advancing Army Group Centre and at the points of junction with its neighbour army groups on the north and south fronts.

To the south, on July 15, the Soviet 21st Army of eight divisions, coming from the Gomel area, attacked across the Dniepr near Rogachev; and simultaneously there emerged from the Pripet marshes a cavalry force, moving north from Mozyr in the direction of Bobruysk on the Berezina. Both movements were aimed at the southern flank of the German II Army. After several days' fighting, the Soviet forces were brought to a standstill. But three corps continued to be engaged in the area, and thus the southern wing of Army Group Centre became pinned down on the Dniepr. This hold-up, combined with the developments on the northern wing of Army Group South, was later to play an important role in the strategy of the German High Command.

Another corps of the German II Army had been given the task—as already mentioned—of getting rid of the Red Army concentration at Mogilev, estimated at six divisions. This was successfully accomplished by July 27. Weichs meanwhile was left with only two army corps to send forward to strengthen the front of II Panzergruppe.

To the north, where the infantry divisions of IX Army had arrived at the Dvina at a relatively early date, and where close contact with the right wing of Army Group North could be maintained, the situation was less critical than it was farther to the south. It was true that IX Army had to defeat strong enemy forces in order to capture the fortress of Polotsk, which fell on July 16. But it was able to detach three corps in good time to help in the fighting around the Smolensk pocket. The enemy groups at Nevel were liquidated by July 24. Mean-

while, the right flank of III Panzergruppe, south of Velikiye-Luki, had been held up by the obstinate resistance of the Soviet 22nd Army.

As long as the fighting for the Smolensk pocket lasted, the Soviet leaders tried desperately to free their trapped comrades; they even hoped to regain this strategically important region from the Germans. With that object, they put strong pressure on the German front from Yelnya to Yartsevo and Belyy. The Desna bridgehead at Yelnya became a focal point in those days, causing great sacrifices of men and material. Thus, in the second half of July, Army Group Centre found itself on the defensive at many points along its 450-mile front. Moreover, the German staff had to take into account a serious dwindling of resources: 40-50% of the armoured units, 20% of the motorised vehicles because of wear-and-tear (even 50% of the tanks). Signs of exhaustion were appearing among the troops, who had now been fighting without a break since the beginning of the offensive. Unexpected crises occurred in the supply system, usually because of the state of the railways (which had now been corrected to narrow-gauge as far as Orsha). A pause for breath was essential. A rest period of 14 days was thought necessary to follow on the arrival of infantry divisions at the front line, during which the armoured units, whose need was the greatest, could be withdrawn for repairs and to be prepared for new operations. Rations and other supplies could be replenished at the same time.

Of course, a rest period was equally valuable to the Red Army, providing time to reconstruct a solid front line. Although substantially weakened in trained personnel, and although most of the cadres now appearing in the front line bore the stamp of improvisation—the Red Army was not yet beaten. Nor was there any doubt about the efforts of the Soviets to mobilise all their potential (the magnitude of which one could not even begin to estimate).

The desperate Soviet attacks on the front of Army Group Centre, and the energy and haste visible in all Soviet movements, made it quite clear that the Soviet leadership was determined to stop any further German advances east of Smolensk on the Desna, to the south of Smolensk on the Sozh and the Dniepr, or to the north of Smolensk among the upper courses of the Dniepr and Dvina. They had obviously realised the danger that threatened their capital city and motherland from this direction. The German leaders rightly suspected that the strongest Russian forces were concentrated in this area. It was here that they made up their minds to seek a rapid conclusion to the whole campaign.

GENERALMAJOR (AD) ALFRED PHILIPPI was born in 1903, and was commissioned into the Reichswehr as an infantry officer in 1924. In the Second World War he served in the Polish, French, and Balkan campaigns; and served in Russia in the field as well as on the General Staff. From autumn 1944 until the end of the war he commanded an infantry division on the Western Front. After the war, he became involved in the study of military history. His publications include *Der Feldzug gegen Sowjetrussland* ('The Campaign Against Soviet Russia'), which appeared in 1962. He has also worked on an edition of the war diaries of General Halder, and in 1957 became Editor-in-Chief of the *Wehrwissenschaftlichen Rundschau* ('Military Science Review').

Then, after the first big victories, the pace slackened

△ A German horse-drawn column brings up the guns to hold the gains won by the Panzer units. In these early days, the Russian roads are dry
▽ Army Group Centre clears Belorussia. **(Left)** The Bialystok salient and the Minsk pockets. **(Right)** The 'land bridge' and the capture of Smolensk

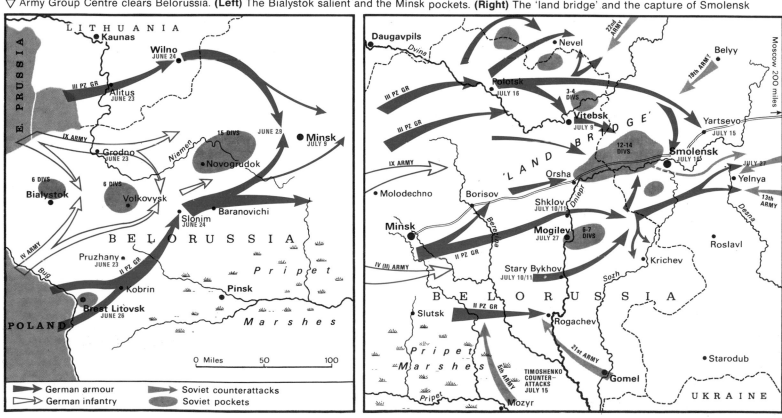

Left map:

LITHUANIA
E. PRUSSIA
Kaunas
Wilno JUNE 24
III PZ GR
Alitus JUNE 23
IX ARMY
Grodno JUNE 23
Niemen
15 DIVS
JUNE 29
Minsk JULY 9
Novogrudok
6 DIVS
Bialystok
6 DIVS
Volkovysk
Baranovichi
Slonim JUNE 24
BELORUSSIA
IV ARMY
Pruzhany JUNE 23
II PZ GR
Bug
Pripet
Kobrin
Pinsk
Brest Litovsk JUNE 26
POLAND
Marshes

0 Miles 50 100

➤ German armour
▷ German infantry
➤ Soviet counterattacks
⬤ Soviet pockets

Right map:

Daugavpils
Dvina
22nd ARMY
Nevel
Belyy
Moscow 200 miles
19th ARMY
III PZ GR
Polotsk JULY 16
3-4 DIVS
III PZ GR
Vitebsk JULY 9
Yartsevo JULY 15
IX ARMY
'LAND BRIDGE'
12-14 DIVS
Smolensk JULY 16
JULY 27
Orsha
Yelnya
Molodechno
Borisov
Shklov JULY 10/11
Dniepr
13th ARMY
Minsk
Berezina
Mogilev JULY 27
6-7 DIVS
Desna
II PZ GR
IV (II) ARMY
Stary Bykhov JULY 10/11
Krichev
Roslavl
Sozh
BELORUSSIA
Slutsk
II PZ GR
Rogachev
21st ARMY
Pripet
5th ARMY
TIMOSHENKO COUNTER-ATTACKS JULY 15
Starodub
Marshes
Gomel
Pripet
Mozyr
UKRAINE

123

The Blitzkrieg in action: the first stages of Barbarossa

After the Luftwaffe's raids, the Panzer spearheads thrust through the main towns lying in the paths of the three advancing army groups **(left)**.The next stage **(above)** — supporting German infantry mop-up and crush local resistance. The speed and progress of the Wehrmacht's advance into Russia depended on the time taken by the long, field-grey columns **(right)** to press eastwards through the bridgeheads won for them by the armour, and to catch up with the impatient Panzer forces holding the loosely tied-off pockets of opposition. Early large-scale destruction of the Red Army was the aim of the Wehrmacht. To achieve this, rapid penetration in depth by the armour was essential; and one of the means to this end was the water-proofed tank, many of which crossed the Bug river demarcation-line underwater on the first day of Barbarossa

Hitler postponed the dash for Moscow—the Ukraine was to come first

The Ukraine was the target area of Army Group South, and the wide areas of the steppe offered superb opportunities for the tacticians of Kleist's Panzergruppe to show their paces. In sealing off the Soviet concentrations at Uman and Kiev, the Panzer and infantry forces of Army Group South won the great battle of annihilation, the 'super-Cannae', that Hitler demanded. This victory was not won by smashing the strong Soviet forces in direct assaults. It was the result of a penetration in such depth that the Soviet strategists did not notice the closing trap until it was too late. **(Right)** Soviet shell-fire in the Ukraine. **(Below)** One of Kleist's Panzer regiments driving across the steppe in ideal conditions. **(Left)** German infantrymen at the exhausting task of eliminating their opposite numbers, and **(bottom)** in a lull during the advance, flushed with what seems to be a gigantic repetition of their earlier swift triumphs in Poland and France

BARBAROSSA

DRIVE TO KIEV

Ukraine
June 22/September 18, 1941

Geoffrey Jukes

As Rundstedt's Army Group South thrust deep into the Ukraine, Hitler halted the central drive on Moscow and decreed—in defiance of his generals' advice—that the Russian capital was not to be the prime military target. Economic factors obsessed Hitler; the wheatlands and industries of the Ukraine were of more importance than the fall of the Soviet capital. The result was the battle of Kiev: it was the greatest military disaster in the Red Army's history; but the Red Army was still in being as autumn approached ▷

△ The meaning of invasion: blazing houses in the town of Zhitomir   ▽ The battle for Zhitomir: a German gun-crew deals with Soviet opposition

The battle of the frontiers was over. In the south it had been fought well to the west of the main Soviet static defence lines, which ran along the old pre-1939 frontier. Many of the rank and file of the disorganised units of the Soviet South-West and South Fronts consoled themselves as they retreated with the idea that once ensconced in the permanent fortifications (which the Germans had christened the 'Stalin Line'), things would be different. Many of their senior officers wondered. They knew the German talent for by-passing permanent defences, proved in Poland, the Low Countries, and France. More disquieting still, they knew that the 'Stalin Line' had not been kept up since the frontier had moved west in 1939-40. There was no sanctuary to be found there.

What the Red Army needed was a doctrine of mobile defence; and this it did not have. Instead, the Supreme Command kept reiterating to shattered formations unrealistic orders to form continuous defence lines, and counterattack an enemy who moved so fast that he was already east of the line they were meant to defend before their orders reached them. Apart from shooting some generals, Stalin had no immediate remedy for the situation.

Sure enough, the 'Stalin Line' proved an illusion. Although some parts of it held, the German Army Group South ruptured it, almost without pausing, in bloody but brief engagements, and by July 9 the bulk of the German VI Army, spearheaded by Colonel-General von Kleist's I Panzergruppe was through it (see maps).

In an attempt to co-ordinate the activities of his armies, Stalin on July 10 appointed three 'Commander-in-Chiefs of Direction'. The man appointed to face Rundstedt and Army Group South was Marshal of the Soviet Union Semyon Mikhailovich Budenny, a former cavalry NCO of the Imperial Army, and already a figure of Soviet Mythology as Commander of the First Cavalry Army in the Civil War. He had been a superb tactician, but as a strategist he was suspect, a man of action rather than a thinker, and a classic 'blood and guts' figure. Not, perhaps, the ideal man to face the old-school, highly professional Field-Marshal von Rundstedt — nor indeed to impress the professional, post-revolution, Red Army generals over whom he was set. But he was an inspiring figure to look at — especially with his bold cavalry-man's moustache. A captive Soviet officer was later to say that this moustache was bigger than the brain behind it.

However, from Stalin's point of view Budenny's very lack of professionalism was a point in his favour. He was a trusted Communist. There would be no nonsense from him about a professional, non-political army; and it was, after all, the 'professional' generals who were yielding up large stretches of Soviet territory. So Budenny became Commander-in-Chief over South-West Front, South Front, and the Black Sea Fleet. To make assurance doubly sure, a reliable Stalinist, Nikita Khrushchev, was appointed as Budenny's 'Member of Military Council' (that is, his political deputy and watchdog). What matter if his new Lieutenant-General's uniform fitted him as a saddle fits a cow? Khrushchev would see that the soldiers were politically sound, and that the population did its bit.

So much for the Soviet side. But, for the moment, the Germans had the initiative. And they, too, had their problems.

Unlike the Soviet ones, the German

problems arose from success. Army Group South had not been viewed as the main potential bringer of victory when the 'Barbarossa' Directive was drawn up. Its thrust was south of the Pripet marshes, whereas the main accumulation of strength (Army Groups North and Centre, with three of the four Panzergruppen) was north of them. Only at its northern end was it strong in German forces. There stood the VI and XVII Armies, and I Panzergruppe, a total of 34½ divisions; while the entire southern sector from the Carpathians to the Black Sea coast had only the XI Army of Colonel-General Ritter von Schobert, totalling eight divisions and the SS motorised brigade 'Adolf Hitler'. There were also two Rumanian armies (III and IV), and a Hungarian corps, but these were mostly armed with old or captured French equipment and given secondary tasks. No bets were to be placed on them.

The tasks were allotted as follows: VI Army was to make a hole through which I Panzergruppe should pour towards the Dniepr below Kiev, then south along the river bank behind the Soviet South-West Front. The XVII Army was to make for Vinnitsa and then continue east or south-east to meet I Panzergruppe. The anticipated result was the annihilation of the entire south-western front west of the Dniepr, and conquest of the north-west Ukraine up to that river. In the south, XVI Army, the Rumanians, and the Hungarians were to protect the Ploesti oilfields, guard the northern wing against any Soviet attempt to outflank it, and then join in exploiting its anticipated success by driving due east, cutting up the Soviet South Front and capturing the south-west Ukraine. Thus all the Ukraine west of the Dniepr (the area known in the Soviet Union as 'right-bank Ukraine') would be in German hands. It was ambitious, but neat. Rundstedt knew his job.

At the Higher Command level, the touch was less sure. Hitler had already said on July 4 that the most difficult decision of the war could be whether to turn north or south after breaking through the 'Stalin Line'. Here the problem was one of deciding between a number of tempting targets — and the key to it was not Army Group South but Field-Marshal von Bock's Army Group Centre.

The essence of Blitzkrieg was deep penetration by the Panzers and motorised infantry into the enemy's rear, followed by a turning inwards so as to cut off a slice, to be minced between the Panzer forces and the infantry armies coming up behind, mostly on foot (see page 18). There were three army groups, but four Panzer groups, since Army Group Centre had two of them (II and III). This meant that any large encirclement in the north or south involved either pinning the enemy against the coast or calling on one of the Panzergruppen of Army Group Centre to provide one claw of the pincer. Encirclements in the centre, on the other hand, could be carried out by Army Group Centre without calling on either of the other army groups for assistance.

A triple choice of targets
There were three particularly enticing prizes, one for each of the army groups. For Army Group North there was Leningrad, birthplace of the October Revolution which had brought the Communists to power in 1917, former capital of the Russian Empire, second city of the Soviet Union, major industrial

centre and the base of the Baltic Fleet. For Army Group Centre there was Moscow, the capital, also a major industrial centre, a Holy City not merely of Communism but of 'Mother Russia' too. Army Group South's major target was Kiev, third largest city in the Soviet Union, the centre of Slav Christianity when Moscow was still a village.

Now Kiev was the capital of the Ukraine, second most important of the Soviet Republics — a republic, moreover, many of whose inhabitants were showing an unusual but gratifying tendency to greet the German army as liberators. More mundanely, Kiev was the key to the huge Kharkov industrial region, a major source of Soviet heavy industry, coal, and oil. Because of the sparseness of the Soviet rail and road systems, most of the oil and petrol from the Caucasus also had to pass through the eastern end of this region on its way to the rest of the Soviet Union.

These were good targets. To those who might say that the business of an army is first of all to destroy the opposing army, and only secondarily to accumulate real estate, there was a ready answer. All of them were so important to the Soviet Union that none would be left undefended. To attack them would mean attacking the main forces of the Red Army. Besides, was not Stalin busily ordering 'Not One Step Back'? Was not STAVKA — the Soviet High Command — helping to place the noose round the Red Army's neck by its insistence on linear defence and futile frontal attacks? Ironically enough, Rundstedt had been among the number of senior German generals who opposed the attack on the Soviet Union. Hitler had taken account of their objections to the extent that he laid down the need to defeat the Red Army before it could retreat into the vast spaces east of the Dniepr. And Stalin and STAVKA, by their opposition to strategic withdrawal, were playing right into his hands.

The German High Command had made no plans to operate in the Pripet marshes, which it considered unsuitable terrain for a modern army. There was, therefore, a broad gap between Army Groups Centre and South, and when I Panzergruppe swept the Soviet 5th Army aside, the latter based itself on the marshy areas, hanging threateningly over the northern flank and rear of the German VI Army, and causing its Commander-in-Chief, Field-Marshal von Reichenau, to glance uneasily over his shoulder from time to time. On July 10 Stalin ordered 5th Army south, and it struck from Korosten towards Novograd Volynski. At the same time, the Soviet 6th Army attacked north-west from Kazatin. The object was to close a pincers on I Panzergruppe west of Kiev, and catch the German in his own trap.

The plan misfired. The German divisions formed defensive fronts to north and south, held firm, then counterattacked; and soon the Soviet assault had degenerated into a fruitless attempt to pinch off the tip of a salient between Zhitomir and Berdichev. Here six very battered Red Army tank corps held up I Panzergruppe for several days, and thus enabled the Soviet 6th, 12th, and 26th Armies to withdraw from the threatened encirclement. But the losses in the tank corps were immense; nor could relief at evading encirclement hide the fact that the object of the exercise had been to inflict a major defeat on I Panzergruppe, not to trade space for men.

Some Soviet units were newly-   ▷

△German tank commanders search the terrain for enemy units
▽German infantry patrol in house-to-house fighting

△Soviet tanks caught and knocked out by direct hits
▽A German section enters a shattered Soviet block-house

equipped with the redoubtable T-34 tank, which outclassed anything the Germans had, and made something of an impression; but for the time being, the Red Army did not have enough of these tanks, nor as yet were the crews sufficiently familiar with this remarkable weapon to extract its full value from it. The Germans improvised an answer to it by using the 88-mm guns of their II Flak Corps. This was an equally remarkable weapon in its way; although designed as an anti-aircraft gun, it had been discovered to be very effective against tanks and had already been used in that role in Africa. With its aid, the Germans were able for the moment to breathe more freely.

When the southern claw of the Soviet pincer had been broken, the Soviet 5th Army recoiled back to the marshes of the Korosten fortified region, where it resumed its role of hanging over Reichenau's left flank. This was to have important consequences later. For the moment, however, that sector of the front remained quiet.

Failure of the Soviet counteroffensive had now placed Kiev in immediate peril. For on July 11 Kleist's XIII and XIV Panzer Divisions (which had been too far east to be caught in the Zhitomir/Berdichev battles) had reached the Irpen river, less than 10 miles from the city.

There could be no question of their taking Kiev. Apart from the inherent unsuitability of Panzer divisions for streetfighting, and the fact that they were too scarce and valuable to be wasted on such tasks, the Soviet administration was doing its best to turn Kiev into an armed camp. Already a militia (opolchenie) of 29,000 men existed, and defence lines were being built to supplement those erected in the early 1930's, when the frontier with Poland had been uncomfortably close. To attempt to fight a way in would have been an unprofitable course for Rundstedt, who believed firmly that towns should be outflanked, not fought over. His optimum course was to create a danger of encirclement, so as to cause the Soviet forces to withdraw into the open steppes, where superior German mobility could exercise its full effect. He therefore told I Panzergruppe that 'A coup de main against Kiev can only come into question when the local commander believes himself to have a favourable opportunity to exploit'—that is, go in if the going is easy, but not otherwise. General Mackensen probed the defences with his XIII and XIV Panzer Divisions, found it was not going to be easy, and, quite rightly, did not go in.

So, on the ground, the war was going well for Germany; to make the picture even more favourable for them, the Rumanians began to move forward on July 10, along with the German XI Army. The Soviet 9th and 12th Armies which comprised the opposing South Front were already in some danger through the retreat of their neighbours of South-West Front. On July 16 Budenny therefore ordered the Commander of South Front, General Tyulenev, to abandon his dangerously exposed positions on the Kishinev/Izmail line, and concentrate his reserves at Uman. This was not too easy; the Zhmerinka/Odessa railway line had already been cut, and the weather was bad (heavy rain fell on most days in the first part of July, turning most of the unsurfaced tracks which did duty as roads in the area, into deep black mud). But somehow it was done.

As a threat to Odessa was now developing from the German/Rumanian thrust, two of the Soviet 9th Army's divisions, which had become separated from the main forces of South Front, were placed under the command of Lieutenant-General G. P. Sofronov under the title of 'Coastal Group of Forces' (later constituted 'Independent Coastal Army'). Plans were set in train for turning Odessa into a 'Black Sea Tobruk', capable of holding out under siege even if completely isolated from the main front. On July 17/18, STAVKA ordered Budenny to hold a line from Belaya Tserkov to the mouth of the Dniestr in front of Odessa, hoping thus to block the threat of encirclement of the inner wings of their South-West and South Fronts, and to restore a continuous front line. Presumably Tyulenev's force at Uman (slightly north of the proposed line's centre) was to be used as theatre reserve, to block any dangerous gaps which might develop.

At this stage, German strategic planning began to show signs of strain, and to follow the course of the argument, it is necessary to go back in time to early July.

German strategy and STAVKA's task

At that time, the Soviet Supreme Command's appreciation of German intentions assumed that Moscow was inevitably the main target. They had therefore decided to concentrate their main forces opposite Army Group Centre, on the grounds that this would not only provide frontal protection for Moscow itself, but would also limit German opportunities for strong offensives in the north or south in two ways. First, it would limit the forces available to them by forcing Army Group Centre to retain strong forces in the middle of the front; and second, any German attempt at deep penetration in the north or south would find a large Soviet force hanging over its inner flank. A strong defence should therefore be combined with counterattacks aimed at the exposed flanks of German forces and at the junctions between them.

If the Soviet troops could carry it through, this was a not unreasonable plan—the more so since enemy troops advancing into Russia from the west are in effect moving out of the neck of a funnel. The farther east they go, the longer the front becomes, and the wider the gaps between their elements. Furthermore, since the essence of German strategy was to achieve deep encirclements by thrusting forward mobile forces, large gaps were inevitably created between the Panzer and motorised infantry divisions rushing on ahead at 20 mph, and the infantry armies following on foot at 3½ mph. The German advance therefore tended to disperse the forces into a series of spearheads and shafts, and STAVKA's task was to sever the one from the other. They had clearly grasped the nature of their problem. The question was whether, after their severe handling in the battle of the frontiers, the Red Army's soldiers could do the job set them.

The attack by Soviet 5th and 6th Armies on July 10 had been an attempt at severing the I Panzergruppe spearhead from the VI Army shaft. The Soviet 5th Army had operated out of the gap between German Army Groups Centre and South, against the north flank of Kleist's Panzers, while Soviet 6th Army was meant to strike against his southern flank. The operation had failed, but it had caused the Germans some anxious moments, and its failure had not removed the threat presented by the Soviet 5th Army, which had merely retreated back to its start line. If this showed anything, it showed that there was still plenty of life in the 'Russian

bear'. Similar incidents had occurred elsewhere on the Eastern Front: here and there, resistance had collapsed with spectacular suddenness, but in many places the Red Army's surrounded formations showed themselves willing to fight their way out with fierce vigour, both receiving and inflicting heavy losses.

It has already been said that many of the senior generals of the German army—including the Commander-in-Chief (Field-Marshal von Brauchitsch), the Chief of General Staff of the Army (Colonel-General Halder), and Rundstedt himself—had opposed the invasion of Russia, and that Hitler had agreed to modify his plan so that it would bring about a quick decision by destroying the main forces of the Red Army before they could retreat across the Dniepr.

This decision brought large problems in its train. It demanded quick encirclement of large forces. This meant large encirclements. But larger encirclements meant that large holes were left in the ring, through which much of the Red Army could punch its way out. To achieve encirclements of the requisite size without leaving such holes, the Panzer forces of two army groups must be used (this was the decision which Hitler had earlier postponed). Otherwise Germany would have to settle for more modest encirclements; but this meant leaving large parts of the Red Army free from encirclement.

The plain fact was that the job was too big for Germany's resources; but this was not yet apparent.

Hitler was already beginning to show a preference for conquering the Ukraine before Moscow and Leningrad, when he said on July 8 that in any case he intended to raze both Moscow and Leningrad to the ground—something which he considered could be done by aircraft without affecting the ground operations—and that for the moment II Panzergruppe, on the southern wing of Army Group Centre, should continue eastwards, so that the Moscow direction would be covered if it was later necessary for part of Army Group Centre to turn south. Thus he shelved a decision for the moment.

On the same day Halder presented to him a highly optimistic Intelligence assessment, claiming that 89 of the 164 known Soviet divisions had already been destroyed, and that of the remainder, 18 were on secondary fronts, 11 unknown, and only 46 known to be still combat-worthy. Brauchitsch then made a modest proposal that the success at Berdichev be exploited by turning Kleist's Panzers south into the rear of the Soviet 6th and 12th Armies, to achieve a 'small decision'.

Hitler, on the other hand, favoured the seizure of Kiev and an advance down the west bank of the Dniepr, so as to achieve a 'big decision'. Brauchitsch objected that this was impossible because of supply difficulties, and Hitler conceded that first of all the strength of the opposition at Kiev would have to be ascertained. And there, for the moment, the matter was allowed to rest in the capable hands of Rundstedt. He dispatched Kleist at Kazatin, which was captured on July 15. South-West Front's only close-up lateral railroad was cut by this manoeuvre, and Budenny began to withdraw into the Dniepr bend.

But the troublesome Soviet 5th Army remained at Korosten, and its presence continued to dim the glittering picture conjured up by Kiev, Ukrainian coal, industry,

Russian *opolchentsy* (militiamen) surrender—the forerunners of the vast numbers of Soviet POWs netted in the battles of Uman and Kiev

and agriculture. Something would have to be done about it, and the matter was raised with Hitler on July 17.

The outcome was OKW Directive 33 of July 19. This ordered that after completing the operations at Smolensk, II Panzergruppe and the infantry of German II Army should turn south-east to destroy the Soviet 21st Army (which was opposite the right wing of Army Group Centre), and then in co-operation with Army Group South should destroy the Soviet 5th Army. At the same time, a concentric attack by Army Group South was to drive across the rear of the Soviet 6th and 12th Armies and destroy them as well. The remaining Panzer forces of Army Group Centre (III Panzergruppe) were to move north-eastwards to assist Army Group North, leaving the advance on Moscow to be continued by the infantry armies of Army Group Centre only.

This decision was tantamount to abandoning the decisive operations against the main Soviet forces in the centre. The collapse of their neighbours on the North-West and South-West Fronts would force the Soviets to continue retreating, but there would be no more major encirclements of them by the Germans in the centre: Fritz might run rings round Ivan in a tank, but he couldn't out-walk him.

Two days later Hitler, paying his first visit to his armies in the east, appeared at HQ Army Group North, where he exposed some of his reasoning. It was essential to take Leningrad soon, in order to stop interference by the Soviet Baltic Fleet with iron ore shipments from Sweden to Germany. The III Panzergruppe would therefore assist Army Group North by cutting the Leningrad/Moscow railway in order to hinder the transfer of Soviet forces to or from the area; this task must be undertaken as soon as III Panzergruppe was available—that is, in about five days time. As for Moscow, he didn't care, as 'Moscow for me is only a geographical concept'. Because of the general situation and the 'instability of the Slav character', the fall of Leningrad could bring about a complete collapse of Soviet resistance.

On July 23 another conference took place between Hitler, Brauchitsch, and Halder, at which Halder reported that the Red Army forces now facing Germany numbered 93 divisions of which 13 were armoured. None of the participants seems to have commented on the fact that in the 15 days since his previous report—15 days of hard and successful operations by the Wehrmacht—the Soviet forces had apparently almost doubled. But clearly, as Halder's own diary shows, the fierceness of the Russian resistance was beginning to make an impression. Despite Hitler's talk two days earlier of the possibility of an imminent Russian collapse, a note of uncertainty began to creep into the conversation. Halder reported that the combat capability of the German infantry divisions was 80%, but that the Panzers were down to 50%, that Army Group South would be over the Dniepr by mid-August, that very strong resistance was to be expected in the Moscow direction—and that the operations of Army Group North seemed to be a failure.

Hitler then emphasised that he believed in destroying the enemy wherever he could be found, but expressed the view that the Panzer formations could come in only at a later stage when there was no longer any great danger to rearward communications. Brauchitsch's disquiet over the more ambitious

encirclements had begun to communicate itself to the Führer; after one month's fighting it was becoming clear that the Russian campaign would perhaps be different from the 'manoeuvres with live ammunition' of 1939 and 1940.

Hitler had that day issued a supplement to Directive 33, laying down future tasks. For Army Group South he ordered the crossing of the Don in the direction of the Caucasus after seizure of the Kharkov industrial region—a task which Army Group South still had to carry out. Brauchitsch protested that the new supplement was quite impossible in view of the current situation at the front, and asked that it be withdrawn until present operations had been concluded; when OKW refused, he raised the question with the Führer.

While Hitler refused to wait until the next battle had been won before contemplating the next but one, he took the opportunity to expound his views on the way mobile battles should be fought, now that there was some experience of fighting the Red Army: While the enemy resists stubbornly, is being decisively led, and has forces available for counterstrokes, no operations with far-reaching aims should be carried out. The Panzer forces should confine themselves to small encirclements, thus giving the infantry a chance to consolidate success quickly, and freeing the Panzer forces for new missions.

In brief, while the aims were to remain grandiose, the means of attaining them were to be scaled down. But while he was no doubt wise to take account of Halder's report that the Panzer forces had been reduced in one month to 50% of the strength with which they had started, it does seem that a commensurate scaling-down of aims was needed if Hitler was to avoid the charge of instability of character which he had himself so recently levelled at the Slavs—not that this would have worried him.

Brauchitsch and Halder went away disgruntled, and wrote a minute, in which they set out their views. To attack Moscow with infantry alone would be difficult but possible, provided quick results were not looked for, but a decisive offensive against the capital would require II and III Panzergruppen, neither of which would now be available until early September. Thus Hitler's plan would present the enemy with a month's grace in which to collect new forces and build and occupy new defence lines. Moreover, the large Soviet group of forces in front of Moscow constituted a threat to the flanks of the other army groups and forced a dispersion of forces to guard against it as long as it remained in being. As to the idea of destroying Moscow from the air, there was no immediate expectation that the Luftwaffe would acquire bases near enough to operate on the necessary scale.

OKH asked once again for a re-examination of the tasks set to Army Group Centre, while admitting that there might be decisive economic factors unknown to them (Hitler was given to saying that his generals knew nothing about economics). Naturally, OKH would do what it was told, but it had great misgivings about the possible consequences: clearly, the Soviet objective was to last out until the winter. If they succeeded, then next spring Germany would have to face more new armies and would be involved in the war on two fronts which it had hoped to avoid. Surely, OKH argued, the best way out would be to attack Moscow. The Soviets would *have* to stand and fight there, so there would be no question of their armies escaping yet again. And if Germany won the battle she would possess the seat of government, the important industrial centre, and the heart of the rail system. Russia would be cut in two. An aim as important as this must take precedence over smaller operations designed to cut up part of the Red Army.

The minute was firm and cogent, though deferential, and argued its case well. General Jodl even tried to strengthen its arguments by remarking that since the Soviets would inevitably stand and defend it, an attack on Moscow would be merely an expression of the Führer's own dictum that the enemy's 'living force' must be attacked wherever it could be found.

But the minute was never sent. Even as the German High Command was debating whether it could kill the Soviet bear in the next two months, or would have to be content with crippling it, Marshal Timoshenko hurled several newly-raised armies into a counteroffensive in the centre, attempting to relieve the large pocket of forces surrounded at Smolensk. All thoughts of Moscow, Kiev, and Leningrad had to be put aside for the time being, and swift improvisation became the order of the day.

The Russian attacks failed in their immediate objective—to wrest the initiative from Army Group Centre and relieve the trapped Soviet 16th and 20th Armies. The Russians were ill-prepared, and there were still too many futile frontal attacks, with new forces committed piecemeal—probably because Timoshenko was not aware of the degree to which the Germans were stretched, and thus was led to overestimate the immediate danger to Moscow. But the mere readiness to attack, and the appearance of large numbers of new formations, intensified still more the divisions of opinion among the German High Command, and led to further diversion of effort.

Opposition from Guderian
The first fruit of the hasty Soviet counteroffensive was a meeting of army commanders of the German Army Group Centre on July 27 at Novy Borisov. Guderian arrived, expecting to be ordered to push on to Moscow—or at least, to Bryansk—but found instead a memorandum from Brauchitsch explicitly ruling out either possibility and stating that the first priority was destruction of the Soviet forces 'in the Gomel area'—that is, the Soviet 5th Army. Again, by continuing to exist in the rear of the German main forces, the 5th Army had succeeded in making the enemy look backwards and diverting their attention from the glittering prospects in front of them.

Guderian was astounded. Here was he, the man whose studies and labour had given Germany the forces with which he himself had then conquered most of Europe, being asked to turn in his tracks and 'advance' back towards Germany, to finish off forces which he had long left behind and which he maintained should be dealt with by infantry. Brauchitsch was, of course, merely implementing Hitler's cautions about ambitious encirclements mentioned in discussion of Directive 33, but Guderian knew nothing of this except for what he gleaned in a disjointed fashion from officers at the Army Group HQs. Of these, the man whom he knew to be least enthusiastic about his armoured dashes was Field-Marshal von

Kluge, Commander-in-Chief of IV Army, to whom Guderian was uneasily and reluctantly subordinate. It is unlikely, therefore, that Guderian realised the full extent of the debate, or all the factors involved in it, and he left the conference in a mood of wounded pride, only partially assuaged by the fact that II Panzergruppe was renamed 'Army Group Guderian', and made subordinate not to Kluge but to the Commander-in-Chief of Army Group Centre, Field-Marshal von Bock.

This new freedom from the restraints imposed by Kluge—a man of some guile, known in the Army as *'Kluge Hans'* ('crafty Hans') and not one to inspire loyalty in his colleagues—was used by Guderian to distort and wilfully misinterpret the directions he had been given at Novy Borisov. He was convinced that the main threat to Army Group Centre was not the Soviet 5th Army in his deep rear, but the forces assembling on his right flank north of Roslavl, and he continued to believe this 'irrespective of any decisions Hitler might now take'.

This threat which he perceived took the form of a grouping described by the STAVKA as the 'Group of Forces of 28th Army', under the command of Lieutenant-General Kachalov, which had been assembled to help relieve the Smolensk pocket. Guderian proposed to Bock that Roslavl be captured, on the grounds that its seizure would give mastery of routes to the east, south, and south-west (thus making available a number of possibilities for continuing the offensive), and was allotted additional forces (the four divisions of VII Army Corps). To relieve Panzer divisions withdrawn from the Yelnya bulge for use in the Roslavl operation, XX Army Corps (two divisions) was earmarked. Guderian was also given a cavalry division.

The necessary preparations took some days, and during this period Guderian received several visitors. On July 29 Hitler's chief adjutant, Colonel Schmundt, arrived, ostensibly to present Guderian with the Oak Leaves to his Iron Cross, but really to discuss his plans with him. He indicated that Hitler had not yet decided between Leningrad, Moscow, and the Ukraine. There is no evidence as to whether Schmundt was being particularly discreet or particularly stupid, since Hitler had in fact been indicating his lack of interest in Moscow for some time and was the very next day to issue Directive 34, which ordered Army Group Centre to cease its advance and go on to the defensive.

Guderian took advantage of the opportunity to urge a direct push on Moscow and also to put in a bid for new tanks and tank engines. On the 31st, the OKH liaison officer, Major von Bredow, turned up to report that 'OKH and the Chief of General Staff are engaged in a thankless undertaking, since the conduct of all operations is being controlled from the very highest level. Final decisions on the future course of events have not yet been taken.' Put more simply, this was a complaint about Hitler's interference, and a tacit invitation to Guderian to influence the decisions not yet taken by his own actions of the present and immediate future.

The attack on Roslavl was launched on August 1. By the 3rd, the town was in German hands, with 38,000 prisoners and 200 guns, and by the 8th all resistance had ceased. It had been a brilliant and rapid victory, but its very ease, and the small number of guns taken, should have shown

Guderian that he had been wrong. This was no force assembled to pose a major threat. Rather it was a hastily assembled scratch team, not much more than three divisions plus support elements—small indeed, by the standards of the Eastern Front—but neither Guderian nor any other German general has to date even remarked on this aspect of the Roslavl diversion.

Eleven days had now elapsed since the decision had been taken to eliminate the Soviet 5th Army, and nothing had been done about it. Not even the closing of the Smolensk battle on August 5—with the Soviet 16th Army and 23rd Mechanised Corps wiped out, along with parts of the 19th and 20th Armies, 300,000 prisoners, 3,200 tanks, and 3,100 guns taken—could compensate for this failure.

Nor had the Roslavl episode contributed to easing the task of Army Group South. All it had done was to keep the Moscow option open, by keeping II Panzergruppe up forward. Its effects on the battle for 'right-bank Ukraine' now remain to be considered.

Hitler had ordered the closing of the Uman pocket on July 24. Although Kleist had wanted something more ambitious—namely to encircle Kiev from the south with one corps, and send his other two corps plunging down across the rear of both South-West and South Soviet Fronts—he complied with the Directive, apparently without protest. On July 30, I Panzergruppe struck deep into the columns of Red Army troops withdrawing from the pocket, wheeled towards the south-west, and on August 3 linked up with the forward elements of Colonel-General von Stülpnagel's XVII Army near Pervomaisk, enclosing two Soviet armies (6th and 12th), and parts of another (18th)—a total of 15 infantry and five armoured divisions. Though some of the Soviet formations succeeded in fighting their way out, resistance in the pocket ended on August 8. About 100,000 prisoners were taken, together with the commanders of the two trapped armies (Generals Muzychenko and Ponedelin), 317 tanks, and 1,100 guns.

At the southern end of the front, where the main weight was to be carried by the Rumanian III and IV Armies, events at first moved more slowly, and such progress as there had been was as much the result of premeditated Soviet withdrawals as of actual fighting gains. However, the withdrawal of Soviet forces into the Uman pocket left South Front very thin on the ground, and by the beginning of August, Odessa was accessible only by sea. The Rumanian III Army settled down to invest it on August 5, leaving the German XI Army to continue the drive eastwards, and with the Uman disaster and beginning of the 73-day siege of Odessa, the Soviet Supreme Command could no longer delude itself that the situation on the South-West Front was under control.

New Soviet plan
Soviet reserves therefore began to pour into the area. But STAVKA was already learning from its earlier mistakes. This time there was to be no piecemeal commitment of half-trained divisions into frontal attacks. The new divisions (ten to South-West Front, 12 to South Front, and two into Front Reserve) were mostly put into preparing a defensive line along the east bank of the Dniepr, and to helping remove industrial equipment. West of the Dniepr, delaying

actions would be fought to gain time for removing or destroying the factories. The Red Army was already painfully aware of the contribution being made by western European industry to the German war effort – and its leaders were determined that Germany should derive no such benefit from captured Soviet industry. What could be moved would be set up again in the Urals or Siberia; even if it rusted away in railway sidings or open fields (and much of it did), it would not be used to kill its true owners. What could not be moved would be destroyed. Even if subsequently repaired by the Germans (and much of it was), the time during which it was out of action was itself worth gaining.

As to the Red Army itself, there must be no repetition of the mass surrenders of encircled formations. The Head of the Political Propaganda Directorate (Army Commissar First Rank L. Z. Mekhlis) issued two directives. One ordered political commissars to emphasise that surrounded units must either fight their way out or, if that proved impossible, must operate against the enemy rear for as long as they could. The other directive exhorted Communist Party and Communist Youth League members to set an example and provide leadership. Stalin still did not believe that the professional soldiers could be trusted to do their best, and he had already restored the political commissars in the forces to a position of equality with their unit commanders – in effect making them responsible for the reliability of the professional military.

Hitler, meanwhile, was, also having his difficulties with generals – particularly those of Army Group Centre, on whom Moscow continued to exert a fatal attraction. On August 4 he arrived at Novy Borisov to hold a rather unusual 'conference': rather than allow professional solidarity to work upon him, he interviewed the army commanders separately, beginning with Halder's representative, Colonel Heusinger, and following with Bock, Guderian, and Hoth.

Though all recommended an advance on Moscow, Bock claimed that he was ready to start at once, whereas both his Panzer commanders admitted that this was not the case. Guderian would not be ready until August 15, and Hoth needed five days more than that, both stressing the need for new tank engines. Hitler reluctantly promised 300 for the whole of the Eastern Front; Guderian rightly described this as totally inadequate, but Hitler refused to budge, and also refused to provide any new tanks, on the grounds that he needed them for equipping new Panzer formations being raised in Germany. Guderian re-emphasised the need to make good the tank losses, as the Red Army, despite its losses, still had a numerical superiority in tanks. Then Hitler made the statement – extraordinary in the context of his refusal to provide more tanks – that if he had believed Guderian's 1937 estimate of Soviet tank strength, he would not have started the war.

Guderian left the meeting determined to prepare the attack on Moscow, whatever Hitler might intend; Hitler returned to his HQ at Rastenburg in East Prussia, in no doubt about his unpopularity with Army Group Centre. He was, however, unaware that a group of Bock's staff officers had in fact planned to arrest and depose him during his visit, but had had to call off the attempt. The principals in the unsuccessful plot

were very close to Bock himself (one, Fabian von Schlabrendorff, was Bock's ADC, and two years later was to make another unsuccessful attempt, by planting in Hitler's aircraft a captured British bomb which failed to explode), and Bock may well have known about the plot.

Hitler's remark to Guderian about Red Army tank strength showed that he was beginning to have doubts, despite the successes so far gained. Many of his generals were now showing signs of disquiet at the continued fierce resistance of the Red Army. And the troops themselves were, as their letters home showed, becoming uneasy when faced with the apparently endless plains and the fact that no matter how many Russians they killed or captured, next day found the Red Army still in business and apparently as vigorous as ever. Though the greatest successes might perhaps still lie ahead, the situation was not altogether as cheerful as the bold arrows on the maps, and the tallies of captured men and material, might indicate.

It had now become a question of nerve. OKH was disgruntled but still obedient; Army Group Centre, hypnotised by Moscow, was openly thwarting the directives it received from OKH; and Guderian was stubbornly trying to keep his Panzers in positions from which they could resume the eastward march. But while he was doing this, most of III Panzergruppe was busily redeploying as ordered, to assist Army Group North in its move against Leningrad – its commander, Hoth, apparently being the only senior officer in Army Group Centre who still believed in doing what he was told.

Kiev remains unattained

The net result was a dispersion of effort and energy which furthered none of the objectives. While Guderian was finding reasons why he should not go back to Gomel to deal with the Soviet 5th Army, and was submitting unacceptable plans to take Moscow, Army Group South stalled yet again in front of Kiev. The Commander-in-Chief of German VI Army (Reichenau) looked once more over his shoulder at the Pripet marshes, and saw that between him and the II Army of Army Group Centre was a gap of 150 miles. Sixty miles of this was covered by only one division (56th Infantry), while facing it were several divisions of Soviet 5th Army. Reichenau's orders were to press ahead with a direct attack on Kiev, but in the circumstances, not unnaturally, he objected to Rundstedt. OKH refused to commit itself either way, so, on August 9, Rundstedt called off the offensive in the Kiev/Korosten area, and VI Army resumed the defensive with its primary operational objective – Kiev – unattained.

An analysis of the situation, made in OKW on the evening of the next day, showed the emergence of an uneasy compromise, designed to pacify the 'Moscow' faction without yielding to it. It was agreed that the main enemy forces were in front of Army Group Centre, and that the most important task was to destroy them and seize Moscow; but, it was argued, the forces facing the other two army groups constituted a threat to Army Group Centre's flanks. Therefore the decisive attack on Moscow must be preceded by operations with limited aims against the forces in north and south.

On the assumption that destruction of these forces would take two weeks, a general offensive against Moscow, with infantry

armies in the centre, and a Panzergruppe on each flank, could begin at the end of August. The enemy would be forced to stand and fight with new and only partially trained forces on an incomplete defence line running roughly from Rzhev to Bryansk via Vyazma. If this plan were adopted, Army Groups North and South would have to deal with their enemies, for the time being, without assistance from Army Group Centre – though with complete assurance that once it had broken through the Soviet defences and begun the pursuit, it would be able to release some of its forces to assist them.

As for Army Group South, its XVII Army was at present free for use, and should be employed in forcing the Dniepr between Kiev and Kremenchug, in order to break up the large Soviet forces forming up on the east bank. When the Dniepr line had been forced, part of Army Group South should turn north into the rear of the Soviet 5th Army, so as to put paid to it once and for all.

On August 12 Hitler again emphasised that the precondition for all future operations was prior destruction of enemy forces on the flanks, in particular those on the right flank of Army Group Centre – that is, the Soviet South-West Front. On the same day Budenny and Khrushchev wrote to Stalin in some uneasiness. They had observed that the German II Army and Guderian's Panzers were making progress towards Gomel and Starodub, and had concluded that their object was to smash down behind South-West Front and cut it off.

STAVKA, however, was just as hypnotised by Moscow as was Army Group Centre. Its assessment was that the object of the movement which worried Budenny and Khrushchev was to exploit the large gap which had opened between Reserve and Central Fronts, and that the Germans would turn east into it, to break through at Bryansk and outflank Moscow from the south. Budenny had asked permission to withdraw 5th Army and 27th Independent Corps from the Korosten Fortified Region, form a front to the north with them, and thus block the German drive across the rear of his South-West Front. STAVKA refused, and instead ordered the formation of Bryansk Front, at first with responsibility only to fill the gap between Central and Reserve Fronts and prevent a German breakthrough to Moscow.

In the light of the information then available to it, it cannot be said that STAVKA's decision was unreasonable: as has already been said, Guderian tried to the last to keep the Moscow option open, and Hitler had not yet firmly ruled it out. Furthermore, the Soviet 5th Army was in fact doing a very important job simply by hovering over the German rear; to withdraw it over the Desna, as Budenny wanted to do, would have relieved OKH and Army Group South of one of their worst headaches, and this was a good reason for keeping it where it was. But the decision, reasonable though it seemed, turned out to be a disastrous mistake in the end. For the Germans were at last making up their minds what to do. And STAVKA's guess – that Moscow would be the target – was wrong.

On August 15 Hitler abandoned the pretence that Army Group Centre could continue its offensive on Moscow with infantry only, for he had by now probably realised the extent to which its generals were abusing the concession. He therefore ordered a complete halt to the advance on Moscow:

THE STEEL CLAWS OF THE PINCER WERE CLOSING FAST

'Mass, not driblets' was Guderian's precept for the use of tanks in battle; but the Red Army's tanks were used in ones and twos—and suffered accordingly. Photographed by German tank crews during the first months in Russia: (Above) A Soviet light tank, knocked out in the steppe. (Below) A Panzer formation moving up for another attack

Army Group Centre was to organise a defence which the Soviets could not encircle, one which could be held without substantial air support and which would be economical in its use of infantry. Three days later Brauchitsch made a last desperate plea for the Moscow operation. He pointed out that the onset of winter in the Moscow area could be expected in mid-October, five weeks earlier than in the Ukraine, and argued that concentration on Moscow would make its capture possible before the bad weather set in, thus freeing forces for use in the South where the campaigning season was longer.

In reply, Hitler rejected Brauchitsch's arguments out of hand, and set out his own views. He repeated his contention that the Panzer columns, by outstripping the infantry and operating too independently, had produced only partial encirclements from which large numbers of the enemy had been able to escape. His rejection of OKW's proposals for a Moscow operation was formalised as a directive, issued on August 21, which laid down, in clear and unambiguous terms, the tasks to be fulfilled before the onset of the winter.

There was nothing surprising in it, given Hitler's known views, but this time there were no loopholes which the generals of Army Group Centre could exploit. The directive stated that the taking of Moscow before the winter was not a primary objective. The first priorities in the south were the taking of the Crimea and the industrial and coal area of the Donets basin, together with the cutting of the supply routes for Caucasus oil. And in the north the aims were to invest Leningrad and establish contact with the Finns.

As for Army Group Centre, it must join Army Group South in a concentric operation against the Soviet 5th Army, with the objective of not merely driving it back across the Dniepr (as would be the case if VI Army alone conducted the operation), but of destroying it, so as to give Army Group South the necessary security for its further operations across the Dniepr and into the Donets basin. Capture of the Crimea was of extreme importance for safeguarding oil supplies from Rumania. (So much for a suggestion by OKW that it would be sufficient to cut it off: Hitler had frequently shown anxiety over the threat to the Ploesti oilfields which Soviet bombers could pose from airfields in the Crimea.)

This, then, was the vital decision. The idea of the actual capture of Leningrad was quietly given up—not surprising in view of Army Group North's stalled offensive—and Moscow was ruled out. Soviet 5th Army was to be disposed of once and for all, and then the main effort was to be in the Ukraine. Nothing could be plainer.

Yet even now there was to be one last attempt to keep the Moscow operation alive. On August 23, a conference was held at HQ Army Group Centre, at which Halder outlined the provisions of the directive. There was then a long discussion of ways in which the Führer's mind might be changed, and it was finally decided that Guderian should go back to Hitler's HQ with Halder. They set off that afternoon, landing at Lötzen (the nearest airfield to Rastenburg) at dusk. Guderian reported immediately to Brauchitsch, who categorically forbade him to reopen the question of Moscow with Hitler. But Guderian was by now not to be stopped by anyone, and in reporting on the state of his Panzergruppe he contrived to lead the

conversation around so that Hitler himself introduced the subject. The Panzer general repeated all the old arguments for an attack on the Soviet capital, adding that the troops were expecting it, and were prepared for it. Army Group Centre was poised ready for it, and a long detour into the south would cause heavy additional wear and tear, as well as loss of time.

Hitler heard him out without challenging any of his statements. (The one that Army Group Centre was poised for an attack on Moscow was particularly dubious: both Panzergruppen were short of the new engines and tanks required for such a major undertaking as the Moscow operation, and neither was suitably deployed, Hoth's tanks being away assisting Army Group North, and Guderian's partly engaged in a southward move around Starodub.) But Hitler was not to be moved; the Moscow offensive was absolutely excluded until the operation in the south had been brought to a successful conclusion.

Guderian bowed to the inevitable, and suggested that his whole Panzergruppe, rather than part of it, be committed to the southern operation to ensure success. Hitler agreed, and Guderian returned at once to Army Group Centre. The next morning he broke the news to Halder, and an angry scene ensued, the details of which will never be known, as there were no witnesses, and the accounts of the two principals differ in a number of important respects. Anyway, it did not matter. There would be no more argument. Kiev it was to be, and the only question now was whether the Red Army could avert the danger which hung over its forces in the south.

It has already been said that the Military Council of Soviet South-West Front had become uneasy as early as August 12. On August 18 General Zhukov, former Chief of General Staff, victor over the Japanese in Mongolia in 1939 and now commanding Reserve Front before Moscow, noticed that the Germans facing him had become less active. On discovering that the same was true on the adjacent Central Front, he began considering why this should be so. Hitler's decision to stop the advance on Moscow had already been taken three days earlier, but had not yet been promulgated in the form of a directive. It is possible that the commanders of the infantry armies (whose enthusiasm for the Moscow offensive had never been as warm as that of Bock and the Panzer generals) had got wind of it through their own unofficial channels and decided to ease off in anticipation of the new orders. Also, part of Guderian's force had been probing around Starodub for some days. Nevertheless, Zhukov was in fact contemplating a fluid situation and his information was incomplete. This mattered less with him than with most: his subsequent career was to show that he was extremely gifted at reading the enemy's intentions; and he was to become the most successful Soviet general, largely through his capacity to foresee what the Germans would do and dispose his forces to foil them.

But in this situation, he had no powers to dictate what STAVKA should do. All he could do was to warn and suggest. So he wrote to STAVKA on August 18, indicating that he thought the Germans might be regrouping for a drive southwards across the rear of Kiev and South-West Front, and suggesting that a strong force be established in the Bryansk area, with the aim of driving

in Guderian's flank as he moved across in front of them. STAVKA replied, accepting his assessment, and claiming that it had already foreseen the danger and had, for this reason, established Bryansk Front a few days before. It is doubtful whether this was true. The front commander, General Yeremenko, has subsequently claimed that his orders were to guard against a breakthrough towards Moscow, and this may well have been his initial directive.

On August 19 STAVKA belatedly granted Budenny's request for permission to withdraw all his forces beyond the Dniepr, ordering only that 37th Army remain in Kiev. The withdrawn forces (5th Army and a new 40th, made up of remnants of other armies) was to form line to the north, defending Chernigov, Konotop, and Kharkov. So far, matters were moving along the right lines: the German intentions had been divined even before they were finalised, and dispositions made to meet Guderian both frontally and on his left flank. But this also meant that Budenny's bolt was shot; his units were thoroughly battered and combat-weary, and he had no reserves left for South-West Front. Everything now depended on Yeremenko.

Yeremenko's stab at the Panzers
On August 24, Stalin spoke to Yeremenko by telephone, offering him two more tank brigades, several tank battalions, some 'Katyusha' rocket batteries, and several air force regiments—'if you promise to beat that scoundrel Guderian'. He also offered another army (the 21st) formed from the tattered 3rd and 21st Armies of the Central Front, and this, too, Yeremenko accepted. The Chief of General Staff, Marshal Shaposhnikov, then came on the line, reintroducing the original STAVKA idea that Guderian might intend to turn through a right-angle and head north of Bryansk, making for Moscow. Thus he introduced a fatal ambiguity into Yeremenko's instructions, by inserting the fear that Bryansk Front might be left high and dry with neither its original nor its second mission accomplished. In an attempt to cover both contingencies, Yeremenko held back his strongest force (50th Army) to protect the routes to Moscow, and it took no part in the attempt to stop Guderian. Shaposhnikov's anxious caution thus inadvertently prejudiced the success of the counteroffensive a week before it began.

Nevertheless, the forces available to Yeremenko for his westward thrust were formidable. Central Front had been disbanded on August 25, and its forces subordinated to him. Thus he had two armies (13th and 21st), plus the entire High Command Reserve of aircraft and the air support forces of Central and Reserve Fronts to add to those of his own front. (So emaciated was the Red Air Force as a result of its earlier losses that even this force totalled only 464 aircraft, half of which were bombers.) STAVKA could do little more now. They, too, had no more reserves to spare.

The Soviet offensive began on August 30, when Yeremenko's troops moved forward to bite at Guderian's flanking force, the XLVII Mechanised Corps. Despite all their efforts, they made little impression, and further north and west the German II Army began to push back Yeremenko's 21st Army. The 21st recoiled back on to the small and hurriedly formed 40th Army of South-West Front, which soon broke and began retreating towards the south-east. Thus the 21st Army was soon completely cut off from the

German assault-troops press home attacks on the Soviet fortifications of the Stalin Line

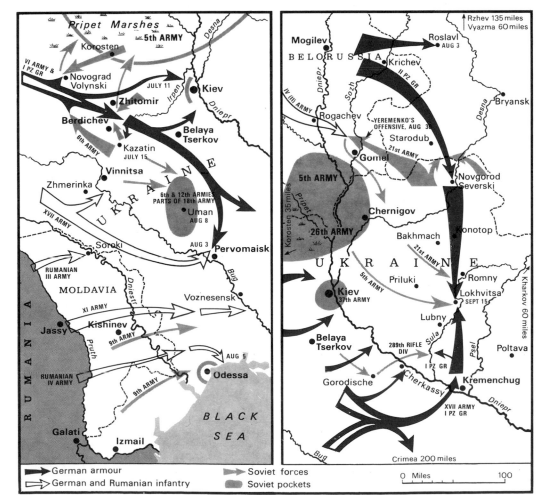

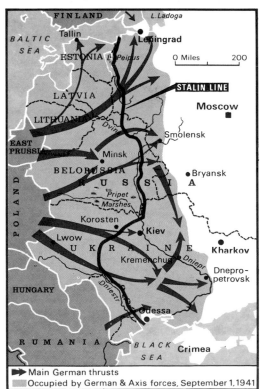

The annihilation-battles of Uman and Kiev, in which the Germans killed and captured 665,000 men —nearly one-third of the entire strength of the Red Army at the outbreak of Barbarossa. The Ukraine, whose industrial and agricultural wealth had obsessed Hitler, was open to the Germans

The Eastern Front by the end of September 1941 had been pushed deep into Russia. The assaults of the three army groups had succeeded in shattering the original dispositions of the Red Army, and Hitler was now ready to resume the advance on Moscow. On the map, Barbarossa seemed well on the way to completion; but now the rains and mud of the Russian autumn were at hand. Barbarossa had not eliminated the Soviet Union in the dry 'campaigning season' of 1941—the Blitzkrieg had met its match

rest of Bryansk Front, having been deeply penetrated on both sides—by the German II Army to the west of it, and by Guderian's Panzers to its east. It began to withdraw hastily to the south-east, completely out of contact with the High Command, and with German troops pouring into the gaps on each side of it.

STAVKA had laid too heavy a task on Bryansk Front, and having done so, was reluctant to believe that Yeremenko could not pull it off. On September 2 Stalin wrote petulantly to him and Petrov (the Deputy C-in-C of the Air Force, who was controlling the air support): 'STAVKA is still not satisfied with your work. . . . You have rattled the enemy just a little, but you haven't succeeded in driving him off his positions. Guderian and all his group must be smashed to pieces. Until this is done, all that you say about successes is worthless. We are waiting for you to report that you have defeated Guderian's group.'

More forces pour in

When it became clear that the Yeremenko counteroffensive was not succeeding, STAVKA's reaction was not to liquidate the undertaking but to pour more forces into it from other sections of the line. The Chief of General Staff (Shaposhnikov) ordered Budenny to hand over his 2nd Cavalry Corps, and this, for the old revolutionary, was the last straw. On September 10 he spoke to Shaposhnikov by radio, pointing out that this was his only reserve for southern front on the whole Dnepropetrovsk/ Kharkov line (a distance of about 125 miles) and saying: 'I ask you to turn your attention to what Yeremenko's doing. He was supposed to stop this enemy group, but nothing's come of it.' Shaposhnikov, however, insisted, and the exasperated Budenny said: 'All right . . . the order to move will be issued right away. Please report my views to the Supreme Commander [Stalin], especially about the operations of Bryansk Front.'

The following day, the Military Council of South-West Front (Budenny, Khrushchev, and Pokrovsky) addressed themselves directly to Stalin. They formally requested permission to withdraw their forces to the east, pointing out that the entire South-West Front was now in serious danger of encirclement from the direction of Novgorod Severski (Guderian's starting point) and Kremenchug (where Kleist's I Panzergruppe and German XVII Army had established a bridgehead over the Dniepr, from which Kleist was hastening north to link up with Guderian). They stated that they had already asked Shaposhnikov for permission to withdraw, and that he had refused, ordering them instead to move two of 26th Army's divisions to block Guderian between Bakhmach and Konotop. Clearly they felt that Shaposhnikov was losing his grip under pressure of events—to carry out this order would have left one remaining division of 26th Army (less than 10,000 men, bearing in mind that it had already seen much action) to guard 100 miles of the Dniepr against German forces which outnumbered it by more than six to one.

Stalin at once contacted the Commander of South-West Front, Colonel-General Kirponos, and sought his views. Kirponos said firmly that his front should be withdrawn from the Kiev salient to the line of the River Psel, some 150 miles to the east. But this Stalin categorically rejected. He ordered Kirponos to hold Kiev at whatever

cost, and to move in all forces that could be brought there. Since Budenny was heading a consensus for withdrawal, Stalin dismissed him, appointing in his place Marshal Timoshenko, a former People's Commissar for Defence (Defence Minister) and so far the most successful of the older generation of Soviet soldiers. But by now it was too late to save the situation. The gap between Guderian and Kleist was less than 60 miles wide, and the Panzergruppen were moving towards each other far faster than the encircled Soviet forces could move towards the shrinking corridor. Even if they started at once, most of them would probably not get through. Yet Shaposhnikov, presumably obeying Stalin's orders, would still not allow them to move. On September 14 Kirponos' Chief-of-Staff, Major-General Tupikov, emphasised to him yet again the dangers inherent in the situation, ending with the words: 'The beginning of the catastrophe about which you know, is a matter of a couple of days.' Shaposhnikov described his report as 'panicky', demanded that the Commands of Direction and Front remain calm, and reminded Tupikov and Kirponos: 'You must carry out the orders [to hold Kiev] which Comrade Stalin gave you on September 11.'

Far from being panicky, Tupikov's assessment was, if anything, optimistic. Guderian, travelling with III Panzer Division at the head of II Panzergruppe, met Kleist's tanks near the school at Lokhvitsa on September 15. Four Soviet Armies (5th, 21st, 26th, and 37th) were trapped. South-West Front was falling apart, and its communications were soon in such a state of chaos that Timoshenko the next day ordered his forces east of the German cordon to hold open the corridor to the east, unaware that there was now no corridor left. He and Khrushchev decided to abandon Kiev in defiance of Stalin's order, and Major-General Bagramyan, of Timoshenko's staff, was sent to give the order verbally to Kirponos at Priluki. Kirponos refused to accept it as authentic, insisting on seeking guidance from STAVKA, so more valuable time was lost.

While Stalin and Shaposhnikov were debating the question in Moscow, the German ring was hardening. Only at 2340 hours on the following day (September 17) did STAVKA reply, authorising the abandonment of Kiev. Two nights which could have been used for extricating troops (movement by day was almost impossible, so complete by now was the German air superiority) had been wasted, and what would in any case have been a major defeat was turned by Stalin's vacillation into a catastrophe. The choice for Kirponos and South-West Front was now only between the frying-pan of Kiev and the fire of the open steppe. There was no safety to be found anywhere.

Kiev: the killing-ground

In the middle of the night of September 17/18, Kirponos ordered all his armies to fight their way out of the cauldron. The 21st Army was to attack towards Romny, where the 2nd Cavalry Corps (yielded up by Budenny a week earlier at Shaposhnikov's insistence) was trying to force an opening through from the east; 5th Army was to make for the junction between I and II Panzergruppen at Lokhvitsa, with 37th Army following it; and 26th Army was to beat its way out through Lubny.

But the breakthrough was fated from the start. Already 37th Army, defending the

city area of Kiev itself, had lost contact, never received the order to break out, and surrendered in the city after fighting on for two days. Within a few hours, Kirponos had lost contact with the other three armies and with STAVKA.

South-West Front now existed only in name; the only part of it still under Kirponos' command was the 289th Rifle Division, to which he and his staff had attached themselves, but even this became dispersed in the course of the night, and by the time it reached Gorodishche only some 3,000 men were left. These were split into several detachments, one of which Kirponos followed, with the Military Councils and Staffs of South-West Front and of 5th Army. That day, they were surrounded in Shumeikovo Grove, and a mere handful of staff officers broke through to the Sula River two days later. They found the Germans already there, but somehow or other a few of them slipped through. They did not include any of the Military Council of South-West Front: all three (Kirponos, Burmistenko, and Tupikov —whom Shaposhnikov had charged with 'panic' a week before) had been killed.

'The greatest catastrophe'

On the eastern side of the cauldron, the Red Army manned its positions and looked west, with dwindling hopes, for some sign of the encircled armies. Soon small groups began to arrive. Major-General Bagramyan, who had taken the order to retreat to Kirponos, came through with 50 men. General Kuznetsov, commanding 21st Army, brought out his survivors in good order, but they numbered only 500. General Kostenko brought out only a few men of his 26th Army. Brigade Commander Borisov came out with 4,000 cavalrymen. Senior Battalion Commissar Gorban led out 52 signallers from the front staff. And there were other detachments, but none were large.

Behind them, dead or imprisoned, were over 500,000 men—more than two-thirds of the strength of South-West Front at the beginning of the war. It was, in terms of numbers, the biggest catastrophe in Russian history, probably in all history, though its strategic consequences were not to prove as fatal as those of many a smaller battle.

The victory of Rundstedt's army group was the greatest single success of German arms. For Guderian (much though he would have preferred to go to Moscow), it was a complete justification of his concept of armoured warfare. Soon he would be able to test his ideas against Moscow itself, and see whether the Soviet preoccupation with that city (which had so harmed their assessments of other threats) would make them capable of defending it more effectively than they had defended Kiev.

But this would be the biggest test of all. And the campaigning season was beginning to run out. Much time had been lost in the south.

GEOFFREY JUKES was born in 1928, and was educated at Queen Elizabeth Grammar School, Carmarthen, and at Wadham College, Oxford. In 1953 he entered the civil service; and from 1956-65 was employed at the Ministry of Defence as a specialist in the affairs of the Soviet bloc, with particular reference to military history and strategy. In 1965 he joined the Foreign Office as a researcher into disarmament problems. He is also a member of the Institute of Strategic Studies.

BARBAROSSA
DRIVE TO KHARKOV

Ukraine, September/December 1941
Geoffrey Jukes

Rundstedt's great victory at Kiev was the prelude to the German invasion of the Ukraine which swept on towards Kharkov, fourth city of the USSR. But precious time had been lost; and as winter drew on, the contemptuous assessment of the Red Army on which 'Barbarossa' had been launched, was proved to be mistaken. Hitler had been terribly wrong: the door had been 'kicked in' at Smolensk, Kiev, and Kharkov all right—but the Red Army and the USSR had not collapsed under the Blitzkrieg, as Hitler had promised

After their victory at Kiev, men of Army Group South proceed with the drive into the southern Ukraine

The great battle for the western Ukraine was over by the end of September. The tiny remnants of four Soviet armies had dragged their way out of the German ring and been merged with other battered units to make up, in name at any rate, new divisions and armies.

The victorious Germans were themselves extremely stretched. Guderian, whose II Panzergruppe had closed the trap by its bold dash south across the front of several Red armies, took himself off to resume the attack on Moscow which he had been advocating all summer over the opposition of Hitler and the German High Command. This left in the Ukraine only the I Panzergruppe of Kleist, now worn down to about 300 tanks (half of its original strength) by three months of hard fighting and long movements over bad roads, together with the three German infantry armies (VI, XI, and XVII), the two Rumanian armies (III and IV), the Hungarian corps, the three divisions of the Italian Expeditionary Force, and the Slovak Light Division.

Though their morale was still high, the forces of Army Group South had taken some hard knocks in carrying out the first part of their task—the conquest of 'Left Bank Ukraine'. Now the autumn rains were beginning, and the second part of their assignment—seizure of the industrial area of eastern Ukraine—still lay before them. It was a daunting prospect.

For the exhausted soldiers of the Soviet Southern and South-West Fronts the outlook was even less cheering. The area which they had to deny to Germany was vital to the Soviet Union. It produced 60% of the Soviet coal, 30% of its iron, and 20% of its steel. Of every four electric power stations in the Soviet Union, three were there. So were two out of every three factories producing chemicals for the Soviet war effort. Three-fifths of the Soviet rail system lay within this area; in particular, the main line along which oil from the Caucasus was distributed ran through its eastern end.

Seizure of eastern Ukraine by the Germans might well cripple the Soviet ability to build up and equip the Red Army through the coming winter, isolate the Caucasus, and lend force to the German blandishments aimed at inducing Turkey to enter the war. Time had to be gained, or the Soviet Union's potential manpower advantage would never be translated into reality—time to evacuate factories from the areas which could not be held, to set them up elsewhere, so that they could begin producing equipment for the new armies being raised in the heartland; time to destroy what could not be moved, not only the machinery which the Germans might use, but the very buildings in which their armies might hope to sit out the winter; time to reorganise the shattered armies which had borne the brunt of the summer disasters and which, mainly through bad handling by their leaders, had lost so many men and so much equipment that they were now seriously outnumbered.

Against the six German and Rumanian Armies of Army Group South, with the Hungarian, Italian, and Slovak components equalling one more army, the Commander-in-Chief of the Soviet South-West Front, Marshal Timoshenko, had seven armies. Until October 16 one Rumanian Army (IV) was tied up besieging Odessa. And from the end of September one of the German armies (XI), was engaged in invading the Crimea, being joined there by IV Rumanian

Army after the Soviet evacuation of Odessa So it was seven Soviet armies against five of the Axis.

But this was not the full story. Even at full strength a Soviet army was much smaller than its German counterpart—and Timoshenko's armies were nowhere near full strength. In the middle of his line, General Feklenko's 38th Army had two infantry divisions, a tank division, and a 'mixed regiment' of 7,000 men. But although one of the infantry divisions was at full strength (about two-thirds the strength of a German division), the other had barely a third of its authorised strength—and only four field guns—while the tank division had just one tank. Most of Timoshenko's other armies were in the same state.

The Red Army had been badly hurt, and had already lost a great part of its experienced cadre. To create formations more easily handled by the many inexperienced middle-rank commanders, the rifle divisions were reduced in size and mechanised corps split up into armoured brigades. Perhaps most humiliating of all was the state of the artillery. Russian armies had always set great store by it, and its intimate association with the infantry was considered so important that each rifle division contained two artillery regiments. But the Red Army was now so short of artillery that its chief gunnery expert, Marshal of Artillery Voronov, could create a High Command Artillery Reserve only by persuading Stalin to authorise the removal from each rifle division of one of its artillery regiments. In time this would make possible a massed use of artillery unequalled elsewhere, but for the moment its short-term effects on the infantry's morale were unlikely to be favourable.

STAVKA no longer had manpower to spare for prodigal counterattacks. It was heavily engaged in the centre, where the German offensive against Moscow was expected any day. South Front had already been ordered to confine itself to firm defence, and on September 27 the same order went out to South-West Front. At the same time a group of senior officers was sent to prepare a belt of defences on the approaches to Kharkov and the Don basin.

The German plan was simple, almost

stereotyped. The I Panzergruppe would break out of its bridgehead on the Dniepr and Samara Rivers between Dnepropetrovsk and Novomoskovsk, and head south towards the shore of the Sea of Azov, behind the Soviet 9th, 12th, and 18th Armies which made up South Front. Kleist had wanted to try this manoeuvre on a larger scale during the battles in the western Ukraine. Now he was to be let off the leash for a 120-mile dash across the Soviet rear with his 300 tanks.

It was an ambitious plan for a force of this size, but not a foolhardy one. The three Soviet armies had between them less than two-thirds as many tanks as Kleist, and were short of anti-tank weapons. If the gamble succeeded, about 100,000 Soviet troops would be ground up between the Panzers and the infantry of General von Manstein's XI Army, which had put off its projected invasion of the Crimea in order to take part in the Azov operation.

The senior officers from STAVKA had no time to organise their belt of defences, for on September 30 I Panzergruppe erupted from its bridgehead at Novomoskovsk and, leaving the Italians to mop up, made straight for the main Soviet lateral supply route—the Kharkov/Zaporozhye railway.

Despite the efforts of a Soviet armoured train the line was reached and cut by the evening of the next day—a success which did not bode well for South Front. The autumn rains had already begun, and they would hinder both sides, as there were few hard-surfaced roads in the area. And now the lateral railway, the only all-weather route by which Soviet troops, supplies, and equipment could be transferred quickly between the various sections of the front, had been cut in two.

It soon began to look as if there would be no Soviet forces left to supply in the area south of the break. The German thrust out of the bridgehead had shattered the right wing of the Soviet 12th Army and there was practically nothing between the Panzers and the coast. The Commander of South Front, Colonel-General Cherevichenko, therefore decided on October 5 to swing his line 45 degrees to the east, pivoting on the coast and presenting a new front to the Germans. This meant abandoning a good

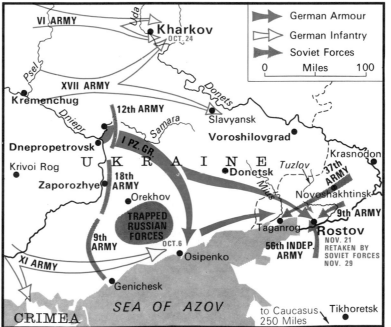

Army Group South's second major target in the 'Barbarossa' plan was the city of Kharkov, which fell without a major battle. The southern Ukraine was over-run, and the Soviet forces in the Crimea were sealed off; but the attempt to capture Rostov, at the mouth of the Don, resulted in Army Group South's first proper defeat. By the end of November, their troops found themselves forced on to the defensive by the enemy which two months before seemed to have been routed

The gun-crew of a German *Panzerjäger* unit, in action against Soviet armour

deal of territory—including the large town of Zaporozhye—but it offered the hope of avoiding another encirclement.

Unfortunately for South Front, the move came too late. As 12th and 18th Armies were attempting to set up defences on the new line, I Panzergruppe broke through at the junction between them, and on October 6 its forward elements met the advance guards of Manstein's XI Army. So the ring was closed, and the Soviet 9th and 18th Armies were herded into an area of steppe between Orekhov and the small port of Osipenko. Their neighbours of 12th Army, already much worn down by the preceding battles, drew away to the north-east, so as not to lose contact with the main Soviet forces on their right. Ninth and 18th Armies were cut off from the landward side; they were cut off from the coast and any possibility of relief by the Black Sea Fleet. Apart from stubborn air support, they were on their own.

They even lacked leaders. On October 6 the SS 'Adolf Hitler' Division captured the entire staff of 9th Army, except for its commander, Major-General F. M. Kharitonov, who was flown out. The 18th Army commander, Lieutenant-General Mirnov, was less fortunate. He was killed while attempting to break out to the north-east.

More than 100,000 POWs
Soviet resistance in the pocket continued to be fierce, but in view of the loss of leadership, it was uncoordinated. Some of 9th Army's right flank units managed to fight their way out, and part of the 18th Army was able to blast a corridor through to Donetsk. But when the fighting died down and the Germans had finished counting they concluded that they had taken 212 tanks, nearly 700 guns, and 106,000 prisoners. They persuaded themselves, over-optimistically, that they had dispersed or destroyed four Soviet armies, and forthwith began to withdraw XI Army, which was needed for the invasion of the Crimea, leaving I Panzergruppe (now essentially reduced to one tank army) to push on to Rostov.

At this point it seems that Army Group South was becoming over-confident. Of the four Soviet armies which it believed it had 'dispersed or destroyed', two (6th and 12th) had been pushed aside and severely handled, but were by no means finished. Of the two encircled armies (9th and 18th), some elements had escaped through the net, and were reorganising. In particular, the 'destroyed' 9th Army was rapidly reconstituting itself, absorbing reinforcements of infantry and cavalry, and settling down to block the approaches to Rostov. Even more ominous for the Germans was that STAVKA was no longer desperately plugging gaps. It was trading space for time and planning an eventual counteroffensive.

At this critical juncture, with Moscow, Leningrad, and Kharkov all seriously threatened, and with the Red Army still in general—though fiercely contested—retreat, STAVKA's response to the Azov coast disaster was to order a withdrawal to a shorter line, with the specific purpose of releasing at least ten infantry divisions and two cavalry corps into reserve. These were made available by the end of October and were formed into a new army (37th), concentrated around Krasnodon, north-east of Rostov. From here it was to mount a counteroffensive against the flanks of any German force attempting to encircle Rostov. What-

ever criticisms might be made of STAVKA, it could not be accused of loss of nerve.

Had it done so, it would have been fully understandable, for nowhere was the situation cheerful. On the South-West Front the three Soviet armies deployed in front of Kharkov (21st, 38th, and 40th) were in little better case than their neighbours to the south. General Popel (Chief Political Commissar of 38th Army) has described what he saw when he entered Kharkov: 'My tankman's heart froze. I saw antediluvian Renaults, Vickers, and Carden-Lloyd tankettes. The implacable people of Kharkov had dug out this ancient armoured rubbish from somewhere or other and turned it into static firing points.'

At Dergachi, north of Kharkov, a regiment had been formed from lieutenants and political officers who had been attending courses. It had one rifle to every two or three men, and its total heavy equipment was four field guns and six mortars. The reason for the weapon shortage was simple: the depots, with their vast stocks of small arms, had been sited too near the frontiers, and there had been no time to evacuate or issue the weapons in them. And so it became necessary to disarm the transport and supply troops in order to issue their weapons to the infantry; inevitably this led to very nervous reactions by the unarmed rear services whenever the Germans were reported or rumoured to have broken through.

Ninety thousand citizens of Kharkov volunteered for the militia. Arms could only be found for them by sending parties of troops out to scour the battlefield for the weapons of the dead. So, amid shortage and desperate improvisation, South-West Front and the people of the Soviet Union's fourth city waited for the Germans to show their hand.

'A forecast of catastrophe'
Army Group South was still advancing, but the headlong offensives of the summer were now a thing of the past. Its VI and XVII Armies were feeling their way forward through the mud while Soviet rearguards harrassed their progress. On most days wheeled transport was next to useless, and both sides were using requisitioned horses and oxen to draw their heavy equipment.

This situation was being actively exploited by the Soviet air force, which was concentrating its attacks on the beasts of burden. On October 11 they killed 238 horses and 196 men in one corps of XVII Army alone, causing an anxious entry to appear in the diary of the German Supreme Command. South-West Front's commanders could not be satisfied that they had yet got the measure of the Germans, and the weather impeded Soviet movement as much as German. Nevertheless, their object was to slow down the pace of the war, and the weather was therefore less of an obstacle to them than it was to Army Group South, whose object was to speed up the pace. The combined efforts of South-West Front and the weather succeeded in slowing down the pace of the German advance from the 12 to 15 miles a day of June to 1 or 2 miles a day by mid-October. As Popel was to remark later: 'Naturally, there was no particular cause for rejoicing. The Germans were advancing, though slowly, and we were retreating. Nevertheless, in the obvious lowering of the speeds planned by the German General Staff was a forecast of the catastrophe which hung over the German

forces in Russia.'

Rundstedt firmly believed that large towns should be by-passed and encircled, not fought over. He had applied this maxim very successfully at Kiev—but this time there could be no great sweep round behind Kharkov, as his Panzer forces were away in the south. Nevertheless it would be advantageous to go through the motions of encirclement in order to force the Red Army to give up Kharkov. So the left wing of XVII Army (XI Corps) seized a bridgehead over the Uda river 5 miles south of the city, and the VI Army pushed out feelers to north and south of Kharkov. STAVKA reacted immediately, and this time Stalin did not insist that the defenders stand fast, so rearguards were left and the main forces pulled out.

Rundstedt had made his point, and could have Kharkov—but he would have to do without his bagful of Soviet armies. Sixth Army entered the city on October 24, and the German advance continued, but as a slow creep forward behind Soviet forces withdrawing slowly and in good order, until even this ceased in early December.

Further south, where I Panzer Army was pressing on the Soviet Southern Front, the weather was better and the Panzers were making faster progress. That it was less spectacular than their usual pace was mainly due to the fact that assimilation of the hard lessons of June and July was now being reflected in much improved Soviet defensive tactics.

Slowing down the Panzers
In the early days of the Soviet-German war, Soviet commanders had relied on linear defences more or less equally strong at all points. These were very vulnerable to breakthrough by tanks at one point, and to being squeezed between the tanks behind and the infantry in front. The Soviet 9th Army, charged with the defence of Rostov, was not alone in seeking better methods. But its solution to the problem is better documented than others. In brief, it consisted of constructing four belts of defences one behind the other, with interlocking fields of fire between the strong points in each. Crews of field, anti-tank, and machine-guns were provided with dug-outs, so that they were protected while not actually serving their guns; and to disperse the enemy effort, large numbers of dummy dug-outs were interspersed among the real ones. Revetments were so constructed as to make it possible for guns to be swung round within them and cover various directions of attack, and flexibility was further assisted by constructing alternative positions to which the guns could be moved quickly if necessary. The infantry trenches were made very narrow, so that they would not collapse when tanks passed over them, thus making it possible for the occupants to remain in position until the tanks had gone by, then engage the German infantry as it followed up.

To slow down the Panzers even more, the banks of streams and creeks were undercut where crossings were likely, and where no natural obstacles existed tank traps were dug—especially on the flanks of units. Troops were deployed on the most likely approach routes at the rate of one battalion to every 1¼ miles in front and depth, while remaining sectors were occupied at half this density. The shortage of land mines made complete mining of approach roads impossible, but all road junctions were mined.

The overall effect was to create four defen-

sive systems, each up to 1½ miles deep, with
good fields of fire in front of each zone, and
with various means of slowing up tanks both
in front of and within each zone. Between the
systems was several miles of open terrain,
and so from front to rear 9th Army's defence
system was nearly 50 miles deep, including
the fortified town of Novoshakhtinsk at its
rear end, where the army HQ was set up.

When I Panzer Army's offensive towards
Rostov burst upon 9th Army on November 1,
only three of the four defensive belts had
been completed. Even so, the new system,
aided to some extent by the bad state of the
roads, proved effective, and if the German
determination to break through was great,
so was the Soviet resolve to stop them. The
battle developed into a slogging match in
the mud and ice of the early winter, and not
until November 12 was I Panzer Army able
to report a daily advance of as much as 4½
miles — a far cry from the headlong dash to
the coast of less than a month before.

On the 14th, the Germans reached the
south bank of the Tuzlov river, near the
coast, which was not part of 9th Army's
defence area, but was being held by the
hastily raised 56th Independent Army. Here
Rundstedt paused for two days of agonising
reappraisal, for the main attack on Rostov
— an outflanking blow through 9th Army's
zone, to envelop the city from the north —
was clearly not going according to plan.
Furthermore, Rundstedt's northern flank
force was beginning to realise the presence
of 37th Army (which, as already mentioned,
was being assembled north and north-east
of Rostov), and the implications of its
presence gave no grounds for complacency.
Although the Germans probably did not
know it, 37th Army was almost ready to
move.

The original German plan was therefore
abandoned. Rundstedt ordered a covering
force to be left behind to guard against a
Soviet counterthrust by 37th Army, and regrouped the bulk of I Panzer Army on the
Tuzlov river line, opposite 56th Independent
Army. Sophisticated encirclement had failed;
Army Group South was now going to try an
old-fashioned frontal assault.

The German regrouping was carried out
with admirable speed, and the offensive
along the coast began on November 17. It
blasted its way through with an ease and
efficiency reminiscent of the battles of the
summer, and the northern edges of Rostov
were reached after only two days of fighting.
But on the very day that the coastal offensive began, the troops left behind to guard
the northern axis ominously reported that
they were under systematic attack.

The scales begin to tip
Soviet 37th Army had at last been ordered
forward — and for the first time in the Second
World War the German army was called on
to face an enemy attack prepared and
launched after adequate advance planning
rather than thrown in as a desperate attempt
to stave off disaster. As a long-term portent,
Hitler's generals would find it disquieting;
in the short term, the troops pouring into
Rostov from the west were putting their
heads into a Soviet noose. The scales of war
had begun to tip, ever so slightly, against
Germany.

For two days the German northern forces
held, and I Panzer Army continued to push
into Rostov. But on the 19th, even while
they were clearing its northern suburbs, the
SS 'Viking' Division began to give ground in

The Germans head into Rostov — and their first defeat

the north-east. An ironic situation resulted, for while on the 21st Rostov fell to III Panzer Corps, the screen force to the north continued to fall back, so that for the first time in the war a Soviet Front Commander could seriously think of encircling a large German formation.

The shock groups of 37th Army had now been joined in the attack by parts of the 9th Army. These were already bearing down on the Tuzlov river line, thus threatening the German flank and rear. The Germans had lost the initiative on their northern and north-eastern flanks, so could not break out there. Neither could they draw off the Soviet forces by a break-out to the south of Rostov, since all bridges had been blown, and 56th Independent Army was now holding firm.

The Commander of South Front, Colonel-General Cherevichenko, was well aware of the possibilities of the situation, and both he and STAVKA were tempted to emulate Kleist's manoeuvre of early October by a swift thrust to the coast behind the main enemy forces. But the Red Army was still short of mobile formations, and its infantry divisions, especially those of 9th Army, were much below strength. It was decided, no doubt reluctantly, to play safe and settle for the recapture of Rostov coupled with a drive along the coast to Taganrog. For if Soviet *defensive* strength had forced the abandonment of the German attempt at encirclement, Soviet *offensive* strength was at this stage adequate only to allow them to adopt the same manouvre that they had forced on Army Group South.

But at least it would be the Red Army which dictated the course of events in this particular battle. And if the outcome was successful, the flanks of the German forces occupying the industrial area between Kharkov and Rostov would be vulnerable to penetration from the south. The effects on the morale of the Soviet people and forces would be beneficial, and on the international plane, salvation of the Caucasus would make manifest the Soviet ability to survive the winter and reduce the attractiveness to Turkey of any German overtures. ▷

Soviet dispositions around Rostov were quickly made. In three groups, 56th Independent Army would attack the southern sector, while 37th Army would move in from the north-west and part of 9th Army from the north-east.

On the night of November 27/28 the operation began. A company of the 33rd Motorised Rifle Regiment crossed the Don on the ice to seize a small bridgehead on Theatre Square, and two battalions of the Rostov militia also made the crossing, seizing the cement factory with the two streets adjoining it. Only light weapons could be brought across, as the ice was not yet thick enough to bear artillery or tanks, but the precarious bridgeheads were held through the night and more troops crossed over in the morning. Simultaneously a fierce assault was mounted along the entire Tuzlov river front. The I Panzer Army succeeded in holding a corridor open, though all its reserves had to be com-

mitted to do so, and Rostov was hastily abandoned before the Soviet 37th Army had even arrived. It had been taken on November 21, and held for only eight days.

With large Soviet forces in hot pursuit, Rundstedt decided to fall back to the more easily defended Mius river line, abandoning Taganrog. Expecting Hitler to oppose the withdrawal, he did not notify the Supreme Command until he had set it in train. Hitler promptly ordered him to cancel the order and stand fast, whereupon he resigned on the spot. Hitler accepted his resignation, and Germany's most eminent soldier left the Eastern Front, never to return to it.

On December 1 OKH issued another assessment of current Red Army strength. It told an ominous story. Despite the brilliant victories of the summer, despite the fact that German armies stood before Leningrad and Moscow, despite the camps bulging with Soviet prisoners of war, OKH estimated

that the Germans were faced by 200 infantry divisions, 35 cavalry divisions, and 40 armoured brigades. Elsewhere in the Soviet Union were a further 63 infantry divisions, $6\frac{1}{2}$ cavalry divisions, and 11 armoured brigades. An unknown number of additional divisions was being formed.

In brief, the Red Army was now over twice as strong as OKH had estimated it to be when its Commander-in-Chief, Brauchitsch, had reported to Hitler on July 23. Furthermore, its tactical leadership and methods were visibly improving, especially in co-ordination of attacks. Vigorous Soviet offensives could be expected during the snowy months ahead, as well as an intensification of partisan and sabotage activity.

It was going to be a hard winter for the German army.

[For Geoffrey Jukes's biography, see p. 118.]

A Soviet counterattack storms through a Rostov street — 'the Red Army dictated the course of events in this particular battle'

United Press

A German attack has surprised and fired a Soviet transport-train

Pearl Harbor THE PLANS

Japan and the Pacific, June 1940/December 1941

Christopher Hart

The touchstone of Japanese strategy was domination of the Far East — and her war with China had been in progress for many months before the conflict in the West began. Moreover, this war had fomented rivalry with the United States. But there was to be no appeasement of Japan, as there had been of Hitler: 'Japan had been drifting towards war with the Western powers since 1931; but in the end she no longer drifted, she leapt'

General Hideki Tojo, who became Japan's Prime Minister and Minister of War on October 17, 1941. His insistence that a bellicose policy be adopted towards the United States made war's inevitability only too clear

For Japan, the sweeping German victories in western Europe in the spring of 1940 seemed to present a golden opportunity. France and Holland, two of the three key colonial powers who barred the way to Japanese domination of the Far East, had been shattered by Hitler's Blitzkrieg. The third, Britain, was desperately close to defeat. Now, if ever, was the time to seize these nations' possessions: Malaya, Burma, French Indo-China, and the Dutch East Indies. These colonies could provide the Japanese with oil, and with a base from which to complete the conquest of China. And they could form the foundation of a 'new order' in Asia, under which the Japanese would free the Asian peoples from European rule.

It was this long-term aspiration—to drive out the Europeans, and establish Japanese hegemony over the Far East—which underlay all Japanese strategic thinking. Since July 1937, Japanese armies had been waging war in China, with only limited success. The United States gave enough aid to Chiang Kai-Shek to keep Chinese resistance going, and could at any time exert intolerable economic pressure on the Japanese by cutting off their supply of oil.

By 1940, the Japanese were faced with an all-or-nothing gamble. If they stepped up their effort in China, they risked the United States imposing a total oil embargo. This would force Japan to seize the oil supplies of the Dutch East Indies. And if a full-scale attack *were* to be mounted against China, her supply lines would have to be bombed— which meant seizing air bases in French Indo-China. Such an assault on the French and Dutch colonies would run the grave risk of a direct intervention by the United States in the war between China and Japan. The choice for the Japanese lay between resigning themselves to a prolonged and fruitless entanglement with China, and making a dramatic bid for domination of the Far East —even if this meant war with America.

Given the state of Japanese politics in 1940, it was scarcely surprising that the 'golden opportunity' was seized. Throughout the 1930's, army officers, encouraged by certain extremist groups, had established an ascendancy over Japanese politicians, to the extent that they could choose their own War Minister. On July 16, 1940, the army brought down the government of the moderate Admiral Yonai, who was replaced by Prince Konoye.

On July 27 a further step on the path of aggression was taken: the Liaison Conference—a policy-making body composed of army and navy officers, and politicians— proclaimed a 'Greater East Asia Co-Prosperity Sphere', over which Japan intended to win control. This 'Co-Prosperity Sphere', which abounded with vital raw materials such as oil, extended over the Dutch East Indies, Malaya, Thailand, Burma, and the Philippines.

To begin with, diplomatic pressure would be exerted—aimed particularly at the Dutch—to establish Japanese control. But it was clearly realised that war with Britain, and America, was a serious possibility, and measures were to be taken at once to re-organise the Japanese economy, and prepare for such a war.

The opening moves on the diplomatic front were encouragingly successful. On August 29 the French gave in to demands that Japanese troops and air squadrons be stationed in northern Indo-China. The

Admiral Yamamoto, C-in-C Japanese fleet

British, too, under pressure from Japan, had no choice but to close the Burma Road (the main supply route to China), and withdraw their garrisons from Shanghai and Tientsin.

As for the threat from the United States, the Japanese Foreign Minister, Matsuoka, believed this could be warded off by aligning Japan with Germany and Italy. On September 27, 1940, the Tripartite Pact, directed against aggression from any power not yet involved in the European or Chinese wars, was signed.

This, however, was the limit of Japanese diplomatic success. Holland, encouraged by America, refused to accede to Japanese requests for massive supplies of oil on long-term contract. On October 18 the British reopened the Burma Road, and at the end of the month began mutual defence talks with the Dutch and Australians. In December, the Americans promised the Chinese a $100 million loan and a volunteer air force; and in January they joined in the Anglo-Dutch-Australian defence preparations. Most important of all, the Tripartite Pact failed to achieve the desired deterrent effect on the United States: the Japanese commitment to Germany—a flagrant aggressor nation—reinforced American determination to resist all Japanese efforts to extract concessions by negotiation.

Expansion through diplomacy still remained the favoured Japanese course, largely because military preparations for war with the Western powers were so woefully inadequate. Not until the autumn of 1940 were preliminary studies begun, and even then it would be some time before Japan was economically and militarily ready for war on a large scale. Consequently, efforts were made to persuade the French to agree to the establishment of Japanese air and sea bases in southern Indo-China (in addition to the ones already in northern Indo-China). At the same time, a new ambassador, Nomura, was dispatched to Washington to resolve Japan's differences with America by direct negotiation with Secretary of State Cordell Hull.

His proposals, presented on May 11, 1941, involved America ceasing to aid China, and resuming normal trade with Japan. These first proposals were unacceptable, but the negotiations continued—Japan was not yet ready for war, and Cordell Hull was not prepared to provide the Japanese with a *casus belli*.

More fruitful was Matsuoka's attempt to keep Russia out of any possible Japanese conflict with America. On April 13, 1941, he signed a non-aggression pact with the Russians—an agreement to which both sides

adhered to the very last. But the effect of this pact was nullified by the sudden German attack on Russia, on June 22. This presented the Liaison Conference with a fascinating choice. Matsuoka pressed for an attack on the traditional Russian enemy—in flagrant contradiction of the non-aggression pact he had just signed—backed up by moves against Singapore, and further onslaughts on Chiang Kai-Shek.

The weight of army opinion, however, favoured a drive to the south, on the grounds that Hitler's attack had removed any fears of Russia striking at Japan's rear. On the other hand, the Prime Minister, Konoye, and the Naval Chief-of-Staff, Admiral Nagano, were fearful of American reaction if Japan invaded the Southern Area (see map).

A compromise was eventually reached on July 2, 1941, when the Liaison Conference, in the presence of the Emperor, decided to reinforce the army in Manchuria, while for the present not attacking Russia; and to seize bases in southern Indo-China in preparation for an advance into the Southern Area. War with Britain and America would not be 'declined', although diplomatic efforts would be made to avoid it.

Indeed, in an attempt to appease America, Matsuoka was replaced by the less bellicose Admiral Toyoda on July 18. But the very next day the conciliatory effect of Toyoda's appointment was nullified by a Japanese ultimatum to the French, demanding air, land, and sea bases in southern Indo-China —which would put Singapore within range of Japanese bombers.

American strategists had for months been debating policy towards Japan. One school of thought argued that Japan was bent on aggression, and the sooner full economic sanctions were imposed, the better. Ranged against this line of argument was the view that the Japanese were still undecided— sanctions would finally push them towards aggression. This new ultimatum to France seemed to settle the argument.

On July 24 the French gave in to Japan's demands. On July 26 President Roosevelt reacted by freezing all Japanese assets in America. Quickly, Britain and Holland followed suit. Japan was faced with a complete halt to all imports of oil and many other vital supplies. If America would not relent, the only way open to Japan was to seize the Southern Area. For Japanese stocks of oil were totally inadequate to sustain a major war. By the middle of 1941 they had declined from the 1939 peak of 51 million barrels to little over 40 million barrels, which would be exhausted in less than a year and a half if Japan went to war against Britain and America. Even the war in China could not be concluded before oil supplies ran out. Some 90% of Japan's oil was imported from America and the Dutch East Indies; this flow would now be staunched by the freezing of Japanese assets. Even home production was restricted because America had withheld technical information since 1939.

The Emperor himself was left in no doubt about Japan's critical situation. The Chief of Naval Staff, Admiral Nagano, told him on July 31 that Japan was 'like a fish in a pond from which the water is gradually being drained away'. Whereas in mid-1940 the Japanese could choose whether or not to bid for supremacy over the Far East, now, in July 1941, they had virtually no choice at all. If Japan were to continue to exist as a major power, her supply of oil had to be guaranteed. If Japan's position on the world

149

stage were not to be dictated by America, the Southern Area would have to be seized. And it was to this objective that the Japanese now applied themselves, with formidable thoroughness.

Serious preparations for large-scale war had not been started in Japan until the autumn of 1940. By the end of 1940 special tropical training had begun in preparation for an invasion of the Southern Area. By July 1941 a complete outline was ready on which to base an operational invasion plan. The American decision to freeze Japanese assets made it imperative that these plans be adapted to the primary objective: oil.

'No alternative but attack'

The mere seizure of oilfields would not be enough: the oil had to be transported safely to Japan. To capture Sumatra, Borneo, and Java — which produced 65 million barrels of oil a year — together with the British and American colonies flanking the route from these islands to Japan, would require nearly all the resources of the Japanese navy and air force, and 15 army divisions. The navy planners estimated the operation would take less than six months.

The army strategists reached their conclusions on August 9. Resisting arguments for an attack on an already beleaguered Russia, and for a stepped-up assault on China, they insisted that there was no alternative but to seize the oilfields of the

Southern Area. And the operation had to be mounted before the end of 1941. By 1942, oil stocks would have sunk too low: there could be no second chance.

The attitude of both services towards negotiations with America was clear. If Japan could secure all she wanted in a peaceful settlement with America, negotiations should continue. But as soon as it became clear that America was only playing for time, negotiations should be broken off. Politicians like Konoye regarded this attitude as desperately dangerous. In an effort to head off the military extremists, Konoye on August 28 asked for a personal meeting with Roosevelt, hoping to win the Emperor's approval of a settlement before the army could lay down its terms — though he risked assassination by the extremists if his plan worked. Cordell Hull, however, advised Roosevelt to reject the request, on the grounds that Konoye was too weak politically to enforce a settlement, even assuming that any kind of settlement could be reached.

By the time Roosevelt's negative response arrived — on September 3 — the Liaison Conference had already laid down a rigid timetable for any negotiations that might take place: the decision for war had to be taken by mid-October. At a crucial meeting on September 5, the Chiefs-of-Staff tried to persuade the Emperor that only drastic action could redeem Japan now. The Em-

peror, reluctant to spread the war, was sceptical about Japan's ability to capture the Southern Area: he reminded his military advisers of the failure to defeat China in the specified time.

On the next day there was a formal meeting of the Liaison Conference in the Emperor's presence. In an almost unprecedented intervention, he went out of his way to stress his desire for peace. This visibly shook the politicians, but the timetable laid down on September 3 was nonetheless approved.

It was left to Konoye to try and reach a settlement before the deadline, and he quickly realised that negotiations with America were hopeless unless Japan showed at least some signs of ending the war in China. But the War Minister, General Hideki Tojo, was not prepared to throw away the fruits of four years of fighting in China. To withdraw now, he argued, would shatter army morale, and would lead to the spread of Communism in Asia, and would encourage the Americans to demand more concessions.

On October 14 Konoye made a final appeal to Tojo to agree to a withdrawal. Tojo refused adamantly, insisting that if Konoye could not decide one way or the other on war, he should resign. Two days later Konoye resigned. He was replaced on October 17 by Tojo.

Yet even Tojo was not quite ready to take the fateful decision. For more than a fort-

A peacetime photograph of the *Kaga*, one of the six fleet carriers available for the Pearl Harbor attack. At a refit in 1935, her flight-deck was extended and the bridge superstructure fitted to starboard

night, he kept the Liaison Conference in almost constant session, reassessing all aspects of policy. On November 5, at a meeting of the Liaison Conference with the Emperor present, there came another crisis. The elder statesmen strongly advised negotiating with America. The army demanded war. And again the decision was postponed, as Tojo extended the deadline for a settlement to November 25. But preparations for the war were by now reaching such an advanced state that it would soon be impossible to keep both options open.

The oil shortage made it imperative to begin operations by December 1941. It also dictated Japanese strategy. The Southern Area oilfields had to be captured intact, and the oil—together with materials like rubber, tin, and bauxite—had to be transported safely back to Japan. Threatening the Japanese line of communications were the British base of Singapore, at the southern tip of the Malayan peninsula, and the American bases in the Philippines, which were rapidly being built up in strength.

In the autumn of 1941 the Japanese army and navy considered four alternative ways of meeting this dual threat. The first was to seize the oil islands, and then attack Malaya and the Philippines: but this would give the British and Americans too much time to prepare their defences. The second envisaged a clockwise sequence of attacks—on the Philippines, then on the oil islands, and

finally on Malaya: but this still gave the British too much time to take countermeasures. Similarly, the third alternative, an anti-clockwise advance, would leave the American Pacific Fleet, and bomber bases on Luzon, to the last, and thus expose the whole Japanese line of communications.

The army and navy therefore agreed by mid-August on the fourth alternative: a sudden co-ordinated attack on the Philippines and Malaya, to be followed—once the primary objectives had been taken—by assaults on the Dutch East Indies and Burma. In this way, all potential threats would be eliminated before the oil islands of Borneo, Java, and Sumatra were seized.

Meanwhile a refinement of this basic strategy was being developed independently by the staff of the Combined Fleet, under their commander, Admiral Yamamoto. The idea was to anticipate, to an even greater degree, American intervention in the war, by attacking the Pacific Fleet base at Pearl Harbor, on the Hawaiian island of Oahu, 3,400 miles from Japan.

Ironically, Yamamoto's staff was encouraged in its planning by the exploit of the American Admiral Yarnell, who had launched a similar dummy attack in a fleet exercise in 1932. Further encouragement came from the British, whose carrier-based attack on the Italian fleet at Taranto in November 1940 convinced the Japanese that torpedoes could be effective in shallow waters

—such as the 40-foot depths of Pearl Harbor. From December 1940, therefore, Yamamoto's staff had been working in the utmost secrecy on a plan. By April 1941 the plan was sufficiently advanced to allow experiments to begin with torpedo dropping during May.

At the end of August 1941 the Pearl Harbor plan was revealed to the Naval General Staff. It met with violent opposition, particularly from the Chief of Naval Staff, Admiral Nagano, who considered it both hazardous and unnecessary. He argued that the American fleet, if it dared enter Japanese waters, could be worn down by light forces, and then destroyed in a fleet action. In early September the plan was tried out in a war game, and earned itself another opponent —the carrier-force commander, Admiral Nagumo, who estimated that the action would cost him two of his six fleet carriers.

Despite the opposition, Yamamoto continued to advocate his plan, and refused to guarantee protection to the southern operations without it. He believed that Japan's only hope was to gain a quick success, and then try to negotiate with America. He was convinced that although Japan might be initially successful, she was bound to lose a long war. Yamamoto had to resort to threats of resignation before Nagano eventually accepted the strategy of striking at the American fleet before it could interfere with the Southern Area operations.

ROUTE OF JAPANESE STRIKE FORCE

LAUNCHING POINT 0600 HRS. DEC. 7

Oahu
Pearl Harbor **Hawaii**
Hawaiian Is.
(U.S.)

Palmyra I. (Br.)

Christmas I. (Br.)

Jarvis

Malden I.

Manihiki I.

Suvorov Is.

Tahiti

ook Is.   **Society Is.**

arotonga

Mercator Projection

December 7, 1941: the Japanese Empire is poised for its war to control the Far East. Her territories in the Marshall, Marianas, and Caroline Islands threaten Wake Island to the east and Guam and the Philippines to the west—all US territory. To the south-west, the Dutch East Indies are another prime target. From her bases in French Indo-China, Japan is prepared for the invasion of Thailand and Malaya. The oil and rubber of the British and Dutch East Indies—the 'Southern Area' in Japanese war plans—are the industrial motives in the Pacific war. The British port of Hong Kong is menaced by the Japanese control of the mainland. ● The Japanese plan consists of a surprise assault on the 'Southern Area', and its defence against subsequent Allied attempts to recover it. There will be no declaration of war: Japan depends on complete surprise, and her war leaders calculate that Japanese resources will be adequate to hold the conquered territories. But the most dramatic Japanese plan is the air strike at the US Pacific Fleet, concentrated in Pearl Harbor, Oahu: Japan's intention is to win unchallenged control of the Pacific Ocean

America Enters the War

1940 **July 27:** Japan proclaims the 'Greater East Asia Co-Prosperity Sphere'—the new order in the east.
August 29: France and Britain yield to Japanese demands for bases in northern Indo-China, and the closing of the Burma Road into China.
September 27: Japan signs the Tripartite Pact, joining the Axis powers.
October 18: Britain reopens the Burma Road.

1941 **April 13:** Japan signs a Non-Aggression Pact with the USSR.
June 22: Germany invades the USSR; the Japanese Army High Command presses for expansion to the south.
July 24: France yields to Japanese demands for air bases in southern Indo-China, within bombing-range of Singapore.
July 26: Roosevelt freezes all Japanese assets in America in reply. Japan is now forced to bid for supremacy in the Pacific to avoid eclipse by the USA.
October 16/17: The moderate Konoye is replaced by the aggressive Tojo as head of the Japanese government.
November 3: Admiral Yamamoto's plan to eliminate the US Pacific Fleet by an air strike is approved.
November 5: Japanese war orders are issued for a general advance in the western Pacific to a set defensive perimeter, and for the air strike against the US Fleet in Pearl Harbor.
November 26: USA demands withdrawal of Japanese forces from China—the end of hopes of a reasonable settlement with Japan. Admiral Nagumo's carrier-force starts on the first leg of its route to Pearl Harbor.
December 7: Pearl Harbor is raided by Nagumo's strike force, but the aircraft-carriers USSs *Enterprise* and *Lexington* escape attack.
December 8: Britain, the USA, and the Royal Netherlands government declare war on Japan.
December 11: Germany and Italy declare war on the USA. The Second World War has now been extended to both hemispheres.

▽ Prince Konoye, the last moderate Japanese Premier, was ousted by the aggressive Tojo

Keystone

On November 3 the plan was approved. It envisaged a stealthy approach across the murky North Pacific to a launching point north of Oahu from which, on a Sunday morning, the Japanese aircraft would take off for the attack on Pearl Harbor. There was to be no attempt to land troops on Oahu: the Japanese could not spare sufficient ships, nor could they risk the almost certain loss of surprise a landing would entail.

If the oil situation restricted Japan's manoeuvring space to the end of December 1941 at the latest, the adoption of the Pearl Harbor plan cut it down even further. Favourable weather conditions could only be expected in the early part of December—when light winds would also favour the Malayan operation—and one day in particular was considered most suitable: December 8, the Sunday in December when moon conditions for the final approach to Pearl Harbor would be best. This, then, was to be 'X-day'; and as it drew closer, the attempts at negotiation became more and more meaningless.

What added to the unreality of the situation was that American Naval Intelligence had broken the Japanese codes, and knew the contents of all messages sent to the ambassador in Washington. Cordell Hull, the Secretary of State, was perfectly aware of Tojo's deadline—later extended to November 29—but could do precious little to avert the final break. The Japanese position left him almost no room to negotiate.

Japan submitted two proposals to Hull. The first, presented on November 7, took a hard line, and entailed Japanese occupation of at least part of China until 1966. It evoked no response. The second—softer—proposal, presented on November 20, offered a promise not to seize the oil islands, if America would not interfere in any settlement of the Chinese war, and would supply Japan with oil until she could obtain sufficient quantities from the Dutch East Indies. Japan, for her part, promised a gradual withdrawal of troops from Indo-China.

Cordell Hull considered this proposal for some days before finally sending a firm reply on November 26, calling for the withdrawal of Japanese troops from China. From this point the negotiations were virtually at an end. Japan's main diplomatic effort was now concentrated on securing in writing Germany's and Italy's promised support in the event of war with Britain or America.

On November 27 Konoye and other elder statesmen pleaded at the Liaison Conference for further negotiations. But on November 29 the Liaison Conference decided on war, and a formal meeting in the presence of a silent Emperor confirmed this decision on December 1. The next day, orders went to the armed forces to expect war on December 8.

The actual war orders had been issued as early as November 5. Operations were to be in three phases. First would come the Pearl Harbor attack, and the operations to capture the Southern Area. A defensive perimeter would be formed from the Kuriles, through Wake, the Marshall and Gilbert islands, the Bismarcks and New Guinea, to Timor, Java, Sumatra, and Borneo. Next, the defensive perimeter would be consolidated, and the resources within it would be exploited. Finally, enemy attempts to pierce the perimeter would be repulsed, until their will to continue fighting had been destroyed. In short, the Japanese hoped to seize the resources of the Southern Area, fence them in, and then force Britain and the United States to make a compromise peace. They did not intend to compel unconditional surrender. This was to be a war of limited object, fought on a grand scale.

Indeed, the scale of the Japanese operations was to be vaster in space, and, in a special way, vaster in time, than in any previous war. A quarter of the way round the world, six operations would be unleashed almost simultaneously on both sides of the International Date Line. The attack was timed for 0800 hours, December 7 in Oahu, when it would be 1330 hours in Washington, 1830 hours in London, and 0330 hours, December 8, in Tokyo.

To be more precise, the Japanese bid for supremacy over the Far East would begin at 0215 hours December 8 (Tokyo time),

when Japanese troops would land on the north-east coast of Malaya at Kota Bharu to capture the British airfield nearby. Then at 0325 hours (0755, December 7, local time), Japanese carrier aircraft would commence action over the waters of Pearl Harbor. At 0400 hours, landings would begin at Singora and Patani on the Isthmus of Kra in Thailand, and these ports would become the main supply bases for the Malayan campaign.

After this point, the operations planned to follow would depend on the success of the initial attacks. If the Pearl Harbor operation had been judged successful, Japanese aircraft would take off from their airfields on Formosa at 0530 hours (0630 in Manila) to attempt to destroy American air power in the Philippines before Japanese landings on

the main island of Luzon began. Similarly, if the initial attacks in Malaya had succeeded, the invasion of the leased territories of Hong Kong would begin at 0830 hours (0800 local time). Small operations would then follow to take Guam, Wake, and the Gilbert Islands.

Strength on land, sea, and air

The cardinal feature of all these operations would be the effort to gain immediate air superiority by destroying enemy aircraft on the ground or by capturing airfields. This would need surprise; and particular difficulty was expected in the Philippines, where, because sunrise was 5½ hours later than over Oahu, the Americans would probably have been alerted by the Pearl Harbor assault before they were themselves attacked, and would be ready to fight back.

If the initial attacks achieved the aim of neutralising enemy air and sea power, bases were to be captured to support further operations. The Japanese did not expect much opposition: Manila, they thought, would fall in 50 days, Singapore in 100, and the Dutch East Indies in 150.

The division of responsibility for these operations was clearly laid out. Southern Area operations were to be under the Southern Army, commanded by Count Terauchi. Only 11 of the 51 operational divisions of the Japanese army would be available for the south (as many as 38 were needed in China and on the Russian frontier). The XIV Army, under Lieutenant-General Homma's command, would take the Philippines. It consisted of the XVI and XLVIII Divisions, the LXV Independent Brigade, and the LVI Regimental Group, and had air support from the army's V Air Division.

Lieutenant-General Iida's XV Army—consisting of the XXXIII and most of the LV Division—would invade Burma and Thailand. In an operation given equal top priority with the Pearl Harbor attack, Lieutenant-General Yamashita's XXV Army—three good divisions, the V, the XVIII, and the Imperial Guards—would invade Malaya. Hong Kong was earmarked for the XXXVIII Division (still under China Command), while Pacific island operations would be undertaken by navy troops, and the remainder of the LV Division. In addition, for the Malayan operations 350 to 450 army aircraft would give air support, and the LVI Division would be held in reserve.

At this time, Japanese divisions varied in size and composition, as the army was being reorganised from 12-battalion formations of over 20,000 men, with animal-drawn transport, into more compact 9-battalion divisions of 12 to 15,000 men, with mechanised transport. Infantry equipment—particularly the mortars—was good, and the Japanese soldiers were tough and fanatically brave, preferring death to capture. They also preferred to attack at night, infiltrating enemy positions and isolating them by roadblocks, for they could not call on lavish artillery support for daylight attacks. Logistical problems were greatly eased by the meagre requirements of the troops, who could live for days on mere rice and water.

In support of the Southern Army, there were some light and medium tanks, 700 army aircraft, and 480 land-based naval aircraft of exceptional range and flown by experienced pilots. The A6M (Zero) fighters—which also equipped the carriers—were the best combat types in the Pacific theatre. They were capable of escorting the G3M

The young Emperor Hirohito (left) with Admiral Togo, who had won the battle of Tsushima against the Russians in 1905 and lived until 1934, symbol of the navy's samurai tradition

Keystone

and G4M twin-engined bombers over the 900-mile round trip from Formosa to Manila and back; unescorted, these bombers could reach Singapore from airfields in southern Indo-China, 700 miles away. Some 96 G3M's reached these airfields in late October, and were joined by 27 of the heavier G4M's in early December—sent with specific orders to attack and sink at all costs the British capital ships *Prince of Wales* and *Repulse*, which had arrived at Singapore, amid much publicity, on December 2.

The navy was organised in task groups. Yamamoto commanded Combined Fleet's 'Main Body', which contained two 16-inch-gun battleships and four with 14-inch guns —soon to be joined by the 18·1-inch gun *Yamato*, the most powerful battleship in the world.

Last-minute negotiations: Japanese envoy Kuruso (right) with America's Cordell Hull

The carrier striking-force which was to attack Pearl Harbor was under Admiral Nagumo's command. It was escorted by two battleships, two heavy cruisers, a light cruiser, 16 destroyers, and three submarines. The six aircraft-carriers, paired in three types, were *Akagi* and *Kaga*, *Hiryu* and *Soryu*, and the newest (commissioned in August and September 1941 respectively): *Shokaku* and *Zuikaku*. All except *Kaga* could make over 30 knots, and they carried from 63 to 75 aircraft each—a total of 423. Four smaller carriers were left behind, two for training, and two for the Southern Area operations, which, in addition, had allocated to them two 14-inch-gun battleships, 11 8-inch-gun cruisers, seven light cruisers, 40 destroyers, and 18 submarines, to protect the troop convoys.

In early December 1941 the Southern Area operations got under way. On the 4th, at 0530 hours, 19 transports carrying 26,000 men left Hainan Island for the landings at Singora, Patani, and Kota Bharu, on the Thailand and Malayan coasts. Next day, seven more transports left for the Thai coast, while the Imperial Guards Division prepared to advance from Indo-China through Thailand to Malaya to support the landings.

In Formosa aircrews were ready for their planned take-off for the Philippines, to be made as soon as news of a successful attack on Pearl Harbor had been received. The XIV Army, on Formosa, Okinawa, and the Palau Islands, prepared to follow up the air attacks with landings. In China, the XXXVIII Division moved towards the Hong Kong leased territories, and on the Japanese Pacific Islands, forces prepared to attack Guam, Wake, and the Gilbert Islands. Southern Army HQ had issued preliminary orders to its forces on November 15, and the final orders designating December 8 as 'X-day' were issued from Tokyo to all forces on December 2.

By this time Nagumo's carriers were already en route to Pearl Harbor. They had assembled in Tankan Bay, in the remote Kuriles, north-east of Japan, by November 22. There they took on extra fuel as deck-cargo, together with special wooden-finned torpedoes for shallow water, and finned armour-piercing shells for high-level bombing. Ahead of the carrier force, an 'Advanced Expeditionary Force' of 27 submarines had left Japan in November to patrol off the entrance to Pearl Harbor. Five of these big 'I-boats' carried midget submarines which were to make a torpedo attack on the anchored American ships. Japanese submarines, like their cruisers and destroyers, carried 24-inch oxygen-fuelled torpedoes— the most powerful in existence.

Nagumo's force gets under way

On November 25 Yamamoto had issued operational orders for the attack. Nagumo's force was to leave next day, refuel on December 3, cross the date line, and turn south-east. He was to keep especial watch for hostile submarines and aircraft, while picket destroyers would patrol well ahead to give warning of any ships encountered, so that the main force could evade them. American, Dutch, or British ships were to be sunk, and others taken over by boarding parties to prevent them from sending radio messages. Strict radio silence was to be maintained, while the remainder of the Combined Fleet ships in Japanese waters increased their own radio traffic as a cover.

If Nagumo's force were detected by the Americans before the final run-in had begun on December 6, the attack was to be abandoned; if detected later, Nagumo himself was to decide on the best course of action. If the last flicker of negotiations with America should suddenly produce a satisfactory settlement, Nagumo's force would stand by to await orders.

The attack was to be launched in two waves. The first wave of 140 bombers, escorted by 50 Zero fighters, was to be launched at 0600 hours (local time), 275 miles north of Pearl Harbor. The targets were five of the six airfields (the Japanese did not know of the existence of the sixth), the Kaneohe seaplane base, the American battleships—and, it was hoped, aircraft-carriers moored beside Ford Island in Pearl Harbor. If, by any chance, the ships had left harbour, the bombers were to fly up to 150 miles south of Oahu in search of them. The second wave would consist of 213 aircraft, leaving 30 to patrol over the Japanese ships, and 40 to be kept in reserve. After the attack, the whole of Nagumo's force was to return to Japan immediately, pausing only to refuel from tankers at a specified rendezvous.

At first, the weather was thick and the seas stormy as the task force, accompanied by its tankers, ploughed east at 13 knots.

On December 4 the weather improved, and after refuelling the force crossed the date line to steam south-east at 25 knots, leaving the tankers behind for refuelling on the return journey.

They sighted only one ship—and that Japanese—during the approach to the launching point. No air searches were flown, and by listening to American radio traffic the Japanese established that all was quiet in the Hawaiian area and that American searches from Oahu were confined to the south-western sector. A series of reports from a spy in the Japanese consulate at Oahu confirmed that eight American battleships—but not the aircraft-carriers *Enterprise* and *Lexington*—were in harbour. The absence of the aircraft-carriers was serious, but the Japanese decided that the sinking of the battleships would justify the operation —moreover, the aircraft-carriers might at any time return to Pearl Harbor.

At 2100 hours on December 6, Nagumo's force reached the point on its route where it had to turn south-east. The night was black, with cloud-base at 6,000 feet, as Admiral Togo's battle-flag from the historic battle of Tsushima in 1905 was hoisted on the *Akagi*, to flutter in a fresh north-east trade wind. After some rousing speeches, the air crews on the aircraft-carriers prepared for the attack, while the cruisers sped on ahead to launch search aircraft. Away to the south, midget submarines started to make their hazardous entry into Pearl Harbor.

At 0500 hours on December 7, two float-planes were catapulted from cruisers to search—unsuccessfully as it happened— Pearl Harbor and Lahaina roads for the missing American carriers. At 0615 hours the first wave of attacking aircraft formed up and flew south, every man knowing his target and task, and all determined to show the Americans that Japanese valour was unsurpassed.

Only one thing was to mar the brilliantly successful operation. The Japanese had intended to give the American government some warning of war by delivering a 14-part note at 1300 hours, Washington time (0730 hours, Pearl Harbor time). The 14th part would declare that negotiations had ended, and it was thought that the Americans would not be able to read it and alert their defences before the attack at 1325 hours, Washington time. No attempt was made to warn the British.

This farcical effort to preserve international law while destroying international peace failed, because the embassy staff in Washington could not type out the 14-part note in time. Indeed, the American decoders were communicating the note to Cordell Hull and Roosevelt faster than the Japanese! When Ambassador Nomura came to see Hull, it was too late. The attack had started. Japan had been drifting towards war with the Western powers since 1931; but in the end, she no longer drifted, she leapt.

 CHRISTOPHER HART was born in 1936. He first became interested in air-sea warfare during the war, and turned to the study of grand strategy after graduating at London University. This led to work for Sir Basil Liddell Hart on the strategy of the Pacific War. He has now widened his field to include contemporary history and the strategic problems of the nuclear age. His recreations include industrial design and travel, and he now divides his time between London and the Channel Islands.

Pearl Harbor:

THE ATTACK

Oahu, Hawaii, December 7, 1941 *Captain Donald Macintyre*

The Pearl Harbor air-strike was an act of ruthless, machine-like destruction: never before had air power virtually wiped out an enemy fleet in one action. True, the Japanese victory was not quite complete: two American aircraft-carriers of the Pacific Fleet escaped to play a vital role in the months ahead. But the main Japanese triumph was unalterable: after Pearl Harbor there could be no immediate American challenge to the Japanese battle fleet

In the original Japanese war plan, the complex multi-pronged southward drive by expeditionary forces to capture Thailand, Malaya, the Philippines, and the Dutch East Indies was to be covered by the whole Imperial Navy. The United States Pacific Fleet, envisaged as hurrying towards the Philippine Sea to the rescue, was to be harried by air and submarine attacks launched from the Marshall and Caroline Islands, before being brought to action by the superior Japanese Main Fleet.

Early in 1941, however, critical eyes had been brought to bear on this plan by the C-in-C of the Japanese Fleet, Admiral Isoroku Yamamoto. Unlike the military faction led by General Tojo, Yamamoto saw clearly that—though the well-prepared Japanese war machine would be able to carry all before it in the initial stages of such a plan—the immense industrial potential of the United States must eventually bring it to a halt. When that time came, a negotiated, compromise peace would be possible only if

Japan had so firmly established herself in her newly-won empire in south-east Asia that eviction would be an insuperable task for the Western Allies. For this, time was needed. Yamamoto wished to gain this time by eliminating the US Pacific Fleet.

An early convert to the decisive role of carrier-borne air power in naval warfare, he had the perfect weapon to his hand in the shape of the six fleet carriers equipped with the most advanced naval aircraft in the world. Rear-Admiral Takijiro Onishi, Chief-of-Staff of the shore-based XI Air Fleet, was instructed to examine the possibility of a carrier-borne air attack on Pearl Harbor. Onishi recruited the best-known hero of such operations in the China War, Commander Minoru Genda. By May 1941, working in great secrecy, Genda had completed a study which promised success—provided that all six fleet aircraft-carriers were committed and complete secrecy imposed.

Put before the Chief of the Naval General Staff, Admiral Nagano, the plan was turned

down on the grounds that the aircraft-carriers were required for the southwards drive, and that an operation depending absolutely on surprise at the end of an ocean passage of 3,400 miles was too much of a gamble. Nevertheless, confident that Nagano's objections would be overcome in time, Yamamoto gave orders for a special training programme to be begun by his carrier air squadrons, concentrating on torpedo, dive-bombing, and high-level bombing attacks on targets in enclosed stretches of water such as Kagoshima Bay in southern Kyushu. Except for a handful of staff officers engaged with Genda in preparing the detailed plan, the object of these practices was revealed to no one.

Technicians at the main naval base of Yokosuka were given the task of adapting airborne torpedoes so that they could be dropped from a greater height than normal and still enter the water in a horizontal attitude, thus avoiding diving deeply at the beginning of their run. The need for such a

Japan's Naval Strike Aircraft

Mitsubishi A6M2 Zero-sen (Zeke)
The Zero outclassed every Allied fighter in the Pacific in December 1941. Light and manoeuvrable, it had a high fire-power, and could also act in a fighter/bomber role. **Max speed:** 351 mph. **Max range:** 975 miles. **Armament:** two 20-mm cannon, and two 7·7-mm machine-guns

Aichi D3A2 (Val)
The *Val* carried home the Japanese dive-bombing attacks at Pearl Harbor. It had been designed in imitation of the pre-war German dive-bombers, and was Japan's first low-wing, all-metal monoplane dive-bomber. **Max speed:** 266 mph. **Max range:** 970 mi. **Bomb load:** 816 lb.

Nakajima B5N2 (Kate)
At the time of Pearl Harbor, the *Kate* was Japan's principal torpedo-bomber, and could also serve as a level bomber. **Max speed:** 235 mph. **Max range:** 1,400 miles. **Weapon load:** one 1,764-lb torpedo

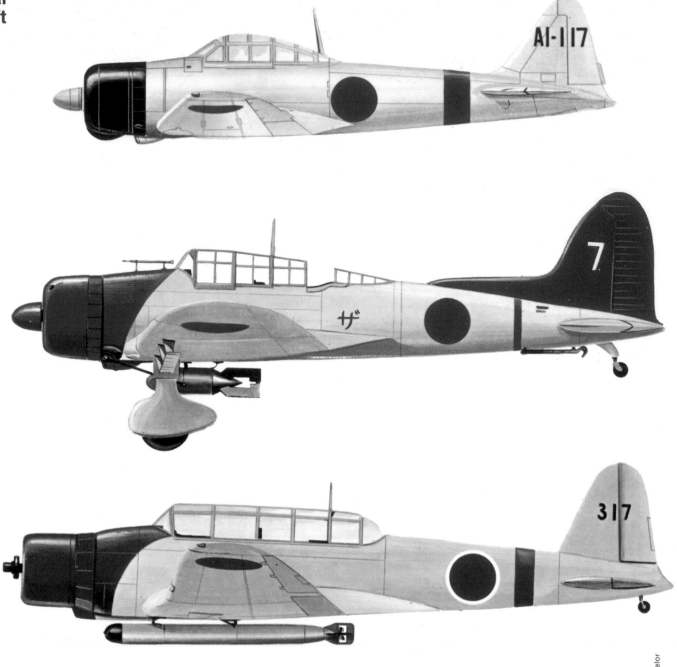

John Batchelor

refinement was not revealed; but by September, torpedoes fitted with special fins which would enable them to be effectively launched in the narrow, shallow waters of Pearl Harbor had been successfully tested and production was being feverishly pressed ahead to meet a deadline in mid-November.

The withdrawal of the Japanese aircraft-carriers to home waters resulted in a cessation of radio messages intercepted by the radio traffic analysis units in Hawaii and Manila. The Japanese carrier-force was for a time 'lost' to the American trackers. These correctly assessed the reason and in due course the aircraft-carriers came on the air again; but the accuracy of this appraisal was to lead to a similar and, this time, faulty assumption later.

The Konoye Cabinet fell on October 16, the new Prime Minister being the aggressive General Tojo. Alarm signals, announcing a 'grave situation' went out from Washington to Admiral Kimmel and General Short —heads of the navy and the army commands

in Hawaii. But now these reports were tempered by the continuing Washington belief that an attack on Russia's maritime provinces was the most probable Japanese move. The fact that the Japanese navy had, as long ago as July, finally won the long argument with the army with regard to war plans, and that the southward drive had been agreed upon, had escaped the US Intelligence organisations.

So far as General Short was concerned, this appreciation greatly reduced the probability of any attack on US territory. He was more concerned with the presence of a large local Japanese population in Hawaii and the need to take precautions against sabotage and subversion.

The possibility of an air attack if and when war should break out had been perfunctorily considered, and occasional drills on a peace-time footing had been concerted with the navy. They had not been very impressive. A few primitive, mobile radar sets had been arriving since August and had been set up

at various points round the coast of Oahu. They suffered many teething troubles and breakdowns. Communications between them and a temporary control centre, and between the control centre and the various commands, was by means of the public telephone system. Operators both of the radar sets and at the control centre were to a large degree untrained or inexperienced; the various units were manned only for a few hours each day, principally for training purposes.

Nevertheless, progress towards efficiency seemed adequate to the general who had informed Admiral Kimmel as long ago as August that the aircraft warning system was 'rapidly nearing completion'.

To the navy, however, both in Washington and Hawaii, the new situation seemed more fraught with threatening possibilities. Although a Japanese attack on Russia was considered the most likely, an attack on the United States or Great Britain was by no means ruled out, and the Pacific Fleet was ordered to take 'due precautions including

◁ Admiral Kimmel, US Navy commander at Pearl Harbor (far left). General Short, the US Army commander there

▷ Admiral Nagano, Chief of the Japanese Naval General Staff (left). Admiral Nagumo, commander of the Japanese carrier force

such preparatory deployments as will not disclose strategic intention nor constitute provocative actions against Japan'.

In case of hostile action by Japan against US merchant shipping, all vessels in the western Pacific were ordered to make for friendly ports. Instructed to 'take all practical precautions' for the safety of airfields at Wake and Midway (the air staging posts on the route to the Philippines), Kimmel dispatched reinforcements of marines, stores, and ammunition to both islands and stationed additional patrol planes there. Extra precautions were also taken against surprise submarine attack in the exercise areas.

The idea of an air attack on Pearl Harbor or its defences appears to have crossed nobody's mind.

Objective: Pearl Harbor

At about this time, aboard the Japanese aircraft-carrier *Akagi*, flagship of Vice-Admiral Chuichi Nagumo, commanding the Fast Carrier Striking Force, a scale model of Pearl Harbor was unveiled under the eyes of the assembled officer pilots of the air groups and of Yamamoto himself. Now, under seal of secrecy, Yamamoto gave them the electrifying news of their intended objective. Training was thereafter resumed at an even fiercer intensity and with added enthusiasm. On November 1 the C-in-C issued the basic operation order, naming Sunday, December 7 (Hawaiian time) as the day of destiny. Two days later Admiral Nagano was at last won over to give his consent.

Between November 10/18, singly or in pairs, the ships of Nagumo's striking force —six aircraft-carriers, two battleships, three cruisers, nine destroyers, and eight oil tankers—slipped away from their anchorages and, by devious routes, steered for a secret rendezvous in the desolate Tankan Bay on Etorofu, the largest of the Kurile Islands far to the north. Strict radio silence was imposed on all from the moment of sailing while the remainder of the fleet at Kure in the Inland Sea kept up a flow of radio messages for the benefit of American radio intelligence.

At about this time, too, and with the same secrecy, 16 submarines of the 'Advanced Expeditionary Force' left harbour and headed eastwards across the wide Pacific. Five of them carried two-man, midget submarines charged with the task of penetrating Pearl Harbor simultaneously with the air attack. The remainder, besides scouting for the carrier force, were expected to find opportunities for attacking any American ships that escaped seawards.

Signs of some impending major Japanese operation were not lacking in Hawaii or Washington. On November 1 the radio traffic analysis unit had reported that all call-signs of Japanese naval units had been changed. In itself, this was not of outstanding significance: change of call-signs from time to time was a normal procedure. But a second change only a month later, on December 1, could only be an indication of preparations for active operations.

In the interval the radio traffic analysis organisation had managed to re-identify a certain number of units, but had lost all contact with the Japanese aircraft-carriers. Relying upon previous correct assumptions on similar occasions, they decided that the latter were in home waters of the Inland Sea.

From the other source of radio intelligence, the 'Purple' diplomatic code, information of a different sort was obtained, information which, if examined alongside the results of traffic analysis, must have been seen to be of the most sinister import. From November 5 onwards, message after message to the Japanese envoys in Washington warned them that the 25th was a deadline for a successful outcome of their negotiations. On the 22nd, Tokyo extended the deadline to the 29th after which, they said, 'things will automatically begin to happen'. Meanwhile, each side conveyed to the other its final terms for a settlement, the Japanese on the 20th, the Americans on the 26th: neither set of terms was conceivably acceptable by both sides and only deadlock was achieved.

So, by the last week of November, negotiations had finally broken down. War was now clearly imminent; but as the Americans were bound to avoid being the first to open fire, or even to take any provocative action, choice of time and place lay in the hands of the Japanese. Intelligence sources, the deciphering system in particular, had to be relied upon to give advance warning. A steady flow of intelligence had, indeed, been reaching the American government and service chiefs, which clearly indicated preliminary Japanese moves for some southwards expedition.

On November 24 American naval commanders abroad were warned that a 'surprise aggressive move in any direction including attack on Philippines and Guam is a possibility'. Three days later a signal from the Chief of Naval Operations opened with the ominous phrase: 'This dispatch is to be considered a war warning,' and went on to list the possible Japanese objectives as 'either the Philippines, Thai or Kra Peninsula or possibly Borneo.' The Hawaiian Islands or even Wake and Midway were not mentioned.

The day before this signal was sent, from the cold windswept waters of Tankan Bay the anchors of Admiral Nagumo's ships had been weighed to rise, streaming mud and water, and thud home in the hawse pipes. A flurry of white foam round the ships' sterns as their screws pointed them to the harbour entrance and then, one by one, they had gathered way and vanished into the stormy northern sea to head due east along the 43rd Parallel, clear of all regular shipping routes.

Aboard the unlovely, flat-topped aircraft-carriers an atmosphere of excitement prevailed. A few hours earlier all but the privileged few already 'informed' had heard, for the first time, the mission on which they were bound—to strike a devastating surprise blow on the sea power of the nation which stood between Japan and the glorious destiny mapped out by her leaders. A feeling of joyful anticipation could be sensed everywhere, except perhaps on the admiral's bridge of the flagship *Akagi,* where Nagumo contemplated the risks of an operation to which he had only hesitantly agreed under the persuasions of his aviation staff officers and his Commander-in-Chief, Admiral Yamamoto.

An unsuspecting target

Some 3,000 miles away to the south-east lay Pearl Harbor, bathed in its perennial sunshine, all unaware of the approaching blow. The only visible results of the war warning signal was a certain amount of movement of army trucks and soldiers as General Short's troops took up their stations for 'Alert No. 1'—precautions against sabotage by the local Japanese population. In naval units, where a minor degree of alert with a proportion of anti-aircraft guns manned had been in force for some time, no additional precautions were taken. The aircraft-carriers *Enterprise* and *Lexington* had been dispatched to carry Marine fighter planes to Wake and Midway. The remainder of the fleet stayed at sea during the week, returning for leave to Pearl Harbor on weekends.

During the first few days of December, the deciphering system revealed that Japanese diplomatic and consular posts had been ordered to destroy most of their codes and ciphers and all confidential documents.

Though this was an added indication that war was imminent, it did not point at Pearl Harbor as a possible Japanese objective. A series of intercepted reports from the Japanese consul at Honolulu on the berthing of ships of the Pacific Fleet might have done so had it not been that similar reports from consuls elsewhere were also being regularly transmitted. The loss of contact with the carriers by radio traffic analysis was another important straw in the wind—but, as mentioned before, this was misinterpreted to indicate that they were lying peacefully in home waters. No long-range reconnaissance flights were ordered, nor was any alteration made in the fleet training programme which would bring the fleet into harbour at the weekend for rest and recreation.

But the overriding reason for discounting any likelihood of an attack on Pearl Harbor was the clear evidence of a huge amphibious operation in the south getting under way. Japanese troop convoys heading into the Gulf of Siam had been sighted and reported by British and American air reconnaissance planes during December 6, and American opinion simply could not conceive that the Japanese had the capacity—or the imaginative boldness—to mount a simultaneous operation elsewhere involving their carrier force.

Far away to the north-west of Hawaii, the Japanese carrier force had advanced unseen, its concealment assisted by foul weather, storms, and fogs which, however, added to the anxiety of Nagumo, who had to have a spell of fine weather in which to replenish from his tankers. Then, on December 1, came the awaited confirmatory signal for the operation—*Niitaka Yama Nobore* ('Climb Mount Niitaka')—announcing that the die had finally been cast. At last, on the 2nd, the weather moderated, the warships' oil tanks were refilled, and the following evening the force turned south-east, heading for a position 500 miles due north of Pearl Harbor, which it was planned to reach on the evening of the 6th. Now the final decision to make the attack lay with Nagumo, a decision which would depend on last-minute messages from

the Japanese agent in Honolulu as to the presence of the US Pacific Fleet.

Meanwhile, messages in the 'Purple' code, indicating Japanese rejection of the American ultimatum of November 6, were being intercepted and deciphered. The main message was a long-winded presentation of the Japanese case transmitted in 14 parts, only the last of which contained anything new—a formal breaking-off of negotiations. This was in American hands by 0300 hours Washington time on the morning of December 7.

At about the same time (the evening of the 6th by Hawaiian time), emotional ceremonies of dedication were taking place aboard the aircraft-carriers of Nagumo's force. All hands had been piped to assemble on the flight decks, patriotic speeches were made; to the masthead of the *Akagi* rose a historic signal flag used by Admiral Togo before the Battle of Tsushima 36 years earlier; and when the excited ships' companies finally dispersed, the force swung

round on to a southerly course and at high speed steered for the flying-off position arranged for dawn on the morrow.

While the ships raced on into the night, another vital message in the 'Purple' code was being read, deciphered, and translated at the Bainbridge Island radio station, Washington. It instructed the Japanese ambassador to submit the message breaking off negotiations to the US Secretary of State at precisely 1300 hours, December 7 (Washington time). Translated by 0600 hours, it was not until 0915 that this reached Admiral Stark, Chief of Naval Operations, and another 35 minutes passed before it was seen by the Secretary of State. It was pointed out to both that 1300 hours would be about sunrise at Honolulu. Yet a further 70 minutes of inactivity passed before General Marshall, Chief of the US General Staff, saw the message on return from his regular morning ride. He at once proposed to Stark that a joint special war alert should be sent out. When Stark disagreed, Marshall drafted

▽Zeros on the flight-deck of one of Nagumo's carriers. (Bottom) A Japanese *Kate* torpedo-bomber prepares for take-off

his own message to army commanders, concluding: 'Just what significance the hour set may have, we do not know, but be on the alert accordingly.' It was handed in for enciphering and dispatch at 1200 hours. But long before it reached Pearl Harbor, the crump of bursting bombs and torpedo warheads had made it superfluous.

At that moment (0630 hours Hawaiian time) the first wave of Nagumo's striking aircraft had already been launched—50 bombers, each armed with one 1,760-pound armour-piercing bomb, 70 more each carrying a torpedo, 51 dive-bombers each loaded with one 550-pound bomb, and 43 Zero fighters to provide escort and to deliver ground-strafing attacks.

It had not been without doubts and hesitation that Nagumo had given the final order—for the agent's report on ships in Pearl Harbor had made no mention of the US aircraft-carriers *Lexington* and *Enterprise* which, in fact, were away on their missions to Wake and Midway. The lure of the eight imposing battleships of the Pacific Fleet and their numerous attendant cruisers and destroyers, however, had been sufficient to harden his decision.

Off Pearl Harbor, indeed, the first acts of war were already taking place. The US minesweeper *Condor,* carrying out a routine sweep, signalled the destroyer *Ward,* on night patrol, that a periscope had been sighted, but no alarm was passed to the harbour control station. After the *Ward* had searched fruitlessly for more than two hours, the periscope was again sighted and marked by smoke bomb from a seaplane, and the destroyer then gained contact with a midget submarine and sank it with depth-charges and gunfire at 0645 hours. A message reporting the encounter reached the Port Admiral at 0712 hours, and, after some delay, was passed to Admiral Kimmel.

At 0750 hours, as Kimmel was hurrying to his office, an explosion on Ford Island, the Naval Air Station, in the middle of the harbour, gave the first startling indication that Pearl Harbor was under air attack.

Since 0615 hours the first wave of Japanese aircraft had been winging their way southwards led by Commander Mitsuo Fuchida, the air group commander, in the leading high-level bomber. A pair of trainee radar operators at the mobile station at Opana, practising with the equipment beyond the normal closing-down hour of 0700 hours, saw them appear on the screen at a range of 137 miles and plotted their approach just as a matter of interest: they were told by the information centre, to which they reported, that the contact could be disregarded as it was probably a flight of Fortresses due to arrive that morning from the mainland.

Fuchida led his swarm of aircraft down the western coast of Oahu, watched with idle curiosity by the many service and civilian families living along the shore, who took them for the air groups returning from the *Lexington* and *Enterprise.* By 0750 hours Fuchida could see across the central plain of the island to Pearl Harbor, its waters glint-

▽ The US destroyer Shaw vanishes as its magazines explode. (Right) A *Val* dive-bomber, just after releasing its bomb   US Navy

US Navy

△ Wrecked navy seaplanes after a raid: the Japanese disposed of any American challenge to their command of the air over Oahu
◁ With her quarter-deck sun awnings still rigged, the *California* keels over as survivors from her crew swarm over the rail

ing in the early sunshine of a peaceful Sunday morning, and through binoculars he was able to count the seven capital ships moored two by two in 'Battleship Row' on the eastern side of Ford Island (see map).

Surprise was complete: he gave the order to attack.

From endlessly repeated practice and meticulous study of maps and models of Oahu and Pearl Harbor, every Japanese pilot knew exactly what he had to do. While the squadrons of dive-bombers split up into sections which were to swoop simultaneously on the several army, navy, and marine airfields, the high-level bombers settled on to their pre-arranged approach course, bomb aimers adjusting their sights, and the torpedo-bombers began the long downward slant to their torpedo launching positions abreast the battleships. A few minutes before 0800 hours, to the scream of vertically plummeting planes, bombs began to burst among the aircraft drawn up, wing-tip to wing-tip in parade-ground perfection on

the various airfields. Simultaneously the duty watch aboard the ships in 'Battleship Row', preparing for the eight o'clock ceremony of hoisting the colours, saw the torpedo-bombers dip low to launch their torpedoes and watched, horror-stricken, the thin pencil line of the tracks heading for their helpless, immobile hulls. Not an American gun had yet opened fire. Not an American fighter plane had taken off.

The absolute surprise achieved by the attack on the airfields, where the bursting of bombs was followed by the tearing chatter of cannon-fire from diving Zero fighters, eliminated any posibility of an effective fighter defence. In the harbour, five of the battleships—*West Virginia, Arizona, Nevada, Oklahoma,* and *California*—were rent open by torpedo hits in the first few minutes; only the *Maryland* and *Tennessee,* occupying inside berths, and the flagship *Pennsylvania* which was in dry dock, escaped torpedo damage. Other ships torpedoed were the old target battleship *Utah,*

and the light cruisers *Raleigh* and *Helena.*

Nevertheless, although to the shudder and shock of underwater explosions was soon added the rising whine of dive-bombers and the shriek and shattering detonation of bombs from them and from the high-flying bombers, the American crews, for the most part, went into action with speed and efficiency, shooting down several of their attackers. Damage-control parties worked manfully to minimise the consequences of flooded compartments, counter-flooding to keep the foundering ships on an even keel, restoring electric and water power and communications, fighting the fires. One battleship, *Nevada,* even succeeded in getting under way and heading for the harbour entrance.

Meanwhile, however, high up above the smoke and confusion, hardly able at first to credit the total absence of any fighter opposition, and little inconvenienced by the sparse gunfire directed at them, Fuchida's high-level bombers were selecting ▷

△Ford Island and 'Battleship Row' under Japanese attack; note explosions on far side of Ford Island, and Japanese aircraft

△How the Japanese saw 'Battleship Row': a neat line of easy targets, rapidly sunk or smothered with bomb-bursts and fires

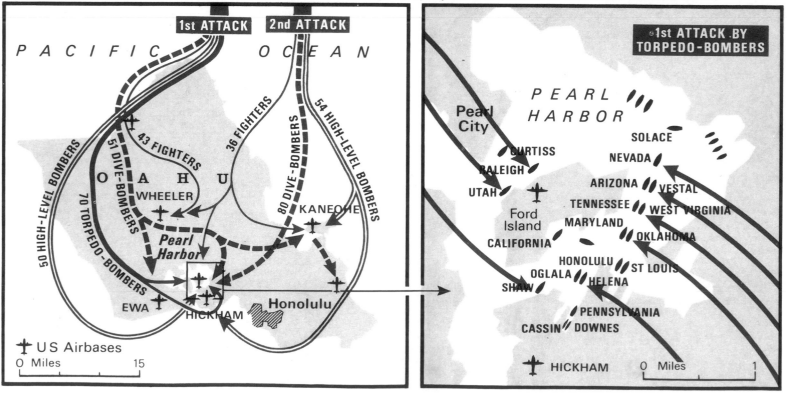

1st ATTACK   **2nd ATTACK**

P A C I F I C   O C E A N

36 FIGHTERS

80 DIVE-BOMBERS

54 HIGH-LEVEL BOMBERS

43 FIGHTERS

51 DIVE-BOMBERS

50 HIGH-LEVEL BOMBERS

70 TORPEDO-BOMBERS

O A H U

WHEELER

KANEOHE

Pearl
Harbor

EWA

HICKHAM

Honolulu

✈ US Airbases

0 Miles 15

1st ATTACK BY TORPEDO-BOMBERS

P E A R L   H A R B O R

Pearl
City

CURTISS

RALEIGH

UTAH

SOLACE

NEVADA

ARIZONA   VESTAL

TENNESSEE   WEST VIRGINIA

Ford
Island

MARYLAND

CALIFORNIA

OKLAHOMA

HONOLULU   ST LOUIS

OGLALA   HELENA

SHAW

PENNSYLVANIA

CASSIN   DOWNES

✈ HICKHAM

0 Miles 1

'A Day of Infamy'

△ The martyrdom of the American battle fleet: the forward bridge superstructure collapses forwards on the blazing hull of the *Arizona,* which sank upright to the bottom with more than 1,000 of her crew trapped below decks with no hope of escape. The *Arizona's* rusting hulk remains today as the base for a national shrine to the memory of the Pearl Harbor dead.

◁ The Japanese air strike consisted of two waves. **First attack:** while the Zeros strafed the airfields at Wheeler, Kaneohe, Ewa, and Hickham, the torpedo strike went in against 'Battleship Row', and achieved complete surprise. **Second attack:** the damage was increased by heavy level- and dive-bombing, but this time the Japanese met with a warmer reception from the defenders. Over-all Japanese losses, however, were slight in comparison: 'for the loss of only nine fighters, 15 dive-bombers, and five torpedo-bombers, the Japanese navy had succeeded in putting out of action the entire battleship force of the US Pacific Fleet'.

▷ Bodies of the slain US crewmen were still being washed ashore weeks later

Associated Press

165

their targets and aiming with cool precision. An armour-piercing bomb sliced through the five inches of armour of a turret in the *Tennessee* to burst inside it; another plunged down through the several decks to explode in the forward magazine of the *Arizona,* which blew up. Both the *Maryland* and the *California* were hit with devastating effect.

When a lull occurred at 0825 hours, as the first wave of Japanese aircraft retired, almost every US aircraft at the air bases was damaged or destroyed, the *West Virginia* was sinking and on fire, the *Arizona* had settled on the bottom with more than a thousand of her crew fatally trapped below. The *Oklahoma* had capsized and settled on the bottom with her keel above water; the *Tennessee,* with a turret destroyed by an armour-piercing bomb, was badly on fire; and the *California* had received damage that was eventually to sink her, in spite of all efforts of her crew. Elsewhere, all that was visible of the *Utah* was her upturned keel. The *Raleigh,* deep in the water from flooding and counter-flooding, was being kept upright only by her mooring wires.

While all this had been taking place, at least one Japanese midget submarine—besides that sunk by the *Ward*—had succeeded in penetrating the harbour, passing through the gate in the boom defences which had been carelessly left open after the entry of two minesweepers at 0458 hours. During a lull in the air attacks this submarine was sighted just as it was firing a torpedo at the seaplane tender *Curtiss.* The torpedo missed and exploded harmlessly against the shore, as did a second one. The submarine was attacked by the destroyer *Monaghan* and sunk by depth charges. Of the other three midgets launched from their parent submarines, two were lost without trace; the third, after running on a reef and being fired at by the destroyer *Helm,* was finally beached and her crew taken prisoner. The parent submarines and the 11 other large boats of the Advanced Expeditionary Force achieved nothing.

The second wave of Japanese aircraft—54 bombers, 80 dive-bombers, and 36 fighters, led by Lieutenant Commander Shimazaki of the aircraft-carrier *Zuikaku*—had taken off an hour after the first wave. They were met by a more effective defence and thus achieved much less. In the breathing space between the two attacks, ammunition supply for the US anti-aircraft guns had been replenished, gun crews reorganised, and reinforced; and a number of the Japanese dive-bombers were shot down. Nevertheless they succeeded in damaging the *Pennsylvania,* wrecking two destroyers which were sharing the dry-dock with her, blowing up another destroyer in the floating dock, and forcing the *Nevada*—feeling her way towards the harbour entrance through the billowing clouds of black smoke from burning ships—to beach herself. Meanwhile the high-level bombers were able to make undisturbed practice and wreak further damage on the already shattered ships.

At 1000 hours it was suddenly all over. The rumble of retreating aircraft engines died away leaving a strange silence except for the crackle of burning ships, the hissing of water hoses and the desperate shouts of men fighting the fires. For the loss of only nine fighters, 15 dive-bombers, and five torpedo-bombers out of the 384 planes engaged, the Japanese navy had succeeded in putting out of action the entire battleship force of the US Pacific Fleet.

To the anxious Nagumo the success seemed so miraculously complete, and the price paid so small, that when Fuchida and other air squadron commanders urged him to mount a second attack, he felt it would be tempting fate to comply. Against their advice, he gave orders for his force to steer away to the north-west to rendezvous with his replenishment aircraft-carriers, and thence set a course for Japan.

This was a bad mistake—but Nagumo, who was no airman, was not alone at that time in a lack of appreciation of the fact that the massive gun armaments of majestic

battleships were no longer the most effective means of exercising sea power. In the vast spaces of the Pacific, only the aircraft-carrier had the long arms with which to feel for and strike at an enemy fleet—and a rich reward would have awaited a second sortie by his exultant airmen. Not only was the *Enterprise* approaching Pearl Harbor from her mission to Wake, and could hardly have survived a massed aerial attack, but the repair facilities of Pearl Harbor and the huge oil-tank farm, its tanks brimming with fuel, still lay intact and now virtually defenceless. Without them the naval base would have been useless for many months to come, forcing what remained of the US Pacific Fleet to retire to its nearest base on the American west coast, out of range of the coming area of operations in the south-east Pacific.

Thus Yamamoto's daring and well-planned attack failed to reap the fullest possible harvest—though undoubtedly the blow it delivered to the United States navy was heavy indeed. But it had one effect even more decisive than that on sea power, for it brought the American people, united, into the war.

Perhaps only such a shock as that delivered at Pearl Harbor could have achieved such a result.

CAPTAIN DONALD MACINTYRE retired from the Royal Navy in 1954 after a career spent partly in the Fleet Air Arm and later, for many years, in command of small ships and destroyers. During the Second World War he was a successful Escort Force commander in the Battle of the Atlantic, gaining the DSO and two bars and the DSC. His experience was described in his book *U-boat Killer,* and in *Jutland* he gave a new account of one of the greatest naval battles of all time. In *Narvik* he told in detail the story of some desperate battles at sea. He has done *The Battle of the Atlantic, The Struggle for the Mediterranean,* and *The Battle for the Pacific* for the Batsford Battles series. Other publications include *Rodney* and *Wings of Neptune* (Peter Davies). Captain Macintyre assisted in the naval television series *Sea War,* was naval adviser to *Mutiny on the Bounty.*

Pearl Harbor A POSTSCRIPT

David Elstein and
Richard Humble

Only the formalities remained. It was an ironic situation: Churchill, who had promised to come to America's aid 'within the hour' if the US were attacked, actually declared war on Japan before Roosevelt did—while the President was debating whether or not to include Germany and Italy in his declaration. He eventually decided to ask Congress to name Japan alone; for even now the American conscience baulked at declaring war without dramatic and direct provocation.

Hitler finally rescued Roosevelt from his predicament by declaring war on the United States on December 11, because of repeated US 'provocations' in the Atlantic. Obviously it was the Japanese attack and not the American 'provocation' which induced Hitler to declare war, for otherwise he would have done so a month before. Possibly Hitler had expected an American declaration of war and wanted to strike the first blow; possibly he felt himself under an obligation to support Japan—though Japan had felt herself under no obligation to come to his aid in Russia.

The 'Grand Alliance' was now complete: Britain, the USSR, and the United States of America were ranged against Germany, Italy, and Japan. Such an alliance amounted to a declaration of war to the death against the feverish aggression of the Axis 'geo-politicians'. The Free World had pledged itself to destroy Germany's hopes of a 'New Order in Europe' and a new 'Greater German Empire' in Russia and central Europe, Italy's hopes of a 'Second Roman Empire', and Japan's 'Greater East-Asian Co-Prosperity Sphere'.

Yet the future looked black for the Allies in December 1941. German armies stood at the gates of Moscow and Leningrad. The Japanese were supreme in the Pacific. Only in the Western Desert had the Allies scored a definite success; and Auchinleck's recovery of Cyrenaica was to have as little permanence as the victories of Wavell and Rommel before him. There seemed no possible immediate counterstroke to halt the run of Axis successes on the land, at sea, or in the air.

In such a gloomy hour, it needed more than unreasoning courage to see a way through to Allied final victory, and the reaction of Churchill to Pearl Harbor was typical of the stature of the man. He recalls that:

'I thought of a remark which Edward Grey had made to me more than thirty years before—that the United States is like "a gigantic boiler. Once the fire is lighted under it, there is no limit to the power it can generate". Being saturated and satiated with emotion and sensation, I went to bed and slept the sleep of the saved and thankful.'

A fireball explodes over the Naval Air Station
at Pearl Harbor after the Japanese air attack
in December 1941

BATTLE FOR MOSCOW: THE GERMAN VIEW

Russia, October/December 1941

Generalmajor (AD) Alfred Philippi

Hitler had had his way: his commanders had been prevented from maintaining the impetus of the central drive on Moscow while spectacular but inconclusive victories and advances were completed in the Baltic states and the Ukraine. When, finally, the orders went out to complete 'Barbarossa' with the capture of Moscow, it was too late in the year: Operation 'Typhoon' foundered in the mud and petered out in exhaustion. This is the German verdict on the failure before Moscow, repeated by German soldiers and historians

Bock: his army group was ordered to end the war by taking Moscow

Guderian: at last he was ordered to advance—but was it now too late?

Hoth: his III Panzer-gruppe closed the ring around six Red armies

Since the end of July 1941, Army Group Centre had been holding a front line which extended for over 500 miles—from Glukhov to the Toropets district—and, weakened by the detachment of much of its strength, had been exposed from time to time to active enemy attack. Our troops had been on active service since June 22, and it had been impossible to grant them any but the shortest leaves. We had suffered considerable losses in personnel—especially officers and NCOs—and in equipment. The fighting strength of the infantry divisions had been reduced by one-third.

The losses in personnel could not be quickly or fully replaced because of the length and inadequacy of the lines of communication; yet—fortunately—the morale of the troops remained unaffected by such difficulties. In the motorised divisions, which had borne the brunt of the fighting, losses had been the most severe, especially in trucks and other motorised equipment, which had deteriorated badly due to the state of the dusty or muddy roads. The

supply of spares was inadequate for maintenance; moreover, an inordinate degree of wear and tear had been caused by the loan of armoured vehicles to the sideshows north and south of the front line, hundreds of miles away from their bases. It was questionable whether their mobility would be sufficient for the new operation, one which would have to penetrate at least 300 miles.

Although our defensive battles during the two months' pause had consumed almost as much in the way of supplies and reinforcements as an offensive, the supply position had been helped out to some extent by the railways, which functioned as far as Gomel, Roslavl, Smolensk, and Toropets. True, their capacity was limited, and motor transport became more and more restricted; but somehow the supply depots near the front line were gradually replenished. But the sufficiency of these supplies during the drive to Moscow depended on that drive going according to plan. And, pending the reconstruction of further stretches of railway, there would likely be another shortage to overcome.

With regard to the Soviet battle order, it was becoming clear that the enemy's strength in personnel and *materiel*, and his powers of resistance, had been greatly underestimated. In this connection General Halder wrote in his war diary for August 11, 1941: 'At the outbreak of war we reckoned on about 200 enemy divisions. By now we have counted up to 360. True, they are not armed or equipped up to our standard, and tactically they are often handled in inferior fashion—but they are there! And as fast as we smash a dozen of them, the Russian replaces them with a fresh dozen. And he gains time from the fact that he is near his sources of supply, while we are always moving farther and farther away from ours.'

The enemy had now succeeded in re-establishing a compact line of defence in front of Army Group Centre and in creating with astounding energy such 'hedgehog' positions as that at Yelnya. Between Moscow and our front line, they had built a system of deep defences in echelon and in several zones, one behind the other. Al-

Operation 'Typhoon' began —
the armour of three Panzer
armies reached out for Moscow —
but now the Wehrmacht was
threatened by 'General Winter'

though some of these fortifications were still under construction, the German Army Group Centre was once again faced with the task of carrying out a full-scale break-through if they were to resume the advance.

Six Russian armies of 55 divisions, under the command of Marshal Timoshenko, with his advanced HQ at Vyazma, had been identified between Pokhep and Toropets, concentrated especially along the Smolensk/Moscow motor road. From the south of Pokhep to Glukhov, General Yeremenko (advanced HQ at Bryansk) was in the process of forming a new front with three armies of some 30 divisions. Farther back, operational reserves, amounting to between ten and 15 divisions, were believed to be in the areas of Kaluga, Vyazma, Gzhatsk, Rzhev, and west of Moscow (see map). Compared to the Soviet deployment on the two flanks, north and south, the battle order in the centre was concentrated, confirming the view of the German army leaders that the main enemy strength would be encountered on the motor road to Moscow, and that the campaign would have to be won there or not at all. The battle order merely illustrated a fact that had long been recognised: the importance which the Soviet leaders attached to an attack on their capital city. Their whole behaviour showed without a doubt that they feared and expected it there.

As regards the operational plan, OKH and Army Group Centre were in general agreement. Two concentrations of armour were formed on either side of Smolensk, under General Hoepner (IV Panzergruppe), and General Hoth (III Panzergruppe) — with a third, born of necessity, in the Glukhov area under Guderian (II Panzergruppe). From the strategic standpoint, II Panzergruppe's attack — from Glukhov via Orel — would be only a second best, because it would have been more effective farther north, by a shorter route with Tula as objective — the area of II Army. But such a lengthy 'castling' by II Panzergruppe, which was being brought from the Kiev battle behind the front line, and the consequent need to regroup II Army in the direction of its southern flank, would have certainly caused a considerable postponement in the date of the whole offensive.

In view of the greater distance he would have to cover through enemy-held territory, Guderian was therefore given an advance of two days, which meant that he would have to start two days before the rest of the front to arrive in time for the main battle. This question of timing was therefore another complication.

On September 24 the plan of operation was discussed in the HQ of Army Group Centre at Smolensk by Field-Marshal von Bock and the commanders-in-chief of the various armies and Panzergruppen, in the presence of the Supreme Army Commander Brauchitsch and his Chief of General Staff, General Halder. The decisions reached at this conference were embodied in army group orders issued on September 26.

The German plan for 'Typhoon'

Kluge's IV Army, with IV Panzergruppe, was to break the enemy front on the line of the Roslavl/Moscow road, while IX Army (Strauss) was to break through on the north side of the Smolensk/Moscow motor road. The two armies were then to swing north and south respectively with the bulk of their forces in order to encircle the enemy and rendezvous near Vyazma. Other units

advancing north-east were to secure the pocket and its flanks from counterattacks. Further south, quite separately from this battlefield, II Army was to break the Desna line north of Bryansk and advance in the direction of Sukhinichi. Attacking the Orel/Bryansk line, II Panzergruppe was to roll up the Desna position from the south and, in co-operation with the flanks of the two attacking groups, contain and destroy the enemy forces around Bryansk. The ultimate objective of II Panzergruppe was an eastward pursuit in the direction of Tula.

To secure the lengthening flanks on the southern and northern sides, the left-wing units of Army Group South were to advance in the direction of Oboyan, while the right-wing units of Army Group North were to move up to the Ostashkov lakes. The whole operation was given the code-name of 'Typhoon'.

The force at the disposal of Army Group Centre consisted of 44 infantry divisions, 14 Panzer divisions, eight motorised infantry divisions, and one cavalry division. Six divisions were allotted the task of mopping up in the rear. The II and VIII Fliegerkorps from Luftflotte II (Field-Marshal Kesselring) were assigned to the operation, their main tasks being to destroy the Soviet air force and assist the troops — especially the Panzergruppen — in every possible way.

Difficulties and delays in transport and the assembly of units coming from a distance faced Bock with a dilemma. Should he postpone the date of the offensive or should he attack before all his troops were ready? He chose the earliest possible date involving the smallest risk, and on September 27 fixed September 30 for the attack of II Panzergruppe and October 2 for the general attack. Army High Command and Army Group Centre, despite Hitler's reproaches and the vain efforts for an earlier start of this, the final offensive of the year, did all in their power to ensure success. According to traditional ideas, they would not have been true soldiers had they acted differently from what was prescribed by the politicians.

But even if they were profoundly conscious that it was now more than ever a race against time, and that success depended on whether the weather would permit uninterrupted operations leading to the final goal. It had to be non-stop from Smolensk to Moscow, and those who held Moscow, the transport centre for all the Russians, would win the campaign. What was to happen afterwards could safely be left till later. Such, in brief, were the thoughts of the army leaders.

But for Hitler, it seemed, the dice were already thrown, when in his daily orders for October 2 he infused the troops with his utter confidence in victory. Favoured by brilliantly sunny weather, the offensive opened according to plan, with a tactical surprise inflicted on the enemy. On October 7, after violent fighting, the spearheads of IV and III Panzergruppen closed the ring around large parts of six Soviet armies (30th, 19th, 29th, 24th, 43rd, and 32nd) in the Vyazma area. Simultaneously further south, II Panzergruppe, in an impetuous rush characteristic of Guderian, thrust towards Orel, diverting some of its Panzers to Bryansk, which was taken on October 6. When the link-up with II Army was made on the 9th, two more Soviet armies (3rd and 13th) were encircled to the south of the town, while to the north of it the encirclement of the 50th Army was begun.

While forces were mopping up the enemy trapped in the pockets, the flanks of II and IV Armies pushed through the wide gap thus created towards Sukhinichi and Yukhnov, while IX Army attained freedom of movement in the Rzhev direction. These considerable successes filled officers and men with renewed hopes.

In order to lose no time, and to give the enemy no chance to build up a new defence line, the German command directed all the troops they could spare from mopping up in the pockets to a pursuit of the beaten enemy in the general direction of Moscow. Bock,

after a conference with the Supreme Commander-in-Chief, issued new orders on October 7. For II Panzer Army (a newly-coined term), Tula was given as its next objective, and it was ordered to advance on a broad front along the River Moskva to the southern outskirts of Moscow. The right wing of IV Army was to advance along the line Kaluga/Medyn, IV Panzergruppe towards the crossings of the River Protva at Maloyaroslavets and Borovsk, and along the motor road via Mozhaysk, where the defences believed to exist were quickly to be disposed of. Mobile units still employed at the pockets were to be released as soon as possible and replaced by infantry divisions.

For IX Army (including III Panzergruppe), Brauchitsch laid down an oblique advance via the line Gzhatsk/Rzhev in the direction of Kalinin, in order to free the flanks of Army Groups Centre and North from enemy pressure. Bock, on the other hand, would have preferred to make a rapid advance on Moscow with all available mobile forces, including III Panzergruppe, which he wanted to send as speedily as possible and by the shortest route into the gap between Moscow and the Volga dam, co-operation with Army Group North being restricted to IX Army. The argument in favour of the Bock plan was that an imminent threat to Moscow would automatically relieve the pressure on the north flank, but he nevertheless adhered to the Brauchitsch directive. The task of II Army therefore was to release the mobile units of II Panzer Army at Bryansk, to mop up unaided the enemy troops in that area as soon as possible, and afterwards to carry on the pursuit in the Tula/Kaluga direction.

▽THE RACE TO MOSCOW

'Typhoon' started with one of the Wehrmacht's biggest victories on the Eastern Front, the double battle of Vyazma/Bryansk – a victory which equalled the earlier triumphs at Kiev and Smolensk. Soviet losses were severe, and the road to Moscow seemed open to the Germans. **Left:** A German mobile gun crew in action. **Below:** A group of Soviet soldiers is trapped in the open, and surrenders to an advancing German patrol. But the Red Army was still in being. **Bottom:** Captured Soviet machine-guns, surrounded by Soviet and German dead

our trying to economise in the use of troops, large numbers of the enemy escaped into the forests, where later, as partisans, they were to prove a serious danger to our supply lines. On the other hand, the fighting around Vyazma was a complete success and terminated on October 14.

The great victory in phase one of the offensive was announced by Bock on October 19, when he reported that as a result of the double battle of Vyazma/Bryansk we had captured 673,000 prisoners, 1,242 tanks, and 5,412 guns of all types. The destruction of eight Soviet armies of 86 divisions (13 of them armoured) might well be considered the greatest defeat suffered by our opponents in this campaign.

Heartened by the victory at Vyazma, which released all the units of IV and IX Armies for further operations – and fondly hoping that the weather-god would soon grant a spell of mild frost sufficient to give us firmer roads and more freedom of movement – OKH issued new orders on October 14 for the close investment of Moscow by II Panzer Army on the south and east, and by IV Army and IV Panzergruppe on the west and north. This objective accorded with the Bock plan, but the constantly recurring mention in the orders of co-operation between the flanks of Army Groups North and Centre in a movement towards Vyshniy Volochek did not, for the aim of this thrust was to relieve pressure from growing enemy strength in that area which, although troublesome, was not crucial – and Bock felt that the proposed manoeuvre was a dangerous dispersal of his forces.

In all the circumstances, he thought it would be much better to use III Panzergruppe to strengthen his forces in front of Moscow, leaving the defence of his northern flank to IX Army alone. He was also anxious about his southern flank, where a gap was forming between the northern flank of Army Group South near Belgorod, and the flank of II Army, which was falling behind. An enemy force penetrating this gap could regain freedom of movement and could well prove a serious danger – and although the Soviets were quiet in that sector, it was only a question of time before they saw their chance and made good use of it. A regrouping of units was therefore put in hand on the southern flank – II Army troops, released from Bryansk, were transferred to II Panzer Army, and II Army took over the command of those troops of II Panzer Army which were left behind south of Orel, with orders to advance on the Kursk/Yelets line for the protection of the southern flank.

Simultaneously with these orders of the OKH came an order from Hitler to the effect that 'any capitulation of Moscow was unacceptable, even if volunteered by the other side'. The encirclement therefore was not to be complete: small gaps had to be left through which the civilian population could escape, for Hitler considered that they would add to the chaos and panic in the interior of Russia.

One fact is certain: the break in the weather was a heaven-sent gift for the Soviets. At the end of 1941, time was on their side, and they were bestirring themselves again – even if only locally and in such counterattacks as those at Mtsensk, Kaluga, and now Kalinin.

Nevertheless there was little confidence in Moscow: on October 16 the Soviet government and the diplomatic corps were evacuated to Kuybyshev on the Volga, though Stalin

Bapty & Co Ltd

The optimism of the army leaders in those days is shown by an entry in Halder's diary for October 8: 'To save Moscow the enemy will try to bring up reinforcements, especially from the north. But any such miscellaneous force, scraped together in an emergency, will not suffice against our superior strength, and provided that our strategy is any good at all (and if the weather is not too bad), we shall succeed in investing Moscow.'

'Stopped by the mud, not the Russians'
As fate would have it, however, just when the pursuit of the enemy, beaten on a wide front, was beginning, the weather suddenly broke: heavy rain set in on October 8, ruining the roads and hampering all movement. There was thus no longer any question of a pursuit 'to the last breath of man and horse', which would deprive the enemy of any chance of rest and recovery. By the middle of the month, the right wing of IV Army had only reached the area east of Kaluga, and its left wing the Borovsk/Mozhaysk line, while IX Army had reached

the Volga near Kalinin and Rzhev. Nevertheless, since October 2 two-thirds of the distance to Moscow had been covered, and what sporadic resistance existed had been quickly crushed.

A period of good weather similar to that when we started would have enabled us to put our forces, in full strength, at the gates of Moscow. It was the weather, not the Russians, which stopped us.

More critical was the situation on the right wing, where the bulk of Guderian's force was tied up in the fighting on both sides of the Bryansk pocket, so that he could not put his full strength into his real objective – the advance on Tula – which had looked so promising. Here he too was stopped by the weather, by fuel shortage, and by other supply difficulties. The resistance of a newly-arrived Soviet armoured brigade also proved awkward, and by the middle of the month the weakened spearhead of our Panzer army had not progressed beyond Mtsensk.

The mopping-up of the Bryansk pocket lasted until October 20, and as a result of

himself remained in the Kremlin and proclaimed a state of siege on October 19. Altogether a million people left the city; workers were mustered into large bands and set to work on the conversion of Moscow into a fortress. The world waited in excitement for the fall of Moscow. Were not the Germans capable of even the impossible? What military commander would conceivably abandon such a vital objective, only two days' march from his front line, so long as there was the slightest chance of success? Moscow was important enough to justify the most dangerous gamble.

Instead of the hoped-for frost, the second half of October turned out to be a 'mud season' *par excellence*. The handicaps which it inflicted on the struggling troops, surprising everyone and exceeding all previous fears, were a veritable disaster. Official geographical descriptions emphasising this characteristic of the country were generally known, and there were many senior officers who had fought in Russia during the First World War. But few expected that mud could prove such a handicap to the mobility of an army with modern equipment.

Roads became morasses, and the movements of units were slowed down or brought completely to a halt. Both the fighting power of the troops, and the efficiency of the supply columns, were badly affected, for the only motor road macadamised throughout was from Smolensk to Moscow, and even that could not stand up to the wear and tear of the concentrated and overloaded traffic. All that pioneers and a whole division of infantry sent to keep the road in repair could do, was to fill with rubble the craters caused by Soviet bombs. All other roads were unpaved and became mud baths in which men and horses sank knee-deep and vehicles up to their axles.

The losses in horses and trucks were horrifying. First of all motor transport failed, then horses perished in hundreds through overwork and starvation. Guns and heavy transport ground to a standstill, and the only transport still capable of movement—and that wholly insufficient—consisted of tracked recovery-vehicles and the local *panye* wagons. The former were used for moving guns and trucks that had foundered, but they had not been built for such heavy jobs and their numbers dwindled rapidly.

Everywhere, divisions were fighting hundreds of miles apart. Front-line units were improvised, many of them lacking anti-tank guns capable of dealing with the enemy T-34 tanks that were now appearing in increasing numbers. Reconnaissance cars could not regain their headquarters, with the result that communications were cut, units became confused or lost through lack of control, and tactical and strategic leadership was impossible. Reinforcements reached the front line in a thin trickle or not at all, while air support was reduced to a minimum. There was not even enough fuel for the motor transport that was still mobile—and the only difference between mobile and infantry units was the presence of a few tanks.

The onset of the cold weather brought great hardship to the troops. Clothing was so badly worn that it provided little warmth in the increasingly cold nights, and units were scattered over wide areas and could not be provisioned by normal methods. Many had to rely on neighbouring villages to save themselves from starvation, and often the men took refuge in them from the weather and the cold. Time and again the front-line officers requested the normal winter uniforms and protective clothing for their men, but there was no transport to move it from the supply depots in the rear—even when it existed—while the railways and other means of transport could hardly cope with the most modest demands for ammunition and fuel. Victims of a natural disaster, the troops and supply services thus suffered a dangerous loss of physical strength and technical efficiency.

Several Soviet advantages

The enemy, on the other hand, was well acquainted with the weather conditions of his homeland, and was prepared and equipped to meet them. He was in his natural element. He had no supply lines to be broken and his sources of supply were close behind his front line. He was more mobile than we were, his horse-drawn wagons were lighter, his trucks had better ground clearance and were more rugged. He had mud-chains, and his tanks were more suited to cross-country work than ours.

At first the Soviets contented themselves with small-scale operations, their aim being to stop or slow down the weakening German spearheads by the use of tank obstacles and other improvised methods, until reinforcements should arrive from the north, the south, and the Far East to save their threatened capital. Nevertheless, in the German officers and men, despite all their sufferings and sacrifices, the will to make a final thrust survived, based on a hope of finding better winter quarters in Moscow and its widespread environs.

Fighting forwards against both nature and the enemy, IV Army front moved slowly and laboriously to the River Oka, north of Aleksin, to the River Nara above Serpukhov, and to the Naro-Fominsk/Volokolamsk line. The IX Army, too, after severe fighting around Kalinin, the cornerstone of the Soviet defences, succeeded in forming a defensive front north of Rzhev and making contact near Ostashkov with the southern wing of Army Group North. Bock reports in his diary for October 25:

Resistance on IV Army front is stiffening. The enemy has brought up fresh forces from Siberia and the Caucasus and is making counterattacks on both sides of the roads leading south-west from Moscow. The southern half of IV Army, which has not yet got up most of its artillery because of the mud roads, is forced on to the defensive. On the northern flank of the army, the left wing of IV Panzergruppe is making some progress in the direction of Volokolamsk. . . . Near Kalinin there are new and fierce attacks by the Russians, who on the west side of the city are pushing south-east across the Volga.

But if one thinks on large lines, all this is nothing. It is the dispersal of the Army Group [he wanted a stricter concentration of all forces on Moscow] *and the frightful weather that have brought us to a standstill. The Russian is winning time to reconstitute his shattered divisions and bolster his defences, and it is he who controls the railways and roads that centre in Moscow. It all looks very bad.*

At last, on October 24, II Panzer Army was on the move again, from Mtsensk. Guderian's memoirs say in this connection:

The only road from Orel to Tula, by which this movement had to be carried out, was quite unsuited for heavy traffic and after a few days it broke up. Moreover, the Russians, masters of the scorched earth policy, had blown up all the bridges as they retreated, and in some places had laid down large minefields on either side of the road. Miles of log roads had to be laid down to transport the scanty reinforcements and supplies that were available. Our fighting power depends less on the number of troops and the amount of armour available than on the feasibility of supplying them with fuel. So most of the tanks that were still usable . . . were assembled, and joined by the 'Gross Deutschland' Infantry Regiment to form a vanguard; and this now moved off towards Tula.*

On October 30 this spearhead approached its first objective, Tula, but was not strong enough to capture the city. About this time the eastern flank of II Panzer Army was heavily engaged, having been suddenly attacked by enemy cavalry; but when our rearguard came up, the enemy were thrown back at Teploye after a battle lasting several days. The enemy transport movements, however, showed that further attacks were pending, so this part of the battle front, with the weak II Army further south struggling slowly forward, remained at full tension. Its right wing had meanwhile reached Kursk, and its left wing was moving on Yefremov; but liaison with the north wing of Army Group South failed to materialise, for this had been held up at Belgorod. Field-Marshal von Reichenau (VI Army) was unwilling to cross the River Donets until the concentration of his divisions was complete and their supplies assured.

At the beginning of November, the German army leaders were faced with two alternatives. Could they continue the offensive, or must they abandon it when so near the goal? It was a difficult decision to have to make, and a ghastly responsibility to weigh the pros and cons.

Even before the beginning of the Moscow offensive, which Hitler's fatal interventions had so long delayed, OKH and Army Group Centre had fully realised that there could be no intermediate halt on the way to Moscow. Either Moscow had to be occupied, and a line reached that would be tolerable in a Russian winter—or the front had to be withdrawn to where it stood on October 2, for the sake of the better facilities there and the partly constructed ground defences. The nearer we got to Moscow, the more exposed was our situation, offering a yet unbeaten enemy every possible advantage for a counteroffensive—with unforeseeable consequences for us.

Then, at the beginning of November, the temperature at last sank below zero, the roads became firmer and transport more mobile. An estimate was now made of the fighting capacity of our forces, and in numbers at least it was better than was expected after the horrors of the mud season. Fighting strength, of course, had diminished, but the infantry divisions (the great majority) still had 65% of their original numbers, although the infantry of the Panzer divisions was down by 50%, and the number of tanks had decreased to 35%.

More serious, however, was the fact that the fighting spirit of the troops had suffered. The boasts of National Socialist propaganda

▷ 'The second half of October turned out to be a "mud season" *par excellence*. The handicaps which it inflicted on the struggling troops exceeded all previous fears.' A German message runner picks his way over shell-blasted trees and rugged terrain

that Russia was already prostrate had
proved an illusion, for the reorganisation of
the Soviet army groups on October 10, and
the appointment of General Zhukov to the
command of the 'West Front' (on both
sides of Moscow) and of General Koniev to
the command of the 'Kalinin Front' (on both
sides of Kalinin) had infused the Soviet
forces with a new spirit of initiative. Soviet
resistance was stiffening, and counterattacks were increasing in intensity, thanks
to the arrival of fresh troops from Siberia
and the Caucasus. Outside Moscow and in
the city itself a system of defences was being
feverishly constructed, and from the civilian
population of Moscow a large number of improvised military units was being formed,
to fill gaps in and behind the fighting line.
Everything showed that the Russians were
ready to defend Moscow to the last gasp.

In spite of all doubts and difficulties, the
senior officers concurred with the opinion
of Bock that the offensive should be resumed as soon as the divisions—especially
the artillery—had been regrouped and the
railways regauged to ensure supply. The
leaders were confident that the overworked
troops would once again give their best so
long as they continued to feel themselves
superior to their opponents. Once Moscow
was invested, the danger to the exposed
German flanks would be lessened—granted
always that the last act of the drama was
concluded before the dreaded winter snows
arrived.

Thus Bock—who had always favoured the
single, concentrated thrust at Moscow—and
the army generals became convinced that
this, the last chance of free manoeuvre
(however short-lived) had to be utilised for a
supreme effort. An important consideration
in their decision was that the fall of Moscow
would be an event of enormous political
significance, both for its effects abroad and
as an encouragement to fresh initiatives at
home. Moreover, not one person on the
German side had the slightest doubt that
for Hitler any hesitation about this final
fling, or alternatively a retreat to Smolensk,
was not even a subject for debate. Finally, it
was not only sober calculation, but anxiety
for the safety of a front line so near the
Soviet capital, that helped them to make up
their minds.

The new German plan named less distant
objectives: in the north, the Volga/Moscow
canal; in the south, the River Moskva—
limited objectives for which supplies would
last until the middle of the month.

● II Panzer Army, under cover of an assault
on Tula, was first of all to occupy Kolomna
on the Moskva, and it was also to secure its
threatened flank on the east from its own
resources, as II Army was still hanging
back and was in any case too weak to take
on the task.

● IV Army was to make a frontal attack,
but as it had previously been forced on to
the defensive by strong enemy counterattacks, only its northern wing, with IV
Panzergruppe—in conjunction with III
Panzergruppe—would advance to the Volga
canal.

● IX Army was to secure its right flank, and
with its right wing advance to the Volga
dam south-east of Kalinin.

When these goals were reached, further
steps would be taken towards the close encirclement of Moscow. The dates for the
attacks would be November 15 for IX Army
and III Panzergruppe, and November 17 for
IV Panzergruppe and II Panzer Army.

'Fresh, tough, and savage fighters'

The offensive started according to plan, in clear and frosty weather, but soon after the initial successes the thermometer dropped to −20°C (−4°F); and so sudden an onset of hard winter paralysed man and beast—and crippled the offensive. The battle broke up into local struggles with an enemy who met the German attacks with fresh troops—tough and savage fighters—as the offensive slowed to a yard-by-yard advance. 'Of 34 fresh divisions brought in from Siberia, 21 are facing Army Group Centre,' wrote Bock in his diary on November 18. And the Soviet air force, operating from nearby bases, was once again very active while the Luftwaffe, whose aid was so sorely needed at this crisis, seemed to be paralysed by cold and by fuel shortage. Temperatures of 30°

of frost were now being recorded, and the morale of the German troops declined at an alarming rate: the cold tore larger gaps in their ranks than the enemy's fire. Machine-guns, motor engines, and locomotives froze up, the paralysing cold slowed down the supply services, and the general situation began to look more gloomy every day.

Nevertheless, the traditional courage of the German army was not dissipated in this struggle against the forces of nature, and its exploits were magnificent. By the end of November the right wing of IX Army had reached the Volga between Kalinin and the dam, and III Panzergruppe, advancing via Klin and Istra, reached the Volga canal south of Dmitrov. On November 27 the II Panzer Division was only 19 miles from Moscow, and the glittering towers of the

Kremlin beckoned to the invaders. On November 28, the VII Panzer Division pushed a bridgehead over the Volga south of Dmitrov, but, counterattacked in front and on the flanks, the armour could make no further progress. The prescribed wheel southwards towards Moscow had to be abandoned, while IV Army at this moment was involved in heavy defensive fighting and could take no part in the attack as had been laid down.

On the southern wing II Panzer Army, in a thrust that took it to the Gorlovo/Mikhaylov line, had first to secure its eastern flank. All that it then had left for a northward thrust was the XVII Panzer Division, which on November 25 forced its way as far as Kashira. Here it remained for two days, attacked from all sides, until Guderian   ▷

As the second phase of 'Typhoon' progressed, the Panzer spearheads were gradually brought to a halt by the worsening conditions—and by stiffening resistance. **Opposite page:** A knocked-out T-34; fortunately for the Wehrmacht, the T-34 was still in short supply with the Red Army, which was forced to employ them singly or in small units. Thus the German tank-killer crews found their task somewhat easier than it was later to become. **Below:** Camouflaged German Pzkw Mk III tanks on the move; the early frosts had improved the going, but the tremendous drop in temperature which accompanied the approach to Moscow crippled all movement. Machine-guns and motor engines froze up in the paralysing cold

'TYPHOON' REACHES ITS LAST GASP

The morale of the German troops was declining at an alarming rate; for the cold tore larger gaps in their ranks than the enemy's fire. By the end of November Bock had realised that Soviet resistance had not been broken, and that Army Group Centre had been pushed to its limits. **Above:** German infantry in a snowstorm. Without the proper winter greatcoats and warm boots with which the Red Army was equipped, there was a limit even to the endurance of the Wehrmacht. **Left:** German infantry prepare for a further advance; the Panzer forces could do no more, and the battle for Moscow now depended on the tenacity of the German infantry armies. **Right:** A German heavy machine-gun position, sited between two buildings on a Soviet collective farm south of Livny; note the method of snow camouflage for the helmets. The German II Army's advance to the Tim/Yelets/Yefremov line marked 'the limits of the possible' for the men and machines of the Wehrmacht

Bapty & Co Ltd

Sado-Opera Mundi

Ullstein

asked on November 27 for assistance, by means of a IV Army attack across the River Oka. The army group could not grant his request and instructed him to abandon the northward attack, and instead to consolidate the position on his western flank, near Tula. Meanwhile, II Army had advanced against slight opposition to the Tim/Yelets/Yefremov line. This situation marked the limits of the possible.

All this meant that the Moscow offensive was definitely a failure, and the army leaders had to admit it. Bock, who had realised the gravity of the situation in the last days of November, now devoted all his efforts to convincing OKH that the offensive had lost all meaning and purpose, if they were not to risk the loss of all the forces engaged. On November 29 he reported to the Chief of the General Staff that 'if within a few days they did not force the north-west Moscow front to collapse, the offensive must be abandoned. It would merely lead to a soulless frontal struggle with an enemy who apparently still had large reserves of men and *materiel*'. And on December 1 he reported to the OKH in writing:

'After further bloody struggles the offensive will bring a restricted gain of ground and it will destroy part of the enemy's forces, but it is most unlikely to bring about strategical success. The idea that the enemy facing the Army Group was on the point of collapse was, as the fighting of the last fortnight shows, a pipe-dream. To remain outside the gates of Moscow, where the rail and road systems connect with almost the whole of eastern Russia, means heavy defensive fighting for us against an enemy vastly superior in numbers. *Further offensive action therefore seems to be senseless and aimless, especially as the time is coming very near when the physical strength of the troops will be completely exhausted.*'

Gloomy days were to elapse, and the events of December 4 and 5 were to pass, before the High Command became convinced of the hopelessness of any further offensive

in 1941. Finally, on December 5, it approved Bock's proposal to withdraw III and IV Panzergruppen from their exposed positions first of all to the Istra/Klin line, and to withdraw II Panzer Army behind the Don and Shat sector. The IV and IX Armies were already in defensive positions.

The Soviet command realised the position and took immediate advantage of their success. They delivered a counterblow which struck Army Group Centre at the moment of its greatest weakness, with its 67 divisions extended over a 600-mile front in a single long line with no reserves, in exposed salients and with no time to regroup.

Nobody could now harbour any illusions regarding the illimitable dangers that resulted from the failure of the German thrust at Moscow. It was still uncertain how the troops would stand up to the consequences; one thing was certain—officers of all ranks would have to exert all their will-power to master the crisis. Only Hitler was still hesitant, and it needed all the persuasive powers of the army leaders, both staff and in the field, to induce him on December 8 to issue his Directive 39, which agreed to a transition to defence 'in strength-economising fronts to be determined by the Supreme Commander-in-Chief of the army'.

Morally and physically, Field-Marshals von Brauchitsch and von Bock were broken men, and shortly afterwards they received their dismissal.

Hitler had proclaimed the political aim of his aggressive war to be the elimination of Soviet Russia as a power factor on the Continent. It was with this object that he gave his armed forces the order to overthrow the Soviet military power. *Both the aim and the order were the illusions of a demoniac personality obsessed by belief in his omnipotence.*

Had the plan of the army leaders been adopted, the German offensive against Moscow would have started by the beginning of September at latest—four weeks earlier than was actually the case. It would have

177

▽ THE GERMAN VERDICT: 'WE WERE STOPPED BY THE MUD'

'The generals' warning had been ignored by Hitler' □ 'The advance on Moscow was resumed too late' □ 'An immediate drive on Moscow after the fall of Smolensk would have been carried through at the most favourable time of the year and would not have been held up by the mud during the first half of October'

been carried through at the most favourable time of the year and would not have been held up by the 'mud period'; and all conditions for movement and fighting would have been far more favourable than they turned out to be a month later. All these considerations were clearly pointed out by the army leaders to Hitler in good time; they are not the product of hindsight.

If anyone still needs to be convinced of the probable success of the offensive had it been carried out on the lines suggested by the military staffs, he should bear in mind that the time required for an advance of 300 miles to Moscow was probably little more than for the 500 miles covered in the first phase of the campaign—about four weeks. One must remember that the offensive as

actually executed—in spite of the mud—came to within a few days' march of Moscow by the end of October. Quite clearly, had it started in good time, the second phase of the campaign would have resulted in the occupation of Moscow and comfortable winter quarters for the Wehrmacht. True, a Soviet counterattack would even then have been possible, but conditions would have been much more unfavourable to them, and we could have met it in carefully planned defensive positions. The supply problem would certainly have been easier to solve.

But such a fundamental alteration in the situation might have offered a real statesman fresh opportunities of producing a political solution to the conflict.

[*General Philippi's biography is on p. 106.*]

BATTLE FOR MOSCOW: THE RUSSIAN VIEW

Timoshenko: he had to take the first shock when 'Typhoon' began

Central Press

Zhukov: his West Front guarded the direct approach to Moscow

Novosti Press Agency

Yeremenko: his Bryansk Front lay in the path of the Panzers

Russia, October/December 1941

Colonel D. Proektor

The Russian view of the Battle of Moscow differs in essential interpretation from the German view. The Russian armies may have been decimated during this retreat, but the Wehrmacht had had to pay for its gains. Moreover, the main German forces never reached Moscow—only a few patrols penetrated the outer suburbs—and the mud was just as much a handicap to Russians, moving out to fight defensive actions, as it was to the Germans. But the extraordinary stubbornness of the Russians had forced the enemy to throw in all his reserves

The battle for Moscow belongs among the most important events of the Second World War. In planning its war against the Soviet Union, the German High Command expected to defeat it within a few weeks and occupy Moscow. In the 'Barbarossa' plan approved by Hitler on December 18, 1940, it was stated that the seizure of Moscow 'will mean decisive success from both the political and economic angles, apart from the fact that the Russians will be deprived of their most important railway centre'. The German strategists expected that, after occupying the Soviet capital, the main forces of their 'Eastern Army' would attain a line from Archangel to the River Volga, and the remaining industrial region in the Urals would be destroyed by bombing.

The surprise attack by Hitler's Wehrmacht against the Soviet Union on June 22, 1941—when the Red Army was incompletely prepared for successful defence—placed the Soviet forces in a very difficult position. In the first months of the war the Red Army underwent the bitterness of severe defeats.

This was a time when combat experience was as yet inadequate and there was not enough modern equipment. The anti-Hitler coalition had not yet been formed, and the resistance movement in Europe had not yet become large-scale.

By autumn 1941, events on the eastern front continued to develop unfavourably for the Soviet Union. The Red Army was forced to retreat and suffered great losses in defensive battles. In the first three weeks alone of the invasion, the enemy put 28 Soviet divisions out of action, and more than 70 suffered losses of 50% or more in men and equipment. The Germans thought that the plan for a 'Blitzkrieg' against the Soviet Union was succeeding.

However, the military failures and heavy losses did not shake the will of the Soviet people or their faith in final victory over the enemy. The Germans also suffered great losses on the eastern front: by mid-July the attacking German forces had already lost over 100,000 men, 50% of their tanks, and 1,284 aircraft.

The Germans firmly retained the strategic initiative throughout the summer months of 1941. The front was drawing inexorably nearer to the Soviet capital. But in the Smolensk battle, the Red Army held the enemy up for two months—and this radically altered the course of the campaign. The German High Command had to carry out a partial regrouping of its forces and temporarily cease the offensive on the central (Moscow) sector. The German offensive on Moscow was delayed by the growing resistance of the Red Army, and only when he had achieved success in the Ukraine did Hitler decide, in early September, that the time had come to strike at Moscow. The German General Staff viewed the offensive against the Soviet capital as 'the last battle of the eastern campaign', one which would bring the war to a successful conclusion. The operational plan received the code-name 'Typhoon'. The Germans intended to pounce on Moscow like a hurricane and seize it, after first defeating the main forces of the Red Army.

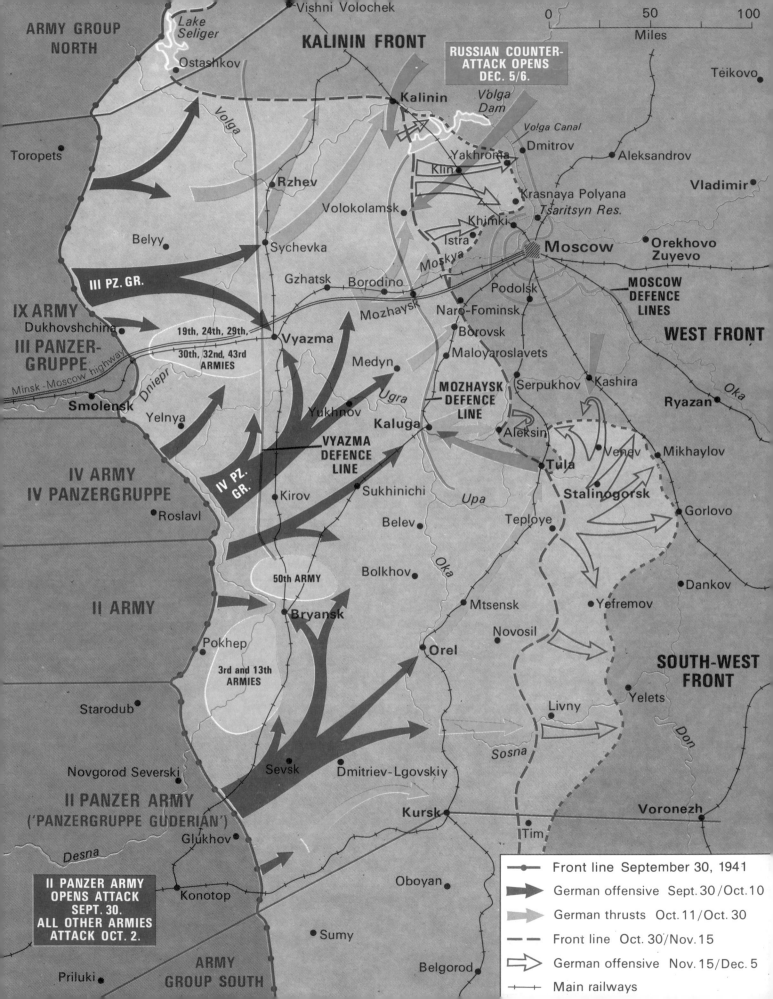

ARMY GROUP NORTH

Lake Seliger

Ostashkov

0   50   100

Miles

KALININ FRONT

Vishni Volochek

Teikovo

Kalinin

RUSSIAN COUNTER-ATTACK OPENS DEC. 5/6.

Volga Dam

Volga Canal

Yakhroma   Dmitrov   Aleksandrov

Klin

Krasnaya Polyana

Tsaritsyn Res.

Vladimir

Toropets

Volga

Rzhev

Volokolamsk

Khimki

Istra

Moskva

Moscow

Orekhovo Zuyevo

Belyy

Sychevka

Gzhatsk   Borodino

Mozhaysk

Podolsk

Naro-Fominsk

MOSCOW DEFENCE LINES

WEST FRONT

III PZ. GR.

IX ARMY

Dukhovshchina

III PANZER-GRUPPE

19th, 24th, 29th, 30th, 32nd, 43rd ARMIES

Vyazma

Medyn

Borovsk

Maloyaroslavets

Serpukhov

Kashira

Ryazan

Oka

Minsk-Moscow highway

Dniepr

Smolensk

Yelnya

Ugra

Yukhnov

MOZHAYSK DEFENCE LINE

Aleksin

Venev

Mikhaylov

IV ARMY
IV PANZERGRUPPE

IV PZ. GR.

Kaluga

VYAZMA DEFENCE LINE

Tula

Stalinogorsk

Gorlovo

Roslavl

Kirov

Sukhinichi

Upa

Teploye

Dankov

II ARMY

Belev

Oka

50th ARMY

Bolkhov

Mtsensk

Yefremov

SOUTH-WEST FRONT

Bryansk

Novosil

3rd and 13th ARMIES

Yelets

Pokhep

Livny

Orel

Starodub

Don

Novgorod Severski

Sevsk

Dmitriev-Lgovskiy

Sosna

II PANZER ARMY ('PANZERGRUPPE GUDERIAN')

Voronezh

Glukhov

Kursk

Desna

Tim

II PANZER ARMY OPENS ATTACK SEPT. 30. ALL OTHER ARMIES ATTACK OCT. 2.

Konotop

Oboyan

Belgorod

Sumy

Priluki

ARMY GROUP SOUTH

•—•—•	Front line September 30, 1941
➤	German offensive Sept. 30/Oct. 10
➤	German thrusts Oct. 11/Oct. 30
– – –	Front line Oct. 30/Nov. 15
⇨	German offensive Nov. 15/Dec. 5
+—+—+	Main railways

The Siege of the Soviet Capital

◁ At the beginning of the German drive on Moscow, Timoshenko's six armies stood on the Vyazma defence line, prepared to defend the Rzhev/Vyazma/Bryansk axis. But 'Typhoon' opened with another disaster for the Red Army: the battle of Vyazma/Bryansk was a classic victory of encirclement, removing some 750,000 men from the Soviet front-line strength. The Red Army fell back on Kalinin/Kaluga/Orel; but meanwhile STAVKA was welding the forces defending Moscow into a reorganised West Front, under the new command of General Zhukov. His shrewd assessment of the Wehrmacht's limitations—plus the construction of 'hedgehog' positions at Tula and the Volga canal—kept the Wehrmacht from making its planned encirclement of Moscow. The capital itself was the centre of a triple line of defences. Even so, the spearheads of II Panzer Division had closed to within 19 miles of Moscow and had reached the outer suburbs by December 5. And on that day, as the Wehrmacht closed in on Moscow from the north, the Red Army went over to the offensive. The German Army Group Centre found itself forced to fight for its life

△ Red reserves in training with machine-guns

1941 September 26: 'Operation Typhoon', the German offensive for the capture of Moscow, is ordered.
October 2: The Moscow offensive begins in ideal weather conditions.
October 7: Panzer spearheads seal off the Soviet forces in the Vyazma and Bryansk pockets.
October 8: Heavy rains set in. The 'mud season' begins to strangle the German mobile units.
October 14: Resistance ends in the Vyazma pocket.
October 19: Stalin proclaims a state of siege in Moscow.
October 20: Resistance ends in the Bryansk pocket, but many Soviet troops manage to escape the net.
October 20/25: Stiffening Soviet resistance and struggling supply-lines halt the original 'Typhoon' offensive. New orders go out for advances on more limited objectives to safeguard the German front line.
November 15: After initial success, the second phase of the Moscow offensive is paralysed by 20° of frost and ever-strengthening Soviet forces.
November 27: Panzer spearheads struggle to within 19 miles of the northern outskirts of Moscow but are halted by fierce counter-attacks. South of Moscow, the advanced German units reach Kashira but are also halted.
December 5: After obstinate argument, Hitler agrees to abandon the Moscow offensive for the winter. Army Group Centre begins to retreat upon safer defensive positions.
December 6: The Soviet counteroffensive begins.

The blow was to be dealt by Army Group Centre, under the command of Field-Marshal von Bock. Its task was to dismember the Soviet defences with three powerful armoured formations striking north and north-east from the areas of Dukhovshchina, Roslavl, and Glukhov; to surround and destroy the formations of Western and Bryansk Fronts in the Vyazma and Bryansk areas; and then to break through to Moscow.

The Germans concentrated the main forces of their eastern front for the 'final blow': 1,000,000 men, 77 divisions—including 14 Panzer and eight mechanised—1,700 tanks and assault guns, 19,500 guns and mortars, and 950 combat aircraft. General Hoepner's IV Panzergruppe was redeployed to Moscow from near Leningrad. From the Ukraine came the II Panzer Army of the very experienced Guderian. General Hoth attacked on the northern flank with his III Panzergruppe. About half the German soldiers, guns, and mortars at that time available on the Soviet-German front were concentrated on the Moscow sector, as were three-quarters of the tanks and one-third of the available forces of the Luftwaffe.

Army Group Centre was opposed by the forces of Western Front (under the command of General I. S. Koniev), Reserve Front (Marshal of the Soviet Union S. M. Budenny), and Bryansk Front (General A. I. Yeremenko). The number of divisions on each side was about the same. However, the Red Army infantry divisions had 5,000 to 6,000 men each, while the German ones had 13,000 to 15,000. The general German superiority in tanks and artillery was more than twofold, and in aircraft was almost threefold.

Hitler and his General Staff had 'sentenced' Moscow in advance. As far back as July 8, 1941, the Chief-of-Staff of OKH, Halder, had written in his diary: 'It is the Führer's unshakable decision to raze Moscow and Leningrad to the ground, so as to be completely relieved of the population of these cities, which we would otherwise have to feed through the winter. The task of destroying the cities is to be carried out by aircraft. In no circumstances are tanks to be used for this. A national catastrophe which will deprive not only Bolshevism, but also Muscovite nationalism of their centres.'

The German Supreme Command issued an order to Army Group Centre on October 12: *The Führer has reaffirmed his decision that the surrender of Moscow will not be accepted, even if it is offered by the enemy.... Everyone who tries to leave the city and pass through our positions must be fired upon and driven back. Small exits left open, providing a possibility for mass departure of the population into the interior of Russia, are only to be welcomed. For other towns, also, the rule must operate that before they are seized they should be destroyed by artillery fire and air sorties, and the population turned to flight. It would be utterly irresponsible to risk the lives of German soldiers to save Russian towns from fires or to feed their populations at Germany's expense. The more the population of Soviet towns is directed into the interior of Russia, the greater will be the chaos in Russia, and the easier it will be to administer the occupied eastern territories and make use of them.*

'All roads to Moscow open'

The Wehrmacht's attack on Moscow began before dawn on October 2, 1941. A very difficult situation at once developed for the

Soviet forces. Faults were noticed in the structure of the defence. The reserves, with whose aid the commander of Western Front was trying to conduct counterattacks, were neither mobile enough nor sufficient in numbers. Counterattacks were mounted by infantry and cavalry without adequate artillery or air support. As a result, the German Army Group Centre succeeded in making deep penetrations in the line of defence. The main forces of Soviet Western and Reserve Fronts—the 19th, 24th, 30th, and 32nd Armies—were surrounded near Vyazma. As Marshal of the Soviet Union G. K. Zhukov wrote in his memoirs: 'By the end of October 7, all roads to Moscow were, in essence, open.'

In this extremely critical situation the Soviet forces fighting within the encirclement tied up 28 German divisions for more than a week. Marshal of the Soviet Union A. M. Vasilevsky has this to say of it: 'This was of great strategic importance, since it gave the Soviet Command the opportunity to take urgent steps to organise a defence on the Mozhaysk line, to which forces were hastily redeployed from the right wing of Western Front, from other fronts, and from the depths of the country.' Some of the surrounded forces broke out of the ring.

In accordance with the STAVKA order forces began to be redeployed urgently from the right wing of Western Front, from North-Western and South-Western Fronts, divisions arriving from the Far East, the Volga, Siberia, and Kazakhstan, and tank brigades and artillery regiments from the reserve. By no means were all the units well-trained or well-equipped, and there was a shortage of arms and ammunition. Nevertheless, it was possible to assemble fairly quickly 14 rifle divisions, 16 tank brigades, 40 artillery regiments, and other units. The Staff of the Supreme High Command of the Red Army combined the forces fighting near Moscow into a single Western Front commanded by Army General G. K. Zhukov, and the so-called Mozhaysk Defence Line became the main line for Moscow's defence. The new front commander was an experienced military leader. Marshal of the Soviet Union K. K. Rokossovsky writes 'In my view G. K. Zhukov remains always a man of strong will and decisiveness, clear and gifted, exacting, persistent and purposeful. These qualities are all, undoubtedly, indispensable to a great military leader, and G. K. Zhukov has them.'

So after the serious failure at Vyazma a new defensive front was being urgently established, and armies were being formed. The Volokolamsk area began to be defended by the newly-created 16th Army of General K. K. Rokossovsky, Mozhaysk by the 5th Army of General D. D. Lelyushenko (General L. A. Govorov from October 18), Maloyaroslavets by the 43rd Army of General K. D. Golubev, and Kaluga by the 49th Army headed by General I. G. Zakharkin. In the Naro-Fominsk area the defence was taken up by the 33rd Army of General M. G. Yefremov.

Fighting began on the Mozhaysk line on October 10. It was especially fierce in the areas of Mozhaysk, Maloyaroslavets, and Kaluga, towards which the German forces had begun to move from Vyazma. The outnumbered Soviet units attempted by stubborn defence to win time for fresh and larger forces to come up. The battles became very fierce. On the historic battlefield of Borodino, where the famous battle with Napoleon had

ВОИН КРАСНОЙ АРМИИ,
СПАСИ!

taken place in 1812, the 32nd Rifle Division, under the command of Colonel V. I. Polosukhin, held up the onslaught of a strong German armoured formation for five days, while the 316th Rifle Division of General I. V. Panfilov made a stubborn defence around Volokolamsk. The Soviet forces were wearing out the attackers and causing them great losses. Nevertheless, Army Group Centre, still possessing superiority in forces, was able to penetrate the Mozhaysk Defence Line in a number of directions, and Kalinin, Mozhaysk, Volokolamsk and Kaluga fell.

The situation had become menacing.

Soviet troops, arriving on the Mozhaysk Defence Line in ever greater numbers, fought against the German divisions with great tenacity and élan. At the cost of supreme efforts they succeeded in stopping the enemy at the end of October and beginning of November; and Hitler's armies, which in October 1941 had made a leap of up to 165 miles, were compelled to go on to the defensive 45 to 75 miles from Moscow. A pause ensued. The Soviet High Command had gained invaluable time to strengthen further the approaches to the capital.

The disruption of the offensive against Moscow came as a complete surprise to Hitler. On November 13 Halder, and the Chiefs-of-Staff of all the army groups arrived in Orsha, where the Headquarters of Army Group Centre then were.

The only question put by Halder to the assembled company amounted to 'What next?' Should the armies of the eastern front dig in until the spring, or could they continue the offensive on Moscow?

The first to speak was Field-Marshal von Rundstedt's Chief-of-Staff, General von Sodenstern. For Army Group South he demanded that the offensive in the Ukraine should stop, and the forces go over to the defensive. After all, his troops stood far to the east, on the Don before Rostov, some 220 miles east of Army Group Centre.

Field-Marshal von Leeb's Chief-of-Staff, General Brennecke, had no need even to think about it. Army Group North was now so weakened that there could be no question of continuing the offensive on Leningrad. Its forces had long gone over to the defensive.

General Greiffenberg, Bock's Chief-of-Staff, then reported: 'The Field-Marshal considers that the capture of Moscow is a military and psychological necessity. The danger that we might not succeed must be taken into account,' he continued, 'but it would be even worse to be left lying in the snow and the cold on open ground 30 miles from the tempting objective.' It was decided to begin a second offensive against Moscow as soon as possible.

The German forces did everything within their power to prepare for this final blow. Their generals addressed them in words full of confidence in imminent and final victory for the Führer and for German arms. The commander of IV Panzergruppe wrote in his order for the offensive: 'The time of waiting is over. We can attack again. The last Russian resistance before Moscow will be smashed. We must . . . complete this year's campaign. Our Panzergruppe has the good fortune to deal the decisive blow. For this all strength, all fighting spirit, and firm resolve to annihilate the enemy are needed.'

Despite the pause in military operations before Moscow, the Soviet Union's position remained very difficult. Germany had already occupied territory on which about 40% of the country's population lived, on

◁ 'Soldier of the Red Army, save us!' — and in truth the fight for Moscow was the fight for Russia's national survival

△ Moscow's defenders throw up makeshift anti-tank defences in the streets of the capital; note the fire to thaw out the ground

▽ Moscow was the vital focus for the Red Army's reinforcements: here fresh troops parade on Red Square in late November

which 69% of its iron, 58% of its steel, and 60% of its aluminium were produced. Gross industrial production had declined by 2·1 times between June and November 1941. To wage war in these conditions was incredibly difficult.

Nevertheless, the first successes had already been achieved. In the north and south — at Rostov and Tikhvin — Soviet forces had gone over to the counteroffensive, thrown the Germans back, and then established a stable defensive front. The pause before Moscow had enabled STAVKA to introduce fresh infantry and cavalry divisions and tank brigades into Western Front. Most of the front's armies had been reinforced with anti-tank and rocket artillery, and on the main sectors an anti-tank defence in depth had been constructed. Altogether, Western Front received an additional 100,000 men, 300 tanks, and 2,000 guns in the first half of November.

But what was happening in the capital?

Moscow: a fortress-city

Moscow had begun preparing itself for defence in the first days of the war. On June 22 the city had been designated as in 'state of threat', because of the danger of air attacks, and barrage balloons were put up. The militia marched about the streets; Moscow formed 12 divisions. Here and there artists and decorators could be seen camouflaging buildings, squares, and streets. From the air the Bolshoi Theatre looked like a group of small houses, and most large buildings looked like gardens or parks. At night the city was shrouded in complete darkness. The wardens looked carefully at windows to prevent even the weakest ray of light getting out. The Muscovites assiduously learned ways of putting out fires, becoming initiated into this skill by the newspapers, by posters stuck on walls and fences, and by special films shown in every cinema. Apartment buildings set up their own volunteer fire-fighting teams, and shop windows, blocked up by boards or sand-bags, were unrecognisable. The inhabitants of the city looked uneasily at the anti-aircraft guns which appeared on the squares and at bridges and most important buildings. Some 25 'destroyer' battalions of militia patrolled the outskirts day and night, ready to liquidate paratroops if they should suddenly appear.

The Luftwaffe's first air raid on Moscow took place exactly a month after the beginning of the war, on the night of July 21/22. The efficient organisation that had gone into building air defence bore fruit at once — 22 aircraft were shot down. In the following weeks Luftwaffe activity increased. When fires began in Moscow, the inhabitants fought them actively and showed not inconsiderable heroism. An extensive fire at the Central Airport was put out by soldiers of the airport guard headed by Chief of Watch Korobchilkin while still under fire from enemy aircraft. (In those days, by the way, the useful experience of Londoners in fire-fighting was disseminated in the pages of the newspaper *Izvestia* by the British journalist Alexander Werth.)

Moscow withstood the test from the air: of the 4,212 German aircraft which took part in 36 raids between July and September 1941, only 120 broke through to the city.

Simultaneously the Muscovites built defensive positions with great zeal on the approaches to the city. First of all they built the so-called Vyazma Defence Line in the

rear of Western Front, and on July 16 the State Defence Committee decided to build the Mozhaysk Defence Line. This line on the near approaches to the capital was built by the efforts of 100,000 inhabitants, two-thirds of whom were women, while more than 250,000 inhabitants of Moscow and district helped to build the Podolsk and Kuntsevo Defence Lines. Besides this the Muscovites built a defensive line along the northern and eastern outskirts of the capital, the most important strongpoints of which were in the area of the Khimki and Tsaritsyn reservoirs.

Defensive lines were built not only on the approaches to Moscow, but also in the city itself. It was divided into two combat sectors, north and south, and each of them had three rings of defences — the first along the Ring Road, the second on the Sadovoye Ring, and the third on the Boulevard Ring. In a short time the city was covered with a dense network of firing points, anti-tank obstacles, barricades, and other defensive installations.

In sum, the Muscovites on the defence lines covering the capital dug 422 miles of anti-tank ditches and 278 miles of breastworks, constructed 238 miles of anti-tank barriers, built more than 30,000 firing points — including foxholes and pillboxes of all types — and put up more than 812 miles of barbed-wire entanglements. Some 955 miles of wooden obstructions were built in the forests of Moscow district. Moscow was turned into a fortress.

The Muscovites subordinated their entire lives to the interests of the front, which now stood a few dozen miles from the city. Despite the fact that 800 large industrial enterprises had been evacuated from the city and that two-thirds of the machine tools had been removed, despite the difficulties caused by shortages of factory equipment, fuel, electric power, and raw materials — the Muscovites undertook production of rocket artillery, mortars, several kinds of field gun, and almost all types of small arms. During the period of the defence of Moscow, its factories and workshops repaired and sent to the front 263 guns, 1,700 mortars, and 15,000 rifles, and repaired and handed over to Western Front 2,000 lorries.

In this difficult time everyone strained every nerve to ensure victory over the enemy. All lived, worked, and fought with the one thought: 'The defeat of the enemy must begin in front of Moscow.'

Many Muscovites became partisans. In the forests of Moscow district there were previously prepared partisan bases with stores of food, medicaments, arms, and ammunition. Special attention was given to the formation of small partisan groups, many of which were formed in Moscow itself — for example, in Timiryazevsky district of Moscow three partisan groups of 48 people were set up, in Leningradsky district five groups, and in Proletarsky two. Partisan groups and detachments were also formed in the other districts of the capital. These partisan groups were armed with rifles and grenades, equipped with warm uniforms and with food, and sent into the rear of the German forces. In all, on the territory of Moscow region, more than 40 partisan detachments, consisting of about 10,000 avengers carried on the struggle against the invaders. In Tula region there were more than 30 partisan detachments. Thus were reborn the methods of conflict which the Russian people had successfully

used at the time of Napoleon's 1812 invasion.

The former Chief-of-Staff of 20th Army, General Sandalov, describes the state of the Moscow defences as follows:

'As soon as it began to get light, I set off for the Army Staff at Khimki. When the car reached the Leningrad motorway I saw the results of the immense work on defences done by the troops of the Moscow Defence Zone and hundreds of thousands of the workers of Moscow. The various anti-tank obstacles on the streets, the powerful defence lines girdling the outskirts of the city, and the Moscow/Volga canal, were ready to give the enemy a fitting reception. The defence lines bristled with metal spikes and dense barbed-wire entanglements. In front of them minefields had been prepared.'

State of emergency proclaimed

The serious situation which developed at the front after the successful beginning of the German offensive against Moscow required emergency measures, as has already been pointed out. On October 19 a Decree of the State Defence Committee was published. It stated that the defence of the capital on lines 60 to 75 miles west of it had been entrusted to the Commander of Western Front, Army General G. K. Zhukov, and that responsibility for defence of Moscow at its approaches had been laid on the Commander of the Moscow Garrison, Lieutenant-General P. A. Artemyev.

With the aims of ensuring security of the rear of the Moscow defences and safeguarding the rear of the forces defending it, and also in order to suppress subversive activity by spies, saboteurs, and other agents of Nazism, the State Defence Committee decreed:

● Introduction of a State of Emergency in the City of Moscow and regions adjacent to it from October 20, 1941.

● Prohibition of all movement in the streets of persons and transport between 12 midnight and 5 am.

● Disturbers of order to be arrested immediately and handed over to a Judge of the Military Tribunal, and provocateurs, spies, and other enemy agents inciting to breaches of order to be shot on the spot.

The State Defence Committee called on all workers of the capital to maintain order and tranquillity.

The entire country provided support for the defence of Moscow. Trains brought troops and military equipment from the central regions of the country, from the Urals, Siberia, the Volga, and Central Asia; and every day the three fronts of the Moscow sector were supplied with everything they needed by 100 to 120 trains. For purposes of comparison, it is interesting to note that in the critical days of the Moscow battle the German Army Group Centre was able to bring up only 23 trains a day instead of the required 70.

STAVKA had adequate information on the new offensive which was being prepared, and on Army Group Centre's preparation of its main blows on the flanks of western Front. General Zhukov was enjoined to prevent the outflanking of Moscow; while the Kalinin and South-Western Fronts (the northern and southern neighbours of Western Front) were given the task of firm defence of their positions and tying up German forces to prevent their redeployment against Moscow.

For the second offensive against Moscow the German High Command allocated to

Army Group Centre 51 divisions, including 13 Panzer and seven mechanised. A powerful armoured formation from III and IV Panzergruppen was aimed at the city from the north-west, and II Panzer Army from the south-west. The IV Army of Field Marshal von Kluge attacked from the west, and the flanks of this armour and infantry 'battering ram' were covered by IX and II Armies.

By mid-November, the Soviet Western Front had a larger number of divisions than the German Army Group Centre. But they were further below strength than the German divisions and had lower fire-power. The Germans therefore continued to maintain a general superiority—$2\frac{1}{2}$ to 1 in guns and mortars, and $1\frac{1}{2}$ to 1 in tanks. The Soviet air forces outnumbered the German $1\frac{1}{2}$ to 1.

After concentrating its main forces along the major roads leading to Moscow, Army Group Centre renewed the assault on the Soviet capital on November 15 and 16.

Bloody battles again broke out. Slowly and doggedly, suffering great losses, the German forces were forcing their way towards Moscow, seeing the seizure of it as their only aim —their final aim—and that which offered salvation. However, the deeply echeloned artillery and anti-tank defences of the Soviet forces prevented them from breaking the front. The Soviet divisions withdrew slowly but in complete order to previously prepared lines already occupied by the artillery, and the Command of the front, and its staff (whose Chief was General V. D. Sokolovski), directed their troops efficiently. Everywhere the Germans met stubborn and heroic resistance. On the Volokolamsk highway the 316th Rifle Division of 16th Army repulsed a massive German tank strike, while in a four-hour battle at Dubosekovo railway sidings, a group of 28 soldiers from this division, using anti-tank rifles and 'Molotov cocktails', destroyed 18 enemy tanks and prevented a breakthrough. Of these men, 23 were killed in this battle, and all who took part were awarded the highest decoration, the title of Hero of the Soviet Union. The tank brigade commanded by General M. E. Katukov destroyed over 30 tanks by fire from ambush in only five days of fighting near Volokolamsk.

On the left wing of Western Front, Guderian's II Panzer Army had already reached the important industrial and communication centre of Tula by the end of October. Its numerous attempts to capture the town had been successfully repulsed by troops of General I. V. Boldin's 50th Army and detachments of the Tula workers, and when the second offensive began, Guderian attempted to by-pass Tula from the northwest, block it off, and then seize it. The defenders of Tula again repulsed the German attacks. They used anti-aircraft guns successfully against the German armour, held out, and Tula became the southern bastion of Western Front. Guderian then left part of his forces to cover his flanks from right and left, and dashed northwards with his main armoured forces, so as to come out *east* of Moscow and join up with the II and III Panzergruppen, which were attacking from the north-west. He struck at the crossings over the Oka River near Kashira.

A critical situation developed. By the end of November the German forces on the northern sector of Western Front had reached the Moscow/Volga canal, and the village of Krasnaya Polyana, where they were 18 miles from Moscow—with their spearheads even closer. In the centre of the front they had

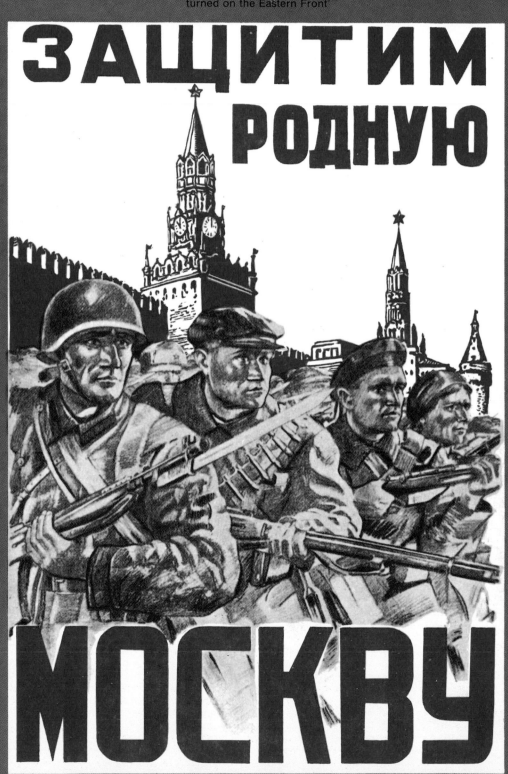

THE RUSSIAN VERDICT: 'HITLER WAS BEATEN BY MISTAKEN STRATEGY AND OUR HEROIC RESISTANCE'

'The heroic resistance of the Soviet people had not been taken into account by Hitler's strategy' □ 'The battle before Moscow was a decisive defeat for the German Blitzkrieg' □ 'Hitler's chances of a quick conquest of the Soviet Union had vanished' □ 'The defeat at the walls of Moscow forced the Wehrmacht on to the defensive for the winter' □ 'The tide had turned on the Eastern Front'

ЗАЩИТИМ РОДНУЮ МОСКВУ

'We will shield our Moscow!'

reached the village of Burtsevo, 25 miles from Moscow, and in the south, Kashira, 69 miles from the capital.

The Soviet defensive front was thus bent into an arc, very weak sectors formed, and it seemed that the last break-through would happen, and then . . . But the defenders of Moscow did not waver, even at this apparently desperate moment.

The German General Blumentritt, former Chief-of-Staff of IV Army during the Moscow offensive recalled: 'As the difficulties increased, the tempo of the offensive by both Panzergruppen slowed down, but all the same they continued to beat through towards Moscow. By throwing into battle their last reserves they captured Klin and reached the Moscow/Volga canal. In this area their northern flank was suddenly attacked by fresh Russian units.

In the last days of November our forward units attacking towards Moscow reached Ozeretsky, and reconnaissance elements of our tank units penetrated even into the western outskirts of Moscow. At this juncture the offensive strength of both our Panzergruppen petered out.'

Marshal G. K. Zhukov gave the following assessment of the state of the German forces at the final stage of their offensive: 'By deploying his striking forces on a broad front and making such long-range gestures with his armoured fists, the enemy extended his forces along the front in the course of the battle for Moscow to such an extent that in the final engagements on the near approaches to Moscow they had lost their capacity to force a way through. The Hitlerite Command had not expected such large losses in the battle for Moscow as were suffered by the task force groups of its elite units, and could not make good these losses and strengthen its group of forces in the Moscow area.'

North of Moscow, where the position was particularly menacing, the Western Front Command had already begun, on November 30, to introduce formations of the 1st Shock Army of General V. I. Kuznetsov, newly received from High Command Reserve. The advance guard of the approaching army — Lieutenant-Colonel V. V. Ryabov's 50th Rifle Brigade — went straight from the march to upset the units of General von Manteuffel's VII Panzer Division which were crossing the Moscow/Volga canal. Here the Germans began hastily to take up the defensive. A little to the south, where the enemy had come closest of all to Moscow, units of yet another fresh army from High Command Reserve — the 20th — were put in in the first days of December. By their counterattacks they forced the I Panzer Division on to the defensive.

Thus the dogged defence by 16th and 30th Armies and the introduction of the fresh 1st Shock and 20th Armies brought about a change in the situation on the north-west approaches to Moscow. The German forces which comprised the stronger, northern, encirclement wing were everywhere brought to a halt. South of Moscow a counterblow by General P. A. Belov's 2nd Cavalry Corps, which had been moved to the Kashira area, succeeded in throwing back Guderian's Panzer units attacking northwards.

And so in the first days of December the offensive against Moscow was finally halted by the counterblows of Soviet forces. In the 20 days of the second offensive German losses were about 155,000 killed, wounded, and frostbitten, about 800 tanks, and 300 guns and mortars — and as Army Group Centre had no reserves, it was compelled to give up any further attempts at taking Moscow.

The capital continued the grim life of a city under siege. The now familiar air raid alarms would sound, the civil defence groups would take up their posts, and many inhabitants would make for the shelters. Things became more difficult with food and consumer goods, and many foods, clothing, footwear, and other goods were rationed. The fuel situation became worse, and public services of all kinds were limited by wartime conditions.

Interesting extracts from the diary of a Moscow woman doctor, E. Sakharova, were published in the Soviet press:

November 14. Today there were two daylight alerts. And while the sirens were howling an air battle was on, the windows in the clinic rattled terribly from the firing of the long-range guns. When the patients began to leave the clinic, they had to wait in the vestibule as there were so many shell fragments flying.

Tonight at 9.30 pm they again announced an air raid. The siren howls and turns your

Novosti Press Agency

△ Cossack cavalry broke through to the rear of Army Group Centre, and operated with great skill and hardihood in the wooded country

◁ 'The well-fed, warmly-clad Siberians, fully-equipped for winter fighting'—an anti-tank rifle squad moves up to the front. As the German thrusts were held to the north and south of Moscow, the Wehrmacht was forced to commit all its reserves; but soon the Red Army, with its fresh troops available, was able to counterattack, and relieve the immediate threat to the capital

▽ A smashed German supply column on the Klin road; German losses during the offensive were 155,000 killed, wounded, or frostbitten, 800 tanks, and 300 guns

whole soul over. In a word, the raids get more frequent every day, life becomes more disturbed. I can't get used to the noise of the siren. People's minds are somehow changing oddly. Nearest relatives tell of the deaths of their kin with indifference, just mentioning the fact, but the real reaction comes afterwards, later on . . . A time not to be repeated, terrible things happen. Hitler must have been born of the devil to a witch. It must be so . . . how much suffering that mad maniac has brought on people.

Of course, not all Muscovites reacted so acutely to the military tone of the situation. Those who were younger, or had stronger nerves, fairly quickly became used to both the noise of the sirens and the enemy air raids, mastering once and for all the rule 'when in war behave as in war'. But what is indicative and important is not this difference in the way they took it, but the fact that all the citizens of the capital believed in victory and were doing everything they could to achieve it as quickly as possible.

The Red Army's stubborn defence during October and November prepared the ground for a counteroffensive before Moscow. The general balance between the forces of both sides had somewhat changed by the beginning of December. The German forces retained their superiority in tanks and artillery. But Hitler had no reserves of manpower. On the other hand, the High Command of the Red Army had 58 infantry and cavalry divisions in strategic reserve. A large part of these was sent to Moscow,

where STAVKA proposed to seize the strategic initiative from the enemy by a decisive blow, and to defeat him. Soviet airmen were more and more actively gaining command of the air. Between November 15 and December 5, the Luftwaffe made about 4,500 sorties; the Soviet air forces made 16,000.

The immediate objective of the counteroffensive was to defeat the enemy strike formations which had pushed forward on the flanks of the front. Further direction of operations was to be carried out by means of orders issued in the course of the counteroffensive and dependent on the way the situation developed, so as to cause the enemy maximum losses, drive him back as far as possible from Moscow, and remove the immediate danger to the capital.

Preparation for the counteroffensive—in which it was planned to use three fronts (Western, Kalinin, and South-Western)—was undertaken while the defensive battles were still going on.

Marshal Zhukov recalled: 'Late on the evening of December 4 the Supremo [Stalin] rang me up and asked "How can we help the front apart from what's already been given?"'

'I replied that we must have support from the air forces of High Command Reserve and Home Air Defence and also tanks with crews, if only 200. The front had an insignificant number of tanks and without them it wouldn't be able to develop the counteroffensive quickly. "There are no tanks, we can't give you any," said Stalin, "but the air forces you shall have. Agree it with the

General Staff. I'll ring them now. Remember that Kalinin Front goes over to the offensive on December 5, and on December 6 so does the operational group of the right wing of South-Western—in the Yelets area."'

The frosts at that time were very severe. Deep snow made it very difficult to concentrate the forces, regroup them, and send them out to their starting positions, but all the difficulties were overcome, and by the morning of December 6 all arms of service were ready to begin the counteroffensive.

By this time the general relationship of forces on the Soviet-German front had changed. By December 1 the German army and those of Hitler's allies amounted to 5,000,000 men, 35,000 guns and mortars, 1,400 tanks, and about 2,500 aircraft; while the Red Army had rather more than 4,000,000 men, 32,000 guns and mortars, about 2,000 tanks, and about 3,700 aircraft. In other words, whereas in October the Germans had a twofold superiority in artillery, it had now almost disappeared, and in tanks and aircraft they had lost it; on the contrary the Red Army surpassed them by $1\frac{1}{2}$ to 1.

The plan for the Moscow counteroffensive envisaged simultaneous operations by the three fronts—Kalinin Front (General I. S Koniev), Western Front (General G. K. Zhukov), and South-Western Front (Marshal of the Soviet Union S. K. Timoshenko). Their immediate task was to defeat the weakened German strike groups. Kalinin Front was to strike at the rear of the forces facing Western

Front. Western Front was to defeat the enemy north-west and south of Moscow. South-Western Front was to defeat the Germans in the Yelets area and help Western Front to destroy the enemy before Tula.

Apart from the fresh 1st Shock and 20th Armies newly received from STAVKA Reserve, Western Front was also given the 10th Army of General F. I. Golikov, which was introduced into the battle south of Moscow, into the flank of Guderian's army. The new reserve armies were to play the main role in the counteroffensive, and in addition to them, STAVKA released to Western Front six armoured brigades and other units.

At the beginning of December the Germans had before Moscow more than 800,000 men, about 10,000 guns and mortars, about 1,000 tanks, and more than 600 aircraft. In the Soviet forces there were 719,000 men, more than 5,700 guns and mortars, 720 tanks, and 1,170 aircraft.

The counteroffensive by Western and Kalinin Fronts began on December 5/6. From the very beginning military operations took on a fierce character, and the troops of Generals I. I. Maslennikov, V. A. Yushkevich, and D. D. Lelyushenko penetrated the German defences north of Moscow and soon cut the Kalinin/Moscow railway. Generals K. K. Rokossovsky and V. I. Kuznetsov's formations threw the German strike forces back from Yakhroma and Krasnaya Polyana. South of Moscow the divisions of Generals P. A. Belov and F. I. Golikov struck at Guderian's II Panzer Army and began to squeeze it. In their retreat the Germans abandoned equipment, wounded, and frost casualties.

The German generals attempted to make their troops hold their positions. Hitler ordered: 'The troops must be compelled by the personal influences of their commanders, commanding officers, and officers to resist fanatically on their present positions, without regard to enemy breakthroughs on the flanks and in the rear. Only by leading their troops in this way can the necessary time be gained for movement of reinforcements from the homeland and the West which I have ordered to be carried out.'

But Western, Kalinin, and South-Western Fronts were pushing Army Group Centre further and further back. Now the Germans were retreating on a front of about 500 miles, losing thousands of killed and wounded, equipment, and transport. The Soviet forces were liberating one town after another. They regained Kalinin, Klin, Volokolamsk, and Kaluga, and advanced from 60 to 155 miles. The German assault forces which had attacked towards Moscow were beaten.

At the beginning of January 1942, the counteroffensive on the Soviet western strategic sector came to an end. The forces of Western, Kalinin, and South-Western Fronts, attacking in the severe conditions of a cold and snowy winter had defeated 38 enemy divisions before Moscow. The Wehrmacht's Panzer armies had suffered a severe defeat. The immediate threat to Moscow and the Moscow industrial area had been removed.

In the prolonged, tense, and especially dramatic struggle, not only was the capital of the Soviet Union, the historic centre of the state, saved, but the basic question of strategy—whether Hitler could, as he supposed, win a 'blitzkrieg' victory over the Soviet Union in 1941—was answered. At the walls of Moscow the myth of the German Army's invincibility was dispelled, and the doctrine of 'blitzkrieg' completely destroyed.

Hitler's plans to conquer the Soviet Union in 1941 by means of a 'short campaign' had therefore failed, and the leaders of the Third Reich had to face the need for a long drawn-out war. The German army's main forces were firmly tied up on the eastern front, so Hitler and his generals had to change their war strategy and all their military-economic estimates. Between December 1941 and April 1942 the German General Staff were to dispatch as reinforcements about 800,000 men and 40 new divisions to the Soviet-German front, and the drain of German forces from Europe now removed all possibility of reviving the 'Sea Lion' plan to eliminate Britain.

In evaluating the results of the Red Army's Moscow victory, Winston Churchill wrote that the Russian army, far from being beaten, was fighting better than ever, and in the coming year its numbers would undoubtedly grow. Winter had come. A prolonged war, he continued, was inevitable. All the anti-Nazi states, great and small, rejoiced in the first failure of the German blitzkrieg. While the German armies were waging a mortal struggle in the East, the threat of an invasion of England was removed. Churchill concluded that no one knew how long this struggle would last.

After the defeat before Moscow, Hitler dismissed almost all the generals occupying the highest posts on the eastern front, including the Commander-in-Chief of the Army, Brauchitsch, and all three army group commanders—Bock, Leeb, Rundstedt 35 men altogether.

The defeat before Moscow showed convincingly how much Hitler's strategy had erred in evaluating the possibilities of Soviet resistance, and the extent to which it had underestimated the patriotism of the Soviet people. Marshal Zhukov emphasised: 'In the war with the Soviet Union the Nazis, despite their careful preparation, had to face a number of important and unforeseen circumstances. For example, they never thought that they would have to fight on two fronts inside the Soviet Union; on the one hand the Red Army, on the other powerful partisan forces, national avengers in their rear, operating energetically under the leadership of numerous underground party organisations. Nor did the Nazis reckon that their forces would be so exhausted and bled white that already in 1941, without having achieved a single one of their strategic objectives, they would be forced to assume the defensive and lose the strategic initiative.'

After the defeat before Moscow the relations between Germany and its allies became significantly more complicated. The German leaders demanded from their vassal countries more and more new soldiers, raw materials, and food, laying a heavy burden on Hitler's allies—who even without it had already borne great losses and fundamentally undermined their economies. Hence the growth of dissatisfaction with the war and passive resistance to German dictation.

The German army was forced to assume the defensive for the whole of the winter and spring following its defeat before Moscow, and was never again able to mount an offensive simultaneously along the entire strategic Soviet-German front.

The victory at the walls of Moscow gave a new stimulus to strengthen the anti-Hitler coalition and enhance co-operation between the great powers fighting against the Axis bloc. In the occupied countries of Europe the scale of the resistance movement grew bigger. Soviet partisans began to strike ever stronger blows on the invaders. Dawn began to break over Europe.

COLONEL D. M. PROEKTOR is a Soviet military historian who fought against Germany in the Second World War. A Doctor of Historical Sciences, he has written two books: *The War in Europe, 1939-41,* and *Through the Dukla Pass;* and a number of articles on military history. He is also a member of the team of authors which wrote the collective works: *History of the Great Patriotic War 1941-45,* Vols I-IV; *World History,* Vol X; *Lessons of History are Irrefutable;* and *The Russo-Japanese War.*

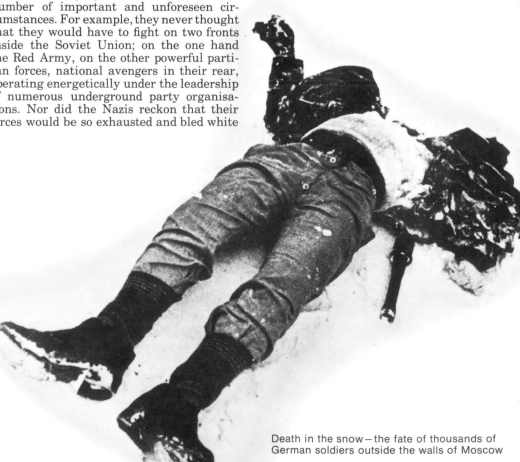

Death in the snow—the fate of thousands of German soldiers outside the walls of Moscow

Novosti Press Agency

'We shall bomb Germany by day as well as by night in ever-increasing measure, casting upon them month by month a heavier discharge of bombs, and making the German people taste and gulp each month a sharper dose of the miseries they have showered upon mankind'
Winston Churchill

THE 1000 BOMBER RAID

Britain and Germany, January 1941/May 1942

Ralph Barker

The first year of the air war – and the sometimes indiscriminate Luftwaffe raids over Britain – had convinced RAF Bomber Command that only a full-scale bombing policy was of any value. In addition to German industry, German morale had to be worn down by heavy, sustained raids. Yet not only were the aircraft lacking for such a full-scale offensive, but it was not until 1941 that the RAF leaders were fully aware of Bomber Command's weakness in finding and hitting its targets. New tactics of saturation bombing were essential – and the first German city singled out for experiment was Cologne

At the beginning of 1941, British hopes of aggressive action against Germany were vested almost entirely in a strategic air offensive, to be mounted by RAF Bomber Command. For the British, still without allies, with their land forces deprived of contact with the enemy following the retreat from Dunkirk, and with their naval blockade largely nullified by Germany's vast conquests in Europe, a bombing campaign offered the only apparent hope of so weakening the industrial and economic structure of Nazi Germany that a landing back on the Continent might one day be contemplated. This situation had been fully recognised by the British War Cabinet in 1940, and when the threat of invasion eased after the Battle of Britain an air offensive – of the greatest possible magnitude – against Germany had been immediately called for, to begin as soon as possible.

Successive directives in the closing months of 1940 had disclosed a twofold aim: the primary object was to be a precision attack on German production of synthetic oil. The secondary object, to be attempted only when the weather was unsuitable for precision bombing, was to be an attack on German morale. This latter aim was to be achieved by the concentrated bombing of Berlin and other large cities, where targets in the middle of industrial areas were to be chosen

as aiming-points. Such raids constituted the first British experiments in area bombing.

From the start of the war the British Air Staff had held to a belief in the efficacy and economy of selective attack on German industrial targets, the most vulnerable of which was believed to be oil. The War Cabinet, on the other hand, believed that the German blitz on British cities ought to be answered by heavy reprisal raids, and some such raids had in fact been carried out. British experience was that morale was toughened rather than weakened by bombing on the German scale, and the German blitz had in any case failed in its intention; but the War Cabinet was led to believe by its economic and political advisers that the situation in Germany was different. Both the German economy and German morale were far more likely, it was thought, to be affected by a bombing campaign.

A compromise between the two viewpoints was not difficult to achieve. Nights when the weather was clear enough for selective attack numbered not more than one in four or five, so if such attacks were to be regarded as exclusive the bombers would remain idle for most of the time. On nights when the weather was unsuitable for precision bombing, the choice of large industrial areas as targets seemed sensible

BIRTH OF THE ALLIED BLITZ

After the fall of France, bombing seemed to be the only way in which Britain could strike back at Germany; but the aircraft with which she began the war had too light a bomb-load to be able to mount an offensive which could really hurt the enemy. The Wellington—an incredibly tough machine—formed the mainstay of the bombing force until the new 'heavies' began to arrive during the summer of 1941. The first of these new aircraft—the Stirling, Manchester, and Halifax—all had their teething troubles, but they gave the RAF new power, and the RAF crews vital new experience for the big raids to come

Handley Page Halifax Mk II The successor to the twin-engined Hampden and Hereford designs (see p. 299), the Halifax was the second of the new RAF 'heavies'. It made its first raid against the docks and shipping of Le Havre, in March 1941. **Max speed:** 282 mph. **Range:** 1,030 miles. **Crew:** seven. **Armament:** nine ·303 Browning machine-guns; up to 13,000 lbs of bombs

Vickers Wellington Mk III Its simple but sturdy 'geodetic' (lattice-work) construction enabled the Wellington to endure an astonishing amount of punishment. **Max speed:** 255 mph. **Range:** 1,325 miles. **Crew:** six. **Armament:** six ·303 Browning machine-guns; up to 6,000 lbs of bombs

Short Stirling Mk I The Stirling was the first four-engined bomber to enter service with the RAF; the first raid flown by Stirlings was in February 1941, against oil-storage tanks in Rotterdam. **Max speed:** 260 mph. **Range:** 1,930 miles. **Crew:** seven or eight. **Armament:** eight ·303 Browning machine-guns; up to 14,000 lbs of bombs

Avro Manchester 1A The twin-engined forerunner of the Lancaster had a short and unsuccessful service life, for its Rolls-Royce Vulture engines proved to be underdeveloped and unreliable. **Max speed:** 265 mph. **Range:** 1,200 miles. **Crew:** seven. **Armament:** eight ·303 Browning machine-guns; up to 10,350 lbs of bombs

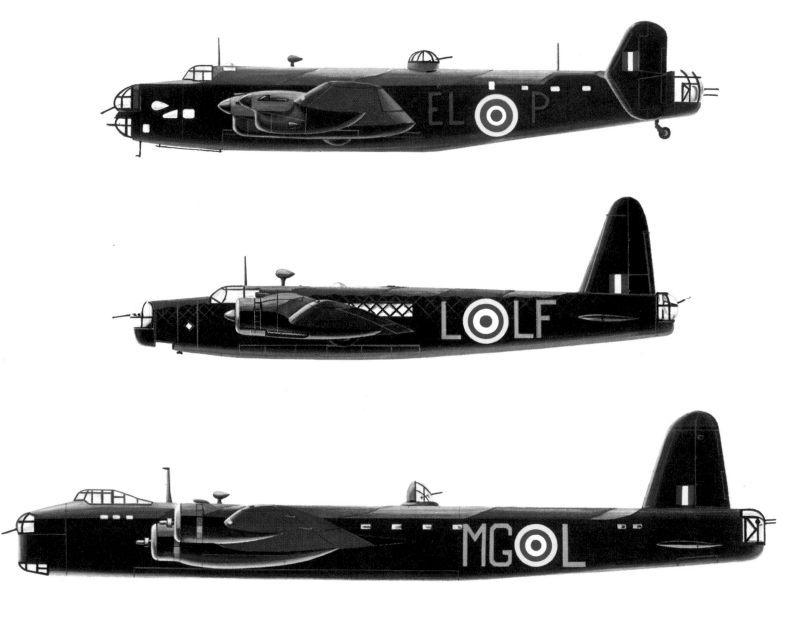

John Batchelor

190

and practicable; there was even the likelihood that, if these targets were carefully chosen, attacks on them might assist and be complementary to the more selective bombing of vulnerable industries.

The fact that a new phase in British bombing had been begun in December 1940, with the decision to attack industrial areas, was known to the British people from the official communiqués, publications, and photographs released in the course of 1941; that these raids were partly designed to cause nervousness and apprehension among the inhabitants of the German industrial centres, and ultimately to undermine morale, was also well publicised.

The question of the moral rectitude of such a campaign hardly arose at this time. Germany, by her unprovoked aggression, and by her bombing of British cities, whatever the purpose of that bombing might be — and the British were led to believe, not merely by British exhortation but by German propaganda, that the purpose had been to break their spirit and bring them to the point of surrender — had brought whatever disaster might befall her on herself. And just as the submarine was the natural weapon of the vastly inferior naval power, so the destruction of industrial capacity and national morale by bombing was the inevitable resort of the power out-classed on land.

Aware that they could never defeat a powerful Continental adversary unless that adversary were first fatally weakened by some indirect means, the British people, in the course of 1941, espoused the weapon of aerial bombardment, knowing the weapon from their own experience in the first six months of that year for what it was — an imprecise weapon likely to be most effective against civil populations.

On June 22, 1941, following the German attack on Russia, the British Prime Minister clearly foreshadowed a bombing offensive aimed specifically at the German people. 'We shall bomb Germany,' said Churchill, 'by day as well as by night in ever-increasing measure, casting upon them month by month a heavier discharge of bombs, and making the German people taste and gulp each month a sharper dose of the miseries they have showered upon mankind.' The British people were thus well aware of the plans for the devastation of Germany by bombing, and it was a policy of which they approved. They expected, and indeed were promised, powerful retaliation in kind, and they braced themselves to absorb it, preferring an attritional warfare in which the whole population shared the dangers to the wholesale slaughter of their young men which they imagined was the likely alternative.

As it happened, Bomber Command was far too weak in 1941 to pursue either of its aims with any chance of success. The diversion of scientific and industrial effort from defensive to offensive channels after the Battle of Britain came slowly. Not only was Bomber Command lacking in modern, high-performance aircraft, effective weapons, and scientific aids to navigation and bombing: it had also suffered, in the first few months of the war, one serious defeat and one severe setback, the implications of which were still not fully appreciated. This setback was the loss of the French airfields, which had greatly increased the length of sorties against Germany; the defeat was the inability, through prohibitive losses, to operate

in daylight. The change to night flights of long duration had revealed, in the course of 1940, operating deficiencies which were not easy to evaluate or rectify.

In spite of the confident tone of official communiqués, and the optimistic intelligence estimates of the effects of British bombing on German oil and morale, the C-in-C Bomber Command, Air Marshal Sir Richard Peirse, was not alone in fearing that far too high a percentage of British bombs missed their targets. In the longer-range attacks, indeed, he believed that only one aircraft out of five found its primary target at all. Such photographic evidence as was available in January 1941 — of the area attack on Mannheim of December 17, 1940, and of two precision attacks on the twin Gelsenkirchen oil plants — could only have aggravated his fears. The Mannheim attack, mounted in retaliation for the German raids on Coventry and Southampton, had failed to achieve any effective concentration; the two Gelsenkirchen oil plants, photographed on December 24 after attacks involving nearly 300 aircraft, were found to have suffered no major damage.

Failure to face the facts

The work of damage assessment, however, was still hampered by a shortage of aircraft cameras and a lack of systematic photographic reconnaissance, so that the truth about Bomber Command's inability to hit its targets remained partly obscured. Bigger and better aircraft were coming into the squadrons, among them the Manchester, the Stirling, and the Halifax; and although for the whole of 1941 the command would have to operate without the radar aids it needed and was demanding, it seemed reasonable to expect that bombing results would improve with experience during the year. In any case, unless the offensive was to be abandoned for the time being, the best would have to be made of it. To fail to look the facts of the war in the face, to view Bomber Command's destructive capacity and Germany's economic vulnerability with optimism, was for Britain a psychological necessity at this time.

The precision attack on oil remained, at the beginning of 1941, the foundation of British war strategy, and a further directive of January 15 put additional emphasis upon it, on the assumption that the critical period for Germany would be the first six months of that year. But this new directive had to be put on one side in the months that followed, first through bad weather, and then through the all-out attack by German submarine and surface raiders on British supply shipping in the Atlantic, forcing Britain on the defensive and resulting in Churchill's Atlantic Directive of March 9, 1941.

From that point until July 1941, when the immediate crisis was over, the command was obliged to concentrate on naval targets, beginning with the battle-cruisers *Scharnhorst* and *Gneisenau,* which sought refuge in dry dock at Brest and thus became the Command's primary target. More than 1,100 sorties were flown against them in the next eight weeks, but in all these attacks only four bombs actually hit the ships. Yet in the period from March to July the bombers, with valuable help from Coastal Command, did accomplish their essential task of neutralising the ships and keeping them immobile at Brest.

After conclusive reports that one at least of the ships had been severely damaged,

Bomber Command turned to the precision attack of targets in Germany connected with the Atlantic battle — such as submarine bases and factories producing long-range aircraft — and to the area attack of ports and naval installations. These area attacks were among the most successful yet undertaken. Hamburg, Bremen, and Kiel all suffered severe damage, much of it in the docks and shipyards; in a ten-week period up to the end of May, 900 sorties were flown against Kiel, where the three main naval shipbuilding yards suffered temporary production losses of 60, 25, and 100%.

These targets, however, shared features which made them comparable to coastal targets, which in good weather the bombers had always been able to find. Precision and area attacks on inland targets were no more accurate than before. Nevertheless, British bombing in this period graduated from being a mere nuisance, ridiculed in German home broadcasts, to something calling for stoicism and ultimate retribution, something for which the German High Command would one day have to find an antidote.

Although the pre-occupation with naval targets had tended to obscure the lessons about precision bombing at night that had seemed about to be learned at the end of 1940, enthusiasm for the oil plan had cooled completely by July 1941, when Bomber Command was at last free to resume the strategic offensive. The command's failure to hit precision targets had in fact left it in danger of operating without a clear strategic aim.

The difficulty was to find an alternative target system which offered a real prospect of damaging the German war machine. Eroded by the needs of Coastal Command, diversions of aircraft and crews to overseas theatres, and the formation and succour of its own operational training units, Bomber Command remained much too small to mount an effective attack on morale, which in a country the size of Germany was such a gigantic task that the British had to seek some alternative target system, the destruction or dislocation of which might be within the bombers' power.

The choice this time fell on transport, and particularly on nine specified rail transport targets in the Ruhr area, which were listed in the new bombing directive of July 9. Germany's military adventures in Russia were believed to be putting an unprecedented strain on her transport system, and if this could be upset in the vulnerable Ruhr area, an important contribution might be made to the disruption of the German economy. Such a disruption would also have an effect on morale, especially as the rail targets were chosen not only for their importance in the transport system but also because of their proximity to industrial areas. Once again a compromise had been reached between precision and area bombing.

The transport plan looked and was a makeshift and attritional plan, the choice of a target system to suit the command's operational capability rather than a target whose destruction might win the war. It was a further significant step towards the acceptance of a tenet already propounded by Sir Charles Portal, Chief of the British Air Staff — that the most suitable object from the economic point of view was not worth pursuing if it was not tactically attainable. Bomber Command remained Britain's only offensive striking force against Germany: therefore, if Bomber Command could not hit its preferred targets, other targets had to be found.

Meanwhile, Germany's ability, in June 1941, to mount a land offensive against Russia had shown that in fact Britain's estimates of her economic vulnerability had been entirely misconceived. And despite the claims made – claims which had been well supported by independent intelligence appreciations – the RAF bombing of Germany could have had little or no strategic effect so far. These two misconceptions – of Germany's vulnerability and of the effect of RAF bombing – while not vital in themselves, were to have considerable influence on the future course of the air offensive. The estimates of the Ministry of Economic Warfare, always subject to conjecture, had been discredited, and confidence in such calculations was inevitably shaken. For the British Chiefs-of-Staff, even the attack on rail transport was looked upon as no more than a transitional policy, to be employed until such time as Bomber Command was strong enough to pass to an all-out offensive against civilian morale, still regarded by the politicians as Germany's weakest point.

June 1941: Wasted opportunities
With the opening of the German offensive against Russia, fresh opportunities seemed to present themselves to the Royal Air Force. First, it seemed, was the chance to take tactical advantage of the pre-occupation of the Luftwaffe in the east by stepping up short-range fighter and day bomber operations over France; second, of more immediate importance, and of potential strategic value, was the belief that such operations might compel the Germans to return some of their fighters to the west, thus relieving the Russians. The aim of Fighter Command, together with No. 2 Group of Bomber Command, became to draw the Luftwaffe into combat over France with the idea of destroying the remnant that had been left there, opening the way for the daylight bombing of precision targets in Germany and at the same time compelling the reinforcement of the west at the expense of the east.

The 'Circus' operations, as they were known, foundered for much the same reasons as the German plans had foundered in the Battle of Britain: an efficient radar early-warning system in the hands of the defenders, the short range of the attacking fighters, and the necessity to defend the slow and lightly-armed bombers (in this case the Blenheims of No. 2 Group). British casualties were heavy, various attempts at daylight bombing proved costly, and the wisdom of a night role for Bomber Command was confirmed. Most significant was the reinforcement of the belief that the long-range fighter would always be at a disadvantage when confronted by the short-range fighter operating within the orbit of ground-controlled radar and within easy reach of its base. This belief, much later and almost by chance, was proved to be erroneous.

In the summer of 1941 it seemed that Bomber Command, with a new group operational (No. 1), with new heavy bombers in service, with heavier and more efficient bombs, with a more realistic target system – and with the Luftwaffe pre-occupied elsewhere – could now mount an effective strategic offensive. Yet the continuing inaccuracy of British night bombing was gradually being confirmed as night photography improved and more and more bombers were

fitted with cameras. Scepticism about Bomber Command's effectiveness culminated in the appointment by Lord Cherwell, the British Prime Minister's scientific adviser, of a member of the War Cabinet secretariat, a Mr Butt, to examine some 600 photographs taken by the night bombers in June and July 1941.

The result, on August 18, was the Butt Report, which revealed that matters were far worse than even the sceptics imagined. Only about a quarter of the crews claiming to have reached their targets actually did so, and in raids over the Ruhr, where Bomber Command's major targets under the transport plan were mostly situated, only one bomber in ten dropped its bombs within 5 miles of its target. The problem was thus shown to be not a bomb-aiming problem at all: it was a problem of navigation. Most

Air Marshal Harris conceived the idea of a massive raid on a major German city – a final gamble with a thousand bombers in the air over Germany in a single night

of the crews were failing even to *reach* the target area.

The significance of the change from day bombing to night, and of the long flights over sea and land necessitated by the loss of the French airfields, was at last fully appreciated. The only task that Bomber Command could hope to accomplish at night was the area bombing of cities – and at the moment it was not often capable even of that.

Even more serious for Bomber Command, in the long term, was the discovery in the course of 1941 that fighter defences could not be completely evaded even at night. The German air and ground defences, at first improvised and rudimentary and still a tiny force in terms of pilots and aircraft, were now efficient and well-organised. To reach targets in the Ruhr, British bombers had to make a sea crossing of at least 100 miles, with another 120 miles of occupied territory to cross before they entered the air space of Germany. These defensive advantages were well exploited by General Joseph Kammhuber when he took over the newly-formed German night-fighter division in July 1940. Starting with three coastal fighter zones

in northern, central, and southern Holland, Kammhuber quickly formed a second line of defences to guard the Ruhr, and by 1941 an unbroken line of radar zones stretched right across the Ruhr approaches. In the course of 1941 this line was extended and deepened, so that detours by the bombers to avoid the defences were no longer possible; as the bombers flew across the contiguous radar zones, one night-fighter after another was guided into the attack, and these defences had to be penetrated twice on each sortie – on the way to the target and again on the way back. There remained the formidable flak, searchlight, and night-fighter defences of the main target areas.

These combined defences, although inadequate to meet the developing threat of a concentrated bomber offensive, began to inflict unacceptable losses on the RAF bombers in the summer of 1941, culminating in the destruction of 37 bombers on November 7 – nearly 10% of the total force employed that night. Such casualties, besides being out of all proportion to the potential results, would have wiped out Bomber Command in a matter of weeks, and the result was that the C-in-C was ordered on November 13 to conserve his force, and to build it up for the renewal of the offensive in the spring of 1942. By that time the new radar navigational aid Gee would be available, many more squadrons would have converted from medium to heavy bombers, the Lancaster would be coming into service, and a real chance might exist of damaging targets in Germany without incurring crippling losses.

This policy of conservation was interrupted, towards the end of the year, by renewed calls for attacks on the *Scharnhorst* and *Gneisenau* in Brest.

Bomber Command's weaknesses
Other factors were meanwhile combining to threaten the very existence of Bomber Command. Throughout 1941 the drain to other commands and other theatres had continued: four more squadrons were lent to Coastal Command (a transfer that later became permanent), and the Middle East Air Force was reinforced with both aircraft and crews, largely at Bomber Command's expense. Thus the expansion that had taken place during the year had almost entirely leaked away. The spread of the conflict to global proportions was making increasing demands on British resources and at the same time reducing the flow of arms from America. Overseas defeats and fears of defeat stimulated a further round of demands for the reinforcement of overseas air forces from the British Admiralty and War Office, whose needs were desperate. A bomber offensive which could not be decisive in the foreseeable future was seen as purposeless and a wanton waste if in the meantime the war might be lost elsewhere.

The strongest argument for a British bomber offensive had always been that it was the only means of taking the initiative against Germany; but in the new circumstances obtaining at the close of 1941 it was by no means certain that this argument still held. The whole war situation had become much more complex. With the enormous access of support from Russia, and the tremendous potential of the United States, it was natural that the British government should have its earlier policy under review.

On February 22, 1942, the post of commander-in-chief, Bomber Command, passed to Air Marshal A. T. Harris. The new C-in-C, whose experience of night bombing went back 20 years and who had commanded No. 4 Bomber Group in peacetime and No. 5 Bomber Group for 12 months in wartime, recognised that Bomber Command's chances of being retained as an effective strategic weapon against Germany depended on some early demonstration of its potential power. Otherwise it was doomed to diversion to a variety of other theatres and other tasks.

But the front-line strength of the command was actually less when he took over than it had been two years earlier, although its striking power was increased by its greater bomb-carrying capacity. The Manchester, however, had proved a failure, the Lancaster, developed from it, was only just coming into service, and the Stirling had been a disappointment. The bulk of the command was still equipped with Wellingtons, with only three Halifax squadrons. Thus, in the early months of 1942, the kind of success that might redeem the command's role in British war strategy, and restore its own morale, seemed beyond its grasp.

In pursuing his aim, however, Harris was greatly assisted by two factors: first, a new bombing directive of February 14, 1942, ante-dating his appointment by eight days, authorised him to take up the offensive with the primary object of undermining the morale of the civil population, and especially of the industrial workers. Second, the retreat of the German battle-cruisers from Brest on February 12 had relieved the command of a liability which had absorbed much of its effort in the previous 12 months.

A third factor, of even more importance in the long term, was the introduction, six months before Harris took over, of scientific analysis of the problems affecting night bombing. In August 1941, following the Butt Report, Sir Richard Peirse had asked for the formation of an operational research section at High Wycombe, similar to those already in being at Stanmore and Northwood for Fighter and Coastal Commands. The new section was formed in September 1941 under a scientist named Dr B. G. Dickins, its ultimate purpose being to assist in getting the maximum number of bombers over their targets with the minimum of losses. The lessons of earlier campaigns, and of the German blitz on Britain, were thus incorporated in the tactics of the new offensive.

These tactics would be, first, concentration of the attacking force over a single target in the shortest feasible time-spread, saturating the defences, both active and passive; and second, incendiarism. There was a limit to the damage that could be caused by a given quantity of high explosive, but the German blitz had demonstrated how fire-raising took advantage of the combustible energy within the target itself to spread the area of destruction. Essential to both these concepts was the new radar aid Gee, with which, when Harris took over, between 100 and 150 bombers — about a third of the force — were equipped. These bombers were to be used as an incendiary force, to identify and mark the targets; but complete concentration could not be achieved until the whole force was Gee-equipped.

The Gee campaign opened on March 8, 1942, with the first of a series of raids on Essen, and a complementary technique, involving the use of a flare-dropping force to lead the raid and a target-marking force using incendiaries to follow up, was em-

ployed. The intention was to produce a concentrated area of fire in the centre of the target into which the bombers not equipped with Gee could aim their high explosives. The limitations of this technique were shown in the next few weeks in eight major attacks on Essen, all involving between 100 and 200 bombers: only one bomb in 20 fell within 5 miles of the town.

Essen, powerfully defended and nearly always partly obscured by industrial haze, was the hardest of all area targets to find, but damage everywhere in this period was scanty and scattered, and it was apparent that defences were not being saturated by this scale of attack. Gee could not solve the problem of target recognition unaided, and the bomber force was still much too small.

The best prospect of early success seemed

General Kammhuber took over Germany's night-fighters in July 1940. By 1941 an unbroken line of radar zones stretched right across the approaches to the Ruhr

to lie in fire-raising raids by moonlight against medium-sized targets — important but not vital — where concentration could be achieved and where the defences were not strong enough to escape saturation. The target chosen for the initial experiment was Lübeck, a town the core of which occupied an island site on a river, easily recognisable by moonlight. Because of its age and the congestion of its buildings it was also highly combustible. The raid was carried out by 234 bombers on the night of March 28, 1942, carrying 300 tons of high explosives (including 17 4,000-pounders) and many thousands of incendiaries. For the British it was a resounding success, proving that in conditions of full moon and good visibility a fire blitz by a medium-sized force could knock out a carefully chosen target at small cost.

In releasing an account of the Lübeck raid, the Air Ministry was more outspoken than was usual at this time. The normal pattern of its bulletins would be an announcement that a certain target had been attacked, a description of the target in terms of size and importance, stressing the chief indus-

trial features, and then a list of the specific objectives of an industrial and military nature that were claimed by the bombers as hit. It would then give a description of the raid in a general way. The fact that the town itself had suffered damage and destruction in the course of the raid was often included, but it was not disclosed that, because of the bombers' inability to hit specific targets, this general damage had been the major aim.

The Lübeck raid, however, mounted to test the theories of incendiarism, inevitably fell largely on the civil population, and the Air Ministry bulletin, while carefully parading the military importance of Lübeck as a shipping, submarine, and communication centre, did not shirk mention of the very extensive damage done to the city itself. 'Crews reported fires of great violence and size in the main city area and spreading rapidly,' said the bulletin.

Still no major victory

A month later, in a series of four moonlight raids on Rostock, the experiment was repeated, and this time the area bombing was accompanied by pinpoint attacks on the Heinkel factory on the outskirts of the town, a pattern which was to become standard procedure in an attempt to get the best of both worlds. But much as these raids encouraged the British and shocked the Germans, neither target was a heavily defended industrial centre vital to the German war machine. Two more raids on Essen, on much the same scale as the raid on Lübeck, failed to achieve a comparable concentration, and similar raids on Hamburg and Dortmund were equally disappointing.

Bomber Command had still to demonstrate its ability to inflict serious damage on important and well-defended targets in Germany, and against such targets it had become obvious that a force of 250 bombers could not break down resistance or produce any great degree of devastation. Thus Bomber Command remained without a major victory, and apparently without the means to achieve one.

Yet the necessity for such a victory was becoming, for Bomber Command, more pressing than ever. Disasters in the Far East and setbacks in the Middle East cried out against the continued hoarding of aircraft in the United Kingdom. In the east the Germans were about to develop a spring offensive aimed at overrunning the Caucasus, gaining possession of Russia's main oil supply, and simultaneously opening the way for a link-up with Rommel's advancing Afrika Korps and for the domination of the entire Middle East. Supplies for Rommel's armies were pouring across the Mediterranean, and the only prospect of stopping them seemed to be by massive air intervention. Above all, the entire strategic situation turned on the supply of shipping; in the first two months of 1942, 117 Allied ships totalling over 750,000 tons were sunk in the Atlantic — the heaviest losses of the war so far. The case for applying every unit of air power to avert defeat seemed overwhelming, and the main pressure, as always, fell on Bomber Command. Everywhere the call was for more bombers.

It was in this atmosphere that Air Marshal Harris and his senior air staff officer, Air Vice-Marshal Saundby, aware that if the bombers were once transferred they would never be returned and might never be replaced, conceived the idea of a massive raid on a major German city, something into which they would throw the whole of their front-line strength and all their reserves in what might be a final gamble. The aim of this gamble would be to strike a political and military blow whose effect would be to preserve the one offensive weapon without which they believed the war would never be won – the strategic air offensive against Germany. This was the raid to be known as the 'Thousand Plan'.

It was Harris who first conceived the idea of putting a thousand bombers over Germany in a single night: he mentioned it to Saundby early in May 1942, hardly imagining that it might be possible. In the next few days Saundby checked the figures with many stations and units and was eventually able to report back to Harris that, given the right support, something might be done.

In Bomber Command in May 1942 there were 37 medium- and heavy-bomber squadrons, made up as follows: 16 Wellington squadrons, six Halifax squadrons, six Lancaster squadrons (two of which were still partly equipped with Manchesters), five Stirling squadrons, and two Manchester and two Hampden squadrons. Allowing for an average rate of unserviceability, this gave a front-line strength of about 400 aircraft. Four other squadrons, all Whitleys, were on temporary transfer to Coastal Command, and if these squadrons could be returned for the raid, the total would be close to 450. If operations were suspended for 48 hours to give the ground crews time to work on unserviceable aircraft, a maximum serviceability state might be reached in which virtually 100% of front-line strength would be available. This would bring the total, from 41 squadrons, to approximately 500 aircraft.

All the new heavy-bomber squadrons had their own conversion flights, and if the aircraft in these flights were added, together with the established conversion units, the figure would be nearer 550. If all suitable Coastal Command aircraft could also be called upon – the Hampdens, Beauforts, and Hudsons – and if the Bomber and Coastal operational training units could be drawn on, using instructor crews, the Thousand Plan could become a reality.

But was such a concentration of aircraft over a single target feasible? Clearly there were certain pre-requisites: it would take time to assemble the force, which meant a break in operations of several days; the target must be an easily recognisable one; good weather was essential; so was a full moon. The problems of concentration would certainly be simplified by Gee, but none of the conversion and training aircraft was Gee-equipped, so a similar technique would be needed to that used at Lübeck and Rostock, the Gee-equipped aircraft going in first to mark the aiming point. Whether it was physically possible to put a thousand aircraft over the same target in so short a space of time as one hour, the period envisaged, was just the sort of question that the scientists and statisticians of the operational research section were established to answer, and Harris passed it on.

The compression of the bomb pattern and the saturation of the defences, which were the objects of concentration, would be pointless if the result was that losses increased through mid-air collisions; but, from their studies of earlier raids, the scientists were able to build up a picture of the density of

A Halifax takes off for Germany. The plan to bomb Cologne with over 1,000 bombers called for an unprecedented concentration of aircraft over the target. But on the night of the raid – despite some confusion and the refusal of some crews to leave the city till they had watched the extensive fires – there were only two collisions

aircraft over a given target at any one moment, and they were thus able to estimate the likely spread of the proposed force in time and space and calculate the collision risk. Their final estimate, based on three main assumptions – that the span of the raid would be increased to 90 minutes, that three separate aiming-points would be chosen, and that heights would be staggered – was that collisions would be unlikely to exceed one per hour.

The staggering of heights raised the fear that aircraft might find themselves bombing each other, but this risk too was investigated and pronounced negligible.

Convinced that the raid was at least feasible, Harris went to see Portal, who asked for a workable plan, warning Harris at the same time that the raid might attract reprisals and that the Chiefs-of-Staff would have to be convinced of its usefulness. To forestall political opposition, Harris then went to see Churchill, who was enthusiastic, and the only doubt that remained was the choice of target. Churchill wanted Essen, as the biggest of all military targets. Harris wanted Hamburg, as the most combustible of major targets and therefore potentially the one where the greatest destruction might be wrought and the greatest impact made. The operational research section, however, advised that the force should stay within Gee range and go to Cologne. Essen was ruled out because of the great difficulty of locating aiming-points beneath the haze, and the final choice was left between Cologne and Hamburg, to be decided on the night according to the state of the weather.

On Monday, May 18, Harris went to Portal with details of the workable plan Portal had asked for, and two days later, on May 20, he received Portal's final approval.

Cologne: the guinea-pig
On the same day Harris wrote to Coastal, Fighter, and Army Co-operation Commands and to the five bomber groups and the two training groups, giving details of the plan and asking for a maximum contribution to it. From Coastal Command Harris hoped for a total of 250 aircraft. From Fighter Com-

mand and No 2 Group of Bomber Command he asked for intruder attacks on German night-fighter airfields, fighter sweeps over the North Sea to protect the bombers, and special air/sea rescue patrols. In his letter he stated his clear intention of annihilating one of Germany's main industrial centres by fire. There were no euphemisms about factories and military targets. The city of Cologne (or Hamburg) was to be wiped out in one night.

The final operation order was issued on May 26. The raid was to take place on the night of May 27/28 or any night thereafter up to the night of May 31/June 1, by which time the moon would be on the wane. This gave a possible margin, to allow for bad weather, of five days.

Sir Philip Joubert, C-in-C of Coastal Command, had meanwhile promised the 250 aircraft, but had then been overruled by the Admiralty, who sensed the political implications of the raid and ordered that Coastal Command, for whom they were operationally responsible, were not in any circumstances to take part. This, after the initial reaction of the First Sea Lord, was a bitter blow to Harris, bringing his thousand-plus down to about 800.

The defection of Coastal Command had not been entirely unforeseen by either Harris or Saundby, and they set to work to make good the deficiency. By a further comb-out of aircraft, and by making up their minds on a decision they had been reluctant to take, to employ pupil as well as instructor crews, they brought the figure up to 940. Thus to the already considerable hazards were added the requisitioning of every possible aircraft and the employment of pupil crews.

Now came the final frustration – the weather. On the morning of May 27, Harris went down to the underground operations room at High Wycombe for his daily planning conference. Waiting for him were Saundby and his air staff officers, together with Magnus T. Spence, who, as Harris's meteorological specialist, now became his most valued counsellor.

Thundery conditions and heavy cloud

existed over most of Germany, and Harris was forced to postpone the operation for 24 hours. The same thing happened on Thursday the 28th, and again on Friday May 29. Two more nights and the moon would be on the wane. But as the week drew to a close the tally of aircraft mounted, until, on the morning of Saturday, May 30, the total was well over four figures. The Thousand Plan, on paper at least, was a reality.

That morning Spence reported the first signs all week of an improvement in the weather. Thundery conditions were persisting, and Hamburg was still under a blanket of cloud, but there was a chance—a 50-50 chance, according to Spence—that the cloud in the Cologne area would clear by midnight.

To Harris it looked very much like the last chance for Bomber Command. If he waited another month, strategic and political decisions which threatened to break up the force might well have been implemented. Conscious of the decisive influence of the weather on all military and naval adventures, and aware of the penalties that follow when armadas fail, he took the decision to dispatch the force that night to Cologne.

In a personal message to his group and station commanders Harris urged that the whole future course and strategy of the war might be altered by the raid. Calculations from British experience of German attacks, he told them, showed that if the force could reach its objective and bomb it accurately, the weight of the attack would be sufficient to destroy it as an industrial centre and to spread apprehension, despair, and panic throughout Germany. 'At best,' he wrote, 'the result may bring the war to a more or less abrupt conclusion owing to the enemy's unwillingness to accept the worst that must befall him increasingly as our bomber force and that of the United States of America build up. At worst it must have the most dire moral and material effect on the enemy's war effort as a whole and force him to withdraw vast forces from his exterior aggressions for his own protection.'

By 1700 hours Spence had forecast that conditions over the bases at take-off would be clear except for local thunderstorms. Thick cloud was likely up to 15,000 feet along the route to Cologne, with more thunderstorms, and the icing index would be high, but conditions would tend to improve for the return flight. Over Cologne itself the cloud would begin to disperse by midnight, and large breaks were hoped for in the target area. Visibility would deteriorate over eastern England during the night, but only about a quarter of the bases would be affected.

A small miscalculation, either about the time or extent of the cloud dispersion over Cologne or the timing of the deterioration over the bases, could still wreck the raid. But Harris did not rescind his order.

At 1800 hours, at 53 different bases scattered down eastern England and across the Midlands, the briefing of the crews began. The tension in the briefing rooms, already heightened by the awareness that something unusual was planned, broke into an uproar of enthusiasm when the scope of the raid was revealed.

The bombers were routed from their bases to the Dutch coast via East Anglia. Those actually based in East Anglia were no more than 300 miles from the target. Others, in Yorkshire and the Midlands, were more than 400. The Dutch coast would be crossed south

of Rotterdam, and the route across Holland and into Germany would touch good pinpoints at Eindhoven and München Gladbach. Crews were recommended to pick out the Rhine north of the target and follow it into Cologne. After bombing they were to steer south-south-west for 20 minutes to Euskirchen, then turn for home on a track parallel to their outward track.

The leading crews of the Gee-equipped squadrons of No. 1 and 3 Groups—Stirlings and Wellingtons—were to comprise the incendiary force. These were the 'pathfinders', though they were not yet styled as such. Their aiming-point was to be the Neumarkt, in the centre of the old town, and the success of the raid would depend on their accuracy. Starting at 0055 hours, they would have the target to themselves for 15 minutes. Succeeding aircraft would aim either a mile to the north or a mile to the south of the Neumarkt, spreading the area of devastation. For an hour after the initial marking period the target would be bombed by the main force of aircraft—the Stirling, Manchester, Wellington, and Hampden squadrons and the aircraft of the training groups; the Lancasters and the Halifaxes would bomb in the final 15 minutes.

The first aircraft to take off, at 2230 that evening, were the outriders of the incendiary force, the Stirlings of No. 15 Squadron, based at Wyton in Huntingdonshire. But on their way across the North Sea they were overtaken by the Blenheims, the Bostons, the Havocs, and the long-range Hurricanes of the intruder force, bound for the German night-fighter airfields that lay in the path of the bombers. Some 88 aircraft, including 50 Blenheims, took part in these operations, bombing airfields and attacking what few German fighters they saw. But these raids, hampered by low cloud, did not succeed in grounding or seriously inconveniencing the German fighters. The intruder force suffered from the same inadequacies as had frustrated the main British bomber force so far: no navigation or bombing aids, dispersed targets that were difficult to find and even harder to put out of action, inadequate weapons, inadequate numbers. The bombers would still have to fight their way through to Cologne.

Cologne: triumph and tragedy

Across the North Sea and central Holland the crews of the incendiary force flew above a blanket of thundery cloud. It was not until they were approaching the German border, about 60 miles from Cologne, that the long tongue of cloud was suddenly withdrawn, discovering the ground in great clarity under the floodlight of the rising moon. Magnus T. Spence had been right.

The first crews to break through the Kammhuber Line made their approach towards the city at 15,000 feet from almost due west. At this early stage there was no collision risk, and contrary to their briefing they got their pinpoint south of the city and then turned north, with the Rhine to their right. Ahead of them were the two central bridges, first the Hindenbergbrücke, then the Hohenzollernbrücke. A mile due west of the first bridge was their aiming-point, in the centre of the old town. Below them the intense moonlight was throwing the old city into braille-like relief. Individual streets could be traced their entire length, honeycombed with buildings, while railways ploughed their furrows round the city and in one instance probed deep into the old town

before passing the cathedral and swinging east across the Hohenzollernbrücke. The crews were looking down on a sight that might never be seen again—the intricate fretwork of the old city of Cologne.

The defences as yet were uncertain, and the first few crews dropped their bombs almost unopposed. Their sticks of incendiaries, 4- and 30-pounders, were right on target.

On the ground in Cologne, the sirens had sounded half an hour earlier. The population was accustomed to aerial bombardment; this was their 105th air raid of the war. At first they stood about in little groups in the streets, waiting to see if it was a false alarm. Then came the first thin rumble of aircraft engines, growing in volume every minute. Hundreds of searchlights quartered the sky, hundreds of guns fired almost simultaneously. While the citizens of Cologne hurried into their cellars, or into the vast air-raid shelters that had been constructed for them, the civil defence and fire-fighting forces, uniformed and volunteer, made ready.

As the first Stirlings turned for home, dummy fires sprang up outside the city; but the target was still so brilliantly illuminated by the moon, with the Rhine snaking through the middle, that the air crews could not be misled. At the end of the first 15 minutes the centre of the old city was ablaze and a column of smoke was pouring skywards.

The main force of bombers, together with the instructor and pupil crews, was now converging on the target. Some crews bombed from under 10,000 feet, unable to climb any higher; others crossed the target at more than 17,000. The experience of individual crews differed widely, even those at the same height and with roughly the same time on target; some were hotly engaged by searchlights and flak, others believed that the defences had already been swamped. In fact, the ground defences were confused and over-strained, and much of the firing was haphazard, a barrage for its own sake. Searchlights found difficulty in concentrating on individual aircraft, but when they did, the flak co-operated well.

Little fighter opposition was encountered in the target area, but across Holland and Belgium and the German border the fighter pilots were energetic and numerous. Every two or three minutes a bomber burst into flames and went down.

Many of the crews, unable to break the habits of independence, were making their bombing runs direct, according to their direction of approach to the target, converging from all directions and thus increasing the collision risk. Others, after dropping their bombs, were so attracted by the sight of the burning city, with extensive fires on both sides of the river, and cathedral and bridges illuminated, that they circled the city to take it all in. Yet the light remained so brilliant that collisions were rare; there were only two incidents of collision over the target throughout the raid: they accounted for four bombers lost.

Meanwhile the people of Cologne were undergoing the inevitable succession of miraculous escapes and tragic misfortunes that were characteristic of the aerial bombardment of a great city. Thousands of fires had taken hold and the whole city shook continually with the blast from the growing weight of high-explosive as the heavy bombers went in. Tens of thousands of people were crowding the aid centres, many of them already evacuated from the blitzed ▷

195

'The Ruhr will not be subjected to a single bomb. If an enemy bomber reaches the Ruhr, my name is not Hermann Göring!'

In 1939 Göring had boasted that no enemy aircraft would survive in the skies above Germany. Now Goebbels, his rival in the Nazi hierarchy, stands in the ruins of Cologne cathedral, inspecting the damage caused by the British bombs. Afterwards he wrote in his diary: 'Naturally the effects of bomb warfare are horrible when one looks at individual cases. But they must be put up with.' The first of the 1,000-bomber raids had destroyed over 600 acres of Cologne—nearly as much as the total estimated area of bomb damage in the whole of Germany up to that time. But it had not eliminated the industrial targets in the city—and the raid could not be repeated until the RAF's strength had been greatly increased. Despite this, the raid was a warning of the destruction which Germany could expect in the future, and as such it was exploited by British propaganda.

▷ **Above:** A leaflet dropped by the RAF announces the beginning of a new phase of the war in the air: 'This proof of the growing strength of the British bomber force is also the herald of what Germany will receive, city by city, from now on.'
Below: The fires of the city took more than a week to die down sufficiently to allow the RAF to take reconnaissance photographs. These showed that although the damage would seriously inconvenience the city for three to six months, vital targets had survived. But not all of them: these two photographs show the extent of the destruction in the railway workshops of Cologne-Nippes

Ullstein

DIE SCHWERSTEN ANGRIFFE DER LUFTWAFFE VON DER R.A.F. WEIT ÜBERBOTEN

Mehr als 1000 Bomber auf einmal eingesetzt

IN der Nacht vom 30. Mai griff die Royal Air Force Köln mit weit über 1000 Flugzeugen an. Der Angriff wurde auf anderthalb Stunden zusammengedrängt. Der deutsche Sicherheits- und Abwehrdienst war der Wucht des Angriffs nicht gewachsen.

Premierminister Churchill sagte in seiner Botschaft an den Oberbefehlshaber des britischen Bomberkommandos am 31. Mai:

„Dieser Beweis der wachsenden Stärke der britischen Luftmacht ist auch das Sturmzeichen für die Dinge, die von nun an eine deutsche Stadt nach der andern zu erwarten hat."

Zwei Nächte darauf griff die Royal Air Force das Ruhrgebiet mit über 1000 Maschinen an.

Die Offensive der Royal Air Force in ihrer neuen Form hat begonnen

G. 30

An unpleasant reminder of Nazi miscalculation — and of growing Allied power

◁ A Halifax comes home: of the 1,046 bombers which took off for Cologne, about 910 reached and bombed the target — but 39 were lost, representing a loss rate of 4%. ▷ Four months after the raid, barges were still clearing rubble from Cologne's dockyard area *(top left)*. Members of a Stirling bomber's ground crew *(top right)* repair the rear-gun turret which was damaged in the raid. *In colour:* Stirlings in flight: the first RAF aircraft to arrive over the target area

areas, others bombed out. Water mains in all areas had been breached, power and telephone cables torn up, gas mains punctured. Seventeen major rail centres were reporting severe damage: railway stations, goods depots, locomotives, trucks, and rails were wrecked. Bombs fell with grim impartiality on factories, industrial estates, empty city offices, crowded hospitals, empty churches, hastily abandoned homes, and crowded shelters. Even so, prompt action by individual and group self-protection forces and industrial civil defence units prevented many fires from developing.

All the time the tale of human tragedy and dramatic rescue went on. Hundreds of people were trapped in cellars; scores had already been killed or suffocated in this way. In one cellar where 150 people were trapped, a high-explosive bomb penetrated the cellar ceiling but miraculously did not explode. Rescue work was intensified and the shelterers, women and children among them, had just been evacuated when the bomb went off. Not all incidents had such a merciful ending.

The crews in the final wave of heavy bombers picked out the target by the glow in the sky from a hundred miles distant. The ground defences were badly disorganised by this time, but the fighters were still active.

It seemed, as the raid drew to a close, as though a single immense fire were raging in central Cologne, throwing up a spiral of smoke to 15,000 feet, with hundreds of smaller fires towards the perimeter. Buildings, when recognisable as such, were mostly skeletons in the midst of fires. The frame-work of white-hot joists was visible at high-altitude; aircraft at a lower height could be seen against the flames.

At 0400 hours that morning, long before the last of the bombers had landed back at their bases, a Mosquito took off to photograph the target at first light, but when it reached Cologne a huge pall of smoke covered the city and it was impossible to get photographs. When at last, nearly a

week later, satisfactory photographs could be taken, the damage revealed was on a far greater scale than anything yet seen in a German city. Some 600 acres — including 300 acres in the centre of the city — had been completely destroyed, nearly as much as the total estimated area of destruction by bombing in Germany up till then.

In spite of extensive damage to factories and industrial buildings, and to rail and other public services, throttling the life of the city for many days, the main weight of the attack had inevitably fallen on the civil population in their homes; 13,000 homes were completely destroyed, 6,000 badly damaged, and over 45,000 people rendered homeless. Past experience, good shelters, and the energetic work of the civil defence forces had combined to keep casualties down, but even so they were heavy, more than in any other raid on Germany up to that time. The total was just over 5,000, of whom 469 were killed.

Cologne, however, had not been destroyed, and the main lesson of the raid was that the destruction of German industry and industrial life was not yet within the power of Bomber Command, and that to achieve conclusive results a massive expansion of the bomber force would be necessary, together with improved aids to target-finding and bomb-aiming. The industrial life of Cologne had been paralysed for a week and seriously inconvenienced for from three to six months, but in time it would recover from a raid that was far beyond Bomber Command's normal capacity, delivered on a specially chosen target in exceptional weather. Thus with the weapons and means available to the RAF at this time, large German industrial areas were virtually indestructible.

Of the 1,046 bombers which took off for Cologne, about 910 reached and bombed the target, and 39 were lost. Most of these fell to night-fighters, which retained their effectiveness in spite of the weight of the attack. The loss rate, about 4% of the

effective force, was about as much as the command could withstand over a period. If the raid provoked the heavy reinforcement of German home fighter strength which had been one of its objects, an unacceptable loss rate might follow.

The Cologne raid had failed to support some of Harris's more ambitious claims ('an abrupt conclusion to the war' and 'spread despair . . . throughout Germany'), but a convincing demonstration had been given of what might be achieved if the strength of Bomber Command were doubled and trebled. Serious damage had been done in the short term to the industrial capacity of Germany's fourth largest city, and although the German leaders were satisfied that raids of such strength would for the present be infrequent, they feared the damage, moral and material, that such raids could do and looked forward to the time when they would once again be able to concentrate their air power in the west. The blow to morale would be absorbed, but the raid had provided an unpleasant reminder of Nazi miscalculation and of growing Allied power.

To judge the raid on its immediate material and moral results, however, would be to ignore its main purposes, which were strategic and political; and political vindication, at least, was not long in coming. 'This proof of the growing power of the British bomber force,' wrote Churchill in a signal to Harris that was published after the raid, 'is also the herald of what Germany will receive, city by city, from now on.' It was this unequivocal declaration of the British government's intention of prosecuting a bomber offensive against Germany's principal cities, no matter how hard pressed the Allies might be in other theatres, which, for Bomber Command, justified the gamble.

For the first time in the war so far, Britain stood in the role of attacker, Germany of defender. It remained for attacker and defender to evaluate the lessons of the raid, and to adjust their plans accordingly.

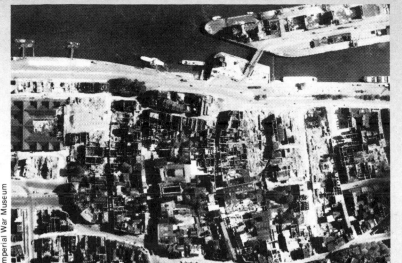

THE FALL OF THE PHILIPPINES

December 1941/April 1942

JOHN VADER

The Japanese Imperial General Staff was supremely confident that they could take the Philippines with little difficulty— so confident that they did not even allot the whole of their XIV Army to the job. At first it seemed that they were justified; for their landings were only lightly opposed, and their troops advanced rapidly against an untrained and ill-equipped enemy. But the siege of Bataan, on which the American and Filipino forces planned to make their last stand, disrupted their progress. Disease and hunger struck both besiegers and besieged, and Japanese victory was delayed for three months until they could bring up fresh reinforcements

On July 22, 1941, with the acquiescence of the Vichy government, Japan occupied naval and air bases in south-east Indo-China, and to counter this threat the armed forces of the Philippines were brought into the service of the United States. On the same day—July 26—the US War Department established a new command: the US Forces in the Far East (USAFFE), based at Manila under the command of General Douglas MacArthur, who was recalled to active duty.

By the first day of December 1941, the line troops in USAFFE comprised ten infantry divisions, five coastal artillery units, two field artillery regiments, and a cavalry regiment equipped with horses and a few scout cars. The élite troops were the Scouts —highly trained members of the cavalry and artillery regiments—and the 45th Battalion.

On Luzon (see map) there were two army groups, the North and South Luzon Forces. Major-General Jonathan M. Wainwright's North Luzon Force was the stronger: there were the 11th, 21st, 31st, and 71st Infantry Divisions, the cavalry regiment, the 45th Battalion, and three field artillery batteries. Brigadier-General George M. Parker's South Luzon Force stood in the area generally south and east of Manila, and consisted of two infantry divisions and a battery of field artillery.

A Visayan-Mindanao Force, under Brigadier-General William F. Sharp, was given the rest of the archipelago to defend. This force consisted of three infantry divisions, and the remaining division, the US Army's Philippine Division, was positioned between North and South Luzon Forces. The defence of the entry to Manila Bay and Subic Bay depended on five small fortified islands and their garrisons, commanded by General Moore.

Major-General Brereton commanded the US Air Force in the Philippines, which was given the title of Far East Air Force. Brereton's most useful aircraft were the B-17s (Flying Fortresses) of Lieutenant-Colonel Eubank's 19th Bombardment Group. All but one of the fighter squadrons in the 24th Pursuit Group were equipped with modern P-40s (Kittyhawks), under the command of Brigadier Clagett. Within 80 miles of Manila there were six airfields suitable for fighters and only one—Clark Field—suitable for heavy bombers; and although there were seven radar sets in the islands, only two had been set up by December. A makeshift system of air-raid watchers communicated by the civilian telephone or telegraph to the interceptor command at Nielson Field on the outskirts of Manila. The two coast artillery anti-aircraft regiments protected Clark Field's B-17s and Manila with 3-inch and 37-mm guns, ·50 machine-guns, and 60-inch Sperry searchlights.

The US Navy in the Philippines was based at Cavite, on the southern shore of Manila Bay. Under Admiral Thomas C. Hart, the fleet consisted of the heavy cruiser *Houston*, two light cruisers, 13 old destroyers, 29 submarines, six gunboats, six motor torpedo-boats, miscellaneous vessels, and an air arm of 32 PBY Catalinas.

Despite the inadequate training the infantry had received, the shortage of air warning devices, and the lack of airfields, there was an expression of optimism in Washington and in the Philippines that the garrison could withstand an attack by the Japanese.

The Japanese Imperial Staff, however, was completely confident that their XIV Army would conquer the Philippines within three months, and that Luzon Island would be in their hands within 50 days. They based their plan on a detailed knowledge of the American and Philippine forces—their equipment, training standards, fighting ability, and displacement. They were so confident that, instead of committing the whole of the XIV Army, its commander, General Homma, was allotted only two divisions, XVI and XLVIII, supported by two tank regiments, two infantry regiments, and a battalion of medium artillery, five anti-aircraft battalions, and various service units.

The Japanese V Air Group (army) and the XI Air Group (navy) were to provide 500 bomber and fighter aircraft for the invasion.

At Formosa on December 1, General Homma received final instructions from Southern Army Headquarters: operations would begin on the morning of December 8 (Tokyo time). The air forces were to open the attack—planned to coincide with the beginning of hostilities against Malaya—soon after the raid was made against the American fleet in Pearl Harbor. The Japanese navy's III Fleet, commanded by Admiral Takahashi, was organised into numerous special task forces which comprised transport and amphibious units supported by cruisers and destroyers. A close cover force of three cruisers would support the main landings.

On Formosa, the experienced and highly-skilled aircrews of the V Air Group readied their *Betty* bombers and Zero fighters. Then at midnight on December 7/8 a heavy fog closed in over the airfields, preventing the scheduled take-offs at dawn. The Japanese commanders were filled with nervous apprehension as they realised that the Americans on Luzon would have news of the raid on Pearl Harbor and could, with the B-17s of the Far East Air Force, attack the planes lined up on the Formosan airfields.

All hope of surprise was lost.

Caught on the ground

'Air raid on Pearl Harbor. This is no drill.' This was the dramatic message tapped out from Hawaii at 0800 hours and received at the US Navy Headquarters in Manila, where it was still dark and the time 0230 hours. A Marine officer passed the message to Admiral Hart, who immediately advised the fleet. General MacArthur was not advised by the navy but heard of the attack from a commercial broadcast shortly after 0330 hours. He then ordered the troops to battle stations.

The man most able to do something about an outbreak of war was General Brereton at Clark Field, but he too only heard the news

from a commercial broadcast, and it was 0500 hours before he could reach Mac-Arthur's office to seek permission to attack Formosa. Warned by a telephone call from General Arnold in the US not to be caught with his aircraft grounded and suffer the same fate as the anchored ships in Pearl Harbor, Brereton sent the heavy bombers on patrol—but without bombs—at 0800 hours. Eventually, at 1045 hours, orders were given for two squadrons of B-17s to attack airfields on southern Formosa 'at the earliest daylight hour that visibility will permit', and the patrolling bombers were brought back to Clark Field to bomb-up and refuel. By 1215 hours the armed bombers and fighters of the 20th Pursuit Squadron were lined up on Clark Field ready for take-off.

On Formosa, the fog had lifted enough by dawn to allow 25 Japanese army bombers to take off for Luzon. At 0930 hours they were over north Luzon, and attacked barracks and other installations at Tuguegarao and Baguio without interference from American fighters. By 1015 hours, the fog had further dispersed to allow the naval aircraft of the Japanese XI Air Fleet to take off.

A force of 108 bombers, escorted by 84 fighters, arrived over Clark Field at 1215 hours, achieving complete tactical surprise and catching the US bombers and fighters, with their tanks full of fuel, perfectly lined up for strafing runs. While anti-aircraft shells exploded 2,000 to 4,000 feet below them, two flights of 27 bombers accurately hit aircraft, hangars, barracks, and warehouses, starting fires that spread to the trees and the cogon grass around the field. The place became a mass of flame, smoke, and destruction, and for more than an hour the Zero fighters sprayed the grounded B-17s and P-40s with bullets. At the Iba Field fighter base, another group of 54 Japanese bombers, escorted by 50 fighters, destroyed barracks, warehouses, and the radar station. Then Zero pilots found P-40s of the US 3rd Pursuit Squadron circling to land at Iba: all but two were shot down.

In the first few hours of the war in the Philippines, the Japanese airmen had therefore achieved success beyond all expectation. For the loss of seven Zeros, they had destroyed 17 B-17s, 56 fighters, some 30 miscellaneous aircraft, and damaged many others, while important installations had been blasted or burned, and 230 men killed or wounded. That afternoon, the US Far East Air Force had ceased to be a serious threat to the invaders.

It is doubtful that even if the Far East Air Force had been spared on the first day of war it would have survived for very long, and if the bombers had raided Formosa it is doubtful if many of them would have returned after a meeting with swarms of Zeros. Losses at Clark Field would have been less had there been sufficient warning; but there had been none. Nielson Field was advised of the approaching Japanese, but the two squadrons that took off covered Manila and Bataan while Clark Field was shattered.

The following day the invaders continued their preliminary tactics of destroying air and naval power, attacking Nichols Field to hit aircraft and ground installations. The next day, December 10, a two-hour attack in the Manila Bay area was made on the Del Carmen Field near Clark, the Nichols and Nielson Fields near Manila, and on the Cavite naval base south of the city. At Cavite the entire yard was ablaze after the first wave of 27 bombers accurately dropped

their loads in the target area. Repair shops, warehouses, the power plant, barracks, the dispensary, and the radio station received direct hits. Casualties amounted to some 500 men. The submarine *Sealion* received a direct hit and a store of over 200 torpedoes was lost. Fortunately, about 40 merchant ships in the bay were unscathed and eventually escaped from the island. As a result of the raid Admiral Hart ordered away two destroyers, three gunboats, tenders, and minesweepers, planning to continue submarine and air operations 'as long as possible'.

Another Formosan fog made December 11 a quiet day but the next day over 100 bombers and fighters swarmed over Luzon, attacking any suitable target without much fear of retaliation: by now the Americans had less than 30 serviceable aircraft left. Seven PBYs were shadowed as they returned from a patrol and were shot down as they approached to alight on the bay. The next day the raiders numbered almost 200. On December 14 Admiral Hart sent the remaining PBYs south to sanctuary; on December 17 the intact B-17s were sent 1,500 miles away to Darwin in northern Australia.

By now the Far East Air Force ceased to exist as a fighting force. Except for a few patched fighters, the army was without air cover and the navy was forced to rely mainly on submarines to protect the thousands of miles of beaches against hostile landings—which had already begun on the northern coast of Luzon.

Six Japanese advance landings.

The first landing on Philippine territory was made on the little island of Batan, about halfway across the strait separating Luzon from Formosa. This was one of six advance landings planned for General Homma's XIV Army—the others were at Aparri and Vigan (on the north and north-west coast of Luzon), at Legaspi (near the southern tip of Luzon), at Davao on Mindanao, and at Jolo Island, between Mindanao and Borneo. The immediate objectives were airfields from which fighters could operate to cover the main landings which would follow. The captured Legaspi base would be a threat to American reinforcements from the south, and the landings at Davao and Jolo Island were designed to secure advanced bases for a later move southwards against the Netherlands East Indies.

The Japanese took a calculated risk in using quite small forces for these first landings—the largest force was only a regiment. On Batan Island a Japanese combat naval unit of 490 men landed unopposed at dawn on December 8. Two days later, Camiguin Island was seized, to provide a seaplane base some 35 miles from Aparri.

Cautiously supported by strong naval and air forces, the Tanaka Force (named after the commander of the II Formosa Regiment) approached undetected, and landed 2,000 men at Aparri and Gonzaga, 20 miles further on. The regiment's other one and a half battalions, known collectively as the Kanno Detachment, landed simultaneously at Pandan, near Vigan, at dawn on December 10. Here the Japanese luck ran out: a patrolling P-40 alerted the Far East Air Force, and the remaining US heavy bombers, with fighter escort, attacked the invaders' convoy at the landing area. The Japanese fighter screen failed to hold the attacks, and two transports were damaged and beached. But

△A Japanese section advances south through the Subic Bay area. By December 24, the Japanese had a firm hold on north Luzon, and Manila was next

△Wreckage and dead in Manila after a Japanese air raid. As the Japanese closed in, MacArthur declared Manila an open city and withdrew to Bataan

the landing was successful, despite rough seas and the air raid, and by the following evening a small detachment had pushed 50 miles north along the coast to occupy the town and airfield of Laoag.

With three airfields in their hands and no signs of a counterattack, the Japanese commanders decided to move the entire regiment down the west coast and join up with the main forces of the XIV Army that were to land on the beaches of Lingayen Gulf. There were delays while bridges were repaired and a light brush with Philippine troops at Bacnotan was resolved, and Colonel Tanaka's regiment arrived a few hours after the main landings began.

The 3rd Battalion of the Philippine Army 12th Regiment was in the Aparri/Gonzaga district, and quickly retreated south down the Cagayán valley, offering no opposition. By the evening of December 12, Tuguegarao airfield (50 miles inland) had been lost, and there was no opposition by the Philippine Army at Vigan, and the nearest American and Filipino force was that at Legaspi – 150 miles away. In south Luzon, General Jones ordered road and rail bridges to be demolished, and outpost defences prepared.

At 0400 hours on December 20, the Japanese landed at Davao. A machine-gun squad of the 101st Regiment inflicted numerous casualties until it was silenced by a direct hit from a Japanese naval gun. Nine bombers from Batchelor Field, near Darwin, made a surprise raid on the Japanese force collected to invade Jolo, but visibility was poor and only near-misses were registered. Jolo fell on Christmas Day.

Within two weeks, General Homma's advanced landing parties had occupied airfields in north and south Luzon, in Mindanao, and Jolo. The Japanese air forces had almost liquidated the Allied opposition, and

the main invasion troops were carried safely to the Lingayen beaches. Here the main strength of Homma's XIV Army began to disembark at 0500 hours on December 22. The XLVIII Division, the IX Infantry Regiment, four artillery regiments with 75-mm, 105-mm, 150-mm guns and 150-mm howitzers, two tank regiments with 80/100 tanks, and a large number of service and special troops were put ashore on the north coast of Lingayen Gulf. Nevertheless, choppy seas, an attack by the Darwin-based B-17s, and shelling from two 155-mm guns provided anxious moments for General Homma and his staff.

Along the 20-mile section of the main Japanese landing strip ran the all-weather Highway 3, which formed part of the road network that led into Manila. South of the landing beaches and between the gulf and Manila Bay, was the central plain of Luzon, a flat area of cleared farmland with many towns and villages. Here – and on the beaches – the Japanese had expected to find the main force of American and Filipino defenders. Yet the only beach resistance was at Bauang, where a ·50 machine-gun inflicted heavy casualties until the Japanese were able to establish a foothold ashore. Then the defenders withdrew.

Colonel Tanaka sent a battalion to take the Naguilian airfield, and at Agoo – at the southern end of the landing front – the XLVII Regiment, supported by artillery, made a sweep inland to Rosario while the XLVIII Reconnaissance and IV Tank Regiments came ashore and routed a battalion of Philippine Army infantry.

Because of poor landing conditions (due to rough seas), General Homma suspended unloading and disembarking operations during the afternoon, and moved his transports further south to a point off Damortis

during the night; and the rest of Lingayan Force was thus ready to land the next day – December 23.

On south Luzon, General Morioka's incomplete XVI Division, numbering 7,000 fighting troops, landed at Siain and Antimonan on the narrow strip of land between Tayabas Bay and Lamon Bay, and at Mauban, further north. By the evening of December 24, the landing was complete, and the only real resistance came from Philippine regulars at Mauban. Army short-range fighter-bombers and aircraft from the seaplane-carrier *Mizuho* gave close and deadly support to the Japanese troops who were in control of the neck of the peninsula by nightfall.

With only a strong action on December 24 to delay them, the Japanese had secured their initial objectives and had established a firm grip on northern Luzon. They were now in a position to march south to Manila along the broad highways of the central plain. Only the southern route to the capital remained to be seized. And MacArthur knew that his defence there was weak. He needed reinforcements and was relying on the convoy of seven ships escorted by the cruiser *Pensacola* to bring in troops, planes, and supplies. But the convoy failed even to test the Japanese barrier of warships and aircraft, and a request by MacArthur to have planes flown in from aircraft-carriers was turned down by a navy which was now so sensitive to the situation that the submarines were also evacuated. Torpedo-boats, minesweepers, gunboats, and tugs were all that remained of the Manila Bay naval force. Marines and sailors ashore were taken into the command of the army, and so too were the remnants of the air force, while the few fighters left were hidden.

Appalled at the inability of the Philippine

202

army to stand up to the Japanese, General MacArthur announced on December 23 a plan for withdrawal to Bataan. He planned to declare Manila an 'open' city after he had moved his headquarters to the island fortress of Corregidor, and the large quantities of ammunition and fuel which had already been stored on the Bataan peninsula, were now augmented as small barges and boats hastily carried more supplies from Manila to Corregidor and Bataan.

By Christmas Day, 1941, when MacArthur moved into Corregidor, the main defence line ran from near Binalonan—where the cavalry had made such a good stand—along the other side of the Agno river and past Carmen to the foothills of the Zambales mountains.

General Tsuchibashi's infantry and tanks attacked the centre of the defence line and soon moved through Villasis and crossed the river to take Carmen by the evening of December 26. With the main road under his control Tsuchibashi forced the Americans to use the railway to evacuate the rest of the 11th Division, and Tsuchibashi's troops then moved quickly along Route 3 to intercept the train at Moncada but a road block of three tanks and a 75-mm half-track delayed them, and the Philippine infantry got through.

After the Americans moved back from their third to their fourth defence line, extending from foothills to foothills across the 40-mile plain, the Japanese XLVIII Division broke through at Cabanatuan, and both the 11th and 21st Philippine Divisions were forced into another withdrawal. Aggressive artillery action by the Filipino gunners slowed down the Japanese advance, but by December 31 General Homma's troops were only 30 miles from Manila.

With the Philippine army forced back to Bataan, General Homma was convinced that the campaign would now be brought to an early and successful conclusion. Another Japanese general, Morioka, believed that the 'defeated enemy' was entering the peninsula like 'a cat entering a sack'—but he did not foresee the consequences of joining the cat in the sack.

Against the line at Porac, Homma sent the IX Regiment, which penetrated 2,000 yards on January 2. The next morning, the Takahashi Detachment, supported by 105-mm guns, moved up to intercept an attack by a battalion of 21st Division. The Japanese found the opposing infantry easy to deal with, but withering fire from the Filipino artillery stopped the Takahashi Detachment from causing a rout. On the marsh flank, the Japanese advance was made along the highway, where fighting was continuous and confused, infantry and artillery battling it out with occasional use of tanks by both sides. The defenders continued to withdraw, and the Japanese followed, harassing the retreating infantry with small-arms and artillery fire. Then, from tanks forming a road-block on the Lubao/Sexmoan road, accurate firing cut some of the Japanese columns to pieces. That night the attack was renewed across an open field in bright moonlight, and again the American guns drove back the Japanese; repeated attempts resulted in more heavy casualties.

As a result of the battering the Japanese had received, their fast pursuit slowed down to cautious probing, while the Americans and Filipinos crossed the Culo bridge at the Layac road-junction in a confused

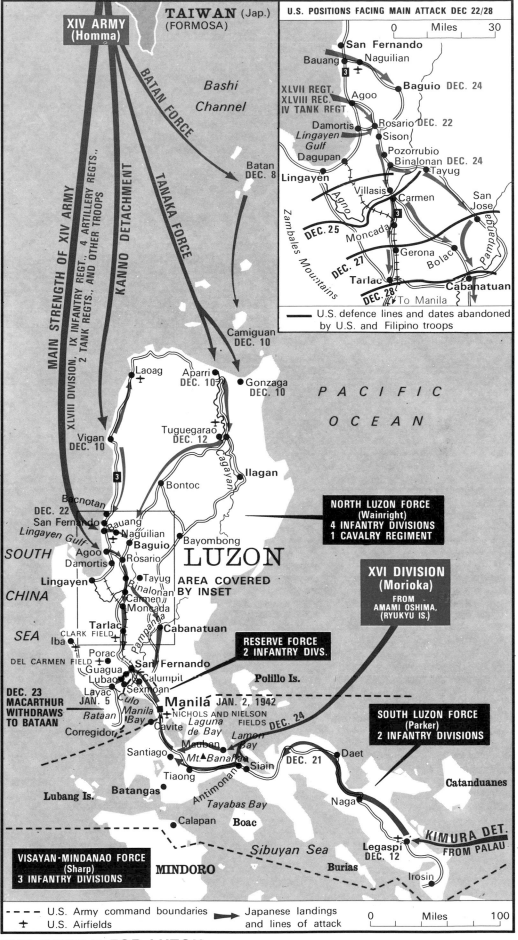

THE BATTLE FOR LUZON

The first Japanese landings on Luzon were a calculated risk, for only relatively small units—the largest was a regiment—were used to make the first landings, and occupy the airfields in north and south Luzon, Mindanao, and Jolo. Not until these were in Japanese hands did the main landings by the remainder of Homma's two divisions follow. Japanese planners had made a shrewd assessment of Allied strength in the Philippines: they were so confident that Homma was not even given the full strength of XIV Army—only two divisions to tackle *eleven* divisions and some of the strongest fortresses in the world

Japanese 'Co-Prosperity' propaganda: these match-box labels were part of the constant Japanese attempts to turn the native populations of conquered territories against the Allies. The matches were circulated through the normal trade channels, and were dropped on Allied-controlled territory as well. Churchill and Roosevelt were main subjects of ridicule

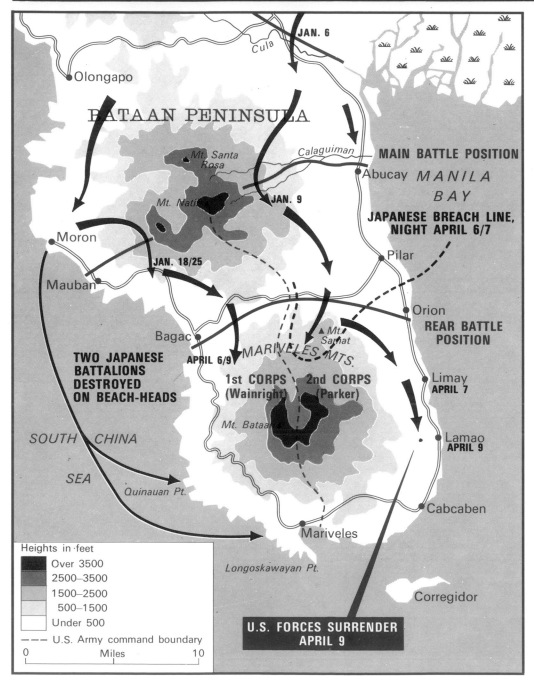

Heights in feet

- Over 3500
- 2500–3500
- 1500–2500
- 500–1500
- Under 500
- - - - U.S. Army command boundary

0   Miles   10

U.S. FORCES SURRENDER APRIL 9

1941 **July 22:** Japan occupies naval and air bases in south-east Indo-China.

July 26: Philippine armed forces are brought under US command. General MacArthur is recalled to active service.

December 8: News of the Japanese attack on Pearl Harbor is received at 0230 hours, but the Japanese still catch the majority of American aircraft in the Philippines on the ground when they attack at 1215 hours. Some 17 B-17s, 56 fighters, and 30 other aircraft are destroyed. First Japanese landing on the island of Batan.

December 10/22: Japanese advance forces land in north and south Luzon, Mindanao, and Jolo, capturing airfields and liquidating local opposition.

December 22: Main Japanese landings at Lingayen Bay and Lamon Bay meet with light resistance. The Japanese now begin to advance on Manila from north and south.

December 23: MacArthur announces a plan for withdrawal to Bataan, leaving Manila as an 'open city'.

December 26: Carmen falls, and Japanese gain control of the main road to Manila.

December 31: Japanese have advanced to within 30 miles of Manila, but their failure to destroy the bridges at Calumpit allows the American and Philippine troops to withdraw and form a defence line between Porac and Guagua.

1942 **January 2:** Japanese attempts to break the Porac line are repulsed by American artillery. The defenders withdraw across the Culo bridge.

January 2/9: American and Philippine troops dig in on Bataan peninsula.

January 9: A concentrated artillery barrage opens the Japanese attack on 2nd Corps.

January 9/February 28: Savage fighting, the Japanese suffer heavy casualties while forcing back the defenders.

February 8: A proposal that the Philippines be granted their independence and declared a neutral area is rejected by President Roosevelt.

March 12: MacArthur, under orders from Roosevelt, leaves for Darwin. General Wainwright takes command of the Philippine forces.

April 3: Japanese artillery bombardment begins the final offensive. Fresh Japanese troops have arrived while the defenders of Bataan have been decimated by disease and lack of food.

April 4: Japanese force a way through the centre, and turn the flank of 2nd Corps.

April 7: Japanese have pushed a salient, 4 miles deep, into the centre of the defenders' line. Both 1st and 2nd Corps have to withdraw quickly.

April 9: General King decides that further resistance is useless, and surrenders the remaining forces on Bataan. About 2,000 persons escape to Corregidor. But some 78,000 are forced to make the 65-mile-long 'death march' from Mariveles to San Fernando.

Once the main Japanese force had landed, their advance was extremely rapid, and the inability of the Philippine army to stand up to them soon convinced General MacArthur that a withdrawal must be made to the Bataan peninsula—which was easily defensible, and on which large quantities of ammunition and fuel had been stored. By January 2, 1942, the Allied cat 'was entering the sack', and the Japanese were ready to finish the campaign quickly. But their first impetuous rush on to the peninsula was met with strong resistance as the 80,000 Allied troops on Bataan prepared to defend a main line on either side of Mount Santa Rosa. The first Japanese attack on January 9 was contained with heavy casualties to both sides and it was not until January 23 that the Allies withdrew to the line running from Orion to Bagac. Here stalemate ensued, for both sides were exhausted by the savage fighting, disease, and lack of food. Only on April 3 were the Japanese sufficiently reinforced to begin the final assault, which brought surrender on April 9

congestion of vehicles, guns, and troops. Once again an obvious target was ignored by the Japanese air force, and the Culo bridge was blown up after the retreating army had crossed.

MacArthur realised that the Japanese success was achieved mainly because of their superiority at sea and in the air, and although he pleaded with his superiors for an Allied effort in the Pacific—the first step would be to land an army corps on Mindanao—he accepted the fact that relief was virtually impossible. He posted his defence across the mountainous peninsula of Bataan and prepared for the final stand.

The first defence line on Bataan extended from the precipitous slopes of the northern mountain, Santa Rosa, down to the sea on

The Philippine army was as ready as it could be, under the circumstances, for General Homma to begin the battle.

A concentrated artillery barrage against 2nd Corps began at 1500 hours on January 9. The defending guns replied effectively against the attacking infantry. The II Battalion crossed the Calaguiman river and managed to reach the cover of a sugar cane farm before midnight, where they were only 150 yards from their enemy's 3rd Battalion. While it was still dark, the Japanese opened up with artillery and mortar fire, then rushed out of the cane field in a screaming banzai charge in the face of intense fire. As the leading men dived across the barbed wire coils those following ran over their backs unimpeded, only to be shot down by the

where fighting became intense. Beginning on January 18, it lasted until January 25, with both sides suffering heavy casualties. One of Wainwright's divisions was forced to escape along the coast without rifles and in complete disorder. Disease and lack of food were beginning to take their toll on the defenders as Japanese pressure forced a general withdrawal, which began on January 23.

In a bold move to open up a front behind the main defence lines and draw away infantry and artillery, two Japanese battalions landed at two points near Mariveles at the tip of Bataan. At first contained in the very rough country by a miscellaneous force of airmen, sailors, and service troops, the two battalions were destroyed after

Japanese flame-thrower attack on an American blockhouse in the main defence-line on Bataan. On January 23, the defenders were forced to fall back

either side. Wainwright had three reinforced divisions, the cavalry, and supporting artillery in his 1st Corps on the left flank, and on the right Parker had four divisions plus a regiment from the Philippine Division. Eight miles behind was the rear battle position served by the Pilar-Bagac road. Preparing this line for a final defence was the USAFFE reserve—the rest of the Philippine Division, the tank group, and a group of self-propelled 75-mm guns. Corps and USAFFE artillery was emplaced to cover the front lines as well as the beach defences in all sectors.

Some 80,000 troops were now on Bataan and about 26,000 civilians had also fled there. Food and motor fuel had been stored to satisfy the requirements of 43,000 men for six months. Now there would only be enough food for a few weeks. There was no mosquito netting and the shortage of quinine tablets was already reflected in the number of malaria cases admitted to the hospital. A few fighter aircraft were miraculously still serviceable and engineers prepared fields for them as well as helping the infantry and artillery to dig in.

defenders—and on the following morning, January 11, between 200 and 300 Japanese lay dead on the field, while the Philippine Army Scouts, who had been rushed up from the reserve, were almost back to their original line.

Colonel Takechi's IX Regiment moved against General Parker's left flank to circle behind the Americans while pressure was maintained at the other end of the line. Little headway was made and both sides suffered heavy losses, yet the pressure was maintained again the following day when II Battalion attacked the 43rd Regiment. Artillery fire helped to prevent the Japanese from gaining ground but the next day's fighting left them in possession of a hill between two Philippine army regiments.

Here, a counterattack took the Japanese by surprise and a Philippine regiment pushed so far into their lines that the Japanese were almost able to surround them. Attacked from three sides the Filipino troops fled to the rear in disorder. Across the peninsula, Japanese attacks against Wainwright's 1st Corps successfully pushed them back to the main defence line

three weeks of bitter fighting.

But General Homma's troops were running into more trouble as they pressed against the last barricade—the Orion-Bagac line. With American artillery shooting accurately from high positions, attacks were costly; but even so they made several intrusions against the long, thinly defended line. General Nara and General Kimura were both successful in making deep penetrations which were then consolidated. But then these strong pockets were gradually wasted by long, arduous fighting in the rough country.

It was now Homma's turn to withdraw and lick his wounds. By the end of February, the XIV Army had suffered 7,000 casualties, including 2,700 dead, and between 10,000 and 12,000 were down with dysentery, beriberi, and various tropical diseases. Homma could barely muster three effective battalions — if the Philippine army had launched an offensive at this time it could have recaptured Manila. But a lull settled over no-man's-land, and sections and platoons patrolled the area between the lines, General Homma awaited reinforce-

△ The first big Allied surrenders in the Philippines: US troops and their Japanese captors

△ An incident on the 'Death March'—American prisoners are bound and posed for the camera. Some 78,000 men were forced to march—with minimum rations—65 miles under the hot sun

ments and the American generals prepared for the final assault.

In Washington on February 8, the War Department received a startling message from Philippine President Manuel Quezon, proposing that the US immediately grant the Philippines their independence, that the islands be neutralised, that American and Japanese forces be withdrawn and the Philippine army be disbanded. At the same time General MacArthur sent a supporting message to the Chief-of-Staff, General Marshall, explaining that the Philippine garrison had sustained a casualty rate of 50%. 'There is no denying the fact that we are near done,' he added.

President Roosevelt repudiated the neutrality scheme, insisting that the fight must continue. He authorised MacArthur to surrender Filipino troops if necessary but forbade the surrender of American troops: 'so long as there remains any possibility of resistance.' Meanwhile, America and its Pacific allies had agreed to place MacArthur in command of a new Allied HQ in the south-west Pacific. MacArthur had earlier advised Marshall that he intended to 'fight to destruction' on Corregidor. When commanded by his President and urged by his senior staff officers, MacArthur accepted the proposed move. He left when the fighting on Bataan had reached a stalemate. With him to Mindanao on four PT boats went his wife and son, and the boy's nurse, Admiral Rockwell, General George (air force), General Sutherland, and 14 other staff members. At Mindanao they were met by General Sharp who took them to Del Monte airfield. In the early hours of March 12 the entire group took off in B-17s and, at 9 am, landed safely at Darwin.

In his first public statement on reaching Australia, MacArthur said that the relief of the Philippines was his primary purpose. 'I came through and I shall return' he pledged.

General Wainwright was appointed the new commander of the Philippine forces, and selected General King to command the Luzon forces on Bataan. Here the most pressing problem was food: army-built rice mills threshed the local palay; Filipino fishermen netted fish; horses, mules, carabao, pigs, chickens, dogs, monkeys, snakes, and iguanas were slaughtered; everything edible on the peninsula was harvested—but the troops' diet became more and more meagre. The absence of sufficient vitamins resulted in outbreaks of beriberi, scurvy, and amoebic dysentery, and malaria and dengue fevers spread with disastrous rapidity.

Before MacArthur left he advised Wainwright to 'give them everything you've got with your artillery. That's the best arm you have'. But on Good Friday, April 3—which was also the anniversary of the legendary Japanese Emperor Jimmu—it was General Homma's guns, howitzers, and mortars which opened up the final offensive.

Homma's XVI Division and 65th Brigade had been reinforced with healthy troops—the IV Division, arriving from Shanghai, and a detachment of infantry, artillery, and engineers also reaching Bataan. Some 60 twin-engined bombers were flown in to Clark Field for a co-ordinated air and artillery assault against the whole American line. The initial objective was Mount Samat, a 2,000-foot rise behind the centre of the Philippine army's coast-to-coast defence line.

On April 3 the awesome bombardment began. For five hours the Japanese guns, mortars, and howitzers pounded the sick and weary troops defending the last few miles of Bataan. More than 60 tons of bombs were dropped on the devastated line in front of Mount Samat. By evening, the stocky brown men of 65th Brigade and IV Division had advanced 1,000 yards; the shell and bomb battering had made the preliminary move much easier than Homma expected, so he repeated the formula the following day, ordering his infantry to continue the attack without bothering to consolidate the earlier gains.

Bombing attacks by the XXII Air Brigade were particularly successful on April 4. By sheer chance the bombs fell among two battalions—the 42nd and 43rd—who stampeded south for 4,500 yards, thus opening the centre for the Japanese 65th Brigade, which pushed deeply behind Mount Samat and threw fresh strength against the flank of 2nd Corps. By dawn on April 7, the Japanese had pushed a bulge 4 miles deep into the centre of the defenders' line, and were commanding the heights of the northern slopes of the Mariveles range.

General King planned to use a counterattack to stop the Japanese offensive. The 45th Brigade, supported by a few tanks, attacked the point of the bulge on the slopes of the Mariveles. But the attempt was futile: there were no flanking attacks to support the brigade, and the corps began to disintegrate. Whole units disappeared into the jungle, communications broke down, and roads and trails became choked with stragglers. Japanese aerial and artillery bombardment was maintained over the whole front, concentrating whenever a stand was made—and as 2nd Corps retreated, 1st Corps became exposed to flanking movements, and also withdrew.

General Wainwright could see that the rout could only be stopped by a strong attack by 1st Corps against the Japanese 65th Brigade and IV Division. He made this suggestion to General King but the Luzon commander refused to issue the order, for he had only a disorganised, routed, decimated, sick and demoralised army which would be slaughtered piecemeal if he did not surrender it. It was his decision, therefore, which ended the fighting on Bataan. On April 9, he sent two emissaries forward with a white flag to meet the Japanese commander.

That night the ammunition dumps were exploded and some 2,000 people—nurses, US army and navy personnel, some Cavalry Scouts, and other Philippine Army troops—escaped in small boats and barges to Corregidor.

On Bataan, 78,000 men of the starved and beaten army went into captivity. The conquerors concluded their victory by forcing their captives into a 'death march', from Mariveles to San Fernando. With the barest rations of food or water, the prisoners were forced to march the 65 miles under the hot sun, and many of them were clubbed and bayonetted on the roadside—a vicious end to a vicious battle. Now General Homma turned to the siege of Corregidor—the formidable 'Gibraltar of the East'—in order to claim possession of Manila Bay and demand the capitulation of the whole of the Philippine Commonwealth.

GENERAL DOUGLAS MACARTHUR, born in 1880, had been associated with the Philippines armed forces since 1928. He had commanded the 42nd 'Rainbow' Division in the First World War, and was wounded and gassed in action. In 1925 he had become the youngest major-general in the US Army, and first commanded the department of the Philippines in 1928/30. President Hoover appointed him US Chief-of-Staff in 1930, but MacArthur retired in 1935 to become an adviser to the Philippine government. Appointed Field-Marshal in 1936, he retired the following year, but he was retained as head of all Filipino military forces by President Quezon. When the Filipino armed forces were incorporated into the US forces in July 1941, Roosevelt nominated MacArthur as C-in-C. On the Allied defeat in the Philippines MacArthur arrived in Australia on March 17, 1942, to assume command of all Allied forces in the Pacific theatre. His counter-offensive in the autumn of 1942 in New Guinea started the Allied reconquest of the Pacific.

US Army

Brown Bros

△ Bodies of American POWs who died on the notorious 'Death March' from Bataan to San Fernando

Associated Press

△ Nearing the end: American and Filipino POWs stagger into Camp O'Donnell with the dead and dying

Japanese troops and their mounted officer move through the long grass during the invasion of Burma in early 1942

THE LONG RETREAT
The First Burma Campaign

Since it had long been thought that a land invasion of Burma was very unlikely, the defences of the country had been seriously neglected. However, by the end of 1941 the Japanese were ready to occupy Burma to protect the north-west flank of their 'Greater East Asia Co-prosperity Sphere'. The author, who commanded the British ground forces during the first part of the campaign, gives a first-hand account of the unequal battle, and the long retreat — the longest ever made by a British army — back to the Indian border. *Brigadier Sir John Smyth*

Japanese tanks cross
a make-shift bridge
during the invasion
of Burma

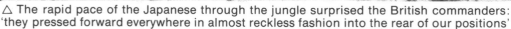

△ The rapid pace of the Japanese through the jungle surprised the British commanders: 'they pressed forward everywhere in almost reckless fashion into the rear of our positions'

△ The British pinned their hopes on river defences—but these did not stop the advance

This short, but extremely important, campaign can be divided conveniently into two parts. The first covers the months of December 1941, and January and February 1942, when the Burma army, under command of General Hutton, fought—and lost—the battle for Rangoon and control of the Burma Road to China. This decided the fate of Burma.

The second part covers the period between March and May 1942, when the remnants of the Burma army, together with the Chinese armies, under command of General Alexander, fought a successful delaying action from Rangoon back to the frontiers of Assam and India. This ensured that there could be no invasion of India before the monsoon broke; and it also enabled the tattered, weary, but very gallant remnants of the Burma army to get safely back to India. General Alexander referred to it as 'The Burma rescue operation'.

It would have been hard to find any country more unprepared for defence in a major war than was Burma in 1941. Yet the importance of Burma to the Allied cause in general, and to the defence of India in particular, in a war against Japan, was fully realised by Winston Churchill and President Roosevelt. From the viewpoint of Allied strategy, it was essential that China should be enabled to continue her struggle against Japan, and thus contain large enemy forces. Through Burma lay the only route by which the Chinese armies could be kept supplied

and any American air bases in China maintained. From India's point of view, so long as Burma was held, Calcutta and the great industrial centres of north-east India were practically immune from air attack, and her eastern land frontiers were secure from the threat of invasion.

The civil administration crumbles

On her separation from India in April 1937, Burma achieved a considerable measure of self-government, though the Governor remained British. Sir Reginald Dorman-Smith became Governor on May 5, 1941. But, in the autumn of that year, U Saw, the Premier, took advantage of Britain's difficulties to press for full self-government immediately after the war.

The population of Burma could hardly have been less geared to resist an invader—particularly one as hardy and brutal as the Japanese. About a million Indians lived in Burma, and provided most of the dock labour in Rangoon. As regards the Burmese, Field-Marshal Slim, in his book *Defeat into Victory,* says: 'The vast majority had no feeling that the war was their business; they wished to avoid it. A small minority, mostly soldiers and officials, were actively loyal to the British; about the same number, nationalist politicians, relics of the old rebels of 1924, students, and some political *pongyis* (Buddhist priests) were actively hostile. These elements were rendered more formidable by the leadership of Japanese-trained

Burmans, imported with the invading Japanese army, and by the flocking to their standards of numbers of *dacoits* [armed thugs] and bad characters attracted by the prospect of loot. As the Japanese advanced, desertion among the police, the subordinates of all services, and clerical staffs, began to spread. The air raids on towns, with their heavy casualties and great destruction by fire and the swarms of Indian refugees, fleeing not so much from the Japanese as from the Burmans among whom they lived, all helped in the breakdown of control and communications. The civil administration was crumbling ahead of the Japanese.'

From the point of view of defence, Burma was nobody's baby. Up to 1937 Burma had been part of India, and its defence, like all its other activities, had been the responsibility of the Indian government. Then, with political separation from India, Burma was made fully responsible for its own military forces. A change came on the outbreak of war with Germany in September 1939, when Burma's forces were placed for operational purposes under the British Chiefs-of-Staff in London, but remained for finance and administration under their own government. Suddenly, in November 1940, operational control was transferred to the newly formed Far Eastern Command in Singapore, while administrative responsibility was divided between the Burma government and the War Office in London. This was obviously a most inefficient and unworkable arrange-

△ As the British fell back, the river bridges were duly blown—but the Japanese army engineers were expert at running up emergency foot- and road-bridges to span the wreckage, and the advance of the infantry columns was rarely hindered by such demolition work

ment, and local commanders and successive commanders-in-chief in India pressed for Burma's return to Indian control. On December 12, 1941, when a Japanese attack was seen to be imminent, Burma was passed back to India. But on the 30th of the same month, just as the Japanese attack had started, it was handed over to the new ABDA (American, British, Dutch, and Australian command), General Wavell's South-West Pacific Command, with its headquarters in Java. When ABDA broke up, following the Japanese invasion of the Dutch East Indies in March 1942, Burma came back to India again. One could hardly imagine a worse administrative muddle.

The Official Inter-Service History of the War Against Japan states: 'The possibility of an attack on Burma across her eastern frontiers had for long been regarded as remote. In August 1940 the Chiefs-of-Staff reviewed the situation in the Far East, and concluded that, though a Japanese occupation of Siam would bring the threat of air attack on Burma close, the invasion of Burmese territory would still be a comparatively remote threat.'

Overall weakness of the defenders
Only very small forces had been maintained in the country after her separation from India in 1937; they consisted of two British battalions, four battalions of the Burma Rifles, and various other units. A demand by the Burmese government for a higher proportion of Burmans in the armed forces caused the Governor, Sir Reginald Dorman-Smith, to form two territorial battalions. But this did not satisfy Burman aspirations, and consequently Burman companies were formed and included in the Burma Rifles, which had previously been recruited solely from the Chins, Kachins, and Karens—generally considered to be the more martial races. But the force on which Burma relied chiefly for her internal security, and for 'watch-and-ward' on her land frontiers, was the Burmese Military Police, consisting of nine battalions.

The only two regular British battalions in Burma at this time were the 1st Battalion of the Gloucestershire Regiment and the 2nd King's Own Yorkshire Light Infantry. Both of these battalions had already sent a number of officers and other ranks to India and to the United Kingdom and, as a result, by December 1941, neither of them could muster more than two companies.

The air force in Burma, as elsewhere in the Far East, was very weak. When war with Japan broke out, the only RAF unit in the country was 67 (Fighter) Squadron with some 16 Buffalo aircraft. The airfields at Victoria Point, Moulmein, Tavoy, and Mergui were essential links on the air reinforcement route to Malaya, since the distance from Rangoon to Singapore was too great for the aircraft then in commission to cover without refuelling. They were therefore of great strategic importance.

But Generalissimo Chiang Kai-Shek had agreed in April 1941 that a number of American air squadrons, manned by volunteers, which became famous as the AVG (American Volunteer Group), formed for service in China, should be made available for the defence of Burma if necessary. In June 1941 the first contingent of the AVG arrived, and by November three squadrons of Tomahawk (P-40) fighters had been formed at Toungoo. When Burma was threatened with invasion in December 1941, the Generalissimo kept his promise, and one squadron was retained in Burma to assist in the air defence of Rangoon.

The superior range and numbers of the Japanese aircraft were not the only handicaps from which we suffered. An efficient warning system was essential if our machines were to escape destruction on the ground. Yet the layout of the Burma airfields made this impossible: they had almost all been sited in a long north-south line facing the Siamese frontier—from Victoria Point in the extreme south, through Mergui, Moulmein, Rangoon, Toungoo, Heho, and Namsang to Lashio. In addition, we possessed only one radio direction-finding set, and the newly-raised Burma Observer Corps had no wireless, and was thus tied to the very scanty and inefficient civil telephone and telegraph system. These were crushing disadvantages for our small air force.

When General Wavell visited Chungking at Christmas 1941, Generalissimo Chiang

Kai-Shek offered to put the 5th and 6th Chinese Armies at his disposal for the defence of Burma. Wavell accepted only the 93rd Division of the 6th Army and moved it into the Shan States; for all sorts of objections had been raised against receiving the whole of the Chinese forces offered—they had practically no supply or transport services, and would have had to live off the country.

Unfortunately the Chinese were bitterly offended at this refusal of their generous offer. A great deal of criticism was levelled at General Wavell for not accepting the two Chinese armies. His hesitation in accepting the Chinese offer of assistance appears to have been based on the assumption that the defences of Malaya would stand firm, which was, of course, the accepted opinion of the Chiefs-of-Staff at that time.

I come now to the first battle of Burma, in which I, as commander of almost the whole of the ground defence forces, had perforce to play a leading part. To understand this campaign, one must realise that the Dunkirk operations, the Battle of Britain, the operations against the Italians in North and East Africa, and now the loss of Singapore and the threat to Burma had stretched the resources of the British Commonwealth to the absolute limit. There just were not the troops, the air and sea forces, and the highly-qualified officers to command them, which were required at this critical time.

And so appointments were made, and actions taken—or not taken—which would have made no sense in normal times, and which are difficult for students of military history to understand. General Tom Hutton, for instance, a brilliant staff-officer and a very gallant man, would probably not have been given command of an army in the field—he was indeed a great loss to India as Chief-of-Staff—nor could it have been foreseen that General Wavell, one of the great commanders of his time, who was certainly in need of a rest after his great endeavours in North Africa, should have had to undertake a vast operational command, and attempt, through General Hutton, to control my battle in the jungles of Burma from his headquarters 2,000 miles away in Java.

Winston Churchill described the efforts he was still making, up to the end of February 1942, to persuade the Australian government to land a division in Rangoon. He said in a letter to Mr Curtin on February 20, 1942: 'It can begin to disembark at Rangoon about 26th or 27th February. There is nothing else in the world which can fill the gap—and save Burma.'

He also cabled to President Roosevelt to the same effect, stressing the vital importance of keeping open the Burma Road and maintaining contact with China.

General Wavell, quite independently, had made a similar request, and had gone further and asked for a whole Australian army corps to be transferred to Burma.

On December 4, 1941, General Wavell ordered me to take command of the 17th (Black Cat) Division. But I was called to Flagstaff House in Delhi for an interview with him on Sunday, December 28, when he informed me that he had sent his Chief-of-Staff, General Hutton, to organise Burma against a Japanese invasion and to command the Burma Army. I was to do the fighting with all the forces which could be put at my disposal, including one remaining brigade of the 17th Division, the 46th (the other two brigades had been lost in the

defence of Malaya).

Although I had the greatest admiration for General Wavell, as a commander and as a man, it did surprise me that he did not consider Burma to be in any immediate danger—he had given the same impression to Brigadier 'Taffy' Davies, whom he had interviewed a few days earlier, before the latter went off to Burma to take up his appointment as BGS (Brigadier General Staff) Burma Army.

Wavell's contempt for the enemy

Wavell's long-established contempt for the Japanese soldier was a 'thing' with him from which he never deviated, right up to the fall of Rangoon. Also it struck me that he regarded the young Indian troops we now had at our disposal, completely untrained and unequipped for jungle warfare, as the equal of those magnificent 4th and 5th Indian Divisions which he had had under his command in North Africa. I think this explains why Wavell could see no reason why our road-bound, untrained Indian and Burmese troops were unable to hold the mobile, highly-trained Japanese divisions on the furthest frontiers of Burma.

A few days later Wavell was ordered to hand over his India command and assume command of all the Allied troops in South-East Asia. He took on this enormous—and impossible—assignment with his usual phlegm, merely remarking as he started off by air to set up his headquarters in Java: 'I have heard of having to hold the baby—but this is twins!'

In the Japanese plans for the capture of what they called 'the Southern Region', the initial role for their XV Army, consisting of the XXXIII Division and the 55th Division, supported by the X Air Brigade, was to occupy Thailand, including the Isthmus of Kra as far south as Nakhon. It was then to capture the British airfields in Tenasserim and protect the right and rear of XXV Army during its advance into Malaya. Later, when Southern Army was satisfied that XXV Army operations in Malaya were developing according to plan, XV Army was to invade Burma by way of the Raheng-Moulmein route with the immediate object of capturing Rangoon.

The XV Army, to which the Imperial Guards Division had been added, entered Bangkok on December 8, 1941, and thereafter was master of Thailand, with its airfields, railways, and assembly areas for the invasion of Burma. On January 16 a Japanese battalion occupied Victoria Point in southern Burma without opposition, the British garrison having been withdrawn.

Rangoon suffered its first air raid on December 23, 1941, and a second one on Christmas Day. RAF fighters and the AVG inflicted heavy losses on the raiders—the estimated losses being 50 Japanese bombers and fighters destroyed, against ten RAF and two AVG aircraft—but were unable to prevent a number of the Japanese bombers from getting through. The effect of the bombing on the Indian dock labourers was disastrous, and for this reason alone it became progressively more and more difficult to work the port and keep the city of Rangoon functioning.

I arrived in Rangoon on January 9, 1942, and went straight into conference with General Hutton—whom I had never previously met. Hutton gave me a clear and—as it turned out—perfectly correct appreciation of the situation. The main Japanese

threat would be likely to come from Raheng via Kawkareik-Paan-Kyaikto, and Sittang. To block this immediate threat the 16th Indian Brigade, under Brigadier J. K. Jones, had already been dispatched to Kawkareik. Brigadier Jones had also been ordered to send one company of the 1/7th Gurkha Rifles to watch the Three Pagoda Pass, which was a fairly well-used track east of Ye, connecting Bangkok with Moulmein. This brigade had only just arrived in Burma. The brigadier, a very tough and reliable Indian army soldier, had reported that he had only taken command a few days before embarkation. His three battalions had been 'milked' to the last drop to send reinforcements to other theatres of war, and had only been made up with new recruits three days before embarkation. They were, therefore, very raw, and had no experience of jungle warfare whatsoever.

The 2nd Burma Brigade, under Brigadier Bourke, consisting of Burma Rifles battalions, plus the 4/12th Frontier Force Rifles attached from 16th Brigade, was spread over 300 miles of jungle country, and was also responsible for the defence of the airfields of Mergui and Tavoy.

There was also another possible line of approach in the north, from Papun on to Sittang; so my total area of responsibility extended from Papun in the north to Mergui in the south, and eastwards to Raheng and the Three Pagoda Pass. This was an enormous area of jungle country—a lot of it with very poor communications—extending for anything between 500 and 800 miles, depending on how the area is measured.

For this I had at the time only two brigades, the 16th Indian and the 2nd Burma, though my 46th Brigade was expected to arrive in Rangoon within a few days. To prevent the possibility of any Japanese advance from the north-east, General Bruce Scott's very weak 1st Burma Division had been located in the Shan States, and though they sent me all the help they could, they were not concerned in this first phase of the campaign.

As the army commander had no line of communication troops available I had to be responsible also for the long line of communications from Moulmein northwards to Bilin and Sittang. First there was the somewhat antiquated steamer ferry service over the 7,000 yards of open water which lay between Moulmein and Martaban. From the railhead at Martaban a good metal road and single track railway ran back through Thaton, over the Bilin river to Kyaikto, but from Kyaikto to Sittang the road became a mere track, almost feet deep in dust. This track led to the big iron railway bridge over the river, which was being planked to make a roadway. There was also a ferry which was slow but quite useful.

The Sittang river was a really formidable barrier lying across the route of the main Japanese advance on to Rangoon—the only real obstacle in the theatre of operations. The Sittang bridge was thus vital to us and to the Japanese, who could have bombed and destroyed it at any time—but they needed it as much as we did. We laid back such troops as we could spare to protect the vital bridge against unforeseen attack and the army sappers prepared it for demolition.

On the west bank of the Sittang the country was open and suitable for the type of operation for which my troops had been trained. In fact it was the only area in which the (so-called) 17th Division could

Paul Popper

Sado-Opera Mundi

Ullstein

△ As Japanese infantrymen break cover and charge, a machine-gun crew prepares to support the attack. Such charges often meant high Japanese losses

△ A Japanese 70-mm howitzer, dismantled for the march and in action

have fought the Japanese on something like level terms. However, it was only 100 miles from Rangoon.

The Japanese 112th Battalion of the Southern Army crossed the Burmese frontier on January 15, and their attack developed rapidly within the next few days. On January 19 they captured Tavoy, overwhelming the garrison of the 6th Burma Rifles and a battery of the Burma Auxiliary force. This resulted in the garrison of Mergui being cut off; it was withdrawn by sea between the 20th and 23rd. Although the operations in Tenasserim were on a minor scale, their importance lay in the fact that the three airfields – Victoria Point, Mergui, and Tavoy – were now in Japanese hands, and could be used to give fighter escort to their bombers attacking Rangoon.

On the 21st it became apparent that the Japanese were advancing in strength against Kawkareik. The army commander had ordered that Brigadier Jones should not get so involved that his withdrawal was rendered so impossible – but this was easier said than done, due to his lack of motor transport. After a hair-raising operation, in which all its transport and most of its supporting weapons were lost, the 16th Brigade arrived back in the Moulmein area very shaken, and in need of considerable reorganisation and re-equipment.

The general pattern of the Japanese advance now became apparent. Taking every advantage of their mobility, compared to

our dependence on the road, they invariably applied 'the hook', to outflank our positions and then attack us from the rear. They continued to develop these same tactics throughout the whole of this first Burma campaign.

My staff and I had come to the conclusion that if we were going to fulfil our purpose and stop the Japanese, we must concentrate as a division and fight on grounds of our own choosing, rather than try to hold widely separated localities in thick jungle country where all the advantages lay with the Japanese. Therefore I advocated an immediate withdrawal to the Bilin-Kyaikto-Sittang area as a preliminary to occupying the Sittang river position.

Ordered to stay put
But I was ordered to stay put. The only course open to me was to co-operate loyally with the plan of the higher command, while making it clear that I did not agree with it. And, of course, I had to fit this in with my duty to save my division from destruction. It was for this latter reason that, without permission, on February 14, I concentrated my whole division behind the Bilin river – which at that time of year was only a ditch, but a good co-ordinating line.

On January 26, Lieutenant-General Iida, commanding the Japanese XV Army, ordered 55th Division to capture Moulmein. I realised full well that the loss of this important town would give the enemy another airfield, and have a bad effect on

morale throughout the whole of Burma. Nevertheless, it was an impossible place to hold – unless, of course, the whole division fought a last-ditch battle there, which was the last thing the army commander wanted. It was a still more impossible place from which to withdraw, as the only method of withdrawal was by river steamer over the broad waters of the Gulf of Martaban.

I advocated holding it with a light screen of skirmishers, but was ordered to hold it 'as long as possible with one brigade'. How Brigadiers Roger Ekin and Paddy Bourke got their troops out of this quite appalling situation I shall never know; after two days of fierce fighting – in which the Japanese suffered heavy losses – I had either to reinforce them or order them to withdraw. By a miracle, and the ineptitude of the Japanese air force, they got away by river steamer under the noses of the Japanese. But they lost 600 men and a great deal of equipment in the process.

I now received a very valuable reinforcement of the 48th (Gurkha) Brigade from my old 19th Division in Secunderabad, India, for which I had asked the army commander previously. They were commanded by Brigadier Noel Hugh-Jones, and were composed of the 1/3rd, the 1/4th, and the 2/5th Gurkhas. I had also asked the army commander to get Brigadier 'Punch' Cowan, an old friend and gallant fighting soldier, for me from India, with the idea of having a spare brigadier. Odd units and battalions ▷

213

Japan reaches out for India

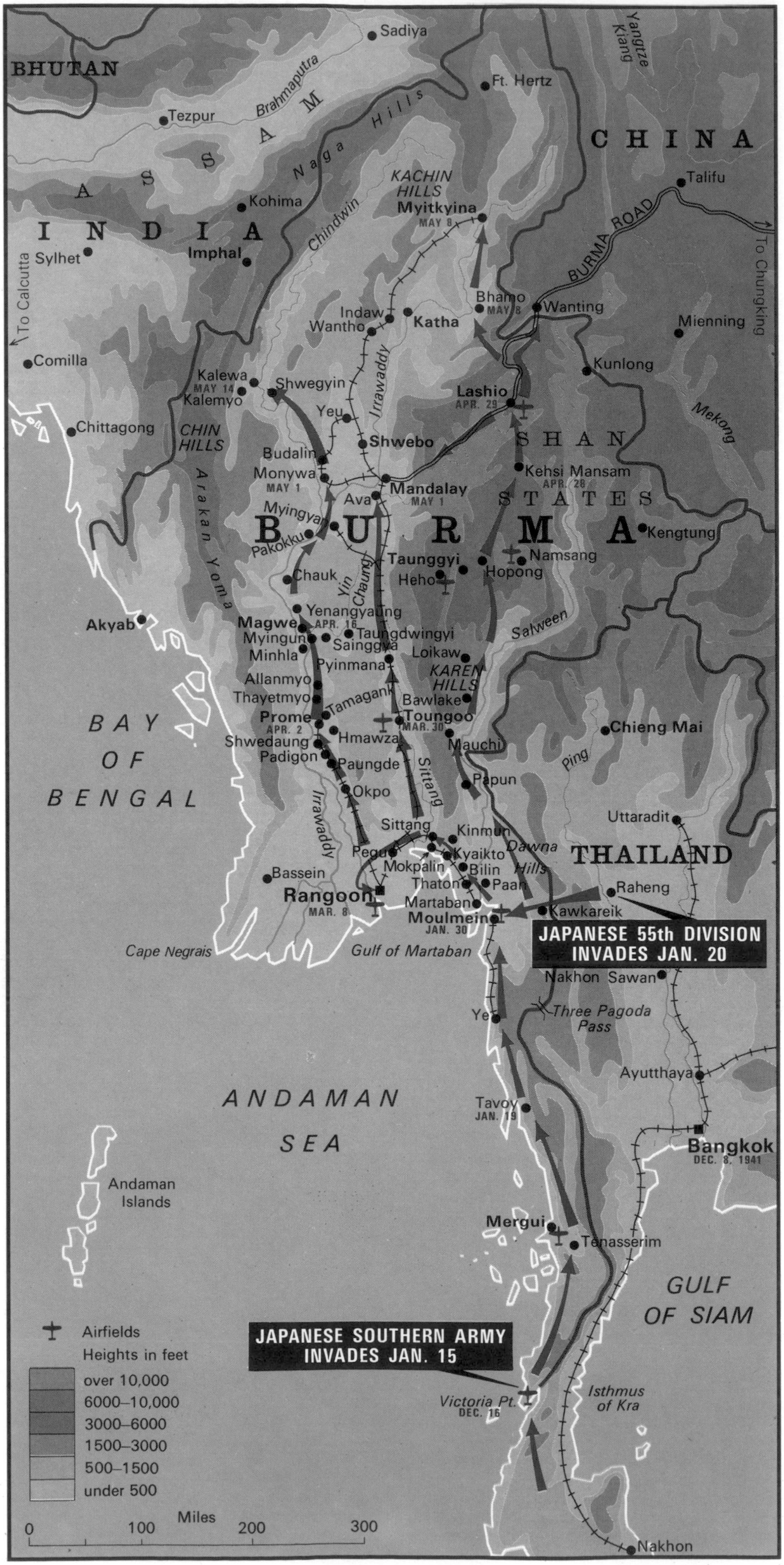

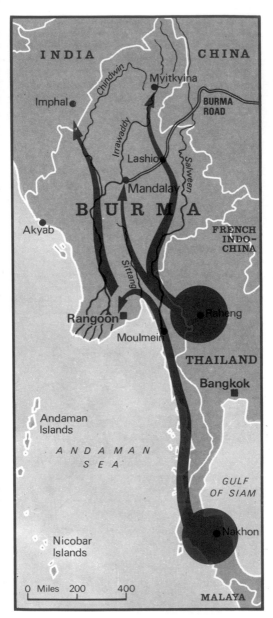

Map labels (left map)

BHUTAN

Sadiya

Tezpur · Ft. Hertz

A S S A M Naga Hills KACHIN HILLS

Kohima · Myitkyina MAY 8

I N D I A CHINA

Talifu

To Calcutta → Sylhet

Imphal Chindwin BURMA ROAD To Chungking →

Comilla

Bhamo MAY 8 · Wanting

Indaw · Katha Mienning

Wantho

Kunlong

Kalewa MAY 14 Shwegyin

Kalemyo Yeu Lashio APR. 29

Chittagong Shwebo

CHIN HILLS Budalin S H A N

Monywa MAY 1 Kehsi Mansam APR. 28

Myingyan Ava · Mandalay MAY 1 S T A T E S

B U R M A Pakokku Chauk Taunggyi Namsang

Yenangyaung APR. 16 Heho · Hopong Kengtung

Magwe Taungdwingyi

Myingun Sainggya Loikaw Salween

Minhla Pyinmana KAREN HILLS

Allanmyo Bawlake

Thayetmyo Tamagank Mauchi

Prome APR. 2 Hmawza · Toungoo MAR. 30 Chieng Mai

Shwedaung Papun Ping

Padigon Paungde

Okpo Mauchi

Sittang Kinmun THAILAND

Pegu Kyaikto Dawna Hills

Bassein Mokpalin Bilin Uttaradit

Thaton Paan

Rangoon MAR. 8 Martaban · Raheng

Moulmein JAN. 30 Kawkareik

Cape Negrais Gulf of Martaban Nakhon Sawan

JAPANESE 55th DIVISION INVADES JAN. 20

Ye

Three Pagoda Pass

Ayutthaya

BAY OF BENGAL

Tavoy JAN. 19

ANDAMAN SEA

Mergui Tenasserim

Andaman Islands

Bangkok DEC. 8, 1941

JAPANESE SOUTHERN ARMY INVADES JAN. 15

GULF OF SIAM

Victoria Pt. DEC. 16 Isthmus of Kra

Airfields
Heights in feet
over 10,000
6000–10,000
3000–6000
1500–3000
500–1500
under 500

Miles 0 100 200 300

Nakhon

Map labels (right map)

INDIA CHINA

Imphal · Myitkyina

Chindwin BURMA ROAD

Irrawaddy Lashio Salween

Mandalay

Akyab B U R M A

FRENCH INDO-CHINA

Sittang

Rangoon · Raheng

Moulmein

Andaman Islands

THAILAND

Bangkok

ANDAMAN SEA

Nicobar Islands

GULF OF SIAM

Nakhon

0 Miles 200 400

MALAYA

Captions

△ Another aspect of the Japanese grand strategy, the invasion of Burma was a development of the Malayan campaign. On December 8/10, 1941, the Japanese Southern Army had occupied the Kra Peninsula, and by January 10 of the new year the position in Malaya was sufficiently secure for its forces to strike north into Burma. This invasion was linked with the operations of 55th Division from Thailand. Apart from its oilfields and the Burma Road to China, the value of Burma was as a bastion against an Allied counterattack from India

◁ The actual invasion was another triumph for the Japanese army planners; and the faulty tactics imposed on the defenders by a remote Allied High Command were fatal. The pattern of Japanese outflanking moves and Allied withdrawals which had already set in in Malaya was repeated in Burma; and by May 1942 the Japanese were on the frontiers of India

The men who fought for Burma

Gurkha soldiers have always been enlisted by private treaty between the British Commonwealth and the King of Nepal, and enjoy one of the highest fighting reputations of any of the native-enlisted units in the British Commonwealth and Empire armies. The national weapon—the *kukri* chopping-knife, with its deadly, razor-sharp half-moon blade—supplemented the standard British infantry weapons (Lee-Enfield rifle and Bren- and Sten-guns) in the Burma campaign. In the long retreat from Burma, the Gurkhas especially distinguished themselves in the battle for the Sittang river-crossing—and in the general tenacity of their performance in action, which was to add to their battle-honours in the years which lay ahead

An Allied assessment of the Japanese soldier (in a wartime manual) stated that: 'he meticulously performs duties allotted to him; he is an efficient cog in the machine, and will carry out instructions to the letter.' This tendency had inherent virtues and vices—but it did not impede the Japanese 'Runaway Victory' in the Pacific. His equipment was sound, but the Model 99 (1939) 7·7-mm rifle (and the 1905 Model 6·5-mm) had a magazine capacity of only five rounds as opposed to the British ten rounds. This slowed down the rate of fire—and the standard Model 92 machine-gun ammunition could not be used in the Model 99 rifle in the same way as the British Bren-gun and Lee-Enfield rifle

The British infantryman in Malaya and Burma was painfully learning the technique of jungle warfare from the Japanese, but his equipment was not inferior. Indeed, it gave far more attention to the comfort of the individual soldier than was to be found in the Japanese army system. The standard British rifle was the legendary Lee-Enfield Mk III, which had so high a rate of fire that the Germans at Mons in 1914 had mistaken it for machine-gun fire; the ammunition-pouches carried by the British infantryman held 60 rounds each—and the ·303-inch ammunition was the same as that fired by the Bren light machine-gun

Deirdre Amsden

were being sent to join me, and I had four brigades—and an armoured brigade due to arrive shortly—so I was glad to have Cowan with me as an addition to my staff.

Requests to withdraw are refused

The Japanese captured Martaban and were everywhere infiltrating between the extended and isolated positions I had been ordered to hold. I felt that I had to make one more urgent appeal to the army commander, if my division was not to be defeated in 'penny packets', without gaining the object which he and General Wavell desired. Therefore, on Thursday, February 12, I sent Cowan, who completely agreed with my appreciation, into Rangoon to explain the position. The Official History says: 'Smyth told him [Cowan] to impress on Hutton the grave danger in which 17th Division stood of being cut off from the Sittang bridge, and to urge that he might be allowed to withdraw the division behind the Bilin river immediately, and that there should be no delay in the next stage of the withdrawal which should be behind the Sittang River.' I wanted to get across the Sittang well before the Japanese could intercept me.

This was the message that Cowan conveyed to the army commander. Even at that late stage, although I was closely engaged by two Japanese divisions, I could have made it, and would then have had the support on the other side of the Sittang of our newly-arrived brigade of light tanks. But seven days later, with the division still locked in close conflict in thick jungle with the Japanese, and utterly exhausted, the cards were stacked heavily against us. No wonder the Official History says: 'In view of the great importance of getting 17th Division safely across the Sittang, Hutton might have been wiser, once action had been joined on the Bilin, to leave Smyth a free hand.'

However, disastrous as I think the army commander's decision—for me to hang on at Bilin—I realised full well the pressure that was brought to bear on him by General Wavell. The latter had just telegraphed to Hutton: 'I have every confidence in judgement and fighting spirit of you and Smyth, but bear in mind that continual withdrawal, as experience of Malaya showed, is most damaging to morale of troops, especially Indian troops. Time can often be gained as effectively and less expensively, by bold counter-offensive. This especially so against Japanese.' Truly Java was a long way from the Sittang river.

The 17th Division gave everything it had at Bilin and surrendered no ground to the Japanese; but, as the pressure increased, every single reserve had to be thrown into the battle—and even then we could not prevent strong parties of the enemy turning our flanks. The 48th Gurkha Brigade, in their first engagement, particularly distinguished themselves in this close-quarter fighting.

Withdrawal to the Sittang

Then, on the 19th, the army commander came up from Rangoon and gave me permission to withdraw across the Sittang. This of course was not possible in daylight, and it says a great deal for the troops and their commanders that they were able to break contact under cover of darkness, with only a few yards separating them from the Japanese.

But their greatest ordeal lay ahead—to withdraw 30 miles, the last part over a single

△ Into central Burma. **Above:** A Japanese patrol in the Mandalay railway yard. **Below:** Japanese seize Yenangyaung oil field—but the huge storage tanks were blown up

dusty track, in face of close pressure from two Japanese divisions and a superior air force. It would have been almost a miracle to have achieved it successfully: and yet—with everything against them—they so nearly did. Tired as they were they had to be kept going, all through the night of the 19th, all day of the 20th, and far into the following night.

The brigades leap-frogged back through one another, imposing considerable delay on the advancing Japanese, and by the morning of the 21st we had got well clear of the XXXIII Japanese Division. But my chief worry was with regard to the Japanese formations which had been reported as having turned our flanks. In actual fact the 215th and 214th Japanese Regiments had done so, and were moving with all speed by cross-country tracks to intercept us at Sittang.

At 0500 hours on February 21, a Japanese raiding party attacked my advanced divisional headquarters at Kyaikto; but, apart from creating some confusion and firing off a lot of ammunition, they achieved little and drew off at daybreak. The 21st was a most unpleasant and disastrous day. It is described in the Official History as follows: 'The 21st was very dry and hot, and dense clouds of thick red dust and a shortage of water added to the trials of man and beast alike. During the day the columns on the main track and the troops in the Boyagyi Rubber Estate were repeatedly bombed and machine-gunned, first by Japanese aircraft, and later

by aircraft carrying Allied markings. As a result vehicles, including ambulances full of wounded men, were ditched or destroyed; mules, carrying weapons and wireless sets, broke loose and vanished with their loads into the jungle; casualties were numerous.'

That evening of the 21st, I had a good look round the Sittang bridge defences. The defence troops consisted of such detachments from three or four battalions as we could spare from the main battle, including a company from the Duke of Wellington's Regiment which had just arrived to join the division.

Danger of paratroop landings

A staff officer from AHQ Rangoon arrived with important news. First, they had received news that the Japanese might make parachute landings at first light next morning on the open ground to the west of the river to try to take the bridge from that side. Secondly, the 7th Armoured Brigade had arrived in Rangoon. This made me all the more angry that 17th Division should not by now be over the Sittang, ready to join up with them for the main battle, with the broad river obstacle as our friend instead of our enemy.

All night long the transport moved forward in a steady stream across the bridge, until a lorry overturned on the narrow railway bridge which had only just been planked, causing a two-hour delay. I had hurried the 1/4th Gurkhas across the river for the anti-

△ The end at Rangoon: this photograph was taken from the last tug to leave, and shows the oil storage tanks near the river front ablaze after the demolitions. At Rangoon, the British were only saved by the Japanese adherence to the letter of their orders

parachute landing role and gone over myself to have a look at them. Brigadier Hugh-Jones had crossed the river also, with his Brigade HQ, and I set up a small Divisional Ops HQ close to him.

Suddenly there was a burst of firing from the jungle east of the bridge, and it became evident that our bridgehead defence troops were being attacked by a considerable force of Japanese. Their first onrush penetrated almost to the bridge itself, killing or capturing among others a number of medical personnel, and taking prisoner my medical officer, Colonel K. P. Mackenzie, with whom I had been talking only a few minutes previously. Had not the 4/12th Frontier Force Regiment and the company of the Duke's stood firm, the bridge might have passed into Japanese hands.

I put in the 1/4th Gurkhas to counter-attack, and the enemy withdrew—but they had interposed a strong body of troops between the bridgehead defences and the 16th and 46th Brigades. The 3rd and 5th Gurkhas, part of Hugh-Jones' brigade, had been just about to cross the bridge but were pushed back in a furious battle.

All that day a close-quarter battle raged on the east bank. It was a dog-fight in the jungle in which the brigades and battalions became broken up into small parties. Both Brigadiers, Jones and Ekin and their staffs, had harrowing experiences, but the battalions, both British and Indian, put up a terrific fight. The bridgehead defences were

once again nearly overwhelmed but were again re-established.

Meanwhile, anxious enquiries had been coming in all day from the army commander, who wanted me to meet him next morning at a conference back on the Rangoon-Pegu road. I realised how vital this conference would be, and that the fates of Rangoon and Burma were hanging in the balance.

The bridge is destroyed

Towards nightfall the fighting died down. I put Hugh-Jones in command of the bridge-head, leaving my GSO-1 with him; and, accompanied by Brigadier Cowan, moved back to Divisional HQ for a meal and a few hours' sleep. We had been on the go at top speed for just over two days and two nights. Before leaving I repeated my orders to Brigadier Hugh-Jones that at all costs the bridge, which had been completely prepared for demolition, with the sappers standing by, must not be allowed to fall into the hands of the Japanese.

At 0430 hours Brigadier Cowan woke me to speak to Hugh-Jones. During the night, pressure on the bridgehead had increased. After consultation with the COs of the 4/12th and 1/4th—both cool and capable commanders, whose opinions I respected—he informed me that he could not guarantee to hold the bridge for more than another hour. He therefore wanted permission from me to blow it.

It was a horrible decision to have to make, knowing as I did that, if he blew, two-thirds of the division would be cut off on the far side of the river; and that if he did not, two Japanese divisions might march straight on to Rangoon. As I had been consulted, the responsibility was mine; and I have always accepted it. Bitter as it was there was only one answer. If the bridge could not be held, it must be destroyed.

I gave the order that the bridge must be destroyed immediately, and it was blown by our sappers at 0530 hours. Hard though the decision was, neither Cowan nor I had any doubt as to its necessity. And what is more, despite the controversy which has always surrounded this operation, neither he nor I have ever had cause to alter our opinion— although it preyed on the mind of Brigadier Hugh-Jones up to the very day of his premature death.

As it turned out, the decision did not have quite such tragic results as it might have done, as the Japanese divisions at once started to move up-river to prepare another crossing place, instead of mopping up our troops at their leisure. And soon, in broad daylight, our troops on the far bank started to swim and ferry themselves across. However, I was not to know all this when I found the army commander and all the chief military and civil officers awaiting me at the rendezvous.

General Hutton took my unpleasant and devastating news with commendable sang-froid, and indeed I never saw him rattled. I sympathised deeply with the heavy burdens he had to bear, for without another two divisions of trained jungle troops no commander could have defeated the Japanese in Burma in 1942.

After the Sittang disaster the infantry of the 17th Division numbered 3,484, which represents about 41% of the total authorised establishment. But most battalions were much below strength before the Sittang action, and the actual casualties there were much less than might have been expected. But guns, transport equipment, and most of the weapons were lost, and the 17th Division had, for the time being, ceased to exist as an effective fighting formation. The real tragedy of this grim little campaign was that the main battle behind the broad obstacle of the Sittang, on the only ground favourable to our arms, was never fought at all.

The divisional and army staffs were now faced with the enormous problem of re-clothing, re-equipping, and rearming the men. The 17th Division withdrew, without any interference from the Japanese, back to Pegu to refit and reorganise. There we were joined by the 7th Armoured Brigade, consisting of the 7th Hussars and 2nd Royal Tank Regiment. This armoured brigade was to be a great source of strength to Generals Slim and Alexander in the second phase of the campaign, but on the other hand the disastrous losses sustained by the 17th Division at Sittang were a great handicap.

It was now obvious that the days of Rangoon's defence were numbered, and the army commander went ahead with his plans for the demolition of the docks, oil tanks, and so forth. Had he and his staff not looked well ahead and laid back supplies, ammunition, petrol, and oil, the remnants of the Burma army would probably never have got back to India at all.

The Australian government, not unnaturally, had definitely refused to agree to the diversion of the 7th Australian Division to Burma, and the only reinforcements available were the partially trained 63rd Indian Infantry Brigade, an Indian Field Regiment, and three British battalions. It was only possible to bring these to Rangoon by reason of the brilliant air victory of the AVG and the few remaining British fighters, over a force of some 170 Japanese bombers and fighters on February 25 and 26.

Reorganisation of the higher command
I now had to go back to India for the rest and treatment upon which the medical officers had insisted. So I handed over command of the 17th Division to Brigadier Cowan on March 2, and flew back to India with General Wavell via Lashio, where he had a conference with Generalissimo Chiang Kai-Shek. Next day we flew straight to Calcutta, where General Alexander—on his way to relieve General Hutton of command of the Burma army—met Wavell at the airport. Wavell had now resumed his appointment as Commander-in-Chief in India—and of course had taken Burma with him.

General Alexander arrived in Rangoon with a very optimistic idea of the situation, which nearly resulted in our Field-Marshal spending the rest of the war in a Japanese prison camp. General Slim described it in his book as follows: 'General Alexander escaped from Rangoon by sheer luck. The whole British force from Rangoon, and with it General Alexander and his headquarters, would have been destroyed had it not been

◁ General the Hon Sir Harold Alexander replaced General Hutton as C-in-C Burma—and was almost captured at Rangoon

◁ Lieutenant-General Iida (XV Army) directed operations during the Japanese conquest of Burma

for the typically rigid adherence to the letter of his orders by a Japanese divisional commander. Coming from the east by paths through hills and jungle in a swoop on the city, he had been told to by-pass it from the north, and swing round to attack it from the west. To cover his flank as he crossed north of Rangoon, he put out a strong block on the main Prome road. He had thus completely bottled up the British force as it tried to get away. Several attacks were made on the road block but Japanese tenacity proved a match for British and Indian valour. The obstacle remained. Nothing could have saved the British, tied as they were by their mechanised transport to the ribbon of road. Luckily for them the Japanese commander withdrew his road block to enter Rangoon from the west according to plan.'

The Japanese had been convinced that the British intended to hold Rangoon. The Official History states: 'About midday on March 8 215th Regiment (of XXXIII Division) entered Rangoon to find to its surprise that the city was unoccupied and deserted. General Sakurai immediately ordered it to pursue the British column which he now realised was the whole of the British forces from the Rangoon area. It was too late and the golden opportunity of destroying the British garrison was lost.'

General Slim had been appointed to command 'Burcorps', which consisted of corps troops (including the 7th Armoured Brigade), the 1st Burma Division, the 17th Indian Division (which now included the 63rd Indian Brigade), and a number of army troops and line-of-communication units. This left General Alexander free to direct the operations of the British and Chinese forces as a whole.

Meanwhile, General Hutton had put into operation his previously planned evacuation of Rangoon, starting with the civilian population, patients in hospitals and mental homes, and civilian prisoners in the jails. Nearly all the police had left, and a wave of incendiarism swept the city, which made it difficult for essential work to be carried out. Finally, the demolition programme of the port was carried out—as far as possible—and the 'last-ditchers' took their leave of the burning city. Launches left the jetty for the three ships waiting downstream to take them to Calcutta; and, at 7.30 pm on March 7, the last train steamed out of Rangoon.

Meanwhile Air-Marshal Stevenson had been putting into effect the plans for the withdrawal of the RAF. About 3,000 airmen had been transferred to India, and at Magwe,

'Burwing' had been formed from 17 (Fighter) Squadron, 45 (Bomber) Squadron, a detachment of 28 (Army Co-operation) Squadron, and an AVG (Fighter) squadron. At Akyab, a smaller 'Akwing' had also been formed.

The long withdrawal begins
The army in Burma now had to fight facing its former base. It was virtually cut off from outside assistance, for only a trickle of reinforcements and supplies could be brought in by air, and there was no through road from India.

While the regrouping of the Allied forces on the general line Prome-Toungoo was taking place, the problem of the Chinese armies entering Burma became a big issue, as the American General J. W. Stilwell, nicknamed 'Vinegar Joe', had arrived in Burma and understood he would be in command of the Chinese armies in Burma.

Generalissimo Chiang Kai-Shek wished him to command the British forces also, since he had lost confidence in the British higher command. But Stilwell himself was in favour of Alexander commanding and readily agreed to serve under him, while remaining himself in command of the Chinese armies. From that time Alexander and Stilwell co-operated with each other loyally until the end of the campaign; but the system of command of the Chinese forces was never satisfactory, since all orders given to them had to pass through so many channels that there were fatal delays in the execution of urgent movements.

On March 30 the 200th Chinese Division, after putting up a most stubborn resistance for nearly a fortnight, was forced to withdraw from Toungoo, without blowing the bridge over the Sittang river which carried the Toungoo-Mawchi-Bawlake road. The Japanese thus gained immediate use of this road, which led into the heart of the Karen hills and Shan States.

Meanwhile, on the Irrawaddy front, the last of the RAF had been forced to leave Magwe and Akyab. From then on Burcorps was totally without air reconnaissance, defence, or support. This forced them to move more by night, and to adopt greater dispersion by day; although the morale of the troops was seriously affected at first, they soon adjusted themselves to the position.

On March 26 Slim received an urgent message from Burma army to stage a demonstration on the Prome front to relieve pressure on the Chinese at Toungoo. Slim gave the task to Cowan's 17th Division, ordering him to advance astride the main road and railway on Okpo. The force became involved in two separate actions, one at Padigon and the other at Paungde; and it was then discovered that a Japanese force had entered Shwedaung behind the British striking forces. Although Cowan's troops eventually forced their way out, this British diversion to help the Chinese resulted in considerable losses. In addition to much transport, they lost two guns and ten tanks, and also 21 officers and 290 men of their already depleted infantry.

On April 1, Wavell and Alexander visited Slim's Burcorps headquarters at Allanmyo, where they agreed that Burcorps should withdraw from Prome to the Thayetmyo-Allanmyo area. The dispositions of 17th Division on this date were: 63rd Brigade (Brigadier A. E. Barlow) at Prome, which was now in ruins as the result of an air attack; 16th Brigade (Brigadier J. K. Jones) east of Prome; 48th Brigade (Brigadier

R. T. Cameron) near Hmawza; and 7th Armoured Brigade at Tamagank. Further north, 1st Burma Division was disposed with 1st Burma Brigade at Dayindabo and 2nd Burma Brigade at Allanmyo. This division was very short of equipment and artillery, and a considerable proportion of its infantry and administrative units were Burmese.

Grave lack of air support
Bringing up their troops in motor transport from Shwedaung, the Japanese launched a strong attack on Prome at midnight on April 1/2 with 215th Regiment. At about 0300 hours, Cowan ordered 48th and 63rd Brigades to disengage before dawn and move back through 16th Brigade to new positions. The 17th Division had a very trying time: they had been fighting all night and much of the day—and April in Burma is one of the hottest months. It was very dusty and water was scarce, and in addition, the Japanese air force gave them no respite, strafing and bombing them incessantly. In spite of this they withdrew successfully, complete, and in fairly good shape.

On April 3 Slim, having concentrated Burcorps, issued an instruction outlining his future plans. His intention was to deny to the enemy the oilfields at Yenangyaung and Chauk, to cover upper Burma, and to maintain touch with the 5th Chinese Army operating in the Sittang river valley.

The lack of air support was creating grave problems for Burma army, as was the fact that the 17th Division had been fighting for three months without relief and without reinforcements. But Wavell simply lacked the air resources to remedy appreciably these two complaints.

The Japanese were quick to take advantage of the capture of Toungoo, and General Iida, the army commander, moved his headquarters there on April 2. He planned to cut the Burma Road—and thus the Chinese line of communications—in the vicinity of Lashio and, by encircling the Allied forces in the Mandalay area, force them to fight with their backs to the Irrawaddy. General Alexander had decided to stand on the line Minhla-Taungdwingyi-Pyinmana-Loikaw. Burcorps was to be responsible for the 40-mile front as far east as Taungdwingyi, and 5th Chinese Army for the Loikaw area.

Burcorps was now operating in the thinly-populated dry zone where the country was generally undulating, though in places steep and rugged, with thin vegetation and scanty patches of forest. Water was scarce, so the dispositions of the troops had to be governed to a large extent by consideration of water supply. By the night of April 13/14, Burcorps was disposed, with the 1st Burma Division, in the Myingun-Sainggya-Yin Chaung area, the 17th Division in depth along the Taungdwingyi road, and the 2nd Burma Brigade at Minhla.

Meanwhile, the Japanese were pressing forward everywhere in their usual, almost reckless, fashion. On the afternoon of the 16th Slim gave the signal for the demolition of the oil storage tanks at Yenangyaung, and the whole storage area, containing millions of gallons of crude oil, became a vast sheet of flame.

The 65th Chinese Army had now begun to enter Burma, and its leading division—the 38th, under Lieutenant-General Sun Li-jen—was placed under Slim's command by agreement between Generals Alexander and Stilwell.

For the next ten days Burcorps and the Chinese were engaged in some fierce fighting south of Mandalay; and to the east the 56th Japanese Division was moving, via Hopong, in the direction of Lashio. The fall of Lashio appeared to be only a matter of time. The condition and numerical weakness of the troops the Chinese had been able to build up south of Mandalay also precluded the possibility of any lengthy stand on the Irrawaddy. In these circumstances Alexander decided that his main object must be the defence of India. He conveyed this decision to Slim on April 26, having been in consultation with General Stilwell the previous day.

The plan to be adopted was for Burcorps, after withdrawal across the Irrawaddy, to fall back on Kalewa. The problem of maintenance was now far from easy; but preparations had been put in hand for making the rough jungle track from Yeu to Shwegyin fit for motor transport. Dumps of rations, water, and petrol were established at staging points, and further supplies were accumulated at Shwegyin.

The Burma Road is cut
Burcorps began its withdrawal immediately. The critical point was the Ava bridge over the Irrawaddy, which the greater part of Burcorps had to use to cross the river. This was threatened by two Japanese divisions, and it was only due to some aggressive counterattacks by 7th Armoured Brigade, 63rd Brigade, and 48th Brigade that the crossing was made successfully.

On the 29th Alexander and Stilwell met in Shwebo, and they then learned that the Japanese had captured Lashio and cut the Burma Road.

The first Burma campaign was entering its final phase. Fortunately, everything was going according to plan on the Burcorps front, and their headquarters had been established at Budalin on the Monywa-Yeu road, when the shattering news was received that a Japanese column had occupied Monywa. The 215th Japanese Regiment, moving rapidly from Pakokku on the evening of the 30th, had succeeded in occupying it next day.

The tremendous thrust and speed of movement of the Japanese had once again taken us by surprise, for the loss of Monywa turned what should have been a controlled timetable retirement into a hurried retreat which might easily have ended in disaster.

Whilst Burcorps was thus laboriously and perilously making its way back to India, the remnants of the 5th Chinese Army fell back from Shwebo to the north. The 5th Army Headquarters, with parts of the 22nd and 96th divisions, after great hardships, eventually staggered through the Hukawng Valley. General Stilwell remained at Shwebo until May 1, and was then forced to proceed on foot to the Chindwin, and then through the hills to Imphal. His gruelling march ended on May 15 when his party reached Assam.

To Burcorps the rains came as a mixed blessing. They caused acute discomfort and made the track infinitely more difficult: but they completely bogged down their Japanese pursuers. Slim wrote: 'On the last day of the retreat I watched the rear-guard march into India. All of them, British, Indian and Gurkha were gaunt and ragged as scarecrows. Yet, as they trudged behind their surviving officers in groups pitifully small, they still carried their arms and kept their ranks. They might look like scarecrows but they looked like soldiers too.'

After the withdrawal
In summing up the lessons of our catastrophic defeat Slim remarked on what a mistake it was not to bring in the Chinese armies when they were offered in December 1941. They alone could have adjusted the numerical balance. That, our completely inadequate air forces, and the entire lack of training and equipment of our ground forces—as compared with the toughness, mobility, and brutality of the Japanese—weighted the odds overwhelmingly against us.

In their five-and-a-half-month campaign the army in Burma had retreated nearly 1,000 miles—the longest retreat ever carried out by a British army. They had suffered some 10,036 casualties, of which 3,670 were killed and wounded, and the remaining 6,366 missing. To these must be added the casualties of the Burmese units, making a grand total of 13,463 casualties. The Japanese casualties are reported to have been 4,597 killed and wounded. In the air the Allies lost 116 aircraft—of which 65 were destroyed in aerial combat—and the Japanese air casualties were almost equivalent.

Only in generalship and leadership did the British compare with, and indeed overshadow, the Japanese: in Generals Alexander and Slim we had two of the finest battle commanders of the Second World War. And the divisional, brigade, and battalion commanders were tough and splendid soldiers, hard to beat in any army in the world.

Slim is bitterly critical in his book of the rather scurvy way his troops were welcomed back to India—as compared with our BEF reaching England after Dunkirk. He wrote: 'They did not expect to be treated like heroes, but they did expect to be met as soldiers, who, even if defeated, were by no means disgraced.

'They were utterly exhausted, riddled with malaria and dysentery, and deserved something better than the complete lack of consideration or help which they received.'

Slim himself was absolutely determined that before taking on the Japanese again he would have troops that were fully trained and equipped for the job, air superiority, and the means to transport troops and supplies by air, so that he should not be constantly subjected to the Japanese 'hook', whereby they sent mobile columns through the jungle, living on the country, round his flanks.

How right he was. And with what wonderful success he put his theories into practice two years later.

BRIGADIER THE RT HON SIR JOHN SMYTH, Bt, VC, MC, has had a varied and exciting career. As a regular soldier he fought in both World Wars and several minor campaigns. He was awarded the Victoria Cross, the Military Cross, the Russian Order of St George, and was six times mentioned in despatches. He was both a student and an instructor at the Camberley Staff College between the wars. In the last war he commanded a brigade at Dunkirk, then raised the 19th (Dagger) Division in Burma at the time of the Japanese invasion in 1942. After the war he became military correspondent for several newspapers, including the *Sunday Times,* of which he was also Lawn Tennis correspondent. He was Member of Parliament for Norwood from 1950 to 1966 and held Ministerial appointments in the Governments of Sir Winston Churchill and Sir Anthony Eden. For political services he was created a Baronet and a Privy Councillor. He has written 20 books since the war.

The USS *Yorktown*'s flight deck showing the damage incurred during the Battle of Midway in June 1942

BATTLE OF MIDWAY

Central Pacific, June 1942

Captain Donald Macintyre

The Battle of Midway must be accounted one of the truly decisive battles of history. In one cataclysmic blow, it wiped out the overwhelming Japanese superiority in naval air strength, the vital key to the successful prosecution of a war in the vast spaces of the Pacific. More than half the Japanese carrier strength—with the élite of their highly trained and experienced aircrews—were eliminated: they were to prove irreplaceable. From now onwards, the Japanese were on the defensive. The early run of victories which Yamamoto had promised had come to a premature end. Now a period of stalemate was to begin during which American production would rise to its overwhelming flood—which Yamamoto had also foreseen. The Rising Sun had passed its brilliant noon

USS *Yorktown* is struck by a Japanese torpedo

Pearl Harbor was a scene of intense activity during the last week of May 1942: a feeling of great impending events pervaded the atmosphere. On the 26th the aircraft-carriers *Enterprise* and *Hornet* of Task Force (TF) 16 had steamed in and moored, to set about in haste the various operations of refuelling and replenishing after a vain race across the Pacific to try to go to the aid of Rear-Admiral Frank Fletcher's Task Force 17 in the Battle of the Coral Sea. On the next day the surviving carriers of TF 17, the *Yorktown*'s blackened sides and twisted decks providing visible signs of the damage sustained in the battle, berthed in the dry dock of the naval base where an army of workmen swarmed aboard to begin repairs.

Under normal circumstances, weeks of work lay ahead of them, but now word had reached the dockyard that emergency repairs in the utmost haste were required. Work was to go on, night and day, without ceasing, until the ship was at least temporarily battle-worthy. For at the headquarters of the C-in-C Pacific, Admiral Chester Nimitz, it was known from patient analysis and deciphering of enemy signals that the Japanese fleet was moving out to throw down a challenge which, in spite of local American inferiority, had to be accepted.

So, on May 28, Task Force 16 sailed again, the *Enterprise* flying the flag of Rear-Admiral Raymond Spruance, and vanished into the wide wastes of the Pacific. Six cruisers and nine destroyers formed its screen; two replenishment tankers accompanied it. The following day the dockyard gave Nimitz the scarcely credible news that the *Yorktown* was once again battle-worthy. Early on the 30th she, too, left harbour and, having gathered in her air groups, headed north-westward to rendezvous with Task Force 16 at 'Point Luck', 350 miles north-east of the island of Midway. Forming the remainder of Task Force 17 were two cruisers and five destroyers.

The main objective of the Japanese was the assault and occupation of the little atoll of Midway, 1,100 miles west-north-west of Oahu, and forming the western extremity of the Hawaiian island chain. Together with the occupation of the Aleutian Islands, the capture of Midway would extend Japan's eastern sea frontier so that sufficient warning might be obtained of any threatened naval air attack on the homeland—Pearl Harbor in reverse. The plan had been given added impetus on April 18 by the raid on Tokyo mounted by Colonel Doolittle's army bombers taking off from the *Hornet*.

Doubts on the wisdom of the Japanese plan had been voiced in various quarters; but Yamamoto, the dynamic C-in-C of the Combined Fleet, had fiercely advocated it for reasons of his own. He had always been certain that only by destroying the American fleet could Japan gain the breathing space required to consolidate her conquests and negotiate satisfactory peace terms—a belief which had inspired the attack on Pearl Harbor. Yamamoto rightly believed that an attack on Midway was a challenge that Nimitz could not ignore. It would bring the US Pacific Fleet out where Yamamoto, in overwhelming strength, would be waiting to bring it to action.

The Japanese plan was an intricate one, as their naval strategic plans customarily were, calling for exact timing for a junction at the crucial moment of several disparate forces; and it involved—also typically—the offering of a decoy or diversion to lure the enemy into dividing his force or expending his strength on a minor objective.

Between May 25/27, Northern Force would sail from Ominato, at the northern tip of Honshu, for the attack on the Aleutians. The II Carrier Striking Force, under Rear-Admiral Kakuta—comprising the small aircraft-carriers *Ryujo* and *Junyo*, two cruisers, and three destroyers—would be the first to sail, its task being to deliver a surprise air attack on Dutch Harbor on June 3. This, it was expected, might induce Nimitz to send at least part of his fleet racing north, in which case it would find waiting to intercept it a Guard Force, of four battleships, two cruisers, and 12 destroyers.

Kakuta's force would be followed two days later by the remainder of the Aleutians force—two small transport units with cruiser and destroyer escorts for the invasion of Attu and Kiska on June 5. Meanwhile, from Hashirajima Anchorage in the Inland Sea, the four big aircraft-carriers of Vice-Admiral Nagumo's I Carrier Striking Force—*Akagi, Kaga, Hiryu,* and *Soryu*—would sail for the vicinity of Midway. There, at dawn on the 4th, their bombers and fighters would take off for the softening-up bombardment of the island prior to the assault landing two days later by troops carried in the Transport Group.

The original plan had called for the inclusion of the *Zuikaku* and *Shokaku* in Nagumo's force. But, like the *Yorktown*,

The moment of greatest danger in carrier warfare, when no retaliation against an enemy strike is possible—Dauntless dive-bombers ranged forward on USS *Enterprise* for refuelling and rearming

US Navy

the *Shokaku* had suffered damage in the Coral Sea battle and could not be repaired in time to take part in the Midway operation, while both carriers had lost so many experienced aircrews that replacements could not be trained in time.

Yamamoto's battle-squadron
In support of the Transport Group, four heavy cruisers under Vice-Admiral Kurita would also sail from Guam. Finally, three powerful forces would sail in company from the Inland Sea during May 28:
● The Main Body, comprising Yamamoto's splendid new flagship *Yamato,* the biggest battleship in the world, mounting nine 18-inch guns, the 16-inch battleships *Nagato* and *Mutsu,* with attendant destroyers;
● The Main Support Force for the Midway invasion force—two battleships, four heavy cruisers, and attendant destroyers—under Vice-Admiral Kondo;
● The Guard Force (mentioned above).

Parting company with Yamamoto's force after getting to sea, Kondo was to head for a supporting position to the south-west of Midway, while the Guard Force would proceed to station itself near the route from Pearl Harbor to the Aleutians. Yamamoto himself, with the Main Body, was to take up a central position from which he could proceed to annihilate whatever enemy force Nimitz sent out. To ensure that the dispatch of any such American force should not go undetected, Pearl Harbor was to be reconnoitred between May 31 and June 3 by two Japanese flying-boats via French Frigate Shoal (500 miles north-west of Hawaii), where a submarine was to deliver them petrol. As a further precaution, two cordons of submarines were to be stationed to the north-west and west of Hawaii by June 2, with a third cordon farther north towards the Aleutians.

Yamamoto's plan was ingenious, if over-intricate: but it had two fatal defects. For all his enthusiasm for naval aviation, he had not yet appreciated that the day of the monstrous capital ship as the queen of battles had passed in favour of the aircraft-carrier which could deliver its blows at a range 30 times greater than that of the biggest guns. The role of the battleship was now as close escort to the vulnerable aircraft-carriers, supplying the defensive anti-aircraft gunpower the latter lacked. Nagumo's force was supported only by two battleships and three cruisers. Had Yamamoto's Main Body kept company with it, the events that were to follow might have been different.

Far more fatal to Yamamoto's plan, however, was his assumption that it was shrouded from the enemy, and that only when news reached Nimitz that Midway was being assaulted would the Pacific Fleet leave Pearl Harbor. Thus long before the scheduled flying-boat reconnaissance—which in the event failed to take place because French Frigate Shoal was found to be in American hands—and before the scouting submarines had reached their stations, Spruance and Fletcher, all unknown to the Japanese, were beyond the patrol lines and poised waiting for the enemy's approach. Details of this approach as well as the broad lines of Yamamoto's plan were known to Nimitz. Beyond sending a small force of five cruisers and ten destroyers to the Aleutians to harass the invasion force, he concentrated all his available force—TF 16 and 17—in the area.

He had also a squadron of battleships under his command, to be sure; but he had no illusions that, with their insufficient speed to keep up with the aircraft-carriers, their great guns could play any useful part in the events to follow. They were therefore relegated to defensive duties on the American west coast.

For the next few days the Japanese Combined Fleet advanced eastwards according to schedule in its wide-spread, multi-pronged formation. Everywhere a buoyant feeling of confidence showed itself, generated by the memories of the unbroken succession of Japanese victories since the beginning of the war. In the I Carrier Striking Force, so recently returned home after its meteoric career of destruction—from Pearl Harbor, through the East Indies, and on to Ceylon without the loss of a ship—the 'Victory Disease' as it was subsequently to be called by the Japanese themselves, was particularly prevalent. Only the admiral—or so Nagumo was subsequently to say—felt doubts of the quality of the many replacements who had come to make up the wastage in experienced aircrews inevitable even in victorious operations.

Spruance and Fletcher had meanwhile made rendezvous during June 2, and Fletcher had assumed command of the two task forces, though they continued to manoeuvre as separate units. The sea was calm under a blue sky split up by towering cumulus clouds. The scouting aircraft, flown off during the following day in perfect visibility, sighted nothing, and Fletcher was able to feel confident that the approaching enemy was all unaware of his presence to the north-east of Midway. Indeed, neither Yamamoto nor Nagumo, pressing forward blindly through rain and fog, gave serious thought to such an apparently remote possibility.

Far to the north on June 3, dawn broke grey and misty over Kikuta's two aircraft-carriers from which, soon after 0300 hours, the first of two strike waves took off to wreak destruction among the installations and fuel tanks of Dutch Harbor. A further attack was delivered the following day, and during the next few days American and Japanese forces sought each other vainly among the swirling fogs, while the virtually unprotected Kiska and Attu were occupied by the Japanese. But as Nimitz refused to let any of his forces be drawn into the skirmish, this part of Yamamoto's plan failed to have much impact on the great drama being enacted farther south.

Setting the scene
The opening scenes of this drama were enacted early on June 3 when a scouting Catalina flying boat some 700 miles west of Midway sighted a large body of ships, steaming in two long lines with a numerous screen in arrowhead formation, which was taken to be the Japanese main fleet. The sighting report brought nine army B-17 bombers from Midway, which delivered three high-level bombing attacks and claimed to have hit two battleships or heavy cruisers and two transports. But the enemy was in reality the Midway Occupation Force of transports and tankers, and no hits were scored on them until four amphibious Catalinas from Midway discovered them again in bright moonlight in the early hours of June 4 and succeeded in torpedoing a tanker. Damage was slight, however, and the tanker remained in formation.

More than 800 miles away to the east, Fletcher intercepted the reports of these encounters but from his detailed knowledge

of the enemy's plan was able to identify the Occupation Force. Nagumo's carriers, he knew, were much closer, some 400 miles to the west of him, approaching their flying-off position from the north-west. During the night, therefore, Task Forces 16 and 17 steamed south-west for a position 200 miles north of Midway which would place them at dawn within scouting range of the unsuspecting enemy. The scene was now set for what was to be one of the great decisive battles of history.

Deadly game of hide-and-seek
The last hour of darkness before sunrise on June 4 saw the familiar activity in both the carrier forces of ranging-up aircraft on the flight-deck for dawn operations. Aboard the *Yorktown,* whose turn it was to mount the first scouting flight of the day, there were Dauntless scout dive-bombers, ten of which were launched at 0430 hours for a search to a depth of 100 miles between west and east through north, a precaution against being taken by surprise while waiting for news from the scouting flying boats from Midway.

Reconnaissance aircraft were dispatched at the same moment from Nagumo's force. One each from the *Akagi* and *Kaga,* and two seaplanes each from the cruisers *Tone* and *Chikuma* were to search to a depth of 300 miles to the east and south. The seaplane carried in the battleship *Haruna,* being of an older type, was restricted to 150 miles. The main activity in Nagumo's carriers, however, was the preparation of the striking force to attack Midway—36 'Kate' torpedo-bombers each carrying a 1,770-pound bomb, 36 'Val' dive-bombers each with a single 550-pound bomb, and 36 Zero fighters as escort. Led by Lieutenant Joichi Tomonaga, this formidable force also took off at 0430.

By 0445 all these aircraft were on their way—with one notable exception. In the cruiser *Tone,* one of the catapults had given trouble, and it was not until 0500 that her second seaplane got away. This apparently minor dislocation of the schedule was to have vital consequences. Meanwhile, the carrier lifts were already hoisting up on deck an equally powerful second wave; but under the bellies of the 'Kates' were slung torpedoes, for these aircraft were to be ready to attack any enemy naval force which might be discovered by the scouts.

The lull in proceedings which followed the dawn fly-off from both carrier forces was broken with dramatic suddenness. At 0520, aboard Nagumo's flagship *Akagi,* the alarm was sounded. An enemy flying boat on reconnaissance had been sighted. Zeros roared off the deck in pursuit. A deadly game of hide-and-seek among the clouds developed, but the American naval fliers evaded their hunters. At 0534 Fletcher's radio office received the message 'Enemy carriers in sight', followed by another reporting many enemy aircraft heading for Midway; finally, at 0603, details were received of the position and composition of Nagumo's force, 200 miles west-south-west of the *Yorktown.* The time for action had arrived.

The *Yorktown*'s scouting aircraft were at once recalled and while she waited to gather them in, Fletcher ordered Spruance to proceed with his Task Force 16 'south-westerly and attack enemy carriers when definitely located'. *Enterprise* and *Hornet* with their screening cruisers and destroyers turned away, increasing to 25 knots, while hooters blared for 'General Quarters' and aircrews

The Cost of Victory

◁ Repair crews at work on the wooden flight-deck of the *Yorktown* after the first attack by Japanese dive-bombers. On this occasion she was struck by three bombs—one burst on the flight-deck and started a fire in the hangar, a second smashed three boiler uptakes, and put five of the six boilers out of action, and the third penetrated to the fourth deck and started another fire. Although the ship was temporarily halted, rapid repairs got her under way again before the second wave of torpedo-bombers arrived.

▽ Their attacks came from four directions, and in spite of violent evasive action, two torpedoes hit her port side, and she began to list heavily

◁ The *Yorktown*'s fuel tanks were torn open, and the flooding caused the 26-degree list; all power was lost, so it was not possible to right her by counter-flooding. Then the order was given to abandon ship.

▷ A salvage party moves along her steeply sloping deck. After the first abandonment, she continued to drift without sinking. So the following day, a salvage party went back on board, and she was taken in tow. But two days later a Japanese submarine, which had been sent to look for her, penetrated her escort screen, and torpedoed her twice. This time she sank— the major US loss at Midway

manned their planes to warm-up ready for take-off. Meanwhile, 240 miles to the south, Midway was preparing to meet the impending attack.

Radar had picked up the approaching aerial swarm at 0553 and seven minutes later every available aircraft on the island had taken off. Bombers and flying-boats were ordered to keep clear, but Marine Corps fighters in two groups clawed their way upwards, and at 0616 swooped in to the attack. But of the 26 planes, all but six were obsolescent Brewster Buffaloes, hopelessly outclassed by the highly manoeuvrable Zeros. Though they took their toll of Japanese bombers, they were in turn overwhelmed, 17 being shot down and seven others damaged beyond repair. The survivors of the Japanese squadrons pressed on to drop their bombs on power-plants, seaplane hangars, and oil tanks.

At the same time as the Marine fighters, ten torpedo-bombers had also taken off from Midway—six of the new Grumman Avengers (which were soon to supersede the unsatisfactory Devastator torpedo-bombers in American aircraft-carriers) and four Army Marauders. At 0710 they located and attacked the Japanese carriers; but with no fighter protection against the many Zeros sent up against them, half of them were shot down before they could reach a launching position. Those which broke through, armed with the slow and unreliable torpedoes which had earned Japanese contempt in the Coral Sea battle, failed to score any hits; greeted with a storm of gunfire, only one Avenger and two Marauders escaped to crash-land on Midway.

Unsuccessful as these attacks were, they had important consequences. From over Midway, Lieutenant Tomonaga, surveying the results of his attack, at 0700 signalled that a further strike was necessary to knock out the island's defences. The torpedo attacks seemed to Nagumo to bear this out, and, as no inkling of any enemy surface forces in the vicinity had yet come to him, he made the first of a train of fatal decisions. At 0715 he ordered the second wave of aircraft to stand by to attack Midway. The 'Kate' bombers, concentrated in the *Akagi* and *Kaga*, had to be struck down into the hangars to have their torpedoes replaced by bombs. Ground crews swarmed round to move them one by one to the lifts which took them below where mechanics set feverishly to work to make the exchange. It could not be a quick operation, however, and it had not been half completed when, at 0728, came a message which threw Nagumo into an agony of indecision.

The reconnaissance seaplane from the *Tone*—the one which had been launched 30 minutes behind schedule—was fated to be the one in whose search sector the American fleet was to be found; and now it sent back the signal—'Have sighted ten ships, apparently enemy, bearing 010 degrees, 240 miles away from Midway: Course 150 degrees, speed more than 20 knots.' For the next quarter of an hour Nagumo waited with mounting impatience for a further signal giving the composition of the enemy force. Only if it included carriers was it any immediate menace at its range of 200 miles—but in that case it was vital to get a strike launched against it at once. At 0745 Nagumo ordered the re-arming of the 'Kates' to be suspended and all aircraft to prepare for an attack on ships, and two minutes later he signalled to the search plane: 'Ascertain ship types and maintain contact.' The response was a signal of 0758 reporting only a change of the enemy's course; but 12 minutes later came the report: 'Enemy ships are five cruisers and five destroyers.'

Nagumo's hopes crushed

This message was received with heartfelt relief by Nagumo and his staff; for at this moment his force came under attack first by 16 Marine Corps dive-bombers from Midway, followed by 15 Flying Fortresses, bombing from 20,000 feet, and finally 11 Marine Corps Vindicator scout-bombers. Every available Zero was sent aloft to deal with them, and not a single hit was scored by the bombers. But now, should Nagumo decide to launch an air strike, it would lack escort fighters until the Zeros had been recovered, refuelled, and re-armed. While the air attacks were in progress, further alarms occupied the attention of the battleship and cruiser screen when the US submarine *Nautilus*—one of 12 covering Midway— fired a torpedo at a battleship at 0825. But neither this nor the massive depth-charge attacks in retaliation were effective; and in the midst of the noise and confusion of the air attacks—at 0820—Nagumo received the message he dreaded to hear: 'Enemy force accompanied by what appears to be a carrier.'

The luckless Japanese admiral's dilemma, however, had been disastrously resolved for him by the return of the survivors of Tomonaga's Midway strike at 0830. With some damaged and all short of fuel, their recovery was urgent; and rejecting the advice of his subordinate carrier squadron commander— Rear-Admiral Yamaguchi, in the *Hiryu*— to launch his strike force, Nagumo issued the order to strike below all aircraft on deck and land the returning aircraft. By the time this was completed, it was 0918.

Refuelling, re-arming, and ranging-up a striking-force in all four carriers began at once, the force consisting of 36 'Val' dive-bombers and 54 'Kates', now again armed with torpedoes, with an escort of as many Zeros as could be spared from defensive patrol over the carriers. Thus it was at a carrier force's most vulnerable moment that— from his screening ships to the south— Nagumo received the report of an approaching swarm of aircraft. The earlier catapult defect in the *Tone*; the inefficient scouting of its aircraft's crew; Nagumo's own vacillation (perhaps induced by the confusion caused by the otherwise ineffective air attacks from Midway); but above all the fatal assumption that the Midway attack would be over long before any enemy aircraft-carriers could arrive in the area— all had combined to plunge Nagumo into a catastrophic situation. The pride and vainglory of the victorious carrier force had just one more hour to run.

When Task Force 16 had turned to the south-west, leaving the *Yorktown* to recover her reconnaissance aircraft, Nagumo's carriers were still too far away for Spruance's aircraft to reach him and return; and if the Japanese continued to steer towards Midway, it would be nearly 0900 before Spruance could launch his strike. When calculations showed that Nagumo would probably be occupied recovering his aircraft at about that time, however, Spruance had decided to accept the consequences of an earlier launching in order to catch him off balance. Every serviceable aircraft in his two carriers, with the exception of the fighters required for defensive patrol, was to be included, involving a double launching, taking a full hour to complete, during which the first aircraft off would have to orbit and wait, eating up precious fuel.

It was just 0702 when the first of the 67 Dauntless dive-bombers, 29 Devastator torpedo-bombers, and 20 Wildcat fighters, which formed Task Force 16's striking force, flew off. The torpedo squadrons had not yet taken the air when the sight of the *Tone's* float plane, circling warily on the horizon, told Spruance that he could not afford to wait for his striking force to form up before dispatching them. The *Enterprise's* dive-bombers led by Lieutenant-Commander McClusky, which had been the first to take off, were ordered to lead on without waiting for the torpedo-bombers or for the fighter escort whose primary task must be to protect the slow, lumbering Devastators. At 0752, McClusky took departure, steering to intercept Nagumo's force which was assumed to be steering south-east towards Midway. The remainder of the air groups followed at intervals, the dive-bombers and fighters up at 19,000 feet, the torpedo-bombers skimming low over the sea.

This distance between them, in which layers of broken cloud made maintenance of contact difficult, had calamitous consequences. The fighters from the *Enterprise*, led by Lieutenant Gray, took station above but did not make contact with Lieutenant-Commander Waldron's torpedo squadron from the *Hornet*, leaving the *Enterprise's* torpedo squadron, led by Lieutenant-Commander Lindsey, unescorted. *Hornet's* fighters never achieved contact with Waldron, and flew instead in company with their dive-bombers. Thus Task Force 16's air strike advanced in four separate, independent groups—McClusky's dive-bombers, the *Hornet's* dive-bombers and fighters, and the two torpedo squadrons.

All steered initially for the estimated position of Nagumo, assuming he had maintained his south-easterly course for Midway. In fact, at 0918, having recovered Tomonaga's Midway striking force, he had altered course to north-east to close the distance between him and the enemy while his projected strike was being ranged up on deck. When the four air groups from TF 16 found nothing at the expected point of interception, therefore, they had various courses of action to choose between. The *Hornet's* dive-bombers decided to search south-easterly where, of course, they found nothing. As fuel ran low, some of the bombers returned to the carrier, others made for Midway to refuel. The fighters were not so lucky: one by one they were forced to ditch as their engines spluttered and died.

The two torpedo squadrons, on the other hand, low down over the water, sighted smoke on the northern horizon and, turning towards it, were rewarded with the sight of the Japanese carriers shortly after 0930. Though bereft of fighter protection, both promptly headed in to the attack. Neither Waldron nor Lindsey had any doubts of the suicidal nature of the task ahead of them. The former, in his last message to his squadron, had written: 'My greatest hope is that we encounter a favourable tactical situation, but if we don't, and the worst comes to the worst, I want each of us to do his utmost to destroy our enemies. If there is only one plane left to make a final run in, I want that man to go in and get a hit. May God be with us all.'

His hopes for a favourable tactical situation were doomed. Fifty or ▷

Turning-point of the Pacific War

Ostensibly the Japanese thrust toward Midway Island and the Aleutians was to extend their defence perimeter so that there would be adequate warning of any US attack. But for Admiral Yamamoto it was the chance to complete Pearl Harbor—the remainder of the US fleet would be destroyed before reinforcements could reach it. But his planning had two vital defects: first it was overcomplicated—with too many units unable to support each other; and second, in spite of his advocacy of carrier-borne airpower and the massive successes it had brought Japan, Yamamoto still saw his lurking battleship force as the vital unit which would intervene to destroy the Americans once they had been lured forward by the invasion fleets. But the Americans were forewarned and realised the trap which was being set. Their forces evaded the enemy patrols and disappeared into the Pacific, to intercept and destroy the Japanese I Carrier Striking Force and withdraw before Yamamoto's battle fleet could get anywhere near them.

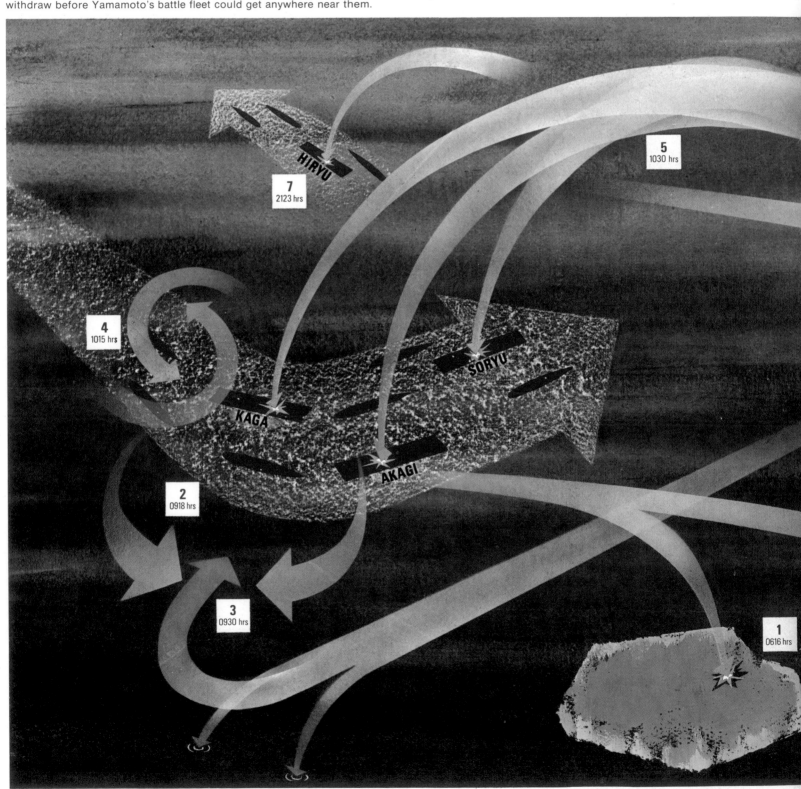

△ Admiral Nimitz, C-in-C US Pacific Fleet, foresaw the enemy moves. Rear-Admiral Spruance (left), Task Force 17, evaded the Japanese trap. **Left:** Vice-Admiral Fletcher: his flagship *Yorktown* was the main US loss

△ Admiral Yamamoto, C-in-C Japanese Combined Fleet: his plan was too complex. Admiral Kondo (right): his Midway support force never saw action. **Right:** Vice-Admiral Nagumo (I Carrier Striking Force): his vacillation was fatal

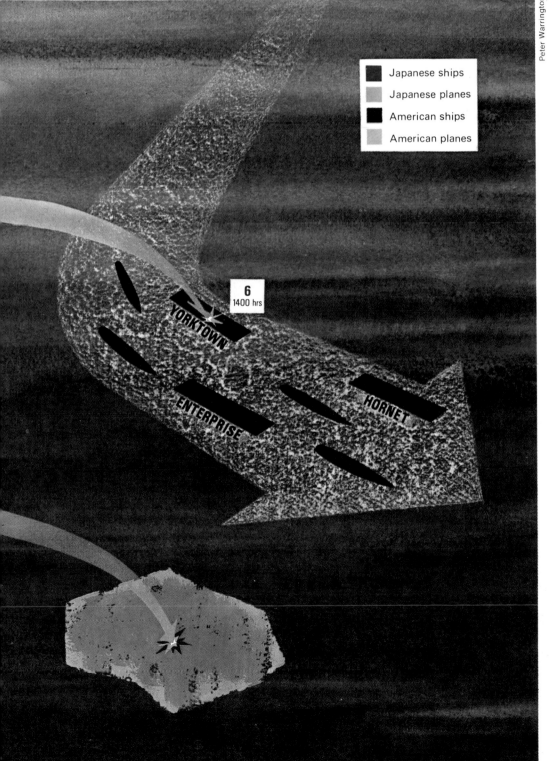

Japanese ships
Japanese planes
American ships
American planes

6
1400 hrs

YORKTOWN

ENTERPRISE

HORNET

At the end of May, 1942, two task forces sailed from Japan—one to attack the Aleutians, and the other to invade Midway Island. Admiral Nagumo's I Carrier Striking Force *(Akagi, Kaga, Hiryu,* and *Soryu)* covered the Midway invasion fleet, while a powerful force of battleships lay to the north waiting to engage the US fleet. But the Americans were forewarned, and their Task Forces 16 *(Hornet* and *Enterprise)* and 17 *(Yorktown)* evaded the Japanese patrol screen and were cruising in a position to intercept the invasion fleet.

1. Japanese carrier aircraft bomb Midway Island.
2. Having recovered the Midway strike force, the Japanese fleet alters course toward the reported position of the approaching American carrier force.
3. This causes the first US strike to miss the Japanese. The US dive-bombers from *Hornet* turn south and the torpedo-bombers from *Enterprise* north to search, while the fighters, out of fuel, have to ditch. Without this fighter escort, the bombers suffer heavy losses from Zeros.
4. The torpedo-bombers from *Yorktown* and *Enterprise* also locate the Japanese, but without fighter support they too are massacred, without damaging the enemy.
5. However, the dive-bombers, having turned north, arrive overhead unseen, and in five minutes they cripple *Kaga, Akagi,* and *Soryu*.
6. A force of dive-bombers from the *Hiryu* locate and damage the *Yorktown*. A second strike of torpedo-bombers cripple her so that she is abandoned.
7. *Hiryu* is located and crippled.

more Zeros concentrated on his formation long before they reached a launching position. High overhead, Lieutenant Gray, leading the *Enterprise*'s fighter squadron, waited for a call for help as arranged with Lindsey, thinking that Waldron's planes were the torpedo squadron from his own ship – a call which never came. From the cruisers and destroyers of the screen came a withering fire. One by one the torpedo-bombers were shot down. A few managed to get their torpedoes away before crashing, but none hit the enemy. Only one of the pilots, Ensign George H. Gay, survived the massacre, clinging to a rubber seat cushion which floated away from his smashed aircraft, until dusk when he could inflate his life-raft without attracting strafing Zeros.

Five minutes later it was the turn of Lindsey's 14 Devastators from the *Enterprise*. Purely by chance, as he was making his attack on the starboard side of the *Kaga*, the torpedo squadron from the *Yorktown* came sweeping in from the other side, aiming to attack the *Soryu*, and drawing off some of the fighter opposition.

The *Yorktown*'s strike group of 17 dive-bombers led by Lieutenant-Commander Maxwell F. Leslie, with 12 torpedo-bombers of Lieutenant-Commander Lance E. Massey's squadron and an escort of six Wildcats, had taken departure from their carrier an hour and a quarter after the strike groups of Task Force 16. A more accurate assessment of probabilities by Leslie, however, had brought the whole of this force simultaneously over the enemy to deliver the co-ordinated, massed attack which alone could hope to swamp and break through the defences. In addition, at this same moment, McClusky's dive-bombers also arrived overhead. McClusky, after reaching the expected point of interception, had continued for a time on his south-westerly course and had then made a cast to the north-west. There he had sighted a destroyer steering north-east at high speed. This was the *Arashi*, which had been left behind to depth-charge the *Nautilus*. Turning to follow her, McClusky was led straight to his objective.

The simultaneous attack by the two torpedo squadrons brought no result of itself. Scores of Zeros swarmed about them, brushing aside the puny force of six Wildcats. The massacre of the clumsy Devastators was re-enacted. Lindsey and ten others of his force were shot down. Of Massey's squadron, only two survived. The few torpedoes launched were easily evaded.

The sacrifice of the torpedo-bombers had not been in vain, nevertheless. For, while every Japanese fighter plane was milling about low over the water, enjoying the easy prey offered to them there, high overhead there were gathering, all unseen and unmolested, the dive-bombers – McClusky's 18, and Leslie's 17. And now, like hawks swooping to their prey, they came plummeting down out of the sky.

In the four Japanese carriers the refuelling and re-arming of the strike force had been almost completed. The decks were crowded with aircraft ranged for take-off. Nagumo had given the order to launch and ships were turning into wind. Aboard the *Akagi*, all eyes were directed downwards at the flight-deck.

Suddenly, over the rumbling roar of engines, the high-pitched rising scream of dive-bombers was heard. Even as faces swivelled upwards at the sound, the black dots which were 1,000-pound bombs were

seen leaving three 'Hell-Divers' as they pulled out from their near-vertical dive. Fascinated eyes watched the bombs grow in size as they fell inexorably towards that most vulnerable of targets, a full deck load of armed and fuelled aircraft. One bomb struck the *Akagi* squarely amidships, opposite the bridge and just behind the aircraft lift, plunged down into the hangar and there exploded, detonating stored torpedoes, tearing up the flight deck, and destroying the lift. A second exploded in the midst of the 'Kates' on the after part of the deck, starting a tremendous conflagration to add to that in the hangar. In a matter of seconds Nagumo's proud flagship had been reduced to a blazing shambles. From time to time she was further shaken by internal explosions as the flames touched off petrol tanks, bombs, and torpedoes. Within a few minutes Captain Aoki knew that the damage and fires were beyond control. He persuaded the reluctant Nagumo that it was necessary to transfer his flag to a ship with radio communication intact. Admiral and staff picked their way through the flames to reach the forecastle whence they lowered themselves down ropes to a boat which took them to the light cruiser *Nagara* of the screen.

Carnage in the Japanese carriers

Only three dive-bombers from the *Enterprise* had attacked the flagship. The remainder of the air group, 34 dive-bombers, all concentrated on the *Kaga*. Of four bombs which scored direct hits, the first burst just forward of the superstructure, blowing up a petrol truck which stood there, and the sheet of flame which swept the bridge killed everyone on it, including the captain. The other three bombs falling among the massed aircraft on the flight deck set the ship ablaze and started the same fatal train of fires and explosions as in the *Akagi*. Within a few minutes, the situation was so beyond control that the senior surviving officer ordered the transfer of the Emperor's portrait to an attendant destroyer – the custom obligatory when a ship was known to be doomed, and conducted with strict naval ceremony. The *Kaga* was to survive for several hours, nevertheless.

Simultaneously, with the *Akagi* and *Kaga*, the *Soryu* had also been reeling under a devastating attack. Leslie of the *Yorktown* was leading veterans of the Coral Sea battle, probably the most battle-experienced aviators in the American navy at that time. With

deadly efficiency they dived in three waves in quick succession from the starboard bow, the starboard quarter, and the port quarter, released their bombs and climbed away without a single casualty. Out of the shower of 1,000-pound bombs, three hit. The first penetrated to the hangar deck and the explosion lifted the steel platform of the lift, folding it back against the bridge. The others landed among the massed aircraft, causing the whole ship to be engulfed in flames. It took Captain Ryusaku Yanaginoto only 20 minutes to decide to order 'Abandon Ship' to save his crew from being burnt alive, though the *Soryu*, like her sisters, was to survive for some hours yet.

Thus, in five brief, searing minutes, half of Japan's entire fleet carrier force, her naval *corps d'élite*, had been shattered. For the time being the *Hiryu*, some miles away, remained untouched. She was to avenge her sisters in some measure before the day was over; but before going on to tell of her part in the battle let us follow the remainder to their deaths in the blue Pacific waters.

On board the *Akagi*, though the bomb damage was confined at first to her flight and hangar decks and her machinery spaces remained intact, the fires fed by aviation petrol from aircraft and from fuel lines were beyond the capacity of the Japanese crew to master. They fought them for seven hours but by 1715 Captain Aoki had decided there was no hope of saving his ship. The Emperor's portrait was transferred to a destroyer and the ship was abandoned. Permission was asked of the C-in-C to hasten her end but it was not until nearly dawn on the following day – when Yamamoto at last fully understood the fullness of the Japanese defeat – that he gave his approval and the *Akagi* was sent to the bottom by torpedoes from a destroyer.

Petrol-fed fires similarly swept the *Kaga* and defeated all efforts to save her. Lying stopped and burning she became the target for three torpedoes from the *Nautilus* which, after her earlier adventure, had surfaced and chased after the Japanese carriers. Even the stationary target, however, was too much for the unreliable torpedoes with which the Americans were at that time equipped. Of three fired, two missed, and the third struck but failed to explode. At 1640 orders were given to abandon the *Kaga*, and at 1925 two great explosions tore her asunder and sent her to the bottom.

The *Soryu*'s story was a similar one, of

US Navy

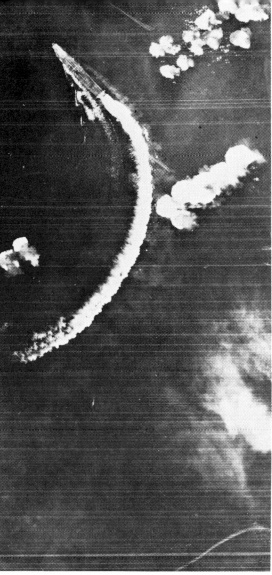

It was not only the Japanese carrier force which suffered at Midway: while taking avoiding action after sighting a US submarine, two heavy cruisers—*Mikuma* and *Mogami*—of the Support Force collided, and became a tempting target for the US aircraft. **Right:** the *Mogami* survived their attentions, and in spite of severe damage was able to reach Truk. But the *Mikuma* **(below left)** was smothered with bombs and sunk, after her speed had been further reduced by an engine-room explosion —petrol fumes from a crashed US dive-bomber had been sucked down into the starboard engine room and exploded, killing the crew there

Eclipse of the Rising Sun
△ In one terrible five minutes Japan's superiority in the Pacific was shattered for ever. While all the Japanese defences were concentrating upon massacring the slow US torpedo-bombers, 35 US dive-bombers arrived overhead, and *Soryu*, *Kaga,* and *Akagi* (seen here taking evasive action) were all reduced to blazing wrecks and had to be abandoned by their crews. Of the fleet carriers only *Hiryu,* cruising separately, was able to launch a counterattack. ▷But she did not last long—about ten hours later, 24 US dive-bombers surprised her, and she was hit four times, one of the bombs blowing the forward lift bodily on to the bridge. She was abandoned and sunk by an attendant destroyer the next morning

intermittent internal explosions from within the great mass of flame and smoke which she had become. When Captain Yanaginoto gave the order 'Abandon Ship', he determined to immolate himself, dying in the flames or going down with her. A party of his men returning on board with the intention of persuading him or, if necessary, of forcing him to save himself, fell back abashed at the heroic, determined figure of their captain, standing sword in hand, facing forward, awaiting his end. They left him to his chosen fate. As they did so they heard him singing the Japanese national anthem. Yanaginoto's resolution held fast till 1913 hours when at last the *Soryu* and the bodies of 718 of her crew slid beneath the surface.

Much had taken place in the meantime before Nagumo's three aircraft-carriers suffered their death throes. The first survivors of the American strike groups to land back on their ships had made it clear that one Japanese carrier had not yet been located. This was the *Hiryu* which, at the time of the attack, had become separated from the remainder. Admiral Fletcher therefore launched a ten-plane search from the *Yorktown,* and sent up a defensive patrol of a dozen Wildcats. It was none too soon. At a few minutes before noon, the *Yorktown*'s radar gave the warning of enemy planes coming in from the west.

These were the *Hiryu*'s attack group of 18 dive-bombers and six fighters, led by Lieutenant Michio Kobayashi, a veteran leader who had taken part in every operation of the Nagumo force. As soon as they had flown off, a further strike of ten torpedo-bombers and six Zeros, to be led by the redoubtable Tomonaga, was ranged up. Kobayashi's force had followed some of the *Yorktown*'s attack planes back and now concentrated on Fletcher's flagship. Wildcats—for once outnumbering the escorting Zeros—broke through to get at the 'Vals', shooting down ten of them, including the leader. Of the eight which remained, two were knocked down by anti-aircraft fire from the cruiser screen.

The six survivors, however, showed that they had lost none of their skill as they screamed down on the carrier. One 'Val' broke up under anti-aircraft fire, but its bomb sped on to burst on the flight-deck, killing many men, and starting a hangar fire below. A second bomb plunged through the side of the funnel and burst inside, starting more fires. With three boiler up-takes smashed and the furnaces of five or six boilers extinguished, the carrier's speed fell away until, 20 minutes later, she came to a stop. A third bomb penetrated to the fourth deck where for a time a fire threatened the forward petrol tanks and magazines.

His flagship immobilised, her radio and radar knocked out, Admiral Fletcher transferred his flag to the cruiser *Astoria,* and ordered the *Portland* to take the aircraft-carrier in tow. The damage-control organization worked wonders, however. Before the towline had been passed, the *Yorktown* was under way again and working up to 20 knots, and the refuelling of the fighters was in progress. Prospects seemed bright. Then a cruiser's radar picked up Tomonaga's air group, 40 miles away and coming in fast. There was just time to launch eight of the refuelling Wildcats to join the four already in the air, but they were unable to get through the screen of fighters to get at the 'Kates'—though they shot down three of the 'Zeros'. A tremendous screen of bursting

shells spread itself in front of the attackers, while the cruisers raised a barrage of splashes with their main armament, a wall of water columns through which it seemed impossible that the skimming 'Kates' could fly.

Yorktown fatally damaged

Five 'Kates' were shot down, but the remainder, coming in from four different angles, displayed all their deadly skill, boring doggedly in to drop their torpedoes at the point-blank range of 500 yards. It was impossible for the carrier to avoid them all. Two hit on her port side, tearing open the double-bottom fuel tanks and causing flooding which soon had her listing at 26 degrees. All power was lost, so that counter-flooding was impossible. It seemed that the *Yorktown* was about to capsize. At 1500, Captain Buckmaster ordered 'Abandon Ship'.

Meanwhile, however, the dive-bombers from Spruance's Task Force 16, operating some 60 miles to the north-east of the *Yorktown,* had wreaked vengeance on the *Hiryu.* Twenty-four Dauntlesses, of which ten had been transferred from the *Yorktown,* arrived overhead undetected soon after the few survivors of *Hiryu*'s attack had been recovered. The aircraft-carrier circled and swerved to avoid the bombs from the plummeting dive-bombers, but in vain. Four of them hit, one of which blew the forward lift bodily on to the bridge. The others started the inevitable fires and explosions, and the same prolonged death agonies as the *Hiryu*'s sisters were still suffering. By 2123 she had come to a stop. Desperate efforts to subdue the flames went on through the night; but at 0230 the following morning she was abandoned to be torpedoed by her attendant destroyers.

When the night of June 4 closed over the four smoking Japanese carriers and over the crippled *Yorktown,* the Battle of Midway was, in the main, over. Neither of the opposing commanders yet knew it, however, and manoeuvres and skirmishes were to continue for two more days. The Japanese commanders, except Nagumo, were slow to realise that the shattering of their four fleet carriers signified defeat and the end of the Midway operation. Admiral Kondo, with his two fast battleships, four heavy cruisers, and the light carrier *Zuiho* had set off to the help of Nagumo at midday on June 4, and soon afterwards Yamamoto was signalling to all his scattered forces to concentrate and attack the enemy. He himself, with the main body of his fleet, was coming up fast from the west bringing the 18-inch guns of the giant *Yamato* and the 16-inch ones of the *Nagato* and *Mutsu* to throw in their weight. Still underestimating his opponent, he was dreaming of a night encounter in which his immensely powerful fleet would overwhelm the American task force and avenge the losses of the previous day. The great 'fleet action' with battleships in stately line hurling huge shells at each other was still his hope and aim.

Such a concept had been forcibly removed from American naval strategy by the shambles of Pearl Harbor. Raymond Spruance, one of the greatest admirals to come to the fore during the war, was not to be lured within range of Yamamoto's battleships, above all at night, when his carriers, at this time untrained for night-flying, would be at a tremendous disadvantage. At sunset he turned away eastwards, aiming to take up a

position on the following day from which he could either 'follow up retreating enemy forces or break up a landing attack on Midway'.

The Japanese C-in-C refused to credit the completeness of the disaster that had overtaken his fleet and the Midway plan until early on June 5 when, at 0255, he ordered a general retirement. Thus, when Spruance, after prudently steering eastwards to keep his distance from the still overwhelmingly superior Japanese surface fleet, and reversing course at midnight so as to be within supporting distance of Midway at daylight, sent a strike of 58 dive-bombers from his two ships during the afternoon of the 5th to seek out Yamamoto's Main Body, his airmen encountered nothing but a lone destroyer sent to search for the *Hiryu.*

Two final incidents remain to be briefly recounted. When Yamamoto ordered his general retirement, the squadron of four heavy cruisers of Admiral Kurita's Support Force, the *Kumano, Suzuya, Mikuma,* and *Mogami,* was to the westward of Midway, steering through the night to deliver a bombardment at dawn. They now swung round to reverse course full in view of the American submarine *Tambor.* As they steadied on their retirement course, from the flagship the *Tambor* was sighted in the moonlight ahead. The signal for an emergency turn to port was flashed down the line but was not taken in by the rear ship, *Mogami.* Failing to turn with the remainder she collided with the *Mikuma,* suffering serious damage which reduced her speed to 12 knots. Leaving the *Mikuma* and two destroyers to escort the cripple, Kurita hurried on with the remainder.

News of this attractive target soon reached Midway. Twelve army Flying Fortresses took off but were unable to locate it; but 12 Marine Corps dive-bombers sighted the long oil slick being trailed by the *Mikuma,* followed it up—and at 0805 dived to the attack. Their bombs failed to achieve direct hits, but the plane of Captain Richard E. Fleming crashed on the after turret of the *Mikuma.* Petrol fumes were sucked down into the cruiser's starboard engine-room and exploded, killing the whole engine-room crew.

The two cruisers nevertheless continued to limp slowly away, until the following day when Spruance, having abandoned hope of delivering another blow on Yamamoto's Main Fleet, was able to direct his dive-bombers on to them. The *Mikuma* was smothered and sunk, but the *Mogami* miraculously survived, heavily damaged, to reach the Japanese base at Truk.

While these events were taking place, far to the east the abandoned *Yorktown* had drifted crewless through the night of June 4/5. She was still afloat at noon the next day and it became clear she had been prematurely abandoned. A salvage party boarded her and she was taken in tow. Hopes of getting her to port were high until the Japanese submarine *I-168,* sent by Yamamoto for the purpose, found her, penetrated her anti-submarine screen, and put two torpedoes into her. At 0600 on June 7 the *Yorktown* sank at last.

At sundown on the previous day Spruance had turned his force back eastwards to meet his supply tankers. That the Battle of Midway was over was finally clear to all.

Captain Donald Macintyre's biography is on page 144.

ALAMEIN: THE

Western Desert, October/November 1942

Major-General Sir Francis de Guingand

Now began what in British eyes has long seemed the most important battle of the war — popularly known as the Battle of Alamein. This title ignores the First Battle of Alamein, fought over virtually the same ground 16 weeks before, at which Rommel's advance was halted and the Afrika Korps given the first inkling of its fate. For now the supply situation favoured the British. Between July and October many changes had been wrought in the 8th Army: the men were rested, conscious of their hard training, aware that for the first time their weapons and equipment were superior in both quality and quantity to the enemy's. And most important of all, they had seen the enemy beaten back at Alam Halfa and knew that he was no Superman. Now it would be demonstrated to the world

When the Axis armies in Africa rose to meet the onslaught of the 8th Army on October 23 they were at a disadvantage in almost every department. Not least of their deficiencies was the absence of their great leader, for Rommel was a sick man and had returned to Germany for rest and treatment on September 23. In his place General Stumme held command — disgruntled in the knowledge that, if an attack came, Rommel would return at once, convinced that he alone was capable of taking the right decisions in an emergency on the Alamein front against the British.

Yet even Rommel regarded a defence against an enemy as strong in material as the British as a 'Battle Without Hope' while, from his masters in Rome and Berlin, he had obtained many promises but little practical help. So, daily, his reserves of men, tanks, guns, ammunition, fuel, and supplies fell lower, making comparison with the British an even gloomier exercise. For instance, Rommel was aware of a British superiority of 2 to 1 in tanks when, in fact, it was nearer 2½ to 1 overall (including 300 Italian tanks) and 5½ to 1 counting Germans alone. And the Royal Air Force now dominated the air, making the Luftwaffe's despairing efforts appear puny by comparison. While in Rome, Rommel told Mussolini that unless the supply position was improved the Axis would have to get out of North Africa, but he sensed his failure to transmit the gravity of the situation and in Berlin he recoiled before a wall of blind optimism and false promises.

At the front, meanwhile, all Panzerarmee could do was prepare an even denser fortified area in the neck between the sea and the Qattara Depression, based on the prime con-

sideration that, if they were driven out into the open, they would be overwhelmed for lack of sufficient vehicles or fuel to withdraw or fight a mobile rearguard action. Thus they planned to hold each piece of ground at all costs, cleaning up each enemy penetration with an immediate counterattack.

The German system of defence which evolved was not unlike that to be found on the Western Front at the end of the First World War — a battle zone spread out in depth behind a screen of outposts, in an effort to acquire time for mobile reserves to assemble and counterattack. One technical feature, in particular, amplified the 1918 concept — anti-tank and anti-personnel mines. Some 500,000 of them, supplemented by buried British bombs and shells, were sown thickly around each defended locality, creating a deep belt along the length of the front.

In each sector Italian troops, well laced with Germans to give stability, waited the impact with mounting anxiety. The pattern they formed contained an invitation to a Battle of Attrition — it only needed the British commander to accept that invitation and a drawn-out battle would be in prospect.

Before the Battle of Alam Halfa was fought, Winston Churchill paid us a visit on his way back from Moscow (August 19) and stayed at our headquarters at Burgh-el-Arab.

General Montgomery took special care to see that the Prime Minister and his party would be comfortable. He gave up his own caravan and sited it within a few yards of the sea, so that our distinguished guest could bathe when he felt so inclined.

TIDE TURNS

Churchill gave us the most vivid description of his visit to Moscow and how he had to talk 'cold turkey' before it was accepted that Great Britain was doing something to win the war, but he had come away with a very deep impression of Stalin's leadership; and enthralled us with details of our gathering war effort, and what we were preparing for the enemy. I well remember him saying: 'Germany has asked for this bombing warfare, and she will rue the day she started it, for her country will be laid in ruins.'

Once Rommel had failed in his last desperate offensive, he was faced with two alternatives. Either to stay and await the attack which he knew would most surely be launched against him, increasing in the meantime the strength of his defences; or to withdraw to some favourable position before we were ready to follow him up in sufficient strength, thereby shortening his lines of communication and so rendering his supply position less precarious.

He chose the first of these courses, no doubt largely because he lacked the necessary transport and petrol for a withdrawal; but in any case a retreat would have been against his character and would certainly have proved very unpopular with the Axis High Command. His decision meant therefore that the longer we waited before launching our offensive, the more formidable his defences would become — particularly with regard to minefields, wire, and the construction of prepared positions.

It was therefore obvious that it was to our advantage to attack as soon as possible and this view was strongly held by Churchill, who started to press General Alexander — Commander-in-Chief Middle East — for an early offensive. He wanted this to take place in September. He had an additional important reason and that was the fact that Operation 'Torch', the Anglo/US landings in North Africa, was due to take place early in November, and therefore hard and prolonged fighting on our front would be of great benefit.

One day Alexander arrived at our headquarters, bringing with him a signal from Churchill saying that he more or less demanded that we should attack in September. After reading the document Montgomery said 'Hand me a pad, Freddie', and seizing it he wrote down these points:

● Rommel's attack had caused some delay in our preparations.

● Moon conditions restricted 'D' day to certain periods in September and October.

● If the September date was insisted upon the troops would be insufficiently equipped and trained, and failure would probably result. But if the attack took place in October then complete victory was assured.

Turning to Alexander, he handed over the pad and said: 'I should make these points in your reply; that should fix it.' A signal was subsequently dispatched on these lines and produced the required result; for what could any Prime Minister do with this clear-cut military opinion before him! Montgomery in his memoirs recalls that he told Alexander 'privately' that if the attack was ordered for September they would have to find someone else to do the job.

Taking all considerations into account, Montgomery decided that we should attack during the October full moon and the exact date fixed was the 23rd. It was essential that we should attack at night owing to the formidable minefield problem.

I now come to the plan itself. There was no way round the enemy positions; the sea and the Qattara Depression saw to that, so a hole had to be punched through their defences. Montgomery had decided to launch the main attack on the right flank with General Leese's 30th Corps, together with a secondary attack on the southern flank by General Horrocks' 13th Corps. The plan was to pass 10th Corps (General Lumsden) through the gap made by 30th Corps to sit astride the enemy's supply line, and so force him to deploy his armour against us, when it would be destroyed. This was in accordance with normal teaching. Having destroyed the enemy's armour, his troops could be dealt with more or less at leisure.

The Army Commander had laid down three basic fundamentals which would govern the preparatory period. These were: leadership — equipment — training. He soon put the first matter in order, and the re-equipment of the army was going well. But early in October he realised that the training of the army was still below what was required, and in view of this weakness made one of his rapid decisions. He would alter the conception of the plan so that instead of first going all out to destroy the enemy's armour, he would eat away the enemy's holding troops — who were for the most part unarmoured — and use our armour to stop the enemy from interfering. Without their infantry divisions to hold the line, providing firm bases for their mobile forces, the enemy's armour would be at a grave disadvantage and their supply routes would be constantly threatened. It was unlikely that they would stand idly by while this 'crumbling' process was going on, and so it was probable that we would force his armour to attack *us,* which, once we were in a position to receive it, would be to our advantage.

The final plan in outline as given out by the Army Commander on October 6 was as follows:
● Main attack by 30th Corps in the north on a front of four divisions [to secure a bridgehead – objective 'Oxalic' – beyond the enemy's main defended zone]. Two corridors were to be cleared through the minefields, and through these lanes 10th Corps was to pass.
● 13th Corps in the south was to stage two attacks. One directed on Himeimat and the Taqa feature. The other into the area of Gebel Kalakh and Qaret el Khadim. These attacks were to be made with the primary object of misleading the enemy and thereby containing forces that might otherwise be used against 30th Corps.
● Both the above corps were to destroy the enemy holding the forward positions.
● 10th Corps was to deploy itself [to a line 'Pierson', just west of 'Oxalic'] so as to prevent 30th Corps' operations from being interfered with. And its final object [by an advance to area 'Skinflint'] was the destruction of the enemy's armour.
● The attack was to start at night during the full moon.

The artillery plan was very carefully prepared. We would go into battle with great gun power and considerable supplies of ammunition. The battle was to open with a very heavy counter-battery bombardment, and then most of our artillery would concentrate on the enemy defences by barrage and concentrations.

The air plan was a good one. Before the battle Air Vice-Marshal Coningham's Desert Air Force had been wearing down the enemy's air effort. On one or two occasions he had shown brilliant leadership by taking advantage of fleeting opportunities when isolated rain storms had grounded portions of the enemy's air force. Low-flying attacks laid on with great rapidity had taken a very heavy toll of the enemy's aircraft and petrol.

During the first night our air forces were to undertake attacks against enemy gun positions, and so help our counter-battery plan. Later they were to switch to the areas where the enemy armoured divisions were located. Our available air strength on 'D' day was 500 fighters and 200 bombers – at that time a considerable force.

The 'going' was one of the matters which gave us a lot of anxiety, and we went to endless trouble to obtain information as to what the ground was like in the area over which we were making our thrusts. Air photos, interrogation of prisoners, questioning of our own troops who had at one time or another traversed the area – these were some of the means employed. We built six tracks leading up to 30th Corps' starting line, and this in itself was a tremendous task, constructed as they were through very soft sand.

Montgomery's dummy army
The deception arrangements were particularly interesting. We had decided quite rightly that strategic surprise was out of the question, for the enemy knew we were going to attack. On the other hand tactical surprise was quite possible. We considered we could delude the enemy as to the weight,

Imperial War Museum

the date, the time, and the direction of our attack. Our plans were all made with this in view, and they proved most successful.

The first problem was to try to conceal our concentration as much as possible from the enemy. The staff worked out the complete layout on the day of the attack – the number of guns, tanks, vehicles, and troops. A very large 'operations' map was kept which showed this layout in various denominations. We then arranged to reach the eventual density as early as possible, and to maintain it up to the last moment, so that the enemy's air photography would show no particular change during the last two or three weeks. To achieve this we used spare transport and dummy transport. These were gradually replaced by those belonging to the assault units and formations as they came up to take over their allotted sectors. These changeovers took place at night, and we had special dummy vehicles made under which guns could be concealed. All moves forward were of course rigidly controlled, and slit trenches were dug and camouflaged at night in which the assault infantry could be concealed.

The next task was to make the enemy think that the main attack would be launched in the southern sector. This, I might add, was not very popular with 13th Corps, but they nobly accepted the plan for the common good. Besides various other methods adopted, we built large dummy dumps away to the south, and also a dummy pipe line and water installations. It was so arranged that the work would appear to the enemy to be aimed at completion a week or two *after* the actual date of our attack. Finally on the night of the attack itself the wireless traffic of the headquarters of an armoured division was so employed as to indicate that a large move of armoured forces was taking place in the southern sector.

On the night of the 23rd we arranged for a feint landing to take place behind the enemy's lines. About 4 pm a convoy sailed westwards out of Alexandria. After dark all but a few fast craft put back, but those remaining staged a dummy landing. Shelling of the coast, mortar and machine-gun fire, and light signals were used. It was timed to take place about three hours after our attack had started, and it was hoped that this would tie down enemy reserves. The loading of the ships was no doubt witnessed by enemy agents, who could see tanks being shipped and troops marching aboard. There is no doubt that all these measures helped materially to confuse the enemy and gained us tactical surprise.

Montgomery was determined not to begin his attack until the 8th Army had overwhelming superiority. Time was on his side, for the Allies now controlled the supply lines, and troops and new equipment – like this Sherman – could be delivered in unprecedented quantities. Meanwhile the Afrika Korps was not only starved of equipment but it would go into battle without Rommel, who was ill

On the administrative side there was a great deal to be done. The whole basis of administration had to be altered. Before, when we were on the defensive, the weight of resources was held back; now that we intended to attack they had to be placed as far forward as possible. The consequent carrying forward of supplies and the camouflaging of the dumps was no small task, and preparations were made to construct the railway forward as rapidly as possible. We also made preparations to open ports when they were captured and perfected our organisation for the recovery and repair of tanks and vehicles.

Montgomery's change in plan as regards the use of our armour nearly caused a crisis between himself and General Herbert Lumsden, who had been selected to command the 'Corps d'Elite' – the 10th Army Corps. Lumsden had fought with conspicuous gallantry when commanding an armoured division in the 'bad old days'. He was a cavalryman through and through and not unnaturally thought in terms of the mobile battle and yearned for the day when his armoured formations, equipped with modern tanks, would be launched through a gap made by the infantry, to roam far and wide. The Army Commander's new instructions were therefore not to his liking.

Shortly after this Lumsden held a corps conference at which he explained his plan and views to all the commanders in his corps. Montgomery was temporarily absent from the army on this occasion and I therefore decided to attend this conference myself.

It soon became clear to me that this new conception of the use of armour had not been fully accepted by the corps commander, and at the end of the meeting I had a talk with Lumsden pointing out the Army Commander's determination to fight the coming battle this way. But I could see that he was anything but happy and there appeared to be a recrudescence of the bad old habit of questioning orders.

On the Army Commander's return, I reported fully on what had taken place and he lost little time in making his views crystal clear to the commander of 10th Corps; and Lumsden, being a good soldier, accepted the position and made the necessary changes in his plans.

Large-scale rehearsals for the coming battle were carried out, and the lessons learned gone into very carefully by the various commanders. And by the end of the third week in October we realised that all these vast preparations were successfully reaching their conclusion. From the staff

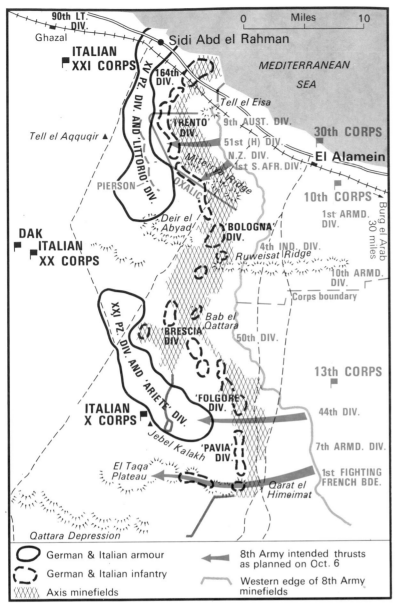

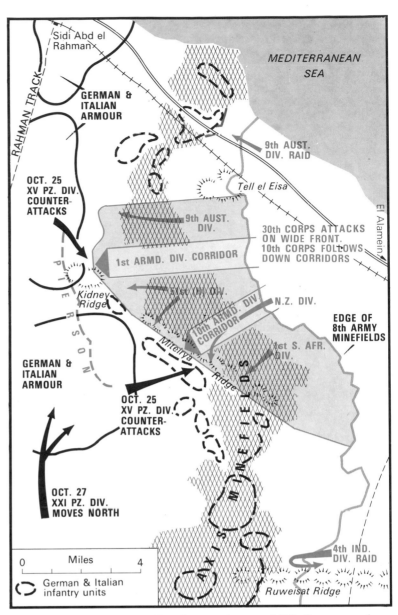

At Alamein in October the 8th Army was faced by an enemy position which could not be turned, but must be breached by direct attack. Montgomery at first intended to use 30th Corps to push two corridors into the enemy lines through which the tanks of 10th Corps would flood to force an armoured battle and cut the Axis supply lines. But weaknesses in his forces' training made him decide to alter this plan: 30th Corps was still to open two corridors through to 'Oxalic', but it was then to concentrate upon 'crumbling' the enemy's holding troops. The tanks were to go no further than 'Pierson', where they would cover the infantry and await the German armoured counter-attacks on ground of their own choosing. Further south, diversionary attacks by 4th Indian Division and 13th Corps would hold a large proportion of the Axis armour during the vital opening phase of the battle. On the Axis side, Stumme had split his armour (XV Panzer in the north, XXI Panzer in the south) to cover both possible lines of attack. This unprecedented step weakened his ability to mount a concentrated counterattack, but General Bayerlein believed that it had been approved by Rommel before he left Africa

After an extremely heavy artillery barrage, troops of 30th Corps, on a four-division front, advanced into the enemy minefields. By dawn on October 24 the infantry had reached most of the objectives of 'Oxalic', but stubborn enemy resistance and congestion in the corridors prevented the tanks from clearing the minefields. At first German reactions seemed hesitant and unsure—not only were Panzerarmee's commanders still uncertain as to where the real attack would come, but Stumme had died of heart failure on the first day, and for vital hours the Axis forces had no leader until General von Thoma was able to take over. It was not until the third day of the attack that a new Axis certainty about counterattacks showed that Rommel had returned. Throughout the 24th and 25th, 30th Corps inched forward, while 13th Corps successfully held XXI Panzer in the south. But Montgomery had realised that the impetus had gone out of the initial attacks, and, using attacks by 9th Australian Division in the north to cut off enemy forces in the salient and force Rommel to concentrate on their relief, he halted and began to redeploy 8th Army for a new breakout attempt

point of view there was a healthy slackening in the tempo of work, denoting that the stage was now set.

Montgomery had been indefatigable, and had satisfied himself that all was in readiness. He very rightly had decided that in order to get the best out of his troops it was necessary for them to know the whole plan so that they would realise how their particular contribution fitted in with the general scheme of things.

On October 19 and 20 he addressed all officers down to lieutenant-colonel level in 30th, 13th, and 10th Corps. It was a real tour de force. These talks were some of the best he had ever given, clear and full of confidence. He touched on the enemy situation, stressing their weaknesses, and

said he was certain a long 'dog-fight' or 'killing match' would take place for several days—'it might be ten'. He then gave details of our great strength, our tanks, our guns, and the enormous supplies of ammunition available. He drummed in the need never to lose the initiative, and how everyone—everyone—must be imbued with the burning desire to 'kill Germans'. 'Even the padres—one per weekday and two on Sundays!' This produced a roar. After explaining how the battle was to be fought, he said that he was entirely confident of the result.

The men were let into the secret on October 21 and 22, from which date no leave was granted, and by the 23rd a tremendous state of enthusiasm had been produced. Those soldiers just knew they would succeed.

On the morning of October 22, Montgomery held a press conference. He explained the plan, his intentions, and his firm conviction of success. Many of the war correspondents were rather shaken by the confidence—this bombastic confidence—which he displayed. They felt there must be a catch in it—how could he be so sure? Some, I think, thought the maze of minefields and deep defences that the enemy had constructed were too difficult a problem to justify such a sanguine attitude.

In the afternoon of the 23rd we drove up to our battle headquarters, tucked away on the coast within a few minutes of 30th and 10th Corps Headquarters. We had well protected buried cables running back to our main headquarters and to the various corps; vehicles

Line-Up for the Battle

Panzerarmee Afrika
Gen Stumme (until Oct 26) and Fld Mshl Rommel

Reserve
German 90th Light Division
Italian **Trieste** Motorised Division
Luftwaffe XIX Flak Division

North
German XV Panzer Division
German 164th Motorised Division
Italian **Littorio** Armoured Division
Italian XXI Infantry Corps—**Trento** Division

Centre
German XXI Panzer Division
Ramcke Parachute Brigade
Italian XX Infantry Corps—**Brescia**
and **Bologna** Divisions

South
Italian **Ariete** Armoured Division
Italian X Infantry Corps—**Pavia**
and **Folgore** Divisions

8th Army
Lieut-Gen Montgomery

30th Corps—Lieut-Gen Leese
51st (Highland) Division—Maj-Gen Wimberley
4th Indian Division—Maj-Gen Tuker
9th Australian Division
New Zealand Division—Lieut-Gen Freyberg
1st South African Division—Maj-Gen Pienaar
23rd Armoured Brigade Group
9th (UK) Armoured Brigade

13th Corps—Lieut-Gen Horrocks
7th Armoured Division—Maj-Gen Harding
50th Division—Maj-Gen Nichols
44th Division—Maj-Gen Hughes
1st Free French Brigade Group
2nd Free French Brigade Group
1st Greek Infantry Brigade Group

10th Corps—Lieut-Gen Lumsden
1st Armoured Division—Maj-Gen Briggs
10th Armoured Division—Maj-Gen Gatehouse
8th Armoured Division—Maj-Gen Gairdner

Rommel
Nehring
Thoma
Bayerlein

Montgomery
Leese
Horrocks
Lumsden

Allied leadership was new and backed by great material resources, but Axis command suffered from changes and resultant indecisiveness. When the offensive began, Panzerarmee was led by General Stumme, but after his death on the first day of the attack it was commanded by General von Thoma until Rommel, who had been ill, returned on October 26

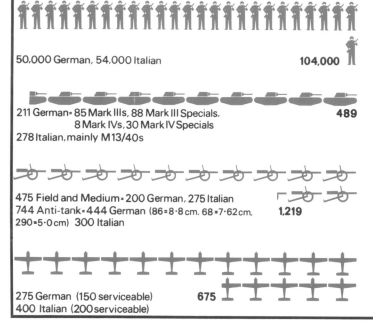

50,000 German, 54,000 Italian — **104,000**

195,000

211 German = 85 Mark IIIs, 88 Mark III Specials, 8 Mark IVs, 30 Mark IV Specials
278 Italian, mainly M13/40s — **489**

1,029 — 170 Grants, 252 Shermans, 216 Crusader 2-pdrs, 78 Crusader 6-pdrs, 119 Stuarts, 194 Valentines

475 Field and Medium = 200 German, 275 Italian
744 Anti-tank = 444 German (86 = 8·8 cm, 68 = 7·62 cm, 290 = 5·0 cm) 300 Italian — **1,219**

2,311 — 908 Field and Medium
1,403 Anti-tank = 554 2-pdrs, 849 6-pdrs

275 German (150 serviceable) — **675**
400 Italian (200 serviceable)

750 — (530 serviceable)

---

were dug in as we were rather far forward and near the desert road, which would undoubtedly become—as it did—a target for enemy air attack. I decided to make this tactical headquarters my base, and it worked very well. My people could talk to me on direct lines and come up for conferences within the hour.

It was a lovely evening, and I drove out after dark to see by the light of the moon the move forward of some of the troops. All was going well, and everyone looked cheerful. This was the day for which so many of us had been preparing and waiting.

As the time drew near we got into our cars and drove to a good view-point to see the opening of the battle. We passed the never-ending stream of tanks and transport—all moving with clockwork precision. This was 10th Corps moving up to its starting line, with the moon providing sufficient light to drive by, but the night protecting them from

the prying eyes of enemy aircraft. We had some of our own machines flying over the enemy's forward positions making distracting noises; otherwise all seemed fairly quiet and normal. An occasional Very light and burst of machine-gun fire, a gun firing here and there, as would happen any night. We looked at our watches, 2130 hours—ten minutes to go. I could hardly wait.

A 1,000-gun barrage begins
The minutes ticked by, and then the whole sky was lit up, and a roar rent the air. Over 1,000 of our guns had opened up. It was a great and heartening sight. I tried to picture what the enemy must be thinking, did he know what was coming? He must do now. How ready was he? Up and down the desert, from north to south, the twinkling of the guns could be seen in an unceasing sequence. Within the enemy's lines we could see an occasional deep red glow

light up the western sky. Each time this happened Brigadier Dennis, the commander of 30th Corps artillery, let out a grunt of satisfaction. Another Axis gun position had been blown up. We checked each change in the artillery plan; the pause while the guns switched to new targets. It was gun drill at its best. Now the infantry started forward. We could see the periodic bursts of Bofors guns which, with their tracer shell, demarcated the direction of advance. Behind us great searchlight beams were directed towards the sky, to help the forward troops plot their positions, and so find out when they had reached their objectives, for few landmarks existed in this part of the desert.

About 2300 hours I crept away and drove back to our headquarters. I knew we could expect to hear little of interest for some time yet, and so I snatched an hour or two's rest before being wakened up to hear the first reports come in.

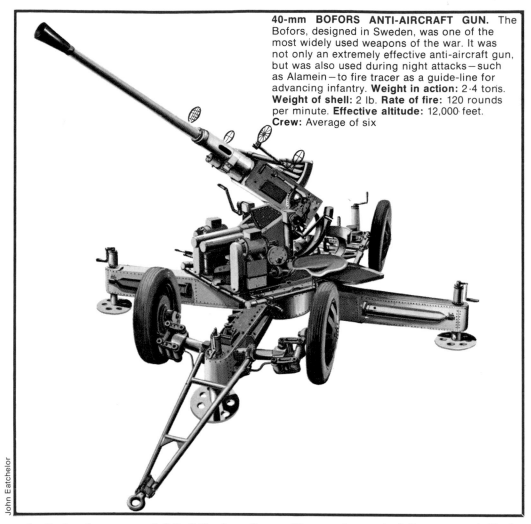

40-mm BOFORS ANTI-AIRCRAFT GUN. The Bofors, designed in Sweden, was one of the most widely used weapons of the war. It was not only an extremely effective anti-aircraft gun, but was also used during night attacks – such as Alamein – to fire tracer as a guide-line for advancing infantry. **Weight in action:** 2·4 tons. **Weight of shell:** 2 lb. **Rate of fire:** 120 rounds per minute. **Effective altitude:** 12,000 feet. **Crew:** Average of six

John Eatchelor

As I closed my eyes I felt full of confidence and hope, but never did I think that this was the opening of a campaign that would bring us in so short a time to the very gates of Carthage.

Although the Battle of El Alamein was a comparatively small affair in relation to later battles fought during the war, for a number of reasons it must rank high in importance. To start with it meant the turn of the tide in Britain's fortunes. In fact the victory stood out as a priceless jewel after a series of depressing defeats. Then it provided a much-wanted stimulus to British morale, for it convinced our armed forces that, given the right leadership and weapons, they could beat the Germans, and it also inspired confidence among the British people in ultimate victory.

By previous standards in the Middle East, however, it was a great offensive and probably some of the bitterest fighting in the whole war took place over those sandy wastes. Our new commander never once lost his confidence or the initiative, while his troops were always convinced that they would win through in the end. I do not propose to give a very detailed description of the operations, but will confine myself to the broad framework of the battle and concentrate upon the highlights.

On that night of October 23/24, 30th Corps attacked with four divisions down two corridors cleared through the minefields. This attack was made on a fairly narrow front of 6 to 7 miles, with the northern flank tied to the Tell el Eisa feature, and the Miteiriya Ridge forming the southern limit.

The enemy's and our own dispositions at the outset of the battle are interesting for three reasons:

● The greater part of the enemy static defences was manned by Italians.
● The German infantry divisions, 164th Division and 90th Light Division, were echeloned in depth, protecting the vital coastal road sector.
● The German armour (Afrika Korps) was held in reserve and distributed equally between the northern and southern sectors.

Besides 30th Corps' main attack, a brigade of the 9th Australian Division carried out a feint between Tell el Eisa and the sea. This, together with the phoney seaborne operation, had a worrying effect on the enemy, while farther south the 4th Indian Division launched a strong raid from the area of the Ruweisat Ridge.

Then, at 0200 hours on October 24, the leading elements of the 1st and 10th Armoured Divisions crossed their start lines.

The Germans reel . . . and recover

Progress was good, and the task of clearing the lanes through the minefields went on well, but by the morning the armour had not managed to get out beyond them. Throughout the night, the Miteiriya Ridge was a very unpleasant place to be, and fierce fighting took place, for once the enemy had recovered from the initial shock, he concentrated his artillery and mortar fire on the corridors, and XV Panzer Division carried out a counterattack. The Army Commander examined the situation on the morning of the 24th, and decided that although a very good start had been made, it was important that there must be no slackening in the efforts to get the armour through, and that the 'crumbling' operations by the New Zealand Division must start at once.

In the south, 13th Corps had started on schedule. The French had successfully assaulted the high ground about Himeimat, but the soft sand had prevented their supporting weapons reaching them in time, and they were driven off again by a German counterattack. The other 13th Corps' attack, after making initial gains, was held up between the belts of minefields. The 24th was, therefore, spent in 'crumbling' operations in this area. These were, however, secondary to the main attack by 30th Corps, and in spite of these small set-backs their main object was achieved, for the XXI Panzer Division was still retained in the southern sector.

Now started a week of terrific fighting. By the evening of the 24th, the 1st Armoured Division had managed to get some elements out of the minefields in positions beyond, but 10th Armoured Division was not so fortunate, and was having a very difficult time. An attack they made at 2200 hours that night, supported by the corps artillery, made little progress.

The Army Commander went to bed in his caravan that night at his usual time – between 2130 and 2200 hours. As things appeared rather uncertain, I decided to stay up and keep in close touch with the corps. Towards 0200 hours on the 25th it was obvious that the situation in the southern corridor about the Miteiriya Ridge was not satisfactory. Congestion was considerable in the cleared lane through the minefields, and a lot of damage was being done by enemy shelling and mortar fire. General Freyberg, as usual in the thick of it, was personally directing operations from his tank in this critical zone.

Altogether I gained the impression that a feeling was developing in some quarters which favoured suspending the forward move, and pulling back under cover of the ridge. I decided, therefore, that this was an occasion when the Army Commander must intervene, and so I called a conference for 0330 hours at our Tactical Headquarters, asking Leese (30th Corps) and Lumsden (10th Corps) to attend. Then I went along to his caravan and woke him up. He appeared to be sleeping peacefully – in spite of a lot of attention from the enemy air force. He agreed with the action I had taken, and told me to bring the two corps commanders along to his map lorry when they arrived.

In due course I led the generals along the little path to the lorry. Montgomery was seated on a stool carefully examining a map fixed to the wall. He greeted us all most cheerfully, motioned us to sit down, and then asked each corps commander to tell his story. He listened very quietly, only occasionally interrupting with a question. There was a certain 'atmosphere' noticeable, careful handling was required, and Lumsden was obviously still not very happy about the role his armour had been given. After a while Montgomery spoke to the commander of the 10th Armoured Division on the telephone, and heard his version of the situation. He then made it quite clear that there would be no alteration to his orders. The armour could and must get through. He also ordered the headquarters of this division to be moved considerably farther forward.

The decision to make no change in the plan at that moment was a brave one, for it meant accepting considerable risks and casualties. But if it had not been made, I am firmly convinced that the attack might

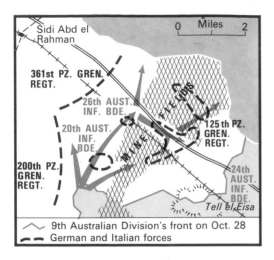

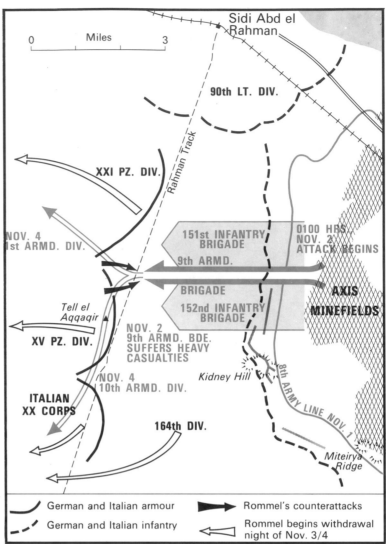

well have fizzled out, and the full measure of success we achieved might never have been possible.

By 0800 hours on October 25 the leading armoured brigade of the 10th Armoured Division was reported to be 2,000 yards west of the minefield area, and in touch with the 1st Armoured Division to the north. In addition, we heard that the New Zealand Division and the 8th Armoured Brigade were clear of the main minefields, and were advancing south-westwards in accordance with the plan, drawing the XV Panzer Division into several counterattacks against us, which were all repulsed with heavy losses.

The attack switches to the north

By about mid-day Montgomery realised that the 'crumbling' operations by the New Zealand Division would prove very expensive and decided to switch the axis northwards, telling the 9th Australian Division to destroy the Germans in the salient. The 1st Armoured Division was ordered to fight its way westwards with the object of threatening the enemy's supply routes in the Rahman track area, where it would also threaten the rear of the enemy holding the coastal salient, but this attack made no appreciable progress until the night of October 26/27.

The Australian attack under General Moreshead went well—ground was gained and heavy casualties inflicted on the enemy. Here the enemy's defences were very strong (the garrison was mainly German) and I believe this area saw the most determined and savage fighting during the whole battle and made a major contribution to ultimate victory.

On the 26th the New Zealand and South African Divisions made slow progress, and the Army Commander decided to regroup. The 30th Corps required a pause to reorganise and, although we had forced our way through the main minefields, the enemy still had well organised anti-tank defences opposing us.

This regrouping produced the reserves required for the decisive phase of the battle. The New Zealand Division was pulled out of the line, their place being taken by moving the 1st South African and 4th Indian Divisions northward. The New Zealanders were given first priority for all tank replacements, and spent a day or so resting and bathing. We could see this cheerful body of men spread out along the beach from our headquarters, the horrors of the Miteiriya Ridge behind them, preparing themselves for the ordeal ahead.

During October 27 news came in that two enemy tankers and a merchantman had been sunk near the entrance to Tobruk harbour, and their loss may have had a considerable influence on the battle. At 1400 hours the Army Commander held a conference at which the regrouping plan was explained, and also plans for the continuance of the Australian attack. The 13th Corps was ordered to make final arrangements for moving the 7th Armoured Division and other troops to the northern sector, for during the night of October 26/27 the XXI Panzer Division had moved northwards, and so these forces could be spared. In the morning we had located, by wireless direction-finding, the headquarters of this German armoured division.

For most of the day, the two German Panzer divisions launched attacks against our positions. This suited us well, and the 1st Armoured Division excelled themselves, claiming 50 enemy tanks knocked out, as well as others damaged. In addition, the RAF was doing good work bombing the enemy as they formed up, so altogether it was an exciting and successful day—from our headquarters we could see the tell-tale pillars of black smoke towering up into the sky when tanks and vehicles were destroyed.

Now Montgomery decided that the 1st Armoured Division needed a rest, and withdrew it into reserve, turning their sector to defence, with infantry brigades, moved up from 13th Corps, and available for subsequent operations.

On the night of the 28/29 the Australian Division attacked again, and drove a wedge into the enemy positions which almost reached the road between Sidi Abd el Rahman and Tell el Eisa, and although on the 29th the enemy did all in their power to destroy this wedge, these attacks made with both tanks and infantry completely failed.

October 29 was a very interesting day as plans and preparations went ahead for the launching of the break-out attack—given the code name of 'Supercharge'.

The Army Commander's intention was to launch this attack as far north as possible, but some of us felt that better results would be gained by adopting a more southerly axis; the farther north we went, the more Germans, mines, and prepared defences would be met.

During the morning we were paid a visit by Commander-in-Chief General Alexander, Minister of State Casey, and Alexander's Chief-of-Staff, Lieutenant-General McCreery. The Army Commander described the situation and his plans, and radiated confidence. He stressed that he had always predicted a ten-day 'dog-fight', and he was quite certain that he would win the battle. However, I soon realised that the Cabinet in London, if not some people in Cairo, were beginning to wonder whether Montgomery would after all fulfil his promise of 'Complete Victory'. It was inevitable therefore that interest was focused upon Supercharge and in discussions with McCreery I found that he also felt that it should be launched farther south.

After Alexander, Casey, and McCreery had departed, I felt more than ever worried about the sector chosen for Supercharge. It appeared to me that Rommel would do all

Far left: The Australian thrust which cut off units of two German regiments and persuaded Rommel to concentrate his reserves in the far north. On the morning of November 2, after a heavy barrage, two infantry brigades began 'Supercharge' **(left),** Montgomery's final thrust: the first armoured unit, 9th Armoured Brigade, was severely mauled, but when the 1st Armoured Division followed it and met XXI Panzer coming from the north, there was a confused tank battle in which the Germans lost much vital equipment. By the morning of the 3rd, Rommel had decided to retreat, only to receive a message from Hitler ordering him to hold the Alamein position at all costs. This order he prepared to obey until the news arrived that his defences in the south had been shattered by 14th Indian and 51st Highland Divisions (not shown on map), and General von Thoma had been captured. He was thus forced to fall back precipitately as the British armour threatened to surround his most precious forces

in his power to protect his main supply dumps and his lines of communication which used the coastal road. He could not afford to take any risks on this portion of his front. So I went along to discuss the problem with Bill Williams (G-1 Intelligence) and found that he shared my views. Fortunately the latest intelligence reports showed that 90th Light Division had been moved to the northern sector, no doubt due to successes achieved by the 9th Australian Division. It became obvious therefore that the Axis front farther south had been weakened. I decided to take Williams along to see the Army Commander, and appraise him of the changing situation. Montgomery had previously been much impressed by Williams' explanation of how Rommel had distributed his German troops in order to 'corset' the Italian units, and he was quick to see that the present situation gave an excellent chance of attacking where the enemy was weakest—where most of the defenders were Italian or at least at the junction of the two Axis allies.

Montgomery was never slow in making up his mind—provided, of course, that he had the necessary facts—and in this case he immediately decided to change the axis of the forthcoming attack. I well remember leaving the map lorry in high spirits, and later on that day I rang up McCreery who was quite delighted at hearing the news. This decision was, I'm sure, a decisive contribution to victory.

The Australians continued their attack on the night of 30/31, crossed the coast road, and at one time it looked as if the bulk of the Germans inside the salient would be cut off and destroyed. They managed, however, to get away with the help of tank reinforcements, but this attack to the north had paid a big dividend, for it kept the enemy's attention focused on the coastal area, besides causing great damage among the Germans themselves.

On November 1 we heard that XXI Panzer Division had moved even farther north, and so everything was set for the final phase. After a delay of 24 hours [to rest the troops, and give more time for reorganisation] Supercharge was launched, helped by a creeping barrage at 0100 hours on the morning of November 2. Some 300 25-pounders and the corps medium artillery supported the attack.

The frontage of attack was 4,000 yards, and the depth of the advance 6,000 yards. The infantry (151st and 152nd Infantry Brigades) attacked, and everything went wonderfully well, so on reaching their objective the armour moved through and formed a bridgehead, through which it was proposed to pass the armoured divisions of 10th Corps. The objectives were reached, but the 9th Armoured Brigade suffered heavy casualties from enemy anti-tank weapons. Then the 1st Armoured Division came through to assist, and an armoured battle was fought.

On November 3 we knew that the enemy was beaten, as air reports came in showing that the retreat had started, and we knew that Rommel had insufficient transport or petrol to get back more than a portion of his force.

Yet November 3 still did not see us right out into the open country, for the enemy were still plugging the hole with anti-tank guns, but on the night of the 3/4 a clean break-through was made by the 51st and 4th Indian Divisions, after mounting a sudden attack with the greatest skill.

The battle had been won in 11 days, which was just about the Army Commander's estimate of how long the heavy fighting would last. The enemy was defeated and in full retreat, and our armour and armoured cars were now operating in open country.

When on November 3 all information showed that the enemy was in full retreat, it was hoped that the Desert Air Force would cause havoc among his transport; for reports described a scene of vehicles, head to tail, four and sometimes eight deep, moving westwards either on or just off the road. Indeed we had visions of the retreat being turned into a complete rout, bearing in mind the fact that we enjoyed virtual air superiority. In the event, the results were very disappointing. When setting out along the road between the Alamein battlefield and Daba, I had expected to see a trail of devastation, but the visible signs of destroyed vehicles were few and far between. The fact is that at this period of the war we had not learned the technique of low strafing, for our fighter bombers had been employed in air fighting and bombing. I believe the attacks on the retreating columns were made mostly with bombs, and that the aircraft were not allowed to come down low; no doubt because our pilots had not been trained in low-flying attacks with cannon. I feel, however, that an opportunity was lost, and that it should have been possible to have produced a form of paralysis in the enemy's rearward movement.

It was also a great disappointment that we were unable to cut off completely Rommel's surviving forces and so save the long and arduous series of operations that took us to Tripoli and beyond. Montgomery, however, knew that it was only a matter of time, and in any case he was very unlucky, for the forces which he had ordered to cut off the enemy at the bottlenecks of Fuka and Matrûh were deprived of fulfilling their object through the interference caused by some most unusually heavy rain storms, which 'bogged' them down within a stone's throw of the retreating enemy.

 MAJOR-GENERAL SIR FRANCIS de GUINGAND KBE, CB, DSO, was educated at Ampleforth and Sandhurst. He joined the West Yorks Regiment in 1920, and served in India, Ireland, Egypt, and the United Kingdom, before going to the Staff College, Camberley, in 1936. From 1939/40 he was Military Assistant to the Secretary of State for War, the Rt. Hon. Hore-Belisha, and became Director of Military Intelligence, Middle East, in 1942. He was Chief-of-Staff to Field Marshal Montgomery from 1942/45, at first with 8th Army and then with 21st Army Group, and Director of Military Intelligence at the War Office from 1945/46. Sir Francis retired in 1947 and emigrated to South Africa. He has written three books—*Operation Victory*, *African Assignment*, and *Generals at War*—and a number of articles on military and other subjects

Bündesarchiv

An Italian machine-gun in action: Italian troops formed the main static element in the Axis line

The Hinge of Fate

1942 October 6: General Montgomery issues his final plan for 8th Army's offensive.
October 23: 2125 hours; artillery bombardment begins in the 13th Corps sector. 2140; 30th Corps bombardment begins. 2200 hours; 30th Corps with four divisions and 13th Corps launch two attacks—on Himeimat and Gebel Kalakh.
October 24: 0200 hours; leading elements of 1st and 10th Armoured Divisions begin to move through the corridors. By dawn most units of 30th Corps have reached their 'Oxalic' line objectives, but 10th Corps has been unable to clear the bridgehead and reach 'Pierson'. After a successful start, 13th Corps is held up between the minefields, but is successful in keeping XXI Panzer Division in its sector. By the evening, 1st Armoured Division has got some units out of the minefields, but 10th Armoured Division's attack at 2200 hours makes little progress.
October 25: 0200 hours; congestion in the southern corridor reaches a dangerous level, but after a conference at 0330 hours, Montgomery confirms that the attempt to break out must continue. 0800; the leading brigade moves clear. The New Zealand Division and 8th Armoured Brigade also clear the main minefield and turn to advance south-westward, fighting off counterattacks by XV Panzer. 1200 hours; Montgomery decides to switch the axis of the attack to the north—9th Australian Division is to strike northward and 1st Armoured Division westward behind the coastal salient.
October 26: The 9th Australian Division gains ground, but all other attacks are held; Montgomery decides to regroup—the New Zealand Division moves back into reserve, and is replaced by the 1st South African and 4th Indian Divisions. Two German tankers—the *Proserpina* and the *Tergesta*—are sunk; Panzerarmee's fuel problem becomes acute.
October 27: XXI Panzer moves northward; the British redeployment continues with 7th Armoured Division being withdrawn from 13th Corps and brought north. A series of German attacks on 1st Armoured Division are thrown back with a loss of 50 tanks.
October 28/29: Further attacks by 9th Australian Division in the northern sector drive a wedge into the enemy position.
October 29: Montgomery decides to launch the break-out (Supercharge) as far north as possible, but revises his decision (on hearing that the German 90th Light Division has also moved north) in order to strike Italian not German troops.
October 30/31: The Australian attack continues in an attempt to cut off the enemy forces in the coastal salient.
November 2: 151st and 152nd Brigades launch Operation Supercharge, they reach their objectives successfully, and at 0615 9th Armoured Brigade advances, but is held up by heavy anti-tank fire. The 1st Armoured Division moves through to eliminate the opposition. At 2015 hours, after a conference with General von Thoma, Rommel decides to begin the retreat to the Fuka position.
November 3: Confused fighting, but during the night the break-through is achieved by the 51st and 4th Indian Divisions in the south.
November 4: After further fighting, Axis troops begin to retreat, followed by 1st, 7th and 10th Armoured Divisions.

Even the most devoted fighting by the men of Afrika Korps could not compensate for lack of equipment and fuel, or hold the continual pressure by 8th Army. Here Australian troops bring in a wounded German

GUADALCANAL:
The Land Battles

The Battle of Midway smashed the Japanese chances of further expansion and forced their planners to concentrate upon consolidating their new empire. But the real defeat of Japan could only begin with the recapture of the Pacific Islands, and the first confrontation came on the island of Guadalcanal. US Marines landed against ominously light resistance, but then began a bitter six-month struggle for the possession of a fever-ridden, almost uninhabitable, yet priceless, piece of land

Imperial War Museum

A landing-craft brings in Marines to reinforce the US beach-head on Guadalcanal

241

Eight months to the day after
Pearl Harbor, US ground forces
were taking the offensive in the
Pacific war. . . .

Guadalcanal is a humid, jungle-covered, hilly tropical island in a remote group known as the Solomons which lie on the north-eastern approaches to Australia and which found themselves in a key strategic position early in 1942. If seized by the Japanese, they could be used to cut the sea supply routes between America and Australia, and in American hands they could in the first instance serve as a shield for the Allied build-up in Australia, and later as a springboard for pushing the Japanese out of the South Pacific. The prize to be won by either side was therefore valuable and tempting.

The reason why Washington did not move in was simply that in early 1942 there were not enough ships, aircraft, men, and guns to do all the things that needed to be done in Europe, Africa, the Middle East, Asia, and the Pacific. Consequently Roosevelt and Churchill laid it down that the war against the Axis in Europe had to take priority, and that no more men and resources were to be allocated to the Pacific than were absolutely essential to prevent further Japanese expansion.

Even in Tokyo there was hesitation about whether to advance further, especially in the army. Deeply committed in China, with 1,000,000 men deployed against the possibility of a Russian move into Manchuria and Korea, and with the recently conquered vast new territories to police, the army's resources were already severely strained. Many senior staff officers argued that Japan's best course at that stage of the war was to go over to the strategic defensive, integrate the newly-won territories into the 'Greater East Asia Co-Prosperity Sphere' and consolidate the 'Resources Area' of South-East Asia acquired at such little cost in blood, time, and treasure. Japan, they maintained, now had enough rice, oil, and rubber to fight a long war. Why take on further commitments which might absorb men and material on a scale none could calculate? Let the Americans and their allies wear themselves out trying to throw the Japanese forces out of the territories they had conquered.

The Japanese navy took a different view. Bubbling over with confidence after the heavy losses they had inflicted on the American and British navies in a series of successful engagements, and proud of the precision with which they had transported vast armies and their material safely to different battle areas across enormous expanses of ocean, the admirals argued that to stand still was an admission of defeatism. By thrusting forward further now, Japan

was in a position to deprive her enemies of any hope of ever striking back effectively.

Eventually the navy's view prevailed, and Imperial General Headquarters authorised a series of offensive operations in the islands north and north-east of Australia, including the establishment of air and naval bases in the Solomons. But these plans were soon to be drastically revised and scaled-down by the severe defeat which the navy suffered during the attempt to invade the Midway islands at the end of May.

Tulagi in the Solomons—an island with a magnificent anchorage—and a few adjacent islands were seized at the beginning of May, and it was not until the end of the month that the Japanese arrived on Guadalcanal. At first their only interest in the island seemed to be the stray cattle which they shot and took back to Tulagi. But their every move—no matter how trivial—was closely observed by members of Commander Eric Feldt's Australian coastwatching organisation, a body of men—traders, colonial officers, and planters—who had volunteered to stay behind in the chain of islands shielding Australia and report back what the Japanese were doing. Each member of this unique intelligence network had been provided with a 'teleradio'—a transmitter, receiver, and generator—together with simple but effective codes.

Confrontation on Guadalcanal
By the middle of June, Martin Clemens, the chief Australian coastwatcher on Guadalcanal, had something more serious to report from his jungle hide-out than the slaughter of stray cattle: the Japanese were building an airfield on the north coast of the island between Tenaru and Kukum on the site of a flat coconut grove on Lunga plantation—virtually the only piece of suitable ground in the whole of the Solomon Islands group.

In the weeks that followed, the tempo of work quickened perceptibly. Coconut trees went down in their hundreds, and the site was protected by a system of slit trenches and machine-gun posts; Japanese strength on Guadalcanal was estimated—accurately—at no less than 3,000 men.

With Clemens' ever more alarming reports arriving almost daily, an anxious Washington decided that something had to be done about that bit of level ground on the north coast of Guadalcanal—and done rapidly, for an airfield there would dominate the whole area. One plan was to raid Tulagi and Guadalcanal in strength, destroy Japanese installations there and then withdraw. Admiral Ernest J. King, recently appointed

head of all US naval forces, opposed the idea on the ground that nothing would be gained in the long run by merely irritating and delaying the Japanese. What he wanted was 'to deny the Japanese' the Solomons once and for all, and although General George C. Marshall and other members of the Joint Chiefs-of-Staff in Washington suspected that their colleague, Admiral King—who had not made a secret of his lack of enthusiasm for the Roosevelt-Churchill directive giving the European theatre of war priority—was after something more ambitious in the Pacific than a mere holding operation, they eventually gave their grudging consent. As a result the United States launched its first offensive against the Japanese in the Pacific only eight months after Pearl Harbor.

On paper the assault plan looked splendid: the 1st US Marine Division, reinforced by Marine Raider and parachute units, was to land in the Tulagi/Guadalcanal area on August 1, and establish a 'permanent lodgement'. In practice it appeared a little less rosy. Although the division was nominally up to war strength and had a hard core of seasoned Marines, who knew their weapons and their tactics, thousands were merely new recruits with no experience beyond elementary drill and weapons training. The division had not taken part in any large-scale exercises, many of its units had no experience of amphibious operations—even under peace-time manoeuvre conditions, and when it was dispatched to the Pacific from its training base in North Carolina in May 1942, its commander, Major-General Alexander Archer Vandegrift, had been assured that he and his division would have plenty of time for training and acclimatisation in the Pacific because they were not likely to see combat until some time in 1943. Indeed, the first that General Vandegrift learned of the task assigned him by the Joint Chiefs-of-Staff was when he called on Admiral Ghormley of the US Navy, the commander of the South Pacific area and overall commander of the expedition, in New Zealand on June 25. Half of his division had then still not arrived, and D-Day was only five weeks away.

Nor did the naval side of the operation look more promising. The aircraft-carriers, cruisers, and destroyers allocated to escorting General Vandegrift's division had not operated together before; they had little or no experience of amphibious operations—and had had no time to make good their deficiencies.

Worst of all, the whole undertaking proceeded in what was virtually an intelligence vacuum. Even elementary information about terrain, sea conditions, and weather was lacking. Available maps and charts were ancient and unreliable; in some cases they were later found to be out by as much as 3 to 4 miles in important essentials. Tide tables showed an erratic rise and fall of a few feet, occurring with unpredictable irregularity, and there were no charts of reefs and other underwater hazards so that it was impossible to calculate how far inshore a ship could safely venture.

All these shortcomings could of course have been put right—as they were in scores of subsequent amphibious operations both in the Pacific and in Europe—given time. But in this instance there was no time. Washington reluctantly agreed to two postponements of D-Day, to August 4 and then August 7, but made it quite clear that August 7 had to be the final date.

It was therefore with an acute awareness of what could go wrong that the admirals and generals commanding the various elements of the expedition rendezvoused with their forces in the 'rehearsal area' off Koro in the Fijis on July 26. And the rehearsals of the next four days—which were designed to perfect air and gunfire support plans, resolve difficulties affecting air-ground and ship-to-shore communications, conduct ground-controlled aerial bombing and ship's gunfire, and practise disembarkation procedures—did nothing to lift their gloomiest forebodings. The rehearsals, in one observer's words, were 'a fiasco, a complete bust'. Coral heads prevented most units from landing on the beaches they had been allocated, many boats broke down from mechanical failure, aerial dive-bombing was wild, and ships' gunfire inaccurate. General Vandegrift consoled himself with the thought that a poor dress rehearsal presaged a good performance and tried to put right the most glaring mistakes as best he could in the circumstances. Further exercises were out of the question: the fleet was now on its way.

'A fleet majestical'

In the early hours of August 7, Clemens, who had first reported the construction of a Japanese airfield on Guadalcanal, was woken by the dull reverberations of distant gunfire. At first light, he had a panoramic view from his mountainside hideout in the jungle of what he called 'a fleet majestical', the most powerful amphibious attack force until then ever assembled. While the grey transport ships of the South Pacific Amphibious Force, commanded by Rear-Admiral

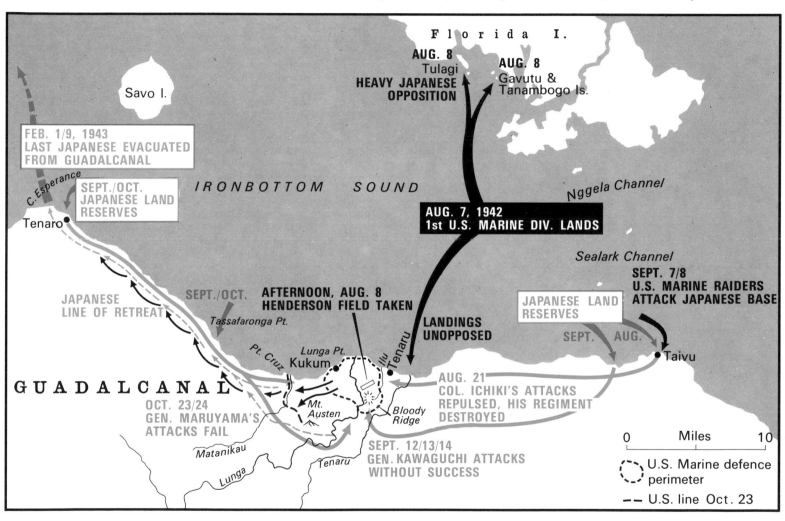

The six-month battle for Guadalcanal

1942 August 7: US Marines land on Guadalcanal, meeting no opposition. But there is savage fighting on the neighbouring islands of Tulagi, Gavutu, and Tanambogo, before they are occupied.
August 8: American forces reach Henderson Field, to find that the Japanese have fled.
August 8/9: The Battle of Savo is fought at sea off Guadalcanal. Admiral Turner's transports are forced to retire, taking much

of the Marines' equipment.
August 18: First Japanese reinforcements, Colonel Ichiki's regiment lands.
August 20: Henderson Field receives its first aircraft—19 Wildcats and 12 Dauntlesses.
August 21/22: *Battle of the Tenaru:* Japanese forces attack across the Ilu and Tenaru rivers. They are driven back with heavy losses but continue to harass the Marines. General Vandegrift sends his reserve battalion around behind them, and the Japanese force is driven into the sea. Colonel Ichiki commits hara-kiri.
August 23/24: The Battle of the Eastern Solomons is fought at sea off Guadalcanal.
September 7: US Marine Raiders land at Taivu, capturing stores and equipment, and gaining intelligence about an impending Japanese attack.
September 12: Japanese bombers attack Henderson Field and the southern perimeter of the defences.
September 13: Japanese launch further heavy

attacks, but they are driven back after losing 1,200 men.
September/October: Japanese II Division and the headquarters of XVII Army HQ are transferred to Guadalcanal. Meanwhile the US 7th Marines, the 164th Infantry Regiment, and other units reinforce the American forces.
October 9: The Battle of Cape Esperance is fought at sea off Guadalcanal.
October 23/24: Two major Japanese assaults are launched on the south of Henderson Field but lack of communication means that they are uncoordinated, and the Americans defeat them piecemeal. Battle of Santa Cruz is fought off Guadalcanal.
December 1/15: US 1st Marine Division is relieved by the 14th Army Corps.
December 31: Appalled by their mounting losses the Japanese begin to plan the withdrawal of XVII Army.

1943 February 1/9: The 'Tokyo Express' takes off the remnant of XVII Army.

To Land The Marines On Guadalcanal

Because of the enormous distances which separated the US Pacific bases from the Japanese-occupied islands, the Americans depended heavily on their ocean-going landing-craft, which had no direct equivalent among the array of British landing-craft. The large illustration shows one of these 'landing-craft (infantry, large)'—the LCI(L)—which did not have an opening bow, but landed its 182 troops by means of twin ramps in the bows. The lighter assault landing-craft (bottom) were the direct equivalent of the British LCAs; they were swung overboard and manned by the troops by means of scrambling-nets from the decks of the parent ship. Like the British at Madagascar and Dieppe, the Americans had many important lessons to learn from the Guadalcanal landings; indeed, the first landing operation was so disorganised that the presence of the Japanese could have spelled disaster. **Specifications for the LCI(L). Capacity:** Six officers, and 182 troops OR 75 tons of cargo. **Range:** 4,000 miles at 12 knots (on 130 tons of fuel). **At beaching draught:** 500 miles at 15 knots. **Armament:** One 40-mm, four 20-mm. **Displacement:** 280 tons (loaded)

John Batchelor

Imperial War Museum

Turner, carrying the landing force moved deliberately to plotted positions off Guadalcanal and neighbouring islands, the British Rear-Admiral Crutchley had disposed the Australian cruisers—*Australia, Hobart,* and *Canberra* and the US cruisers *Chicago* and *San Juan* plus nine destroyers north-east and north-west of Savo Island on the most likely Japanese avenue of approach. In the meantime, out of Clemens' view, the American Vice-Admiral Fletcher's three carriers *Saratoga, Wasp,* and *Enterprise,* manoeuvring 100 miles south of Guadalcanal and screened by the battleship *North Carolina,* six cruisers, and 16 destroyers, provided air cover for the Marines.

The attackers had achieved complete tactical surprise. The Japanese on Guadalcanal and the neighbouring islands of Florida, Tulagi, Gavutu, and Tanambogo did not know that the enemy was upon them until the first shells and bombs burst on the positions.

At 0641 came the order in the transports off Red Beach on Guadalcanal: Land the landing force'. Thousands of tense Marines, grouped in 36-man 'boat teams', streamed down the cargo nets suspended from the decks of the transports. The sea was calm; disembarkation fast and orderly. Loaded boats pulled away from the transports to assembly areas, formed there into 'boat groups' and moved toward the beach in regulated waves. As the hulls of the boats in the first wave jarred to a stop on the white sand, ships' gunfire and aerial bombardment lifted to targets further inland. The ramps of the boats splashed into the warm greenish-blue water, and the Marines, their weapons held high, waded ashore. This was the moment everyone dreaded, expecting to be met with withering fire from the shattered coconut groves that fringed the beach—but there was none. Indeed there was no sign of the Japanese either then or later in the day.

If there had been, the landing operation might well have run into disaster. For by early afternoon, the disembarkation of men and supplies which had started so smoothly was little short of chaotic. As artillery, tanks, jeeps, trucks, and amphibious tractors moved inland, crated equipment, boxed supplies, and drums of fuel piled up alarmingly on Red Beach; untrained navy coxswains brought boats loaded with rations to beach points marked to receive fuel; medical supplies were unceremoniously dumped with ammunition; Marines, landed in late waves, wandered around the beach waiting for someone to tell them what to do; and scores of boats hovered in confusion off shore, their crews looking for a spot to dump

▷Luckily for the Marines, the landing on Guadalcanal met no initial resistance. The Japanese had been taken completely by surprise and not all of them managed to escape into the jungle ▽ But on the islets of Gavutu and Tanambogo, seen here under a US air attack, it was a very different story. It took the 1st Marine Raiders most of August 8 to crush the fierce Japanese resistance

their supplies.

Nor could the progress of the units that pushed inland towards the airfield be called encouraging. Many of the officers as well as the men lacked training and experience. After more than two weeks in the cramped conditions of a combat troop-transport, and now weighed down with heavy equipment in a hot, humid, jungle climate to which they were completely unaccustomed, they were soon near the point of total exhaustion. Moreover, their maps and much of their communication equipment proved unreliable, giving them a feeling of isolation, and when night fell, many nervous sentries, unused to the sounds of the jungle, fired hundreds of rounds at imaginary targets. The Japanese, who had made no attempt anywhere on Guadalcanal to engage the Americans, were greatly puzzled by the uproar.

While there was no fighting on Guadalcanal in the first 24 hours, it was a different story on the neighbouring islands. On the larger island General Vandegrift had, as events had shown, picked as his point of disembarkation a spot where there were no Japanese and his men could go in unopposed. On the smaller islands he could expect no such bonus and it was therefore against these that he threw his more

seasoned units led by officers with previous combat experience.

Colonel Merritt Edson, of 1st Marine Raiders, who was to seize Tulagi, ordered his men to strip down to minimum combat equipment – 'Don't worry about food,' he told them, 'Japs eat it too. All you have to do is get it.' Although their swift landing tactics got them established on the island before noon, stiff Japanese resistance made it impossible to capture the whole island before nightfall, and during the night the Japanese, liberally equipped with light mortars, grenade throwers, and heavy and light machine-guns, counterattacked. Four times they threw themselves against the Raiders and four times they were thrown back. Although most of the Japanese garrison died in these night attacks, it took the Raiders most of August 8 to eliminate the survivors.

The fighting was even tougher on the islet of Gavutu. The islet had been bombed from the air and shelled by ships' guns, but as the paratroops moved inshore, it became clear that the bombardment had had no effect on the defending Japanese in their reinforced dugouts and caves. The paratroops were met by a hail of fire. Their commanders asked for covering gunfire from the warships offshore, but because the waters around Gavutu

were uncharted, none of the warships could move in close enough to give pin-point cover. Only after heavy losses did the paratroops secure a foothold.

On the neighbouring islet of Tanambogo, connected to Gavutu by a causeway, the story was grimmer still; the assault troops and their boats were shot to pieces by the defending Japanese before they touched land. Reinforcements were asked for and arrived on the morning of August 8. The Japanese were blasted and blown out of the caves and dugouts on Gavutu but there remained the problem of Tanambogo. Before crossing over from Gavutu, the American commander asked for two preliminary airstrikes to soften up Tanambogo's defenders, but neither air-strike made any impression. The heaviest casualties were suffered by the American assault troops poised on Gavutu, by bombs that fell short of their target. In despair their commander called on the US destroyer *Buchanan* to open fire on the Japanese in their caves and let go with everything she had. The bombardment was devastating and within minutes assault parties had captured Tanambogo.

On Guadalcanal the Americans had still encountered no Japanese but progress towards the airfield continued to be slow. Only as a result of General Vandegrift's unrelenting drive did the first American patrols eventually reach the airfield late in the afternoon of August 8. The Japanese construction teams and their Naval Landing Force protectors had fled into the jungle after the bombardment in the early hours of August 7. The Japanese had obviously been taken completely by surprise, for there were signs of panic everywhere – uniforms, shirts, caps, chopsticks, helmets, mosquito netting, rifles, teacups, and rice bowls, their contents half-consumed, littered the ground.

It had taken the Americans much longer to reach the airfield than General Vandegrift had hoped, and the speed and control of unloading at the main disembarkation point had shown up serious shortcomings. Moreover, the heavy casualties the Americans had suffered on Tulagi, Gavutu, and Tanambogo – in some cases higher than 20% – showed what tough and resourceful fighters the Japanese were in defence even when outmanned and outgunned.

Still the airfield on Guadalcanal and the islands in the immediate vicinity of the part of the coast of Guadalcanal where the airfield was situated, were in American hands. Despite delays, deficiencies, and mistakes the operation had achieved its objective of denying the Japanese a base from which to cut Allied supply lines and isolate Australia. There was immense relief in Australia, Washington, and London. But the feeling was not to last long. For, on the night of August 8/9, a Japanese cruiser force shattered the Allied naval forces under Admiral Crutchley, and the transports were forced to withdraw.

By the late afternoon of August 9, the last of Admiral Turner's ships had disappeared. The Marines were on their own.

Could the Marines hold out?

The position facing General Vandegrift after Admiral Turner's departure was unenviable. He and his 1st Marine Division held an enclave consisting of a partially completed airfield surrounded by a few acres, on an island covered with dense, inhospitable jungle, in which lurked the remnants of the original Japanese construction and occupation forces. The waters around Guadalcanal were dominated by the Japanese navy. Indeed, in the days that followed, Japanese warships usually patrolled just off his enclave outside the range of his guns. On one occasion a Japanese submarine surfaced and in a leisurely fashion shelled the Marines' position on the beach and on another a Japanese cruiser landed a 200-strong advance echelon and supplies along the coast in broad daylight. Moreover, constant Japanese bombing attacks on 'Henderson' (as the airfield came to be known) and the American-held area around it, never allowed General Vandegrift and his men to forget for long who was in control of the skies above Guadalcanal. Above all, the general knew that the Japanese were bound to try and annihilate his division sooner or later.

His main concern, therefore, was to build up his defences against assault both from the sea and from inland, and to complete the airfield so that it could be used by American aircraft to give him his own air cover. His difficulties in pursuing both these aims were immense, largely because so much essential equipment had sailed away in the holds of Admiral Turner's transports – only 18 spools of barbed wire had been landed; there were no anti-tank or anti-personnel mines, and no tools like axes, saws, shovels, machetes, or picks. Fortunately the equipment left behind by the Japanese – which included four heavy-duty tractors, six road-rollers, 12 trucks, and two petrol locomotives with hopper cars – made good these deficiencies to some extent and within days the airfield was completed and work was begun on two subsidiary strips. On August 20 the first American aircraft – 19 Wildcat fighters and 12 Dauntless dive-bombers launched from an aircraft-carrier well to the south of Guadalcanal – landed on Henderson Field. A few hours later, shortly after midnight, before the aircraft could go into action, the Japanese attacked from the east.

Radio Tokyo had made no secret of its answer to the question of what fate had in store for the Marines on Guadalcanal. Admiral Mikawa (the area commander), it announced in triumph, had routed 'the remnants of Anglo-American naval strength in the Pacific and isolated Australia'. The Marines on Guadalcanal were like 'summer insects which have dropped into the fire by themselves'.

Such exaggerated claims may be excusable in propagandists intent on bolstering the morale of their own side and striking fear into the heart of the enemy. But what was

▷ Major-General A. A. Vandegrift, the commander of 1st US Marine Division on Guadalcanal. By August 9, the US naval close support forces had withdrawn, and his Marines were on their own. The Japanese were strong in the air and at sea—and the general knew that they were bound to try to annihilate his division by land

△ By November, fatigue and strain were lining the faces of Vandegrift's Marines

△ One of the Stuart light tanks which won the Battle of the Tenaru for the Marines

△A US platoon crosses the Lunga, which ran through the Marine defence perimeter
◁ Violent tropical rainstorms added to the difficulties of movement on Guadalcanal
▽ On guard against snipers, a Marine patrol advances cautiously out of the defence zone

Paul Popper

▷ Japanese troops in the Shortland Island base embark for Guadalcanal. The Japanese High Command was contemptuous of the US landings on Guadalcanal, and thought that the Americans would be thrown back into the sea with ease. But once the first US aircraft were flown in to the vital Henderson Field (bottom) on August 20, the Japanese naval support forces could only operate safely by night. Six months later the field was still in American hands – and it was the Americans who were attacking on Guadalcanal

US Navy

astonishing in this instance was that these claims reflected the attitude of many senior Japanese staff officers. Men trained to assess every given situation coolly and without passion and then to lay their plans with care and attention to detail, refused to take the Marines on Guadalcanal seriously. It could, in their view, be no more than a reconnaissance in force, a manoeuvre to distract and annoy, and as such it was an insolent affront to the hónour of Japanese arms which had to be washed away in blood without delay. No attempt was made to obtain an accurate picture of American strength and dispositions. Lieutenant-General Hyakutake, in command of XVII Army in the South Pacific area, was ordered to 'eliminate' the Americans, and he allocated the XXXV Infantry Brigade under Major-General Kawaguchi for the purpose but since the brigade had still to be assembled, it was decided to send in at once, in two echelons, the only units immediately available – Colonel Ichiki's regiment and a special naval landing force.

Colonel Ichiki landed with the first echelon on August 18. He was a distinguished officer who had fought in China in the 1930s, with years of experience as a battalion and regimental commander, but on this occasion he disregarded all he had learned. Japanese Intelligence had told him that the Marines were no more than 2,000 strong and that their morale was low. In any case, Colonel Ichiki was one of many Japanese officers who believed firmly that man for man the Japanese were infinitely superior to the Americans who were only effective when they had superior equipment. He therefore decided that he had no cause to wait even for his second echelon; he could wipe out this

pitiful American 'jungle beach-head' at one stroke.

In the early hours of August 21, after a brief preparatory mortar bombardment of the American positions on General Vandegrift's eastern perimeter, Colonel Ichiki's men who had waded across the Ilu and Tenaru rivers, threw themselves at the Marines in a bayonet charge. They were met and stopped by a deadly wall of fire from carefully sited positions, but somehow Ichiki managed to rally his men and launch a second bayonet charge, only to be stopped again. This time he decided to withdraw across the Ilu.

Only a crack formation like Ichiki's could have survived such a mauling without disintegrating, but the accurate and often telling fire to which the Marines were subjected from across the river on the following morning, told them that they were still facing a fighting unit that had to be reckoned with. General Vandegrift, who had had reports that further Japanese reinforcements were on the way, decided that Ichiki's men constituted too great a danger to be left where they were. He ordered one of his reserve battalions to cross the river further upstream and swing north in an enveloping movement.

By early afternoon Ichiki's men were encircled, and the final phase of what came to be known among the Marines as the 'Battle of the Tenaru' began. Bombed and strafed by the American aircraft that had landed at Henderson Field on the previous day, and bombarded at short range by artillery, the Japanese were pushed back slowly towards the sea from three sides. Finally, the few light tanks which had been landed with Vandegrift's division moved in, their steel treads mangling and crushing the living, the dying, and the dead. But still the Japanese refused to surrender. 'The rear of the tanks,' General Vandegrift wrote in his report, 'looked like meat grinders.' Even after organised fighting had ceased, the Japanese survivors did not allow themselves to be taken prisoner. 'The wounded will wait until men come up to examine them,' Vandegrift wrote, 'and blow themselves and the other fellow to pieces with a hand grenade.' At 'the Tenaru' the Marines learned what the Japanese meant by total resistance, resistance to the last breath of the last man.

Only a handful of men, led by Colonel Ichiki, got away to Taivu further along the coast to the east. There the Colonel ceremoniously tore up his regiment's colour, poured oil over its shreds, set them alight, and committed *hara-kiri*.

The victory at the Tenaru lives on in the history of the US Marine Corps, but General Vandegrift knew that it did not answer the question of whether the Marines could hold out. It was merely the prelude to other stronger attempts by the Japanese. In fact, in the last ten days of August, a far more menacing force consisting of the late Colonel Ichiki's second echelon and General Kawaguchi's XXXV Brigade were waiting to be taken to Guadalcanal to finish the job. The main problem was how to get them there. Rear-Admiral Tanaka, who had been made commander of the Reinforcement Force with his base in the Shortlands to the north-west of Guadalcanal, understood the difficulties. The second echelon of Ichiki's detachment which he had been ordered to take to Guadalcanal in transports screened by a light cruiser and destroyers, had been spotted by aircraft from Henderson Field, bombed, and had had to turn back.

The arrival of the aircraft on Henderson Field had drastically altered the situation: the Japanese, Tanaka pointed out to General Kawaguchi, could only use the waters around Guadalcanal safely between dusk and dawn, and he therefore planned to move the Japanese army to Guadalcanal in a series of what were aptly named 'Rat runs', using fast destroyers as transports at night. Kawaguchi at first insisted on slower and more cumbersome barges being used as transport, and one barge 'run' that was organised against Tanaka's advice, ended in disaster. In the end Tanaka had his way and by the end of August, the 'Rat runs' were dashing back and forth with the precision of express trains, while the Marine positions were regularly bombarded from the sea.

General Vandegrift was aware of the gradual Japanese build-up to the east and west of his position. He brought Colonel Edson's crack Marine Raiders and the paratroops over from Tulagi and after dark on September 7 sent the Raiders by sea on a reconnaissance in force to Taivu, one of the main Japanese bases. Their foray was a complete success: they found only communications and headquarters personnel at the base who promptly fled into the jungle. They also found valuable stores and provisions which they brought back with them. But the most valuable thing they brought back was information about the strength of the forces they would soon have to face and the news that General Kawaguchi had already moved off into the jungle with the bulk of his force. The second Japanese attack could not be long delayed, and General Vandegrift calculated that the

In December 1941 the
US Marines had won
their first battle
honours of the Second
World War in the deter-
mined but doomed
battle to save Wake
Atoll. Eight months
later they were on
the offensive—and
the ordeal of Guadal-
canal, justly, became
another Marine legend

main assault would be launched against the ridge to the south of Henderson Field. It was to this ridge that Vandegrift moved the Raiders and the paratroops, with his reserve —a Marine battalion—immediately behind them. He had no other uncommitted troops.

The Battle of Bloody Ridge

At noon on September 12, when Japanese bombers heavily bombed not Henderson Field, but the ridge south of the airfield, Vandegrift knew that his calculations about Japanese intentions had been correct. Shortly after darkness a Japanese cruiser and three destroyers started shelling the ridge, and when their gunfire ceased, Kawa-guchi's troops began their probing. They cut off one Raider platoon but it fought back into the American lines.

When daylight came the Americans assumed that the Japanese had only been testing. They would have been heartened if they had known that Kawaguchi had intended his attack of the previous night to be decisive. His plan had been to attack the ridge with three battalions while his other units pinned down the Americans on the western and eastern flanks of his perimeter. But his long and arduous march had exhausted his troops, cut his communi-cations with other units of his command, and deprived him of effective control. Despite these handicaps, however, he plunged ahead as recklessly as Ichiki had done before him and rigidly stuck to the order to attack on September 12.

At 2100 hours on September 13, Kawa-guchi renewed his assault. As his two battalions—almost 2,000 men—rushed up the slopes of the ridge, Marine mortars sited in defilade poured shells into the assault waves as fast as loaders could slide them down the hot tubes. Marine artillery just to the rear of the Raiders pumped round after round into the attackers while seven Japanese destroyers shelled Henderson Field, which was illuminated by Japanese flares. On the ridge the Raiders' defences were bent but not broken, and eventually the Japanese fell back. Before long they returned in an assault as fierce as the first. Again the defences were dented but not broken; and again the Japanese fell back.

Two hours later, after a preparatory mor-tar bombardment which cut the Raiders' communications with Vandegrift and sup-porting artillery, the Japanese swept for-ward to within 1,000 yards of Henderson Field, only to be beaten back after some of the most ferocious fighting on Guadalcanal. They launched two more attacks before daybreak noticeably weaker than the first three, and when cannon-firing fighters from Henderson Field strafed the fringes of the jungle below the ridge, Kawaguchi decided to withdraw. He had over 1,200 officers and men killed, missing, and wounded. Hungry and plagued by disease the disorganised remnants of the XXXV Brigade, carrying only their rifles, clawed their way through the jungle for eight grim days to Point Cruz, west of Henderson Field.

The Raiders and the paratroops, too, had suffered heavily. Of slightly over 750 men who had landed on August 7, the Raiders had lost 234 casualties, and of 377 para-troops, 212 had been killed or wounded. But as far as the Marines were concerned, the question whether they could hold Guadalcanal, had been answered in the affirmative.

Imperial General Headquarters in Tokyo

did not share the Marines' view. The XXXVIII Division, veterans of Hong Kong, Java, and Sumatra, were ordered to proceed to the South Pacific to join Lieutenant-General Hyakutake's XVII Army. In the meantime, the II Division under Lieutenant-General Maruyama, which was already in the area, was to be transported to Guadalcanal. Operations on New Guinea against Port Moresby were to be suspended so that all naval, air, and military resources could be concentrated on recapturing Guadalcanal, and General Hyakutake transferred XVII Army HQ to the island, to control a total force of some 20,000 men—including a regiment and three batteries of heavy artillery, a mortar battalion, and a tank company. In the next six weeks Admiral Tanaka's 'Rat run' or 'Tokyo Night Express' was busier than ever, and the Marines were bombarded every night from the sea.

Fortunately General Vandegrift, too, received reinforcements: the 7th Marines, an artillery battalion, motor transport companies, communications personnel, and later 164th Infantry Regiment, US Army—more than 6,000 men altogether, bringing his total strength to over 23,000. And equally vital the air force on Henderson Field was strengthened considerably. On paper Vandegrift's force looked impressive; in practice, it was less so. Although battle casualties had not yet reached 1,000, large numbers of Marines suffered from malnutrition, dysentery, virulent fungus infections, exposure, and plain exhaustion. In other less exposed battle areas more than a third of the men would have been declared unfit for combat.

On October 23 the Japanese II Division —consisting of some eight battalions totalling 5,600 troops, attacked the eastern perimeter in force with tanks across the Matanikau river. Concentrated artillery fire brought their advance to a bloody halt. Then, 24 hours later, General Maruyama attacked with the main force of more than 7,000 men from the south. For two days the Japanese flung themselves against the ridges to the south of Henderson Field—at one stage there was a Japanese enclave inside the perimeter—and then, like Kawaguchi's brigade, they sank back into the jungle, decimated and exhausted, having lost 3,500 men.

What had happened was that Japanese communications had broken down once again. Maruyama's approach march through the jungle—which had begun on October 16—had been slower and more arduous than he had expected, and the artillery and mortars had had to be abandoned. Twice Maruyama had to postpone his offensive, and the second time, news of the postponement did not reach the Japanese commander on the Matanikau. Instead of being simultaneous, the two assaults took place 24 hours apart and General Vandegrift, operating on interior lines, was able to defeat each in turn.

General Vandegrift had now defeated three attempts by the Japanese to dislodge him, and both the Americans and the Japanese had to face the problem of what to do next. For Vandegrift and Admiral Halsey, who had recently replaced Admiral Ghormley as Area Commander, there was no doubt about the answer: it was time to go over to the offensive and drive what remained of the XVII Army out of Guadalcanal. It was equally obvious to both officers that the 1st Marine Division, after all it had been through, was not the ideal instrument for a long, harsh, and bitter offensive. Fresher and bigger units were required. And so after spending November in extending the perimeter and reducing threatening Japanese outposts around it in preparation for future offensive action, General Vandegrift and the 1st Marine Division were relieved at the beginning of December, and their place taken by the 25th Infantry Division, US Army, the 2nd Marine Division, and the America Division—all combined as 14th Corps under General Patch.

For the Japanese the problem was whether to go on trying to wrest Henderson Field and the shattered coconut groves around it from the Americans. Imperial General Headquarters refused to accept defeat; fresh divisions and brigades from distant parts of the Empire were allocated to XVII Army and Lieutenant-General Sano's XXVIII Division was ordered to Guadalcanal, in preparation for a fourth determined attempt to drive out the Americans to be launched about the middle of January 1943. But in mid-November 1942 a US naval squadron, despite crippling losses, stopped a Japanese squadron from bombarding Henderson Field, and neutralising its air force, and the Henderson Field aircraft, saved by this gallant action, pounced on a convoy of 11 transports in which the bulk of General Sano's division was being taken to Guadalcanal. Six transports were sunk, one was crippled, and four had to be beached. Only 2,000 men, most of them without equipment, reached Guadalcanal. The drain in men and resources, Imperial General Headquarters decided reluctantly after much argument, was too great to sustain any longer. Since August 7, the Japanese had lost 65 combat ships and more than 800 aircraft. On December 31, 1942, the Emperor gave his approval to the withdrawal of the XVII Army from Guadalcanal.

General Hyakutake accepted the order reluctantly. As he withdrew to the east, 14th Corps learned how tough and resourceful even starving and ill-equipped Japanese troops could be in defensive jungle warfare. At no time during January and early February were the Americans able to upset the pace and timing of the withdrawal, and between February 1 and 9 the destroyers of the 'Tokyo Night Express' took off what remained of the XVII Army—11,000 men, only a fraction of those who had arrived to drive the Americans into the sea but still a fighting force destined to return to do battle another day.

For the Americans and their allies the successful seizure and defence of Guadalcanal brought immense advantages. Australia and New Zealand were safe, and Allied forces now stood on the flank of the Palau/Truk/Marshalls line, the outer cordon of the Japanese empire.

CHARLES ROETTER was educated at Merchant Taylors' and later read law at London and Cambridge. During the Second World War he served in the Political Intelligence Department of the Foreign Office, where he was concerned with political warfare and propaganda operations. Since the war he has travelled widely in Europe, the United States, and the Soviet Union. He writes and broadcasts regularly on current affairs, history, geography, and the mechanics of government.

US Navy

The end of the US carrier *Wasp*, after being torpedoed by the Japanese submarine I-19

South-West Pacific, August/October 1942 *Captain Donald Macintyre*

The struggle of the Marines on Guadalcanal was accompanied by an equally bloody campaign at sea to intercept the 'Tokyo Express', and secure control of the approaches. In one disastrous action off Savo Island the Allied naval force had been shattered, and thereafter the Japanese controlled 'The Slot' at night—bringing in supplies and shelling the Marines with impunity

GUADALCANAL:
The Sea Battles

The Battle of Midway checked the overweening Japanese ambitions which had been engendered by the previous run of easy victories, and only slightly marred by the strategic set-back of the Coral Sea Battle. The Japanese High Command now reverted to its original plan, which at this stage called for a halt to expansion while the perimeter of Japan's vast new possessions was consolidated.

In the South Pacific, plans to occupy New Caledonia, Fiji, and Samoa were abandoned. From Rabaul on New Britain—which was to be built up into a main naval and air base—a firm grip on the Solomon Islands, the Bismarck Archipelago, and Papua was to be established. In command of the area was appointed Vice-Admiral Gunichi Mikawa.

The Allies, by now gathering strength in the South Pacific to counterattack after the unbroken retreat of the first six months of the war, were meanwhile planning to advance up the Solomon Islands chain, starting with the occupation of the Santa Cruz Islands and going on to recapture Tulagi and the area adjacent to it.

But this plan was swiftly changed when it was realised that the Japanese were building an airfield on Guadalcanal. Everything must be subordinated to its speedy capture.

Nevertheless, in spite of the most furious efforts, it was not until August 6 that, after making rendezvous south of Fiji and spending a few days in impromptu landing rehearsals for the unfledged Marines of the 1st US Marines Division, a hastily gathered armada approached the eastern entrance of Indispensable Strait between Guadalcanal and Malaita to make simultaneous landings at Lunga Point and Tulagi at dawn the following day (see map on page 1095).

A fanatical but hopeless defence

Surprise was an essential feature if the amphibious force was to avoid being attacked at that most vulnerable moment. Fortune favoured it by providing rain and low cloud to shroud its approach; and so, when Mikawa was woken early on the 7th by an urgent radio message from Tulagi, the US Marines were already landing there and on Guadalcanal. At Tulagi the little Japanese garrison put up a fanatical but hopeless defence against overwhelming numbers. At Guadalcanal only a Japanese labour battalion opposed the invaders, and the airfield was quickly occupied.

Disembarkation of the Marines' equipment, artillery, ammunition, and food was the next essential for permanent occupation of the airstrip, now christened Henderson Field after a Marine hero of Midway. Mikawa's immediate object was to prevent this by attacking the throng of transports in Lunga Roads: within two hours of receipt of the alarm from Tulagi, his bombers with fighter escort were on their way. Warnings of their approach reached the Allied command from the Australian naval lieutenants, P. E. Mason and W. J. Read on Bougainville Island—two of the numerous 'coast-watchers' left behind on the various islands with portable radio sets when the Australians had been forced by the Japanese advance to evacuate, and who were to supply invaluable intelligence in the months to come. From Fletcher's aircraft-carriers, operating to the south of Guadalcanal, 60 Wildcats were flown off. A furious battle developed over the Roads in which 14 Japanese bombers and two Zeros were shot down for

the loss of 11 Wildcats. The transports remained unscathed.

The following day the bombers returned, armed now with torpedoes. But Rear-Admiral Turner, forewarned, had his ships under way. The only torpedo hit scored was on the US destroyer Jarvis, which was severely damaged; a burning bomber crashed into a transport and set it ablaze to become eventually a total loss. For these meagre results the attackers paid with the loss of 17 bombers.

Nevertheless disembarkation of vital equipment had been disrupted; when the transports returned to their anchorage at dusk another day of unloading still lay ahead. As the black, tropical night settled down, Admiral Crutchley's force of cruisers and destroyers took up their defensive stations. To the west the approaches were divided by the steep jungle-clad little island of Savo. To the east, a less likely route for an approaching enemy threaded the Lengo and Sealark Channels between Florida Island and Guadalcanal. To each of these lines of approach, Crutchley allocated a squadron of cruisers and destroyers. A Southern Group, composed of the Australian cruisers Australia (Crutchley's flagship) and Canberra, each mounting eight 8-inch guns, the US heavy cruiser Chicago with nine 8-inch, and the destroyers Patterson and Bagley, were to patrol between Guadalcanal and Savo. To the north and east of Savo were stationed the 8-inch-gun cruisers Vincennes, Quincy, and Astoria and the destroyers Helm and Wilson; while in the eastern approaches were the US light cruiser San Juan, flagship of Rear-Admiral Scott, the Australian light cruiser Hobart, and two destroyers. Beyond Savo, as distant pickets, the destroyer Blue covered the southern route, the Ralph Talbot the northern, each equipped with an early type of radar with limited surface capabilities.

There was no great expectation that any of these forces would see action that night. Although air reconnaissance had reported some naval activity in the vicinity of Rabaul, and although it was also learned that the American submarine S-38 had seen two destroyers and three larger ships of unknown type emerging from the St. George's Channel between New Britain and New Ireland at 2000 hours on the previous evening, nothing further had been heard from the scouting aircraft covering the waters between Rabaul and Guadalcanal. Even when a much delayed report came in at 1845 hours of 'Three cruisers, three destroyers, and two seaplane tenders' north of Bougainville during the forenoon of the 8th, Admiral Turner assumed that this was simply an expedition proceeding to set up a seaplane base somewhere among the islands.

It was for quite another reason that, early in the evening, Turner summoned Crutchley to a conference aboard the former's flagship, the transport McCawley, in Lunga Roads. Turner had just heard that Admiral Fletcher was withdrawing his aircraft-carrier force and wished to discuss the implications. Giving orders for the Australia to be taken into the Roads, Crutchley turned over the tactical command of the Southern Group to Captain Bode of the Chicago.

The Battle of Savo

All unknown to anyone in the Allied force, towards them through the night was racing the whole of Mikawa's cruiser strength.

These were the ships which had been belatedly and inaccurately reported first by the S-38 and later by an aircraft which had seen them as they were 'marking time' north of Bougainville. While doing so, Mikawa from his flagship Chokai had catapulted scout seaplanes to reconnoitre. By mid-day they had reported the transports clustered off Tulagi and Lunga Point. They also claimed to have seen—besides six cruisers and a large number of destroyers—a battleship. Nothing daunted, however, Mikawa had signalled for 24 knots and set course through the Bougainville Strait into 'The Slot', the long strip of water between the two island chains, timing his approach to arrive off Savo at 0100 hours.

The Japanese were supremely confident—and with good reason. Though they had no radar, their crews had been for years intensively trained in night fighting, great risks being taken in the process and accidents accepted. They were provided with huge night binoculars with which they had developed night vision of an excellence only attainable through constant practice. Every cruiser and destroyer carried the weapon best suited to night action—the deadly 'Long Lance', 24-inch liquid-oxygen propelled torpedo, which carried a 1,000-pound warhead at 36 knots for 44,000 yards or at 49 knots for 22,000 yards.

Opposed to them was a recently assembled mixed force with different signal systems and night-fighting procedure and which, in any case, had had no recent night encounter practice; nor had they fired their guns at a target by night during the previous eight months. The professional, indeed, was matched with an amateur.

At 2313 hours, with 90 miles to go to reach Savo, Mikawa again launched his seaplanes to reconnoitre and illuminate the enemy when the right moment came. They were seen overhead, with their navigation lights burning, by the Allied ships an hour or so later and were dismissed as 'friendly'. Shortly before 0100 hours, look-outs in the Chokai reported first the destroyer Blue and then the Ralph Talbot. Mikawa's seven cruisers and one destroyer slipped unsighted and unsuspected between them. At 0130 hours, as the Japanese force was entering the channel between Savo and Guadalcanal, another destroyer steering slowly on an opposite course was sighted and avoided—the damaged Jarvis, leaving for Sydney and dockyard repairs. A minute or two later the silhouettes of the Canberra and Chicago of the Southern Group were in sight. The order to attack was given and at 0138 hours the first of a wave of torpedoes sped away towards their victims, steaming on a roughly opposite course through the calm, oppressive tropical night at 12 knots, the cruisers in line ahead with the Canberra leading and a destroyer on either bow.

The false calm was brusquely shattered when, almost simultaneously, look-outs in the Canberra and the destroyers shouted the warning of ships in sight ahead; astern of them an aircraft flare blossomed whitely, and down each side of the Canberra torpedo tracks were seen. Before the Australian cruiser could even bring her guns to bear on the dimly seen enemy, a storm of shells, 8-inch and smaller, smothered her upper-works and tore open her high, unarmoured hull. Steam-power lost, she came to a halt, a blazing wreck.

Astern of her the Chicago shuddered when a torpedo exploded against her   ▷

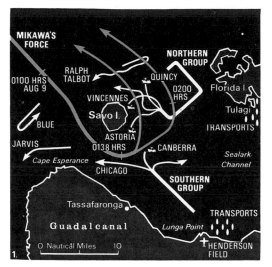

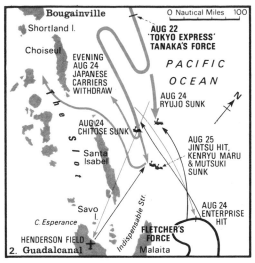

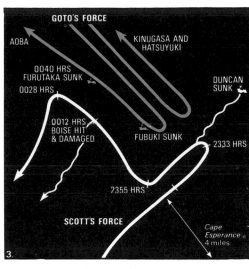

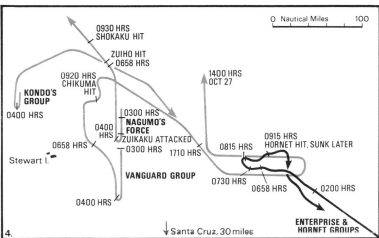

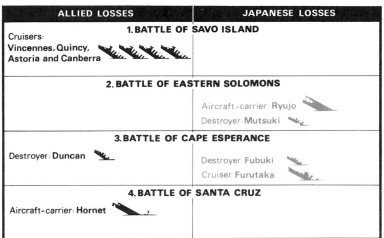

ALLIED LOSSES	JAPANESE LOSSES
1. BATTLE OF SAVO ISLAND	
Cruisers: **Vincennes, Quincy, Astoria and Canberra**	
2. BATTLE OF EASTERN SOLOMONS	
	Aircraft-carrier: **Ryujo**
	Destroyer: **Mutsuki**
3. BATTLE OF CAPE ESPERANCE	
Destroyer: **Duncan**	Destroyer: **Fubuki**
	Cruiser: **Furutaka**
4. BATTLE OF SANTA CRUZ	
Aircraft-carrier: **Hornet**	

1. SAVO ISLAND—August 8/9, 1942

A Japanese cruiser force under Vice-Admiral Mikawa advances down 'The Slot' to attack the American transports unloading off Guadalcanal. An Allied cruiser force under Rear-Admiral Crutchley RN, divided into three squadrons, patrols the approaches around Savo Island. 0100 hours: The Japanese cruisers slip past the destroyers *Blue* and *Ralph Talbot*. 0138 hours: The cruisers *Canberra* and *Chicago* are sighted and disabled with accurate gunfire. When the *Vincennes, Quincy,* and *Astoria* intervene, they too are disabled. The Japanese then retire, damaging the *Ralph Talbot* as they go.

2. EASTERN SOLOMONS—August 23, 1942

An attempt to run supplies to the Japanese troops on Guadalcanal is supported by the aircraft-carriers *Shokaku, Zuikaku,* and *Ryujo*. Vice-Admiral Fletcher's Task Force 61, patrolling to the east of the Solomon Islands, sights the Japanese fleet. The Japanese reverse course, and avoid the American strike aircraft.
August 24: *Ryujo,* sailing ahead of the main Japanese fleet, is sighted by an American flying boat. An armed reconnaissance is flown off from *Enterprise,* and followed, at 1345 hours, by a strike force from *Saratoga*. *Ryujo* launches her aircraft to attack Henderson Field. Just as the American strike flies off, another reconnaissance aircraft sights *Shokaku* and *Zuikaku,* who have launched a massive striking force. An attempt to divert the US aircraft to the new target fails, but the *Ryujo* is sunk. *Enterprise* is hit three times by dive-bombers, but is able to continue recovering her aircraft.

3. CAPE ESPERANCE—October 11/12, 1942

American supply convoy sails for Guadalcanal. It is escorted by a cruiser squadron commanded by Rear-Admiral Scott, which is also to ambush any Japanese forces moving down the Slot.
October 11/12: A Japanese convoy, covered by Rear-Admiral Goto's cruiser squadron, moves down the Slot. Scott receives information of its approach, and steers to intercept it. 2325 hours: The cruiser *Helena*'s radar detects the Japanese at a range of 14 miles but she fails to inform Scott. At 2333 hours he decides to reverse course, but in the confusion the cohesion of his force is broken. Scott then learns of the enemy's approach. The destroyer *Duncan* attacks independently, and the *Helena* opens fire, followed by the other cruisers. An order to cease fire does not take effect until the *Aoba* and *Furutaka* have been severely damaged. The Japanese turn and retreat, and during the pursuit they damage the *Boise* and lose the destroyer *Fubuki*.

▷ **Left:** Vice-Admiral Gunichi Mikawa, who was responsible for the Solomons area. His rival was Rear-Admiral W. Halsey **(right)**, who replaced Ghormley as commander, South Pacific

4. SANTA CRUZ—October 24/26, 1942

The Japanese Combined Fleet moves to the north of Guadalcanal, ready to fly aircraft in to Henderson Field as soon as it is captured.
October 24: US Task Force 16 *(Enterprise)* rejoins Task Force 17 *(Hornet),* and is ordered to sweep in a wide circle around the Santa Cruz Islands to intercept any Japanese forces approaching Guadalcanal.
October 25: At noon an American flying boat sights two Japanese aircraft-carriers, but an American strike fails to make contact.
October 26: The Japanese fleet is again sighted and the *Enterprise* launches 16 dive-bombers to make an armed reconnaissance. At 0658 hours the Japanese aircraft-carriers *(Shokaku, Zuikaku,* and *Zuiho)* launch a first striking force. As a second force is being ranged up, two of the *Enterprise*'s dive-bombers attack *Zuiho* and put her out of action. 0730/0815 hours: *Enterprise* and *Hornet* launch three small strike forces. 0822 hours: *Shokaku* and *Zuikaku* launch their second strike. The main Japanese attack falls on *Hornet,* which is struck by two torpedoes and six bombs. Meanwhile *Shokaku* is seriously damaged by American dive-bombers. The second Japanese strike concentrates on the *Enterprise;* her forward lift is put permanently out of action, but her speed and manoeuvrability are unaffected. A third Japanese strike fails to achieve any results. The American forces then withdraw. *Hornet* is sunk by the Japanese when they find her burning hulk.

253

CRUISERS: KEY WARSHIPS IN THE GUADALCANA

When the battle for Guadalcanal began in August 1942, the sea approaches to that vitally important island were dominated during the daylight hours by air power. And since two-thirds of the Japanese carrier fleet had been shattered at the Battle of Midway, and the Americans held the only air base in the Solomon Islands, air power was largely in American hands. No Japanese surface forces dared operate by day in those waters, but as darkness fell, the surface forces of both sides—particularly the cruisers and destroyers—moved in and clashed in savage combat in the narrow straits between the islands. In these skirmishes the Japanese showed themselves initially the masters. The Americans had radar, but the Japanese crews were trained to the highest pitch of night-fighting efficiency, and they had the superb 'Long Lance' torpedo—better than any torpedo in the American armoury. Japanese tactics were also superior to those used by the Americans. During the long battle for the Solomon Islands, every one of the pre-war American cruisers involved was sunk or damaged. But the Americans had enormous reserves of ships and men to throw into the fight, whereas the Japanese ships and their crack crews, exhausted by battle after battle, were irreplaceable

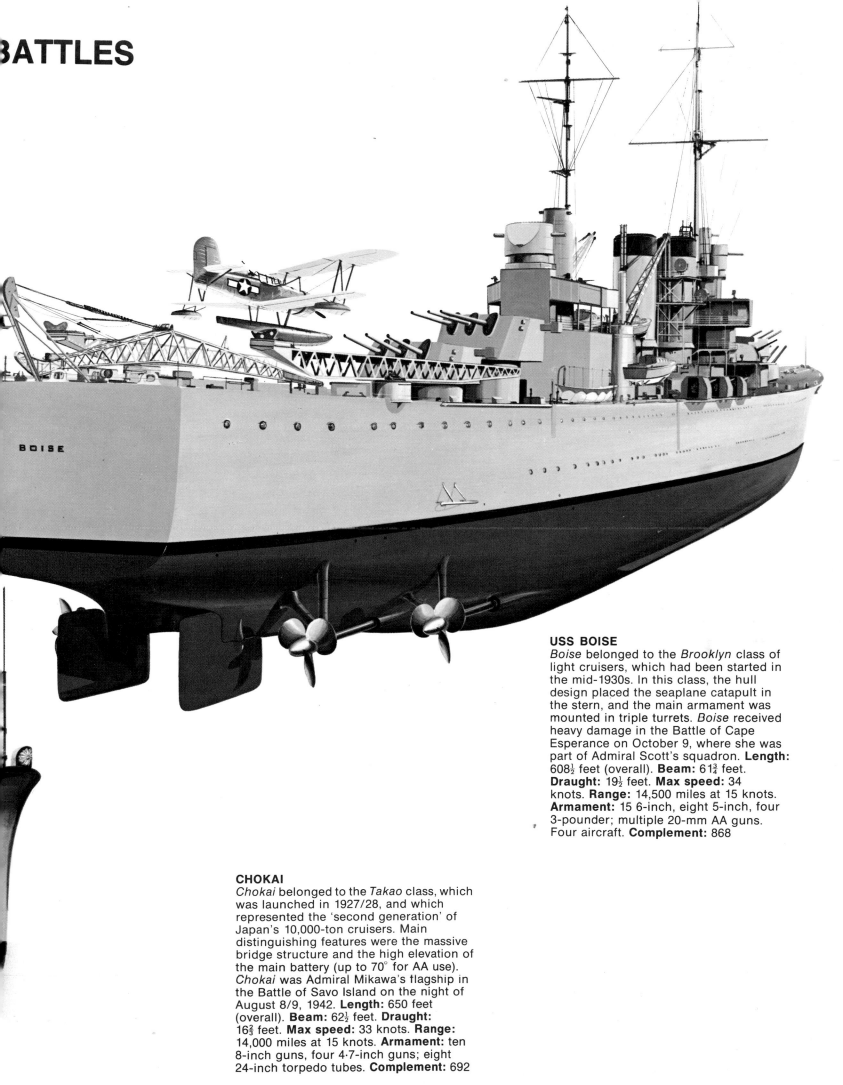

USS BOISE

Boise belonged to the *Brooklyn* class of light cruisers, which had been started in the mid-1930s. In this class, the hull design placed the seaplane catapult in the stern, and the main armament was mounted in triple turrets. *Boise* received heavy damage in the Battle of Cape Esperance on October 9, where she was part of Admiral Scott's squadron. **Length:** 608½ feet (overall). **Beam:** 61¾ feet. **Draught:** 19½ feet. **Max speed:** 34 knots. **Range:** 14,500 miles at 15 knots. **Armament:** 15 6-inch, eight 5-inch, four 3-pounder; multiple 20-mm AA guns. Four aircraft. **Complement:** 868

CHOKAI

Chokai belonged to the *Takao* class, which was launched in 1927/28, and which represented the 'second generation' of Japan's 10,000-ton cruisers. Main distinguishing features were the massive bridge structure and the high elevation of the main battery (up to 70° for AA use). *Chokai* was Admiral Mikawa's flagship in the Battle of Savo Island on the night of August 8/9, 1942. **Length:** 650 feet (overall). **Beam:** 62½ feet. **Draught:** 16⅔ feet. **Max speed:** 33 knots. **Range:** 14,000 miles at 15 knots. **Armament:** ten 8-inch guns, four 4·7-inch guns; eight 24-inch torpedo tubes. **Complement:** 692

port bow, though without inflicting crippling damage. Unable to see the enemy, she opened fire with star shells which failed to ignite, and blundered blindly on to the westward—and out of the action. For Mikawa's force had raced by and, sighting the Northern Group to the north-east, turned to engage. There, the senior officer, Captain Riefkohl of the *Vincennes,* leading the *Quincy* and *Astoria* with a destroyer on either bow, had been called from his berth with the report of aircraft flares overhead and gunfire to the southwest. In the other cruisers, too, the captains were still trying to discover what was going on when the blinding bedlam of night action broke out around. A hail of shells shattered them, setting them furiously ablaze before they could do more than make a brief and ineffective reply.

All three were left in a sinking condition as the Japanese raced past and away, circling Savo Island, briefly savaging the *Ralph Talbot* before disappearing into the night on their way back to base. Behind them were left four cruisers sunk or sinking, another and a destroyer damaged. It was but a small measure of revenge that was exacted by the submarine S-44 when she intercepted the Japanese cruisers on the morning of August 10 and sent the *Kako* to the bottom.

Mikawa had given a brilliant display of night-fighting. But he had not achieved his main objective—the destruction of the transports. With enemy aircraft-carriers in the vicinity, as he believed, he had not dared to linger. Yet, in fact, Turner was forced to order a retirement of his amphibious force on the evening of the 9th, partly on account of the annihilation of its defensive squadron, but equally because Fletcher had withdrawn his aircraft-carriers, a decision which was to be subsequently much criticised.

A six-month struggle begins
Both sides now entered on a six-months struggle for possession of the almost uninhabitable fever-infested island of mountain, jungle, and swamp, the outcome of which was to mark the turn of the tide of Japanese expansion. And while ashore the troops fought fierce battles under appalling conditions, at sea an equally bloody campaign to secure control of the approaches was played out.

Japanese land forces in the South-West Pacific were commanded by General Hyakutake at Rabaul. The majority of his troops were committed to an operation to capture Port Moresby across the Owen Stanley Mountains of Papua. But, underestimating the American strength on Guadalcanal, he believed that a small reinforcement of the troops which had been ejected from Henderson Field would be sufficient to recapture it. Loading 815 troops into six destroyers, he landed them to the east of the field during the night of August 18/19. This was the first of many night runs—which were to be known to the exasperated Americans as the 'Tokyo Express'—by ships under the command of Rear-Admiral Raizo Tanaka, whose stubborn persistence in the face of great odds and heavy casualties was to earn him the sobriquet of 'Tenacious Tanaka'.

It was wasted effort on this occasion. Engaged by the US Marines in the Battle of the Tenaru River, the Japanese force was wiped out. Failing to profit by this experience, the Japanese decided to run another small reinforcement; this time the Tokyo Express, escorted by Tanaka in his

light cruiser flagship *Jintsu* and destroyers, would be given support by a powerful fleet including the big aircraft-carriers *Shokaku* and *Zuikaku* operating to the north of the Solomons. The Japanese C-in-C, Admiral Yamamoto, thus hoped to draw the weaker American fleet in the area into close action, a bait being offered in the shape of the light aircraft-carrier *Ryujo* operating ahead of the main body to send her bombers to harry the Marine positions on Guadalcanal.

As soon as these moves became apparent, Admiral Ghormley ordered Fletcher's Task Force 61, centred on the aircraft-carriers *Saratoga, Enterprise,* and *Wasp* to the east of the Solomons. On August 23, scouting planes reported part of the Japanese fleet, and from the *Saratoga* a striking force of dive-bombers and torpedo aircraft was flown off. The Japanese, however, realising they

△ Rear-Admiral Raizo Tanaka, master tactician of the cruiser/destroyer night actions in the Slot

△ Santa Cruz: the Americans attack. The Japanese cruiser *Chikuma* takes evasive action

▽ Santa Cruz: the Japanese attack. A Kate makes a torpedo run on the *South Dakota*

▽ Santa Cruz: *Hornet,* the fourth US carrier lost in 1942, ablaze after a Japanese attack

had been discovered, reversed course and, in rain and low cloud, the American aviators failed to find a target. Suspecting a mare's nest, Fletcher now detached the *Wasp's* group to refuel at a rendezvous 240 miles to the south.

The Battle of the Eastern Solomons

Early the next day the sacrificial goat *Ryujo* was sighted and reported by an American scouting flying boat. Fletcher steered to close this contact as much as possible and launched an armed reconnaissance of 29 bombers and torpedo-planes from the *Enterprise*. Then, at 1345 hours, a striking force of 30 dive-bombers and eight Avenger torpedo aircraft took off from the *Saratoga* to attack the *Ryujo* which, by this time, had herself launched her strike aircraft to bomb Henderson Field.

As at the Coral Sea, Fletcher had committed the majority of his strike force to attack a subsidiary target. When the scout planes from the *Enterprise* discovered the *Shokaku* and *Zuikaku*, he tried to divert his main strike on to them but communication difficulties arose. The *Ryujo* was set upon and, torn open by 1,000-pound bombs and a torpedo, was sent to the bottom. The *Shokaku* was attacked by only a few of the aircraft from the *Enterprise* which inflicted only minor damage.

Meanwhile the two big Japanese aircraft-carriers had launched a massive striking force in two groups. Their targets, Fletcher's two aircraft-carriers, awaited the onslaught as they manoeuvred separately, each with her circular screen of cruisers and destroyers, the *Enterprise's* escort including the new battleship *North Carolina* mounting a huge array of anti-aircraft guns. Fletcher had prudently retained a large defensive force of Wildcat fighters so that no less than 51, stacked in three layers, were aloft when the approach of the first strike was detected by radar.

Fighter direction, however, had not reached the standard of later periods of the war. Friendly aircraft returning mingled on the radar screens with enemy aircraft. Towering cumulus clouds screened attackers during the approach and baffled the questing defensive fighters. Lack of good radio discipline filled the air with an excited jumble of 'Tally-ho's' and gossip. Amid the confusion, though a number of Japanese aircraft were intercepted and shot down — and not a single torpedo-plane broke through — the main body of Val dive-bombers, some 30 strong, arrived undetected at 18,000 feet over the *Enterprise* and plunged to the attack. The storm of gunfire that met them accounted for many; but others survived long enough to release their bombs accurately. Three hit the flight deck of the *Enterprise*, two of them penetrating to lower decks before exploding.

Damage control technique had greatly improved since the time similar damage had proved fatal to the *Lexington*, and within an hour the *Enterprise* was steaming at 24 knots into wind, recovering her aircraft. Nevertheless she was in mortal peril again later when her steering gear broke down and she lay immobilised at the very moment the second Japanese strike appeared on the radar screen. Fortune smiled, however: the Japanese failed to find their targets, and after a fruitless search turned back to their aircraft-carriers.

The *Saratoga* had meanwhile been left unmolested and a small force of dive-bombers and torpedo-planes flown off from her had found and seriously damaged the seaplane-carrier *Chitose*. The aircraft-carriers of both sides retired at sundown, bringing the Battle of the Eastern Solomons to an indecisive end.

The main objective of the Japanese, the reinforcement of their troops on Guadalcanal, was frustrated the following day when Tanaka's squadron, pressing stubbornly on though his covering force had retired, was pounced on by Marine dive-bombers from Henderson Field. His flagship, *Jintsu*, and the ex-light cruiser transport *Kenryu Maru*, were both hit and set on fire. When further attacks by Flying Fortresses from Espiritu Santo sent one of his destroyers as well as the transport to the bottom, Tanaka was ordered to retire to the advanced base in the Shortland Islands whence the night runs of the Tokyo Express would be resumed.

Attrition and attempted intervention

At sea attrition was exacting its toll principally from the Americans at this time. Several destroyer-transports or escorts were sunk in clashes with the Tokyo Express. The *Saratoga* had been torpedoed by a Japanese submarine on August 31 and put out of action for three months. Two weeks later the aircraft-carrier *Wasp*, part of an escort for a transport convoy, was sunk, and the *North Carolina* and a destroyer damaged, by torpedoes from two submarines.

When the next large American reinforcement, embarked in two big transports and eight destroyer types, sailed for Guadalcanal on October 9, Ghormley decided to send a cruiser striking force to cover it from the west and at the same time to ambush the almost nightly Japanese excursions down the Slot. This force, commanded by Rear-Admiral Norman Scott, was composed of the 8-inch-gun cruisers *San Francisco* and *Salt Lake City*, the 6-inch-gun cruisers *Boise* and *Helena*, and five destroyers.

At the same time, as yet unknown to the Americans, the Japanese had at last woken up to the overriding importance of recapturing Guadalcanal as opposed to that of taking Port Moresby. During the night of October 9/10, General Hyakutake himself landed from a light cruiser to take command of operations, accompanied by several hundred fresh troops. The trickle of supplies and reinforcements being run in by small fast craft was obviously insufficient. Transports would have to be used, accepting the risk of air attack during their approach down the Slot. As a first step, however, two seaplane-carriers and six destroyers were to bring in troops and supplies, including heavy artillery, during the night October 11/12. To cover this convoy, Rear-Admiral Goto was to bring his cruiser squadron, the *Aoba*, *Kinugasa*, and *Furutaka* and two destroyers, from Rabaul and, as soon as the landings had been accomplished, carry on to bombard Henderson Field.

Information of their approach reached Scott during the 11th to the south of Guadalcanal, where he had been waiting for three days for just such news. He steered at once to intercept and when night fell, dark and clear, with only a light breeze ruffling the surface of the sea, he was running at 29 knots up the western end of Guadalcanal.

Scott had been present, an appalled spectator, at the calamitous Battle of Savo, the outcome of which he had ascribed largely to the lack of concentration and the divided command of the Allied force. He had decided,

therefore, to keep all his ships under his tight, personal control. Although he had given them intensive training in night action, signalling shortcomings and inexperience of night encounter were still such as to make single line ahead the only safe formation. It was therefore with three destroyers, *Farenholt*, *Duncan*, and *Laffey*, leading his flagship, with the three other cruisers followed by the destroyers *Buchanan* and *McCalla* bringing up the rear, a single line at least 2½ miles long, that he advanced. He possessed the inestimable advantage over the Japanese of up-to-date radar; but unfortunately this was housed in his two light cruisers only and not in his flagship.

An hour before midnight Scott was some 8 miles north of the western tip of Guadalcanal, steering north-east at 20 knots across the expected line of advance of the Japanese force. Goto, unaware of Scott's presence in the area, was hurrying forward at 26 knots down the middle of the Slot, his three cruisers in line ahead with a destroyer on either bow. At 2325 hours the *Helena's* radar detected him at a range of 14 miles but failed to inform the flagship where the admiral, at 2333 hours, deciding he had gone far enough to the north-east, ordered a reversal of course.

For some reason the manoeuvre ordered was neither a simultaneous turn by every ship nor a wheel in succession, either of which would have kept Scott's force in a single, orderly body. Instead the leading destroyer and the leading cruiser (*San Francisco*) altered course to port together so that the three destroyers in the van would have to increase speed and overtake the main body to regain their assigned station. Thus when Scott at last learned from the *Helena* of the enemy's presence, well within gun range at about 5 miles, the van destroyers were steering to pass between him and the enemy — or, rather, two of them were: the *Duncan*, having gained radar contact with the enemy during the turn, had charged off to the attack on her own.

The cohesion of Scott's force had broken down at the most critical moment. When the *Helena*, from which the enemy had come in sight at the close range of 5,000 yards, opened fire, she was quickly ordered to cease fire because Scott feared the target might be his own destroyers. Fortunately the order was disregarded long enough for the total surprise achieved by the American force to reap its reward.

The Battle of Cape Esperance

The Japanese, accustomed to having the Slot to themselves by night, and displaying an unwonted lack of alertness, had been caught with their gun-turrets still trained fore and aft when the *Helena's* first salvo erupted on and around the bridge of the *Aoba*, followed seconds later by shells from the other American cruisers which set the *Furutaka* ablaze. Goto had only time to order a wheel to starboard before he was mortally wounded. The *Furutaka* followed the *Aoba* round and both ships were mercilessly hammered by a concentrated fire before Scott's order took effect. In the respite this afforded them, they limped away, the *Furutaka* to sink later. The destroyer *Fubuki* had already gone to the bottom.

The rear Japanese cruiser, *Kinugasa*, and the destroyer *Hatsuyuki* had prudently turned to port and so escaped this punishment. In doing so they encountered the lone *Duncan*, which was quickly knocked out of action and left blazing, to be abandoned two hours later.

The action now developed into a confused chase of the retreating Japanese ships in the course of which the American destroyers came under fire from their own cruisers. These had up to now suffered hardly any damage when, to identify a target detected by radar, the *Boise* switched on a searchlight. The Japanese, who lacked radar, had for the first time a clear point of aim. Both the *Aoba*, still full of fight, in spite of her heavy damage, and the unscathed *Kinugasa* concentrated on it, shattering the *Boise*, whose forward magazine was only saved from blowing up by the inrush of sea water which swamped the flames.

She was saved from further punishment by the *Salt Lake City* which steered to interpose herself, while the *Boise* turned away to fight her fires and patch up her wounds. A desultory running fight continued for a little while longer with the American ships swerving out of line to avoid torpedoes fired by the retreating enemy, until at 0028 hours Scott broke off contact, leading away to the south-west and re-forming his line.

Although, while this Battle of Cape Esperance was in progress, General Hyakutake's artillery and reinforcements were safely landed, the battle itself was hailed by the Americans as a notable victory and a demonstration that the Japanese could at last be mastered in night action, an opinion supported by a false belief that four Japanese cruisers and four destroyers had been sunk. The unusual Japanese lack of alertness which had led them to be taken by surprise and prevented the timely use of their most potent weapon, the torpedo, was not appreciated. This was to encourage an unjustified confidence in the rigid single-line formation and in the pre-eminence of gunfire.

Unopposed bombardment
That the dark hours were still the preserve of the Japanese navy in the waters north of Guadalcanal (Ironbottom Sound as it had been grimly dubbed from the number of sunken ships already littering it) was made clear when, during the night of October 13/14, the battleships *Kongo* and *Haruna*, unopposed except for a spirited but ineffective attack by four motor torpedo-boats from Tulagi, delivered a 90-minute bombardment of the Marines' positions with their 14-inch guns. Aircraft, petrol supplies, and the runways of Henderson Field were all pounded; and on the following night, Mikawa's two remaining cruisers, *Chokai* and *Kinugasa*, added to the destruction with a storm of 752 8-inch shells. Air raids during the 13th and 14th inflicted further damage, leaving so few aircraft serviceable and petrol in such critically short supply that a Japanese supply convoy of six transports boldly advancing in daylight down the Slot was able to reach the beaches at Tassafaronga to put 3,500 fresh troops ashore with ammunition and supplies. Although, by getting every flyable aircraft into the air the following morning, partially fuelled and armed from hidden reserves which had escaped destruction, the US Marines forced three of the transports to beach themselves, by the end of the day the Japanese were ashore for the first time in strength roughly equal to that of the Americans.

The next night Japanese cruisers appeared off Lunga Point again, the *Myoko* and *Maya* this time, and once again the Marines cowered under a hail of 800 8-inch shells and 300 5-inch ones from accompanying destroyers. With Henderson Field partly neutralised, the Americans had lost even their daytime domination of the sea approaches. Supplies were reduced to a trickle brought in by transport aircraft and submarine.

Morale afloat and ashore was at a low ebb. Urgent steps to restore it were now taken. Ghormley was replaced by Admiral William Halsey, who had a reputation for aggressiveness. The South Pacific aircraft-carrier force which, since the torpedoing of the *Saratoga* and *Wasp*, had been reduced to the *Hornet* only, was reinforced by the hastily repaired *Enterprise* and the fast new battleship *South Dakota*. A surface task force under Rear-Admiral Willis A. Lee, flying his flag in the battleship *Washington*, with three cruisers and six destroyers was formed to stop the Tokyo Express.

Away to the north of the Solomons, the Japanese Combined Fleet under Vice-Admiral Kondo had been hovering since October 22, the date General Hyakutake had predicted that Henderson Field would be captured by Maruyama's II Division, ready to fly in aircraft to consolidate the capture. Since then, Kondo's patience had been wearing thin and on the 24th he had warned Hyakutake that he must soon withdraw to replenish. A signal from the naval liaison officer on Guadalcanal announcing victory early on the 25th had induced Kondo to be patient a while longer—just long enough, as it turned out, to bring on another of the aircraft-carrier battles which, in their sum, were to decide the outcome of the war in the Pacific.

For on the 24th, to the east of the New Hebrides Islands, the *Enterprise* group, Task Force 16 under Rear-Admiral Thomas Kinkaid, had joined the *Hornet*'s Task Force 17; and, though this joint force was still greatly inferior to the Japanese fleet, Halsey ordered it to sweep in a wide circle round the Santa Cruz Islands into the Coral Sea 'to be in a position to intercept enemy forces approaching the Guadalcanal-Tulagi area'. Kinkaid was still to the east of the Santa Cruz Islands when scouting Catalina flying-boats located two Japanese aircraft-carriers 360 miles north-west of him at noon on the 25th and steering south-eastward. He at once launched his own reconnaissance aircraft, followed by a striking force of bombers and fighters. They failed to locate the enemy who had reversed course: but Kinkaid pressed on through the night to the north-west where the Japanese fleet was again reported at midnight some 300 miles ahead and now once again steering south to be in a position to send aircraft to Henderson Field the following morning.

The Battle of Santa Cruz
Day broke in fair weather over the two fleets with a light south-easterly breeze, though columns of cumulus cloud sailed in the blue tropical sky, occasionally loosing their watery contents in a local rainstorm. It was good dive-bomber's weather; and with first light 16 Dauntless aircraft, each with a 500-pound bomb, roared off the deck of the *Enterprise* to fan out in an armed reconnaissance, just as renewed reports of enemy aircraft-carriers at a distance of 200 miles came in and a brief unambiguous signal from Halsey at Nouméa—'Attack!' Nevertheless Kinkaid decided to wait for reliable reports from his own search aircraft before committing his striking force.

The Japanese fleet was divided into several separate groups. Nearest to the enemy was the Striking Force commanded by Vice-Admiral Nagumo with his flag in the aircraft-carrier *Shokaku*. This force was itself divided into two groups. A Vanguard Group under the command of Rear-Admiral Hiroaki Abe—composed of two battleships, three cruisers, and escort screen—was stationed some 60 miles to the south of the Carrier Group, the two large aircraft-carriers, *Shokaku* and *Zuikaku* and the smaller *Zuiho*, screened by a cruiser and eight destroyers. Some 120 miles farther to the north-west was a third group comprising Kondo's flagship, the cruiser *Atago*, three other cruisers, two battleships, and the new aircraft-carrier *Junyo*.

The Catalinas which had located the Japanese aircraft-carriers around midnight had shadowed them for the next three hours and, shortly before dawn, had launched torpedoes which closely missed the *Zuikaku*. Admiral Kondo, impatiently waiting for the victory message from Guadalcanal, and still uncertain of the presence of American aircraft-carriers in the area, had once again reversed the course of the fleet to the north, while his reconnaissance aircraft probed to the south.

The lessons of Midway still fresh in his mind, Nagumo had a striking force of 65 aircraft, half of them Zero fighters, ranged on his three aircraft-carriers before daylight. So, when at 0658 hours final confirmation of the position of one American aircraft-carrier reached him, the strike was on its way within 12 minutes. And, as the last aircraft roared off, the lifts went clanging down to range up a second force. Preparations had not gone far when suddenly out of the cloud-dappled sky plummeted two American dive-bombers.

Taken by surprise, not a Japanese gun opened fire to distract the aim of the two pilots, Lieutenant-Commander Strong and Ensign Irvine of the *Enterprise*. Their two bombs both exploded on the flight deck of the *Zuiho*, punching a huge jagged hole which put her out of action for flying operations.

Two of the *Enterprise*'s scouting bombers had first located the Japanese Vanguard Group at 0630 hours. Some 20 minutes later two others had discovered the aircraft-carriers, and Strong and Irvine had intercepted their report. On its receipt in the *Enterprise*, Kinkaid gave the order to launch his striking force. By 0730 hours 15 dive-bombers, six Avenger torpedo-planes, and an escort of eight Wildcats were taking off from the *Hornet*; 30 minutes later they were followed by the *Enterprise*'s smaller force of three Dauntless dive-bombers, eight Avengers, and eight Wildcats. Finally, at 0815 hours, a second striking force was launched by the *Hornet*—nine dive-bombers, nine torpedo-planes, and nine fighters.

Thus it was in a strung-out succession of separate units, comparatively small and weakly escorted, that the American striking force passed, on an opposite course, the compact Japanese strike with its high proportion of fighters. Selecting the small *Enterprise* group, 12 Zeros, circling to come in unseen from the direction of the sun, pounced on them to shoot down four Avengers and four Wildcats at the cost of three of their own numbers. Meanwhile the second Japanese strike of 44 planes from the *Shokaku* and *Zuikaku* had taken off at 0822 hours and a further 29 were being prepared aboard

US Navy

Right: Japanese strike aircraft attack the *Hornet* from all directions in the Battle of Santa Cruz. She was hit by two torpedoes, three 500-lb bombs, and two 'suicide' aircraft
Below: *Hornet*'s signal bridge, wrecked by the second suicide plane-crash

Imperial War Museum

the more distant *Junyo*.

Both sides now prepared to receive the coming onslaught. The two American aircraft-carriers, following their usual custom at that stage of the war, were operating in separate groups – the *Hornet* 10 miles south-east of the *Enterprise* – each surrounded by its circular screen of cruisers and destroyers, strengthened in the latter's case by the battleship *South Dakota*. Soon after the Japanese air group was detected, the *Enterprise* group steamed into a rain squall, and the *Hornet* was left to take the brunt of the attack.

Equipped with the latest type of radar, the *Enterprise* was the first to gain contact and might have been expected to develop a more efficient fighter control than on the last occasion the opposing aircraft-carriers had met; but the technique lagged behind the weapon and radar screens were soon too cluttered for proper interpretation. The Japanese dive-bombers were only a few miles away when the first American fight-

ers, Wildcats from the *Hornet*, sighted them at 17,000 feet. They ripped into them at once; but they could not prevent about 15 of them from breaking through. At the same time some 20 torpedo-planes came skimming low over the water to co-ordinate their attack with that of the bombers.

It was too much even for the well-directed fire of the huge number of guns to master entirely. Though more than half the torpedo planes were shot down before they reached a launching position and though 12 of the 15 plummeting Vals were fatally hit on their way down, the *Hornet* was hit by two torpedoes and six bombs, two of which were delivered by the Japanese squadron commander who, his plane hit, deliberately crashed on to the flight deck and plunged through it. Another suicidal crash was made by a blazing torpedo aircraft. In ten catastrophic minutes the aircraft-carrier had been reduced to a blazing wreck.

At almost the same moment, 200 miles to the north-west, the attack on the Japanese fleet was developing. From the start it was less well concentrated and organised than the Japanese strike. On passage it had lost some of its strength to fighter attack as recounted earlier. The torpedo section of the *Hornet*'s first wave lost touch with the air group commander, Lieutenant-Commander Widhelm, leading the 15 dive-bombers, and, on sighting the Vanguard Group, expended their efforts fruitlessly on it, as did the survivors of the *Enterprise* striking force. The *Hornet*'s second wave similarly attacked Abe's squadron, one dive-bomber heavily damaging the cruiser *Chikuma*.

These meagre results, however, were compensated for by Widhelm's section. The four Wildcats with him fought off attacks by Zeros sent up from the *Junyo* while he pressed on until smoke from the still-burning *Zuiho* led him to the vital target. More Zeros shot down or damaged four of his Dauntless bombers including his own, in which he force-landed. From his dinghy, he and his gunner watched what followed.

Arriving over the *Shokaku*, ignoring the Zeros on their tails and the curtain of vicious black shell-bursts, the remainder of his group dived down to drop between three and six – the number is uncertain – 1,000-pound bombs on the carrier's deck. Plunging through to the hangar below they set it ablaze. With damage which was to put her out of action for nine months she was sent, in company with the crippled *Zuiho*, limping back to base. Had the American torpedo-planes been able to co-ordinate their attack with that of the dive-bombers, her fate must

have been as conclusive as that of the *Hornet*.

That ship was lying immobilised with her crew struggling manfully to save her – while winging towards her was the second wave of aircraft from the *Shokaku* and *Zuikaku*. Wisely ignoring the temptation of this easy target, however, they concentrated instead on the *Enterprise* which had now emerged from the rain smother into the open. Detecting them by radar at a range of 55 miles there was ample time for the fighter director to concentrate the defensive Wildcats on them; but the control was again found wanting and the bombers reached their diving position unopposed.

Few survived the curtain of gunfire which met them as they screamed vertically down to drop their bombs; nevertheless two hit the *Enterprise*'s flight deck and her forward lift was put permanently out of action. Fortunately her speed and manoeuvrability were unaffected, so that when the torpedo-carrying Kate bombers attacked she was able to avoid the nine torpedoes fired at her.

Temporary repairs to her flight deck were put in hand so that the swarm of aircraft waiting to land on could be recovered. While this was in progress yet another Japanese striking force approached undetected – 29 planes from the *Junyo*, 20 of which suddenly broke out of the overcast in shallow dives. They failed to achieve anything: but the remainder, selecting ships of the screen, hit the *South Dakota* on her forward turret and sent a bomb clean through the cruiser *San Juan* to explode beneath her hull, though neither ship suffered much damage.

As soon as the *Enterprise* had gathered in the waiting aircraft, Kinkaid decided the time had come to withdraw. With both his aircraft-carriers virtually eliminated he had little with which to oppose the large Japanese surface fleet. Efforts to tow the *Hornet* to safety were abandoned. Attempts to sink her by torpedo and gunfire were ineffective and it was left to the Japanese to give her the *coup de grâce* when they came up with her burning hulk after dark.

For Japan, another Pyrrhic victory
Once again the Japanese naval air arm in this Battle of the Santa Cruz Islands had won a tactical victory over its American opponent. The *Shokaku* and *Zuiho* had been put out of action; but they would live to fight another day, while the *Zuikaku* and *Junyo* had been untouched. With the loss of the *Hornet* and damage to the *Enterprise*, not a single aircraft-carrier remained operational in the US Pacific fleet. Once again, however, it was a Pyrrhic victory for the Japanese, with about 100 planes and their irreplaceable, experienced crews paying the price. Indeed, the *Zuikaku* was virtually out of action owing to lack of aircrews of which enough remained to man only the two small aircraft-carriers *Junyo* and *Hiyo*, less than 100 planes in all. The Americans had not only lost many less, but they would have no difficulty in replacing losses from the huge training organisation in operation in the United States. Meanwhile the *Enterprise* was receiving hasty repairs at Nouméa.

Strategically, the Japanese had failed in their plan to recapture Guadalcanal. But much hard fighting on land and sea was yet to take place before either side could claim decisive victory in the struggle for that loathsome yet priceless island.
[*For Captain Macintyre's biography, see page 144.*]

By the middle of 1942, British and American leaders—despite the reluctance of the US Chiefs-of-Staff—had agreed that their first positive move against the Axis powers should be a landing in French North Africa (Operation 'Torch'). But before this could take place, there were awkward political problems to be solved.

Prompt action by the Vichy régime in 1940 had scotched any hope that the struggle against Germany would be continued from North Africa; and the result had been public apathy throughout the French possessions, together with apparent official agreement in the Vichy policy of collaboration. There was, however, some clandestine opposition by a small minority—and this opposition slowly increased. First contact between French North Africa and the United States had been made—while the United States was still neutral—in order to arrange the importation of food supplies; gradually and secretly, the arrangement extended to include the smuggling of arms and the advance preparation for an invasion. The American leaders demanded that large-scale intervention in North Africa must be supported by some highly-placed French official before any move could take place —while on their side the French leaders insisted that the exact relationship between their leaders and those of any invader must be defined.

General Juin, C-in-C of the French forces in North Africa, was ruled out as leader of the French allies because of his reluctance to act

General Sir Alan Brooke, the British CIGS, doubted Allied prospects to the east of Algiers—yet another inhibition for the 'Torch' planning

General Marshall, US Army Chief-of-Staff: not enthusiastic about the planned invasion of North Africa, he pressed for a descent on northern France

General de Gaulle was unsuitable for the opposite reason: his defiance of Vichy since 1941 had alienated him from too many Frenchmen

Admiral King, the US Navy Chief-of-Staff, agreed with Marshall that the Allies should concentrate on the Pacific if Europe could not be invaded

Admiral Darlan, the Vichy C-in-C, was ready to negotiate with the Allies—but he had long ago forfeited the confidence of both the French and the British

General Clark, of the US General Staff, was to land in Algeria for secret talks with the leaders of the resistance—and pave the way for 'Torch'

General Giraud— 'King-Pin', as he was known to Churchill and Roosevelt in their communications—was the most promising head for the French allies

OPERATION TORCH

Imperial War Museum

For political reasons US participation was emphasised throughout the landings

Even without Stalin's demands for a second front, the western Allies knew that they must make some positive move against Germany during 1942. But here the difficulties arose, for the Americans still hoped for a landing in France, while the British were determined to pacify North Africa. After much argument, it was decided to invade Morocco and Algeria and establish a base from which Axis supply lines across the Mediterranean could be cut, and from which eventually an attack could be launched at the 'soft under-belly of Europe'. But this decision seemed only to redouble the difficulties, for the relationships between the various leaders in French North Africa, their government in Vichy France, and the Allies, were extremely complex. And the success of Operation Torch might be said to have been the triumph of political machination over military inexperience

The Allied landings in French North Africa took place on November 8, 1942. This entry into north-west Africa came a fortnight after the launching of the British offensive on Rommel's position at Alamein, in the extreme north-east of Africa, and four days after the collapse of that position. By the time that the new Allied expedition, a joint American and British force, landed in Morocco and Algeria the remnants of Rommel's army were in full retreat to the frontier of Cyrenaica. The menace to his rear base and sea communications, although a long-range threat, nullified his hope of renewing the fight in Cyrenaica, or in Tripolitania. The reinforcements needed for that purpose were sent, instead, to check the Allied advance from the Atlantic.

This new Allied move – Operation 'Torch' – had been in preparation for three months, but in conception much longer. It had been mooted at the Atlantic Conference in August 1941 when President Roosevelt met Winston Churchill off the coast of Newfoundland, along with their respective service advisers, and the British Chiefs-of-Staff had there emphasised the value of using American forces for a combined entry into French North Africa as a means to 'revolutionise' the military situation in this theatre.

Then at the Arcadia Conference in Washington at Christmastide – the first Allied conference following the Japanese stroke at Pearl Harbor which brought the United States into the war – Churchill put forward the 'North-West Africa Project' in a more explicit way as a step towards 'closing and tightening the ring around Germany'. He told the Americans that there was already a plan, 'Gymnast', under which 55,000 British troops were earmarked, with the necessary shipping, for a landing in Algeria if the 8th Army gained a sufficiently decisive success in Cyrenaica for it to push westward to the Tunisian border. He went on to propose that 'at the same time United States forces, assuming French agreement, should proceed to land on the Moroccan coast by invitation'.

Roosevelt was immediately favourable to the project, being quick to see its political advantages in grand strategy, but his service advisers were dubious about its practicability while anxious lest it should interfere with the prospects of an early and more direct attack against Hitler's hold on Europe. They estimated that a force of over 200,000 men, rising to 300,000, would be needed for such an operation, compared with the British figure of 100,000 – and they saw no possibility of providing the shipping for such a large expedition so early after their entry into the war. The most they were willing to agree was that study of the operation, now rechristened 'Super-Gymnast', should continue. But then in January 1942 Rommel's counterstroke from the border of Tripolitania dislocated the 8th Army's westward advance and produced a retreat of more than 200 miles before it rallied on the Gazala Line. Super-Gymnast was then classed as an 'academic study', and the plan shelved.

During the next few months discussion concentrated on the project of an early cross-Channel attack, to be launched in August or September with the aim of relieving German pressure on Russia, and meeting Stalin's demand for the opening of a 'Second Front', by establishing an Anglo-American lodgment on the north coast of France. The sites considered were the Pas-de-Calais, and the Brest, Cotentin (Cherbourg), and Le Havre peninsulas. The Cotentin peninsula came to be the most favoured site, as urged by General Marshall, the Chief-of-Staff of the United States army, and by Major-General Eisenhower, whom he had chosen and sent to London as commander of the American forces in the European theatre.

The British emphasised the drawbacks of a premature landing in Europe with inadequate strength, pointing out the risks of such a bridgehead being bottled up, or overwhelmed, without bringing appreciable relief to the Russians. But President Roosevelt swung his weight in support of the project, and committed himself, when Molotov visited Washington at the end of May, to an assurance that he 'hoped' and 'expected' to create 'a Second Front in Europe in 1942'.

The British had been more cautious in their discussions with Molotov the week before, when he was on his way to Washington. They had gone no further than to say, noncommittally: 'We are making preparations for a landing on the Continent in August or September 1942. . . . Clearly, however, it would not further either the Russian cause or that of the Allies as a whole if, for the sake of action at any price, we embarked on some operation which ended in disaster and gave the enemy an opportunity for glorification at our discomfiture. It is impossible to say in advance whether the situation will be such as to make this operation feasible when the time comes. We can therefore give no promise in the matter . . .'

Ironically, a sudden reversion to the project of a landing in north-west Africa was produced by the unexpected British collapse in north-east Africa which occurred in June, following Rommel's forestalling attack on the Gazala Line. Instead of resuming its westward advance as planned, the 8th Army was thrown back in disorder a further 400 miles before it rallied on the Alamein Line – the last possible stop-line in Egypt short of Alexandria, Cairo, and the Nile Delta.

The battle of Gazala had already taken a bad turn when Churchill flew to Washington on June 17, with his Chiefs-of-Staff, for a fresh conference. On arrival Churchill went on by air to Hyde Park, Roosevelt's family home on the Hudson, for a private talk. Here he re-emphasised the drawbacks and dangers of a premature landing in France, while suggesting the revival of Gymnast as a better alternative. He had reminded Roosevelt of this in a message of May 28, and found the President much inclined to agree, particularly in view of the British objections to an early attempt to land on the north coast of France.

Meanwhile the British and American Chiefs-of-Staff, meeting in Washington, had disagreed over the Cherbourg project – but found themselves in complete agreement that the North Africa project was unsound!

So, in a dubious way, they suggested a further study of other possible operations: against Brest, the Channel Islands, the Iberian peninsula, or northern Norway – a project which Churchill had long cherished and urged, although neither his own service advisers nor the Americans thought that its effect was likely to be worth the effort involved. But their agreed conclusion was that: 'Any of these plans would be preferable to undertaking Gymnast, especially from the standpoint of dispersing base organizations, lines of communication, and air strength.'

Their combined negative conclusion about this project was soon reversed by the pressure of events, combined with Roosevelt's pressing desire for some positive action in 1942 that would fulfil, even if not so directly as intended, his promise to the Russians. On June 21, while the argument proceeded in Washington, news came that the fortress of Tobruk had fallen to Rommel's assault and that the remains of the British 8th Army were in retreat to Egypt. Before Churchill flew home to grapple with the crisis, Roosevelt and his service chiefs discussed ways and means of helping the British to meet it. The President's first suggestion was that of providing a direct reinforcement 'by dispatching substantial US forces to the Middle East'. Marshall, more cautiously, proposed the dispatch of an armoured division, and then, as a more immediate aid, offered to provide the British with 300 of the new Sherman tanks. (This offer was gratefully and promptly accepted. Although the tanks did not arrive in Egypt until September, after Rommel had been

Operation Torch was the first Allied experience of joint planning and operations. Before the planning could start, the British and American chiefs-of-staff had to reconcile their very divergent strategic aims, and even when the landings with all their complicated political subterfuge had been completed, there were major problems to be solved with the French. Lieutenant-General Eisenhower, relatively unknown commander-in-chief of the Allied forces, discusses the plans with Admiral Sir Andrew Cunningham

definitely checked, they were of invaluable, and decisive, service in the Second Battle of Alamein—Montgomery's October offensive.)

Sledgehammer versus Gymnast

During the weeks that followed, the British situation worsened, and the argument for direct or indirect American intervention in Africa was correspondingly strengthened. By the end of June, Rommel reached and started to attack the Alamein Line, following on the heels of the British retreat. On July 8 Churchill cabled to Roosevelt that 'Sledgehammer', the plan for a landing in France that year, must be discarded, and went on to urge, once again, the case for Gymnast. He followed it up with a message through Field-Marshal Sir John Dill, who was now head of the British Joint Staff Mission in Washington: 'Gymnast affords the sole means by which the U.S. can strike at Hitler in 1942', and that otherwise both the western Allies would have to remain 'motionless in 1942'. The American Chiefs-of-Staff reacted to this contention with renewed objections to Gymnast—Marshall's condemnation of it as 'expensive and ineffectual' was supported by Admiral King's declaration that it was 'impossible to fulfil naval commitments in other theatres and at the same time to provide the shipping and escorts which would be essential should that operation be undertaken'.

They also agreed in viewing the British refusal to attempt a landing in France in 1942 as clear evidence that the British did not really want to risk it even in 1943. So Marshall, readily supported by King, proposed a radical change of strategy—that

unless the British accepted the American plan for an early cross-Channel attack 'we should turn to the Pacific and strike decisively against Japan; in other words assume a defensive attitude against Germany, except for air operations; and use all available means in the Pacific'.

But the President objected to the idea of delivering such an ultimatum to his British allies, and the Chiefs-of-Staff admitted, in answer to his searching questions, that they had not thought out the problem of meeting such a drastic switch, and had no plan ready to meet it. He thereupon expressed his disapproval of the proposed strategic switch, and told his Chiefs-of-Staff that unless they could persuade the British to undertake a cross-Channel operation in 1942 they must either launch one into French North Africa or send a strong reinforcement to the Middle East. He emphasised that it was politically imperative to take some striking action before the year ended. While leaving the choice to them, and telling them to settle it with the British, he indicated that the former was his own preference, either in the form of a combined American-British operation or a purely American one in Morocco.

Faced with the President's decision, the American Chiefs-of-Staff might have been expected to choose the course of temporarily reinforcing the British in the Middle East, rather than embarking on the Gymnast plan which they had so strongly and persistently opposed. Moreover, Marshall's planning staff after reviewing the two courses reached the conclusion that the former was. the lesser of two evils. But contrary to expectation, he and King swung

round in favour of Gymnast. This became their preferred alternative when they flew to London in mid-July along with Harry Hopkins, as the President's representatives, and found that the British Chiefs-of-Staff were firmly opposed to Eisenhower's plan for an early landing near Cherbourg. The British, as Brooke's diary records, urged that such a small bridgehead would be overwhelmed by the Germans long before it could be expanded in the spring, and that 'such action could only lead to the loss of some six divisions without achieving any results'—a conclusion that looks even more probable in historical retrospect.

In choosing north-west Africa as the alternative, rather than a reinforcement to the Middle East, Marshall's prime reason, according to Harry Hopkins, was 'the difficulty of mixing our troops with the British in Egypt'. While a mixture would also occur in the case of a combined operation in north-west Africa, it was obvious that American reinforcements to the Middle East would have to come under a British Commander-in-Chief, as the British had such a large army there, whereas in opening up a new theatre the supreme command might reasonably be claimed for an American. Another reason for their choice, and the one which Marshall and King gave to the President on returning to Washington, was that north-west Africa provided a more flexible line of operation for adaptation to circumstances—both to the plan of mounting the cross-Channel attack in 1943 and the danger of a 'Russian collapse this fall'—and was therefore 'the logical line of action'.

The adoption of Super-Gymnast was for-

mulated at two further meetings of the Combined Chiefs-of-Staff, American and British, in London on July 24 and 25 – and promptly endorsed by Roosevelt. Moreover, he emphasised in his cable that the landing should be planned to take place 'not later than October 30th' – a directive that Hopkins had suggested, in a personal message, as a means 'to avoid procrastination and delays'. On Churchill's initiative the operation was rechristened Torch, as a more inspiring name. It was also agreed that the supreme command should be given to an American – an ointment for the sore feelings of the American service chiefs that Churchill was very ready to provide – and on the 26th Eisenhower was told, by Marshall, that he was to have the post.

But under the surface of agreement there were still reservations. In London, Marshall had got the British Chiefs-of-Staff to agree to the insertion of a clause in the agreement specifying that a final decision should be put off until September 15, to see how the struggle in Russia turned. That loophole had been closed by the President's cable. Nevertheless, on returning to Washington, Marshall and King still argued that they had not regarded the decision as final, and urged on July 30 that it should be deferred a week until a detailed study of the logistical problem and 'of all implications of Torch' had been completed. Their plea for a deferment was promptly overruled, that evening, by the President – who 'stated very definitely that he, as Commander-in-Chief, had made the decision that Torch would be undertaken at the earliest possible moment'. In justice to them, it should be noted that their prime reason for stalling was their conviction that the adoption of Torch would lead to a prolonged diversion of the Allied effort, to the Mediterranean, and annul the prospect of launching the cross-Channel attack in 1943. This was the main 'implication' which they felt that the President had not taken into account.

While the decision for Torch was now definite, it had been made before the questions of time and site were settled, or even fully examined. Thus fresh conflicts of view arose over both these problems.

On the question of time the British Chiefs-of-Staff, spurred by Churchill, proposed October 7 as the target date. But the American Chiefs-of-Staff recommended November 7, as being 'the earliest reasonable date for landing of the forces based on availability of combat loaders'. Actually, nine out of ten of the transports that were being modified for combat loading would be ready in mid-September, and the tenth by October 1. But Marshall wanted a margin of time sufficient to complete amphibious training, and insisted on rehearsals, whereas the British were willing to curtail these 'for the sake of speed'. When the issue was referred to Roosevelt, he urged his Chiefs-of-Staff to hasten the target date, and make it October 7, or at least the 14th, but did not succeed in moving them.

On the question of site, the respective views were even wider apart. The British urged that the landings should be made on

Keystone

Torch was not only the first appearance of the US army in Europe, but it also introduced one of the most flamboyant and successful generals of the Second World War to a public which was to admire his exploits but suspect the aura with which he surrounded himself. Major-General George Patton was one of the few Americans to have gained combat experience with tanks in the First World War, and between the wars he became a leading US exponent of armoured warfare. His debut as commander of the Western Task Force which took Casablanca was marked with all the energy and controversy which were to make him the *'enfant terrible'* of Allied commanders

the north coast of Africa, inside the Mediterranean, so that a quick advance to Tunisia would be possible. But the American Chiefs-of-Staff stuck to the limited objective of the original Gymnast plan, when it was envisaged as a purely American operation, and were anxious to confine the landings to the Casablanca area on the west coast – the Atlantic coast – of Morocco. They feared not only the dangers of French opposition but of hostile Spanish reaction and a German counterstroke to block the gateway into the Mediterranean by seizing Gibraltar. There would be no such risk, they cautiously argued, if the operation was limited to securing Casablanca as a base port for transatlantic convoys, and then developing an eastward advance into Algeria and Tunisia in turn.

The British on this issue were dismayed by such a cautious approach to the strategic problem. They argued that it would allow the Germans time to seize Tunisia, stiffen or replace French opposition in Algeria and Morocco, and thus frustrate the aim of the Allied operation.

I was asked for my views on the question of the north-west Africa project on June 28, immediately after the Washington Conference when its revival was mooted. On being told that the main landing was then intended to be at Casablanca, on the Atlantic coast, I pointed out that this site was 1,100 miles distant from Bizerta and Tunis, the strategic keys, and that the best chance of early success lay in capturing them as quickly as possible, which meant that the landings

should be made as near them as possible. I also emphasised the importance of landing on the north coast, in Algeria, 'on the backs of the French' as a means to diminish the opposition that was likely to develop in face of a frontal attack at, and slow advance from, Casablanca.

The British also expressed doubt of the success of a landing at or near Casablanca if there was any serious opposition, pointing out that there is usually a heavy surf on the Atlantic coast, whereas landing conditions inside the Mediterranean are easier and ports more numerous.

Eisenhower and his staff were inclined to agree with the British view. His first outline plan, formulated on August 9, was devised as a compromise. It proposed simultaneous landings inside and outside the Mediterranean, but not farther eastward than Algiers – because of the risk of enemy air attacks from Sicily and Sardinia – except for a minor one at Bône to seize the airfield there (Bône is 270 miles east of Algiers but 130 miles short of Bizerta). This compromise did not satisfy the British planners, as it did not seem likely to fulfil the principal condition of success, which they defined as being: 'We must have occupied the key points of Tunisia within 26 days of passing Gibraltar and preferably within 14 days'.

Even that was a slow time-schedule, and a too leisurely requirement, in the light of experience about the Germans' quickness in reacting to threatening developments. The British Chiefs-of-Staff declared that 'the whole conception of Torch may stand

Roosevelt urged: 'I feel very strongly that the first attacks must be made by an exclusively American ground force'

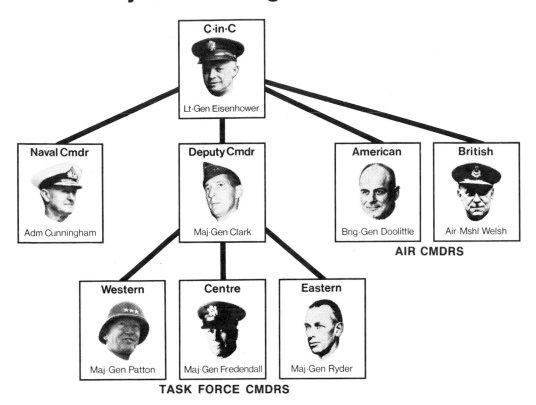

C·in·C — Lt·Gen Eisenhower

Naval Cmdr — Adm Cunningham

Deputy Cmdr — Maj·Gen Clark

American — Brig·Gen Doolittle

British — Air·Mshl Welsh

AIR CMDRS

Western — Maj·Gen Patton

Centre — Maj·Gen Fredendall

Eastern — Maj·Gen Ryder

TASK FORCE CMDRS

Although Eisenhower had insisted that Torch was to be a truly Allied venture, the command structure for the landings was exclusively American. But once these had taken place, all the forces in Algeria were to become the basis of 1st Army commanded by the British Lieutenant-General Anderson. Mark Clark was Deputy C-in-C, to ensure that, in case of any injury to Eisenhower, the C-in-C would remain an American

or fall on this question of early occupation of Tunisia'. In their view, a major landing at Bône, or even farther east, was essential to achieve a quick enough advance to Tunisia, and a landing at Casablanca ought to be dropped or postponed, as it could have no early influence on the main aim.

These arguments impressed the President, who directed Marshall and King to restudy the project. They had also impressed Eisenhower, who reported to Washington that the American members of his staff were now convinced of the soundness of the British reasoning, and that he was now drawing up a new plan that would eliminate the Casablanca landings, and advance the date of the others. But when Marshall said in reply that the operation now proposed would have 'less than a fifty-fifty chance of success' Eisenhower concurred with this view.

His staff, however, produced (on August 21) a second outline plan which largely followed the British idea. Discarding the Casablanca landing, it provided for an American landing at Oran (250 miles east of Gibraltar) as well as for British landings at Algiers and Bône. But Eisenhower's own endorsement of it was tepid, and emphasised that such an expedition, wholly inside the Mediterranean, would be badly exposed on its flank. He went on to say, as a personal view, that a landing at Casablanca would make a great difference to the chances of success of the operation as a whole, if the Allied navies could manage to provide the additional cover that would be required. That tuned in with Marshall's opinion.

The second outline plan was as unpalatable to the American Chiefs-of-Staff as the first had been to the British. Marshall told the President that 'a single line of communication through the Straits is far too hazardous' and he was against any landing being made inside the Mediterranean farther east than Oran (600 miles short of Bizerta). Moreover he and his fellow Chiefs-of-Staff proposed that the objective of the operation should be limited to the domination of the north-west corner of Africa. This extremely cautious and modest proposal produced dismay in London—all the more because the British Chiefs-of-Staff had just previously agreed to accept the American wish to defer the landing until November 7, in order to carry out the second plan in full, although Churchill still urged an earlier date.

Churchill received the news of this cautious turn after returning from his flying visit with Brooke to Egypt and Moscow—where Stalin had taunted them about the failure of the Western powers to open a 'Second Front', with such scornful questions as 'Are you going to let us do all the work while you look on? Are you never going to start fighting? You will find it is not too bad when you once start!' That had, naturally, stung Churchill, but he had managed to arouse Stalin's interest in the potentialities of Torch, and had vividly depicted how it could indirectly relieve the pressure on Russia. So he was shocked to find that the Americans were proposing to whittle down the plan.

On August 27 he sent off a long cable to

Roosevelt protesting that the changes which the American Chiefs-of-Staff suggested might be 'fatal to the whole plan', and that 'the whole pith of the operation will be lost if we do not take Algiers as well as Oran on the first day'. He emphasised the bad impression that a narrowing of the aim would have on Stalin, in view of what he had been told. Less wisely, Churchill said: 'The occupation of Algeria and the movement towards Tunis and Bizerta is an indispensable part of the attack on Italy, which is the best chance of enlisting French co-operation and one of the main objects of our future campaign'. For that sentence implied that the British were aiming to exploit Torch in a way that diverged from the direct line of approach to Germany, so that the cross-Channel attack would be shelved once again. That was the very implication of Torch which Marshall had feared all along.

Roosevelt's reply, on the 30th, insisted that 'under any circumstances one of our landings must be on the Atlantic'. So he proposed that the Americans should carry out the Casablanca and Oran landings, leaving the British to make the eastward ones. But he went on to say that these would have to depend on the provision of additional ships, as 'it is essential of course that all ships now assigned to Eisenhower for his two landings remain intact'.

Moreover, he raised a fresh issue:

I feel very strongly that the initial attacks must be made by an exclusively American ground force . . . I would even go so far as to say I am reasonably sure a simultaneous landing by British and Americans would result in full resistance by all French in Africa, whereas an initial American landing without British ground forces offers a real chance that there would be no French resistance, or only a token resistance. I need a week, if possible, after we land to consolidate the position for both of us by securing the non-resistance of the French . . . Then your force can come in to the eastward . . . It is our belief that German air or parachute troops cannot get to Algiers or Tunis in any large force for at least two weeks after the landing.

The British were appalled at the idea of a week's pause before making eastward landings, more important and urgent for the strategic goal than the westerly ones, and were far from happy about the Americans' optimistic estimate that the Germans could not intervene effectively in less than two weeks.

Churchill was very willing to profit from the persuasive influence of the American ambassador to the Vichy government, Admiral Leahy, towards easing the way politically and psychologically—although he did not 'wholly share the American view that either they were so beloved by Vichy or we so hated as to make the difference between fighting and submission'. While he was 'anxious to preserve the American character of the expedition', and therefore willing to keep the British forces 'as much in the background as was physically possible', he did not believe it possible to conceal the

US Navy

fact that the larger part of the shipping, the air support, and the naval forces would be British – and these elements would become visible first, before the ground forces.

He touched on these points in a tactful reply to Roosevelt on September 1, and emphasised that if 'the political bloodless victory, for which I agree with you there is a good chance, should go amiss, a military disaster of very great consequence would ensue. We could have stormed Dakar in September 1940 if we had not been cluttered up with preliminary conciliatory processes. It is that hard experience that makes our military experts rely so much on the simplicity of force'. That remark was characteristic and self-revealing. He continued: 'Finally, in spite of the difficulties it seems to us vital that Algiers should be occupied simultaneously with Casablanca and Oran. Here is the most friendly and hopeful spot where the political reaction would be most decisive throughout North Africa. To give up Algiers for the sake of the doubtfully practicable landing at Casablanca seems to us a very

serious decision. If it led to the Germans forestalling us not only in Tunis but in Algeria, the results on balance would be lamentable throughout the Mediterranean.'

An omission of fateful consequence

This good argument for maintaining the landing at Algiers as part of the plan did not mention the importance of landings farther east, and nearer Bizerta – an omission, and concession, which was of fateful consequence. It was prompted by Brooke, who, in a conference with Churchill at Chequers the previous weekend, had advocated 'doing Casablanca, Oran, and Algiers, instead of Oran, Algiers, and Bône' – and wrote in his diary: 'This is, I think, a much wiser plan and conforms much nearer to the U.S.A. outlook.' Brooke had always been dubious about Torch, while having an innate tendency himself to take a cautious, and apprehensive, view.

Replying to Churchill's cable, on September 3, Roosevelt agreed that a landing at Algiers should be included in the plan, while

suggesting that American troops should land first 'followed within an hour by British troops'. Churchill immediately accepted this solution, provided that there was such a reduction in the force earmarked for Casablanca as to make the Algiers landing effective. To this Roosevelt agreed, in a modified form, suggesting a reduction of 'one regimental combat team' at Casablanca, and another at Oran, to provide '10,000 men for use at Algiers'. Churchill cabled back on September 5: 'We agree to the military lay-out you propose. We have plenty of troops highly trained for landing. If convenient they can wear your uniform. They will be proud to do so. Shipping will be all right.' That same day, Roosevelt replied in a one-word cable 'Hurrah!'

Thus the matter was finally settled in this exchange of cables between Roosevelt and Churchill. Three days later Eisenhower specified November 8 as the date of the landings, while declining Churchill's offer to put the British Commandos in American uniform, as he wanted to preserve an ▷

Despite the length of the voyages, there was little enemy interference: tracer during a practice for the Axis attack which never came

British troops of the Eastern Task Force. Throughout the operations their part was played down to avoid antagonising the French

Men of the American assault groups during the approach to the beaches; most US troops were over-loaded, with nearly 90 lbs of equipment

Imperial War Museum   Imperial War Museum   US Army

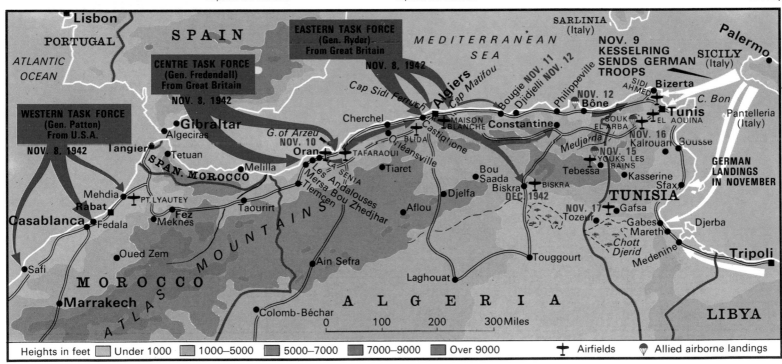

Heights in feet Under 1000 1000–5000 5000–7000 7000–9000 Over 9000 ✈ Airfields Allied airborne landings

New Tide from the Atlantic

1942 July 24/25: The combined British and American Chiefs-of-Staff decide to adopt the 'Super-Gymnast' plan—a major Anglo-American invasion of north-west Africa. Churchill renames the operation Torch; General Eisenhower is given overall command.
October 22/23: American General Mark Clark makes a secret landing on the Algerian coast for talks with key French officials. The first assault forces for Oran and Algiers sail from Britain.
November 2: Rommel gives Afrika Korps orders to withdraw from El Alamein.
November 3: On receiving Hitler's refusal of permission to withdraw, Rommel orders his units to take up new defensive positions.
November 3/4: 8th Army breaches the German defence line, Afrika Korps loses about 200 tanks and armoured vehicles.
November 5: Rommel establishes a new halt-line at Fuka, where his units can reorganise, but it is penetrated by the 8th Army.
November 6: Heavy rain slows up the 8th Army's pursuit.
November 7: French General Giraud, principal

candidate to lead the French in Africa, is picked up on the south coast of France by a British submarine, and taken to Gibraltar to await the results of the landing.
November 8: The Allied assault forces land near Casablanca, Oran, and Algiers. At Casablanca, landing troubles delay the invaders, but the other forces are not opposed until they begin to move toward their objectives.
November 9: Following discussions with General Clark in Algiers, Admiral Darlan issues an order to cease fire. After pressure from the Germans this is countermanded by the Vichy government, but the French forces in North Africa obey. On hearing of Torch, Rommel decides to retreat in one bound to El Agheila. Sidi Barrani is evacuated.
November 11: German forces overrun the unoccupied part of France, and begin to pour into Tunisia, as the British 1st Army begins to advance towards Tunis and Bizerta. Afrika Korps evacuates Halfaya Pass. 36th Brigade lands at Bougie.
November 12: Paratroops of British 1st Parachute Brigade occupy Bône Airfield.
November 13: Advance guard of the 8th Army enters Tobruk.

November 16: Souk el Arba airfield is captured by the 1st Parachute Battalion; it begins to advance towards Tunis. The head-quarters of 78th Division is established at Bône.
November 20: 8th Army reaches Benghazi.
November 23: Afrika Korps falls back from Agedabia; Montgomery slows up the pursuit in order to reorganise his fighting forces and supply lines.
November 26/30: Medjez is evacuated by the Germans and occupied by 11th Brigade. 36th Brigade reaches Tamera, and continues to probe towards Mateur. It meets strong resistance, and 1st Army's advance is held up on a line Mateur/Medjez. Djedeida is occupied for a short time, but the Germans recapture it.
November 29: The 2nd Parachute Battalion lands at Depienne airfield, and marches to Oudna, but it has to withdraw when 1st Army fails to break through at Djedeida and link up with it.
December 12/13: 8th Army attacks the German line at Mersa Brega, the Afrika Korps withdraws to avoid a major struggle.
December 14/18: Rommel evades an attempt to surround his forces at El Agheila.
December 24: Admiral Darlan is assassinated.

all-American look in the initial landings. Churchill reconciled himself to the delay, and to the modification of the plan. Indeed, in a subsequent cable to Roosevelt on September 15, he submissively said: 'In the whole of Torch, military and political, I consider myself your lieutenant, asking only to put my view-point plainly before you.'

Roosevelt's 'Hurrah' cable on September 5 settled what was aptly called 'the transatlantic essay competition'–although Marshall continued to express doubts, while his immediate political chief, Henry Stimson, the Secretary for War (that is, for the army), made a bitter complaint to the President about the decision to land in North Africa. But the President's decision enabled detailed planning to be pushed on in a hurried effort to catch up the effects of procrastination. The plan, however, carried the two-edged effects of a compromise. By diminishing the chances of a quickly decisive success in North Africa it made more certain the prolonged diversion of Allied effort in the Mediterranean–as American official historians have recognised and emphasised.

In the final plan, the Atlantic coast landing to capture Casablanca was to be made by the all-American Western Task Force under Major General George S. Patton, with 35,000 troops, carried by a naval task force under Rear-Admiral H. Kent Hewitt. It sailed direct from America–the main part from Hampton Roads in Virginia–and consisted of 102 ships, of which 29 were transports.

The capture of Oran was entrusted to the Centre Task Force, which comprised 39,000 American troops under Major-General Lloyd R. Fredendall, but was escorted by a British naval force under Commodore Thomas Troubridge. It sailed from the Clyde, as it was composed of American troops who had been brought over to Scotland and Northern Ireland early in August.

For the operation against Algiers, the Eastern Naval Task Force was also entirely British, commanded by Rear-Admiral Sir Harold Burrough, but the assault force consisted of 23,000 British and 10,000 American troops, and its commander, Major-General Charles Ryder, was American. Moreover American troops were incorporated in the British Commando units. This curiously mixed composition was inspired by the hope that putting Americans in the front of the shop-window would lead the French to assume that the assault force was all-American. On November 9, the day after the landings, overall command of all the Allied troops in Algeria was to be taken over by the commander of the newly-created British 1st Army, Lieutenant-General Kenneth Anderson.

The assault forces for both Oran and Algiers sailed together from Britain in two large convoys, a slow one starting on October 22 and a fast one four days later. This timing was arranged so that they could pass through the Straits of Gibraltar simultaneously during the night of November 5, and from there they were covered by part of the British Mediterranean Fleet under Admiral Sir Andrew Cunningham. Its pre-

sence sufficed to deter the Italian fleet from interfering, even after the landings–so that, as Cunningham regretfully remarked, his force had 'to be kept cruising idly'.

But Cunningham had plenty of work on his hands, as he was Allied Naval Commander, under Eisenhower, and thus responsible for the whole of the maritime side of Torch. Including storeships that had come in advance convoys early in October, over 250 merchantmen sailed from Britain, of which some 40 were transports (including three American), while the British naval force employed in the operation, as escort and cover, amounted to 160 warships of various types.

The diplomatic prelude to the landings was akin to a mixture of a spy story and a Western, with comic interludes, carried into the field of history. Robert Murphy, the chief American diplomatic representative in North Africa, had been active in preparing the way for the landings by discreet sounding among French officers whom he felt were likely to be in sympathy with, and give aid to, the project. He relied particularly on General Mast, commander of the troops in the Algiers sector (and previously Chief-of-Staff to General Juin, the Commander-in-Chief), and General Béthouart, who commanded the troops in the Casablanca sector–although that sector as a whole was under the command of Admiral Michelier: a fact that the Americans failed to realise.

Mast had urged that a senior Allied military representative should come secretly to Algiers for back-stage talks, and discussion of plans, with Juin and others. Accordingly General Mark Clark (who had just been appointed Deputy Commander-in-Chief for Torch) flew to Gibraltar with four key staff officers, and the party were carried on by a British submarine, HMS *Seraph* (Lieutenant N. A. A. Jewell), to a rendezvous at a villa on the coast some 60 miles west of Algiers. The submarine arrived off the coast early on October 21 but too late to land Mark Clark's party before daylight, so had to stay submerged all day, while the puzzled and disappointed French party went home. A message from the submarine to Gibraltar, relayed to Algiers over a secret radio chain, brought Murphy and some of the French back to the villa the next night, when Clark's party came ashore in four canvas canoes–one of which upset when they embarked. They had been guided to the meeting place by a lamp, with a white blanket behind, shining through a window.

General Mark Clark told Mast, in a broad way, that a large American force was being prepared for dispatch to North Africa, and would be supported by British air and sea forces–a statement which was lacking in frankness. Moreover he abstained, in the interests of security, from giving Mast a clear idea of the time and places of the Allied landings. This excess of secrecy in dealing with a man whose help was of key importance was unwise, since it deprived him and his associates of the information and time necessary to plan, and take, co-operative steps. Clark authorised Murphy to inform Mast of the date immediately before the land-

ings, but even then not of the places. That was too late for Mast to notify his associates in Morocco.

Yet the French officers who took part in the conference showed their good will by providing many valuable details about the layout of the French forces. One significant item was that the garrison and airfield at Bône were controlled by an associate of theirs–news which would have been more valuable if the Bône landing had not been dropped in deference to the objections of the American Chiefs-of-Staff. While Mast was unaware of this, or of the intended landing places, his own grasp of the problem was shown by the way he urged the crucial importance of preparing for the swiftest possible advance into Tunisia to forestall the arrival of airborne Axis troops, which he expected to begin within 36 hours of the Allied landings.

The conference was temporarily, and dramatically, interrupted by the appearance on the scene of suspicious French police. Mark Clark and his companions were hurriedly hidden in an empty wine cellar while the police searched the villa. Danger became more acute when one of the British Commando officers who had piloted the party began coughing. Mark Clark passed him a bit of chewing gum as a remedy, but he soon asked for more, saying that it had not got much taste–to which Clark replied: 'That is not surprising, as I have been chewing it for two hours!' After the police at last went away, still suspicious and likely to return, Clark and his party ran into fresh trouble when they tried to re-embark at dusk, for the surf had become heavy, and he had a narrow escape from drowning when his canoe overturned. At a further attempt shortly before dawn, the others capsized, but all of the party got through the breakers in the end and reached the submarine, safe though soaked. The next day they were transferred to a flying-boat, which carried them back to Gibraltar.

Search for a suitable French leader
An important issue which came into further discussion at this conference was the choice of the most suitable French leader to rally the French forces in North Africa to the Allied side. While Juin, their Commander-in-Chief, had privately expressed a favourable inclination, he showed a tendency to 'sit on the fence' as long as possible, and a reluctance to take the initiative. His chief subordinate commanders lacked sufficient prestige, and were no less reluctant to take any definite step in disregard or defiance of orders from the Vichy government.

Admiral Darlan, the Commander-in-Chief of its forces as a whole, and potential head of the government if the aged Marshal Pétain were to die, had hinted to Leahy in 1941 and more recently to Murphy that he might be willing to break away from the policy of collaboration with Germany and bring the French over to the Allied side if assured of American military aid on a sufficiently large scale. But he had played in with Hitler so long that his hints did not inspire confidence. Moreover he had an anti-

British bias, which had naturally been increased by the British action against the French fleet at Oran and elsewhere, after the collapse of France in 1940. This made his attitude all the more doubtful in view of the difficulty of disguising the fact that the British were playing a large part in Torch.

De Gaulle was ruled out for the opposite reason – that his defiance of Pétain in 1940 and subsequent part in Churchill's moves against Dakar, Syria, and Madagascar would make all French officers who had remained loyal to the Vichy government unwilling to accept his leadership – even those who were most eager to throw off the German yoke. That was emphasised by Murphy and readily assumed by Roosevelt, who had developed a deep distrust of de Gaulle's judgment and dislike of his arrogance. Indeed, Roosevelt insisted that all information about Torch should be withheld from de Gaulle – and when Churchill pleaded that he should at least be allowed to inform de Gaulle 'some time during D minus 1', Roosevelt replied:

I am very apprehensive in regard to the adverse effect that any introduction of de Gaulle into the Torch situation would have on our promising efforts to attach a large part of the French African forces to our expedition.

I therefore consider it inadvisable for you to give de Gaulle any information in regard to Torch until subsequent to a successful landing. You would then inform him that the American commander of an American expedition with my approval insisted on complete secrecy as a necessary safety precaution.

Churchill, who had recently dubbed himself 'your lieutenant', bowed to his master's voice, and de Gaulle was given no information of the project until the landings had taken place. That de Gaulle obtained no inkling of the expedition before then was remarkable testimony to the security value of that 'British reserve' of which other people so often complain. For it became evident to anyone who knew the project that a broad awareness of it was spreading to a widening circle in London, including the press, during the preceding weeks. That nothing leaked out showed that a habit of restraint in discussion can be more effectively leak-proof than any formal security precautions.

In these circumstances the Americans, from the President downward, readily accepted the view of General Mast and his associates that General Giraud was the most desirable and acceptable candidate for the leadership of the French in North Africa – as Murphy had already conveyed before the conference took place. Giraud, an army commander in May 1940, had been taken prisoner by the Germans, but had managed to escape in April 1942 and reached the unoccupied part of France, where he was allowed to stay on promising to support Pétain's authority. He took up residence near Lyons. From there, although under surveillance, he got into communication with many officers, both in France itself and in North Africa, who shared his desire to organise a revolt against German domination with American help. Giraud's viewpoint was expressed in a letter

to one of his supporters, General Odic: 'We don't want the Americans to free us; we want them to help us free ourselves, which is not quite the same.'

Moreover, in his private negotiations with them Giraud made it one of his conditions that he should be Commander-in-Chief of Allied troops in French territory wherever French troops were fighting. From a message he received he understood that his conditions were accepted by Roosevelt, but they came as a complete surprise to Eisenhower when Giraud arrived at Gibraltar to meet him on November 7 – the eve of the landings.

Giraud had been picked up, at a rendezvous on the south coast of France, by the same British submarine, HMS *Seraph,* that had carried Mark Clark on his secret mission to the Algerian coast. He was then transferred to a flying-boat, though nearly drowned in doing so, and carried on to Gibraltar. On reaching there, he was staggered at the news that the Allied landings in North Africa were taking place early next morning – as he had been told that they were planned for the following month – and also by the discovery that the command of them was in the hands of Eisenhower, instead of his own. This led to a heated argument, in which he based himself on his higher rank as well as on the assurances he had received, and constantly reiterated that to take anything less than supreme command would be a surrender of his country's prestige and his own.

The argument went on until midnight, and when it was broken off he was still declaring that unless his claims were conceded he would refuse to co-operate and remain 'a spectator in this affair'. But when talks were resumed in the morning (November 8) he reconciled himself to the situation, after explicit assurances that he would be head of the French forces and administration in North Africa – a promise that was soon to be set aside on grounds of expediency and the superior assets of Admiral Darlan.

In bringing the 'Torch' of liberty to French North Africa, the Americans had achieved surprise too fully, throwing their friends and helpers into confusion – more confusion than was caused on the enemy's side. The benefit of surprise was enjoyed in the unhindered ocean passage and safe arrival off the landing places of all the convoys. But in the final stage, when the Allied forces moved inshore, the military advantages of such complete surprise were offset, for a time, by the political and psychological disadvantages. Their French collaborators were caught unready to aid effectively in clearing the way, and under the shock of the sudden invasion most of the French commanders reacted in the way that was natural in such circumstances, and in conformity with their loyalty to legitimate authority, embodied in Marshal Pétain at Vichy. Thus the landings met resistance initially – although less at Algiers than at Oran and Casablanca.

At Casablanca, General Béthouart received a message late in the evening of the 7th that the landing would take place at 0200 hours on the 8th. He sent off parties of his troops to arrest the German armistice commissions, and posted some of his officers

to welcome the Americans on the beach at Rabat, 50 miles to the north, as he assumed that they would land there, since it had no coastal defence batteries and was the seat of French government in Morocco. (Rabat had originally been an intended landing site, but the planners of the Western Task Force preferred Mehdia, 20 miles farther north, and Eisenhower had bowed to their wishes.)

After these preliminary steps, Béthouart himself went with a battalion to occupy army headquarters at Rabat, and sent the army commander off under escort. Béthouart had also dispatched letters to General Noguès, the Resident-General (and overall Commander-in-Chief) in Morocco, and to Admiral Michelier, informing them that the Americans were about to land, that Giraud was coming to take over command of French North Africa as a whole, and that he himself had been appointed by Giraud to take over command of the army in Morocco. His letter to Noguès and Michelier asked them to back the order he had issued allowing the Americans to land unopposed – or else to keep out of the way until it was more convenient for them to accept the *fait accompli.*

On receiving the letter, Noguès tried to 'sit on the fence' until the situation was clearer. His state of uncertainty and hesitancy was the greater because neither he nor any of the French commanders in Morocco heard, or received news of, President Roosevelt's broadcast announcements – which were repeated at half-hourly intervals from 0130 hours onwards.

While Noguès hesitated, Michelier took prompt action. His air and submarine patrols had not spotted the approaching armada before nightfall, so he jumped to the conclusion that Béthouart was deluded or hoaxed. Michelier's assurance that no strong force had been sighted off the coast so impressed Noguès that even when the first reports of the landings reached him, shortly after 0500 hours, he believed that they were no more than Commando raids. He therefore jumped down off the fence, on the anti-American side, and ordered the French forces to resist the landings, while putting Béthouart under arrest on a charge of treason.

The American armada lands

Patton's main landing was made at Fedala, 15 miles north of Casablanca, with subsidiary ones at Mehdia, 55 miles farther north, and Safi, 140 miles south of Casablanca. Fedala offered the nearest suitable landing beaches to that city and its strongly defended harbour – the only large and well-equipped one on the Atlantic coast of Morocco. Mehdia was chosen because it was the nearest landing place to the Port Lyautey airfield, the only one in Morocco with a concrete runway. Safi was chosen because a right flank force operating there might ward off the strong French garrison of the inland city of Marrakech from intervening at Casablanca, and also because it had a harbour where medium tanks could be disembarked – for the new LSTs (Landing Ships Tank) then being produced were not ready in time.

As the American armada approached the coast of Morocco on November 6, after a

smooth ocean passage, heavy seas were reported there and the forecast for the 8th was that the surf would be so high as to make landings impossible. But Admiral Hewitt's own weather expert predicted that the storm would pass away, and he decided to take the risk of pursuing the plan of landing on the Atlantic coast. On the 7th the sea began to subside, and on the 8th it was calm, with only a moderate ground swell. The surf was slighter than on any morning in the month. Even so, many mishaps and delays arose from inexperience. At Fedala the first landings were an hour later than the original H-hour (0400 hours), while 18 of the 25 boats in the initial attack waves were wrecked in the approach or on the beach, and many more in the follow-up. Indeed, there were more miscarriages after daylight than in the dark, and nearly half of the 347 landing boats with this main group were lost on D-day.

But things at least went better than Patton had forecast in a characteristically bombastic 'blood and guts' speech at the final conference before embarkation, when he had caustically told the naval members that their elaborate landing plans would break down 'in the first five minutes' and gone on to declare: 'Never in history has the navy landed an army at the planned time and place. But if you land us anywhere within fifty miles of Fedala and within one week of D-day, I'll go ahead and win.'

It was fortunate that the confusion and hesitation among the French were such that the landing attack waves were safely ashore before the defenders' fire became serious, and by then the light was good enough to help the American naval gunners in subduing the coastal batteries. But fresh trouble developed in the beach-head, and in extending it, from the inexperience and muddles of the army's shore parties, so that Patton switched his explosive criticism to the faults of his own force and service.

Both the troops and the boats had been overloaded. Although the advance on Casablanca got going on the second day, and met no serious opposition, it was abruptly halted by the pull on its tail that was caused by lack of equipment—which was piling up on the beaches but failed to come forward to the combat troops. Little progress was made on the third day, and there was an increase of opposition, so that the outlook became gloomy.

On Patton's left wing, his Northern Attack Group not only suffered from similar landing troubles and muddles but also met stronger opposition—which was the more disconcerting because a welcome 'with brass bands' had been expected. Even on the third day the troops were still engaged in clearing the thinly defended coastal strip around Mehdia, and not until the evening did they succeed in capturing the airport, which was the D-day objective and only 5 miles inland.

On Patton's right wing, his Southern Attack Group had an easier run. Profiting from surprise, they had occupied the harbour and the town before daylight on D-day—the harbour being captured by the old destroyers *Bernadou* and *Cole*, which audaciously dashed into the harbour with picked parties of assault troops. *Bernadou* raced in first, was hailed by bursts of fire as she entered the narrow mouth but escaped being hit, swept the quays with her own fire, and landed her troops on a small beach at the far end. *Cole* was then called in, and berthed beside a quay, closely followed by waves of landing boats. Other troops landed on neighbouring beaches.

The weak defences—the whole garrison of Safi numbered less than 1,000 men, with two four-gun batteries, and 15 obsolete light tanks—were soon overrun or subdued, and the tank carrier came in soon after midday to unload her 50 Shermans. Only one landing craft was destroyed, and eight damaged, out of 121 employed. But unloading was slow, through inexperience, and it was not until the night of the 10th that the tank column made a start on its long move north to aid the assault on Casablanca. It would have been much too late to affect the situation if the fight there had continued.

The situation would have been more serious if the French naval threat had not been quelled on the first day. This was achieved in a battle off Casablanca that had an old-style flavour. It started just before 0700 hours, when the coastal defence battery on Cap El Hank and *Jean Bart* in the harbour—this was the newest French battleship but still uncompleted, and unable to move from her berth—opened fire on Rear-Admiral R. L. Giffen's Covering Group, which comprised the battleship *Massachusetts,* two heavy cruisers, and four destroyers. These suffered no hits, although there were several near-misses, and their reply was sufficiently effective to silence temporarily both the El Hank battery and *Jean Bart*.

But they became so absorbed in this lively action that they neglected their task of keeping the other French ships penned there. By 0900 hours one light cruiser, seven destroyers, and eight submarines had slipped out, and the destroyers headed for Fedala, where the American transports were 'sitting ducks'. Fortunately they were headed off and driven to withdraw by a heavy cruiser, a light cruiser, and two destroyers which Admiral Hewitt had ordered to intercept them, and then, on Hewitt's summons, the Covering Group came up to cut off their retreat. Thanks to able seamanship, the skilful use of smokescreens, and the disturbing effect of a relief attack by their submarines, the French managed to survive this overwhelming concentration of heavyweight fire with the loss of only one destroyer, and then made another gallant effort to reach the transport area. In this second engagement, however, another was sunk, and only one of the eight French ships returned to harbour undamaged. There two more sank and others were further crippled by bombing.

But the result was not decisive, as the El Hank batteries and *Jean Bart*'s 15-inch guns had come to life again, while the American ships had used up so much of their ammunition that they might not have been able to drive off the French warships based on Dakar if these had come up, as was feared.

Fortunately, the situation at Casablanca, and on the Atlantic coast as a whole, was decisively changed by favourable political developments in Algiers. In the late afternoon General Noguès heard indirectly that the French authorities there, headed by Admiral Darlan, had issued an order to stop fighting. Noguès was prompt to act on this unconfirmed report, and ordered his own subordinate commanders to cease active resistance pending an armistice—which was arranged the following morning.

Complete surprise at Oran

Meanwhile, the American landings at Oran had met somewhat stiffer opposition than those of the Western Task Force in the Casablanca area. Yet there was remarkably good joint planning and co-operation between the American military task force and the British naval force which brought it to the scene and delivered it ashore. Moreover, its spearhead, the 1st US Infantry Division, commanded by Major-General Terry Allen, was a highly trained formation, and it was backed up by half the 1st US Armoured Division.

The plan was to capture the port and city of Oran by a double envelopment—two of Terry Allen's regimental combat teams landing on beaches in the Gulf of Arzeu, 24 miles to the east, while the third (under Brigadier-General Theodore Roosevelt) landed on beaches at Les Andalouses, 14 miles to the west of the city. Then a light armoured column was to drive inland from the beachhead at Arzeu, and a smaller one from a further landing point at Mersa Bou Zedjhar, 30 miles west of Oran, to capture the airfields south of Oran and close on the city to the rear. To shut it off quickly was the more important because, as estimated, its garrison of 10,000 troops could be almost doubled within 24 hours by reinforcement from inland stations.

The operation started well. At nightfall on November 7 the convoy had deceptively passed Oran, heading east, but then doubled back in the dark. The landings began promptly to time (0100 hours) at Arzeu and only half an hour later at Les Andalouses and Mersa Bou Zedjhar. Surprise was complete and no opposition was met on the beaches. Although 13 coast-defence batteries covered this stretch, there was no harassing fire until after daylight, and even then it caused very little damage, thanks to effective naval support and the cloak it provided with smoke-screens. Disembarkation and unloading went smoothly on the whole, although slowed down by the overloading of the troops, who were carrying nearly 90 pounds' load apiece of equipment. The early landing of armour benefited from the use of three 'Maracaibos'—prototypes of the LST produced by conversion of shallow-draught oil-tankers designed for use on Lake Maracaibo in Venezuela. The two at Arzeu beached about 0400 hours, and their vehicles were all ashore by 0800. The medium tanks were carried in transports and unloaded on the quay after the harbour at Arzeu was captured.

The only serious reverse was suffered in an attempt to storm Oran harbour by direct assault, to forestall sabotage of its apparatus and the ships lying there. Two small British

Roosevelt had predicted: 'An initial US landing offers a real hope that there will be no French resistance'

cutters, HMS *Walney* and *Hartland,* carrying 400 American troops, and accompanied by two motor launches, were employed to carry out this daring plan—which the American naval authorities had deprecated as rash. The outcome confirmed their view that it was a 'suicide mission'. Unwisely, it was timed to start two hours after H-hour, just when the French had been aroused by the landings elsewhere. The precaution of displaying a large American flag failed to deter the French from replying with sustained blasts of fire which crippled both cutters and killed half of their crews and troops, while the remainder, mostly wounded, were taken prisoner. This success inspired the French to send out four warships in search of larger targets, but these were speedily repelled and two of them sunk.

The advance from the beach-heads got going by 0900 hours or earlier, and soon after 1100 Colonel Waters's light armoured column from Arzeu reached Tafaraoui airfield, which was reported an hour later as ready to receive aircraft from Gibraltar. But when the column turned north it was checked short of La Sénia airfield, and so was Colonel Robinett's column from Mersa Bou Zedjhar. The converging infantry advances from Arzeu and Les Andalouses also became hung up when they met resistance as they approached Oran. No help was provided by the Paratroop Task Force, which came from Cornwall in 38 transport planes, as its plan miscarried and the bulk of it was dropped or landed 40 miles distant from Oran, while a number of planes went far astray.

On the second day little progress was made, as French resistance stiffened and a counterattack on the flank of the Arzeu beach-head dislocated the whole plan of operations through the threat being magnified by lurid reports—which led General Fredenhall to divert forces from other missions. While La Sénia airfield was captured in the morning, most of the French aircraft had already flown off and it could not be used because of persistent shellfire. A concentric attack towards Oran was mounted on the third morning, after some of the islands of resistance on the approach roads had been by-passed during the night. The infantry attacks from east and west again met checks, but helped to fix the attention of the defenders, while advance parties of the two light armoured columns drove into the city from the south without being opposed, apart from occasional sniping, to reach the French Military Headquarters before mid-day. The French commanders then agreed to surrender. The American casualties in the three days' fighting on land were under 400, and the French even less. These light losses, and particularly the diminishing resistance on the final day, were influenced by the French commanders' awareness that negotiations were proceeding at Algiers.

The landings at Algiers had run a smoother and shorter course, thanks largely to the local commander, General Mast, and his collaborating associates. No serious resistance was met anywhere, except in trying to force an early entry into the harbour.

One transport, USS *Thomas Stone,* was

△ French sailors watch with scepticism as American troops clear a damaged blockhouse

△ Resistance was sporadic: here US soldiers escort a column of French troops

△ An American half-track in Oran after Centre Task Force had occupied the town

temporarily disabled at daybreak on the 7th by a torpedo fired by a U-boat when 150 miles short of Algiers, but after that the seaborne approach deeper into the Mediterranean met no further trouble. Although sighted by a few enemy observation planes, no air attack came before the convoy made its southward turn after dark to the landing beaches. One group of these was near Cap Matifou, some 15 miles east of Algiers, another near Cap Sidi Ferruch, 10 miles west of the city, and the third group 10 miles farther west near Castiglione. For political camouflage the landings nearest Algiers were made by the Americans, with an admixture of British Commandos, and the main British one was on the more westerly beaches near Castiglione.

Here the landings began promptly at 0100 hours, and proceeded without mishap despite rough and dangerous beaches. French troops who were met a short way inland said that they had been instructed to offer no resistance. Blida airfield was reached about 0900. On the eastern side of Algiers the landings were a little late and suffered some confusion, but 'in the absence of resistance it was possible to straighten out the situation quickly'. The important Maison Blanche airfield was reached soon after 0600 hours and occupied after a few shots had been fired as token resistance. The advance on Algiers itself, however, met a village strongpoint that refused passage, and was then brought to a complete halt by a threat of attack from three French tanks. The coast battery on Cap Matifou also rejected calls to surrender, and only yielded after being twice bombarded by warships and dive-bombed.

The attempt to rush the port of Algiers fared worse. The British destroyers, *Broke* and *Malcolm,* flying large American flags and carrying an American infantry battalion, were used for this venture—which was planned to enter the harbour three hours after the landings in the hope that the defenders would have been drawn off, even if their acquiescence had not been secured. Instead, the destroyers came under heavy fire as soon as they approached the entrance. *Malcolm* was badly hit and withdrew. *Broke,* at the fourth try, succeeded in running the gauntlet, and berthed alongside a quay, where her troops disembarked. At first they were allowed to occupy installations unopposed, but about 0800 hours guns started to shell *Broke,* forcing her to cast off and withdraw. The landing party was hemmed in by French African troops, and surrendered soon after mid-day, as its ammunition was running low and there were no signs of relief by the main force. The French fire, however, had been directed to keep the landing party in check rather than destroy it.

In the landings west of Algiers near Cap Sidi Ferruch there was much more delay and confusion, while a number of the landing craft went astray and arrived on the British beaches farther west. Components of each battalion were scattered over 15 miles of coast, while many of the landing craft were wrecked in the surf or delayed by engine trouble. Fortunately, the troops had a passive reception at first, ▷

WORKHORSE FOR THE ALLIES

Debut of the Parachute Regiment. By the time of the Torch landings, the British had recruited a small force of airborne troops which was to prove vital during the opening stages of the race into Tunisia. The operations to capture the airfields at Bône and Souk el Arba were among the first occasions in which the new parachute battalions were used in action, and since at this stage they had not acquired a new badge, the men wore the distinctive red beret with the badges of their old regiments. A parachute battalion at this time consisted of about 538 men of all ranks—a headquarters company and three rifle companies—and would be accompanied into action by a variety of specialists: troops from the Royal Engineers, Royal Signals, and Royal Army Medical Corps. The operations in Tunisia were also the first time that the airborne troops used the aircraft which was to become their standard mount for the rest of the war—and the workhorse of almost all the Allied forces in every theatre.

Douglas C-47 Dakota. A military version of the DC-3 airliner, the Dakota had a strengthened floor and larger cargo-handling door on the port side. Rugged and extremely reliable, over 10,000 Dakotas had been produced by the end of the war—1,200 of them being supplied to the RAF—and many were still in use 20 years after the war ended. **Speed:** 230 mph (maximum), 167 mph (cruising) **Range:** 1,300 miles. **Crew:** Three. **Load:** 9,028 lb of cargo, or 18/24 paratroops

(Below) Dakotas in flight during the advance into Tunisia
(Below right) British paratroops inside a Dakota en route to Bône airfield

John Batchelor

LE COURRIER DE L'AIR

APPORTE PAR LA RAF — LONDRES 10 NOVEMBRE 1942

EDITION SPECIALE

LE GENERAL GIRAUD

COMMUNIQUE OFFICIEL

DU COMMANDANT EN CHEF

DES FORCES ALLIEES

EN AFRIQUE DU NORD

VOIR AU VERSO →

Message du Président des Etats Unis

Le Président des Etats Unis m'a chargé comme Général Commandant en Chef des Forces Expéditionnaires Américaines de faire parvenir aux peuples de l'Afrique française du Nord le message suivant:

Aucune nation n'est plus intimement liée, tant par l'histoire que par l'amitié profonde, au peuple de France et à ses amis que ne le sont les Etats Unis d'Amérique.

Les Américains luttent actuellement, non seulement pour assurer leur avenir, mais pour restituer les libertés et les principes démocratiques de tous ceux qui ont vécu sous le drapeau tricolore.

Nous venons chez vous pour vous libérer des conquérants qui ne désirent que vous priver à tout jamais de vos droits souverains, de votre droit à la liberté du culte, de votre droit de mener votre train de vie en paix.

Nous venons chez vous uniquement pour anéantir vos ennemis — nous ne voulons pas vous faire de mal.

Nous venons chez vous en vous assurant que nous partirons dès que la menace de l'Allemagne et de l'Italie aura été dissipée.

Je fais appel à votre sens des réalités ainsi qu'à votre idéalisme.

Ne faites rien pour entraver l'accomplissement de ce grand dessein.

Aidez-nous, et l'avènement du jour de la paix universelle sera hâté.

Dwight D. Eisenhower

DWIGHT D. EISENHOWER
Lieutenant Général, Commandant en Chef
des Forces Expéditionnaires Américaines.

A poster which announced the support of General Giraud for the Torch operations. His influence was to be short-lived

A message from Roosevelt emphasising the ties between France and America, and appealing to French 'realism and idealism'

Eisenhower and Mark Clark with Admiral Darlan, whose support was to clinch acceptance of the invasion in North Africa.

Generals Juin (right) and Noguès, commanders of the French North African Forces who followed Darlan in supporting the Allies

Mast and some of his officers coming to meet them and clear the way – otherwise these landings would have turned into a costly fiasco. But when, after hasty reorganisation, columns pushed on towards Algiers they encountered resistance in several places. For Mast had by now been relieved of command, his orders for co-operation cancelled, and his troops bidden to oppose the Allied advance.

The Allies' collaborators in Algiers had played their part remarkably well under the difficulties caused by the very short notice they had been given of the landing, and the little they had been told about its objectives. Their own plans to aid such a landing were promptly put into action. Officers were posted along the coast to welcome and guide the Americans, control points seized by organised parties, the telephone service largely blocked, police headquarters and outlying stations occupied, unsympathetic higher officials locked up, and the radio station taken over in readiness for a broadcast by Giraud or on his behalf which they hoped would be of decisive effect. In sum, the collaborators achieved enough to paralyse opposition by the time that the landings took place, and they kept control of the city until about 0700 hours – longer than they had reckoned on doing or had regarded as necessary. But the advance from the landing beaches was too slow to match the need.

When the Americans failed to appear by 0700, the limitations of the collaborators' influence on their countrymen became manifest. Moreover, when they broadcast an appeal in the name of Giraud, who had also failed to arrive as expected, this fell so flat as to show that the weight of his name had been overestimated by them. They soon began to lose control of the situation, and were brushed aside or put under arrest.

Breaking the news to General Juin

Meanwhile fateful discussions were proceeding on a higher level. Half an hour after midnight Robert Murphy had gone to see General Juin, broken the news to him that overwhelmingly strong forces were about to land, and urged him to co-operate by prompt instructions that they were not to be resisted. Murphy said that they had come on the invitation of Giraud, to help France in liberating herself. Juin showed no readiness to accept Giraud's leadership or regard his authority as sufficient, and said that the appeal must be submitted to Admiral Darlan – who was, by chance, in Algiers at that moment, having flown there to see his son, who had fallen dangerously ill. Darlan was awakened by a telephone call and asked to come to Juin's villa to receive an urgent message from Murphy. On arrival, his first reaction was to exclaim angrily: 'I have known for a long time that the British were stupid, but I always believed that the Americans were more intelligent. I begin to believe that you make as many mistakes as they do.'

After some discussion he eventually agreed to send a radio message to Marshal Pétain reporting the situation and asking for authorisation to deal with it freely on the Marshal's behalf. Meanwhile the villa had been surrounded by an armed band of anti-Vichy French, so that Darlan was virtually under guard. But a little later they were driven off by a detachment of *gardes mobiles,* who put Murphy under arrest. Then Darlan and Juin, eyeing one another like suspicious cats, went off to the headquarters in Algiers. From here Juin took steps to regain control, releasing General Koeltz and other officers who had been arrested by Mast and his associates, while putting the latter under arrest in their turn. Darlan, however, sent a further telegram to Marshal Pétain, just before 0800 hours, in which he emphasised that 'The situation is getting worse and the defences will soon be overwhelmed' – a palpable hint that it would be wise to bow to *force majeure.* Pétain's reply gave the authorisation requested.

Just after 0900 hours the American Chargé d'Affaires in Vichy, Pinkney Tuck, had gone to see Pétain and deliver Roosevelt's letter requesting his co-operation. Pétain handed him a reply, already prepared by then, expressing 'bewilderment and sadness' at American 'aggression', and declaring that France would resist attack on her empire even by old friends – 'This is the order I give.' But his attitude to Tuck was very pleasant, and he seemed to be far from sad. Indeed, his behaviour conveyed the impression that his formal reply was really meant to allay German suspicions and intervention. But a few hours later Laval, the Prime Minister, accepted under Hitler's pressure an offer of German air support – and by evening the Axis powers were preparing forces for dispatch to Tunisia.

Meanwhile Darlan, on his own responsibility, had issued orders to the French troops and ships in the Algiers area to cease firing. Although this order did not apply to the Oran and Casablanca areas, Darlan authorised Juin to arrange a settlement for the whole of North Africa. Moreover it was agreed early in the evening that control of Algiers should be transferred to the Americans at 2000 hours, and that the Allies should have the use of the harbour from first light the next morning, the 9th.

The afternoon of the 9th saw the arrival of General Mark Clark to conduct the fuller negotiations necessary, and of General Kenneth Anderson to assume command of the Allied troops for the advance to Tunisia. Giraud also arrived, a little earlier, but found that he was far from welcome among his chief compatriots there, and took refuge with a family who lived in an out-of-the-way place. Mark Clark remarks 'he practically went underground' – although he emerged next morning for Clark's first conference with Darlan, Juin, and their chief subordinates.

Here Clark pressed Darlan to order an immediate cease-fire everywhere in French North Africa, and when he hesitated – arguing that he had sent a summary of the terms to Vichy and must await word from there – Clark began pounding the table and said that he would get Giraud to issue the order in his place. At that, Darlan pointed out Giraud's lack of legal authority or sufficient personal weight. He also declared that such an order 'would result in the immediate occupation of southern France by the Germans' – a forecast that was soon borne out. After some more argument, with an accompaniment of table-pounding, Clark pungently told Darlan that unless he issued the order immediately he would be taken into custody – Clark having taken the precaution of posting an armed guard around the building. Darlan then, after a brief discussion with his staff, accepted this ultimatum – and his order was sent out at 1120 hours.

When it was reported to Vichy, Pétain's own reaction was to approve it, but when Laval heard of it en route to Munich, in response to a brusque summons from Hitler, he got on the telephone to Pétain and induced him to disavow it. Early in the afternoon, Clark received the news that Vichy had rejected the armistice. When Darlan was told of this by Clark, he dejectedly said: 'There is nothing I can do but revoke the order I signed this morning.' Thereupon Clark retorted: 'You will do nothing of the kind. There will be no revocation of these orders; and, to make it certain, I shall hold you in custody.' Darlan, who had already hinted at this solution, showed himself very ready to accept it – and sent the reply to Pétain: 'I annul my orders and constitute myself a prisoner' – the annulment being only for Vichy and German ears.

Next day, under pressure from Hitler via Laval, Pétain announced that all authority in North Africa had been transferred from Darlan to Noguès, but had already sent Darlan a secret message that the disavowal had been made under German pressure and was contrary to his own wishes. Such double-talk was a subterfuge compelled by the perilous situation in France, but left the situation and French commanders in North Africa, outside Algiers, still confused.

Fortunately, Hitler helped to clarify it and resolve their doubts by ordering his forces to invade the unoccupied part of France that, by the 1940 armistice agreement, had been left under the control of the Vichy government. On November 8 and 9 Vichy had stalled on the offers of armed support which Hitler pressed on them, making reservations which inflamed his suspicions. On the 10th Laval arrived in Munich to face Hitler and Mussolini, and that afternoon Hitler insisted that the ports and air bases in Tunisia must be made available to the Axis forces. Laval still tried to hedge, saying that France could not agree to the Italians moving in, and that in any case only Pétain could decide. Hitler then lost all patience, and soon after the talk ended gave orders for his forces to drive into the unoccupied part of France at midnight – a move already mounted in readiness – as well as to seize the Tunisian air and sea bases, along with the Italians.

The Wehrmacht takes over

Southern France was speedily overrun by the German mechanised forces while six Italian divisions marched in from the east.

German aircraft had started to arrive on an airfield near Tunis in the afternoon of the 9th, together with an escort of troops to protect them on the ground, but had been confined to the airfield by a ring of French troops. Now, from the 11th onward, the airlift was multiplied, the adjacent French troops disarmed, while tanks, guns, transport vehicles, and stores were brought over by sea to Bizerta. By the end of the month 15,000 German troops had arrived, with about 100 tanks, although a large proportion were administrative personnel to organise the base. Some 9,000 Italians had also arrived, largely by road from Tripoli, and were primarily used to cover the southern flank.

For a hastily improvised move, at a time when the Axis forces were hard pressed everywhere, that was a fine achievement. But such a scale of force was very small compared with what the Allies had brought to French North Africa, and would have had slight chance of resisting them if the Torch plan had provided for a larger proportion of the Allied expeditionary force to be used for the advance to Tunisia, or if the Allied Command had developed the advance more rapidly than it did.

The German invasion of southern France did more than anything else to help the Allied situation in Africa by the shock it gave to the French commanders there. On the morning of the 11th, before the news came, there had been another see-saw in Algiers. The first sign was when Clark went to see Darlan, and pressed him to take two urgent steps—to order the French fleet at Toulon to come to a North African port, and to order the Governor of Tunisia, Admiral Esteva, to resist the Germans' entry.

Darlan was first evasive, arguing that his orders might not be obeyed in view of the broadcast announcement that he had been dismissed from command of the French forces—and, when further pressed, he refused to comply with Clark's demands. Clark marched out of the house, slamming the door to relieve his feelings. But in the afternoon he had a telephone message ask-ing him to see Darlan again, and Darlan now agreed to comply with Clark's wishes, in view of developments in France—although his message to the commander of the fleet at Toulon was worded as urgent advice rather than as an order. Another favourable turn was that General Noguès, Darlan's Vichy-nominated successor, agreed to come to Algiers for a conference next day.

But in the early hours of the 12th Clark had a fresh jolt on hearing that Darlan's order for resistance in Tunisia had been revoked. Summoning Darlan and Juin to his hotel, it soon became apparent that the change was due to Juin, who argued that it was not a revocation but only a suspension of the previous order pending the arrival of Noguès, who was now his legitimate superior. Such scruples about legality, while characteristic of the French military code, appeared to Clark as merely legalistic quibbles. Although they bowed to his insistence that the order to Tunisia must be reissued immediately, without waiting for the arrival of Noguès, his suspicion was renewed by their reluctance to accept Giraud's participation in the conference. Clark was so exasperated at their procrastination that he spoke of putting all the French leaders under arrest, and locking them up aboard a ship in the harbour, unless they came to a satisfactory decision within 24 hours.

Meanwhile, Darlan's position in relation to the other French leaders in Africa had been strengthened by the receipt of a second clandestine message from Pétain reaffirming his confidence in Darlan and emphasising that he himself was in *accord intime* with President Roosevelt, although he could not speak his mind openly because of the Germans' presence. This helped Darlan, who had a shrewder sense of realities than many of his compatriots, to secure the agreement of Noguès and the others for a working agreement with the Allies, including the recognition of Giraud. Their discussions at a further conference on the 13th were expedited by a fresh threat by Clark that he would lock up the lot.

That afternoon it was settled, and promptly endorsed by Eisenhower who had just flown over from Gibraltar. Under its terms, Darlan was to be High Commissioner and Commander-in-Chief of Naval Forces; Giraud to be Commander-in-Chief of Ground and Air Forces; Juin, Commander of the Eastern Sector; Noguès, Commander of the Western Sector, as well as Resident-General of French Morocco. Active co-operation with the Allies in liberating Tunisia was to begin immediately.

Eisenhower endorsed the agreement all the more readily because he had come to realise, like Clark, that Darlan was the only man who could bring the French round to the Allied side, and also because he remembered Churchill's remark to him just before he left London: 'If I could meet Darlan, much as I hate him, I would cheerfully crawl on my hands and knees for a mile if by doing so I could get him to bring that fleet of his into the circle of the Allied forces.' Eisenhower's decision was no less promptly endorsed by Roosevelt and Churchill.

But such a 'deal with Darlan', who had so long been presented in the press as a sinister pro-Nazi figure, aroused a storm of protest in Britain and America—a worse storm than either Churchill or Roosevelt had foreseen. In Britain it was the greater, since de Gaulle was there, and his supporters did their utmost to increase the outburst of popular indignation. Roosevelt sought to calm the tumult by a public statement of explanation in which he adopted a phrase from Churchill's private cable to him, saying that the arrangement with Darlan 'is only a temporary expedient, justified solely by the stress of battle'. Moreover, in an off-the-record press conference, he described it as an application of an old proverb of the Orthodox Church: 'My children, it is permitted you in time of grave danger to walk with the devil until you have crossed the bridge.'

Roosevelt's way of explaining away the arrangement as 'only a temporary expedient' naturally came as a shock to Darlan, who felt that he had been tricked. In a letter

Once Darlan had agreed to support the Allies, French resistance in Algeria was at an end, and Allied forces were able to move out from the main cities, and complete the occupation of the country swiftly and easily

United Press

of protest to Mark Clark he bitterly remarked that both public statement and private word appeared to show that he was regarded as 'only a lemon which the Americans will drop after they have squeezed it dry'.

Roosevelt's statement was still more hotly resented by the French commanders who had supported Darlan in reaching an agreement with the Allies. Eisenhower, very perturbed, cabled to Washington emphasising that 'existing French sentiment does not even remotely resemble prior calculation, and it is of utmost importance that no precipitate action be taken which will upset such equilibrium as we have been able to establish'. General Smuts, who flew to Algiers on his way back from London to South Africa, cabled to Churchill: 'As regards Darlan, statements published have had unsettling effect on local French leaders, and it would be dangerous to go further on these lines. Noguès has threatened to resign, and as he controls the Moroccan population the results of such a step may be far-reaching.'

Meanwhile, Darlan had made a definite and detailed agreement with Clark for co-operative action. He also induced the French leaders in West Africa to follow his lead, and make the key port of Dakar, together with the air bases, available to the Allies. Then, on Christmas Eve, he was assassinated by a young man believed to be a fanatical Gaullist. That helped to solve the Allies' awkward political problem, and to clear the way for de Gaulle's advent, while the Allies had already reaped the benefit of their 'deal with Darlan'.

Churchill commented in his memoirs: 'Darlan's murder, however criminal, relieved the Allies of their embarrassment in working with him, and at the same time left them with all the advantages he had been able to bestow during the vital hours of the Allied landings.' Mark Clark remarks in his: 'Darlan's death was to me an act of providence. It is too bad he went in that way, but, strategically speaking, his removal from the scene was like the lancing of a troublesome boil. He had served his purpose,

and his death solved what could have been the very difficult problem of what to do with him in the future.' His assassin was promptly tried by court-martial on Giraud's orders, and quickly executed. On the following day the French leaders agreed to choose Giraud as High Commissioner in succession to Darlan. He filled the gap—for a short time.

If the Allies had not succeeded in enlisting Darlan's help their problem would have been much tougher than it turned out. For there were nearly 120,000 French troops in North Africa—about 55,000 in Morocco, 50,000 in Algeria, and 15,000 in Tunisia. Although widely spread, they could have provided formidable opposition if they had continued to resist the Allies.

End of the French fleet

The only important respect in which Darlan's aid and authority failed to achieve the desired effect was over bringing the main French fleet across from Toulon to North Africa. Its commander, Admiral de Laborde, hesitated to respond to Darlan's summons without confirming word from Pétain, and a special emissary sent by Darlan to convince him was picked up by the Germans. Laborde's hesitation was prolonged, and his anxiety lulled, by the Germans' shrewdness in halting on the outskirts of the Toulon naval base and allowing it to remain an unoccupied zone garrisoned by French troops. Meanwhile they prepared a plan for a coup to seize the fleet intact, and launched it on November 27, after blocking the harbour exits with a minefield. But although delay had forfeited the chance of breaking out, the French managed to carry out their prepared plan for scuttling the fleet quickly enough to frustrate the German attempt to capture it—thus fulfilling the assurance that Darlan had given in his initial conference with Clark at Algiers on November 10: 'In no circumstances will our fleet fall into German hands.' The Allies' disappointment that it had not come to North Africa was outweighed by their relief that the danger of it being used against them had vanished with its sinking.

Another cause of relief during this critical period, and especially the first few days, was that the Spanish had abstained from any intervention and that Hitler had not attempted to strike back through Spain against the western gateway into the Mediterranean. The Spanish army could have made the harbour and airfield at Gibraltar unusable by artillery fire from Algeciras, and could also have cut communications between Patton's force and the Allied forces in Algeria, as the railway from Casablanca to Oran runs close to the border of Spanish Morocco—as close as 20 miles. When Torch was being planned the British had said that if Franco were to intervene it would be impossible to preserve the use of Gibraltar, while Eisenhower's planning staff reckoned that a force of five divisions would be necessary to occupy Spanish Morocco and that the task would take three and a half months. Fortunately Franco was content to stay quiet, as a 'non-belligerent' ally of the Axis—and the more contentedly because the Americans were both buying Spanish products and allowing him to obtain oil from the Caribbean. Moreover, the Axis archives show that Hitler, after his earlier experience of Franco's skill in evading his desires for a move through Spain against Gibraltar, did not really consider attempting such a counterstroke in November 1942. The idea was only revived, and then by Mussolini, the following April—when the Axis forces in Tunisia were hard pressed and an early Allied invasion of Italy was feared.

Even then Hitler turned down Mussolini's plea, both because he feared that a move through Spain would be fiercely and stubbornly resisted by his 'non-belligerent' ally, and because he remained confident that the Axis forces could maintain their hold on Tunisia. That confidence of his was bolstered by the remarkable success of the very slender Axis forces sent to Tunisia by the end of November in holding up the Allied advance at that time.

[*For Sir Basil Liddell Hart's biography, see jacket flap.*]

THE END IN AFRICA

Tunisia, April 1943 *Major K. J. Macksey*

The Axis forces in North Africa had been pressed back into a small perimeter in which they waited, without hope of relief, for the final overwhelming Allied attacks. After a false start—a fruitless attempt by 8th Army to win the last triumph and break through to Tunis—1st Army inched forward, fighting bitterly over a close-knit series of peaks, seeking to break out into the plain where its full strength could be deployed

PART 1

Never at any other time during the North African campaign were the issues more clearly defined than during the last three weeks. With 19 well-manned and equipped divisions at their disposal the Allies sought to overthrow 13 sadly depleted Axis divisions: nearly 1,200 Allied tanks were concentrated against 130 belonging to the Axis: in artillery 1,500 guns were opposed by just under 500; and in the air over 3,000 aircraft dominated 500. But although even the most optimistic Axis forecast could not ignore the inevitability of final engulfment, this did not mean that Hitler or Mussolini could cut their losses, still less withdraw: to them every month spent holding the north-eastern corner of Tunisia imposed crucial delay on the launching of an Allied offensive across the Mediterranean.

If Tunisia could be held until late in the summer, the Axis leaders reasoned, it might be that the Allied invasion of Europe would be delayed until autumn when the worsening weather and rough seas would intervene to hamper amphibious operations. Much work had been expended by German engineers building inter-locking nests of strongpoints on all the principal Tunisian heights overlooking the exiguous routes into the plain, and although the Allied 1st Army's attacks in March and early April had captured important ground, particularly that overlooking the entrance to the Medjerda valley, the German defence still presented a formidable array. To take any one hill invariably demanded other co-ordinated attacks on its fellows: to fail in one sector often threatened failure in the rest. Before the more open 'tank country' could be reached, a close-knit series of peaks had still to be overcome.

From the coast just to the east of Cap Serrat to the bottleneck to the west of Pont du Fahs, the line ran very much as it had before Arnim's February offensive, but south of Pont du Fahs, where 8th Army waited below the ramparts overlooking Enfidaville and the sea, there was a new front guarding the narrow route leading along the coast to either Tunis or Cap Bon (see map).

Without doubt the comparatively broad approach through the Medjerda valley still offered the most promising entrance to Tunis via Massi-cault or Tebourba. Clear the last enemy-occupied hills on either side of Medjez el Bab, and the way was open for the armour to pour eastwards. Nowhere else could such a concentration of force be employed at once and only by using his resources in mass was Sir Harold Alexander likely to achieve the rapid conquest of the ports he desired as a prerequisite to the invasion of Sicily in July. For this reason, on April 12, he ordered General Anderson, commanding 1st Army, to aim a large-scale offensive on April 22 at Tunis from between Medjez el Bab and Bou Arada, co-ordinating his activities the meantime with those of the US 2nd Corps, which was to attack across the difficult northern sector in the direction of Bizerta via Mateur. To Montgomery's 8th Army, full of aggressive fire after its breathtaking lunge from Akarit, was allotted only a subsidiary role, that of mounting holding attacks in the vicinity of Enfidaville, to deflect the enemy's attention from 1st Army before the main blow fell.

It would appear that this minor role did not satisfy Montgomery and that the large-scale assault he now proposed to Alexander was meant to garland 8th Army with the last victory. An attack by three infantry divisions supported by massed artillery, to be followed up by an armoured division to a depth of at least 20 miles, smacks not of a holding attack but, instead, a full-blooded offensive—clearly intended by Montgomery to sieze the Cap Bon peninsula before it could be converted into a last bastion by the enemy. And, perhaps more to the point, before 1st Army took the last laurels. By allowing Montgomery to pursue his course, Alexander set aside his original intention to concentrate everything in 1st Army's area—with results which will soon become apparent.

Strong in their hillside emplacements with their backs to the plains and the sea, the German and Italian soldiers waited on events with an unnatural outward confidence. Yet they mistook their prospects and had forgotten their aim. Formerly, to hold Tunisia and maintain a temporary bridgehead into which Rommel could escape had represented sound strategy. Now the Axis sought merely to postpone the inevitable with woefully inadequate materials. Even if the Axis powers had land resources to spare from the immediate needs of the defence of Europe, they could never contrive to overcome the Allied sea and air blockade of the Straits of Sicily; the reinforcements they dribbled across were automatically being denied the chance of defending Europe—and yet imposing no worthwhile delay on the date of the invasion. In short, the Germans never fully understood the logistics of North Africa as conditioned by the air and sea power being applied against them.

8th Army: out of its element

Montgomery spoke at one time of 'bouncing' the enemy out of the Enfidaville position—a term redolent with the supreme confidence which permeated the whole of 8th Army. By April 16, when the strength of the enemy defences was better known, he had revised his estimate and substituted a heavy attack for the 'bouncing' operation. But the 'bouncing' spirit was not so easily dispelled from the minds of Lieutenant-General Horrocks and his colleagues in 10th Corps, upon whom fell the task of planning the operation, and with Montgomery giving only part of his attention to the preparations (because he was also planning the invasion of Sicily), a somewhat unrealistic operation of war hatched out.

For a start, 10th Corps was led to believe that only six Axis battalions barred its way: in fact there were 23, low in strength but revived in spirit. Next, with the notable exception of the GOC 4th Indian Division (Major-General Tuker), each commander in the corps thought in terms

CLOSING THE TUNISIAN BRIDGEHEAD

1943 **April 19/20:** 8th Army launches an attack on the Enfidaville position which makes little progress.
April 20/21: A German spoiling attack on 1st Army positions between Goubellat and Medjez is turned back with heavy loss.
April 22: Montgomery abandons the 8th Army attack. 1st Army moves forward for its offensive—British 5th Corps to capture the hills around Longstop and Peter's Corner, and advance to Tunis via Massicault; US 2nd Corps to attack towards Mateur; and British 9th Corps towards the Goubellat plain.
April 23: British troops reach top of Longstop but bitter fighting continues, while in the north the US 9th Division makes steady progress.
April 26: Longstop is finally secured, and 5th Corps troops reach Djebel Bou Aoukaz.
April 28/30: Final Axis armoured attack recaptures Djebel Bou Aoukaz. US troops fight bitterly to gain possession of Hill 609.
April 30: Montgomery offers to dispatch 7th Armoured and 4th Indian Divisions, and 201st Guards Brigade to 1st Army.

▷ After abortive attempts by 8th Army to break through the Axis defences in the south, and thus earn the glory of ending the Tunisian campaign, the rest of the battle to liquidate the bridgehead falls into two distinct parts. In a series of attacks from April 26/30 the 1st Army attempted to seize the last Axis strong-points which barred the way to the plain; but it met such stubborn resistance that the offensive halted, having threatened to lose all momentum and degenerate into a series of local attacks. It was now that Alexander stepped in and, taking advantage of Montgomery's offer of help, shifted several of 8th Army's units north to prepare for the final breakthrough

Although disappointing as an interceptor, the Curtiss Kittyhawk—which had been widely supplied to the RAF under lend-lease—came into its own during the North African campaign. Its ruggedness made it one of the most widely used aircraft for the new close-support techniques the RAF was developing there.
Maximum speed: 362 mph at 15,000 feet. **Range:** 700 miles.
Armament: Six ·50-inch machine-guns and two 250-lb bombs

John Batchelor

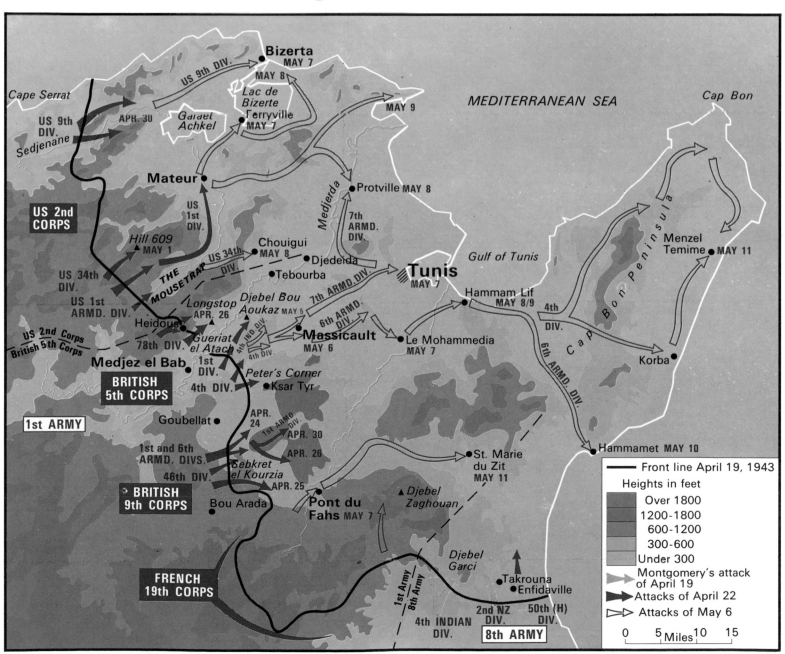

Cape Serrat

Bizerta
MAY 7

US 9th DIV.

MAY 8

US 9th DIV.
Sedjenane
APR. 30

Lac de
Bizerte

Garael
Achkel

Ferryville
MAY 7

MAY 9

MEDITERRANEAN SEA

Cap Bon

Mateur

US 2nd
CORPS

US
1st
DIV.

Hill 609
MAY 1

US 34th
DIV.

THE
MOUSETRAP

US 34th
DIV.

Chouigui
MAY 8

Djedeida

Protville MAY 8

Medjerda

7th
ARMD.
DIV.

Gulf of Tunis

Menzel
Temime ● MAY 11

US 34th
DIV.

US 1st
ARMD. DIV.

Tebourba

Djebel Bou
Aoukaz MAY 5

7th ARMD. DIV.

Tunis
MAY 7

Longstop
APR. 26

Heidous

Gueriat
el Atach

4th IND DIV.

6th ARMD.
DIV

4th DIV.

Massicault
MAY 6

Hammam Lif
MAY 8/9

Le Mohammedia
MAY 7

4th
DIV.

6th ARMD. DIV.

Korba

US 2nd Corps
British 5th Corps

78th DIV.

1st
DIV.

Medjez el Bab

BRITISH
5th CORPS

4th DIV.

Peter's Corner
● Ksar Tyr

1st ARMY

Goubellat ●

APR.
24

1st ARMD.
DIV.

APR. 30

APR. 26

St. Marie
du Zit
MAY 11

Hammamet MAY 10

1st and 6th
ARMD. DIVS.

46th DIV.

Sebkret
el Kourzia

APR. 25

BRITISH
9th CORPS

Bou Arada ●

Pont du
Fahs
MAY 7

Djebel
Zaghouan

Front line April 19, 1943
Heights in feet

Over 1800
1200-1800
600-1200
300-600
Under 300

Montgomery's attack
of April 19

Attacks of April 22

Attacks of May 6

FRENCH
19th CORPS

Djebel
Garci

Takrouna
● Enfidaville

0   5   10   15
Miles

1st Army
8th Army

2nd NZ
DIV.

50th (H)
DIV.

4th INDIAN
DIV.

8th ARMY

of desert time and space by envisaging sweeping advances even up steep mountainsides and along enemy-dominated valleys. Of the formations available to Horrocks, only 4th Indian Division was attuned by its training and its inherent psychology to mountain warfare: 2nd New Zealand, 50th, and 56th Divisions had no such experience, and 7th Armoured Division was totally unsuited to confined conditions such as these.

Horrocks's plan called upon 4th Indian and 2nd New Zealand Divisions to assault side-by-side into the hills, wheeling across the enemy rear to the coast (as once they did in the desert) while flank protection was given on the left by 7th Armoured Division and on the right (on the coastal road) by 50th Division. Thereafter the plan envisaged a rhythmic advance, gathering speed as the enemy was shattered and the armour broke through in the traditional manner. But, as Horrocks explained, everything depended on what they met—emphasising the tentative under-tone of the whole operation.

On the night of April 19/20, the men of 4th Indian Division threw themselves at the first range of hills, Djebel Blida and Djebel Garci, and the New Zealanders struck at Takrouna Hill. Everywhere they each met an unexpectedly stubborn resistance. The savagery of the fighting, in which the Italians fought as well as the Germans, is caught in this short excerpt from a contemporary Indian source and is typical of the New Zealanders' experience as well:

In the darkness men grappled and slew each other. The survivors went to earth as bombs burst about them, rose and rushed forward in the dust and smoke, and fastened upon enemies.... Every gain drew a counterattack from desperate men pledged to hold the heights at all costs. Yard by yard the assailants worked upwards, around rocky knolls, across mountain wadis, surging over crests to face other crests from which mortar and small arms fire swept down incessantly upon them.

At dawn on the 20th hardly any ground vital to subsequent extensions of the offensive had been taken in its entirety. Far from rolling forward in a grandiose left hook, the initial penetration had stuck in the outer fringe of the Axis defence at a severe toll in men's lives. To press onwards invited decimation: to stay half on and half off the high ground presaged a mounting toll of casualties but at least increased opportunities for inflicting greater losses upon the enemy. But, whichever course was adopted, the theme was slow attrition at a time when a quick decision was in demand.

A sort of mental stagnation

Throughout April 20/21, both sides hung on the hills while 50th Division made slight progress up the coast, taking Enfidaville in the process. But no decisive advance could be made. A sort of mental stagnation began to haze over an already complete physical exhaustion as Montgomery re-cast his plans—determined, so it seems, to maintain the prestige of the 8th Army—making ready to attack again on the 24th through the narrow coastal defile. For a moment he was out of character, the inspiration of Mareth absent from him.

Despite heroic efforts by 8th Army to win for themselves the last triumph, the point of decision had shifted irrevocably to the fronts of General Anderson's 1st Army and General Patton's US 2nd Corps. From the positions reached on April 18, at the end of their preliminary offensive, the British and Americans had cut their way, as it were, deep into the hard, outer crust of a pie but were held back from the soft meat beyond by one last layer of half-cooked pastry. In the American sector in the extreme north, the enemy positions on the high ground on either side of the River Sedjenane and, somewhat farther south, guarding the approaches to Mateur, were the last heights barring the way to Bizerta. For the British, the bitterly contested bridgehead across the Medjerda river scored deep into an enemy system which could hold up only so long as the hills on either side of the river, at Longstop on the northern flank, and in the hills around Peter's Corner on the southern one, remained in German

A Hurricane prepares to take off to provide close support for the initial attacks

A Churchill covers some of the infantry moving

Infantry advance through smoke in a preliminary attack on the German positions

280

...orward for an attack
...n Longstop

Guardsmen pinned down by enemy fire on
Longstop as artillery engages the enemy

Climax of much bitter fighting:
troops approach the crest of Longstop Hill

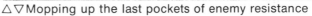

△▽ Mopping up the last pockets of enemy resistance

hands. Still further south of Medjez, the Gou-bellat plain, held weakly and enticingly by the enemy, looked ripe for penetration, although easily sealed at its eastern end by the broken and readily defensible ground between Sebkret el Kourzia and Ksar Tyr.

Against each of these sectors Alexander projected his offensive of April 22. If the Americans could force their way to the gates of Bizerta via the incredibly formidable country to their front, well and good: if the British 9th Corps could break into and through the Goubellat plain and turn north to capture Massicault in the enemy rear, better still. But the thrust by the British 5th Corps—to be aimed straight along the direct line of approach from Medjez to Tunisia via Massicault, once Longstop Hill and Peter's Corner had been cleared of the enemy—was intended to be the decisive one. Moreover, it was the obvious one—made more obvious because there seems to have been no devious or cunning plan to deceive the Germans. Even as the divisions concentrated in their assault positions, warnings were received that German spoiling attacks were to be expected.

The warnings were not mistaken. On the night of April 20/21, on both 9th and 5th Corps's fronts, tanks and infantry from the 'Hermann Göring' Division and X Panzer Division rolled forward between Goubellat and Medjez, glancing off 46th Division—on the left of 9th Corps—to become deeply imbedded within the boundaries of 1st and 4th Divisions, on the right of 5th Corps. But 46th Division was scheduled to be the first to attack at dawn on the 22nd, and so the defensive fighting which developed on its front throughout the 21st carried with it the sort of shock that could lead to failure next day. It was a tense situation.

Sheer weight of Allied numbers

Against 4th Division the velocity of the German stroke carried it to within half a mile of Divisional HQ where desperate fighting broke out, tank versus tank and man against man, across a wide arc of country. Here sheer weight of numbers began to tell against the Germans, for they could hardly eliminate two well-poised divisions supported by a brigade of Churchill tanks with the equivalent of only one division of their own. The scale of casualties bore testimony to the failure of their attempt—33 German tanks with 450 prisoners, against less than half that number of British tanks and men.

Nor was the British offensive it was meant to check materially delayed. True, a brigade of 46th Division was somewhat late advancing on the morning of the 22nd, but the whole of 5th Corps heaved forward in the evening while US 2nd Corps made its last preparations for the morning of the 23rd. Once again, as at Alam Halfa and at Medenine, the Germans had critically weakened their mobile arm by attritional attacks immediately before they were needed to repel a major offensive.

Only marginal success attended the advance of British 9th Corps, however, as (rather as General Anderson had expected) it was blocked by an anti-tank screen and prevented from breaking out to the north. It forced a minor redeployment upon Arnim but at a high price to the British. The 5th Corps once more pitted itself against the heights close to Peter's Corner and, above all, against the most celebrated and sinister of the Tunisian hills: Longstop. At Longstop, complete success was essential: so long as Germans remained upon its double peak they would be able to direct fire not only upon the British in the Medjerda valley but also on the Americans moving towards Mateur.

Resting on the shoulders of the well-seasoned 78th Division, founder members of 1st Army, lay the task of scaling the slopes of Longstop on 5th Corps's left. The 1st Division went for Gueriat el Atach in the centre, and 4th Division secured the right flank at Peter's Corner. During the eve of Good Friday, April 22, two battalions from 36th Brigade of 78th Division closed to the lower slopes of Longstop while just to the north another element of the division, its Irish Brigade, passing through the exhausted 11th Brigade, flung itself

against the last of the hills associated with Long-stop—Tanngoucha, the Kefs, and the village of Heidous. Through the night, while the rest of the Christian world prepared for its greatest religious celebration, the massed artillery of 1st Army enveloped the hillsides in fire and the infantry entered the swept zone of the German counter-barrage.

On Good Friday morning—a fine, still day—Churchill tanks of the North Irish Horse joined the assault with a battalion of Argyll and Sutherland Highlanders, followed by the East Surreys, making for the first crest through a curtain of fire. Soon, in thick scrub cut by a torrent of machine-gun and mortar fire, the Highlanders lost formation but yet continued to climb on up with unyielding determination, regardless of order or formation. When their CO lay dead, the 2nd IC, Major Anderson, took over and at last he and the remnants of the Argylls, a mere 40 men, held the summit—a deed for which he received the VC.

It was the night of the 22nd. To the left of Longstop the Irish Brigade prepared to assault Tanngoucha and the Kefs. From Longstop's ancillary peak, Djebel el Rhar, the Germans struck back with fire against their assailants. In the valley below, 1st and 4th Divisions worked forward, opening the way into the more open, tank-bearing territory beyond. Now the Americans also stood ready to attack on the 23rd as the whole Tunisian front sprang aflame from end to end.

Up the valley of the Sedjenane and lapping over the slopes of Bald and Green Hills, the US 9th Infantry Division made steady if unspectacular progress. Across the heights, their vehicles set forlornly aside, the US 1st Infantry Division tackled the forbidding jumble of peaks separating the Djoumine and Tine rivers with a verve and skill which might have drawn approval from the mountain fighters of 4th Indian Division. On the southern boundary of the American attack, 78th Division remained locked in close combat at Heidous and on Longstop—everywhere holding grimly to what they had taken, nowhere yet in possession of all they must take. South of the Medjerda the remorseless advance of 5th Corps approached Djebel Bou Aoukaz barring the way to Tebourba. East and north-east of Sebkret el Kourzia, 9th Corps—and notably the tanks of the British 6th Armoured Division, fought a see-saw battle with X Panzer Division at great loss to both. The French 19th Corps made ready to spring to the south of Bou Arada while, close to Enfidaville, Montgomery's 8th Army struck again into the hills, but this time closer to the coast, reaching for less ambitious objectives than in the past.

With such enormous strength bearing down upon them, the Germans could not expect to retain their forward positions indefinitely. Everywhere they were forced slowly and painfully back, and with each retirement there was lost to them their strongest positions, irreplaceable equipment, their best fighting men, and, gradually, the will to persist. Each redeployment to plug the gaps gouged out of his defences left Arnim with a thinner crust in front of Tunis and Bizerta. Each counterattack to seal off a new penetration invariably made him draw upon his dwindling tank force, causing his mobile arm to bleed to death without necessarily drawing blood of the same group from the enemy. Yet during that last week of April there were no obvious signs that the Axis troops were fighting with less vigour or skill than ever they had before; they doggedly counter-attacked each incursion, and never surrendered lightly. The cost to the Allies was heavy—an advance of 1,000 yards a day was in the highest order of progress.

Defeat a matter of days

No hill was fought for as was Longstop, but to those of both sides who struggled in the peaks to north and south of Longstop a comparison would have seemed academic. On Easter Monday—April 26— British infantry with tanks finally blasted the Germans out of their last strongpoint at Longstop, just a few hours after Heidous had fallen and the Americans had begun to come to the end of the first phase of their assault. In the Medjerda valley, 5th Corps reached and took Djebel Bou Aoukaz. At this moment—perhaps for

the first time—Arnim began to realise that the inevitability of defeat (for he had always understood that) lay no longer several months away. It was now a matter of just a few days. Unless he could block the Medjerda valley.

And so once more, and almost for the last time, he sought to seize the initiative and strike back hard. As the battle near Sebkret el Kourzia died away, he concentrated his remaining armoured forces, making them into one solitary unit—VIII Panzer Regiment—under a Colonel Irkens. Then under the direct supervision of V Panzer Army he flung the armour into its last ride in Tunisia, on April 28. Preliminary results looked promising—the British sustained heavy losses and with them possession of Bou Aoukaz—but when all was said and done, by the evening of April 30 nothing of enduring value had been achieved. Only 69 German tanks remained battle-worthy, and these were stopped in their tracks from a total lack of fuel.

Meanwhile, as the dust flew up from the tanks, the mountain battle went on, the Americans finding their Longstop at Hill 609 and the peaks in its vicinity, where their 34th and 1st Infantry Divisions bled for five days closely interlocked with an incredibly fierce German defence. Men fought with everything to hand, turning the weapons of one side against the other as they were captured, hurling bundles of grenades from the high crags on to those scrambling up from below, attacking, digging, counterattacking, holding, and lunging. But gradually the perseverance of the Americans found its reward in ground won by a display of guts and adaptability to varied conditions which turned them into veterans overnight. By April 30, as the last heights on either side of the Mousetrap fell, it looked as if the US 1st Armoured Division might soon be able to advance from there up the Tine valley. Once clear of the suffocating hills fast-moving mechanised warfare could start again.

This, to General Alexander, was the moment to assert his overall authority. On April 29 it was evident that the general offensive was beginning to stall by reverting into unco-ordinated local attacks. The 1st Army had virtually come to a halt; US 2nd Corps, while making measurable progress, exhibited no assurance that it was going to break out of the mountains in the immediate future, and the private war being waged by 8th Army at Enfidaville looked less promising with every day that passed, and had ceased to magnetise the enemy reserves.

Partly, 8th Army's troubles sprang from the intractable nature of the ground, partly they were increased by the Army Commander having to look ever more intently towards his next task—Sicily: but not least the men of 8th Army suffered from being in transition, those destined to land in Sicily being in course of relief by fresh, inexperienced divisions.

Indeed, it was the failure of 56th Division under its first dose of artillery fire when preparing for its baptism of action on April 28 that finally convinced Montgomery that his men had temporarily shot their bolt. He had persevered to the last against the advice of Horrocks, Freyberg, and Tuker in his determination to break through at Enfidaville—it is hard to dismiss the thought that, for a short, ill-considered moment, Montgomery had been ready to hazard the well-being of 8th Army for the glory of its participation in the final victory. Horrocks had said to his chief: 'We will break through, but I doubt whether at the end there will be very much left of the 8th Army.'

Now, at the moment of truth, Montgomery asked Alexander to visit him on April 30, offering 7th Armoured and 4th Indian Divisions with 201st Guards Brigade as additions to 1st Army for the last offensive.

In fact, Alexander had already decided that 8th Army had no useful role in the forefront of the battle, but that it must give a healthy infusion to the body of 1st Army—but Montgomery's offer of three of his best formations arrived before the order was issued. Thus it gained in importance and generosity because it was unsolicited and illustrated, once again, the innate sympathy that linked Alexander and Montgomery.

The fact that intercepted Allied radio messages had revealed to Arnim the transfer of strength from 8th to 1st Army, and that he was perfectly aware that the blow must fall in the Medjerda valley, was of no assistance, because not only was he powerless to launch another disruptive move, he could not even build a viable defence and plug the holes. In Rome, Kesselring could only implore the Italians to greater endeavours in supply, well knowing they could not do so and that nothing could circumvent a rapid and total collapse. On April 30, Mussolini wrote to Hitler: 'Today we have lost three destroyers — two of them carrying German troops and the third munitions, in consequence of attacks by great enemy air formations accompanied by 70 to 120 escorting fighter planes.'

Alexander planned to strike with overwhelming force backed by crushing air power in great depth on a comparatively narrow front along the road from Medjez el Bab to Tunis on May 6. Thereafter his force was to diverge, half turning north to assist the Americans in taking Bizerta and the rest turning rapidly south to cut the base

Tunisia, April 30/May 13, 1943
Major K. J. Macksey

THE END IN AFRICA

PART 2

By the end of April 1943 there was no more hope for Army Group Afrika. Sooner or later, the Allies were going to break through to Bizerta via Mateur, and to Tunis via the Medjerda valley — but for the Axis defeat was inevitable. This is the story of the dramatic fortnight which brought the desert war to its close

of the Cap Bon peninsula (in conjunction with pressure by 8th Army towards Hammamet from the south), prior to completing the round-up of the enemy taking refuge in the peninsula. Off the coast the Royal Navy was waiting to deal with any bold spirits who might take to the water on what was now, indisputably, a British lake.

Events were moving at such a speed that Alexander's directive when issued on May 3 did not, in one important detail, reflect the true position at the front. The concentration of 1st Army went on smoothly and apace, coincident with diversionary displays by the British 1st Armoured Division designed to (and partially succeeding in) deceiving the Germans that a strong attack would come through Pont-du-Fahs. But on the American sector there came a sudden dramatic transformation which promised to distract the enemy far more than might any simulated manoeuvre.

In the extreme north, the US 9th Infantry Division had renewed its attacks on the night of April 26/27, guided now by a new corps commander; for Patton left that day to take command of the US 7th Army destined for Sicily, and Omar Bradley took his place at the height of the battle. Faster than before, but still at great peril in the face of the tough resistance of Manteuffel's division, the 9th Division at last forced a way along the coast until, on April 30, it directly threatened to cut off the enemy on Bald and Green Hills not only from Bizerta but also from Mateur (see p. 253). Simultaneously the remainder of the US 2nd Corps conquered Hill 609 at last, after a night assault, as 1st Armoured Division came battling down the Mousetrap until stopped dead by the enemy rearguard on May 1.

It was 9th Division's success in the north which was decisive, because now the enemy had to retreat or be encircled. From Hill 609 on May 2, observers looking far across the plain of Mateur witnessed a systematic withdrawal in progress. There was a great fire in Mateur while round and about there erupted explosions galore as bridges and the equipment that could not be carried back were feverishly demolished by the Germans. Yet, regrettably, they could do no more than watch because none of the American infantry divisions were, for the moment, fit for rapid pursuit after their arduous and costly adventures in the hills; and 1st Armoured Division remained locked in the Mousetrap for another two days until the opposition withdrew and let it burst out unopposed.

Efficient German retreat
The Germans handled their retirement with typical thoroughness and skill. Not much was left for the Americans to pick up and, despite the terrific speed with which 1st Armoured Division followed when it could, it was not in time to brush aside the new German defence before it had settled into fresh positions between the coast and the Garaet Ichkeul in the north and due south from Garaet Ichkeul towards the British front on Djebel Bou Aoukaz in the Medjerda valley.

Nevertheless, there was far less reason now for Alexander to tell 1st Army to help the Americans take Bizerta. Instead, Bizerta was within the grasp of the Americans by their own endeavours and it was a determined Bradley who set his divisions the task of assaulting side-by-side with the British when the last drive for Tunis opened on May 6.

The British 9th Corps, to which General Anderson entrusted the great offensive in the Medjerda valley, had just lost its commander, General Crocker, wounded. To take Crocker's place came Horrocks, fresh from his rebuff at Enfidaville but eager and adept at the sort of operation Anderson was planning against Tunis. Placed under Horrocks's command were 6th and 7th Armoured Divisions, 4th British and 4th Indian Divisions, four battalions of Churchill tanks, 201st Guards Brigade, and some 400 pieces of artillery.

To assist Horrocks, 5th Corps—told to establish at the outset a defensive base behind which 9th Corps could assemble in security—was to capture Djebel Bou Aoukaz on May 5 before 9th Corps jumped off on the 6th, and then line the walls of the corridor opened into the enemy rear. On the left, the US 2nd Corps was to make a complementary thrust through the Chouigui Pass to Djedeida as well as pressing on to Bizerta: to the right the French 19th Corps was to distract the enemy's attention on

May 4 by an assault on the formidable Djebel Zaghouan. Nowhere was the enemy to be allowed a respite: practically the entire Allied army was to be set in motion at once.

As 2nd Corps reorganised and refreshed itself for another effort after its gruelling battle before Mateur, the elements of 1st and 8th Army mingled on the threshold of action in the Medjerda valley. The men of the 1st Army viewed with respect the battered appearance of the yellow painted desert-camouflaged vehicles, and looked in wonder on the bizarre dress of 8th Army—the suède shoes, corduroy trousers, and gaudy scarves—the epitome of Jon's caricatures. And 8th Army commented with slight envy upon the sprucer, olive-drab 1st Army equipment while maintaining a somewhat condescending air to what appeared to them to be almost another foreign army, and one which still had much to learn—from them. Ironically and rashly, perhaps for consumption in Berlin alone, a high-ranking German officer is said to have reported at this moment:

'The Americans up to now have shown but little fighting spirit; the 1st Army is good but has not yet got any fighting experience and the 8th Army, best of all, has become tired.'

But the carefully concealed concentration of vehicles and men, the dumping of 450 rounds by each gun, the reconnaissance and planning for joint battle—all went on with unified efficiency and speed. The 9th Corps adopted an operational plan familiar to old 8th Army troops if not to those of the 1st Army because Horrocks was never too proud to repeat a successful formula. After 1st Division had cleared Djebel Bou Aoukaz on the 5th, the sort of 'blitzkrieg aerial assault' which blasted a pathway through the Tebaga Gap to El Hamma in March was to be repeated on twice the scale. In the air the Luftwaffe had to all intents and purposes disappeared, and so the full weight of the Allied air forces could deluge the battlefield with impunity.

Patchwork German defences
In fact, subsequent statements by the Germans suggested that they were amazed at the pause in operations after May 1, since by then they had virtually no power to resist. Those divisions in the line were often formations in name rather than being: elsewhere improvisation with mixed *ad hoc* units, flung into battle regardless of their condition, engineered a patchwork defence which barely warranted the title of an organised system. Supplies of all kinds were on a hand-to-mouth basis. Alone of the soldierly virtues, the will to fight remained, but this will was of such sterling quality that, alone, it came to persuade the staff of 1st Army that resistance to their offensive would continue to be heavy and prolonged. By their courage the Germans deluded the British into an unwarranted spirit of caution.

By the evening of May 5 (the day Hitler regarded Tunisia as lost), Djebel Bou Aoukaz fell swiftly into the hands of the British 1st Infantry Division after a brisk assault. To their rear, 9th Corps was rolling forward, 4th Indian Division on the left of the Medjez to Massicault road with 7th Armoured Division stretched out in column behind it; the British 4th Division on the right of the road with 6th Amoured Division keeping in step with the 4th Indian and 7th Armoured. Of the infantry divisions, 4th

Indian had the harder task and needed to penetrate to greatest depth in order to unbar the way for its attendant armoured division. Possibly for this reason the voice of its commander, Major-General Tuker, had been heard loudest in the councils of war preceding the battle, taking a critical part in shaping the artillery plan and, above all, the decision to attack before first light.

When, at 0300 hours on the 6th, the sky to the east lit up with gun flashes, the earth shook and German positions vanished behind a wall of flame, smoke and dust, something new happened. For the first time, in a body, the Axis troops stopped fighting and either ran or surrendered after firing hardly a shot. The Allied divisional and regimental histories all comment on how few were the enemy dead to be counted, how thin the opposition, how light their own losses, and how punctually they arrived according to plan on their objectives, having overrun even the Axis artillery positions as they surged ahead. Only where the remnants of old Afrika Korps formations were met was a protracted stand attempted.

By 0900 hours the way was clear for both armoured divisions to pass through a corridor carpeted by the fire from waves of bombers and fighters and, in the view of General Tuker, to advance to Tunis itself that day, with armoured cars only if necessary. But the commander of 7th Armoured Division was less hasty—in fact he appears to have conducted operations with a somewhat cautious and ponderous method, fearing a trap, rather than with the dash for which the occasion called. Difficulties in replenishment and the need for rest (on the first day of what had not been an exacting advance) were cited as reasons for halting just beyond Massicault on the night of May 6/7. When an armoured breakthrough loses momentum, it sacrifices its greatest advantage by giving the enemy time to patch up a new defence. Premature pauses had been fatal in the past, but this time the measure of the enemy's collapse could be taken from the fact that next morning no new defence had been erected.

From daybreak on the 7th the tanks rolled faster and faster until, that afternoon, to the astonishment of Germans walking with their girl friends in the streets of Tunis, they were passed by a joint party of armoured cars from the 11th Hussars and Derbyshire Yeomanry. The street fighting which ensued was of a perfunctory nature: the hysterical outbursts of delight by the inhabitants of Tunis who bombarded the armoured cars with flowers transcended everything else, and there were some in 7th Armoured Division, as they took the curtain call after a three-year run in the desert theatre, who perhaps overlooked that they, and the 6th Armoured Division on their right, had split the Axis armies in Tunisia in two.

Tunis had been totally subdued by the morning of May 8: to the south of the city 6th Armoured Division, with 201st Guards Brigade, was racing for the Cap Bon peninsula: to the north the 7th was curling up to meet the Americans near Bizerta. For the Americans had been no less successful than the British. The US 9th Infantry Division had barely halted its easterly advance along the coast, and on May 7 had its reconnaissance elements probing round the outskirts of Bizerta itself. As if by arrangement, a mere 30 minutes after the 11th Hussars and Derbyshire Yeomanry

Collapse of the German Machine

By a natural instinct the men sought the preservation of the last thing left to them—their own lives. The prisoners I saw—and I suppose I passed 30,000 on the first day, mostly Germans—were not exhausted; they were not hungry or shell-shocked or wounded; they were not frightened. I saw their dumps under the trees from Soliman to Grombalia and away up the Peninsula, and the weapons they had thrown away; they had ammunition and food and water, they had enough weapons and supplies to make a series of isolated stands in the mountains for weeks had they chosen to do so.

But they did not choose because they had lost the power of making military decisions. From the moment of our breakthrough on May 6 orders had stopped flowing through the German machine.

It appeared to me as I travelled among the prisoners, especially the Germans, that they lacked the power of individual thought and action. They had been trained as a team, for years the best fighting men in the world. They had never been trained to fight in small groups or by themselves. They were seldom forced to make adaptations and makeshifts on the spur of the moment, because they were usually on the winning side and their almost perfect supply machine had placed the finest weapons in their hands. The German army organisation had been a miracle of precision in every phase of the African war. The fighting men always got their ammunition and their food. It used to come by air while we were still using carts. They even got their mail twice a week from home. And so they leaned heavily on the machine and trusted it. They never tried out the odd exciting things that we did—things like the Long Range Desert Group. They were never much good at guerilla fighting or patrolling at night. From May 6 onwards the Germans were for ever in doubt, and doubt created despair.

I stress the Germans in all this. The Italians at the end showed far more initiative. Indeed, the Young Fascists were indignant at several places when their German companions gave up. A few of the Italians at least wanted to fight it out, guerilla fashion, to the death.

The extraordinary thing was that once the enemy troops had decided to surrender they had no thought whatever of taking up arms again. Two days before they were concentrating all their minds and bodies on killing Englishmen and Americans. At this moment they were entirely free to pick up their rifles and shoot us. But they did not seem to be morose or resentful.

[From *The Desert War* by Alan Moorehead, published by Hamish Hamilton]

had slipped into Tunis, 9th Reconnaissance Troop and some tanks were rushing the centre of Bizerta. Such opposition as there was centred around clusters of mines and booby-traps—resistance by Axis soldiers collapsed suddenly, illuminated by the last dying sparks of individual belligerence.

As the remainder of US 2nd Corps, with its 1st Armoured Division leading, left Mateur behind on the 6th, it ran straight into a screen of 88-mm guns drawn from the anti-aircraft defences of Bizerta, which was soon brushed aside. On the 7th, Ferryville, in the neck of land separating Garaet Ichkeul and Lac de Bizerte, fell as, across the breadth of the American front, the advance went on against spasmodic and dying resistance, some of it heavy in the old traditions but more and more of it only of a token nature. The 34th Division, attacking through the Chouigui Pass on the left of the British 9th Corps, had to fight hard at all times, acquiring only minimal

benefit from the British success on their immediate right. In the north the Germans were seen to burn their tanks as the Americans advanced—this, beyond doubt, signified the end.

By reason of their careful preparation of the drive along the Medjerda river, the British reaped considerable benefit, although at the expense of pace, whereas the Americans, hardly less successful in the outcome, nevertheless suffered from greater opposition because of the shorter time available to arrange for the obliteration in detail of enemy positions. Regardless of the methods employed, by noon on May 9 Vaerst had to concede that his contracting and cracking perimeter to the south-east of Bizerta was only a perimeter in name. He and his army, some 40,000 strong, surrendered unconditionally to the Americans.

The French corps had captured Pont-du-Fahs on the 7th and was still advancing.

Now only those Germans who had fled to the Cap Bon peninsula remained at liberty under their fugitive commander Arnim, encouraged alone by a desperate plan to hold the neck of the peninsula and prolong resistance a little longer so that an attempt might be made to stage a miniature Dunkirk evacuation to Sicily. Nothing could have been more devoid of realism, if only because the Royal Navy and the air forces dominated the straits: but quite simply the Axis forces had virtually stopped fighting and were pouring of their own accord by the tens of thousands into the POW cages. Here and there determined pockets of Germans fought to the last, but even the Teutons had largely given up and the Italians had ceased to care to the extent that they barely seemed capable of looking after their own welfare when in captivity.

On the morning of May 8, the 6th Armoured Division by-passed Tunis in the direction of Hammam Lif, at the base of the peninsula, there to suffer a rude check on the 9th in the face of the almost inevitable screen of 88s. But this was the last check of all. Lit by the moon that night, tanks and infantry burst, regardless of risk, into Hammam Lif and tackled the Germans in house-to-house fighting while other tanks turned the flank by driving along the sea shore through the surf on to the enemy rear.

By dawn the town was in British hands, the defile funnelling the route to the base of the peninsula cleared, and the tanks set loose on a race for Hammamet. Through the gap opened by the armour followed the British 4th Division, dividing in two immediately after to send a brigade round the peninsula via Cap Bon itself, thence to rejoin the rest of the division crossing to and coming along the opposite coast. And 4th Indian Division too, following 6th Armoured Division to Hammamet, peeled off to link up with 10th Corps (commanded at the last by Freyberg) advancing from Enfidaville. Corps and divisions criss-crossed each other at will—there was nothing left to stop even the most extravagant risk.

For the staffs of the advancing divisions, fighting was rapidly receding in priorities. Although the enemy had ceased to offer coherent resistance, he now constituted—in his thousands—a major administrative problem. Utterly broken but still soldierly in bearing and behaviour, the Germans were marching into captivity under well-ordered discipline, continuing to administer themselves in the prison camps until the Allies had time to muster a big enough organisation to do it themselves. A few managed to take to the sea for Sicily, of whom 77 were scooped out of the water by the Royal Navy and 126 found marooned on Ile Zembra.

It was claimed by the Allies that 250,000 surrendered on land—a legendary figure which can never be checked, and one not in the least commensurate with earlier estimates of Axis fighting strengths. Probably it was related to the ration returns submitted by the German quartermasters who, like all quartermasters, inflated the true figure for the good of the units they were feeding. But the total victory now bore scant relationship to mere numbers. What had taken place was the disruption of a legend of German invincibility, imparting a revolution to the strategic wheel.

From isolated pockets among the last to surrender came the military commanders—commanders in name only, since they no longer possessed the means to communicate with their broken troops, even to tell them to stop fighting. First to Major-General Keightley of 6th Armoured Division, who passed him to Lieutenant-General Freyberg, came the commander of 90th Light Division, Freyberg's old rival. Almost simultaneously, an officer of 4th Indian Division stumbled across General von Arnim and his staff and brought them to Major-General Tuker. Last of all, on the 13th, there came Field-Marshal Messe (promoted to the rank but 24 hours before) to surrender in person, and as unconditionally as the rest, to Freyberg.

Three hours later Alexander signalled to Churchill:

'Sir, it is my duty to report that the Tunisian campaign is over.

All enemy resistance has ceased.

We are masters of the North African shores.'

△ A column of British armoured cars rolls into the outskirts of Tunis on May 7

△ Bren-gunner and rifleman in position during the probe towards Cap Bon

△ General Tuker's ADC ushers Arnim into captivity after the last surrenders

△ Crowds of citizens throng the streets of Tunis to welcome the Allied forces

SALERNO AND THE FIGHT FOR SOUTHERN ITALY

Southern Italy, August/October 1943
Martin Blumenson

When the Allies decided to invade Italy rather than southern France or the Balkans, they hoped for an easy task. The Italians were not going to fight, and the Allied High Command doubted whether the Germans could transfer sufficient troops into Italy to impede an Allied drive to the north. But there was a severe shock in store: Italy was no 'soft underbelly' geographically, and despite easy successes at Taranto and Messina the landing at Salerno was the Anglo/American forces' most desperate and closely-run battle yet

September 3, 1943: Amphibious DUKWs take the water at Messina in Sicily for the short voyage to the Italian mainland

Would the Germans move in and fight to repel the landings? Or would they pull back to the north?

The Anglo-American invasions of North Africa and Sicily, the latter employing token French forces, were concerned primarily with ensuring the safety of the sea lanes between Gibraltar and Suez, thereby making voyages around Africa unnecessary. The invasion of southern Italy marked a new strategic phase, in which, General Sir Harold R. L. G. Alexander later wrote: 'The Mediterranean theatre would no longer receive the first priority of resources and its operations would become preparatory and subsidiary to the great invasion based on the United Kingdom.'

The decision to invade southern Italy stemmed from the Casablanca Conference, held in French Morocco during January 1943, while the Tunisian campaign was still in progress. Having decided to invade Sicily in hopes of securing Mediterranean lines of communication, diverting German strength from the Russian front, and forcing Italy out of the war, Prime Minister Churchill and President Roosevelt, together with their principal military advisers, the Combined Chiefs-of-Staff (CCS), discussed what to do after conquering Sicily.

Since they had agreed to seek ultimate victory in Europe by means of a cross-Channel operation, was any other Mediterranean undertaking feasible? Because the available resources precluded simultaneous major campaigns in both areas, Mediterranean ventures would draw off the build-up being accumulated in the United Kingdom for the cross-Channel attack—and would probably postpone the decisive action. Yet the southern shoreline of Europe between Spain and Turkey, occupied by Axis troops, was close at hand and a tempting target for invasion. Was it, then, better to halt after Sicily and conserve resources for a quicker thrust into north-west Europe—or to employ against the European underbelly the men and material gathered in the Mediterranean?

The Americans, more conscious of the war in the Pacific, inclined toward an early cross-Channel invasion, while the British, who generally regarded a cross-Channel operation as the decisive strike against a weakened Germany, favoured continuing the war in the Mediterranean. As it became clear during the spring of 1943 that shortages of assault shipping and the German strength would prevent a cross-Channel effort that year, Mediterranean ventures beyond Sicily became increasingly practicable and attractive.

Where to go? The Americans generally looked toward the western Mediterranean, with conquest of Sardinia and Corsica leading to an invasion of southern France in order to complement a main effort across the Channel. The British generally looked to the eastern Mediterranean, with landings on the foot of Italy leading to an invasion of the Balkans in order to support the Yugoslav Partisans, draw Turkey into the war, and open a shorter sea route to the USSR for lend-lease supplies. Both courses of action had serious disadvantages.

One hope intrigued the Allies: if invasion of Sicily failed to force Italy, the weaker European Axis partner, out of the war, would an additional blow do so? If Italy surrendered, the Germans would be doubly stretched over the periphery of Europe; they might even withdraw from Italy, thereby giving the Allies airfields for intensified bombing attacks. But if the Germans chose to fight in the rugged Italian terrain, they might provoke a protracted campaign that would probably require the Allies to increase the resources in a theatre relegated by the Combined Chiefs to subsidiary importance.

When the Allied leaders met in Washington for the Trident Conference during May 1943, as the North African campaign was ending in triumph, they confirmed their plans to invade Sicily, scheduled the operation for July, and decided on their Mediterranean goals: they would try to knock Italy out of the war, and at the same time engage and contain the maximum number of German forces. But when they tried to define how to attain these aims, they could reach no agreement.

Planning for Italy

To find a specific solution, Mr Churchill, General George C. Marshall, the US Army Chief-of-Staff, and General Sir Alan Brooke, Chief of the Imperial General Staff, travelled to Algiers to meet with the Mediterranean commanders: General Dwight D. Eisenhower, the Commander-in-Chief, Allied Force; General Alexander, his deputy commander; Air-Chief-Marshal Sir Arthur Tedder; and Admiral Sir Andrew B. Cunningham.

The commanders concluded that heavy pressure during the next few months might well force the Italians to surrender. But the choice of operations after Sicily would have to depend on two Axis reactions impossible to know in advance: whether the Italians would disintegrate during the Sicily campaign, and what the Germans would do about continued Italian demoralisation. Eisenhower felt that if conquest of Sicily failed to eliminate Italy from the war, the Allies ought to go directly to the mainland. Churchill agreed. But Marshall, fearing that an Italian campaign would absorb resources needed for the cross-Channel attack, proposed that Eisenhower set up two separate planning staffs, one for an operation against Sardinia and Corsica, the other against southern Italy. The recommendation was accepted, and Eisenhower assigned planning for Sardinia and Corsica to the US 5th Army HQ, and for southern Italy to the British 10th and 5th Corps HQ.

The easiest way to get on to the mainland and into southern Italy was to cross the Strait of Messina. But because the troops at the end of the Sicily campaign might be too exhausted—or because a crossing might be desirable before the Sicily campaign ended—Eisenhower instructed British 10th Corps to plan an assault ('Buttress') launched from North Africa and landed on the toe of Italy near Reggio. If British 10th Corps was unable to advance, British 5th Corps was to be ready to make an amphibious assault ('Goblet') near Crotone. On the other hand, if Sardinia was selected, British 10th Corps would add its 'Buttress' troops to the US 5th Army's assault divisions; for Corsica, Eisenhower requested General Henri Giraud, Commander-in-Chief of French forces in North Africa, to plan a wholly French operation.

In June, a month before the invasion of Sicily, the British Chiefs-of-Staff began to see a campaign in southern Italy as far north as Naples, even Rome, as complying

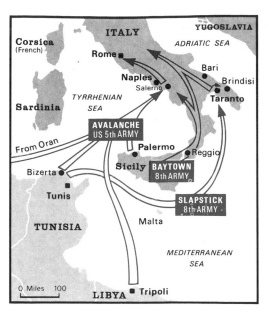

better with the CCS goals but — disturbed by
the drift into a major land campaign that
would adversely affect a cross-Channel
attack — the American Joint Chiefs preferred Sardinia and Corsica, which required
fewer resources.

When the relatively easy invasion of Sicily
showed the extreme deterioration of Italian
military power, the CCS asked whether a
landing on the west coast of Italy near
Naples was feasible in lieu of Sardinia. The
principal risks were limitations of air cover
and assault shipping, for Naples was just
outside the effective range of single-engine
fighter aircraft operating from Sicily's airfields, while available assault shipping
seemed altogether inadequate to support a
substantial landing.

American planners disliked a Naples
operation: success might accelerate Italy's
collapse, but a setback would prejudice the
cross-Channel build-up and disrupt the
global strategy. British planners nevertheless searched the shore of Italy from
Rome to the toe for suitable landing sites
and code-named the concept 'Avalanche'.

On July 18, when Eisenhower requested
approval (which he quickly secured) to
carry the war to the Italian mainland soon
after the Sicily fighting, he had in mind a
landing on the toe, but on July 25, when
King Victor Emmanuel III removed Benito
Mussolini from power, Avalanche — a landing by the US 5th Army somewhere on the
Italian west coast above the toe — seemed
feasible. To reduce the risks of Avalanche,
which required the use of the Buttress
forces, Eisenhower decided to have the
British 8th Army rush troops across the
Strait of Messina and seize a bridgehead on
the toe ('Baytown').

Because the phase of the moon between
September 7/11 would facilitate both the
naval approach to the Avalanche beaches
and airborne drops, and because landing
craft and ships could not be released from
Sicily earlier for refitting and redeployment,
the British 8th Army would cross the strait
in the earliest days of September, while
Avalanche — with the US 5th Army controlling the British 10th Corps and the US 6th
Corps — would go on the 9th.

The Avalanche planners rejected the Gulf

of Naples as a landing site — the beaches
were unsuitable, the slopes of Mount
Vesuvius dominate the shore, and the sea
approaches were strongly fortified. They
also rejected the Gulf of Gaeta just north of
Naples — the beaches were soft and beyond
the effective range of fighter aircraft based
on Sicily's airfields — selecting instead the
20-mile stretch of beach below Salerno,
south of Naples — though the Sele river cuts
the Salerno plain into two distinct sectors
and would split the invasion forces. Though
nearby hills dominate the shore, and the
mountains filling the Sorrento peninsula
would bar immediate access to Naples,
fighter aircraft could cover the landings,
the excellent airfield of Montecorvino was
close to the shore, and the port of Salerno
and the harbour of Amalfi would be helpful
for receiving supplies.

Surrender negotiations changed the plans
The risks deriving from the problems of air
cover and seaborne lift, as well as from the
strength of the Germans who had successfully evacuated their forces from Sicily,
then brought a subtle shift in outlook. The
Allied blow at the Italian mainland had
originally been conceived as a means of
forcing Italian capitulation — but now it
became contingent upon the prior elimination of Italy by military diplomacy. Fortunately, the Italian government under Marshal
Pietro Badoglio, successor to Mussolini,
while assuring the Germans that Italy would
remain in the war, was negotiating secretly
with the Allies to surrender, and the Allies
could obviously lessen the risks of Avalanche by turning the Italians against the
Germans.

During the surrender negotiations the
Italians offered to open to the Allies the
ports of Taranto in the heel of Italy, and
Brindisi on the east coast. The few Germans
in the region were expected to withdraw,
and by seizing these excellent harbours,
and Bari as well, the Allies would gain
another complex of entry points which
would facilitate the build-up in Italy. They
would have two lines of communication,
one based on Salerno and Naples for the
US 5th Army, another based on the other
side of the Italian peninsula for the British

8th, which would be freed of the limited
unloading capacities of the minor ports of
Calabria and long overland truck hauls.
Eisenhower decided to move troops on warships into Taranto as soon as the Italians
capitulated. The code name 'Slapstick',
Alexander later remarked, well illustrated
the makeshift nature of the planning.

Thus, the invasion of southern Italy came
to have three distinct parts: Baytown in the
toe early in September; Avalanche at Salerno, and Slapstick at Taranto, both on the
9th.

Would the Germans fight to repel the
landings, or would they retire to the north?
The Germans were suspicious of Italy's intentions, and their uncertainty with respect
to their ally complicated their preparations
to defend in the Mediterranean area. If Italy
collapsed, Hitler would have to fill a vacuum
in the Balkans and in southern France,
where Italian troops occupied coastal
regions. He would have to assume the
defence of all of Italy, withdraw to the
Alps, or hold along some geographic line to
retain the rich agricultural and industrial
resources of the north. His earliest thought
was to occupy and defend the entire country, and in May 1943, he instructed Field-
Marshal Erwin Rommel, recently returned
from North Africa, to activate in Munich a
skeleton army group headquarters for this
mission. But when operations in the USSR
made it impossible to furnish Rommel with
adequate forces, Hitler decided to defend
only part of Italy by establishing a fortified
line in the northern Apennines.

While Hitler and Rommel made plans in
anticipation of Italian defection, Field-
Marshal Albert Kesselring, Commander-in-
Chief South (the senior German officer in
Italy), worked in close co-operation with the
Italians to turn back any Allied invasion.
Shocked by Mussolini's fall from power in
July, he accepted in good faith Badoglio's
declarations that Italy would stay in the war.

Not so Hitler, who decided in August to
occupy Italy unobtrusively by sending additional forces into the country, ostensibly to
augment the defences. If the Italians capitulated to the Allies, Rommel was to move
into northern Italy while Kesselring pulled
his forces out of southern Italy and became

289

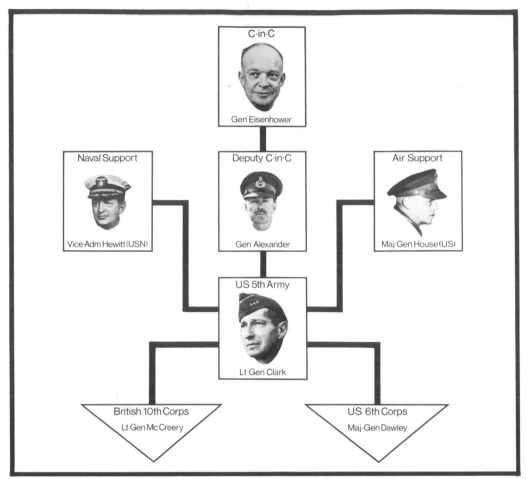

C-in-C
Gen Eisenhower

Naval Support
Vice-Adm Hewitt (USN)

Deputy C-in-C
Gen Alexander

Air Support
Maj Gen House (US)

US 5th Army
Lt-Gen Clark

British 10th Corps
Lt-Gen McCreery

US 6th Corps
Maj-Gen Dawley

△ The leadership of Avalanche, which would be the most hazardous of the Allied landings
▽ They saved Avalanche from near disaster: *(left to right)* Alexander, Clark, McCreery

as Hitler put it, 'operationally connected' with those of Rommel, who was then to assume overall command.

In August, increasing numbers of German divisions entered the mainland of Italy as Rommel moved troops in from the north and Kesselring withdrew the units that had fought in Sicily. To relieve Kesselring of the details of tactical control in the south, the Germans activated the X Army HQ under Generaloberst Heinrich von Vietinghoff.

Despite increasing tension between Germans and Italians on the upper echelons of command, neither wished to be responsible for an open break. The Italians felt insecure because they had been unable to reach a surrender agreement with the Allies. They had no doubt that the German troops in the north were an occupation force, but, too weak to protest, they pretended to accept the German explanation that Rommel's units were a strategic reserve for the Balkans, southern France, and Italy.

By the end of August, Hitler had reached a firm decision. If the Allies landed in Italy or if the Italians turned on the Germans, Kesselring was to withdraw to the Rome area, holding there only until the troops in the south had safely retired and those on Sardinia and Corsica had reached the mainland. Then he was to move to the north and join Rommel's forces. If the Allies invaded the mainland before an Italian capitulation, Vietinghoff, with Italian support, was to repel the landings in order to guarantee the routes of withdrawal to Rome.

At the beginning of September, Allied strategic bombing attacks had forced the Axis to remove their planes from all the major fields in southern Italy except the important Foggia complex. But a respectable force of ground troops remained in place: about 30,000 men of the XXVI Panzer and XXIX Panzer Grenadier Divisions under the 76th Panzer Corps HQ in the toe; and about 45,000 men of the Hermann Göring, XV Panzer Grenadier, and XVI Panzer Divisions along the west coast between Gaeta and Salerno under the XIV Panzer Corps HQ. Both corps, as well as 17,000 men of the I Parachute Division around Foggia, were under the X Army HQ. In the Rome area, under the XI Fliegerkorps HQ, directly under Kesselring's control, were about 45,000 men of the II Panzer Grenadier and II Parachute Divisions.

No opposition to a massive invasion

At 0430 hours on September 3, four years to the day after Britain had gone to war, Montgomery's 8th Army, with massive artillery, naval, and air support, invaded the continent of Europe, as the British 13th Corps, with Canadian 1st and British 5th Divisions reinforced by armoured brigades, infantry brigades, and Commandos, crossed the Strait of Messina to the toe of Italy. There was no opposition. Some Italian troops volunteered to unload the landing craft and ships.

When the two German divisions in the toe began at once to withdraw, it became apparent to the Allies that the natural obstructions of the terrain, intensified by German demolitions, would be the main obstacles to the advance. Roads were few and inferior, the units lacked transport, and the farther the troops advanced the more difficult their progress would become. A small amphibious attack to Pizzo, about 50 miles from Reggio, on September 8 almost caught some Germans, but the withdrawal continued, prompted at least partially by observation of Allied ships on their way to Salerno.

The amphibious movement had started on September 3. The British 10th Corps troops, loaded into many different types of ships, departed from Tripoli and Bizerta in a series of convoys of various speeds and compositions, some stopping at Sicily. The US 6th Corps sailed from Oran in a single convoy. By September 6, practically all the convoys were at sea, and an Axis air raid of about 180 aircraft against Bizerta had no effect on the operation.

All vessels, steaming through narrow, mine-swept lanes, were to pass west of Sicily, go north on the 8th, then turn east toward Salerno after sundown. They comprised the Western Naval Task Force, commanded by Vice-Admiral H. Kent Hewitt, USN. Under him were the Northern Attack Force (Commodore N. G. N. Oliver, RN), which transported the British 10th Corps; the Southern Attack Force (Rear-Admiral John L. Hall, Jr, USN), carrying the US 6th Corps; a Naval Air Support Force (Rear-Admiral Sir Philip Vian) of one fleet aircraft-carrier and four escort-carriers to give air cover; and a Naval Covering Force (Vice-Admiral Sir Algernon Willis) of four battleships, two aircraft-carriers, and a cruiser squadron to protect against the Italian fleet.

The Coastal Air Force, composed of British, French, and American units, protected the convoys for part of the voyage. The Tactical Air Force, specifically Major-General Edwin J. House's US 12th Air Support Command, was to provide cover during the latter part of the voyage and at the assault area.

At least 15 naval aircraft would be aloft constantly during the first two days of the invasion. But since the pilots were short on training and experience in ground support operations, and since the Spitfire, the best Allied land-based fighter, could operate from Sicily only as far as Salerno, could, with an extra fuel tank, patrol over Salerno for 20 minutes, but could remain only 10 minutes if engaged in combat, the Montecorvino airfield was an important objective of the invasion.

To get ashore and take Naples was the mission of Lieutenant-General Mark W. Clark, who headed the US 5th Army and who would have his first battlefield command in the Second World War. 'Clark impresses me, as always,' a senior officer wrote at the time, 'with his energy and intelligence. You cannot help but like him. He certainly is not afraid to take rather desperate chances which, after all, is the only way to win a war.' Under him were the British 10th Corps, commanded by Lieutenant-General Sir Richard McCreery (who had replaced Lieutenant-General Sir Brian G. Horrocks, wounded during an air raid), and the US 6th Corps, under Major-General Ernest J. Dawley.

The British 10th Corps, with the 46th and 56th Divisions, three Ranger battalions, and two Commando units, was to land north of the Sele river, seize the port of Salerno, capture the Montecorvino airfield, take the road and rail centre of Battipaglia, secure Ponte Sele 14 miles inland, and gain possession of the mountain passes leading to Naples (see map). The British 7th Armoured Division was to come ashore on the fifth or sixth day of the invasion.

The US 6th Corps, with the 36th Division,

8th Army lands on Italian soil: the Baytown landings met little or no resistance, and drove rapidly inland

Imperial War Museum

British machine-gunners in action during the swift and easy drive through the toe of Italy, which forced a rapid German withdrawal towards Naples – and Salerno

Imperial War Museum

NEAR DISASTER AT SALERNO

Once the news of the Italian capitulation was broadcast to the troops on their way to the beaches of Salerno for Avalanche, few men in 5th Army anticipated much trouble. But they had bargained without Kesselring's lightning deployment of his troops. All the Allied landings in the Gulf of Salerno established themselves on the beaches—but the first attempts to push inland were thrown back by devastating German fire. Vietinghoff, the German commander in the Salerno sector, launched such a deadly counterattack that he nearly drove clean through 8th Army to the sea. As it was, Clark's US 6th Corps and British 10th Corps were separated and tied down by German attacks all along the Allied front, while Clark himself almost decided to cut his losses and re-embark 5th Army. But the front held; reinforcements poured into the beach-head—and Kesselring could not ignore the steady advance of 8th Army in the east. German strategy demanded a withdrawal, regardless of the outcome at Salerno; and after a ten-day crisis for the Allies, the Germans fell back. As they did so, Clark's forces broke out of the beach-head, driving north-west towards Naples

Aftermath: British troops of 56th Division probe towards Montecorvino

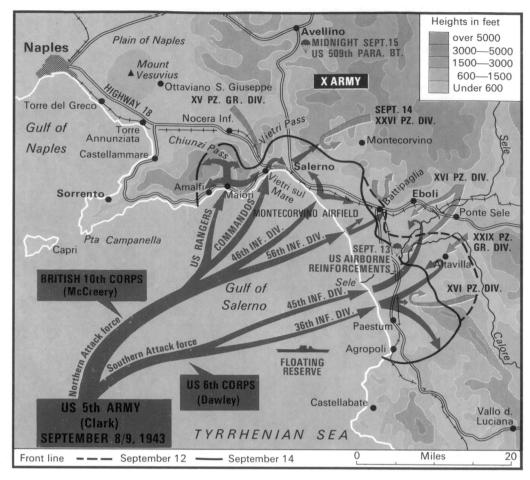

Imperial War Museum

was to land south of the Sele river, protect the army right flank by seizing the high ground dominating the Salerno plain from the south and east, and make contact with the British at Ponte Sele. Two regiments of the 45th Division comprised a 'floating reserve' available immediately offshore. After the 45th Division came across the beaches, the 1st Armoured and 34th Divisions, later the 3rd, were to enter Italy through the captured port of Naples, which the Allies hoped to have by the 13th day of the invasion, September 22.

Since the available airlift was sufficient to transport only one division, the British 1st Airborne Division was nominated for seaborne movement to Taranto in Slapstick. The US 82nd Airborne Division was to drop 40 miles north of Salerno and 20 miles north of Naples along the Volturno river to destroy the bridges from Capua to the sea and impede German reinforcement of the defenders of Salerno. But when the Italians, during the surrender negotiations, expressed fears that the Germans would occupy Rome and capture the royal family and the government, Eisenhower agreed to send the 82nd to the capital to help Italian military forces safeguard the city. He withdrew the airborne division from the Avalanche troop list on September 3. When the Italians failed to give a satisfactory guarantee of co-operation, Eisenhower cancelled the Rome drop on the evening of September 8. By then it was too late to employ the division in Avalanche.

Proceeding north in calm seas and good weather, the Avalanche convoys turned east toward the Gulf of Salerno at nightfall of the 8th. Minesweepers ahead made contact with a British submarine, on station more than a week. At 2200 hours, the convoys sighted the beacon lights of ships sent ahead to mark the assault transport area 12 to 20 miles off the Salerno beaches.

To guard the northern flank against sneak attack, a picket group of 16 PT (patrol torpedo) boats headed into the Bay of Naples to cause a diversion. A larger diversionary group entered the Gulf of Gaeta to demonstrate near the mouth of the Volturno river and captured a German radar station on Ventotene Island.

Meanwhile, at 1830 hours on September 8, Eisenhower had announced the surrender of Italy. Ships' radios carried Eisenhower's words over loudspeakers and brought an immediate reaction. 'I never again expect to witness such scenes of sheer joy,' an observer later wrote. As cheers rang out, 'speculation was rampant and it was all good . . . we dock in Naples harbour unopposed, with an olive branch in one hand and an opera ticket in the other.' A holiday mood took possession of most of the soldiers in the invasion force, and there was an 'immediate general let-down among the troops.'

Officers who anticipated that Germans instead of Italians would now oppose the landings tried to warn of increased resistance. But thoughts of a painless landing dulled the troops' fighting edge. Any resistance, no matter how light, because of its unexpectedness, would seem worse.

Should there be a preliminary naval bombardment of the shore defences? Because the Northern Attack Force had been bombed and strafed by enemy aircraft, though with little effect, the British decided that surprise had been lost, and they opted for a bombardment. The Americans, hoping

still to attain surprise, decided to the contrary.

As the troops prepared to land, they wondered whether the beaches would be deserted, whether jubilant Italians would receive them with open arms, or whether grim Germans would seek to repel them.

Germans caught off guard
The Germans, having recognised the invasion of the toe as a subsidiary operation, expected a major landing elsewhere. Lacking reliable strategic Intelligence, they looked to all possible sites. Hitler expected an assault in Yugoslavia, Kesselring anticipated a 'decisive fight' near Rome, Vietinghoff looked to the extensive shoreline between Gaeta and Salerno. When pilots observed the Avalanche convoys and reported their 'destination unknown', Hitler decided to issue an ultimatum to Italy in order to sweep away the uncertainties. If the Italian reply was unsatisfactory, Hitler would withdraw his troops from southern Italy immediately. The ultimatum was ready to be sent on September 8, when the Italian surrender was announced.

Had the invasion of Salerno come several days later, the Germans would probably have been in the process of retiring to the Rome area. Instead, they moved to man the coastal defences previously occupied by Italians. A battle became inevitable on the beaches of Salerno.

Vietinghoff picked up a London broadcast of the surrender, and Kesselring soon confirmed the event. 'If we retain our fighting spirit and remain dead calm,' Kesselring declared, 'I am confident that we will continue to perform the tasks entrusted to us by the Führer.' The German naval command in Italy was less dramatic: 'Italian armistice does not apply to us. The fight continues.'

Italian army units allowed themselves to be disarmed by the Germans or simply dissolved themselves, many soldiers throwing away their weapons and uniforms and disappearing into the countryside. In Naples, a hungry population threatened a German anti-aircraft installation until combat troops arrived and put down rioting. In the Rome area, Kesselring faced several hostile Italian divisions, but after a few days of confrontation and skirmish, he dissipated the threat. The Italian resistance that the Allied command had hoped to turn against the Germans, particularly those defending at Salerno, failed to materialise.

Off the Salerno shore, the darkened ships were in position by midnight on September 8. Loudspeakers called the boat teams to their stations, assault boats and nets were lowered, and men clambered from transports into landing-craft. The initial boat waves headed for the rendezvous area 3 to 5 miles off the beaches; forming behind the red tail lights of boats with navigational equipment, they began to circle slowly. Behind them came more craft and amphibious trucks (DUKWs) carrying tanks, guns, heavy weapons, artillery and anti-tank pieces, crews, and ammunition. At 0200, on September 9, when enemy shore units opened fire on the Northern Attack Force, Allied warships replied with a steady bombardment.

On the left flank of the invasion force, three US Ranger battalions under Colonel William S. Darby hit the beach at Maiori at 0310, 20 minutes before H-Hour. There were no Germans. Some Americans moved

along the winding coastal road toward Salerno; others marched westward to Amalfi. Against a surprising absence of resistance, Rangers quickly pushed inland and seized the Chiunzi pass at the top of the mountain. By dawn of D-Day, they firmly held the peaks on both sides of the pass, with a breathtaking view of the Bay of Salerno behind them and excellent observation of Highway 18 going north to Naples.

At H-Hour—0330 hours—British Army Commandos came ashore to the right of the Rangers at Vietri sul Mare. There was no opposition. But half an hour later, when Marine Commandos landed, the British found themselves up against Germans who had infiltrated into town and were placing mortar fire on the beach. With subsequent assault and support waves prevented from landing, the Commandos, under Brigadier Robert Laycock, fought at close range against the most determined kind of resistance. Expanding their beach-head, they forced their way into Salerno and established a tenuous hold over the city.

On the right of the Commandos and separated from them by a gap of several miles was Major-General J. L. T. Hawkesworth's British 46th 'Oak Tree' Division. A brigade went ashore just south of Salerno with little difficulty and secured the beaches by 0445 hours. But as men moved inland, they met increasingly bitter resistance. Beating back recurring counterattacks, British troops headed toward the Montecorvino airfield and partially surrounded it, while others moved toward Salerno under heavy fire.

On the British 10th Corps' right flank, Major-General Douglas A. H. Graham's 56th (London) Division committed two brigades abreast, each with two battalions abreast. The men had no trouble getting ashore but soon ran into German tanks, which were dispersed only by strong naval gunfire. Patrols advanced into Battipaglia, but were soon driven out. An attempt to take the Montecorvino airfield failed.

South of the Sele river, Major-General Fred L. Walker's US 36th 'Texas' Division put two reinforced regiments ashore near the ancient town of Paestum. In contrast with the noise and flashes of gun and rocket fire in the northern area, the beaches were dark and silent as troops stepped into the shallow water along the shore. But flares suddenly illuminated the beaches, and German fire began to rain down. As boats grounded, men stumbled ashore in the darkness. Frightened, tense, they blundered across the loose sand, some running, others crawling toward the dunes for cover. The assault waves became disarranged, and an orderly advance impossible. Landing-craft coxwains who judged the fire too strong turned round and headed back toward the transports. Boats struck by fire burned near shore or drifted helplessly.

Yet somehow in the mêlée of boats and men and weapons, soldiers found their wits, exercised self-discipline, and got on with their jobs. Most infantrymen worked their way toward the railroad running parallel to the beach a mile and a half inland. When daylight arrived, training, discipline, and organisation had taken hold. With the usual 'orderly confusion,' the division moved to its initial objectives. By 1800 hours, the men had reached positions designated as objectives for the following

morning and had no contact with German troops.

For the moment, a success

Allied commanders aboard ships in the gulf had only the vaguest notion during most of the day of what was happening. The shore had been obscured at first by darkness, later by smoke. By the end of the day they judged that the invasion was, for the moment at least, a success. The Germans had withdrawn. Though some beaches remained under direct artillery fire, most of the shoreline was usable for landing additional troops, equipment, and supplies.

There were two ominous developments. Neither corps had been able to establish its flank on the Sele river; a gap of about 7 miles separated them. And Allied pilots reported enemy units moving out of the toe toward Salerno; some German reinforcements could be expected at the beach-head on the following day.

With only the most meagre news from Salerno, Eisenhower was particularly concerned by the German troops hurrying from Calabria. Feeling that Montgomery would be unable to help Clark 'for some days', he expected 'some very tough fighting'. Avalanche would be 'a matter of touch and go for the next few days'.

Slapstick had gone much better. The Italian surrender, which included turning over the fleet, made it possible on September 7 to divert four cruisers from the task of screening the Italian warships to the task of transporting the British 1st Airborne Division to Taranto. Additional strength would soon be available to build up the forces on the east coast: the British 78th Division in Sicily, the Indian 8th Division in Egypt and already loading for movement to Italy, and other divisions in the Middle East and in North Africa. Lieutenant-General Sir Charles Allfrey's British 5th Corps HQ was at hand to direct the troops in the new area until Montgomery could move from Calabria to the east coast.

Sailing in light cruisers and minelayers, preceded by minesweepers, 3,600 airborne troops entered Taranto on September 9. No German forces were there, and Italians manning the defences welcomed the arrivals. The only incident was the tragic sinking, with heavy loss of life, of the British minelaying cruiser *Abdiel,* which struck a mine in the harbour.

Taranto was in excellent condition. While some troops organised the port facilities, others moved off in search of Germans and two days later occupied Brindisi without opposition. The German I Parachute Division, dispersed over a large area vulnerable to Allied invasion, withdrew toward Foggia, maintaining light contact with the pursuing British and delaying where possible.

At Salerno, Vietinghoff had realised as early as 0800 hours on September 9 that the extent of the invasion made another major assault unlikely. But without word from Kesselring—the civilian telephone system was not entirely secure, and atmospheric disturbances interfered with radio communications—he had to decide himself whether to repel the invasion or withdraw to Rome. He chose the former and ordered XIV Panzer Corps to make a 'ruthless concentration of all forces at Salerno'. Kesselring approved at noon.

The XIV Panzer Corps commander was on leave, and the acting commander had telephone contact with neither Vietinghoff nor Kesselring and only intermittent radio contact with both. Lacking good Intelligence, he felt too insecure, despite Vietinghoff's order, to rush troops to Salerno.

The XVI Panzer Division, as a consequence, met the Allied invasion alone. Not quite at full strength with 17,000 men, somewhat more than 100 tanks, and 36 assault guns, the division was short in combat experience and fuel, had a long front of more than 20 miles to defend, and lacked strong defensive works. Hampered not only by numerous irrigation and drainage canals and fences and walls, but also by the fire from Allied artillery, tanks, rocket-launchers, warships, and aircraft, the troops carried out small, piecemeal counterattacks by tank/infantry teams. At the end of D-Day, the division had only 35 tanks in operating condition.

Expecting the XXIX Panzer Grenadier Division to start arriving near Salerno

AT SALERNO, EIGHT DESPERATE DAYS ON A DANGEROUSLY SHALLOW BEACH-HEAD . . .

during the night, Vietinghoff instructed the XVI Panzer Division to withdraw from the US 6th Corps area and to concentrate against the British 10th Corps. The pressure increased even more when Kesselring, on the 10th, shifted a division from Rome to the Gulf of Gaeta and permitted Vietinghoff to move portions of two other divisions also against the British 10th Corps.

Though British 46th Division units and Commandos cleared the town of Salerno and advanced 2 miles to the Vietri pass, they did so with great difficulty. The British 56th Division, against rising opposition, was denied high ground near Battipaglia necessary to control Montecorvino airfield.

In contrast, US 6th Corps had hardly any contact with the Germans; troops took the ring of high ground in their zone, and the floating reserve came ashore. The reason for the absence of pressure was the failure of the XXIX Panzer Grenadier Division to arrive as expected. A panicky naval commander had destroyed a coastal tanker and a fuel depot at the head of the Gulf of Policastro, and the division was stalled for lack of fuel. It took emergency measures, including an air shipment of fuel, to get the division rolling, and it would be several days before the bulk of the troops reached the beach-head.

To counter the increased German strength in the British 10th Corps zone, Clark moved the corps boundary to the left, inserted Major-General Troy H. Middleton's US 45th

Division north of the Sele river, and sent an American infantry battalion to reinforce the Rangers holding the Chiunzi pass.

Fighting in the British 10th Corps area became intense on September 11, particularly around Battipaglia. Supported by effective naval bombardment, British troops finally captured the Montecorvino airfield, but German infantry on nearby hills and German artillery within range denied its use. On that day alone, the German X Army took almost 1,500 prisoners, most of them British. An attack by the US 45th Division toward Eboli to try to loosen the German pressure was stopped almost at once.

A step-up in German air attacks was also remarked, observers counting no less than 120 hostile aircraft over the beaches. Barrage balloons, anti-aircraft artillery, and fighter aircraft reduced the effect of the raids, but inability to capture the Montecorvino airfield put a strain on naval pilots, who became concerned about their diminishing fuel supplies.

During the first three days of the invasion, German pilots flew more than 550 sorties, their prime target being the invasion fleet. They sank four transports, one heavy cruiser, and seven landing-craft, as they scored a total of 85 hits. Particularly successful were new radio-controlled glider and rocket bombs, which had been available since July but which Hitler had held off using, as he said, 'lest we give away our secret'.

Hewitt requested assistance from Cuningham, who promptly dispatched from Malta the cruisers *Aurora* and *Penelope*. To remove the most conspicuous target in the gulf, his flagship *Ancon,* Hewitt put out to sea for the night, returning at daylight of the 12th to resume both fighter direction control and his place in the command network.

Enough of the XXIX Panzer Grenadier Division had reached the Salerno area to make its presence felt against the US 6th Corps. An attack drove the US 36th Division from Altavilla, gained easily a day before. A reinforced XVI Panzer Division prevented the US 45th Division from threatening Eboli, and Germans drove contingents of the British 56th Division back from Battipaglia.

That the beach-head was still dangerously shallow and unstable undoubtedly contributed to Clark's decision to establish his headquarters ashore. But there was no good location for it. The army command post was within range of German artillery, and during several uncomfortable hours when American troops were briefly forced out of their positions north of the Sele river, the headquarters was menaced by German infantry.

That night Hewitt moved to a smaller ship and dispatched the *Ancon* to Algiers. He also released Vian's carrier force, even though Montecorvino airfield was still under hostile fire and unable to be used.

Some of Vian's Seafire pilots flew to a strip constructed near Paestum and became the first land-based fighters in the beach-head.

Vietinghoff makes his move

On the morning of September 13, Vietinghoff suddenly discovered the gap between the two Allied corps. Inferring that the Allies had voluntarily 'split themselves into two sections', he believed they were planning to evacuate the beach-head. He construed the arrival of additional ships as those necessary for the withdrawal. He regarded the Allied use of smoke near Battipaglia as designed to mask a retirement. An intercepted radio message seemed to indicate an intention to abandon the beach-head. German propaganda broadcasts claiming another Dunkirk supported his conviction. Sensing victory, he ordered attack.

Shortly after mid-day, Germans struck from Vietri, Battipaglia, Eboli, and Altavilla. They soon reported being in pursuit of the enemy. They inflicted a sharp defeat on Americans seeking to regain Altavilla, overran and destroyed an American battalion in the Sele corridor, came close to splitting the main British 10th Corps body from the Rangers, briefly reaching the coastal road near Vietri, and threatened to retake Salerno, where the port, opened two days earlier, had to be closed. Glider bombs damaged the British cruiser *Uganda* and the US cruiser *Philadelphia* and struck two hospital ships, setting one on fire.

At the end of the afternoon, German troops were headed toward the juncture of the Sele and Calore rivers, where only a few Americans stood between them and the sea. Less than 5 miles from the shore and a stone's throw from the US 5th Army HQ, miscellaneous troops—cooks, clerks, and drivers—hastily built up a firing line to protect two battalions of artillery firing at point-blank range. Though the German advance halted at the confluence of the rivers, Clark arranged to evacuate his headquarters on ten minutes' notice and take a PT boat to the British 10th Corps area where conditions seemed to be somewhat better.

That evening, US 5th Army staff officers prepared plans to evacuate the beach-head if such drastic action became necessary. They drew two plans, code-named 'Sealion' and 'Seatrain', one for each corps. Whether one corps was to be withdrawn to reinforce the other, as was later claimed, or whether this was the ostensible rather than the real purpose, Clark directed his chief-of-staff to alert Hewitt to the possibility that the beach-head might have to be abandoned.

After voicing his objection to a withdrawal on the ground that it was technically impracticable to beach an empty landing craft and retract it full, Hewitt prepared to comply should Clark give the order. He recalled his flagship, which was proceeding to Algiers. But since it might be necessary to re-embark the army staff before the *Ancon* could return, Hewitt asked Oliver whether his flagship, the *Hilary,* could take part of the army headquarters aboard.

Shocked by the requirement, Oliver protested. Re-embarking heavily engaged troops from a shallow beach-head, he said, was 'simply not on, quite apart from other considerations'. He thought it would be 'suicidal' to allow enemy artillery 'to rake the beaches'. Had McCreery been consulted, he asked?

McCreery was furious. Going to see Clark personally, he learned that Clark had not actually ordered evacuation but was rather trying to be prepared for all contingencies, including the worst.

Clark, meanwhile, after meeting with his senior American commanders, had decided to shorten the front in the US 6th Corps sector by pulling back to a line where a last-ditch stand was possible. That night the Americans moved back about 2 miles to new defences that were dug in, wired, mined, and to be held at all costs. As Walker said, the US 36th Division would 'fight it out on this position'.

Sure of victory, Vietinghoff sent a telegram to Kesselring: 'After a defensive battle lasting four days, enemy resistance is collapsing. X Army pursuing on wide front.' The entry in the war diary was a simple notation: 'The battle of Salerno appears to be over.'

The crisis had already prompted Allied efforts to redress the balance. Cunningham ordered the battleships *Valiant* and *Warspite* from Malta. He informed Hewitt he would send the battleships *Nelson* and *Rodney* if necessary. He instructed three cruisers to sail at top speed to Tripoli to pick up British replacements and rush them to the beach-head. Eisenhower ordered Tedder to divert the strategic air forces temporarily from their long-range hammering of railroads, dumps, and bridges in the distant rear of the enemy. They were, instead, to start on the 14th to slam targets closer to the beach-head. Alexander seized ships and landing craft that were to transport service to Salerno and sent them instead to Sicily to carry the US 3rd Division to the beach-head.

Could Montgomery get overland in time to help? As early as the second day of the Salerno invasion, on September 10, Alexander had radioed Montgomery that it was essential for him to tie down the Germans and prevent them from reaching Salerno; to do so, Alexander made explicit, Montgomery had to maintain firm contact and exert great pressure. To emphasise the urgency, he sent his chief-of-staff to Montgomery's headquarters. Alexander's message and his chief-of-staff arrived early on the 11th. Though Montgomery felt that his army 'was administratively very stretched', he thought that by taking what he saw as 'considerable administrative risks' he could move some troops forward about 75 miles in four days. A move of that distance would get his leading elements to a place 75 miles still short of Salerno. By September 13, the day of crisis at Salerno, Montgomery was more than 100 miles away, too far to help.

The only hope for quick assistance lay with the US 82nd Airborne Division, which was in Sicily and available for commitment. On the morning of September 13, Clark had sent a letter by plane to the division commander, Major-General Matthew B. Ridgway. Informing him that the fighting had taken a turn for the worse, Clark wrote: 'I want you to accept this letter as an order. I realize the time normally needed to prepare for a drop, but . . . I want you to make a drop within our lines on the beach-head and I want you to make it tonight. This is a must.'

Recalling the tragic incident at Sicily two months earlier when anti-aircraft guns of the invasion fleet and the ground troops had shot down transports filled with para-

ALLIED BLITZ ON NAPLES
While 5th Army was fighting for survival in the Salerno beach-head, Allied bombers were smashing at Naples —first major Italian city in the Allies' path. The bombings were intended to prevent the Germans from using the base during the battle for the south—but by the time the Allies eventually entered Naples *(above)* the port and much of the city lay in ruins—an inauspicious start to Allied bombing policy in the Italian theatre

troops, Ridgway replied: Vitally important that all ground and naval forces . . . be directed to hold fire tonight. Rigid control of anti-aircraft fire is absolutely essential for success.'

That evening two battalions of paratroops boarded planes, and shortly before midnight on the 13th, about 1,300 men jumped into the beach-head near Paestum and were quickly trucked to positions along the final line of defence.

'Nothing of interest to report'

The Germans, bolstered on the morning of September 14 by the XXVI Panzer Division, now arrived from Calabria, concentrated pressure first against the town of Salerno. Then came an attack, supported by a heavy volume of artillery fire, from Vietri, which gave McCreery, he later admitted, 'several anxious moments'. The British 46th Division, dug in on the hills around Salerno, had every unit committed in defence. And when it seemed that the Germans might break through, they shifted to Battipaglia, where the British 56th Division held grimly in turn. At the end of the day, the situation remained unchanged. With perhaps some studied nonchalance, McCreery informed Clark: 'Nothing of interest to report.'

German attacks against the US 6th Corps had also come to naught. At the end of the day the Americans were in firm command of

the front and claimed to have knocked out almost 30 tanks.

On the beaches, all unloading had ceased, as men working the supply system joined the combat troops and helped improve the defences. Naval gunfire was particularly effective along the Battipaglia/ Eboli road. And heavy bombers operating over the Salerno plain—187 B-25s, 166 B-26s, and 170 B-17s—prompted the Germans to make liberal use of smoke to screen their positions and movements.

Clark toured the front to encourage the troops, while Alexander, who made his first visit to the beach-head, found the defences impressive. By evening, plans to evacuate the beach-head were no longer under consideration. Contributing to a new optimism was the arrival of the British 7th Armoured Division, which came ashore in the British 10 Corps area. The last regiment of the US 45th Division also arrived and assembled in army reserve. After darkness, about 2,100 more men of the US 82nd Airborne Division jumped into the beach-head.

That night the Americans launched a daring airborne operation designed to assist the British 10th Corps. The US 509th Parachute Infantry Battalion dropped near Avellino, far behind the Germans' front, to harass lines of communication and disrupt the movement of reinforcements from the north. About 600 men jumped around

midnight and were terribly dispersed, some coming to earth as far as 25 miles from the drop zone. Broken terrain, thick woods, and vineyards made it impossible for the scattered troops to concentrate. Most of the equipment was lost or hopelessly entangled in trees. Quickly coalescing into small groups of five to 20 men, the paratroops raided German supply trains, truck convoys, and isolated outposts. Eventually, more than 400 men trickled back to safety. They had been too small a force and too dispersed to be more than a minor nuisance to the Germans, and their operation had no effect on the battle at Salerno.

German attacks became less than effective in the beach-head. Battle in the US 6th Corps area turned into 'minor contacts and engagements'. Clark congratulated all his troops: 'Our beach-head is secure,' he announced, 'and we are here to stay.'

Concluding he could no longer hope to destroy the beach-head, Vietinghoff asked for permission to break off. 'The fact,' he reported, 'that the attacks (which had been fully prepared and carried out with spirit, especially by the XIV Corps) were unable to reach their objective owing to the fire from naval guns and low-flying aircraft, as well as the slow but steady approach of the [British] 8th Army' made it necessary that he move into good defensive positions. He recommended a general

On the left of the Salerno beach-head: US Rangers tackle the heights around Salerno which dominated the battle

Upper hand in Salerno: a Bren-gun carrier heads into the ruined town

withdrawal. Kesselring consented.

By afternoon of the 17th, resistance in the US 6th Corps area had obviously lessened, and McCreery began to feel better about the British 56th Division, though he was 'still anxious' about some 'very tired' battalions of the British 46th Division. On September 18, as the Germans withdrew, British tanks entered Battipaglia, and American troops moved to Ponte Sele. By then Major-General Lucian K. Truscott Jr's US 3rd Division was going ashore, and a liaison party from the British 5th Division, part of Montgomery's 8th Army, arrived to arrange a meeting some 20 miles south of the beach-head.

Vietinghoff praised his troops. 'Success had been ours,' he declared. 'Once again German soldiers have proved their superiority over the enemy.'

Only Darby's Rangers, Laycock's Commandos, and the British 46th Division fought defensively on September 19. The British 56th Division eliminated German artillery firing on the Montecorvino airfield, and the US 45th Division entered Eboli. The roads in the beach-head became jammed with traffic.

'Some would like to think—I did at the time,' Montgomery's Chief-of-Staff, General de Guingand, wrote several years later, 'that we helped, if not saved, the situation at Salerno. But now I doubt whether we influenced matters to any great extent. General Clark had everything under control *before* 8th Army appeared on the scene.'

Actually, the slow movement of the British 8th Army disappointed many commanders who had hoped that Montgomery would get rapidly to Salerno and help. Clark, for example, described 8th Army's progress as 'a slow advance toward Salerno, despite Alexander's almost daily efforts to prod it into greater speed'.

The fact was that the mere presence of the 8th Army had weighed heavily on the Germans. No matter how slowly Montgomery moved, he would eventually reach Salerno. Because Hitler was unwilling to expend more troops to reinforce those fighting at Salerno and because those committed were unable to dislodge the US 5th Army, the Germans had to give way. The British 8th Army gave them a good excuse to do so, and the Germans implemented their original strategy of withdrawing from southern Italy. Montgomery, exercised an influence, though his troops took no direct part in the battle.

Could he have done more? As early as September 10, the Germans noted the pattern of his advance: 'The withdrawal of our troops from Calabria continues according to plan. The enemy is not crowding after us.'

The Germans failed to dislodge the US 5th Army because their strategic planning projected a withdrawal from southern Italy regardless of the outcome of the battle at the beach-head. They would have liked to repel the invasion, and a victory would doubtless have changed their strategic plans, but their resistance was aimed at covering their withdrawal—and the Germans denied themselves the possibility of committing additional strength, for example, from northern Italy.

'An important German success'

Hitler, Kesselring, and Vietinghoff were satisfied. They had denied the Allies quick access to Naples, inflicted severe losses on Allied units, extricated their forces from southern Italy, and prohibited the Allies from fully exploiting the Italian surrender. 'The Germans may claim with some justification,' Alexander admitted, 'to have won if not a victory at least an important success over us.' Fighting with limited forces for a limited objective, the Germans had sustained casualties of probably 3,500 men. In contrast, the Americans lost about 3,500, the British around 5,500.

On September 20, British 8th Army forces occupied Potenza, 50 miles east of Salerno, cut the lateral highway between Salerno and Bari, and met American units at Auletta, 20 miles east of Eboli. By then, the Canadian

The scene after the explosion of a German time-bomb in the Naples post office on October 7. In Italy, as in North Africa, the Allies were constantly plagued by such devices and suffered considerable losses from them

1st Division coming up from Calabria had made contact with the British 1st Airborne Division to bring together the Slapstick and Baytown elements. The British 5th Corps HQ had come ashore at Taranto on September 18 and prepared to receive additional forces at Bari. Now Montgomery would concentrate his widely dispersed units for an attack to Foggia, while Clark prepared to drive to Naples to secure the port.

Additional gains of the invasion of southern Italy were Sardinia and Corsica, abandoned by the Germans. By virtue of their strategic location, the islands were a great prize. They made the Mediterranean even more secure for shipping, and airfields, particularly on Corsica, would place Allied bombers closer to the German homeland.

When Kesselring gave Vietinghoff permission to break off the battle at Salerno, he ordered a slow retirement to the north. If Vietinghoff could gain enough time, Kesselring would fortify a naturally strong line through Mignano—about 50 miles north of Naples and 90 miles south of Rome—for a more protracted defence. A dozen miles north of Mignano, the terrain around Cassino provided even better prospects for a prolonged defensive battle.

If Kesselring could get Hitler to change his mind, he might be able to halt the Allied forces far below the northern Apennine positions. He therefore instructed Vietinghoff to realign his forces and form a front across the entire peninsula, then pull back slowly through a series of defensive lines, the first one along the Volturno river, 25 miles north of Naples, and the Biferno river, about 40 miles north of Foggia. While withdrawing, Vietinghoff was to destroy methodically all installations of military value in order to deny their use to the Allies.

In compliance, Vietinghoff deployed the XIV Panzer Corps on the west coast, the 76th Panzer Corps on the east. By the end

of September he had extended a front across the peninsula of Italy.

Clark now moved to take Naples, but he wanted his troops to continue, without stopping, to the Volturno river, which would give him a large buffer zone to protect the port from raids and incursions. The US 6th Corps under a new commander, Major-General John P. Lucas, moved from the Salerno beaches into the interior on September 20, hoping to outflank Naples and to reach the Volturno above Capua. The US 3rd and 45th Divisions immediately struck rugged terrain that was more than adequately defended by small rearguard units employing demolitions and mines with skill to impede progress. Sluicing rain washed away bridges and turned roads into quagmires. The arrival of Major-General Charles W. Ryder's US 34th Division made little difference, and the corps slogged slowly toward the river.

McCreery's British 10th Corps carried the main effort. After shifting his forces to the left to position the British 46th Division at Vietri and the British 56th at Salerno to place them at the two major passes through the Sorrento hill mass, McCreery attacked on September 23, but made little progress. Clark then reinforced the Rangers at Chiunzi, eventually placing the entire US 82nd Airborne Division under McCreery's control. On the 28th, when the corps attacked again, the troops penetrated through the passes and reached the Naples plain.

Vietinghoff had been ready to give way. While his troops hastily fortified the Volturno river line, he fell back grudgingly. On October 1, British troops entered the eastern outskirts of Naples, then continued up the coastal road to the Volturno. The US 82nd Airborne Division moved into Naples to police the city. Against decreasing resistance, the British divisions closed to the Volturno river, arriving there in strength

by the 7th. By then, the US 6th Corps had also reached the Volturno.

The US 5th Army had taken Naples and made it secure. The cost of the 21-day campaign was more than 12,000 British and American casualties, of whom approximately 2,000 were killed, 7,000 were wounded, and 3,500 were missing.

Putting Naples back into shape
But the prize of Avalanche, the city of Naples, was destroyed by Allied bombing and by more systematic German demolitions. Industrial Naples was a mass of twisted girders, the port a pile of wreckage, the harbour a hazard choked with sunken ships and miscellaneous rubble.

Allied troops, assisted by Italians, cleared the streets of obstructions, mended breaks in sewers, repaired the aqueduct, installed a power plant, and rehabilitated the port. In the midst of the work, a delayed-fuse bomb exploded in the post office around noon, October 7, killing and injuring about 35 soldiers and an equal number of civilians; a bomb or mine exploding on the 11th in a barrack killed 18 soldiers and injured 36. Later in the month, German air raids would inflict casualties on troops and civilians.

While the port was being restored, it was also being used. At first a fleet of DUKWs brought supplies from transports anchored offshore. As early as October 3, landing craft were docking at berths. On October 4, a Liberty ship was unloaded. Eventually, berthing was provided for 26 Liberty ships, six coasters, and 11 landing ships. Two weeks after the capture of Naples, 3,500 tons of cargo were being unloaded daily, not quite half the average 8,000 tons discharged per day before the war. By the end of October, with about 600 DUKWs being used in port operations, Naples was receiving 7,000 tons daily, while the ports of Salerno, Torre Annunziata, and Castellam-

John Batchelor

THE GLIDER BOMB: IDEAL FOR LUFTWAFFE COUNTERSTRIKES

As the Allied armies moved into southern Italy, Luftflotte II did everything in its power to disrupt the Allied build-up of supplies. The Luftwaffe bomber crews had a new and potent weapon in the glider bomb, which was released out of range of the anti-aircraft defences of the target area and found its own way to the target—the first true stand-off bomb. Healthy respect for the Allied fighters caused the Germans to equip the Dornier Do-217 K3 *(left)* with a heavy defensive armament. These Dorniers had the right length of wing-span to accommodate the glider bombs which—although ready for use by the spring of 1943—had been kept back from active service by failure to produce an effective carrier-plane. And the Dornier/glider bomb combination continued to be a constant hazard to the Allies, proving especially deadly against shipping.

Dornier Do-217 K3

Max speed: 345 mph. *Range:* 1,550 miles. *Crew:* five. *Armament:* twin 7·8-mm machine-guns in nose; two 7·9-mm machine-guns in beam mountings; one 13-mm machine-gun in dorsal mounting; one 13-mm machine-gun in lower rear mounting; four fixed 7·9-mm machine-guns in tail cone.

Henschel Hs-293 Glider Bomb:

Length: nine feet. *Weight:* 1,500 lb.

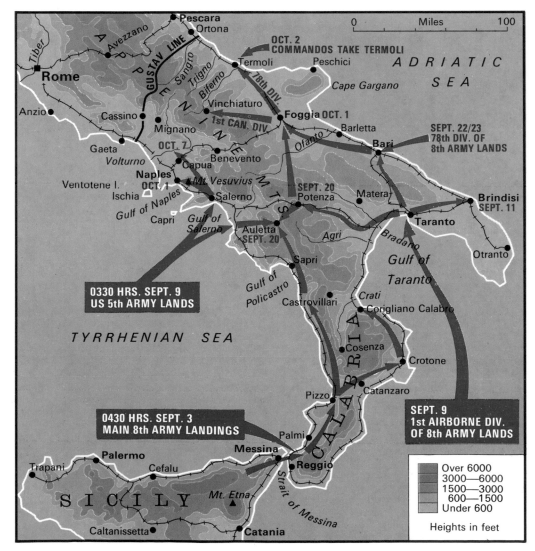

1943 **September 3:** Operation 'Baytown' begins: Montgomery's 8th Army invades Italy across the Straits of Messina. Convoys carrying the troops for 'Avalanche' (Salerno) and 'Slapstick' (Taranto) leave North Africa.
September 8: German troops have pulled back into the Salerno area from the south; the Allied troopships arrive off Salerno. Italy surrenders, but German forces prepare to hold Italy against the Allied forces.
September 8/9: Anglo-American troops hit the beaches at Salerno but are pinned down by heavy German fire. The attack on Taranto, however, meets no German resistance and the port falls to the Allies in excellent condition.
September 9: At Salerno, the XVI Panzer Division has to deal with the Allied attacks by itself. Vietinghoff orders it to concentrate against the British 10th Corps; in a fighting withdrawal, the Germans fall back 2 miles from Salerno. The US forces have an easier task as XXIX Panzer Division has not arrived; but for the next two days the beach-head remains dangerously shallow and the US and British corps remain separated.
September 13: Vietinghoff counterattacks the Allied beach-head; rapid German successes threaten to reach the sea and split the Allied force into two pockets. The Germans are stopped within 5 miles of the beaches, but US Army HQ prepares for an emergency evacuation.
September 13/15: Allied troops are rushed into the beach-head by night; the Salerno front stabilises and German attacks meet ever-strengthening resistance. US paratroops drop behind the German lines, but make little impression on the course of the battle.
September 17/18: Vietinghoff receives Kesselring's permission to withdraw from the Salerno area; Allied forces pursue.
September 20: 8th Army forces, fighting their way up from the south, join up with US forces east of Eboli.
October 1: British troops enter Naples.
October 7: Allied troops are halted by the German defence line on the Volturno.

Aftermath: the battered waterfront of Naples, after 5th Army had moved on to the north. Within a month of the first landings, the Allies had conquered southern Italy – but Naples had been laid in ruins, and Allied forces were already meeting stiff German resistance on the line of the Volturno river. It was clear that there was not going to be a rapid drive on Rome

mare, as well as the beaches of Salerno, contributed additional amounts.

Despite a violent, two-day wind and rain storm, which destroyed 84 landing craft and three landing ships, drove a merchant ship ashore, and swamped six unloading ramps, the Allied forces landed 200,000 men between September 9 and October 10, about 35,000 vehicles of all sorts, and close to 150,000 tons of supplies on the west coast of Italy.

On the other side of the Italian peninsula, British 8th Army's advance elements had almost no contact with the enemy as they pushed to Foggia, which the Germans abandoned on September 27. By October 1, British patrols had taken and secured the nearby airfields.

Montgomery then sought to reach the Biferno river, and he sent the British 13 Corps forward on a two-division front, with the British 78th Division marching along the coastal road to Termoli, the Canadian 1st Division moving inland to Vinchiaturo. The British 5 Corps followed, protecting the

inner flank. While Canadians fought rugged terrain as well as Germans, the British 78th Division had no trouble until patrols reached the outskirts of Termoli, where they met serious resistance. Launching a quick amphibious strike to secure the small port, Montgomery dispatched Commando forces, which were ferried by landing craft from Sicily, to the town. Gaining surprise, the Commandos landed during the night of October 2 and soon captured and cleared Termoli. On the following night, a brigade of the British 78th Division arrived by water to reinforce them.

Because the capture of Termoli invalidated the Biferno river defensive line, the Germans reacted swiftly. Vietinghoff rushed the XVI Panzer Division across the mountains from the west road. Arriving at Termoli on October 4, the division counterattacked on that day and on the succeeding two.

Flood waters interfered with British bridging operations and prevented tanks and artillery from making firm contact with the beach-head. But on October 7, when an

additional brigade of the British 78th Division was transported to Termoli by sea, the Germans fell back toward the Trigno river.

Montgomery reorganised his front on October 9, assigning the British 5th Corps the coastal area and control of the British 78th Division and Indian 8th Division, giving the British 13th Corps responsibility for an interior zone with the Canadian 1st and British 5th Divisions. The New Zealand 2nd Division was due to arrive soon in Taranto.

Two days later, with British 8th Army formations in firm possession of Termoli and Vinchiaturo, the Foggia airfields were secure, and Allied air forces were preparing to base heavy bombers on the fields for attacks against targets in Austria, southern Germany, and the Balkans.

With sizeable forces of the US 5th Army standing at the Volturno, and with the bulk of the British 8th Army able to move beyond the Biferno, the Allies had successfully concluded their invasion of southern Italy.

Italy, May/June 1944　　　　　　　　*Martin Blumenson*

At the end of the bitter winter fighting, Kesselring, the German C-in-C in Italy, had had good reason to be satisfied. He had repulsed the frontal Allied attacks on the Cassino defences and had cramped the Anzio landing force into a narrow beach-head. But Alexander's great spring offensive caught the Germans off balance, and cracked their front. As the battered German forces pulled out of the Gustav Line, Hitler insisted—as he had done at Stalingrad—on fanatical delaying actions to 'bleed the Allies white'. But this deluded policy, as at Stalingrad, bled only his own forces white—and led inevitably to the Allied capture of Rome

DRIVE TO ROME

PAVED WITH SKULLS!

A German warning which almost came true for Clark's men. The Italian front was notable for the quantity and savagery of its propaganda: all the combatants were far from their homes and fighting amid an unwilling population so the battles could be made to seem useless sideshows

Early in May 1944, a stillness hovered over the battlefields in Italy. Both sides, each with 22 divisions, rested, trained, regrouped, patrolled, replenished their resources, and awaited good weather. During the preceding eight months, from the Allied invasion of southern Italy in September 1943, Germany had fought the Allies to a standstill. The suitability of the winter weather and the rugged terrain for defence had more than offset German deficiencies in artillery ammunition and air support. There were two fronts, the main one across the Italian peninsula at Cassino and a perimeter enclosing the Allied beach-head at Anzio.

Having established an active if not extensive front on European soil, the Allies were tying down a large German force and inflicting steady losses in casualties. The German ground forces, having kept the Allies in southern Italy, had delivered three humiliating defeats on them at Cassino and had contained the Anzio beach-head; they were determined to retain Rome, which had become a symbol of prestige, and Cassino, which had acquired a semi-sacred character.

Field-Marshal Albert Kesselring, the German commander-in-chief, with an essentially defensive outlook, tried to divine whether the Allies would attack:

● In the Cassino area, in order to gain entrance into the Liri valley for a link-up with the Anzio beach-head;
● At Anzio, in order to cut Highways 7 and 6, in that sequence, and sever the German lines of communication south of Rome;
● Or somewhere along the west coast in the form of an amphibious landing.

In the Cassino area, the X Army, under General Heinrich von Vietinghoff, held the formidable Gustav Line anchored on Monte Cairo, 5,415 feet high, and naturally strong by virtue both of the Monte Cassino massif and the continuous water line formed by the Rapido and Garigliano rivers. Though Allied troops had crossed the lower reaches of the Garigliano in February, German positions in the high ground effectively barred expansion of the bridgehead. The Gustav Line remained intact.

Behind the Gustav Line was the Adolf Hitler Line, running from Terracina on the coast along the Fondi/Pico road to Pontecorvo and across the Liri valley through Aquino and Piedimonte to Monte Cairo, where it joined the Gustav Line. More elaborate in its defensive works, the Adolf Hitler Line had concrete fortifications and nearly 200 'armoured crabs' or portable steel

pillboxes that were actually turrets of Panther tanks converted for a static role. The only trouble with this line of defence was that the Allied troops at the Anzio beach-head were already behind it. If they broke out and reached Highway 6 near Valmontone, at the head of the Liri valley, the Adolf Hitler Line would be lost.

Manning the perimeter containing the Anzio beach-head was General Eberhard von Mackensen's XIV Army, which had built excellent field fortifications in ground wrinkled by a network of ditches and canals.

In case Allied pressure made it necessary to fuse the X and XIV Armies and establish them along a single, continuous front across the Italian peninsula, Kesselring built the Caesar Line. These positions crossed the Alban Hills and went through Valmontone into the mountains above Avezzano. From there the Germans could continue to deny Rome to the Allies.

Unable to make what they called 'a conclusive estimate of enemy intentions', the Germans considered it 'highly probable' that the Allies were preparing for 'a large-scale offensive'. Observing simulated amphibious exercises, they judged that the Allies had enough troops and landing

The Race to Rome

Alexander had planned that the Dora Line should be broken by frontal attacks, while a thrust out of the Anzio beach-head towards Valmonte cut the German line of retreat. But Mark Clark was more interested in the glory of reaching Rome first, than in destroying the German army; after breaking through out of Cisterna he swung the majority of US 6th Corps north towards Rome along Highway 7. The attack stalled and the Germans were able to stabilise their front along the Caesar Line. It was not until the rest of the US 5th Army plus the British 8th Army came up to break the line, that Clark was able to achieve his ambition

1944 May 11: Alexander launches the Allied offensive intended to break through the Gustav Line, join up with the Anzio force, and capture Rome.
May 11/14: 8th Army's attacks are pinned down, but Juin's Fighting French penetrate the Gustav Line in two days.
May 15: Germans begin withdrawal from the Gustav Line. Kesselring authorises a fighting withdrawal to the Adolf Hitler Line.
May 17: Germans finally evacuate Monte Cassino, occupied by Polish troops on the 18th.
May 19: American troops advance to Gaeta and Itri.
May 22: Canadian troops break the Adolf Hitler Line.

May 23: American troops begin the breakout from the Anzio beach-head against stubborn German resistance.
May 25: Allied forces from the Anzio force meet patrols of 5th Army north of Terracina—four months after the original Anzio landing.
May 25/27: Clark attacks towards Rome; his attacks are held, giving the Germans time to dig in around Valmontone.
May 30/31: American troops break the Valmontone defences and threaten to break through the last defences of Rome.
June 3: Kesselring receives Hitler's authorisation to withdraw from Rome.
June 4: Allied troops enter Rome.
June/July: Allied troops advance as far as the line of the Arno.

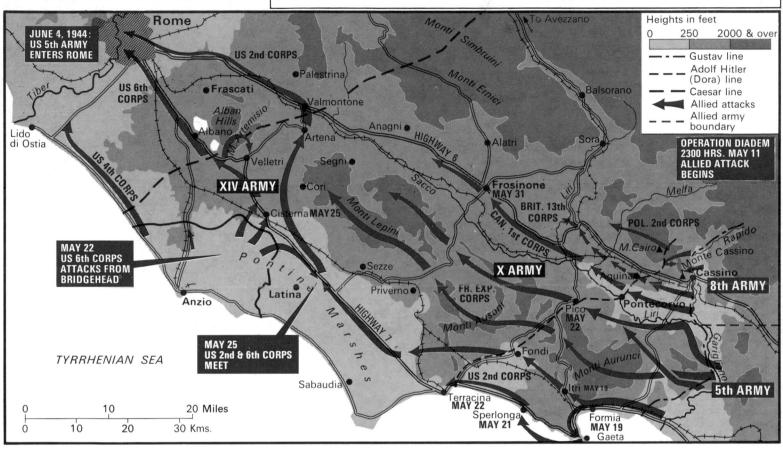

craft 'to carry out landing operations on both sides of Gaeta'.

As the calm continued, the commander of the XIV Panzer Corps, who had defended Cassino, went to Germany on leave. So did Kesselring's able Chief-of-Staff.

On May 10, Colonel Fritz Wentzell, the X Army Chief-of-Staff, just returned from leave, was talking on the telephone with Colonel Dietrich Beelitz, who was temporarily acting as Kesselring's Chief-of-Staff. 'To my great pleasure,' Wentzell said, 'everything is quiet. Only I do not know what is going on. Things are becoming ever more uncertain.'

Beelitz agreed, adding that Kesselring 'was looking very intently toward the coast'.

'I think it not impossible,' Wentzell observed cautiously, 'that things are going on of which we have no idea.'

On the following morning, May 11, at 0905 hours, Vietinghoff telephoned Kesselring. 'There is nothing special taking place,' he said. 'Both corps commanders told me that they did not yet have the impression that anything was going to happen.' That evening, as the quiet continued, Vietinghoff departed Italy for Hitler's headquarters, where he was to receive a decoration. A few hours after he left, a roar of Allied artillery

opened the spring offensive.

Alexander attacks

General Sir Harold R. L. G. Alexander, the Allied ground forces commander, planned to make his decisive attack at the Cassino front. As early as February 28, he announced he would concentrate the US 5th and British 8th Armies west of the Apennines while holding the Adriatic sector with as few troops as possible. To ease administrative matters, he would place all British and British-equipped divisions— Indian, Dominion, and Polish—under the 8th Army; American and French divisions would be under the 5th.

Starting his regrouping on March 5, Alexander left minimum forces under the British 5th Corps on the east coast. He moved Lieutenant-General Sir Oliver W. H. Leese's British 8th Army to the Cassino sector to assume an 85-mile front, much of it in virtually impassable mountains. He shifted Lieutenant-General Mark W. Clark's US 5th Army to a narrow front of 13 miles on the west coast.

Ahead of the US 5th Army was a chain of three distinct mountain ranges, all rugged and steep, named Aurunci, Ausoni, and Lepini Mountains in turn. About 15 miles

wide, bounded by the sea and by the valley of the Liri and Sacco rivers, the high ground stretches about 60 miles toward Rome. Because of the forbidding peaks, Alexander expected little in that area.

He looked for progress by the British 8th Army, which was to break the Cassino defences, penetrate the Gustav Line, enter the Liri valley, and advance toward the Anzio beach-head. When junction appeared imminent, he would have Major-General Lucian K. Truscott, Jr, who commanded the US 6th Corps at Anzio, attack out of the beach-head, strike through Cisterna and, at Valmontone on Highway 6, block the German X Army's escape route. What he hoped to do, he said, was 'to destroy the right wing of the German X Army; to drive what remains of it and the German XIV Army north of Rome; and to pursue the enemy to the Rimini/Pisa Line, inflicting the maximum losses on him in the process'.

Early in April, Alexander set the attack for the 15th. Delays in regrouping forced postponement. Finally, on May 5, Alexander instructed the armies to attack simultaneously at 2300 hours, May 11. Since the moon would rise at 2331 hours, the attacking troops would have several hours of darkness to move into assault positions and

'We had won the race to Rome by only two days.
Even while I stood there, Ike's army was
embarking for Normandy . . .' *General Mark Clark*

British troops pinned down during the offensive on the Gustav Line

Italian participation: an informal end to the Pact of Steel

German POWs bring in a British casualty at Anzio

Their line shattered, German POWs are searched before going to the rea

Objective Rome: as the race begins, US transport passes through a ruined Gaeta

Anticipation: US troops rush through the suburbs of Rome early on June 4

Triumph: US armour passes the Colosseum as the first Axis capital falls

sufficient light to consolidate their initial gains.

Strategically, the spring offensive, code-named Operation 'Diadem', was designed to engage and wear down German divisions that might otherwise he moved to France to meet the cross-Channel invasion of Normandy, scheduled for June 6. But foremost in the minds of the commanders in Italy was the desire to smash the Cassino defences and gain the Eternal City.

Leese issued a short directive to his corps commanders on April 11, then amplified his instructions by verbal orders delivered in a series of conferences.

● **Lieutenant-General Sir Richard L. McCreery's British 10 Corps** (with several British units in approximate division strength, the 2nd New Zealand Division, and the division-size Corps of Italian Liberation), on the right and in mountainous terrain, was to tie down the opposing Germans;

● **Lieutenant-General W. Anders' 2nd Polish Corps** (with the 5th Kresowa and 3rd Carpathian Divisions) was to attack the the Cassino massif and take the abbey of Monte Cassino;

● **Lieutenant-General S. C. Kirkman's British 13th Corps** (with the 4th British and 8th Indian Divisions in line and the 6th Armoured and 78th Divisions in reserve) was to secure a bridgehead across the Rapido river, clear the town of Cassino, and open up Highway 6 in the Liri valley toward Rome;

● **Lieutenant-General E. L. M. Burns' Candian 1st Corps** (with two Canadian divisions, the 1st Infantry and 5th Armoured) was to remain in reserve, ready to pass through the British 13th Corps.

The Liri valley, the main approach to Rome and the most suitable place to deploy Allied tanks and artillery, was so narrow that entrance could be forced only by frontal attack against prepared positions; it was so obviously the best route to Rome that obtaining tactical surprise would be difficult. But if the Poles took Monte Cassino and dominated Highway 6, the British 13th Corps could sweep up the valley.

In the US 5th Army zone:

● **Major-General Geoffrey Keyes' US 2nd Corps** (with 85th and 88th Divisions in line and the 36th in reserve) would attack in a narrow coastal area.

● **General Alphonse Juin's French Expeditionary Corps,** with elements of all four of its divisions in the line (1st Motorised, 2nd Moroccan, 4th Mountain Moroccan, and 3rd Algerian), would strike into the trackless mountains forming the southern wall of the Liri valley.

Both Allied armies counted on the efficacy of a concentrated 40-minute artillery preparation, and at 2300 hours on May 11, more than 1,600 guns of all calibres emplaced between Cassino and the sea began to pound the German defences. During the first 24 hours of the attack, US 5th Army artillery pieces alone would fire more than 180,000 rounds. On May 12, the air forces would give massive support, fighter-bombers flying 294 sorties, medium bombers 429 sorties, and heavy bombers 728.

For two weeks before the attack, the two divisions of the Polish Corps had, like their predecessors, undergone hardships on the Cassino massif. The rocky ground prevented the construction of proper positions and compelled the men to live in the cramped quarters of shallow hollows protected by small sangars. The slightest movement drew accurate fire from the Germans, who had almost every yard of ground under observation, and Polish casualties ranged between ten and 30 every day. It was impossible to reconnoitre attack routes, even to have hot food prepared or brought up to the troops; water was strictly rationed. The divisions were provided with 72 4·2-inch mortars, 7,000 camouflage suits for snipers, special entrenching tools, and 16 flamethrowers. Five Cypriot mule-pack companies were allotted, and one Indian and five Italian labour companies were assigned the mission of repairing the trails in the high ground.

Jumping off at 0100 hours on May 12, the Polish assault battalions had lost one of every five men by 0230 and were taking twice as long as expected to get to their initial objectives. Communications were already disrupted, and control and discipline started to slip. Dense thorn-scrub, together with a profusion of rocks and boulders, increased the normal difficulties of night fighting. Engineers clearing lanes through mine-fields took heavy casualties, and tanks were consequently unable to come forward to give close support. By morning the situation was thoroughly confused. Twelve hours later, having suffered serious losses, the Polish divisions were withdrawn, the attack was temporarily abandoned. Several days of rest and reorganisation were needed to recover.

Setbacks for 8th Army

The British 13th Corps sent two divisions across the Rapido river in assault boats at 2345 hours on May 11. The swift current swept assault boats downstream and capsized many. German automatic weapons and small-arms fire was heavier than expected. As soon as troops set foot across the river, they found themselves among a thick and continuous network of pillboxes, wire, mine-fields, and concrete emplacements. Both divisions secured bridgeheads by daylight. Though the 4th Division's on the right was too shallow to permit bridging, the 8th Indian Division near Sant'Angelo had two bridges spanning the stream by 0900 hours on May 12.

Despite the success of the river crossing, the attack was disappointing. By the end of May 12, the British 13th Corps had seized only half of its initial objectives, which were to have been captured within the first two hours of the infantry assault. Not until the following morning, at 0500 hours on May 13, could the 4th Division get a bridge in. That afternoon, the corps had a consolidated bridgehead 1,500 to 2,500 yards deep, and three bridges in operation. But both divisions were taking heavy casualties, and it became necessary to commit the 78th Division. Traffic congestion and soft ground delayed the forward movement of the 78th, which crossed the Rapido on May 14.

After three days of fighting, the British 8th Army still lacked a proper entrance into the Liri valley; it had failed to break through the Gustav Line in convincing fashion.

In the coastal area, where the US 2nd Corps had attacked, the battle swirled in indecision for three days, the Americans making little progress. Then, suddenly, on May 15, the Germans began to retreat.

The reason for the German withdrawal was a spectacular achievement by Juin's French Expeditionary Corps, which smashed the Gustav Line. Major-General André W. Dody's 2nd Moroccan Division made the actual penetration in the first 24 hours of the attack. Continuing to advance over ground the Germans had judged impassable, the division moved 4 miles and, by the end of the second day, (May 13) took Monte Maio. The Germans never recovered from this breakthrough, and every step they took thereafter to plug the gap was always too late. By the evening of May 14, French troops everywhere in their zone had broken through the defences, and the 1st Motorised Division was on high ground near Sant' Apollinare, 4 miles from its line of departure, and overlooking the Liri valley.

Kesselring caught off balance

The Allied attack had caught Kesselring off balance. In the Liri valley, the two British divisions had struck five German battalions while reliefs were in progress and while a division headquarters was moving to take control of these miscellaneous units, an action never completed. The X Army reported its defences near Sant'Angelo penetrated early on May 12, and Kesselring sent piecemeal elements of three divisions to meet the British thrust.

Greater was the surprise attained by the French. Their ability to operate across the barren and trackless Aurunci Mountains was incredible to the Germans, who kept calling their effort 'a diversionary and holding attack'. Kesselring was reluctant to divert reserves to meet the recklessly advancing French even though the German 71st Division had withdrawn to the Adolf Hitler Line by May 14.

'I must demand of the divisions,' Kesselring that day told Vietinghoff, who had hastily returned from Germany, 'that they obtain a clear picture of their own situation and of that of the enemy. It is an intolerable condition when a division remains in the dark for one and half days about the events in its own sector. It is equally intolerable for a division to be in fighting contact with the enemy for two days without knowing whom they are fighting. I demand a clear picture by noon.'

A clear picture revealed that the German 71st Division had had its centre pierced and both flanks enveloped, that it had been hurled back with a loss of 2,000 men taken prisoner and very heavy casualties in killed and wounded. 'The French, particularly the Moroccans,' Kesselring later declared, 'fought with great *élan* and exploited every local success.' On May 15 he authorised a fighting withdrawal to the Adolf Hitler Line, quickly renamed the Dora Line. 'Every man must realise,' he announced, 'that with arrival in the Dora position, withdrawal has come to an end, and that the position will be held to the last man.'

Though Kesselring still wanted Monte Cassino to be defended, the success of the French, now 6 miles beyond the Rapido and on high ground overlooking the Liri, tugged along Americans, who followed retreating Germans, and British, who passed exploiting troops through an enlarged bridgehead and started up the Liri valley.

On the 16th, Kesselring moved a division from Anzio to reinforce the X Army. His action came too late to bolster the crumbling units. The German 71st Division had virtually disappeared as a result of the French onslaught, and the German 94th Division facing the Americans was on the verge of disintegrating as it relinquished Formia, 9 miles beyond the mouth of the Garigliano, and told its men to scatter and make their way to the rear as best they could. 'I can tell you quite frankly,' Kessel-

ring told Wentzell, 'I can't call anything like that tactics.'

On May 17, the Poles again attacked the Cassino massif in waves of battalions supported by 200 air sorties. By nightfall, the Poles were exhausted, and they had failed again – but the Germans were outflanked by virtue of the French and British advances, and they withdrew during the night to avoid having their escape route severed. On the following morning, at 1030 hours, the Polish standard flew over the ruins of the Benedictine monastery and British troops entered and cleared lanes through the rubble of the devastated town of Cassino at the foot of the hill. When a Polish patrol made contact with British troops in the Liri valley, the German defensive position that had withstood bitter attack for four months was finally eliminated.

On that day, the 18th, Vietinghoff phoned Kesselring to tell him that 100 infantrymen remained of the 71st Division. He needed reinforcement. If he took any more strength from the XIV Army, Kesselring answered, he would 'have to listen to Mackensen's reproaches'.

But as the X Army's right flank was being driven rapidly back in disorder and as the rest of the army was falling back into the Dora Line, he ordered a division to start moving down from Civitavecchia.

'Everything appears to be too late,' Wentzell told Beelitz. 'We are no longer able to contain the enemy.'

Alexander and Clark having agreed that it was now possible to think of attacking at Anzio, Alexander informed Winston Churchill he would soon 'punch out [from the beach-head] and get astride the enemy's communications to Rome'. He released the US 36th Division for water movement to Anzio to bolster the US 6th Corps' attack. He ordered Leese to 'use the utmost energy to break through the Adolf Hitler Line in the Liri valley before the Germans had time to settle down in it'.

In compliance, the British 8th Army sprinted to the Hitler Line only to realise that the Germans were already well entrenched. It would take a full-scale assault to dislodge them – and as the Canadian 1st and British 13th Corps prepared an attack, heavy rains delayed them for several days.

American units took Gaeta and Itri on May 19. French troops, 20 miles beyond the Garigliano, crossed the Itri/Pico road, the main lateral connecting Highways 6 and 7 below Rome, and entered the Ausonia Mountains. The advance continued on the 20th, Americans taking Fondi, French troops driving towards Pico, where they would threaten to trap the X Army in the Liri valley. On the 21st, an American infantry battalion embarked at Gaeta in amphibious trucks (DUKWs) and sailed 11 miles to Sperlonga, where the men came ashore unopposed and Terracina, 10 miles away at the southern edge of the Pontine Marshes, was the last place where the Germans could block Americans from joining the Anzio beach-head forces. On the 22nd, as Americans took Terracina and the French captured Pico, Alexander signalled: 'The battle has now reached a critical stage.' He wanted British, French, and American troops – not only those on the main front but also those at the beach-head – to attack simultaneously on the following day, the 23rd.

Kesselring, who began a systematic withdrawal of the X Army out of the Liri valley through Valmontone on May 22nd, was sure

he had done all he could. He had bolstered the X Army over protests of the XIV Army, and he had only a single division at Leghorn in reserve. It was about to become apparent that X Army had received too little, too late; that XIV Army had lost too much, too soon.

What Alexander visualised at the Anzio beach-head was a US 6th Corps thrust through Cisterna and a drive eastward to Valmontone, the only manoeuvre, he thought, that would produce 'worthwhile results'. Churchill agreed, expecting 'a decisive battle, fought to a finish, and having for its object the destruction and ruin of the armed force of the enemy south of Rome'. Alexander confirmed 'our object, namely the destruction of the enemy south of Rome'.

Clark, in contrast, was interested less in destroying the German armies than in entering Rome. He instructed Truscott to be ready to execute any one of four plans, each projecting a strike in a different direction: north-west along the coast, north along Highway 7 through Albano, east to Valmontone, and south-east to juncture with the main US 5th Army forces. The marshy terrain along the coast made only two advances practical: to Valmontone, and along Highway 7 directly into Rome. Both had disadvantages. Though the ground around Cisterna is fairly open and level and suitable for tanks, a relatively narrow corridor, obstructed by scattered patches of trees, steep ravines, and deeply-cut streams, leads to the upper end of the Liri valley at Valmontone. An advance along Highway 7 directly towards Rome would strike the strongest German positions along the Caesar Line.

As the Allied main forces came within 40 miles of the Anzio perimeter on May 19, Alexander told Clark it was time to order Truscott to break out of the beach-head. Clark procrastinated. Deciding he had to obey Alexander's wish for an attack to Valmontone, he determined to have Truscott strike directly towards Rome, regardless of Alexander's desire, if the German defences began to crumble. He instructed Truscott to be ready to attack to and through Cisterna towards Valmontone, but to be alert to the possibility of shifting his forces north to Rome after he took Cisterna.

Breakout from Anzio

Two days later, as the US 5th Army's main forces continued to advance towards the beach-head, Clark told Truscott to launch his attack at 0630 hours on May 23rd, at the same time as a major attack scheduled by the British 8th Army to break through the Adolf Hitler Line in the Liri valley. The two pincers conformed with Alexander's concept: trap the German forces and squeeze them to destruction.

The attack to dissolve the confinement imposed by the XIV Army at Anzio began on the evening of May 22nd with preliminary action. Since Alexander had asked that the American divisions of the US 6th Corps be used in the main effort – he cited the difficulty of obtaining individual troop replacements from Britain – the two British divisions in the beach-head opened Truscott's endeavour. At 2030 hours the British 1st Division launched a feint attack, and at 0215 hours on May 23rd, the British 5th Division demonstrated with artillery. At daybreak, as a slight drizzle fell, more than 500 Allied guns opened fire and 60 light bombers struck Cisterna to launch the main blow. Despite a concentrated attack by three divisions that gained initial tactical surprise, the corps failed to rupture the line. Mackensen's resistance was tenacious. American troops captured almost 1,500 prisoners and reached the Cisterna/Rome railroad, but they lost 100 tanks and serious casualties in men – the US 3rd Division alone sustaining the staggering number of 950 killed, wounded, and missing in a single day. 'More opposition there [in Cisterna],' the division commander reported, 'than we thought.'

The struggle continued on the 24th, and though the Germans stubbornly refused to give up Cisterna, the US 6th Corps reached and cut Highway 7. This opened a wedge between the X and XIV Armies.

By then, the Adolf Hitler Line had been pierced. The Canadian 1st Corps, launching a preliminary attack during the night of the 22nd, penetrated the defences, and the major attack launched by the British 8th Army on the 23rd broke the line completely. The Germans executed violent counterattacks with the XXVI Panzer and 305th Infantry Divisions, and both sides incurred heavy casualties, the Canadian 1st Division alone losing more than 500 men, but it became obvious that Kesselring would have to withdraw into the Caesar Line.

The climax of the battle
As Kesselring ordered his last reserve division south from Leghorn, he began arrangements to link the X and XIV Armies, both beaten by now, for a final stand in defence of Rome. On the 24th, Hitler gave him permission to pull back into the Caesar Line but instructed him to hold there fanatically.

The climax of the battle occurred on the 25th. The US 6th Corps reduced the German 362nd Division, which had made a gallant stand in Cisterna, to the size of a regiment and finally took the ruined town. On that day, American troops of the US 2nd Corps crossed the marshland above Terracina and met a US 6th Corps patrol coming down Highway 7 from the north. This meeting, four months after the initial Anzio landings, brought the epic Allied stand on a lonely beach-head to an end. The US 6th Corps was again joined to the main US 5th Army forces.

On that day too, Canadian units crossed the Melfa river in the Liri valley, the 78th Division went through Aquina, the British 10th Corps took Monte Cairo, and the Polish Corps, which had advanced along the high ground constituting the northern shoulder of the Liri valley, entered Piedimonte and began to be pinched out by the British 13th Corps.

During the early afternoon of May 25, Clark wrestled with his conscience. Should he throw the weight of the US 6th Corps' five American divisions towards Valmontone? Should he turn them immediately north from Cisterna towards Rome? Or should he go in both directions? Believing that the Germans would be unable to stop Truscott no matter where he struck, Clark doubted that a thrust to Valmontone would trap many Germans. The X Army was already streaming out of the Liri valley, and the British 8th Army seemed to be lagging far behind. If the US 6th Corps continued to Valmontone, it would have to make a complicated shift at Highway 6 to get to Rome across the Alban Hills.

Clark decided to send the US 6th Corps directly up Highway 7 to Rome. But because he was unable to ignore Alexander's categorical instruction for movement to Valmontone, he split Truscott's forces. He ordered Truscott to drive on Valmontone but to make his main effort along the axis of Highway 7. This message Clark sent by his G-3, who told Truscott: 'The Boss wants you to . . . block Highway 6 and mount that assault you discussed with him to the north as soon as you can.' Truscott protested. He had built up considerable momentum to the east. He had no evidence that Kesselring had weakened his defences around Albano. He was sure that Highway 7 would be blocked.

But Clark had made his decision. The Germans, he announced, had been 'decisively defeated', and the overwhelming Allied success made it possible 'to launch a new attack along the most direct route to Rome'.

Having no recourse but to obey, Truscott called together his division commanders that evening and explained the new plan. Loyally carrying out Clark's instructions, Truscott made an enthusiastic presentation. 'The Boche is badly disorganised,' he said, 'has a hodge-podge of units, and if we can drive as hard tomorrow as we have done the last three days, a great victory is in our grasp.' His division commanders were quizzical, but they said little.

The new attack on May 26 was stopped cold. By having Truscott shift his main weight towards Albano, where the Caesar Line was strongest, Clark permitted the Germans to stabilise their positions around Valmontone.

'It is the Führer's explicit order and also my belief,' Kesselring told Vietinghoff on the 26th, 'that we must bleed the enemy to exhaustion by hard fighting. . . . You have always been optimistic; why has your attitude changed?' Vietinghoff made no answer. He knew full well who was being bled to exhaustion on the approaches to Rome.

Clark had asked his Chief-of-Staff, Major-General Alfred M. Gruenther, to inform Alexander of his new attack. Gruenther did so and added, 'We are shooting the works.'

On the 27th, when Alexander visited the US 5th Army command post, he told Gruenther: 'I am for any line which the army commander believes will offer a chance to continue his present success.' But he added: 'I am sure that the army commander will continue to push towards Valmontone, will he not?' Gruenther assured him that he could depend on Clark 'to execute a vigorous plan with all the push in the world'. Alexander accepted the explanation with his usual good grace.

But Clark neither unlocked the door to Rome nor cut the German withdrawal through Valmontone. The XIV Army in the Caesar Line lost the 715th Division, which ceased to exist, but halted five days of bitter effort by the Americans to open Highway 7; and the X Army retired through Valmontone, exposed and threatened but never trapped.

On May 28, Clark inserted the newly arrived US 4th Corps on the coast and shifted the US 2nd Corps to Artena, on the eastern side of the Alban Hills. Trying to stretch the German defences, Clark would now have the US 2nd Corps take Valmontone and strike along Highway 6 towards Rome while the US 6th Corps made a twin thrust towards Rome along Highway 7. But by May 30, the US 5th Army attack had stalled again, the Caesar Line still intact.

The British 8th Army, its principal route of advance, Highway 6, pre-empted by the US 5th Army, moved slowly up the Liri valley, clearing scattered opposition in a narrowing zone, the Canadian corps moving towards Frosinone, which it would enter on May 31.

By then, the US 5th Army had cracked the Caesar Line at last. In a surprise infiltration during the night of May 30, Major-General Fred L. Walker's US 36th Division moved silently up Monte Artemisio and took possession of the height by morning. When the division then cut in behind Velletri, it broke the Valmontone defences and doomed the German positions in the Alban Hills. As the French Expeditionary Corps exerted pressure in the Lepini Mountains and the US 2nd Corps pressed towards Valmontone, the final defensive line barring entrance into Rome began to crumble.

On June 2, Kesselring asked permission to give up Rome. When consent came 24 hours later, a general disengagement was already under way. Kesselring ordered continued fighting south and south-east of Rome as long as possible to permit units to evacuate the city and the XIV Army to withdraw across the Tiber. Covered by rearguard actions of the IV Parachute Division, the Germans slipped out of Rome.

A German broadcast offered to make Rome an open city. But the Allies were already in the outskirts, and the German promise 'to carry out no troop movements in Rome' sounded both 'belated and insincere'.

Pressing forward on all roads came flying columns of the US 5th Army's 2nd and 6th Corps. On the afternoon of June 4, while the last Germans departed from Rome along deserted streets, American troops entered amid cheers of welcome from Italians who lined the thoroughfares. By midnight the US 5th Army had closed to the Tiber. Every bridge in the city was intact; every bridge outside the city had been destroyed.

The first Axis capital falls
As soon as roads were cleared, both Allied armies would go northward, the British 8th Army passing east of Rome. Alexander wished to hurry to the northern Apennines before the Germans had time to organise defences. By dusk of June 5, the sounds of battle had rolled far beyond Rome. Kesselring had started what would be a masterful withdrawal that would continue for 150 miles up the Italian peninsula. The Allies would follow in close pursuit for almost two months, reaching the Arno river at the end of July. There they would have to pause in order to prepare for another battle.

The spring offensive, which had cost the US 5th Army close to 30,000 men, the British 8th Army about 12,000, and the Germans at least 25,000, had succeeded in driving the Germans from southern Italy and in liberating the first Axis capital city of the war. King Victor Emanuel abdicated his throne and installed his son as Regent. Field-Marshal Pietro Badoglio resigned as Premier on June 9, and Ivanoe Bonomi, a prominent anti-Facist politician, formed a new government.

In larger perspective, the most important achievement of the spring offensive was to have tied down and worn out German formations. This contribution to Allied victory would become clearer when the Allies crossed the Channel.

FORTRESS

EUROPE

R. W. Thompson

Build-Up for D-Day

'I am the greatest fortress builder of all time' boasted Hitler; 'I built the West Wall; I built the Atlantic Wall. . .' But the much-vaunted Atlantic Wall, against which the invading Allies were intended to dash themselves into ruin, was only a figment of Hitler's imagination. He had never visited the invasion coast; and despite Rommel's frantic efforts to create a strong defence system, it was only in the Pas de Calais that the 'Wall' existed in anything like its intended form. And the Pas de Calais was not the Allied target area . . .

From the moment of Germany's offensive against Russia her forces had been totally inadequate for the defence of the 3,000 miles of western coastline she controlled. Field-Marshal von Rundstedt, transferred from his command in the West in April 1941, to command Army Group South in the attack against Russia, confessed that the bareness at his back gave him a feeling of chill. He expected Britain to walk in. This is not only illustrative of the Nazi weakness in the West, but of German ignorance of the true condition of the almost unarmed remnants of the British army that had survived Dunkirk. Such thinking helped to save Britain from invasion.

Returning to command in the West in 1942, Rundstedt found the situation little more to his liking. Throughout that year France had been used as a rest area for divisions badly mauled on the Eastern Front. The 50 or 60 divisions available at all material times on paper seldom mustered 25 field divisions of reasonable quality, and seldom at full strength. A Nazi decision that it would be more profitable to use prisoners of war as soldiers rather than to exterminate them, or induce them to rot in their 'Belsens' led to a complex situation, but it relieved the growing strain on German manpower. In 1942, foreign battalions were being drafted into German divisions, and in one German regiment no fewer than eight different kinds of 'Pay Book' were in use, covering at least a score of Eastern 'tribes'. A hotch-potch of races under German officers made up at least 10% of the strength of many divisions, and up to 25% of the strength of a few.

It can be seen at a glance—and it was seen at a glance by Rundstedt—that 50 or 60 divisions, even of the highest quality, will 'go' at least ten times too many into 3,000 miles of coastline. One division to 3 miles was not excessive in defence; one division in 50 or 60 miles was hopeless. One of the main enemy problems, therefore, was to decide where as well as when a major assault from the West might be expected. Whatever decision is made, wide areas must be left bare. The problem of reserves becomes insoluble.

The appreciation of Field-Marshal von Rundstedt, which remained constant, was that the Western Allies would assault against the Pas de Calais area, probably astride the Somme, not only because it was the shortest route from shore to shore, simplifying sea and air cover and a quick turn-round, but because it offered the shortest route to the Rhine, and on into the heart of the Reich. The fact that it was obvious could not exclude it, and the view from France was very different from the view from Britain. While the Allies saw the strength of the enemy positions, Rundstedt was acutely aware of the weaknesses. If the 'Atlantic Wall' was more than the 'propaganda structure' Rundstedt considered it, it was also much less than Hitler had led himself or the Allies to imagine. The materials and labour were never available to carry out his dreams, and even had the dreams been practical the fate of the immensely powerful Maginot Line had proved that defences were no stronger than their weakest links, or their defenders. The 'Atlantic Wall' existed in something like its 'propaganda strength' in the Pas de Calais, and nowhere else.

Throughout 1943, as the Nazi armies were bled white in the East, and the Allied strategic bombing offensive moved steadily towards its terrible crescendo, Rundstedt strove to reorganise the meagre and poor quality troops at his disposal. Static coastal divisions were formed, carrying a high proportion of second grade troops, but with the virtue of gaining familiarity with their allotted areas.

Hitler's invasion fears

The Allied landings in North Africa in the late autumn of 1942 put Hitler 'constantly on the jump', in the words of General Blumentritt. He expected landings anywhere and everywhere. His anxieties included Holland, Portugal, Spain, and the Adriatic. The fall of Tunis led him to believe that the south of France was immediately threatened. At the same time his fears for the vulnerability of Norway matched Churchill's recurrent desire to make these fears come true. It was an impossible situation for his generals, almost all of whom were kept in ignorance of the progress of war outside their immediate command areas. In April 1943, Geyr von Schweppenburg, then commanding the 86th Corps, was ordered to prepare Operation 'Gisela' in which five mechanised divisions would fan-out through Spain, four divisions making a 'dash' for Madrid while the fifth anchored on Bilbao. It is not to be wondered at that Geyr described the project as 'This folly'.

But although the generals did not share the wide range of their Führer's haunting apprehensions they were compelled to act upon his hunches, especially when they pointed to the region of the Somme and Normandy.

In September 1943, the elaborate exercise carried out in Britain, partly as a rehearsal of the massive and complex troop movements and loadings problems for Overlord, and partly to mislead the enemy, failed in its second purpose. The bluff, Rundstedt thought, was 'too obvious', and it seems that the Germans were misled and alarmed more by the natural rumours abounding in the occupied countries than by the stories planted by the Allies.

The autumn of 1943, bringing with it the first heavy seas and the promise of winter, limited the areas of possible Allied attack, and a respite to the enemy. All was probably secure until the spring of 1944. All that could be done was to strengthen the 'Atlantic Wall', increase the minefields guarding the approaches, and improve the training and rather miscellaneous weapon strength of the available troops. The placing and use of the armoured reserve was already looming as difficult matter, and one which the suspicions of Hitler, combined with the air power of the Allies, would make impossible.

Through the year the quality of the French Resistance had greatly improved, the quarrels of the various groups had abated, and the whole movement had responded well to British aid and organisation. By the winter of 1943/44 the Resistance had become a serious problem for the Germans, sabotaging railways and transport, and undermining morale with the fears that there might always be a bomb under the bed or in the wardrobe, that trains might leave the rails, or mysteriously blow up. And these things happened with growing frequency. The signs that the moment of crisis in the West was approaching could not be misread. 1944 would be the year, Western Europe the place, the spring or summer would bring the hour.

Information reaching the Axis through a German Foreign Office report dated January 8, 1944, by way of Ankara, gave the code name of 'Overlock' to the Allied plans, and provided 'conclusive evidence that the Anglo-Saxons are determined to force a show-down by opening a "Second Front" in 1944. However, this Second Front will not be in the Balkans.'

An Intelligence analysis by the Chief of Western Military Intelligence followed a month later:

For 1944 an operation is planned outside the Mediterranean *that will seek to force a decision and, therefore, will be carried out with all available forces. This operation is probably being prepared under the code name of OVERLORD. The intention of committing large forces becomes clear from the fact that the operation is expected to produce the final military decision within a comparatively short period of time.*

The exact area to be attacked eluded the enemy, but an Intelligence report dated February 21 re-affirmed that:

The frequently expressed determination to bring the war to an end in 1944 *is to be considered* the keynote of the enemy's operational

Rommel faces the facts . . .

Illusion and reality: when Hitler spoke of his Atlantic Wall, he saw it in his mind's eye—the greatest rampart in history. When Rommel saw it as it was—with all its blatant weaknesses—he knew that only time, labour, and vast amounts of material could begin to make reality of the Führer's dream

Alfredo Zennaro

planning. *It is also repeatedly mentioned as a definite fact that the decision will be sought by a* large-scale attack in Western Europe.

The Germans expected the attack either in the first or the third quarter of the year. Their Balkan fears were at an end. Time had narrowed down to May-August, 1944; place could be narrowed perhaps to the Pas de Calais . . . or Normandy.

The appointment of Field-Marshal Rommel in November 1943, to inspect and improve the defences of the Western coastline from Denmark to the Spanish border complicated an already difficult command situation. Possibly General Blumentritt exaggerated when he said that 'soon the armies did not know whether they were under command of Rundstedt or Rommel'. Rommel's direct line through to Hitler certainly invested him with great influence, but equally there is no doubt that he respected Rundstedt, C-in-C West, and observed the proper etiquette. Rundstedt, while holding a poor opinion of Rommel as a strategist, has paid tributes to his courage and loyalty. In the hands of one of the Nazi upstarts the appointment would have rendered the position of the C-in-C intolerable.

It was, inevitably, an uneasy situation, eased over the months by Rommel's appointment to command Army Group B, with responsibility under Rundstedt for the vital sectors of the Channel coast from the Dutch-German border to the Loire. Later, the appointment of Colonel-General Blaskowitz to command Army Group G covering the Biscay and Mediterranean coasts of France, clearly, if unsatisfactorily, clarified the 'Ground Force Command'.

But the Ground Force Command, even in isolation, and it was virtually in isolation, remained subject to powerful influences, arising not only out of the divergencies of opinion between the C-in-C West and the Commander of Army Group B, but also from General Guderian, Inspector General of Armour since March 1943, and from General Geyr von Schweppenburg, commanding Panzer Group West, and controlling the armoured reserve.

Rommel, sharing Hitler's view that Normandy would be the main Allied target, and believing that the enemy must be annihilated, if possible on and in the sea, and certainly on the beaches, wanted the armour close up under his hand ready to deliver an immediate and massive counterstroke. He had had painful experience of Allied air supremacy in the Western Desert, and knew well the fate of armoured columns attempting to move by daylight under 'open bomb sights'. If the armour was not 'there' he doubted its ability to get there, and certainly not in time. It was, in any case, virtually impossible to move armour on the stricken roads by day.

None doubted the magnitude of the Allied air threat, of which they were having daily and nightly experience, but at the same time neither Rundstedt nor the Panzer generals agreed with Rommel's tactics, or shared his beliefs about the site of operations. First, Rundstedt visualised delivering massive counterstrokes after the Allies had broken through the outer crust of the sea defences; second, he did not share Rommel's views on Normandy; third, he could not agree to the commitment of the armoured reserve close up before the event. The air argument which rendered the armour difficult to move might easily trap it and destroy it if Rommel had his way, and the main assault should come in against the Pas de Calais, or elsewhere.

Guderian, greatly worried about the situation in both the East and West, breakfasted alone with Hitler in early January 1944, and urged upon him the necessity to strengthen the Eastern defences and release much needed reserves to the West. This touched off a typical Hitler outburst:

'Believe me! I am the greatest builder of fortifications of all time,' Hitler ranted. 'I built the West Wall; I built the Atlantic Wall . . .' He then began to deluge Guderian's ears with 'tons of concrete' and a mass of statistics. In fact, Hitler had never visited the 'Atlantic Wall', and it existed, like the Emperor's clothes, largely in his imagination.

Guderian then toured the West, and was at once alarmed by Rommel's intended dispositions, and his intention to commit the Panzer divisions close up before the 'Day'. 'Disposed thus,' he wrote, 'they could not be withdrawn and committed elsewhere with sufficient rapidity.'

Back at Supreme Headquarters, Guderian took the opportunity to point out 'this error' in conference. Hitler refused to countermand the orders of the 'man on the spot', and advised Guderian to 'go to France and discuss the matter once more with Rommel'.

Guderian and Schweppenburg then visited Rommel at his Headquarters at La Roche Guyon. The Field-Marshal explained his views fully, but was not disposed to argue. Apart from his belief that Normandy would be the sector of assault, he was convinced that the enemy must be destroyed without gaining a foothold. Given his own way he might deliver such a blow to the enemy in the shallows and on the beaches that it would be impossible to mount a further assault, at least in that year. And if he were right in these beliefs, which he shared with Hitler, then he must be right about the disposition of the armour close up. The risk admittedly was great, but there was no escape from that. Clearly Rommel did not share Rundstedt's view that a battle of mobility might be won.

Hitler, meanwhile, clung to his intuitions, reinforced by his reasonable deductions from Allied troop placings, especially in the south-west of England, that Normandy would be the main target, and that Cherbourg would be the natural port for the Allies to aim at. But the nagging possibility of a second assault—even a major effort—elsewhere, began to divide his mind, disposing him far more than the commanders on the spot to the ultimate disasters of compromise.

Guderian had made a third attempt to convince Hitler of the dangers of Rommel's armoured dispositions, but early in May, Schweppenburg, fearing that Rundstedt was moving closer to Rommel's views, appealed to Hitler on his own account. He wanted to hold the bulk of his armour north and south of Paris, and at last Hitler dithered. The result was a disastrous compromise whereby four Panzer divisions were held as an assault reserve under the command of OKW, Supreme Headquarters. This weakened Rundstedt's command, for the old Field-Marshal, already thwarted in his attempts to organise an infantry reserve in Normandy by withdrawing strength from south of the Loire, now found himself deprived of the means to deliver an effective counterstroke against the beaches, or later, without seeking permission from OKW.

Thus Schweppenburg had unwittingly brought about a situation which was to prove fatal.

These were worries enough, but they were but one expression of a general weakness based on suspicion and decay at the top.

Whereas Rommel, in his natural desire to have full control of the battle his armies must fight, was in a position comparable with Montgomery's, Rundstedt's position was not in any way comparable with Eisenhower's. Not only was Rundstedt deprived of full control of his ground forces, but he was also forced to 'request' air and naval support when he might need them. There was no machinery for combined planning between the services. Worse, the German navy controlled the coastal batteries which must play a major part in repelling an assault. The fact that naval and air strength had been reduced to very small, almost negligible proportions, strengthened rather than weakened the need to co-operate and co-ordinate all available defences.

Admiral Theodor Krancke, C-in-C, German Naval Group West, had his small fleet of some 60 miscellaneous craft, hemmed into port under incessant Allied air attack. Clashes in the Channel reduced his destroyer flotilla to two operational vessels. For the rest he could muster two torpedo boats, 31 motor torpedo-boats, and a handful of patrol vessels and mine-sweepers. In addition 15 of the smaller U-boats in Atlantic ports were to be made available, but were not under his command.

In the event, even this small 'fleet' was virtually unable to put to sea.

The German Luftflotte III, commanded by General Hugo Sperrle, was equally a broken reed. Compelled to use half-trained pilots its effectiveness, even with its dwindling numbers, was poor, and it was harried constantly on the ground as well as in the air. At the beginning of June 1944, Luftflotte III mustered some 400 aircraft operational 'on paper'. Again on paper these were divided between Jagdgeschwader IV and V under II Fliegerkorps. Those of Jagdgeschwader IV had the priority task of intercepting Allied bombers bound for the Reich, but could be diverted in the event of Allied assault landings. In the event none of the units of II Fliegerkorps had aircraft available to make their presence felt on the 'Day'. The promised fighter 'wings' on the way from Germany mostly failed to arrive. Few pilots knew France; few could read maps. The Chief-of-Staff of II Fliegerkorps estimated that he had no more than 50 aircraft under command.

Thus, the Western Allies could not be challenged at sea or in the air, and Rommel had few illusions about his task. It was, in a sense, simple: the German armies in the West, battered incessantly from the air, short of training, short of essential transport, and of poor quality, deprived by the disruption of their radar installations of the full use of their 'eyes' and 'ears', stood alone, waiting.

For nearly six months Field-Marshal Rommel devoted his tremendous energies to the task of making the coastal defences impregnable from Cherbourg to the Somme, giving as much attention as was permitted to the problems of Normandy. Moved by a profound pessimism, untrammelled by the limitations of the orthodox military thinking which patterned the minds of Rundstedt and the older school, perhaps even sub-consciously aware that there could be no compromise for Germany while Germany was Hitler, he knew that the enemy must be beaten on the beaches. Perhaps he knew also that it was a forlorn hope: there was no other.

In the Pas de Calais there were huge guns which could hurl their shells across the Channel—but elsewhere along the Channel coast isolated belts of half-finished defences were scattered in threadbare and almost haphazard confusion. . . .

There is no evidence to suggest that Rommel would have disliked a battle of manoeuvre. It was simply that he knew it would be too late, and lost. There was no room, therefore, for Rundstedt's belief that the Allies were bound to gain a foothold, and that the battle for Normandy would then be fought.

To Rommel such optimism was another name for despair, and Hitler, with the shadow of disaster already darkening his door, knew it also. Blumentritt remarked that messages from OKW at this time invariably began: 'The Führer fears . . .' He was full of fears, centring on Normandy where the Valkyrie rode the skies. But whereas Rommel was a realist concerned with men and materials, concrete and mines, guns and ammunition, Hitler was a visionary, seeing figures in a glass darkly. His support for Rommel was split too many ways, and never effective. He stated clearly, to Warlimont and others: 'If we do not stop the invasion and do not drive the enemy back into the sea, the war will be lost.' He had the greatest faith in Rommel, yet apart from ordering a few anti-tank and anti-aircraft units to reinforce Western Normandy, he did almost nothing about it. US troop concentrations and assault landing

exercises in south-west England pointed ever more clearly to Normandy, and to Cherbourg, but Hitler vacillated. Neither he, nor anyone else, had conceived the possibility of the harbours the Allies planned to tow in their wake.

A powerful factor in the indecision in regard to the armoured reserve was the haunting fear that Normandy might not be the place, or only one place. The extreme lack of mobility of the German armies in the West haunted the minds of the Commanders. The Allied air forces would not only be able, in Rommel's considered opinion, to prevent troop movement in battle, but they had already knocked the wheels from under the ground troops, condemning them to static rôles.

It was impossible to make the best of it. In spite of repeated demands Rommel did not receive the command control essential to the carrying out of his basic plans even on a minimum basis. His demands for labour and materials could not be 'orders', but merely 'requests' through the normal channels. Denied the help of the Todt Organisation, fully extended on fortress work mainly in the Pas de Calais, and unable to cope with the sustained Allied

air attacks which were wrecking the transport services, Rommel used his troops as labourers to the detriment of their essential training. Some units were employed for three full days a week on labouring tasks, and much of the remainder of their time was taken up with special guard duties.

In February, Rommel issued a directive to his army commanders, and repeated it again towards the end of April:
In the short time left before the great offensive starts, we must succeed in bringing all defences to such a standard that they will hold up against the strongest attacks. Never in history was there a defence of such an extent with such an obstacle as the sea. The enemy must be annihilated before he reaches our main battlefield. We must stop him in the water, not only delaying him but destroying all his equipment while it is still afloat.

Repeatedly he emphasised to his commanders and staff that the first 24 hours would be decisive. He conceived an elaborate system of obstacles between high and low water marks covering the beaches, which would make the passage even of flat-bottomed boats perilous in the extreme, if not impossible. He planned to lay 50 ▷

million mines as the first line of sea defence, and sow minefields over the beaches. The mines were never available, and when at last inadequate deliveries were made, the minelayers were immobilised by Allied air attack and unable to put to sea. In the event not more than 6 million mines were laid, little more than one-tenth of the minimum programme.

Regarding Rundstedt's 'Zweite Stellung', or second line of defence as 'a waste of time', Rommel ordered all work upon it to cease, and the entire effort concentrated upon strengthening the forward positions. Innumerable 'hedgehogs' and anti-tank obstacles were moved forward to reinforce the massive concoctions of angle iron, the 'Tetrahydra' and 'Belgian Gates', which with thousands of mined stakes slanted seaward, mazed the approaches to the beaches. So grave was the shortage of labour that the 352nd Division, covering the vital stretch of beach from Grandcamp to Arromanches, had to cut and haul its own stakes from the Cerisy forest, 11 miles inland, and drive each stake by hand into position.

In the areas behind the Cotentin, Rommel had planned an extensive network of poles linked by wires and mined as a defence in depth against airborne landings. When the work should have been completed in the middle of May he visited the site and found that the task was only in its opening stages. The 13,000 shells necessary to set off explosions were not available.

The acute shortage of labour, mines and materials of all kinds, and the reduction of transport to the horse and cart and the bicycle, made the carrying out of a massive defensive plan impossible. Of 10 million mines needed for the 30-mile front of the 352nd Division only 10,000 were forthcoming, and these did not include any Teller mines. The situation of the 716th and 711th Divisions covering the vital frontage behind the Normandy beaches was no better. Not more than two-thirds of the coastal guns covering the army group front had been casemated by the end of May. A system of strongpoints spaced from 800 to 1,300 yards apart were in the main unprotected. 'Of the installations in the sector of the 352nd Division only 15 were bombproof; the remainder were virtually unprotected from air attack.' The 716th Division regarded its situation as even worse.

The minimum daily need of the VII Army in Normandy to fulfil its construction tasks was for 240 carloads of cement alone. In one typical three-day period the records show that it received 47 carloads. The forced closure of the Cherbourg cement works for lack of coal aggravated the extreme shortage. This was, above all, due to the Allied attacks on road and rail transport.

These desperate shortages sharpened the edge of Rommel's bitter criticism of the Luftwaffe. He pointed out that the Luftwaffe employed 50,000 men to maintain its communications, and engaged a further 300,000 on ground services. This worked out at 100 men on the ground to every man in the air. That Hugo Sperrle, commanding Luftflotte III, largely shared his views availed nothing. The situation existed to feed the grandiose dreams of Göring.

Rommel's repeated attempts to gain the services of the III Flak Corps in Normandy were thwarted, and it remained under the Luftflotte III, subject to the whims of Göring, and useless in defence. It might have done much to counter the overwhelming air strength of the Allies, and would have given some comfort and a sense of 'hitting back' to the battered troops in their dug-outs. Even the II Parachute Corps, tactically under VII Army, remained administratively and for training under the Luftwaffe. Göring refused to permit these troops to be used to help in defence works.

Thus, as June opened, the gaps in the defences were frightful, and each new device had been observed by the Allies, and often tested through the courage of the small teams of men who explored the shallows by night. By abandoning the 'Zweite Stellung' the defences had been deprived of depth, and reduced to an outer crust too fragile to withstand the immense weight of assault in store for it. Nevertheless, the fault was not Rommel's. He had attempted the impossible, and had achieved much. He had inherited a myth, and had given it 'teeth' to inflict a dangerous, if not deadly, bite. He had also greatly improved the dispositions of his troops.

On the eve of 'D-Day', Field-Marshal von Rundstedt's command in the West numbered 60 divisions, one of them, the XIX Panzer Division, refitting after a severe hammering on the Eastern Front, another in the Channel Islands, reducing the effective total to 58 divisions (see map).

Of these, 31 divisions were in static rôles, and 27, including 10 armoured divisions, were as mobile as the suspicions of the Führer and the available resources allowed. They were disposed from Holland to the Atlantic and Mediterranean coasts, five divisions in Holland in the 88th Corps, including the 'lame' XIX Panzer, 19 in the Pas de Calais between the Scheldt and the Seine, 18 between the Seine and the Loire. The remainder were south of the Loire.

Some 43 divisions out of the grand total of 60 were grouped under

Field-Marshal Rommel's Army Group B, the 88th Corps in Holland, the powerful XV Army in the Pas de Calais, the VII Army in Normandy. The XV Army, commanded by Salmuth, was virtually anchored in its positions mainly by the incapability of the German military mind to disengage itself from a pre-conceived idea. The Western Allies did their best to nurture the illusion.

By the eve of D-Day, Field-Marshal Rommel had succeeded in improving and strengthening the dispositions of the VII Army under Dollmann which, he believed, must fight the decisive battle on the beaches. The 352nd and 716th Infantry Divisions lay in their dug-outs and resistance 'nests' along the coast of Calvados from the Vire river to the Orne. On the German left flank the 91st Division, with the VI Parachute Regiment under command, covered the left flank of the 352nd in the area of Carentan. The 709th Division covered the eastern coastline of the Cherbourg Peninsula. Behind its right flank positions, known to the Allies by the code name 'Utah' beach, the extensive marshes and the flooded areas following the courses of the rivers Dives and Merderet from Carentan to le Port Brehay, were regarded as safeguarding the rear, and blocking the exits from the beaches. The 243rd Division faced west in the Peninsula.

On the German right flank the 711th Division with one regiment of the 346th Division under command covered the coast from the River Orne to the Seine Estuary opposite Le Havre.

The 709th, the 352nd, and the 716th Infantry Divisions would, therefore, meet the Allied assaults on the beaches codes named 'Utah', 'Omaha', 'Gold', 'Juno', 'Sword'. Against the will of Rundstedt, Rommel had succeeded in bringing up the XXI Panzer Division to the Caen area, poised to strike against the Allied left flank. The three armoured divisions, the XII and 116th Panzer, and the Panzer Lehr, the Army Group B reserve, capable of delivering a massive punch, lay in the rectangle Mantes-Gassicourt, Chartres, Bernay, Gacé, the 116th forward. But the fears of Rundstedt, Guderian, and Schweppenburg had placed the force under OKW, subject to the will of Hitler. Thus, the outcome of the day of decision lay with the coastal batteries and with the three divisions entrenched along the Normandy coast, the 91st Division and its parachute regiment on the left, and the XXI Panzer Division on the right. If these should fail to hold and destroy the Allies in the shallows and on the beaches the fate of Nazi Germany would be sealed, and in the pattern of the remaining days the future of Europe would be formed.

The Allied assault had been expected in the middle of May, and in spite of warnings from the German Naval Command in the West, the military view was that the assault would be at high tide. When the middle of May had safely passed there was a tendency to relax, in the belief that the attempt would be delayed until August. Enemy appreciations continued to be governed by the belief that the Allies must gain the use of a port or ports, and naval opinion moved away from the Pas de Calais, hardening in the belief that Le Havre and Cherbourg would be the main objectives. Allied troops and shipping concentrations in the south and south-west of England strongly supported this view, as also did the comparative freedom of the two ports from air attack, and the general pattern of Allied bombing at the end of May. The navy also believed that the rocky shallows covering the eastern sector of the Normandy coast would rule out landings, and expected that a major effort would come in against the Cotentin, together with airborne landings.

By the end of May, Admiral Krancke, Navy Group West, had lulled himself into an optimism, the more remarkable in view of the almost total immobilisation of his naval force. He believed that his coastal batteries could blow the Allied armada out of the water, and noted that Allied air attacks on the batteries had accounted for only eight guns, five of them between Le Havre and Le Treport, and three in Normandy. The Admiral began to believe that the massed shipping in British ports, the immense activities, the assault exercises, of which the enemy had some knowledge from isolated air reconnaissance and the reports of agents, were all part of a gigantic bluff. In effect he plumped for 'Rankin C', the Allied plan to move in as the Germans moved out.

The rapid deterioration of the weather in the first days of June ruled out the possibility of invasion in the mind of the enemy. The interceptions of warning messages broadcast to the Resistance and handed to Admiral Dönitz, failed to weigh against the high winds and rising seas in the Channel. On June 4, while General Eisenhower met with his admirals, air marshals, generals, and weather forecasters at Portsmouth, and the approaches to the Channel already seethed with the ships of the spearhead troops, Admiral Krancke in Normandy reached the view that no attack was or could be imminent. General Blumentritt, Chief of Staff, OB West agreed with him.

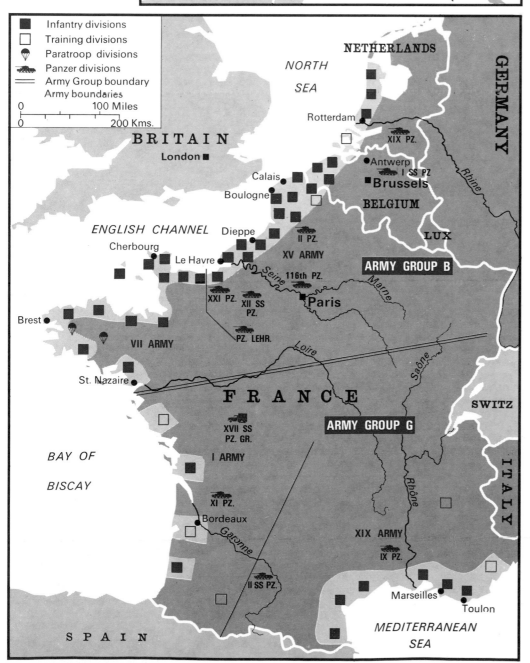

Norway, France, Portugal, Greece: Where would the blow fall? And when?

Left: Hitler's guessing-game
By June 1944 the Germans knew that the launching of the Allied Second Front could not be long delayed, and that the main blow would be a cross-Channel invasion. But Hitler expected supplementary invasions everywhere—and even Rommel came to believe that the Allies would follow up their first landings with other operations in France. And so the West was allocated some 58 divisions—but they had to be spread from the Netherlands to the Italian frontier, and divided between two separate army groups.

Left: Hitler's garrison in the West
Rommel could not believe that the Allies would ignore the Pas de Calais, and therefore he did not try to diminish the German forces already massed there. But he knew that if the Allied beach-heads were to be smashed before they could be built up into secure jumping-off points, the Panzer divisions would have to be stationed near the beaches; for Allied air superiority would prevent all large-scale reinforcement from moving up to the front. And he had lost his battle to put the Panzers where he wanted them: OKW insisted on retaining the armour inland, as an inner ring of strategic defence—the classic pattern of mobile reserve. Rommel lamented:
At one time they (OKW) looked on mobile warfare as something to keep clear of at all costs, but now that our freedom of movement in the West has gone, they're all crazy after it . . . thanks to the Allied air forces we will have nothing there in time. The day of the dashing cut-and-thrust tank attack of the early war years is past and gone. . . .

317

D-DAY
THE GREAT
GAMBLE

Normandy, June 6, 1944
R. W. Thompson

The day had dawned: the first Allied troops drifted down from the sky and struggled from the sea to begin the battle for Europe. For some it was to be an anti-climax to the months of waiting, training, thinking, wondering. For others it was to be chaos, confusion, and death. On one beach men walked ashore with next to no opposition, on its neighbour they were pinned down and massacred. There were moments of near disaster when a resolute German attack might have shattered the Allied beach-heads, but the Germans too were confused and bewildered by the weight of the massive attack. By evening the Allied foothold was secure: the great gamble had paid off

Below: Airborne Pathfinders, leaders of the paratroop drops which heralded the invasion, check their watches before take-off

By June 4, the weather was so bad that the invasion had to be delayed for one day. On the 5th, though conditions were still terrible, there was some slight hope of improvement. Appalled by the chaos which would ensue if there were more delay, Eisenhower decided that the risk must be taken: D-Day would be June 6

THE WAITING

Sunrise at two minutes to six on the morning of June 5, 1944, was an arbitrary statement rather than a visible fact marking the progress from dark stormy night to grey blustery day. The Channel heaved in a chaos of cruel pinnacles flecked white upon steel grey, and waves rose steeply to test the seamanship and try the stomachs of all those afloat in little ships. Clouds fled in tormented tattered shrouds over a cold sky. A gusty westerly, veering WSW to WNW at Force 5, whipped the spume into the faces of look-outs and helmsmen as scores of small craft reared and bucked towards their meeting place. By sunrise, 5,000 ships of half-a-hundred shapes and sizes had begun to move from their anchorages, and the wakes of many convoys already patterned the coastal waters of Britain from Fowey to the Nore. It was four years almost to the day since the remnants of an army had struggled back from Dunkirk, and the coastal waters of England had known any comparable activity. Admiral Ramsay had commanded then, and he commanded now, on this morning.

This fifth day of June is not one of those landmarks in history to be covered by easy generalisation. It was many things to many men. 287,000 men and a host of armoured fighting vehicles had been preloaded into ships, some of them since the first day of the month, some of them had been already shuttled and shunted, blind to sea and sky, daylight or darkness, sick, weary, wondering, aware that a moment would come when they would be spewed up like Jonahs upon an alien shore, bristling with devices of death and beaten with shot and shell.

The many thousands on deck, however sick and cold, could count themselves fortunate that they were not of the many thousands below, huddled in the great caverns of the LCTs (Landing Crafts, Tank), in the cramped quarters of the LSIs (Landing Ships, Infantry), in the dull yellow electric glow, and the stench of vomit.

While thousands waited in a grey limbo, thousands worked, manning the little ships and the great ships of war, alert in hundreds of gun turrets, crouched astride swivel seats behind a great array of weapons pointing to the sky, cloud ceiling 4,000 feet, and above that the sustained roar of 10,000 aircraft. Hundreds more wrestled with towing gear and hawsers, tugs grappling and towing strange ungainly shapes out of the estuaries in the wake of the Armada massing south of the Isle of Wight.

Towards evening there was a break in the weather, and in that brief hour a soldier wrote: 'It was a perfect summer's evening, the Isle of Wight lay green and friendly, and tantalisingly peaceful behind the tapestry of warships.' And in the dusk when the convoys began to move towards their date with destiny, men were answering cheer with cheer across the water, the pennants flew from the ships of war, and a British Admiral threw his cap in the air. Yet what a travesty of the truth this is to the thousands who seemed to inhabit a grey ante-chamber to a morgue, dull sickness upon them to eke out the miseries of the long blind ordeal of waiting.

Force U2a, part of Force U for Utah, had had the worst of it. 128 tank landing craft, crowded with men and armour, sailed out of the west through the hours of indecision, easted down Channel, turned about, plunged back into the teeth of the westerly to seek shelter in Weymouth Bay and in the lee of Portsmouth, easted again down Channel at last in the dusk of June 5 to set course for France.

Force O for Omaha had had also a long haul from the south-west, a turn and turn-about, an agonising drawing out of the hours of confinement. Already men on deck had kept watch upwards of 50 hours, and perhaps 50 more lay ahead before sleep. For these no cheers, no happy vision of the Isle of Wight, for their 'green and pleasant land' lay beyond the Atlantic.

Through the hours of darkness the immense convoys moved steadily, unmolested, on their courses in the buoyed channels cleared by the mine-sweeping flotillas, a wedge more than 50 miles wide, and with scores of small fighting ships ranging far out on the flanks probing for the enemy. There was nothing. The long lines of ships seemed to unwind on fabulous spools, drawing their component threads from a hundred havens of the English coast, to weave them into thick skeins to the Bay of Seine. The fierce turbulence of wind and sea failed to mask the strange 'unnatural' silence of the night. The sustained thunder of the fleets of bombers overhead, quenched for those below by the drenching sounds of sea, and the shuddering stresses of steel plates, seemed to accentuate the absence of the enemy. It seemed impossible that such an avalanche of ships and men could muster through the months, at last to fill the English Channel from shore to shore, and remain undetected. Surely no instrument more 'scientific' than the human ear would be needed to hear so vast a throb of power!

No signs of detection

Before the sun had set on the evening of the 5th, two flotillas of mine-sweepers stood off the coast of Normandy, well within sight, and easily able to distinguish houses on shore with the naked eye. The midget submarines of Lieutenant Honour's command were at their stations, close inshore marking the eastern flank and the dangerous rocks. There were no signs of detection. From 0200 hours on the 6th, the HQ ships of the assault moved into their transport areas, and prepared to put their assault craft into the water. The only interference came from the unfriendly sea, and the weather was not alone to thank, or blame, for this.

The sustained attacks from the air on the elaborate Early Warning System of the enemy had succeeded almost too well. In the entire Neptune Area from Cap d'Antifer to Barfleur, 74 radar stations were out of action, and the 18 still capable of working were silent. But it was not enough simply to blind the enemy, it was important also to mislead. For this purpose ten stations were deliberately left in working order north of the Seine, and on to these screens the Royal Navy contrived to produce a misleading web of shapes and echoes. It seems extravagant that such a claim is made, for it reveals a predominance over the enemy that reduces his forces to a stricken body, lacerated on all sides, unable to fly or float, but capable of inflicting grievous, even crippling, wounds upon those seeking to deliver the *coup de grâce*.

But there was no inclination on the part of the Allies to underestimate the powers of the German army in the west. Thus all through June 5 and the night, 105 aircraft of the RAF and 34 little ships of the Royal Navy contrived by means of weaving patterns over the sky and sea, and flying barrage balloons, to produce the 'echoes' in the enemy radar ears of a substantial fleet approaching the Pas de Calais. At the same time jamming operations and diversions were carried on against Cap d'Antifer and Barfleur. The silent approach of the great armada to spread out in a fan from 8 to 12 miles offshore enclosing the Bay of Seine is the measure of success.

Soon after 9 o'clock, the unusual length and content of the BBC broadcast warning to the French Resistance alarmed the Germans, and the XV Army in the Pas de Calais was alerted, while the VII Army in Normandy remained undisturbed. Nothing, it seemed, could prise von Rundstedt's mind away from its preconceived fixations, even the deadly facts of the elements of three airborne divisions dropping in the midst of his forces. Well before the first assault craft of the seaborne forces were in the water, the battle on land was joined.

AIR DROP IN THE WEST: 'CHAOS WILL REIGN'

Within half-an-hour of sunset on the night of June 5, while the leading ships of the seaborne assault moved into the buoyed channels to steer for France, the Pathfinders of the United States and British air forces took off from their English fields to light their beacons in the fields of Normandy. Soon after midnight these small vanguards of élite troops were moving silently in the midst of the enemy, the British to mark the dropping zones for the 6th Airborne Division to the north-east of Caen on the eastern flank, the Americans astride the Merderet river, and the road Carentan-Montebourg-Cherbourg in the area of Ste Mère-Église. Behind them more than 1,200 aircraft bore nearly 20,000 men into battle;

behind them the gliders for which the paratroops must clear the way.

The last warning of the brigadier commanding the British 3rd Parachute Brigade may well serve for all: 'Do not be daunted if chaos reigns: it undoubtedly will.'

The drop of the US 101st Airborne Division, as fully plotted as all subsequent information has made possible, spatters the map over an area 25 miles long by 15 miles broad, and with small isolated elements even further afield. Very few of these had even an outside chance of becoming part of the division. The men had been loosed, as it seems, recklessly upon the winds of Heaven, and thence to the flooded hinterlands, and maze of closed country, behind Utah Beach.

The US 82nd Airborne Division, largely due to the arrival of one regiment reasonably on its objectives, fared a little better, but of the remainder of the division only 4% were dropped in their zones west of the Merderet river. Thus the tasks of the division west of the Merderet, and the crossings of the Merderet and Douve rivers, could not be fulfilled. The division had become a regiment.

At dawn, when the seaborne landings were coming in on Utah Beach, the 101st Airborne Division mustered 1,100 men out of 6,600. By evening its strength had grown to 2,500 men. The 82nd Airborne Division, at least 4,000 men short on the day, was still only at one-third of its strength three days later. Both divisions had lost great quantities of equipment, and almost their entire glider-borne artillery, much of it in the floods of the Merderet and Douve rivers. Neither division was able to prepare adequately for the arrival of its glider-borne follow-up, the losses were severe and tragic.

Yet the remarkable fact is that so great a confusion was created in the enemy by this incoherent scattering of men in their midst that there was no possibility of reserves supporting the beach defenders. By the time the US 4th Infantry Division came in to land the battle of Utah Beach was virtually won.

No coherent pattern has ever emerged from the struggles of the isolated remnants of the airborne divisions on that day; nor will such a pattern ever emerge. The individual contributions of many men who fought bravely alone or in twos and threes will never be assessed. Even those who gave up without a fight added to rather than subtracted from enemy bewilderment. The Pathfinders of the airborne divisions did not do well. Many failed to find and to mark the dropping zones; some beacons were missing entirely, especially west of the Merderet in country infested by enemy; others were wrongly placed. Pilots under fire for the first time, many of them 'inadequately briefed', took wild evasive action, lost direction in the cloud banks, and overshot the dropping zones. Many came in too fast and too high, and spilled out their 'sticks' of men, adding greatly to the normal hazards of jumping.

Major-General Maxwell Taylor, commanding the 101st, dropped with a nucleus of his divisional HQ, and struggled all through the day to make contact and to bring some sort of order out of chaos. He felt 'alone on the Cotentin'. In the upshot the pattern may be seen dimly in the struggles of half-a-dozen colonels, each managing to group between 75 and 200 men round him, aided by the tell-tale click-clack of the toy 'crickets' with which every man was provided.

By a stroke of remarkable fortune a small band of men ambushed and killed the commander of the German 91st Division, returning from an 'exercise' conference to his headquarters. Thus the 91st Division, trained in the role of defence against airborne attack, and forming almost the sole available reserve behind the defenders of the Cotentin coast, was deprived of its commander and severely handicapped. There was no 'shape' or dimension to the airborne enemy, no focal point or points to counterattack, no time to think, no commander with the temerity to commit troops with the strength and purpose of knowledge.

While many German officers were sure that this must be the beginning of the main Allied assault — so long awaited and expected — and that the battlefield was Normandy, others, including Lieutenant-General Speidel, Rommel's Chief-of-Staff, and Lieutenant-General Blumentritt, Chief-of-Staff to Rundstedt, were doubtful. Thus the German military machine remained hesitant and palsied, its slender reserves uncommitted, its armour waiting, Rommel out of touch, Hitler sleeping. These things gave the airborne troops on the western flank an initial advantage of which, perforce, they were unaware, and saved them from the possibility of annihilation.

Throughout the whole day and night the 101st Airborne Division, reduced to much less than the effective strength of a single regiment, was not only isolated from its own widely scattered units, but also in complete ignorance of the fate of the 82nd Airborne Division. Ironically, it may have achieved at least as much in its confusion as it could have hoped for in coherence, for chaos bred chaos.

The one effective landing

The story of the 82nd Airborne Division is simple. Two of its regiments with the tasks of clearing the area west of the Merderet river and in the angle of the Douve, were not in the fight. It fell to one regiment to save the day, and to fight the one clear-cut battle fought by the US airborne forces on D-Day. While scores of men struggled in the swamps of the Merderet, dragging themselves towards the dry land of the railway embankment, concerned in the main with the problem of survival, the third regiment had dropped in a fairly tight group to the north-west of Ste Mère-Église. This was not due to chance, but to the determination of the pilots to find their targets. Long before the dawn, Lieutenant-Colonel Krause, finding himself on the outskirts of Ste Mère-Église with roughly a quarter of his battalion, bounced the town without waiting for more, and taking the enemy completely by surprise began to establish a solid base. By the afternoon the town was securely held, and four recognisable actions had developed, apart from a score or more of fragmentary encounters in the hopeless wilderness west of the Merderet.

The 82nd Airborne had dropped on the fringe of the assembly area of the German 91st Division, and its position from the outset was much more precarious than that of the 101st. All troops, however fragmentary, were at once in the midst of the enemy, and fighting for their lives within minutes of finding their feet. Some small groups up to 50 or 60 strong fought all day in the ditches and hedgerows within 1,000 yards of others with whom it was impossible to make contact. Often they were unaware of their nearness.

The performance of the 101st and 82nd Airborne Divisions on D-Day may only be seen in fragmentary terms. At the end of the day the divisions had not made contact. Each believed it had lost some two-thirds of its troops. Neither one had cause for satisfaction, or the haziest idea of what was happening. All that they could do was to wait for the morning.

Fortunately, the enemy's confusion was equivalent to almost total breakdown. Hammered savagely and incessantly from the air, handicapped by the chance of a conference at Rennes of their senior commanders coinciding with the assault, their communications disrupted, and with, as it seems, a premonition of inevitable doom, their resistance was as fragmentary as that of the airborne troops infesting their imaginations as well as their fields. Many surrendered almost without a fight. Major von der Heydte, commanding the German VI Parachute Regiment, probably the finest enemy troops available in the Carentan area, has told of his difficulties in getting orders from his senior commanders. From the church steeple of St Côme-du-Mont he had a personal view of the seaborne armada on the western flank. It seemed to him curiously detached from reality, almost peaceful. At noon the sun was shining, and the whole scene reminded him 'of a summer's day on the Wannsee'. The immense bustle of landing craft, and the warships fading into the horizon, lacked to his ears the orchestration of battle.

Von der Heydte sent his three battalions into battle, one to the north to attack Ste Mère-Église, another to the north-east to protect the seaward flank in the area Ste Marie-du-Mont, the third back on Carentan. Von der Heydte almost at once lost contact. Organised defence on the western flank had crumbled.

322

A host of men and vehicles had been loaded into ships . . . soon they would be spewed up like Jonahs upon an alien shore

287,000 men and a host of armoured fighting vehicles were pre-loaded into ships, some of them as early as the first of the month

△Grim-faced American troops file aboard a landing ship
▽British soldiers pass the time learning about their target

UTAH BEACH: 12 MEN KILLED

At 0200 hours on June 6, the leading ships of Force U, organised in 12 convoys comprising 865 vessels commanded by Rear-Admiral Moon, USN, moved into their assembly area 12 miles off the western coast of the Cotentin Peninsula, opposite the dunes of Varreville—Utah Beach. The assault upon Utah Beach on the extreme western flank was virtually an isolated operation. If all else failed it might have been reinforced to establish a bridgehead, to cut off the Cotentin Peninsula, gaining Cherbourg as a major port from which to mount some subsequent effort. In that event Overlord would be no more.

Field Order 1 states: '7th Corps assaults Utah Beach on D-Day at H-Hour and captures Cherbourg with minimum delay.'

Steadily in the hours before dawn the orders to 7th Corps reduced down to those few who would debouch into the shallows of the unfriendly sea. The 4th Infantry Division would establish the bridgehead; the 8th Infantry Regiment leading—the 1st Battalion on the right, 'Green beach'; the 2nd Battalion on the left, 'Red beach'; two companies of each battalion forward; 30 men to each landing craft; five landing craft to each company, 20 landing craft carrying 600 men in the van, with two companies of the 70th Tank Battalion in the first wave (see map on pages 1806/07). Behind them, wave upon wave of their fellows and the waves of the sea, H+5, H+15, H+17, H+30, on and on through all the day and night, and beyond; infantry, armour, engineers, into the shallows, through the obstacles, the mine-fields, over the beaches, the sea wall, the causeways, the floods, inland to the villages and fields; 27 miles across the neck of the peninsula, Carentan to Lessay; north to Cherbourg.

H-Hour on the western flank was 0630 hours, but along the invasion beaches tidal-variations decreed four different H-Hours from right to left, from Utah Beach to Sword Beach, a span of one hour and 25 minutes. But the men on the right were in their own cocoons of loneliness. Now, in the bitter morning, they were being buffeted in the shallow draft vessels, the dark sky above them wild with the roar of aircraft, the crescendo rising, the blasting roar of the main armament, the scream of shells, and all around a turbulence of men and craft.

To the left, for nearly 50 miles, variations on the theme were unfolding over the waters, Omaha, Gold, Juno, Sword, and over the dark shore-line from end to end the dust was rising, blasted in towering columns by shells and bombs to hang, an opaque and ominous curtain, above the stage.

Enemy shells air-bursting over the water, the spasmodic explosions of mines, the shouts of men floundering, arms flung out, weighed down by equipment, created an uproar in the mind and senses in which the last cries of the lost, the total personal tragedies, were no more than the plaintive squeakings of mice in a cage of lions. The 60 men of Battery B, 29th Field Artillery Battalion, became a statistic on the debit side, dark shadows threshing in the water, under the water, part of the pattern at the bottom of the sea.

But the pattern advanced, untroubled by calamity, the second wave, the bulldozers on their craft, the special engineer units, all in position, the heavy armament of the bombarding squadron blasting the grey dawn to crimson shreds, 40 minutes to go. Some 276 aircraft of the US 9th Air Force roaring in over the beach defences, delivering their bombs, 4,404 bombs each of 250 pounds upon seven targets, 'according to the book'.

Seventeen of the 33 supporting craft seemed to tear the crackling scalp off the universe in an unbearable rasping agony as their mattresses of rockets shuddered inshore. Other craft were machine-gunning, perhaps in the hope of detonating mines, perhaps simply to boost morale, but all 'drenching the beaches with fire'.

About 700 yards to go, and on time, ten assault craft, 300 men on the left, ten assault craft, 300 men on the right; in their wakes 28 DD tanks, swimming, slopping the choppy water across their grey backs, the long muzzles of their guns like snouts, a seeming miracle thanks to the bold initiative and swift decision of their commander to launch close in at 3,000 yards, 'not according to the book'.

The beach was almost invisible behind the sand pall, blasted by gunfire and bombs, joining it to the sky, and in it, under it, the enemy—if there could be an enemy!

Some 67 of the bombers had failed to release their bombs, one-third of the remainder had fallen between high and low water mark, the bulk of the rest on the fortifications of La Madeleine.

A swift, painless landing

Out of the leading wave of the assault craft smoke projectiles hurtled to the sky, demanding silence from the gunners of the bombarding force. About 300 yards to go, and the ramps down, 300 men of the 2nd Battalion, waist deep in water, floundering, finding their feet, wading in, rifles held high, to the dry sand, and the sudden upsurge of spirit. Normandy, the first men ashore, and not a shot out of the haze of battle, the grey shapes of the tanks crawling up out of the sea in their 'skirts', striking terror to the few who still lifted up their heads in the defences and dared to fire, a few wavering shots, 'desultory fire'.

These few men, and their comrades in the van, landing within minutes on their right, did not know that the south-easterly set of the tide had carried them more than a mile south of their target. It was a fortunate chance. Two hours later the leading troops were off the beach. The enemy strongpoints yielded to mopping-up operations in company strength, and the sea wall did not demand assault. Six battalions of infantry had begun to move off the beach by 1000 hours, and little more than an occasional air burst hampered the engineers at their toil, or reminded them of their extreme vulnerability as they placed their charges by hand. By noon the beach had been cleared at a cost of six men killed and 39 wounded out of the 400 involved in static roles, all of them sitting ducks without cover, and without armour.

Shortly after midday three battalions of the 22nd Infantry Regiment were moving north to open the northerly exit, the 3rd Battalion along the coast road to anchor a flank on Hamel-de-Cruttes, the 1st and 2nd Battalions wading diagonally, and miserably, waist deep, and often armpit and neck deep, across the floods all the way to St Germain-de-Varreville.

The 12th Infantry Regiment found the going worse, wading from the Grand Dune position immediately backing the beach, and crossing the line of march as they reached dry land, many of them soaked to the ears.

In all that day, the 8th and 22nd Infantry Regiments lost 12 men killed. Twenty times the number would have been counted fortunate; 100 times the number a misfortune to be looked for. A single resolute man armed with a flint lock could have accounted for more than 12 men on the beach in the first half-an-hour, including a brigadier-general and a colonel. The struggle of the 4th Infantry Division was mainly against the forces of nature, which were considerable. Eastwards it was different.

OMAHA BEACH: THE BLOODBATH

The beach of Omaha lies between the outcropping rocks of Pointe de la Percée in the west, and Port-en-Bessin in the east, a shallow arc of sand enclosed inland by bluffs rising in a gentle slope 150 feet to a plateau of tiny hedge-enclosed fields, deep lanes, and scattered hamlets built solidly of stone. It is a thinly populated region, the largest village, Trévières, 3 or 4 miles inland on the south side of the Aure river, counting not more than 800 inhabitants.

Three coastal villages, Vierville, St Laurent, and Colleville lie behind the beach at regular intervals a mile and a half apart, and linked by a narrow lane from 500 to 1,000 yards in from the shore line. A stretch of paved promenade along the 'front', and with a score or more of good houses between Vierville and St Laurent, backs a low sea wall of masonry and wood. Gullies opening from the beach give access up narrow lanes to the villages.

At low tide the sands slope gradually to the sea wall, and in places to a heavy shingle bank of stones 3 inches in diameter, a barrier 8 to 10 feet high between the beach and the reedy grasses of the bluffs.

War had become a battle
of machines against machines

For months before D-Day, the crews of the specialised armour of British 79th Armoured Division had practised their techniques for breaching the German defences. On The Day they were highly successful, as British and Canadians rushed ashore.
(1) The swimming Duplex Drive Sherman tanks were first ashore, taking up positions at water's edge from which they could engage and control enemy pillboxes.
(2) They were followed by Crab flail tanks, which advanced up the beach in echelon, overlapping to ensure that *all* the mines in their path were cleared.
(3) When the flails had reached the sea wall an AVRE with an SBG bridge would place its bridge; a DD tank would mount the sea wall to attack the pillboxes at closer range. This would be followed by an AVRE carrying a fascine to fill the anti-tank ditch. By now the infantry (red arrows) would be crossing the beach.
(4) The flails continued to clear the minefields to open lanes through which the beach-head could be extended. Petard tanks would advance to destroy the last pillboxes by firing through the embrasures. At all times, reserves would be held to ensure that the loss of individual machines did not disrupt the whole landing

Seaward the stresses of the sea and the strong currents carve runnels in the wet ribbed sands.

The rocky shoulders of the bluffs of Omaha, flanking the crescent of the beach, provided concealed gun positions to enfilade the fore shore and the sea approaches, and behind the obstacle of the heavy shingle bank and the wall, the enemy defended entrenchments linking strongpoints, pillboxes, and concrete gun emplacements sited to bring devastating cross-fire to bear upon the beach. Theoretically, at least, light and heavy machine-guns, 75- and 88-mm artillery pieces, would make a beaten zone of the entire beach area from end to end. And behind the forward defensive positions the terraced slopes of the bluffs gave cover to further trench systems, machine-gun nests, and minefields.

The beach itself was moderately mined, especially in the areas between the gullies, and from low to high water mark an elaborate system of staggered lethal obstacles seemed to defy the passage of any craft larger than a matchbox. But all these things had been studied in some detail by small parties visiting the beaches by night, and from countless air photographs.

Omaha Beach held no mystery and no surprises. Even the bringing in of a new and vastly superior division – 352nd – had been observed by British Intelligence, and passed on to US 1st Army. Unhappily, this piece of information had seemed suspect to the 1st Army Command, and the assault troops were not informed. Yet it is inconceivable that they had been briefed to expect less than the worst the enemy could be expected to perform. To attack this superb defensive position General Bradley had rejected Hobart's magnificent array of assault armour, and had accepted DD tanks only with reluctance.

A terrible confusion

At 0300 hours on June 6, Force O, commanded by Rear-Admiral Hall, USN, and carrying 34,000 men and 3,300 vehicles and with a follow-up force, almost its equal, a few hours astern, began to put its assault craft into the water 12 miles off shore. There followed four hours of a macabre Dantesque confusion, through which men struggled blindly with the sea, a prey to despair, knowing the dregs of misery. While the larger vessels moved forward, finding difficulty in maintaining their stations in the heavy sea, the smaller craft were exposed to the full force of the north westerly, fighting seas up to 6 feet high, unstable and making water too fast for the pumps.

Some of the larger ships had put their assault craft into the water fully loaded, but others had put their men over the side into craft pitching and rolling wildly, an ordeal for men wracked with sea sickness. The sea, unfriendly through all the hours of the long passage, became in minutes a dark heaving formless jungle upon which men and boats wrestled like the damned in a labyrinthine maze of driven spume.

Almost at once ten small craft foundered, and upwards of 300 men struggled for their lives in a darkness which seemed to contain a kind of uproar in its relentless impersonal violence. Rudderless, foundering small craft and the sodden wreckage of equipment added to the menace, buffeting the men in their life jackets.

In nearly 200 assault craft, the crews and troops who must presently assault the enemy across open beaches in the face of withering fire, baled with their tin hats for their lives, in some boats 100% sea-sick, in all boats sodden, cramped, and cold. At last on the verge of nervous and physical exhaustion the assault troops neared the shore, and their craft strove to manoeuvre for the final run-in.

These men in the vanguard were more naked than they knew or greatly cared. Behind them the seas had stripped them steadily of guns and armour, and the teams of combat engineers had suffered no less than they. With a reckless irresponsibility the commander of the tank landing-craft carrying 32 DD tanks due to land at H−5 launched his massive vehicles into the steep seas 6,000 yards off shore. Even with well-trained crews there would have been small hopes for the tanks; as it was 27 were swamped within minutes and sank. Two, by brilliant seamanship and chance, ▷

'A foothold has been gained on the continent of Europe'

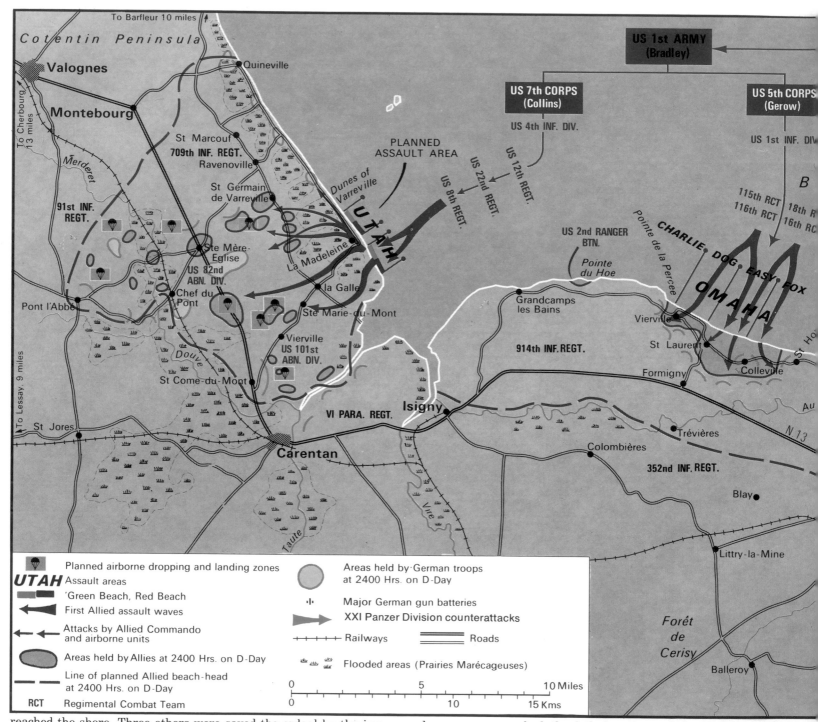

reached the shore. Three others were saved the ordeal by the jamming of the ramp of the landing craft, and were carried in. Thus the 96 tanks planned to provide vital close support for the 1,450 men of eight companies, and the first wave of the engineer teams, in the moment of assault had dwindled by almost a third of their number.

Disaster had also met the attempts to ferry the supporting artillery ashore in DUKWs. The small overloaded craft, almost unmanageable, quickly foundered. The 111th Field Artillery Battalion lost all its 105-mm howitzers save one. The 16th Infantry Cannon Company shared the same fate, and the 7th Field Artillery was very little better. The engineer teams, off-loading their heavy equipment from LCTs to LCMs, also had their troubles and losses. Nevertheless, in the last hour a great concourse of men, guns,

and armour approached the lethal regions of the shallows, their initial losses far less than must have been inflicted by an enemy capable of even a moderate challenge on the sea and in the air. But the sea and air belonged to the Allies. With 40 minutes still to go the powerful bombarding squadron opened fire on the coastal defences with a great armament from the 16-inch guns of the battleships to the 5-inch guns of the destroyers, deluging the line of the bluffs with fire and smoke. At the same time 329 out of the 446 Liberators sent to do the job attacked 13 targets on and about the beaches with more than 1,000 tons of bombs.

The leading assault craft were some 800 yards out when the barrage behind them lifted and the vast uproar muted to the violent staccato sounds of the guns in the close support craft in their wakes.

Overlord began with the paratroop drops: in the west to isolate the Cotentin peninsula by holding the Merderet/Douve line, in the east to shield the left flank by holding the line of the Orne. Despite scattered landings, both objectives were achieved: widely dispersed US paratroops prevented coherent German attacks on the Omaha sector, while the British destroyed the Orne bridges and pinned down the German armoured reserves in the Ranville area. Opposition to the landings varied considerably. On Utah Beach the troops went ashore at 0630 hours with negligible losses, and were off the beaches by 1200 hours. On Omaha, lack of specialised armour allowed very strong defences to hold the troops on the beach and slaughter them. By midnight the deepest penetration was hardly a mile. In the central sector, specialised armour brought the British and Canadians swiftly over Gold and Juno Beaches and by the afternoon they were probing inland towards Bayeux and Caen. The Sword assault was equally rapid: by 1400 hours leading troops had reached Biéville and the Commandos were linking up with the paratroops. This proved a vital factor, for it was through the gap between Juno and Sword that the Germans made their one major counterattack—a battlegroup of XXI Panzer Division swept towards the coast, but turned back when British reinforcements were flown in to the airborne troops behind it. From the beginning, the main weight of German resistance was on the Allied left flank, and it was there that the German armour was pinned down, fortunately far from the precarious toe-hold at Omaha, which could have turned from a local disaster to a major crisis

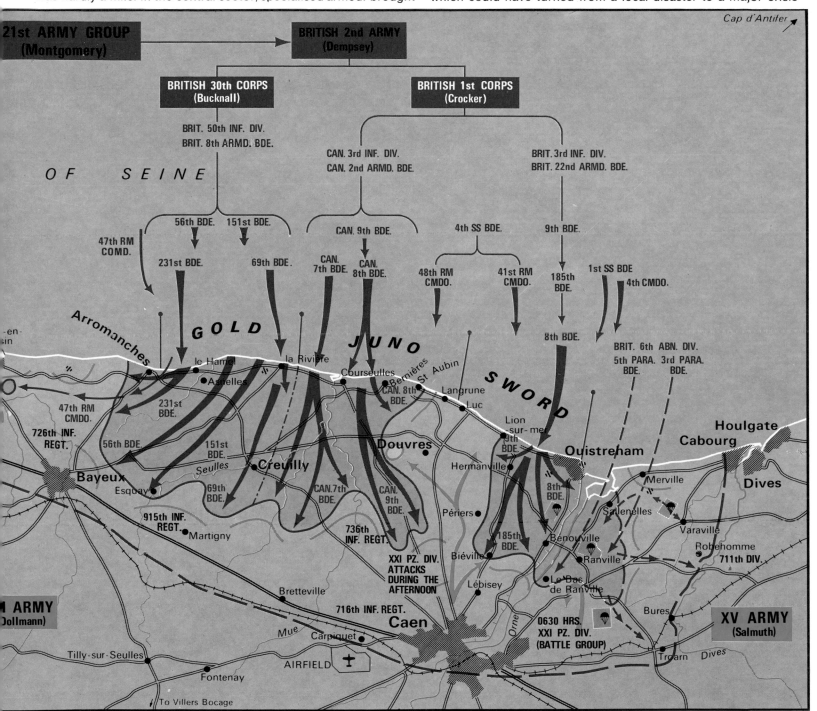

The crash of bursting mortar bombs, of shells, and the smash of machine-gun bullets against the ramps warned the assault troops that the enemy held them in his sights. The cries of men in the water, the sudden searing sheets of flame, the thunderous explosions as craft were hit by enemy shell and mortar fire, caught them up and splintered their isolation to fragments, and the ramps went down.

There is a devastating simplicity about disaster. There were no dry landings. The assault craft, and the larger LCVPs and LCMs grounded on the sandbanks, slewed in the sand runnels, and cast scores of men knee, waist, and neck deep into seas lashed not only by the wind, but by mortar bombs, shells, and machine-gun bullets. While isolated groups waded to the shore, dazed and bewildered by their loneliness on that 5-mile-long wilderness of sand, blinded by the smoke of many fires raging on the bluffs, uncertain what to do, others, the great majority, were in the midst of infernos of exploding ammunition and engineer charges set off by direct hits. Here and there craft blew up in ferocious ovens of flame.

The LCTs of the 743rd Tank Battalion leading in the van on the right flank surged on with men diving from stricken craft on either side, seeking the shelter of the waves, while others fought for footholds, clawing their ways to the beach, weighed down with equipment, some on hands and knees, others dragging forward on their bellies, with their wounded and their wounds. But it was safer in the sea.

A direct hit on the leading LCT killed all the company officers,

'Do not be daunted
if chaos reigns.
It undoubtedly will'

save one, but eight of the DD tanks landed on the rim of the sea to open fire on the Vierville strongpoint: range 200 yards. The tanks of the 743rd were getting in further east, but the men without armour had little chance. When the ramps of the leading assault craft went down the enemy machine-guns tore through living flesh so that the front cavities of the vessels became in seconds raw wounds, thick with blood. Dozens leaped this way and that for their lives.

Within half-an-hour of H-Hour there were at least 1,000 assault infantry and engineers alive on the beach and in the shallows, but they were not fighting the enemy; they were fighting quite simply for survival, many exhausted, all too weary to drag their equipment across the beach, very few among them able to run, to assault, head-on, the enemy strongpoints.

Some went back to the water, and came in with the tide until at last it brought them, like flotsam, to the meagre shelter of the sea wall or the shingle bank. Very few of those scattered, almost at random, along the length of that beach, and all trained for the specific tasks with which, it was planned, they would be faced, knew where they were. Very few had come in on those 'stages' for which they had rehearsed. Boat teams, organised as fighting units, were miserably scrambled, and often alone, a detachment here, another 200, 300, even 1,000 yards away. For all many of them knew they were alone on the beach known as Omaha. The sea was behind them, and the blinding smoke, saving them from enemy fire in the lucky places, dazed them. The few officers were often slow to get their bearings, or to make up their minds what to do. Few found the leadership in that first hour which alone could have got them off the beach. Above all they were exhausted, and there was no refuge.

The engineer combat teams, coming in on the heels of the assault infantry, had suffered severely on the run-in, losing much of their vital equipment. Direct hits had blown some of their craft to pieces. Of 16 teams, each trained for its special role in its sector, only five came near to their assignments, and of these, three were utterly alone, unprotected by man or gun, naked to the enemy. Within minutes only three bulldozers out of 16 survived for the work of heaving aside the heavy barriers of angle iron and obstacles, and these lost their ability to manoeuvre as men took cover behind them.

Yet despite their crippling losses, and their exposure to the full force of enemy fire, the engineers salvaged what gear they could and strove to clear lanes through which the follow-up forces hoped to pass. Heavy mortar and shell fire detonated chains of fuses painfully laid by hand, and blew up whole detachments of engineers before they could get clear. The swiftly rising tide foamed round their feet, their waists, submerging the outer obstacles, and forcing the survivors to the sea wall and the shingle before their tasks were a tenth-part done. On the whole sector of the 116th RCT they had cleared two gaps. Far to the east, where scarcely a man had landed, they had cleared four gaps, but of them only one was marked. The effort had cost more than 40% of the engineer strength, most of it in the first half-hour.

But always behind the engineers, not only the rising tide, but the tremendous tide of men and vehicles pressed on, steadily wave upon wave, building up on the beaches, in the shallows, demanding an outlet. After three terrible hours the foreshore was a wilderness of wreckage, of burning vehicles, of shattered craft, and shattered men. Not one of the exits from the beach was open, not one of the defensive positions had been stormed, and a message went back to the sea to land no more vehicles, but only men.

Nevertheless, long before the destroyers of the naval force came close inshore to blaze away at the enemy strongpoints at little more than 1,000 yards, a desperate beginning of order was growing out of chaos, and men, tried to the limits of endurance, regained their feet, lifted up their heads, and began to fight for more than their lives. They had paid a terrible price for General Bradley's rejection of the specialised armoured fighting vehicles Montgomery had offered him, for these were the 'tin openers' to Normandy.

Only 100 tons out of 2,400 tons of essential supplies needed on D-Day went ashore. But at last men, reinforced by the waves of

the follow-up battalions, were moving off the beaches. It did not look very hopeful to the generals in the command ships, but the hard outer crust of the defence had broken, and the enemy was without reserves. By night-fall the Germans had lost the battle of Omaha Beach, but the Americans did not know that they had won it.

On the eastern flank the British fought their different battles.

AIR DROP IN THE EAST: ALMOST OVERWHELMED
The task of the British 6th Airborne Division was to establish a bridgehead across the Orne river and the Caen Canal, midway between the city of Caen and the Normandy coast, and to protect the eastern flank of the seaborne landings. In its initial stages the task was both complex and of a desperate simplicity; complex because the pieces in the pattern were many, simple because there was no room for finesse, no time. A number of coups de main must succeed, and become one simple tour de force.

Two parachute brigades would land in the very midst of the enemy, on the boundary of the German VII and XV Armies, seize the vital objectives, and at all costs prevent reinforcements from reaching the main battlefields.

Powerful elements of the German 711th and 716th Divisions defended every village, strongpoint, and bridge; the XXI Panzer Division poised and ready to strike was on their right flank, and behind them the whole weight of the German armoured reserve lay within striking distance. Unless, therefore, the two leading brigades of paratroops could strike their blows like lightning out of the sky, and consolidate, unless they could clear landing places for the glider-borne brigade, and could have with them anti-tank guns, mortars, and the bulk of their heavy equipment, their task would be beyond hope. Whatever might be won by lightning strokes must inevitably be lost, even before the sun was up, and assuredly before the sun was down.

The 5th Parachute Brigade would seize the bridges across the Orne and the Caen Canal north of Ranville, clear and protect landing zones for their gliders, and establish a firm bridgehead.

The 3rd Parachute Brigade would demolish the bridges across the flooded Dives river at Troarn, Bures, Robehomme, and Varaville. They would block and hold all routes leading in from the south-east. They would destroy the powerful Merville battery of 155-mm guns and its garrison before it could enfilade the left flank of the seaborne attack with devastating fire. For this latter task there would be a maximum time of one hour.

It was 2330 hours on the night of the 5th when the first of six Albemarle aircraft of the Pathfinder force took off from their English field with 60 men who must light the beacons to lead the way. At the same hour, six gliders bore a small force of the 2nd Battalion, the Oxford and Bucks Light Infantry, and Royal Engineers to seize crossings of the Caen Canal and the Orne. It was a night of drizzling rain and gusty winds, and lit by tattered patches of moonlight; a night filled with the roar of aircraft, the bombers, the transports, the tugs and their gliders in their thousands teeming through the Channel sky from Le Havre to Cherbourg. Below them the wakes of 5,000 ships cleaving the gun-metal sea into greenish-white trails of foam.

At 0030 hours, the first of the Pathfinders touched down on the soil of France, two-thirds blown awry by the winds, beacons lost, equipment damaged, but enough on their targets to do the vital minimum as best they might. Within minutes the leading glider of the first of the coup de main parties crash-landed 47 yards from its objective, overwhelmed the enemy with the sleep still in their eyes, and seized intact the bridges over the Caen Canal and the Orne. Already the enemy tracer looped the sky, and the flak streaming up into the cloud-banks exacted a price in gliders and transports over the coast. A hot reception met the men of the 7th, 12th, and 13th Battalions of the 5th Brigade tumbling out of the cloud-banks. While many landed fighting, at once at grips with the enemy, others hung suspended in the trees, sitting ducks, few to survive.

A flare lighting up the medieval tower of Ranville Church pinpointed the position, and nearly half of the 7th Battalion was able to move swiftly to reinforce the bridgeheads. Civilians, possessed of an awful optimism, both hindered and inspired the British. By 0230 hours, the 7th Battalion was engaged desperately on both banks of the Orne against units of the German 716th Division and two battalions of Feuchtinger's XXI Panzer Division, which had been committed soon after 0100 hours. One company of the 7th, hard pressed at Bénouville, held on, fighting against time, knowing that relief could not reach them until early afternoon, but the colossal detonations of the naval bombardment preceding the seaborne landings brought inspiration.

The 12th Battalion, having seized Le Bas de Ranville, found itself in need of luck as well as inspiration. Its forward platoons, outnumbered twenty to one, faced 88-mm guns firing point blank at 70 yards, and with the breech block of their solitary 6-pounder smashed on landing, their only hope lay in the uncertainty of the enemy, and fortunately this was great. While Blumentritt strove to arouse an adequate sense of urgency in the German High Command, and obtain the release of the armoured reserve, Speidel was advising Rommel of the situation with equal urgency, and receiving orders for the employment of the XXI Panzer Division.

But Feuchtinger had committed a battle group of the XXI Panzer Division on his own initiative soon after 0600 hours. Had this battle group pressed its attack it must have overwhelmed the defenders of Le Bas de Ranville, and greatly restricted the bridgehead. As it was, the confusion in the enemy command, the widespread threats developing over the entire Normandy coast, was the luck the paratroops needed. At about mid-morning the German armour turned its back upon Le Bas de Ranville leaving the battered defenders in possession.

The effects of the struggle in the early hours on the extreme left flank were to have a vital significance in the crises developing on Omaha Beach, for when Feuchtinger was ordered to move his infantry battalions to counterattack the Americans, he was unable to extricate them from their fight with the 5th Parachute Brigade. His anti-tank battalion was also deeply committed in an attempt to save the 716th Infantry Division from the seaborne infantry and armour. Thus no reserves were available to move against 'Omaha' at the vital hour.

In the hours before dawn the enemy was unable to form a clear idea of the forces coming against him out of the sky from end to end of the Cherbourg Peninsula.

Meanwhile the third battalion of the 5th Parachute Brigade, the 13th, had landed well in a tight perimeter, and a strong force had advanced upon Ranville, leaving one company to clear stakes and mines against the coming of the glider-borne reinforcements. But the brigade was very thin on the ground, too many of its men lost in the trees, and many more engaged in a score of local savage encounters, which, in the end, could and did strengthen the position.

When the first of the Commandos fought through from the beach at Ouistreham, reaching the Orne bridgehead only two-and-a-half minutes behind schedule, the small force of the Oxford and Bucks Light Infantry, with the help of the 7th Battalion, had held for 12 hours against powerful counterattacks supported by artillery and mortars. One company, with all its officers killed or wounded, held on without relief for 17 hours. It was 1400 hours when No. 6 Commando crossed the Orne bridge on its way to reinforce the 9th Battalion of the 3rd Parachute Brigade. The Commando had then fought its way through enemy strongpoints, destroyed a battery in full blast against the beaches, and marched 9 miles.

Daring of a high order

It seemed impossible that a coherent pattern could emerge from the complex missions of the 3rd Parachute Brigade, or that seven major tasks, covering a 7-mile front from the town of Troarn, due east of Caen, to the coast at Merville, could be successfully fulfilled. Each demanded daring of a high order, meticulous planning, impeccable timing, and above all the ability to improvise if, as was almost certain, things went wrong.

The Albemarles carrying advance parties with the urgent role of clearing a way for a small glider-borne force with anti-tank guns, dropped their cargoes reasonably near their objective, but the brigadier, wounded and wallowing in the flooded Dives with his HQ, and elements of the 1st and 9th Battalions, did not regain the main body of the brigade before dusk. The 3rd Brigade had a bad drop. The smoke and dust from the heavy bombing of the Merville battery position obscured dropping zones on which many beacons were damaged, and failed to show up. Flak and the strong wind gusts played their parts; gliders parted from their tugs, many were hit, but above all, perhaps, 46 Group in particular had lacked the time for training. Now, on the day, on sea and land, the miserable and bitter battles waged by the Overlord planners for air and sea landing-craft, always denied until the last moment, were reaping a harvest in lives from end to end of the Peninsula.

On the left the Canadians of the 1st Battalion found sufficient strength to press home immediate attacks on their objectives at Varaville and Robehomme. While all kinds and conditions of civilian men, women, and children, including a boy of eleven and a Cockney woman of 55, a native of Camberwell, helped stragglers to rejoin their battalion, the solid nucleus of one company attacked Varaville, destroyed the bridge, and at once became too heavily engaged to extricate itself until late in the morning. Meanwhile a captain of Royal Engineers, with elements of the battalion, blew the Robehomme bridge.

These exploits, performed with satisfactory speed in spite of the chaos predicted by the brigadier, were outshone by a deed of a different order. This was the assault on the Merville Battery position.

The 150-mm guns of Merville were housed in concrete emplacements 6 feet 6 inches thick, reinforced by 12 feet of earthworks, and protected by steel doors. The perimeter fence, lined with a concertina barbed wire barrier 15 feet wide and 5 feet high, enclosed an area of some 400 square yards defended by a garrison of 130 men. At least 20 weapon pits and machine-gun positions were sited to protect every possible avenue of approach through surrounding minefields, and with no cover from fire for attackers over the open fields and orchards. At least one 20-mm dual-purpose gun completed the known armament of a battery which threatened the left flank of the seaborne assault at close range. It was imperative that the Merville guns should be destroyed. Direct hits by heavy bombs had failed to penetrate the casemates, and the naval gunfire, to be directed against the battery if all else failed, could only hope to put the guns out of action by direct hits through the embrasures or up the 'spouts'. Such hits occur by mere chance, and are not to be looked for.

A force of 1,000 Lancasters unloading a deluge of 4,000-pound bombs shortly after midnight failed to hit the target, but killed a number of cattle and provided some deep craters which might be useful cover for the attackers.

In the last four or five minutes of the flight from England, enemy flak forced pilots to take evasive action, and tumbled the battalion commander of the assault force into the garden of a German headquarters. The rest of the force lay scattered over an area ten times as large as it should have been. Yet at 0250 hours the battalion commander had assembled 150 men, one Vickers heavy machine-gun, a bare minimum of signals equipment, and 20 lengths of bangalore torpedo. Jeeps, 6-pounders, mortars, sappers, mine detectors, had all gone astray. With this force, organised in groups 30 strong, each with a special mission, the commander attacked. Within a minute or two of 0430 hours the assault went in. Half an hour later, after a hand to hand mêlée of a desperate and deadly intensity, the success signal blazed out. It had been a fight of gaunt shadow shapes against a spasmodic background of smoke, flame, and violent explosion. One of the battery guns had been destroyed by firing two shells simultaneously, and the other three by gammon bombs. A lieutenant, dying of his wounds, checked the destruction and was added to 66 British dead. Some 30 men were wounded, 20

(Top) Landing ships close in on the
British beaches as fresh waves of tanks
and troops go ashore to consolidate the
beach-head which was already expanding
(Bottom) The scene ashore: burning tanks
of the first waves lie among the obstacles
they had so efficiently overcome

(Top) The bloodbath on Omaha: assault
troops shelter behind beach obstacles
and the few tanks which had managed
to get ashore through the heavy seas
(Bottom) The scene in the British sector:
men fall wounded while a few yards away
others move without any hurry

A sense of chaos on the edge of the sea. . .

(Top) In some places the British assault troops had to fight their way ashore, in others they cleared the beach swiftly (Bottom) For many, the sea was more deadly than the enemy: survivors of a sunken US landing craft give artificial respiration to a friend

Imperial War Museum

Fox Photos

seriously. Not a man of the party was over twenty-one years of age, and few had fought before.

By early evening, the two brigades of the British 6th Airborne Division, anxiously awaiting their glider and seaborne reinforcements, had carried out their tasks, and established bridgeheads across the Caen Canal and the Orne. They had been strengthened by the arrival of the 1st Commando Brigade, and had blocked all roads from the east. Their future—if they were to have a future—must depend on the success or failure of the British 3rd Infantry Division, spearheading the left flank assault on the beaches.

By evening it had become clear that the advance out of the beachhead was too slow. Infantry had dug in too soon, when they should have pressed on. Traffic jams building up on the beach prevented the British from shaking loose until early afternoon, and Feuchtinger's armour, at last with its orders, was driving down, nearly 90 tanks strong, to the sea at Lion-sur-Mer. Nevertheless, the diversion of the German armour to meet the major threat of the British landing had saved the airborne from being overwhelmed.

SWORD BEACH: HITLER WAKES UP

The battle for the Orne bridgehead was already six hours old when Hobart's armour led the British and Canadian seaborne assaults to the rock-enclosed strips of beach fronting Ouistreham and Lion-sur-Mer, Langrune and Courseulles, la Rivière and le Hamel. Far away on the right, beyond the outcropping rocks of Port-en-Bessin, the Americans had suffered for a full hour under the guns of the enemy strongpoints on the long bare stretch of Omaha. The hopes of surprise in the east had seeped away, but it appeared to make no difference to an enemy hammered from the sea and sky.

A smoke screen veiled the whole British left flank from the powerful guns of the Le Havre batteries, which had withstood a hundred batterings from the air, and were a graver menace than the rough sea to the convoys assembling 7½ miles offshore, and putting their hordes of small craft into the water. Enemy E-boats, choosing their moment to venture out of Le Havre, emerged momentarily from the smoke to discharge four torpedoes, one to sink a Norwegian destroyer, another to force the command ship, HMS *Largs,* full astern in evasive action, the remaining two to pass harmlessly between the warships.

Torrents of bombardment from the air soon after dawn were followed by greater bombardments from the sea, concentrating an enormous weight of metal and explosive upon the narrow coastal strips, the grey lines of buildings protruding like desolate crusts out of the mists of smoke and flame which tore the amphitheatres to shreds. The helmsman of an assault craft was seen to be hanging out over the stern acting as a human rudder. Men floundered to death by drowning; the assault and landing craft surged on, as if borne on the screaming, crashing ferocity of their own gun craft, which blazed away with 4·7s, rockets, Oerlikons, and machine-guns, while the armour and field artillery went into action from their carrying craft. Mines, mortar bombs, and shells erupted small craft out of the water to fill air and sea with falling wreckage; explosions tore the entrails out of larger vessels, and leapt into furnaces in which, miraculously, men survived.

The high wind was piling the rising tide above the outer belts of obstacles, and there was nothing for it but to ride in, attempting to navigate the lethal forest of angle iron, stakes, and steel, and crash down in the foam of waves breaking on the shore.

H-Hour was 0730 hours, with the armour leading in at H−5. Force S for Sword had put its DD tanks into the water 3 miles out, and it was clear that only fine seamanship on the part of their crews, the 13/18th Hussars, would bring them in on time, or at all. Low in the water, beaten by waves 4 feet high, the grey upper works were almost invisible, and a line of tank landing craft cutting across their bows sank two, and might have swamped a score but for a mattress of rockets falling short, and forcing the tank landing craft to alter course.

When the bombardment of the warships began to lift, the shore approaches were a turmoil of weaving craft and wreckage, and almost to the minute the flail tanks crawled on shore in the lead, eight assault teams, beating up towards the beach exits, engaging enemy guns point blank, followed by the whole strange 'menagerie' of armoured monsters, the bridging tanks, the bobbins, the petards, and 33 out of 40 DD tanks crawling up out of the water in time to shoot the infantry over the hazardous stretch of beach.

Within minutes, the wreckage of armour added a grotesque dimension to the inferno. A flail, losing its tracks, continued to engage an enemy 88, another brewed, a bridging tank lost its bridge, and somewhere a DD tank foundered in a bewildering mass of steel. Sappers leaving their armoured vehicles pressed on, clearing by hand. Men leapt from blazing craft in the shallows, and struggled

If the men could hurl
themselves off the beaches
they must win. There was no
other place to stop them. . .

A tremendous tide
of men and vehicles pressing on,
steadily wave upon wave,
building up on the beaches,
in the shallows, demanding an outlet

towards the beach through the crumpled ruins of men and equipment.

On the right, the 1st Battalion of the South Lancashire Regiment, spearheading the 8th Infantry Brigade, quickly cleared the beach in the wake of the armour, and began to assault the strongpoints. The 2nd Battalion, the East Yorkshire Regiment, their brothers-in-arms on the left, fought their way more slowly to a foothold. Over all the beach, left and right, enemy mortar and small-arms fire was intense, thickened by the anti-tank guns sited on Périers Ridge, and the divisional artillery ranging on the barrage balloons.

Order out of chaos

Out of the seeming chaos and confusion, and the increasing wreckage on the beach, the threads of order began to emerge. By 0930 hours, Hobart's armour – manned by the 22nd Dragoons, the Westminster Dragoons, and two squadrons of the 5th Assault Regiment, Royal Engineers – had cleared seven out of the eight lanes through the exits. At La Riva Farm, the squadrons were rallying, some to aid Commando troops fighting for possession of the Ouistreham Locks, and for Lion-sur-Mer, others making ready to spearhead the infantry on the road to Caen.

The South Lancashires reached Hermanville in good time, one-and-a-half miles inland, confronting the vital Périers Ridge, bristling with Feuchtinger's anti-tank guns and defended by infantry of the 716th Division. But the 8th Infantry Brigade had lost its vital momentum. Enemy guns broke up armoured sorties, and the infantry dug in at Hermanville.

Meanwhile, by 1100, the 185th Brigade was assembling its three battalions in the orchards beyond Hermanville, and an immediate attack should have been pressed home against the Périers Ridge, not only to open the road to Caen, but for the urgent relief of the Orne bridgehead. Where Commando troops had marched boldly through, the infantry, dourly led, performed its slow set-piece gyrations.

A contributory cause of the slowness in front was, however, the growing mass of men and armour, striving to break loose from the beaches, and the impossible tangles of traffic in the narrow streets, the laterals, and leads out of the exits. The tanks of the Staffordshire Yeomanry, with the role of carrying the men of the King's Shropshire Light Infantry on the road to Caen, could not be prised loose from the mêlée. It was late when the guns of the Périers Ridge were silenced, and the Shropshires took the road alone.

The infantry of the line did all that its leaders demanded of it, but it was not enough. The East Yorkshires had taken a severe hammering, losing five officers and 60 men killed, and more than 140 wounded, in gaining their objectives. The Shropshires on the lonely road out of Hermanville were marching boldly into the midst of the enemy, their flanks bare. At 1600 hours, the battalion, joined by the self-propelled guns and armour of the Staffordshire Yeomanry, reached Biéville, barely 3½ miles short of Caen.

It was, in fact, a position of extreme difficulty, for at last Feuchtinger had his clear orders, Rommel was speeding on his way to his command, Hitler had awakened from the effects of his sleeping pills, and the German armour was on the move. At Biéville 24 tanks leading a powerful battle group of the XXI Panzer Division, probing for a crevice in the British assault, clashed head-on with the Shropshires and their armour. Self-propelled guns accounted for five enemy tanks, and the enemy withdrew. In spite of the armoured threats the Shropshires strove to press on, only to be halted by intense fire from the thickly wooded Lébisey Ridge. Casualties were growing steadily; a renewed armoured attack might develop at any moment, and the flanking battalions of the 185th Brigade were making very slow progress. Caen was a fading dream.

But Feuchtinger's armour was not coming that way again. The British, now in command of the Périers Ridge, had pushed the battle group further west, and the spearhead, bouncing off the Shropshires, and again off the British guns, was pounding northward down the wide gap between the British and Canadian landings, 90 tanks strong. There was nothing to stop them.

GOLD BEACH: HOBART'S SPEARHEAD WORKS

The main weight of the British seaborne assault fell on the right, on the beach code-named Gold, a shallow arc streaked with treacherous strands of soft clay, and behind that to the west the powerful strongpoints and fortified villages of Arromanches and le Hamel, and to the east, la Rivière.

It was 0725 hours when the leading flotillas carrying the flail tanks and armoured fighting vehicles of the Westminster Dragoons and the 81st and 82nd Assault Squadrons, Royal Engineers, closed the beaches of le Hamel and la Rivière. It was at once clear that the heavy air and naval bombardment had failed to silence the enemy guns, especially on the right. Only one of the flails serving the 231st Brigade's right flank succeeded in beating a lane up and off the beach, while in its wake others foundered, losing their tracks to mines and heavy machine-gun fire. On-coming craft, driven like surf boats by the strong wind and heavy seas, fouled obstacles and armour, creating a sense of chaos on the edge of the sea.

The squadron commander of the right flanking teams was killed at the outset in the turret of his AVRE, but many armoured vehicles, temporarily unable to crawl, engaged the enemy with their main armament, and were a valuable cover. But further to the east, beyond the immediate beaten zone of fire from the le Hamel strongpoints, the three assault teams serving the left flank of the brigade made good progress. While flails lashed the beach, lumbering on in the midst of eruptions of mines, mud, and sand, to gain the coast road, the bobbins laid mattresses over patches of soft blue clay, and fascine bridging tanks crawled over the beach with their huge unwieldy burdens, finally to fill craters, to make anti-tank barriers crossable, to pave the way for infantry, armour, and the great mass of vehicles bearing down, with a pressure impossible to deny, upon the beaches.

The DD tanks, finding the sea passage to the beach hopeless under their own power in the rough conditions, had been held back, later to beach dry shod, and add greatly to the early armoured firepower. Meanwhile, the spearhead role belonged to the flails and their supporting AVREs.

Well within the hour Hobart's armour had emerged from the turmoil of the water's edge and cleared four safe lanes out of six over the le Hamel beaches, and spearheaded the leading battalions of the 231st Brigade on to their objectives. Petard tanks all along the line were dealing out murderous treatment to fortified houses and strongpoints which would have tied up infantry platoons and companies, perhaps for hours, and taken a steady toll in dead.

On the 69th Brigade front facing la Rivière the flails and AVREs of the assault teams fought their way with infantry across the beaches in the face of intense mortar, anti-tank, and machine-gun fire directed from well-sited pillboxes, and houses linked together in systems of strongpoints. Three clear lanes were opened out of six from the edge of the sea to the edge of the marshland beyond the coast road. While petard tanks supporting the infantry blasted the coastal crust of strongpoints with their giant mortars, like ancient cannon, AVREs filled craters and anti-tank ditches with fascines, provided soft landings for armour behind walls, bridged culverts, and bulldozed tracks for the host of vehicles and men coming in fast on the rising tide. Within the hour armour and infantry were more than a mile inland, and the hard outer crust of the defence was broken.

Saved by the 'specials'

On the right flank of le Hamel there might have been a 'little Omaha' but for Hobart's armour. The 1st Battalion of the Hampshire Regiment, leading on the right flank, had had an uneasy passage. For them the sea-sick pills had not worked. They debouched from their assault craft 30 yards out into waves beating about their thighs and dragging at their feet as they struggled to dry sand. If they were grateful for anything it was simply that the movement of the sea had stilled, no longer to rack their guts with sickness. They had come in supported by self-propelled guns and field artillery firing from their carrying craft, aware of mortar and machine-gun fire from the enemy over the last half-mile. It had been uncomfortable rather than deadly. Smoke and flame obscured the beaches, but it seemed that the terrific bombing, followed by the naval bombardment, had failed to silence the enemy.

On the beach, in their first moments of comparative immunity before they came within the traverse of the le Hamel guns, they saw only the confusion of disabled armour, and swiftly discovered that for two-thirds of their numbers there were no safe lanes across the shambles of the beach. An immense weight of fire stopped them in their tracks as they strove to move up the beach, and no gunfire from the sea could bring them aid. With their battalion commander twice wounded and forced out of action, their second-in-command soon killed, there was nothing for it but to abandon the direct approach. Moving east the left flanking companies of the battalion gained les Roquettes, an objective of the 1st Dorsets on their left, and then swung right handed, seized Asnelles-sur-mer, and prepared to assault the le Hamel sanatorium. But it was afternoon before the sanatorium, resisting all infantry attacks, finally caved in to the devastating 'dustbins' of a petard, not the least of Hobart's 'specials'.

Meanwhile the 1st Dorsets, out of reach of the le Hamel guns, had stormed over the beach, covered by the guns of the 'specials', and swung right handed to gain the slight rise of Arromanches.

On the beach of la Rivière the 5th Battalion of the East Yorkshire Regiment and the 6th Battalion the Green Howards, leading the assault of the 69th Brigade, were in no doubt about the value of the armour. From the first, infantry and armour, greatly aided by close-support fire from gun craft, stormed the beach defences in complete co-ordination, and fought a tight battle through the streets, eliminating 88s and pillboxes, cutting out the enemy like a canker, and moving inland. Things had been bad, but not bad enough to curb their momentum on landing, and if men could hurl themselves over the first obstacle of the beach they must win. There was no other place to stop them but in the shallows and on the beaches.

By 1100 hours, seven lanes had been cleared on Gold Beach, the DD tanks were moving fast inland, and with them the 56th and 151st Brigades, carving out the centre, keeping the enemy off balance at all costs. Long before the le Hamel sanatorium had fallen the bridgehead was 3 miles in depth, the 56th Brigade was going well astride the la Rivière-Bayeux road, the 151st, on its left, racing for the high ground, and beyond into the Seulles valley, while left again the 69th pressed on for Creully. Even the right flank, delayed at le Hamel, had cut the Arromanches-Bayeux road, while the 47th Royal Marine Commando was working round to assault Port-en-Bessin.

The Commando had outstripped them all. Coming in to land west of le Hamel they had come under fire from the cliffs and lost four out of their 14 assault craft. Finally, forced eastward, they had run in east of the le Hamel position, hoping to find the way cleared ahead. It wasn't. They had had to fight their way through the coastal villages, each man humping 88 pounds of equipment, and covering 10 miles by early afternoon. By the time the 231st Brigade began to ease their sense of isolation they were occupying the high ground south of Port-en-Bessin. No men on their feet had done more.

JUNO BEACH: SOLID FOOTHOLD

By the time the Canadians stormed ashore with two brigades up astride the Seulles estuary, and raced for the sea walls, the rising tide had reduced the gauntlet of the beaches to as little as 100 yards at the narrowest point, and the battles of the beaches on the flanks were already from one to two hours old. The Canadians had no intention of being left behind.

The Canadian 7th Brigade, the Royal Winnipeg Regiment and the Regina Rifles leading, came in on the right, west of the Seulles river, beating the Canadian 8th Brigade to the beach by a minute or two. With them were eight, possibly ten, DD tanks manned by the Canadian 1st Hussars. The tanks had taken to the water 800 yards

out, threatened by the turbulent sea, in constant danger of swamping, threading their ways through a maze of scantlings jutting out of the water like the stumps of some petrified forest.

On the left, the Queen's Own Regiment of Canada and the North Shore Regiment led the Canadian 8th Brigade without armour, and raced for the sea wall, the heavy machine-guns of the enemy cutting swathes out of the Queen's Own in the 30 seconds or so it took them to reach the shelter of the wall. The landing craft carrying the assault armour of the engineers were still battling with the heavy seas and obstacles, and the DD tanks were coming in to land dry-shod when the spearhead infantry were well away, blasting the enemy out of Courselles and Bernières, and pressing on. When the Régiment de la Chaudière came in 15 minutes later there was scarcely a shot.

The Canadian battalions were borne in on a rough sea driven by the wind which flung them onto the beaches, and in one bound across them. The dangerous reefs and rocks of that narrow coast forced the assault craft to wait for the tide, and when at last they were clear of the reefs the larger craft had to charge the obstacles, hoping for the best, while the small craft strove to swerve and weave through tangles of angle iron and stakes. At one point 20 out of 24 assault craft blew up, and men struggled for the shore with the splinters of their landing craft falling from the skies about their ears. According to the record, 'chunks of débris rose a hundred feet in the air and troops, now hugging the shelter of a breakwater, were peppered with pieces of wood'.

Driven by the wind, the rapidly rising tide piling up the heavy surf, the helmsmen of the assault craft could only hang on and pray. The first three craft coming in on the Canadian left blew up, but their entire complement, save two killed, struggled out of the débris and water to make the beach and fight.

There were many brave men manning the landing craft all along the line from Sword to Utah, men fighting lone battles against outbreaks of fire and exploding ammunition, one man at least, a man named Jones, saving wounded from drowning in a flooded hold and amputating two horribly mangled legs. He was no doctor, merely a sick-berth attendant, but he did the job. And there were scores of 'Joneses' at sea that day off the beaches, but none had a struggle as grim as that of the men who carried the Canadians ashore on Juno.

The LCOCU (landing craft obstacle clearance units) of the naval demolition teams, and the beach units, striving to sort out the horrible muddle of mined obstacles, machines, and men, were under shell fire from enemy corps and divisional artillery long after the last mortar, machine-gun, and 88 of the beach defences, even the last sniper, had been silenced. Bulldozers not only bulldozed débris out of the way, but bulldozed beached craft back into the sea, giving them a start on the way back.

When the engineer assault armour of the 22nd Dragoons and the 26th Assault Squadron, Royal Engineers, reached the beach on the Canadian 7th Brigade front, the DD tanks which had landed with the infantry had settled the score with the worst of the enemy strong-points mounting the 75-mm guns and the heavy mortars and machine-guns, but there was plenty of mortar and automatic fire coming in from a bit further back. The flails were urgently needed to carve clear lanes through to the exits for the mass of armour and vehicles building up, and the petards and bridging tanks lumbered up behind them, to keep the infantry going at high pressure.

East of the Seulles the going was good, and on both sides of the river the flails had opened the exits before 0930 hours, the fascines and bridging tanks had bridged the worst of the craters and culverts, and opened the sluices of the Seulles to drain a crater as large as a village pond, and twice as deep.

On the left at Bernières, flails and petards had smashed exits through the 12-foot-high sea wall, and cleared lanes and laterals well in time to work in with the infantry against the pillboxes and strongpoints. Before noon on the right flank the flails were advancing inland under command of the Canadian 2nd Armoured Brigade.

Twelve lanes were cleared that day on the Juno beaches by

US troops begin to move off Utah Beach: by nightfall their beach-head was secure with 20,000 men ashore, and the leading units moving towards the areas held by the paratroops

On Omaha Beach there was no security: troops were still held on the beach—the deepest penetration was hardly a mile—and a determined counterattack could have swept them away

Hobart's armour, and the exits linked right through to join the brigade fronts. The DD tanks, beaching dry shod an hour behind the infantry, were swiftly off the beach, adding their firepower to the men storming on inland to keep the enemy off balance and not giving him a chance to form a second line. By late afternoon the Canadian 7th Brigade was challenging the 69th Brigade of '50 Div' for the lead, its armoured patrols probing for the main Bayeux-Caen road at Bretteville, while on the left, the Canadian 9th Brigade, breaking loose from the chaos and confusion on the beach, was through the 8th Brigade, and going well astride the Courselles road to Caen.

The centre bridgehead from Langrune to Arromanches was solid, 12 miles wide and growing deeper every hour. The bottleneck was behind, in the congestion of the narrow beach, the struggle of armour, vehicles, and men, to break loose from the appalling traffic jams. And on the right, there was the growing awareness of an ominous gap, the dangerous toe-hold of Omaha, the Americans inching slowly off the beach, their progress measured in yards.

Whatever happened the enemy reserves must be prevented from reaching Omaha, and it was this above all which made Dempsey pause, ready to reach out a helping hand, holding back his armour.

THE END OF THE DAY

It was late afternoon before the German High Command began to emerge from confusion. The lack of air reconnaissance, the blocking of radar, the dislocation of communications of every kind, had reduced observation almost to the eyes and ears of men. Reports could not be quickly confirmed, or information co-ordinated. Uncertainty inhibited the violent counterblows which alone could have driven the British and Americans back into the sea. And the instrument was lacking. The I Panzer Corps lay west of the Seine, immobilised, awaiting the decision of the Führer.

Field-Marshal Rommel had been right about the first 24 hours: they would be decisive. He had made repeated efforts to move the XII SS Panzer and the Panzer Lehr Divisions on a line St Lô-Carentan. Had these divisions been there, the Omaha beach-head must have been smashed; even had Rommel himself been there on the day, able perhaps to rouse Hitler out of his early morning dreams, it might not have been too late. It was too late when Hitler held his

afternoon conference, and released the XII SS Panzer Division.

All that could be done against the Allied air and seaborne assaults had been done by the forces immediately available. Feuchtinger, commanding the XXI Panzer Division, the only counterattacking force within reach, had reacted swiftly against the British airborne landings on the Orne, according to his standing orders. But at once there followed a long period of uncertainty, due partly to a breakdown in communications. When at last the division was put under command of the 84th Corps, General Marcks, the corps commander, was right in his appreciation that the British 3rd Division was the more potent threat, and that Caen must be at once powerfully screened. Nevertheless, too much time had been wasted, and he might have done better to commit the division against the airborne bridgehead. Had that been done the great glider-borne force might have arrived to a terrible reception.

As it was, Feuchtinger could not disengage his infantry battalions from the British, nor his anti-tank guns from the German 716th Division. He had been shot away from the Périers Ridge by British guns when he might have shot the British armour out of the way with his own guns—if he had had any.

But XXI Panzer Division did very well in view of its difficulties. Had they not taken fright at the impressive spectacle of 250 airtugs towing their gliders full of reinforcements for the airborne divisions on their flank, and at the evening sky black with the fighter escorts, the battle group, powerfully and swiftly reinforced, might have disrupted the British right flank on Sword Beach, and driven a dangerous wedge between the British and Canadians, down to the sea. Instead it withdrew to take up a position to the north of Caen. There was no second chance.

But it is unlikely that the XXI Panzer could have prevailed, even the first time. Air power had done its work for the Allies, sealing off the battlefield, holding the ring, denying mobility to the reserves, making of each day a hideous nightmare, and of each night a tortured crawling progress. Of the more than 11,000 sorties flown by the Allied air forces on June 6, not one single aircraft was lost to the Luftwaffe. Air superiority, it has been estimated by some staff authorities, multiplies superiority on the ground by three. On D-Day, Allied air power was overwhelming, and decisive.

The pattern of the Battle for Normandy was beginning to set

'Then, out of all the confusion, a certain desperate order began to emerge'

The British prepare to move off Sword Beach: by noon units were probing inland to Bénouville and Ranville, and during the afternoon the one serious German counterattack was neutralised

Bottlenecks in the coastal villages delayed the British advance out of Gold, and many units dug in too soon—but the German armoured reserve was pinned down far from vulnerable Omaha

by the end of the first day, with the British and Canadians thickening a stout shoulder on the left, holding off the entire enemy armoured reserve, while the Americans made ready to exploit the open right flank. If—if that right flank could have been smashed at the outset, vulnerable, almost defenceless, on the long beach of Omaha, then a terrible, nagging battle of attrition might have gone on and on, the British bridgehead virtually sealed off. But the 6th Airborne, and then the British 3rd Division, and then the Canadian 3rd Division, had made that 'if' impossible. General Bradley may have feared a German counterattack, but General Kraiss, commanding the German 352nd Division, knew that counterattack was impossible.

And the maintenance of an 'open right flank' was essential to Allied victory. That was the point and purpose of General Montgomery's strategy, and by the end of the day he knew that he would win; that he would impose his will on the shape of the Battle for Normandy. He didn't care much for 'phase lines' and estimates of progress. He was concerned with the end result.

Meanwhile, by taking a chance, Rundstedt had dared to move a powerful force of the XII SS Panzer Division to Lisieux, and as soon as the release order came through from the High Command, this group, under Kurt Meyer, was ordered at once to the battlefield. By midnight, constantly harassed and desperately short of fuel, it reached Evrecy, 9 miles south-west of Caen, to find its petrol dumps a burned-out ruin. When it was able to move it had to counter a powerful Canadian threat, for it was opposite the line of advance from Juno Beach. Thereafter, the British and Canadian 3rd Divisions absorbed its offensive power, and sapped its defensive strength.

The Panzer Lehr Division was nowhere near the battlefield on D-Day; or the day after.

'As a result of the D-Day operations a foothold has been gained on the continent of Europe,' General Montgomery was able to report.

For General Bradley, commanding the US 1st Army, it must have been a night of grave anxieties, even—but there is no evidence —of some self-questioning. For General Dempsey, commanding the British 2nd Army, there was cause for some satisfaction, but not for jubilation. Dempsey, of whom very little has ever been written, is a quiet, gentle man, a good strategist and a sound tactician. He confined himself absolutely, and with a remarkable devotion, to his work of soldiering. On that night of June 6, Dempsey knew that his

army had done enough. It was a good army, perhaps the last real 'army' Britain would ever produce. The dreams had faded; as they had been almost sure to fade. The vital momentum which might— might—have carried the Canadians and the British into the open country beyond Caen was never there. Beyond the Caen-Bayeux road there was no open country, only the bocage, the close-hedged, deep-ditched fields, the narrow lanes, the steep wooded valleys. The real open country had never been truly 'in the sights'. Perhaps it did not matter. The pattern of the struggle would have been different, but not necessarily more favourable to the Allies.

The bottlenecks, checking the forward troops, dragging at them, were the beaches, the coastal villages, the narrow exits and lateral roads choked with vehicles and armour, and behind the beaches the sea, rough, unpredictable.

The first of the landing craft, turning about, had reached the hards of England, the small ports, the estuaries, in the afternoon, swiftly replenishing ammunition, stores, men, cleaning and greasing the guns, setting forth a second time through the great maze of shipping. Through all the day and night the Mulberry tows were breaking loose, the tugs fighting scores of desperate battles with hawsers, winches, and chains, clawing at the huge unwieldy objects they sought to drag through the seas. Some 40% of the 'Whale' units broke away and were lost. But it would go on, and on.

It was a strange day and night on and off the beaches. Men clung marooned to obstacles and debris, on rocks, on the tops of drowned vehicles, while naval and small craft, DUKWS and outboard motors, buzzed and weaved about their business, impervious to croaking cries for help, and to the full-blooded curses of frustrated, angry, frightened men. Many of those picked up by craft on the 'turnabout' were carried straight back to England whether they liked it or not. There were a good many men wandering about for days in Normandy trying to find their units.

There was not much chance to rest in the bridgehead. The smoke rose from the burned-out houses lining the battered sea fronts from Ouistreham to Arromanches, and beyond to the desolation of Omaha and the isolation of Utah, the dunes of Varreville. In the midst of the monstrous chaos of the beaches, in the jungles of shattered craft, tank tracks, wheels, and twisted masses of iron and steel, the bodies of men lay under gas capes, awaiting burial. ▷

337

Rommel had been right about the first 24 hours: they were indeed decisive...

At Sallenelles on the left, in the 3-mile gap between Sword and Juno, and in the chasm between Gold and Omaha, there was no rest. The airborne and the Commandos were having a rugged time. Yet some lay in the meadows, and wrote home about 'butterflies' and 'bird song', which seemed the oddest things of all in the day.

Morale was high. To most of those not 'in contact', and not 'fighting' – and a minority is 'in contact' doing any 'fighting' – it seemed an anti-climax. One man called it 'a crashing anti-climax'. In a sense it was an anti-climax not to be dead, after so much waiting, training, thinking, and expecting 'God knew what'.

Some thought that the French were warm and friendly, others that they were suspicious and unfriendly, still others that they were indifferent. Many were startled by the extreme youth, or age, of the captured enemy and inclined to believe that it was going to be, what they called in those days, 'a piece of cake'. But the men who had charged the strongpoints, and gone into the cellars behind grenades, knew better. The German 716th Division had been cut to pieces, but its isolated 'bits' fought on.

The men, above all, who felt themselves to be 'out on a limb' that night were the US 82nd Airborne, holding on in Ste Mère-Église and with the 101st in scores of tiny 'pockets', wondering when their small seaborne 'attachment' was going to catch up. They didn't realise that many of their small bits and pieces would presently come together and give a much greater length and depth to the Utah bridgehead than it looked.

But the Utah bridgehead was sound. The entire 4th Division was on shore well before midnight, and much more besides, 20,000 men and 1,700 vehicles in round figures. The two leading regiments had lost twelve men killed between them. General Collins, the corps commander, was far more worried about the possible actions – or lack of actions – of Admiral Moon, than about the bridgehead. The General wanted to go on shore, but he dared not leave the *Bayfield*. The Admiral, worrying about his losses, wanted to suspend landing operations through the night, and General Collins had 'to hold down Admiral Moon', as Bradley put it.

General Gerow, commanding the US 5th Corps, with no such sea cares, but with plenty on shore, had set up his command post on the bluffs of that desolate stretch of coast. There were 'no rear areas on Omaha' that night, according to the record, no comfort, no feeling of security. Enemy were still firing from beach positions, sniping all night, and all through the next day. Barely 100 tons of supplies had come on shore, and the men were hungry, weary, hanging on grimly, short of ammunition, sleep, short of most things. At the deepest point the penetration on Omaha was not much more than 1,500 yards, and there wasn't a line, not even the planned 'Beach Maintenance Line'. It was a miracle that they had gained a foothold, but they had. Men without armour.

No one may ever know what General Bradley thought about it. Why had he refused the flails, the petards, and all the rest of Hobart's armour? Chester Wilmot believed that it was Bradley's contempt for British 'under confidence and over-insurance'. Captain Sir Basil Liddell Hart summed up: 'Analysis makes it clear that the American troops paid dearly for their higher commander's hesitation to accept Montgomery's earlier offer to give them a share of Hobart's specialised armour.'

And the Supreme Commander's report states:

Apart from the factor of tactical surprise, the comparatively light casualties which we sustained on all beaches, except 'Omaha', were in large measure due to the success of the novel mechanical contrivances which we employed and to the staggering moral and material effect of the mass of armour landed in the leading waves of the assault. It is doubtful if the assault forces could have firmly established themselves without the assistance of these weapons.

The cost of the day in killed was not more than 2,500 men, 1,000 of them on Omaha Beach. At Towton Field, on 29th March, 1461, 33,000 men perished by the sword and were buried there. Nearly 20,000 British troops were killed on the first day of the Battle of the Somme in 1916. War had become a battle of machines against machines. Tens of thousands of tons of explosive, of copper, tungsten, bronze, iron, steel, bombs, bricks, mortar, concrete, guns, tanks, vehicles, ships, all 'blown to smithereens'. Bridges, railways, dumps, factories, whole towns, flattened to rubble, a war for bulldozers.

And presently the men controlling the bombers sensed their power, making it almost impossible for men on their feet to get through. It will be an unhappy day for the world when men on their feet cannot get through.

The cost of the day in killed was not more than 2,500 men . . . nearly 20,000 British troops were killed on the first day of the Battle of the Somme in 1916

THE LIBERATION OF PARIS

France, August/September 1944. As the Allies swung east out of Normandy, the prize of Paris beckoned to the spearheads racing for the Seine. But which forces could Eisenhower afford to detach for Paris? What of the political consequences of leaving the job to the Fighting French? And could Paris be freed before the Germans razed the city as Hitler had ordered?

Jacques Mordal

▽ At the barricades— equipped with captured German helmet and grenades

▷ 'One fight for one country': a Free French poster stresses the links between the Fighting French and the people still under German Occupation

Bapty & Co Ltd

LIBERTÉ
ÉGALITÉ
FRATERNITÉ

UN SEUL COMBAT
POUR UNE SEULE PATRIE

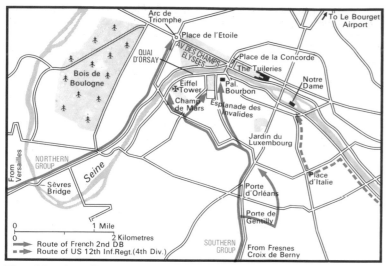

The drive into Paris, with French tanks in the van

It appeared that Paris was the least of the worries of the Overlord planners. No one on the SHAEF General Staff appears to have thought of proposing a plan to attack Paris—even after the termination of Operation 'Cobra', and the successful repulse of the German counteroffensive on Mortain. The operational idea was to bypass Paris on the north and south and calmly leave the German forces encircled in the 'Gross Paris' area to their fate. No one had any desire to get involved in a street battle to liberate the French capital. No one likes street fighting. Already, in September 1939, the German generals who remembered the very recent example of Madrid, had refused to attack Warsaw frontally, preferring to reduce it with artillery shelling and aerial bombing. And since then, Stalingrad had taken place.

No, General Eisenhower had no intention of taking Paris, district by district, at the cost of extremely heavy losses, not only to the Allied forces, but also to the inhabitants, not to mention the irreparable damage that would be inflicted on monuments and other works of art.

Also, reasoning calmly, there would be a terrible problem in supplying the great city following its capture. During the planning, the figure of 4,000 tons a day was quoted—and this merely to prevent the Parisians dying of hunger. In other words, each day, there would be 4,000 tons of supplies or ammunition less for Montgomery's and Bradley's troops, since, naturally, Paris was not going to be liberated merely to reduce all its inhabitants to famine. Was it not better to leave this care to the Germans? Soon, Paris would no longer have any strategic importance, since the Seine had already been crossed downstream near Mantes by the American 79th Infantry Division (August 20) and it was shortly going to be crossed upstream, between Melun and Troyes, by Patton's 3rd Army (August 26).

Finally, military problems were not the only ones involved. Politics were also involved, since the liberation of France was obviously going to bring about a change of régime. In General Eisenhower's entourage, there was no lack of people sufficiently well-read in history to remember that the Bourbons after Waterloo had never been able to clear themselves entirely of the accusation of having 'returned to France in the foreigner's baggage-waggons'. The Supreme Commander had no desire to get involved in the settlement of a dispute between Frenchmen, at the very moment when General de Gaulle would present himself to take up Marshal Pétain's succession. If the Allies entered Paris, it was obvious that de Gaulle would follow them in, and that people in France or elsewhere in the world might well reproach the American army for this intervention in French internal affairs. The later the problem could be examined, the better it would be. General Eisenhower was in no hurry to tackle it, and he had everything to gain from shelving it as long as possible.

Naturally, no one in France would have agreed with this reasoning, and the Parisians less than anyone else. Paris had not the least intention of letting herself be bypassed by the current of the Allied invasion. Aware or unaware of Eisenhower's General Staff's proposals, her inhabitants were going to take the necessary measures to induce the Allies to change their plans.

Actually, Paris had been astir since the beginning of August. First the railwaymen, then the postmen, and now the police—with the undertakers still to come—had gone on strike. From August 16, no policeman in uniform could be seen in the streets. Dressed in civilian clothes, they stormed the police prefecture on the 19th

and all the resistance movements rose as if on a single watchword.

The new German commander of the 'Gross Paris' area, infantry General Dietrich von Choltitz, had commanded the 84th German Army Corps in Normandy at the time of the breakthrough by General Bradley's American 1st Army, west of Saint Lô. His decisions had not pleased Hitler, who removed him from his command but did not keep him idle for long, since he required an energetic leader in Paris to replace General von Stülpnagel, who had been compromised by the '20th of July' plot. Choltitz took up his new post with the order to turn Paris into a veritable fortress. He was also given the right of life and death over everyone, German soldiers or French civilians, throughout the territory he was required to defend. Paris was to be defended to the bitter end and all bridges were to be destroyed—without any consideration of the damage these demolitions would inflict on the surrounding areas.

Even though the German garrison was far from being as formidable as has often been stated, it was certainly strong enough to allow Choltitz to put down any riot or insurrection organised by the resistance. Had the FFIs been alone, their rising would have been drowned in a river of blood, exactly like the rising which was taking place in Warsaw at the same time. Without any doubt, Paris was unable to liberate herself alone from the German army. But she could free herself from the far too narrow frame in which she had been enclosed by the Allied plans. And she was going to succeed in doing just this by inducing the Supreme Commander into changing his plans by launching his forces against Paris instead of bypassing the capital.

And thus it came to pass that 'Paris freed herself'... This phrase is naturally somewhat excessive, since the regular forces did play their part, but it is also true that 1,500 of her children gave their lives as the price of this deliverance—and this figure is considerably higher than the dead of the French 2nd Armoured Division and of the American 4th Infantry Division.

Let us add that Paris was lucky that General von Choltitz had not the slightest intention of prolonging a battle which was lost from the start, nor of linking his name to her destruction.

From 1943, it had been understood that a major French formation would take part in the deliverance of Paris and it was with this aim in mind that the French 2nd Armoured Division, commanded by General Leclerc, had landed at Utah Beach on August 1 to operate with General Haislip's US 15th Corps, to begin with. The French 2nd Armoured Division had been fighting in the Sarthe region and had taken part in the reduction of the Falaise pocket, while French tanks of the Langlade tactical grouping, put at the disposal of the American 90th Infantry Division, completed the sealing of the pocket by meeting the tanks of General Maczek's Polish 1st Armoured Division at Chambois.

However, from mid-August, Leclerc had the impression he was marking time. While he was thinking only of Paris, he had watched, with disappointment, two American divisions of the 15th Corps being launched in the direction of Dreux, leaving him idle. When he went to General Patton to complain of this, Patton received him fairly cavalierly, stating that he had little interest in knowing who would be first on the Seine; what mattered to him was to drive to the east those divisions which were best placed to do it rapidly. In any case, the French 2nd Armoured Division was withdrawn from US 3rd Army on August 16 and placed in US 1st Army, where General Hodges attached it to the 5th Corps (Gerow) with the American 80th and 90th Divisions. It was then that Leclerc had had to put the Langlade grouping under the orders of the 90th Division for the end of the Falaise battle.

Together with General Collins' US 7th Corps, Gerow's US 5th Corps had been one of those most closely engaged in the fighting since D-Day. Both on Omaha Beach and at the time of the German counterattack at Mortain, its troops had suffered severe losses. Therefore General Gerow did not consider that the Leclerc division, in comparison with his own, had earned or deserved preferential treatment, and the fact that Leclerc was allowed to enter Paris first was obviously a favour. In any case, for the moment, there was no question of entering Paris before September 1 at the earliest. In addition, Leclerc was controlled directly by de Gaulle, who was in a hurry to get him to Paris, with or without the agreement of the Americans. This Gerow did not like in the least: for him, all these political considerations were of no importance; and he could not be expected to be pleased that one of his divisional generals should receive directives from some other authority. All this explains the difficult relationship which was soon to develop between the American general and his French subordinate.

In the meantime, Paris was involved in a rising that began on August 19. But Choltitz did not try to crush this insurrection by force; he even signed a truce with resistance representatives on August 20. Although this was a precarious truce—which the French extremist leaders refused to recognise and which could be interrupted at any moment by serious incidents, despite all the efforts of M Raoul Nordling, the Swedish consul-general in Paris—it was nevertheless a real windfall for Parisians during those stirring days.

On August 21, de Gaulle urged Eisenhower to send Leclerc straight to Paris. Then General Juin visited Patton, who was no longer directly involved since the Leclerc division had been transferred to Hodges' army. At that very moment Patton was receiving a delegation from Paris led by Rolf Nordling, the brother of the Swedish diplomat, who had come to describe the explosive situation prevailing in Paris and the urgency of Allied intervention. Once again, on August 22, Paris had covered herself with barricades, while fiery posters called the population to arms, alongside Marshal Pétain's last appeal, which had been posted on the walls following the news of his abduction in Vichy by the retreating Germans. There were no longer any electricity, gas, or metro services . . . nor even grave-diggers! But nothing irremediable had occurred so far, and the information brought to the American 3rd Army HQ raised hopes that 'Choltitz was not the man to undertake systematic destruction in Paris unless things got out of hand before the arrival of regular troops'.

Leclerc decides to move

Happily, on the previous day (August 21), Leclerc, losing all patience, had decided on action without waiting. He was then in the area of Argentan, over 60 miles behind the American advance-guards which had already reached Mantes and Rambouillet; and he told himself—not unreasonably—that if General Eisenhower changed his mind about not attacking Paris, he would loose on the capital those units which were closest without worrying about whatever promises he may have made to Leclerc. There was no shortage of candidates! When going to plead his cause at Patton's headquarters, Leclerc found there the ardent General Wood, commander of the American 4th Armoured Division, to whom Patton had said, when seeing Leclerc coming in: 'He is even more annoying than you!' Everyone wanted to go to Paris.

And now, to cap it all, Leclerc received a service letter from General Koenig naming him, in the name of the provisional government of the French Republic, interim governor of Paris. Was it not his duty to do everything to take up his post at the earliest?

He therefore set up a small 150-man detachment, with ten tanks and ten armoured cars, which he entrusted to Lieutenant-Colonel de Guillebon with the order to drive straight to Paris, getting himself mixed up with the Americans if they looked like entering first. Having left Fleuré on the 21st, Guillebon arrived the next day at Rambouillet—but not without having been spotted the previous evening while crossing Senonches and being reported to the 5th Corps. Gerow got angry. What were these elements of the French 2nd Armoured Division doing outside their area? Leclerc was ordered to recall this detachment at once and to report in writing as soon as he returned to his division's camping area.

But Leclerc did not give up. Before executing this order, he decided to appeal to the commander of 1st Army and took a Piper Cub aircraft to Hodges' headquarters. There, late in the afternoon of the 22nd, Bradley had come from Granville after a long meeting with Eisenhower, to announce—without wasting time on Leclerc's dispute with Gerow—that the Supreme Commander had decided to engage the French division in the liberation of Paris without delay.

It was nearly nightfall when Leclerc landed at Fleuré close to his headquarters and brought back the good news. This was confirmed shortly afterwards by a telephone call from Gerow ordering the French 2nd Armoured Division to get on the move at once. Unfortunately, it was not ready and only left at 0630 hours the next morning (August 23), after a reminder from 5th Corps.

The plans drawn up by Bradley and Hodges at 1st Army HQ, in application of Eisenhower's new directives, were designed to make the Allied forces intervene in Paris at the very moment when the interim truce between Choltitz and the resistance leaders expired, that is at noon on the 23rd. In fact, this wholly relative truce had not lasted beyond the 21st.

On the other hand, the French 2nd Armoured Division was not to present itself alone in Paris. A British contingent was to take part while the Americans would send a reconnaissance cavalry group, all flying their national flags. Finally, the American 4th Infantry Division (General Barton), received the mission of capturing the Seine bridges upstream from Paris and constituting a reserve for the Leclerc division. The whole group was commanded by Gerow.

Being wary of difficulties which could arise between Allied forces in a sector so sensitive for French hearts, the British preferred to abstain, despite General Eisenhower's openly expressed wishes. In consequence, the 5th Corps General Staff divided its forces along two axes of advance:

● In the north, via Sées, Mortagne, Châteauneuf-en-Thymerais, Rambouillet, Versailles—the bulk of the French 2nd Armoured, a group of American engineers, and the 5th Corps artillery;
● In the south, via Alençon, Nogent-le-Rotrou, Chartres, Limours, Palaiseau—a group belonging to the Leclerc division, the 5th Corps General Staff, the US 4th Division, reinforced by two battalions of tank destroyers and two battalions of heavy tanks.

The French had been given the leading position in the two columns, together with a request not to cross the Versailles-Palaiseau line before noon on the 23rd—which they were not likely to do, in any case, owing to their late departure. Besides, the road was still not entirely clear since the Germans were still holding on the Trappes-Guyancourt-Châteaufort line, in front of which they had tank patrols.

As commander of these defenders, General von Choltitz had chosen Lieutenant-Colonel Hubertus von Aulock, whose brother Andreas had opposed the Americans with an extraordinary resistance at St Malo. Promoted, in view of the circumstances, to the rank of Major-General, Aulock was going to exert himself to be worthy of his brother. He had 20,000 men of the most diverse origins under his command: elements from the Flak, the 325th and 352nd Infantry Divisions, and other isolated Wehrmacht service units which had fallen back from Normandy. Their fighting value was debatable.

Choltitz had kept about 5,000 men in Paris itself, with about 50 artillery pieces, a company of tanks from the Panzer Lehr Division, and enough machine-guns to put down any rising. The Luftwaffe still had about 60 aircraft available at Le Bourget.

We already know in which spirit Hitler had given his orders to Choltitz when entrusting him with the defence of Paris. He had not changed his mind by August 20 when he told Field-Marshal Model that he considered Paris as the bastion of the Seine-Yonne line. It is certain that if it was desired to hold on to that waterway, it would be necessary to fight in Paris, or else, as Model advised, to organise a solid defence position east and north of the capital. But the OKW did not want to hear any talk of this latter position. Ordered peremptorily by Hitler, General Jodl confirmed to Choltitz his obligation to defend himself in Paris itself, whatever the consequences to the capital and its inhabitants.

Did the Führer really ask the famous question 'Brennt Paris?' ('Is Paris burning?'). Not everyone is convinced of this. But whether or not he used this phrase, it is true that his instructions dated August 23—at the very moment when the Allied forces were approaching the barriers—ended with these words: 'Paris is not to fall in the hands of the enemy, except as a heap of ruins.'

A heap of ruins . . . Paris had never been so marvellously seductive as on the eve of her liberation. The weather was fine and hot; the Parisian women competed in charm and elegance. In the Champ de Mars, children played innocently, practically in the shadow of the Wehrmacht soldier stationed close to his machine-gun aimed at the Pont d'Iéna. . . . Even the barricades looked innocent. Paris, though living on top of a powder-magazine, almost exuded a fairground atmosphere.

The final word lay with the head of the German defence. A loyal soldier, Choltitz would certainly have scrupulously obeyed reasonable orders. Even the truce he had accepted had concrete advantages for the German formations which had to find a withdrawal route across Paris. But the instructions he was now given were both excessive and impractical. Unwilling to speak of this to Model, who, he believed, could only confirm them, he wanted to know the opinion of Rommel's former chief-of-staff, Speidel, who had not yet left his post at Army Group B.

Many descriptions of these telephone conversations have been given, during which the two generals, convinced the Gestapo was listening in, found ingenious ways to explain to each other points of view which no longer had anything to do with Hitler's orders. Choltitz gave a highly-coloured description of his preparations for destruction, but obviously the other could not believe a single word of it. On his part, Speidel was able to make it perfectly clear that Army Group B HQ expected no drastic decisions from him.

Finally, in Paris itself, the German general was being seriously pressed by intermediaries, and first of all by Raoul Nordling, to whom the Parisians can never be too grateful. It goes without saying that on the French side, all those who intervened with Choltitz —resistance members or representatives of the French state— are convinced that their intervention was not of negligible effect. All the arguments used must have had their effect, but it is not very easy to state which was the most important. Paris, however, was not destroyed.

Nevertheless, it was time for the Allies to intervene, since things could turn sour, and the fairground atmosphere could change into tragedy. The approach to Paris was no military picnic: ▷

mines and the German batteries seriously delayed the Leclerc division, which thought it could gain time by making the bulk of its forces pass through Arpajon and *Route Nationale 20* (Paris-Orleans) instead of sticking to the road set by the US 5th Corps orders. But it met just as much resistance on this route, especially at Longjumeau where the Billotte group had a fairly tough fight. German 88s posted at Massy and at Wissous held the highway under their fire, and the way was not completely clear until noon on the 24th. There was still another battery to reduce at the Croix de Berny crossroads and then the Fresnes prison garrison, which finally consented to surrender at the end of the afternoon.

Because of these delays, Gerow had ordered General Barton to drive his 4th Division to Paris without worrying any longer whether the French or the Americans reached Paris first. Leclerc was informed that Barton would start at 0200 hours on the morning of the 25th from Villeneuve-le-Roi and that the two divisions were to give each other all possible support during this final advance.

The enemy was not the only factor responsible for the slowing-down of the advance. As they penetrated deeper into this densely populated suburban area, the soldiers, hardly rid of the Germans, fell into the arms of the enthusiastic population. Flowers, drinks, girls' kisses . . . all this contributed to blocking the roads as surely as a good anti-tank gun; tactical liaison had become practically impossible and it had become just as difficult for Leclerc to find out exactly what was happening as to inform the American command.

With all this, he only asked to move forward, without regard for his losses, which were already mounting: 71 killed, 225 wounded, 35 tanks, six self-propelled guns, and 111 vehicles of various sorts destroyed or put out of action. This was, as Martin Blumenson writes, 'a rather high ratio of losses for an armoured division'.

Spurred on by de Gaulle, harassed by calls for help which the resistance was sending him by all possible means, Leclerc had every difficulty in sending a message of encouragement into Paris: 'Hold on, we are coming!', which was only dropped by a Piper Cub on the police prefecture at 1830 hours after a first unsuccessful attempt. The aircraft, violently attacked by flak, landed at Longjumeau with a dozen holes in it.

But finally, four hours later, a small detachment led by Captain Dronne, which had entered Paris by the Porte de Gentilly, reached the police prefecture to demonstrate that the message of encouragement was not in vain. All together, the bells rang out to hail the arrival of these French soldiers in arms, the first to walk the ground of the capital, for four years, two months, and ten days. It was half past ten in the evening of August 24, 1944.

But the business was not yet over. Determined to maintain the material integrity of the French capital, General von Choltitz was, however, not inclined to capitulate without fighting, and the liberation of Paris, on August 25, was not completed without some serious clashes. Nevertheless, it was clear that German resistance could no longer be anything but sporadic. At dawn, the Billotte group penetrated, via the Porte de Gentilly, in the direction of the Cité, ready to intervene in the area of the Tuileries and Place de la Concorde and to attack the Hotel Meurice, General von Choltitz's command post. Having entered at the Porte d'Orleans, Dio followed the Boulevard des Maréchaux to advance towards the Champ de Mars, the Invalides, the Palais Bourbon, and the Quai d'Orsay. From the Sèvres bridge, Langlade reached the Place de l'Etoile via the Avenue Mozart, and Massu captured by force of arms the Hotel Majestic, while a French tank at the Arc de Triomphe enfiladed the Champs Elysées and destroyed with a single round a Panther stationed in the Place de la Concorde.

Having been raised in Morocco at the beginning of 1944, the French 2nd Armoured Division offered a practically complete picture of all that France overseas could send to the help of *la Patrie*: the Chad March Regiment, Moroccan Spahis, Algerian artillerymen, the armoured Marines regiment, people who had escaped from France via Spain. The welcome was delirious, but the cries of enthusiasm were still mingled with the sharp crackling of machine-guns and the more muffled sounds of tank shells exploding. Here and there the bullets of snipers lodged on rooftops transformed cries of joy into cries of agony . . . We must not forget that those days cost the Parisian population and the FFI 1,483 dead and 3,467 wounded, while the German defenders suffered 2,788 dead and 4,911 wounded. Besides these, the losses of the French 2nd Armoured Division rose to a total of 130 dead and 319 wounded, to which we must add the losses of the American 4th Division.

Here, General Barton had designated the 12th Infantry Regiment as the first to enter Paris, since it was the best placed geographically and — as a unit which had gone through the toughest fighting in Normandy — it appeared ready-made to deserve this satisfaction. Led by scouts of the 102nd Cavalry Group, the 12th Motorised Infantry Regiment advanced via Athis-Mons and Villeneuve-le-Roi,

and then left the Seine to protect itself from the fire of German cannons posted on the right bank. After this, the only obstacles it met were from rejoicing crowds, through which it had to make its way to reach Notre Dame at noon after passing through Porte d'Italie and Place d'Italie.

During the morning of the 25th, Colonel Billotte sent Major de la Horie to Nordling asking him to send an ultimatum to Choltitz. It was rejected. In these conditions, there remained only to assault the German headquarters, which was done at 1315 hours. After a fairly fierce resistance, the defenders began to give way, and at 1500 hours General von Choltitz was taken prisoner. He was taken to the police prefecture where Leclerc had gone to receive his surrender, in which Colonel Rol-Tanguy, commander of the Ile de France FFIs, had insisted on being included. Unfortunately, there was a slip-up and General Barton was not invited, and the fact that the capitulation was signed in the name of the provisional government of the French Republic — which no Allied authority had yet recognised — and not in that of the Supreme Commander of the Allied Expeditionary Forces, was to create many difficulties.

With all this, General von Choltitz's capitulation did not yet solve the problem everywhere. There was a certain delay in informing all isolated points of resistance, some of which surrendered rather disconsolately. The most important knot of resistance was at the senate, where 700 men with tanks occupied the Luxembourg palace and garden. On the other hand, there remained in the Bois de Boulogne 2,600 armed soldiers equipped with artillery who had not been included in the cease-fire order, and these did not surrender till the next day, the 26th. In the four corners of the capital, various incidents — often picturesque, sometimes tragic — marked the last stages of the liberation. The reconquest of the Eiffel Tower was the object of a homeric race as to who would be the first to reach the top and raise the Tricolour. But everywhere else, many small marble plaques, still piously wreathed with flowers after over 20 years, mark on the city walls the spot where one of her sons fell.

A windfall for de Gaulle
Paris represented only a stage in the pursuit of the retreating Germans — a stage which was a much happier one for the Parisians since it took place earlier than forecast. It was much more favourable for de Gaulle, since it allowed him to enter the capital as a liberator in the midst of general enthusiasm, install himself more solidly in power, and enabled him to overcome much more easily the many intrigues which had been woven during this transition period — a revolution in the real meaning of the word.

The change of régime was facilitated by the disappearance of the Pétain government a few days before the liberation of Paris, precipitated by the retreat of the German I Army.

Even before the Normandy landing, M de Renthe-Fink, German minister-plenipotentiary at Vichy, had urged the Marshal many times to move to the Voisins château near Rambouillet. The latter had always refused and had only accepted a quick visit to Paris and Nancy. Having returned to Vichy on May 28, he hastened to inform the diplomatic corps of the pressures he was being subjected to and his intention: not to submit to them.

On the other hand, he wanted to put an end to the mandate he held from the National Assembly meeting of July 10, 1940, and had considered possible solutions aimed at this: he would personally return to Paris as the Allies got closer, denounce the armistice of June 25, 1940, and decree general mobilisation, convene the National Assembly, and hand over his powers. Foreseeing the possibility that he might be arrested, he had designated a sort of regency council comprising nine members. Admiral Auphan was given the mission of representing Pétain with the Allied military authorities or the first representatives of the French Committee of National Liberation and examining with General de Gaulle the question of a regular transfer of government authority.

None of this was to amount to anything, both because of material impossibilities created by the Germans themselves, and because of opposition in principle to these ideas in resistance circles, as well as that of de Gaulle himself. In Vichy on August 19, General von Neubronn, representing the German Commander-in-Chief in the West (and visibly disgusted with the role he was being forced to play), came to Marshal Pétain. In the presence of Renthe-Fink, the Swiss minister Stucki, and some members or high officials of the government, he announced that he was ordered to take him — by force if necessary — to Belfort where, so it was claimed, there was already M Laval, head of the government. At the same time, Laval was invited to go there on the pretext that the Marshal was already there.

This flagrant lie, for which Neubronn was not responsible, aroused general indignation and a sharp reply from Admiral Bléhaut, Secretary of State for the Navy, but Marshal Pétain, refusing to allow bloodshed at Vichy, declared he would make only passive re-sistance. Very early in the morning of the next day, SS units pene-trated the Hotel du Parc, smashing in all the doors including that of the Marshal's bedroom, whom they carried off as a prisoner to Belfort and from thence to Sigmaringen.

Thanks to Stucki's intervention—as effective in Vichy as Nord-ling's in Paris—the liberation of the provisional capital of the French state took place without too much trouble, at least after the departure of the German forces and of some hundreds of militia-men who had rivalled the Gestapo in cruelty. It was the Swiss minis-ter in person who, on the 26th, chaired a meeting dealing with the transfer of power between representatives of the fallen government and those representing the new régime. . . .

For de Gaulle, the German action in removing Marshal Pétain and his government cleared the ground wonderfully well; but while all complications of that sort had been removed, there were serious anxieties caused by the most advanced elements of the resistance who did not easily renounce the chance to profit from the circum-stances in order to create a 'people's government'. The Council of the Resistance, the Parisian Committee of the Liberation, patriotic militias, whose pretensions after the battle were often totally out of proportion with the sacrifices made during the action . . . all this constituted the other side of the medal of the acclama-tions which the population did not stint de Gaulle. Having reached Paris on the afternoon of the 25th, he made contact with Leclerc in the hall of the Montparnasse station, then installed himself at the War Ministry before going to the Town Hall to contact the leaders of the resistance. On the 26th, de Gaulle intended to go down the Champs Elysées on foot on the way to Notre Dame and mingle with the crowd, and for this he demanded the presence of the French 2nd Armoured Division, as much for prestige as for security.

General Gerow, who had to chase the Germans to the north-east of Paris, did not intend to lose a division which was still under his orders. Leclerc received a formal order to continue his present mission without accepting orders from anyone else. Naturally, he obeyed de Gaulle and disobeyed Gerow. He could hardly do other-wise, but this time Bradley's General Staff wisely decided to end this ill-assorted union. Held back in Paris at the formal request of General de Gaulle, since its presence was indispensable for the maintenance of order and the liquidation of the last islets of Ger-man resistance in the outskirts, the French 2nd Armoured Division only resumed active operations on September 7, when it was placed under the orders of the 3rd Army, not the 1st.

Knowing General de Gaulle's character, it is not surprising that during those days he openly demonstrated his determined inten-tion to be master in Paris, without worrying any more about whom he owed the position to. The incidents we have described—and some others which it is unnecessary to mention—derived from this determination. The Americans showed themselves to be very understanding. 'We cannot blame the French,' wrote Eisenhower, 'that they were a little nervous!' The SHAEF services made a con-siderable effort to supply Paris and when, on August 29, General de Gaulle, still rather uncertain at the trend of events in Paris, asked General Eisenhower to show Paris some American troops, the latter accepted, not without some satisfaction, and sent the 28th Infantry Division to parade down the Champs Elysées, in order to impress the population—a very impressive performance which ended with the division boarding its trucks at the gates of Paris to go up the line that very evening.

Finally, order was not disturbed in Paris, in the streets at least, though perhaps it had not yet been re-established in certain spirits. The government apparatus was progressively coming back into operation, and the FFIs were soon invited to choose between being incorporated in a regular formation or returning to their civilian occupations. There was some grinding of teeth but no serious incidents. And, on September 7, the French 2nd Armoured Division was able to leave the capital to take its place alongside the Ameri-can 79th Infantry Division on the right wing of the US 15 Corps.

Four days after its return to the battlefield, it linked up in Bur-gundy with de Lattre's army which had landed in Provence, finally joining together Operations 'Overlord' and 'Dragoon' and complet-ing the encirclement of all the remaining German forces in the west of France. A few days earlier and the entire German I Army could have been cut off, which would have made things a lot easier for the Allied divisions driving towards the Rhine.

This was the ransom of that nearly miraculous deliverance. But at that time no one could be aware that, had the original plans been followed to the letter, the Normandy-Provence junction would have taken place earlier and the pincers would have closed on a much greater mass of German forces.

THE END FOR CHOLTITZ, THE GENERAL WHO REFUSED TO RAZE PARIS

THE BEGINNING FOR DE GAULLE, NOW POPULAR OVERLORD OF THE CAPITAL

THE GAMBLE AT ARNHEM

Holland, September 1944   *Christopher Hibbert*

After much argument, General Eisenhower was at last persuaded to back Montgomery's bold and imaginative plan for an armoured and airborne thrust across Holland to outflank the German defences. But 'Market Garden' was not given all possible support, and a crucial failure at Arnhem nullified the other considerable successes. Lack of transport aircraft meant that the British paratroops were dropped piecemeal—in the midst of far stronger German forces than had been anticipated. Such troops as reached the vital Rhine bridge were wiped out, and their sacrifice marked the end of any hopes of ending the European war during 1944

As the Allied armies slowly closed up towards the frontiers of the Reich, the enemy resistance stiffened. General Dempsey, directing the operations of the British 2nd Army, was given constant evidence of this increasingly determined opposition to his advance. His leading units were being repeatedly held up by young Nazis, men from convalescent depots and garrison battalions, even Luftwaffe pilots whose squadrons had been grounded through lack of petrol. In groups of isolated houses, from streams which cut across the sandy heath, hidden in inaccessible marshes, these fierce patriots, well aware that they were defending the gateway to the Fatherland, fought back with frantic bravery.

British Intelligence reported the existence of the enemy's ill-trained and hastily-formed units with sardonic irreverence: 'Both as regards quality and diversity the enemy force opposing us shows the effects of the recent measures in Germany to step up the national effort. Paratroops and pilots, policemen and sailors, boys of 16 and men with duodenal ulcers' had all recently been taken prisoner; and now 'some deep sea divers' had been captured. The depths had 'indeed been plumbed'.

Diverse and inexperienced they may have been; but there could be no doubt that these troops were playing an important part in the unmistakable faltering of the Allied advance.

It was in these circumstances that Montgomery formed his plan of quickly breaking through the crust of German opposition after a series of airborne landings. By seizing a succession of bridges between the Dutch frontier and the Neder Rijn river (see map), he hoped to be able to make the way clear for a rapid advance by the 2nd Army through Holland and on to the north German plains, thus both avoiding the problems posed by a crossing of the Rhine and the Maas and outflanking the Siegfried defences which ended in the area of the Reichswald.

Montgomery had already suggested to General Omar Bradley, commanding the United States 12th Army Group, that his own 21st Army Group and Bradley's 12th 'should keep together as a solid mass of 40 divisions, which would be so strong that it need fear nothing. This force should advance northwards'.

But Eisenhower, for reasons both military and political, refused to agree to this. Recognising the value of a push to the north which would secure a good sea port for an eventual

347

thrust towards the Ruhr, he realised, too, the inadvisability of stopping General Patton, the hero of the American public, whose US 3rd Army was racing away with great élan in the south. He therefore rejected the idea of what he was later to term Montgomery's 'pencil-like thrust', and confirmed the broad front policy which would take the whole Allied force up to the Rhine and would leave open the question of future advances until the dangerously long lines of communication had been shortened and the whole matter of supply and reinforcements had been re-established on a firmer base.

Eisenhower was, nevertheless, prepared to give some priority to Montgomery; for an essential prerequisite to the successful development of any future advance into Germany was the capture of the Channel ports and Antwerp. So the 21st Army Group was given the support of both the US 1st Army and the Allied Airborne Army which had recently been formed under the command of Lieutenant-General Lewis H. Brereton (US).

at Wesel than to go 'off at a tangent into Holland' alone.

On September 10 Dempsey went to see Montgomery to press his point of view. But Montgomery told him that he had just had a signal from the War Office asking what could be done to capture or cut off the bases near The Hague from which the V-2s—which had landed on London two days before—were launched. After this there could be no further discussion; the northern attack must be made.

Dempsey could at least take heart from the fact that the route which his army was to follow was an unlikely one and, therefore, the enemy might be taken by surprise; also the preliminary airborne operations could be carried out within reasonable distance of English bases.

Eisenhower himself was at first reluctant to agree to Montgomery's plan, for it involved the withdrawal of transport aircraft from supply duties and, as he wrote afterwards: 'It was difficult to determine whether

gomery told Eisenhower that the airborne operation could not take place as planned by September 17. He would be obliged to postpone the attack until September 21 at the earliest and, because of the delay, 'stronger resistance and slower progress' must be expected.

This blunt warning had the desired effect. The day after Eisenhower received it, his Chief-of-Staff flew to Montgomery's headquarters with the promise of several American truck companies, the daily delivery of 1,000 tons of supplies to Brussels, the undertaking that the drive to the Saar would be stopped, and that most of the US 12th Army Group's supplies would then be allocated to its 1st Army, which would consequently be able to give 30th Corps adequate support on its right when the advance began. Eisenhower's prompt reaction to the British representations seems to have been largely due to his now urgent desire to get the vital port of Antwerp into commission. At that time its approaches were still blocked by German

'A 60-mile salient driven up a side-alley to the Reich' *Bradley*

Now, as the initially swift Allied advance ground to a halt towards the end of the first week of September, Montgomery felt sure the time had come to use the airborne forces. After capturing the Dutch bridges he could launch the 2nd Army in an attack which would establish it on an extended line facing east between Arnhem and Zwolle; and, with a deep bridgehead across the IJssel, he would be in a strong position from which to launch that 'powerful full-blooded thrust into the heart of Germany' on which he was set.

There were five major bridges to capture, two over canals, and three over rivers. The canals were the Wilhelmina Canal, about 20 miles beyond the Dutch frontier, and the Zuid Willems Vaart Canal, 10 miles farther north; the rivers were the Maas, the Waal, and the Neder Rijn. One division of the Airborne Army would have to be landed in the 20-mile stretch between Eindhoven and Uden to capture the two canal bridges and to open up the road between them; a second division would have to be assigned to the Maas bridge at Grave and the Waal bridge at Nijmegen; while a third would have to be dropped at Arnhem to secure the crossing of the 150-yard-wide Neder Rijn.

It was an ambitious plan, but an imaginative one; and if it succeeded, the advantages gained would be incalculable. Not only would the Siegfried Line be outflanked and a firm springboard obtained for an attack into the Reich, but once the 2nd Army had rolled forward to the Zuider Zee all the German troops in western Holland would be cut off.

Naturally the plan had its critics. General Bradley spoke disdainfully of 'a 60-mile salient to be driven up a side-alley route to the Reich', and was concerned by the dangerous gap which would be opened up between the British 2nd Army and the US 1st Army which was already heavily committed. General Dempsey, whose Intelligence staff was reporting mounting German activity in central Holland, particularly around Arnhem and Nijmegen, thought it would be better to strike out alongside the Americans in an easterly direction towards the Rhine

greater results could be achieved by continuing the planes in supply activities. Unfortunately the withdrawal of planes from other work had to precede an airborne operation by several days to provide time for refitting equipment and for briefing and retraining of crews.'

Furthermore, he refused to give the airborne operation and the northern route absolute priority over Patton who was, in fact, already extending his front even further south and would soon, if undisturbed, have firm contact with the US 6th Army Group coming up from the Mediterranean.

Only 'limited priority'
The 'limited priority' which Eisenhower *was* prepared to give the airborne operation in the way of additional supplies and transport from American sources seemed to both Montgomery and Dempsey quite inadequate. The Americans thought that even this 'limited priority' was unjustified, for they themselves were not in a position to spare either supplies or transport. But Montgomery, less than sympathetic towards Eisenhower's political problems, continued to insist that he must have priority over all other operations.

Already all the reserves of 21st Army Group were in use; new transport companies were promised from Britain but had not yet arrived; even tank transporters, with lengths of airfield track welded to their sides, were conveying essential supplies; most of the 2nd Army's heavy artillery and anti-aircraft guns had consequently been grounded for some time.

Lieutenant-General Brian Horrocks's corps, which was to lead the 2nd Army's attack once the airborne troops had captured the bridges, could not rely for support on the US 1st Army so long as Patton was advancing in the south, and would have to be supported, therefore, by the British 8th Corps brought up on its right. Yet most of 8th Corps' transport was already in use by other units of the 2nd Army, and the additional transport promised by the Americans would not be enough to make up the lack.

Accordingly, on September 11, Mont-

troops firmly dug in along the banks of the Scheldt estuary; and any delay to Montgomery's operation meant a delay in freeing the port which *must* be freed before any deep thrust into Germany could be made.

But Eisenhower's plans were baulked by the ebullient Patton who, as soon as he heard that it was likely he would be ordered to assume the defensive, ensured that his forces became fully committed beyond the Moselle. Authorised merely 'to carry out a continuous reconnaissance', Patton, as he himself admitted, used this order as an excuse to 'pretend to reconnoitre, then reinforce the reconnaissance, and finally put in an attack—all depending on what gasoline and ammunition' he could secure. And, as one of his officers commented, they 'secured plenty'. Already the capture of over 100,000 gallons of petrol from the Germans had been concealed from Eisenhower; now some of Patton's officers went so far as to represent themselves as members of the 1st Army 'and secured quite a bit of gasoline from one of the dumps of that unit'.

Bradley tacitly supported Patton. So Eisenhower's order that the 12th Army Group's supplies should be allocated with priority to General Hodges's US 1st Army—and thus, to the support of Montgomery's operation—went by default.

American support for the British operation soon, indeed, became negligible. For as soon as Hodges crossed the German frontier near Prüm he met the same defiant defenders that Patton encountered beyond the Moselle.

In fact, all along the Allied line, German resistance grew stronger with each September day and although on the 4th of the month, Field-Marshal Model, Kluge's successor as Commander-in-Chief in the West, had informed the Führer that 'the unequal struggle cannot long continue', he was not now feeling so depressed. The Wehrmacht was recovering some of its former power; and the longer the airborne operation in the north was delayed the less likely it was to succeed.

On the day that General Dempsey went to

see Montgomery in an effort to persuade him to abandon the operation altogether, detailed discussions of its execution began at the Allied Airborne Army's headquarters in Britain.

There were four divisions in the army available for the operation, two British and two American, together with a Polish Independent Parachute Brigade, commanded by the gallant and gifted Major-General Stanislaw Sosabowski.

The two American divisions were Major-General James Gavin's 101st and Major-General Maxwell Taylor's 82nd. Both Gavin, later to become his country's ambassador in Paris, and Taylor, a future Chief-of-Staff of the United States Army, were men of high attainments and wide experience. The two British divisions were the 52nd (Lowland) Division and the 1st Airborne Division, commanded by Major-General R. E. Urquhart.

General Urquhart, unlike his American counterparts, was relatively new to airborne forces. A big, energetic, and extremely popular Scotsman of 42, he had fought bravely in Africa, Sicily, and Italy. But, as he said himself, no one could have been more surprised than he had been when he was given command of the division nine months previously. He suffered badly from air sickness, had never made a parachute jump or a glider landing, and had been advised, when he suggested that he ought to have some parachute training, that his job was to prepare for the invasion of Europe and that, in any case, he was too big and too old.

In fact, his division had not taken part in the Normandy landings, being kept in Britain as a strategic reserve, and for the past three months he and his men had been preparing for a series of operations which never took place, sometimes because of the weather, sometimes because their wild impracticability had been admitted in time, or more often because the Allied armoured columns had been so successful that by the time the operation had been fully planned the need for it had gone. The result of this disappointment at seeing their rivals of the 6th Airborne Division gain all the laurels of the Normandy landings, followed by weeks of training, planning, and recurrent anticlimax, had been that the division, in the words of one of its officers, was now 'restless, frustrated, and ready for anything'. It was, so Urquhart said himself, 'battle-hungry to a degree which only those who have commanded large forces of trained soldiers can fully comprehend'.

'The British,' Eisenhower told Captain Butcher, one of his staff officers at SHAEF, 'insisted that their airborne division take the toughest, most advanced assignment.'

And this they were given. When General Urquhart was summoned to his corps headquarters in the club house on Moor Park Golf Course, he realised immediately just how tough the assignment was. The Corps Commander, Lieutenant-General F. A. M. Browning, told him that the US 101st Division was to land north of Eindhoven to capture the town, the four railway and road bridges over the Aa river and the Zuid

Willems Vaart Canal at Veghel, together with the bridges over the Dommel at St Oedenrode and over the Wilhelmina Canal at Son. The US 82nd Division was to capture the bridges over the Maas at Grave and over the Waal at Nijmegen. Then, with what Urquhart called a 'grand sweep of the hand', Browning drew another large circle on the talc-covered map. 'Arnhem bridge,' he said, 'and hold it.'

Although it involved the largest airborne operation which had ever yet taken place, Operation 'Market Garden' as it was to be called—Market referring to the airborne corps's activities, Garden to the follow-through by the 2nd Army—had all to be planned in six days. And the difficulties of planning were extreme.

So far as Urquhart's division was concerned, there were two main problems: the shortage of aircraft, and the belief that the flak in the Arnhem area was too heavy for a landing immediately around the bridge and on both sides of the river.

Priority in aircraft—as Browning pointed out when Urquhart asked for more transport for the British division—must be given to the Americans. There would obviously be no point in capturing the bridge at Arnhem if the Americans failed to capture the bridges over the Maas and the Waal. So the paratroops of both American divisions would have to be taken in one lift. But, since there were just no more aircraft available, the British division would have to be sent to Arnhem in three separate lifts.

The dangers of separating the division in this way were very great. The men taken in the first lift would have the double duty of seizing the bridges and of protecting the landing zones which were to be used for the men to follow. And even if a surprise attack could be made by the first lift, by the time the later lifts arrived the enemy would have had time to make preparations to resist the subsequent landings. To offset this risk it was suggested that the available aircraft should make two trips to Holland on the same day; but this was rejected by the troop carrier commanders on the grounds that 'there would be insufficient time between missions for spot maintenance, repair of battle damage, and rest for the crews'. A further suggestion that the first lift should be taken in by night, and the second as soon after dawn as possible, also had to be rejected because the American crews, who were to fly in a large proportion of the paratroops, had not had enough training in night work and on two previous occasions—in Sicily and the Cotentin Peninsula—when they had operated at night, the results had been alarming.

A series of daylight landings, widely separated in time, had therefore to be accepted. And the success of the British operation would, accordingly, depend on there being a relatively small force of enemy defenders in the area, on initial surprise, and on a wise choice of landing zones.

The landings of the British 6th Airborne Division in Normandy had demonstrated the advisability, if not the necessity, of landing on or close to the objective. And it had long

been accepted that General Gavin's maxim—'it is in general better to take landing losses and land on the objective than to have to fight after landing in order to reach the objective'—was an undeniable truth.

The British 1st Airborne Division, however, had suffered heavily in Sicily, when a poor choice of landing zones had been made; and Urquhart was understandably concerned to get as much as possible of it down in Holland 'all in one piece and able to function properly on landing', particularly as it would be 'functioning some 60 or 70 miles away from our nearest troops'.

Moreover, the RAF, after carrying out several reconnaissance flights—which confirmed the impression of bomber crews who flew by that route to the Ruhr—was insistent that the flak likely to be encountered in the Arnhem area made dropping close to the main road bridge out of the question. There was also the danger, if the unwieldy, unarmed, and vulnerable glider-towing tugs came in too far, that they would either run into more flak over Dutch airfields on making a homeward turn to the north, or would become entangled with the American tugs over Nijmegen on turning to the south.

Landing zones far from the town

Urquhart felt obliged, therefore, to select landing zones well outside the town when the danger from flak would be minimal and where a neat and tidy drop could be made. He had to reject the open heath about 4 miles north of Arnhem, for, although the land was dry and screened from the town by woods, it was too cut up by dunes and scrub and too constricted for the landing of any considerable number of gliders. He also had to reject the inviting-looking open area around the main bridge just south of the river, not only because of the 'almost prohibitive' flak which the RAF warned he would encounter there, but also because both Intelligence officers and Dutch resistance reports agreed that it was low-lying, swampy polderland, very exposed and cut up by deep ditches, unsuitable for both glider landings and the quick deployment of large bodies of troops.

Urquhart decided, nevertheless, that by the time the third lift came in the flak batteries near the bridge should have been put out of action; and he therefore marked this area on his map as allocated to Sosabowski's Polish paratroops, who were to be flown in on the third day of the operation.

All the other dropping zones and glider landing zones, which were to be used on the first and second days, he marked out on his map well to the west of the town, where the ground was firm and dry and relatively spacious.

He drew in five zones—three of them to the north of the Arnhem to Utrecht railway line on Ginkel Heath, two others to the south of it on Renkum Heath. All these zones would be marked out on the ground with strips of coloured nylon tape by the men of the 21st Independent Parachute Company, who were to be dropped two hours before H-Hour. At H-Hour the 1st Parachute Brigade, and most of the gliders of the 1st

'Springboard for a powerful full-blooded thrust to the heart of Germany' *Montgomery*

Airlanding Brigade would come in with divisional troops, leaving the 4th Parachute Brigade and the rest of the 1st Airlanding Brigade to come in with supplies on the second day, and the Poles to come in on the third day.

The Polish commander, General Sosabowski, could not help wondering, though, if the weather would hold long enough for all three flights to take place as planned, and, if the weather did not hold, how Urquhart would fare should the 2nd Army not be able to drive through to his relief as quickly as expected and should the German reactions prove immediate and forceful.

At this stage of the planning it was, however, believed that the German forces in the area were incapable of such decisive action.

Facing Horrocks's 30th Corps, the waiting spearhead of the 2nd Army along the Dutch border, there were — it was believed — no more than six infantry battalions supported by 25 guns and only 20 tanks. Behind this weak front line, in the Nijmegen area, Dutch resistance agents reported six further battalions of low medical category and beyond these, in the Arnhem area, a few battered armoured units being reorganised and refitted. The enemy was also supposed to be as weak in numbers as in morale. On September 12, the Intelligence summary of 21st Army Group, which made no reference to troops in the Arnhem area, said that the German retreat had been both disorderly and dispirited: 'Several hundred thousand soldiers are moving backwards, among them there stream along, together with now superfluous headquarters, columns which have been routed, which have broken out from their front and which for the moment have no firm destination and no clear orders.'

Six days later 21st Army Group Intelligence were still maintaining this optimistic note; and despite its earlier warnings which had disturbed Dempsey at the time of his meeting with Montgomery on December 10, 2nd Army Intelligence, too, now inclined to the belief that behind the crust of fanatic but spasmodic opposition there was no formidable German strength in Holland. An Intelligence officer at SHAEF believed that armoured units reported to be in the Arnhem area might be the IX (Hohenstaufen) and the XX (Frundsberg) SS Panzer Divisions which had been pulled out of the Normandy beach-head so as to escape the final rout. But this belief was discredited; while the prophetic warnings of Major Brian Urquhart, Chief Intelligence Officer at Airborne Corps Headquarters, were disregarded. From the generally optimistic reports which were otherwise received it seemed safe to assume — and 1st Airborne Army Headquarters did assume — that there was no 'direct evidence that the area Arnhem/Nijmegen' was 'manned by much more than the considerable flak defences already known to exist', that the strength in the Arnhem area in particular was 'nothing larger than a brigade with a few guns and tanks'.

A Dutch resistance radio's message sent to London on September 15 which said that 'SS Div Hohenstruff [obviously Hohenstaufen] along IJssel, sub-units observed between Arnhem and Zutphen — Apeldoorn road', was not passed on to the 1st Airborne Division until September 20, long after the paratroops had learned this distressing information for themselves.

Even if the Intelligence summaries had been far more realistic than they were,

The British insisted that their airborne division take the toughest, most advanced assignment

Urquhart: he felt obliged to select drop zones well outside Arnhem

Sosabowski: he was appalled by the nonchalant and confident British

Gavin: 'better to accept losses and land on target than have to fight for it'

Taylor: his troops were the first to be reached by units of 2nd Corps

◁ Troops of the British 1st Airborne Division in their aircraft during the flight to Arnhem
▽ The possibility of heavy flak in the area of the bridge had persuaded the planners to choose dropping zones far from the town. Allied Intelligence had reported few German units in the vicinity—but it turned out that two Panzer divisions and the 'Führer's Fireman' Field-Marshal Model were ready for the British

though, the determination of the Airborne Corps to get into the battle would have been little diminished.

Brigadier J. W. Hackett, the clever young commander of the 4th Parachute Brigade, warned his battalion commanders that they would expect heavy casualties. But the other officers in the division, General Sosabowski thought, seemed unduly confident. At Urquhart's Order Group, not one of them spoke. Sosabowski wrote afterwards: 'Most of them sat nonchalantly with legs crossed, looking rather bored and waiting for the conference to end.'

Eventually one officer asked how long they were expected to hold the bridgehead at Arnhem.

General Browning had asked Montgomery the same question a few days before; and Montgomery had said: 'Two days. They'll be up with you by then.'

'We can hold it for four,' Browning had replied, and then he had added, 'But I think we might be going a bridge too far.'

On Sunday morning, September 17, 1944, Operation Market Garden began. The weather was as forecast: winds were light, visibility was good, the few patches of stratus cloud had lifted by 1000 hours.

At eight British and 14 American airfields stretching from Dorset to Lincolnshire, the troops began to board the aircraft.

The plans for carrying them to Holland had been carefully laid by the joint planning staff of 38 Group RAF and 9th United States Troop Carrier Command, which had decided that the base airfields for the complete operation should form two distinct groups. Aircraft from bases in the southern group should form up over Hatfield in Hertfordshire and those in the northern group over March in Cambridgeshire.

The US 101st Airborne Division was to fly by the southern route towards the North Foreland and then due east across the Channel to Geel, turning north then for Eindhoven. The US 82nd Airborne Division and the British 1st Airborne Division were to fly by the northern route, over Aldeburgh and Schouwen Island to a rendezvous above 's Hertogenbosch where the stream would diverge, the Americans making for their targets, at Grave and Nijmegen, the British for Arnhem.

The routes would be marked by beacons and occults at all rendezvous and turning-points; by more beacons and coded lights on ships in mid-Channel; and eventually by ground strips, coloured smoke signals, and beacons on the dropping and landing zones. Full air cover was to be provided by about 1,000 British and American fighters both during their flight and after the landings; armed reconnaissance would be carried out over the target areas; and diversionary missions would be made beyond the operational area. Enemy fighter airfields and anti-aircraft positions had already been bombed; just before the landings barracks near the landing zones would also be attacked; and soon after the landings dummy parachutes would be dropped west of Utrecht, at Emmerich, and east of Arnhem.

It was thought that the greatest danger would be from flak; and although the routes had been chosen so as to avoid the heaviest flak areas, losses of up to 40% of the gliders and transport aircraft involved were predicted.

In the event flak was not nearly as heavy as had been feared. Very few of the 1,545 aircraft and 478 gliders were lost;   ▷

and the isolated Focke-Wulfs and Messerschmitts that were seen, attacked the high fighter cover but did not interfere with the main formations. It was, one of the Stirling pilots said afterwards, 'no trouble at all – a piece of cake'.

Looking down from the aircraft, the men thought how peaceful everything looked – people standing in the streets of villages, looking upwards and waving handkerchiefs, the little air-sea rescue craft in the calm, brown-looking water of the North Sea, the coastal defences of Holland quiet and seemingly abandoned, then the countryside around the dropping zones like air photographs suddenly come to life.

Gavin's US 82nd Division landed without undue mishap around Grave and Nijmegen. One of his battalions, by landing astride the bridge over the Maas at Grave, captured it within an hour. Six hours later other units of his division captured a bridge across the Maas-Waal Canal and advanced far to the east towards the edges of the Reichswald. The enemy opposition was rapidly overcome and it was not until he sent a battalion north for the Waal bridge at Nijmegen that General Gavin came up against more formidable opposition.

Meanwhile, further south, Maxwell Taylor's US 101st Division had been equally quick and had enjoyed the same initial success. As they had approached Eindhoven, the aircraft of the division had come under heavy fire but little damage was done, and once they had landed, the Americans moved fast, overwhelming what scattered opposition they encountered. All the bridges across the Zuid Willems Vaart Canal at Veghel were captured and although the bridge across the Wilhelmina Canal at Son was blown up before they could reach it, one parachute regiment – about the same in strength as a British parachute brigade – was able to cross the canal during the night, and early the next morning, while repair work began on the bridge at Son, this regiment advanced south into the outskirts of Eindhoven, opening up the narrow route for the British armoured attack.

That attack had already begun. Sitting on the roof of a factory on the bank of the Maas-Scheldt Canal, General Horrocks had seen the streams of aircraft pass overhead towards the landing zones, and had issued his final orders to 30th Corps. Soon his artillery had opened their bombardment and then the tanks of the Irish Guards, supported by 200 Typhoons of the RAF, began to blast their way up the narrow road towards Valkenswaard and Eindhoven. Before nightfall the Americans and British were shaking hands in Eindhoven and the narrow corridor north to Arnhem was open as far as Nijmegen.

Hold-up at Nijmegen
At Nijmegen, however, the capture of the vital bridge over the Waal was proving a difficult and dangerous task. General Gavin had intended making an assault upon the bridge on Monday morning, but before he could do so the enemy counterattacked from the Reichswald and overran the landing zones where his glider-borne artillery and infantry reinforcements were shortly due. After a fierce struggle the Germans were driven back and the gliders, fortunately delayed two hours by fog, were able to land without serious loss.

But the next day the second wave of glider-borne infantry reinforcements were prevented by fog from leaving at all; and when

Gavin was joined on the outskirts of Nijmegen by the Grenadier Guards Group (the spearhead of the Guards Armoured Division), he was under such heavy pressure from the Germans in the east that he was able to spare only one of his three parachute regiments for an attack with the Grenadiers' tanks on the road and rail bridges across the Waal. By then the approaches to these bridges were strongly defended – the approaches to the road bridge, in fact, had been so well fortified before the war that the Germans had been held here for three days in 1940 – and successive attempts by the Guards and American paratroops during Tuesday afternoon to break through the defences had all been repulsed. Indeed, the German command believed that the road bridge was impregnable and had ordered that it must not be destroyed since it 'could certainly be defended successfully'.

On Wednesday morning, despite the heavy losses the previous day and the seemingly unbreakable strength of the German perimeter, the attacks were renewed. In execution of a plan prepared jointly by General Horrocks and General Browning, who had landed near Nijmegen to direct the Airborne Corps' operations, assaults were made on the bridges from north and south simultaneously.

The northern attack was made by the US 504th Parachute Regiment which, after the Germans had been cleared from Nijmegen in the morning, began to cross the river a mile downstream at 1500 hours, launching their storm-boats into the fast-flowing water under a furious fire.

Although less than half the boats of the first wave reached the far bank, the Americans managed to establish and hold a small bridgehead while the subsequent waves crossed the 400 yards of swirling, bullet-swept water behind them. By the late afternoon they had broken out of their bridgehead, had raised the Stars and Stripes on the northern end of the railway bridge, and were advancing towards the road bridge.

Seeing the flag flying through the smoke, the Guards on the southern bank of the river took it as a signal to begin their final attack. Battering their way through the remaining German stronghold and under heavy fire from German 88s, the British tanks rattled down towards the Waal bridge while the other parachute regiments in Gavin's division continued to hold back the enemy's forces pressing in from the Reichswald. Just after 2100 hours that evening, four tanks reached the bridge. Two of them were knocked out by anti-tank guns concealed behind the thick steel girders, but two others reached the far end, smashed their way past the road block there and linked up with the American paratroops on the northern bank. An hour later the bridge was securely held.

This operation by the Guards Armoured Division and the US 82nd Airborne was one of the most dashing and brilliant of the entire war. After it was completed General Dempsey said to Gavin: 'I am proud to meet the commander of the greatest division in the world today.' It was not an exaggerated compliment.

The way to Arnhem was now open; and spearheads of 30th Corps were given their orders to race on to the relief of the 1st British Airborne Division at dawn.

For more than three days now the British troops at Arnhem had been fighting a desperate and isolated battle.

While Horrocks had been watching the

streams of aircraft carrying the Americans to Eindhoven, Field-Marshal Walter Model, commander of German Army Group B, had been sipping a glass of wine in the Tafelberg Hotel at Oosterbeek as an aperitif before lunch.

The Tafelberg Hotel was his headquarters. It was scarcely 2 miles west of Arnhem.

If the British had not expected to find this formidable opponent so close to the centre of their intended operations, neither he nor Colonel-General Kurt Student, commanding the I Parachute Army, whose headquarters were further south at Vught, had expected the Allied airborne attack.

Student's command, which included German forces already in Holland together with parachute regiments and Luftwaffe battalions formed into infantry units, was being hourly increased by scattered but considerable remnants of the XV German Army, which had been edging for several days past the slowly extending pincers of the Allies along the Belgian frontier and had been crossing the Scheldt estuary north-east of Antwerp. Student did not doubt that these troops would soon come under attack from the British 2nd Army, but he was, as he admitted himself, taken 'completely by surprise' by Operation Market Garden. He had 'never considered the possibility of an airborne attack' in that area. 'Actually, it was obvious to use airborne troops in this situation in order to gain possession of bridges before their demolition. However, both the command and the troops, particularly my staff and I, were all so overtaxed and under such severe strain in the face of our difficult and many-sided mission that we thought only in terms of ground operations.'

The Germans utterly surprised
Even when the aircraft roared over the roof of his headquarters on the morning of September 17 in an 'immense stream', the danger of the situation did not at first occur to him. He merely recalled with some regret his own earlier airborne operations at Rotterdam and Crete, and when his Chief-of-Staff joined him on the balcony, he 'could only remark, "Oh, how I wish I had ever had such a powerful force at my disposal"'.

Field-Marshal Model was equally surprised. Only three days before a senior staff officer at his headquarters, in an attempt to consider the problems of a thrust into Germany from the Allied point of view, had composed an imaginary order from General Eisenhower which envisaged an attack by the British 2nd Army across the Maas and into the Ruhr through Roermond, later to be combined with a large-scale airborne landing north of the Lippe river in the area south of Munster. Not all the German generals agreed that this was the most likely form for the Allied attack to take; but when General Rauter, Polizeiführer (Chief of Police) in Holland, told Model that he thought an airborne landing in the Arnhem area was 'a distinct possibility', neither Model, nor his Chief-of-Staff, General Krebs, was convinced. Airborne forces were a precious commodity, they insisted, and Montgomery, 'tactically a very prudent man', would not use them on so reckless a mission; certainly not until the port of Antwerp was in use and the Allied lines of communications could be shortened. Besides, Arnhem was far too far in advance of the spearheads of the 2nd Army; an airborne force landed there would be almost certainly defeated before these spearheads could get through to it.

And as soon as he was told that British paratroops were tumbling out of the sky scarcely 2 miles to the west, Model reacted with characteristic speed to ensure that they certainly were defeated. He put down his aperitif, gave rapid orders for the evacuation of the headquarters, and ran upstairs into his bedroom to cram his belongings into a suitcase while his driver in the road below nervously tooted the horn of his staff car. His officers, too, grabbed what they could from their rooms before running out into the road; but they were obliged to leave much behind, including several plans and many files of secret documents.

Soon a convoy of cars was racing out of Oosterbeek and down the road towards Arnhem. It had covered less than a mile when it overtook an SS major pedalling furiously towards Arnhem on a bicycle.

'Which is the way to General Bittrich's headquarters?' Model shouted from the front seat of the leading car.

'The Doetinchem road,' the major shouted back and was almost knocked into the ditch as the car accelerated past him.

A formidable reception committee

General Willi Bittrich, for whom Field-Marshal Model had asked, was commander of the II SS Panzer Korps. Two divisions of this corps, the IX and X SS Panzer Divisions, were, as SHAEF had feared and as Dutch resistance had reported, refitting and re-grouping to the north and east of Arnhem. The IX, commanded by Lieutenant-Colonel Walter Harzer, had its main bivouac area around Zutphen. The main bivouac area of the X Division, commanded by SS Major-General Heinz Harmel, was between Zutphen and Ruurlo. Both divisions had several units in villages nearer to Arnhem; while in the suburbs of the town, in the woods and Dutch army barracks just to the north of it, and in the open fields beside the Nijmegen road were still further units of these two crack divisions—comparable to the Hermann Göring and Alpine Divisions.

Camouflaged between green and khaki nets, concealed beneath trees and tarpaulin, and in railway sheds and garages were their tanks, self-propelled guns, and armoured troop-carriers. Although neither division had received any replacements either in men or material since the battles in Normandy and although most of their armoured vehicles were under repair, they were both still fighting formations with several excellent mortar platoons which were almost intact. The IX, indeed, was unexpectedly well equipped with armour. For Lieutenant-Colonel Harzer had disobeyed an order from Berlin to hand over all his serviceable tanks and vehicles preparatory to a move back into Germany. Instead, he had had the tracks and guns taken off several of his tanks so that they appeared to be disabled and he described them as such in his returns.

In addition to these two divisions, there were also in the Arnhem area at this time three fairly strong and competent infantry battalions, as well as various scattered 'Fliegerhorst' battalions (comprising Luftwaffe ground staff), Schiffstammabteilungen (German naval personnel from abandoned coastal defences), gunners (many of them also from abandoned coastal defences), Dutch SS (originally formed to guard the concentration camp at Amersfoort, and commanded by a German officer, Paul Helle), together with several anti-aircraft batteries. The three competent infantry battalions were Colonel Lippert's training battalion of SS Unteroffizier cadets and two SS depôt battalions, commanded by Majors Kraft and Eberwein. One of these, Sepp Kraft's battalion, was actually stationed just outside Arnhem on September 17.

It was not these troops, however, which formed the real threat to the British division's success, but the 8,500 men of the IX and X SS Panzer Divisions under the command of General Willi Bittrich.

Bittrich, tall, stiff, handsome, and highly intelligent, was one of the most respected Waffen SS generals in the German army. Unlike most of them he had a cultivated taste, a kindly manner, and a pleasant sense of humour. He also had a very quick mind, and when Model arrived at his headquarters at about 1500 hours on that Sunday afternoon he had already understood the nature of the Allied threat and taken the necessary steps to contain it.

A battle group of the IX SS Panzer Division was on its way towards the landing zones with orders to 'destroy the enemy troops landed at Oosterbeek, west of Arnhem'. 'It is necessary to strike immediately,' the orders continued. 'The most important task is to occupy and secure the bridge with strong forces.'

Units of the X Division were also on the move, but not to Arnhem. For Bittrich had immediately realised that it was as important to prevent the obviously intended link-up with spearheads of the 2nd Army as to destroy the airborne troops that had landed north of the Neder Rijn. And since the 2nd Army would naturally try to get through to Arnhem by way of Nijmegen, the X Division was ordered there.

'We shall soon be able to discount the threat of the British north of the Neder Rijn,' Bittrich said confidently. 'We must remember that British soldiers do not act on their own initiative when they are fighting in a town and when it consequently becomes difficult for officers to exercise control they are amazing in defence, but we need not be afraid of their capabilities in attack.'

The success of his plan rested to a large extent on the ability of the troops who would first come into contact with the advancing British paratroops being able to check their initial advance from the landing grounds. It was, therefore, fortunate for him that the troops on whom this task would fall were the keen and fresh recruits, mostly between 17 and 19 years old, who comprised Major Sepp Kraft's SS depôt battalion, stationed between Oosterbeek and Wolfheze.

'The only way to draw the teeth of an airborne landing with an inferior force,' Kraft believed, was 'to drive right into it.'

And this he determined to do. Sending a company towards the landing grounds with orders to fight a delaying action, he drew up the rest of his 400 or so men into a forward defensive line across the roads leading into Arnhem and ordered them to hold their positions there until the IX Division came to their assistance with armoured cars, light tanks, and artillery.

'Almost before the British had touched the ground,' General Bittrich commented afterwards with justifiable satisfaction, 'we were ready to defeat them.'

A dangerously slow advance

Immediately on landing, the men of the British Airborne Division met the first of their misfortunes. The 21st Independent Parachute Company had landed without serious mishap and had unrolled the coloured nylon strips across the fields without interference. But although no more than seven aircraft of the first lift were hit by flak and not one was shot down, several gliders had been lost on the journey, mainly through broken tow ropes. And in these missing gliders were nearly all the vehicles of the 1st Airborne Reconnaissance Squadron, whose task it was to lead the race for the road and railway bridges.

The advance into Arnhem did not begin, therefore, until about 1445 hours. It was led by the 2nd Battalion of Brigadier G. W. Lathbury's 1st Parachute Brigade.

Lieutenant-Colonel J. D. Frost, who commanded this battalion, remarked on the numbers of Dutch people, men, women, and scores of children, who crowded round the troops as soon as they began to march off from the landing zones. They offered them apples, pears, jugs of milk, and cups of tea. The British soldiers, too polite to refuse, lingered to accept the gifts and to show their appreciation to these friendly people who seemed to believe that the war must now be as good as over. Some soldiers took politeness so far as to deferentially ask permission before searching homes where German ambushes were suspected, and to take special care not to damage the flower-beds or the high, wire-mesh fences which surrounded many of the neat gardens. This politeness and respect for property slowed up the advance as much as the soldiers' natural caution.

Then, as a cause of further delay, some of the maps which had been issued were wildly inaccurate, showing, so one company commander complained, 'few of the roads that actually existed'.

The road along which Colonel Frost's men advanced was the most southerly of those that ran into Arnhem through Heelsum and south of Oosterbeek. It was the one least well covered by the Germans' immediate dispositions; but although the opposition encountered was by no means strong or well-directed it was sufficiently persistent to slow Frost's men down and occasionally to bring them to a halt. General Urquhart, whose radio sets were already proving totally inadequate as a means of communication with his subordinate commanders, felt compelled to go forward personally to urge the 2nd Battalion to increase its speed. It would soon be dark and the Arnhem bridges were still a long way off.

The 3rd Battalion of Lathbury's brigade, commanded by Lieutenant-Colonel J. A. C. Fitch, was also in difficulties and moving slowly. This battalion was advancing into Arnhem along a more northerly road which would take them through Oosterbeek. But having reached a cross-roads about 2 miles west of the town—and having there shot Major-General Kussin, regional commander of Arnhem, who came racing down from the village of Wolfheze in a Citroën staff car—the leading platoon, and then the whole battalion, came to a halt under heavy mortar fire.

For several minutes the 3rd Battalion remained in this dangerous and heavily bombed locality, where men on all sides were killed or wounded by the bombs which burst in the trees and sent fragments flying through the air and the undergrowth. Then Brigadier Lathbury decided that it would be 'suicide to stay any longer on that infernal cross-roads', and gave Colonel Fitch orders to move on.

The 3rd Battalion, however, could not get

US paratroops unload a wrecked glider:
their part of the operation succeeded brilliantly

The advance into Arnhem: troops were
dropped too far out and moved in too slowly

far. Sepp Kraft's men, now reinforced by the IX Division's battle group, were fighting well and were supported by several self-propelled guns. On the outskirts of Oosterbeek they brought the British to a halt again; and, it now being dark, Lathbury suggested to Fitch that his men should take a few hours' rest. Patrols were sent out in the direction of Arnhem, and a message dispatched to Colonel Frost to tell him that the 3rd Battalion would not now try to reach the bridge till morning.

Nor would the 1st Battalion of Lathbury's Brigade reach the bridge till morning. This battalion, commanded by Lieutenant-Colonel David Dobie, had originally been ordered to make for the high ground north of Arnhem and to close the route leading into the town from Apeldoorn and Zutphen. But

just north of Wolfheze the battalion had become involved in a savage fight with German tanks, guns, and infantry. 'Everywhere we turned or moved,' a young soldier from Northumberland, Andrew Milbourne, remembers, 'we were swept with a withering fire. Dead lay all around, wounded were crying for water, groans and shrieks of pain filled the air. . . . Time and again they overran our positions and had to be driven out with the bayonet.'

By the time what remained of the battalion had fought its way through the woods, past Johanna Hoeve, to the northern outskirts of Arnhem, casualties were pitifully heavy. Colonel Dobie could have no doubt that the Germans held the ground north of the town in far too great a strength for him to occupy it as planned; and he gave orders for an

advance on the bridge as soon as it was light.

Colonel Frost, who had now reached the bridge, was desperately in need of Dobie's support. He had only about 500 men with him—parts of his own battalion, some men of one of the 3rd Battalion's companies, others of the reconnaissance squadron, a detachment of engineers, a platoon of the Royal Army Service Corps, and brigade headquarters. Frost's own C Company had been detached to secure the railway bridge, which had been blown up in their faces before they could reach it, and were now held fighting in the town by the railway station.

With the troops at his disposal Frost had managed to secure the northern end of the bridge and occupy the buildings around it.

The only battalion which fought its
way to the bridge was cut off and destroyed

But two gallant attempts to capture the southern end had been beaten back by Harzer's Panzers. And although the enemy was already being reinforced from Army Group B with infantry, artillery, and modern King Tiger tanks, it seemed as yet unlikely that Frost could be reinforced with any troops at all.

General Urquhart, as he himself afterwards confessed, was already aware that he 'was losing control of the battle'. Since he could not direct the operations of the division by wireless, he had decided to remain with General Lathbury who himself was with the advanced troops of the 3rd Battalion. On Monday morning, when this battalion resumed its advance into Arnhem, it was soon engaged in heavy and confused fighting with tanks and self-propelled guns around

the massive Gothic structure of the Roman Catholic St Elizabeth Hospital.

The confusion was aggravated when Colonel Dobie's 1st Battalion, trying to break through to the bridge, came under fierce fire from mortars, armoured cars, tanks, and snipers in the area of the railway station, which is close to the hospital. 'The Jerries seemed to have hundreds of tanks,' one British soldier said. 'You could hear them and see them everywhere. They had more mortars than we did too; and they knew how to use them, all right. Bombs were going off around us all the time.'

And not all the bombs were enemy ones. For the British units were so muddled and split up in the maze of narrow streets and conglomeration of buildings in this part of the town that it was no longer possible to

tell friend from enemy or which houses contained paratroops and which Germans.

In the midst of this confusion, Brigadier Lathbury was hit and paralysed by a Spandau bullet which struck his spine; and General Urquhart, surrounded by Panzer Grenadiers, was forced to conceal himself in the attic of a terraced house in Zwarteweg. There with a platoon commander of the 3rd Battalion and an Intelligence officer on Lathbury's staff he was obliged to remain all night, with the German crew of a self-propelled gun immediately below the window.

At Divisional HQ, Brigadier Hicks was now in command. His 1st Airlanding Brigade had spent the previous day protecting the landing zones; but now that Lathbury's brigade was in the process of dissolution,

An American paratroop rushes through enemy fire during the battle to seize the bridge at Nijmegen

A German self-propelled gun moves towards Arnhem

German troops dash across a street during fighting in Arnhem

the time had obviously come to reinforce those parts of it still trying to get through to the bridge.

Exactly how many cohesive parts of Lathbury's Brigade still remained in existence, Hicks could not determine. For there were still virtually no wireless links working satisfactorily. Several sets had been destroyed by enemy action; and most of those which were still in use were designed for communications over limited distances (not much more than 3 miles) so that the irregular, faint, and crackling messages which reached Divisional HQ (which was still 8 miles from the bridge) were as often as not incomprehensible.

When, therefore, Hicks sent two companies of the 2nd South Staffordshire Regi-

ment off into Arnhem, he had no clear idea of the situation they would find there. Stronger reinforcements Hicks felt unable to send, for, despite the hopeful weather forecast that had been issued before the operation began, low fog was drifting over the airfields in Britain. Consequently the second lift was delayed, and Hicks dared not reduce any further the numbers of troops defending the landing zones until that lift arrived with the urgently needed troops of the 4th Parachute Brigade.

Aware that the lift was due – since the Germans had found a set of the plans for Operation Market Garden on the body of a dead British officer – Bittrich now made a determined effort to drive the British off the landing zones, so that when Brigadier

Hackett did arrive with his 4th Parachute Brigade, he found them only tenuously held. He also found what he described himself as 'a grossly untidy situation'.

Although Hackett did what he could at Divisional HQ to impose some sort of order on this situation, when Urquhart managed to escape from his attic and returned to reassume command, confusion still prevailed.

Colonel Frost's men, Urquhart was told, were still bravely maintaining their fight at the bridge under increasing pressure; while parties from four battalions were making attempts to fight their way through the German cordon in the town to his relief. Three other battalions under Hackett had gone off to the north and might or might not be entering the town from that direction.

'Almost before the British had touched the ground, we were ready to defeat them'
General Bittrich

Südd Verlag

Sado Opera Mundi

Slowly the British were forced away from the bridge into a perimeter at Oosterbeek

The ninth battalion in the division was the only one left in the immediate area.

That Tuesday was a day of disaster. Concerted attacks by the units in the town all failed with heavy loss of life; and Hackett's battalions, deeply involved with increasingly strong German forces between Johanna Hoeve and Lichtenbeck, were forced to withdraw south of the railway line when the one battalion left in the divisional area behind him came under an attack which threatened to cut it entirely loose from the rest of the division. The withdrawal was drastic, resulting in fearful loss of both life and vehicles; and before it was completed the exhausted men were dismayed to see the RAF supply aircraft fly into heavy flak to drop their supplies on predetermined tar-

gets which had not yet been captured from the enemy.

As darkness fell British troops were still fighting in the town with undiminished energy and dash but in increasing confusion; while others were falling back, disillusioned and dismayed. The colonels of all four battalions engaged in the town had been wounded and had lost more than half their officers. And Colonel Frost's troops at the bridge, worn out by their exertion, could not be expected to hold out much longer.

They did hold out, however, for the whole of the next day and night. They had no food or water, and little ammunition left; the dark cellars of the scarred and blackened buildings were crammed with wounded and dying men; there seemed now, amid the dust

and smoke and the blood-splashed ruins, no hope of victory. Yet when the final assault was made by the Germans at dawn on Thursday morning, the fighting, a German who took part in it recorded, was of 'an indescribable fanaticism . . . the fight raged through ceilings and staircases. Hand grenades flew in every direction. Each house had to be taken in this way. Some of the British offered resistance to their last breath'. By 0900 hours, however, the area was cleared.

By then the rest of the division had formed an irregular horseshoe-shaped perimeter of defence to the west of Oosterbeek, north of the Heveadorp ferry. Urquhart had hoped that if he could hold on here, there might yet be a chance of the 2nd Army crossing the river to reach him even if Frost failed

357

to maintain his grasp on the north end of the bridge.

Everything depended upon the speed of the 2nd Army's advance. And once news reached the division that the Americans and the Guards had captured the bridge at Nijmegen, only 10 miles to the south, there seemed every reason to believe that relief would very soon come. Indeed, at dawn on Friday Urquhart received a message from 30th Corps HQ which read: '43rd Division ordered to take all risks to effect relief today.'

But the Germans defended those last 10 miles between Nijmegen and Arnhem with great skill and tenacity, exploiting all the advantages which the countryside afforded them, using a concealed lateral road for the movement of vehicles and armour, while the British tanks could not move off the narrow axis of their advance because of the dykes and drainage ditches which lay on each side of it. Moreover the single road behind 30th Corps' spearhead was under constant threat from the artillery and infantry of Model's rapidly recuperating and growing army; traffic conditions along it were chaotic; ammunition was delayed in the congestion; and when aircraft support was needed the radio sets in the only two RAF contact cars were found to be out of order. 30th Corps' advance was accordingly much slower than had been predicted.

'A collection of individuals holding on'
Urquhart, distressed by the plight of his division—now no more, as he put it himself, than 'a collection of individuals holding on' —felt that all risks were not being taken; and, as hour followed hour, his hold on the northern bank of the river weakened. All along his defended line and in the constantly bombarded area inside it, which the Germans called 'The Cauldron', his men were given no respite, no opportunity for sleep. There was little food or ammunition left, scarcely any water or medical supplies. Tanks and infantry patrols, snipers, and self-propelled guns firing phosphorus shells were repeatedly infiltrating between the extended outposts causing heavy casualties among the exhausted, hungry, and burningly thirsty defenders, whose suffering was aggravated by the sight of the RAF and USAF transport crews bravely and unhesitatingly flying into the ferocious German barrage, mistaking the Airborne Division's position, and dropping their supplies outside its reach.

Some men broke down completely; but most fought doggedly on, inspired by those many heroic figures of the Arnhem legend whose fine example and individual deeds have elsewhere been commemorated.

After fierce fighting the Border Regiment of Hicks's brigade was driven off the high ground at Westerbouwing, which commanded the Heveadorp ferry; and when at last the weather permitted the dropping of Sosabowski's Polish Brigade south of the river near Driel, the British had been driven off the northern end of the ferry. The ferry itself was destroyed and the crossings were dominated by German guns.

Despite the appalling dangers and difficulties, however, an attempt was made by the Poles to cross the river on Friday night; but when the dawn bombardment of 'The Cauldron' began on Saturday morning, less than 50 Poles had been able to get across. Another attempt was made to cross on Saturday night by the 4th Battalion of the Dorset Regiment, a spearhead unit of 30th Corps

which had reached the Neder Rijn at last. But this attempt, too, failed, many of the men being killed in the boats which were, in any event, borne downstream by the fast current to land well beyond the edge of the perimeter.

This crossing by the Dorsets was not so much intended as an attempt to reinforce the Airborne Division, as a means of ensuring that the line of the perimeter held while it was evacuated. For it had now been decided that the precarious bridgehead north of the river could not be held any longer; and what remained of the Airborne Division would have to be brought back.

On Monday night the evacuation began. The Germans, quiet at first, soon realised what was happening and, after midnight, the withdrawal was continued under heavy fire both from Spandaus and heavy guns on the high ground at Westerbouwing. Then German tanks began to roll into the perimeter and for the first time in a week they were unopposed.

Over 300 wounded were taken prisoner inside the perimeter; almost ten times that number were already in German dressing stations and Dutch hospitals outside it. Hundreds of these were later sent back to freedom by the Dutch resistance, but for many more there could be no return. Over 1,200 British soldiers were dead, and more than 3,400 German soldiers were killed or wounded.

A great prize almost won
Several reasons can be advanced for the ultimate failure of the operation. The most comforting is that bad flying conditions not only prevented the supply and reinforcement of the Allied troops but also prevented the break-up of German supply and reinforcement columns moving towards the battle area. There are other explanations, however, which are more disturbing.

The pressure in the immediate operational area of such skilful generals as Model, Student, and Bittrich could scarcely, perhaps, have been foreseen; and the remarkable speed with which they acted to concentrate their forces could hardly have been predicted. But the undeniable fact remains that the British were landed at Arnhem with very little guidance from Allied Intelligence officers as to the kind of opposition they might be likely to meet there, although much of the material upon which this guidance could have been based was, in fact, available.

As well as being supplied with inadequate Intelligence reports, they were supplied with inadequate signals equipment. As the Cabinet Office Papers show, the range of battalion, brigade, and divisional sets were nearly all insufficient and the signallers were sometimes badly trained. Wireless communications throughout the battle were either intermittent or non-existent, and not until the last day was it possible to call effectively for close air support. One of the reasons for the breakdown in wireless communications was that—in view of the limited number of aircraft available for the operation—to take more powerful and more bulky sets would have meant fewer fighting men.

The aircraft shortage was also partly responsible for what the Germans themselves gave as one of the main reasons for the British defeat: the spreading of the landings over three days so that the full strength of the Airborne Division was never felt.

Had a more concentrated landing been

made, had General Urquhart insisted, against all the advice that was offered to him, on landing closer to his objective, and had he—when the capture of the bridge seemed impossible—concentrated on holding the high ground at Westerbouwing, the operation might perhaps have succeeded.

But even so the doubt remains. For by nightfall on September 22, it was clear that the appalling congestion on the Eindhoven-Nijmegen road and the increasing enemy pressure on either side of it, had made it not only impossible to increase and adequately supply the forces in the foremost areas but had also made it unlikely that, even if a bridgehead across the Neder Rijn were to be successfully established, it could be successfully held.

The direction of the attack was not a mistaken one. A quick and triumphant conclusion to Operation Market Garden followed by an operation against the German defences along the Scheldt to free Antwerp, would have had incalculable consequences. As Churchill said, a 'great prize was so nearly within our grasp'.

Whether or not the heavy risks taken to seize that prize were justified in view of the limited priority which Eisenhower felt able to give Montgomery may, however, be doubted.

But Operation Market Garden was not a complete failure. Passages across the Maas and Waal had been secured, together with what General Kurt Student called 'an excellent spring board from which to launch the final attack upon Germany'.

And although that final attack could not now be made as soon as once had been hoped, it was clear that one day soon it would come. [*Christopher Hibbert's biography is on page 46.*]

Operation 'Market Garden'

1944 September 17: Operation Market Garden begins with the British 1st Airborne Division landing near Arnhem; the US 101st Airborne Division near Eindhoven; the 82nd near Grave and Nijmegen; and the British 30th Corps advancing north from the Dutch border. The 82nd lands without difficulty and captures the Maas and Maas-Waal canal bridges, but meets heavy resistance at Nijmegen. The 101st also captures its bridges, but the British paratroops find their way to Arnhem blocked by strong German forces, and only one battalion manages to reach the bridge, where it is cut off.
September 18: A German counterattack forestalls an American attempt to capture the bridge at Nijmegen. The Germans mount heavy attacks on the Arnhem DZ to try and prevent reinforcements from landing.
September 19: The leading troops of British 30th Corps reach the US paratroops at Nijmegen. At Arnhem, all attempts to break through to the troops at the bridge fail.
September 20: The bridge at Nijmegen is captured in a combined assault by the US 82nd Airborne Division and the British 30th Corps.
September 21: At Arnhem, the British troops at the bridge are overwhelmed; the remainder form a defensive perimeter on the northern bank of the Neder Rijn to the west of Oosterbeek.
September 22: The advance of 30th Corps is slowed down by German resistance. The Polish Brigade begins to land south of the river.
September 23: Attempts by the Poles and advance troops of 30th Corps to cross the river are driven back.
September 25: Evacuation of the surviving paratroops begins.

'I think we may be going one bridge too far . . .'

Montgomery's plan for Market Garden envisaged the dropping of three airborne divisions to seize the bridges on the Eindhoven-Arnhem road to enable units of the 2nd Army of 21st Army Group to outflank the Siegfried Line. The first part of the plan went well: the US 101st Airborne Division, dropping between Veghel and Eindhoven, captured the two southern bridges and 2nd Army raced on to link up with the US 82nd Airborne at Grave and Nijmegen. But at Arnhem things had gone badly from the start: the British 1st Airborne, landing a long way from the town, found that there were large German forces in the neighbourhood which reacted swiftly to protect the bridge and to block the relieving force at Nijmegen. The one British battalion which was able to fight its way to the bridge was cut off, and the remainder were forced back into a bridgehead near Oosterbeek, where they hoped to be able to hold out until relieved. But the US 82nd Airborne had found that the Nijmegen bridge was strongly held, and it was only after a combined attack with the lead units of 2nd Army that it was cleared. The Germans then contested every mile to Arnhem fiercely, aided by deteriorating weather, and although the Polish Brigade was dropped south of the British bridgehead in an attempt to relieve it, few troops could get across. Even when 2nd Army arrived, it was only with difficulty that the survivors of the 1st Airborne Division could be brought back, having held out for more than a week. The prophecy of General Browning, commander of the Airborne Corps was amply justified. This diagrammatic representation depicts the key events of the operation.

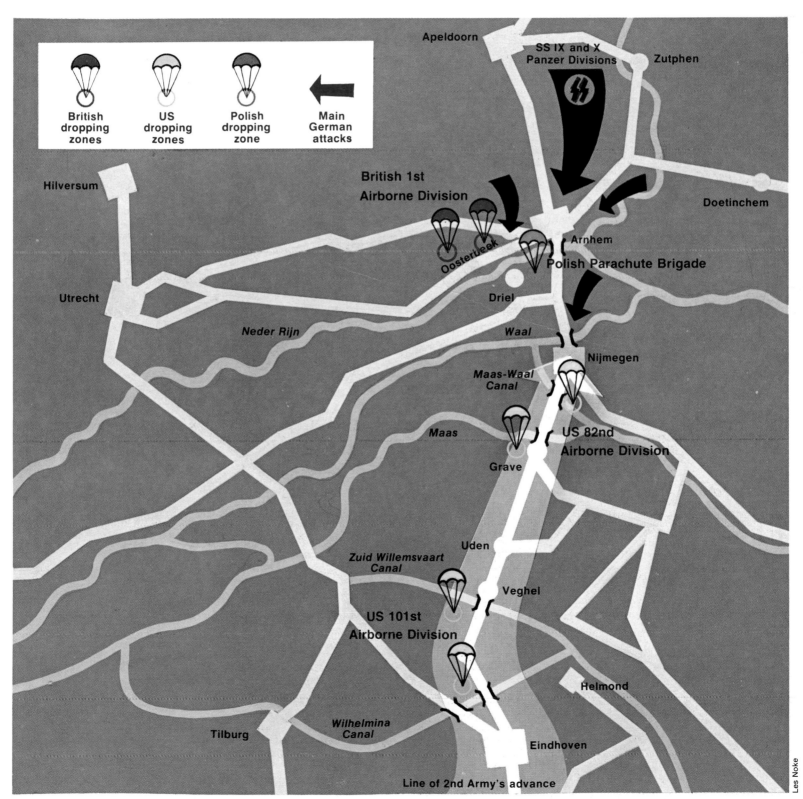

Les Noke

BATTLE OF LEYTE

Philippine Islands, October/December 1944
Stanley L. Falk

When the US armada—the greatest yet seen in the Pacific theatre—descended on Leyte Gulf in the southern Philippines, the Japanese were ready. Their navy had been ordered to combat any invasion with a desperate plan—Operation *Sho* (Victory). The last surviving battleships and carriers of the Imperial Japanese Navy were to stake all for victory, and they duly steamed out to do battle when the news of the invasion came. The result was the Battle of Leyte Gulf, a mighty three-day struggle which resulted in the virtual annihilation of the Japanese fleet

Right: **MacArthur returns to the Philippines**
Below: **US rocket bombardment before the Leyte landings**

US Army

US Navy

Leyte Gulf: the rival fleets

The Japanese *(left)* were gambling on the surprise arrival of their imposing battleship force, including the huge *Yamato* and *Musashi.* Ozawa's carriers, starved of planes, were to be the bait

Halsey's 3rd Fleet had the bulk of the US strike carriers; Kinkaid's 7th Fleet had the lighter force of escort carriers, backed by a stronger battleship force than Halsey's

US Navy

US Navy

American
Right: Halsey, C-in-C US 3rd Fleet: he commanded the main US carrier and strike forces in the action
Far right: Kinkaid, C-in-C US 7th Fleet: he had the task of guarding the invasion fleet in Leyte Gulf
Bottom right: Oldendorf, Kinkaid's subordinate, whose battle squadron smashed the Japanese attempt to break into Leyte Gulf through Surigao Strait
Bottom far right: Sprague, commander of the 7th Fleet's small escort carrier force which narrowly escaped annihilation off Samar

Japanese
Top left: Kurita, the commander of the main Japanese battle squadron, whose premature retreat off Samar cost him a great victory over an inferior force
Bottom left: Ozawa, the cool, gallant commander of the decoy carrier force which drew Halsey's 3rd Fleet away from Leyte Gulf

Fox Photos

US Navy

US Navy

US Navy

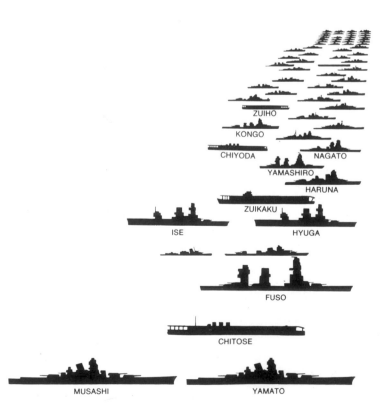

ZUIHO
KONGO
CHIYODA   NAGATO
YAMASHIRO
HARUNA
ZUIKAKU
ISE   HYUGA
FUSO
CHITOSE
MUSASHI   YAMATO

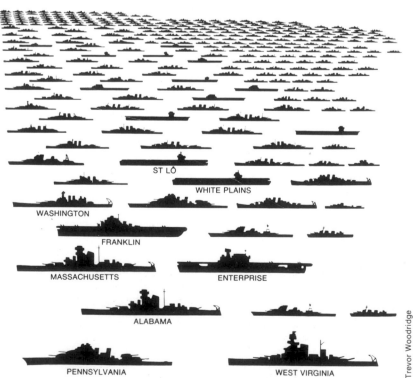

ST LÔ
WHITE PLAINS
WASHINGTON
FRANKLIN
MASSACHUSETTS   ENTERPRISE
ALABAMA
PENNSYLVANIA   WEST VIRGINIA

Trevor Woodridge

When the sun rose over Leyte Gulf in the central Philippines on the morning of October 20, 1944, it disclosed the largest and mightiest fleet of amphibious assault vessels and warships yet assembled in the Pacific. Over 700 transports, combat ships, and service and support craft were concentrated in the waters east of Leyte Island, or guarding the entrance to the gulf. Further east and north, four powerful task groups of carriers and battleships provided distant cover in the Philippine Sea. Scores of aircraft maintained a constant vigil overhead, while many more prepared to support the assault that morning of four American divisions against the shore of Leyte. The presence of this huge armada signalled the fulfilment of General MacArthur's pledge to return to the Philippines.

The island of Leyte in the central Philippines is some 115 miles long but only 45 miles wide at its broadest and barely 15 at its narrow waist. Its eastern shore, washed by Leyte Gulf, boasts some of the finest landing beaches in the Pacific. Most of the island is mountainous save for the flat, marshy Leyte Valley in the northeast and, in the west, the Ormoc Valley, a narrow corridor running north from the port of Ormoc.

For the seizure of Leyte, General MacArthur had under his command the 200,000 men of General Krueger's 6th Army, Lieutenant-General George C. Kenney's Far East Air Forces, with over 2,500 combat aircraft, and Vice-Admiral Thomas C. Kinkaid's 7th Fleet — often called 'MacArthur's Navy' — which included more than 100 combat vessels, over five times as many transports, supply vessels, landing ships, and other support craft, and 500 planes. In a supporting role, but not under MacArthur's control, was Halsey's 3rd Fleet, one of the largest and most powerful naval striking forces ever assembled, containing nearly 100 of the most modern warships and over 1,000 aircraft.

Kinkaid was responsible for carrying the 6th Army to Leyte and putting it ashore. Halsey meanwhile would cover the landings with pre-invasion airstrikes on the Philippines, Formosa, and the Ryukyus. Close air support for the landings would come from Kinkaid's escort carriers, but only for the first few days. By the end of this period, General Krueger would have captured the east Leyte airfields and Kenney could move in his fighters and light bombers to take over the air-support mission from the navy. The 6th Army could then proceed with the business of occupying Leyte, and MacArthur could use the island as a base from which to move on to other conquests.

The Leyte invasion represented a significant departure from previous MacArthur operations in that it was to be attempted beyond the range of land-based air cover. If carrier protection was lost before Kenney could bring his planes in, then the entire operation might be jeopardised. Naval support was therefore extremely important. Yet Halsey, who was still operating under Nimitz, had as his primary mission not the protection of the beachhead but, if the opportunity arose or could 'be created', the destruction of the Japanese fleet. This left Halsey with the option of withdrawing his support of the invasion whenever he wished. MacArthur could neither prevent this nor could he ever be certain for just how long he could rely on Halsey's presence.

There was still, to be sure, the 7th Fleet. But Kinkaid's small escort carriers could boast only a fraction of the planes that Halsey had. Furthermore, without Halsey, Kinkaid would be hard put to defend himself and the beach-head against a major Japanese fleet effort while at the same time providing Krueger with close air support.

American success, therefore, might well rest on just how soon General Kenney could establish his air units on Leyte. And here the weather entered the picture. From September until early spring, eastern Leyte is subject to frequent heavy rains and, for much of this time, to typhoons. The ground, naturally soft and marshy in many areas, becomes almost completely saturated. Constructing airfields on the spongy Leyte soil under these conditions would be extremely difficult, and without adequate airfields there would be no place for Kenney to put his planes.

MacArthur's staff was well aware of these problems. But the only way to avoid them was to postpone the Leyte invasion, either until bases could be seized on Mindanao or until the weather cleared. And this would mean passing up the opportunity to hit the Japanese while they were weak and off-balance. Better instead to take some risk in order to win a swift and important victory. Besides, Halsey's September raids had shown that the Japanese were in no shape to put up much of a fight. A bold stroke might capture Leyte before the Japanese could even respond to the invasion.

The lack of resistance to Halsey's raids had been in part the result of Japanese weakness. But it had also been based on Japanese determination to husband their main strength for use against a major American offensive. The Japanese, indeed, had developed an elaborate and, as it turned out, dangerously complicated scheme of

manoeuvre by which they hoped to throw massive sea, air, and land forces into a 'decisive battle' to crush the Americans.

The Japanese plans — code-named Sho ('Victory') — were aimed at defending important territories from the Kuriles to the Philippines. An American invasion — but only one which was clearly a major operation — would be met by a combined air and sea attack launched just as the enemy landings were getting under way. It would be an all-out effort to destroy transports and covering warships in a single blow at the last possible moment. The sadly reduced strength of Japanese carrier airpower, however, meant that the carriers could contribute little to this attack. So they were, instead, to be used as a decoy force to draw off American carriers and expose the rest of the invasion force to Japanese land-based air assaults and naval firepower. Any of the invaders who survived to carry out a landing would be dealt with by the Japanese army.

Timing and close co-ordination were essential features of the Sho plans. But unfortunately for the Japanese, their confused and divided command structure denied them the central control so vital to their hopes. This was particularly true for Sho-1, the defence of the Philippines. In those important islands there was no single command to integrate land, air, and sea operations. Ground warfare was the responsibility of the XIV Area Army, whose newly appointed commander, General Tomoyuki Yamashita, did not, in fact, reach the Philippines until early October. Under Yamashita, and charged with the defence of the central and southern Philippines, was Lieutenant-General Sosaku Suzuki's XXXV Army. But Yamashita had no control over the Philippine-based IV Air Army of Lieutenant-General Kyoji Tominaga.

Both Yamashita and Tominaga reported on an equal basis to Field-Marshal Count Hisaichi Terauchi who, as Southern Army commander, was responsible for the area from the Philippines through the Indies to Burma. Among his many other duties, then, was the task of co-ordinating army, air, and ground activities in the Philippines.

Naval forces operated completely independent of any of these commands. Practically all Japanese naval units belonged to Admiral Soemu Toyoda's Combined Fleet. The main combat elements, each operating separately and responsible directly to Toyoda, were: Vice-Admiral Takeo Kurita's I Striking Force, battleships, cruisers, and destroyers, based at Lingga Roads, across from Singapore, where they were assured a ready supply of fuel; Vice-Admiral Jisaburo Ozawa's Main Body, a carrier force located in the Inland Sea; and Vice-Admiral Kiyohide Shima's II Striking Force, a few cruisers and destroyers, also in northern waters. Major naval air units in the Philippines and elsewhere were linked to the other fleet elements and, for that matter, to each other only through Toyoda.

The Combined Fleet commander thus had the herculean responsibility of co-ordinating all Japanese naval elements assigned to Sho, even as Marshal Terauchi had the same broad task for major army units. But neither Toyoda nor Terauchi were required to have much to do with each other. And Imperial General Headquarters, which theoretically linked the two commanders in Tokyo, did little to achieve this end. Instead of being a joint overall headquarters, it was in fact two separate commands, with independent army and navy sections split by animosities too strong to permit any close co-operation or integration of operations. From top to bottom, then, co-ordinating execution of Sho would be extremely difficult, if not impossible.

Overwhelming display of airpower

Clear evidence of this was provided by events in mid-October. To soften the Japanese for the coming Leyte assault, on October 10 Halsey's carriers began a sustained attack against Japanese bases from the Ryukyus to the northern Philippines. In an unprecedented and overwhelming display of sea-borne airpower, Halsey sent as many as 1,000 planes at a time into action, smothering the Japanese defences, destroying ground installations, and driving Japanese aircraft from the sky. To Admiral Toyoda, the weight of these blows indicated the imminence of a major American invasion. After some confusion, he directed naval air units to execute operations under both Sho-1, the defence of the Philippines, and Sho-2, the defence of Formosa and the Ryukyus.

The result of this premature commitment of Japanese naval air strength was the involvement of practically all of Toyoda's planes in a fruitless effort to halt a non-existent invasion. General Tominaga, meanwhile, did practically nothing in response to Halsey's blows and, for that matter, was probably unaware of Toyoda's unilateral issuing of the 'Sho-execute' orders. Thanks to this restraint, he suffered few losses.

But Toyoda's forces were severely battered. In less than a week of action, over 600 Japanese naval aircraft were destroyed.

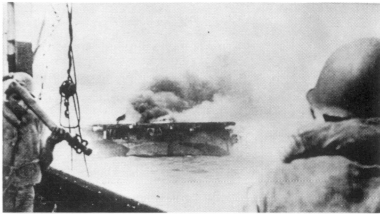

Japanese naval air strength on Formosa and in the Philippines was badly crippled and even the small body of planes assigned to Admiral Ozawa's carriers had been committed to the fight and dissipated. American losses were not quite 100 planes.

To add insult to injury, Japanese aircrews had been making ridiculous and completely unfounded claims of success against the US 3rd Fleet. Radio Tokyo announced that as many as 19 American carriers had been sunk, along with a great number of battleships, cruisers, and destroyers. The Emperor issued a special rescript, and mass celebrations were held throughout Japan.

Toyoda too was completely fooled. When Halsey decided to use two damaged cruisers—the only ships in his entire fleet to be hurt at all—as a lure to trap the Japanese fleet, Toyoda rose to the bait. Convinced that he had victory in his grasp, he committed additional air power to the attack and simultaneously directed Admiral Shima's II Striking Force to pursue the supposedly crippled Halsey and mop up. 'Needless to say,' wrote one Japanese commander later, 'all this pursuit business ended in fiasco.' More Japanese planes were lost and Shima barely escaped destruction when Toyoda, finally realising something of the truth, directed the II Striking Force to withdraw.

Toyoda's blunder was a serious blow to Japanese chances of successfully executing the *Sho* plan. Without the hundreds of naval aircraft now lost, it would be impossible to carry out the all-important air phase of the plan. There were still about 300 navy planes on Formosa, some 150 more planes of the IV Air Army widely scattered throughout the Philippines, and perhaps 100 carrier aircraft, flown by inexperienced and ill-trained pilots, gathering again with Admiral Ozawa. But the best planes and pilots were gone.

The strength of Japanese naval surface forces was somewhat more reassuring. Yet without adequate air power, even Admiral Kurita's powerful battleship force at Lingga Roads would have a difficult time when he sortied to meet the Americans. And in the face of uncontested American air operations, General Yamashita would be equally hard pressed to redeploy his forces to meet the expected landings. He had, altogether, some 300,000 troops in the Philippines. But only a third of these were in the southern Philippines, while Leyte was defended by but 20,000 men.

The first landings in the American return to the Philippines took place on October 17 and 18 on three small islands guarding the eastern approaches to Leyte Gulf. Ranger and infantry elements swept the islands with little difficulty, destroyed Japanese radio installations, and set up navigation lights to guide the Leyte invasion convoy. Minesweepers and underwater demolition teams checked and cleared the approaches on the 18th and 19th and

warships and planes of the 7th Fleet began a heavy pre-invasion bombardment of beaches and inland installations on the morning of the 19th. To this activity came almost no Japanese response.

The Japanese were experiencing their usual co-ordination difficulties. Admiral Toyoda had the fastest reaction. When the first alert reached him on the 17th, he ordered his main combat elements to sea and, on the 18th, directed an all-out attack on the invasion force in Leyte Gulf. The other Japanese were more sceptical. Bad weather limited initial observation of the Leyte Gulf area and, unlike Toyoda, they were still under the impression that heavy 3rd Fleet losses the previous week would delay a major American operation for some time. Any American shipping in Leyte Gulf was probably the crippled remnant of Halsey's armada.

By noon of the 18th, however, the Southern and IV Air Army commanders, Field-Marshal Terauchi and General Tominaga, were convinced that the invasion had come. Their recommendations and those of Toyoda convinced their respective superiors in Tokyo. Just after 1700 hours, after reporting their decision to the Emperor, the army and navy sections of Imperial General Headquarters issued separate orders activating *Sho*-1.

The Combined Fleet was already moving to the attack. At noon on the 20th, Kurita's powerful I Striking Force reached Brunei Bay, Borneo. From here, Kurita would lead the bulk of it through the central Philippines and San Bernardino Strait to the Philippine Sea and then rush south to attack Admiral Kinkaid's invasion force in Leyte Gulf. For this purpose, Kurita had five battleships—including the 64,000-ton behemoths *Musashi* and *Yamato*—12 cruisers, and 15 destroyers. A smaller and slower force under Vice-Admiral Shoji Nishimura—two old battleships, a cruiser, and four destroyers—would take a southern route and enter Leyte Gulf through Surigao Strait. Kurita and Nishimura would, hopefully, arrive simultaneously at dawn of the 25th, three days later than called for by the *Sho* plan, but the earliest they could make it. Admiral Shima's II Striking Force of three cruisers and four destroyers, now in Formosan waters, would follow Nishimura (see maps).

There was, however, no plan to co-ordinate their movements. Meanwhile, Admiral Ozawa's Main Body would move south from the Inland Sea. It included four carriers, two battleships partially converted to carry aircraft, three cruisers, and eight destroyers. Yet with barely 100 planes aboard and pilots so poor that many could not even make a carrier landing, the force had no real offensive capability. Its mission was to decoy Halsey's covering fleet away from Leyte and, if possible, engage and destroy it.

The difficulty and danger of the whole complicated manoeuvre against Leyte Gulf was greatly increased by the fact that the earlier Japanese air losses now deprived the fleet of precious air cover.

Far left: US bombs
burst around the
battleship *Yamashiro,*
Nishimura's flagship
Top left: US carrier
Princeton, abandoned
and blazing beyond
hope of recovery
Bottom left: The
mighty 18-inch-gun
battleship *Yamato*
under air attack

Right: US battleship
West Virginia, firing
a broadside in the
night battle of
Surigao Strait

Whatever Japanese planes were available would concentrate on the invasion force and beach-head. There were no air elements left to protect Kurita, Nishimura, and Shima against air and submarine attacks during their long voyage to Leyte Gulf.

Kurita's mighty flotilla left Brunei on the morning of the 22nd. Nishimura, following a shorter course, sailed that afternoon. A few minutes after midnight, two American submarines patrolling west of Palawan spotted Kurita and radioed a contact report. They attacked him just after dawn of the 23rd. Their torpedoes sank two heavy cruisers, and so badly damaged a third that it had to return to Brunei, taking two destroyers with it as a screen. In manoeuvring, however, one of the submarines grounded on a reef and had to be blown up by its escaping crew. But Kurita's 32 warships had been reduced by five, and his approach route was now evident to the Americans. He continued to advance, nevertheless, and on the morning of the 24th entered the Sibuyan Sea and came into range of Halsey's planes.

Halsey had spent the 23rd deploying his carrier forces to launch airstrikes against both Kurita and Nishimura, who had also been detected. But it was Japanese air power that drew first blood. Early on the 24th, from bases on Luzon, nearly 200 navy planes set out to attack the nearest American carrier group. Detected by radar as they approached, they met skilful and determined opposition from American fighters. In an hour's engagement, nearly half the Japanese planes were downed and the rest driven off. Only a few of the defenders were lost. Not a ship had come under attack.

Just after 0930 hours, however, a lone Japanese dive-bomber emerged from a low cloud, made a shallow approach on its target, and dropped a 550-pound bomb through the flight deck of the light carrier *Princeton.* The bomb exploded within the ship, setting off other explosions, and sending flaming gasoline throughout the *Princeton*'s interior.

For a few hours it seemed as if the holocaust might be contained. But in mid-afternoon a huge blast rent the carrier, shattering her stern and sending great deadly fragments of steel into the firefighters and across the loaded deck of the cruiser *Birmingham,* which had drawn in close to assist. The *Birmingham,* her topsides strewn with the dead and mutilated, was forced to pull clear, and all efforts to save the *Princeton* were abandoned. Late in the day, American torpedoes sank the blazing ship, the first fast carrier to be lost in two years. But this, and the damaging of the *Birmingham,* was all the Japanese had accomplished. The *Sho* mission of the naval air units—to sink any American warships that might block the approach of the Japanese fleet—had failed.

Nor had General Tominaga's IV Air Army done any better in attacking 7th Fleet units in Leyte Gulf that day. Nearly all of Tom-

inaga's planes struck repeatedly at the landing area throughout the 24th. So frequent were these attacks that aircraft from the escort carriers had to suspend ground-support missions in order to defend the anchorage. But few of the American ships were hit, and Tominaga lost nearly 70 planes to US fighters and AA fire.

Admiral Halsey, on the other hand, had been exacting a heavy revenge. A single strike that morning inflicted light damage on a battleship and cruiser in Nishimura's force. Then the entire weight of the 3rd Fleet carrier planes was thrown against Kurita. Beginning about 0900 and lasting till mid-afternoon, five separate attacks hit his ships as they doggedly made their way through the narrow, reef-filled waters of the Sibuyan Sea. At a cost of only 18 aircraft out of well over 250 sorties, Halsey's bombers and torpedo planes sank the mighty *Musashi*—although it took 19 torpedoes and 17 bombs to do it—and sent a crippled heavy cruiser limping back to Brunei. Other Japanese warships also sustained damage, particularly to their exposed communications and fire-control equipment.

Kurita, moreover, was badly shaken by the fury of the assaults. 'We had expected air attacks,' said his chief-of-staff later, 'but this day's were almost enough to discourage us.' Finally, at 1530, after several false submarine alarms, and in anticipation of continued air attacks in the narrow waters of San Bernardino Strait that lay just ahead, Kurita decided to reverse course temporarily. An hour and three-quarters later, when he felt that no more American airstrikes could be launched that day, he turned again and resumed his original course. A little later he received an order from Admiral Toyoda: 'All forces will dash to the attack, trusting in divine assistance!' Kurita replied that he would 'break into Leyte Gulf and fight to the last man'.

Meanwhile, Admiral Ozawa's decoy force had finally attracted Halsey's attention. That morning he had sent his planes in an unsuccessful strike at Halsey's northernmost carrier group. About half were shot down and the rest, since their pilots were incapable of making carrier landings, continued on to Luzon. Then, in the afternoon, Halsey's search planes found Ozawa, giving the 3rd Fleet commander the final 'pieces of the puzzle', as he put it.

For Halsey, Ozawa was the main threat and thus his primary target. The Nishimura and Shima forces seemed to constitute no real danger, certainly nothing that could not be handled by Kinkaid's more numerous and heavier units. Kurita's armada was obviously stronger, but it appeared to have suffered considerable damage—Halsey, like Toyoda earlier, was at the mercy of exaggerated reports by his pilots—and Kurita's vacillations before San Bernardino Strait raised doubts about whether or not he would continue to advance. Even if he did, he could only hit and run, and Kinkaid could probably take care of both Kurita and Nishimura/Shima.

In any event, Ozawa's force contained most of Japan's carriers and, as far as Halsey had any way of knowing, a full complement of aircraft. It seemed to be the strongest and the most dangerous of the Japanese forces approaching Leyte Gulf. To wait for it near Leyte would leave the initiative with the Japanese and allow them to shuttle planes back and forth between their carriers and Luzon, with Halsey's ships in the middle. His best course, he reasoned, was to go after Ozawa with sufficient force to destroy him completely. He would thus wipe out the major threat to the Leyte invasion and achieve his primary mission: 'the destruction of a major portion of the enemy fleet'.

Shortly before 2000 hours on the 24th, Halsey ordered the entire 3rd Fleet north after Ozawa. Assuming that Kinkaid was keeping San Bernardino Strait under aerial observation and that the 7th Fleet commander would notice and be able to handle any attempt of Kurita's to break through, Halsey left not even a single destroyer to watch the strait. Ozawa had thus succeeded in opening the way for Kurita's attack. The Japanese plan, for all its weaknesses, seemed to be working.

While these events were taking place, Admiral Nishimura had been steaming toward Surigao Strait. Kurita's hesitancy before San Bernardino Strait now denied Nishimura the support he would have received had both Japanese elements attempted to penetrate Leyte Gulf simultaneously. Nishimura's smaller force would have to make the effort unaided. To make matters worse, Admiral Kinkaid was well aware of Nishimura's—and, by now, Shima's—approach, and he had sent the entire 7th Fleet Bombardment and Fire Support Group under Rear-Admiral Jesse B. Oldendorf to intercept and destroy the Japanese warships.

Oldendorf positioned his six battleships—most of them survivors of the Pearl Harbor attack—in a line across the northern end of Surigao Strait. Eight cruisers extended the flanks of this battle line, while 21 destroyers took their place on and ahead of both flanks. And at the southern entrance to the strait, 39 motor torpedo-boats deployed to make the first contact. Nishimura and Shima would have to run a gauntlet of torpedoes from the PT boats and destroyers and then come under the punishing weight of heavy shellfire from the battleships and cruisers that crossed the 'T' of their advance. It was a beautiful example of a classical naval tactic.

And it worked almost perfectly. Nishimura reached the entrance to Surigao Strait about an hour before midnight on October 24. He brushed aside the PT attacks with little difficulty and turned into the strait itself around 0200 hours on the 25th. Then, an hour later, the first of three separate but well coordinated destroyer torpedo attacks hit him. Performing their traditional role flawlessly, the American destroyers blew one Japanese battleship in two, damaged another, and sank two destroyers. The American cruisers and battleships then finished the job, sending Nishimura and most of his ships to the bottom. A damaged cruiser and destroyer, *Mogami* and *Shigure,* fled south. In the confusion, the American shelling also heavily damaged the destroyer *Grant* before Admiral Oldendorf could give the order to cease fire.

No sooner had Nishimura been disposed of, than Shima's force arrived. Unaware of the fate of Nishimura, Shima took a PT's torpedo in one of his cruisers, exchanged signals but little information with *Shigure,* and then suffered the ignominy of a careless collision between his flagship and *Mogami.* By 0500 hours, he was convinced that only complete destruction lay ahead: soon the surviving Japanese ships were in full retreat. Not all escaped, however, for American planes continued to harry them and exacted further losses. Of the two battleships, four cruisers, and eight destroyers that entered Surigao Strait with Nishimura and Shima, only a single cruiser and five destroyers were still afloat two weeks later.

At about 0530 hours on October 25, Admiral Kurita received word from Shima of the Japanese defeat in Surigao Strait. By this time, Kurita had passed through San Bernardino Strait and was speeding down the east coast of Samar towards Leyte Gulf. His passage was undetected, thanks to the fact that poor communications and misunderstood messages had left both Halsey and Kinkaid unaware that neither of them was guarding the vital strait.

An hour or so later, at daybreak, Kurita suddenly came upon what he believed to be a 'gigantic enemy task force', including many large carriers, cruisers, and destroyers, and perhaps even a battleship or two. Throughout the engagement that followed, he was never aware that the only force standing between him and Leyte Gulf consisted of half a dozen slow and tiny escort carriers, three destroyers, and four puny destroyer escorts. These ships, commanded by Rear-Admiral Clifton F. Sprague, were the northernmost of three similar task units operating under Kinkaid in support

Samar: 'We were saved by the definite partiality of Almighty God' Sprague

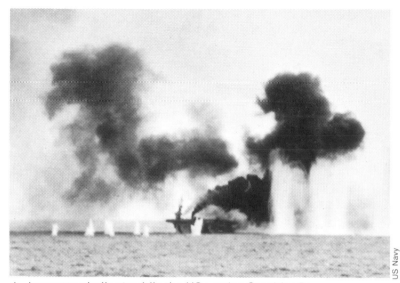
△ Japanese shells straddle the US carrier *Gambier Bay*

△ Scene aboard another US carrier at the height of the chase
▽ An Avenger is prepared for take-off aboard the *Kitkun Bay*

Cape Engaño: 'I turned my back on the opportunity I had dreamed of since my days as a cadet' Halsey

This map shows the triple Japanese threat to the US landings in Leyte Gulf, with the dispositions of the two US fleets. Of the four Japanese admirals only Ozawa played his role correctly; but his success in drawing off Halsey's 3rd Fleet was wasted by Kurita's premature retreat and the defeat of the Nishimura/Shima force

△ Japanese carrier *Zuiho,* completely open to attack
▽ One of Ozawa's carriers dodges US bombs

of the Leyte landings.

Kurita was momentarily confused by the sudden encounter, but Sprague wasted no time. He ordered his planes aloft and called back those out on missions, headed for the cover of a nearby rain squall, and sent out a frantic plain-language radio call for help. A moment later Kurita's powerful flotilla attacked, sweeping down on the fleeing American vessels and discharging a murderous barrage of fire. To Sprague it seemed improbable that any of his command 'could survive another five minutes'.

What followed was an incredible series of events. The American ships used smoke, rain squalls, and excellent seamanship to dodge and evade their pursuers. Sprague sent his destroyers and destroyer escorts in repeated and remarkably courageous attacks on the heavier Japanese vessels, while overhead the American planes, unopposed in the air, made strike after strike at the increasingly frustrated Japanese. These counterblows caused great confusion in Kurita's units. They forced the Japanese to take evasive action, split their formations, crippled three cruisers, and all but destroyed Kurita's control of his forces.

But Sprague's men paid heavily for their boldness. Despite remarkably poor Japanese marksmanship, the volume and weight of fire was too much to allow the exposed American vessels to remain unscathed. By about 0900 hours, one of the fleeing escort carriers had been sunk along with three of the gallant destroyers and destroyer escorts. A similar fate for the rest of Sprague's command seemed imminent.

At this moment, what Sprague later referred to as 'the definite partiality of Almighty God' took a hand. Kurita—confused about the situation, believing that he had done as much damage as he could to a powerful and swift American battle force which was now outrunning him, anticipating continued airstrikes, and still determined to reach Leyte Gulf—broke off the action. He ordered his scattered warships to fall back and reorganise. 'I could not believe my eyes,' Sprague was to recall. 'It took a whole series of reports from circling planes to convince me.'

But the agony of his small force was not yet over. Two hours after Kurita gave up his pursuit, Sprague's vessels came under a new and no less fearsome type of attack. That morning Japanese suicide planes had carried out the first organised *Kamikaze* strike of the war against some of the other 7th Fleet escort carriers. Now it was Sprague's turn. Nine of these macabre craft swept in low over the water to avoid the American radar, climbed swiftly at close range, and then hurled themselves down on their surprised targets. American gunners destroyed some of them, but several scored hits on the vulnerable escort carriers, sinking one and badly damaging others. A second *Kamikaze* attack, 20 minutes later, sank no ships but inflicted heavy damage and casualties.

Kurita, meanwhile, was headed back toward San Bernardino Strait. After briefly resuming his advance on Leyte Gulf, he had finally concluded that the game was no longer worth the candle. Not only did he believe that he would be faced with a mighty combination of aroused American naval and air power, but—and this was the decisive factor in his reasoning—he felt that by now most of the American transports in Leyte Gulf had unloaded and withdrawn. He had, he thought, already destroyed a large American carrier unit. To risk his country's last major naval striking force for the sake of a few empty cargo vessels seemed ridiculous. It was about 1230 hours when he gave the order to turn north. Leyte Gulf was then but 45 miles away.

Far to the north, Halsey had finally come to grips with Ozawa. From early morning of the 25th until late afternoon, 3rd Fleet carrier pilots under the tactical direction of Vice-Admiral Marc A. Mitscher pounded away at the all but defenceless Japanese decoy force. By the end of the day, of his original 17 ships, Ozawa had lost all four carriers, a cruiser, and two destroyers. That the destruction was not greater was the direct consequence of Halsey's attention being diverted sharply elsewhere.

Beginning shortly after 0800 hours, Halsey had received from Admiral Kinkaid a series of increasingly desperate reports on Sprague's situation accompanied by sharp pleas for aid. He continued to chase Ozawa, nevertheless, in the firm belief that the Japanese carriers still represented the major threat and primary target. But at 1000 hours he received a sharp message from Admiral Nimitz, who had been monitoring Kinkaid's communications from his headquarters at Pearl Harbor. Nimitz's message, a query about the situation rather than an order, finally caused Halsey to change his mind. Just before 1100, he directed most of the 3rd Fleet to turn south after Kurita, leaving Mitscher with a carrier striking force to finish off Ozawa from the air. 'At that moment,' Halsey was to write, 'Ozawa was exactly 42 miles from the muzzles of my 16-inch guns. . . . I turned my back on the opportunity I had dreamed of since my days as a cadet.'

Leyte Gulf: the Four-Stage Epic

Phase One: Battle of Sibuyan Sea. Kurita, Shima, and Nishimura *(orange tracks)* head for Leyte Gulf. US air strikes sink battleship *Musashi* in Kurita's force and damage others. Nishimura is also attacked. Land-based Japanese attacks from Luzon airfields sink carrier *Princeton* in US 3rd Fleet. Halsey, locating the southerly approach of Ozawa's force, concentrates 3rd Fleet and sets off to engage Ozawa, leaving 7th Fleet to cover Leyte Gulf; Kurita and Nishimura continue toward San Bernadino and Surigao Straits

Phase Two: Battle of Surigao Strait. Without Shima's support, Nishimura heads directly into Surigao Strait in line-ahead. US destroyers on both sides of the strait savage the Japanese line with torpedoes, sinking battleship *Fuso*. Oldendorf deploys his US cruisers and battleships across the mouth of the strait, crossing the Japanese 'T'; and a heavy barrage of gunfire halts and repulses the Japanese remnants. Nishimura goes down in *Yamashiro*; Shima arrives too late to be of any assistance and his ships play no further part

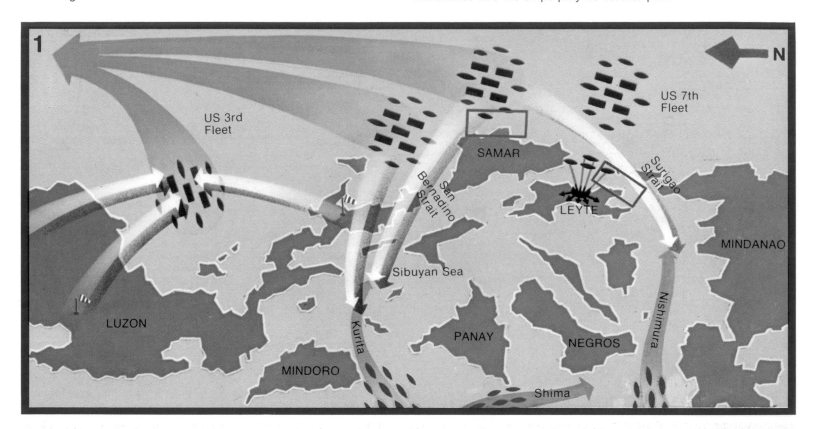

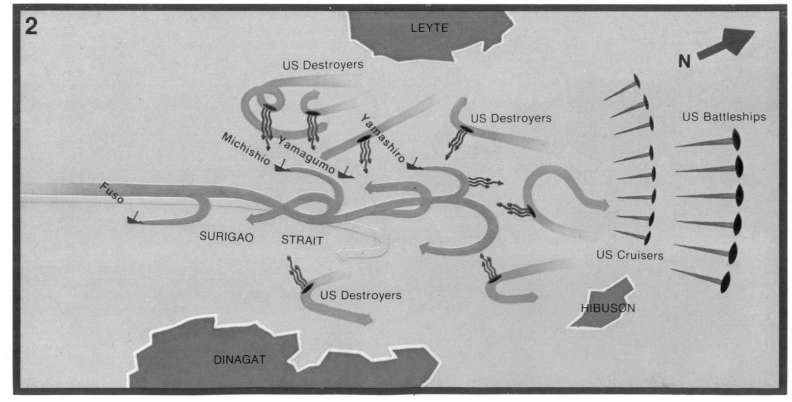

Phase Three: Battle off Samar. Kurita's force emerges from San Bernadino Strait and swings south toward Leyte Gulf, surprising Sprague's small carrier force which turns and runs south. Japanese cruisers *(orange track at top)* steadily overhaul the fleeing US carriers and Sprague is only saved from annihilation by Kurita's retreat, pursued by repeated US air strikes. But Sprague's ships still have to cope with long-range *Kamikaze* attacks *(diagonal white track)* which sink the carrier *St Lô* and damage several other 7th Fleet vessels

Phase Four: Battle of Cape Engaño. Halsey and Mitscher, with an overwhelming superiority, head north to finish off Ozawa's carrier force. Ozawa's ships are defenceless against the US carrier attacks and he loses three carriers to repeated strikes. Halsey is forced to head back toward Samar due to the crisis caused by Kurita's arrival there, but he is too late to engage Kurita. Mitscher launches further air strikes against the remnants of Ozawa's force, but his planes only succeed in sinking a light cruiser as Ozawa retires north

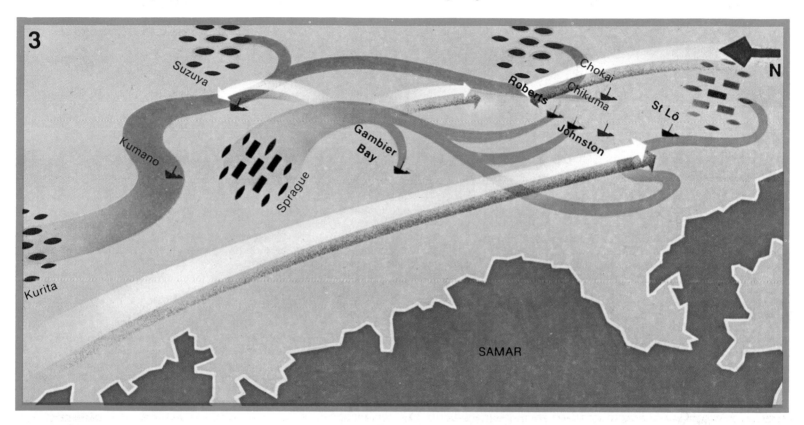

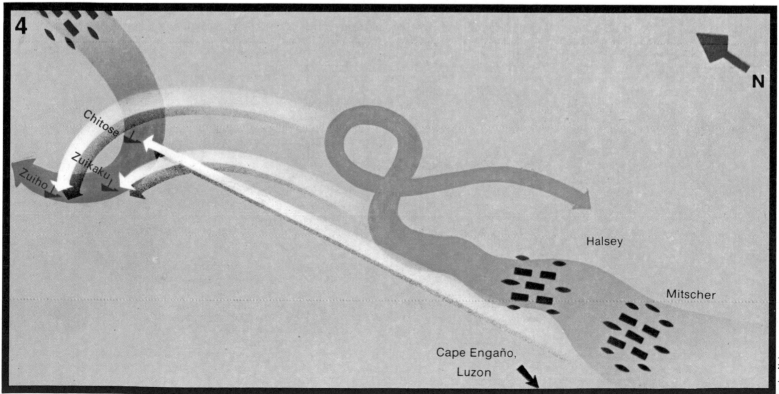

Lesley Noke

369

Leyte: end of the land battle

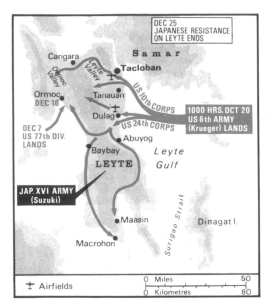

The campaign on the ground

A 155-mm 'Long Tom' bombards the Carigara sector in northern Leyte

But it was now too late to catch Kurita, who escaped practically unscathed through San Bernardino Strait. All that Halsey's mighty force of battleships and cruisers was able to overtake and sink was a single Japanese destroyer. The huge armada had covered a total distance of 600 miles in a futile race north and then south, without actually engaging either Ozawa or Kurita.

While the Battle of Leyte Gulf ended in the destruction of a major portion of the Combined Fleet and the removal of the primary threat to the Leyte beach-head, it also served to nurture a growing body of criticisms, recriminations, and second-guessing. Yet out of the welter of confusion and argument that surround the battle, certain conclusions suggest themselves.

First, given what he knew, Halsey was justified in going after Ozawa. Had the Japanese carriers been loaded with planes—as he had every reason to believe—he would have been foolhardy to ignore them. Nevertheless, he should have left at least a destroyer patrol to watch San Bernardino Strait. Second, if the decision to go after the carriers was correct, then Halsey was probably wrong to turn south just when he was about to make the kill. And finally, even if Halsey's chase north had permitted Kurita to fight his way into Leyte Gulf—and this is debatable, in light of the presence of Admiral Oldendorf's battle line and the planes from Kinkaid's escort carriers—it is doubtful if Kurita could have done significant damage or held up American operations ashore more than a week or two.

The American naval victory had secured MacArthur's communications and supply line and the seaward flank of the 6th Army. By the end of October, Krueger's troops had completely occupied the Leyte Valley and all of the airfields in the east-central part of the island. But now the invaders encountered a more difficult foe than even the Japanese, an enemy that increasingly frustrated the American effort. This was the weather: continuous drenching rain and high winds that soaked men and supplies, blew over shelters, and turned the ground into a morass of mud and giant puddles. Thirty-five inches of rain in the first 40 days of the campaign proved far too much for the low, poorly drained ground to absorb.

The worst that MacArthur's staff had feared came to pass when it proved impossible to put the newly captured airstrips into any reasonable shape. One field, at Tacloban, was operational. The strip at Dulag was able to handle a few planes by the end of November. But it was not until December that a new field could be built on more solid ground at Tanauan, in time to support the end of the campaign.

Until then, however, only a few American fighters could be advanced to Leyte, and these were too busy fighting off Japanese airstrikes—staged from dryer bases in the central and northern Philippines—to do much in the way of supporting the infantry.

Nor could General Kenney's bombers be moved forward to the primitive, muddy Leyte fields. So the bulk of support missions had to be flown from Kinkaid's battered escort carriers and Halsey's tired and overworked larger ships. It was late November before direct-support missions could take off from Leyte airstrips, and no more than a dozen strikes were made from these fields before the end of the year.

With the weather as their ally, the Japanese, who by now had determined to make an all-out defence of Leyte, were able to bring in enough additional troops through the western port of Ormoc to prolong the struggle for many weeks. Before the battle was over, more than 45,000 Japanese reinforcements reached General Suzuki's embattled XXXV Army, despite the valiant and at times extremely successful efforts of American aircrews to knock out the Japanese convoys. Japanese air strength in the central Philippines also increased somewhat as both army and navy planes staged forward to the area. These aircraft harried the American airstrips, struck at the beach-head, and launched *Kamikaze* attacks in growing numbers at American shipping.

The Japanese never really won air control over Leyte itself, but they kept the Americans from achieving it until the campaign was just about over. They could not, however, prevent a 6th Army ground build-up, as General Krueger brought in additional divisions to strengthen his own forces, nearly doubling his combat elements by mid-December.

During November, a bitter struggle took place on the ground. The American 10th Corps secured north-eastern Leyte but ran into stubborn Japanese defences along the steep ridges and rough, rocky hills that blocked the northern entrance to the Ormoc Valley. The 24th Corps cleared the southern portion of the island. It had little luck, however, in its attempt to penetrate the mountain barrier in central Leyte. Elements of the 7th Division finally pushed overland along an unguarded trail that crossed the island's narrow waist. But as these units turned north toward Ormoc in the middle of the month they were halted and thrown back by an aggressive Japanese defence of a series of spiny ridgelines running inland from Ormoc Bay.

In all of these operations, Krueger was seriously hampered by the continued tropical downpour which blinded men and inundated supply areas, turned roads into streams of slippery mud, frustrated construction efforts, and made a quagmire of the island. The Japanese, shielded by the central mountains from the full force of the north-east monsoons, were hampered only slightly less. Yet they were operating on shorter lines and, since this sort of weather always favours the defence, they had more to gain than to lose from the heavy rains.

Still, the XXXV Army was gradually being squeezed in a tightening

A surprise Japanese air raid smashes a Liberty Ship

US infantrymen close in on a Japanese machine-gun nest

vice between the northern Ormoc Valley and the ridges south of Ormoc. From Manila, therefore, Yamashita ordered Suzuki to make a major effort to recapture the Leyte airfields and regain the initiative on the island. General Tominaga agreed to help with a paratroop drop on the airstrips and all available army and navy planes were also to be thrown into the offensive.

The operation began in late November with a series of heavy but largely unsuccessful airstrikes. A small Japanese raiding party attempted to crash-land four transports on the airfields, but one plane was shot down and the others missed their mark and came down in Leyte Gulf or on the beach, where they did no damage. A larger airdrop—planned in brigade strength but actually carried out by barely 350 men—took place with somewhat more success on the night of December 5. The paratroops succeeded in occupying Buri airstrip and destroying supplies and installations there, but superior American forces wiped them out within a few days.

Suzuki's ground offensive, meanwhile, had been delayed by rough terrain, the poor condition of the Japanese units, and the swift reaction of the Americans. Of two divisions assigned to seize the airfields, only about two infantry battalions were able to advance far enough to make a disorganised and confused attack. Like the paratroops, they caused little real damage.

Ironically enough, the targets of the Japanese offensive, including the one airstrip temporarily occupied, had been all but abandoned by the end of November. American engineer officers had concluded that rain, poor drainage, and unstable soil conditions made the muddy strips all but unredeemable. The Japanese assault thus achieved almost nothing, except to throw a fright into some of the rear-echelon 6th Army troops. Yamashita failed completely to disrupt American air operations or to delay appreciably Krueger's advance. Indeed, by dissipating Suzuki's strength, he helped to ensure continued American success.

The final American offensive on Leyte began on December 5 with a drive by the 10th Corps into the northern Ormoc Valley, and simultaneous attacks by the 24th Corps in central and south-western Leyte. Two days later, the 77th Division landed virtually unopposed just below Ormoc. Despite Japanese attempts to disrupt the landing from the air, the division pushed into the city against increasing resistance and finally secured it on the 10th. The commitment of Japanese troops to the abortive attack on the airfields had made it difficult for General Suzuki to shift forces to meet this new threat.

Further north, the American 10th Corps' drive had less initial success, since most of XXXV Army remained dug into the rough terrain across the top of the Ormoc Valley. Still, the increased American pressure here tied down Suzuki's units, easing the going for the 24th Corps and 77th Division. American success in the

south now denied the Japanese their main supply port on Leyte, cut off many XXXV Army troops still operating inland, and compressed the remainder in the narrow corridor of the Ormoc Valley. American artillery and aircraft pounded the trapped Japanese.

The battle for Leyte was all but over. General Krueger continued to tighten the vice on the stubborn, courageous, but all but helpless defenders. Pressed from three sides, Suzuki was slowly forced out of the Ormoc Valley and into final positions in the rugged wilderness of western Leyte. On December 19, he learned from General Yamashita that he would receive no more reinforcements or other aid. By now there was little left of the XXXV Army but scattered elements, harried from position to position by the overwhelming American pressure. Of the more than 65,000 Japanese troops that had fought on Leyte, no more than 15,000 were left.

Final messages from Yamashita reached Suzuki on the 25th. These directed him to evacuate those troops that he could to other islands in the central Philippines, and then bid the XXXV Army commander a sad farewell. On the same day, General MacArthur announced the end of organised resistance on Leyte. The grim and dangerous business of mopping up continued for several months, however. Suzuki himself, with part of his staff, did not leave the island until late March 1945. Three weeks later he was dead, the victim of an American airstrike.

The Leyte campaign in all its phases—air, sea, and land—cost the United States approximately 5,000 dead and 14,000 wounded and a relatively light toll in planes and warships. It had taken longer than planned, less because of Japanese resistance than as a result of the fierce opposition of the elements. The bad weather and unsuitable soil conditions on the island also prevented Leyte from becoming the major base that American strategists had hoped to make of it. Yet the accomplishments at Leyte far outweighed the costs and disappointments of the victory.

The Japanese defeat at Leyte, the failure of the *Sho* plan, was a heavy blow to Japan's fortunes. In the abortive attempt to hold the island, a major portion of Japanese airpower, the bulk of the Japanese fleet, and an important segment of the Japanese army were all destroyed. Japan's air force was reduced to the terrifying but indecisive strategy of *Kamikaze* attacks, the fleet was no longer capable of significant offensive action, and the army was isolated on hundreds of Pacific islands without hope of support or rescue. Finally, the American return to the Philippines cut the Japanese supply line to the resources of the Indies and denied the home islands the means to wage effective warfare.

'Our defeat at Leyte,' said Admiral Mitsumasa Yonai, the Navy Minister, 'was tantamount to the loss of the Philippines. And when you took the Philippines, that was the end of our resources.'

BATTLE OF THE BULGE: THE ONSLAUGHT

**Ardennes, Belgium
December 16/19, 1944**

Peter Elstob

By early December 1944, Hitler had achieved a near-impossible: out of the armies which had fought, lost, and disintegrated in Normandy, France, Belgium, and the approaches to the German frontier, he had built up a new army group on the Western Front. What was more, this new force was intended not merely to hold the front, but to hurl itself on the weakest American sector, sweep westward to the Meuse as in 1940, and reach the Channel in one of the most daring armoured counteroffensives in history. The onslaught was the heaviest Panzer attack ever seen on the Western Front, and its success depended on the strictest adherence to a taut timetable of vital objectives. This is the story of how the disorganised and often panic-stricken American defenders met the full fury of what soon became known as the 'Battle of the Bulge'.

Right: German soldiers advance on the first day of the Ardennes offensive

As early as August 19, 1944, just after the successful Allied landings on the Mediterranean coast of France and on the actual day that almost the last of the German armour in the West was destroyed in the Falaise pocket, Hitler issued the following order: 'Prepare to take the offensive in November . . . some 25 divisions must be moved to the Western Front in the next one to two months.'

But how? Where, after the gigantic losses of men and material, could Germany find 25 divisions? The Führer's generals told him it would be a miracle if the Wehrmacht could replace half its losses; to create a whole new army group was impossible. Hitler replied that he would once again show them how to achieve the impossible.

For the first time Germany was put on a total war footing. Dr Goebbels was given dictatorial powers to increase war production and direct men into the army. The call-up age was lowered to 16, and no one escaped the scraping of the manpower barrel: non-essential workers, small shopkeepers, civil servants, university students, officer candidates in training, men formerly listed as unfit, prisoners from the jails—all were sucked into the great maw. Despite the heavy bombing, German war production actually increased to all-time records. After six to eight weeks' concentrated training, these new soldiers, *Volksgrenadiers* (People's Infantry), were equipped and ready to go into the line; and by the beginning of November Hitler had, to the amazement of his generals, replaced his lost mobile reserve and sent 18 new divisions to the West.

The problem of where to mount his great offensive occupied a lot of Hitler's thinking, but one area had long attracted him—the heavily wooded hills where Luxembourg, Belgium, and Germany meet, known in Germany as the Eifel and in Belgium and Luxembourg as the Ardennes. It was an historic German invasion route, the scene of his great success in 1940. And—miraculously—it was the weakest-held section of the entire 450 miles of the Western Front.

That fact was decisive: once again it would be the Ardennes.

This time Hitler planned everything himself and although, for the sake of morale, the old but still much respected Field-Marshal Gerd von Rundstedt was persuaded to come out of retirement and assume nominal command, the Führer actually directed the battle from a new headquarters in the West.

Three armies—two armoured and one infantry—were joined to make Army Group B, commanded by Field-Marshal Model, an aggressive attacker and master of improvisation, who had prevented total defeat on the Eastern Front three times. The VI SS Panzer Army, which would spearhead the attack, was given to one of Hitler's oldest comrades, Josef 'Sepp' Dietrich, ex-sergeant-major in the regular German army, the Führer's personal bodyguard in the early street-brawling days of the Nazi Party, and former commander of the famous I SS Panzer Division, 'Leibstandarte Adolf Hitler' (Hitler's Bodyguard).

Moving alongside VI SS Panzer Army and adding weight to the left hook would be V Panzer Army commanded by another of Hitler's 'fighting generals' from the Eastern Front, Hasso von Manteuffel. The important task of throwing up a wall to cover the southern flank of the attack was given to the German VII Army commanded

by Erich Brandenberger, a general of the old school, unimaginative but dogged.

Hitler also decided to use the shattered German Parachute Corps once more to seize important crossroads behind the American lines and hold them open for his beloved SS Panzer divisions, and Colonel von der Heydte, a veteran of Crete, was ordered to get a force together. Also the Führer had one of his famous unorthodox ideas and sent for Otto Skorzeny, the man who had 'rescued' Mussolini. Skorzeny was ordered to train special units of German commandos dressed in Allied uniforms who would travel in captured vehicles ahead of the main force to seize bridges over the Meuse, the first big obstacle, and, as well, cause chaos behind the American lines by giving false orders, upsetting communications, and spreading rumours of great German successes.

An 85-mile sector of the front from Monschau in the north to Echternach in the south was chosen for the breakthrough. After a tremendous opening barrage, infantry in overwhelming strength would breach the American line in a dozen places through which the Panzers would pour in a classic Blitzkrieg, racing for the Meuse crossings before the Allies could regain their balance.

Once across the Meuse the second phase of the offensive, a double-pronged drive northwest to Antwerp, would begin. Army Group B's attack would be supported by one from General Student's XV Army in Holland, and when Antwerp and the Scheldt estuary had been taken the Allied forces in Europe would be cut in two and their four armies in the north—US 9th, US 1st, British 2nd, and Canadian 1st—could be destroyed. Then, Hitler thought, the Western Allies would be ready to make a separate peace, and Germany could switch all her forces to the East.

The German commanders in the field protested that the plan was far too ambitious. Old Field-Marshal von Rundstedt was scathing. 'Antwerp? If we reach the Meuse we should go down on our knees and thank God!'

But Hitler refused even to consider any of their alternative plans, insisting on his own and reminding them that their sole duty was to obey his orders. The field commanders' opposition and the tremendous logistic problems involved made the original date impossible and Hitler was forced to agree to several postponements. In the end he lost his patience, saying that generals are never ready to attack, and set a last unalterable hour, 0530 hours on Saturday December 16, 1944.

The final German strength was less than had been promised but more than the generals had expected, and their mood changed from deep pessimism to mild optimism. Without alerting Allied Intelligence, they had been able to move 20 divisions, including seven armoured, into the attack front which the Americans were holding with only six divisions, of which one was armoured.

The overall superiority in manpower was no more than five to two, which is about the minimum required for a successful attack. But the attacker chooses the ground as well as the time, and the main weight of the offensive—eight *Volksgrenadier* divisions and five Panzer divisions—was concentrated on 45 miles of the Ardennes held by two American infantry divisions, a squadron of reconnaissance cavalry, with the only reserve a single combat command of an untried armoured division.

In the north, this blitz front took in the

extreme right wing of 1st Army's 5th Corps, held thinly by the US 99th Infantry Division, six weeks in the line and yet to experience battle; and an inexplicably unguarded 2-mile gap between 5th Corps and General Middleton's 8th Corps front, the northernmost two-thirds of which was included in the mammoth breakthrough.

Next to the inter-corps gap, thinly stretched across a classic easy entry from Germany into Belgium known as the Losheim Gap (see map), were some 900 men of the 18th Cavalry Squadron who had not yet tied in with a newly-arrived division on their right. This was the 106th Infantry who, after a gruelling journey across France and Belgium, had taken over positions three days before on the forward or eastern slope of a high ridge known as the Schnee Eifel. Completely inexperienced and suffering from frostbite and 'trench foot' they were to prove easy meat for the attacking Germans.

The southern half of the blitz front, which was to be hit by V Panzer Army with three *Volksgrenadier* divisions, one parachute infantry division, and two Panzer divisions, was held by the 28th Infantry Division, holding US 8th Corps' centre. This veteran division had been badly mauled in the recent heavy fighting around Aachen, where it had lost 6,184 men, and had been sent to the quietest part of the Ardennes for rest and refitting.

Were five objectives possible?
The rest of Army Group B was to be committed on either side of the main thrust to destroy the American line and to supply flank protection for the advance. On 8th Corps' right General Patton's US 3rd Army was in the last stages of preparation for an all-out offensive through the Saar; on their left 5th Corps had begun, three days before the German attack, an attack north towards the Roer dams. Part of this attack entailed an unusual manoeuvre: the 2nd Infantry Division, greatly experienced and recently rested, had pushed an attack column through the middle of 99th Infantry Division and captured an important crossroads 4 miles inside Germany. The unexpected presence of this division and its supporting artillery was to help to upset VI SS Panzer Army's plans.

Army Group B would have to achieve five initial objectives, and achieve them quickly if there were to be any chance at all of reaching Antwerp. The first two objectives were the setting up of 'hard shoulders' at both ends of the assault front to secure the flanks and make sure that the attack could not be pinched out. Thirdly, Sepp Dietrich's crack SS Panzer divisions must quickly overrun the lightly held American line and race for the Meuse, securing the bridges within 24 or at the most 48 hours. Fourth, General von Manteuffel's right-hand armoured punch must move alongside the SS Panzer divisions and, even though their route was longer, keep up with them, and also capture the important road and rail centre of St Vith along the way. Fifth, Manteuffel's left-wing attack must first capture Bastogne, the equally vital communications centre in the south, and go on to seize bridges over a third section of the Meuse.

The long night of December 15, 1944, was one of the darkest and coldest of that dark, cold winter. By midnight everything was ready on the German side—some 200,000 men with more tanks, guns, and ammunition than for many months past, waited to start

The 'blitz front' of the Ardennes

The German plan *Wacht am Rhein* ('Watch on the Rhine') gambled on a surprise breakthrough against US 8th Corps, strung out weakly along the Ardennes front. Some 80,000 unprepared Americans were to be struck by 200,000 keyed-up Germans

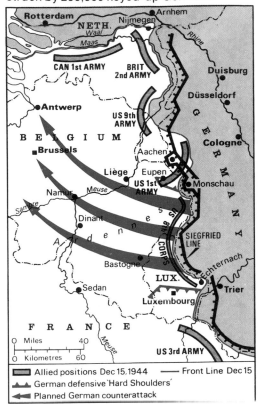

Allied positions Dec 15, 1944 ——— Front Line Dec 15
▲▲ German defensive 'Hard Shoulders'
◀━ Planned German counterattack

the biggest German offensive on the Western Front since 1940. Far to the rear Colonel von der Heydte's 1,250 paratroops, many about to jump for the first time, waited for trucks to carry them to the airfields. Skorzeny's men, in Allied uniforms and driving Allied vehicles, were lined up behind the leading tanks of the I SS Panzer Division, joking among themselves about it being too late to learn any more English and privately wondering if they would be shot if captured. The assault troops, many going into battle for the first time, tried to get some rest before the opening barrage. They had been thrilled by a multitude of stirring 'Orders of the Day'—from their own commanders, from the famous Field-Marshals von Rundstedt and Model and from the Führer himself. Many of them believed that they were about to take part in a great battle which would somehow miraculously win the war for Germany after all.

In the path of this mighty force were about 80,000 Americans, most of whom were sleeping peacefully, completely unaware of the storm that was about to break over them—for German security had been superb, Allied Intelligence sadly deficient. Some of these soldiers had not yet heard a shot fired in earnest; some had heard too many, and had been sent here so that their shattered nerves could recover. Most were thinking about their chance for leave at the many rest centres in the Ardennes or the promised Christmas festivities, a Christmas that many would never see.

Promptly at 0530 hours, the concentrated German artillery opened fire and almost all American positions were pounded heavily for periods from 20 minutes to an hour and a half. The startled Americans behind the front line tumbled out of their sleeping bags into shelters. At the forward outposts, where

the wire communications were quickly knocked out, the soldiers peered into the pre-dawn murkiness and asked each other what the hell had happened to this quietest of all fronts.

When the barrage stopped, hundreds of searchlights flicked on, reflecting off the low cloud to create 'artificial moonlight'. Moments later, before the dazed Americans could recover, German shock troops surged forward to make gaps for their tanks or to seize their own first-day objectives.

Tactically the most important of these was the securing of the flanks by setting up 'hard shoulders' at either end of the attack front. While not as dramatic as the Panzer thrusts these defence lines were absolutely vital, for without them the strong Allied forces north and south of the Ardennes could pinch out the offensive.

The northern 'hard shoulder' was to run from the town of Monschau along a ridge road to Eupen (see map). Sepp Dietrich decided first to attack on either side of Monschau, and after his other three infantry divisions had breached the American front lines and launched the SS Panzer divisions on their dash westwards, they would wheel right and continue the defence wall as far as Liège.

A first, fatal setback

The attack north of Monschau was halted at a roadblock before dawn by the 102nd Cavalry Squadron who, in the light of star shells, inflicted 20% casualties on the *Volksgrenadiers,* and stopped the assault dead. South of Monschau the *Volksgrenadiers* hit a battalion of the 99th Infantry Division in good defensive positions on high ground. As soon as the barrage stopped, German assault troops, closely packed, advanced steadily on to the American dug in positions. The result was not battle, but slaughter, yet the young Germans kept coming—in at least three verified instances their bodies fell into the American foxhole line. They could not possibly succeed for they were too few (the unexpected US 5th Corps attack towards the Roer dams, which had started three days before, tied down most of the German troops assigned to the attack around Monschau) and without armoured support. The assault was broken off and an attempt later in the day to get it rolling again was repelled.

At the end of the first day the plan to set up the 'hard shoulder' in the north had failed completely—and this was a failure that was to become increasingly serious for the Germans.

Some 85 miles to the south, General Brandenberger's tactics called for one of his four *Volksgrenadier* divisions to cross the Sauer river before dawn east of Echternach (the Sauer runs west to east here) and another to cross west of the town. After joining up south of Echternach they would then seize high ground behind the American artillery, so forcing the guns to pull back. Once they had done so, pontoon bridges could be put in over the Sauer and the heavy guns and equipment needed to set up the southern 'hard shoulder' could be brought across. At the same time, a third *Volksgrenadier* division would cross the river further up and, after overrunning an unexperienced American armoured infantry battalion, wheel left to continue the southern 'hard shoulder'.

The Echternach sector of the American front was held by 4th Infantry Division's 12th Infantry Regiment, still about 500 to

600 men under strength. The *Volksgrenadiers* attacking them would number about 12,000—a four to one advantage—but many were newly-raised 17-year-olds, and they had few vehicles, no tanks, and only a handful of self-propelled guns—which helped to even out the odds.

The Sauer runs fast in December, and the German assault troops in rubber boats found the crossing difficult; some had to try several locations before getting across, thus upsetting the timetable; but the opening barrage knocked out communications and deluged the forward posts with shells. Many were overrun before they had time to give the alarm and at first—as elsewhere along the Ardennes front—there was complete confusion. Villages were taken, lost, and retaken with captors and prisoners changing rôles. In some places small bodies of American troops held out against the odds: 21 men turned a thick stone farmhouse into a fort and beat off all attacks for four days. Elsewhere, 60 Americans with only one machine-gun made a tourist hotel into a strongpoint, and held up the German advance long enough for relieving infantry to besiege the besiegers. But in many places the small American forces were simply overwhelmed.

The 60th Armoured Infantry Battalion, which had been given a small section of front a few days before for 'battle indoctrination', had about an hour's warning because the *Volksgrenadier* division sent against them was delayed by fog. Although greatly outnumbering the defenders, the Germans had no self-propelled guns, while the American armoured infantry—whose job is to protect its division's tanks—were fully equipped and wrought terrible damage on the German horse-drawn artillery and unarmoured transport. Although the American main line of resistance was penetrated several times the arrival of their reserves saved the situation and by nightfall the armoured infantry were still in position, blocking the *Volksgrenadiers*' attempt to join the Echternach attackers in forming a southern wall.

On this front, too, the Germans had failed to reach their main objectives. The American forward outposts had been overrun and the Germans were in force west of the Sauer, but they had failed to dislodge 4th Infantry Division's artillery, whose gunners were able to knock out the temporary bridges and prevent self-propelled guns or heavy mortars from being brought into play. Although the position of the American troops at the extreme southern flank of the Ardennes front was precarious, and would become more so before reinforcements arrived, the German advance had slipped behind schedule. Like the failure in the north, it was to have far-reaching effects on the battle.

Heady successes, serious setbacks

Along the line of the main attack the first 24 hours brought the Germans two main successes, one partial success, one serious failure, and three temporary setbacks which the plan could not afford.

The major success, like the major failure, took place on VI SS Panzer Army's front: a battlegroup spearheading I SS Panzer Division got through the gap between US 5th Corps and US 8th Corps and broke out into the unguarded rear areas. On the other hand XII SS Panzer Division and two divisions of *Volksgrenadiers,* who were to open gaps for the tanks, were held up all day.

The other major success was achieved by Manteuffel's force north of the Schnee ▷

375

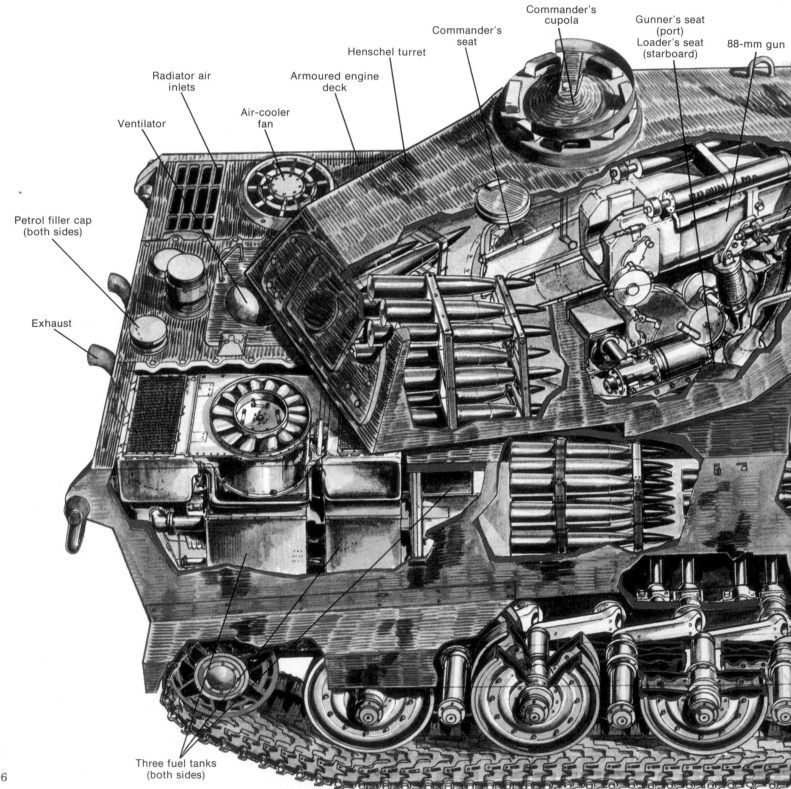

Commander's cupola

Commander's seat

Henschel turret

Gunner's seat (port)
Loader's seat (starboard)

88-mm gun

Radiator air inlets

Armoured engine deck

Air-cooler fan

Ventilator

Petrol filler cap (both sides)

Exhaust

Three fuel tanks (both sides)

John Batchelor

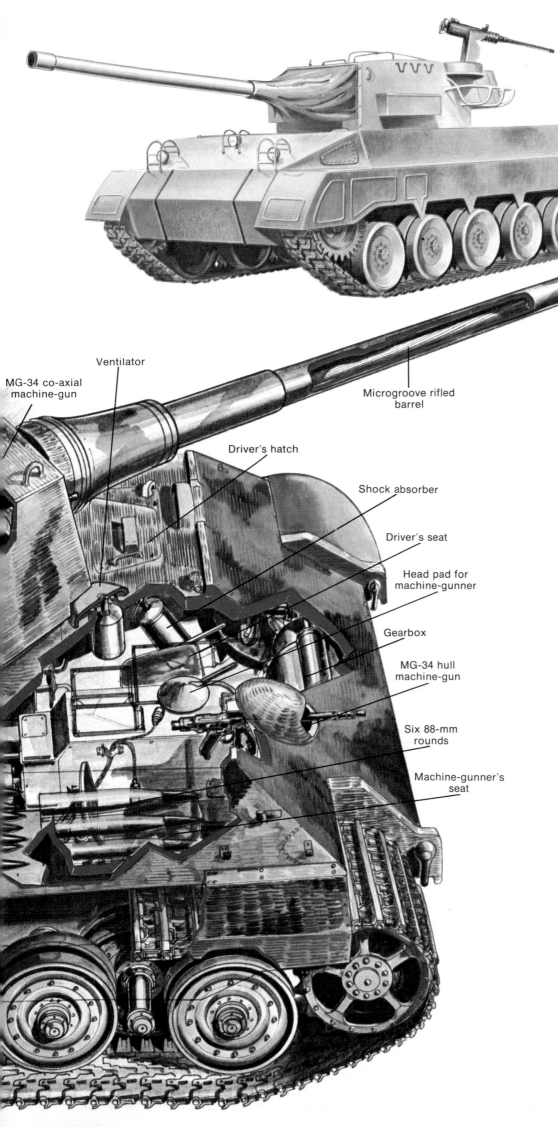

MG-34 co-axial machine-gun

Ventilator

Microgroove rifled barrel

Driver's hatch

Shock absorber

Driver's seat

Head pad for machine-gunner

Gearbox

MG-34 hull machine-gun

Six 88-mm rounds

Machine-gunner's seat

A new breed of tiger

'King Tiger' *(left)*. The Pzkw Mk VI Tiger II ('Königstiger') entered service in mid-1944 — and was one of the best protected, hardest-hitting tanks of the war. It was manufactured under the most difficult circumstances: Allied bombing of factories and the sources of essential materials produced a series of delays which limited the total production figure to 485 machines. Tiger II appeared with two different types of turret, Henschel (shown here), and Porsche. Both were used in a machine which was a vast improvement over Tiger I — with a longer gun, well-sloped armour, and a larger engine giving better all-round performance. Even so, Tiger II was underpowered and difficult to manoeuvre, particularly when crossing bridges. *Weight:* 68 tons. *Crew:* five. *Armour:* 185-mm (max), 40-mm (min). *Armament:* one 88-mm gun, two 7·9-mm MGs

'Hunting Tiger' *(top left)*. The Jagdpanzer VI ('Jagdtiger') was next in line of succession to the 'Elephant' heavy tank destroyer (see Vol 4, p. 1386). It was the heaviest armoured vehicle in use with the German army — but its manoeuvrability was hampered by excessive weight, and was in no way compensated by its immensely thick armour — or by its 128-mm gun, with its low rate of fire. *Weight:* 70 tons. *Crew:* six. *Armour:* 250-mm (max), 30-mm (min). *Armament:* one 128-mm gun, one 7·9-mm MG

'Hellcat' *(top right)*. The American M-18 ('Hellcat') was a lighter, high-powered version of the M-10 3-inch-gun motor carriage (see Vol 4, p. 1611). With a top speed of 55 mph, this fast, elusive tank-destroyer was used to hit and run rather than to stand and fight it out; and so it was the antithesis of the German Jagdpanzer. *Weight:* 20 tons. *Crew:* five. *Armour:* 25-mm (max). *Armament:* one 76-mm gun, two ·50-inch MGs

Eifel, which swept through the strung-out positions of the 18th Cavalry Squadron in the Losheim Gap and reached the main road to St Vith less than 10 miles from that vital communications centre. But again, his centre thrust, intended to go round the south of the Schnee Eifel and join up with his right-wing attack, thus entrapping two regiments of newly-arrived infantry along the top of the hill, was held up all day only a mile or so from their start line.

General Manteuffel's main effort to reach the Meuse came from his left wing, where the élite XLVII Panzer Corps of one Panzer and two infantry divisions (plus a division of parachute infantry from Brandenberger's VII Army) planned to cross the Our, cut the main north/south highway, and seize bridges over the next river to the west (the Clerf) in the first 24 hours. This would enable them to take Bastogne the next day and also to get their Panzers on good roads to the Meuse.

His centre thrust also fumbled when a Panzer division and its supporting infantry division were unable to cross the Our in their sector at all and the armour had to be sent south to get over by another bridge. But the II Panzer Division, destined to advance further than any other troops in the Battle of the Bulge, got across the Our and moved up the wooded slopes to seize the main highway (known as 'Skyline Drive' to the heavily-shelled drivers of the lorries who used it to carry supplies to the American 9th Army in the north) thus achieving a partial success. Somehow the outnumbered and exhausted 28th Infantry Division was able to prevent them from crossing the Clerf for the whole of the second day, a gallant stand which bought the precious hours needed to reinforce Bastogne.

Although, at the time, neither side was able to see it, the pattern that emerged at the end of the first two days' fighting determined the outcome of the battle, and these events are worth examining a little more closely.

In VI SS Panzer Army confidence ran high, for it had not only the best and shortest route to the Meuse but had been given the most tanks, guns, and men. Two main armoured punches were planned: XII SS Panzer Division ('Hitler Jugend') was to lead the right-hand one and its great rival, I SS Panzer Division ('Leibstandarte Adolf Hitler') the left. Each waited behind a *Volksgrenadier* division which was to make the initial breakthrough; these four divisions were opposed by four *battalions*—less than half a division—of the green 99th US Infantry Division. But, because of the Roer dams attack going in just to the north, there was an exceptional concentration of American artillery on this front.

The German barrage here was the heaviest of all. A few days before, a US Intelligence report had said that the German front opposite one of 99th Infantry's battalions seemed to be very lightly held, adding that there were only two horse-drawn guns there. After an hour's non-stop shelling the battalion executive officer reported: 'They sure worked those horses to death.'

As soon as the shelling stopped, assault troops hit every American forward position in strength and most of the riflemen were killed or captured. But when the *Volksgrenadiers* tried to exploit this success they were hammered by heavy howitzer and artillery fire and went to ground. Some of the 'Hitler Jugend' Division, impatient at the delay, tried to advance their tanks alone, but were stopped by large-calibre, high-explosive shells.

By dusk, about 1630 hours, the American survivors had formed strongpoints around their battalion command posts in the woods and, though reduced to half strength, somehow preserved a front. After only six weeks in the line these young soldiers had held up two élite SS Panzer divisions for an all-important 24 hours, the time needed to bring in other troops to hold the high ground behind the Elsenborn Ridge against which the 'Hitler Jugend' division was practically to destroy itself in the next few days before giving up and being moved to another part of the front.

But the leading battle group of the 'Leibstandarte Adolf Hitler' was commanded by one of Germany's toughest, most ruthless, and most daring SS Panzer leaders, Colonel Joachim Peiper, who demanded and got almost suicidal devotion from his men.

Disgusted at the failure of the *Volksgrenadiers* to open a breach for his battle group, he went forward and personally led his Panzers through the snarled-up rear areas, ordering them to run down anything that did not get out of their way. Breaking out into no-man's-land after dark, his spearhead lost five Panzers to old German mines. Carrying on all through the night, they seized the town of Honsfeld, far behind the American lines, at dawn on Sunday, December 17, capturing many vehicles and anti-tank guns and shooting down 19 unarmed American soldiers, the first of a number of atrocities perpetrated by these veterans from the bitter no-quarter fighting in Russia.

Peiper's vital breakthrough

In need of fuel, Peiper's men swung 2 miles off route into the 'Hitler Jugend' Division's zone and seized a large petrol dump at Büllingen, forcing 50 American soldiers to fill their tanks and then shooting them down in cold blood too, before swinging back on to their own route and pushing west as fast as possible.

Just after noon Peiper's men pierced an American column moving down from the north as reinforcements. This was part of the US 7th Armoured Division, on its way to St Vith. Only half an hour earlier Peiper's column would have run head on into their Armoured Combat Command and a great tank battle would have developed, but this had passed through and blind chance brought a field artillery observation battery of 125 men to the Malmédy crossroads at that precise moment. They could do nothing against the tanks and guns of a Panzer division and all were quickly captured. A couple of hours later, while standing in a field waiting to be marched back, these prisoners were machine-gunned by passing SS. Some were unconscious or feigned death but 86 died and the news of this massacre, reaching the Americans in front line positions that night by 'latrine telegraph', was responsible for a stiffening of the will to resist and an unwillingness to surrender.

Having apparently achieved a clean breakthrough, Peiper hoped to reach his objective—the bridge over the Meuse at Huy—by late that night or early the next morning. A few miles ahead of him lay Stavelot, and from there a good road ran almost due west 40 miles to the Meuse.

What happened next is something of a mystery still. His spearhead, racing on, was stopped when the leading half-tracks were knocked out; but this was no more than had been expected; and German countermoves knocked out two American tanks and captured more prisoners. But the encounter bred caution in the leaders, and the battle group's advance guard did not get to the high ground across the river from Stavelot until dusk. There they saw hundreds of American vehicles and jumped to the conclusion that they had reached a heavily defended position.

In fact the only combat troops in Stavelot were a single battalion of engineers who were constructing a roadblock: there were no tanks or anti-tank guns at all. The vehicles were trucks engaged in moving fuel out of a huge dump a few miles away. The leading German tanks ran on to a newly-laid American minefield and the commanders who, after all, had been on the move for 36 hours and advanced 25 miles, must have decided that they had pushed their luck far enough for they greatly exaggerated the strength of the defences. Uncharacteristically, Peiper did not come up to see for himself but consented to a halt—probably realising that he must now wind up his tail anyway.

Whatever the explanation the stopping of Battle Group Peiper at Stavelot on the second night of the offensive was the turning point in VI SS Panzer Army's offensive, for although in the next week this strong force would remain the main threat on the northern front, lack of support and particularly lack of fuel prevented its breaking out to the west. American reinforcements from the 82nd Airborne Division, the 30th Infantry Division, the 3rd Armoured Division, and other units bore down heavily on Battle Group Peiper, which became isolated from the rest of I SS Panzer Division.

The unexpected stiff resistance of the US 99th Infantry Division in front of I SS Panzer Corps and the delay caused by the extensive minefields on that front brought about colossal traffic jams behind the German attack front as horse-drawn artillery, supply trains, bridging equipment, reserves, and huge siege guns all pressed forward trying to keep to their time-tables.

Skorzeny—master of confusion

Otto Skorzeny personally led his group through this tangle, bypassing clogged roads by cutting across fields (and losing his most experienced commander on an old German mine) and so was able to dispatch three of his disguised commando teams towards the Meuse crossings. One actually got to the bridge at Huy and 'guarded' it all day, doling out terrifying rumours to passing American units. Other teams blew up ammunition dumps and destroyed communications but the main result of the presence of German soldiers in American uniforms far behind the front was to set in motion the most elaborate measures to check on everyone's identity. All jeeps or staff cars were stopped and passengers asked the names of comic strip characters, the league positions of baseball teams, or details of the private lives of film stars. Often the more senior American officers did not know the correct answer and many spent a few hours in custody. All this, combined with the stories of German paratroops dropping everywhere, tied up troops who were desperately needed in the fighting.

In fact, like Skorzeny's operation, the parachute drop was something of a farce, for lack of fuel for the transport trucks stopped the paratroops on the first night and postponed their drop for 24 hours, when the element of surprise was lost and it was almost certain that American reinforcements would be moving through the drop zone.

Strong crosswinds scattered the aircraft and the paratroops came down at widely separated spots. Many of these young, courageous volunteers, jumping in the black, freezing night for the first time, came down in remote parts of the Ardennes, far from houses or roads. Some broke arms or legs on landing and although some were found by American search parties or local people others lay in the snow and slowly died. Bodies were still being found the following spring.

Only ten or 15 bombers found the drop zone and Colonel von der Heydte discovered that he had only about 350 men, little food, no blankets, no weapons larger than small mortars and machine-pistols, and no radios working. Just after first light the paratroops heard the noise of heavy trucks climbing towards them from the north and moments later trucks crammed with American infantry rolled through their position. This was the 1st Infantry Division, the most experienced in the American army, veterans of three beach assaults—Africa, Sicily, and Normandy. Now they were on their way to reinforce the 99th Infantry Division and the 2nd Infantry Division, now being pulled back from the Roer dams attack to screen 99th Infantry's withdrawal to the Elsenborn Ridge. 'The Big Red One' Division would arrive just in time to shore up the southern flank and help block VI SS Panzer Army's attack in which Hitler had such high hopes.

In the next few days Colonel von der Heydte had to watch two more American divisions, the 7th Armoured and the 30th Infantry, move into the attack zone without his being able to do anything about it. What Omar Bradley has described as America's 'secret weapon', mobility, was being brought into play.

After four days, out of rations and suffering severely from the intense cold, Colonel von der Heydte ordered his men to break up into small parties and find their own way back. He sent back his American prisoners and, with them, his own wounded with a request to the American commander to look after them. Two days later, exhausted and ravenous, he surrendered himself. It was the end of the once-great German Parachute Corps, whose exploits had won the admiration of soldiers everywhere.

On VI SS Panzer Army's left General von Manteuffel planned a double-pronged drive around the Schnee Eifel, which would first trap the green 106th Infantry Division's troops there and would then go on to take St Vith, whose road and rail communications were absolutely essential to the second phase of the German offensive.

Attached to the 106th Division and guarding its left flank were 900 men of the 18th Cavalry Squadron in village strongpoints across the Losheim Gap. At dawn they were hit by both Manteuffel's right-wing attack of reinforced Volksgrenadiers and Sepp Dietrich's left, a division of parachute infantry whose main axis ran from Germany to Manderfeld, the reconnaissance cavalry's headquarters.

The 18th Cavalry Squadron was part of the 14th Cavalry Group, whose commander, Colonel Mark Devine, went forward from Manderfeld to try to discover what was happening on his front. In some places the first German assaults had been beaten off,

but other small groups had been overwhelmed before they could do much more than radio for artillery support. Realising that this was a major attack and that his outposts were hopelessly outnumbered, Devine ordered those who were able to do so to disengage and fall back. He got through to his superiors at 106th Division HQ in St Vith and proposed a new flank defence line across the western end of the Losheim Gap to be followed by a counterattack as soon as his reserve squadron arrived. This was agreed to, for no one at divisional headquarters realised that both proposals were quite unreal in the light of the strength of the German attack.

Rumours, confusion—and panic

When Devine got back to his headquarters in Manderfeld about 1100 hours, he found it a shambles, with his staff frantically packing and trying to destroy their records. Floods of refugees had been pouring in with stories of terrible disasters and German successes. Their terror was unnerving. Panic swept through 14th Cavalry Group HQ and the staff piled into their vehicles with what personal possessions they could grab; and, in an attempt to destroy anything which might aid the Germans, they simply set fire to the whole town, destroying it completely. It was the beginning of a series of disorganised retreats which became a long nightmare, only ending some 60 hours and four commanding officers later, 25 miles to the rear, when the 14th Cavalry Group's survivors were attached to the 7th Armoured Division as part of the defence of St Vith.

When the cavalry broke off action and pulled back, Manteuffel's right wing raced through the Losheim Gap until it was halted by artillery near the village of Auw in front of St Vith. Here the commander of the 106th Infantry Division, General Alan Jones, only recently arrived on the Continent, was involved in his first battle. His main worry was the fate of his two regiments stuck out on the eastern side of the Schnee Eifel ridge. Wrongly believing that the 14th Cavalry was guarding his left flank, he sent one of his reserve battalions to stiffen his right flank and the other to engage Manteuffel's right wing, a mixed force of infantry and assault guns attacking the field artillery at Auw. These guns were then able to withdraw and take part in the all-important defence of St Vith itself, which took place over the next few days.

The southern prong of Manteuffel's attack around the Schnee Eifel had come under killing fire from 106th Division infantry on the southern slope of the hill, and after fierce hand-to-hand fighting in the streets of Bleialf, key to the road network there, the Germans had been halted less than 2 miles from their start line. Displeased, General Manteuffel ordered them to renew their attack at dawn, take Bleialf 'at all costs', and advance to join the northern prong, closing the trap on the two regiments of American infantry on the Schnee Eifel.

The 106th Division had lost little actual ground on the first day of the offensive and its inexperienced staff probably failed to realise the precariousness of their position. All through the night the Germans continued to move infantry and guns into the breaches they had made, in preparation for the next day's onslaught.

In answer to the 106th Division's request for reinforcements, 8th Corps gave it an armoured combat command, no longer needed for the Roer Dams attack, and during the evening of the 16th, promised that the 7th Armoured Division from the north was on its way and that its leading combat command would arrive at 0700 hours the next morning. This estimate was hopelessly out, for it had not taken into account either the winter road conditions or the traffic jams being caused by the disorganised headlong retreat of many rear troops. In fact the main body of tanks of the 7th Armoured did not arrive at St Vith until late on Sunday afternoon, too late to save the two regiments on the Schnee Eifel. It took the tanks five hours to cover the last 12 miles against a tide of panic-stricken staff and rear area troops.

By nightfall on December 17, some 8-9,000 American troops were surrounded in the Schnee Eifel. Two days later, without having incurred more than a few casualties or inflicted any serious damage on the encircling Germans who did not outnumber them but who did have tanks and self-propelled guns, they all surrendered. It was, as the official American history says, the most serious reverse suffered by American arms in the European theatre.

Jubilantly the Germans moved in for the kill at St Vith.

The central blow

The V Panzer Army's main effort, an attack by two Panzer corps in the centre, although destined to be the most successful of all, did not get off to the flying start planned. On the German right 58th Panzer Corps of a division of Volksgrenadiers followed by the 116th Panzer Division, planned to roll through a single regiment of the 28th Infantry Division (the 112th), holding trenches east of the Our river, and go flat out for the Meuse through the vacuum between Bastogne and St Vith, which it was expected the attacks on both those places would create.

South of this thrust XLVII Panzer Corps' XXVI Volksgrenadier Division would seize bridges over the Our for the armour of the élite II Panzer Division, and both infantry and tanks would smash through the centre of US 28th Infantry Division's front, held by their 110th Regiment, get across the Clerf river 6 or 7 miles further west, and go on to capture Bastogne. As an added precaution, one of General Brandenberger's divisions of parachute infantry would move alongside this attack, cutting the 110th Infantry Regiment off from the 109th further south.

It was a good plan and should have succeeded quickly, for the Germans numbered about 50,000 while the American defenders consisted of 14 companies of riflemen (about 3,250 combat troops) supported by artillery and howitzer positions, and one battalion of tanks. But, of course, only a part of the total German strength could be brought to bear at the beginning of the attack.

On 58th Panzer Corps' front the American defenders, being east of the Our, maintained intact bridges behind them capable of taking tanks and self-propelled guns. If these could be taken by surprise, the Panzers could get off to the flying start they needed to reach the Meuse.

To make sure of surprise General von Manteuffel ordered that this section of the front would not receive the pre-dawn opening barrage but, instead, white-clad Volksgrenadiers would quietly penetrate the rear areas of the American front line before dawn and, when the attack began, move swiftly to seize the two bridges.

Had the *Volksgrenadiers* on this front been more experienced or the defending infantry less so this plan might have succeeded, but the German division were a scratch lot of ex-garrison troops from Norway and Denmark, most of whom had never seen action. The first part of the plan worked—shock companies of *Volksgrenadiers* penetrated the American forward line during the night and, as soon as the barrage began—an hour later here than on the rest of the front—moved through the gaps in the long, deep, barbed-wire defences which the Americans had left open for moving up supplies at night.

The Germans achieved complete surprise. In one case they burst into a clearing just as a platoon was lined up for breakfast. The sudden fire of machine-pistols and exploding grenades killed a number of Americans and the rest broke. The white-clad shock troops moved swiftly towards the bridges—and here their inexperience was their undoing. Flushed with success they advanced openly on to defended pillboxes and manned trenches. The veterans of the US 112th Infantry Regiment, who had lost 2,000 out of 3,000 in the bitter Hurtgen Forest fighting the month before, picked the invaders off with rifle fire, sprayed them with machine-guns and, when they took refuge in gullies, plastered them with mortar fire. German casualties were very heavy here and elsewhere on this part of the front and by nightfall all the bridges were still in American hands.

The *Volksgrenadiers* had been badly mauled and the Panzer division had lost six tanks. Manteuffel's centre thrust was badly behind schedule and, in an attempt to catch up, the 116th Panzer Division was ordered to send a battalion of light tanks (Mk IVs) 5 or 6 miles south and cross the Our over a bridge which had been established by the XLVII Panzer Corps. The Mk IVs were then to turn north, come back along the American side of the Our, and take the bridges on 58th Panzer Corps' front from the rear.

The Panzer schwerpunkt

General Hasso von Manteuffel's main hope of reaching the Meuse lay with his XLVII Panzer Corps, the Wehrmacht's 'Number One Reserve' on the Western Front. For the Ardennes offensive this consisted of a first-class infantry division from the Eastern Front ('The Old XXVI', renamed the XXVI *Volksgrenadiers*) and the famous II Panzer Division, which had fought the Allies with spirit and courage all the way from Normandy to Germany. In reserve another crack division, Panzer Lehr, was to be thrown in to add weight to the *schwerpunkt*.

The XXVI *Volksgrenadiers* were given a particularly difficult rôle: they had to force the Our river, advance 7 or 8 miles and force the Clerf river, hold both these open for the armour to cross, and then follow the Panzers on foot 15 more miles to Bastogne, which it was then their task to take.

In order not to alert the Americans, *Volksgrenadier* shock troops were not allowed to cross the Our before the opening barrage but XXVI *Volksgrenadier's* commanding officer, Major-General Kokott, pointed out that he had been in the habit of putting men over the river at night and holding a line of outposts on the American side until dawn and not to do so would arouse sus-

Imperial War Museum

At the tip of the 'Bulge': SS Colonel Peiper with a scout team of his group. It was Peiper's battle group which committed the Malmédy massacre of US POWs in the early days of the breakthrough

picion. He was given permission to continue this practice on the night before the attack and, taking advantage of the concession, slipped two of his three regiments over the Our and moved them silently up through the woods to the north/south highway, 'Skyline Drive', on which the American 110th Infantry Regiment had based its main line of resistance. This highway was one of XLVII Panzer's first objectives.

General von Manteuffel's main armoured punch, II Panzer Division, was to cross the Our at Dasburg, move rapidly up 4 miles through wooded country to the small town of Marnach on Skyline Drive, seize this, and then move another 3 miles and capture the town of Clervaux, principal crossing place of the Clerf and headquarters of the 28th Division's 110th Infantry Regiment. From here good roads ran to Bastogne and beyond.

The German schedule called for all the Clerf river crossings to be held by nightfall of the first day—less than 12 hours after the opening barrage. It would be a tight schedule and unit commanders were impatient to get their men moving.

The 28th Infantry Division's 110th Regiment, holding this 10 miles of the Ardennes front, had based its defences on a series of fortified villages held in company strength and backed up by artillery positions. It was realised that the Germans could not be prevented from crossing the Our, and the ground between Skyline Drive and the Our was virtually no-man's-land used by both sides for patrolling. In the event of an attack, which as elsewhere in the Ardennes was regarded as almost an academic problem, it was intended first to hold Skyline Drive, the principal tactical feature, and next to deny the Germans the Clerf river bridges.

Fierce US resistance

On this front as elsewhere the opening barrage knocked out wire communications but the first contact was made, not at the front line, but at Holzthum west of Skyline Drive, 5 miles from the Our and only 4 miles from an important Clerf bridge. The attackers, of course, were some of the XXVI *Volksgrenadiers* who had quietly moved up during the night. They were beaten off by the Americans who had been alerted by the opening barrage and word was flashed at 0615 hours to regimental headquarters at Clervaux enabling 110th Infantry's other strongpoints to prepare to resist attack.

Failing to clear Holzthum by direct assault the XXVI *Volksgrenadiers* tried to work round north but came under fire from an artillery battalion which caused them to go to ground. Annoyed, the German commander ordered an attack against the guns which were without infantry support but this too failed. Again and again the *Volksgrenadiers* attacked the villages of Holzthum and Consthum, which barred their way to the Clerf crossing, but were unable to get past. It was an unexpectedly stubborn defence and it cost these German troops, who had hoped to be the first to cross the Clerf, all the time advantage they had gained by their night crossing of the Our. Desperately they attacked the American artillery position but the gunners put their shells on one-second fuses and fired over open sights—in some cases parts of the shells blew back on the gun positions. Although the battery commander and 15 of his gun crews became casualties, the position was held.

Other positions on this part of the American front also put up unexpectedly fierce resistance. At Wahlhausen, a cluster of houses on top of a hill with an all-round view, an American observation post of a single platoon beat off attack after attack until their ammunition ran out. After dark the Germans shelled them with anti-aircraft guns and came on in force. The last message from Wahlhausen was a request for American artillery fire on top of them; only one man survived. The rest of the company to which this platoon belonged were in the village of Weiler near the German start line, and they too beat off successive waves of brave but largely inexperienced young *Volksgrenadiers* all day, and were not eliminated until nightfall. The troops who finally captured these two positions should by then have been across the Clerf.

General Kokott had ordered his assault troops to bypass the defended village of Hosingen on Skyline Drive but a company of riflemen and another of combat engineers sallied out and engaged the German columns on either side and drew them into a pitched battle for the village. This threw the German timetable out here, too, and the outnumbered Americans held out for two and a half days when, cut off and out of ammunition, the survivors surrendered.

The tough defence of the 110th Infantry Regiment's right flank stopped the XXVI *Volksgrenadiers* from getting across the Clerf until the third day and undoubtedly enabled Bastogne to be reinforced—and so later to resist all the German efforts to capture it.

The left half of the 110th Infantry Regiment's sector, based on Clervaux, also put up an unexpectedly fierce fight. At Marnach, midway between the Dasburg crossing and the key town of Clervaux, a company of American infantry held off the German assault all the first day, only going down when the tanks of II Panzer Division crashed into the little town. At Clervaux itself a particularly spirited defence held up the combined German armour and infantry for two days, the regimental commander himself remaining in his headquarters until the attackers had broken into the downstairs rooms. With survivors of his staff and some walking wounded he got out of an upstairs back door which led up the hill behind, but he was later captured.

The 28th Infantry Division's centre regiment, the 110th, lost about 2,750 men in two and a half days holding the Clerf crossings—but in doing so enabled Bastogne to be reinforced and later held, which in turn stopped General von Manteuffel from reaching the Meuse.

This then was the situation, after nearly 100 hours of continuous fighting in the Ardennes. On the northern flank the Elsenborn Ridge was securely held by four American infantry divisions and concentrated artillery—but it had been a near thing. The 99th Infantry Division was forced back by overwhelming infantry and tank attacks; the 2nd, breaking off its own offensive, had had to fight a desperate withdrawing action through the crumbling front. The 9th Division had moved in from Eupen to back up the Monschau position where no ground had been yielded despite wave after wave of attackers; and the veteran 1st Division had arrived just in time to hold the right of the ridge line against renewed SS Panzer attacks. Thus, with most of VI SS Panzer Army held almost at the start line and their

one success, Peiper's Battle Group (spearheading the 'Leibstandarte Adolf Hitler' Division) in a pocket, the main hope of a quick, unbroken advance to the Meuse in the north had failed. And with St Vith and Bastogne under attack but still in American hands, the original timetable had to be torn up.

'Our forces must now prepare to defend the territory we have already taken,' Field-Marshal von Rundstedt said as early as December 18. Although Hitler overruled him and ordered the Panzers to smash through regardless of casualties, even he was forced to face reality. On the 19th he cancelled the supporting attack from the German XV Army in the north.

The first crisis passes

But on the American side it was only after four days that some sort of order emerged from the confusion caused by the mass of small actions, the breakdown of communications, and the near panic in some of the rear areas. Now major decisions could be taken. Although at first General Bradley had thought the Germans were mounting a spoiling attack to stop General Patton's projected Saar offensive, he had immediately moved an armoured division into the attacked front from either side, the 7th from the north which saved St Vith, and the 10th from the south which got one combat command into Bastogne and another to the hard-pressed defenders around Echternach.

Also 9th Army's General Simpson voluntarily sent his 5th Armoured Division and his 30th Infantry to his old friend General Hodges' aid, and SHAEF's sole reserve, two airborne divisions, were also thrown into the battle. They had been resting and refitting at Rheims after nearly two months' fighting in Holland and were not supposed to be operational for another month: but after a wild 100-mile ride through the night the 101st came into Bastogne on December 19 and the 82nd arrived near the point of 'Liebstandarte' Division by the evening of the 18th.

Although the offensive was taking place entirely on the American front, Field-Marshal Montgomery moved part of his only reserve, 30th Corps, to backstop positions west of the Meuse.

When the full seriousness of the situation was realised at SHAEF on December 19, the offensive through the Saar was called off and General Patton was ordered to counterattack the German left flank as soon as possible with two of 3rd Army's corps.

This, it was realised, would take time, and orders were given for Allied forces to fall back if necessary—but not further than the Meuse. General Eisenhower told General Bradley to 'choose the line he could hold most cheaply' and he asked Field-Marshal Montgomery to examine the possibility of giving up ground in Holland to shorten the line and amass a reserve.

While General Patton worked furiously to turn his whole front through 90°, and while Bastogne and St Vith waited for all-out assaults, General von Manteuffel drove his armour straight through the vacuum between these towns. This threatened to split the front in two, making it increasingly difficult for General Bradley to exercise control over both halves.

It was a situation which faced General Eisenhower with one of his most difficult command decisions.

BATTLE OF THE BULGE:
THE ALLIED COUNTERBLOW

Ardennes, Belgium, December 22, 1944/January 28, 1945
Charles B. MacDonald

On December 22, the Allies still seemed on the edge of disaster—the Germans were still advancing towards the Meuse, still confidently demanding the surrender of Bastogne. But in reality, despite the disagreements which were rending the Allied command, the worst was over: incredibly stubborn American resistance had sapped the strength of the German drive and soon the US forces would begin their counterattack—unfortunately settling for the 'small solution' of squeezing the Germans out of the Bulge instead of amputating it cleanly. *Below:* American infantrymen advance towards beleaguered Bastogne

No one could have discerned it with any certainty at the time, but the day of December 22, 1944, saw the beginning of the climax of the battle in the Ardennes.

On that day, in a blinding snowstorm, General Patton made good his promise to counterattack. While rushing an infantry division into the line north-east of Luxembourg city to bolster a weakening American position at the southern base of the bulge, he threw another infantry division and the veteran 4th Armoured Division into a drive to break through to encircled Bastogne. The 3rd Army had withdrawn in the face of the enemy and executed a 90° shift in direction of attack with a speed unparalleled in military history.

On that day, too, the Germans surrounding Bastogne tightened their encirclement and delivered a surrender ultimatum, only to be left to ponder the meaning of the reply that came back in American slang: 'Nuts!'

Also on the 22nd, the Germans launched what they hoped would be the last leg on the drive to the Meuse—the II Panzer Division already across the west branch of the river and the 116th Panzer Division driving from Houffalize along the north bank of the main branch with plans to cross the river where it swings north near

Out of the east emerged what weathermen call a 'Russian high', bringing in the wake of the day's heavy snowfall sharply dropping temperatures that froze the ground, allowing tanks—both American and German—to manoeuvre freely, but also bringing weather that allowed aircraft to operate again.

Given the overwhelming Allied superiority in aircraft, the advantage of clear skies rested fully with the Allied side. As December 23 dawned, fighter-bombers and mediums would be out in force, wreaking havoc on German columns that heretofore had enjoyed virtual immunity to punishment from the air. Out in force, too, would be big C-47 transport aircraft, looking like pregnant geese against the sky and dropping multi-hued parachutes bearing critical supplies to the troops in beleaguered Bastogne.

For all the assistance from the air, by mid-day of December 23 a hasty line thrown up by the 84th Division beyond the Ourthe around Marche was in serious trouble. So was the American line between the Salm and the Ourthe, where the II SS Panzer Division attacked alongside the 116th Panzer Division. So devastating were the German strikes against the combat command of the 3rd Armoured Division that contingents of another infantry division ear-

American armour deploys during a counterblow against the 'Bulge'. Within ten days of the initial German thrust, the American forces were again on the offensive, but their efforts were much hampered by weather conditions like this

Hotton. General von Manteuffel was hoping to reinforce these two divisions, the II Panzer with the Panzer Lehr once the latter could shake loose from Bastogne, the 116th Panzer with the II SS Panzer Division, shifted from Dietrich's army.

Yet the Germans had lost too much time getting through Noville, waiting for fuel beyond the Ourthe, and countermarching to Houffalize to enjoy the same free wheeling they had experienced in earlier days: for the divisions scheduled to 'flesh out' Joe Collins' 7th Corps for counterattack were now arriving. First, a combat command of the 3rd Armoured Division, which Hodges committed astride the Houffalize-Liège highway to extend westward all the way to the Ourthe the southward-facing positions assumed by the 82nd Airborne Division between the Salm and the Ourthe. Second, the 84th Infantry Division, which in assembling behind the Ourthe near the town of Marche would lie full in the projected path of the II Panzer Division, north-westward from Ourtheville toward the Meuse. And before the battle south of the Meuse was over, the other two divisions joining Collins' corps also would enter the fight.

Another move began on the 22nd—American withdrawal from the St Vith horseshoe. Having lost 8,000 out of some 22,000 men, not counting the regiments of the 106th Division that had been trapped on the Schnee Eifel, the defenders of St Vith came back under orders from Montgomery. They were orders laced with the kind of accolade that had long ago endeared the Field-Marshal to the British Tommy: the heroic defenders of St Vith were authorised to withdraw 'with all honour . . . They put up a wonderful show'.

The last of them would make it before daylight on December 23, not to return to some warm, safe haven but to re-enter the line; for by this time the positions of the 82nd Airborne and 3rd Armoured Divisions between the Salm and the Ourthe were under heavy attack.

One final event on the 22nd would have an authoritative impact on the continuing battle. As darkness fell, chill winds began to blow.

marked to join Collins' counterattacking reserve were pulled into this fray, leaving only one division of armour from the counterattacking force still uncommitted. Once the remnants of the St Vith defenders were safely within American lines, Montgomery aided this fight by ordering the 82nd Airborne Division to withdraw from what had become a sharp corner at Vielsalm, along the Salm river west of St Vith.

Crisis there was between the Salm and the Ourthe; but to American commanders the most serious crisis was developing in what represented the tip of the bulge, beyond the Ourthe where the II Panzer Division bounced off the flank of the 84th Division and continued toward the Meuse. Here, by mid-day of the 23rd, the last of the units that Montgomery had hoped to assemble as a reserve, the 2nd Armoured Division, was arriving.

This development was destined to bring to a head a kind of covert contest of wills that since the day Montgomery had assumed command had been running between Montgomery and the commander of the US 1st Army, Courtney Hodges. As demonstrated by Montgomery's early wish to withdraw from St Vith and the Elsenborn Ridge, the British commander believed in a policy of rolling with the punches. The Americans, for their part, shocked at what a presumably defeated German army had done to them, were reluctant sometimes to the point of fault to give up any ground unless forced, particularly ground that American soldiers had bought with blood.

Montgomery's theory was that by holding the most economical line possible in the north and amassing a reserve in the process, he might force the Germans to overextend themselves, whereupon he would strike with Collins' 7th Corps. Montgomery was relatively unconcerned about the Germans reaching or even crossing the Meuse: by this time he had moved a British armoured brigade to cover the critical bridges on either side of the big bend at Namur. Furthermore, even should the Germans cross the Meuse, he had a reserve corps in position to annihilate them.

Possessed of no ready reserve, American commanders could hardly be so sanguine. As late as the 22nd, both Patton and Middleton were still concerned lest the Germans suddenly swing south-west in the direction of Sedan and the site of their triumph in 1940. Remembering 1914 and 1940, Paris had the jitters, and military police were enforcing a strict curfew in the French capital while guarding Eisenhower closely lest Otto Skorzeny's disguised raiders try to assassinate the Supreme Commander. Hodges and the staff of the 1st Army were still unconvinced that the Germans would not turn north to take Liège. Even the British were concerned enough to station guards and erect roadblocks on the outskirts of Brussels.

Having had close personal experience with the power of the German drive, Courtney Hodges remained most concerned of all. That he had been forced, contrary to Montgomery's plan, to keep committing incoming divisions as the Germans continued to work westward seemed to him under the circumstances the only way to run the fight. He saw the tip of Manteuffel's striking force embracing or soon to embrace four Panzer divisions—Panzer Lehr in the south, II Panzer and 116th Panzer in the centre, and II SS Panzer

The 'big' solution—severing the bulge completely—was rejected in favour of the 'small' solution: squeezing it out

1944 **December 22:** The Germans launch their last attempt to reach the Meuse. US forces withdraw from the St Vith area.
December 25: US 2nd Armoured Division attacks and turns back II Panzer Division 4 miles from the Meuse.
December 26: US 4th Armoured Division relieves Bastogne. Word reaches Hitler that Antwerp can no longer be reached.
December 30: A US attack north-east from Bastogne towards Houffalize is stalemated by a German attack on the corridor to Bastogne.

1945 **January 3/4:** The last German attack on Bastogne is defeated. The US counterattack begins.
January 8: Hitler authorises withdrawal to Houffalize.
January 16: US 1st and 3rd Armies link up at Houffalize.
January 20: General Patch's withdrawal from the north-eastern sector is complete.
January 22: The weather clears, allowing US pilots to take the air against German convoys.
January 28: The last vestige of the Bulge disappears.

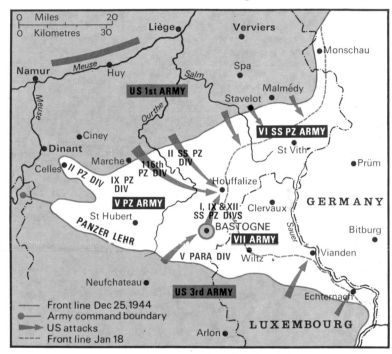

in the north, while to the right of II SS Panzer, Sepp Dietrich was at last bringing his two remaining SS Panzer divisions to bear.

To Hodges, to withhold reserves while forces of such power were still on the move—even in view of radio intercepts indicating that the Germans were running short of fuel—was to flirt with disaster.

Without asking approval, the commander of the 2nd Armoured Division, Major-General Ernest Harmon, sent one of his combat commands southward on December 23 to investigate reports of German tanks passing south of Marche. Yet word came back of no contact except with British armoured patrols already working the area with no sign of the enemy.

Yet, in reality, the II Panzer Division had found free passage south of Marche and was toiling toward the Meuse at Dinant. (The only one of Skorzeny's disguised patrols to reach a Meuse bridge gained Dinant that night but was quickly captured by British guards.) By mid-afternoon of December 24—Christmas Eve—it was all too apparent to General Harmon that German tanks were present a few miles farther south in strength. He put in a call to Collins, his corps commander, for authority to turn the entire 2nd Armoured Division to the attack.

With Collins away from his headquarters, the 7th Corps' staff relayed the request to 1st Army HQ. Courtney Hodges was torn. Although still under Field-Marshal Montgomery's dictum to amass a reserve, and specifically to keep from getting the 2nd Armoured Division involved, Hodges' heart was with Collins and Harmon.

The word that came from Hodges was that Collins was 'authorised' to roll with the punch, to peel back to the north-west; but along with the failure specifically to order withdrawal, Hodges included no proviso denying attack. That was all the licence General Collins needed. That night he and Harmon mapped out an attack to begin early on Christmas Day, employing all of the 2nd Armoured Division.

Collins' decision represented the high-water mark of the German counteroffensive in the Ardennes. In conjunction with contingents

of British armour and American fighter-bombers enjoying another day in the sun, the 2nd Armoured Division on Christmas Day began to wipe out a II Panzer Division that at the height of its achievement had run out of gasoline at the town of Celles—only 4 miles from the Meuse and not quite 60 miles from the start line along the German frontier.

The Germans paid a price of more than 80 tanks. They left not only their spearhead but their ambition broken in the snow.

Bastogne relieved at last
There were two other events on Christmas Day equally disconcerting to the Germans. The first was in the north-west, where the US 3rd Armoured Division with help of infantry reinforcements brought to a halt an all-out attack by the II SS Panzer Division to break through between the Salm and the Ourthe, while on the west bank of the Ourthe other American troops dealt roughly with the 116th Panzer Division.

The second was at Bastogne.

Obsessed with the idea that the II Panzer Division was out on a limb, General von Manteuffel saw Bastogne as a boil that had to be lanced if the Panzer division were to be reinforced and if the entire German counteroffensive were not to be disrupted by Patton's counterattack. Rather than send the Panzer Lehr Division immediately to II Panzer's assistance, Manteuffel held on to it and ordered an all-out attack by Lüttwitz's XLVII Panzer Corps to be launched on Christmas Day to capture Bastogne. This time Lüttwitz was to hit a previously untested and presumably soft rear—or western—arc of the American perimeter.

Preceded by a heavy air bombardment of Bastogne the night before, the new attack posed such a threat that as the morning dawned many an American paratrooper shook hands with his buddies in a final gesture of salute. The farewells were premature. Before night came, the paratroops of the 101st with their *pot-pourri* of reinforcements had either held or quickly sealed off every penetration.

The next day, December 26, as dusk descended, an engineer battalion manning a portion of the southern fringe of the perimeter reported the approach of 'three light tanks, believed friendly'.

The 4th Armoured Division had arrived.

The siege was ended.

On this day after Christmas, the word reaching Hitler from Manteuffel, Model, and Rundstedt was that no chance whatever remained of reaching Antwerp. The only hope of salvaging any sort of victory from the Ardennes was to turn the V and VI Panzer Armies north to cross the Meuse west of Liège and come in behind Aachen. This presupposed the capture of Bastogne and a secondary attack from the north to link with the Panzer armies. Yet if these prerequisites were to be met, Hitler would have to abandon a new project he had been contemplating: a second counteroffensive in Alsace.

This was, in effect, a return to what Hitler earlier had labelled the 'Small Solution', a proposal his generals had championed when he first had broached the idea of a counteroffensive in the Ardennes. Deeming German resources too limited for taking Antwerp,

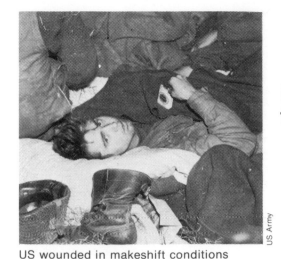

US wounded in makeshift conditions

Bastogne: 'bastion of the battered bastards of the 101st'...

POWs dig mass graves, also makeshift

A vital communications centre, Bastogne was the key to the Ardennes—and the target of an all-out German attack

they had wanted instead a limited attack to take the American supply base of Liège and cut in behind the 1st and 9th US Armies around Aachen. Hitler long ago had scorned the 'Small Solution'. Again he rejected it.

'We have had unexpected setbacks,' the Führer acknowledged, but that was 'because my plan was not followed to the letter'.

So stretched had the Americans become in Alsace in order to release Patton for counterattack, Hitler believed, that the second counteroffensive he contemplated there would score such gains as to turn Patton away from the Ardennes. Given the code name *Nordwind* ('North Wind'), the counteroffensive was to begin on New Year's Day.

Nor would Hitler accept the contention that Antwerp lay beyond reach. While agreeing that, once Bastogne was captured, the two Panzer armies might turn northward to clear the east and south banks of the Meuse, he saw this as no switch to the 'Small Solu-

tion' but as a temporary diversion to trap the American units that had rushed to the north shoulder of the bulge. This would prepare the way for renewing the drive on Antwerp.

On the Allied side, Bradley on Christmas Day and Eisenhower a few days later urged Field-Marshal Montgomery to turn the 1st Army quickly to the offensive in order to take some of the pressure off Bastogne and Patton's efforts to carve a viable corridor into the town. Montgomery responded that he expected the Germans to hit the 1st Army one more blow; but if that failed to come he would attack on January 3.

Montgomery's reluctance to attack annoyed the American commanders. The British field-marshal, they knew, had an entire corps in reserve. Although neither Bradley, Hodges, nor Patton asked commitment of British troops, they believed that so long as Montgomery had this reserve he need fear no further German thrust.

Another German blow in the north never came, primarily because

POWs: German casualties neared 100,000

...and the rock which broke the German offensive

The wrack of the receding German tide

Turret torn off by anti-tank fire, this shattered German tank symbolises the ferocity of the American defence of Bastogne

Patton's troops at Bastogne and on either side of the relief corridor that he opened on the 26th fought the V Panzer Army to a standstill. The battle reached a climax on December 30 when Patton, his forces around Bastogne swollen now to six divisions, tried to resume his attack north-east toward Houffalize. At almost precisely the same moment, General von Manteuffel launched another major attempt to cut the corridor into Bastogne and take the town.

Casualties on both sides mounted, and bitterly cold weather took an inevitable toll; but the American troops held firm, even after the Germans had driven a salient into the east side of the corridor. It was a struggle for survival such as Bastogne had not known even in the critical days of encirclement.

Threat to the 'Colmar Pocket'
As events strode to a climax at Bastogne, a crucible similarly demanding was beginning to develop for troops of the US 7th Army,

commanded by Lieutenant-General Alexander M. Patch, and some of their compatriots in General Jean de Lattre de Tassigny's French 1st Army, which together made up General Devers' 6th Army Group. Undermined by any standards of comparison with Bradley's 12th Army Group or Montgomery's 21st Army Group, Devers' forces had had to stretch already thin lines even thinner to absorb former positions of two of the 3rd Army's corps in order to release Patton for counterattack.

The new arrangement charged General Patch's 7th Army with 124 miles of front, the bulk of it along the German frontier facing the Saar industrial region, 40 miles of it along the Rhine to include the city of Strasbourg. From that point southward General de Lattre's French took over, containing what Allied troops called the 'Colmar Pocket', an expansive German bridgehead on the Rhine's west bank around the town of Colmar, a hold-out position that Devers' undermanned forces had yet been unable to eliminate and one that had posed a constant threat in General Eisenhower's mind ever since the counteroffensive had begun in the Ardennes.

Because General Patch's positions formed a right angle where the Franco-German border meets the Rhine, those American divisions in this extreme north-east corner of France would be threatened by entrapment should the Germans launch converging thrusts against them or should the Germans strike swiftly to deny the few passes through the Vosges Mountains, which stood behind them. Recognising that little of strategic importance lay in this low plain alongside the Rhine, General Eisenhower had told Devers at the meeting in Verdun to yield ground rather than endanger the integrity of his forces.

To withdraw all the way to the Vosges would nevertheless involve giving up Strasbourg, a city which the French looked upon symbolically as the capital of Alsace and Lorraine, the provinces lost to the Germans from 1870 to 1918 and again from 1940 until late 1944. To the French, to abandon Strasbourg was to relinquish a part of the soul of France.

Yet to defend 124 miles of front, including Strasbourg, the 7th Army had only seven divisions, plus the infantry regiments of three new divisions, only recently arrived from the United States in response to Eisenhower's call for assistance at the start of the Ardennes counteroffensive. Also available as a last resort were two divisions that Eisenhower had managed to cull from the line to recreate a Supreme Headquarters reserve; but these might at any time have to be sent into the Ardennes.

That left the stratagem of withdrawal in the event of a major German attack perhaps the only recourse.

That the Germans planned to attack either on New Year's Day or soon thereafter became clear to the 6th Army Group during the last week of December. The attack actually was to begin an hour before the first stroke of the New Year.

The American soldier, victor of Bastogne...

When Hitler had first proposed a counteroffensive in Alsace, the idea had been a heavy strike all the way to the American supply base of Metz, but even Hitler had to accept that this was too ambitious for the available resources. As in the Ardennes, the Führer himself planned the blow actually delivered—Operation *Nordwind*.

Attacking west of the Vosges Mountains, two divisions under the aegis of Army Group G (Generaloberst Johannes Blaskowitz) were to make a penetration, whereupon a reserve of two armoured divisions was to strike swiftly southward to seal from the rear the vital Saverne Gap, which separates the High Vosges in the south from the less imposing Low Vosges in the north. At the same time a supporting effort by three infantry divisions was to push down the spine of the Low Vosges. A few days later, a lone division was to cross the Rhine north of Strasbourg, while two divisions were to attack northward from the Colmar Pocket, link with the Rhine bridgehead (encircling Strasbourg in the process), then swing westward to the Saverne Gap.

The net effect would be to trap all American units east of the Low Vosges, the equivalent of five divisions, and those French troops guarding the northern periphery of the Colmar Pocket.

Sharply conscious of this possibility, General Eisenhower moved swiftly once the German attack began, and ordered General Devers to pull back from his north-eastern salient all the way to the Vosges, leaving only delaying forces on the low-lying plain.

That meant abandoning Strasbourg, a condition that prompted the head of the provisional French government, Charles de Gaulle, to send an emissary to Eisenhower's headquarters to express his dismay. Rather than relinquish the city, the word was, de Gaulle already had ordered General de Lattre to extend his lines north and take over the defence.

Struck by this defiance, Eisenhower's Chief-of-Staff, Lieutenant-General Walter B. Smith, threatened to cut off American supplies and equipment, without which the French army would be powerless —to which de Gaulle's man responded that the French were prepared to withdraw their troops from Eisenhower's command.

Although it sounded like an argument in a schoolyard, it was a serious confrontation. De Gaulle even went so far as to cable the

American President and the British Prime Minister for support; but intercession proved unnecessary. When apprised by General Smith of the fervour of de Gaulle's objections and when apprised, too, by the end of the second day (January 2) of the success of Patch's troops in constraining the German main effort toward the Saverne Gap, Eisenhower withdrew the order. While directing the French to take responsibility for defending Strasbourg, he told General Devers to withdraw from the north-eastern salient only as far as the little Moder river, some 20 miles behind the existing lines.

By January 20 this withdrawal was complete. The Germans, meanwhile, had succeeded in establishing a Rhine bridgehead north of Strasbourg, advancing to within 8 miles of the city, and inducing near panic in the civilian population before commitment of a portion of General Eisenhower's reserve brought them to a halt. The attack northward out of the Colmar Pocket got within 13 miles of Strasbourg, but the French stopped it at the last bridge short of the city.

While Devers' 6th Army Group retained its integrity, Strasbourg stayed French. Having committed so much to the Ardennes, the Germans had simply been unequal to a second blow: ten under-

Thick fog and low clouds, combined with high winds, deprived the American armour and infantry of much-needed air support. Here men of the 82nd Airborne Division move through typical Ardennes Forest terrain

Although both Model and Rundstedt gave their endorsement, Hitler refused. The counteroffensive under the original concept of taking Antwerp and trapping Allied armies, he at last admitted, no longer had any chance of success; but he had arrived at definite ideas of how the bulge in the Ardennes might be turned to German advantage.

In creating the salient, Hitler reasoned, he had forced General Eisenhower to employ almost all his resources. That Eisenhower used élite airborne divisions to do the brutal defensive work of infantry was proof enough of that. By holding the bulge, he might keep the Allies widely stretched while pulling out some German units for spoiling attacks elsewhere—like Operation *Nordwind.* That way he might prevent the Allies from concentrating their forces in the north for a renewed offensive to cross the Rhine and capture the Ruhr industrial region.

Yet even this strategy begged the capture of Bastogne, for Hitler required the town both to anchor the southern flank of the bulge and to deny its nexus of roads to the Americans.

To American troops, Manteuffel's final offensive at Bastogne, aimed at severing the corridor into the town, appeared less a concerted attack than reaction by counterattack to Patton's efforts to drive on to Houffalize. Lasting two days—January 3 and 4—the German offensive delayed the drive on Houffalize; but it was too feeble either to pose any genuine threat to Bastogne or to thwart the American offensive entirely. What was more, it operated on borrowed time, for it opened on the same day that Field-Marshal Montgomery at last released Hodges' 1st Army to attack from the north.

The pattern of the drive to eliminate the bulge had been set at the Allied conference in Verdun on December 19 with the decision to send the 3rd Army to Bastogne. Although Patton insisted, once Bastogne was relieved, on shifting to the classic though venturesome manoeuvre for eliminating a deep penetration—culling it off

...and of the whole Ardennes campaign

at its base—he found no support from either Hodges or Bradley. They were concerned about the limited roadnet at the northern base and about the effect of winter weather in the more sharply compartmented terrain along the German frontier. Montgomery conformed, moving parts of two British divisions to the tip of the bulge to enable General Collins to shift his 7th Corps slightly northward and drive from the north-west for Houffalize. Once the 1st and 3rd Armies met at Houffalize, both were to sweep, after the manner of synchronized windshield wipers, on to the German frontier.

In other words, they were going to push in the bulge rather than cut it off. It was—Field-Marshal von Rundstedt would observe after the war—the 'Small Solution'.

The nadir of winter
The snow was deeper than ever in the Ardennes, the temperatures lower; the fog thicker, the winds more penetrating when, early on January 3, General Collins sent two armoured divisions backed by infantry south-east toward Houffalize across ground featured by stretches of high marshland, dense patches of firs, and deep-cut streambeds. Only three of Sepp Dietrich's badly damaged divisions barred the way, including fragments of the mauled II Panzer Division. But that was enough, in view of the weather and the terrain, to slow the Allied advance to a crawl.

So murky was the atmosphere that not a single tactical aircraft could support the attack all day, and sorties by little artillery observation aircraft were possible for no more than an hour. It was a pattern that would undergo little change for a fortnight. On only three days would fighter-bombers be able to take to the air at all. Much of the time the men advanced through snow flurries, followed on the fourth day by a heavy snowfall that piled drifts in places to a depth of several feet.

Tanks stalled on icy hillsides in long rows. Trucks towing anti-tank guns or artillery pieces skidded, jack-knifed, collided, and blocked vital roads for hours. Two trucks towing 105-mm howitzers plunged off a cliff. Deliberate roadblocks formed by felled trees with anti-tank mines on the approaches could be eliminated only by

strength divisions were not enough. The fighting in bitter cold and snow nevertheless cost the Americans 15,600 casualties; the Germans, 25,000.

As the 6th Army Group was meeting its test in Alsace, the Germans managed two last spasms in a dying effort in the Ardennes.

One came from the air, an extraordinary effort by the Luftwaffe. Early on New Year's Day, 700 German planes struck at Allied airfields in Belgium and the Netherlands. The blow took Allied airmen by surprise and cost 156 planes, most of them destroyed on the ground.

The second blow again was aimed at Bastogne, where General von Manteuffel had seen his offensive of December 30 collapse in the face of Patton's renewed attack. It was a blow of which Manteuffel himself disapproved. The time had long come, he believed, to abandon all attempts at maintaining the offensive in the Ardennes. Lest the troops in the tip of the bulge be trapped between Patton and what appeared to be a pending attack by the US 1st Army from the north, he appealed to Field-Marshal Model late on January 2 for permission to pull back to a line anchored on Houffalize.

These POWs, promised a quick victory in December, were humbled by defeat and capture in February

dismounted infantry making slow, sometimes costly flanking moves through deep snow. Bridges everywhere were demolished, the sites defended, so that, just as with the roadblocks, winter-weary infantry had to plod upstream or down to find an uncontested ford, then wade the icy stream to take the Germans in flank, finding in most cases that the foe at the last moment pulled back to fight again another day. The Germans occasionally counterattacked: five or six tanks, a company or a battalion of infantry at a time. Under these conditions, to advance 2 miles a day was a major achievement.

The 3rd Army had it as hard and more so, for the defences in the vicinity of Bastogne reflected the large concentration of German forces there for the various efforts to take the town. Bitterly cold, stung by biting winds and driven snow, nostrils frozen, Patton's troops saw little change in a pattern too long familiar. The Germans opposing them were old and dreaded foes — such units as the I, IX, and XII SS Panzer Divisions, the V Parachute, the Panzer Lehr. Accustomed too were the place names, the same towns and villages where little clots of tanks and infantry a fortnight before had thwarted the Germans in the race for Bastogne, although these were less towns and villages now than macabre monuments to the destructiveness of war.

Yet for all the rigour of the fighting, it became apparent on January 5 that the final crisis at Bastogne had passed. When Field-Marshal Model pulled out one of the SS Panzer divisions to go to the aid of the VI Panzer Army in the north, General von Manteuffel took it upon himself to pull another of the SS Panzer divisions from the line to form a reserve. Three days later, on January 8, Hitler himself authorised withdrawal from the tip of the bulge, not all the way back to Houffalize as Manteuffel had asked, but to a line anchored on a series of ridges 5 miles west of Houffalize.

This was the Führer's first grudging admission that the counteroffensive in the Ardennes had failed utterly. Dietrich's VI Panzer Army, he directed, was gradually to relinquish control of all but the SS Panzer divisions to Manteuffel's V Panzer Army, whereupon these four divisions were to assemble in the rear at St Vith. There they were ostensibly to guard against attacks near the base of the bulge: but in reality they were executing the first step in leaving the Ardennes entirely. As Hitler's advisers in the East had long been warning, a powerful new Russian offensive was destined to begin any day. It would actually start on January 12, and Hitler on January 22 would order the VI Panzer Army to move with all speed to the Eastern Front.

Meanwhile, early on January 16, patrols of the US 1st and 3rd Armies met at Houffalize. Rent apart by the counteroffensive, the two armies had joined hands at the waist of the bulge, failing to trap many of the elusive foe but setting the stage for the return of Hodges' 1st Army to General Bradley's command. This General Eisenhower would order, effective the next day, at the same time retaining Simpson's 9th Army under Montgomery with an eye toward renewing an Allied offensive toward the Ruhr.

It would take another eight days to push in what was left of the bulge in a slow contest against weather and long-proven German ingenuity on the defence. Back to St. Vith, back to Clerf, back to Echternach, back to the Skyline Drive, back to many another spot where American infantrymen, surprised, frightened, but determined, had purchased a commodity called time.

On January 22 the clouds finally cleared dramatically. A brilliant sun came up, its rays dancing on a new snow cover. Pilots were early in the air, jubilant to find German vehicles stalled bumper to bumper waiting their turn to cross ice-encrusted bridges over the Our river into Germany. Astride the Skyline Drive, infantrymen cheered to see the carnage that both air and artillery wrought.

By January 28 the last vestige of the bulge in the Ardennes had disappeared.

The cost of the campaign

Of some 600,000 Americans who fought in the Ardennes — more than participated on both sides at Gettysburg — 81,000 were killed, wounded, or captured, and the British incurred 1,400 casualties. The Germans probably lost 100,000 killed, wounded or captured.

Both sides lost heavily in weapons and equipment, probably as many as 800 tanks on each side, and the Germans 1,000 aircraft. Yet the Americans could replace their losses in little more than a fortnight, while the Germans could no longer make theirs good. The Germans nevertheless had managed to extricate almost all

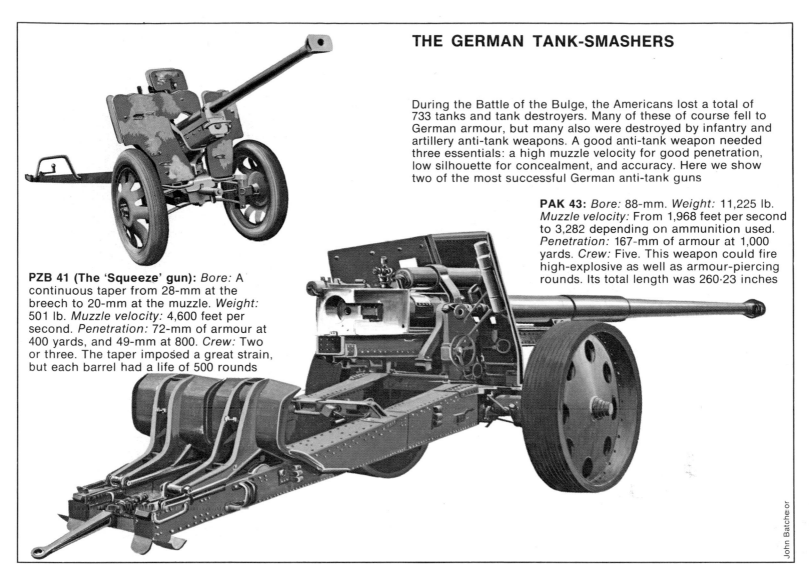

THE GERMAN TANK-SMASHERS

During the Battle of the Bulge, the Americans lost a total of 733 tanks and tank destroyers. Many of these of course fell to German armour, but many also were destroyed by infantry and artillery anti-tank weapons. A good anti-tank weapon needed three essentials: a high muzzle velocity for good penetration, low silhouette for concealment, and accuracy. Here we show two of the most successful German anti-tank guns

PAK 43: *Bore:* 88-mm. *Weight:* 11,225 lb. *Muzzle velocity:* From 1,968 feet per second to 3,282 depending on ammunition used. *Penetration:* 167-mm of armour at 1,000 yards. *Crew:* Five. This weapon could fire high-explosive as well as armour-piercing rounds. Its total length was 260·23 inches

PZB 41 (The 'Squeeze' gun): *Bore:* A continuous taper from 28-mm at the breech to 20-mm at the muzzle. *Weight:* 501 lb. *Muzzle velocity:* 4,600 feet per second. *Penetration:* 72-mm of armour at 400 yards, and 49-mm at 800. *Crew:* Two or three. The taper imposed a great strain, but each barrel had a life of 500 rounds

John Batcheror

that they had taken into the Ardennes except that destroyed in the fighting—a combination of weather, the 'Small Solution' of reducing the bulge, and German ingenuity had seen to that.

Not only did the Germans fail to come close to achieving their strategic objective of Antwerp: they fell short even of the interim objective of the Meuse. Although they had failed to wring from General Eisenhower any 'Backs to the Wall' order like that proclaimed by Sir Douglas Haig in 1918, they had provided the American command many an anxious moment. Yet neither Patton, Bradley, Eisenhower, nor even Hodges—once the first brutal impact of what had happened to his command had passed—had displayed any indication but that matters would be settled their way in the end. That the Germans under Hitler's tutelage should act irrationally and come out of their defences into the open would in the long run do nothing to aid their plight.

In deluding himself that the Wehrmacht of 1944 had the power to repeat the performance of 1940, Hitler had accomplished nothing other than to assure swift victory for the new Russian offensive and possibly delay for a few weeks a final offensive by the Allies. Yet in delaying that offensive he probably speeded the final act, for he retained fewer resources with which to oppose it.

The victor in the Ardennes was the American soldier—he who had given his Allies some sharp concern almost two years before at the Kasserine Pass but who had come a long way since that first battle experience in North Africa. Purportedly pampered, lacking in motivation, he had met the test when it came, giving his commanders—for all their Intelligence failure—time to bring their mobility and reserve power into play. Although Allied power would have told in the end in any case, the American soldier in the Ardennes made the outcome a certainty by his valour and determination at the Elsenborn Ridge, St Vith, Echternach, Clerf, Stavelot, Bastogne, Celles, and countless untold places.

Footnote to the battle
One unfortunate footnote to the battle remained. Perhaps as a reflection of a campaign that had begun in the British press to revive the old issue of making Montgomery overall ground commander, the Field-Marshal in a press conference on January 7

indulged in an exaggeration that the record could hardly sustain. 'As soon as I saw what was happening,' he said, 'I took certain steps myself to ensure that if the Germans got to the Meuse they would certainly not get over that river.' He was 'thinking ahead'. When 'the situation began to deteriorate . . . national considerations were thrown overboard' and 'General Eisenhower placed me in command of the whole northern front'. He had, he claimed, 'employed the whole available power of the British Group of Armies', bringing it into play gradually and then finally 'with a bang'. The operation was 'one of the most interesting and tricky I have ever handled'.

While denigration of American commanders was probably far from Montgomery's mind, his remarks had much the same effect, particularly after the Germans broke in on a BBC wavelength to imitate a British broadcast and give a distorted version of Montgomery's remarks. So upset was General Bradley that he told Eisenhower that rather than serve under Montgomery he would ask to be relieved. Patton said that if Bradley went, so would he.

Bradley saw Montgomery's remarks as a reflection on his own ability as a commander, yet Eisenhower had called in Montgomery only because he hesitated to shift Bradley's headquarters from Luxembourg city to a point farther west and because he wanted to ensure the use of British reserves if needed. While those reserves had been conveniently at hand, few of them had been employed, certainly in no such force as Montgomery intimated in saying he had committed 'with a bang' the 'whole available power of the British Group of Armies'. At most, an armoured brigade and parts of two divisions had briefly entered the fight.

That Montgomery had withheld undermanned British units consciously to save them for the coming offensive against the Ruhr was, in the American view, fully justified. But to have withheld them and then boast otherwise was unjustified.

It remained for that splendid orator, Winston Churchill, to heal the wound. In an address before the House of Commons, he paid full tribute to the American soldier and made abundantly clear that the Ardennes was an American battle and one, he believed, that would be regarded as 'an ever famous American victory'.

391

THE FIGHT FOR IWO JIMA

Pacific Theatre,
February 16/April 7, 1945
Don Yoder

Before the Marines even set foot on
Iwo Jima the island citadel had been
given the heaviest bombardment of the
entire Pacific war. Yet the 36-day battle
for the island was the bloodiest in
Marine Corps history, a campaign that
cost the lives of more than 6,000
Americans and 22,000 Japanese. 'This
fight,' said Marine General Holland
Smith, 'is the toughest we've run across
in 168 years.' *Right:* The Marines hit
the beach and the ordeal begins. In the
background is Mount Suribachi, Iwo
Jima's dominating feature

Did Iwo Jima *have* to be taken by force? Could it not, like certain other Japanese-held strongholds in the Pacific, have been bypassed, cut off, and left 'to wither on the vine'? The answer is no, and for four good reasons, most of them dictated by Allied air strategy:

● First, heavy B-29 bomber losses over Japan emphasised the need for fighter escorts, and since the 2,800-mile round trip from US air bases in the Marianas to Japan and back was beyond the range of the fighters, a nearer staging point had to be captured.

● Second, Iwo Jima, with its two completed airbases and its proximity to Tokyo (660 nautical miles or three air hours) would itself make an excellent base for Allied bombers.

● Third, since Iwo Jima was traditional Japanese territory, administered by the Tokyo prefecture, its conquest would mean a severe psychological blow to the homeland, as well as a vital strategic outpost denied to the Japanese.

● Fourth, Iwo Jima was a necessary link in the air defences of the Marianas. So to isolate Iwo Jima would not be enough: it would have to be seized.

Preliminary planning for the invasion of Iwo Jima began as early as September 1943, and 13 months later, after the Marianas had been secured, Admiral Chester Nimitz informed Lieutenant-General Holland M. ('Howling Mad') Smith, one of the leading exponents of amphibious warfare and commander of all the Marines in the Pacific, that he would be in charge of an operation to take Iwo Jima. Handling the invasion itself would be Major-General Harry Schmidt's 5th Amphibious Corps, veterans of the Gilberts, the Marshalls, and the Marianas campaigns. Schmidt would control three divisions:

● The 3rd Marine Division (Maj-Gen G. B. Erskine), a veteran unit that had seen action on Guam, would be held offshore Iwo Jima as a floating reserve.

● The 4th Marine Division (Maj-Gen C. B. Cates) was also a battle-hardened unit, one that had been in on the Saipan and Tinian landings. It would take part in the initial assault along with the 5th Division.

● The 5th Marine Division (Maj-Gen K. E. Rockey), though yet untried in combat as a unit, was composed of 40% seasoned veterans.

Longest bombardment

Once the target had been selected, the Marines began a rigorous training programme for the invasion: practice landings were made on beaches as similar to Iwo's as possible, and a hill shaped much like Mount Suribachi, Iwo Jima's dominating feature (see map), was taken time and time again in mock assault. Meanwhile, as preparations continued, the air force had begun, on December 8, 1944, the longest and heaviest aerial bombardment of the whole Pacific war, a 72-day 'softening-up' by B-24s and B-25s. A few optimists thought that the island had been neutralised. Only the Marines who had to hit the beaches would be able to verify this.

The US navy, too, laid down its bombardments, which began in November 1944 and continued with intervals until February 16, 1945, when it began its pre-assault barrage. For three days US warships pounded the island from the sea in an attempt to pulverise, or at least neutralise, the Japanese guns capable of hitting the

Marine firepower

In the amphibious landings the worst moment of all was at the moment of contact with the shore, when the first wave of the landing force came under the fire of enemy beach defences with no heavy firepower of their own in support. The British met this problem with the DD swimming tank—but in the Pacific war the Americans preferred to improve on the well-tried 'Landing Vehicle, Tracked'—the Buffalo. Two armed versions helped the Iwo Jima landings, one armed with twin cannons for light support and one with a 75-mm howitzer for heavy support. The former was able to fire at ground targets while acting as a troop transport, while the howitzer version played the same role as the DD tank

The course of the battle. The Marines landed on Iwo Jima without much opposition and within five days had conquered the southern part of the island, including Mount Suribachi. But the drive to the north was an agonising battle of attrition against an enemy who had sworn to kill ten Americans for each Japanese before dying. US casualties after the 36-day fight totalled almost 25,000

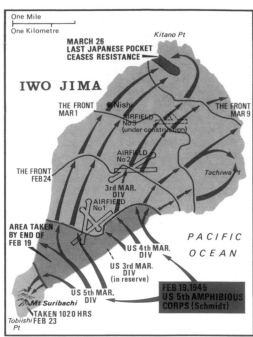

LVT(A) (Howitzer)
Weight: 13·7 tons. *Crew:* four. *Speed:* 20 mph on land, 7½ mph afloat. *Armament:* one 75-mm M-3 howitzer, two ·50-inch Browning machine-guns

LVT(A) (Twin Cannons)
Weight: 12·5 tons. *Crew:* six. *Troop capacity:* 15. *Speed:* 20 mph on land, 7½ mph afloat. *Armament:* two 20-mm cannon, two ·50-inch Browning machine-guns

beaches. Like their counterparts in the air force, the navy too believed they had succeeded. Again, the verdict of the Marines would be the one that counted.

On February 17, two days before the actual invasion was scheduled to begin, LCI gunboats and rocket boats came close inshore to cover the frogmen clearing the beach approaches and checking beach and surf conditions. Suddenly, at 1100 hours, the Japanese, who felt certain that this was the invasion they had so long awaited, opened fire with their heaviest artillery. Some 170 casualties were suffered in this action, but the frogmen did return with a full report of beach and surf conditions. Moreover, by revealing their carefully concealed positions the massive coastal guns had marked themselves for certain destruction. They could have raised havoc on D-Day itself.

The morning of D-Day, February 19, found 450 vessels of the US 5th Fleet gathered offshore the tiny island—the largest collection of ships yet for a Pacific operation. And around and among these vessels swarmed the 482 LVT(A)s, packed with troops, that would carry the eight Marine battalions into action. The bombarding warships closed in to 1,000 yards and began firing. Then the air strikes began and the navy laid down a creeping barrage, the first time it was used in the Pacific. The first wave, 68 LVT(A)s, aligned itself for battle. Every few minutes one of these waves would begin the 4,000-yard dash to the shore and certain violence. If all went according to schedule, the first seven battalions of fighting Marines would be ashore within 45 minutes.

At 0902 hours the first wave of Marines hit the beach, the 5th Division on the left, the 4th on the right, and for the first few minutes reported only light resistance and scattered Japanese fire. Could the defences have been exaggerated? Had the preliminary bombardment really worked after all? It seemed too good to be true. Then, after 20 minutes, the deadly fire of all the Japanese weapons—all the artillery and mortars so carefully sited beforehand—opened up in a vicious barrage. Suddenly, the Marines, by now 200 to 300 yards inland, found themselves pinned down. Then the small-arms fire opened up—from underground pillboxes, from harmless looking sand hummocks, from apparently everywhere. The most costly operation in Marine history had begun in earnest.

Fatal Japanese mistake

The Japanese plan had been clever, but they had made one mistake, a fatal one: they had allowed the Marines to get ashore with all the equipment they would need. By 1030 hours elements of all eight assault battalions were ashore and the bigger LSMs were following up with tanks, bulldozers, and artillery. By the end of the day some 30,000 Marines had been landed and although their casualties had been high, very high, they knew they were there to stay: the entire neck of the island was now secure. By the end of the second day the Marines were at the foot of Suribachi. The next move was obvious.

For three days the Marines fought for control of Suribachi, and at 1020 hours on February 23 a 40-man patrol clawed its way to the summit and raised the American flag. But the fall of Suribachi by no means meant the fall of Iwo. The 4th and 5th

Divisions had now to turn north and face the first line of the main Japanese defence belt, and the savage days that followed were evidence of how carefully it had been prepared. The advance had been stopped cold: a battle of attrition, fought with bayonet, flamethrower, rifle, and grenade, had begun. Each time the Marines managed to penetrate one defence line they would find themselves facing another, seemingly more formidable than the last. Artillery was useless against these positions, and the terrain handicapped the tanks. To escape the Marine artillery barrages the Japanese would hug the US front lines as close as possible. So convincing was their camouflage that time after time they would deliberately allow the Marines to overrun their positions, holding their fire until the last possible moment not to give themselves away. By D+10 it had become clear that US strength was being bled off just as relentlessly as Japanese: casualties, and sheer exhaustion, had reduced many combat units to only 50% efficiency.

Not until D+18 (March 9) was a final breakthrough to the north-east shore of the island made by patrols of 3rd Division. But elsewhere on the island the 4th Division was forced to deal with a Japanese counterblow which, if not a formal Banzai charge, was definitely suicidal in nature: 650 Japanese were found dead in one area alone, and reports from other sectors brought the total to nearly 800. In no way had the

Marine advance been blocked. From now on it was 'simply' a case of mopping up.

It was during this phase that the Marines discovered what the Japanese had been doing since they first occupied the island. Complex mazes of interwoven caves; networks of underground bunkers; ridges, gorges, ledges: the island was one vast lattice of defensive positions. In one area, 1,000 yards wide by 200 deep, 800 separate fortifications, pillboxes, and blockhouses were counted. Entire hills had been hollowed out and rebuilt to house hundreds of defenders, all of whom had sworn to kill ten Marines before dying. It was like nothing the Marines had ever encountered before.

An Intelligence officer of 4th Division described the action like this:
The enemy remains below ground in his maze of tunnels throughout our preliminary artillery fire. When the fire ceases he pushes OPs out of the entrances not demolished by our fire. Then, choosing a suitable exit, he moves as many men and weapons to the surface as he can, often as close as 75 yards from our front. As our troops advance toward this point he delivers all the fire at his disposal, rifle, machine-gun, and mortar. When he has inflicted sufficient casualties to pin down our advance he then withdraws through his underground tunnels most of his forces, possibly leaving a few machine-gunners and mortars. Meanwhile we have delivered a concentration of rockets, mortars, and artillery. Our tanks then push in, supported by infantry. When the hot spot is over-run we find a handful of dead Japs and few if any enemy weapons. While this is happening, the enemy has repeated the process and another sector of our advance is engaged in a vicious fire fight. And so the cycle continues.

It was not until D+25 that the Marines dared declare organised resistance on Iwo to have ceased, but even so, the actual mopping up lasted until D+34. On the night of March 25/26 the Marines witnessed the last convulsions of the desperate Japanese forces: a 300-man Banzai attack on a bivouac area. It had no effect.

Bloodiest prize in the Pacific

Iwo was the bloodiest prize in the Pacific, but its value had not been exaggerated. On March 4, twelve days before the island was declared secure, the first B-29 landed there. On April 7, 108 P-51 Mustangs left from Iwo for the first time to escort a daylight B-29 attack on Tokyo, and within three months of the island's fall more than 850 B-29s had made emergency landings there; without Iwo most of them would have been lost.

Yet the price of Iwo had been extraordinarily high, and whether the dead were Japanese or Americans they had died with the utmost violence. Of the 23,000 men defending Iwo only 1,083 were ever taken prisoner. As for the Americans, some 6,821 soldiers and sailors lost their lives in the struggle for the 8 square miles of Iwo: 24 Medals of Honor were won; 12,600 pints of blood were transfused; 2,650 men were classified 'casualties of combat fatigue'. It had been a fight with a fury unprecedented in the Pacific, and must have left America's military leaders with one haunting thought at least: if to conquer tiny Iwo it took a 72-day air bombardment, a three-day naval hammering, and 36 days of the best the Marines could offer, how long would it take to overwhelm Japan herself? And at what cost?

One month of the bloodiest fighting in US Marine history

1944 October 9: Admiral Nimitz informs General Smith that Iwo Jima will be his target in the Volcano-Bonin Islands.
November 11/12: US navy bombards Iwo Jima for the first time.
November 24: First B-29 raid on Tokyo from the Marianas.
December 8: US air force begins its 72-day bombardment of Iwo Jima, the longest and heaviest of the Pacific war.
1945 February 16: US navy begins a three-day concentrated bombardment of Iwo Jima.
February 17: US frogmen suffer 170 casualties while investigating Iwo Jima's beach defences.
February 19: The 4th and 5th Marine Divisions land on Iwo Jima and gain a foothold.
February 23: Marines raise the US flag on summit of Mt Suribachi.
February 25: The 3rd Marine Division is committed to the battle.
March 4: First B-29 lands on Iwo Jima.
March 16: Iwo Jima is declared secured after 26 days of combat.
March 26: Some 300 Japanese, last of the island's defenders, launch an early morning Banzai charge against Marine and army bivouac areas.
April 7: 108 P-51s flying from Iwo Jima escort B-29s to Japan—the first US land-based fighters to fly to the Japanese homeland.

Far left: A wounded Marine is rushed to an aid station. But in the early days of the battle there were no safe areas, even for the wounded

D+1: Marines move up during the fight for an airfield— the *raison d'être* of the whole Marine invasion

D+4: Suribachi falls. This is one of several famous photos celebrating its capture

D+5: The drive to the north begins. In most areas the US tanks were handicapped by the terrain, and artillery was often quite useless against the carefully prepared defence positions

BERLIN: THE BATTLE

The Berlin Operation, April/May 1945

Major-General I. V. Parotkin

The drive to Berlin started with one of the greatest slogging-matches ever waged on the Eastern Front: the Germans were not only fighting for utter survival, but some of their generals and leaders were hoping to slow down the Russian advance in the hope that the Western Allies would get to Berlin before the Russians. And so the Red Army—although it had never enjoyed such superiority in men and material—found itself locked in battle with Heinrici's desperate divisions on the Oder. Yet it was only a matter of time before the front broke and the Russian masses flooded through, carrying the war into the wrecked streets of Berlin and there repeating many of the grim scenes of Stalingrad. *Below:* Russian troops before the blazing Reichstag, core of the defence in 'Fortress Berlin'

The Berlin operation, one of the largest of the war, saw the final defeat of Hitler's forces on the Eastern Front, and the end of the war followed soon afterwards. It had three stages:
● The breakthrough on the Oder and Neisse (April 16/19).
● The attacks in which the German force was split into three and encircled, some in the city, others in the forests south-east of it (April 19/25).
● The annihilation of the encircled forces, capture of the city, and advance to the Elbe (April 26/May 8).

Germany had already lost the war, but her leaders, above all Hitler, would not admit it: they were hoping to find a way out by prolonging it in the expectation that the Alliance would disintegrate, and their plans were based on this assumption. They tried to encourage the rift by attempting to negotiate separately with the Western Allies, and ordering the Eastern Front to be held even at the expense of letting the British and Americans in behind them.

To strengthen the Eastern Front even further, Himmler was removed from command of Army Group Vistula, his place being taken by General Heinrici, acknowledged in the German army as a master of defensive fighting. In late March General Guderian was replaced as Chief of General Staff at OKH by General Krebs, a former military attaché in Moscow and now regarded as Germany's greatest expert on the Red Army, and General Hauenschild was appointed to command III Military District, responsible for defence behind the front line.

The Germans began working on the Berlin defences early in February and by mid-April three belts had been set up between the Baltic and the Sudeten foothills, making a system 12½ to 25 miles deep, with all towns and villages adapted for all-round defence. A major obstacle to attack from the east was presented by the Seelow Heights, stretching north to south behind the Old Oder Channel, some 4 to 6 miles ahead of 1st Belorussian Front's forward positions in the Küstrin bridgehead. These heights rise in a ridge some 130 to 160 feet above the Oder valley, sloping steeply, broken by ridges and gullies, and with gradients as steep as 1 in 2¼ at Seelow. The Germans regarded the heights as the key position of the Berlin defences, and fortified and manned them accordingly.

Berlin itself was converted into a strongpoint, and the defence system, including the Berlin defence zone, was 62 miles from front to rear.

The German forces comprised four armies—III Panzer Army and IX Army of Army Group Vistula, IV Panzer Army and XVII Army of Army Group Centre—totalling 62 divisions, four of them Panzer and ten motorised, with many smaller units. For defence of the city were in addition about 200 *Volkssturm* battalions, security and police formations, while OKH Reserve possessed eight divisions. German forces came to about 1,000,000 men, with 10,400 guns and mortars, 1,500 tanks or assault guns, and 3,300 combat aircraft. It was a formidable and a desperate force.

Stavka knew well that the fight would be fierce and, as described in Marshal Konev's account, made its preparations very carefully. The operation was to begin on April 16 and last 12 to 15 days. The III and IV Panzer and IX Armies were to be smashed quickly, Berlin seized, and the Elbe reached on a broad front, so as to link up with the Anglo-American forces, split the strategic front in two, and thus force Germany to surrender. The forces employed would be 1st and 2nd Belorussian and 1st Ukrainian Fronts, the Long Range Air Force, Dniepr Flotilla, and two Polish armies—a total of 2,500,000 men with 41,600 guns and mortars, 6,250 tanks and self-propelled guns, 7,500 combat aircraft, and a great deal of other equipment.

The offensive was opened by Zhukov's and Konev's forces on the appointed day, April 16. Marshal Zhukov had decided to achieve surprise and make aimed German fire difficult by attacking before dawn under searchlights. So at 0500 hours his guns poured a hail of fire down on the German positions, while his air forces simultaneously attacked the first and second lines, artillery positions, and command posts; 140 searchlights were then switched on and infantry and tanks went in under an artillery screen. From the very beginning the offensive was a matter of breaking through one line of positions after another, and by midday the second line had been reached. This line ran along the crest of the Seelow Heights and, despite commitment of forward elements of 1st and 2nd Guards Tank Armies, proved impossible to storm off the march.

The German command regarded the second line as the main one, and reinforced it with three divisions; all Soviet attempts to break through in daylight on the 16th failed. The Soviet troops were ordered to maintain action during the hours of darkness, so that the break could be completed the next morning, and tanks and artillery were brought forward during the night. In the morning 800 bombers attacked the German strongpoints, and the attack went in after a 30-minute artillery bombardment. Four more German divisions had arrived during the night, and resistance was fierce, with one counterattack after another coming in. Nevertheless, the Seelow line had been breached by the evening and the Soviet advance was resumed. Large German forces were brought out from Berlin itself, including anti-aircraft artillery, and the tempo of the Soviet advance was slowed. In two days, Marshal Zhukov's forces had advanced only 7 or 8 miles, less than planned, while the penetration north and south of the Küstrin bridgehead had been somewhat less—3 to 7½ miles only.

The 'Last Battle' begins

Marshal Konev's crossing of the Neisse began at 0615 hours on the 16th, when his guns opened up, and as soon as they did so aircraft laid a smoke screen along the entire line, so that the Germans could not see what the Soviets were doing or where they intended to cross. Forward elements came over on assault bridges, boats, and rafts, captured a foothold on the west bank, and dug in. The engineers then erected bridges and main divisional forces crossed in an hour, after which a 40-minute artillery bombardment preceded the assault on the west bank at 0840 hours.

By 1000 hours several breaches had been made, and at 1400 hours armour was committed. A gap about 16 miles wide was made in the main German line, and the assault force advanced about 8 miles, penetrating the second line in places. In an attempt to hold the second line, the Germans threw in four Panzer divisions and several smaller formations, but when the Soviet offensive resumed on the morning of the 17th the main tank forces were committed, so that by evening the Soviets had broken the second line and advanced up to 11 miles.

On the Dresden axis, the main defence line was breached and the second penetrated 1½ to 2 miles on a number of sectors during the first two days.

Konev's main attack therefore had broken the second line of defences and caused the Germans to expend their Cottbus area reserves in two days, so conditions favoured development into the German rear. The Germans decided to stand on their third line, on the west bank of the Spree, and began to move formations from reserve and elsewhere in the line. By April 18 they had manned it with retreating forces reinforced by one Panzer and two infantry divisions, concentrated most densely in defence of Cottbus and Spremberg, while a strong force had begun to assemble around Görlitz, with the ambitious task of breaking through to Spremberg, rolling up the flank of the Soviet force, getting athwart its communications, and threatening it from behind.

Stavka was seriously concerned at the hold-up to Zhukov's forces, and to ensure encirclement of Berlin ordered Konev to turn his 3rd and 4th Guards Tank Armies north, to attack Berlin from the south, while Rokossovsky's force, due to attack on April 20, was ordered to by-pass Berlin from the north not later than April 22. Thus even if Zhukov's offensive failed to develop momentum, encirclement of Berlin was assured.

Zhukov's troops resumed their offensive on the morning of April 18 after 10 to 30 minutes of artillery bombardment, and on their main axis succeeded in levering the Germans off the Seelow Heights. But still every village, hill, or passage between lakes had to be fought hard for. During April 18/19 large reinforcements were brought in by the Germans, and fighting was very fierce; but by the evening of the 19th the Oder Line had been ripped open on a 44-mile front. The 1st Belorussian Front's greatest success was on the right, where 3rd Shock and 47th Armies seized a position from which they could either attack Berlin from the north-east or by-pass it to north or north-west.

The secondary assaults to right and left of the main one also met a most dogged resistance, with the Germans exploiting the forests and lakes skilfully. But by the 19th the secondary assault forces had also broken through the main line, advanced up to 5 miles, and penetrated the second line in places. On the left wing, the German bridgehead east of the Oder at Frankfurt was eliminated, and the eastern part of the town captured.

Thus in the first four days, 1st Belorussian Front advanced 19 miles, and split IX Army into three—in the south V SS *Gebirgskorps*, the Frankfurt garrison, and units of II SS Panzer Corps; in the centre 56th Panzer Corps; and in the north 101st Army Corps. The Germans made numerous attempts to close the gaps between these with reserves, but unsuccessfully. The IX Army's and Army Group Vistula's operational reserves lost heavily, and the transfer away of III Panzer Army's reserve (the 'Nederland' and 'Nordland' Motorised Divisions) to face 1st Belorussian Front facilitated 2nd Belorussian Front's breach of the German defences on the west bank of the Oder.

By April 20, German resistance on the Oder had been smashed, and the offensive towards Berlin could proceed. But it had been a hard fight for Zhukov's troops. They had had to overcome three defensive belts, each of two or three lines, with intermediate lines between the second and third belts, the numerous villages turned into strongpoints, and the whole occupied by the Germans in good time. Every day the Soviet guns had had to be dragged up to the infantry positions for a preliminary bombardment before the attack could begin again.

Meanwhile Konev's forces were manoeuvring to attack Berlin as ordered. He had decided to attack the German third belt at its weakest point, between the large concentrations at Cottbus and Spremberg, with his 3rd and 4th Guards Tank Armies. The Spree was reached on the morning of the 18th, crossed at once, and bridgeheads seized north and south of Spremberg. The third belt had been broken. On the Dresden axis the important strongpoint of Niesky had been captured, and the Soviet troops were near Bautzen, despite a counterattack by the Görlitz force which pushed them back some 2 to 2½ miles northwards. Thus Konev, too, had split his opponent—IV Panzer Army—into three parts, inflicted heavy casualties on it and the German reserves, broken the Neisse and Spree lines, and prepared the ground for an outflanking movement round the German forces south of Berlin and into the city with the tank armies.

Furthermore, German Air Fleets VI and 'Reich' had suffered heavily in air battles with the Soviet air forces. Army Groups Vistula and Centre had committed all their reserves—more than 12 divisions—to no avail, and over 20 German divisions had been smashed, while the Oder-Neisse defence belt had been broken. Konev's mobile forces began their outflanking movement against Berlin on the 18th, and that day advanced 25 to 31 miles, getting 12 to 15 miles ahead of the infantry. Forward elements of 3rd Tank Army captured Baruth on the 20th and moved up to the Zossen area so fast that the OKW Operations Staff and the OKH General Staff had to flee to Wannsee in great confusion, while some sections were flown out to south Germany.

The Red Army bursts through

Marshal Konev now wanted to develop his offensive on Berlin and also to encircle the German Frankfurt-Guben force, so he committed his 28th Army from second echelon, using two divisions of it to reinforce 3rd Guards Army. With this aid, 3rd Guards Army burst the outer defence perimeter of Berlin without a pause, and by the evening of the 22nd was in Marienfelde and Lankwitz, in the southern outskirts of the city, astride the rear of IV Panzer Army. By then 4th Guards Tank Army, making to outflank Berlin from the southwest, had captured Saarmund and Beelitz.

But the large German forces left behind in Cottbus and Spremberg were still fighting hard, and by holding on were splitting Konev's front, making it difficult for his armies to co-ordinate operations and hindering their supply. They had to be disposed of, and this was done, Spremberg falling on April 21 and Cottbus the next day. Army Group Centre was now completely cut off from Army Group South, and as April 22 drew to a close the line of retreat of the Frankfurt-Guben force was cut, while 4th Tank Army took up good positions from which to close a tight ring on Berlin.

Marshal Zhukov's offensive was going slowly but well. On the 20th his troops breached the outer defensive perimeter northwest of Berlin, and at 1350 hours the assault on the capital began when long-range guns of 79th Rifle Corps (3rd Shock Army) opened fire on it. Next day 3rd and 5th Shock Armies broke into the city in the north-east, followed in the south-east on April 22 by 8th Guards Army. That day also saw 2nd Guards Tank and 47th Armies outflank the city from the north-west and cross the Hafel river. General Weidling (56th Panzer Corps) later admitted that April 20 was the worst day of all for his corps, and perhaps for all the German forces.

By the evening of April 22, therefore, IX Army and most of IV Panzer Army were ripe for encirclement. Konev's 4th Guards Tank and Zhukov's 47th Armies were both west of Berlin and less than 25 miles apart, while 8th Guards Army of Zhukov's front was less than 10 miles away from Konev's 3rd Guards Tank Army southeast of the city.

But if the Germans in Berlin were to be smashed, Rokossovsky's 2nd Belorussian Front had to do well against III Panzer Army on the Oder north of the city. And conditions here were difficult. The Oder here has two wide channels each separated by steep earth dikes rising some 5 to 8 feet above the plain, which the Germans had flooded. The flooding made it impossible for wheeled or tracked vehicles to move off the dikes, and seriously impeded the infantry. It also limited the capacity of the assembly areas, so that forces could only be committed to battle piecemeal, and the artillery had to remain east of the east channel, some 3 to 4 miles from the front line, leaving the infantry to be supported ▷

'Two eyes for an eye' — the Red Army's motto as the Berlin drive begins

One sector of the massive Russian artillery-line at the start of the offensive. Zhukov and Konev enjoyed an artillery density of one gun every 13 feet

Russian assault-guns and infantry head in to the attack. Massive thrusts gave the over-stretched forces of Army Group Vistula no chance

The Russians had mastered every technique of modern armoured warfare: this pontoon bridge speeded the Soviet armour over the Spree river on the outskirts of Berlin

Berlin was no fortress
—its defences were
rudimentary, appalling
all the regular army
officers entrusted with
its defence. And the
Russians knew that
they could afford to
surround Berlin until
it lay in the jaws of
a gigantic vice.

When the attack
finally came—on April
26—it came as a
pattern of relentless,
concentric drives by
the armies of both
Zhukov and Konev.
The Red Air Force
held complete control
of the sky, and opened
the battle with heavy
air attacks. The ground
drives—ironically—
encountered the worst
resistance in the
suburbs and blocks
which had been
wrecked by the Allied
bombing, where the
rubble tended to
cancel out the
difference between
the veterans of the
Red Army and the
unskilled but fanatical
elements among the
defenders.

By the evening of
the 27th, 'Fortress
Berlin' was reduced
to an east-west belt
10 miles long but
never more than 3
miles wide—and on
the following day the
attack on the heart of
Berlin, the Reichstag
area, began

BERLIN

2nd GDS TK ARMY

3rd SHOCK ARMY

Siemensstadt

To Spandau

SPANDAUER CHAUSSEE

Westend

KAISER

CHAR   DAMM

Charlottenburg

BURG

KURFURSTEN

Grunewald

Schmargendorf

MOTORISED

BERLINER

DIV

Wilmersdorf

Spree

Moabit

TURM   STRASSE

ALT   MOABIT

CHARLOTTENBURGER

Tiergar

TIER

STR

FLAK TOWERS

ZOOLOGICAL
GARDENS

DAMM

KLEIST

STR

STR

Schön

Steglitz

To Zehlendorf

To Lichterfelde

To L

3rd GUARDS TANK ARMY

28th ARMY

Russian attacks

Front line
Apr 26, 1945

Front line Apr 28

City defence
perimeter

IV   Defence sector

0   Yards   1000

0   Metres   1000

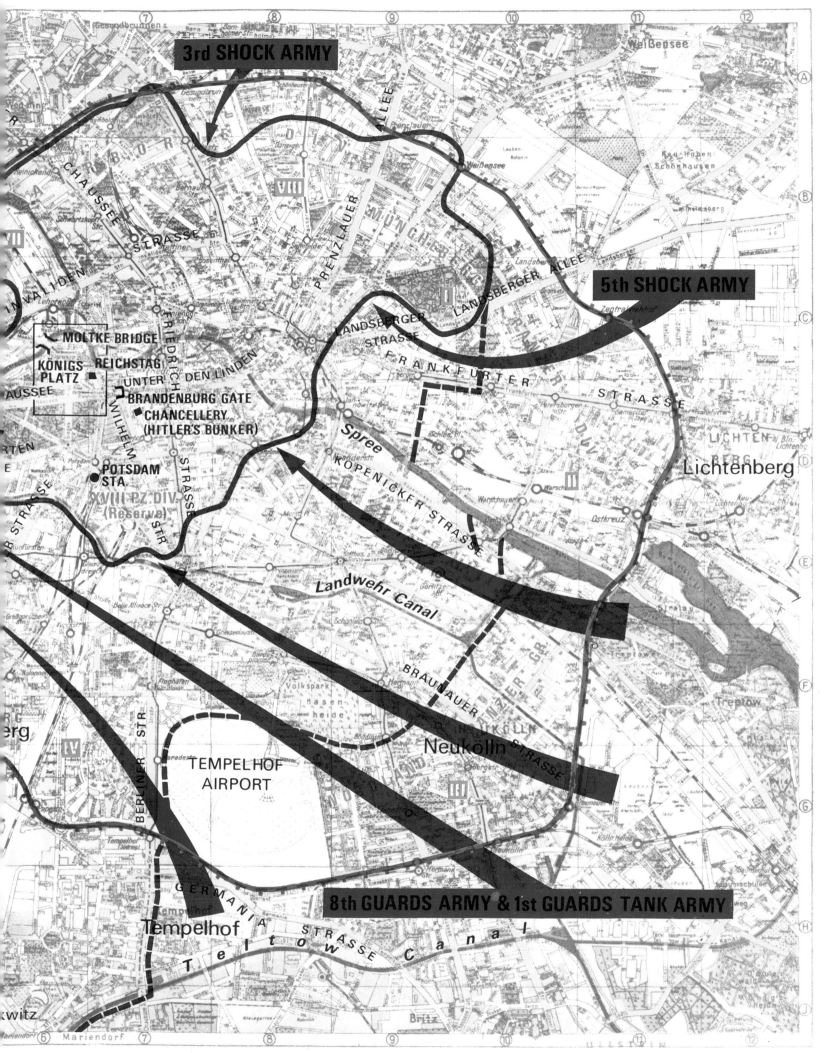

3rd SHOCK ARMY

5th SHOCK ARMY

MOLTKE BRIDGE
KÖNIGS PLATZ
REICHSTAG
UNTER DEN LINDEN
BRANDENBURG GATE
CHANCELLERY (HITLER'S BUNKER)

POTSDAM STA.
XVIII PZ. DIV. (Reserve)

Spree

KOPENICKER STRASSE

Lichtenberg

Landwehr Canal

BRAUNAUER

Neukölln

TEMPELHOF AIRPORT

GERMANIA

8th GUARDS ARMY & 1st GUARDS TANK ARMY

Tempelhof

STRASSE

Teltow Canal

△In the Panzerfaust we trust: Hitler Youth and Volkssturm

△ Berlin street scene, April 1945: German refugees move out

△ Mass Allied bombing did not stop when the Russians attacked

△Clearing up: Russian shellfire added to the havoc of the bombs

mainly by the 82-mm mortars which they could take with them.

During April 18 and 19 small German forces between the two channels were wiped out, and a jumping-off point for crossing the West Oder secured. That evening the troops began to deploy along the dikes on the east bank of the West Oder, and on the morning of the 20th, after night bombing and a dawn artillery bombardment, 65th and 70th Armies crossed, seizing footholds on the west bank to which reinforcements were ferried. Over the next three days they linked their three bridgeheads, overcame stiff opposition, and penetrated deeply into the main German defences in several places. But on 49th Army's sector, all was not well. Most of it was still on the east bank, and it held only some small bridgeheads west of the river.

Since Zhukov's troops had now advanced to the area north-west of Berlin, Stavka on April 23 cancelled the order to 2nd Belorussian Front to by-pass Berlin from the north, and it reverted to the original plan. By late on the 25th, 65th and 70th Armies had advanced to the Randow river, where the Germans were unable to set up a stable defence to hinder them. The III Panzer Army had been severely battered and cut off from Berlin. Zhukov's encirclement manoeuvre north and north-west of Berlin was thus facilitated, as 2nd Belorussian Front had frustrated the German intention to use III Panzer Army to block it.

At this point Stavka took a crucially important decision, when it ordered Zhukov and Konev to complete the encirclement of the Frankfurt-Guben force in the forests south-east of Berlin by April 24, to prevent their breaking through to Berlin, and also urged the utmost energy in closing the ring west of the city.

To fulfil this directive Zhukov committed 3rd Army from second echelon on the night of April 22/23, with orders to isolate IX Army from Berlin by advancing from west of Fürstenwalde, and sent 47th Army out towards Potsdam to meet Konev's forces. Konev in turn ordered his 3rd Guards Army to capture Buckow (a southern suburb of Berlin) and link up with 1st Belorussian Front, 4th Tank Army to strike north-west to meet Zhukov's forces west of Berlin, and other elements to take up a series of positions on routes which the Frankfurt-Guben force might use to retreat westwards.

At 1500 hours on April 22 Hitler held his last extended operational conference in the Chancellery, and the OKW Diary, confirmed by Jodl, shows that it was then that he finally decided to stay in Berlin and conduct the defence in person. He ordered Keitel to 'withdraw all forces from the front facing the Anglo-Saxons and throw them into the battle for Berlin' to prevent its encirclement by the Red Army.

Link-up with the Americans
His intention was, however, frustrated, for on April 24 Zhukov's 8th Guards and 1st Guards Tank Armies linked up on the south-east edge of Berlin with Konev's 3rd Guards Tank and 28th Armies, thus encircling the Frankfurt-Guben force (200,000 men, over 2,000 guns and mortars, more than 200 tanks), while on the following day Konev's 4th Guards Tank Army met Zhukov's 2nd Guards Tank and 47th Armies at Potsdam, closing the ring on the Berlin force of about 200,000 men, 3,000 guns and mortars, and 250 tanks. Also on that day (April 25) elements of Konev's 5th Guards Army crossed the Elbe at Torgau and met American 1st Army, thus cutting the front in two.

The first ten days of the operation had seen the three Soviet Fronts split Army Groups Vistula and Centre into three isolated groups and set the stage to annihilate them, a task performed between April 26 and May 2.

The German High Command was desperate. It determined to try and postpone the impending catastrophe, if only for a few days, by using all available resources, including troops who were fighting the British and Americans, to break through to the city, and an OKW directive issued on the night of April 24/25 ordered: 'Throw all available forces against the mortal enemy, Bolshevism. In doing so ignore the considerable territorial gains which the Anglo-American forces may make.'

The XII Army (withdrawn from the Western Front), IX Army, and Operational Group Steiner were to be used for this: XII Army was first to relieve the encircled IX Army by an attack from Belzig towards Luckenwalde, and the two armies would then attack north towards Berlin, while Operational Group Steiner would attack south towards the city from Oranienburg. Grand Admiral Dönitz would also fly in sailors to reinforce the Berlin garrison. He now controlled the forces in northern Germany, while Staff B, headed by General Winter, took charge of those in the south.

Marshals Zhukov and Konev used part of their strength to establish a solid front against the Germans in and south-east of Berlin, as soon as they had encircled them, and decided to wipe out the force in the forests south-east of the city by two convergent attacks.

To avert any attempt at a breakout westwards towards XII Army, Konev also set up defences in depth along their most likely escape routes.

The conditions in which the Soviet attack was launched on April 26 were extremely unfavourable — the terrain was a mixture of forests, lakes, and marshes, and the German resistance strong, with passages between forests and lakes very stubbornly defended. On the night before the attack the Germans in the pocket regrouped and formed a strong assault force of one Panzer, one motorised, and three infantry divisions. This force attacked at 0800 hours on the 26th, broke through, and began spreading out to the west, but the Soviets closed the gap, and the assault force, isolated from the troops in the pocket, had largely been wiped out by evening. Nevertheless, Marshal Konev expected further attempts, and so he deployed five divisions with tanks and artillery along the most likely escape routes, in three lines facing east.

The further attempts made on April 27/28 all failed, but General Busse decided that despite the poor state of his force and the likelihood of heavy casualties another attempt must be made. This was launched at 0100 hours on April 29, and by dawn the Soviet line had been broken, but when the Germans came up against the prepared positions they made no further headway. Additional German forces were brought up from the pocket, bringing the assault force up to 45,000 men. Three days of bloody fighting ensued, and the Germans advanced somewhat, but they could not break through, nor could XII Army get through to them. The Görlitz force tried to drive south, but was repulsed, and had to revert to the defensive with its objectives unattained.

The Frankfurt-Guben force had meanwhile been split into small isolated groups, and the last of these was wiped out on May 1 at Beelitz, with 5,000 killed and 13,000 captured. This brought the total German losses here to 60,000 killed and 120,000 taken prisoner. Soviet booty comprised over 300 tanks and assault guns, 1,500 field guns, 2,180 machine-guns, 17,600 vehicles, and large quantities of supplies. Only small groups of Germans succeeded in slipping through the lines of demarcation between Soviet forces and escaping west through the forests.

Heavy fighting had now broken out in Berlin itself. This city, one of the largest in the world, had been preparing to fight since January, with a special Berlin Defence Staff in charge of the day to day work. Hitler had appointed Goebbels, his closest henchman, as Reichskommissar for Defence of the Capital, and General Reimann as City Commandant.

By the time the attack began there were three defensive perimeters. The outer perimeter ran mostly along the banks of lakes, rivers, and canals, and through wooded hills, some 15 to 25 miles from the city centre, and here the German High Command hoped to disorganise the attacking Soviet forces and impose maximum casualties on them. The *inner* perimeter, the main one, ran mostly through the outskirts of the suburbs, which had been made into strongpoints linked by three to five trenches, with machine-gun and artillery positions, while the *city* perimeter ran along the ring railway. The city had been divided into nine sectors, eight in a ring and the ninth in the centre. The central one was especially important, as it contained the state political and administrative apparatus, and therefore was particularly heavily fortified. Each sector was to be defended by two or three regiments — an overall count of not less than 24,000 men in the Berlin garrison.

Fortress Berlin: strongpoint after strongpoint
Within the sectors were mutually supporting strongpoints, and maximum use was made of all kinds of obstruction. Garrisons of the strongpoints varied with the importance of the objective, up to a company or sometimes a battalion. Not only intact buildings but entire blocks destroyed by British or American bombing were used, especially basements and semi-basements of ruined houses, as these were usually intact. All approaches to the centre were permanently barricaded, with tanks dug in or reinforced concrete pillboxes built at intersections to give an all-round field of fire. There were over 400 perimeter reinforced concrete structures in the Berlin defences. Extensive use was also made of the underground railways and sewers, which were considerably improved and extended during the period of preparation.

The Nazi leaders intended to hold Berlin at whatever cost, since its fall meant the collapse of their régime, and they were indifferent to the dangers to which their policy exposed the city's 2,000,000 civilian inhabitants, including many children and old people.

In addition to fortifying the city, the German High Command increased the number of troops allocated to its defence. General Weidling, commanding 56th Panzer Corps, was appointed to command the garrison when it was encircled, and on April 24 received a personal order from Hitler to hold the city at all costs. He ▷

The spectre of Stalingrad haunts the Reich capital, as a Soviet armoured division rolls deeper into the stricken city. For the most part, however, the Russians advanced not only through the streets but through courtyards, basements, and buildings. In this way they captured entire sections of the city: Zhukov's men alone cleared over 600 city blocks in the course of one day

took a number of steps to improve the defences, dispatching the 'Müncheberg' Panzer Division to Sectors 1 and 2 (in the east), the 'Nordland' Panzer Grenadier Division to Sector 3 (south-east), IX Airborne Division to Sectors 7 and 8 (north), and elements of XX Motorised Division to Sector 5 (south-west). Weidling kept his most intact and battle-worthy division (XVIII Panzer) as a reserve.

Whatever he might do, there was no hope for Berlin. It was tightly encircled, and each day the Soviet advance pushed possible relieving forces further west. Food stocks were negligible—two or three days only—as the majority of the warehouses were in the suburbs and had been destroyed during fighting or by the Germans themselves before withdrawing. From April 22 rations were severely cut. There was no water and no public transport. The best way out was to end the war: no honour or glory or victory could be got from fighting in the Berlin streets.

The Military Council of 1st Belorussian Front offered surrender terms on April 23, but the Germans rejected this humane proposal, even though it was pointless to carry on. Marshals Zhukov and Konev had therefore no choice but to proceed with the assault on the city.

Strong attacks from all sides

The Soviet offensive was concentric, with strong attacks launched from all sides simultaneously: from the south, between Potsdam and Tempelhof, by Konev's 3rd Guards Tank Army, attacking from Zehlendorf and Lichterfelde towards Wilmersdorf, and 28th Army from Lankwitz towards Schöneberg; and from south-east, east, north, and north-west by six of Zhukov's armies (8th Guards, 1st and 2nd Guards Tank, 3rd and 5th Shock and 47th) deployed on the line Tempelhof-Lichtenberg-Wedding-Siemensstadt-Spandau-Potsdam. The general assault was preceded by heavy air attacks by bombers of 16th and 18th Air Armies during daylight on April 25 and the night of the 25th/26th, and on the morning of the 26th fierce fighting began all along the perimeter of Berlin. Everywhere the German resistance was fierce, but especially in the bomb-damaged areas, where small units of troops in the ruins impeded the Soviet sappers and demolition parties which were clearing a path for the infantry, tanks, and artillery.

By the evening of the 27th, 47th Army had reached the bank of the Hafel from Spandau to Gatow, isolating Potsdam from Berlin, while 2nd Guards Tank and 3rd Shock Armies broke through the city defence perimeter, cleared Siemensstadt, crossed the Spree, and established several small bridgeheads on its south bank. The 5th Shock, 1st Guards Tank, and 8th Guards Armies, attacking from east and south-east, captured hundreds of city blocks, overran Tempelhof airport, and were in the city centre by evening. General Weidling was not pleased with the outcome of the fighting, especially the loss of the airport, and dismissed the Sector 3 Commander, SS-*Brigadeführer* Ziegler, replacing him with SS-*Brigadeführer* Krumberg. But reshuffles of this sort could no longer affect the issue.

Konev's armies coming up from the south were over the Teltow Canal and in full control of the southern suburbs of Stenglitz, Schmargendorf, and Grünewald. His 3rd Guards Army advanced 5½ miles on April 26, reached the inner perimeter in Schmargendorf, and was only 1¼ miles from Zhukov's 2nd Guards Tank Army. Weidling had to dispatch his last reserve, XVIII Panzer Division, to close the ominous gap in his line, but when he evaluated the day's results, he could not deny that his position had become materially worse, for his lines had been deeply penetrated in Spandau, the western harbour, Friedrichsheim, and Zehlendorf. Consolation, however, was now offered. 'Tomorrow, at the latest,' said Krebs, 'we shall contact Wenck's XII Army, which is attacking from the south-west.' But this, of course, was pure wishful thinking.

On the morning of the 27th, after preliminary artillery bombardment, the Soviet attack was renewed at 0500 hours, the day's objective being to wipe out the German force cut off in Potsdam and split up those in Berlin.

The German command had counted on bleeding the Soviets white and stalemating their attack by fighting for every block, building, floor, and workshop, as well as underground. But they had fundamentally miscalculated, for the Soviet assumption was that most German effort would go into the defence of the mined and barricaded streets, and they therefore resorted to bold out-flanking movements, advancing not through the streets but through courtyards, basements, and buildings, making holes in the party walls. In this way they captured entire sections of the city on the 27th: Zhukov's men alone cleared over 600 city blocks in the course of the day. By evening the Germans had been squeezed into a narrow east-west belt, 10 miles long but only 1¼ to 3 miles wide, and the Potsdam force had been wiped out.

With 47th Army's arrival on the Hafel, and elimination of the German bridgeheads in Spandau and Wilhelmstadt, breakout from Berlin to the west became practically impossible. Attempts were made to supply it by air, but without success, as most of the aircraft were shot down before they reached the city, and most of the loads which were dropped fell in the Soviet positions. The endeavour to use the broad tarmac of the Charlottenburger Chaussee as an airfield also failed, as it was considerably cratered by shelling and bombing, and came under Soviet artillery fire. Naturally all this had a bad effect on German morale, and there were cases of mass desertion and suicide, including that of Major-General Schultz, in charge of the southern part of the city.

However, the Nazi leaders continued to seek ways of using IX and XII Armies to lift the siege, and at 0300 hours on the 28th Krebs demanded, on Hitler's orders, that Keitel speed up the relief operation, saying that if help did not come within 48 hours it would be too late. But neither army was in any fit state to give help. The IX Army was surrounded and its end was near, while XII Army was on the defensive and under flank attack. By the evening of the 29th the Berlin garrison had been cut into three parts, one in the north-east, one in the Tiergarten (Zoo), and one in Westend and Ruhleben.

The Nazi leadership began to disintegrate. Hitler sensed his end was near, so on the 29th he composed his 'Testament', expelling Göring and Himmler from the Party and all their posts, and designating Grand Admiral Dönitz as his successor. Keitel dismissed the Commander of Army Group Vistula, General Heinrici, for allegedly 'sabotaging' Hitler's order to help Berlin. Events then took a most bizarre turn—nobody wanted Heinrici's job. Colonel-General Student was appointed, but was unable to take it up for a variety of reasons, so it was then offered to General Manteuffel (III Panzer Army), who refused on the grounds that he could not leave his army at such a critical moment, and began an energetic withdrawal to the west in order to surrender to the British as quickly as possible. General Tippelskirch also demurred stoutly, but under pressure from Keitel he took the job just the same.

General Weidling considered the situation critical, and in his routine report to Hitler on the 28th presented a plan for a breakout to end the incredible sufferings of the civilian population. Hitler turned it down. Weidling presented a similar plan on the following day, and this time Hitler approved it, scheduling it for the next day, so Weidling's staff began to work on it. Hitler confirmed his decision at 1430 hours, but between 1700 and 1800 hours sent a new order, cancelling the previous one and demanding that the city be defended to the last man.

By now the battle for the central sector, above all for the Reichstag—the final battle—had begun. This building was the focal point of all Soviet attacks, and every formation from Front down to section was out to get there first to fulfil the Red Army's assignment of raising the flag of victory over Berlin.

Best placed to win the contest was Colonel-General V. I. Kuznetsov's 3rd Shock Army, which had captured the Moabit area and by the evening of the 28th was a mere 550 yards north-west of the Reichstag, separated from it only by the Spree river and the Königs-platz, and that night it began to prepare to storm it. Routes from the north had to cross the Spree, here about 80 feet wide, and those from the south had to cross the Landwehr Canal. Both had granite-faced banks rising about 10 feet above water level. Most of the bridges over the Spree had been blown up, and the surviving Moltke Bridge was covered by anti-tank obstacles, artillery, and machine-guns. There was a permanent barricade at each end of it, kept under multiple cross-fire by machine-guns sited in nearby buildings. The massive stone buildings of the Imperial Theatre and the Ministry of the Interior, so solid that not even large-calibre shells could penetrate their walls, had been turned into strong-points, while the Reichstag itself had been adapted for all-round defence.

The walls of the lower storeys had been strengthened with rails, reinforced concrete, and earth. Windows and doors had been bricked up, and loop-holes made to fire through. Some 220 yards from the building were three trenches, linked with the Reichstag basement, and in front of these were anti-tank ditches filled with water. The streets leading to the Reichstag were barricaded, and the intersections mined. South-west of the Reichstag, in the Zoo-logical Gardens, was a powerful strongpoint with reinforced concrete bunkers. The garrison of the Reichstag consisted mainly of picked detachments of SS *Volkssturm* battalions, and small units from the Naval School, flown in from Rostock—some 5,000 men altogether. It was clear from all this that the men of 3rd Shock Army would have a tough fight on their hands, and that for the sake of the final victory over Nazism many would give their lives in the last days of the war.

The job of capturing the Reichstag was entrusted by the ▷

Russian snipers man a captured barricade. Resistance was savage everywhere, but especially so in ravaged areas like this one, where small numbers of troops could impede the Soviet advance

The Red Flag flies from the Brandenburg Gate, Berlin's most famous landmark

THE TOP RUSSIAN GENERALS

These were the men who strove to stem the tide of the German invasion of Russia; who masterminded the great Red Army counter-offensives from the gates of Moscow to 'Fortress Berlin'. Geoffrey Jukes selects five of the top Russian generals

Marshal of the Soviet Union
Georgy Konstantinovich Zhukov

Zhukov first became prominent in 1939 when he defeated a Japanese attempt to invade Outer Mongolia, and was appointed Chief of the General Staff in January 1941. His first major battle of the war was the defence of Moscow in the winter of 1941, and the subsequent counter-offensive which inflicted on the Germans their first serious defeat of the war and which had brought Army Group Centre to the brink of catastrophe before it petered out for lack of resources in the spring of 1942. After a relatively quiescent period in the summer of 1942 (he disagreed with Stalin's planned offensive), he was dispatched to Stalingrad as leader of the Stavka team sent to retrieve the situation there. Here he supervised the organisation of a counteroffensive which ended with the encirclement and destruction of German VI Army—a total of 330,000 Axis troops being killed or captured and 22 divisions wiped out. When Manstein's counteroffensive led to serious defeats being inflicted on the Soviet South-Western and Voronezh Fronts, he was again sent to retrieve the situation, and when the front had been stabilised he led the Stavka team which organised the defence of, and counteroffensive from, the Kursk salient, the success of which placed the outcome of the war in the East beyond further doubt. He was obliged to take over command of 1st Ukrainian Front when its C-in-C, General Vatutin, was ambushed and mortally wounded by Ukrainian Nationalist guerrillas on March 1, 1944, and in this capacity took part in the operations in which the Ukraine was cleared of Germans and Rumania invaded. He then moved to the northern sector of the front, where he co-ordinated the operations to liberate Belorussia and Poland, and commanded 1st Belorussian Front, which advanced at high speed from the Vistula to the Oder, and mounted the direct assault on Berlin in April/May 1945.

Zhukov performed simultaneously and highly successfully as a field commander, a member of Stavka, and Deputy Supreme Commander. Though he did not always achieve all his objectives, no battle with which he was associated was ever lost. His ruthlessness in pursuit of his objectives in the battles which he conducted, both offensive and defensive, sometimes led to heavy casualties, but in general his methods were economical in expenditure of forces by Soviet standards, and he was noted for his ability to inspire his subordinates and their troops to extraordinary efforts. He was not popular with his senior colleagues because of a certain arrogance, which in view of his record is understandable. He was intimately involved in almost all the major Soviet victories, and his record of success was on a scale unmatched by any other general in any army throughout the war. He is now living in retirement outside Moscow.

Marshal of the Soviet Union
Fedor Ivanovich Tolbukhin

As Chief-of-Staff of Transcaucasus Military District, Tolbukhin (then a major-general) organised the occupation of Northern Iran by the Red Army in the autumn of 1941, and planned the landing of two armies on the Kerch peninsula, in the rear of German XI Army which was besieging Sebastopol. When this operation failed to develop successfully, Tolbukhin was relieved of his post on March 10, 1942, and summoned to Moscow. After satisfying the Chief of General Staff that he was not responsible for the failure in the Crimea he was appointed, in July 1942, to command of 57th Army in the Don bend. This army took part in the general withdrawal to the Volga and the subsequent Stalingrad counteroffensive. For his handling of it Tolbukhin was promoted to Lieutenant-General and sent to command the newly-formed 68th Army on the North-West Front. In March 1943 he was appointed to command South Front, and in April was promoted again, to Colonel-General. In July his forces unsuccessfully attacked the Germans on the strongly fortified Mius river line, but in a second attempt in August/September they succeeded in breaking through and jointly with South-West Front freed the Donbass industrial area. His forces (now renamed 4th Ukrainian Front) liberated the Crimea in April 1944. In May Tolbukhin was transferred to command of 3rd Ukrainian Front, and he remained in this post until the end of the war. His forces took part in the encirclement of five German corps at Jassy-Kishinev, invaded Rumania and Bulgaria, liberated Belgrade and captured Budapest and Vienna, in joint operations with the 2nd Ukrainian Front of General R. Y. Malinovsky, with whom Tolbukhin established a very effective working relationship.

Tolbukhin was revered in the Red Army for his organising abilities, attention to detail, care for his subordinates, and avoidance where possible of excessive casualties. He suffered from ill health throughout his war service, and died in 1949.

Army General Ivan Danilovich Chernyakhovsky

One of the relatively few Jews to take up regular service in the Red Army, Chernyakhovsky emerged as an outstanding senior commander. As Commander-in-Chief 60th Army he recaptured the city of Voronezh in January 1943, and held the centre of the western face of the Kursk salient in July. After General Sokolovsky's failure to break through the German defences at Smolensk, Chernyakhovsky was appointed to succeed him as commander of Western (later renamed 3rd Belorussian) Front. In June and July 1944 his forces and those of 1st Belorussian Front encircled 105,000 Germans (the bulk of IV Army) at Minsk. He captured both that city and Vilnyus (the capital of Lithuania) on July 13, and then advanced at high speed to Kaunas on the border of East Prussia. In January 1945 he opened his advance on Königsberg against very heavily defended German positions, which he nevertheless overcame. In February 1945, while visiting front line positions, he was killed by a shell fragment. Thus, at the age of 38, ended the career of one of the Red Army's most brilliant younger generals, renowned for his dash and unorthodoxy.

Marshal of the Soviet Union
Semen Konstantinovich Timoshenko

Timoshenko belonged to the older generation of Red Army commanders, having served in the Civil War in the 1st Cavalry Army. After the débâcle in the Finnish War of 1939-40, he was appointed People's Commissar for Defence with the task of reorganising the army. He re-established the primacy of military commanders over their political commissars, introduced a new set of field regulations to replace the outdated ones in use at the time of the war with Finland, and tightened discipline by introducing a new code with very harsh punishments for minor offences.

Though his reforms were introduced hurriedly, and were too sweeping to be absorbed by an army soon to be faced by a major war, they were in general on the right lines. However, they had not fully taken effect by the time the Germans attacked, and Timoshenko has been blamed for the Red Army's unreadiness in June 1941. It is probably fairer to say that he was appointed too late, and was hamstrung by Stalin's unwillingness to allow him to take steps (such as firing on German reconnaissance aircraft) which Hitler might regard as provocative. Nor had Timoshenko the grasp of the concepts of armoured warfare necessary for a thoroughgoing modernisation.

On July 2, 1941 Timoshenko took command of the enlarged 'Western Front' and shortly thereafter of the 'Western Axis', the central of the three strategic 'axes' into which the Soviet-German front was divided. In this post he fought the Smolensk battle in which the German advance on Moscow was halted for two months, though at immense cost. In September 1941 he superseded Marshal Budenny as Commander-in-Chief South-Western Axis. Though too late to prevent the destruction of four Soviet armies in the Kiev pocket, he succeeded in slowing down the German advance until it eventually petered out. In the following spring, however, his attempted major strategic offensive, though initially successful, ended in disaster and the Soviet front in the south collapsed, letting the Germans through to Stalingrad and the North Caucasus. His command was abolished; but after his dismissal from command in the south, he was sent to command North-Western Front, and was downgraded even further in July 1942 by being dismissed from that post. However, he remained a member of Stavka, and as such co-ordinated the operations of 2nd and 3rd Ukrainian Fronts in their successful drive into the Balkans.

Marshal of the Soviet Union
Vasily Ivanovich Chuikov

In June 1941 Chuikov was Soviet Military Attaché in China, and was not recalled to the Soviet Union until March 1942. In May he was given command of the Reserve Army, which was renamed 64th Army and moved to the Don bend in July. After the retreat to Stalingrad and subsequent reshuffles of the command, he was appointed to command 62nd Army on September 12, 1942, thus becoming responsible for the defence of the city area itself. Under conditions of extreme difficulty, particularly over supplies (all of which had to be brought across the Volga under constant air and artillery bombardment), he conducted the defence with such skill and determination as to tie down numerically superior German forces (VI Army and part of IV Panzer Army) and make it possible for a subsequent Soviet counteroffensive to encircle them. His army then took part in their destruction (total Axis losses being 330,000) and after the surrender of the remnants of VI Army on February 2, 1943, it received the title of 8th Guards Army. Chuikov commanded it until the end of the war, taking part in a number of major offensives through Belorussia and Poland. On April 21, 1945 his forces penetrated into Berlin, and on May 1 the Chief of General Staff of the German Army, General Krebs, arrived at Chuikov's headquarters to negotiate the surrender of the German capital.

Chuikov was Commander-in-Chief of the Soviet Land Forces from 1960-64, and has headed the Civil Defence programme since 1964.

THE TOP GERMAN GENERALS

These were the men who commanded on the decisive front of the war; who perfected every technique of modern land warfare from daring armoured thrust to skilful rearguard withdrawal. Geoffrey Jukes selects five of the top German generals on the Russian Front

Zhukov

Rundstedt

Tolbukhin

Guderian

Chernyakhovsky

Halder

Timoshenko

Manstein

Chuikov

Heinrici

Field-Marshal Gerd von Rundstedt

Rundstedt had already retired, on grounds of age, before the outbreak of war, but was recalled in August 1939 to command Army Group South in the invasion of Poland, Army Group A in the campaign in France, and Army Group South again in the attack on the Soviet Union. An aristocratic Prussian of the old school, he was strongly opposed to the attack on Russia, but despite his reservations his army group achieved the greatest successes of 1941, killing or capturing at least 1,500,000 Soviet troops, occupying the Ukraine (the Soviet Union's richest agricultural area), the third and fourth largest Soviet cities (Kiev and Kharkov), and the extremely important industrial and mining areas of Kharkov and the Donbass. In December 1941, as winter set in and the Red Army counterattacked, he withdrew his forces from their exposed position at Rostov on Don to the more defensible Mius river line. When Hitler ordered him to countermand the withdrawal, he resigned his command, and never returned to the Eastern Front, though his military qualities and standing in his profession made him indispensable to Hitler, who appointed him Commander-in-Chief West early in 1942.

Colonel-General Heinz Guderian

It was Guderian more than any other who created the Panzer forces, often against the bitter opposition of his more conservatively-minded superiors. After the abilities of the new forces had been brilliantly proved by the Polish and French campaigns (in both of which he commanded Panzer forces in the field), he headed II Panzergruppe of Army Group Centre in the invasion of Russia. In the summer of 1941 he achieved outstanding results, the summit of his achievement being his dash across the front of General Yeremenko's army group to link up with Kleist's I Panzergruppe of Army Group South and encircle four Soviet armies in September. Personal and professional friction with his immediate superior, Field-Marshal von Kluge, led to his dismissal following the failure of the German offensive against Moscow, and he was not re-employed until February 1943, when he was appointed Inspector-General of Armoured Troops, with the tasks of restoring the morale of the Panzer forces and bringing order into the chaos of German armoured vehicle production. He achieved striking results in a few months, but the forces so laboriously recreated were largely squandered in the disastrous offensive at Kursk.

In July 1944 he succeeded Zeitzler as Chief of General Staff of the Army (OKH), but proved not an unqualified success. He was probably temperamentally unsuited to the task, the war was clearly lost, and Hitler had become impervious to military advice. Guderian urged withdrawal from the Baltic states, Italy, and the Balkans in order to furnish reserves for the Eastern Front, but to no avail. He was dismissed from his post in March 1945, for discussing with other leading Nazis the possibility of seeking an immediate peace.

Colonel-General Franz Halder

Halder became Chief of the General Staff of the Army High Command in August 1938, and was mainly responsible for the planning of the successful German offensives against France and Poland, as well as the invasion of the Soviet Union in 1941. In the late summer of 1941 he attempted to change the plan in order to exploit an apparent opportunity of destroying the main Soviet forces defending Moscow and capturing the city, but was overruled by Hitler, who did not sanction the offensive against Moscow until September, by which time its success was no longer possible. Though he survived the mass dismissal of generals which followed the German defeats at Rostov and Moscow, Halder's position became increasingly precarious. His design for the summer offensive of 1942 envisaged the Caucasus oilfields as the main objective, and when Hitler changed the emphasis to the capture of Stalingrad, relations between them became increasingly strained. As the German offensive began to grind to a halt, Halder advocated its abandonment, and at the end of September 1942 Hitler dismissed him.

Although Halder had been an early opponent of Hitler (he was the key figure in an abortive plot to remove the Nazi leader late in 1938), he appears to have become so impressed by Hitler's successes of 1939-41 that he became temporarily his supporter. He took no part in the attempt of July 20, 1944, on Hitler's life, but was nevertheless arrested, placed in solitary confinement in darkness for several months, and narrowly escaped execution. Despite his fine strategic brain he was no more successful at influencing Hitler than the many other generals who attempted to do so.

Field-Marshal Erich von Manstein

Manstein (born Lewinsky) devised the idea of a tank attack through the Ardennes which proved so important a factor in the German defeat of France in 1940, and was then appointed to command the landing force in the contemplated invasion of England. When this project was abandoned he headed 56th Panzer Corps of Army Group North, which in June 1941 advanced 200 miles in four days and captured the very important bridges over the Dvina. In September 1941 he became Commander-in-Chief XI Army, which invaded the Crimea, besieged Sebastopol (the main base of the Soviet Black Sea Fleet), and in July 1942 captured it after a 250-day siege. He was then chosen to command the attack on Leningrad, but when VI Army was surrounded at Stalingrad he became Commander-in-Chief of Army Group Don and planned the unsuccessful attempt to relieve Stalingrad. After the failure of this he executed Germany's last successful counterattack in the East, which in March 1943 threw the Red Army back to the Donets river. As Commander-in-Chief Army Group South he took part in the unsuccessful Kursk offensive, and it is likely that if his proposals for this operation had been accepted by Hitler, the damage done to the German forces would have been on a lesser scale. After its failure he conducted a skilful step-by-step retreat to the Polish border, but in March 1944 was dismissed by Hitler for advocating a long withdrawal to a shorter and more easily defended line.

Colonel-General Gotthard Heinrici

Heinrici commanded IV Army after the promotion of Field-Marshal von Kluge to command Army Group Centre, and during his holding of the Rogachev-Orsha line in autumn of 1943 gained an outstanding reputation as a winner of defensive battles against great odds. By use of a system in which very heavy concentrations of troops and artillery were achieved on narrow sectors, and by breaking the traditional system of the divisional unit through constant rotation of fresh troops from quiet sectors into the line, he succeeded in withstanding attacks by forces up to 12 times as numerous as his own, and occasionally even more. In May 1944 he took command of I Panzer Army and Hungarian I Army and conducted the retreat through the Carpathians to Silesia. In March 1945 he was given command of the defences on the Oder, where he held up Marshal Zhukov's advance for several days, despite the overwhelming weight of the Soviet forces. His methods of defence depended essentially on gaining good Intelligence of enemy intentions, so that force could be concentrated in good time in the right places, and on saving manpower by withdrawing his forward line in time for the Soviet artillery bombardment to dissipate itself on empty positions. By the end of the war he had become the German army's outstanding expert on defensive battles, a field in which it had initially proved itself surprisingly weak because of the pre-war training emphasis on attack.

411

army commander to Major-General Perevertkin's 79th Rifle Corps. General Perevertkin decided to carry it out by stages: first, to seize the Moltke Bridge, and then to capture the Ministry of the Interior so as to gain a good starting position for the storming of the Reichstag itself. Preparations for the attack were completed by the evening of April 28, and the divisions (171st under Colonel A.P. Negoda and 150th under Major-General B. M. Shatilov) took up their positions. Two assault groups supported by self-propelled guns had been formed in each battalion, and the artillery had been deployed close up to fire over open sights.

Closing in on the Reichstag

The Moltke Bridge was captured on the night of April 28/29 in a daring action by 1st Battalion, 756th Rifle Regiment of 150th Division (Captain S. A. Neustroyev) and 1st Battalion, 380th Rifle Regiment of 171st Division (Lieutenant K. Y. Samsonov). The Germans fought back stubbornly and put in furious counterattacks in an attempt to destroy the Soviets who had broken through on the left bank of the Spree. To make matters worse, the right bank had not been completely cleared of Germans. Those remaining there mounted a number of counterattacks during the night, and tried to blow the bridge up. But all the counterattacks were beaten off, and the rest of 756th and 380th Regiments crossed the river, together with 525th Regiment from 171st Division and 750th Regiment from 150th Division, accompanied by their artillery, tanks, and flamethrowers of 10th Independent Motorised Flamethrower Battalion.

Under cover of darkness the assault groups which had crossed attacked the corner house on Kronprinzenufer. By 0200 hours on the 29th it was in their hands, but further progress was stopped by heavy fire from the Ministry of the Interior ('Himmler's House', as the Soviet troops called it), the Kroll Opera, and houses on Alsenstrasse, which made it very difficult to get troops across the bridge and prevented development of the attack on the Reichstag. General Perevertkin therefore ordered that these strongpoints be captured as quickly as possible.

The attack began again at 0700 hours on the 29th, after a ten-minute bombardment. Although there was no practical point in it, German resistance was fierce everywhere, especially at the Ministry of the Interior, which was defended by a picked force of SS. The battle here raged all day, and the assault groups frequently fought hand to hand. Only after 674th Regiment (Colonel A. D. Plekhodanov) was committed from second echelon of 150th Division, during the night of April 29/30, was the German opposition broken. By 0430 hours on the 30th 'Himmler's House' had been cleared by the assault groups, and by that time small units from 525th Regiment had captured a number of enemy strongpoints adjoining it on the north-east, to come out on to Alsenstrasse. Captain Neustroyev (now a Lieutenant-Colonel and a Hero of the Soviet Union) writes in recalling the battle: 'We had to work in small groups, and fight literally for every room. Smoke, smoke, smoke . . . it was stifling. Hardly any of the wounded left the battlefield—if field is the right word to apply to the offices of Himmler's butchers.'

The fall of the main strongpoint—the Ministry of the Interior—and the clearing of the area between Kronprinzenufer and Alsenstrasse seriously weakened the defence of the Reichstag, and attacking units of 150th and 171st Divisions got to between 330 and 550 yards of it, but the nearer they were, the harder it was to go on. Development of the assault was especially hindered by the Kroll Opera strongpoint. Machine-guns and light artillery had been emplaced on the roof and second floor landings. These kept under fire both the Moltke Bridge (thus impeding the crossing of units from 79th Rifle Corps) and Königsplatz, where units of 380th, 674th, and 756th Regiments had taken up positions for the final assault on the Reichstag.

To avoid a postponement of the assault on the Reichstag itself, General Perevertkin, entirely reasonably, decided to storm it and the Kroll Opera simultaneously, the Reichstag with 150th and 171st Divisions from north-west and west, while 207th Division (Colonel V. M. Afasov) attacked the Kroll Opera to pin down the German forces there and thus facilitate the main attack. About 90 guns were brought close up, and *Katyusha* rockets were used as well. On the initiative of the corps command and political department, two volunteer groups of Communist Party and Youth League members,

Before the survivors in the *Führerbunker* accepted the fact that further resistance was hopeless, there occurred the last great engagement in Berlin: the battle for the Reichstag

Top: Katyusha rocket batteries pound the Reichstag area at long range. *Bottom:* Soviet infantry, headed by the Red Flag, storm through the rubble towards the battered citadel

each consisting of 20 men, were formed to raise the flag over the Reichstag, and each was placed under command of a daring and energetic officer, Major M: M. Bondar and Captain V. N. Makov.

The actual assault on the Reichstag began early on the morning of April 30, and lasted without a moment's pause until the morning of May 2. The garrison resisted doggedly, paying no regard to losses or to whether it was sensible to fight on. Attacks undertaken by 150th and 171st Divisions at 0430 and 1130 hours had no success. Small units of 674th and 756th Regiments which reached the last obstacle—the anti-tank ditch—came under a hail of fire and had to go to ground. Apart from the fierce fire, the Germans also mounted a number of counterattacks in an effort to disrupt the Soviet assault. At midday about one battalion of infantry, supported by machine-guns and artillery, counterattacked 525th Regiment in the Alsenstrasse area, and then a flank attack was put in against 380th Regiment. Fierce hand-to-hand fighting took place before the German attacks were beaten off.

The artillery bombardment preceding the storming of the building began at 1300 hours on April 30. All the guns which had been brought over to the south bank of the Spree, the tanks, self-propelled guns, and *Katyushas* fired over open sights and were supported by the artillery on the north bank, while the infantry joined in with captured bazookas. A cloud of smoke and dust hovered over and around the Reichstag.

At 1330 hours the assault began. While a storm of fire poured down on the attacking infantry from machine-guns and automatic weapons in the building, heavy guns and anti-aircraft artillery fired on them from the Zoo, and most of the assault force was pinned to the ground, so that only isolated groups broke through. The assault had failed yet again, and preparations had to be made afresh. The new assault went in at 1800 hours under artillery cover. In the front ranks were the 1st Battalions of 380th, 574th, and 756th Rifle Regiments. This time the garrison of the Reichstag could not restrain the onslaught of the Soviet troops, who took only a few minutes to reach the building.

Among the first to raise himself up to the steps of the main approach was Sergeant Peter Pyatnitsky, with the flag of 1st Battalion, 756th Regiment, but he was mortally wounded by a machine-gun burst. The flag was picked up by Junior Sergeant P. D. Shcherbina and placed on one of the columns of the main entrance.

Battle for the Reichstag

Breaking into the building proved a very arduous task for the Soviet troops. At first they infiltrated into the circular vestibule through gaps in the walls, and then after hard fighting began to spread out into the other rooms. They met desperate resistance. The battle for the Reichstag was literally a fight for every storey, staircase, corridor, and room, with the Germans using everything they had—grenades, bazookas, automatic weapons, and machine-guns—setting the rooms on fire, and counterattacking frequently. Men were suffocating in the smoke. Captain K. Y. Samsonov later recalled: 'Under cover of the smoke the Germans began to press us, but we stood our ground. The fighting became fiercer and fiercer, and the barrels of our weapons grew too hot to touch. There was no water, we were tormented by thirst, the smoke gnawed at our eyes, and many men's uniforms were on fire.'

The Soviet onslaught was growing all the time; they smashed the resistance on the ground floor and proceeded to storm the first floor. By the end of the day they had captured most of it, but the Germans kept up a fierce resistance in the basement. Soldiers from Captain Makarov's group broke out on to the roof and set up the flag which had been entrusted to them. On the night of April 30/May 1, by order of Colonel F. M. Zinchenko, commanding 756th Regiment, Sergeants M. A. Yegorov and M. V. Kontary raised the flag given to the regiment by the Military Council of 3rd Shock Army on the dome of the Reichstag. The flag of victory waved proudly over the prostrate city.

Although the fighting in the Reichstag continued throughout May 1 the garrison's will to resist was broken, and individual groups began to put out white flags. The position of those who had been driven into the basement became hopeless, and on the morning of May 2 they capitulated. Some 2,500 of the Reichstag garrison had been killed, and 2,600 taken prisoner.

While the battle for the Reichstag was on, Soviet troops ▷

One of the 2,600 German defenders of the Reichstag who surrendered on the morning of May 2. Another 2,500 had been killed in the bitter fighting against dedicated Soviet units

Top: Russians exult in front of the Chancellery—under which lay the *Führerbunker*. *Bottom:* Sergeant Shcherbina *(right)* raised the Red Flag on the steps of the Reichstag

413

Zhukov sums up:
This was not like Moscow or Leningrad, or even Stalingrad . . . During the first years of the war, we often had to fight against fearful odds; nor did our officers and soldiers have as much experience as they have now In this Battle of Germany we had great superiority in men, tanks, aircraft, guns, everything. Three-to-one, sometimes even five-to-one. But the important thing was not to take Berlin— that was a foregone conclusion—but to take it in the shortest possible time. The Germans were expecting our blow and we had to think out how to introduce the important element of surprise.

I attacked along the *whole* front, and at night. As prisoners later told us, the great artillery barrage at night was what they had least expected. They had expected night attacks, but not a *general* attack at night. After the artillery barrage, our tanks went into action. We had used 22,000 guns and mortars along the Oder, and 4,000 tanks were now thrown in. We also used 4,000 to 5,000 planes. During the first day alone there were 15,000 sorties.

The great offensive was launched at 4 am on April 16, and we devised some novel features: to help the tanks to find their way, we used searchlights, 200 of them. These powerful searchlights not only helped the tanks, but also blinded the enemy, who could not aim properly at our tanks.

Very soon we broke through the German defences on the Oder along a wide front. Realising this, the German High Command threw what reserves it had outside Berlin into the fray, and even some reserves from inside Berlin. But it was no good. These reserves were smashed from the air or by our tanks, and when our troops broke into Berlin, the city was largely denuded of troops. Most of Berlin's anti-aircraft guns had been thrown into the Oder battle, and the city was defenceless against air attack.

More than half a million German soldiers took part in the Berlin operation. 300,000 were taken prisoner even before the capitulation, 150,000 were killed; the rest fled.

It was an interesting and instructive battle, especially as regards tempos and the technique of night fighting on such a scale. The main point is that the Germans were smashed on the Oder, and in Berlin itself it was, in fact, just one immense mopping-up operation. It was very different from the Battle of Moscow.
[From *Russia at War* by Alexander Werth (Barrie & Rockliffe).]

414

were fighting for central Berlin. They suppressed fierce German opposition to reach the Chancellery, the Potsdam station, and the Zoo, thus tightening the ring around the encircled Berlin garrison and breaking it up into small isolated groups. When the High Command communication centre on Bendlerstrasse fell into Soviet hands the situation became hopeless for the Nazi supreme leadership. Besides, the Chancellery, beneath which Hitler and his entourage were still skulking, was by now less than half a mile from the line of battle.

On April 28 Hitler learned that Mussolini had been caught and executed by the Italians, and fearing to share the same fate, or to fall into Soviet hands and be made to answer for all his crimes, he put an end to himself at midday on the 30th. In accordance with his 'Testament' Grand Admiral Dönitz became head of a hastily created new government of the Reich. Field-Marshal Schörner was appointed Commander-in-Chief of the Army, Colonel-General Jodl Chief-of-Staff of OKW, and General Krebs Chief of the Army General Staff.

The purpose of the new government was to save the Wehrmacht from final defeat and maintain the reactionary Nazi circles in power in Germany, and it took a number of steps to that end. On the one hand, Dönitz, who was at Flensburg, gave the governing circles of Britain and the USA to understand from his broadcasts that Germany was continuing to fight only in the name of the struggle against Bolshevism, and began negotiating with the Anglo-American command about a separate capitulation of the German armed forces in the West, thus attempting to keep the Wehrmacht in being to some extent. On the other hand, Goebbels and Bormann in Berlin tried to play for time by entering into negotiations with the Soviet command. Late on April 30 they sent Colonel Seiffert with a flag of truce. At 2330 hours he came out to the Soviet forward troops in the Potsdam Station area, and was taken to 8th Guards Army HQ, where he declared that the leadership of Nazi Germany requested that its representative be received by the Soviet command to make an important statement.

At 0300 hours on May 1 the Chief of General Staff of OKH, General Krebs, accompanied by the Chief-of-Staff of 56th Panzer Corps, Colonel von Dufving, an interpreter, and one soldier, passed through the front line and were taken to 35th Guards Rifle Division HQ, from which after half an hour they were taken on to the command post of 8th Guards Army, where the commander, Colonel-General V. I. Chuikov, received them. Shortly afterwards the Deputy Commander of 1st Belorussian Front, Army General V. D. Sokolovsky, arrived, and he and General Chuikov entered into negotiation with Krebs on behalf of the Soviet command. The document which Krebs handed over was signed by Goebbels and Bormann. It stated officially that Hitler had committed suicide, a new government had been formed, and Krebs was authorised to negotiate with the Soviet command.

In the interests of gaining time the Nazi leaders proposed a temporary cease-fire in Berlin. The Soviet command replied that a cease-fire could come about only if Germany surrendered unconditionally to *all* the Allies, and warned the Germans that further resistance by the Berlin garrison would lead only to useless bloodshed and to entirely unjustified casualties among the population of Berlin. If the conditions were accepted all personnel of the garrison were guaranteed their lives, retention of medals and personal effects, and, in the case of officers, their swords. The discussion lasted about five hours, and Krebs left to report to Goebbels at 1400 hours. The Nazi leaders did not hurry to answer, and it was 1800 hours before Goebbels and Bormann replied, rejecting the terms. Yet again they had shown their recklessness, egotism, and complete indifference to the lives of millions of ordinary Germans.

There was no alternative for the Soviet command but to proceed to the final storming of the city, and at 1830 hours all the artillery opened heavy fire on the German forces which were still resisting. Dense clouds of smoke, dust, and ash covered the centre of the city, and at 1915 hours the general assault began. Fighting went on throughout the night. The 3rd Shock Army, attacking from the north, linked up south of the Reichstag with 8th Guards Army advancing from the south, while 2nd and 3rd Guards Tank Armies linked up in the Zoo, so that by the morning of May 2 the surviving remnants of the Berlin garrison were in an absolutely hopeless position.

However much Goebbels and Bormann might demand heroism, there was nothing left for the Germans but to lay down their arms. And indeed at 0040 hours on May 2 the radio station of 79th Guards Rifle Division (8th Guards Army) picked up a message in Russian from the commander of 56th Panzer Corps, requesting the Soviets to cease fire at 0050 hours and receive truce negotiators at the Potsdam bridge. The Soviet forces complied with this request and ceased fire. Colonel von Dufving arrived again, accompanied by

two majors, and stated on behalf of the corps commander, General Weidling, that it would cease fighting and surrender.

Marshal Zhukov demanded that the whole corps disarm and surrender by 0700 hours. This demand was met, and at 0600 hours General Weidling, who was also commandant of Berlin, crossed the front line and surrendered. It was proposed to him that he should at once order the entire garrison to capitulate. He wrote out an order, in which he declared that the general situation made further fighting senseless, and 'every hour of fighting increases the terrible sufferings of the civilian population of Berlin and of our wounded. Everyone who falls for Berlin is making a useless sacrifice. In agreement with the Supreme Command of the Soviet Forces, I order an immediate cessation of the conflict'.

The end in Berlin

A similar order was issued somewhat later by Fritsche, Goebbels' principal deputy. The orders were issued over the radio, through amplifiers, and by specially dispatched German officers in cars. But while these orders were being written and announced, German troops had already begun surrendering on their own initiative. All resistance had ceased by 1500 hours, and by the evening of that day (May 2), the whole city was occupied by Soviet forces.

Goebbels, following his Führer's example and fearing a just vengeance, took his own life on May 1, first killing his young children and his wife. Bormann vanished. There are various versions of what happened to him, but according to recent information it is by no means impossible that he is still alive and in hiding in South America.

The 1st Ukrainian Front's forces then began to prepare for the Prague operation. They were replaced south of Berlin by 1st Belorussian Front, which went in pursuit of German XII Army and reached the Elbe on May 7. A large part of XII Army crossed the Elbe and surrendered to the Americans.

While the last battles were being fought in Berlin, 2nd Belorussian Front to the north was continuing its successful offensive to shatter III Panzer Army. The Germans had maintained a dogged resistance from prepared second and rear defence lines throughout April 26/27, but unavailingly, because by the evening of the 27th both lines had been broken on the west bank of the Oder and not only their main forces but also all the reserves dispatched to them had been smashed. The beaten remnants of III Panzer Army were retreating at high speed, with 2nd Belorussian Front hard on their heels.

During the pursuit 2nd Belorussian Front's operations may be summed up as fights with individual covering units and reserves, by whose aid the German command was trying to hold up the Soviet advance and withdraw its forces across the Elbe. As the Germans withdrew they blew the bridges and mined the roads behind them, but in spite of that the Soviet pursuing force managed to cover 12 to 18 miles a day, and by the evening of May 2 it had destroyed or captured the Germans retreating before it and reached the shores of the Baltic. During the two succeeding days the centre and left of the front reached the Elbe from Wismar to Wittenberg, where they met the forward elements of British 2nd Army, and on May 5 they cleared the islands of Wollin, Usedom, and Rügen.

So Berlin fell, and the victory flag raised over the Reichstag by Soviet troops marked the end of Hitler's military order in Europe.

The Berlin operation was one of the greatest and most important of the war. Altogether 3,500,000 men took part in it on the two sides, with more than 52,000 guns and mortars, 7,500 tanks and self-propelled guns, about 11,000 combat aircraft and around 280 large army formations. But not only the scale of it was remarkable: the results were, too. Soviet forces smashed a strong German force, of about 90 divisions, took 480,000 prisoners, and captured over 1,500 tanks or self-propelled guns, 4,500 aircraft, and about 11,000 guns or mortars. It was another illustration of the skill of Soviet commanders and the bravery of their troops, in preparing such a large operation in less than 14 days and solving all the problems which arose in the course of it.

But let it not be forgotten that the victory was not cheaply won. Between April 16 and May 8, 1st and 2nd Belorussian and 1st Ukrainian Fronts lost about 300,000 men, killed, wounded, or missing, over 2,000 tanks or self-propelled guns, and more than 500 aircraft. The remains of the Soviet dead lie now in the quiet of communal graves in Treptow Park and Pankow, their memory crowned by an impressive statue of the soldier-liberator, holding in his arms a child he has saved.

The defeat of the German forces at Berlin, and the capture of the city, paralysed the state and military administration of Nazi Germany, and forced its armed forces to capitulate, thus ending the war in Europe.

THE DEATH OF HITLER

Berlin, April/May 1945
Alan Bullock

By April 1945, the atmosphere in the 'Führerbunker' was tense to the point of hysteria. The presence of the Red Army in the city, the bombing, and the lack of any coherent Intelligence all combined to make Hitler even more unpredictable than usual. He wavered between unreasonable extremes of hope, and rather more reasonable extremes of despair. With the Red Army only a mile away, he maintained a daily routine of conferences, keeping alive as long as possible the pretence of power. After Göring's 'betrayal' Hitler's mind turned increasingly to suicide. Vacillating and unbalanced, he remained constant only in his decision to remain in Berlin and, finally, to take his life

This picture, taken just ten days before Hitler died, reflects his mood of tension and despair before the *Götterdämmerung*

By the middle of April 1945, the Nazi empire, which had once stretched to the Caucasus and the Atlantic, was reduced to a narrow corridor in the heart of Germany little more than a hundred miles wide. Hitler had reached the end of the road.

Shortly after Hitler's hopes had been raised and dashed by Roosevelt's death, Eva Braun arrived unexpectedly in Berlin and, defying Hitler's orders, announced her intention of staying with him to the end. For some time Goebbels had been urging Hitler to remain in Berlin and make an ending in the besieged city worthy of an admirer of Wagner's *Götterdämmerung*. Goebbels scorned any suggestion that by leaving the capital he might allow the 2,000,000 people still living there to escape the horrors of a pitched battle fought in the streets of the city. 'If a single white flag is hoisted in Berlin,' he declared, 'I shall not hesitate to have the whole street and all its inhabitants blown up. This has the full authority of the Führer.'

None the less Hitler's mind was not yet made up. Preparations were in train for the government to leave Berlin and move to the 'National Redoubt' in the heart of the Bavarian Alps, round Berchtesgaden, the homeland of the Nazi movement, where the Führer was expected to make his last stand. Various ministries and commands had already been transferred to the Redoubt area, and the time had come when Hitler himself must follow if he was still to get through the narrow corridor left between the Russian and American armies.

Hitler's original plan was to leave for the south on April 20, his 56th birthday, but at the conference on the 20th, following the reception and congratulations, he still hesitated. For the last time, all the Nazi hierarchs were present — Göring, Himmler, Goebbels, Ribbentrop, Bormann, Speer — together with the chiefs of the three services. Their advice was in favour of his leaving Berlin. The most Hitler would agree to, however, was the establishment of Northern and Southern Commands, in case Germany should be cut in two by the Allied advance. There and then he appointed Admiral Dönitz to assume the full responsibility in the north, but, although Kesselring was nominated for the Southern Command, Hitler left open the possibility that he might move to the south and take the direction of the war there into his own hands.

On April 21 Hitler ordered an all-out attack on the Russians besieging Berlin. Every man was to be thrown in, and any commander who withheld forces was to be shot. The direction of the attack Hitler confided to an SS general, Obergruppenführer Steiner, and he built the most exaggerated hopes on the success which he anticipated from the operation. It was the disappointment of these hopes which led him finally to make up his mind and refuse to leave the capital.

For Steiner's attack was never launched. The withdrawal of troops to provide the forces necessary allowed the Russians to break through the city's outer defences in the north, and Hitler's plan foundered in confusion. Throughout the morning of April 22 a series of telephone calls from the Bunker failed to elicit any news of what was happening. By the time the conference met at three o'clock in the afternoon there was still no news of Steiner, and Hitler was on the verge of one of his worst outbursts.

The decision to stay
The storm burst during the conference, which lasted for three hours and left everyone who took part in it shaken and exhausted. In a universal gesture of denunciation Hitler cursed them all for their cowardice, treachery, and incompetence. The end had come, he declared. He could no longer go on. There was nothing left but to die. He would meet his end there, in Berlin; those who wished could go to the south, but he would never move. From this resolution he was not to be moved. Telephone calls from Himmler and Dönitz, and the entreaties of his own staff, had no effect. Acting on his decision, he dictated an announcement to be read over the wireless, declaring that the Führer was in Berlin and that he would remain there to the very last.

The implications of Hitler's declaration were more far-reaching than may appear at first sight. For, since 1941, Hitler had taken over the immediate day-to-day direction of the war as the active commander-in-chief of the German army. Now that he was forced to admit the fact of defeat, however, the man who had insisted on prolonging the war against the advice of his generals refused to take any further responsibility. Instead, he instructed his two chief assistants, Generals Keitel and Jodl, to leave at once for Berchtesgaden and declined to give them further orders. All the grandiloquent talk of dying in Berlin cannot disguise the fact that this petulant decision was a gross dereliction of his duty to the troops still fighting under his command and an action wholly at variance with the most elementary military tradition.

Jodl later described to General Koller, the Luftwaffe Chief-of-Staff, their unavailing efforts to persuade Hitler to change his mind:

Hitler declared that he had decided to stay in Berlin, lead its defence and then at the last moment shoot himself. For physical reasons he was unable to take part in the fighting personally, nor did he wish to, for he could not run the risk of falling into enemy hands. We all attempted to bring him over from this decision and even offered to move troops from the west to fight in the east. His answer was that everything was falling to pieces anyway, and that he could do no more: that should be left to the Reichsmarshall (Göring). When someone remarked that no soldier would fight for the Reichsmarshall, Hitler retorted: 'What do you mean, fight? There's precious little more fighting to be done and, if it comes to negotiating, the Reichsmarshall can do better than I can.' The latest development of the situation had made the deepest impression on him, he spoke all the time of treachery and failure, of corruption in the leadership and in the ranks. Even the SS now told him lies.

By the time Jodl and Keitel left Hitler on the evening of April 22 he had recovered his self-control and talked calmly to Keitel of the possibility of the XII Army, then fighting on the Elbe under General Wenck, coming to the relief of Berlin. But his decision to stay in the capital was irrevocable; as a logical consequence he began to burn his papers and invited Goebbels, the advocate of a 'world-historical end', to join him in the Führerbunker.

The setting in which Hitler played out the last scene of all was well suited to the end of so strange a history. The Chancellery air-raid shelter, in which the events of April 22 had taken place, was buried 50 feet beneath the ground, and built in two storeys covered with a massive canopy of reinforced concrete. The lower of the storeys formed the Führerbunker. It was divided into 18 small rooms grouped on either side of a central passageway. Half of this passage was closed by a partition and used for the daily conferences. A suite of six rooms was set aside for Hitler and Eva Braun. Eva had a bed-sitting-room, a bathroom, and a dressing-room; Hitler a bedroom and a study, the sole decoration in which was a portrait of Frederick the Great. A map-room used for small conferences, a telephone exchange, a power-house, and guard rooms took up most of the rest of the space, but there were two rooms for Goebbels (formerly occupied by Morell) and two for Stumpfegger, Brandt's successor as Hitler's surgeon. Frau Goebbels, who insisted on remaining with her husband, together with her five children, occupied four rooms on the floor above, where the kitchen, servants' quarters, and dining-hall were also to be found. Other shelters had been built near-by. One housed Bormann, his staff, and the various service officers; another Mohnke, the SS commandant of the Chancellery, and his staff.

Exhaustion and near-hysteria

The physical atmosphere of the bunker was oppressive, but this was nothing compared to the pressure of the psychological atmosphere. The incessant air-raids, the knowledge that the Russians were now in the city, nervous exhaustion, fear, and despair produced a tension bordering on hysteria, which was heightened by propinquity to a man whose changes of mood were not only unpredictable but affected the lives of all those in the shelter.

Hitler had been living in the bunker for some time. Such sleep as he got in the last month appears to have been between 8 and 11 am. As soon as the mid-morning air attacks began, Hitler got up and dressed. He had a horror of being caught either lying down or undressed.

Much of the time was still taken up with conferences. The midday or afternoon conference was matched by a second after midnight which sometimes lasted till dawn. The evening meal was served between 9 and 10 pm, and Hitler liked to drag it out in order not to be left alone during a night air-raid. Sometimes he would receive his secretaries at six in the morning, after a late-night conference. He would make an effort to stand up and greet them, but rapidly sank back exhausted on to the sofa. The early-morning meal was the one he most enjoyed, and he would eat greedily of chocolate and cakes, playing with his dog Blondi and the puppies which she produced in March. To one of these puppies Hitler gave his own old nickname, Wolf, and brought it up without anyone's help. He would lie with it on his lap, stroking it and repeating its name until the meal was over and he tried to get some sleep.

Between April 20 and 24 a considerable number of Hitler's entourage—including Göring, Hitler's adjutant Schaub, and Morell—left for the south. In the last week of his life Hitler shared the cramped accommodation of the Führerbunker with Eva Braun; the Goebbels and their children; Stumpfegger, his surgeon; his valet, Heinz Linge; and his SS adjutant, Günsche; his two remaining secretaries, Frau Christian and Frau Junge; Fräulein Manzialy, his vegetarian cook; and Goebbels' adjutant. Frequent visitors to the Führerbunker from the neighbouring shelters were Bormann; General Krebs, who had succeeded Guderian as the army's chief-of-staff; General Burgdorf, Hitler's chief military adjutant; Artur Axmann, the leader of the Hitler Youth (a thousand of whom took part in the defence of Berlin); and a crowd of *aides-de-camp,* adjutants, liaison officers, and SS guards.

On Monday, April 23, having at last come to a decision, Hitler was in a calmer frame of mind. Keitel, who talked to him in the afternoon, reports that he appeared rested and even satisfied with the position. This was borne out by his reception of Speer, who flew back from Hamburg to say farewell, and made a full confession of the steps he had taken to thwart Hitler's orders for scorching the German earth. Hitler undoubtedly had a genuine affection for Speer, but it is still surprising that he was moved, rather than incensed, by his frankness. Speer was neither arrested nor shot, but allowed to go free, and like everyone else who saw Hitler that day he was impressed by the change in him, the serenity which he appeared to have reached after months of desperate effort to maintain his conviction, in the face of all the facts, that the war could still be won. Now that he had abandoned the attempt to flog himself and those around him into keeping up the pretence he was more philosophical and resigned to facing death as a release from the difficulties which overwhelmed him. He repeated to Speer what he had told Jodl and Keitel the day before: that he would shoot himself in the bunker and have his body burned to avoid its falling into the hands of the enemy. This was stated quietly and firmly, as a matter no longer open to discussion.

While it is true, however, that Hitler never varied this decision, his moods remained as unstable as ever, anger rapidly succeeding to resignation, and in turn yielding to the brief revival of hope. This is well illustrated by the incident of Göring's dismissal, of which Speer was also a witness before he

left the bunker for good in the early hours of April 24.

Göring's last message to Hitler

When Göring flew to the south he left behind as his representative General Koller, the Chief-of-Staff of the Luftwaffe. On April 23 Koller appeared at the Obersalzberg and reported the decisions of the fateful conference in the bunker the day before. Believing that Hitler had abandoned the direction of the war, and interpreting literally his remark that 'if it comes to negotiating the Reichsmarshall can do better than I can', Göring assumed that he was now the Führer's successor, as he had been designated by the decree of June 1941. He wirelessed to Hitler for confirmation. The message, sent on the evening of April 23, read as follows:

My Führer,

In view of your decision to remain at your post in the fortress of Berlin, do you agree that I take over, at once, the total leadership of the Reich, with full freedom of action at home and abroad, as your deputy, in accordance with your decree of June 29, 1941? If no reply is received by ten o'clock tonight I shall take it for granted that you have lost your freedom of action, and shall consider the conditions of your decree as fulfilled, and shall act for the best interests of our country and our people. You know what I feel for you in the gravest hour of my life. Words fail me to express myself. May God protect you, and speed you quickly here in spite of all.

Your loyal
Hermann Göring

When Göring's message reached the bunker it did not take long for Bormann, Göring's sworn enemy, to represent it as an

Outside the Chancellery, in one of the last pictures taken of him, Hitler decorates some of Berlin's defenders

ultimatum. Speer, who was present, reports that Hitler became unusually excited, denouncing Göring as corrupt, a failure, and a drug addict, but adding: 'He can negotiate the capitulation all the same. It does not matter anyway who does it.'

The addition is revealing. Hitler was clearly angry at Göring's presumption – the habits of tyranny are not easily broken – he agreed to Bormann's suggestion that Göring should be arrested for high treason, and he authorised his dismissal from all his offices, including the succession – yet 'it does not matter anyway'. As Speer pointed out at Nuremberg, all Hitler's contempt for the German people was contained in the off-hand way in which he made this remark.

To try to make too much sense out of what Hitler said or ordered in those final days would be wholly to misread both the extraordinary circumstances and his state of mind. Those who saw him at this time and who were not so infected by the atmosphere of the bunker as to share his mood regarded him as closer than ever to that shadowy line which divides the world of the sane from that of the insane. He spoke entirely on the impulse of the moment, and moods of comparative lucidity, such as that in which Speer had talked to him on the 23rd, were interspersed with wild accusations, wilder hopes, and half-crazed ramblings.

Hitler found it more difficult than ever to realise the situation outside the shelter, or to grasp that this was the end. Conferences continued until the morning of the day on which he committed suicide, and as late as the evening of April 29 Hitler was demanding news of General Wenck's XII Army which he had ordered to relieve Berlin. On April 24 he sent an urgent summons for

Colonel-General Ritter von Greim, in command of Luftflotte VI, to fly from Munich to Berlin. Greim made the hazardous journey into the heart of the capital, with the help of a young woman test-pilot, Hanna Reitsch, at the cost of a severe wound in his foot. To get there they had to fly at the level of the tree-tops, in the face of heavy AA fire and constant fighter attacks which cost the escorting aircraft considerable losses. When Greim arrived it was to find that Hitler had insisted on this simply in order to inform him personally that he was promoting him to be commander-in-chief of the Luftwaffe in succession to Göring, an appointment that he could perfectly well have made by telegram. The only result of Hitler's action was to imprison the new commander-in-chief in the bunker for three days and to cripple him with a wounded foot.

The scene when Hitler greeted Greim and Hanna Reitsch was marked by the theatricality of Hitler's behaviour. Hanna Reitsch describes the tears in his eyes as he referred to Göring's treachery:

His head sagged, his face was deathly pallid, and the uncontrolled shaking of his hands made the message [from Göring] flutter wildly as he handed it to Greim.

The Führer's face remained deathly earnest as Greim read. Then every muscle in it began to twitch and his breath came in explosive puffs; only with effort did he gain sufficient control to shout: 'An ultimatum! A crass ultimatum! Now nothing remains. Nothing is spared to me. No allegiances are kept, no honour lived up to, no disappointments that I have not had, no betrayals that I have not experienced – and now this above all else. Nothing remains. Every wrong has already been done me.'

Later that night Hitler sent for Hanna Reitsch and gave her a vial of poison. 'Hanna, you belong to those who will die with me. Each of us has a vial of poison such as this. I do not wish that one of us falls into the hands of the Russians alive, nor do I wish our bodies to be found by them.' At the end of a highly emotional interview Hitler reassured her: 'But, my Hanna, I still have hope. The army of General Wenck is moving up from the south. He must and will drive the Russians back long enough to save our people. Then we will fall back to hold again.'

Hitler's resentment found expression in constant accusations of treachery, which were echoed by Goebbels and the others. Hanna Reitsch describes Eva Braun as 'raving about all the ungrateful swine who had deserted their Führer and should be destroyed. It appeared that the only good Germans were those who were caught in the bunker and that all the others were traitors because they were not there to die with him.' Eva regarded her own fate with equanimity. She had no desire to survive Hitler, and spent much of her time changing her clothes and caring for her appearance in order to keep up his spirits. Her perpetual complaint was: 'Poor, poor Adolf, deserted by everyone, betrayed by all. Better that ten thousand others die than that he should be lost to Germany.'

On the night of the 26th the Russians began to shell the Chancellery, and the bunker shook as the massive masonry split and crashed into the courtyard and garden. Resistance could scarcely last much longer. The Russians were now less than a mile away, and the army which had once goose-stepped before Hitler's arrogant gaze on the Wenceslas Square of Prague, through the ruins of Warsaw, and down the Champs Elysées, was reduced to a handful of exhausted companies fighting desperately street by street for the barely recognisable centre of Berlin.

Himmler – the last betrayal

The climax came on Saturday night, April 28/29. Between nine and ten o'clock on the Saturday evening Hitler was talking to Ritter von Greim when a message was sent in to him which determined him to end at last the career which had begun 27 years before, at the end of another lost war. Brought by Heinz Lorenz, an official of the Propaganda Ministry, it consisted of a brief Reuter report to the effect that Himmler had been in touch with the Swedish Count Bernadotte for the purpose of negotiating peace terms.

Since the beginning of 1945 Himmler had been secretly urged by Walter Schellenberg, the youngest of his SS generals, to open negotiations with the Western Powers on his own initiative, and when Count Bernadotte visited Berlin in February to discuss the release of Norwegian and Danish prisoners on behalf of the Swedish Red Cross, Schellenberg arranged for Himmler to meet him in the hope that this might provide the opportunity he sought. At that stage the reluctant Reichsführer-SS, much troubled by his loyalty to Hitler, had been unwilling to commit himself. Even when Bernadotte paid a second visit to Berlin in April Himmler could not make up his mind to speak out. But the dramatic scene at the conference of April 22 and Hitler's declaration that the war was lost, that he would seek death in the ruins of Berlin, made   ▷

'Once again the long march through an underground passage to the Führer's bunker, which must have been two storeys below ground. Again check-point after check-point. At one of the last guard posts my pistol and belt were taken away. Through the kitchen we reached a sort of mess, where a lot of SS officers were having supper. Another flight led down to the Führer's anteroom.' General Weidling's account of a visit to the bunker shows the thoroughness with which Hitler sealed himself off from the outside world during his last days. Buried two storeys deep, the bunker had a concrete ceiling 8½ feet thick. The outer walls were 6½ feet thick, and the whole bunker was designed on two levels (joined by a staircase), the lower level containing the living quarters of Hitler and his immediate entourage, while the upper level contained the kitchen, living quarters for the staff, and rooms for Goebbels' family. From this self-contained unit Hitler rarely stirred, and his grip on events and contact with reality became increasingly tenuous

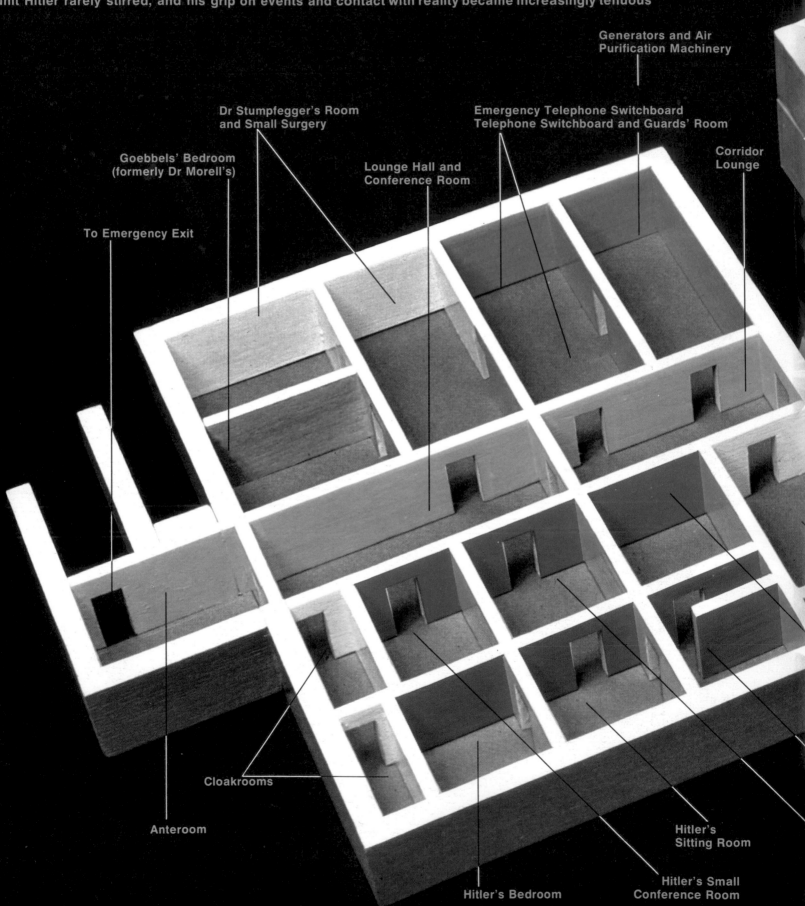

Generators and Air Purification Machinery

Dr Stumpfegger's Room and Small Surgery

Emergency Telephone Switchboard
Telephone Switchboard and Guards' Room

Goebbels' Bedroom (formerly Dr Morell's)

Lounge Hall and Conference Room

Corridor Lounge

To Emergency Exit

Cloakrooms

Anteroom

Hitler's Bedroom

Hitler's Sitting Room

Hitler's Small Conference Room

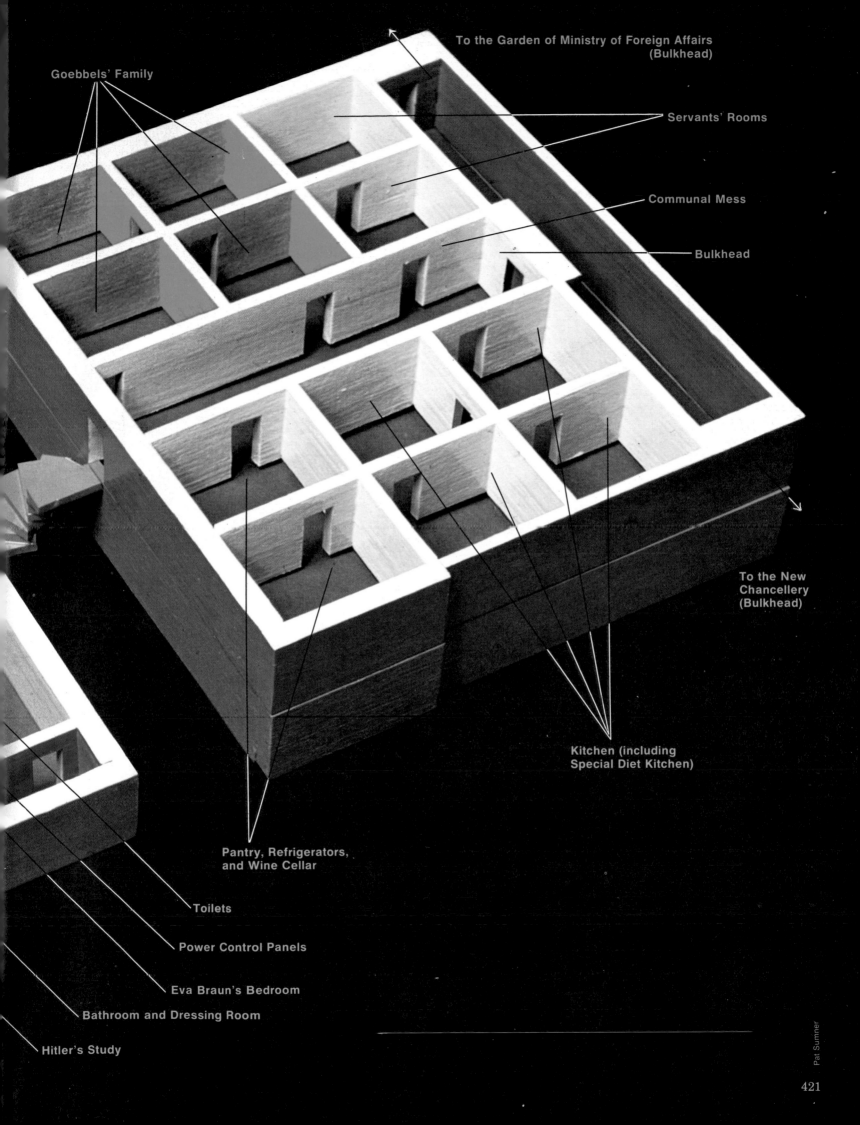

Goebbels' Family

To the Garden of Ministry of Foreign Affairs
(Bulkhead)

Servants' Rooms

Communal Mess

Bulkhead

To the New
Chancellery
(Bulkhead)

Kitchen (including
Special Diet Kitchen)

Pantry, Refrigerators,
and Wine Cellar

Toilets

Power Control Panels

Eva Braun's Bedroom

Bathroom and Dressing Room

Hitler's Study

Pat Sumner

421

much the same impression on Himmler that it had made on Göring. Both men concluded that loyalty to Hitler was no longer inconsistent with independent steps to end the war, but while Göring telegraphed to Hitler for confirmation of his view, Himmler more wisely acted in secret.

On the night of April 23/24, while Hitler was raging at the disloyalty of Göring, Himmler accompanied Schellenberg to Lübeck for another meeting with Count Bernadotte at the Swedish Consulate. This time Himmler was prepared to put his cards on the table. Hitler, he told Bernadotte, was quite possibly dead; if not, he certainly would be in the next few days.

'In the situation that has now arisen,' Himmler continued, 'I consider my hands free. I admit that Germany is defeated. In order to save as great a part of Germany as possible from a Russian invasion I am willing to capitulate on the Western Front in order to enable the Western Allies to advance rapidly towards the east. But I am not prepared to capitulate on the Eastern Front.'

On condition that Norway and Denmark were included in the surrender Bernadotte agreed to forward a proposal on Himmler's lines through the Swedish Foreign Minister, although he warned the two Germans that he did not believe there was the least chance that Britain and the USA would agree to a separate peace.

While Bernadotte left for Stockholm, Himmler began to think of the ministers he would appoint to his government when he assumed power, and to discuss with Schellenberg the new 'Party of National Union' which was to take the place of the Nazi Party.

On April 27, however, Bernadotte returned from the north with the news that the Western Allies refused to consider a separate peace and insisted on unconditional surrender. This was a heavy blow, especially to Schellenberg. But worse was to follow: on the 28th the fact that Himmler had been taking part in such negotiations was reported from London and New York. Himmler was now to discover, as Göring had before him, that it was unwise to discount Hitler before he was really dead.

Hitler was beside himself at the news. Göring had at least asked permission first before beginning negotiations; Himmler, in whose loyalty he had placed unlimited faith, had said nothing. That Himmler should betray him was the bitterest blow of all, and it served to crystallise the decision to commit suicide which Hitler had threatened on the 22nd, but which he had not yet made up his mind to put into effect. This final decision followed the pattern of all the others: a period of hesitation, then a sudden resolution from which he was not to be moved. So it had been before the decision to stay in Berlin; and so it had been in the succeeding week over the question of suicide. Throughout the week Hitler spoke constantly of taking his own life, and on the night of the 27th—if Hanna Reitsch's report is to be believed—he held a conference at which the plans for a mass suicide were carefully rehearsed and everyone made little speeches swearing allegiance to the Führer and Germany. But still he waited and hoped—until the night of the 28th. That was the night of decisions.

Shortly after he received the news from Lorenz, Hitler disappeared behind closed doors with Goebbels and Bormann, the only

two Nazi leaders in whom he now felt any confidence. Hitler's first thought was revenge, and Bormann had at least the satisfaction of removing Himmler as well as Göring before the Third Reich crumbled into dust.

Himmler's representative with the Führer, Fegelein, had already been arrested after it had been discovered that he had slipped quietly out of the bunker with the apparent intention of making a discreet escape before the end. The fact that he was married to Eva Braun's sister, Gretl, was no protection. He was now subjected to a close examination on what he knew of Himmler's treasonable negotiations and then taken into the courtyard of the Chancellery to be shot. Himmler was more difficult to reach, but Hitler ordered Greim and Hanna Reitsch to make an attempt to get out of Berlin by plane and entrusted them with the order to arrest Himmler at all costs. 'A traitor must never

The 'Nazi beasts lair'. Behind the battered Chancellery is the bunker where Hitler died. On the left is the bunker entrance, and on the right the cone-topped ventilation shaft

succeed me as Führer,' Hitler shouted in a trembling voice. 'You must go out to ensure that he will not.'

Greim and Hanna Reitsch left between midnight and 1 am on the morning of Sunday, April 29, and Hitler now turned to more personal matters. One human being at least had remained true and she should have her reward. Now that he had decided to end his life, the argument he had always used against marriage—that it would interfere with his career—no longer carried weight. So, between 1 am and 3 am on the 29th, Hitler married Eva Braun. The ceremony, performed according to civil law, was hurriedly carried out by one of Goebbels' staff, Walter Wagner, then serving in the *Volkssturm,* who was brought into the shelter for the purpose. The Führer's marriage took place in the map-room which was used for small conferences. Goebbels and Bormann were present as witnesses and signed the register after the bride and bridegroom. Eva began to write her maiden name of Braun, but struck out the initial

B and corrected her signature to 'Eva Hitler, *née* Braun.' Afterwards, the bridal party returned to their private suite, where a few friends—Bormann, Goebbels and his wife, Hitler's two secretaries, his adjutants, and his cook—came in to drink champagne and to talk nostalgically of the old days and Goebbels' marriage at which Hitler had been one of the witnesses before they came to power.

The celebration went on while Hitler retired to the adjoining room with his secretary, Frau Junge. There, in the early hours of April 29 he dictated his will and his political testament. Both documents are of such interest as to justify quotation at length.

Facing death and the destruction of the régime he had created, this man who had exacted the sacrifice of millions of lives rather than admit defeat was still recognisably the old Hitler. From first to last there is not a word of regret, nor a sugges-

tion of remorse. The fault is that of others, above all that of the Jews, for even now the old hatred is unappeased. Word for word, Hitler's final address to the German nation could be taken from almost any of his early speeches of the 1920s or from the pages of *Mein Kampf.* Some 20 years had changed and taught him nothing. His mind remained as tightly closed as it had been on the day when he wrote: 'During these years in Vienna a view of life and a definite outlook on the world took shape in my mind. These became the granite basis of my conduct. Since then I have extended that foundation very little, I have changed nothing in it.'

The first part of Hitler's political testament consists of a general defence of his career:
More than thirty years have now passed since in 1914 I made my modest contribution as a volunteer in the First World War, which was forced upon the Reich.

In these three decades I have been actuated solely by love and loyalty to my people. . . .
It is untrue that I, or anyone else in Ger-

many, wanted the war in 1939. It was desired and instigated solely by those international statesmen who were either of Jewish descent or worked for Jewish interests. I have made too many offers for the control and limitation of armaments, which posterity will not for all time be able to disregard, for the responsibility for the outbreak of this war to be laid on me. I have further never wished that, after the fatal First World War, a second against England or against America, should break out. Centuries will pass away, but out of the ruins of our towns and monuments hatred will grow against those finally responsible for everything, International Jewry, and its helpers. . . .

I have also made it plain that, if the nations of Europe are again to be regarded as mere shares to be bought and sold by those international conspirators in money and finance, then that race, Jewry, which is the real criminal of this murderous struggle, will be

of the realisation of a true community of nations. . . .

. . . I beg the heads of the Army, Navy, and Air Force to strengthen by all possible means the spirit of resistance of our soldiers in the National Socialist sense, with special reference to the fact that I myself, as founder and creator of this movement, have preferred death to cowardly abdication or even capitulation.

To this Hitler could not refrain from adding a gibe at the officer corps:

May it at some future time become part of the code of honour of the German officer – as it already is in the case of our navy – that the surrender of a district or of a town should be impossible and that the leaders should march ahead as shining examples faithfully fulfilling their duty unto death.

The second part of the testament contains Hitler's provisions for the succession. He began by expelling Göring and Himmler

while the last Commander-in-Chief of the German army was Field-Marshal Schörner, who commanded the still undefeated army group in Bohemia.

The last paragraph returned once more to the earliest of Hitler's obsessions: 'Above all I charge the leaders of the nation and those under them to scrupulous observance of the laws of race and to merciless opposition to the universal poisoner of all peoples, international Jewry.'

The testament was signed at four o'clock in the morning of Sunday, April 29, and witnessed by Goebbels and Bormann for the party, by Burgdorf and Krebs as representatives of the army. At the same time Hitler signed his will, which was again witnessed by Goebbels and Bormann, with the additional signature of Colonel von Below, his Luftwaffe adjutant. This was a shorter and more personal document:

Although I did not consider that I could take

Hitler's last-minute marriage to Eva Braun astonished even his most intimate circle, as the nature of their relationship had always been equivocal. As Speer remarked, 'To all writers of history, Eva Braun is going to be a disappointment'

Keystone

saddled with the responsibility. . . .

Hitler then turned to defend his decision to stay in Berlin and to speak of the future:

After six years of war, which in spite of all setbacks will go down one day in history as the most glorious and valiant demonstration of a nation's life-purpose, I cannot forsake the city which is the capital of the Reich. . . . I have decided, therefore, to remain in Berlin and there of my own free will to choose death at the moment when I believe the position of Führer and Chancellor can no longer be held. . . .

I die with a happy heart aware of the immeasurable deeds of our soldiers at the front. . . . That from the bottom of my heart I express my thanks to you all is just as self-evident as my wish that you should, because of that, on no account give up the struggle, but rather continue it against the enemies of the Fatherland. . . . From the sacrifice of our soldiers and from my own unity with them unto death will spring up in the history of Germany the seed of a radiant renaissance of the National Socialist movement and thus

from the Party and from all offices of state. He accused them of causing immeasurable harm to Germany by unauthorised negotiations with the enemy and of illegally attempting to seize power for themselves.

As his successor he appointed Admiral Dönitz President of the Reich, Minister of War, and Supreme Commander of the Wehrmacht – and promptly proceeded to nominate his government for him. Goebbels and Bormann had their reward, the first as the new Chancellor, the second as Party Minister. Hitler's choice for Foreign Minister was Seyss-Inquart, once a key figure in the annexation of Austria and since 1940 Reich Commissioner for the Netherlands. Himmler's successor as Reichsführer SS was Hanke, the Gauleiter of Lower Silesia, and, as Minister of the Interior, Paul Giesler, the Gauleiter of Upper Bavaria. The influence of Bormann is evident in the appointment of Party Gauleiters to both posts. Ley, Funk, and Schwerin-Krosigk kept their offices; Speer was replaced by Saur, his chief assistant at the Ministry for Armaments;

the responsibility during the years of struggle of contracting a marriage, I have now decided, before the end of my life, to take as my wife the woman who, after many years of faithful friendship, of her own free will entered this town, when it was already besieged, in order to share my fate. At her own desire she goes to death with me as my wife. This will compensate us for what we have both lost through my work in the service of my people.

What I possess belongs – in so far as it has any value – to the Party, or, if this no longer exists, to the State. Should the State too be destroyed, no further decision on my part is necessary.

My pictures, in the collection which I have bought in the course of years, have never been collected for private purposes, but only for the establishment of a gallery in my home-town of Linz on the Danube.

It is my heartfelt wish that this bequest should be duly executed.

As my executor I nominate my most faithful Party comrade, Martin Bormann. He is given full legal authority to make all *decisions. He is permitted to hand to my relatives anything which has a sentimental value or is necessary for the maintenance of a modest standard of life ['eines kleinen bürgerlichen Lebens']; especially for my wife's mother and my faithful fellow-workers who are well known to him. The chief of these are my former secretaries, Frau Winter, etc, who have for many years helped me by their work.*

I myself and my wife choose to die in order to escape the disgrace of deposition or capitulation. It is our wish to be burned immediately in the place where I have carried out the greater part of my daily work in the course of my twelve years' service to my people.

Hitler's choice of Dönitz as his successor is surprising, and to no one did it come as more of a surprise than to Dönitz himself. Since Dönitz had replaced Raeder as commander-in-chief, however, Hitler had come

lost, but, as the political testament shows, he was making a clumsy attempt to save something for the future. As a legacy to a new generation of National Socialists, however, it was a singularly unimpressive document. The game was played out and when the prestige of power was stripped away nothing remained but the stale and unconvincing slogans of the beer-hall agitator of the 1920s.

Characteristically, Hitler's last message to the German people contained at least one striking lie. His death was anything but a hero's end. by committing suicide he deliberately abandoned his responsibilities and took a way out which in earlier years he had strongly condemned as a coward's. The words in the testament are carefully chosen to conceal this: he speaks of his 'unity with our soldiers unto death', and again of fulfilling his duty unto death. It is worth noting that when General Weidling, the Commandant of

gandist did not desert him. Despite Hitler's order, he declined to leave his leader's side and finished his apologia with the promise 'to end a life which will have no further value to me if I cannot spend it in the service of the Führer'.

In the course of Sunday, the 29th, arrangements were made to send copies of the Führer's political testament out of the bunker, and three men were selected to make their way as best they could to Admiral Dönitz's and Field-Marshal Schörner's headquarters. One of the men selected was an official of the Propaganda Ministry, and to him Goebbels entrusted his own appendix to Hitler's manifesto. At midnight on April 29 another messenger, Colonel von Below, left carrying with him a postscript which Hitler instructed him to deliver to General Keitel. It was the Supreme Commander's last message to the Wehrmacht, and the sting was in the tail:

'So this was the end.' General Weidling leaves the bunker after hearing of Hitler's death

'In these three decades I have been actuated solely by love and loyalty to my people'

to look upon the navy with different eyes. He attached the greatest importance to the U-boat campaign, and contrasted the 'National Socialist spirit' of the navy under Dönitz with what he regarded as the treachery and disaffection of the army and Luftwaffe. In the last year of his life Hitler showed more confidence in Dönitz than in any of his senior commanders, and this was repaid by an unquestioning loyalty on the admiral's part. With Göring and Himmler excluded, Goebbels was the obvious choice as Hitler's successor, but Goebbels would never have been accepted by the soldiers. To command the Wehrmacht – which, in effect, meant to negotiate a surrender – someone else, preferably a serving officer, must become head of the State and Minister for War. Goebbels was thus to succeed Hitler as Chancellor, but Dönitz was to become head of the State and Supreme Commander. By choosing an officer from the navy, rather than from the army, Hitler offered a last deliberate insult to the military caste on whom he laid the blame for losing the war.

Hitler knew very well that the war was

Berlin, discovered that Hitler had committed suicide shortly after refusing the garrison permission to fight its way out of the city, he was so disgusted that he at once released his soldiers from their oaths. None the less the fiction was maintained in the official announcement, and Dönitz, in his broadcast of May 1, declared that the Führer had died fighting at the head of his troops.

After he had finished dictating the two documents Hitler tried to get some rest. Goebbels too retired, but not to sleep. Instead, he sat down to compose his own last contribution to the Nazi legend, an 'Appendix to the Führer's Political Testament'.

For days Goebbels had been talking in extravagant terms of winning a place in history. 'Gentlemen,' he told a conference at the Propaganda Ministry on April 17, 'in a hundred years' time they will be showing a fine colour film describing the terrible days we are living through. Don't you want to play a part in that film? . . . Hold out now, so that a hundred years hence the audience does not hoot and whistle when you appear on the screen.' Goebbels' genius as a propa-

The people and the Wehrmacht have given their all in this long and hard-struggle. The sacrifice has been enormous. But my trust has been misused by many people. Disloyalty and betrayal have undermined resistance throughout the war. It was therefore not granted to me to lead the people to victory. The Army General Staff cannot be compared with the General Staff of the First World War. Its achievements were far behind those of the fighting front.

The war had been begun by the Jews, it had been lost by the generals. In neither case was the responsibility Hitler's and his last word of all was to reaffirm his original purpose: 'The efforts and sacrifice of the German people in this war have been so great that I cannot believe they have been in vain. The aim must still be to win territory in the east for the German people.'

During the 29th, while the messengers were setting out from the bunker, the news arrived of Mussolini's end. The Duce, too, had shared his fate with his mistress; together with Clara Petacci, he had been caught by the Partisans and shot on the shore of Lake Como on April 28. Their bodies were taken to Milan and hung in the Piazzale Loreto. If Hitler made any comment on the end of his brother dictator it is unrecorded; but the news can only have confirmed him in the decision he had taken about his own end. Even when dead he was determined not to be put on show.

He now began to make systematic preparations for taking his life. He had his Alsatian bitch, Blondi, destroyed, and in the early hours of Monday, April 30, assembled his staff in the passage in order to say farewell. Walking along the line, he shook each man and woman silently by the hand. Shortly afterwards Bormann sent out a telegram to Dönitz, whose headquarters was at Plön, between Lübeck and Kiel, instructing him to proceed 'at once and mercilessly' against all traitors.

On the morning of the 30th Hitler was given the latest reports on the situation in

which was soaked in blood: he had shot himself through the mouth. On the right-hand side lay Eva Braun, also dead: she had swallowed poison. The time was 3.30 pm on Monday, April 30, 1945, ten days after Hitler's 56th birthday.

Hitler's instructions for the disposal of their bodies had been explicit, and they were carried out to the letter. Hitler's own body, wrapped in a blanket, was carried out and up to the garden by two SS men. The head was concealed, but the black trousers and black shoes which he wore with his uniform jacket hung down beneath the covering. Eva's body was picked up by Bormann, who handed it to Kempka. They made their way up the stairs and out into the open air, accompanied by Goebbels, Günsche, and Burgdorf. The doors leading into the garden had been locked and the bodies were laid in a shallow depression of sandy soil close to the porch. Picking up the five cans of petrol, one after another,

cast on the evening of May 1 to the solemn setting of music from Wagner and Brückner's 7th Symphony: the impression left was that of a hero's death, fighting to the last against Bolshevism.

An attempt at a mass escape by the men and women crowded into the network of bunkers round the Chancellery was made on the night of May 1/2, and a considerable number succeeded in making their way out of Berlin. Among them was Martin Bormann: whether he was killed at the time or got away has never been established. Goebbels did not join them. On the evening of May 1, after giving poison to his children, Goebbels shot his wife and himself in the Chancellery Garden. The bodies were set fire to by Goebbels' adjutant, but the job was badly done, and the charred remains were found next day by the Russians. After Goebbels' death the Führerbunker was set on fire.

In the following week Dönitz attempted to negotiate terms of surrender with the Western Allies, but their reply was uncompromising. The German army in Italy had already capitulated and the British and Americans refused to be drawn by Dönitz's clumsy efforts to secure a separate peace and split the Grand Alliance. On May 4 Admiral von Friedeburg signed an armistice providing for the surrender of the German forces in north-west Europe, and early on the morning of the 7th General Jodl and Friedeburg put their signatures to an unconditional surrender of all the German forces presented to them jointly by the representatives of the USA, Great Britain, the USSR, and France at Rheims.

The Third Reich had outlasted its founder by just one week.

[From *Hitler: A Study in Tyranny* (Odhams, 1952).]

ALAN BULLOCK, born in 1914, is the Master of St Catherine's College, Oxford. He was educated at Bradford Grammar School and Wadham College, Oxford, where he achieved a 'First' in Classics and 'First' in Modern History. From 1940 to 1945 he worked in the BBC European Service, latterly as diplomatic correspondent. After the war he was elected fellow of New College, where he was Dean and tutor in Modern History, and in 1952 he was appointed Censor of St Catherine's Society, pending its establishment as a college. He edited *The Ribbentrop Memoirs*, and is co-editor of *The Oxford Modern History* of Europe. His other works include *The Liberal Tradition* (1956) and *The Life and Times of Ernest Bevin*, Vol I (1960). He is married with four children, and lives in Oxford.

In the garden of the Chancellery Red soldiers indicate Hitler's alleged grave

Berlin at the usual conference. The Russians had occupied the Tiergarten and reached the Potsdamer Platz, only a block or two away from the Chancellery. Hitler received the news without excitement, and took lunch at 2 pm in the company of his two secretaries and his cook. Eva Hitler remained in her room and Hitler behaved as if nothing unusual were happening.

In the course of the early afternoon Erich Kempka, Hitler's chauffeur, was ordered to send 200 litres of petrol to the Chancellery Garden. It was carried over in jerricans and its delivery supervised by Heinz Linge, Hitler's batman.

Meanwhile, having finished his lunch, Hitler went to fetch his wife from her room, and for the second time they said farewell to Goebbels, Bormann, and the others who remained in the bunker. Hitler then returned to the Führer's suite with Eva and closed the door. A few minutes passed while those outside stood waiting in the passage. Then a single shot rang out.

After a brief pause the little group outside opened the door. Hitler was lying on the sofa,

Günsche, Hitler's SS adjutant, poured the contents over the two corpses and set fire to them with a lighted rag.

A sheet of flame leapt up, and the watchers withdrew to the shelter of the porch. A heavy Russian bombardment was in progress and shells continually burst on the Chancellery. Silently they stood to attention, and for the last time gave the Hitler salute; then turned and disappeared into the shelter.

Outside, in the deserted garden, the two bodies burned steadily side by side. It was 12 years and three months to the day since Hitler had walked out of the President's room, Chancellor of the German Reich.

The rest of the story is briefly told. Bormann at once informed Dönitz by radio that Hitler had nominated him as his successor, but he concealed the fact of Hitler's death for another 24 hours. During the interval, on the night of April 30, Goebbels and Bormann made an unsuccessful effort to negotiate with the Russians. The Russian reply was 'unconditional surrender'. Then, but only then, Bormann sent a further cable to Dönitz, reporting Hitler's death. The news was broad-

Hitler's Last Two Weeks

1945 April 21: Steiner's attack on the Russian forces besieging Berlin comes to nothing.
April 22: Hitler, goaded to a tantrum by Steiner's failure, announces his resolve to remain in Berlin and defend it to the last.
April 20/24: Göring and others of Hitler's entourage leave for the south.
April 23: Göring wirelesses to Hitler announcing his intention to negotiate with the Allies on Hitler's behalf. Hitler denounces him as a traitor. Colonel-General Ritter von Greim succeeds Göring as Commander-in-Chief of the Luftwaffe.
April 23/24: Himmler attempts to sue for peace with Sweden's Count Bernadotte.
April 29: Greim leaves Berlin charged with the arrest of Himmler. Hitler publishes his 'Political Testament', nominates Admiral Dönitz as his successor, blames International Jewry for his plight, and marries Eva Braun.
April 30: Hitler and Eva Braun kill themselves.
May 4: German forces in north-west Europe surrender to the Allies.

On the evening of May 1, 1945, Hamburg radio alerted its listeners for 'a grave and important announcement'. The news of the Führer's death was accompanied by the slow movement of Brückner's Seventh Symphony. Then his appointed successor, Admiral Dönitz, broadcast these words: 'My first task is to save Germany from destruction by the advancing Bolshevik enemy. It is to serve this purpose alone that the military struggle continues.'

A continuation of the war at this stage seems suicidal, but Dönitz's motives in taking this decision are not difficult to follow. During the Ardennes offensive, a plan of the Allied occupation zones projected for Germany had fallen into German hands and the exact delineation of the east/west border was therefore known to Dönitz. As yet his forces still controlled territory on both sides of it and, while they did, the eastern armies and their accompanying hosts of refugees, now running to millions in number, had some hope of making their way to refuge under the less vengeful of their enemies. It was not enough, however, for Dönitz to order continued resistance against the Russians alone, for he rightly feared that the British and Americans might be bound to close their zonal borders, once secured, to passage from the east. Germany then still needed those five minutes of time past midnight into which Hitler had boasted he would prolong the fight. But not to win victories, merely to hold open a pocket of sanctuary on the west bank of the Elbe.

But had Dönitz the means to continue a war on all fronts? In his first hours of office, he surveyed the situation. The German army was on paper and indeed in numbers still a powerful body. It counted over 6,000,000 men under arms and 300 divisions in its order of battle.

In fact it was a dismembered skeleton. Three formations still dignified as Army Groups—those in Courland, East Prussia, and Holland—were quite cut off and had almost exhausted their stocks of munitions. That in the Ruhr—Army Group B of invasion memories—had been dissolved in mid-April and its commander, Model, had taken poison. Army Group C in Italy was negotiating a local surrender, which would take effect on May 3. And those on German soil were fighting almost back to back. Army Group Vistula (a river to which it had long bade farewell) was retreating through Mecklenburg, encumbered with long columns of refugees and under fierce Russian attack. Army Group Schörner, strung out along the Sudeten Heights in Czechoslovakia, was holding its front only with the greatest difficulty and was threatened with the breakdown of civil order in its rear. Army Group North-West, facing the British and Americans, was on the point of collapse. Army Group South (Ostmark) was seeking a local capitulation to the Americans and French. Army Group F was making what haste it could from the vengeance of the Yugoslavs.

The Luftwaffe now counted its aircraft in handfuls and scarcely dared show those to the enemy. The navy's effort was reduced to the evacuation of refugees from the Baltic coast, behind Russian lines, to north German ports. All the main centres of production were in Allied hands and the population of the as yet unoccupied fragments of the Reich were helpless against air attack.

Dönitz, then, had little prospect of winning time by military initiatives. What other

Right: A hasty, huddled conference under the trees. Admiral von Friedeburg and his delegates confer outside Montgomery's headquarters

THE SURRENDER

Germany, May 1945
John Keegan

No German dared speak of surrender while Hitler lived. But on the afternoon of April 30, with Russian shells falling into the gardens overhead, Hitler made an end of himself. Now it could be up to others to make what end they could to his war . . .

means remained? The best he could hope was that, by offering the Western Powers a series of local and partial surrenders, and protracting the negotiations over them, he might delay the final collapse for another eight to ten days—enough to gather in the vagrant hosts from the east. But this, in view of the Allies' all too often repeated insistence on simultaneous unconditional surrender, was doubtful of realisation. It was true that an arrangement of that sort had proved possible in Italy; but that front fell outside the provisions of the inter-Allied occupation agreement. He resolved, nevertheless, to try.

The area in which an accommodation was most urgent lay in the north, where Army Groups Vistula and North-West were squeezed almost back to back under concentric British and Russian pressure. This urgency became extreme on May 2 when British armour broke across the Elbe and raced almost unopposed to Lübeck on the Baltic, thus severing Army Group Vistula's line of escape into Schleswig-Holstein, and refuge within the British zone. Any movement of civilians en masse would now depend upon engaging British good will. Dönitz resolved, therefore, to put himself in immediate touch with Field-Marshal Montgomery and sue for a standstill. He sent

accordingly for Admiral von Friedeburg, his successor as Commander-in-Chief of the Navy, whom he had alerted a day earlier to 'proceed on a special mission'. The commander of the Hamburg district was meanwhile ordered to have a flag of truce sent to the British at 0800 hours on May 3 and to ask for parley.

Dönitz's instruction was that Friedeburg was to offer Montgomery the military surrender of all north Germany. At the same time he was to 'invite the Field-Marshal's special attention to the problem of the refugees and troops in retreat on the eastern boundaries of the area occupied by the British' and was to seek his permission for the continued evacuation by sea of the population from the Baltic coast.

No news came in from Lüneburg during the day, which Dönitz spent in conference with the military and political leaders of what was left of the Greater Reich. Frank, from Czechoslovakia, warned how near to collapse his authority was, asked that Prague be declared an open city, and suggested the opening of negotiations for its surrender to the Americans. The head of administration in south Germany warned that only in upper Austria was the government in control; elsewhere the population showed itself hostile to the army and in

gomery's demands, nevertheless declared himself ready to endorse them when he returned to Dönitz. Montgomery then gave him a document promising to accept the surrender of all Germans appearing from the east and he left for Murwik, with orders to be back by 1800 hours at latest the following day, May 4. Kinzel and Wagner remained at Montgomery's headquarters.

Friedeburg's news came as a 'great relief' to Dönitz, particularly Montgomery's promise that he would be 'no monster' over the refugee problem. The admiral was dejected by the demand that the surrender extend to the navy but, despite OKW's protests at what appeared to them a slur on professional honour, decided that the threat of renewed air attack, to say nothing of a possible nullification of the capitulation itself, outweighed whatever hope the navy still had of completing the evacuations. He therefore authorised Friedeburg to return to Lüneburg and meet Montgomery's demands. He was then to seek onward passage to Eisenhower's headquarters at Rheims and offer him a similar separate surrender of the German forces facing the Americans.

On his return, Friedeburg and his party were again made to wait, while Montgomery concluded a press briefing, and then paraded beneath the Union Jack. When the Field-Marshal appeared, he first took Friedeburg into his caravan to ask if he were ready to sign and then had the party moved into a tent which had been pitched to house the ceremony. The appointments were characteristically simple: 'a trestle table covered with an army blanket, an inkpot, an ordinary army pen that you could buy in a shop for twopence. There were two BBC microphones on the table. The Germans stood up as I entered,' said Montgomery, 'then we all sat round the table. The Germans were clearly nervous and one of them took out a cigarette. . . . I looked at him and he put the cigarette away.'

Montgomery then had the English version of the instrument of surrender read out, warned the Germans of the penalties of failing to sign, then called on each to do so. He then signed for the Supreme Commander.

The terms were those they had already agreed. Remorseless though they were, Montgomery's verbal glosses encouraged Friedeburg to set off for Rheims in better heart than he had come to Lüneburg. But, as Dönitz well knew, the Supreme Commander was likely to prove less flexible than a subordinate commander. He, to some extent, could settle affairs as between soldiers. At Rheims the German delegation must treat as representatives of a government, and under the surveillance not merely of the western capitals but of Moscow also. Those who faced them might wear uniforms but would speak for their political superiors who, if finding other issues on which to differ, had shown a frightening degree of unity on the principle of Germany's unconditional and simultaneous surrender on all fronts.

Eisenhower indeed had already made it clear to his Chief-of-Staff, Bedell Smith, that there would be no bargaining with the Germans and that he himself would meet them only after they had signed. Smith and Strong, the British officer who had handled the Italian surrender in 1943, would conduct the negotiations. And to allay any Russian suspicion or German hope that the Western Allies were open to offers of a separate

Bavaria the old national flag was reappearing. There had been an attempt at a *putsch* in Munich. And there were other meetings about the conduct of affairs in Scandinavia and the Netherlands and over the local surrender of Kesselring's forces to the Americans in the south.

The most troublesome of these interviews was with Schörner, commanding in Czechoslovakia, who resisted Dönitz's order to retreat on the grounds that his army would disintegrate as soon as it left its positions. But Dönitz was adamant that every German soldier who could be saved from the Russians must be given the chance, whatever the ruin of military organisation that entailed.

These affairs consumed most of the day and much of the evening. Just before midnight Friedeburg returned from Lüneburg. How had he been received?

He and his party—Kinzel, Wagner, Polek, and Friedel—had been taken to Montgomery's tactical headquarters and left to wait under a Union Jack flying in front of the Field-Marshal's caravan. After a few minutes, he emerged and demanded of his interpreter: 'Who are these men? What do they want?' When credentials had been established, Friedeburg began by offering the surrender of Army Group Vistula. This

Montgomery refused, emphasising that it could be surrendered only to the Russians but adding that individual soldiers surrendering would automatically be taken prisoner. Friedeburg then raised the fate of the refugees who had put themselves under its wing and asked whether Montgomery might adjust the pace of his advance to that of Army Group Vistula's retreat, so that they would have a chance of escaping across the zonal border.

Montgomery, who was perfectly familiar with the provision of a SHAEF instruction of August 1944 forbidding any commitment by military commanders to the enemy, dismissed this proposal. Instead he suggested that the delegation surrender to him all forces on his northern and western flanks. If so, he would accept it as a tactical surrender, without prejudice to later negotiations. The delegation had of course no power to do any such thing nor, as yet, the will. But after an inspection of the situation map, which revealed a state of affairs whose hopelessness they had not guessed at, and a solitary lunch over which Friedeburg wept and his staff kept silence, they were in a more tractable mood.

When Montgomery threatened to reopen his offensive, Friedeburg, though still protesting his powerlessness to meet Mont-

peace, General Suslaparov, the Russian representative at SHAEF, must be summoned to participate at once. Eisenhower had already signalled Moscow that the surrender would be purely military in character and extend to all fronts.

Friedeburg and Polek met therefore an unnervingly rigid reception when they reached Rheims next afternoon, May 5. As at Montgomery's headquarters the admiral began by offering to surrender the German forces in the west alone. But Smith left him in no doubt that a surrender must apply to all fronts and, to emphasise how desperate their situation was, had the Germans shown the situation maps—a number of broad red arrows, indicating projected offensives, had been added to heighten their effect. Again Friedeburg quailed but had to declare himself unempowered to sign. Nevertheless he agreed to signal Dönitz asking for permission to do so and for the naval and air representatives to join him.

Since he had neglected to bring a code book, he was lent facilities by SHAEF (presumably to keep affairs secret at least from the world press) and it was by this makeshift means that Kinzel brought the message from Lüneburg to Murwik next morning. It was a bitter disappointment to Dönitz. He and Schwerin von Krosigk nevertheless thought it worthwhile concocting another time-wasting formula which they entrusted to Jodl, chief of the operations staff and bitterest opponent of surrender. His instructions were:

To try once again to explain why we wish to make this separate surrender to the Americans. If you have no more success with Eisenhower than Friedeburg had, offer a simultaneous surrender on all fronts, to be implemented in two phases. In the first phase, all hostilities will have ceased but German troops will still be allowed liberty of movement. During the second phase this liberty will be withheld. Try to make the period elapsing before phase two as long as possible and, if you can, try to get them to agree that individual German soldiers will be allowed to surrender to the Americans. The greater your success in these directions, the greater will be the numbers of German soldiers and refugees who will find salvation in the West.

Jodl was given plenipotentiary powers in these terms but only these, and then only if a separate surrender proved unattainable. Then he too set off, first to be put under escort at Lüneburg and then to journey to Rheims.

During these comings and goings, two other German groups had followed Army Group C in making their own approaches to the Allies. On the middle Elbe, the remnants of IX and XII Armies found the US 9th Army uncompromising and broke into small groups which made their own way across the river. In the south, Army Group G surrendered untidily to the Franco-American 6th Army Group, Kesselring proving unable to carry all his subordinates with him. But the ultimate outcome was distinctly gratifying, particularly to the French, for the haul of prisoners included the authors of most of Germany's early victories, Rundstedt, Leeb, List, and Göring.

While fighting continued on that front Jodl arrived at Rheims, accompanied by General de Guingand, Montgomery's Chief-of-Staff, and Brigadier Williams, his Chief of Intelligence. He was taken at once to Friedeburg's room, greeted him with a cryptic 'Aha', and closed the door on some unashamed eavesdroppers. 'Soon the Admiral came out, asked for coffee and a map of Europe. Jodl could be seen marching up and down.'

Playing for time

Shortly after 1800 hours, the Germans emerged and were taken to Bedell Smith's office where they stayed for over an hour. At the end of it, Smith reported to Eisenhower that he suspected them of playing for time. He was told to report the state of talks to the Russian representative, who as yet had not met the Germans, and he then rejoined them. After another 15 minutes, however, Strong, who was interpreting, telephoned Eisenhower to say that the Germans were still asking for a delay. Butcher, the chief of public relations, overheard his reply: 'You tell them that 48 hours from midnight tonight I will close my lines on the Western Front so that no more Germans can get through. Whether they sign or not—however much more time they take.'

This, though an ultimatum, offered the Germans at least a little of the time they wanted. It was, in that sense, a concession and the last, Jodl judged, that they would be granted. He at any rate was convinced that they must sign on these terms and signalled Dönitz at once for permission.

Dönitz was strongly impressed by this sudden reversal of mood in the most intractable opponent of surrender and, while characterising Eisenhower's attitude as 'sheer extortion', nevertheless instructed Keitel, the Chief of OKW, to signal Rheims that 'full power granted to sign in accordance

After much hesitation, playing for time, and trying to secure terms, the Germans finally succumbed to General Eisenhower's threat to seal the Western Front. Here General Jodl signs the unconditional surrender while Admiral von Friedeburg watches

with conditions as given'.

This message went off at 0100 hours in the morning of May 7. At about 0200 hours, the parties to the surrender assembled in the war room. Its walls were now covered with situation maps, charts of current air operations, casualty lists, records of supplies landed, diagrams of road and rail systems, and meteorological plots. Most striking of the displays was a giant mock thermometer, mounted on a background of swastikas, which showed the running total of prisoners in Allied hands.

Much of the floor space was now taken up by the impedimenta of cinema photographers and broadcasters. Among it stood seventeen correspondents who had been chosen to witness the ceremony. They faced a large table which had once been used to mark papers.

Bedell Smith arrived first; then the Germans, escorted by Strong. The signatories seated themselves formally: on the outside of the table, Friedeburg, Jodl, and Oxenius, his ADC; facing them, General Morgan, the British Deputy Chief of SHAEF staff, General Sevez, representing France, Admiral Burrough, the American commander of the naval expeditionary force, General Suslaparov, representing Russia, and General Spaatz, commander of the American Strategic Air Force.

Smith asked the Germans whether they were ready to sign. Jodl indicated that they were and was passed copies of the surrender document in German and English. Its main clause read:

We the undersigned, acting by authority of the German High Command, hereby surrender unconditionally to the Supreme Commander, Allied Expeditionary Force and simultaneously to the Soviet High Command all forces on the land, sea and in the air which are at this date under German control.

This act of surrender is without prejudice to, and will be superseded by, any general instrument of surrender imposed by, or on behalf of, the United Nations and applicable to Germany and the German armed forces as a whole.

Butcher had provided Smith with one of two gold pens which an admirer had given Eisenhower long before this day. He handed the other to Jodl and, after he had signed the first copy, substituted his own pen for the second signature. The two in gold were to go to the President and Prime Minister.

When Jodl had finished, the documents were signed in turn by Smith, on behalf of Eisenhower, by Suslaparov, on behalf of the Soviet High Command, and by Sevez as a witness.

Into the victor's hands

At this point Jodl rose and said in English: 'I want to say a word.' Then in German to Smith: 'General! With this signature, the German people and the German armed forces are, for better or worse, delivered into the victors' hands. In this war, which has lasted more than five years, both have achieved and suffered perhaps more than any other people in the world. In this hour I can only hope that the victor will treat them with generosity.' General Smith made no reply.

An hour later, having seen Jodl and warned formally of the penalties attendant on any breach of the act he had just signed, Eisenhower cabled the British and American

Chiefs-of-Staff: 'The mission of this Allied Force was fulfilled at 0241, local time, May 7, 1945. Eisenhower.'

The final surrender of Germany was not quite complete. The Russians requested and the Germans had been charged to provide representatives at a separate ceremony in their sector on the following day. Keitel, Stumpff (representing the Luftwaffe), and Friedeburg were accordingly transported to Berlin and, in the presence of Zhukov, Tedder, Spaatz, de Lattre de Tassigny, and Vishinsky (who overheard Keitel mutter: 'The French are here! That's all we need') signed similar articles early in the morning of May 8.

In Flensburg, Dönitz broadcast a last message to the officer corps: 'Comrades, we have been set back a thousand years in our history. Land that was German for a thousand years has now fallen into Russian hands . . . [but] despite today's military breakdown, our people are unlike the Germany of 1918. They have not been split asunder. Whether we want to create another form of National Socialism or whether we conform to the life imposed upon us by the enemy, we should make sure that the unity given to us by National Socialism is maintained under all circumstances.'

'The personal fate of each of us,' he concluded, 'is uncertain.' A fortnight later, he and the rest of the German High Command were taken into captivity. None of the men to whom he had delegated powers of surrender survived. Friedeburg died by his own hand, Jodl and Keitel on the gallows at Nuremberg.

Generals Suslaparov, Morgan, Smith, and Eisenhower, with Air Chief-Marshal Tedder, smile for the cameras after receiving the capitulation of the Third Reich. A subsequent surrender in Berlin confirmed unconditional surrender on all fronts

US Army

FIRE RAIDS

Marianas Islands and Japan, December 1944/May 1945
John Vader

Imperial War Museum

By winter 1944, the US bomber pilots in the Far East were carrying the air war to Japanese targets in the biggest bombers of the war: Boeing B-29s, the Superfortresses, intended to unleash a non-stop bombing offensive on the Japanese islands from their new bases in the Marianas. But the B-29 crews soon found that accurate strategic bombing offered far more problems than had been envisaged; and so began the terrible fire raids on Japanese cities, directed by General LeMay, the 'Bomber Harris' of the Pacific War. Never before in the history of warfare had such undiscriminating damage been inflicted with such pitiless regularity—and the raids were steadily built from strength to strength as the summer of 1945 drew on

Top left: A B-29 Superfortress formation unloads its incendiaries over Yokohama. *Top right:* Bombing triumvirate (left to right): Brigadier-General 'Rosie' O'Donnell, who led the first B-29 raid on Japan; Major-General Curtis LeMay, advocate of the mass fire raids; and Lieutenant-General Barney Giles

On November 1, 1944, and for the first time since General Doolittle's intrepid raid in April 1942, an American aircraft flew over Tokyo. Flying too high and too fast to be intercepted on its surprise reconnaissance, the B-29 Superfortress returned safely to its base in the Marianas. The air war had at last reached the Japanese homeland, where those who could see high enough into the sky were able to observe the flight of a new aircraft that was to hasten the end of the conflict.

The B-29 was a most formidable bomber, designed from its inception to carry a 2,000-pound bombload 5,000 miles. Designed for war in the Pacific and the great ocean wilderness to be crossed on the way to far-distant targets, the B-29 also had crew compartments which were pressurised to provide comfort and freedom of movement during long flights at high altitude. Continuing a practice that began in the South-West Pacific where B-24s and B-25s were the star 'heavies', lurid emblems and comic names were painted on the sides of the Superfortresses. Two, *Enola Gay* and *Bockscar,* are ensured of their place in the annals of history, for they were to carry the two ugly containers, 'Little Boy' and 'Fat Boy', to Hiro-

430

Keystone

shima and Nagasaki. Some that displayed colourful paintings of near-nude girls possibly spoiled the aim of surprised Zero pilots. 'Supine Sue', 'Horezontal Dream', 'Battlin Betty III', 'Strange Cargo', 'Over Exposed' and 'Lassy Too' were titles of some of the fuselage 'pop art' exhibited over Japanese targets.

This gaily-decorated super-bomber was the most important instrument that the Allies possessed when the war against Japan entered its fourth year.

With the B-29 in existence, the Joint Chiefs-of-Staff decided that large-scale landings in China would be unnecessary and that Japan itself could be invaded: the essential softening-up prelude could be made by the huge bombers based on suitable Pacific islands. Thus the Marianas became an objective for the Central Pacific forces. It was also decided to send B-29s to China despite the difficulties of maintenance and service and the doubtful protection afforded to bases by the Chinese army. After deliveries of the planes to training units in the autumn of 1943, enough crews were ready in early 1944 to form two groups, the 20th and 21st Bomber Commands, both under the direct control of General H. H. Arnold and the Joint

Chiefs-of-Staff in Washington.

Hundreds of thousands of labourers were employed in constructing four fields in China, and five were constructed in India to accommodate planes of the 20th Bomber Command which flew from America in April 1944. Supplies of fuel and bombs from India were accumulated in China by using the B-29s as transports to augment the hard-worked Transport Command. The first bombing mission was a raid from India on targets at Bangkok and a few days later, on June 15, Yawata in southern Japan was bombed by B-29s operating from a Chinese field. Flying fuel 'over the Hump' into China was a misuse of the Superfortresses, but it was the only way the Command could build up enough fuel to launch attacks on the Japanese mainland. The raid against the iron and steel works at Yawata registered the beginning of the strategic bombing of Japan, although on this raid the estimated damage of the target amounted to a mere 2%. On July 7, Sasebo on Kyushu was ineffectively attacked. After a night raid with incendiaries against Nagasaki there were no signs of fires. On August 20, Yawata was again attacked by day: anti-aircraft fire and fighters shot down 18 of the 70 bombers and

After the raid: midget submarines in a wrecked dry-dock at Kure base

the target was only slightly damaged.

The standard of bombing improved after Brigadier-General Curtis LeMay, an experienced leader from the 8th Air Force which had taken part in the strategic bombing of Europe, took over command of the 20th and intensified its training: LeMay firmly believed that strategic bombing would destroy the industrial potential of Japan, that it would destroy its fuel supplies and aircraft factories, its ports and communications. In a land assault on Japan, against a Japanese army of some 2,000,000 front-line troops and swarms of missiles and planes manned by suicide pilots, the cost could be higher than a million American casualties and most of the invasion ships sunk. LeMay was prepared to lay waste all the Japanese cities that contributed to their war effort. And he believed that the huge bombers could do the job, that bombing alone could force Japan into unconditional surrender.

LeMay's bomb-aimers improved with experience but they still required the right weather conditions for success. In clear skies the bombers attacked an aircraft depot at Okayama on Formosa and destroyed the target; the Rangoon marshalling yards were destroyed in one raid; and a raid that took the bombers 3,800 miles during an 18-hour flight wrecked the dock gate and blasted the stern off a ship in the Singapore Dock. In these operations the B-29 crews proved that they could fly long distances and bomb accurately from a great height.

During the decisive first seven months of 1944, the central Pacific islands of Kwajalein, Eniwetok, Guam, Saipan, Tinian, and Pelelieu were invaded by the Americans. In the Marianas, Guam, Saipan, and Tinian were developed as bases for B-29s of the 21st Bomber Command, which was formed under the leadership of Brigadier-General H. S. Hansell. The task of constructing bases for the Superfortresses was gigantic, yet five bases were developed in a very short time. On Saipan the airstrips were 200 feet wide and 8,500 feet long, served by 6 miles of taxiways and parking bays. On Tinian the engineers constructed 8,000-feet-long strips in the coral, and at one point a valley was filled across to complete the length; 90 miles of hard-surface roads connected various parts of the island. On Guam the asphalt plant, which looked like an open-air factory, mixed 90,000 tons of crushed rock with 1,200,000 gallons of asphalt oil for the hard-surfacing of the runways and taxiways. Although the fighting for these islands lasted until August, Superfortresses were able to land in October and begin operations against Truk at the end of the month.

The first bombing raid against a target in Tokyo, 1,500 miles from the Marianas, was made on November 24. Brigadier-General Emmett O'Donnell, flying in *Dauntless Dotty*, led 111 Superfortresses in an attack against the Musashina engine factory, but only 24 planes found the target and the bombing from 30,000 feet was inaccurate. Despite intensive training and the excellent Norden bombsight, high-level bombing was to prove unreliable—from results in China and Japan it appeared that it was not going to be of much use faltering about at 30,000 feet, losing bombers to flak and fighters, and missing the target. This was not the fault of pilots or aircraft but a result of weather conditions that existed at high altitudes over Japan. Sometimes there were jet-stream winds of over 100 and 200 mph, there was severe icing, and often fog so covered the target that unreliable radar-bombing was resorted to or alternative targets chosen and concentration dissipated.

In order to bring the full weight of the B-29s against the main industrial areas of eastern and central Japan, the 20th Bomber Command was transferred from India and China to the Marianas.

The big raids begin

In January, General LeMay flew to the islands to take charge of the 21st Bomber Command, and when the 20th arrived he was given command of both groups, combined as the 20th Air Force. Until February the formations consisted of about 100 Superfortresses and as more runways were completed strikes were made by nearly 200 and, in March, by over 300 bombers. The heavy fire-power of the big planes amazed the Japanese fighter pilots. The central sighting systems and remote control turrets of the B-29 proved their effectiveness when on one occasion a lone bomber on a photographic mission was jumped by 90 fighters. The bomber was able to use its great unladen speed at a high altitude, and, after a running fight that lasted half an hour, seven fighters were shot down and the bomber escaped. It was perhaps fortunate that there were few Japanese aces still about.

However, the fire from 12·50 machine-guns and a cannon did not stop the fighter attacks, and despite the high losses of Japanese fighter aircraft in the south-west Pacific, in Luzon, and Burma, there were still thousands of aircraft reserves in Japan. Many of their pilots were inexperienced, yet they were fanatically determined and their courageous attacks brought down considerable numbers

of B-29s. The new 'George' and 'Jack' fighters were particularly dangerous as they were fast and mounted four cannon, which were highly destructive even against the heavily armoured bombers. As the strikes increased in size losses rose proportionately and the bombing effect was certainly not worth the casualties and loss of aircraft. Sometimes the opposition over a target was as strong as 200 fighters, all of them determined to bag a B-29 regardless of the withering fire from hundreds of machine-guns and cannon, or the bursting shells of their own anti-aircraft defences.

A vital benefit that resulted from the capture of Iwo Jima in March was the introduction of fighter escorts for the bombers. The most important fighter was the improved P-51 Mustang—a fast, long-range aircraft that could fly rings around anything the Japanese might send up. Radar-equipped P-61 'Black Widows' night fighters used their eight cannon and guns to destroy Japanese planes that raided after dark. On April 7, over 100 Mustangs escorted Superfortresses in a daylight raid on Japan and the defenders lost more aircraft than they shot down—a pattern which was to continue in the Americans' favour.

During the unescorted daylight raids in February the bomber losses rose to 5·7%, badly affecting the morale of air crews. When losses reached these proportions, as the USAAF experienced in Europe, bombing results and general efficiency were inclined to deteriorate rapidly. Losses of over 5% meant that the average expectancy was about 16 raids before a crew 'got the chop'; such statistics and the sight of bombers blowing up in the air or falling in blazing spirals were damaging to the morale of the airmen. The escorting Mustang pilots had often sat cramped in their small cockpits for up to nine hours on the long escort flights to Japan, but fighter presence altered the situation in the air over Japan and the high-level raids were increased in number and strength.

Start of the fire raids

The demolition-bomb effect on Japan's industries, however, was still negligible compared with the quantity of bombs dropped and the effort to get them there. The lesson learned in Europe was that it was possible to destroy individual targets by bombing from the comparative safety of a great height—but that it usually took several raids or a massive one to saturate the target *area*. LeMay had quite a problem on his hands. He possessed a powerful force of bombers designed to fly high over long distances, but the enormous amount of fuel needed for such operations meant that the bombloads were relatively small; when they reached the target it was uncertain if it would be destroyed; at this rate the process of whittling down the Japanese manufacturing capability would be a lengthy one, as many factories would be quickly moved to hidden sites. There were thousands of fighter and bomber aircraft reserved by the Japanese for the day the Allies invaded the country; fighter aircraft were still being manufactured and many parts were turned out in the widespread 'cottage industry' that could not be pin-pointed on the Intelligence maps.

A radical variation in tactics had to be made, and the general's experience of one particular raid on Hankow could have brought about the decisive change in operations which was to alter the course of the war. It was a combined raid by Chennault's 14th Air Force and the 20th Bomber Command, at the end of 1944, when it was decided to send in some of the B-29s at a lower altitude than their customary 30,000 feet and to drop incendiary bombs on Hankow. This raid had been considered very successful, due primarily to the incendiaries, and LeMay decided to see if they could set Japan's major cities alight.

The target for the first big incendiary attack was heavily-defended Tokyo. A night attack was planned and there was a strong possibility that the anti-aircraft gunners would be confused by the height of the bombers' approach—between 5,000 and 8,000 feet. Less fuel was needed for the distance at this height and, since little opposition was expected from night fighters, no guns or ammunition were to be carried and crew numbers reduced. Altogether the saving in weight allowed each plane to carry over 6 tons of bombs. As the objective was the great expanse of urban Tokyo, there was no need for the exacting task of forming up behind the leader, and aircraft could make individual attacks. Chosen for the first series of incendiary experiment as well as Tokyo were Nagoya, Osaka, and Kobe, each one a centre of large and small industries. The destruction of the cottage workshops which served as feeder plants would halt the flow of many vital parts to major assembly plants. Also it was feasible that the big factories would either be hit in the widespread bombing or be caught up in the general conflagration LeMay hoped to generate in each city.

The M-69 fire bombs weighed 6 pounds each and were dropped in a cluster of 38 within a container. A time fuse was set to release the small bombs from the cluster at 5,000 feet and they exploded on

△ A B-29 after crash-landing on Iwo Jima. Many bombers would have been lost without this vital staging-post. ▽ Looking down on vast burned-out areas created by previous incendiary raids

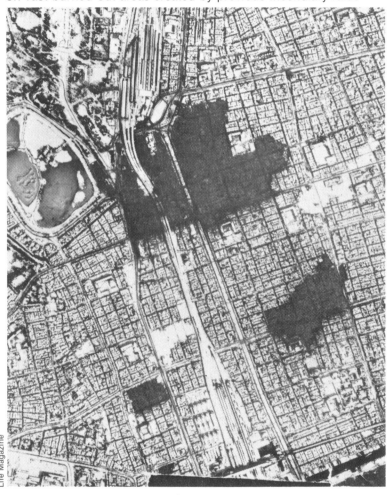

contact, spreading a jelly-gasoline compound. The B-29s usually carried 37 of the 500-pound clusters, fuse vanes held in place by an arming wire that was withdrawn after take-off. To fan the fires it was necessary to have a good ground wind blowing across the target.

The night of March 10 was chosen for the incendiary raid on Tokyo. Loaded with 1,667 tons of cluster bombs, over 300 Superfortresses took off from the Marianas runways, flying at about 7,000 feet and estimated to arrive over the target just before dawn, when they would have the cover of darkness over Tokyo and daylight for possible ditching on the way home.

The results of the raid were incredible. No one could have estimated the inflammability of the city. A photo-reconnaissance made a few hours after the raid showed that 16½ square miles of the city had burned out. Along with the many 'home industry' workshops 16 targets scheduled for future daylight high-level demolition attacks had also gone up in smoke. The fierce fires started by the incendiaries consumed so much air that strong thermal winds were sucked across the city, spreading the flames and making them burn more fiercely. The fire storm raged until nothing was left to burn.

Such a fire had only burned once before – at Hamburg in 1942 – but the death toll in the Tokyo blaze was more than double: over 100,000 people were killed and at least 100,000 injured. The Americans lost 14 Superfortresses over the target.

Two nights later the bombers again took off with their loads of incendiaries, this time headed for Nagoya. Fires were started all over the city but, since they did not join up, the firestorm was averted and only about 1½ square miles were destroyed. Osaka was the next target, attacked on March 13 by over 300 bombers which destroyed 8 square miles of the city. A few nights later 2·4 square miles, including 11,000,000 square feet of dock area, were burned out in Kobe. The last attack in the ten-day period was a return to Nagoya when another force of 300-plus dropped 2,000 tons of incendiaries on a more compact area but again the city refused to ignite and only ·65 of a square mile was destroyed. In these five raids the bombers had dropped 9,365 tons of incendiaries and burned out more than 29 square miles of Japan's main industrial cities.

With the careless bombing of civilians and the callous, cowardly forms of total war already established as their standards early in the war by the Axis, the Allies had few qualms about the coarse approach to destroying military and industrial installations in Europe. There is no evidence that the appalling possibilities of fire raids on Japan might encourage the Joint Chiefs-of-Staff to revert to target-only bombing. There would have been few aircrew too horrified to continue the bombing – they were conditioned by their knowledge of the Allied prisoners who had been bayonetted to death, the hospital ships bombed and shelled, the shot-down pilots who were beheaded, the numerous atrocities that had been committed by their enemy. The general mood was expressed in a simple attitude: 'They've only got themselves to blame – they started it.' The burning of Tokyo probably killed more people, and in a more frightful way, than the two atom bombs that ended the war, yet the fire raid is rarely mentioned in the probing of man's conscience that has gone on ever since.

The morale of the B-29 crews quickly improved when they found that these night raids were much safer than the daylight high-level bombing; only 22 bombers (1·4%) were lost over the target in the ten-day period. There was sanctuary at Iwo Jima and ditching at sea was made safe by the presence of 'Dumbos' (B-17s and PBY Catalinas) and 'Superdumbos' (B-29s) which flew in the vicinity of the target, carrying extra life rafts and emergency kits and monitoring the bombers' frequencies so that if one went down the position would be located and rescue planes, ships, or submarines would be sent to pick up the airmen.

For the Joint Chiefs-of-Staff and for General LeMay fire raids were a successful means of destruction; they became the prime operation in the air war against Japan. For the Japanese military and political leaders the ominous result of the visit by B-29s to four cities within a period of ten days proved that their country was virtually defenceless and that there was little that they could do to improve the state of affairs. Their Axis partner was about to collapse and their Kamikaze ('divine wind') was ineffective against bombers that flew at night.

For the 20th Air Force, the pattern had been established. All that was required now was to choose the cities, build up a large stock of fuel and clusters of jelly-gasoline bombs, and begin the assault. After the ten-day incendiary concentration the force began a new series of daylight attacks. In order to carry a heavier bomb load the B-29s reduced their altitude to between 12,000 and 18,000 feet where weather conditions allowed greater bombing accuracy. The expected fighter attacks continued but were no more effective than they were at 30,000 feet. As with the bombardiers hitting their targets, experience improved the aim of the defensive gunners and Japanese fighters suffered as a result. The long-range P-47 Thunderbolt fighters joined the Mustangs in bomber escort flights to establish a fighter superiority over the heart of Japan. They had been assisted in achieving this by the extensive sweeps made by navy aircraft from Task Force 58. Sailing to within 175 miles of Tokyo, Admirals Spruance and Mitscher provided a short range for their fighters and bombers, which shot dozens of Japanese fighters out of the sky and strafed and bombed many more on the ground. They also contributed their share of bombs to industrial targets, primarily aircraft plants. They made their first attacks on February 16 and 17, returning for more strikes on February 24.

By the end of March the end of the war was in sight. There could only be one result of the conflagration being wrought by LeMay's B-29s – bigger and more frequent incendiary bombing that would completely raze the Japanese factories. Since Japan's fanatical leaders did not capitulate after the awful loss of life in Tokyo's fire, something more dramatic would possibly enable them to save face and bow to surrender.

USA, December 1941/ August 1945

David Elstein
Ending the Japanese war was by no means the only reason for using the world's first nuclear bomb against Japan. America's new President, Harry Truman, desperately needed a potent diplomatic weapon to back up his toughening attitude towards Russia. This was why – although his Chiefs-of-Staff tended to the view that Japan was already hopelessly beaten – Truman was determined, even before the first vital test had revealed its dreadful power, to use the atomic bomb against Japan

DECISION

President Harry Truman (left) with Secretary of War Henry L. Stimson. The new atomic bomb was reported to have been the main topic of their conversation

On April 24, 1945, 12 days after the death of Franklin Roosevelt, the new President, Harry Truman, received an urgent note from his Secretary of War. It concerned 'a highly secret matter', which 'has such a bearing on our present foreign relations and has such an important impact upon all my thinking in this field that I think you ought to know about it without much further delay'.

The 'highly secret matter', which was always referred to by the code names 'Tube Alloys' or 'S-1', was the atomic bomb. The man who wrote the note, Henry Stimson, knew better than anyone else the military and diplomatic implications of this terrible new weapon – and even now, weeks before the first test, he was 99% sure of its success. Harry Truman, when Vice-President, had known nothing of the project, and although Stimson had mentioned it to him soon after Roosevelt's death, it was only on April 25 that the new President became fully aware of the tremendous possibilities of atomic power.

For Roosevelt, the culmination of the atomic programme had been too distant to affect his strategic outlook. But for Truman the atomic bomb was a potent diplomatic weapon. It could be used to exert the maximum pressure on the Russians, and so reverse the tendency to defer to Russian demands which had characterised the last months of Roosevelt's administration.

It was also left for Truman to decide on the military use of the bomb. Clearly, the fighting in Europe would be over months before the first combat weapon would be available. But in the Pacific arena, although the Japanese position was hopeless, it was estimated that an invasion of the home islands would take 18 months. To use the bomb against Japan was a natural decision to take: indeed, it was scarcely a decision at all.

Secretary Stimson later wrote: 'At no time from 1941 to 1945 did I ever hear it suggested by the President or any other responsible member of the government that atomic energy should not be used in the war.' Given the assumption that the bomb would be used, the only remaining questions were: when and where? To take these decisions, the President set up what was called the 'Interim Committee', made up of key political, scientific, and military advisers. The one question the committee was not asked to decide was: did the United States need to use the bomb?

During the month it took the Interim Committee to report back, Truman was already anticipating the advent of the bomb in formulating his foreign policy. Even before the April 25 meeting with Stimson, all Truman's top advisers were intent on moving away from Roosevelt's conciliatory attitude towards the Russians. Truman himself felt he had to dispel the feeling, which had built up since the Big Three meeting at Yalta in February, that America would 'win' the war, but 'lose' the peace – to Russia.

The agreements which had acknowledged Soviet interest and influence in Central and Eastern Europe had been interpreted by Russia in ways which aroused American suspicions. Truman wanted to take a strong line, and told his cabinet on April 23 that 'our agreements with the Soviet Union so far had been a one-way street and that he could not continue . . . it was now or never.'

The next day, Truman complained bitterly to Soviet Foreign Minister Molotov of Russian actions in Poland, and of a general failure to implement the Yalta agreements. Molotov's response was: 'I have never been talked to like that in my life.'

The news of the atomic bomb development encouraged Truman in his stiffened response to Soviet diplomacy. Where Roosevelt had always been suspicious of Churchill's inclination to play power politics, Truman quickly took up the Prime Minister's tactic of exploiting Allied occupation of Soviet zones of Germany to try and extract concessions from the Russians. And as soon as the European war ended, Truman abruptly cut off Lend-Lease shipments to Russia.

With the European war over, one of the major reasons for conciliating Stalin – the need to co-ordinate wartime operations – therefore disappeared. The only other sphere in which America needed Russia's help was in the Far East, and for many months past the United States Joint Chiefs-of-Staff had been planning ahead for Russian entry in the war against Japan; but by the end of April 1945 they had decided that this would make practically no military difference. Of course, a Russian declaration of war would have a severe psychological impact on Japan. But at the same time, American politicians were beginning to wonder whether it might not be better to forestall any expansion of Soviet influence in South-East Asia by ending the war while Russian troops were still on the other side of the Manchurian border.

In this way, the atomic bomb was to take on an extra, and very particular, significance. In strategic terms, the bomb would bolster America's more belligerent diplomacy, while tactically it could be used to pre-empt a Russian declaration of war against Japan, which, since October 1944, had been promised within three months of VE-Day. The European war ended on May 8. A shadow was already looming over Hiroshima.

By June 1, the Interim Committee's report was ready. Its scientific advisers had discovered widespread doubts among the atomic scientists over the military use of the bomb, but in the end the committee's recommendations were unanimous:

● The bomb should be used against Japan as soon as possible.

● It should be used on a dual target – that is, a military installation or war plant surrounded by or adjacent to houses and other buildings most susceptible to damage.

● It should be used without prior warning.

The idea of warning Japan, or demonstrating the weapon, was rejected, in case the demonstration failed, or the Japanese moved war prisoners into the designated area. So far as the committee was concerned, if the object of using the bomb was to end the war, then there was 'no acceptable alternative to direct military use' Truman was informed by Stimson that a gun-type Uranium 235 bomb would be ready by August 1, and that a plutonium bomb would be available for combat use within a month of successful testing. The test was scheduled for July.

Because two types of bomb were being developed, two groups of crews were designated for training, which started in the late summer of 1944. The crews were sent out to the giant air-base at Tinian, in the Marianas, some 1,400 miles from the main Japanese island of Honshu. Between May and mid-July 1945, the parts of the combat bombs were sent out to Tinian, to await the go-ahead from President Truman. The precise target was still undecided.

Since November 1944, a team ▷

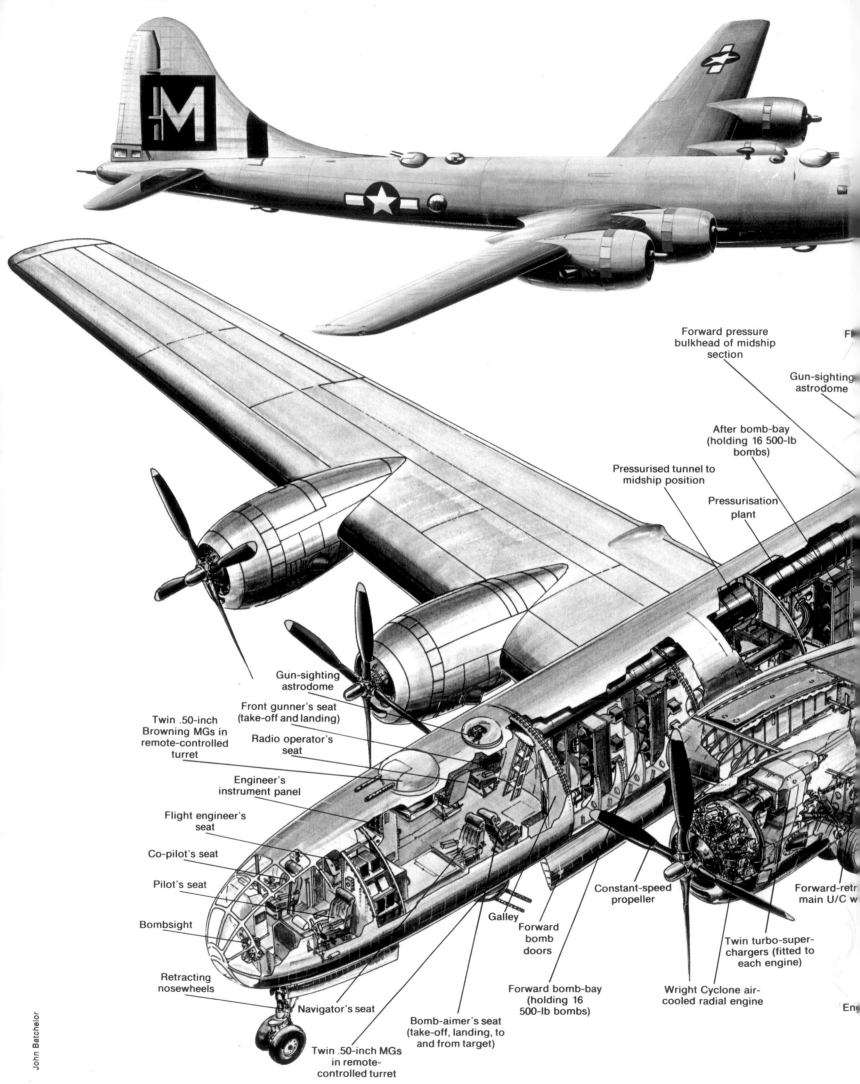

Forward pressure
bulkhead of midship
section

Gun-sighting
astrodome

After bomb-bay
(holding 16 500-lb
bombs)

Pressurised tunnel to
midship position

Pressurisation
plant

Gun-sighting
astrodome

Front gunner's seat
(take-off and landing)

Twin .50-inch
Browning MGs in
remote-controlled
turret

Radio operator's
seat

Engineer's
instrument panel

Flight engineer's
seat

Co-pilot's seat

Pilot's seat

Bombsight

Galley

Forward
bomb
doors

Constant-speed
propeller

Forward-retr
main U/C w

Twin turbo-super-
chargers (fitted to
each engine)

Retracting
nosewheels

Navigator's seat

Forward bomb-bay
(holding 16
500-lb bombs)

Wright Cyclone air-
cooled radial engine

En

Bomb-aimer's seat
(take-off, landing, to
and from target)

Twin .50-inch MGs
in remote-
controlled turret

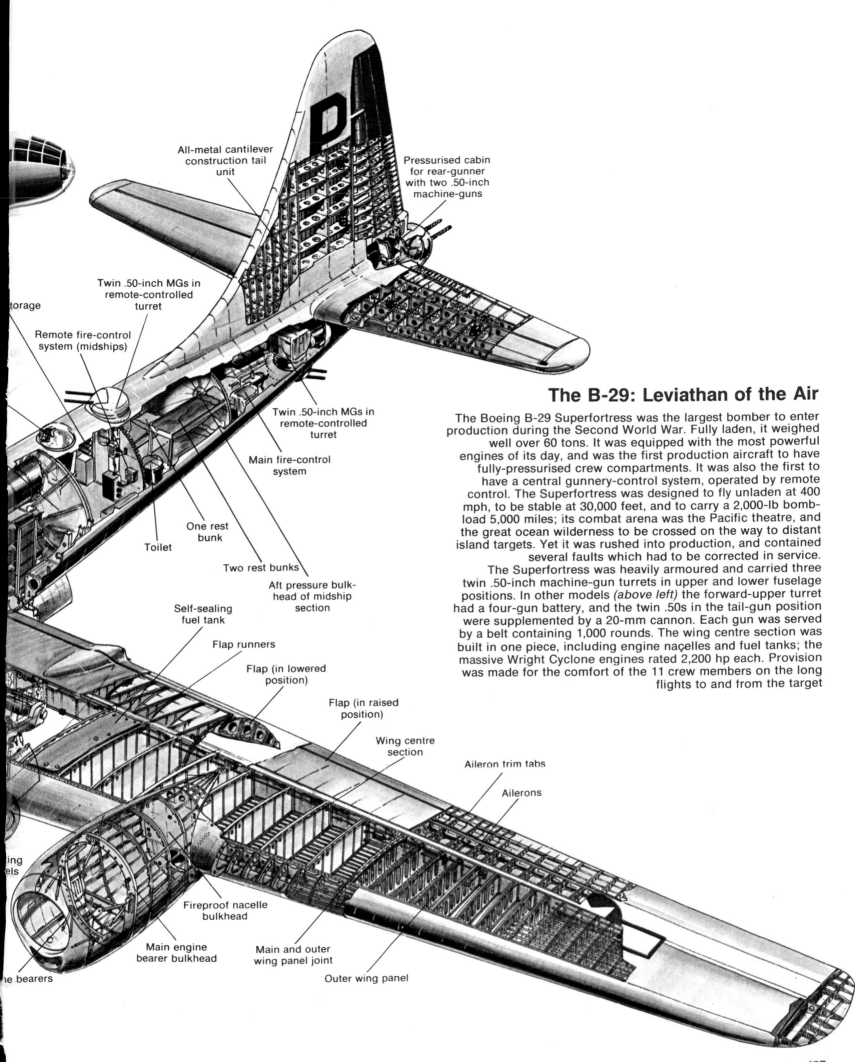

All-metal cantilever construction tail unit

Pressurised cabin for rear-gunner with two .50-inch machine-guns

Twin .50-inch MGs in remote-controlled turret

...torage

Remote fire-control system (midships)

Twin .50-inch MGs in remote-controlled turret

Main fire-control system

One rest bunk

Toilet

Two rest bunks

Aft pressure bulk-head of midship section

Self-sealing fuel tank

Flap runners

Flap (in lowered position)

Flap (in raised position)

Wing centre section

Aileron trim tabs

Ailerons

...ing ...els

Fireproof nacelle bulkhead

Main engine bearer bulkhead

Main and outer wing panel joint

Outer wing panel

...e bearers

The B-29: Leviathan of the Air

The Boeing B-29 Superfortress was the largest bomber to enter production during the Second World War. Fully laden, it weighed well over 60 tons. It was equipped with the most powerful engines of its day, and was the first production aircraft to have fully-pressurised crew compartments. It was also the first to have a central gunnery-control system, operated by remote control. The Superfortress was designed to fly unladen at 400 mph, to be stable at 30,000 feet, and to carry a 2,000-lb bomb-load 5,000 miles; its combat arena was the Pacific theatre, and the great ocean wilderness to be crossed on the way to distant island targets. Yet it was rushed into production, and contained several faults which had to be corrected in service.

The Superfortress was heavily armoured and carried three twin .50-inch machine-gun turrets in upper and lower fuselage positions. In other models *(above left)* the forward-upper turret had a four-gun battery, and the twin .50s in the tail-gun position were supplemented by a 20-mm cannon. Each gun was served by a belt containing 1,000 rounds. The wing centre section was built in one piece, including engine naçelles and fuel tanks; the massive Wright Cyclone engines rated 2,200 hp each. Provision was made for the comfort of the 11 crew members on the long flights to and from the target

reporting to Stimson had begun to draw up a list of possible targets for the atomic bomb. Ideally, they were looking for large towns, with military installations, which had not yet been seriously affected by conventional bombing. Ten cities were chosen. Number four was Nagasaki. Kokura, not far distant, was number three. Second on the list was Kyoto, which was later eliminated because of its historic and cultural importance in Japan. At the head of the list was the seventh largest Japanese city, Hiroshima.

The only hold-up in the programme was the failure to supply casting moulds and firing circuits for the bomb on time. As the test fell behind schedule, Truman's diplomatic offensive had to be delayed, but in response to the urgings of his own advisers, and of Churchill, Truman had asked for another meeting of the Big Three, at which to stage a showdown with Stalin on all outstanding issues. Stimson, however, warned strongly against a premature showdown. He regarded it as 'a terrible thing to gamble with such big stakes in diplomacy without having your master card in your hand'. He urged Truman to postpone any meeting until after the atomic test in New Mexico.

Accordingly, Truman held off the meeting till mid-July, and meanwhile conducted an elaborate, backtracking manoeuvre, during which he sent Harry Hopkins, Roosevelt's close friend, to Moscow, to patch up relations with Stalin. Meanwhile, along with James Byrnes, soon to be his Secretary of State, Truman looked forward to the time when the bomb would 'put us in a position to dictate our own terms'.

But before the bomb could be diplomatically effective, it had to be demonstrated. And the prospect of using the bomb against Japan led to a growing divergence of views between Truman's military and political advisers. For some months, the planned invasion of the Japanese home islands had been subject to second thoughts by the military chiefs, and as early as April 1945 there is evidence that they were inclined against it.

The military situation of Japan was desperate. Since the fall of Okinawa, the Japanese had known that there was no prospect of winning the war, and they turned their main efforts to defending the home islands. These, too, were taking a terrible battering. Each month, the US Air Force dropped 40,000 tons of bombs on Japan; nearly half the buildings in 60 cities and towns had been destroyed; 90% of the navy and merchant shipping had been sunk, and the main island, Honshu, was practically cut off from Hokkaido to the north, and Kyushu to the south. Practically no resistance was offered to the continuous B-29 bombing raids, because the Japanese needed to conserve all their aviation fuel in case of invasion.

No one under-estimated the problems of invasion. The Japanese still had over 2,000,000 soldiers on the home islands, and even with 5,000,000 men at their disposal, the American Joint Chiefs-of-Staff reckoned that the fighting would continue into the winter of 1946. Estimates of possible Allied casualties ranged from 200,000 to a million, and the feeling that dropping the bomb would stop the war and save millions of lives naturally affected the issue.

But long before the bomb was dropped, all Truman's military advisers were agreed that an invasion was unnecessary, for saturation bombing and naval blockade were hav-

ing an overwhelming impact on the Japanese. Even the most cautious of the Chiefs-of-Staff, General Marshall, thought it needed only a Russian declaration of war to force Japan into capitulation, and the other chiefs were more emphatic. In the opinion of Admiral Leahy, 'the Japanese were already defeated and ready to surrender'.

Of course, the military advisers may well have been wrong. Although the Emperor of Japan and three of his most important ministers were in favour of early peace negotiations, the army leaders were still obstinately clinging to the war which they had started. The Foreign Minister, Togo, was allowed to explore the possibility of Russian mediation, but in public the cabinet was united behind the war effort. In fact, the army would never have surrendered of its own accord, and even after the Emperor finally decided to accept America's terms, elements in the army tried to continue the struggle.

But even if their assessment of the Japanese mentality was at fault, the fact remains that Truman's military advisers reckoned that Japan would surrender without an invasion, and without the use of the atomic bomb. General Eisenhower summed up the feelings of the military when he saw Stimson at the Big Three meeting in Potsdam at the end of July: 'I voiced to him my grave misgivings, first on the basis of my belief that Japan was already defeated and that dropping the bomb was completely unnecessary, and secondly because I thought that our country should avoid shocking world opinion by the use of a weapon whose employment was, I thought, no longer mandatory as a measure to save American lives. It was my belief that Japan was, at that very moment, seeking some way to surrender with a minimum loss of "face".'

The efforts made by the Japanese to negotiate a surrender were well known to the American government. All the messages that Togo sent to Sato, the Ambassador in Moscow, were intercepted by the Americans, and it was clear from an early stage that if the peace party could eliminate the 'unconditional surrender' clause, they might persuade the Emperor to overrule the cabinet. The only condition they really held out for was that the position of the Emperor should remain untouched. Secretary of the Navy Forrestal noted in his diary Togo's telegram to Sato on July 12: 'Togo said further that the unconditional surrender terms of the Allies was about the only thing in the way of termination of the war.'

In marked contrast to the alacrity with which they had responded to German peace feelers, the Americans took no notice of Japan's efforts to start negotiations. The Russians also ignored them: they did not want the Pacific war to end before they had a chance to share in the spoils. But why should the Americans, if they really did want to shorten the war, make no attempt to take up the Japanese initiative – especially as, when the crunch came, they did allow the Japanese to retain their monarchy?

The answer emerged clearly during the Potsdam Conference, at which Eisenhower had lodged so strong a protest against the decision to drop the bomb on Japan. This was the place scheduled for the showdown with Stalin, at which Truman could bring to bear the diplomatic weight of atomic weaponry. And Potsdam was also to be the place where Truman would make his one gesture to allow the Japanese to surrender

before an atomic attack – by issuing an ultimatum.

Truman arrived at Potsdam, just outside Berlin, on Sunday, July 15. The next evening, he heard the first news of the long-awaited atomic test at Alamogordo. The cryptic message read: 'Operated on this morning. Diagnosis not yet complete, but results seem satisfactory, and already exceed expectations.' The next day, an elated Truman opened the conference with a pungent statement of American demands in Europe. On the 21st, Stimson received a full report on the test, and read it to Truman and Byrnes: 'The President was tremendously pepped up by it . . . he said it gave him an entirely new feeling of confidence.'

When Churchill was told the news, he, too, immediately recognised the diplomatic implications of the test: 'From that moment, our outlook on the future was transformed.' For the British, as for the Americans, the decision to use the bomb was scarcely a decision at all. Churchill, on July 1, had given the formal approval required under the Quebec agreement of 1943, and although he, too, realised that Japan's 'defeat was certain before the first bomb fell', the question of not using the weapon never arose.

For Truman, however, the question did arise. But for him it was not really a moral question, as the destructive power of the atomic bomb was no greater than that of conventional bombing. In fact, the B-29 raids on Tokyo on March 10 devastated four times the area, and resulted in 50,000 more casualties, than did the atomic raid on Hiroshima. The question for Truman was, could he justify militarily the atomic attack he felt to be so advantageous to his diplomacy?

For it transpired, at Potsdam, that the atomic test was not enough. It had been decided to tell Stalin about the bomb, but when Truman mentioned it to him on July 24, the message was so casual and enigmatic that Churchill for one was convinced that Stalin had no idea of what he was being told. Truman at the last moment had felt that only an actual atomic raid would convince Stalin of the irresistible force behind America's diplomacy.

As a result, although he had stated America's position so forcibly a week earlier, Truman did not press the arguments to conclusion. Indeed, he chose to wait for a final showdown until after the bomb had been 'laid on Japan', and on July 25 he instructed Stimson that the order to use the bomb 'would stand unless I notified him that the Japanese reply to our ultimatum was acceptable'.

This ultimatum was issued by Truman, Churchill and Chiang Kai-shek the next day. It threatened Japan with prompt and utter destruction, but made no mention of the bomb. It stated the terms for surrender, but still insisted on the word 'unconditional', and made no mention of the Emperor's status. It is at this point that it becomes clear that the decision to bomb Hiroshima was not taken purely and simply to end the war as soon as possible.

For there were a number of things Truman could have done to hasten the surrender. He could have encouraged the Russians to declare war, which would have ended the last hopes of the Japanese army that Russia would stay neutral, and of the Japanese peace party that Russia would mediate. Many American advisers thought a Russian declaration of war would in itself bring about a surrender. But Truman actually tried to delay Russian entry during the last days of July, because he wanted to keep Soviet troops out of Manchuria.

Also, now that the bomb had been successfully tested, he could have afforded to warn Japan of the nature of the new weapon; but he chose not to. Most important, he could have taken much more notice of the evident Japanese desire to end the war. But again Truman chose to interpret the Japanese reaction to the Potsdam ultimatum in an unfavourable way. On July 28, the Japanese Prime Minister, Suzuki, announced that his cabinet would *mokusatsu* the ultimatum — which could be translated to mean either 'ignore' or 'withhold comment on'. Truman took it to mean 'ignore', and confirmed instructions that the first bomb should be dropped as soon as possible after August 2.

Yet, on that day, August 2, Togo sent an agonized cable to Sato in Moscow, in a final bid to get Russian help in seeking peace terms based on the Potsdam ultimatum: 'Since the loss of one day relative to this present matter may result in a thousand years of regret, it is requested that you immediately have a talk with Molotov.' But Molotov refused to see Sato until the 8th, when he calmly announced Russia's declaration of war on Japan — exactly three months after VE-Day.

'The greatest thing in history'

For Truman, all that remained after Potsdam was to sail home and await the event which would mark the final emergence of America from isolationism. For the decision to drop the bomb was not a military one — the Allied Supreme Commander in the Pacific, General MacArthur, was not even asked his opinion. Truman's decision was political. In the short term, he wanted to end the war in the Pacific before the Russians could join in — it was hoped that the psychological impact of the bomb might achieve this.

But Truman ignored other ways of ending the war because, in the long run, he needed a military use of the bomb to reinforce his new diplomacy. In May 1945, one of the atomic scientists who went to see James Byrnes about the bomb recorded the future Secretary of State's point of view: 'Mr Byrnes did not argue that it was necessary to use the bomb against the cities of Japan in order to win the war.' His view was 'that our possessing and demonstrating the bomb would make Russia more manageable in Europe'. The United States, which had only been shocked into its international responsibilities by Pearl Harbor, announced on August 6, in the most dramatic way possible, its new, world-wide commitments — to Europe, to democracy, to 'lasting peace'. In an astonishing throwback to the days of Woodrow Wilson, America, by means of atomic supremacy, was going to put the world to rights.

In the early hours of August 6, after three days of delay through bad weather, after three other B-29s carrying weights similar to the bomb had crashed in practice takeoffs, *Enola Gay* rose from the specially lengthened runway at Tinian, and headed towards Hiroshima to deliver her fatal payload of Uranium 235. President Truman was aboard the cruiser *Augusta* when he heard the news, and announced to those around him: 'This is the greatest thing in history.'

THE NUCLEAR RAIDS

August 1945

Hiroshima and Nagasaki

Louis Allen

The explosion of the first nuclear bomb over Japan in 1945 was the climax of the Second World War. The nuclear bomb was born in war; it had been prepared in one of the most rapid scientific revolutions of all time, which could only have taken the form it did under the impetus of the war. The most brilliant brains of the scientific world had contributed to forge a weapon of frightful power; and the sufferings which it had inflicted on the people of Hiroshima and Nagasaki have mercifully never been repeated elsewhere. For those who survived the two nuclear raids, the memory of the *Pikadon* has a scarring permanence which can never be forgotten

At 0245 hours, August 6, 1945 (local time), the Superfortress *Enola Gay* lifted off the specially lengthened runway at North Field, Tinian, with just a few yards to spare—she was 7 tons overweight—and headed for Japan. She carried a crew of nine, with four passengers, all of them scientists, and a single bomb which bore the incongruous code name of *Little Boy*. 'General Bombing Mission 13' was under way. Her captain, Colonel Paul Tibbets, had been training his hand-picked crew for over a year and now, as the spearhead of 509 Composite Group of 20th Air Force, they were preparing to launch the first atomic bomb— though only Tibbets himself, of the crew members, had any accurate idea of the type of bomb it was.

Electronically complex enough to require its own dashboard and wiring system, the bomb had already posed one problem before the plane left the ground. Some B-29s had already crashed when taking off from Tinian on conventional bombing missions, and if the *Enola Gay* had a similar accident, the whole island might well disappear in smoke. Could the bomb be rendered harmless for the take-off and then armed during the flight? Captain William Parsons thought it could. A naval ordnance expert who had been associate director at the Los Alamos bomb laboratory, and who was flying with Tibbets as one of the scientific observers, he spent some hectic hours on August 5 practising the insertion of the conventional explosive trigger. By the time he had finished, his fingers were bleeding from the sharp edges of the bomb's components, but he was confident he could repeat the process in flight. When the plane reached 8,000 feet, Parsons went down into the bomb bay and reported to Tibbets, less than half an hour later, that they were now carrying a 'final bomb'.

They were not the first plane to take off. At 0130 hours three weather planes had left Tinian to report visibility over the possible targets, Hiroshima, Kokura, and Nagasaki. The bomb had to be dropped visually. Hiroshima was the primary target, but if there was too much cloud cover Tibbets was to select one of the other cities. Washington had already provided him with a long-term weather forecast; four months before, a meteorologist had confidently predicted that the most suitable period would be between August 6 and August 9. Understandably, Tibbets had been taken aback by his assurance, but the event justified it.

Major Claude Eatherly, in the weather plane *Straight Flush*, 32,000 feet above Hiroshima, saw a rim of cloud round the edge of the city, but there was a clear gap 10 miles wide which gave perfect visibility. He radioed to the *Enola Gay* the Morse code message which sealed the fate of Hiroshima: 'Y2.Q2.B2.C1'. In cloud terms this meant '2/10 lower and middle and 2/10 at 15,000 feet', so visibility was good over the primary target. At 0809 hours, Hiroshima time, the city was in sight and the crew put on their arc-welder's goggles to protect their eyes from the flash. At 0811 Tibbets started the bomb run and 2½ minutes later handed over to his bomb-aimer.

Major Thomas Ferebee knew by heart the shape of Hiroshima, with the fingers of the Ota river delta reaching out into the sea, and he soon had the aiming-point in

his bomb sight: a bridge over the widest branch of the Ota. The orders were to drop the bomb at 0815 hours, local time, and Tibbets' skill and the excellent conditions had brought the *Enola Gay*, now travelling at 285 mph, over the target within a margin of seconds. At 17 seconds past 0815 hours, the bomb bay doors opened, and *Little Boy* fell out, from a height of nearly 6 miles. As the B-29 and its accompanying observation plane streaked away in a turn of 150 degrees, to put as great a distance as possible between themselves and the explosion, the crew counted. Fifty-one seconds later, *Little Boy* exploded, 1,850 feet over the city, and only 200 yards from the target point.

Purple clouds, seething flames

As the plane turned, the crew saw a flash, and then felt a double shock wave hit the aircraft. They were 15 miles away by this time, and suddenly below them was a ball of fire, with a temperature, for an imperceptible fraction of a second, of 1,000,000°, changing to purple clouds and seething, boiling flames which swept upwards. A turbulent cloud of dense white smoke, mushrooming at the top, shot up and up into the sky, reaching a height of 40,000 feet in a matter of minutes. The crew could still see it 360 miles away on their flight back to Tinian. The whole city, except for the dock areas on its fringes, lay under a pall of dark grey dust 3 miles across, in which they could make out flashes of red and orange fire.

But there was no appreciable sound, and accounts differ as to the sound heard by those in the city. Dr Hachiya, of the Hiroshima Communications Bureau Hospital, recalled a strong flash of light, and his colleague, Dr Tabuchi, saw a blinding white flash. Those who survived inside the city referred to the bomb as the *Pika* ('flash'). Those outside called it *Pikadon* ('flash-boom'), for there seems to be more agreement about the sound of the explosion many miles away than in Hiroshima itself. An army officer boarding the train at Iwakuni heard a huge *Don* and saw a great mass of smoke as he looked east to Hiroshima; and a fisherman in his sampan 20 miles away in the Inland Sea near Tsuzu saw the flash and heard a tremendous explosion.

Then Hiroshima began to die. In a matter of seconds, the thermal radiation from the fireball in the centre of the city vaporised thousands of people. Others some distance from the epicentre were fearfully burned, and the blast which followed, like a typhoon, whipped clothes and skin from their bodies as they screamed and writhed in agony. The shock wave, lasting about a second, flattened factories, offices, and houses, burying thousands more under the débris. Trains were overturned in Hiroshima station 2,000 yards away, trams were hurled into the air with their grisly load of already charred corpses. One or two reinforced concrete buildings in the centre remained standing, otherwise the whole of the commercial and residential core of the city was simply annihilated in an instant. Trees and grass burned like straw, and as the overturned *hibachis* or charcoal stoves in the devastated houses ignited the walls and partitions, the fire spread rapidly, fanned by a violent wind that swept through the city.

The people of Hiroshima had been caught unawares. Apart from four or five bombs

Central Press

earlier in 1945, their city had been spared the raids which had reduced nearly every other major city in Japan to ruins in the past few months. But they had no illusions. As a big military base, containing the headquarters of the II Army Command, the V Division, and many other units, they felt they must be a target sooner or later, and plans had been drawn up and partly carried out to evacuate useless mouths and knock down houses to make east-west firebreaks through the city. Some 70,000 houses had been demolished, and the peak population of 380,000 was now less than 300,000.

There was a nightly exodus from the city, too. Towards sunset people would form up with their belongings in carts, and make their way to the outskirts, to return the following morning. In fact this 'unplanned' evacuation had reached such proportions that the Army HQ and the Prefectural Office were seriously concerned lest a heavy raid find the firebreak programme incomplete and the streets possibly blocked with streams of people, horses, and carts.

Like the rest of the Japanese cities, Hiroshima had an air-raid warning system, an alert on the approach of aircraft, and a rapid alarm if the city itself was threatened. At 0731 hours on August 6, the alert had been sounded as *Straight Flush* was spotted coming in for its weather observation flight. As the plane turned out to seaward again, 22 minutes later, the 'all clear' sounded. Few people paid any attention when two more planes were sighted, but some cheered when they saw parachutes break from one of them. The crews, they thought, must be bailing out. Most people were either in their offices, or on their way to factories in the industrial outskirts. Men unfit for military service and school children who had been mobilised for the firebreaks were already at work. So the estimate of probable casualties—20,000—made by J. R. Oppenheimer, on the assumption that the bomb would be dropped in a city whose population had already taken shelter, bore no relation to what actually occurred.

Men vaporised, shredded, charred
There were innumerable ways of dying. Those close to the epicentre were vaporised, burned to nothing, in less than an instant. All that remained of them, if they had been standing near a concrete wall, was the imprint of their shadow upon it. The whole centre of Hiroshima, 2 miles across, became for a brief moment of time a lethal oven. Then it disintegrated, and what had been an industrial and commercial city of a quarter of a million people was a dust cloud made up of millions and millions of splinters of wood, glass, metal, and flesh, blown outwards and upwards with tremendous force. More than 2 miles from the explosion, bare skin was burned, telegraph poles were charred. Nearly 400 yards from the epicentre, the mica on granite gravestones—melting point 900°C—had fused. Grey clay tiles—melting point 1,300°C—had melted at a distance of 600 yards. The bomb's heat at ground zero, immediately beneath the epicentre, was later believed to have been around 6,000°C. The force of the blast reached a pressure of 8·0 tons per square yard.

But the bomb had other deaths in store. Thousands of those who survived the burns and shock from blast had been bombarded by neutrons and gamma rays. Nearly all those who survived within half a

441

US Air Force

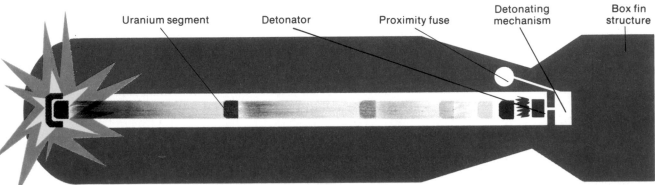

Uranium segment   Detonator   Proximity fuse   Detonating mechanism   Box fin structure

Peter Warrington

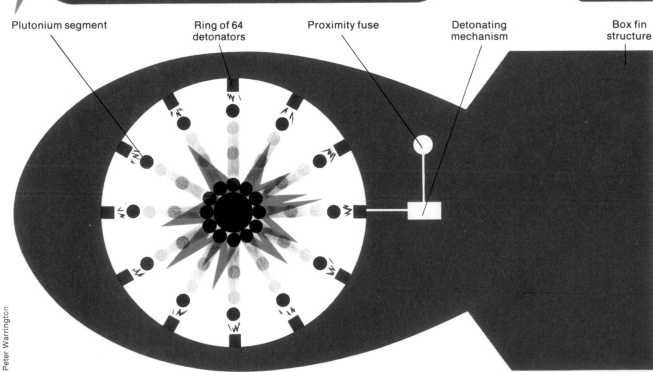

Plutonium segment   Ring of 64 detonators   Proximity fuse   Detonating mechanism   Box fin structure

Above: The bomber which carried out one of the most accurate —and destructive— raids of the war, delivering 'Little Boy' to within 200 yards of the aiming point in the heart of Hiroshima.

Left: 'Little Boy', the bomb dropped on Hiroshima. Weighing about 9,000 lbs, 28 inches in diameter and 10 feet long, it was a 'gun-type' weapon, shooting a piece of sub-critical U-235 into another, cup-shaped piece to create the super-critical mass—and the nuclear explosion

Left: The 'Fat Man' bomb was dropped on Nagasaki. This bomb used the implosion method, with a ring of 64 detonators shooting segments of Plutonium together to obtain the super-critical mass. It weighed about 10,000 lbs, was 10 feet 8 inches long, and had the destructive power of approximately 20,000 tons of high explosive— roughly the same as 'Little Boy'

Below left: 'Little Boy'
Below right: 'Fat Man'

Fred Wolfe

US Air Force

442

mile of the epicentre died later from the effects of radiation.

Major-General Shūitsu Matsumura had been in Hiroshima just one month. He had been transferred from GHQ Tokyo as Chief-of-Staff to the Hiroshima Military District, and it was a pleasant change to come from the incinerated metropolis to Japan's almost untouched seventh city, where some of the comforts of life were still obtainable. He lived with a Mr and Mrs Kurota, and on the morning of August 6 had taken tea with them, and was about to change into his uniform to make his way to the District HQ in Hiroshima Castle. Hiroshima had been the site of the Imperial GHQ in the Sino-Japanese War, and since 1941 thousands of troops had left its docks for the campaigns in the South Pacific and South-East Asia.

As General Matsumura went into his room, he was suddenly aware of a brilliant flash, followed by a huge PHWATT!! He was hurled through the roof and found himself floating in the air above a Chinese lotus-tree. He saw a dazzling, glowing ball of fire, and then, in what seemed the same instant of time, he was lying in the garden, bleeding from cuts all over his body, with his clothes in tattered shreds. The house collapsed round him, chunks of timber, roof-beams, and pillars came hurtling down. He thought at first that a bomb had exploded directly on top of the lotus-tree, then, as a red glow shone over the house, he feared he was going to be burned alive and covered his head with his hands. Oddly enough, he felt no heat. He spied a crack in the roof above his head, and scrambled out through broken planks and tiles to find himself outside in the street, naked save for a loincloth.

All around, houses were falling down, people were crawling out from cracking roofs, bathed in blood. His first thought was to bring the army in to help, and, oblivious of his own wounds, he decided to fetch troops from the Castle. Unfortunately he did not yet know the town well, the collapsing houses had filled the streets with débris, and he lost his bearings. He came out in front of the blazing radio station where two people lay in a state of shock in the entrance, one of them with blood pouring from a huge wound in the thigh.

An announcer, whose face Matsumura vaguely recognised, dashed out of the building, and Matsumura called out 'Do you know Hiroshima well?' 'I was born here,' was the answer. 'Take me to District HQ,' asked Matsumura, but the announcer found it hard to get his bearings too, so they began to clamber on the roofs of collapsing houses to see where they were. On every side were visions of catastrophe, cars overturned and burning, horses bucking in their death-throes, people screaming with agony, or dazed from shock and loss of blood. When they finally reached the corner of the West Parade Ground, tongues of flame were licking up from the buildings on every side, the C-in-C's residence was already surrounded by fire, and the infantry, artillery, and medical barracks were ablaze. The five-storey castle was not there any more.

But the most horrifying sight was the centre of the parade ground. The troops had just come out to do drill or PT, and the blast had blown them down and crushed them to death. Those whose sleeves were rolled up

or who had taken their shirts off were covered with fearful blisters. The groans of wounded men came from the air-raid shelters. Matsumura turned along the moat towards the castle gates, while troops ran screaming out of the hutments, all with burned hands or forearms raised above the level of the heart to lessen the pain of the burns. Collecting a few men, he made his way towards the Asano Sentei Park. They noticed how badly he was bleeding, and prevailed on him to let them roughly bandage his wounds with their puttees. Using the tramlines as guides they moved along, in the stream of naked or half-naked people with bodies raw-red from burns, or crippled from the blast.

Apart from groans of pain the endless procession went forward in silence. They passed houses where they could see frantic parents scrabbling at tiles and timber to reach children whose voices could still be heard from within, before the devouring flames reached them. The regional governor's house was near Matsumura's. Trapped by a beam and unable to move, the governor screamed to his wife to cut off his legs, then realised it was hopeless. As the flames came nearer, he called to her 'I'm done for, get away as fast as you can!' At the time of the explosion General Fujii, of the District GHQ, had just put on his uniform, and was about to leave the house, carrying his sword. The burned sword was found beside his black charred remains, with the general's gold fillings. His groom, waiting by the side of the porch, had been calcinated in an instant, along with the horse he was holding.

A strange, viscous rain . . .

When they reached the pinewoods by the river, Matsumura could go no further, and sat down among a group of wounded, exhausted from fatigue and shock. The whole front of his body by this time was covered with a sheet of dried blood, and he peeled it off like a sheet of cellophane. There were scores of badly wounded soldiers lying everywhere. Many of them had been drafted into Hiroshima from the surrounding country, and they were begging people to take messages for their relatives. There were still men who kept their heads: one warrant-officer, with his back torn to pieces, pulled a pocket-book from his map-case and began scrupulously noting down the messages.

Then the fire moved on to the pines in the park, and as the wind changed direction, Matsumura's shelter was covered with thick black smoke. He saw the Nigitsu Shrine begin to burn. As both river banks were now alight, boats went back and forth ferrying people to the island in the middle. Then the convection from the intense heat brought a whirlwind whistling along the banks, spreading the fire further, but those who were lying along them were too far gone to move. Many of those who survived the flames were drowned by the rising waters. Matsumura made towards a bridge. As he paused, leaning against a pillar, rain began to fall—a strange, viscous rain, full of the aspirated dust of the city—and the rising tide reached up to his waist.

It occurred to him that it might be possible to contact other units, in Yamaguchi or Shimane prefectures; and perhaps the Akatsuki Unit in the port of Ujina had not been affected. So he made his way up the Ushita hillside, to contact Lieutenant-

General Yamamoto, commanding the Ordnance Depot, reached Yamamoto's house, and collapsed on the verandah. He did not notice the passing of time, but was vaguely aware that someone cooked some rice for him, which tasted full of sand. But Matsumura had been in the Canton campaign and sand in his rice was the least of his worries. You simply had to eat from the top. Yamamoto went down the hillside and came back with some nurses and a naval medical officer, who had just reached Hiroshima from the base at Kure. By candle light they ferreted out the splinters of broken glass from 36 places in Matsumura's body, and stitched a deep wound in his neck, using mercurochrome as disinfectant. It was all they had.

Matsumura later learned he was not the only survivor of his staff. Most of them had been killed at once by the blast, but one, Lieutenant-Colonel Kigi, had been standing at the foot of a flight of stairs, and had come off with only light wounds. Kigi's house happened to be near the epicentre, and his wife, her sister, and their two children had been annihilated. The sister had been washing the children's clothes, and had died face downwards in the wash-tub. Curiously enough, the clothes themselves had remained intact, and Kigi wandered round the charred remains of the HQ, clutching this solitary reminder that he had once had children.

Later the troops from Ujina moved in. Roads had to be cleared of rubble and opened, and the innumerable corpses removed from beneath collapsed buildings and walls. With the summer heat, the stench had become unbearable, and mass cremations took place, but since it was feared the fires from the cremation pyres might be seen and used by enemy bombers, they had to be restricted to the hours of daylight. So the cremations went on, day after day. At Kure, once the news of the Truman broadcast filtered through and put an end to the various rumours about the type of bomb which had been used, the Army Medical Service began to carry out examinations of the blood of casualties. On August 10, the Atomic Bomb Observation group arrived from Tokyo, and by triangulation measurements determined the epicentre of the explosion to be about 1,000 yards from Matsumura's house. The height of the explosion they estimated to be about 500 yards, and the ground temperature immediately beneath it as 5,000°C.

Tortured, melted features

Asano Sentei Park, where Matsumura, with thousands of others, had sheltered from the flames, was the scene of countless strange and horrible incidents. In his book *Hiroshima* John Hersey tells how Father Kleinsorge, a German priest from the Jesuit mission house, himself cut and bleeding from splinters, answered a call for help from a soldier who could not move and begged for water. As Fr Kleinsorge came up to give him some, he saw the soldier was not alone. Behind a row of bushes lay other soldiers, with their faces completely burned, and hollow eye sockets from which the melted eyes had run, liquid, down their cheeks. Their mouths were mere suppurating holes. One of the boatmen ferrying casualties across the river to the Park stopped in midstream to help a girl out of the water. As he pulled her up, he saw her nose and eyes had been burned away; her ▷

Hiroshima/Nagasaki/Tokyo/The Casualties

It has frequently been pointed out that the casualties from the Tokyo fire-raid on the night of March 9/10, 1945, were greater than those from the atomic bomb, but comparison of overall casualties is not the best way to show the effectiveness of the atomic bomb. If the (rounded) figures are shown in relation to the density of population per square mile destroyed, a different picture emerges: the rate of casualties per square mile is shown to be four times greater in Hiroshima than in Tokyo.

The original Japanese figures for Nagasaki were based on verified cases only, and were considered too low by the US Strategic Bombing Survey. On the other hand, the Japanese themselves later began to raise casualty figures. The Nagasaki Prefectural Office later proposed a figure of 87,000 for the dead alone, and a municipal publication *Hiroshima Today* (1953) declared that the total figure for that city was 260,000. This is lower than the figure of 306,545 given in Toshikazu Kase's *Eclipse of the Rising Sun*, where it is pointed out that the original death roll in

Hiroshima took no account of the military casualties, which must have been high, the estimate being half the military population of the city.

For this particular figure the American Air Force historians give 6,769 troops killed or missing of a total of 24,158. A broadcast early in 1968 by the Japanese Broadcasting Corporation gave a figure for Hiroshima of 240,000 to 270,000 killed outright or from radiation sickness within five years. On the other hand, the same broadcast put the population of the city at the time as 400,000, which is far higher than usual estimates. Over 4 square miles of Hiroshima were obliterated. Within a 2-mile radius of the epicentre, 10,000 buildings were annihilated by blast and 50,000 by fire. In Nagasaki, nearly 2 square miles were destroyed, a figure smaller than that of the average area for incendiary raids on Japan (2·97 square miles). But the Hiroshima bomb fell into a commercial and administrative area. At Nagasaki, *Fat Man* hit a much more heavily industrialised zone, nearly 70% of which was destroyed.

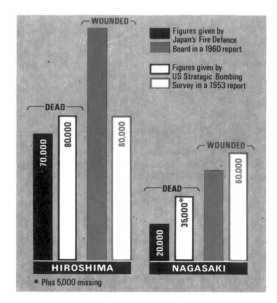

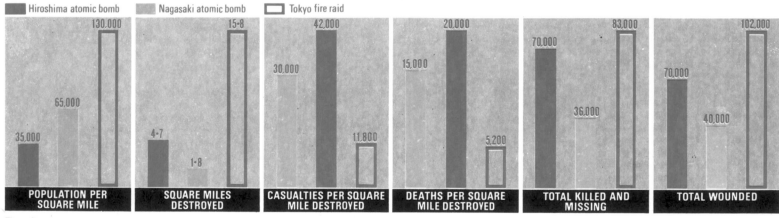

These figures were given by the US Atomic Energy Commission in *The Effects of Nuclear Weapons*

ears looked as if they had melted. Then the round, featureless face fell back into the water, to drown with thousands of others.

Perhaps the strangest incident that day, and one which sheds light on the mood of wartime Japan, was one related by Dr Hachiya in his *Hiroshima Diary*. A portrait of the Emperor was kept in a special place in the Communications Bureau, and Mr Yasuda, the employee responsible for the safe keeping of the picture in emergencies, was on a tram going to work when the bomb fell. His first thought was for the portrait, and he left his shattered tram and made his way on foot through the burning streets, the corpses, and the dark clouds of fiery dust. Running up to the fourth floor, he forced open the iron door behind which the picture was kept. His colleagues thought the Castle would be the safest place for it, so with four of them (one in front, one behind, one on either side), Yasuda carried the picture on his back out of the grounds and made for the Castle. At the Castle gates, a sentry warned them fire was spreading everywhere, so they turned towards the Asano Sentei Park.

As the little procession made its way through the dense crowds of dead and wounded, the cry 'The Emperor's picture!' went up, and those who were still on their

feet, however badly burned they might be, saluted or bowed low. Those who were too seriously wounded to stand clasped their hands in prayer. When the party reached the river, the crowds made way and the picture was entrusted to Mr Ushio, a senior Bureau official, who climbed into a boat with it. As the boat drew away from the shore an officer drew his sword and rapped out an order. The burned and bleeding troops lining the banks stood to attention and saluted. Just after Ushio reached the opposite bank with his precious charge, the whole river bank he had just left turned into a maelstrom of flames. The great pine trees of Asano Park caught fire too, and thousands tried to escape the flames by jumping into the river, where they drowned. But the Emperor's portrait was brought to safety.

Hiroshima was not the only city in Japan to report damage that day. On August 5, USAAF bombers had raided a number of cities, among them the port of Kobe, and reports from these were coming into the capital when the news from Hiroshima arrived. But it was soon evident that what had happened there was exceptional both in the scale and speed of the catastrophe, and the number of aircraft involved. Telephone communication between the city and the Japan Broadcasting Corporation in

Tokyo was cut; the telegraph line to Hiroshima had ceased to function, according to the Tokyo railway signals centre; and Army GHQ could not contact II Army HQ.

Finally a message came through from the Army Transportation Office at Ujina: Hiroshima had been annihilated by a single bomb (Tokyo Radio, in spite of this, was to refer on August 7 to 'a small number of bombs'). The city itself had been full of rumours: a plane had sprayed petrol from the sky and ignited it by dropping incendiaries; the city had been sprinkled with magnesium powder which exploded when it came into contact with the electric tram wires. To many of the Japanese on the ground, as to the navigator of the *Enola Gay*, the first effect had been that of an enormous photographic flash.

A rapid realisation

But there were those in Japan who had a shrewd idea of what was involved. As early as February 1944, the nuclear physicist Yoshio Nishina, the constructor of Japan's first cyclotron in 1937, and a former pupil of Niels Bohr, had been introduced to the Prime Minister, Tojo, by the head of the Second Bureau (Intelligence), General Seizo Arisue. Nishina had proposed the manufacture of a bomb employing the principle of nuclear fission. Tojo refused: there were simply not enough funds available for the industrial installations such a bomb would require. Arisue remembered Nishina's proposal when he was told to go down to Hiroshima with an investigation team on August 7, and he asked Nishina to go with him. Arisue had received a message from the naval base at Kure which referred to a new weapon of unprecedented destructiveness, and the following day his monitors picked up the phrase 'atomic bomb'.

An air-raid siren sounded as he was about to take off from Tachikawa airport outside Tokyo, and he told Nishina to follow later. At 1800 hours he was flying at 4,500 feet over devastated Hiroshima. Arisue was no stranger to bombed cities, but this calcinated desert with its few blackened trees gave no sign of life at all. He landed in a field close to the port, about 2½ miles from ground zero, and as he jumped down, he noticed the mud-coloured grass was all bent seaward, as if it had been pressed flat by a gigantic iron.

An officer ran to meet the aircraft, sword in hand. The right side of his face was perfectly normal, the left was a hideous mass of deep burns. Arisue made his way by launch to the Army Transport HQ in Ujina, where he was met on the quayside by General Baba. There was no light, no electricity, no water, and the staff was working by candlelight in a backyard. General Baba began to tell Arisue what had happened, then burst into tears. He had seen his daughter leave for school that morning, and a few minutes later found her dead body lying in the street, cut to pieces by flying glass. Baba's own personal agony had not prevented him making observations: people in reinforced concrete buildings or deep shelters had survived; shade and white clothing had provided some protection from burns.

The next day, August 8, Arisue went round Hiroshima. Corpses of men and horses lay everywhere, and after two days in the summer heat, they were already decomposing. In the afternoon Nishina arrived with his team of scientists and declared at once that a bomb using uranium had been used. Arisue arranged an interservices conference at Kure for the following day, but on hearing of the Russian declaration of war he returned to Tokyo, bidding farewell to the 70-year-old Field-Marshal Shunroku Hata at his command post on a hillside outside Hiroshima. Arisue could see that the old Marshal had no hope left.

The second bomb
At least two Americans—Admiral Purnell and General Groves, who had been the military 'midwife' of the atomic bomb project—were convinced that a rapid 'double dose' of atomic warfare would end the war; and some of the Los Alamos scientists who had tested another type of bomb, using plutonium, wanted to know if the device would work in battle. August 11 had been fixed as the date for dropping this second bomb, then the weather reports showed good weather could be expected for August 9, with bad weather for the following five days, so it became imperative to bring the date forward. Of the three targets remaining, Kokura, Nagasaki (put on the list when Kyoto was removed because of its cultural and religious associations), and Niigata, the last was deleted because of the extra distance involved. Now part of the in-

dustrial complex known as Kitakyushu, Kokura was a large war arsenal extending over 200 acres.

Nagasaki was a big shipbuilding and repair centre and a major military port, but considered less suitable as a target both because it had been bombed five times in the previous 12 months and because its topography would limit the blast effects and make the damage harder to assess: it was broken by hills and valleys, where Hiroshima had offered a relatively smooth, flat surface.

Instead of being a gun-type bomb, triggering off a Uranium 235 reaction, the second bomb—*Fat Man*—employed the implosion method, a circle of 64 detonators to drive pieces of plutonium together into the supercritical mass. There was no question of arming it in flight.

Where Tibbets had had a smooth run, everything seemed to go wrong with Major Sweeney's trip. Just before take-off at 0349 hours his strike plane, *Bockscar*, was found to have a faulty fuel pump, which meant that the bomb bay could not pump its 800 gallons of fuel to the engines. The plane would not only be deprived of the use of the fuel, it would have to carry a useless load to Japan and back.

The strike plane and observation planes flew separately, and one of the latter (carrying two British observers who had obtained last-minute authorisation from Washington to accompany the flight, William Penney, the scientist, and Group Captain Leonard Cheshire) muffed its rendezvous over the island of Yakushima. Sweeney waited over Yakushima at least 15 minutes, then made for the primary target, Kokura, where it was obvious that visual bombing was impossible. Sweeney made three runs over the city, shortening his fuel still more, but the bomb-aimer could find no break in the cloud. It was Nagasaki's bad luck.

On the way to the secondary target, they worked out what fuel they had left: enough for one run only, and even then they would not be able to return to Tinian, but would have to drop short at Okinawa. Commander Ashworth, operations officer of 509 Group, and a naval atomic weapons expert, was Sweeney's weaponeer and took the responsibility of cancelling the Washington order that only visual bombing be permitted. He told Sweeney to go ahead on radar, if Nagasaki was covered with cloud. It was. There was 8/10 cloud cover when they reached it, and most of the bomb run was made by radar. At the last moment, the bomb-aimer found a break in the cloud, lined up on a race-track, and let go the bomb from 28,900 feet. It was 1058 hours, Nagasaki time.

A second holocaust
Nagasaki was different in several ways from other Japanese cities, with a longer history of western contacts. Founded by a local Christian *daimyō* ruler in the 16th century and then presented by him to the Society of Jesus, it was a port to which Spanish and Portuguese ships had brought traders and missionaries, and was later the scene of the martyrdom of thousands of Japanese Catholics during the persecutions under the Shōgun Hideyoshi. Nagasaki still had a large Catholic population, centred chiefly round the industrial and residential district of Urakami. Wide of its aiming point, *Fat Man* fell on Urakami.

As in Hiroshima three days before, Naga-

saki had sounded the alert when Sweeney's weather plane was spotted at 0745 hours, and the alarm went five minutes later. But the alert had often been sounded when planes were attacking other targets in Kyushu, and the citizens had grown sceptical and careless. When the second alert was sounded at 1053 hours, after the strike plane had been observed, very few people bothered to take shelter. As it happened, Nagasaki was well off for shelters: tunnels had been dug into the surrounding hillsides, and these would have been very effective. In the event, the casualties from fire were less than in Hiroshima, as the large water areas prevented the fires spreading so ruthlessly. A firestorm, which had terrorised Hiroshima, did not occur in Nagasaki.

On the other hand, the plutonium bomb was more efficient than *Little Boy,* and the blast was greater. Because of the bowl-shaped terrain, the damage extended roughly in an oval 2·3 by 1·9 miles, and it was uneven, as the buildings in Urakami were less congested and more irregularly spread. Within the oval nearly every building was destroyed or made uninhabitable, and minor damage occurred up to 16,000 feet from ground zero. On the other hand there was not the same total disorganisation of medical services which had so increased the Hiroshima casualties, although some of the finest hospitals in the Far East—Nagasaki University and Nagasaki Medical College—were destroyed. Oddly enough, the train service was not interrupted. But the individual tragedies were very much like those of Hiroshima.

Matsu Moriuchi, an elderly woman, was in Yamazato Grade School air-raid shelter when the bomb fell. Many people in the shelter were killed, and almost all those in the immediate area outside it. When she peered out, she saw half-naked people, lying around the mouth of the shelter, their bodies swollen to a monstrous size, and the skin peeling off like pieces of torn rag. She realised they were the school teachers who had been outside digging a new shelter. They were not dead and moaned pitifully for water. Sadako Moriyama was in the same shelter and was petrified with horror when she saw two foul, croaking, lizard-like monsters crawl into the shelter mouth. She was even more terrified when the light revealed them to be human beings, their skin stripped to the raw flesh by burns and their bodies shattered where the blast had hurled them against a wall.

In a pathetic heap on a sand-pit outside the shelter lay four children who had been chasing dragon-flies a few minutes before, now naked and burned, the skin hanging from their fingertips like gloves turned inside out. Then she saw the yard was covered with the still twitching bodies of other dying children. On the Koba hillside, 3½ miles away, Fujie Urata saw a flash of red then blue light of intense and unbearable brilliance, but she was separated from the explosion by a mountain and so felt no blast and was exposed to no radiation.

As she watched the black smoke boiling up into the sky, the wounded began to file past her from Urakami, young children with black and swollen faces, workers from the Mitsubishi Urakami Ordnance Plant, naked too, sobbing with shock, faces, necks and hands bleeding or covered with blisters, the skin peeling off in great sheets that flapped in the black dust. On her way to

Urakami she saw a woman's head lying grotesquely by itself in a pumpkin field, with a single gold tooth gleaming in the open mouth, and burned black holes where the eyes had been. A mile from Urakami her sister Tatsue came upon a woman lying in the road with two babies, her face one huge blister, her hair burned to the roots, begging passers-by to take her dying children with them.

From the mountain tops, St Francis' Hospital could be seen blazing, and the hills around Urakami were stripped bare of foliage—the trees had been blasted down to the stumps. About 30 nuns from the Urakami Orphanage who had been working outside on the orphanage farm lay in a huddle behind some rocks, saying the Rosary. They had been burned all over, and the blast that followed the heat had whipped both clothing and skin off their bodies.

Some 'double' survivors

In the hospitals, the scenes from Hiroshima were repeated, living and dead lying together in heaps of burned and mangled flesh, blood, and skin everywhere, uncontrollable diarrhoea cases pouring excreta over hospital floors and down stairs covered in filth and blood. By what must seem the most tragic of coincidences, there were even a number of people in Nagasaki who had survived the Hiroshima bomb, and who lived through the terror of Nagasaki as well. A newspaper publisher, a naval architect, an accountant, an engineer, a dock labourer, and, most improbably, four kite-makers, were 'double' survivors, and there were no doubt others. They were all born in Nagasaki or had family connections there, and all worked in Hiroshima, with the exception of the newspaper publisher who had stopped in the city on his return from a business trip to Tokyo. Within three days of the Hiroshima bombing they were back in Nagasaki. Their experience warned them and their families to take shelter when the B-29s were spotted approaching the city, and so they escaped death a second time.

Perhaps the most poignant story is that of Kenshi Hirata, the accountant, who had only been married a few weeks and had brought his new bride to Hiroshima ten days before the bomb fell. He had been on duty in his office throughout the night August 5/6, and after the bomb fell began searching for his wife, only to find their house crushed flat and her dead body inside. Sadly bearing his wife's ashes back to the city of her birth, he arrived in Nagasaki just in time for the second atomic bomb.

Apathy, defiance, despair, and joy

The reaction of the people of Hiroshima to the bomb did not follow a straightforward pattern. Immediately after the first terror, they made for the suburbs and hills, broken in spirit, unable to think of anything except following the silent, mournful files moving along the railway lines, footpaths, or riverbeds out of the doomed city.

Then life began to re-assert itself. When the news of Nagasaki arrived, the rumour began to spread that Japan too had the atomic weapon but had refrained from using it. Once the Americans had dropped it, a special naval squadron of six-engined bombers had crossed the Pacific and delivered it on San Francisco and Los Angeles. As this rumour spread, it cheered up those suffering from wounds and sickness, patients in hospital began to laugh and sing,

and prayers were offered for the pilots who were supposed to have made the gallant suicide flight.

On August 15, those listening in to the Emperor's broadcast at Hiroshima Station or in the Communications Bureau could hardly make out what he was saying, and not everyone realised at first that he was telling them the war was over. The shock made some of them almost faint, and Dr Hachiya felt cold sweat running down his back as he returned to his bed with the words 'Haisen da!' ('We've lost the war') ringing in his ears. The other patients in his ward were weeping in despair. Then suddenly their tears gave way to anger, and even those who had been hoping for peace were shouting that the war must go on, that it was better to die for Japan than live in disgrace. The following day, when news came that a Japanese air force unit from Kure, 25 miles away, was dropping leaflets encouraging resistance to the surrender, some of the patients shouted for joy.

But side by side with this passionate rejection of the unendurable, radiation sickness and moral disintegration made their way. No one in Hiroshima knew the symptoms or treatment of radiation sickness, a hazard brought by no other weapon of war, and which struck at those who had lived through blast and fire. Those who had been within 500 yards of the epicentre began to show a low blood platelet count, leading to fatal haemorrhages. Two to 15 days after the explosion, many of those who had been within 500 yards of it, but had been shielded by buildings from flash burns and the shock wave, began to develop the fatal signs: loss of appetite, vomiting, spitting of blood, abnormally low white blood cell counts. Those nearest to the epicentre developed *petechiae* (subcutaneous haemorrhages of tiny blood vessels). In the next 500-yard zone the death rate was high, but the symptoms developed later. Even many of those who were up to 3,000 yards from ground zero fell ill and died.

American historians attribute 7 to 20% of the deaths to radiation sickness, but point out that thousands of those who were vaporised or burned to death must have been so close to the explosion that they would have been among the severest radiation casualties had they not died in some other way.

Years after the bomb, there were several cases involving scientists and doctors which gave the Japanese furiously to think. Three men had come to Hiroshima and Nagasaki to examine the after-effects: the nuclear physicist Yoshio Nishina, an expert on the medical aspects of radiation, Masao Tsuzuki, and a radiobiologist, Koichi Murachi. Nishina died in 1951 of liver cancer, Tsuzuki in 1960 of lung cancer, Murachi in 1961 of leukemia. All these men had handled radioactive substances for many years during their researches, but they undoubtedly were exposed to exceptionally high doses of radiation in the bombed cities, and whatever the causality involved in the three cases, they seemed more than coincidental to the ordinary Japanese and pointed up the concealed dangers of lingering radiation sickness decades later.

The damage was not merely physical. The huge dumps left by the Japanese army in the hills behind Hiroshima were soon raided when the surrender was announced,

and in the disordered state of the city in the following months, looting, gangsterism, and black marketeering flourished. Later still, the reconstruction of the city and the focussing upon it of a rather gruesome tourist industry brought to the town many thousands of people on the make, so that the survivors gradually found themselves to be a minority in a city that had once been theirs.

Spiritual wreckage beyond repair

On the individual plane, there were many who had not only suffered unspeakably but had also, they obscurely felt, let down some deeply loved person in a moment of great need. The sufferings inflicted by the bombing and the state of utter despair it left behind had drawn men's courage up to—and frequently beyond—the extremes it could bear, and the best of wills had often snapped. Those who stayed in shelters, fearful of what might happen if they emerged to look for parents or brothers and sisters, felt later a remorse they would never overcome.

Dr Nagai, the author of *We of Nagasaki*, who slaved in a hospital for days after the explosion while his wife died, unattended, from burns, accused himself not only of her death but also of creating a gap or 'fissure' between himself and those of his *tonarigumi* ('neighbourhood group') who —he knew—had relied on him to help them during air raids, and to whose help he had not come. All those who survived, he claimed, were like him: those who ignored calls for help, those who could not bear to stay and care for the horrible, twisted, charred sub-human objects which had once been their sons and daughters, their fathers and mothers, those who had failed in their duty, were not merely lucky, they were selfish, driven by a savage instinct of self-preservation.

Dr Nagai later wondered whether those who decided the fate of nations and who seemed already to have classified the atomic bomb as merely one weapon among others, if slightly more frightful and effective, realised what the bomb had done, not just to the bodies, but to the hearts and minds of those who had survived. Those who visited the incinerated wastelands of Hiroshima or Nagasaki and later saw fine modern cities growing there may have marvelled at the power of recuperation the communities had shown in rebuilding their shattered surroundings.

But they did not see the stubborn spiritual wounds in the hearts of those who could not look their neighbours or friends in the eye because, in the last extremity, they had failed them. These were the victims of a spiritual wreckage which was, he believed, quite beyond repair.

LOUIS ALLEN was born in Yorkshire in 1922, educated at the Universities of Manchester, London (School of Oriental Studies), and Paris. He served in Indian Army Intelligence as Japanese language officer in India and Burma, and was mentioned in dispatches. After the surrender, he lived in Japanese army camps in Burma, Siam, Malaya, and Indo-China, interrogating Japanese commanders and staffs on the Burma campaign, and writing divisional histories. Mr Allen is co-translator of a Japanese account of the end of the war and its aftermath in Burma: Yuji Aida's *Prisoner of the British*. He now teaches French literature in the University of Durham.

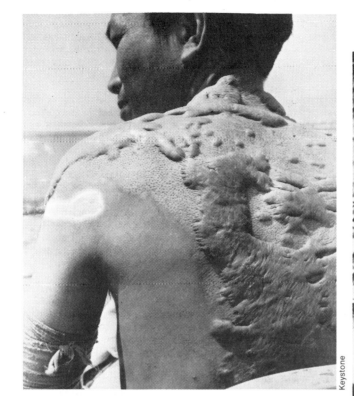

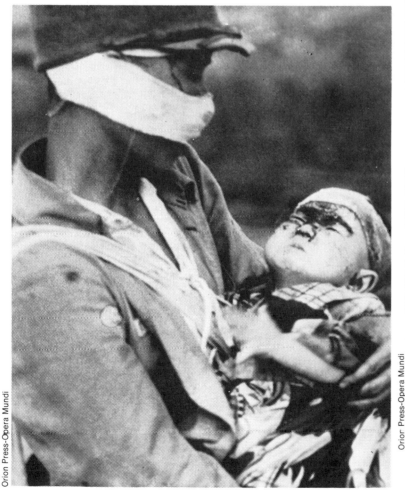

And yet the damage was not merely physical

THE WAR: AN OVERVIEW

A quest for certainty has been an integral part of mankind's occupation ever since the discovery that two and two made four began the pursuit of science, a pursuit based on quantitative values. The arts, however, being based on qualitative values, permit no such comforting certainties, and in the pursuit of historical truth the practitioners are all only too aware of the frailty of the evidence upon which they must base their judgements. Four eye-witnesses of any simple event will all give differing versions of what they saw — as any policeman investigating a car accident will confirm — so what reliance can be placed upon those immediate 'I was there' reports concocted immediately after the dreadful stress and confusion of battle has died away?

It is for this reason that throughout this history we have endeavoured to present opposing accounts of many events, and that the soldiers and historians chosen to write the main body of the work were, in general, men who had devoted many years to the examination and analysis of the evidence in connection with their subjects. It often occurs that such examination and analysis produces an entirely different picture of events to that which has long been popularly accepted and, as a result, a large proportion of the readers' letters which have poured into the editorial offices have contained that note of indignation which marks the reaction of honest men to the destruction of long-held and cherished beliefs — for beliefs can be more enduring that events, and often persist even after it has been demonstrated that evidence to support them is faulty or indeed lacking.

One such belief — which we trust we have exploded — is that the Second World War did not inflict such dreadful wounds upon mankind as did the First. This belief is mistaken. The Second World War lasted longer than the First, and was conducted with unparalleled ferocity over a larger proportion of the world's surface, using weapons of far greater destructive power than had been conceived in the earlier war. It engaged the attentions and energies of a larger number of people and, in the end, it killed or damaged far more of them; it seems likely that well over 50,000,000 perished as a result of the Second World War — a figure which includes the victims of the deliberate attempts at genocide by the German leaders — against the 8,634,300 lives lost between 1914 and 1918.

The reason for the popularity of this widespread belief is not far to seek. Although the world as a whole suffered greater loss in the Second World War, Europe and especially Britain suffered more in the First. The First World War was fought in great part in Belgium and northern France, and in the swathe of misery and massacre which stretched from Switzerland to the Belgian coast, an average of 2,000 British, French, and German soldiers died every day as a result of 'normal activity' while during the vast setpiece battles such as at Verdun, on the Somme, or at Passchendaele, hundreds of thousands of lives were consumed as though with the appetite of Moloch. Other fronts in the Balkans, or in Russia after 1916, were regarded as secondary, and although casualties suffered in these outer theatres served to drain strength from the main protagonists, these were the 'sideshows' — outside the main contest.

In the Second World War, the Verduns and Passchendaeles were fought on the Eastern Front at Kiev and Stalingrad (even the First War's Jutland and Dogger Bank were fought out in the Pacific at Midway and in the Coral Sea) and once the giants, Germany and Russia, Japan and the United States, became fully engaged in the conflict, it was Europe that was the sideshow.

Was it really 'Hitler's War'?

At the beginning, of course, it did seem that the war against Hitler was to be a European war — conceived in Europe out of Europe's politics and launched originally out of Europe's economy and industry — which soon proved unable to sustain it. In order to feed the war machines, the war became global, the centre of balance shifted eastwards, and as a result neither France nor Britain had in the end to pay the awful price of widespread destruction which modern war inflicts on the battlefield, and which history may well decide they should have paid in view of the part they had in its outbreak.

For many years it was fashionable to say that the Second World War was 'Hitler's War' — and it is certainly true that only his demonic genius could have led the German people so swiftly and so ruthlessly into such a prolonged and violently conducted conflict; but it should also be remembered that Winston Churchill gave it another name. He called it 'The Unnecessary War', and when one considers the chances the Western democracies were given to halt Hitler's career, this name is seen to be apt.

From the earliest days of his political career, Hitler made it perfectly clear that his main ambitions for the German people lay in generous eastward expansion. Three days after he became Chancellor of the Reich, he addressed the German High Command in conditions of no particular Top Secret security, and informed them that their prime duty would be to obtain Lebensraum — 'living space' — in the east and the unqualified Germanisation of the occupied territory. At the same time, he repudiated the terms of the various treaties which had endeavoured to limit Germany's armed strength and made it perfectly clear that in addition to holding unqualified expansionist aims, he had every intention of possessing the means by which to attain them.

As he would also need heavy industrial capacity to arm his expanding forces, he re-occupied the Rhineland — the heart of German industry which after 1918 had been placed under Allied control — using the few partially trained military units available to him, in spite of the earnest protests of his military advisers.

To Hitler's coldly megalomaniac mind, there can have been only one explanation for the fact that his first military gamble met with success. France and Britain had not only the right, but also the means to hold the Rhineland, to prevent German soldiers entering in the first place, to eject them once they had entered — tasks which the armies of either nation could have carried out with the greatest ease. As neither country made the slightest attempt to oppose or eject the re-occupation forces, Hitler could only assume that they sympathised — not only with the return of thoroughly German provinces to the German Fatherland, but also with the oft and loudly repeated ambitions of the man who led the nation.

And indeed this sympathy was openly expressed. When in early 1935, conscription was reintroduced in Germany as the means of the expansion of the German army, *The Times*, though it spoke soberly of the dangers posed to European peace, also pointed out that Germany's action was not in defiance of agreements cordially arrived at between free contracting parties, but of one which had been 'forcibly imposed' on her, and which she could be expected to find 'intolerable'. French newspapers were just as guarded in tone, and the *de facto* acceptance of these violations of agreed principles could have no other result than to make those responsible for them believe that their course of action was approved.

Hitler continued with the expansion of his armed forces, and of territory under his control, in part at least because he believed that the French and British governments wished to see that large eastward German expansion, at the expense of Communist Russia, which he was still vociferously proclaiming.

The process continued.

In March 1938, German troops marched into Vienna, and Austria was again fitted snugly into her Prussian-ordained position of subservience – and by this time Hitler had no apprehensions of intervention from the west, and could hardly be blamed for thinking that he acted with a degree of western approval – approval which was to grow six months later into political collaboration when Britain and France agreed to the cession to Germany of those western provinces of Czechoslovakia which alone could serve as a shield against German domination of the rest of that country.

In effect, having apparently granted full right to Germany to evolve again from a relatively small and militarily weak country in 1933 into the dominant European power by 1939, it seemed that Britain and France were now co-operating in the clearance of the eastern borders which would allow that attainment of *Lebensraum* in the east, which the Führer had been demanding from the advent of his political career. To Hitler – who believed the French, and especially the British, to be politically astute and indeed as logically ruthless as he was himself – it seemed that these countries were pursuing a sound and consistent policy which would in the end rid the world of Communism; and if they were using him to achieve their ends for the moment, he had his own ideas as to who would foot the ultimate bill.

The resolution of this misconception occurred – perhaps appropriately – on April 1, 1939, when the world's press announced that the British Cabinet under the direction of the Prime Minister, Mr Chamberlain, had reversed its policy of detached appeasement and 'with the aim of ensuring peace in Europe' had pledged Britain to defend Poland against any aggressive action on the part of Germany – a move which despite its significance as an emergence from the gloomy twilight of self-deception in which British and French politics had floundered for ten years, was in itself a disastrous piece of muddleheadedness: of all countries for the western democracies to offer protection, Poland was almost the most inaccessible, besides being in many ways among the least deserving. She too, had profited from the dismemberment of Czechoslovakia. Aptly was Winston Churchill later to write:

There was sense in fighting for Czechoslovakia in 1938 when the German army could scarcely put half a dozen trained divisions on the western Front, when the French, with nearly sixty or seventy divisions, could most certainly have rolled forward across the Rhine or into the Ruhr. But this had been judged unreasonable, rash, below the level of modern intellectual thought and morality. Yet now at last the two Western Democracies declared themselves ready to stake their lives upon the territorial integrity of Poland. History, which we are told is mainly the record of the crimes, follies and miseries of mankind, may be scoured and ransacked to find a parallel to this sudden and complete reversal of five or six years' policy of easygoing placatory appeasement, and its transformation almost overnight into a readiness to accept an obviously imminent war on far worse conditions and on the greatest scale. . . .

Hitler was astonished and indeed affronted by this sudden *volte-face* on the part of Britain, and it is difficult to see what other reaction could have been expected. And with the knowledge which western diplomats should by now have acquired of Hitler's character, it should not have been difficult to prophesy his next move.

Chamberlain's reversal of policy appeared as a direct challenge to Hitler's political supremacy in Europe – and it was a challenge which Hitler could accept without one-tenth of the risk he had accepted when he sent his forces into the Rhineland or into Austria or even when he took over Czechoslovakia. The only country which could possibly underwrite Britain's support of Poland, was Russia – and Russia was the country with which British statesmen, for a variety of reasons both traditional and religious, would not co-operate despite urgent representations from the Russian leaders themselves.

Over the edge of the abyss

Five months after Britain's guarantee to Poland, Hitler's troops crossed the Polish frontier and the European War which was to develop into the Second World War had begun. Given that Hitler's evil genius provided the explosive power which dragged the world over the edge of the abyss, the western democracies cannot evade all responsibility for its outbreak. As Sir Basil Liddell Hart has written: 'If you allow anyone to stoke up a boiler until the steam-pressure rises to danger-point, and you then close the safety-valve, the real responsibility for the resultant explosion will lie with you.'

If the parallel is not exact, it is still close enough to cast doubt on the justification for calling the tragic events which now followed – just 'Hitler's War'.

For the next two years, however, it did seem that there was an entirely different justification (from that of moral responsibility) for calling the conflict 'Hitler's War', for it followed a course largely dictated by his ambitions and appeared likely to end with their fulfilment. Rarely has the course of war run so smoothly, and it almost seems that when Fate appeared to offer some temporary check to Hitler's progress, she was in fact offering him a permanent advantage. When, in January 1940, the plan for the German attack in the west fell accidentally into Allied hands, the changes made necessary by this apparent misfortune resulted in the conservative

Stalin: He failed at first to grasp the threat of Nazi Germany

mediocrity of the original gradually being replaced by the revolutionary brilliance of General Manstein's plan, which took the German armour through the Allied defences and on to the Channel coast in ten days.

France fell, Poland was already under the Nazi heel, and the end in Norway was evidently at hand: 15 months after Mr Chamberlain's announcement of the Polish guarantee 'with the aim of ensuring peace in Europe', there was indeed peace in Europe – so long as one subscribed to the common viewpoints that the reality of peace is an absence of armed conflict and that the British Isles is a non-European entity.

But so far as Hitler was concerned, whatever role Britain decided to assume – Imperial or solitary – there could still be peace in Europe. Whatever misunderstandings may have recently occurred, he had no immediate designs on Britain, on British life, or even on the position which Britain held in the world outside Europe. So long as Britain recognised German domination inside Europe and – far more important – so long as she allowed him now to turn his full attention to the solution of that problem which bedevilled the world, posed by the existence of Communist Russia, then Britain could go her own way, with Hitler's blessing and indeed under whatever protection she may care to ask from him.

It was at this point that Britain played her greatest part in the defeat of Nazi Germany. She alone could still offer defiance to German power and rejection to Nazi philosophy, for she alone of the powers who had at last taken up arms against Hitler remained unconquered. The only other powers who could offer him practical resistance, Russia and the United States, were prevented from doing so by blindness where power lay in their respective political systems: neither Stalin nor the American public saw as yet why the existence of Nazi Germany posed threats to their own ways of life.

Britain therefore stood alone. Had she fully appreciated the enormous power against which she was pitted, and had she then believed that no one would ever come to her aid and that she really would have to abide by her slogan to 'Go it alone!' then assuredly her courage must have faltered and her acceptance of Hitler's domination followed. But the British are an unmilitary race and do not understand military reality. In their imaginations they conjured forth hundreds of divisions from the peoples of the Empire (which was never able to produce more than a maximum of 40 divisions throughout the entire war) – and used a long-departed industrial supremacy to equip them. Armed with this spurious hope and confidence, Britain stood in 1940 and defied Hitler – and after a few months of exasperated gestures against her, he angrily turned his back on the stubborn islanders to gaze again at the snowy reaches past the Carpathians which have haunted Teutonic imaginations for centuries.

During the months which followed, Hitler's attention was sporadically diverted from his main and cherished ambition by the antics of his jackal, Mussolini. As a result of these, he was drawn first into North Africa and then down through the Balkans into the Mediterranean, but these expeditions – attended almost casually by brilliant military success – were to him but irritating distractions. What to

the British were campaigns of honour, enterprise, and desperate gallantry – such as the Siege of Tobruk, the Greek Campaign, or the Battle for Crete – were to their opponent matters of almost trifling account. So must Napoleon and his armies have felt about the Peninsula War 130 years before, and it is interesting to see how little even Hitler was prepared to learn from history: he too turned his back on the British and advanced across the steppes to his eventual doom.

The greatest military spectacle since 1914

June 22, 1941, was surely the apocalyptic date of the military calendar. 'When Operation Barbarossa is launched,' Hitler proclaimed, 'the world will hold its breath!' – and the extent to which this did not in fact happen is merely a measure of mankind's disinterest in matters much removed from personal and almost domestic circles.

The opening moves of Barbarossa, as some of the most brilliant articles in this work have demonstrated, presented the greatest military spectacle since the events of August 1914, and Western Europe and America watched them with the casual disinterest of cattle watching the passing of an express train. Even those whose profession was the analysis of large affairs were mostly concerned with estimating the degree of attrition to which German strength would be subject before the inevitable and early collapse of Russian resistance.

At first, it must be admitted that there was much evidence to support this gloomy view. No military plan of the scope of Operation Barbarossa had ever before been launched, for never before had techniques of organisation, transport, and communication been available for application on such a scale. 'We have only to kick in the front door,' Hitler had boasted, 'and the whole rotten Russian edifice will come tumbling down!' – and as day followed day and the black lines extended ever further eastward, the only exaggeration the statement appeared to possess was with regard to the effort needed against the 'front door'. Moreover, the doubt which had always arisen in military minds when they had watched such swift advances in the past, did not arise. Here, it seemed, was no spectacle of skilful tactical retreats tempting the aggressor ever deeper into a trap – for whole Russian armies were being caught and annihilated. The prison-camps were full to overflowing, and within the wide sweeps of the armoured columns the soil was soaked in Russian blood.

When German Army Group Centre was seen to pause on the Desna, therefore, the west took little hope from the sight, for it was not unreasonable to believe that Russia's armed might was now smashed or at least trapped, and that the Germans were engaged in mopping up, reinforcing tired but triumphant troops, and preparing for the last easy sweep ahead into Moscow. This view was by no means amended by immediately subsequent events, for although the German spearheads now surprisingly swung away from the Russian capital, it was only to deliver yet another shattering blow against Russian armies – this time in Kiev, where in terms of loss in both men and material, Russia suffered the biggest catastrophe in her history.

Churchill: He called the struggle 'The Unnecessary War'

Roosevelt: He died with victory in sight

But Russia had, in fact, won something more vitally important – time; and when the German columns turned again to seek safe and comfortable winter quarters in Moscow, they found the way securely blocked. Russian labour had been building defences since June, Russian armies had been marshalled for specific duties; perhaps most important of all, a Russian soldier whose subsequent achievements entitle him to serious consideration as the greatest general of this century, Georgy Konstantinovich Zhukov, was in command not only of the defence of Moscow, but also of plans for the counterattack.

By the time winter had frozen the Eastern Front with both Leningrad and Moscow still beyond the invader's grasp, the world began to perceive the scale of events which had been taking place between the Baltic and the Black Sea. By this time, the Germans had totally annihilated 200 Soviet divisions – and Stalin had thrown in another 160!

Japan's bid for power

It was at this point that the war underwent its last and greatest expansion. When Japan went to war against China in 1937, she did so with the tacit permission and indeed encouragement of the United States, who wanted Japanese ambition diverted from the Pacific and also as much commercial advantage as could be obtained from any situation. As month followed month, the Japanese armies by their very success moved farther and farther away from the homeland, needing more and more lorries to move the men, more armoured vehicles to protect thin-skinned transport, and more air cover to protect them all. And much more oil to fuel everything.

At first Japan had little difficulty in securing everything she needed, and her military adventure prospered, driving deeper and deeper into China, occupying more and more territory. Then came 1940 and a sudden, severe curtailing of essential supplies; in September America imposed an embargo on rubber and in July 1941 America froze all Japanese assets in the United States and announced an oil embargo against 'all aggressors' – letting Japan know quite clearly that this was a category in which she herself was included.

Almost 90% of Japan's oil supplies vanished at a stroke, together with important proportions of other essentials. Japan was faced with either abandoning her hardly-won gains of two years' fighting together with a loss of prestige and face which no eastern nation could afford, or else attaining other sources of supply. As it happened, other sources of the essential oil were not far away: Borneo, Java, and Sumatra could supply Japan's foreseeable needs and there was also what could be regarded as a reserve supply farther north in Burma – but the only way in which to obtain them was by the rapid, comprehensive, and successful military occupation of a vast area.

Different nations possess different philosophies and different attitudes to such matters as war, because they have experienced different histories. As a result of the tradition of western thought, we of the west tend to look upon December 7, 1941 – the day of the attack on Pearl Harbor – as The Day of Infamy, and on February 15, 1942 – the day when Singapore surrendered – as a Day of Tragedy.

There is a different point of view. To the Japanese, December 7, 1941, was the day on which they chose enormous risk, with valour and honour, instead of weak capitulation with cowardice and shame; and February 15, 1942, was The Day of Infamy, when to their incredulous eyes, beings wearing the uniform of soldiers were so lost to all shades of honour that they gave up fighting while still in possession of their faculties, *while they still possessed arms with which to defy their foes*. One Japanese soldier was so stricken by the sight that even while his spirits were buoyed up by victory, he was ashamed of his humanity that human beings could act so basely.

Japan attained the sources of oil, and the equally essential clear passageway for the oil back to the homeland, in an astonishing explosion of military energy which menaced the borders of India, completely contained the Dutch Eastern Empire and brushed the north coast of Australia, besides controlling almost half of the Pacific Ocean. Domination over this vast area was almost all achieved within six months of the attack on Pearl Harbor, but at the end of this period Japan was extending her military strength to its utmost limit: she resembled a man lying on a floor, holding the four doors of a room shut, one with each foot, one with each hand, hoping that the pressures on the doors would not be enough to force any of them open.

This was, obviously, a weak posture, but it did not appear so to the hard-pressed Allies, who during 1942 experienced Fortune's ebb and who by the middle of the year appeared to be in desperate straits. In North Africa, Britain's 8th Army had lately been thrown back once again from Cyrenaica and was digging defensive positions south of El Alamein; in Russia Stalingrad was apparently about to fall and indeed Hitler had already announced its seizure by his triumphant armies, while in Allied naval circles the news of the Battle of Midway was received with sober consideration, for its significance was not immediately obvious.

Stalingrad: no Verdun on the Volga

But this period was, of course, what Mr Churchill was to call the Hinge of Fate – and the place where most pressure was being applied to the door in order to swing it the other way was undoubtedly Stalingrad.

It is just possible that had the Soviet leaders not seen fit to change the name of the small country town on the Volga from Tsaritsyn to Stalingrad, it would not have become the most famous city of the Second World War. True, the northern flank of the German thrust down into the Caucasus needed a guard, and that short gap between Upper Don and Lower Volga had to be covered; but the necessity to possess a bridge across the Volga *at that particular point* was not so great that over 1,000,000 men should have to be fed into the attack by Hitler. The truth of the matter was that he saw in this battle the chance to humiliate his most hated opponent, and the propaganda point became more important than military objectivity. The result was a battle which tore the guts from the German army, and tossed to the wind the fragments of the myth of German invincibility.

Stalingrad has been compared with Verdun in intensity and significance, and there is much to support the comparison; but in one vital matter it was different. The French in 1916 accepted Falkenhayn's challenge and exchanged soldier's life for soldier's life, feed-

Hitler:
His avowed intention — 'Lebensraum' in the east

ing an endless stream of reinforcements into that cramped arena on the Meuse until both sides fell back sickened by the slaughter and bled almost white. The effect of the desanguination on French life revealed itself most clearly in 1940, and may still be with us today.

But at Stalingrad during that crucial winter of 1942/43, the Red Army leaders showed an appreciation of military reality, and an ability to learn from the past, which should act as a model for all. Again under the shrewd direction of General Zhukov, they refused to be tempted by the emotive implications of the city's name, reinforced the defenders inside along lines dictated by the *minimum necessary* instead of the *maximum possible,* and used the power and strength thus preserved to launch the great encircling movements which eventually throttled the German army within.

Thus Stalingrad is the name of a great victory, won at reasonable cost; Verdun is just the name of a battle which devoured millions of lives to no effect, leaving both sides weaker and poorer. And in the same way, the Battle of Alamein—which has been compared to Mons—was really the battle which turned the scales for Britain in her fight with Hitler; and from that moment, victory seemed certain.

So 1943 saw the tilting of the scales. North Africa was cleared of Axis troops, Italy invaded and persuaded to change her alliance, the Balkans became the scene of growing resistance to the Occupation Forces and a growing danger to the flank of the German armies in Russia. And in Russia itself, reality was at last growing behind the age-old legend of the 'Russian steamroller'. Inexorably, the German armies which had achieved such magnificent triumphs for their Führer, at such bitter cost throughout two Russian winters, were pressed back—and on this front the battle was grim and ruthless indeed. There was no chivalry in Russia for the fallen foe, no quarter asked or expected, for too much Russian blood had been spilt during the German invasion and occupation, and revenge on one side and fear on the other gave the battle the fanaticism of a religious war. Human life was of no value, and death the commonest of occurrences; hundreds of divisions had already been destroyed in battle, hundreds were now engaged, and hundreds more would break and then disintegrate before the Russian homeland was again free of the invader —and then there were yet more weeks of slaughter to follow.

But perhaps the most astonishing spectacle presented to the Western world was the reorganisation and expansion of Soviet industry. This had suffered a near disaster during the opening months of the war, for much of Russia's industrial potential was based west of the Don, and so fell into German hands. Thus Russia lost the output of some 31,000 big and small industrial enterprises, a quarter of a million electric engines, 175,000 machine tools, nearly 300 blast or open-hearth furnaces, and electric powerplant with a capacity of 5,000,000 kw.

Yet all had not been lost, for by prodigious effort some vital plant and machinery had been transported back from the invaders' path, and in some cases entire factories had been bodily carried eastwards out of danger. With a measure of urgency and improvisation which will live in history as a spectacle of human achievement, these factories were resited and rebuilt, new ones created and thrown into production, and by March 1942 production was in growth—and

growth which was soon to outstrip even that of the carefully nurtured and cultivated German war industry. By the time of Stalingrad, the Red Army was as well equipped as any in the world, and never again would Russian soldiers find themselves pitted against superior numbers armed with more, or better, weapons.

The Allied reply to 'Totalkrieg'

In Europe, the greatest effort was in the air, and Britain's bombing offensive against Germany was growing in operational numbers and in weight of bombs dropped; although doubts were already growing as to the moral justification for so indiscriminate a method of warfare, and indeed even a few doubts as to its effectiveness. But on the whole, despite their own experience under Hitler's bombing— when the greater the danger, the greater grew their determination to resist—the British people illogically believed that this was the method by which Germany would be subdued. A large part of the nation's energies was thus devoted to supporting the bombing offensive, a great number of her best and bravest young men gave their lives to carry it out, though in the end it did little to hamper the German *'Totalkrieg'* but much to sow seeds of postwar hatred. It also undermined Britain's standing in the world as arbiter—or even upholder—of civilised standards of behaviour.

The main effort of the British naval and military services however, together with those of her allies, was devoted to preparations for the Second Front. There was, of course, considerable pressure from Russia for this vast enterprise to be launched in 1943 but, aided by the rather specious argument that a Second Front did already exist in Italy, the moment was postponed until adequate preparations could be completed, and the invasion of Normandy was launched on June 6, 1944.

If the launching of Operation Barbarossa was the greatest military spectacle of all time, that of the launching of Operation Overlord was the greatest exhibition of technical ingenuity and organisation. The actual number of forces engaged was not so large, but owing to the amphibious nature of the operation, the physical difficulties were much greater and moreover there was a far greater degree of expectation of attack by the German defenders in 1944 than there had been by the Russian defenders in 1941.

The formation of the Allied bridgehead on the French coast was thus a task of infinite complexity, and the breakout from that bridgehead a matter of urgency and of large-scale but precise organisation. It was not until August that the Allies began to tear themselves free from the north coast of France, after appalling slaughter in what became known as the Falaise Gap, and later in the month they launched another amphibious operation on the Mediterranean coast of France. By the beginning of September, American armoured columns were driving deep into France and some drove eastwards to cross the German border near Triers on September 11. For the first time since the unification of Germany under Bismarck, foreign troops were invading the Fatherland in the face of fierce national resistance.

The resistance was not to wane.

The hold that National Socialism had on the German people was

Mussolini: Hitler's 'jackal', who diverted him from his main aim

Tojo: The only Axis head of state to be hanged by the Allies

retained right up until almost every separate German individual came under Allied control – whether this was a matter of patriotic valour until the end, or fear of resistance towards Hitler's dictatorship until Allied protection was at hand, is immaterial. There were a few Germans of astounding moral and physical courage who resisted the immorality of Hitler's regime – as was shown by the attempt to assassinate him on July 20, 1944 – but the vast majority of the nation were either hypnotised by his personality, or dutifully acceptant of his political creed.

And they remained so until the end; most of the battles across Germany until the gap closed between Eastern and Western Fronts were as bitterly fought and as destructive of human material as those at the beginning of the war, and on the Eastern Front especially, Russian hatred of the German aggressor and German fear of Russian vengeance resulted in conflict of astounding ferocity and violence.

A man of enormous but demonic gifts

On April 30, 1945, Hitler committed suicide and the war in the west was over except for the formalities; a man of enormous but demonic gifts had lifted his country from weakness and chaos to unparalleled power, and then dropped her back into chaos again, all in the space of twelve short years. Fortunately, men of such quality are rare.

In the east, the days of Japanese power were numbered, and indeed they had always depended upon the success of her Axis partners – in effect upon German victory. To return to the simile of the man lying on the floor, Japan could only hold the doors shut while the attentions of those trying to open them were largely engaged elsewhere. Once Britain and America could release some of their energies from the war in Europe, Japan could no longer hold the circumference of her conquests.

As it happened, geography determined that those doors could not be forced open in the most logical order. The great naval campaigns mounted by the Americans in the Pacific were at first attacking Japan in the most unimportant area; she could afford to lose the myriad Pacific islands so long as the areas in the west – Java, Sumatra, Borneo, and the seaways north of the Philippines – remained under her control.

But, inexorably, the Allied attacks crept nearer and nearer to the vital area, and at the end of October 1944 – by which time German troops were defending their own Fatherland – American divisions were landed at Leyte; by December they had reached Mindoro and the following month they invaded Luzon itself.

One quickly exhausts superlatives when describing the bravery and stubborn determination of Japanese troops, for they fought with fanaticism on every field and every occasion – but even their self-sacrifice could not hold back the tide. On February 4, 1945, the Americans reached Manila and by the time Germany finally admitted defeat, Japan was completely cut off from all sources of oil. Her gamble had failed, her choice of risk with honour had been in vain.

Now she was to be given her excuse to capitulate by science. The theory of nuclear fission had been known before the war, but it had needed the desperation of war to persuade the nations to afford the expense in time, money, and effort to put the theory into practice. Germany's attempt to exploit the theory in the form of a bomb had failed – ironically enough because her anti-Semitic policy had driven abroad many of the brains she needed. Axis loss proved to be the Allied gain – and the Manhattan Project which eventually produced the first atomic explosion at Alamogordo on July 16, 1945, was in its way just as intricate and monumental an operation as those of Barbarossa or Overlord. Certainly July 16, 1945, is just as apocalyptic a date, in the scientific and political calendars, as June 22, 1941, in the military one.

On August 6 and August 9, atom bombs were dropped on Hiroshima and Nagasaki respectively and on August 10 the Japanese government announced its willingness to negotiate with the Allies. Whether it had been necessary to release this last engine of mass destruction is a matter for argument which will probably for ever remain unresolved. But with regard to its immediate effect it should be remembered that more people were burned to death in the RAF firestorm in Dresden on February 13 and 14, 1945, than perished at Hiroshima, that sudden death is the same to its victims whatever its method of administration, that a lingering death from the effects of gas or liquid fire is even more unpleasant than one from leukemia, and that the effects of five years of conventional warfare on generations then unborn is still unknown, but likely to be considerable if only for the mental stress suffered by the parents during that time.

The most violent injury in history

On September 2, 1945, the Japanese signed the surrender document, and the Second World War was officially over. It had lasted almost six years (fighting was, in fact, to continue for some months), had been waged in the end by a total of 56 combatant nations (though some had been more vitally engaged than others) and caused the loss of well over 50,000,000 lives.

It was thus the most violent and prolonged self-inflicted injury upon mankind of which history has record, and will probably remain so – for if any future war is likely to be more violent, it is hardly likely also to be more prolonged.

Yet this was not a period of universal folly. Given that political ineptitude had allowed Hitler to rise to power, it would surely have been even greater stupidity to have allowed him to remain there and eventually to dominate the world, reducing its abundance to within the narrow limitations of his own political and social vision. As Dr Roger Manvell pointed out, Hitler possessed the attributes of greatness while remaining destitute of human quality; the world is better for his leaving it.

But the cost of ridding the world of his unbalanced qualities, in human pain and exhaustion, in courage, fortitude, and endurance, and in sheer mental and physical effort, will remain for ever a matter of wonder and speculation. How can a species so inept as to allow so gross a danger to arise, still find within itself such vast reserves of human greatness?

Mankind is the eternal enigma.

WW I

The two world wars have often been compared in the minds of the generations who experienced both. The Second World War was immeasurably more destructive than the First, but because of the horrors of the fighting in Flanders between 1914 and 1918, this is not always realised. The purpose of these pages is to compare the two wars in terms of areas involved in warfare, lives lost, and the destruction of seaborne commerce.

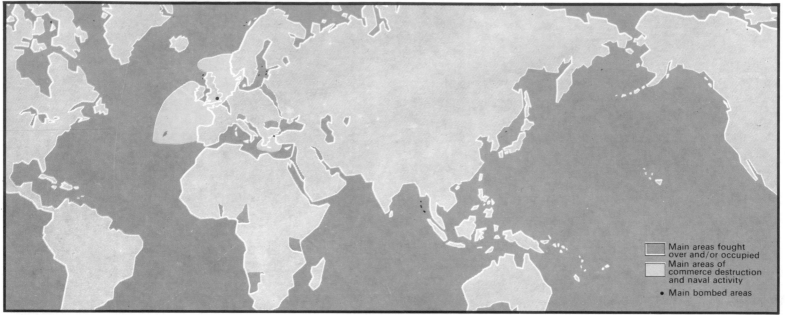

- Main areas fought over and/or occupied
- Main areas of commerce destruction and naval activity
- Main bombed areas

PEAK WARTIME STRENGTHS

Number of men under arms

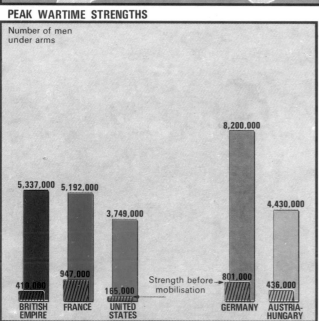

BRITISH EMPIRE	5,337,000
FRANCE	5,192,000
UNITED STATES	3,749,000
GERMANY	8,200,000
AUSTRIA-HUNGARY	4,430,000

Strength before mobilisation:
- BRITISH EMPIRE 410,000
- FRANCE 947,000
- UNITED STATES 165,000
- GERMANY 801,000
- AUSTRIA-HUNGARY 436,000

ALLIED MERCHANT SHIPPING LOSSES

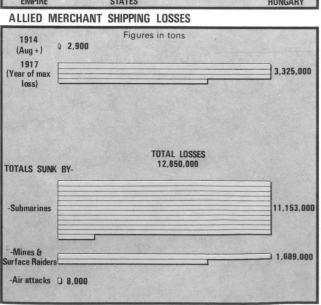

Figures in tons

1914 (Aug +)	2,900
1917 (Year of max loss)	3,325,000

TOTAL LOSSES 12,850,000

TOTALS SUNK BY —
- Submarines 11,153,000
- Mines & Surface Raiders 1,689,000
- Air attacks 8,000

ALLIED AND CENTRAL POWERS' KILLED (Combatants only)

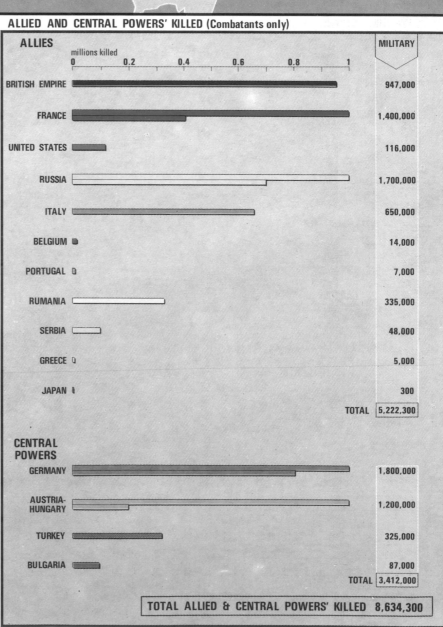

ALLIES

millions killed

	MILITARY
BRITISH EMPIRE	947,000
FRANCE	1,400,000
UNITED STATES	116,000
RUSSIA	1,700,000
ITALY	650,000
BELGIUM	14,000
PORTUGAL	7,000
RUMANIA	335,000
SERBIA	48,000
GREECE	5,000
JAPAN	300
TOTAL	**5,222,300**

CENTRAL POWERS

	MILITARY
GERMANY	1,800,000
AUSTRIA-HUNGARY	1,200,000
TURKEY	325,000
BULGARIA	87,000
TOTAL	**3,412,000**

TOTAL ALLIED & CENTRAL POWERS' KILLED 8,634,300

WW II

Always bearing in mind that there are three kinds of lies—lies, damned lies, and statistics—and the fact that there are no reliable figures for civilian deaths for the First World War, it can be seen that the scope and cost of the Second World War was far greater. Also included are the comparative peak strengths of the forces involved, with their mobilisation strengths beside them. Mobilisation strengths for Russia are available in neither case

Areas fought over and/or occupied
Main areas of commerce destruction and naval activity
• Main bombed areas
● Atomic bomb explosions

PEAK WARTIME STRENGTHS

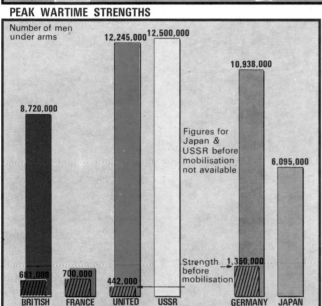

Number of men under arms

BRITISH EMPIRE	8,720,000
FRANCE	12,245,000
UNITED STATES	12,500,000
USSR	10,938,000
GERMANY	6,095,000
JAPAN	

Figures for Japan & USSR before mobilisation not available

Strength before mobilisation

681,000 — BRITISH EMPIRE
700,000 — FRANCE
442,000 — UNITED STATES
1,360,000 — GERMANY

ALLIED MERCHANT SHIPPING LOSSES

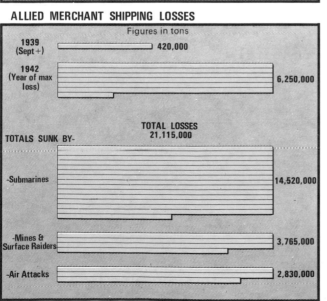

Figures in tons

1939 (Sept +)	420,000
1942 (Year of max loss)	6,250,000

TOTAL LOSSES 21,115,000

TOTALS SUNK BY—

-Submarines 14,520,000
-Mines & Surface Raiders 3,765,000
-Air Attacks 2,830,000

ALLIED AND AXIS KILLED (Combatants and civilians)

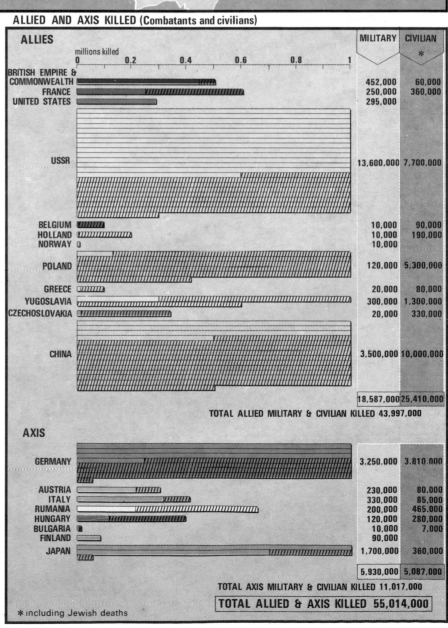

ALLIES

millions killed
0   0.2   0.4   0.6   0.8   1

	MILITARY	CIVILIAN *
BRITISH EMPIRE & COMMONWEALTH	452,000	60,000
FRANCE	250,000	360,000
UNITED STATES	295,000	
USSR	13,600,000	7,700,000
BELGIUM	10,000	90,000
HOLLAND	10,000	190,000
NORWAY	10,000	
POLAND	120,000	5,300,000
GREECE	20,000	80,000
YUGOSLAVIA	300,000	1,300,000
CZECHOSLOVAKIA	20,000	330,000
CHINA	3,500,000	10,000,000
	18,587,000	25,410,000

TOTAL ALLIED MILITARY & CIVILIAN KILLED 43,997,000

AXIS

	MILITARY	CIVILIAN *
GERMANY	3,250,000	3,810,000
AUSTRIA	230,000	80,000
ITALY	330,000	85,000
RUMANIA	200,000	465,000
HUNGARY	120,000	280,000
BULGARIA	10,000	7,000
FINLAND	90,000	
JAPAN	1,700,000	360,000
	5,930,000	5,087,000

TOTAL AXIS MILITARY & CIVILIAN KILLED 11,017,000

TOTAL ALLIED & AXIS KILLED 55,014,000

*including Jewish deaths

CHRONOLOGY

1939

March 15: German troops march into Prague and take over Bohemia and Moravia.
March 16: Hitler declares that 'Czechoslovakia has ceased to exist.'
March 22: Germans annex Memel; Lithuanians forced to sign treaty.
March 23: Poland rejects German proposals on Danzig.
March 31: Chamberlain announces Anglo-French guarantees to Poland.
April 7: Italy invades Albania. Spain joins Germany, Italy and Japan in Anti-Comintern pact.
April 13: Britain, France guarantee independence of Rumania and Greece.
April 28: Hitler rejects Roosevelt's peace proposals, denounces Anglo-German Naval Pact and German-Polish Non-Aggression Pact.
May 22: Germany signs 'Pact of Steel', a military alliance with Italy.
August 12: Anglo-French Mission to Russia begins talks in Moscow.
August 23: Germany signs non-aggression pact with Russia; secret clauses partition Poland. Chamberlain warns Hitler that Britain will fulfil guarantees to Poland. Hitler states that Germany's interest in Danzig and the Corridor cannot be waived.
August 25: Anglo-Polish Mutual Assistance Pact signed. Mussolini informs Hitler that Italy is not ready for war.
September 1: Poland invaded 0445 hours; Germany annexes Danzig; France, Britain demand withdrawal of German troops.
September 3: Britain, France, Australia, New Zealand declare war on Germany.
September 5: German troops cross the Vistula River.
September 10: Canada declares war on Germany. BEF, under Lord Gort, begins move to France.
September 17: Red Army invades Eastern Poland.
September 19: Soviet troops occupy Vilna.
September 22: Red Army occupies Lwow.
September 23: German troops withdraw to the demarcation line agreed with Russia.
September 27: Warsaw surrenders.
September 29: Soviet-German Treaty of Friendship partitions Poland. Russia signs pacts with Estonia and Finland.
October 12: Stalin presents territorial demands to Finns. Chamberlain rejects Hitler's peace plan. First deportation of Austrian, Czech Jews to Poland.
October 27: US Neutrality Bill passed in Senate.
November 9: Finns finally reject Soviet demands.
November 13: USSR decides on war against Finland and plans to set up puppet Finnish government.
November 18: German magnetic mines sink 60,000 tons of shipping off English east coast in one week.
November 30: USSR invades Finland; Helsinki bombed; fighting north of Lake Ladoga.
December 7: Russians reach main Karelian defence line.
December 13: Battle of the River Plate.
December 17: *Graf Spee* scuttled;

captain commits suicide.
December 22: Strong Finnish counterattack.

1940

January 2: Heavy Russian attacks on Karelian Isthmus.
January 8: Russian 44th Division destroyed in Karelian 'waistline'.
January 15: Belgium refuses Allied request to pass through Belgian territory.
February 1: Russians attack on Karelian Isthmus.
February 5: Allied War Council decide to send aircraft and guns to Finland.
February 11: German-Soviet economic pact signed. Fierce fighting in Karelia.
February 12: Finnish cabinet favours peace; Karelian Isthmus defences crack. Australians, New Zealanders land at Suez.
February 15: Germany announces all British merchant ships will be treated as warships.
February 17: Finns withdraw in Karelia.
February 24: First German plans for Western offensive completed.
March 1: Hitler issues Norway, Denmark invasion plans.
March 3: Russians on outskirts of Viipuri.
March 5: Finns decide to accept Russian peace terms as basis for negotiation.
March 11: Chamberlain announces plans for Allied aid to Finland.
March 12: Russo-Finnish pact signed in Moscow.
March 13: Treaty of Moscow concludes Winter war.
March 28: Britain, France agree not to conclude peace separately. Allied War Council decides to mine Norwegian waters, occupy bases in Norway.
March 29: Molotov announces USSR neutrality.
April 2: Hitler orders preparation for invasion of Norway, Denmark— *Weserübung.*
April 7: Allied force sails for Norway.
April 8: RN lays mines in Norwegian waters. HMS *Glowworm* sunk by German cruiser *Hipper.*
April 9: *Weserübung* begins: German troops occupy Denmark and invade Norway.
April 10: First battle of Narvik. Rapid German advance from Oslo.
April 11: In Norway, King and government appeal to all Norwegians to fight.
April 13: Second battle of Narvik; seven German destroyers sunk.
April 15: British troops land in Norway near Narvik.
April 21: Fighting near Namsos, Trondheim, and Narvik.
April 27: Himmler orders construction of Auschwitz concentration camp.
April 30: German force advancing from Oslo link up with Trondheim force.
May 1: Norwegians surrender in Lillehammer.
May 2: Germans reach Andalsnes; Allies evacuate Namsos.
May 10: Germany attacks Holland, Belgium, Luxembourg. Chamberlain resigns, Churchill becomes Prime Minister. British troops land in Iceland.
May 11: Rapid German advances; Albert Canal crossed; Fort Eben-Emael taken by airborne troops.
May 13: Churchill makes 'blood and toil' speech.
May 14: German air raid on

Rotterdam; Dutch troops cease fighting. Heavy fighting on Moselle.
May 15: Holland capitulates. Rommel's tanks defeat French in breakthrough at Sedan.
May 18: Germans capture Antwerp, cross Sambre, and reach Amiens. Pétain becomes Vice-Premier of France.
May 19: Weygand becomes C-in-C Allied Forces.
May 20: Somme battlefield reached. Kleist's tanks break through to Channel at Abbéville, cutting off Allied forces in the north.
May 21: Germans claim French 9th Army defeated; BEF and French counterattack at Arras.
May 26: Operation 'Dynamo', the evacuation of Allied troops at Dunkirk, begins.
May 27: Belgian Army capitulates at midnight. Calais falls.
May 29: Rumanian arms and oil pact with Germany. Germans in Ypres, Ostend, Lille.
May 31: Roosevelt's 'million-dollar' defence programme.
June 3: Paris bombed. Dunkirk evacuation ends; 224,585 British, 112,546 French and Belgians evacuated. British troops begin to evacuate Narvik.
June 4: 40,000 prisoners taken at Dunkirk. Churchill's policy speech: 'We shall fight on the beaches'.
June 5: Battle of France begins.
June 7: Berlin bombed by French aircraft.
June 8: HMS *Glorious* sunk during withdrawal from Narvik.
June 10: Italy declares war on Britain and France. Norway capitulates.
June 14: Germans enter Paris. First attack on Maginot Line.
June 15: Germans capture Verdun.
June 16: British offer Anglo-French union; Reynaud resigns, Pétain forms new government.
June 17: Pétain asks for armistice terms. Russians begin to occupy Baltic states.
June 18: French army in general retreat. Hitler, Mussolini meet in Munich. De Gaulle broadcasts resistance appeal from London. Churchill's 'finest hour' speech.
June 21: Italians attack between sea and Mont Blanc.
June 22: Franco-German armistice signed at Compiègne.
June 23: Germans advance along Atlantic coast. First British Commando raid, on French coast near Boulogne.
June 24: Franco-Italian armistice signed in Rome.
June 25: Hostilities end in France. Churchill states France not relieved of her obligations.
June 28: Britain recognises General de Gaulle as Free French leader.
July 1: French government moves to Vichy.
July 2: Hitler orders plans for invasion of England.
July 3: RN destroys French naval squadron in Oran. French warships in British ports taken over.
July 5: New Rumanian cabinet announces friendship with Axis powers.
July 9: RAF begins night bombing of Germany. French warships in Alexandria neutralised.
July 10: Battle of Britain begins; 70-aircraft raid on South Wales docks.
July 16: Hitler orders preparations for the invasion of England to be completed by mid-August.
July 21: Czechoslovak government established in London. Hitler orders preliminary preparations for attack on Russia.
August 1: Molotov attacks UK, USA; reaffirms Russo-German pact.

Japanese New Order in East.
August 3: Italians invade British Somaliland.
August 5: Anglo-Polish military agreement.
August 7: Britain agrees with de Gaulle's organisation of Free French forces.
August 12: Portsmouth bombed. Battle of Britain intensifies.
August 13: 'Eagle Day' of the Battle of Britain.
August 17: Germany announces 'total blockade' of Britain.
August 19: British withdraw from Somaliland.
August 20: Churchill's 'so much owed to so few' speech. Italy announces total blockade of Britain's Mediterranean, African possessions.
August 23: All-night raid begins London Blitz.
August 25: RAF makes first raid on Berlin.
August 26: Luftwaffe intensifies operations against RAF airfields.
September 3: Britain cedes bases in Western Hemisphere to USA for 50 destroyers. Operation Sea Lion fixed for September 21.
September 13: Italians invade Egypt and occupy Sollum.
September 15: At least 60 German aircraft shot down over Britain.
September 17: Air raid casualties in Britain 10,000; 2,000 killed during first half of September.
September 18: Italians occupy Sidi Barrani.
Sepember 22: Japanese forces enter Indo-China.
September 26: US bans iron export to Japan.
September 27: Germany, Italy, Japan sign pact.
October 4: Hitler, Mussolini meet at the Brenner Pass.
October 7: German troops enter Rumania.
October 23: Hitler meets Franco; discuss Spain's entry into war, attack on Gibraltar.
October 24: Hitler meets Pétain.
October 28: Italians invade Greece.
November 1: Italians reach Kalamas River. British mine Bay of Biscay.
November 3: British troops land in Greece.
November 5: *Admiral Scheer* sinks HMS *Jervis Bay* in attack on Atlantic convoy.
November 7: RAF raids Krupp works at Essen.
November 8: Greeks capture 5,000 Italians.
November 11-12: Fleet Air Arm attacks Taranto, cripples Italian battle fleet.
November 14: Greeks push Italians back into Albania.
November 19: Birmingham bombed. Italians driven back across the Kalamas; heavy fighting near Koritsa.
November 22: Greeks take Koritsa, defeating Italian IX Army.
November 29: German High Command issues Draft Plan for Eastern campaign.
December 4: Greeks enter Premeti; capture Albanian port of Sarandë.
December 9: Operation 'Compass', first British offensive in Western Desert begins; Wavell's 'Thirty Thousand' cut off Graziani's army at Sidi Barrani.
December 11: British capture Sidi Barrani.
December 12: 20,000 Italians taken in desert.
December 17: British occupy Sollum; 38,000 Italian prisoners.
December 18: Hitler issues secret memo on Operation 'Barbarossa'.

1941

January 1: British sea and air bombardment of Bardia, continuing until night of January 2.
January 3: Australian 6th Division breaks through Bardia defences. Luftwaffe arrives in Italy. Italian counteroffensive in Albania.
January 5: Australians and British capture Bardia; over 30,000 prisoners taken.
January 9: HMS *Illustrious* brings convoy to Valetta harbour; HMS *Southampton* lost.
January 19: British advance in Eritrea, occupy Kassala in Sudan.
January 20: Roosevelt's third inauguration.
January 21: British and Australians break through Tobruk defences.
January 22: Tobruk falls; 25,000 prisoners, 50 tanks taken; Allied casualties under 500.
January 30: Wavell's force takes Derna.
February 3: German battlecruisers *Scharnhorst, Gneisenau* break out through Skagerrak to North Sea. British occupy Cyrene.
February 4: British armour leaves Mechili to intercept Italians south of Benghazi.
February 5: British armour engages Italians; fierce fighting near Benghazi.
February 6: British and Australians enter Benghazi.
February 7: Italians collapse at Beda Fomm.
February 8: Lend-Lease Bill passed by 260 to 165 in US House of Representatives. First German transports leave Naples for North Africa. El Agheila occupied by British and Australians.
February 9: Genoa bombarded by RN. Churchill broadcast to US: 'Give us the tools and we will finish the job.'
February 10: Mussolini accepts Hitler's offer of a German armoured divison. Cunningham's forces commence advance into Italian East Africa.
February 11: German bombers attack convoy off Azores, sinking five ships.
February 12: General Rommel arrives in Tripoli.
February 14: German units arrive in Tripoli. South Africans capture Gobuen in Somaliland.
February 19: Australian 8th Division lands at Singapore.
February 20: British cross the Juba into Somaliland.
February 22: Rommel attacks at El Agheila.
February 23: Free French forces land in Eritrea.
February 24: British Cabinet agree to send force to Greece. Darlan forms Vichy Cabinet.
February 25: British Nigerian troops occupy Mogadishu.
March 1: Bulgaria joins Axis.
March 2: German troops occupy Bulgaria.
March 4: British commando raid on Lofoten Islands. British force leaves Egypt for Greece.
March 5: Hitler decrees that Japan must actively participate in Far East.
March 6: British force in Somaliland enters Ethiopia.
March 7: Australian, British, New Zealand troops land at Piraeus, Volos.
March 8: US Senate passes Lend-Lease Bill by 60-31.
March 9: Italians launch offensive in Albania.
March 11: Roosevelt signs Lend-Lease Bill.
March 12: Roosevelt requests

Lend-Lease appropriation of $7,000,000,000. Churchill thanks America for 'a new Magna Carta'.
March 15: Roosevelt's broadcast, 'The end of compromise with tyranny'.
March 16: Hitler's speech: war to be won by Axis this year.
March 19: Germany gives ultimatum to Yugoslavia.
March 24: Germans capture El Agheila. British force Marda Pass. British Somaliland clear of Italians. USSR assures Turkey of neutrality.
March 25: Yugoslavia signs Tripartite Pact.
March 27: Revolution in Yugoslavia; King Peter takes over, forms new cabinet. Lease of Atlantic, Caribbean bases in exchange for 50 destroyers agreement signed.
March 28: Battle of Cape Matapan.
March 30: German, Italian, Danish ships in US ports seized. Rommel launches offensive in Cyrenaica. HMS *York* sunk. RAF attacks *Scharnhorst, Gneisenau* at Brest.
April 1: Raschid Ali seizes power in Iraq.
April 2: British withdraw from Mersa Brega.
April 4: Germans capture Benghazi, Msus.
April 6: Germans invade Greece, Yugoslavia. British occupy Addis Ababa.
April 9: Rommel takes Bardia. German armour enters Thessaloniki.
April 10: Australian 9th Division withdraws to Tobruk.
April 11: Blitz on Coventry. Italian and Hungarian troops enter Yugoslavia.
April 12: Belgrade surrendered to Germans. RAF daylight sweeps over Europe.
April 13: Rommel encircles Tobruk. Stalin signs neutrality pact with Japan.
April 14: Germans repulsed at Tobruk. Germans force Kleisoura Pass.
April 19: Bulgarians enter Macedonia. Heavy raids on London.
April 20: Germans cut off Greek forces in Epirus and Macedonia.
April 21: RN bombards Tripoli. Japanese occupy Foochow.
April 22: Greek Army capitulates in Thessaloniki; withdrawal of British forces begins.
April 24: German breakthrough at Thermopylae.
April 25: Germans capture Halfaya Pass; invade Lemnos; British pushed back to Mersa Matruh.
April 27: German troops enter Athens.
April 28: Rommel captures Sollum. British evacuate last forces from Greece.
April 30: Iraqi troops surround RAF base at Habbaniyah.
May 1: Attack on Tobruk repulsed.
May 2: Iraq demands withdrawal of British forces; British occupy Basra.
May 3: Hamburg bombed, the first of five raids in May.
May 6: British and native levies defeat Iraqi troops around Habbaniyah.
May 10: Hess flies to Scotland.
May 15: British retake Sollum and Halfaya Pass as part of Operation 'Brevity'.
May 16: Last British reinforcements arrive in Crete.
May 18: *Bismarck, Prinz Eugen* sail from Gdynia.
May 20: German Operation 'Merkur' begins against Crete. 120 German divisions now on Soviet front.
May 21: Germans capture Máleme airfield.

May 22: Cruisers *Gloucester* and *Fiji* sunk, battleships *Warspite* and *Valiant* damaged near Crete.
May 23: Admiral Darlan announces no surrender of French fleet or colonies.
May 24: *Hood, Prince of Wales* engage *Bismarck, Prinz Eugen* at 17 miles; *Hood* sunk.
May 25: *Bismarck* escapes pursuers.
May 26: *Bismarck* located, stopped by aircraft torpedo. HMS *Formidable* damaged by Stukas.
May 27: *Bismarck* sunk. Germans take Caneá.
May 28: British evacuate Heraklion.
May 30: Iraq revolt collapses.
May 31: British finish evacuation of Crete.
June 1: British enter Baghdad.
June 8: British, Australian, Indian, Free French forces invade Syria, supported by RAF and naval forces.
June 11: USSR-Japan trade pact signed. First of 20 consecutive RAF night raids on Germany.
June 14: Operation 'Battleaxe', to relieve Tobruk, begins.
June 15: British attack Sollum.
June 21: Damascus occupied by Free French forces. Auchinleck replaces Wavell as C-in-C Middle East.
June 22: Germany invades Russia; Italy, Rumania declares war on USSR; Churchill promises aid.
June 23: Germans cross the Bug.
June 26: Finland declares war on USSR.
June 27: Sir Stafford Cripps and British Military Mission arrive in Moscow. Japan proclaims 'Greater East Asia Co-Prosperity Sphere'.
June 29: Stalin, Malenkov, Voroshilov, Beria form defence committee.
June 30: Germans capture Lwow.
July 1: Germans capture Riga.
July 3: Stalin calls for 'scorched earth' policy.
July 4: Tito announces resistance.
July 7: US Marines in Iceland, Trinidad, British Guiana.
July 8: Germany, Italy partition Yugoslavia. Hitler plans to raze Moscow, Leningrad.
July 9: Germans take Minsk pocket and Vitebsk.
July 10: Germany urges Japan to fight Russia. Panzers cross Dniepr.
July 11: Cease-fire in Syria. USSR appoints Voroshilov, Timoshenko, Budenny commanders of North, Central, and South Fronts.
July 12: Anglo-Soviet Mutual Assistance Agreement signed.
July 15: Smolensk captured by Army Group Centre.
July 18: USSR-Czech agreement signed in London. Stalin requests Second Front.
July 21: Moscow bombed.
July 22: Germans stopped at Lake Ilmen as a result of exhaustion.
July 24: Vichy agrees to Japanese occupation of Indo-China bases.
July 25: Japanese assets in US, UK, and Dominions to be frozen.
July 27: First London raid since May 10.
July 28: Japanese troops land in Indo-China.
July 30: USSR-Polish agreement signed.
August 1: US oil embargo against Japanese 'aggressors'.
August 3: Kleist, Stülpnagel seal Uman pocket. Mannerheim continues attacks to recover Karelian Isthmus, independently of German plans.
August 5: Rumanian forces begin 73-day siege of Odessa. Soviet resistance in Smolensk pocket ends.
August 7: Stalin becomes Supreme

Commander. Red Air Force begins raids on Berlin.
August 12: Atlantic Charter signed by Churchill, Roosevelt. Army Group North advances on Leningrad.
August 16: Novgorod taken by Army Group North.
August 19: German encirclement of Leningrad continues. British, Polish troops begin relief of Australians and Indians in Tobruk.
August 21: Voroshilov calls for Leningrad defence to the last man.
August 24: Russians counterattack at Gomel; inflict heavy losses on Rumanians at Odessa; Finns surround Russians at Viipuri.
August 25: British, Russians enter Persia.
August 28: Cease-fire in Persia; Ali Furughi forms government.
August 29: Russians evacuate Karelian Isthmus.
September 1: Timoshenko counterattacks in Gomel sector. Japanese Army Press announces that Japan must break out of Allied encirclement.
September 3: First use of gas chamber at Auschwitz.
September 4: Finland reoccupies prewar frontier. Heavy air raids on Malta.
September 5: Germans complete occupation of Estonia.
September 6: Japanese Imperial Conference decides to accept risk of war.
September 8: Leningrad cut off by German tanks.
September 15: Kleist's and Guderian's Panzers meet at Lokhvitsa, trapping four Soviet Armies. Siege of Leningrad begins.
September 19: Germans take Kiev, Poltava.
September 23: Timoshenko counterattacks.
September 25: German paratroops drop in Crimea.
September 26: Hitler orders offensive against Moscow. Winter conditions halt heavy fighting east of Kiev.
September 28: Japanese occupy Chang-Sha. First Arctic convoy to Russia leaves Iceland.
September 29: Massacre of Jews in Kiev.
October 2: Hitler issues Order of Day to troops facing Moscow. Germans launch fierce attack against Moscow.
October 7: Panzer spearheads seal off Soviet forces in Vyasma, Bryansk pockets.
October 8: Germans take Orel.
October 10: Britain to supply Russia on Lend-Lease terms.
October 16: Soviet government leave Moscow for Kuybyshev. Odessa falls to Germans.
October 20: Resistance ends in Bryansk pocket; Germans capture Stalino. Japanese navy prepares for Pearl Harbor attack.
October 21: General Zhukov appointed commander of outer defences of Moscow.
October 24: Germans take Kharkov.
October 26: Final relief of Australians in Tobruk.
October 27: Russians counterattack in Moscow area.
October 29: German breakthrough in Crimea.
October 30: Bock attacks Moscow from the north-west.
November 1: Germans capture Simferopol. Marshal Shaposhnikov new Russian C-of-S.
November 3: Germans capture Kursk. Yamamoto's plan to attack US fleet is approved.
November 6: Russian casualties given as 350,000 killed, 378,000

missing, 1,020,000 wounded. US to lend USSR $1,000,000,000.
November 9: Germans capture Yalta, Tikhvin railhead. RN annihilates two Italian convoys.
November 10: Churchill announces Britain's parity in the air; Britain will join US if Japan attacks; powerful naval forces ready to be sent to the Far East.
November 14: HMS *Ark Royal* sinks off Gibraltar after previous torpedo attack; one casualty. Russians counterattack at Moscow.
November 15: German second-phase offensive at Moscow paralysed by 20° of frost.
November 16: Germans capture Kerch.
November 18: Operation 'Crusader', second Western Desert campaign, launched by 8th Army.
November 19: British reach Sidi Rezegh.
November 20: Tank battle at Sidi Rezegh.
November 22: Panzers blunt British attack. Germans enter Rostov.
November 23: Rommel destroys South African 5th Brigade, prepares 'dash to the wire'.
November 24: Auchinleck orders 'Attack and pursue'.
November 25: All-out German attack on Moscow. HMS *Barham* sunk off Sollum.
November 26: Japanese carrier fleet sails. US demands Japanese withdrawal from China. Tobruk garrison linked up near Sidi Rezegh. US forces receive 'war alert'. Panzers stopped 19 miles from Moscow.
November 28: Germans forced out of Rostov.
November 29: Rommel counterattacks.
November 30: Fighting in Tobruk-Sidi Rezegh corridor.
December 1: Russians counterattack at Tula.
December 5: Hitler abandons Moscow offensive for winter. UK declares war on Hungary, Finland, Rumania.
December 6: Soviet counteroffensive begins.
December 7: Japan declares war on UK, US. Pearl Harbor attacked; Japanese land in Thailand, Malaya; Singapore bombed.
December 8: Allies declare war on Japan. Russia remains neutral. Japanese begin land, sea attacks on Hong Kong, bomb Guam, Midway, Wake Island, and Philippines.
December 9: Russians recapture Tikhvin.
December 10: *Repulse* and *Prince of Wales* sunk. Japanese land on Luzon.
December 11: US declares war on Italy, Germany.
December 15: British withdraw in Malaya, Burma, Kowloon. Rommel decides to evacuate Cyrenaica.
December 17: British advance to Gazala line. Japanese land in North Borneo. In Malaya British withdraw to Perak River.
December 18: *Scharnhorst, Gneisenau* bombed. Japanese land on Hong Kong.
December 19: Italian frogmen damage HMS *Queen Elizabeth, Valiant*. British retake Derna and Mechili.
December 22: Japanese land in Gulf of Lingayen. First Washington Conference starts.
December 24: Japanese capture Wake Island. British retake Benghazi.
December 25: Hong Kong surrenders.
December 29: Russians retake Kerch, Feodosia.

1942

January 2: Japanese occupy Manila, Cavite. British, South Africans recapture Bardia.
January 4: Russians retake Borovsk.
January 5: Further Japanese landings on west coast of Malaya.
January 7: Heavy fighting between Chinese, Japanese at Changsha. Japanese break Slim's river defences in central Malaya.
January 8: Rommel forced to retreat from Agedabia.
January 9: Russians enter Smolensk Province.
January 11: Japanese enter Kuala Lumpur; Japanese campaign in Dutch East Indies begins with capture of Tarakan. British recapture Sollum.
January 16: Japanese invade Burma from Thailand. Heavy US losses on Bataan Peninsula.
January 17: Rommel's last garrisons in Cyrenaica surrender.
January 18: Germany, Italy, Japan sign new military pact. 'Wannsee Conference' under Heydrich announces 'Final Solution of the Jewish Problem'.
January 21: Rommel surprises Allied outposts and begins the reconquest of Cyrenaica.
January 22: Americans retreat on Bataan.
January 23: Japanese land at Rabaul, Kavieng, and Balikpapan. Australia appeals to UK, US for reinforcements. Heavy Japanese raids on Rangoon. Russians break through between Lake Ilmen and Smolensk.
January 24: Battle of Macassar Strait. Australians evacuate Lae, Salamaua.
January 28: Timoshenko advances into Ukraine. Rommel recaptures Benghazi.
January 30: British forces withdraw into Singapore; causeway destroyed.
February 3: Japanese begin bombing of Port Moresby. Japanese make pre-invasion air attacks on Java, capture Paan in Burma.
February 4: Japanese demand unconditional surrender of Singapore. Rommel captures Derna.
February 7: General Percival declares Singapore will be held to last man. Japanese land on Singapore Island.
February 11: *Scharnhorst, Gneisenau, Prinz Eugen* escape from Brest, proceed up Channel.
February 13: German resistance on Eastern Front stiffens as vanguard of Red Army enters White Russia.
February 15: Singapore surrenders; Allied losses for campaign totalled 9,000 killed and wounded, 130,000 captured.
February 19: Japanese invade Bali, cross Bilin in Burma, bomb Darwin.
February 20: Japanese land on Portuguese Timor. US grants billion-dollar loan to USSR.
February 22. General MacArthur ordered to leave Philippines; appointed C-in-C Allied Forces in Australia.
February 23: Mutual Aid Agreement signed between US, UK, Australia, New Zealand.
February 27: Battle of Java Sea; Allied force destroyed.
February 28: Japanese invade Java.
March 1: Russians launch offensive in Crimea.
March 2: Japanese land at Mindanao.
March 6: *Tirpitz* stopped from attacking PQ-12 convoy by aircraft from *Victorious*.
March 8: Japanese land at Lae and Salamaua; enter Rangoon.
March 9: General Yamashita appointed C-in-C Philippines. Dutch East Indies government capitulates.
March 12: British garrison withdraws from Andaman Islands.
March 18: Admiral Mountbatten appointed Chief of Combined Operations.
March 23: Japanese occupy Andaman Islands.
March 28: Allied raid on St Nazaire.
March 30: Pacific War Council established in Washington.
April 1: Japanese begin landings on Dutch New Guinea.
April 3: Japanese open all-out offensive against last line of defence on Bataan.
April 4: Japanese sink HMSs *Dorsetshire, Cornwall, Hermes, Hollyhock* in Indian Ocean.
April 9: General King surrenders Bataan; Wainwright escapes to Corregidor.
April 16: George Cross awarded to Malta.
April 18: Colonel Doolittle leads bombing raid on Japan.
April 29: Japanese take Lashio. Hitler and Mussolini meet at Salzburg.
April 30: Japanese complete conquest of central Burma.
May 1: British evacuate Mandalay.
May 2: All British troops withdrawn from Irrawaddy.
May 5: Japanese land on Corregidor. British land on Madagascar; little opposition from Vichy troops.
May 6: Garrison of 11,000 surrenders on Corregidor; Wainwright surrenders all forces in Philippines.
May 7: Battle of Coral Sea begins. USN sinks Japanese carrier *Shoho*.
May 8: Main action of Battle of Coral Sea. USS *Lexington* sunk. Japanese occupy Akyab, Myitkyina. Germans begin summer offensive in Crimea.
May 11: Japanese launch offensives in Yünnan, Chekiang Provinces.
May 15: Russians make strong attack in Kharkov area; withdraw in Kerch Peninsula.
May 15: Retreating British forces cross Burma-India frontier.
May 16: Germans capture Kerch; Red Army continues offensive towards Kharkov.
May 17: Germans halt Russian offensive east of Kharkov.
May 20: Germans recapture whole of Kerch Peninsula. Japanese take up defensive positions in Burma.
May 26: 20-year Anglo-Soviet Treaty signed. Rommel atacks Gazala Line. Heavy fighting in this area for one month.
May 27: Heydrich assassinated in Prague.
May 28: Germans destroy large Russian forces in Kharkov area.
May 30: US task force leaves for Midway. First RAF 1,000-bomber raid (on Cologne).
June 4: Battle of Midway; Japanese suffer heavy losses, four carriers sunk.
June 5: Germans besiege Sebastopol.
June 7: Japanese invade Aleutians.
June 10: Free French forces withdraw from Bir Hakeim. Lidice wiped out to avenge Heydrich's death.
June 17: British withdraw towards Egypt; leave garrison in Tobruk.
June 19: Churchill, Roosevelt confer on problems of second front, atomic bomb.
June 21: Tobruk falls. Germans drive wedge into Sebastopol defence.
June 24: Rommel advances to Sidi Barrani.
June 25: Auchinleck takes commands in Desert. 8th Army retreats to Mersa Matrûh. Eisenhower appointed US C-in-C Europe.
June 27: Germans advance to Mersa Matrûh.
June 28: German offensive at Kursk. British begin withdrawal to El Alamein area.
June 30: Rommel reaches Alamein.
July 2: British force German withdrawal from Alamein.
July 3: Sebastopol falls.
July 4: Germans reach Don on wide front. PQ-17 convoy to Russia attacked by German aircraft; escort ordered away; convoy scatters.
July 7: Germans capture Voronezh.
July 12: Australians reach Kokoda.
July 22: Japanese reinforcements for Kokoda Trail move to Buna.
July 30: Stalin orders 'not another step back'.
July 31: Germans cross Don on front of 150 miles.
August 7: US Marines land in Guadalcanal-Tulagi area of Solomons.
August 8: Battle of Savo Island.
August 9: Germans capture Krasnodar and Maikop.
August 11: Violent attacks on 'Pedestal' convoy to Malta; HMS *Eagle* sunk.
August 12: First Moscow Conference.
August 13: Montgomery takes command of 8th Army. Germans advance in Caucasus.
August 15: General Alexander takes over command of MEF from General Auchinleck.
August 16: USAAF bomb German installations in Desert.
August 17: Germans establish bridgeheads in Kuban Peninsula. British, Canadians raid Dieppe.
August 19: General Paulus orders German VI Army to attack and take Stalingrad.
August 24: Sea Battle of Eastern Solomons. Russian offensive south of Lake Ladoga begins.
August 26: Japanese land at Milne Bay; engaged by Australians.
August 28: Fierce fighting around Stalingrad.
August 31: Battle of Alam Halfa begins.
September 3: Fierce fighting south of Stalingrad.
September 5: Australians force Japanese to evacuate Milne Bay.
September 11: Japanese halted in Owen Stanley range at Ioribaiwa.
September 16: German Army Group B penetrates Stalingrad suburbs. Australians hold Japanese on Imita Ridge, 32 miles from Port Moresby.
September 30: First British liaison mission arrives in Greece. Limited offensive launched by 8th Army at El Alamein.
October 11: Battle of Cape Esperence off Guadalcanal.
October 14: Australians advancing along Kokoda Trail meet stubborn opposition near Templeton's Crossing. Hitler orders all troops on Eastern Front to stand fast.
October 17: Bitter fighting at Eora Creek on Kokoda Trail.
October 19: US War Department agrees to equip 30 more Chinese divisions.
October 23: Battle of Alamein opens. Japanese suffer heavy losses in Guadalcanal attack.
October 24: Battle of Santa Cruz off Guadalcanal; USS *Hornet* sunk.
October 25: El Alamein battle intensifies. Another Japanese attack repulsed on Guadalcanal.
October 30: 8th Army assault on northern flank of 30th Corps;

Australians drive to sea, trapping large enemy force; RAF attacks accurately with tactical support.
November 1: Marines launch attack on Guadalcanal.
November 2: Operation 'Supercharge', the breakout from Alamein, begins.
November 4: Start of Axis retreat from Alamein.
November 6: 8th Army approach Matrûh as heavy rains begin.
November 8: Operation 'Torch' begins. Roosevelt broadcasts to people of France. French North Africa; Pétain orders resistance, but Vichy troops disobey; Algiers falls.
November 10: Rommel's rearguards evacuate Sidi Barrani and retreat to Buq Buq. US troops take Oran.
November 11: Axis troops enter Unoccupied France and Corsica. Allies occupy Casablanca, Bougie. 8th Army takes Bardia.
November 12: USN loses two cruisers, four destroyers in night naval battle at 1st Battle of Guadalcanal.
November 13: 8th Army reaches Tobruk.
November 15: In naval action off Guadalcanal Japanese lose seven transports, a battleship, and a destroyer; remaining four transports sunk by navy, army and air forces; defeat almost isolates Japanese on Guadalcanal.
November 18: 8th Army enters Cyrene.
November 20: 8th Army reaches Benghazi.
November 23: Red Army closes ring round German VI Army at Stalingrad; Hitler orders 'dig in and await relief'.
November 28: Wide Russian offensive on Central Front.
November 30: Naval battle of Tassafaronga.
December 13: Rommel withdraws from El Agheila.
December 16: Italians routed on the Don as Russian offensive begins.
December 17: UN to avenge Nazi crimes against Jews.
December 18: Australian, US troops in fierce fighting in Papua; Japanese strongly defend Sanananda front.
December 21: 8th Army advance units overtake German rearguard at Sirte. British, Indian troops cross Burma frontier, advance towards Akyab.
December 24: Admiral Darlan assassinated.
December 25: 8th Army occupy Sirte.
December 28: Hitler agrees to withdrawal of Army Group A from the Caucasus.

1943

January 3: Germans start withdrawal from Caucasus.
January 4: Japanese begin evacuation of Guadalcanal.
January 8: Rokossovsky sends ultimatum to Paulus to surrender German VI Army.
January 11: Roosevelt asks Congress for Budget of $100,000,000,000.
January 14: Casablanca Conference begins; continues for 10 days; Roosevelt demands 'unconditional surrender'.
January 15: 8th Army opens offensive against Buerat.
January 18: Siege of Leningrad raised by Russian attack. Germans use Tiger tanks in Tunisia.
January 19: 8th Army occupies Homs, Tarhuna. Russians advance in centre and Caucasus. Japanese retreat from Sanananda.

January 23: 8th Army enters Tripoli.
January 26: Russians complete capture of Voronezh; take 52,000 prisoners.
January 27: USAAF makes first attack on Germany, bombing docks at Wilhelmshaven.
January 31: Paulus surrenders southern group of VI Army at Stalingrad.
February 1/19: Japanese XVII Army evacuated from Guadalcanal.
February 1: Churchill arrives in Cairo from Adana.
February 2: Remaining German forces at Stalingrad capitulate.
February 6: Russians reach Sea of Azov at Yeisk, isolating German Army Group A.
February 8: Russians take Kursk.
February 14: Germans launch strong counterattack in Tunisia. Chindits cross the Chindwin unopposed. Russians take Rostov.
February 16: Russians capture Kharkov, Voroshilovgrad; 8th Army occupies Mareth Line outpost.
February 17: Germans reach Feriana, Kasserine, Sbeitla.
February 20: Germans break through Kasserine Pass.
February 25: Allied troops recover Kasserine Pass.
March 2: Battle of the Bismarck Sea starts.
March 5: Bismarck Sea Battle ends; 12 Japanese ships sunk.
March 6: Rommel leaves the Afrika Korps.
March 12: Opening of Military Conference on Pacific in Washington.
March 13: Chinese throw Japanese back across Yangtze.
March 15: Germans recapture Kharkov.
March 17: Japanese attack on Arakan front.
March 20: 8th Army opens attack on Mareth Line. Attempt to assassinate Hitler.
March 28: 8th Army takes Mareth, Toujane, Matmata.
March 29: 8th Army occupies Gabes, El Hamma.
April 6: 8th Army attacks at Wadi Akarit.
April 7: 8th Army links up with US II Corps. Hitler, Mussolini meet at Führer's HQ.
April 16: Announcement in London of discovery of mass graves of Polish officers at Katyn Wood.
April 18: Admiral Yamamoto's plane intercepted and shot down; Yamamoto killed.
April 19: Rising in Warsaw Ghetto begins.
April 21: 8th Army takes Enfidaville.
April 22: 1st Army attacks at Bou Arada towards Tunis.
April 23: Hitler orders 'utmost severity' in treatment of Jews in Warsaw Ghetto.
April 24: US warships bombard Japanese positions in the Aleutians.
April 26: USSR breaks off relations with Polish government in London over demand for investigation of Katyn graves.
April 30: New RN command formed to co-ordinate convoy protection. Beginning of aircraft carrier convoy escort, long-range bomber support and special 'Support Groups'.
May 7: 18th Army Group overruns Tunis and Bizerta.
May 9: Axis forces in US II Corps Zone in Tunis surrender.
May 10: 1st Army cuts off Cape Bon Peninsula.
May 11: US infantry achieve complete tactical surprise in landing on Attu.

May 12: Arnim and Axis forces surrender in N. Africa. 2nd Washington Conference starts.
May 13: General Messe surrenders. Japanese begin new series of heavy air attacks in New Guinea.
May 16: Rising suppressed in Warsaw Ghetto.
May 17: RAF Lancasters breach Möhne and Eder Dams. Japanese retreat on Attu.
May 21: Japanese launch attack in Central China.
May 23: Heaviest RAF raid to date: 2,000 tons dropped on Dortmund.
May 25: 2nd Washington Conference ends.
May 27: First dropping of British liaison mission to Tito's partisans.
May 29: Chinese launch new counteroffensive on Hupeh-Hunan border, supported by USAAF.
May 30: Organised resistance collapses on Attu.
June 4: Russians bomb Karachev, Bryansk; Luftwaffe bombs Gorki.
June 8: Japanese order abandonment of Kiska.
June 11: British invade Pantelleria virtually unopposed.
June 16: Tojo informs Japanese Diet that the war situation has become tense. Japanese lose almost 100 aircraft in attack on Guadalcanal.
June 20: Japanese launch attacks on Australian positions on Mubo-Lababia Ridge area in New Guinea.
June 25: Allies continue bombing of Sicily, concentrating on Messina.
July 1: Americans capture Viru Harbour, New Georgia Island; consolidate positions in Nassau Bay area, New Guinea.
July 4: General Sikorski, several other Polish leaders killed in air crash.
July 5: Germans launch last major offensive of Eastern Front in Kursk sector. Battle of Kula Gulf.
July 9: US, British airborne troops make night landing on Sicily. Russians hold Axis forces north and south of Kursk.
July 10: Main Allied landing on Sicily.
July 12: 'Greatest tank battle in history' fought near Prokhorovka. Russians go over to counter-offensive.
July 15: Russian offensives launched near Orel. Japanese lose 45 aircraft in air battle over Central Solomons; three US aircraft lost.
July 22: Americans capture Palermo.
July 24: King of Italy invited to command armed forces. 'Window' tinfoil strips used to confuse German radar; 20,000 killed in raid on Hamburg by RAF.
July 25: Mussolini resigns and is arrested; Marshal Badoglio takes command of Italian army, and forms government.
July 26: Martial Law in Italy; Fascist Party dissolved.
July 28: Roosevelt broadcasts Allies' terms to Italy.
August 1: De Gaulle becomes President of French Committee of National Defence; Giraud C-in-C French armed forces. UK, US, USSR governments warn neutral countries not to give shelter to war criminals.
August 5: Russians take Orel, Belgorod.
August 6: Battle of Vella Gulf. Russians close in on Kharkov.
August 12: Large-scale German evacuation from Sicily.
August 14: Rome declared an 'open city'.
August 17: Americans enter Messina. All resistance in Sicily

ends. RAF bombs Peenemunde.
August 22: Germans evacuate Kharkov.
August 23: Russians capture Kharkov. Japanese raid Chungking.
August 28: All Japanese resistance in New Georgia ends.
September 3: Allies land in Italy opposite Messina. Armistice with Italy signed but not announced.
September 4: Allies land east of Lae. Allied bridgeheads in Italy link up.
September 7: Himmler and Göring order total evacuation of the Ukraine. V-weapon sites bombed.
September 8: Eisenhower and Badoglio announce surrender of Italy. Russians finish recapture of entire Donets Basin.
September 9: Allies land at Salerno. British 1st Airborne Div. lands at Taranto.
September 10: Germans occupy Rome. 8th Army takes Taranto.
September 12: Skorzeny rescues Mussolini.
September 13: Germans push 5th Army back at Salerno. Chiang Kai-shek elected President of Chinese Republic.
September 22: Allies land at Bari. Poltava taken by Russians. First units of Central Front cross Dniepr. RN midget submarines damage Tirpitz in Altenfjord.
September 25: Russians take Smolensk.
October 1: 5th Army captures Naples.
October 2: 5th Army takes Benevento. British commandos land at Termoli, link with 8th Army.
October 3: Japanese attack successfully in Central China.
October 5: USN begins two-day sea and air bombardment of Wake Island.
October 13: Italy declares war on Germany. Allies cross Volturno.
October 18: Second Moscow Conference.
October 19: Third (London) Protocol: aid to Russia.
November 5: US Task Force aircraft and USAAF damage five Japanese cruisers, two destroyers, bomb wharf area at Rabaul.
November 6: Russians recapture Kiev.
November 7: Japanese reinforcements land on Bougainville.
November 20: US troops land on Makin and Tarawa Atolls. 8th Army crosses the Sangro.
November 22: First Cairo Conference.
November 23: Organised resistance ends on Tarawa.
November 28: Teheran Conference begins.
December 3: Russians advance on wide front. 5th Army offensive begins. 2nd Cairo Conference begins.
December 7: Cairo Conference ends.
December 12: Czech-Soviet alliance signed in Moscow. Rommel appointed C-in-C Fortress Europe.
December 14: Russians open winter offensive.
December 17: 5th Army take San Pietro.
December 21: Russians destroy German bridgehead over Dniepr at Kherson.
December 25: Allies land on New Britain.
December 26: Russians launch new offensive on Kiev salient. American Marines land at Cape Gloucester. RN sinks the Scharnhorst.

1944

January 5: 5th Army begins final assault on Winter Line, east of Cassino.
January 6: Russians advance into Poland.
January 7: Russians advance in Ukraine.
January 15: 5th Army takes Mount Trocchio; Germans withdraw across Rapido. Russians open offensives for Leningrad and Novgorod.
January 16: Eisenhower assumes duties as Supreme Commander, Allied Expeditionary Forces.
January 17: 5th Army's British 10th Corps crosses the Garigliano.
January 19: Russians take Novgorod.
January 20: Americans reach the Rapido.
January 22: 5th Army landings at Anzio.
January 24: 5th Army occupies Anzio and Nettuno.
January 26: Russians announce complete relief of Leningrad.
January 27: Russians trap large German force in pocket behind front line at Kanyew.
January 30: 5th Army break into Gustav Line.
January 31: US troops make successful invasion of Kwajalein Atoll and other islands in Marshall Group. Australian and Dutch troops engage Japanese in Dutch New Guinea.
February 3: Russians surround 10 divisions of German VIII Army. Night counteroffensive launched by Germans at Anzio.
February 4: Japanese open offensive on Arakan front to force Allies back to India.
February 5: Americans mop up in Kwajalein. Chindit 16th Brigade begins move towards Indaw.
February 7: Allied force cut off in 'Admin Box' on Arakan front.
February 8: Plan for Overlord confirmed at Allied HQ. Australians clear Huon Peninsula.
February 11: Supplies dropped by air to 'Admin Box'.
February 14: Eisenhower establishes SHAEF headquarters.
February 15: Air and artillery bombardment destroys Cassino Abbey.
February 16: Germans launch second counteroffensive at Anzio, almost cutting Allied positions in two.
February 19: US troops land on Eniwetok Island. Allied air strikes halt German attacks at Anzio.
February 21: Tojo becomes Chief of Japanese Army General Staff.
February 25: British clear Japanese from Ngakyedyauk Pass in Burma; 'Admin Box' relieved.
March 3: Greek resistance groups co-operate to fight Germans.
March 4: US and Chinese troops make pincer movement against Japanese in Hukawng Valley. First bombing raid on Berlin by USAAF.
March 5: Chindits dropped on Broadway and Piccadilly strips north of Indaw.
March 6: Russians advance on 100-mile front in Ukraine.
March 9: Japanese attack on Bougainville.
March 13: British, West African troops land on Arakan coast. Russians capture Kherson.
March 14: Germans trapped in Nikolayev pocket. British withdraw from from Tiddim to Imphal Plain.
March 16: Japanese cross Chindwin River to cut Kohima-Imphal road.
March 18: RAF drops over 3,000 tons of bombs on Hamburg; heaviest raid to date.
March 24: Japanese decisively

beaten during counteroffensive on Bougainville. All resistance in Admiralty Islands ceases.
March 26: British paratroops retreat to Imphal after delaying Japanese advance.
March 29: Siege of Imphal begins. Imphal-Kohima road cut.
March 31: Russians capture Ochakov on the Black Sea.
April 2: Russians enter Rumania.
April 3: Fleet Air Arm damages *Tirpitz* in Altenfjord.
April 4: Japanese begin assault on Kohima.
April 8: Russians approach Czech border; open final offensive in the Crimea.
April 10: Odessa falls to Red Army.
April 11: Russians seize Kerch; German XVII Army retreats into Sebastopol; Russians advance on Simferopol.
April 14/17: Russians liberate Tarnopol and cut Axis front in two.
April 22: Americans make unopposed landing at Hollandia, Dutch New Guinea.
April 27: Americans control all airfields in Hollandia sector. Indaw occupied.
April 28: Japanese advance in Honan Province. US and Chinese troops move up Mogaung valley towards Myitkyina.
May 5: 14th Army begins attack on Assam.
May 7: Russians begin attack on Sebastopol.
May 8: Eisenhower decides on June 5 as D-Day for Normandy invasion.
May 9: Sebastopol taken by Russians. Japanese capture Lushan and cut last sector of Peiping-Hankow railway. Allied air forces begin large-scale attacks on French airfields in preparation for D-Day.
May 11: 5th and 8th Armies open offensive to break through Germans on Gustav Line.
May 12: Allies cross Garigliano, Rapido Rivers; advances in several sectors. Last German forces evacuated from Crimea.
May 13: Allies take St Angelo, Castelforte; open way to Rome.
May 15: Germans begin withdrawal from Gustav to Adolf Hitler line.
May 16: 5th and 8th Armies overrun Gustav Line south of the Liri. Last Japanese troops cleared from Kohima Ridge.
May 17: US forces land on Wakde and Insoemanai Islands. Kesselring orders Cassino evacuated.
May 18: Poles capture Cassino monastery.
May 22: Canadians break through Adolf Hitler Line.
May 23: Allied offensive from Anzio beachhead begins with large air support: Operation 'Buffalo'. 8th Army opens general assault.
May 25: Troops from Anzio link up with 5th Army patrols at Terracina.
May 27: Americans land on Biak Island. Monsoons restrict operations in Burma.
May 29: First tank battle of SW Pacific is fought on Biak.
May 31: Germans launch heavy counterattacks against Russians north of Jassy.
June 2: Chinese besiege Myitkyina.
June 3: Hitler authorises Kesselring to withdraw from Rome. End of battle of Kohima.
June 4: 5th Army enters Rome.
June 5: Airborne troops dropped in Normandy.
June 6: D-Day. Allied naval forces land troops on French coast between Cherbourg and Le Havre.
June 7: Allies reach Bayeux.
June 10: Allied bridgehead expands; Montgomery establishes HQ in Normandy. Russians break

through on Karelian Isthmus.
June 12: All Normandy beachheads linked up; front extends to 50 miles.
June 13: First V-1 flying-bombs land in England.
June 15: US Marines land on Saipan, press inland against strong opposition.
June 16: USAAF raids Japan (Kyushu Island) from Chinese bases for first time.
June 18: Russians break through Mannerheim Line. 8th Army takes Assisi. US troops reach west coast of Cotentin Peninsula and cut off Cherbourg.
June 19: Naval air battle in Marianas: Battle of the Philippine Sea: Japanese lose about 400 aircraft.
June 20: US carrier aircraft attack retiring Japanese fleet; total Japanese losses are 14 warships sunk or damaged including 3 aircraft carriers.
June 22: 14th Army clears Kohima-Imphal road and relieves Imphal. Chindits begin attack on Mogaung.
June 24: Russians reach the Dvina.
June 26: Mogaung taken. British launch drive west of Caen; halted after heavy losses.
June 27: Russians cross Dniepr; German force destroyed near Vitebsk.
June 29: Cherbourg taken.
July 3: Russians recapture Minsk. USN aircraft sink several destroyers, cargo ships in 2-day attack on Iwo Jima, Roata, and Haha Islands.
July 7: Japanese Admirals Nagumo, Yano killed in fighting on Saipan; annihilation of Japanese garrison on Saipan.
July 9: 2nd Army takes Caen, Bretteville-sur-Odon. Admiral Turner declares Saipan secure. Russians cross the Vuoksi in Finland.
July 16: 8th Army takes Arezzo, reaches the Arno.
July 17: Russians cross Bug into Poland. 8th Army crosses the Arno, drives towards Florence.
July 18: US forces enter St Lô. 2nd Army launches Operation 'Goodwood'. Japanese retreat from Imphal-Kohima area.
July 20: The July Bomb Plot; attempt to assassinate Hitler.
July 21: US Marines land on Guam.
July 24: US Marines land on Tinian; heavy fighting on Guam.
July 26: Russians take Narva in Estonia and reach Vistula east of Radom. Heavy Japanese counterattack on Guam defeated.
July 27: 1st Army breaks through west of St Lô. Russians capture Lwow, Stanislavov, Daugavpils and Rezekne.
August 1: Russians cut communications between East Prussia and Baltic states. Polish underground army fights openly in Warsaw.
August 9: Eisenhower sets up HQ in France.
August 10: Japanese garrison on Guam annihilated.
August 13: Germans begin withdrawal from Falaise-Argentan trap.
August 14: Soviet offensive from Vistula bridgehead begins.
August 15: Operation 'Anvil': Allies invade Southern France: Americans and French in US 7th Army land between Toulon and Nice.
August 17: Russians reach East Prussian border.
August 18: Roosevelt announces agreement reached between Allies on military occupation of Germany.
August 20: US 3rd Army

establishes bridgehead across the Seine near Mantes-Gassingcourt. Falaise Gap closed completely. Revolt in Paris. French enter Toulon. De Gaulle in France where eight *départements* have been freed by FFI. Russians open offensive against Rumania, and break through toward the Danube.
August 22: Beginning of Fleet Air Arm attack on *Tirpitz* and other German naval units in Altenfjord.
August 23: FFI takes over control of Paris. Allies take Melun, Evreux, Grenoble, Hyères, Marseilles.
August 25: Allied forces liberate Paris.
August 26: Allied forces begin the advance eastward from Seine bridgeheads.
August 27: Last Chindits evacuated to India.
August 28: Last garrison in Marseilles surrenders and Toulon cleared of Germans.
August 29: US 1st Army liberates Soissons. French troops cross the Rhône.
August 30: Russians take Ploesti.
August 31: US 5th Army crosses the Arno.
September 1: British enter Arras; Canadians take Dieppe, Rouen.
September 3: British 2nd Army liberates Brussels; French capture Lyons.
September 4: British 2nd Army liberates Antwerp. Cease-fire on Russo-Finnish front.
September 5: US 3rd Army spearheads cross the Meuse; Ghent taken. Russia declares war on Bulgaria; Bulgaria requests armistice with Russia.
September 6: Russians reach Yugoslav border.
September 8: Russians enter Bulgaria unopposed. First V-2 lands at Chiswick, West London.
September 10: Operation 'Market Garden' planned to secure Rhine bridgehead at Arnhem. Russians capture Prague.
September 12: US 1st Army crosses German frontier near Aachen. German garrison in Le Havre surrenders.
September 14: Russians enter Warsaw suburb.
September 16: Russians enter Sofia.
September 17: 1st Allied Airborne Army lands in Holland near Eindhoven and Arnhem. Russians advance into Estonia.
September 18: Germans mount heavy counterattacks in both sectors of Arnhem operation. End of German resistance in Brest.
September 21: British force at Arnhem bridge destroyed.
September 22: Russians enter Tallinn in Estonia and Arad in Rumania. Boulogne surrenders. US troops land on Ulithi Atoll.
September 23: Russians reach Gulf of Riga.
September 24: British 2nd Army reaches Lower Rhine.
September 25: Canadians launch heavy attack on Calais. Hitler orders formation of *Volkssturm*.
September 26: Estonia occupied by Russians.
September 30: Germans surrender Calais.
October 1: Red Army enters Yugoslavia.
October 2: Russian offensive against Germans in North Finland. Warsaw patriots capitulate to Germans through lack of food and arms.
October 4: Russians and Tito's forces link up. Operation 'Manna': British troops land in Greece.
October 5: British troops land in Albania and on Greek islands.
October 6: Russians enter

Czechoslovakia.
October 9: Third Moscow Conference.
October 10: Russians reach Baltic coast; also cross Carpathians. US 3rd Fleet aircraft attack shipping and airfields on Okinawa.
October 10/29: Huge tank battle near Debrecon; three Soviet Corps destroyed.
October 11: US 3rd Fleet aircraft attack Luzon.
October 12: British paratroops capture Athens airfield. US 3rd Fleet commences 7-day air operations against Formosa.
October 13: Germans launch V-bombs against Antwerp. US 1st Army enters Aachen.
October 14: British liberate Athens.
October 15: Chinese begin offensive in North Burma.
October 17: US Rangers land on islands in approaches to Leyte Gulf.
October 19: British capture Japanese supply depot at Mohnyin in Burma. Moscow Conference ends. Hitler orders annihilation of Warsaw. Spain closes French frontier. Germans evacuate Belgrade.
October 20: US 6th Army invades Leyte; two beach-heads established. Belgrade and Dubrovnik liberated.
October 23: Battle of Leyte Gulf; 3-day naval-air battle begins. Russians enter East Prussia.
October 25: US 3rd, 7th Fleets continue to attack Japanese fleet at Leyte.
October 27: Kamikaze attacks on US TF 38 in Philippines. Russians open new offensive in Latvia.
October 28: Russo-Bulgarian armistice signed in Moscow. Germans begin evacuation of Albania.
October 30: Last extermination gassing at Auschwitz.
November 2: Germans evacuated from Greece.
November 10: Russians and partisans cross the Danube.
November 11: USN bombards Iwo Jima.
November 12: RAF Lancasters sink the *Tirpitz* in Tromso Fjord.
November 16: 14th Army captures Kalemyo, cutting Japanese communications with south.
November 18: US 3rd Army crosses German frontier.
November 22: US 3rd Army clears Metz.
November 23: Germans evacuate Finnish Lapland and Macedonia.
November 24: Allies cross the Saar and French take Strasbourg. B-29s raid Tokyo from bases in the Marianas for first time.
November 29: Russians cross the Danube north of the Drava. Russians cease operations in North Finland.
December 6: US 3rd Army crosses the Saar.
December 7: US forces land near Ormoc on Leyte Island.
December 8: USAAF begins 72-day bombardment of Iwo Jima.
December 9: Budapest almost encircled by Red Army.
December 15: Western Visayan Task Force lands on Mindoro, commences airfield construction. Chinese take Bhamo in Burma; Indaw taken.
December 16: Battle of the Bulge: German V and VI Panzer Armies under Rundstedt begin counterattack against US 1st and 9th Armies in the Ardennes.
December 19: Montgomery to command Allied forces north of the Ardennes, Bradley all forces to the south. Heavy fighting in US 1st Army area; German column reaches Houffalize and Bastogne.

December 22: Final German attempt to reach the Meuse in Ardennes offensive.
December 25: German Panzers turned back four miles from the Meuse. Japanese resistance on Leyte ends.
December 27: Budapest encircled.

1945
January 1: Luftwaffe employs over 800 aircraft to attack Allied airfields in France, Belgium and Holland in the last major Luftwaffe attack. Germans launch Operation 'Nordwind' against US 7th Army. US 8th Army begins four-month mopping up operations on Leyte.
January 2: Germans counterattack at Budapest.
January 3: US 1st Army counterattacks in Germans' Ardennes salient.
January 9: US 6th Army lands at Lingayen Gulf on Luzon Island.
January 11: Russians enter Warsaw. Bridgeheads across the Irrawaddy north of Mandalay established.
January 12: Russians begin winter offensive in South Poland.
January 16: Ardennes salient eliminated by join-up of American 1st and 3rd Armies at Houffalize.
January 17: Germans evacuate Warsaw.
January 18: Germans break through Russian lines and reach Danube south of Budapest.
January 19: Russians take Tilsit and Cracow.
January 22: Burma road reopened.
January 25: Americans capture Clark Field on Luzon.
January 27: Russians take Memel; Lithuania freed. Vistula is crossed.
January 28: Last vestige of German salient in Ardennes removed. Russians enter Pomerania. Supply convoy reaches China over the Ledo-Burma Road.
February 1: US 7th Army reaches Siegfried Line: US 6th Army drives towards Manila.
February 4: Yalta Conference opens.
February 6: Russians cross the Upper Oder.
February 8: British and Canadians launch operation to clear region between the Maas and the Rhine.
February 9: British and Canadians break through Siegfried Line, reach the Rhine.
February 12: Yalta Conference ends.
February 13: 14th Army establishes bridgeheads over Irrawaddy south of Mandalay. RAF terror raid on Dresden, worst firestorm raid of European war.
February 14: USAAF raids Dresden. US 6th Army begins operations on Bataan Peninsula.
February 15: Russians attack towards Danzig and complete encirclement of Breslau. Heavy fighting continues in Manila.
February 16: Pre-invasion naval and air bombardment of Iwo Jima. Indian brigade lands on Arakan coast to block Japanese withdrawal. US paratroops land on Corregidor.
February 17: Americans occupy Bataan Peninsula.
February 17/24: Germans wipe out Russian Hron bridgehead.
February 19: US Marines land on Iwo Jima.
February 23: Russians take Poznan. Marines take Mt Suribachi on Iwo Jima.
February 24: Americans complete occupation of Manila except for isolated pockets.
February 26: Canadian 1st Army

begins Operation 'Blockbuster'.
February 28: Corregidor declared secure.
March 3: Manila finally secured; US infantry land on Burias, Ticao Islands.
March 5: Cologne captured. Russians approach Stettin. Germans destroy bridges as US 9th and 1st Armies reach the Rhine.
March 6: Germans launch major counter-offensive towards Budapest. Russians advance towards Danzig. Most of Cologne cleared by US 1st Army.
March 7: US 1st Army crosses the Rhine over Remagen railway bridge. US 3rd Army thrusts towards the Ahr. Chinese occupy Lashio.
March 8: Americans enter Bonn. US troops land at Samboanga on Mindanao.
March 9: US 3rd Army completes drive to the Rhine. Japanese attack French forces in Indo-China.
March 10: Superfortress fire-raid burns out over 16½ acres in Tokyo. Japanese and French fight in Hanoi. US 1st and 2nd Armies link up on Rhine.
March 13: 14th Army captures Maymo, cutting Japanese escape route from Mandalay.
March 16: US 3rd Army begins assault across the Moselle. Iwo Jima declared secure.
March 17: US 3rd Army captures Coblenz.
March 19: Japanese evacuate Mandalay.
March 22: Russians besiege Danzig and Gdynia. US 3rd Army overcomes resistance in Mainz.
March 25: US 3rd Army crosses Rhine, establishes bridgehead, captures Darmstadt; US 9th Army makes contact with British. Russians advance towards Austria on broad front after breaking through German counter-offensive.
March 26: British 2nd Army expands bridgehead towards the Ijssel.
March 28: Allied objective for final drive altered from Berlin to Leipzig; Gdynia falls to Russian troops. Russian troops reach Austrian border.
March 30: Russians capture Danzig.
April 1: US 1st and 9th Armies complete encirclement of Ruhr, linking up at Lippstadt; US 1st Army enters Hamm; French 1st Army reaches Linkenheim. Okinawa invaded by US 10th Army which moves rapidly inland against light opposition.
April 4: Hungary is cleared of Germans. Japanese resistance increases on Okinawa.
April 5: Russia denounces Russo-Japanese Neutrality Pact.
April 7: Russians break into Vienna. Battle of East China Sea: US TF 58 sinks *Yamato.* RN aircraft attack Japanese targets in the Sakadina Group. First US land-based fighters from Iwo Jima fly over Japan.
April 9: Russians take Königsberg fortress. RAF bombers sink the *Admiral Scheer* at Kiel.
April 10: US 9th Army takes Hanover; Canadians cross the Ijssel.
April 12: Death of President Roosevelt; Harry Truman sworn in as President. Canadians assault Arnhem.
April 13: Vienna occupied by Russians. Belsen and Buchenwald concentration camps taken by British and Americans.
April 14: 5th Army opens offensive toward the Po Valley.
April 15: Canadians reach the sea in North Holland; Arnhem captured.

April 16: Russians begin offensive towards Berlin along the Oder and Neisse. RAF sinks the *Lützow.*
April 17: US extend further Lend-Lease agreements with Russia.
April 18: Ruhr pocket is neutralised; 370,000 prisoners taken. British 2nd Army reaches Lüneberg; US 3rd Army crosses Czech border near Prex; 9th Army takes Magdeberg. Allies advance in Italy.
April 19: British begin assault on Bremen; US 1st Army captures Halle and Leipzig. Japanese hold out on Bloody Ridge, le Shima.
April 20: Nuremberg falls to US 7th Army.
April 21: Russians develop pincer movement against Berlin; outer suburbs penetrated; German counterattack fails. French take Stuttgart; Americans of US 5th Army and Poles of 8th Army enter Bologna. After taking Bloody Ridge, Americans secure le Shima.
April 22: Hitler decides to stay in Berlin to the end.
April 23: US 8th Army ends Central Philippines campaign with the capture of Cebu. 5th and 8th Armies reach the Po. Himmler offers to surrender German forces to western Allies only. Hitler orders Göring to resign. Troops of 1st White Russian Front and 1st Ukrainian Front break into Berlin.
April 24: Red Army Fronts join forces inside Berlin. British and Canadians enter Bremen; Dessau taken. Dachau concentration camp liberated. 5th and 8th Armies cross the Po; Spezia taken. Hitler has Göring arrested.
April 25: US 1st Army patrols make contact with Soviet forces near Torgau. Russians complete encirclement of Berlin. 5th Army takes Verona.
April 26: French occupy Swiss border from Basle to Lake Constance; Bremen taken. Red Army takes Stettin and Brno. Allies cross the Adige. US 3rd, 7th Armies establish bridgeheads across the Danube. Italian partisans take over in Genoa, flight in Milan. Intense fighting on Okinawa.
April 27: UK, US refusal of armistice delivered by Count Bernadotte from Himmler.
April 28: Mussolini captured near Swiss border; killed by Italian partisans. US 7th Army takes Augsburg and reaches Austrian border. 5th Army takes Venice.
April 29: German army representatives sign terms of unconditional surrender at Caserta; hostilities to cease on May 2. 8th Army advances towards Trieste; 5th Army enters Milan, contacts 8th Army at Padua. US 3rd Army reaches the Isar; 7th Army reaches Munich, overruns Dachau concentration camp.
April 30: Hitler commits suicide in Chancellery bunker. Russians reach the Reichstag building in Berlin. US 1st Army meets Russians at Eilenburg; US 7th Army clears Munich. In five days Japanese air attacks, mostly kamikaze, have sunk 20, damaged 157 US and Allied ships at Okinawa.
May 1: Australians land on Tarakan Island. British airborne troops land south of Rangoon.
May 2: Berlin held by Red Army. German armies in Italy surrender; Turin, Milan, and Trieste taken. British 2nd Army reaches the Baltic; US 9th Army contacts Russians near Abbendorft. Mosquitoes bomb Kiel: last RAF raid in Europe. Prome and Pegu in

INDEX

Page numbers in italics refer to index entries that are illustrated.